ARCHBISHOP CHARLES AGAR

Archbishop Charles Agar

Churchmanship and Politics in Ireland, 1760–1810

A.P.W. MALCOMSON

FOUR COURTS PRESS

Published by
FOUR COURTS PRESS LTD
Fumbally Lane, Dublin 8, Ireland
email: info@four-courts-press.ie
http://www.four-courts-press.ie
and in North America by
FOUR COURTS PRESS
c/o ISBS, 5824 N.E. Hassalo Street, Portland, OR 97213.

ISBN 1-85182-694-7

A catalogue record for this title
is available from the British Library.

Printed in Great Britain
by MPG Books, Bodmin, Cornwall

We are ruled by Englishmen and the servants of Englishmen, whose object is the interest of another country, ... and these men have the whole of the power and patronage of the country.

Declaration of the United Irishmen of Dublin, 9 November 1791

Now, my dear Lord, you see what these English are!

Unnamed Roman catholic bishop
to William Alexander, bishop of Derry,
just after Disestablishment in 1869

In memory of Tessa,
a great lady

Contents

List of illustrations xi
Acknowledgments xiii
Introduction 1

PART ONE: BACKGROUND, CHARACTER AND CONNECTIONS

1 Charles Agar's ancestry, c.1660–1802 13

A confused pedigree: the Agars, c.1660–c.1700 13
The rise of the Agars, 1692–1746 17
The Ellis family, c.1660–1734 26
Welbore Ellis, 1st Lord Mendip (1713–1802) 30

2 Charles Agar's family, friends and foibles, c.1760–1809 40

Charles Agar's three brothers, 1747–1805 40
Other members of the Agar family, 1768–1809 53
Charles Agar's aesthetic interests and intellectual friendships 58
Clonmell, Carleton and Clare: Agar's political circle 64
Lord Macartney, Mrs Agar and the Agars' family life 78
Agar's physiognomy and personality 86

3 The Agar power-base in Kilkenny, 1715–1800 92

Power vacuum and power struggles, 1715–27 92
The Agar boroughs of Gowran, Thomastown and Callan, 1727–c.1770 95
James Agar and the representation of Co. Kilkenny, 1755–61 102
James Agar's interest in Kilkenny, 1761–78 107
Kilkenny politics, 1778–90 116
The disposal of the Gowran and Thomastown seats, 1761–1800 125
'The enormous folly' of contesting Co. Kilkenny, 1789–1801 129

4 The Agar political connection, 1763–1800 134

Agar's rise in the Church of Ireland, 1763–78 138

The proposed 'removal of the Dublin custom house', 1773–8   143
The contest for the archbishopric of Dublin in 1778   148
Compromise over the custom house, 1780–86   158
The Agar connection divided between Pitt and Fox, 1783–8   160
The Regency Crisis of 1788–9   164
The longer-term consequences of the Regency Crisis, 1789–94   170
The 'borough annexed to the primacy'   175

PART TWO: ECCLESIASTICAL IMPROVEMENT

5 **Agar as improving and reforming churchman, 1768–1801**   185

Improving or inactive?: the Irish episcopate   186
Agar as bishop of Cloyne, 1768–79   197
'Approaching desolation': Cashel in 1779   199
Agar's improvements and reforms in Cashel, 1779–1801   204
Agar's promotion of clerical residence, 1777–1801   211
The board of first fruits, 1763–1801   220
Reform by a 'critical stranger': Lord Buckingham's proposals of 1788   230

6 **Agar as improving and reforming churchman, 1801–9**   242

'In such a see as Dublin'!   243
Agar's achievements as a diocesan, 1801–9   252
Church and glebe-house building in Ireland, 1802–6   257
Clerical residence legislation for Ireland, 1806–8   269
The church and glebe-house bonanza, 1808–23   276

7 **Cashel city and cathedral, 1694–1801**   286

Cashel borough, 1694–1779   287
Agar and the town and neighbourhood of Cashel, 1779–1801   292
Kingston College, Mitchelstown, 1768–1801   295
Agar and Cloyne cathedral, 1768–79   301
Agar and Cashel cathedral, 1779–1801   303
The economics of cathedral restoration, 1766–1809   310
The Cashel cathedral organ and choir, 1783–1801   317
Architectural emulation by the Catholic Church in Munster, 1782–96   323
Agar's Cashel and Robinson's Armagh, *c*.1770–*c*.1820   329

PART THREE: SACRED AND PROFANE

8 **The Cashel and other palaces, 1728–1833**   334

Pearce's palace, 1728–44   334
Improvements and dilapidations: the economics of the episcopal palace,
1713–1819   338
The Bolton Library, 1732–1836   347
Agar's 'improvements' to the Cashel palace, 1779–97   350
Agar's improvements to the palace gardens, 1779–1801   355
The palace's 'ruinous condition', 1798–1801   360
The archbishop of Dublin's 'old and miserable mansions', 1778–1821   365
Brodrick's alterations to the Cashel palace, 1803–14   370
The survival of Pearce's palace   377
The 'edifying' archbishops   381

9 **See estates and Agar's 'love of lucre', *c.*1750–1833**   384

The 'odium' incurred by the bishops as landlords   384
The Tenantry Act of 1780 and 'the Archbishop of Cashel's Act' of 1795   393
The leasing strategies of bishops, *c.*1740–1809   399
Agar's acquisition of Cashel see leases, 1792–1804   406
The see lands of Dublin, 1778–1806   412
The Cashel see lands estate after Agar, 1809–90   416
Agar's making of a great estate to his family, 1762–1809   422
Agar's accounts as treasurer to the board of first fruits, 1787–1803   430
The 'love of lucre'   434

10 **Three 'accidental' archbishops from England: Robinson,
Fowler and Newcome, *c.*1760–1800**   437

Primate Robinson (1709–94)   437
Archbishop Fowler (1726–1801)   461
Primate Newcome (1729–1800)   467

11 **'Making such men bishops': the Irish episcopal bench,
*c.*1760–*c.*1810**   475

The political prelate, *c.*1760–1806   475
The alleged superiority of the Englishmen on the Irish bench,
*c.*1760–*c.*1800   483
A mixed bag of bishops, 1758–1822   491
The case for coadjutors, 1770–1819   499
A disruptive and divisive system of pay and promotion, 1772–1809   504

PART FOUR: SURVIVAL OF THE ESTABLISHMENT

12 **Emancipation, rebellion and union, 1795–9**   510

Agar's unionist tradition   510
Agar and Catholic Emancipation, 1791–5   515
Agar and security policy, 1795–8   521
Agar's relations with Cornwallis   525
The rough wooing of Agar, July–November 1798   529
Tithe commutation and Agar's other misgivings   533
Compensation for suffering loyalists and the clergy   544
Agar's conversion to Unionism   550
Agar's motives   554

13 **Agar and the Union, 1800–1: 'a bright example to
the Irish bench'**   559

The Church's post-Union representation and constitution   559
Compensation for the bishops' boroughs   568
Tithes and curates   574
Agar's contribution to other aspects of the Union   581
A 'negligent' and nominal union of the Churches   584
'The vacant primacy'   587
'The ministry have made the Archbishop of Cashel primate'   598
Primate Stuart is not 'as temperate as could have been supposed'   609

Conclusion   615
Bibliography   625
Index   647

Illustrations

1 Thomas Burgh's Dublin custom house of 1704–7: detail of the illustration in Walter Harris's *The history and antiquities of the city of Dublin* (Dublin, 1766).

2 Welbore Ellis, 1st Lord Mendip: mezzotint after the portrait by Gainsborough painted in 1763 and later presented by Ellis to Christ Church.

3 Bust of James Agar, 1st Viscount Clifden, by Edward Smyth, 1789?, in Leighlin cathedral, Co. Carlow.

4 Engraving of Henry Welbore, 2nd Viscount Clifden and 2nd Lord Mendip, from a portrait of *c.*1815.

5 George Macartney, Earl Macartney, painted for Archbishop and Mrs Agar by Gilbert Stuart in 1787, and now in the collection at Somerley.

6 John Scott, 1st earl of Clonmell, painted for Agar by Gilbert Stuart in 1790.

7 Hugh Carleton, Viscount Carleton, by Stuart, *c.*1790.

8 Mrs Agar by Stuart, *c.*1790.

9 Agar, after Stuart, *c.*1790: mezzotint by William Say, 1803.

10 Agar's daughter, Frances?, *c.*1798?, possibly by Frederick Prussia Plowman.

11 Agar's unmarried sister, Diana?, *c.*1790?, possibly by Hoppner.

12 Ellis Agar, countess of Brandon, by Philip Hussey, 1758?.

13 'Copperplate' of the cathedral on the Rock of Cashel, after a drawing by Jonas Blaymires, 1739.

14 Engraving of the cathedral on the Rock after a drawing by Anthony Chearnley, *c.*1740.

15 Sketch by 'R. Gibbs', 1813, of Gowran Castle as it looked after its re-modelling or rebuilding of *c.*1715.

16 Lawrence photograph of the garden front of the Cashel palace, 1880–1900.

17 Agar's funeral monument in Westminster Abbey, by John Bacon junior, 1815.

18 Archbishop Charles Brodrick by Hugh Douglas Hamilton, possibly painted in 1795 at the time of Brodrick's elevation to the bishopric of Kilmore.

19 Archbishop Charles Agar: 'nose portrait' by George Dance; engraved and published by Dance, 1809.

20 Agar's son and successor, Welbore Agar, Viscount Somerton and 2nd earl of Normanton, by Sir Thomas Lawrence, begun 1815.

21 'The Union fishery': caricature of January-July 1800 mainly about the vacant primacy.

Acknowledgments

In the course of researching, writing and seeking permission to publish material for this book, I have incurred heavy obligations to many helpful and generous people. In order, therefore, to keep this Acknowledgements section within reasonable bounds, I have confined myself to acknowledgements of a general kind. Where my obligation relates to a particular point in the text, I have recorded it in a foot-note at that place.

My first and biggest debt of gratitude is to Agar's direct descendant, the present earl of Normanton. Lord Normanton has given me the free run of his family papers deposited in the Hampshire RO, has allowed me to quote from them as I pleased, has invited me twice to Somerley to look at family portraits and other relevant material and to give a lecture on his ancestor, and has given me permission to use in the book any pictures I needed from the famous collection at Somerley. These include the five Gilbert Stuarts which are here reproduced for the first time. While taking an interest in the book and giving me every help and encouragement in the writing of it, Lord Normanton has not sought to influence my views in any way, and is unimplicated in any errors of fact or judgement which I may have committed.

My next debt is to my former place of work, the Public Record Office of Northern Ireland. It is literally true that the research for this book began when I joined the staff of PRONI in 1967, even though the book itself has been in preparation only for the last three years. Over the thirty-one years between 1967 and my retirement in 1998, I have been collecting and calendaring, always for other purposes and in other connections, the archival material which has proved to be the foundation for the book. I am fully aware of the privilege and unique opportunity I enjoyed through working in PRONI during that dynamic period in its history. To my PRONI and Departmental colleagues, past and present, I record my thanks for their contribution to that experience.

During 1998–2001, I have incurred huge debts of hospitality to friends who had the misfortune to live near some key archive, or who provided a congenial retreat where I could work in peace. In this connection, I should particularly like to express my thanks to: Mrs Peig and Mr David Butler; Mr and Mrs Ian Campbell; Mr and Mrs S.B.J. Corballis; Professor and Mrs L.M. Cullen; Miss Rosemary Dunhill (former County Archivist of Hampshire and, quite as important, a model hostess); the earl and countess of Dunraven; Desmond FitzGerald, Knight of Glin, and Madam FitzGerald; Mr J.H. Green; the staff of the Kildare Street and University Club, Dublin; Mr and Mrs James King; the Very Rev. Philip Knowles, dean of Cashel; Mr and Mrs Robert Molony (whose three addresses not only inspire confidence in tradesmen, but afford a range of amenities to authors); Mr and Mrs Noel McMullan; Mr and Mrs Thomas Pakenham; Mr and Mrs Kieran Thompson, Ms. Catherine Flynn and the staff of Newport House, Co. Mayo; and Mr and Mrs James Villiers-Stuart.

In addition I have received kindness and invaluable assistance in numerous different ways from a remarkable range of friends and colleagues. Among these, I hope I will be forgiven if I single out: Professor Thomas Bartlett; Mr Mark Bence-Jones; Ms Susan E. Pack-Beresford; Ms Margot Bosonnet; Dr Maurice J. Bric; Mrs Linda Brown; Mr David Butler; Mr P.L. Cavan; Mr Tom Desmond; Sister Eileen Fahy; Mr David Fleming; the Rev. Dr B.A. Follis; Dr Patrick Geoghegan; Dr D.W. Hayton; Dr Welby Henry; Miss Esther Hewitt; Dr Stephanie Holmes; Ms. Aideen Ireland; Professor E.M. Johnston-Liik; Dr Colum Kenny; Mr Barry McMullan; the Rev. Canon W.A. Lewis; Dr John Logan; Mr James McGuire; Mr Neil McGleenon; Mr David McKeown; Dr Eoin Magennis; Mr Brendan O'Donoghue; Miss Shirley Reid; Mrs Margaret Riddels; Sir John Sainty; Mr R.B. Spence; and Mr F.A.J. Emery-Wallis. Most of my close friends have cheerfully endured lengthy discourses on 'the Archbishop' and offered sensible comments and correctives; in this connection, I should particularly like to mention Mr P.L. Cavan (again) and Mr J.R. Eyre-Maunsell. Professor B.M.S. Campbell, while always stressing that this was not his kind of history and 'that the answer lies in the soil', was supportive and encouraging, and made a number of specific suggestions which have considerably improved the book.

A number of experts devoted much time to reading chapters relevant to their particular expertise and giving me comments and feed-back. Mr John Kirwan was inexhaustibly helpful with information about his native Co. Kilkenny. Dr W.E. Vaughan gave me the benefit of his unrivalled knowledge of landlord-tenant relations in the nineteenth century. Dr Edward McParland commented minutely and constructively on the chapters mainly devoted to architecture. The Knight of Glin and Sir Charles Brett also vetted the architectural chapters, and the Knight of Glin helped and advised in more ways than I have space to acknowledge. Dr T.C. Barnard, the Rev. Patrick Comerford, the Very Rev. Dr R.B. McCarthy, dean of St Patrick's, the Rev. Dr W.G. Neely and Mr J. Frederick Rankin steered me out of error in, and made helpful suggestions for, the chapters on ecclesiastical administration. Dr Kenneth Milne, historiographer to the Church of Ireland, read and commented on all the chapters relating to the Church, listened patiently to my out-pourings, either *viva voce* or on the telephone, and always responded with advice, encouragement and help. Professor P.J. Jupp and Dr James Kelly read and commented on just about everything, and were forbearing when they received chapters in the wrong order or were told that what they had read was now superseded! I am much beholden to them for their comments and for the friendship they have shown me throughout the gestation of this book. I am also grateful to Professor Thomas Bartlett for his support and comments when it was in its final stages. While all these colleagues have effected improvements, I alone am responsible for the imperfections which remain.

As something of a technophobe, I have needed all manner of practical assistance from others. Mrs Deborah Duffy word-processed PRONI's calendar of Archbishop

Agar's correspondence (T/3719/C) with her customary expedition and faultless accuracy. Mr T.D. Scott of WP Plus word-processed the text of the book, draft after draft, second thought after second thought. His good humour, de-coding skills and ability to spell have earned my respect and regard, and I thank him warmly for taking such a keen interest in what has been very much a joint project. I have been spared some of the horrors of on-line access by the help and knowledge of Mrs Karen Latimer, the then architectural librarian at the Queen's University of Belfast, and of Mr Gerry Healy, Ms Bernadette Kane and the staff at the Irish desk of the Linenhall Library, Belfast. Since my retirement from PRONI, its Public Search Room staff have taken delight in sparing me nothing (!), but in spite of computerised document-ordering, I have been very well and efficiently treated, and would like to thank all concerned. Late on in the writing of the book, I was made an honorary senior research fellow of the Modern History Department, QUB; this is not only an honour, but confers practical advantages, such as access to a user-friendly xerox machine. Finally, I owe a great deal to Mr Michael Adams and the staff of Four Courts Press who have been efficient and uncomplaining, though I have no doubt that they are glad to see the end of this sizeable tome.

For permission to quote from archive material in their keeping, I should like to thank the following office-holders and/or institutions: the Armagh County Museum; the Armagh Public Library; the Bedfordshire and Luton Record Office; the Bolton Library, Cashel; the British Library Board; the Cheshire Record Office; the Derby-shire Record Office; Down County Museum; Dublin Roman Catholic Diocesan Archives; the Durham University Library; the Hampshire Record Office; the History of the Irish Parliament; Hull University Archives; the Henry E. Huntington Library; the Irish Architectural Archive; the Keele University Library; the Centre for Kentish Studies; the Lambeth Palace Library; Limerick Regional Archives; the National Archives of Ireland; the Trustees of the National Library of Ireland; the Northamptonshire Record Office; the Nottingham University Library; the Pennsylvania Historical Society; the Public Record Office; the Deputy Keeper of the Records, Public Record Office of Northern Ireland; the Registry of Deeds; the Representative Church Body Library; the Royal Irish Academy; the Royal Society of Antiquaries of Ireland; Sheffield Archives (the Sheffield City Library); the Comptroller, H.M. Stationery Office; the Surrey History Centre; the Board of Trinity College, Dublin; the West Sussex Record Office; and the Yale University Library.

I should also like to thank the following owners and/or depositors of archive material: the Most Rev. Lord Eames, archbishop of Armagh, and the diocesan registrar of Armagh; the Marquess Camden; Mrs Ian Campbell; the trustees of the Chatsworth Settlement; the trustees of the Chevening Trust; the Most Rev. Joseph Duffy, bishop of Clogher; Mrs Hazel Dolling (in respect of the Staples papers); the Lord Egremont; Sir Adrian FitzGerald, Bt; the Earl Fitzwilliam and the trustees of the Fitzwilliam Settled Estates; Mr John Fowler; Mrs John Hamilton and Stella, Lady Durand (in respect of the Wynne of Hazelwood papers); the Viscount Harberton; the Lord Hotham; Professor P.J. Jupp; Mr Andrew Kavanagh; Mr James King; Colonel

A.L. King-Harman; the Viscount Massereene and Ferrard; George Mealy & Sons Ltd; the Viscount Midleton; Mr Hugh Montgomery; the duke of Northumberland; the late Miss Faith O'Grady; Mr Dermot O'Hara; the duke of Portland; the Lord Rathdonnell; the earl of Rosse; the earl of Shannon; the Hon. Mrs Jonathan Sykes; the marquess of Tavistock; Major-General M.E. Tickell; Mr Simon Woodworth; and Mr O.C.R. Wynne (in respect of the Primate Stuart papers).

I have already acknowledged, in the list of illustrations on pp xi-xii, most of the help I have received with illustrative material and the permissions to publish it which I have been given. To this I must add my appreciation of the care and skill which Ms Moira Concannon has brought to bear on improving the quality of several of the most unpromising originals.

I am profoundly grateful to the Esme Mitchell trust for a most generous subvention, which has made it possible for the book to be sold at a price which is reasonable in relation to its size.

Finally, I must record my deepest debt, which is to Bruce Campbell and Minnie. They had to coexist with 'the Archbishop' for what must have seemed three long years; they constituted most of the working environment in which the book was written; and when the writing of it veered towards obsessiveness, they reinstated my sense of proportion and sense of humour. I have dedicated the book to Tessa, who died during the early stages of its writing.

A.P.W. Malcomson
February 2002

Introduction

Archbishop Charles Agar, 1st earl of Normanton (1735–1809), was the third son of Henry Agar (1707–46) of Gowran, Co. Kilkenny, by his wife, Anne (1707–65), daughter of Welbore Ellis, bishop of Meath. The Agars of Gowran owned *c.*20,000 statute acres in Co. Kilkenny, and controlled the two Kilkenny boroughs of Gowran and Thomastown. This gave them a minimum of four seats in the Irish House of Commons, plus a fifth when an Agar was elected for the county of Kilkenny (Chapter Three). On the strength of this considerable parliamentary influence, Charles Agar's eldest brother, James (1734–89), was created Baron Clifden in 1776 and Viscount Clifden in 1781.

Charles Agar's ecclesiastical career began with his appointment in 1763 as second chaplain to the lord lieutenant, the 2nd earl of Northumberland, and as rector and vicar of Ballymagarvey and Skreen, diocese of Meath. He was then, successively, dean of Kilmore (and rector of Annagh, alias Belturbet, and vicar of Ballintemple, Co. Cavan, in the same diocese), 1765–8, bishop of Cloyne, 1768–79, archbishop of Cashel, 1779–1801, and archbishop of Dublin, 1801–9. He was the Church's leading improver, administrative reformer and legislator during the period *c.*1775–1800. He was also the Church's leading spokesman in its efforts to resist the dismantling of the Penal Laws against catholics and dissenters, and he was the leading defender of a Church Establishment under frequent political attack from anti-clerical or greedy Anglicans in the Irish House of Commons, as well as from catholics and dissenters (the former of whom remained outside parliament until twenty years after his death, but were restored to the parliamentary franchise in 1793). For the quarter of a century and more between *c.*1770 and 1800, he was very prominent in the cabinets of successive lords lieutenant of Ireland and a formidable speaker, man of business and tactician in the House of Lords (Chapters Four and Eleven). His highest ambition, the archbishopric of Armagh, eluded him; but he did have the consolation of a remarkable accumulation of temporal as well as spiritual honours, to say nothing of the accumulation of great wealth. He was created Baron Somerton in 1795, Viscount Somerton in 1800, and earl of Normanton in 1806, and died possessed of an estate which his wife reckoned was worth £10,000 a year. This was a considerable underestimate, because in addition to landed property of nearly that annual value, it comprised something like £350,000 in investments. Agar's wife was Jane Benson (1751–1826), a member of a clerical family which had been prominent in the diocese of Down and Connor.[1] Agar married her in 1776 and they had three sons and a daughter.

1 Agar's obituary in the *Gentleman's Magazine* for 1809.

I

For the younger son of a substantial squire, whose origins, even by Irish standards, were recent (Chapter One), this was a quite remarkable achievement. In the process of making it, Agar needless to say made enemies: fellow-churchmen and fellow-politicians who were envious of his almost universally acknowledged ability; country gentlemen with parliamentary influence who resented the way in which he frustrated their efforts to fleece the Church; catholics and dissenters who hated him for his efforts to oppose or at the very least delay measures for placing them on a footing of religious, civil and political equality with Anglican protestants; English ministers, whether holding office in Great Britain or, more usually, Ireland, who leaned on him – because of his endlessly praised ability, judgement and sound advice – and yet feared him, and who recognised that, while generally amenable to their behests, there were some issues on which he was likely to dig in; opposition politicians, again in Great Britain as well as Ireland, who thought the contrary, and that he was time-serving and a trimmer; and so on. He also, it should be emphasised, had many admirers, as will be shown in Chapter Two.

Expression to the wildest contemporary animosities against him was given in the obituary published in Watty Cox's *Irish Magazine* for September 1809 (Agar had died on 14 July of that year), and in a mock-epitaph on him in verse form, published in the same issue of that journal.[2]

> The history of this man's political and religious life forms a disgusting picture of avarice, ambition and an abject servility to the measures and politics of the English cabinet. The unfortunate catholics, in other words the people of this prostrated country, were the objects of his contempt and ridicule, ... whom he designated as so stupid a race that they professed a religion only fitted for knaves and fools.[3]   So sordid was his mind that to accumulate wealth, after his passion for power and titles, was the most prevailing feeling of his heart

And so on, with increasing coarseness and virulence. The mock-epitaph is in places too excruciating as poetry to be reproduced, and in other places not altogether comprehensible. The memorable lines are:

> Adieu, thou mitred nothingness, adieu!
> Thy failings many and thy virtues few.
> More true to speak: to every vice a slave,
> A niggard, bigot and a wily knave. ...
> Affliction never bade your heart expand,
> And love of lucre clenched your griping hand. ...
> In early youth the leech-like avarice tore
> Your little heart and sucked the yielding gore,

2 I am grateful to both Professor Kevin Whelan and the Knight of Glin for (almost simultaneously) drawing my attention to this source, and to the latter for kindly sending me a photocopy.   3 For a discussion of this episode, see pp 515-16.

Dried each fine fibre, shrivelled every vein,
And filled the vacuum with deceit and spleen.
The sordid wretch life's fleeting treasure prized,
And lived detested as he died despised.[4]

It should be emphasised that Watty Cox was a former United Irishman and specialised in obituaries which de-constructed 'establishment' figures. His victim immediately prior to Agar had been the 1st marquess of Sligo, an officiously zealous promoter of the Union, especially in his native Connaught. 'His Lordship' wrote Cox 'outlived his country nine years, whose independence he laboured to extinguish, and enjoyed his new title but seven years, the wages of his political labours.'[5] Cox's obituary of Lord Sligo is actually more effective as propaganda than that of Agar, because it is more humorous, restrained and tongue-in-cheek. But it is relevant in that it establishes Cox's motivation and technique, and places in context his character-assassination of Agar.

Character-assassination or not, Cox's obituary has had a major influence on how Agar has been viewed by subsequent writers. Cox's better lines have been re-cycled, for example by the mid-nineteenth century nationalist compiler of biographical *pot-pourris*, W.J. Fitzpatrick;[6] and, stripped of offensive language, some of Cox's charges have a grain of truth in them, particularly the charges of 'avarice, ambition ... [and a] passion for power and titles'. These are not attractive, far less romantic, failings; and the repeated attribution of them to Agar has served to dampen interest in him. In any case, the most important outcome of Cox's indecent attack was that Agar's son and heir, the 2nd earl of Normanton (1778–1868), who must have been familiar with the obituary, became hypersensitive on the subject of his father's reputation and irrationally unhelpful to historians. Nothing else can explain the response of this well educated and civilised man, to requests for access to archival material. In 1815, he was most uncooperative (at least initially) when approached by William Monck Mason, who was researching an archiepiscopally sanctioned *History of St Patrick's Cathedral* (which was published in 1820).[7] John D'Alton, author of *The memoirs of the archbishops of Dublin* (Dublin, 1838), also had cause to complain, which he did very bitterly, of 'the inability or reluctance of his Grace's relatives to afford any materials for this memoir'. More generally, but clearly with Lord Normanton in mind, D'Alton explained:

4 The *Irish magazine or monthly asylum for neglected biography for September 1809.* 5 Page from the *Irish Magazine* for February 1809, preserved – as if by premonition – among the Normanton papers in the Hampshire Record Office (21 M 57/A8/23). 6 Fitzpatrick, *'The Sham Squire'* [*Francis Higgins*] *and the informers of 1798, with a view of their contemporaries* ... (3rd ed., Dublin, 1866), p. 198. 7 *The history and antiquities of the collegiate and cathedral church of St Patrick, near Dublin ..., 1190 to ... 1819* (Dublin, 1820); Monck Mason to Normanton, 14 Mar. and 24 July 1815, with retained copies of Normanton to Monck Mason, 19 Mar. and 10 Aug. 1815, Normanton papers, Hampshire RO, 21 M 57, unreferenced correspondence of the 2nd earl. See also 'A list of books, papers, *etc.*, belonging to the see of Dublin delivered to' Agar's successor, Archbishop Cleaver, by the 2nd earl of Normanton, [1809], NLI, Midleton papers, Ms. 8886.

The brevity of these memoirs, in reference to the later archbishops, is not to be attributed to any neglect or omission of their compiler in applying, both by public advertisement and by private letters, for fuller and authentic materials; ... [but] the individuals applied to either refused to answer; or, as in the instance of one other more intimately connected with a memoir, absolutely refused to communicate what he could not but have well known.[8]

D'Alton did not indulge in the venomous style of denunciation characteristic of Watty Cox. But he did allude to a controversial episode in Agar's career of which Cox had made no mention, the allegedly large amount of money Agar had made out of one lease of the see lands of Cashel (a transaction which D'Alton completely misunderstood – see Chapter Nine). More damningly, D'Alton concluded: 'Ambitious and avaricious, he entirely neglected his episcopal duties for affairs of state and, while the curates of Dublin were starving on £50 per annum, he amassed so much wealth himself that he died worth £400,000.'[9] This was demonstrably unfair as regards the pay of curates (see pp 578–81) and the alleged neglect of episcopal duties. In short, it looks as if Lord Normanton unintentionally did his father a disservice, and that D'Alton's memoir of Agar was the more unfavourable for Lord Normanton's non-cooperation.

Perhaps made wiser by this experience, Lord Normanton welcomed with open arms Sir Charles Ross, the editor of the forthcoming *Memoirs and correspondence of Charles, 1st Marquess Cornwallis* (lord lieutenant of Ireland, 1798–1801), published in 1859. When approached by Ross in 1856, he conducted a search for Agar-Cornwallis letters, and found and actually lent no less than thirty-two. Clearly, he was anxious to predispose Ross to make favourable mention of Agar. He quoted to Ross the somewhat improbable sentiments of the late duke of Wellington (a Hampshire associate of Lord Normanton) that Agar 'had the clearest and soundest head of a[ny] statesman in Ireland from the time of the duke of Portland [1782] to the time of the duke of Richmond, when I was there in office [as chief secretary, 1807–9]'. Ross, on receipt of the 32 letters (which he returned, because they are among Agar's papers today), commented reassuringly that 'there are none which do not do credit to both parties'.[10] This was true, as far as it went. However, as Cornwallis had been slow to appreciate Agar's good points and enlist him in the campaign to carry the Union, and as the archbishopric of Armagh had fallen vacant at the beginning of 1800 and been the subject of not a little lobbying in Agar's favour, the references to Agar in the lord lieutenant's letters to other people are not uniformly creditable.

His one minor attempt at the rehabilitation of Agar having fallen flat, Lord Normanton died, at an advanced age, in 1868. His son, the 3rd earl (1818–96), appears to have been the first of Agar's descendants to take any interest in Agar's papers. Lord

---

8 D'Alton, *Archbishops of Dublin*, pp 351 and 363. 9 Ibid., pp 350–1. 10 Ross to Normanton, 16 Jan., N.D. and 20 Feb. 1856, and Normanton to Ross, 20 Jan. 1856, 21 M 57, 2nd earl's unreferenced correspondence. See also 21 M 57/D58. Ross makes full acknowledgement to Normanton in *The Cornwallis correspondence* (2nd ed., 3 vols., London, 1859), i, p. vi.

Normanton went through them, scribbling attempted identification of writers on them and making other comments, many of them misleading or actually mistaken. His contributions, however, do at least denote some interest in the subject. Nevertheless, in his time Agar's reputation suffered further damage. In 1871, the distinguished, late nineteenth-century, Liberal-Unionist historian, W.E.H. Lecky, devoted a hostile and misleading footnote to Agar in his *Leaders of public opinion in Ireland*. In this, Lecky describes Agar's conversion to the Unionist cause in 1799 as 'amusingly characteristic' of the low political morality of the day. He continues:

> Archbishop Agar was also remarkable for the zeal with which he advocated sanguinary measures of repression during the rebellion of 1798 (Grattan's *Life*, vol. iv, p. 390); for the large fortune which he made by letting the Church lands on terms beneficial to his own family ...; and for having allowed the fine old church at Cashel to fall into ruins, and built in its place a cathedral in the worst modern taste, which he ordered to be represented on his tomb (Stanley's *Westminster Abbey*, p. 324). There is an extremely eulogistic inscription to his memory in Westminster Abbey, and a fine bas relief representing the angels bearing the mitre to the saintly prelate.[11]

As a matter of fact, there is no reference on p. 324 of the first, second or third editions of *Historical memorials of Westminster Abbey by Arthur Penrhyn Stanley, D.D., dean of Westminster* ... (London, 1868 *et seq.*), or anywhere else in the book, to Agar's monument. Lecky was possibly writing from memory, and confused the inscription to Agar with that to Primate Boulter (which was indeed quoted by Stanley). This latter states that Boulter 'was translated to the archbishopric of Armagh, 1724, and from thence to heaven, 1742'. The inscription to Agar, on the other hand, though eulogistic, was not unreasonably so, as will be argued on p. 185 *et seq.* It may be that Lecky thought better of some of these aspersions on Agar, because the footnote does not appear in the revised, two-volume edition of *Leaders of public opinion* published in 1903.

Nevertheless, the damage to Agar was done; for, Lecky's attack undoubtedly encouraged another. In 1876, the Harleian Society published Colonel Joseph Lemuel Chester's *The marriage, baptismal and burial registers of the collegiate church or abbey of St Peter, Westminster* (i.e. Westminster Abbey, where Agar is buried). In a footnote to the entry for Agar's burial, Chester wrote:

> It is to this prelate that the world is indebted for completing the destruction, commenced by his predecessor [actually by Arthur Price, archbishop, 1744–52], of the magnificent old cathedral on the Rock of Cashel; for, there is no evidence to sustain the assertion of his friends that he made a vain attempt to restore it, and felt compelled to supplant it by the erection of a new cathedral. The devotion to this purpose of a comparatively small portion of the immense

11 Lecky, *Leaders of public opinion in Ireland* ... (new ed., London, 1871), pp 157–8*n*. The first edition, published in 1861, had made no impact.

fortune which he acquired in a most extraordinary manner, the loss of which he could scarcely have felt, would have sufficed to preserve for future ages one of the greatest medieval relics of the three kingdoms.[12]

As will be demonstrated in Chapter Seven, most of this was incorrect. But because Chester, and Lecky, did not display the obvious animus and the deplorable taste of Watty Cox, their attacks were the more damaging for their pseudo-magisterial tone. Moreover, in a broader historiographical sense, Lecky and his predecessor and *bête noire* as an interpreter of eighteenth-century Ireland, J.A. Froude, dealt Agar a much heavier blow than these glancing, superficial footnotes. 'The received opinion of the application, or indeed the misapplication, of the [eighteenth-century] bishops [of the Church of Ireland] to matters spiritual and ecclesiological has, in the main, been formed by the nineteenth-century strictures of Froude and Lecky, whose standards of expectation had been very much widened [*sic* – raised?] by the many evangelical and theologico-reformational changes which protestantism had undergone throughout the first half of that century.'[13]

Watty Cox had bracketed Agar with 'the FitzGibbons, Fosters, Beresfords and other scourges that irritated and humbled a suffering country'. By the late nineteenth century, all of them had fared decidedly better in reputation than had Agar. John FitzGibbon, 1st earl of Clare, lord chancellor of Ireland, 1789–1802, had won some grudging praise from J. Roderick O'Flanagan in O'Flanagan's *Lives of the lord chancellors*, published in 1870; and a succeeding, but very different, lord chancellor of Ireland, the 1st Lord Ashbourne, devoted a fulsome chapter to FitzGibbon in his *Pitt: some chapters of his life and times*, published in 1898. (Ashbourne on FitzGibbon is like a mouse's life of a lion.) John Foster, speaker of the Irish House of Commons, 1785–1800, had been praised as well as criticised in Henry Grattan Junior's hagiographic, five-volume *Life and times of the Rt Hon. Henry Grattan*, published in 1839–46 (and the source of Lecky's accusation that Agar had been 'sanguinary' during the 1798 Rebellion); essentially, Grattan Junior did for Foster what O'Flanagan was to do for FitzGibbon. A mid-1870s proposal to publish a *Life of Foster* sub-titled 'The last days of the old Irish parliament', came to naught;[14] but Foster, as the leader of the opposition to the Act of Union, was always receiving vicarious tributes from confused nationalist writers.[15] Finally, John Beresford, chief commissioner of the revenue,

12 Chester, *Westminster Abbey registers*, p. 479.   13 Jeremiah Falvey, 'The Church of Ireland episcopate in the eighteenth century: an overview', *Eighteenth-Century Ireland*, viii (1993), p. 104. 14 Correspondence of Chichester Arthur Skeffington, Speaker Foster's great-grandson, with Samuel Ferguson, John T. Gilbert, Arthur Blennerhassett Leech (the author of the proposed *Life*) and others, Dec. 1874–Dec. 1875 and 27 Apr. 1878, Public Record Office of Northern Ireland (hereafter PRONI), MIC/680/L/11. This correspondence recently came to light in a small, detached section of Foster/Massereene papers preserved at Springfield Castle, Drumcollogher, Co. Limerick. I am grateful to the Hon. Mrs Jonathan Sykes for drawing it to my attention and allowing PRONI to microfilm it.   15 Draft speech proposing that the Newry Repeal Club should be called 'The Foster Club', c.1845, Ross of Bladensburg (Rosstrevor) papers, PRONI, D/2004/2/19; Malcomson, *John Foster: the politics of the Anglo-Irish Ascendancy* (Oxford, 1978), p. 351. The

1780–1802, had an adroit grandson who published a two-volume *Correspondence of the Rt Hon. John Beresford* in 1854. This portrayed its hero as an astute politician, a diligent administrator and the centre of a wide circle of intelligent and agreeable correspondents.[16] One little unpleasantness in which Beresford had been implicated, and which at the time Agar had investigated (see p. 146), was suavely glossed over. Beresford's point of view was also fully represented in *The ... correspondence of William [Eden, 1st] Lord Auckland ...* , published in 1861–2, as was FitzGibbon's and, to a very slight extent, Agar's. But, broadly speaking, not a good word was said for Agar in the whole nineteenth-century historiography. The 3rd earl of Normanton's annotations may have been preliminary to a *Memoirs and correspondence of Archbishop Agar* which never materialised: in the absence of that or any other Agar-orientated publication, Agar's reputation sat by the close of the nineteenth century, and sits today, at the low level to which it had been sunk by Watty Cox, John D'Alton and Colonel Chester. He is still regarded as a good example of what was worst and worldliest in the late eighteenth-century Church of Ireland. He is seen as a political prelate, as having neglected his ecclesiastical responsibilities in the pursuit of political power and personal advancement, and as having been avaricious to the point of misappropriating part of the see lands of Cashel.

And yet, all along, the corrective lay in Agar's own papers, and was not applied because of the misguided protectiveness and/or ignorance of his descendants. Agar's, like most people's, papers on the whole speak well of him. They also include indications that he regarded his archive as the insurance policy for his reputation. This is not to suggest that it is in any way doctored or concocted. Agar was an exceedingly meticulous man of business, to whom it was second nature to make memoranda of transactions in which he was concerned, and *précis* of the contents of letters he received which he endorsed on, or docketed with, those letters. What is significant is that, in these memoranda and *précis*, he almost always uses the third person – 'The Archbishop did such-and-such', 'On receipt of this letter, the Archbishop wrote such-and-such'. This way of recording things denotes an eye to posterity. It looks as if the 2nd and 3rd earls of Normanton not only did Agar a disservice, but failed to follow his fairly clear intentions, by not allowing his archive to speak for itself. However, from at least the start of the twentieth century, there can have been no difficulty about access to Agar's papers. The late Professor Arthur Aspinall sought and obtained it on behalf of The History of Parliament, probably in the early or mid-1950s. But no Irish historian seems to have bothered – perhaps because the earls of Normanton, though eminently traceable to Somerley, near Ringwood, Hampshire, which has been their seat since 1829, were by this time completely divorced from any connection with Ireland. From 1957, when the 5th earl of Normanton deposited all his family and estate papers in the Hampshire Record Office (ref. 21 M 57), the existence and

punch-line of the speech is: 'Yes, gentlemen, he carried a Repealer's heart into the British senate, and that at a time when all were anxious to give the Union a fair trial.' 16 The Rt Hon. William Beresford (ed.), *The correspondence of the Rt Hon. John Beresford, illustrative of the last thirty years of the Irish parliament ...* (2 vols., London, 1854), ii, pp 49–120.

whereabouts of Agar's archive ought to have become widely known. For Irish historians, access has been easier still since the mid-1980s, when the 6th and present earl of Normanton allowed the Public Record Office of Northern Ireland (PRONI) to obtain photocopies of the correspondence section of Agar's papers, which has recently been fully calendared.

Nevertheless, Agar is now probably the most important figure in late eighteenth-century Irish public life who has received no kind of biographical treatment. His papers have been dipped into for other and particular purposes; an awareness of his importance and of his ability has become widespread; but though his name has been frequently mentioned, it has usually been with the qualification that, as well as being able, he was ambitious, avaricious, unscrupulous, worldly, wily, and so on, or any combination or permutation of such epithets. It may be that historians, without giving the matter much thought, have been fearful that his failings were too many and his virtues too few to make for a rounded biography. It may be that political historians have been deterred from attempting his biography because he was a churchman, and the unfamiliar waters of Church history were beyond their navigational skills; this was certainly a consideration which for a long time gave the present writer pause. For whatever reason, an important subject has been for too long unattempted and an important archive untapped.

The correspondence section of Agar's archive alonecontains *c.*1,500 documents, 1767–1809, but unevenly spread over that period. In general, the correspondence becomes more voluminous as time goes on, with the earlier years being particularly sparse in their documentation. But it is not obvious why – for example – there should be 51 letters for 1779, 6 for 1782, 56 for 1788, 12 for 1790 and 24 for 1791. The explanation may be provided by a remarkable letter which has turned up among the papers of the 2nd earl of Normanton. Writing to him in May 1836, a man called Henry Carter, who seems to have been a former servant, confessed that many years ago (perhaps in 1817), when he was clearing the attics of Agar's house in St Stephen's Green, Dublin, he came upon a 'large' trunk of considerable weight full of papers. They had been labelled 'important' by Agar himself, included letters from Pitt and 'were very voluminous'. Carter, having previously assured Lord Normanton that there were no more papers in the house, was loath to admit his error, and so burnt the lot![17] (It is not clear why he was now prepared to make this much more serious admission; perhaps it was because he had ceased to be in the employment of the family or was in the process of making his peace with his Maker as well as with Lord Normanton.) The gaps in Agar's correspondence are certainly redolent of random destruction of this kind.

Yet the material which remains is wide-ranging and important, with its particular emphasis falling on local and national politics and the affairs of the Church of Ireland. Throughout the period 1767–1800, there are important references to the local politics of Co. Kilkenny, where the inherited electoral influence of the Agar family, and their

17 Carter to Normanton, 13 May 1836, 21 M 57, 2nd earl's unreferenced correspondence. Agar's fully referenced, and calendared, correspondence is Hampshire RO, 21 M 57/C: PRONI, T/3719/C).

two boroughs, Gowran and Thomastown, were located. The earliest letters, however, relate to the borough of Callan, Co. Kilkenny, where the principal electoral interest belonged to Agar's uncle, James Agar of Ringwood, Co. Kilkenny, who was killed in an election duel with his rival for control of Callan, Henry Flood, in 1769.[18] During the lord lieutenancy of the 2nd earl of Buckinghamshire (1776–80), there are important letters from Agar to his maternal uncle, former guardian, and political mentor, Welbore Ellis, 1st Lord Mendip (1713–1802), criticising the Catholic Relief Bill of 1778, the repeal of the Test Act in 1780 and Buckinghamshire's general mishandling of the Irish situation.[19] These letters are inextricably mixed up with Agar's campaign to get himself promoted to the archbishopric of Cashel or, preferably, to that of Dublin (pp 148–58). In the mid-1780s, with Cashel the ecclesiastical province affected by the Rightboy movement, the correspondence is occasionally revealing about that movement and highly revealing about the measures proposed in consequence of it in the period 1786–8 (pp 230–40, 444 and 449–54).[20] The correspondence of 1788 also reveals the long-standing and growing tensions between Agar and his ecclesiastical superior, Richard Robinson, archbishop of Armagh, 1765–94. Events leading up to the 1798 Rebellion are well documented, as is the whole process of decision-making in 'the Irish cabinet' of the 1790s. Agar's lengthy and very precise endorsements are particularly valuable in this latter respect, as they often state precisely when cabinets (and he uses the term) were held and who attended them.[21] He himself was the only member of the inner cabinet who had no *ex officio* reason for being there (other members were the lord chancellor, the speaker of the House of Commons, the law officers, the chancellor of the exchequer and the chief commissioner of the revenue) – proof in itself of Agar's political importance. His contribution to the crucially important 'Coronation Oath' argument and to its inculcation in the mind of George III in early 1795 is also fully documented, as is his (belated) contribution to the passing and provisions of the Act of Union in 1799–1800 (Chapters Twelve and Thirteen).[22]

Agar's papers other than correspondence run from 1741 to 1809 and are also very important. They include, for example, accounts (in both the financial and narrative senses of the word) of the dioceses of Cloyne, Cashel and Dublin, 1755, 1771 and 1779–1809. The papers on Cashel, as might be expected, are particularly full. They document Agar's completion of the new cathedral (Chapter Seven), his improvements to the palace (Chapter Eight), his building of churches and glebe-houses (Chapter Five), and his management of the see estate and of his own private estate under the see (Chapter Nine). Moreover, as the quotations so far made from them illustrate, the

18 Ellis Agar, countess of Brandon, to Rev. Thomas Bushe, 25 Oct. 1767, Normanton papers, Hampshire RO, 21 M 57/C/1/1 (hereafter cited, when they have been photocopied by PRONI, under their PRONI reference number, in this instance T/3719/C/1/1); memo. by the 4th Viscount Townshend, [pre-31 Dec. 1769], and letter from Townshend to Sir George Macartney, 31 Dec. 1769, both printed in Thomas Bartlett (ed.), *Macartney in Ireland, 1768–72: a calendar of the chief secretaryship papers of Sir George Macartney* (Belfast, 1978), pp 40–41; and James Kelly, *Henry Flood: patriots and politics in eighteenth-century Ireland* (Dublin, 1998), pp 40–61. 19 Agar to Ellis, 13 Sep. 1776 and 27 Dec. 1779, T/3719/C/10/1 and 13/50. 20 T/3719/C/20–22 *passim.* 21 21 M 57/A41–2. 22 Ibid., A45–6 and T/3719/C/32–4 *passim.*

papers of his successors, the 2nd and 3rd earls of Normanton, have proved unexpectedly relevant. The Normanton estates in Ireland were sold in the late 1880s and very early 1890s, but up to that time, the correspondence and accounts relating to them, and particularly to Agar's controversial Cashel see lands lease, are highly revealing (Chapter Nine). Other sections of the archive which do not pertain to individual members of the family are also important – title deeds, leases, settlements, wills, rentals, accounts, picture inventories, and so on. Agar's career is not comprehensible except in terms of family history before his time (Chapters One and Three) and family history thereafter.

One effect of an immersion in Agar's archive is a refreshing re-assessment of his role in Irish Church history. His achievements as an ecclesiastical improver, administrator and legislator are the main theme of Chapters Five to Eight. One of his acts of parliament, passed in 1795, was actually known as 'the Archbishop of Cashel's Act' (pp 397–9). Chapters Twelve and Thirteen mainly discuss his contribution to the terms of the Act of Union, as they affected the Church of Ireland, and more generally to the survival of the Establishment during the period 1795–1801. In spite of his leadership role in the Church and in the House of Lords, he was twice passed over for the top job in the Church, the archbishopric of Armagh – once in 1794 and once in 1800 (Chapters Four, Ten and Thirteen) – mainly because Armagh in the eighteenth century was sacred to Englishmen. Nevertheless, until his very last years his energy and motivation did not significantly flag, in spite of the frustration of having to carry – in fact to fill the void created by – the inferior men who were archbishops of Armagh or Dublin in the period c.1775–1801 (Chapters Ten and Thirteen). His papers establish other important facts about him and dispel other myths. They show (Chapter Seven) that the medieval cathedral on the Rock of Cashel was too far gone by Agar's time to be capable of restoration, and that he did the next-best thing by shoring it up against further deterioration and by completing, partly at his own expense, the half-built Georgian cathedral in the town of Cashel which was another of the problems he inherited in 1779. They show that, though he made a huge fortune, he did not do so by alienating Church lands, or abusing any of his ecclesiastical trusts (Chapter Nine). Instead, he made it on the stock market. The riches amassed by a number of contemporary ecclesiastics are not so capable of innocent explanation. His papers also show that his politics were not as bloodthirsty before and during the 1798 Rebellion and not as self-interested at the time of the Union, as has hitherto been believed (Chapter Twelve). His papers do not reveal him as a 'saintly prelate' – for example, his will is a damming document, in that it contains not a single bequest to the Church or to a charity. But they permit a balanced, rounded and on the whole favourable assessment of him to be made.

The study which follows is not, however, a biography. To an extent, it might be called a thematic biography – as indicated by the chapter headings. The disregard of chronology may seem at first perverse; but the emphasis is consistently placed on the different contexts in which Agar operated, and lateral comparisons are frequently made between Agar and his contemporaries and near-contemporaries. The Agar of

Gowran family motto was 'Spectendur agendo' – 'Let us be judged by our actions'. But, except to simple, scurrilous souls like Watty Cox, judgement is an exercise in the comparative. Following such comparison, some important conclusions about Agar suggest themselves – for example, that the political influence which he derived from his family hindered as well as helped his ecclesiastical career (Chapter Four), and that, far from being the last of the bad old eighteenth-century ecclesiastics, he (and others) anticipated by three decades the 'graceful' administrative reformers who have hitherto been regarded as a phenomenon of the early nineteenth-century Church (Chapters Five to Seven and Thirteen). Generalizing about a longer period, the near-century between 1730 and 1822, a recent historian of the Church of Ireland has commented:

> The Georgian bishops have suffered from the generalisations that their era is wont to attract. ... Their antecedents, functions and reputation were quite different from those of the Victorian bishops, whose backgrounds were usually academic or, less often, pastoral ... . The Georgian bishops were, by definition, the lords spiritual of Ireland, with responsibilities and residences in the capital, generally men of culture and liberal education ... . The best-known among them, with but few exceptions, made their mark in fields other than the theological or conventionally episcopal. ... Much detailed research has yet to be undertaken, and conclusions now being tentatively drawn can be attested only on the basis of such research. But in order to understand the Georgian Church as it was, rather than as perceived by high-minded Victorians, it is useful to set it in the context of its age and to delineate those features which influenced it.[23]

This, in a sense, is the starting-point for the present study.

Its focus is on administration and politics: Church administration at episcopal level; internal Church politics; and local and national politics as they affected Agar and the Church. The book is not about theology or even religion; it is not about the missionary, evangelical or even educational role of the Church. Instead, it is a study, through the medium of Agar, of what has been summarised in the sub-title as 'churchmanship and politics in Ireland, 1760–1810'. The book concludes, tentatively, that Agar and most bishops of his day were surprisingly zealous and well intentioned, but were deflected from their purpose by the variety of extra-ecclesiastical duties imposed upon them by the system – for example, managerial responsibility for see estates, financial liability for episcopal palaces and even political superintendence of bishops' boroughs. To these enforced distractions was added the influence of political patronage on senior ecclesiastical appointments – an influence of which the bishops were victims as well as beneficiaries, and by which bishops of Irish birth were disproportionately victimised because, right up to the Union, it continued to operate in favour of Englishmen.

23 Alan Acheson, *A history of the Church of Ireland, 1691–1996* (Dublin, 1997), pp 69 and 81. The reader will have to get used to the confusing fact that, of the recent historians of the Church of Ireland, one is called Acheson and the other Akenson.

Writing about 'The making of protestant Ireland, 1660–1760', Professor Connolly has remarked, pithily and wisely: 'The task of the historian ... is to strike a balance between teleology and antiquarianism.'[24] There is certainly much apparent antiquarianism in a study of the mysteries and minutiae of see estates, episcopal palaces, bishops' boroughs and the episcopal promotion system (for which 'system' is far from being the right word). But these things, it will be demonstrated, occupied an inordinate amount, if not the lion's share, of the bishops' time: which perhaps suggests that the historian has to undertake another task – *viz.* that of making sure that his priorities and agenda are not hopelessly out of kilter with those of the group or age which he is studying. This book tries to do more than *study* its subject – certainly to do more than study it from a great distance and from a great height. It tries to evoke Agar's world. In this process of evocation, frequent quotation has been made from Agar's hard-hitting, colourful and literific correspondence; and if this produces a 'life and letters' flavour, that is intentional. The observation of contemporary nuances is fundamental to sound historical conclusions; the past must first be recreated before it can be pronounced upon with any degree of confidence.

In 1997, an obituarist of the late Sir Geoffrey Elton referred to Elton's 'no longer fashionable' view that the past 'must be studied and written on in its own terms and even for its own sake, which meant "giving the past the right to exist within the terms of its own experience".'[25] Perhaps this view is more fashionable, at least in some recent writings on Irish social and political history, than the obituarist knew. Connolly's already-cited work on the entire Protestant *élite* in the age before Agar, is a good example. There is no better expression of the view, or apter conclusion to this introduction, than the few key sentences in which Connolly outlines his own aim

> to look at the protestant *élite* primarily in its own terms: to reconstruct the way in which its members saw the society in which they lived and the issues that seemed to them to matter most. ... None of this means that what follows should be read as an apology or a defence. The point is, rather, that beliefs and attitudes that were shared by all or most of the members of a particular society cannot, by definition, have been either stupid or immoral.[26]

---

24 S.J. Connolly, *Religion, law and power: the making of protestant Ireland, 1660–1760* (Oxford, 1992), p. 3. 25 Patrick Collinson, 'Geoffrey Rudolph Elton, 1921–94', in *Proceedings of the British Academy*, xciv (1997), p. 441. 26 Connolly, op. cit., p. 4.

Charles Agar's ancestry, *c.*1660–1802

There is, to say the least, some doubt about the antiquity of the Agar family. According to one theory, the Agars are of Saxon origin. According to another – that of Agar's great-nephew, the Hon. George James Agar-Ellis, 1st Lord Dover – they originated in the Comté Venaissin, moved to Yorkshire during the French wars of religion in the second half of the sixteenth century, and settled in Co. Kilkenny about 1660.[1] John Hotham, bishop of Clogher, 1782–95, a waspish and witty Englishman on the Irish bench, in a letter of 1785 ridiculing the antecedents of some of his Rt Reverend Brethren, claimed that Agar was 'grandson to a livery-stable ostler in Dublin'.[2] Now, Hotham – though clearly no friend of Agar, whom he elsewhere described as 'a most violent, ambitious, hot-headed Irishman' – was a connection of the Agars by marriage, his cousin, Gertrude Hotham, having married Agar's elder brother, Welbore Ellis Agar. Moreover, Hotham was a Yorkshireman, and Yorkshire was the Agars' reputed county of origin. So, Hotham ought to have been in a position to know. He is clearly out by at least a generation, as enough is known about Agar's grandfather to establish that he had never been an ostler. But some uncertainty envelops Agar's *great*-grandfather, Charles Agar, as will be seen. Interestingly, at about this time just such an allegation was made against Agar's colleague in the lord lieutenant's cabinet, Speaker Foster, another of Watty Cox's 'scourges that irritated and humbled a suffering country'.[3] In Foster's case, too, the allegation was out by at least a generation.

A CONFUSED PEDIGREE: THE AGARS, *c.*1660–*c.*1700

In 1788, Agar's eldest brother, the 1st Viscount Clifden (1734–89), who was certainly neither an historian nor a genealogist – Agar had to restrain him from wantonly changing the family motto[4] – gave Agar the following simplistic (and inaccurate) account of the early history of the Agars in Ireland:

1 Lord Dover (ed.), *Letters written during the years 1686, 1687, 1688, and addressed to John Ellis Esq., secretary to the commissioners of his majesty's revenue in Ireland* (2 vols., London, 1829), i, xxiii.   2 Hotham to his brother, Sir Charles Hotham Thompson, 8th Bt, 5 Oct. 1785, Hotham papers, Hull University Archives: photocopy in PRONI, T/3429/2/9.   3 Malcomson, *John Foster*, pp 2–8.   4 Agar to Clifden, 1 Nov. 1788, T/3719/C/22/40. As a matter of fact, Agar himself adopted a new motto when he was raised to the peerage in 1795, and the 2nd Viscount Clifden assumed the Ellis family motto in 1802.

Our grandmother told me that during the Civil Wars in England it happened in our family as in many others that the husband and wife, father and son, etc., took different sides of the question, that Charles Agar was persuaded by his mother to join the king's party, though his father was a strong Cromwellian, and for his so doing was disinherited by his father, and the estate went to the second son. Charles joined the king's forces here, and by marrying into the Blanchville [also spelt Blanchfield] family acquired an establishment at Gowran, which his son, James, surprisingly [*sic*] improved. ... You recollect the circumstance of King William's having delivered the ... [rod, mace], etc., of the corporation of Gowran to Charles Agar as he passed through the town, and desired him to keep the town for him and his successors until they demanded it of him again, which the family have since held and will I hope long continue to do so.5

Another version of family history connected the Agars of Gowran with the 'Eagars' of Co. Kerry. The armorial bearings registered in the office of arms in Dublin Castle for the two families are different. Yet, according to a history of the Eagars of Kerry, they had a common ancestor in 'Major Robert Eagar of the army of Charles I, [who] resided in Queen's County and married a Miss Hamilton. He left issue two sons, Alexander and Charles. Charles, [the] second son, was the ancestor of the Agars of Kilkenny'.6 When Archbishop Agar's promotion to Cashel was announced in August 1779, his new neighbour, at Dundrum, Co. Tipperary, Sir Cornwallis Maude, 3rd Bt, wrote a letter of congratulation in which he spelt Agar 'Eagar'.7 The difference in the spellings must have worried Agar, particularly after he took up residence in Cashel and became familiar with the Munster as opposed to the Leinster usage, the Kerry as opposed to the Kilkenny. 'About 1784', perhaps in a short-lived attempt to connect the two families, Agar, at a 'visitation' (which sounds heraldic rather than ecclesiastical) of his metropolitan province 'held a general meeting of the family or clan [of Eagar], and the spelling of the name was discussed. As the Irish pronunciation of the name made no distinction between the diverse spellings, it was urged that "Agar" should be the general form to be used.'8

G.D. Burtchaell gives yet another account of the early history of the Agars in Ireland in his *Genealogical memoirs of the members of parliament for [the] county and city of Kilkenny* (Dublin, 1888): 'Charles Agar, who was a native of Yorkshire, appears to have come into Ireland in the parliamentary army [i.e. not the royalist]. In 1664 he paid 2*s*. hearth money for his house in Gowran.' (This squares with the evidence of a late

5 Clifden to Agar, 20 May 1788, T/3719/C/22/17.   6 Jeremiah King, *A history of Co. Kerry, part two* (Liverpool, c.1910), pp 168–9. I am grateful for this reference to Mr Terence Finley of Benton Lodge, Newcastle-on-Tyne. Mr Finley has a female descent from the Rev. Henry Agar (1743–98), youngest brother of Lord Clifden and the Archbishop. He has carried out a great deal of research into family history, the results of which he has generously made available, as frequent acknowledgements and attributions in the text which follows make plain.   7 Maude to Agar, 10 Aug. 1779, T/3719/C/13/31. Maude should have known better, as his father had sat for Gowran, 1703–13.   8 Jeremiah King, op. cit.

eighteenth-century endorsement on a title deed of 1692 among the Clifden estate papers,[9] which states that Charles Agar was 'the first of [the] Agar family resident at Gowran'.) 'He became a member of that corporation and on 3rd May 1687 signed the formal act of surrender by the corporation of its charters, liberties, etc., to James II, addressed in submissive terms to [the duke of] Tyrconnel, lord lieutenant of Ireland. Either on account of this submission, or because he then held no previously forfeited property worth re-confiscating, he escaped being attainted in 1689.'[10] A recent account of 'The Agars of Gowran', partly based on Burtchaell, continues the story of Charles Agar as follows:

> On April 10th 1690, Agar was appointed one of the commissioners for the county of Kilkenny 'for applotting £20,000 per month on personal estates and the benefit of trade, according to the ancient custom of the kingdom, used in time of danger' (*5 James II*). The total raised was £1,932–4–3*d*. Other than expediency, there is little reason to believe that Agar was ever truly a Jacobite. Later in 1690 events had changed in favour of King William and both Gowran corporation and Charles Agar managed to change sides successfully. At a meeting of the corporation held 6th October 1690, ... [he was unanimously elected portrieve, or mayor, of Gowran (following the favour shown him by King William during the royal visit, and remained portrieve for the rest of his life.] In 1695, Charles Agar was appointed a commissioner of Co. Kilkenny for putting in execution an act 'for granting a supply to his Majesty, by raising money by a poll or otherwise' (*7 William III, cap. 15*). ... In 1695, ... he loaned £150 to the corporation of Kilkenny to build the new tholsel. ... He died on February 14th 1696.[11]

Burtchaell was a herald – he held the offices of Athlone pursuivant and register of the college of arms. He also had local knowledge, as a Co. Kilkenny man and the great-grandson of the Clifden agent (from *c.*1795),[12] Peter Burtchaell (1744–1815), whose son and successor, David, lived at Brandondale, a property on the Agar estate at Graiguenemanagh which took its name from nearby Mount Brandon. So G.D. Burtchaell's account, and derivatives from it, of Charles' politic deviation into Jacobitism is much more convincing than the purely Williamite allegiance attributed to him by Lord Clifden.

Other evidence about the protean Charles Agar is meagre and somewhat contra-dictory. No information is forthcoming about his origins and his career prior to 1664.

9 Provisional lease from the 2nd duke of Ormonde's commissioners to Charles Agar of Gowran, 14 Mar. 1691/2, National Archives of Ireland (hereafter NA), D 20062. 10 Burtchaell, op. cit., pp 114–15. 11 Mary Moran, 'The Agars of Gowran (Lords Clifden and Callan)', in *In the shadow of the steeple* [: *the journal of the Duchas-Tullaheerin Heritage Society*], no. 2 (1990), pp 110–11. I am most grateful to Mr and Mrs S.B.J. Corballis of Castlefield House, Gowran, for drawing my attention to this important source. 12 Diana Agar to Agar (her brother), 15 May 1796, T/3719/ C/30/16.

In 1800, Francis Evans of Rathcormack (Co. Cork), who was compiling a *Peerage of Ireland*, wrote to Archbishop Agar seeking more information about Agar's great-grandfather, Charles, and some information about Charles Agar's ancestors.[13] Archbishop Agar was unable (or unwilling) to help;[14] and a pedigree which he himself had drawn up in 1795 (the date of his elevation to the peerage, and required for that purpose) began with Charles Agar.[15] When promoted to an earldom in 1806, Archbishop Agar took 'Normanton' as his title; and Normanton is a small town outside York. Charles Agar is alternatively described as 'of Yorkshire' and 'of York', which strongly suggests that he was actually 'of Normanton' and that Archbishop Agar was aware of the fact and in general knew more about the early Agars than he cared to admit.[16] Charles Agar, regardless of whether he fought for king or parliament, is unlikely to have been the disinherited heir to a landed property. Burtchaell implies, gently, that he came to Ireland as a trooper, not an officer, and less gently that he had nothing worth confiscating in 1689. Both assumptions are borne out by the fact that no Restoration grant, or confirmation, of lands to Charles Agar survives. A hearth tax assessment of 2s. does not suggest that his house in Gowran was impressive.

'About 1660', he married Ellis, daughter of Peter Blanchville, or Blanchfield, of Rathgarvan (near Gowran) and Rathcash, Co. Kilkenny, who came from 'a junior branch of the house of Blanchvillestown', or Blanchfieldstown.[17] Through her he is supposed to have 'acquired a claim to the property of that family'.[18] It can have amounted to nothing more than a claim, since the Blanchville/Blanchfield family were not restored to their estates in the Gowran area at the Restoration. What may have caused confusion is that Rathgarvan, by a transaction of uncertain date and unconnected with the marriage, was afterwards acquired by the Agars of Gowran. At some point subsequent to the 1740s, they renamed it 'Clifden' (a name which has not stuck), and Archbishop Agar's eldest brother took his peerage title from it in 1776.[19] Other lands formerly belonging to the Blanchvilles/Blanchfields which were later absorbed by the Agars of Gowran were: 220 acres in Bennetsbridge, part of the former manor of Blanchvillestown, which James Agar acquired in fee farm from Edward Worth, chief baron of the court of exchequer, in 1710;[20] and the 552-acre Blanchfield's Park, near Gowran, bought by the 2nd Viscount Clifden, *c.*1815–20.[21]

---

13 Evans to Agar, 4 Oct. 1800, 21 M 57, 2nd earl's unreferenced correspondence.   14 Notes on family history by Agar, *c.*1790s, 21 M 57/D48/1–9.   15 Draft of the pedigree lodged 'in the office of arms in the Parliament House', 1795, 21 M 57/D49.   16 I am grateful to the present earl of Normanton for telling me where Normanton is! Because it was an Irish peerage, its territorial designation had to be Irish, so it is described in the patent as 'Normanton, Co. Kilkenny'. Archbishop Agar said it was 'a title taken from part of my own estate in the county of Kilkenny'. He owned the townland of Newtown, barony of Fassadinin, Co. Kilkenny, and claimed that Normanton was an alternative name for Newtown – see 'The state of Earl [*sic*] Normanton's property, 1806', 21 M 57/D23, and Agar to Alexander Marsden, 6 Nov. 1805, T/3719/C/39/18.   17 Moran, 'The Agars of Gowran', p. 110.   18 Burtchaell, op. cit., p. 114.   19 Oral information from Mr John Kirwan of the Kilkenny Archaeological Society; Monica Brennan, 'The changing composition of Kilkenny's landowners, 1641–1700', in William Nolan and Kevin Whelan (eds.), *Kilkenny history and society* (Dublin, 1990), p. 184.   20 Conveyance from Worth to Agar, 5 Dec. 1710, Registry of Deeds, Dublin (hereafter ROD), memorial no. 1681.   21 Release from the 2nd Viscount Clifden to Lord

Confusing though all this is, the 1st Viscount Clifden cannot have been correct when he claimed that Charles Agar 'acquired an establishment at Gowran' through his marriage: he acquired it by leasing the old castle and demesne of Gowran from the 2nd duke of Ormonde.[22]

In fact, Charles Agar's marriage to Ellis Blanchville was mainly important for the children it produced. There were four: James, the heir, who died in 1733; Peter, who died in 1716; Elizabeth; and Margaret. James Agar must have been born in about 1671: 'Both James and Peter appear on the register of Kilkenny college for the years 1685–86 and 1694 respectively. James was aged fourteen and Peter twelve years.'[23] Of the daughters, Elizabeth was the one who, through her marriage, was to be of some significance in subsequent family history, and particularly in relation to Co. Kilkenny elections (Chapter Three). She married, in September 1692, Samuel Bradstreet of Tinnescolly, Co. Kilkenny, by whom she was the mother of Charlotte Bradstreet, who in 1744 married the 10th Viscount Mountgarret, a major Co. Kilkenny magnate.[24] Charles Agar's wife, Ellis Blanchville, died on 10 October 1703.

Like the family of Speaker Foster, the Agars leased or bought all their land, sometimes in small units (particularly in their early days), and received none of it by patent from the crown. Also like the Fosters, they had the good luck or good sense to establish themselves in and around a parliamentary borough – in the case of the Fosters, Dunleer, Co. Louth, and in the case of the Agars, Gowran. In both cases, the advantages of location outweighed the disadvantages of birth. Charles Agar was of sufficient local standing in Gowran to offer himself, unsuccessfully and against the interest of his landlord, Ormonde, as a candidate for the borough at the general election of 1692.[25] Significantly, the letter which documents his candidature also mentions that he had until recently been the postmaster of Gowran – a less than gentlemanly employment. On the whole, it is not incredible that he should have started civilian life in Ireland as a 'livery-stable ostler in Dublin'. 'The evidence suggests ... that it was James Agar, eldest [*sic*] son of Charles, who acquired the lands which gave his family a firm footing in the country ... and was the real founder of one of ... [its] most important gentry families.'[26] Where the Agars differed from the Fosters and most other 'new' families is that their land was mainly of prime agricultural quality.

THE RISE OF THE AGARS, 1692–1746

Once the eighteenth century is reached, Agar family history becomes more firmly based on documentary evidence, taken in part from the corporation records of

Callan's executors, 22 May 1839, NA, D 10149. 22 D.W. Hayton, 'Dependence, clientage and affinity: the political following of the 2nd duke of Ormonde', in T.C. Barnard and Jane Fenlon (eds.), *The dukes of Ormonde, 1610–1745* (Woodbridge, 2000), p. 233. 23 Moran, 'The Agars of Gowran', p. 111. 24 Burtchaell, op. cit., p. 115. 25 Patrick Melvin (ed.), 'Letters of Lord Longford [the head of the then commission for managing Ormonde's estates] and others on Irish affairs, 1689–1702', in *Analecta Hibernica*, xxxii (1985), pp 100–1. 26 Brennan, op. cit., p. 184.

Gowran.[27] Burtchaell's account continues: '[James] Agar ... first entered parliament in 1703 as MP for Old Leighlin, which he represented till 1713. He was MP for Gowran, 1713–14, Callan, 1715–27, and St Canice, 1727 till his death in 1733, thus in each successive parliament sitting for a different constituency. ... He belonged ... to the Tory faction',[28] but like almost all Irish Tories, he was without Jacobite leanings and was swift to transfer his allegiance to the Whigs following the collapse of Irish Toryism in 1715.[29] This partly explains why his own grandson, the 1st Viscount Clifden, born in 1734, was in no doubt of the impeccable and uninterrupted Whiggery of Lord Clifden's forebears.

James Agar's first wife, and his children by her, all died young. 'He married secondly [*c.*1706] Mary, eldest daughter of Sir Henry Wemys of Danesfort [Bennetsbridge, not far from Gowran], MP for the county, and by her (who died 18th April 1771 aged 106) had two sons and two daughters: ... Henry [of Gowran (1707–46)] and ... James [of Ringwood, Co. Kilkenny (1713–69)] ..., of whom hereafter; ... Ellis ... [who married, in 1726 and 1745 respectively, the 7th Viscount Mayo, who died in 1742, and the 21st Lord Athenry, who died in 1749] ..., by whom she had no issue ..., [and] was created a peeress in her own right as countess of Brandon, ... [in] 1758, but died ... in 1789, when her title became extinct; ... [and] Mary, [who] married in 1742 James Smyth of Tinny Park, [Delgany], Co. Wicklow'.[30] As an influence on their nephew, Archbishop Charles Agar, Mary Smyth was completely overshadowed by her forceful sister, Ellis, countess of Brandon. But the marriages of Mary Smyth's daughters – one to Francis Mathew of Thomastown, Co. Tipperary, later 1st earl of Landaff, and another to John Preston of Bellinter, Co. Meath, later Lord Tara – were to be of significance to the career of their cousin, the archbishop.

The countess of Brandon (1708–89) was a *femme formidable*. Her first marriage took her to the west of Ireland, where Lord Mayo inhabited a Gaelic-speaking world of 'riots and irregularities'.[31] Three companies of foot and the building of a permanent barrack were needed in the late 1750s before his cousins, the O'Flahertys of Eyre Connaught, Co. Galway, could be reduced to order.[32] In this alien, and potentially hostile, environment, Ellis Agar acquired survival skills. She was painted twice by the Irish portrait-painter, Philip Hussey, once when married to Lord Mayo, and the second time almost certainly to mark her elevation to the earldom of Brandon in 1758 (fig. 12).

27 Extracts by Agar from the corporation book starting with the year 1687, [*c.*1770?], 21 M 57/A4/1–2. These are of especial interest because the one surviving corporation book starts only in 1736. This latter is in the keeping of the Royal Society of Antiquaries of Ireland (hereafter RSAI), Merrion Square, Dublin (Ms. C7A5).   28 Burtchaell, op. cit., pp 114–15.   29 Hayton, 'The political following of the 2nd duke of Ormonde', pp 211–41.   30 Burtchaell, op. cit., p. 115.   31 Report of the law officers of the crown on the claim of David Bourke to the viscountcy of Mayo, 1770 (which includes evidence back to 1698, some of it from Lady Brandon), National Library of Ireland (hereafter NLI) reports on private collections, no. 138.   32 Edward Willes, lord chief baron of the Irish exchequer, to 1st earl of Warwick, 1761, printed in James Kelly (ed.), *The letters of ... Willes to ... Warwick, 1757–62: an account of Ireland in the mid-eighteenth century* (Aberystwyth, 1990), pp 84–6.

In this second portrait, now part of the collection at Glin Castle, Co. Limerick (where she is irreverently known as 'the hatchet-faced countess'), she is narrowly saved by her *fichu* from being too *décolletée* for a woman of her age (fifty in 1758).[33] It seems that she continued to be a lady of fashion for many years thereafter. In 1783, Bishop Hotham of Clogher (that scourge of the Agars) observed that, though a 'centurian' (he meant a centenarian), she was 'in good health and for aught I know, as handsome as ever. ... Queen Anne's motto (or Queen Elizabeth's?) will suit her Ladyship admirably: "*Semper eadem*" – which a wicked wag once put into English ... [as] "Worse and worse".'[34] Her taste for commemorative portraiture remained with her to the end. When she died at the age of eighty in 1789, it was found that she had stipulated in her will that £300 was to be spent on a 'handsomely executed' monument to her in St Mary's church, Gowran. Furthermore, her legacies to her principal heir were to be hugely reduced unless he built the monument.[35] Archbishop Agar inherited almost nothing from her. But there was a marked physical resemblance between them, particularly in respect of the Agar nose (see pp 86–7). Agar liked and admired her so much that when, later in 1789, he first solicited a peerage, he asked for the title of Brandon.[36]

Though they were probably unusual in the humbleness of their origins, the Agars in other respects conformed to type in Co. Kilkenny. In Kilkenny, the gentry of the eighteenth century 'did not stem, as was the case in some Irish counties, from a base dominated by the older aristocracy, augmented by successive planters, but from one dominated by post-Cromwellian settlers'.[37] Charles Agar, though not

> an original Cromwellian grantee ..., very quickly allied himself to that group and for all intents and purposes can be regarded as one of their number. ... Many of the original grantees sold out immediately, often without even having seen their property. These small parcels of land were subsequently bought up by a few of the more industrious, aggressive and determined ... settler families.

---

33 I am grateful to the Knight of Glin for showing me the portrait and also his file on the portrait. 34 Hotham to Buckinghamshire, 7 Nov. 1783, *H.M.C. Lothian Mss.*, p. 423. 35 'Substance of Lady Brandon's will' of 2 May 1787, in Archbishop Agar's handwriting (he was an executor), 21 M 57/D51/5. The splendid monument to her by Edward Smyth (1749–1812) – Irish Architectural Archive (hereafter IAA), neg. S/859/5 – has the courage to depict her as she was, a characterful old woman. It is currently being restored along with the rest of the church interior by Duchas (the Heritage Service). Three hundred pounds was a lot of money: the monument to the 2nd duke of Argyll in Westminster Abbey states that it had cost £500 half a century earlier, in 1743. 36 Memos. by Agar of his conversation with the lord lieutenant, the 1st marquess of Buckingham, on 25 Mar. 1789, T/3719/C/23/18–19. Confusingly, there was also a barony of Branden (spelt with an 'e'). Ellis Agar took her title from Mount Brandon, Graiguenamanagh, which was part of the Agar of Gowran estate: the Crosbies of Ardfert, Co. Kerry, took their title from Mount Brandon, Co. Kerry. It was actually unusual for two different families to hold two such similar titles at the same time, particularly since the peerages were conferred on two successive days, 15 and 16 September 1758. When Agar was finally created a peer in 1795, he took the title 'Somerton', perhaps because the 3rd Lord Branden, who was also 2nd earl of Glandore, had objected to 'Brandon'. Ellis Agar's peerage narrowly preceded the barony of Branden and was not hereditary, whereas Agar's was subsequent to the barony of Branden and was hereditary. 37 Brennan, op. cit., pp 182 and 187.

Thus, in the eighteenth century, instead of an extensive occupying yeomanry [as envisaged in the Cromwellian settlement of the county], there emerged a numerically small landed aristocracy ... . The Agars were one such family.[38]

Meanwhile, the older aristocracy of Kilkenny, the Ormonde Butlers in particular, were on the wane. The Agars were beneficiaries of this process, even though their gains, initially, were modest by comparison with those of other local families. Gowran had been the chief seat of the Butlers until 1391, when they acquired Kilkenny Castle. At the Restoration, nearly all the Gowran estate (which had been granted to Henry Ireton, then lord deputy of Ireland) was granted to the duke of York, later King James II: only Gowran Castle and its demesne were restored to James Butler, 1st duke of Ormonde. They may have been settled on Lord John Butler, Ormonde's fourth son, because he was created earl of Gowran in 1676. He died without issue in 1677, when his earldom became extinct and his estate was presumably reunited with that of the senior branch of his family. As has been seen, his nephew, the 2nd duke of Ormonde, let Gowran Castle and demesne to Charles Agar at some date prior to 1692.

No version of this lease survives among the Clifden estate papers in their different locations. Among these, the earliest surviving title deed which concerns the Agars (as distinct from previous owners), is a lease to Charles Agar granted in 1692 by the commissioners set up to try to manage the 2nd duke of Ormonde's much-encumbered estates, of the 273 Irish acres of Haggard Street, in the barony of Gowran and the Ormonde manor of Gowran, for three lives at a rent of £50 per annum.[39] Later, in 1711, this lease, along with another of the adjoining 100 acres of Castle Ellis, was converted into a fee farm grant to James Agar, who in the following year bought out the small, fixed fee farm rents, and so became the owner in fee simple.[40] Other acquisitions of Ormonde lands in the manor and barony of Gowran were Bramblestown and Ballyshanemore, sub-let to James Agar by an Ormonde tenant in 1700,[41] and Ballyquirk (284 Irish acres), sold to him 'for a valuable consideration' in 1711.[42] Part of the Agar estate in Kilkenny City also derived from the 2nd duke of Ormonde, under a conveyance to James Agar of 1705.[43] Further afield, 'Agar acquired lands in Fassadinin barony in the area of Kilmocar [*c.*1710], which ... had been Ormonde property. Here he owned eight townlands in the hill country between [two major estates in Fassadinin, the] Wandesford and [the] Mountgarret ..., totalling 3,888 [statute] acres.'[44] In 1881, the rental of the 'Kilmocar estate' was £1,812. Deliberately excluded from the acreage figure were three or four townlands – Coolnambrisklaun, Tomakeany and the two Maudlins – which had been let in fee farm by Ormonde before his sale to James Agar.[45]

38 Moran, 'The Agars of Gowran', p. 127.   39 Provisional lease, 14 Mar. 1691/2, NA, D 20062. 40 Conveyance of the fee by the Ormonde trustees to Agar, 12 Mar. 1711/12, ROD, memorial no. 2875.   41 Finding list made by the late Edmond Keane of NLI of the contents of the 10,000 boxes in the Irish Land Commission archive, in this case Box LC 1752, documenting sales under the Land Acts of 1881–1909.   42 Lease for a year of Ballyquirk, 3 Oct. 1711, NA, D 20056.   43 Deed, 24 Sep. 1705, Annaly/Clifden papers (in the possession of James King Esq., Rademon, Crossgar, Co. Down), F/8/1.   44 Moran, 'The Agars of Gowran', p. 111.   45 Rental of the Clifden estates, 1881, Annaly/Clifden papers, G/1/1. The townlands comprising the Kilmocar estate were:

However, James Agar's biggest, single purchase of land came from another branch of the Butler family, the Jacobite Viscounts Galmoy (the 2nd duke of Ormonde did not declare himself a Jacobite until much later, in 1715). The vendor to James Agar was the trustees of the forfeited estates (who had been set up by an act of the British parliament in 1700), and the purchase was so big that it made him 'the largest individual purchaser of forfeited lands in Kilkenny'.[46] The trustees of the forfeited estates conducted between 1702 and 1703 what with hindsight was the sale of the century. But, at the time, there were doubts about the goodness of the title they were able to convey. Moreover, the market was glutted and money was scarce. In 1703, James Agar bought from the trustees 3,776 profitable Irish acres in Co. Kilkenny, which included the lands formerly belonging to Duiske Abbey (Graiguenamanagh). Most, and perhaps all, of these acres were part of the 11,356–acre estate in that county of the forfeiting Jacobite general, Piers Butler, 3rd Viscount Galmoy.[47] There is some doubt about the provenance of *c.*1,000 of them (the poorish grazing lands of Castlewarren, etc., barony of Gowran), because the deed whereby the trustees sold these to James Agar for £812 mentions another forfeiting Jacobite, Sir Redmond Everard, as the previous proprietor.[48] The Everard family were not old-established landowners in this part of the county, so it looks as if Everard may have derived his title in some way from the 'Dame Elizabeth Butler' who was the Restoration grantee and whose husband succeeded as 3rd Viscount Galmoy in 1667.[49] In making this large, 3,776–acre purchase, James Agar must have temporarily over-stretched himself; for, it looks as if he immediately sold *c.*800 of the Duiske Abbey/Galmoy acres to Capt. Ralph Gore (*c.*1653–1721) of Barrowmount, Goresbridge. Although Gore gave the town or village of Goresbridge its name, the Agars continued to own most of it.[50] By 1709, James Agar was again in funds. In that year, he bought from the Hollow Blades, an English company who had stepped in to relieve the trustees of over 250,000 acres all over Ireland which had failed to find resident or local purchasers,[51] no less than 3,114 acres in the Graiguenamanagh/Thomastown area (the lands of Cooleroe, Old Grange, Raheendonore, etc., also the former property of Lord Galmoy, and all in the barony of Gowran), for the large sum of £2,228.[52]

James Agar's temporary shortages of ready money are understandable in one who was financing each purchase out of its predecessors. Their most serious consequence for the future was that they prevented him from buying 'part of the town and the greater part of the lands of Gowran'. This property amounted to 1,278 Irish acres (the corporation's lands, which James Agar's son, Henry, eventually came to control,

Byrnesgrove, Kilmocar, Moyne, Rathkyle, Sleveen, Tinnalinton, Toorbeg and Toormore. **46** Brennan, op. cit., p. 184. **47** J.G. Simms, *The Williamite confiscation in Ireland, 1690–1703* (London, 1956), pp 179 and 182. **48** Trustees' conveyance, 19 June 1703, NA, D 20046. **49** I am grateful to John Kirwan for keeping me right about the Everards. **50** Mary Lightbown, 'The Gores of Barrowmount and their memorials', in John Kirwan (ed.), *Kilkenny studies in honour of Margaret M. Phelan* (Kilkenny, 1997), p. 104. I am indebted to John Kirwan for drawing this essay to my attention. **51** Simms, *Williamite confiscation*, pp 150–154. **52** Conveyance, 23 June 1709, NA, D 20108A.

amounted to 1,300), and it had been granted to the future James II at the Restoration and so had been forfeited and sold by the trustees. It was bought by the Hollow Blades, who re-sold it in 1704 to Lewis Chaigneau, a Dublin merchant, and other Huguenot-sounding associates.[53] In 1714, Lewis and David Chaigneau granted the Hollow Blades property in fee farm to one Joseph Bayly, who thus became in effect the owner, subject to a fixed rent of £210. James Agar bought out the Chaigneau interest for £4,620 in 1725,[54] but this now consisted only of the head rent and whatever rights and reservation had been retained by the Chaigneaus under the 1714 fee farm grant. In 1771–2, James Agar's grandson and namesake, the future Viscount Clifden, was fighting a lawsuit with Bayly's grandson and successor, John, over rights of way through Bayly's land to the corporation land controlled by Agar. Even a century later, it was a problem for the administration of the Agar estate in Gowran 'that Lord Monck [whose ancestor had bought Paulstown, near Gowran, in 1718, and presumably other land in the area besides] possesses some isolated property within the town'.[55] The franchise in Gowran (and in Thomastown) did not depend on owning or leasing property within the borough boundaries, but on being a burgess or freeman of the corporation. Nevertheless, it was more convenient for aspiring patrons like the Agars to control such boroughs by means of resident voters and to reward (or punish) them in the various ways available to a landlord. One key part of the once united Gowran estate which James Agar did succeed in buying, 'some time after 1710', was the castle and demesne of Gowran.[56] Built *c.*1385, the original castle was virtually destroyed by Cromwellian artillery in 1650. What it consisted of *c.*1710 is a matter of conjecture.[57] Then, 'in 1713, after a disastrous fire, James Agar made great alterations to it by casing it with stone and making a front two storeys high of nine windows with a pediment in the centre'.[58]

In 1713, James Agar's total estate rental was estimated as £700 per annum.[59] He made further purchases of land post-1713, but the lion's share of these did not pass under the terms of his will to his elder son. His major purchase, apparently made in May 1718, was of the Rower estate in the baronies of Knocktopher and Ida in south-east Kilkenny, formerly the property of Thomas Crawford of New Ross, Co. Wexford, who had been MP for that borough from 1692 until his death in 1707. In 1881, the Rower estate amounted to 3,361 Irish acres at a rental of £3,741 per annum.[60] It

53 Conveyance, 9 Feb. 1703/4, and case papers, 26 Aug. 1771 and 3 Apr. 1772, NA, D 20080, M 3242 and M 3244.   54 Conveyance, 5 May 1725, NA, D 20097.   55 Report on the future management of the Clifden estates in Ireland by the head agent, Charles William Hamilton, c.1870, PRONI, Register of Irish Archives, Hamilton of Hamwood (Dunboyne, Co. Meath) papers, A/25/3. The original is now in NLI.   56 Hayton, 'The political following of the 2nd duke of Ormonde', p. 226.   57 Again, I am grateful to John Kirwan for his guidance.   58 Moran, 'The Agars of Gowran', pp 111–12. For a sketch by 'R. Gibbs' of this house as it looked in 1813, just before it was replaced by the present building, see fig. 15; the original is in the collection of the Knight of Glin.   59 Estimates of the rentals of members of the Irish House of Commons in 1713, Blenheim Palace papers, BL: photocopy in PRONI, T/3411. It is a coincidence that this information should come from Blenheim, since James Agar's great-grandson, the 2nd Viscount Clifden, married a daughter of that house in 1792.   60 Rental, 1881, Annaly/Clifden papers, G/1/1.

comprised some 25 townlands, including Ringwood, and the income from 'the ferry and boats of Old Ross and New Ross', i.e. the bridge and ferry at Mountgarret, which crossed the River Nore from the Rower to New Ross.[61] At James Agar's death in 1733, the Rower estate (including the ferry), and premises in Kilkenny and Waterford Cities and elsewhere, passed under the terms of his will[62] to his second son, James Agar of 'The Roar'. 'The Roar' was probably an earlier name for Ringwood, which became the seat of this cadet branch of the family and remained so until the late 1780s. James Agar of Ringwood later, in 1765–6, purchased the Callan estate of the 2nd Lord Desart, some twenty miles from and to the north-west of the Rower, and with almost as high a rental in 1881 – £3,241 per annum as compared to £3,741.[63] But this was an acquisition of his own and not an inheritance from his father. The rest of James Agar of Gowran's estate passed at his death in 1733 to his elder son, Henry. Henry, too, was a purchaser of land, though on a more modest scale. In particular, he bought and leased lands and tithes belonging to the financially straitened corporation of Kilkenny, who in 1741 still owed him £800 on foot of a loan made to them by his father.[64] However, most of Henry Agar's acquisitions did not become permanent additions to the Agar of Gowran estate, but were used as a provision for his younger children.

After 1713, no reliable eighteenth-century figures for the acreage and/or rental of the Agar of Gowran estate are available. A list of the chief interests in Co. Kilkenny and the size of their rentals was drawn up in 1775, the year before a general election was due, for the use of the Agars' then partners (and rivals) in the representation of the county, the Ponsonby family headed by the absentee 2nd earl of Bessborough.[65] Lord Bessborough was by then the largest landowner in Kilkenny, and the list states his rental as £14,000 per annum. However, the reliable figure given for the gross rental of his estates in all parts of Ireland, not just Kilkenny, twenty years later, in 1793, was £11,600.[66] Since the 1775 list is unreliable in respect of the county interest for whom it was compiled, it is not likely to be more accurate about the Agars. In their case, it gives £4,000 as the rental of the Gowran branch and £7,000 as that of the Ringwood. It is inherently improbable that the junior branch of the family was much better-off in terms of landed income than the senior; the figures would be more convincing if they were the other way round. In 1802, William Tighe of Woodstock, Inistioge, Co. Kilkenny, in his *Statistical observations relative to the county of Kilkenny* (Dublin,

61 Conveyance, 29 May 1718, Annaly/Clifden papers, F/7/1.   62 Contemporary copy of the will, 9 Sep. 1733, 21 M 57/T285.   63 Annaly/Clifden papers, F/6/1, F/7/1, F/81–2 and G/1/1. 64 List of deeds relating to Lisnafunshin, barony of Fassadinin, Co. Kilkenny, sold by the corporation of Kilkenny to Henry Agar in 1736–41, 21 M 57/T358; assignment of mortgage affecting the tithes of New Ross and various townlands, all held by the late Alderman Thomas Barnes under the corporation and sold by him to the late Henry Agar, 3 Jan. 1769, 21 M 57/T363. After Henry Agar's death, Lisnafunshin went to the future archbishop and the corporation property to the archbishop's sister, Diana Agar.   65 Thomas U. Sadleir (ed.), 'Manuscripts at Kilboy, Co. Tipperary, in the possession of the Lord Dunalley', in *Analecta Hibernica*, xii (1943), pp 144–7.   66 Ben. Caldwell to 4th Earl Fitzwilliam, 17 May [1793], Fitzwilliam papers, Sheffield Archives (the Sheffield City Library): photocopy in PRONI, T/3302/2/68.

1802), credited the Gowran branch, then headed by the 2nd Viscount Clifden, with *c.*20,000 statute acres in Kilkenny[67] – an estimate which is believable. In 1815, the estates of the two branches merged, when the Agars of Ringwood became extinct in the legitimate male line.[68] The only thoroughly reliable estate office evidence dates from the last third of the nineteenth century onwards,[69] long after this merger (and other distorting, intervening events), and is of little help in reconstructing the situation in the eighteenth century.

What is fairly clear about that situation is that, by the 1730s–1740s, settlement and other charges on the estate were becoming burdensome. This is understandable, in view of the fact that James Agar had inherited little from his father and had had to buy – partly with borrowed money – most of the *c.*20,000 acres. He also, as a *nouveau riche*, had to expect to pay disproportionately highly in order to make 'good' marriages for his two daughters – not that the two marriages of his elder daughter, Ellis, the future Countess of Brandon, were in reality all that 'good'. Her successive husbands were two peers of distinguished Old English lineage (Lord Athenry was the bearer of the oldest title in Ireland), but in addition to being Connaught backwoodsmen, were so impoverished that they and/or other members of their families (Ellis Agar included) were in receipt of 'aristocratic dole' from the Irish pension list. Worse still, Athenry seems to have been a crypto-catholic rather than a clearcut convert to the Church of Ireland.[70] James Agar's younger daughter, Mary, was still unmarried at the time of his death in 1733, but his will, made in the same year, establishes that her marriage portion was £8,000[71] – a large sum in comparison, say, with the £4,000 which the 1st earl of Bessborough gave with his daughter in 1739.[72] Ellis Agar had received £4,000 on her first marriage in 1726.[73] But, as she had to be re-portioned on the occasion of her second marriage in 1745,[74] and as it was unusual to portion daughters differentially, it was probably the premature death of her first husband which forced the portions of both sisters up to £8,000. By contrast, James Agar's elder son and principal heir, Henry, received only £5,500 with his wife, Anne Ellis, only daughter of Welbore Ellis,

67 Quoted in Moran, 'The Agars of Gowran', p. 126. The figure is repeated (or perhaps arrived at independently) in Edward Wakefield, *An account of Ireland statistical and political* (2 vols., London, 1812), i. 264.   68 Will of George Agar, Lord Callan, son and successor of James Agar of Ringwood, 1809, and probate, 1815, NA, T 10997.   69 Rental of the Clifden estates, 1881, Annaly/Clifden papers, G/1/1. In the archive recently established in Kilkenny Castle, there are other Clifden rentals, some of them of earlier date, which I have not had an opportunity of consulting. These comprise two rental fragments for the 1840s, and two runs of rentals, 1873–95 and 1898–1920. I am grateful for this information to John Kirwan.   70 Ms. civil list establishment of Ireland, 1749 (author's collection); Patrick McNally, *Parties, Patriots and Undertakers: parliamentary politics in early Hanoverian* Ireland (Dublin, 1997), pp 100–01; Connolly, *Religion, law and power*, p. 153.   71 Copy of James Agar's will, 9 Sep. 1733, 21 M 57/T285.   72 I am grateful to John Kirwan for suggesting this comparison.   73 Deed of re-settlement, 28 Feb. 1729/30, NA, D 20069.   74 The settlement made on the second marriage has proved elusive. By a deed of 6 May 1746 (ROD, memorial no. 83380), James Agar seems to have conveyed to Lord Athenry a 'great house, offices and three gardens' on Lazar's Hill, Dublin, worth £500–plus (perhaps a great deal more than £500?). This may be a post-nuptial settlement. Ellis Agar's financial contribution to the second marriage would also have included (notionally)

bishop of Meath, whom Henry Agar married on 29 May 1733.[75] The Bishop's other children, with the exception of one son, Welbore Ellis, the future Lord Mendip, had all died young; so the Bishop must have been in a position to portion Anne Agar more generously had he so wished. Presumably, he took the view that he had already 'condescended'[76] sufficiently to the *parvenu* Agars in allowing her to marry among them. The other obvious reason for the level of charges falling upon the Agar of Gowran estate was James Agar's decision to establish his younger son, James Agar of Ringwood, as a considerable landowner in his own right with the Rower estate as his appanage. If borrowed money had contributed to its purchase, that borrowing probably remained a charge on the estate of the senior branch of the family.

There is one indication that, even before his death, James Agar of Gowran was beginning to feel the pinch. In 1730, he found it necessary to substitute the lands of 'Cloghlen' (probably Cloghala, near Gowran) and Huntingstown, Co. Kilkenny, for £2,500 of his daughter, Ellis', £4,000,[77] which suggests that he had over-reached himself in the buying of land. Surprisingly, this did not cause him to trim his testamentary dispositions, which included unnecessary bequests of £3,000 to James Agar of Ringwood, £1,000 to his new daughter-in-law, Anne Agar, and the interest on £1,500 to his daughter, Ellis. His elder son, Henry Agar of Gowran (husband of Anne), provided adequately, but not lavishly, for his younger children. After all, the family were on a more secure footing socially by his generation, and he did not need to bid as high as his father in the marriage market. However, Henry Agar did spend lavishly on electioneering in the Agar boroughs of Callan, Gowran and Thomastown, Co. Kilkenny, as will be seen in Chapter Three. Plainly, in spite of having made a more modest provision for his family, he was somewhat strapped for cash when he in turn came to make his will, in September 1743, to which he added a codicil in September 1746, just before his death. To his eldest son and heir, James Agar Junior, the future Viscount Clifden (b.1734), he left the Agar of Gowran estate; to his next two sons, Welbore Ellis Agar and the future Archbishop (both b.1735), he left £4,000 and a couple of Co. Kilkenny townlands each; and to his fourth son, Henry Agar (b.1743) and his posthumous daughter, Diana (b.1746), he left £4,000 each, charged on the land and cash which constituted his not-otherwise-disposed-of personal estate.[78] This last proved barely sufficient to answer the legacies to Henry and Diana.[79] In the end, after some interfamilial juggling, it was arranged that Henry should get his £4,000 in cash in 1767, and that Diana should be assigned all the land.[80]

the capital value of her widow's jointure charged on the estate of her late first husband.   **75** Deeds of lease and release on the occasion of the Agar-Ellis marriage, 3–4 May 1733, ROD, memorial no. 50711; Burtchaell, op. cit., p 135.   **76** For this notion of 'condescension', see Malcomson, *The pursuit of the heiress: aristocratic marriage in Ireland, 1750–1820* (Belfast, 1982), p. 11.   **77** Deed of re-settlement, 28 Feb. 1729/30, NA, D 20069. I am grateful to John Kirwan for identifying Cloghala.   **78** Copy of Henry Agar's will, 22 Sep. 1743, and codicil, 26 Sep. 1746, 21 M 57/T363.   **79** Case for counsel's opinion, 24 May 1766, 21 M 57/T363.   **80** Conveyances, mainly to Diana Agar, of parts of the lands constituting the personal estate, 24 Oct. and 18 Nov. 1766, 30 Nov. 1770 and 15 July 1773, ibid. and T364; articles of agreement between Henry and Diana Agar, 12 Sep. 1767, ibid., T363.

THE ELLIS FAMILY, *c.*1660–1734[81]

If Anne Agar (*née* Ellis) was a somewhat disappointing marriage connection from the narrowly financial point of view, in other respects the contribution of her family to the future of the Agars, and particularly to that of her third son, Archbishop Charles Agar, was of crucial importance. First, the connection with the Ellises inaugurated the Agar family tradition of being educated at Westminster school and 'the greatest college' in England, Christ Church, Oxford,[82] which was also 'much patronised by those born into or designed for the higher reaches of the Church of Ireland' (see pp 186–7). Second, the presence of two Anglican divines among his maternal ancestors must have had a bearing on Agar's choice of career and on the starting-point of that career; while it was standard practice for English clergymen like Agar's grandfather, Welbore Ellis, bishop of Meath, to come to Ireland as viceregal chaplains and thence be preferred to Irish bishoprics, it was much more unusual for an Irish clergyman like Agar to pursue this course. Third, it is important to an understanding of Agar's role in Irish politics to bear in mind that one side of his ancestry was not Anglo-Irish but very largely English. Finally, the presence of one Roman catholic divine in Agar's Ellis ancestry may have had a bearing on the good personal relations with Irish catholic ecclesiastics which were later to be characteristic of him (see pp 324–8).

The Ellises were originally from Yorkshire, where families of that name were prominent in the Doncaster/Leeds/Pontefract/Wakefield area and are thought to have been of Norman extraction ('Ellys') from the area of Lisieux. The Rev. John Ellis (1606–81), grandfather of Anne Agar and her brother, Lord Mendip, appears to have been the son of a younger son of a branch of the Ellises seated since the fourteenth century at Kiddal Hall, near Leeds. The Rev. John Ellis had been a fellow of St Catharine's College (then Hall), Cambridge, and was rector of Waddesdon, Buckinghamshire, from 1659 or 1660 until his death. His eldest son, John Ellis (1643–1738), was secretary to Sir Leoline Jenkins, British representative at Nimeguen during the negotiations with the Dutch in 1676–9. Later, he was secretary to Thomas Butler, earl of Ossory (1678–80), and then to Butler's father, the 1st duke of Ormonde. Ellis was secretary to the commissioners of the revenue in Ireland, 1682–8, and then seems to have returned to London to consolidate his position with the new *régime*. This he did with success, having been known personally to William III, then Prince of Orange, in the second half of the 1670s. In 1689 he became 'English' (as opposed to Irish) secretary to the young 2nd Duke of Ormonde, and remained so until 1695.[83] In 1691 he was appointed commissioner for transports and in 1695 under-secretary of state,

---

81 The information on the Ellises which follows has been kindly communicated – unless otherwise attributed – by Mr Terence Finley.   82 3rd duke of Portland (the home secretary) to 1st Marquess Cornwallis (the lord lieutenant of Ireland), 28 June 1799, PRO, Home Office papers (microfilmed by PRONI, ref. MIC/224), HO 100/87, ff. 23–4. However, it should be noted that Henry Flood, another Kilkenny man and a slightly older contemporary of Agar, had preceded him to Christ Church.   83 Hayton, 'The political following of the 2nd duke of Ormonde', p. 228.

serving in this latter office for ten years. He was appointed comptroller of the mint in 1701 at a salary of £500 per annum, was confirmed in this position in 1702, but was deprived of it in 1711. In 1710, under the last of a series of private acts of parliament and increasingly desperate measures to retrieve Ormonde's hopeless financial situation, Ellis became one of the trustees of the Ormonde estates.[84] In that capacity, he was party to at least one conveyance of Ormonde land to James Agar of Gowran.[85] Ellis died unmarried in 1738, aged 95, at his house in Pall Mall.

The famous Ellis correspondence in the British Library consists of five large volumes of correspondence, 1642–1712, between and among the Ellises, principally John.[86] In 1829, George James Agar-Ellis, Lord Dover, son and heir of the 2nd Viscount Clifden, edited and published the letters covering the years (1686–8) leading up to the Glorious Revolution, which are mainly addressed to John Ellis, then in Ireland. They describe the gradual build-up to the invasion by William of Orange and the abdication of James II. Ellis' nephew, Lord Mendip, must have been fully conversant with this archive; and Mendip took the view that Ellis – 'by an uncommon share of modesty and of political timidity' – failed to take advantage of his early contact with William III and of that monarch's high opinion of him and desire to promote him.[87] But it was also said of Ellis that 'By making good use of his opportunities he amassed enormous wealth'; and that he 'was a man of excellent business habits, industrious, ... and obliging'. Exactly the same might have been said of his great-nephew, Archbishop Agar.

John Ellis' next brother was Sir William Ellis (1647?–1734). In 1678, through the influence of the 1st duke of Ormonde (lord lieutenant of Ireland, 1676–85), he was appointed with his brother, Welbore, later bishop of Meath, to 'a lucrative sinecure' in the Irish customs, which gave him the wherewithal to acquire a considerable estate in Ireland. He was secretary to Tyrconnel, James II's Roman catholic lord lieutenant, and was knighted at this time (1687). In 1688 he was appointed, and served briefly as, clerk to Ormonde's palatinate court of Tipperary.[88] He was attainted in 1691 and went into exile as treasurer to James II and then to his son, the 'Old Pretender'. His estate in Ireland was forfeited; but, as he had borrowed £1,231 on its security from his Williamite brother, John, the latter received a grant of the forfeited estate. John Ellis, finding that it 'was encumbered to near its value', petitioned parliament for relief, which was granted in 1702. According to Lord Mendip, the estate was originally worth £3,000 per annum, but was reduced by fraud and chicanery to £900.[89] In its reduced state, it comprised the Kildare and Meath estates which were inherited by Lord Mendip: the Brownstown estate, near The Curragh, comprised nearly 1,000 statute acres in 1883, and the Clondelee estate, near the Hill of the Down, Co. Meath,

84 Ibid., p. 218. 85 The already-mentioned conveyance of Haggard Street and Castle Ellis, 12 Mar. 1711/12, ROD, memorial no. 2875. 86 Described as follows by Terence Finley: BL, Add. Mss. 28930–34; vol. i (28930), 1642–86; vol. ii (28931), 1687–99; vol. iii (28932), 1700–6; vol. iv (28933), 1707–9; vol. v (28934), 1709–12. 87 Ellis to Agar, 25 Aug. 1788, T/3719/C/22/32. 88 Hayton, 'The political following of the 2nd duke of Ormonde', p. 230. 89 Ellis to Agar, 25 Aug. 1788, T/3719/ C/22/32.

comprised 500 acres. Sir William Ellis died in Rome in 1734, unmarried and a
protestant. Philip Ellis (1651?–1726), the third brother, was emphatically not a protestant. He ran away from Westminster, joined the Benedictine order and became a
monk at Douai. He was the senior of the Benedictines who officiated in James II's
private chapel at St James', and it was in this chapel royal that, according to Lord
Dover, he was 'consecrated a titular bishop of the English Roman catholic Church ...
on Sunday, May 6th, 1688'.[90] Philip Ellis was a confidant of James II, and after a brief
spell in Newgate prison, joined the King in exile, receiving from him a gift of £1,500.
He subsequently became bishop of Segni, near Rome, and founded a seminary there.
Compared to the Jacobitism of these two Ellises, that of Charles Agar of Gowran was
token indeed.

Welbore Ellis, bishop of Meath (1652?–1734), the fourth brother, was educated at
Westminster and Christ Church (BA, 1684; MA, 1687; DD, Trinity College, Dublin,
1732). He became a prebendary of Winchester in 1696. Welbore was the family name
of the Rev. John Ellis' wife, Susanna (1623–1700), whose father, William Welbore, was
a merchant in Cambridge. Through the influence of his brothers, Welbore Ellis was
appointed chaplain to the 2nd duke of Ormonde in 1693 and accompanied the latter
to Ireland when he was appointed lord lieutenant in 1703. But letters from Welbore
Ellis in the Ellis correspondence in the British Library show that he was in Dublin a
good deal between 1700 and 1702; in particular, one of 8 June 1702 describes the start
of a dispute over the rights and immunities of Christ Church Cathedral, Dublin, in
which Ellis was soon to become a protagonist. In 1705, again through Ormonde's
influence, he was appointed bishop of Kildare and *ex officio* dean of Christ Church.
He was not made bishop of Meath until 1732.

During his time at Christ Church, the dean and chapter were engaged in a series
of protracted and unsuccessful lawsuits which continued for nearly a quarter of a
century, when they were ended by a decision of the supreme appellate authority, the
British House of Lords, in 1724. They had come to a head with the appointment of
the domineering William King as archbishop of Dublin in 1703. King claimed the
right to be enthroned in whichever of the two Dublin cathedrals he chose; he also
claimed the right to conduct a full visitation of Christ Church, though Christ Church
considered itself exempt from episcopal visitation because it was 'a peculiar of the
crown's own making' or, more simply, a chapel royal. The previous dean had hoped
that his successor would 'take up the gauntlet that I lay down', and was not
disappointed: 'the pace of confrontation if anything accelerated under Welbore Ellis'
from 1711 onwards.[91] Apart from the jurisdictional matters in dispute, there were
factious, politico-theological differences between the chapter and their archbishop.
Christ Church, Oxford, from which Ellis and 'two of the most formidable spokesmen
for the "High Church" party among the bishops' haled, was the 'citadel of Oxonian

90 *Ellis correspondence*, i, xviii.   91 Kenneth Milne (ed.), *Christ Church Cathedral, Dublin: a history*
(Dublin, 2000), pp 257 and 282–4; Raymond Kennedy, 'The administration of the diocese of Dublin
and Glendalough in the eighteenth century' (unpublished University of Dublin Ph.D. thesis, 1968),
p. 144 and, for the dispute more generally, pp 127–49.

Toryism', and the members of the chapter were 'generally "High Church" or "Tory" '. Archbishop King was by contrast (insofar as he can be categorised as anything) a 'Low Church' Whig.[92] Although his comments on the chapter are very damning ('they have turned their chapter house into a toyshop, their vaults into wine cellars', etc.), and although he affected magisterial *gravitas* ("'Tis an uncomfortable thing that all assemblies of men come to some conclusion and agreement, only churchmen'), it has to be remembered that he was 'incurably quarrelsome' and 'the very model of an overbearing bishop'. His visitation methods were strongly resented by all his diocesans (Ferns and Ossory as well as Kildare). The other archbishops, when conducting their triennial visitation, 'inhibited' (i.e. suspended) their bishops' authority for 'but a few months, and as soon as they have visited the dioceses of their suffragans, they immediately relax their inhibition'. But King maintained his for 'the whole year, ... by what law I can't tell', thus depriving his bishops not only of their jurisdiction but of their income from fees and proxies.[93] Although they lost in the end, 'the entire chapter of Christ Church were united in resisting what they regarded as the unjustified assertions of authority made by King'.[94] However, the story had an unexpectedly happy ending. 'The opponents became reconciled and ... by 1725 the dean and chapter were willing to accept the archbishop's reasonable authority and join with him in making provision for the cures dependent upon them.'[95]

Bishop Ellis, quite as much as his older brothers, Sir William and John, laid the foundations of the somewhat scattered Ellis, later Agar-Ellis, estates in Ireland, which had the considerable rental of £2,237 per annum in the 1770s.[96] It was almost certainly he, with the local knowledge and contacts he must have possessed as dean of Christ Church, who bought the Ellis estate along the quays in Dublin city and county (part of it held on long lease from the corporation of Dublin),[97] in the process giving the name 'Ellis' to one of the quays. For the future, the most important component of this Dublin estate was the site of the custom house erected in 1707 to the design of Thomas Burgh, engineer and surveyor general of Ireland (fig. 1). The later history of the estate, which in the 1770s impinged on national politics, will be discussed on pp 143–8 and 158–60. Bishop Ellis also acquired, probably in the 1720s, a rural Co. Dublin estate – the lands of Barberstown and Pickardstown, barony of Coolock (comprising 820 statute acres in 1883), and Kilsallaghan, barony of Uppercross. For

92 Hayton, 'The High Church party in the Irish convocation, 1703–1713', in H.J. Real and H. Stover-Leidig (eds.), *Reading Swift: papers from the third Münster symposium on Jonathan Swift* (Munich, 1998), pp 121 and 127–8.   93 Rev. Philip Ridgate to Sir Thomas Vesey, 1st Bt, bishop of Ossory, 14 Jan. 1720/21 and 18 Nov. 1727, De Vesci papers, NLI, J/23 and 24; Kennedy, 'Dublin and Glendalough', p. 60.   94 Hayton, 'The High Church party', pp 122 and 134; Sir Charles Simeon King, Bt (ed.), *A great archbishop of Dublin: William King, D.D., 1650–1729, his autobiography, family and a selection from his correspondence* (London, 1908), pp 210 and 245–7.   95 Walter Alison Phillips (ed.), *History of the Church of Ireland from the earliest times to the present day* (3 vols., Oxford, 1933), iii, pp 199–200. The two chapters drawn on in this book were actually the work of Dr D.A. Chart. For Archbishop Charles Agar's contentions with the dean, though not the chapter, while archbishop of Dublin, 1801–9, see pp 256–7 and 282.   96 21 M 57/D26/2.   97 Ellis to Agar, 28 May 1786, T/3719/C/20/9.

this last, the bishop paid £5,250; his only surviving son, and heir, Lord Mendip, sold it in 1747–8.[98] Lord Mendip became the heir because, by the time of Bishop Ellis' death in 1734, six of the Bishop's eight children by his wife, Diana Briscoe of Broughton, Northamptonshire, had pre-deceased him. The Bishop was buried 'with great ceremony' in Christ Church, where a monument (by Nollekens) was erected to his parents by Lord Mendip in 1791. Lord Mendip's survival, against this background of heavy sibling mortality, betokens a strong constitution – and perhaps a strong will. In spite of a tendency to hypochondria and an unhealthy interest in the illnesses of others, he lived to be nearly ninety.

WELBORE ELLIS, 1ST LORD MENDIP (1713–1802)

The earliest and most important influence on Archbishop Agar, his most frequent correspondent and his point of reference in British politics, was his maternal uncle, Welbore Ellis, Lord Mendip. Since Agar's father had died when Agar was only ten, his mother, Anne Ellis, must also have been an important influence on him in his early years; but this is impossible to assess, in the absence of any surviving correspondence between them and even of any reference to her in Agar's correspondence. Because there was ill-feeling between the two branches of the Agar family, the role of guardian to Henry Agar's young children, which would normally have been performed by a paternal uncle – in this case James Agar of Ringwood – fell to Welbore Ellis. In 1753, that close student of parliamentary form, George Stone, archbishop of Armagh, 1746–64, observed: 'That family of Agar, when it appears [i.e. when the eldest son came of age], will from their property be considerable. A simple marriage of the mother's throws the management of their affairs upon Ellis, and he may be very instrumental in serving us.'[99] Later, because of Ellis' sustained, if secondary, position in British politics, he continued to be an influence upon his Agar nephews and was their link with British ministers and even the king. Though the most obvious bene-ficiary of his backstairs influence was Agar, the second Agar brother, Welbore Ellis Agar, must have owed at least his first step on the ladder of English office-holding to his uncle and (obviously) godfather. Moreover, Welbore Ellis Agar's wife, Gertrude Hotham, whom he married in 1762, was a cousin of the first Mrs Ellis, Elizabeth Stanhope.

Welbore Ellis entered the British House of Commons in 1741, and in six years' time had made himself sufficiently useful to obtain junior ministerial office. He was a lord of the admiralty, 1747–December 1755; joint vice-treasurer for Ireland, December 1755–December 1762; a privy councillor, 20 March 1760; secretary at war,

98 Map of part of Barberstown, the estate of Welbore Ellis, bishop of Kildare, 1731, NLI, Ms. 8796/1; agent's letters from Henry Moore of Dublin to Welbore Ellis, the Bishop's son, 23 June 1746, 1 Aug. 1747 and 16 Apr. 1748, Agar-Ellis papers, Northamptonshire RO: photocopies in PRONI, T/3403/1/4, 29 and 52.   99 Stone to Lord George Sackville (the chief secretary), 30 Jan. 1753, *H.M.C. Stopford-Sackville Mss.*, i. 189.

December 1762–July 1765; joint vice-treasurer for Ireland (again), April 1770–June 1777; treasurer of the navy, June 1777–February 1782; and secretary of state for the colonies, February–March 1782. At various times, he aspired to higher offices, but his very short-lived secretaryship of state was the highest he ever attained. His *History of Parliament* biography[100] includes the comments: 'Without any parliamentary interest of his own, he sat in the House of Commons for over fifty years [1741–94], and held office for over thirty [1747–82]. Ambitious and industrious, his name became a byword for a placeman prepared to serve any administration – which is hardly fair to him.'

He first obtained office through the influence of his sometime friend, Henry Fox, and preserved himself in office by shifting his allegiance, first, to the duke of Newcastle and then, in November 1760, to the new king's favourite, the 3rd earl of Bute. In the secretaryship at war, 'an onerous and difficult post ..., Ellis acquitted himself well', making a 'masterly' speech on the army estimates in March 1763. An Irish listener thought it far from 'masterly': 'Ellis made a speech ... about the military establishment, declaring that nothing was so much wished for in Ireland as to have the forces raised there to 18,000. When asked how he could say so, he answered he did not know how it was, only was instructed to say so.'[101] During the years 1763–5, 'he supported administration loyally, but never identified himself with the ministers. "I would serve your Majesty in the station of your footman, to procure your ease of mind or to promote the good of your affairs", he told the king on 21 May 1765.' From then until 1770 he was out of office. The king remarked '[in] May 1766: ... "Poor man, he belongs to nobody, and therefore nobody [is] for him."' In the following year, on the formation of the Chatham administration, Ellis made a rather abject tender of his support. Clearly, he had the interests of his Irish nephews in mind as well as his own, because he made his overture to the 2nd earl of Bristol, lord lieutenant of Ireland, October 1766–August 1767, and 'the real and confidential friend of Lord C[hatham]'.[102] Notwithstanding Ellis' assurances of goodwill, Lord Bristol gave priority to making his own brother, Frederick Hervey (who will feature frequently in these pages) a bishop, and did nothing for Ellis' clerical nephew, Charles Agar.

'Wraxall wrote about Ellis: "In his figure, manner and deportment the very essence of form, he regularly took his place on the treasury bench dressed in all points as if he had been going to the Drawing Room at St James'." ... . His precise and formal manner was the reflection of a rigid and authoritarian mind, unable to adapt itself to new ideas. He "always had a dislike to doing anything which altered the constitution"; and his conception of the constitution was static and literal, taking no account of new trends. "He did not think the House of Commons an assembly calculated for the discussion of state affairs", he said on 25 May 1778. "It was the business of parliament to raise supplies, not to debate on the measures of government." ... In February 1782,

100 Sir Lewis Namier and John Brooke, *The History of Parliament: the House of Commons, 1754–1790* (3 vols., London, 1964), ii, pp 397–400.   101 Diary kept by Robert FitzGerald, MP for Dingle, Co. Kerry, during a visit to London between 25 Feb. and 7 Mar. 1763, FitzGerald (Knight of Kerry) papers, PRONI, MIC/639/1/60.   102 Paper endorsed by Ellis, 'Minute of what I said to Lord Bristol, March 9th 1767', Agar-Ellis papers, PRONI, T/3403/2/1.

... [on accepting] the post of secretary of state for America ..., [he expressed the wish] that, when he shall receive his Majesty's commands to retire, he may be raised in dignity and have his title granted in remainder to his nephew [Lord Clifden]." ' Shortly afterwards, the collapse of North's American policy and his administration ended Ellis' official career.

Ellis' hopes of a peerage revived when the Fox-North Coalition came to power. But they were dashed in July 1783, in spite of the regard which the king was supposed to have for him. 'In the parliament of 1784–90, he voted regularly with opposition, and was a frequent speaker (e.g. on the ... Regency)', but seemed 'out of his place' in the anti-government camp. Nevertheless, Agar's friend, John Scott, Lord Earlsfort, wrote in July 1788 that Ellis was 'literally as young, as perpendicular, as well dressed, as attentive and as well accommodated with all good things as I saw him six years ago'.[103] 'Ellis broke with Fox over the French Revolution, and obtained his peerage in 1794 (at the age of eighty), when the Portland Whigs went over to Pitt.' He 'was created baron of Mendip in the county of Somerset on August 13th, with a collateral remainder to the issue male of the body of his sister, Anne, wife of Henry Agar Esq. of Gowran'.[104] This prompted the witticism: 'Ellis never would believe the American colonies could be lost; [and] from the long list of remainders for which he has now provided, he seems to be equally sanguine respecting the eternal duration of the English aristocracy.'[105] After 1794, he was (in the words of Wraxall) 'considered as the Nestor of the ministry and of the House of Commons, ... but he was neither listened to with enthusiasm nor regretted when he ceased actively to exert his abilities in support of the measures of the administration.'[106]

In private life, the new Lord Mendip devoted himself to 'learned ease and dignified retirement, contenting himself with the society of his private friends, and reaping the fruits of a good education and a well-spent life. ... His Lordship was an excellent Classical scholar, and on every subject a well-informed man; and the library which he left behind is said to have been one of the most numerous and valuable private collections in the kingdom.'[107] Charles Jenkinson, 1st earl of Liverpool, who must have known Ellis since *c.*1760, described him in 1802 as 'a worthy, honourable, respectable man, but of no parts [i.e. ability. Liverpool] ... had often heard of his scholarship and believed him to be a good scholar, but ... had never seen or heard of any composition of his.' ('As to his political opinions and notions concerning government, he had formed them in Sir R[obert] Walpole's [actually, Henry Pelham's]

103 Earlsfort to Agar, 21 July 1788, T/3719/C/22/30.   104 *Collins' peerage of England* ... [*edited*] *by Sir Egerton Brydges* ... (9 vols., London, 1812), viii, pp 360–66. Brydges was not entirely correct: her fourth and youngest son was excluded from the special remainder (see pp 52–3).   105 1st Lord Auckland to Lord Henry Spencer, 14 Aug. 1794, printed in Bishop of Bath and Wells (ed.), *The journal and correspondence of William [Eden, 1st] Lord Auckland* (4 vols., London, 1861–2), iii. 230. Terence Finley has suggested that the original (Add. Ms. 34453, f. 6) actually reads 'electoral disposition', not 'eternal duration'. This makes sense in view of the exclusion of one of Mendip's nephews (see pp 52–3). But it does not sit happily with the preceding reference to the American War.   106 Terence Finley's notes.   107 *Collins' peerage*, viii, pp 360–6.

time, with whom he was connected, and had never altered them.')[108] Ellis was elected a fellow of the Royal Society in 1745, and was appointed a trustee of the British Museum in 1780. Gainsborough painted him in 1763, and the portrait, which Ellis presented to Christ Church in 1769 (fig. 2), is considered a fine example of Gainsborough's work; he also painted Ellis with Ellis' second wife. To judge from the affectionate tone of a letter from Ellis reporting Gainsborough's death in August 1788, the two men were on fairly close terms.[109]

Ellis 'married, first, Elizabeth, daughter of Sir William Stanhope, K.B., who died August 1st, 1761, without issue. In right of her, he enjoyed [for his life] Pope's Villa at Twickenham, which was bought by Sir William after Pope's death [in] 1744. He married, secondly, ... [Anne], sister and [co-]heir of the late Rt Hon. Hans Stanley, in right of whom he enjoyed, after Mr Stanley's death [in 1780], the beautiful seat of Paultons in the New Forest, Hampshire. This lady survived him' by a year.[110] Of the first of these two houses, Pope's Villa, the versifier and minor politician, Robert, Earl Nugent, himself a serial marrier of rich wives, wrote:

> Fancy now displays a larger scope,
> And Stanhope's plans unfold the soul of Pope.[111]

Ellis, too, continued to put into effect plans for the garden and pleasure grounds at Pope's Villa until the very end of his life. The life interest he inherited in right of his second wife comprised, not just Paultons, but half of the Stanley estates in Hampshire, Wales and Chelsea.[112] Ellis, now Lord Mendip, died on 2 February 1802.

The Ellis who emerges from the correspondence with his favourite nephew is less stiff, solemn and 'emptily important' than the 'Don Welbore Ellis'[113] of the stereotype. Somewhat surprisingly, he even makes little jokes. In September 1786, for example, he 'earnestly' advised Agar 'to take Mr Fuller's word for the comet, without endeavouring to trace its march at the hazard of a fit of the rheumatism'.[114] Referring in March 1788 to a recent measure to reduce the tithe payable on hides in Ireland, he quipped: 'I am sorry that you have been obliged to lose some leather in order to save the rest of your hide'; and in May 1791, he wrote to his archiepiscopal nephew to inform him, with obvious glee, that Agar's eldest son, Welbore, knew as little of the bible as he did of the Koran.[115] There are many lectures on politics, and the tone is

108 Jupp/Aspinall transcript from the diaries of Sylvester Douglas, 1st Lord Glenbervie, *sub* 4 Feb. 1802.   109 Ellis to Agar, 25 Aug. 1788, T/3719/C/22/32.   110 *Collins' peerage*, viii, pp 360–6. 111 Memorandum book kept by Agar, c.1790s, 21 M 57/D56. Nugent was also for some time Ellis' colleague as vice-treasurer for Ireland.   112 3rd Lord Cadogan to 2nd earl of Buckinghamshire, 15 Jan. 1780, *H.M.C. Lothian Mss.*, p. 360.   113 Quoted from Horace Walpole in Terence Finley's notes.   114 Ellis to Agar, 22 Sep. 1786, T/3719/C/20/29. 'Mr Fuller' was Stephen Fuller of St George's, Bloomsbury, the father-in-law of Hans Sloane of South Stoneham, Hampshire, who was heir to Paultons on the death of Mrs Ellis. Fuller was then on a visit to Broadlands, near Paultons, the Hampshire seat of the 2nd Viscount Palmerston. For these particulars about Fuller and Sloane, see Sloane's marriage settlement, 1772, Sloane Stanley papers, Hampshire RO, 46 M 48/99. 115 Ellis to Agar, 19 Mar. 1788 and 30 May 1791, T/3719/C/22/4 and C/25/16.

often pedagogic and self-conscious. But Ellis is surprisingly open-minded on some issues, certainly for a man reared in the 'citadel of Oxonian Toryism'. For example, his defence of Lord North's Quebec Act of 1774 is startling (though it must be remembered that Ellis was a devoted Northite and that Canada was conveniently far away). He denied that the act had established the Roman catholic religion by

> authorising the secular priests to receive and recover all their accustomed rights and dues of all their catholic parishioners. ... [Had the subsistence of the clergy been left] to the voluntary contribution of their communicants ..., it would then become the necessary and immediate interest of the clergy to exert their utmost industry to preserve or to extend if possible their influence over the minds of the people: whereas experience shows that independence makes men indolent, and the wrangles for tithe and dues wean the minds of the people from their clergy in all countries and will most likely have that effect in that country, where the people are poor and litigious; and it is sound policy to diminish in that province the close connection between the priest and people as far as you fairly may. The crown has the right to present to most of the livings, so that would help to make the clergy rather court the favour of government rather than of their parishioners.[116]

It would be hard to find a more persuasive argument against Established Churches of any kind, particularly in Ireland (where 'the wrangles over tithes and dues' certainly 'wean[ed] the minds of the people from their clergy' – see pp 190–1, 480–1 and 536–7), or by implication a more persuasive argument in favour of binding the Irish catholic priesthood in some way to the state.

Again, it becomes apparent from his letters to Agar that Ellis was surprisingly well versed in current works on political economy and, though deeply conservative in constitutional and parliamentary matters, much more *avant garde* in his views on economic affairs. For a man of his landed, clerical and southern English background, he waxed positively poetical about the Industrial Revolution, 'the rapid and wonderful' effects of which he saw first-hand when 'making a tour as far as to Manchester' in July 1787. 'These are objects worthy the contemplation of a statesman and will furnish us with subjects of frequent conversation when we shall meet.'[117] In March of the following year, he gave Agar what amounted to a short lecture in political economy:

> I saw with great satisfaction that you adopted [in the Irish House of Lords] the right side of the question upon the bill for the reduction of interest, and that principally upon the great principle that by its nature it cannot be controlled by any law, as it depends upon plenty or scarcity, neither of which depend upon any law. Laws in such cases embarrass dealings and drive men to contrive expedients to elude the law, and the government is forced to lead the way, when

116 Ellis to Agar, 23 June 1774, T/3719/C/8/4. 117 Ellis to Agar, 11 July 1787, T/3719/C/21/26.

money is scarce, by contrivances of lottery tickets and tontines, etc., to give advantages to the amount of eight or nine per cent, while they affect to borrow within the terms of the law.[118]

On the other hand, Ellis' correspondence about his Irish estates shows that his economic practice was less flexible than his economic theory – or, perhaps, that he had a lot to learn about Ireland. Letters written to him in the late 1740s by his then Irish agent, Henry Moore, suggest that ignorance of Ireland may have been the problem. In December 1748, Moore tactfully pointed out to Ellis that 'The laws here [concerning landlord-tenant relations] are much the same as in England, but the gentlemen of the profession tell me the practice differs very much.' Shortly afterwards, Moore expounded to him 'the abominable custom which universally prevails here of not paying one half year till another becomes due, [and which] makes the arrears so great in all my returns, and if a tenant fails, makes the loss to the landlords much greater than it would be, could this custom be abolished, which is impossible to be done.'[119] Thirty years later, in 1777, Ellis was still finding that the ways of Irish agents and tenants jarred against his exaggeratedly English punctiliousness. His agent was now Thomas Tench, a Dublin attorney from Co. Kilkenny who had probably been recommended to him by Agar, since Tench had drawn up Agar's marriage settlement in 1776.[120] 'Tench', exclaimed Ellis, 'is intolerably slow [and] will do nothing without orders .... Lord Clifden ... is very good, but he ... doth not love business and is so often in the country, is not very decisive, and abhors writing; so that he is no great quickener.'[121] Soon afterwards, Tench was sacked. Ellis went into minute detail about the terms of appointment of his successor, John Forde. There was to be a 'fixed appointment of £60 a year. As to leases, I shall allow him to take one guinea and no more from the tenants upon each, which includes the expense of parchment, etc.' But only six months later, in September 1779, Forde was pronounced 'either more negligent or more inactive than even Tench'.[122] Sooner or later, he was succeeded by Thomas Prendergast of Golden Lane, Dublin, deputy-register of the court of chancery, a paragon who gave complete satisfaction.[123]

Assisting in the running of Ellis' Irish estates cannot have been one of Agar's favourite tasks; and, in general, Ellis lacked imagination and dynamism and introduced Agar to political principles and practices which reflected these defects. All the same, if Agar imbibed some of his uncle's conservatism, he also learned from him the importance of detail and draughtsmanship. In the more limited sphere of Irish politics, these were of particular value to a man who wanted to make his way to the top. His debt to Ellis was in some other respects profound. The very combination of a Westminster and Christ Church education was, as has been seen, introduced into the

---

118 Ellis to Agar, 19 Mar. 1788, T/3719/C/22/4.   119 Moore to Ellis, 27 Dec. 1748 and 28 Jan. 1749, Agar-Ellis papers, PRONI, T/3403/1/65 and 68.   120 21 M 57/T358.   121 Ellis to Agar, 27 Dec. 1777, T/3719/C/11/9.   122 Ellis to Agar, 1 Mar. and 20 Sep. 1779, T/3719/C/13/6 and 37.   123 Mendip to Agar, 9 and 12 Jan. 1802, T/3719/C/36/2–3.

Agar family by the Ellises. The Agars, with their *parvenu* background and aggressive concentration on acquiring land and political influence, had no university or intel-lectual tradition of their own. Unfortunately, there is no surviving correspondence between the young Agar and his uncle and guardian. But it must be significant that the curriculum and education of a succession of little Agars, both Agar's sons and Lord Clifden's, were later a frequent preoccupation in Agar's correspondence with Ellis. For example, Ellis wrote to him in January 1793: 'Your son, W[elbore], has passed his vacation with me. He tells me that he has had a dancing master, and I immediately saw it, for beside [*sic*] his natural growth, he was an inch and [a] half taller by holding himself upright. He certainly has made progress [at Westminster] in Latin, but as to Greek, he is not as ready in declension of nouns or conjugations of verbs as I could wish, or as I conceive he ought to be if he is to stand [*sic*] out in six weeks hence or little more for college.'[124] All these little Agars passed vacations from school and university with Ellis, and Agar is bound to have done the same. When he went up to Christ Church in May 1755, it must have been under the tutelage of Ellis.

Ironically, the college's reputation was at that time still at a temporary low, following a 'drunken frolic' and near-'ravishment' which had been perpetrated some three and a half years previously by 'four or five Christ Church students ... at the New Inn in Oxford'.[125] As far as is known, Agar's undergraduate career was innocent of such an 'excessively silly and at the same time wicked action'. Well prepared – by Ellis quite as much as by Westminster – Agar was almost certainly a powerfully motivated and purposeful student.[126] A book which must have been one of the earliest volumes in his library, contains a bookplate which he had had engraved while an Oxford under-graduate in the years 1755–9 and which bears, under his coat of arms, the legend 'Charles Agar Esq., Ch.Ch., Oxon.'[127] This was a remarkable piece of grandiosity for the younger brother of an Irish squire, and an Irish squire, moreover, whose greatest assets – the boroughs of Gowran and Thomastown – had yet to appreciate fully or be fully appreciated and, more important, had only recently been secured to the nomina-tion and control of Agar's eldest brother (see pp 95–100). Clearly, from his undergraduate days, and with every encouragement from Ellis, Agar was an ambitious young man who intended to go places.

Nevertheless, he was not a young man in a hurry. He had gone up to Oxford late, and obtained his BA in 1759, his MA in 1762, and his first preferment in the Church

124 Ellis to Agar, 14 Jan. 1793, T/3719/C/27/1. For Ellis' letters about the education and development of the future 2nd Viscount Clifden, in which Ellis took a keen interest because Clifden was his ultimate heir, see Ellis to Agar, 6 May and 17 Nov. 1784, T/3719/C/18/6 and 48. 125 John Cocks to his mother, Mrs John Cocks of Castleditch, Herefordshire, 15 Nov. 1751, Joseph Smith papers in the possession of Mrs Ian Campbell, Moot Farm, Downton, Wiltshire. 126 'Other than purely administrative material, e.g. admission registers, battels books, disbursement books, etc., there are no references to the Agar family in the [college] archive.' I am grateful to Mrs Judith Curthoys, the Christ Church archivist, for this information, and to her and to Mr Dennis Harrington, research assistant to the curator of pictures at Christ Church, for information about college portraits. 127 [James Ralph], *A critical history of the administration of Sir Robert Walpole, now earl of Orford* (London, 1743) – author's collection.

of Ireland in the following year, 1763. The canonical age for ordination was then, as now, twenty-four, and he had attained that age at the end of 1759. This raises the question, why did this well connected and ambitious young man take so long to embark on his career. Again, the influence of Ellis was probably responsible, and inclined Agar towards theological study and thorough intellectual preparation. Years later, in 1788, Agar gave what was plainly autobiographical advice for the benefit of his nephew, John Ellis Agar, who had just decided to go into holy orders:

> I do not scruple to say that I think men in general go into orders too soon, and that whenever I have been consulted on that subject, I have advised that, instead of going into orders first, and then sitting down to qualify himself for his profession, a young man should begin by enabling himself to execute the duties of a well informed clergyman, and then take upon him the profession. Is not this the practice in every other line? A lawyer is not called to the bar until he has studied his books for some years; a physician goes through the same course of probation before he assumes the care of our bodies. ... Were John my son, I should advise him ... to return to Christ Church [for two or three years longer] ... . He will there have the use of a noble library, [and access to] men of skill and great knowledge within his own walls, who will at all times be ready to explain and remove all difficulties and refer him to proper books on every subject. Compare these advantages with the situation of a very young man possessed of a curacy or a parish, not yet master of his business, and yet called upon daily to execute it; without the assistance of able ecclesiastics ... [and] an ecclesiastical library ... . Add to these the avocations which necessarily arise from the very execution of parochial duties – the amusements which youth renders too powerful to be withstood and which are recommended possibly by the practice of too many of his clerical neighbours, the squire of his parish and all, or the greatest part of, the country gentlemen who live near him. Under these circumstances, how is a young man to fulfil the duties of the office he undertakes, not merely in a manner to escape censure, but so as to acquire credit and reputation?[128]

In Agar's case, the scholarly habits which he acquired as a young man at Christ Church were with him for the rest of his life. For all that time, he maintained an interest in his *alma mater* (and not only because two of his sons were also educated there), corresponding regularly with Ellis and sundry dons about academic and architectural developments in the college.[129]

In general, the culture he shared with Ellis and which informs their correspondence, was not a dead thing, fossilized in the Classics. Rather, it expresses itself in comments on, and recommendations to each other of, the latest publications on

128 Agar to Clifden, 25 May 1788, 21 M 57/D53/1.   129 For example, Jos. Berkley to Agar, 13 Mar. 1772, and Dr William Hemington to Agar, 12 Feb. 1783 (both writing from Christ Church), T/3719/C/6/3 and C/17/1.

science, horticulture, literature, philosophy, and so forth – subjects which it might be imagined that two highly political animals would not have had leisure to continue to study.[130] Ellis and Agar really were reading men; and even at times of high political crisis, they break off from whatever they are writing about to comment on some recent book, whether in English, French or Italian – James Harris' *Tract* [*sic – Treatise*] *upon happiness* (1771), Abraham Tucker's *Light of nature* (1771), Lord Monboddo's *Ancient metaphysics* (1779), a French translation of Zoroaster's *Bible of the Parsees* (1779), Bishop Watson's *Essays on chemistry* (1786), the Rev. Dr William Vincent's book on *Niarchus' journal* (1797), etc., etc. Ellis was a friend of the first-named author, James Harris (who lived in Malmesbury House, Salisbury, and was therefore nearly a neighbour). Both knew Dr Vincent, who taught at Westminster school for many years, and was headmaster, 1788–1802. Another of Ellis' literary connections was the minor politician and theological writer, Soame Jenyns.[131] Agar, for his part, explicitly stated the view that men of business should make a conscious effort to keep up their literary and other aesthetic interests. His papers include some pages of autograph reflections headed 'The cultivation of taste':

> The most busy man, in the most active sphere, cannot be always occupied by business. Men of serious professions cannot always be on the stretch of serious thought. Neither can the most gay and flourishing situations of fortune afford any man the power of filling all his hours with pleasure. Life must always languish in the hands of the idle. It will frequently languish even in the hands of the busy, if they have not some employment subsidiary to that which forms their main pursuit. ... [And what better] than in the entertainments of taste and the study of polite literature? ... The pleasures of taste refresh the mind after the toils of the intellect and the labours of abstract study, and they gradually raise it above the attachments of sense and prepare it for the enjoyments of virtue.[132]

These 'Reflections' may have been written for the instruction of Agar's eldest son, Welbore, later 2nd earl of Normanton (who was to become one of the greatest British picture-collectors of the period *c.*1815–60).

Ellis respected male primogeniture, so in material terms his heir was his great-nephew and Agar's nephew, Henry Welbore, 2nd Viscount Clifden (1761–1836), who succeeded in 1802 to the already-mentioned Ellis estates in Ireland, to the manor of Hydon in Somerset (whence the title 'Mendip' must have been taken), to property in London, Twickenham and Westminster, and to a great deal of cash.[133] Lord Clifden

130 For a memorandum book of the 1790s in which Agar made notes of and on books he had been reading, see 21 M 57/D56.   131 Ellis to Agar, [mid-Sep.] 1771, 15 July and [pre-Aug.] 1779, 31 July 1786 and 18 Mar. 1797, T/3719/C/5/1A, C/13/16 and 21–6, C/20/18 and C/31/23. For Soame Jenyns, see 21 M 57/B23/1–2.   132 Reflections by Agar on 'The cultivation of taste', [c.1790?], 21 M 57/A8/23.   133 Probate (1802) of Lord Mendip's will (1799) and codicils (1799 and 1801), PRO, Prob. 11/1370.

(fig. 4) also succeeded as 2nd Lord Mendip, double-barrelled his name to Agar-Ellis and took the Ellis family motto (so appropriate to a partly clerical dynasty), 'Non haec sine numine' – 'These things come from above'! However, in political, intellectual and personal terms, Ellis' heir and successor was Agar. Seven years after Ellis' death, Agar joined him in the same grave in Westminster Abbey; and today, with the extinction (in 1974) of the viscountcy of Clifden, it is the present earl of Normanton who holds the barony of Mendip under the special remainder attached to its creation in 1794.

2

Charles Agar's family, friends and foibles, c.1760–1809

Welbore Ellis, Lord Mendip, lived so long that he in effect spanned two generations of the Agar family. It is therefore necessary to return to the generation to which Charles Agar himself belonged, the children of Henry Agar of Gowran (d.1746) and Anne Ellis (d.1765). They were, in the language of Burtchaell: 'James, MP [1st Viscount Clifden] ...; ... Welbore Ellis, born 1735, died 30th October 1805, a commissioner of the customs and deputy muster-master general [both in Great Britain, who] married 21st October 1762 Gertrude, third daughter of Sir Charles Hotham, 5th Bt, MP for Beverley, but [by her, who died on 14 August 1780] had no issue; ... Rev. Charles [the Archbishop] ...; ... Rev. Henry, [born 1743], died 14th May 1798 ... [leaving] issue three sons and a daughter; ... [and] Diana, [born 1746], died unmarried in July 1814.'[1] The early death of his eldest brother, James, 1st Viscount Clifden, in 1789 meant that Charles Agar, in spite of the generation gap, had to defer for the last twenty years of his life to a new and comparatively youthful head of the family, Clifden's son, Henry Welbore, the 2nd viscount (1761–1836). The 2nd viscount's younger brother, the Hon. and Rev. John Ellis Agar (1764–97), also played a part in the Archbishop's life, as did the Archbishop's considerably younger cousins, George Agar of Ringwood, later Lord Callan (1751–1815), and the latter's younger brother, the Rev. Charles Agar (1755–89). All these family members, therefore, feature in this Chapter and/or Chapters Three and Four. Two of the Archbishop's brothers, James and Welbore, and his sister, Diana, were among his closest friends. His other friends he chose out of a wide circle of literary, political and 'society' acquaintances, and in some cases the choice, and the way in which the friendship developed, are revealing of his character and personality. His most important relationship was with his wife, Jane Benson (1751–1826). She was in worldly terms a surprising choice for Agar, but the marriage was a great success. His family life meant a great deal to him and, in turn, provides numerous glimpses into the private *persona* of an otherwise public man. More generally, relationships, connections and personalities were important to him and to his career, and therefore deserve the attention devoted to them in this Chapter.

CHARLES AGAR'S THREE BROTHERS, 1747–1805

The earliest surviving reference to Charles Agar's siblings dates from June 1747, when a letter to their guardian reports that 'the two Master Agars' are off to England,

1 Burtchaell, *Kilkenny* MPs, p. 135.

presumably to Westminster school, accompanied by someone who must be a tutor.[2] These 'two Master Agars' are likely to have been James and Welbore. 'The eldest son', writes Burtchaell, 'James, 1st Viscount Clifden (1734–89), was MP for Gowran, 1753–60, for Co. Kilkenny, 1761–76, and for Gowran, 1776. He was a commissioner of the revenue in Ireland, 1771 [*sic* – 1772]–84, was created Baron Clifden in July 1776 and Viscount Clifden in 1781. He was a privy councillor, and was joint postmaster-general for Ireland, 1784–9. He married in 1760 Lucinda, widow of the Hon. Henry Boyle-Walsingham, first daughter of John Martin of Dublin. He was buried at Gowran in 1789. His widow lived until 1802, when she died at the age of seventy.'[3] James Agar's choice of title requires comment. His 'Clifden' has nothing to do with the more famous Clifden in Connemara, Co. Galway, a town built specifically as a seaside resort in the early nineteenth century, and not by the Agars, who owned no land in that part of Ireland. James Agar's 'Clifden' was the re-named townland of Rathgarvan (see p. 16) in his Gowran estate (though why it was re-named 'Clifden' is unclear). He could not take his title from Gowran itself, because that was a subsidiary title held by the earls of Upper Ossory.

His elevation to the peerage notwithstanding, it would seem that James Agar's leading characteristic was that he was a good, gregarious, fairly efficient, resident country gentleman. In May 1772, his brother, Charles, then bishop of Cloyne, drafted an anonymous newspaper polemic defending him from an attack in the *Freeman's Journal* which, though also anonymous, was plainly by Henry Flood, their Co. Kilkenny rival. In this draft defence, Bishop Agar described his brother as

> a gentleman ... who is as much loved and respected in the county where he lives as you are feared by your inferiors and despised by your equals and superiors. ... I shall pass over as altogether unworthy of notice your insinuations with regard to roads and bridges, for every road in the county of which Mr A. was one of the overseers, and every bridge built under his direction, are so many incontestable proofs to the public of his strict attention to, and honour in the execution of, those trusts.[4]

There was in James Agar's day plenty to occupy the energies of a good country gentleman in Co. Kilkenny. In *c.*1763, for example 'about £12,000 [was] granted [by parliament] for bridges at Castlecomer, Kilkenny and Gowran, and as much more for the [Nore] navigation',[5] a canal which was intended to connect Kilkenny City to Inistioge (where the Nore became tidal) and promised great economic benefit to the landowners of the southern half of Co. Kilkenny. James Agar was a commissioner appointed by the board of inland navigation to oversee the very sluggish progress of the canal, into which the Irish parliament poured *c.*£36,000 between 1755 and 1768

2 Henry Moore to Welbore Ellis, 13 June 1747, PRONI, T/3403/1. 3 Burtchaell, op. cit., pp 156–7. 4 Incomplete draft squib or pamphlet in Agar's handwriting, [*c.*May 1772], 21M 57/A4 /3 and 5–6. 5 William Lane to Sir William Barker, [3rd] Bt, [1763?], Barker Ponsonby papers, TCD, P1/9/33.

and which in the end got nowhere.[6] More usefully, he was a major subscriber in 1767 to the building of a Co. Kilkenny infirmary.[7] He was also, for a man of considerable corpulence, a literally active country gentleman, riding about at all hours at the head of either the Gowran or Thomastown Volunteers in pursuit of Whiteboys in the late 1770s.[8] Added to all this were attractive personal qualities – 'an uncommon share ... [of] affection and good nature', 'honour' and 'good sense'.[9] He features prominently in Chapters Three and Four.

For all his good points, he was not an entirely satisfactory head of the family, mainly because he was in straitened financial circumstances. The system of primogeniture worked tolerably well from the point of view of younger children, if the eldest son was in a position to pay their portions, bale them out of financial difficulties and generally look after their interests. But James Agar, as has been seen, had to struggle under a burden of inherited debt, some of it attributable to expensive (and ongoing) lawsuits over Gowran and Thomastown boroughs; and, although he bowed out of Callan borough and left that fatal pursuit to his uncle, James Agar of Ringwood, he plunged into expensive, and successful, electioneering for Co. Kilkenny (Chapter Three). Another of his inheritances was his grandmother, Mary Agar (*née* Wemys), who lived to be 106 and drew a widow's jointure from the estate from her husband's death in 1733 until her own death in 1771. For the period 1746–65 Lord Clifden was also paying a jointure to his widowed mother, Anne Agar (*née* Ellis), who died in the latter year. Paying two jointures over a twenty year period would have been regarded as a serious misfortune by any landed family. In the case of the Agar family, it made it difficult for Clifden to meet the next generation of settlement charges. Only his youngest brother, Henry, who was the least successful of the brothers in making his way in the world, was paid the principal of his portion of £4,000 with reasonable promptitude.[10] Welbore and Charles received only the interest, and were not paid the principal until 1796–7,[11] years after Clifden's death. Diana's situation would have been particularly precarious if Charles had not advanced Clifden *c.*£2,000 in 1769 to pay off a mortgage affecting the lands which had become the sole security for her £4,000 and which, in the end, she accepted in lieu of cash.[12]

Clifden's financial difficulties were well known, even at this early stage. One of the sneers made at his expense in Henry Flood's attack on him in the *Freeman's Journal* in 1772 was that 'his fortune being too narrow to compass his selfish views, the

6 Rev. Dr W.G. Neely, *Kilkenny: an urban history, 1391–1843* (Belfast, 1989), pp 192–4.   7 Ibid., p. 234; James Kelly, *Henry Flood*, pp 231–2.   8 Clifden to Agar, 28 Oct. 1779, T/3719/C/13/41; George Bushe, Thomastown, to [Lord Luttrell], 24 Aug. 1786, *H.M.C. Rutland Mss.*, iii. 337. There is in St Mary's Church, Gowran, a magnificent bust of Lord Clifden by Edward Smyth, fronting a eulogistic funeral inscription, and paid for out of money earmarked for the purpose in Lord Clifden's will. The bust shows that Lord Clifden was a fatty, in marked contrast to Agar, who was lean and angular. There is a replica of Smyth's bust in Leighlin cathedral (fig. 3).   9 Ellis to Agar, [pre-27 Aug. 1773] and 5 Nov. 1773, T/3719/C/7/3 and 5.   10 Articles of agreement between Henry and Diana Agar, 12 Sep. 1767, 21 M 57/T363.   11 2nd Viscount Clifden to Agar, 25 Mar. 1796, T/3719/C/30/ 10B.   12 Assignment of mortgage to Agar, 3 Jan. 1769, 21 M 57/T363.

properties of others, both public and private, were made subservient to them'.[13] Yet, Clifden persisted, regardless, in the family tradition of buying land whenever something adjacent to his existing estate came up for sale. He made at least two significant additions to his inherited property. In 1773 he bought Dunbell and Maddoxtown, both in the barony of Gowran, from William Knaresborough, an 'Old English' catholic belonging to one of the mediaeval 'tribes' of Kilkenny City, who held these 905 Irish acres in perpetuity. The price was £5,400.[14] In 1775 he spent a further £2,300 on Moneroe, in the same barony.[15] The first transaction is of interest because Clifden had acted as a protestant trustee for Knaresborough at the time the latter acquired the perpetuity lease (which legally he could not have done in his own name) and, when making the purchase, was fearful of 'the hazard of the popery laws'. This reinforces the suggestion that, at a personal level, the Agars were open-minded on 'popery' issues. (However, it would be interesting to know if Bishop Charles Agar, a strong critic of subterfuges by which catholics became 'real purchasers by *collusion*',[16] was aware of what Clifden had done for Knaresborough.) The second transaction is ominous, because Clifden had to borrow £2,000 of the purchase money on a mortgage granted to John Cradock, archbishop of Dublin, 1772–8 (the archbishop whose death created a vacancy which Charles Agar aspired to fill). This mortgage debt, after two assignments, was not discharged until 1794.[17] Buying land with borrowed money was as big a 'hazard' as 'the popery laws'.

Finally, Clifden multiplied his difficulties by unwarily acting as security for two office-holders – 'bad men' who, one after the other, defaulted, leaving him unexpectedly liable for a demand of just over £13,000. This gave rise to distraught letters to Agar from Lady Clifden and to an apparently secret loan from Agar to her. In October 1780, she wrote urging him to try to stop proceedings in the case of 'G. Martin's' forfeited security and so avert the 'infinite distress this will bring on me, already at my wits' end on account of the heavy burthen of debt with which we are encumbered'.[18] Her maiden name was Martin, so this defaulter was probably a relation of hers – perhaps a brother holding a colonial office in Jamaica.[19] At the end of December 1780, she wrote to Agar still more urgently (and strongly implying that Clifden had a mistress):

13 21 M 57/A4/3 and 5–6. 14 Case of the 1st Viscount Clifden (then James Agar), arising out of his purchase of Dunbell and Maddoxtown, 16 June 1773, NA, D 20130; Neely, *Kilkenny*, p. 28. 15 Power of attorney in connection with the purchase of Moneroe, 10 July 1775, NA, D 20121. 16 Agar to Ellis, 24 June 1778, T/3719/C/12/10b. In that year, 1778, Knaresborough conformed – an outcome to which his association with the Agars may have contributed. I am indebted to Dr James Kelly for this information, as also for a reference to correspondence of April–May 1778 on the subject in the Dartmouth papers, Staffordshire RO, D/(W) 1778/III/369, 371 and 373. 17 Bond and mortgage re Moneroe, 13 Oct. 1775, two assignments of the mortgage, 26 Apr. 1781 and 1 May 1789, and reconveyance (i.e. discharge) of the mortgage, 21 June 1794, NA, D 20125, 20127A and 20128–9. 18 Lady Clifden to Agar, 14 Oct. 1780, T/3719/C/14/29. 19 Lord George Germain to Edmond Sexten Pery, 21 Oct. 1779, Emly/Pery papers, PRONI, T/3052/82; [Colonel, later General Sir] Alured Clarke, [acting?] governor of Jamaica, to Agar, 13 Sep. 1789, 21 M 57/D53/31.

The melancholy picture (of which I only gave you a slight sketch) respecting your brother's affairs must have affected you [deeply], and however surprising it may be, it is nevertheless perfectly true. To take upon me to say what is, or has been, the whole cause of all this, I must beg to be excused. ... The manner of my life and conversation the world can judge of; and, as to the rest, Lord Clifden himself must be responsible for it, and your Grace knows too well the management of a family not to know, that if married people do not reside together, expenses increase most amazingly! Which is saying more than I believe in strictness I ought to do to anybody ... . I must request all payments be applied to Balinaboola rent until that is cleared off.[20]

'Balinaboola' refers to the 400-acre townland of Ballynaboley, two miles from Gowran, which Agar had been left under his father's will (see p. 423) and which he had let to Clifden for £177 per annum.[21] Agar was still owed a large sum of money in May 1784. In that month, Lady Clifden wrote to him expressing hopes of soon being able to reduce 'our' debts, and referring to 'the various and accumulated misfortunes that have for the last three years overwhelmed us and have driven our affairs into such embarrassments as have made it hardly possible for us to keep up even the appearance of credit'.[22]

All of this was contrary to text-book notions of primogeniture and the implicit obligations of the head of the family to his younger siblings. Agar rose in his profession with some help from Clifden and the family connection (see pp 138–41), but without the benefit of the capital left him by his father. Indeed, he provided financial help to his eldest brother instead of the other way round. Things went better for Clifden from 1784 onwards (see p. 163), and presumably the money borrowed from Agar was repaid? But the situation was still far from satisfactory. When Clifden died at the beginning of 1789, Henry Welbore Agar, now 2nd viscount, gloomily informed Agar: 'All I hope for, in truth, from the estate left by Lord Clifden is that there may remain, after all and every necessary demand is answered, some little sinking fund to liquidate the encumbrances.' This was before he returned to Ireland and had a chance to look 'a little into my own affairs', which he subsequently described as 'not as bad as I feared'. His father's debts, however, still amounted to £48,000, and the new Lord Clifden embarked on a strict economy drive (made easier by the fact that he was a bachelor until 1792). This economy drive dictated, among other things, that he give up all thought of Co. Kilkenny electioneering and consider selling the seats for his boroughs.[23] Welbore Ellis was horrified at the thought of this latter indignity. Indeed, it was partly to avert 'his wretched intention with regard to his boroughs' that Ellis urged, and Agar acquiesced in, the ill-starred presentation of Clifden's younger brother, John, to the best living in Agar's gift (see pp 54–7).[24] This meant that Agar

20 Lady Clifden to Agar, 30 Dec. 1780, T/3719/C/14/44.   21 Agar's account book, 1778–1808, which among other things records the rent due from Ballynaboley, 1779–84, 21 M 57/D16. 22 Lady Clifden to Agar, 22 May 1784, T/3719/C/18/9.   23 Lord Clifden to Agar, 19 Jan. and 2 Feb. 1789 and 9 Oct. 1795, T/3719/C/23/12 and 14 and C/29/37.   24 Ellis to Agar, 30 May

was still subsidising the head of his family as surely as if he had lent him money. Indeed, lending him money would have been preferable, because it would not have involved Agar in compromising the standards he had set himself as a churchman. By the time his fortune was at last paid over to him, in 1796–7, the money meant little to him because he was already rich in his own right and through his own exertions.

Much the same applied to his elder brother, the Rt Hon. Welbore Ellis Agar (1735–1805), the commissioner of customs and deputy muster-master general in England. 'Welby', as he was known in the family (and using that pet name helps to distinguish him from all the other 'Welbores' in the story) was clearly well off: his wife, Gertrude Hotham, brought him a marriage portion of over £4,000, and one of his offices alone, the commissionership of customs, £1,000 per annum.[25] John Scott, on a visit to London in 1783, joked to Agar: 'Welby is as magnificent and hospitable as an archbishop'.[26] Because his career lay in England, obviously under the patronage of his uncle and godfather, Welbore Ellis, Welby did not suffer like the Archbishop and the Irish Agars as a result of the financial and other vagaries of the 1st Lord Clifden. He was also in a good position to save out of his official income, because he had no legitimate children and his wife predeceased him by twenty-five years. Moreover, his official situations, which he held from probably the late 1770s until his death, required that he live in London, so there is no mention of his incurring the expense of a country house. After his death in October 1805, the painter-diarist, Joseph Farington, recorded that he had 'left £100,000 to two natural sons, one of whom is a colonel in the Guards'.[27] Farington was mistaken about the colonelcy: Emmanuel Felix Agar, Welby's second son, was a lieutenant in the first regiment of Guards, and was stationed in Hyde Park barracks. The elder son, Welbore Felix Agar, lived with Welby in the latter's house in New Norfolk Street.[28] They had the same mother, who had been 'dead some years'.[29] All this suggests that they were young men, born of a relationship which was formed after the death of Welby's wife in 1780. However, there may well have been other women in his life. In September 1758, it was rumoured that 'our dear Dainty' (who sounds like the pensioned-off mistress of an English duke) was 'going to be ... married to young Agar. They are only in dread of Ellis' preventing it, which he will certainly do if he can.'[30] 'Young Agar' was probably Welby.

Agar and Welby 'had lived during our whole lives in the most perfect friendship and confidence'.[31] Welby, as will be seen (pp 125–6), gave advice to Lord Clifden on the management of his political interest in Ireland, and occasionally used the access which his customs commissionership gave him to the first lord of the treasury[32] to put

1789, T/3719/C/23/23. **25** Peter Roebuck, *Yorkshire baronets, 1640–1760: families, estates and fortunes* (Oxford, 1980), pp 91 and 103. **26** Scott to Agar, 19 May 1783, T/3719/C/17/15. **27** James Greig (ed.), *The Farington diary* ... (8 vols., London, 1922–8), iii. 130. **28** Copy of Welby's will, dated 24 June 1804 and probated, 2 Nov. 1805, T/3719/C/39/22. **29** Diana Agar to Agar, 9 Nov. 1805, T/3719/C/39/20. **30** Richard Rigby to 4th duke of Bedford, 14 Sep. 1758, printed in Malcomson (ed.), *Irish official papers in Great Britain: private collections*, vols. i–ii (Belfast, 1973 and 1990), ii. 201. **31** Agar to 'James Agar of the Temple', 4 Nov. 1805, T/3719/C/39/17c. This James Agar, who is generally described as 'of the Temple' to distinguish him from the others, cannot

in a word for Clifden or the Archbishop with Lord North. Since he was a commissioner for some twenty-five years and had been rewarded with a privy councillorship by 1790, he must have been an at least competent man of business. But, not surprisingly, he did not come up to Ellis' exacting standards. Writing about a blunder which Welby had made in 1797 in connection with a family matter, Ellis, now Lord Mendip, complained: 'Our friend is zealous and kind in undertaking, but not as clever in executing, business.'[33] There are frequent references, from the 1780s on, to Welby's being ill. In 1788, for example, a visitor to London reported to Agar: 'Welby we found surprisingly recovered – indeed to all appearances quite well – though he moans a little if you say he has no complaint.'[34] Towards the end of his life, ill-health made him something of a recluse and valetudinarian. He explained that 'I never dine out, nor can I bear the night air'; and his sister, Diana, observed that 'he must have a most wonderful constitution to stand the number of physicians and medicines he deals in'.[35] Nevertheless, he remained a popular and well known man about town. At his funeral in 1805, which was to be, at his own request, 'as private as circumstances would permit, ... the line of carriages extended from his house to the place of interment ... near a mile'.[36]

Welby's great claim to fame was his picture collection, 'formed mainly through Gavin Hamilton [(1730–97), a dealer and a painter of vast neo-classical canvasses], who brought many fine pictures to England from Italy'.[37]

> The Agar collection was celebrated for its eight paintings by Claude [Lorraine] ... . The largest of the Agar Claudes were the *Sermon on the Mount* and the *Adoration of the Golden Calf*, but the most highly esteemed were the serenely pastoral *Morning* and the hauntingly nostalgic *Evening*. The Agar collection also included Velazquez's *Don Baltasar Carlos*, works by Andrea del Sarto, Sassoferrato, Berchem, Hobbema, Van de Werff and Van Dyck, and the psychologically penetrating *Expulsion of Hagan* by Rubens [1618].[38]

There was a good deal of rivalry among the leading English collectors of the day, and in October 1786 Sir Joshua Reynolds gloated rather unpleasantly over a recent coup

---

so far be fitted into the pedigree, and may have sprung from an illegitimate branch. The countess of Brandon left him ten guineas in her will, made in 1787, when he was already a 'counsellor-at-law' in London. He had known Welby well for twenty years (he says), but had just got married; so he must have been relatively young in 1805. Almost certainly, he was the James Agar who had embraced radical politics, become a friend of Valentine Lawless, 2nd Lord Cloncurry, and acted as the latter's second in a duel. On 1 June 1798, a series of arrests of suspected United Irishmen was made in London; they included Lawless and 'Mr Agar, barrister-at-law, at his chambers in the Temple' (*Dublin Evening Post*, 5 June 1798). I am indebted for this reference and most of the preceding information to Sir Richard Aylmer, Bt.   32 Welby to 3rd duke of Portland, 7 Apr. 1783, Portland papers, Nottingham University Library, PWF 68.   33 Mendip to Agar, 24 June 1797, T/3719/C/31/78.   34 Scott, now Lord Earlsfort, to Agar, 21 July 1788, T/3719/C/22/30. 35 Welby to Agar, 30 Jan. 1804, T/3719/C/31/78.   36 James Agar of the Temple to Agar, 6 Nov. 1805, T/3719/C/39/19.   37 *The Farington diary*, iii. 130*n*.   38 Peter Boughton, 'Ducal art: a study in changing tastes', in *National Art Collections Fund Art Quarterly*, *no. 12* (winter 1992), p. 40.

at Welby's expense. Reynolds had just bought eight Poussins for the 4th duke of Rutland, then in Ireland as lord lieutenant, and reported that, after the application of a new technique of picture-cleaning, they were

> now just as they came from the easel. As to their originality, it is quite out of all question. They are not only original, but in his very best manner, which cannot be said of the set in the duke of Orleans' collection. ... Welbore Ellis Agar told me they were offered to him some years ago for £1,500, but he declined the purchase by the advice of Hamilton ..., on account ... of their being in bad condition. It is very extraordinary that a man so conversant in pictures should not distinguish between mere dirtyness and what is defaced or damaged. Mr Agar dined with me a few days since with a party of connoisseurs; but the admiration of the company ... so mortified him at having missed them that he was for the whole day very much what the vulgar call down in the mouth, for he made very little use of it either for eating or talking.[39]

After Welby's death, his 'collection ... was catalogued for sale at Christie's on May 2, 1806, and purchased privately before that day by Lord Grosvenor for 30,000 guineas'. Farington recorded in his diary on 17 May 1806 that the initial asking price was £40,000.[40] The Grosvenor collection was 'transformed' by this purchase, and the purchaser, Robert, 2nd Earl Grosvenor (created marquess of Westminster in 1831), held sales in 1807 and 1812 to dispose of paintings which were now outclassed by components of the Agar collection. He had just (1805) acquired Grosvenor House, Park Lane, 'where the majority of the family's pictures were displayed until 1924 ..., [and which now became] one of the greatest private galleries in nineteenth-century London'.[41] From the gap in time between Welby's death and this transaction, it looks as if the £30,000 was additional to the £100,000 which his natural sons had reputedly received.

Welby was the first collector in a family notable for its collectors. Agar himself seems to have had no more than a discerning interest in painting (see pp 62–4). But his eldest son, the 2nd earl of Normanton (fig. 20), who must have been familiar with his uncle's collection, was later to become one of the most important private collectors of his day. Agar's great-nephew (the 2nd Viscount Clifden's eldest son), Lord Dover, was to be another major collector, starting just a little later than his second cousin. However, Lord Dover's collection, like Welby's, was dispersed – in 1895: of the Agar collections, only that of the 2nd earl of Normanton remains. It is at Somerley to this day.

The Rev. Henry Agar (1743–98), the youngest brother, was the black sheep of the family. Before this became apparent, he had entered the Church under Agar's

39 Reynolds to Rutland, 7 Sep. and 4 Oct. 1787, *H.M.C. Rutland Mss.*, iii, pp 343 and 346–7. **40** *The Farington diary* ..., iii, pp 130, 189 and 232. **41** Boughton, op. cit., p. 40; see also John Young, *A catalogue of the pictures at Grosvenor House, London* ... (London, 1820), which notes the provenance of each.

patronage, and been beneficed in the diocese of Cloyne. For this reason, and because Lord Clifden was in no financial position to make alternative provision for Henry, Henry became Agar's problem, and an embarrassment and reproach to him as a churchman. Henry received his first preferment in the diocese, the prebend of Subulter, in 1768. Then came further promotion in the cathedral chapter until, by 1770, he was prebend of Inishcarra and rector and vicar of Aghabullogue, with a combined income of £560 per annum.[42] The first scandal in which he was involved occurred in February 1772, when a post-chaise boy in his service killed himself at Inishcarra by drinking a large quantity of brandy at a swallow, and the boy's mother endeavoured to stir up trouble or extort money by blaming Henry for her son's death.[43] In 1773, Welbore Ellis referred darkly to 'most scandalous enormities' committed by somebody, probably Henry.[44] In December of the following year, Agar's friend, John Scott, warned him: 'This cursed brother of yours, I fear, will be in New-gate before your Lordship receives this [letter]. Some rumour of a cookmaid's lately disappearing who was his servant, and a quarrel with all the rest of his servants.'[45] Of these youthful 'enormities' it was noted years later: 'Besides a general reputation of his profligacy, it stands on record that he was arraigned at the assizes of Cork for a rape and murder. He escaped trial on a point of law, the examination against him having been taken by the magistrate in the city of Cork instead of the county at large.'[46] About this time, Henry married a local north Cork lady, Mary Tyrrell, daughter of one Benjamin Tyrrell.[47] It was presumably hoped that marriage would render him more stable and less liable to involvement in sensational happenings. But this was to prove absurdly optimistic.

In July 1792, the then bishop of Cloyne, Richard Woodward, who was absent from his diocese drinking the waters at Bristol Hot Wells,

> received from a very respectable quarter information that H. Agar has lately attempted, if not perpetrated, a crime exceeding all the other enormities of his life, in endeavouring to seduce, or rather violate, his own daughter. If the assault could be proved, I should think a process [for depriving Henry Agar of his preferments] could be instituted against him, which, if it did not remove the scandal of his being a member of our body, would at least remove the scandal of our being suspected of acquiescing in his remaining so. On this occasion I would exert myself to the utmost, and hope to be seconded by the

42 W. Maziere Brady, *Clerical and parochial records of Cork, Cloyne and Ross* (2 vols., Dublin, 1863), 239; notes made by Terence Finley. Inishcarra is north of Cork, and Aghabullogue lies to the north-west of Inishcarra, between Cork and Macroom.   43 William Lumley, Ballymaloe, Co. Cork, to Agar, 25 Feb. 1772, T/3719/C/6/1.   44 Ellis to Agar, [pre-27 Aug. 1773], T/3719/C/7/3.   45 Scott to Agar, 10 Dec. 1774, T/3719/C/8.7.   46 Richard Woodward, bishop of Cloyne, to John Moore, archbishop of Canterbury, 14 Sep. 1793, Moore papers, Lambeth Palace Library, vol. 6, ff. 230–33. I am hugely indebted to Terence Finley for a transcript of this and other documents in the Moore papers, and to Professor G.C. Bolton for drawing the source to my attention in the first place. 47 Anthony Greene, 'The Church of Ireland: Aghabullogue', in the *Coachford Record*, iv (Dec. 1993), p. 74. I am indebted for this reference to Terence Finley. Coachford is near Macroom.

principal clergy, who might endeavour to procure the necessary evidence on this, or any other of his public crimes ... . I most sincerely pity the Archbishop, but a case like this does not admit the intrusion of any considerations of a private nature.[48]

Henry denied the charge 'in the most explicit terms', and the king's advocate in England, the country's leading ecclesiastical lawyer, Sir William Scott, considered 'the evidence ... not sufficient for conviction'.[49] It was notoriously difficult to convict and punish peccant clergymen for anything – as witness the impunity with which Frederick Hervey, successively bishop of Cloyne and Derry, pursued his lengthy career of profligacy and absenteeism.[50] Bishop Woodward believed that, over the years, Henry had been guilty of 'drunkenness, whoredom, profaneness, neglect of duty and contumacy as well as incest'.[51] But the last and most 'horrid' charge depended for proof on the evidence of Henry's wife and daughter, who almost certainly would not have testified against him.

It also depended, to a lesser extent, on 'the evidence which Sir N[icholas Conway Colthurst, 3rd Bt] and his lady can give of the daughter and mother applying to them for refuge';[52] and Sir Nicholas was not an unimpeachable witness, because he had a grudge against Archbishop Agar. Sir Nicholas' father had been (rightly) accused of abetting and encouraging the Rightboy disturbances of 1785–7 by a pamphleteer called Dominick Trant who had written a defence of the Munster clergy at Agar's instigation. Stung by this accusation, Sir John Conway Colthurst had challenged Trant to a duel in February 1787, and Trant had shot him dead.[53] Against this background, not only was Sir Nicholas' testimony suspect, but so also was the spontaneity of the subsequent boycott of Inishcarra church which was mounted by Henry's parishioners; they had refused to pay tithe long before 1785 and all or nearly all of them were tenants of the Colthurst estate. Moreover, the parishioners did more than desert the church. In December 1793, Henry, in an appeal to Bishop Woodward for leave of absence, claimed that, while in his stables at Inishcarra, he had been

> shot at, struck several times on the head with the butt end of a musket, my rooms broke into, rifled and plundered of a gun and other articles of value ..., [and] my watch dog ... shot ... . [They] afterwards attacked the windows of my bedchamber with stones. In short, I am not safe inside or outside my house ... .

48 Woodward to the Hon. and Rev. Charles Brodrick (his son-in-law), 30 July 1792, Midleton papers, NLI, Ms. 8870/3. 49 Archbishop Agar to Rev. George Lee (Henry's curate), Cork, 12 July 1792, and Woodward to Brodrick, 30 Oct. 1792, ibid., Ms. 8861/1 and Ms. 8870/3. 50 Akenson, *Church of Ireland*, pp 30–33 and 121–3. See also pp 385–6 and 406. 51 Woodward to Moore, 14 Sep. 1793, loc. cit. 52 Woodward to Brodrick, 8 Aug. and 30 Oct. 1792, Ms. 8870/3. 53 Trant, *Considerations on the present disturbances in the province of Munster* ... (Dublin, 1787); Woodward to Brodrick, 16 Feb. 1787, Ms. 8870/1; Maurice J. Bric, 'Priests, parsons and politics: the Rightboy protest in Co. Cork, 1785–8', in *Past and Present*, no. 100 (Aug. 1983), pp 101–4 and 119–20; James Kelly, *'That damn'd thing called honour': duelling in Ireland, 1570–1860* (Cork, 1995), pp 145–6.

[This] set of villains ... I have every reason to believe live near me and are
encouraged by some of my good neighbours to answer some sinister motives.
Whatever may be the cause, I am not conscious to myself of having deserved
such inhuman treatment in a Christian kingdom. I have ... been too lenient in
regard to tithe matters. ... I never wilfully absented myself, my Lord, from my
residence till, by another such act made against me, I was dragged from my
house, cruelly and most unwarrantably confined for a long space of time.[54]

The rights and wrongs of the incest charge (and of the preceding 'enormities')
will never be known. All the information about it comes from Woodward's letters:
there is no statement by either Agar of the case for the defence. Woodward reported
that eighteen (or ten? – his handwriting is hard to decipher at this point) of the clergy
of Cloyne had petitioned him in July 1793 to conduct an investigation, and five had
presented him with another petition in September (which suggests a declining level of
belief in Henry's guilt).[55] But he also mentioned the existence of clergymen 'who have
publicly abetted Mr Agar'[56] – i.e. who might genuinely have believed in his innocence.
Woodward seems to have taken the view that it was 'for the advantage of the clerical
profession ... to clear them of a suspicion of compromising the crimes of one brother
from respect to the other', and – even if the case fell to the ground – was 'content if it
ends in our being able to manifest our principles and feelings'.[57] Presumably, it was
permissible to take the opposite view – that proceeding unsuccessfully against Henry
would give additional publicity to the matter without getting rid of the suspected
party. Woodward privately accused Archbishop Agar, not only of reluctance to bring
Henry before the metropolitan and consistorial court of Cashel, but also of so timing
his metropolitan visitation as to interrupt Woodward's attempted proceedings against
Henry. He also accused the Archbishop of instigating a proposal made by a third party
that Henry should be allowed 'to retire into some distant and private retreat', never to
be seen again in Cloyne (though presumably retaining his emoluments in the
diocese).[58] When, however, an alternative proposal was made by Thomas Percy, bishop
of Dromore – that Henry should be presented to a living of equivalent value elsewhere
(presumably in Dromore) and some other clergyman be nominated by Archbishop
Agar to Henry's preferments in Cloyne – Woodward made no demur, provided
Henry's successor was not one of the Cloyne clergymen who had 'publicly abetted'
him.[59]

What casts doubt on Woodward's objectivity and motives are his failure ever to
mention the obvious prejudice of Sir Nicholas Colthurst; also, his determination to

54 Henry Agar, Inishcarra, to Woodward, 28 Dec. 1793, Midleton papers, Ms. 8861/3.
55 Woodward to Moore, 14 Sep. 1793, loc. cit.   56 Woodward to Brodrick, 10 Mar. 1794, Ms.
8870/5.   57 Woodward to Brodrick, 24 Nov. 1792 and 11 Feb. 1793, Ms. 8870/3 and 4.   58
Woodward to Brodrick, 4 Nov. 1792, Ms. 8870/3; Archbishop Agar to Woodward, 9 July 1793, Ms.
8861/2; Rev. Dr Francis Atterbury to Woodward, 21 Nov. 1793, and to Brodrick, 4 Feb. 1794, Ms.
8861/3; Woodward to Brodrick, 10 Mar. 1794, Ms. 8870/5.   59 Brodrick to Woodward, 24 Apr.
1794, and Woodward to Brodrick and to [the Hon. John Hewitt], dean of Cloyne, 26 Apr. 1794 and
[same date], Ms. 8870/5 and 1.

bring the matter to the attention of the 10th earl of Westmorland (lord lieutenant, 1789–94), John Moore (archbishop of Canterbury, 1783–1805), and through the latter to that of George III. Woodward claimed that, because he was 'the patron [of Henry's livings] as well as the ordinary', it was necessary for him to establish 'that no disgrace ... [had arisen] to the episcopal character from my conduct'.[60] This suggests 'a prudery [rather] than a chastity of sentiment'.[61] In Bristol and Bath, where Woodward was for most of 1792–3, he was constantly in the company of the aged and ailing primate, Richard Robinson, who was to die in October 1794. Woodward could perfectly well have explained himself to Robinson, without raising the matter at the unprecedently high level to which he took it. The suspicion must be strong that Woodward, with the first-hand knowledge he had of Robinson's state of health, was taking the opportunity to establish his pretensions to the primacy and at the same time discredit the leading rival contender on the Irish bench, Archbishop Agar. (In the event, Woodward died in May 1794 and so was out of the running when Robinson died in October.) What is significant is that, although Archbishop Moore did show the king a lengthy letter from Woodward to Moore,[62] nobody seems to have accepted Woodward's extreme view of Henry's delinquency and, by implication, of Archbishop Agar's 'compromising [of] the crimes'.[63] When Lord Westmorland came to enumerate the rival qualifications and claims of individuals to the primacy in September 1794, he did not mention the Henry Agar affair. A little later, Archbishop Moore's brother-in-law and intimate, William Eden, 1st Lord Auckland, who was bound to have been consulted by Moore because he was a former chief secretary and knew Archbishop Agar well, was of the view that Archbishop Agar would be made primate. At the beginning of 1795, after Archbishop Agar had failed in that pursuit (for reasons which were almost certainly unconnected with Henry Agar), the king intervened personally to promote Archbishop Agar's wishes in another important respect.[64] And in late 1801, when Archbishop Agar was promoted to Dublin, Moore went out of his way to offer his congratulations.[65]

If Woodward's motives were probably less conscientious than at first sight appears, Archbishop Agar's may not have been as discreditable. He presumably took the view that there was insufficient evidence to convict Henry and that Sir Nicholas Colthurst had his own reasons for wanting 'to propagate the obloquy'.[66] The financial consideration of how Henry and his family were to be supported in the future must also have weighed with him. Henry's livings had been under sequestration for debt in 1790, when Archbishop Agar had intervened to effect a settlement between Henry and Henry's creditors. Under the terms of this, the income from the livings was vested in

60 Woodward to Moore, 14 Sep. 1793, loc. cit. 61 Thomas Barnard, bishop of Killaloe, to 2nd earl of Buckinghamshire, 8 May 1784, Heron papers, NLI, Ms. 13047/3. Though the expression is apt, it was of course used in a quite different context. 62 Woodward to Moore, 24 Mar. 1794, Moore papers, vol. 6, ff. 234–5, and to Brodrick, 24 Mar. [1794], Ms. 8870/5. 63 Woodward to Brodrick, 24 Nov. 1792, Ms. 8870/3. 64 The evidence for all these statements will be found on pp 172–5. 65 Welby to Agar, 2 Nov. 1801, T/3719/C/35/26. 66 Woodward to Brodrick, 30 Oct. 1792, Ms. 8870/3.

a trustee, the Rev. Dr Francis Atterbury of Great Island, Co. Cork, vicar of Kilmahon, diocese of Cloyne, who was to allow Henry £300 per annum and his wife another £100 as a provision for herself and the children, and was to devote the rest to the paying off of Henry's debts.[67] Henry, however, in spite of the desperateness of his financial plight, began to fire furiously on his rescuer. In September 1790, he repaid 'all the kindness and trouble Dr A[tterbury] had been taking for him and his family' by almost bringing an action 'against the Doctor for an illicit commerce with his wife'.[68] Later, in 1793, Henry did bring an action against Atterbury, this time for an alleged arrear in Henry's allowance; he obtained a one-off payment of £114 and an undertaking that the allowance would be increased by £50 per annum.[69] (Possibly this increase was given on condition that he went to live elsewhere, handing over the care of his livings to his curate.) All this suggests that Henry was not an easy man to deal with. Even if Archbishop Agar had thought it appropriate to call upon him to resign his livings, and even if the Archbishop had been prepared to take on himself the financial consequences, it seems doubtful if Henry would have complied. The tone of his letter to Woodward suggests a defiant as well as a frightened man.

The all-important, though unspoken, issue was Henry's mental health. Ellis had described Henry as 'that foolish and bad man' in 1776.[70] But it is probable that Henry was mad rather than bad; and Ellis later described him as 'incapable' – i.e. mentally ill. The fact that he is barely mentioned by name in the letters of Ellis and the other Agars, even when he died in 1798,[71] suggests embarrassment, if not some degree of revulsion. The same anonymity descends on Henry's 'eldest boy', who was apparently called Charles Welbore and was presumably the Archbishop's godson. In 1790, it was feared that he would prove 'utterly incapable, by the defect of his mind', of acquiring even manual skills.[72] The Agars – like most eighteenth-century families – found it impossible to be open about mental illness, not just from misplaced delicacy, but because of the threat it constituted to the marriage prospects of their young.[73] However, in the case of Henry Agar this had the unfortunate effect of making it look as if they – and particularly the Archbishop – were condoning crime instead of covering up the 'sad catastrophe' of what was probably some form of intermittent insanity. The unusually worded special remainders annexed to the creation of the barony of Mendip in 1794, and the terms of Lord Mendip's will, confirm the supposition that Henry was, in some sense, mad. The gossipy Sylvester Douglas, 1st Lord Glenbervie, noted at the time of Mendip's death in 1802 that his title and estates were limited 'to all his nephews by name and their heirs male of the body, instead of ... the heirs male of the body of his grandfather'. Glenbervie had been told that the object was 'to pass over one of the nephews ..., a man of an infamous character and addicted

67 Deed of trust, 2 July 1790, ROD, memorial no. 276570. 68 Ellis to Agar, 20 Sep. 1790, T/3719/C/24/8. 69 Deed, 10 June 1793, ROD, 299308. 70 Ellis to Agar, 13 Apr. 1776, T/3719/C/10/102. 71 Ellis to Agar, 23 June 1791, T/3719/C/25/18; 2nd viscount Clifden to Agar, 7 Mar. 1798, T/3719/C/32/14; and Mendip to Agar, 15 and 23 May 1798, T/3719/C/32/58 and 60. 72 Ellis to Agar, 20 Sep. 1790, T/3719/C/24/8. 73 Malcomson, *Pursuit of the heiress*, p. 33.

to an unnatural vice'.[74] But there would have been no reason to exclude Henry's male children, as well as Henry, unless Henry's problem had been deemed to be of a transmissible nature and had actually been transmitted to his eldest son.

Henry himself predeceased Mendip, dying in May 1798. Woodward's successor, who was not noted for zeal and activity (see pp 487–9), took no further action against Henry between 1794 and 1798, so Henry died still in possession of his Cloyne livings. Before and after Henry's death, Archbishop Agar behaved generously to Henry's family. He not only got Henry's widow admitted to the north Cork charitable foundation, Kingston college, Mitchelstown (see p. 300), but paid her an allowance of £80 per annum. He used his influence, and spent some money, to establish Henry's third son, Henry Junior (b.1776), in the East-India Company's service and regularly received lengthy progress reports from Henry Junior in India.[75] Until he reached the canonical age for ordination and Archbishop Agar could provide for him in the Church, Agar paid an allowance to the second son, Welbore Ellis Agar (1774–1810), without which the young man acknowledged that he would have been 'left destitute in the world'.[76] According to family tradition among Henry's descendants, Agar and his wife took Henry's daughter, Mary, to live with them, which she continued to do until she married.[77] Finally, Agar left 'Charles Agar' (presumably Henry's 'utterly incapable' eldest son) a comfortable annuity in his will.[78]

OTHER MEMBERS OF THE AGAR FAMILY, 1768–1809

The last of Agar's siblings, the only girl in the family, and a posthumous child, was Diana (fig. 11). Like their aunt, the countess of Brandon, she was a 'character'. She adored Agar. But she stood up to him, and sometimes offered him sound, common-sense advice – mainly about his health and lifestyle, but a few times about politics.[79] On one occasion, she lectured their brother, Welby, 'much more fully than I suppose was very palatable'.[80] She had a good brain and a considerable sense of humour, and would have made more of an impression within the family if she had not accepted the stereo-typed role of her sex; also, if she had not been an invalid from roughly the mid-1790s until her death. A rare glimpse of her in her early days (the autumn of 1768) is provided by a visitor to Agar at Cloyne, who found her presence 'was a great improvement, both to the house and house-keeping. She is a sensible, cheerful, well tempered young woman, and has other qualities that become her.'[81] Thirty years later, writing from what was to become her principal place of residence, Clifton, outside Bristol, a health resort 'congenial ... to my constitution and complaints', she described to Agar, in a manner which anticipated the case of Elizabeth Barrett Browning, the advice given her by

74 G.E. C[ockayne], Vicary Gibbs and others, *The complete peerage* (revised ed., 13 vols., London, 1913–40), *sub* 'Mendip'; Jupp/Aspinall transcript from the Glenbervie diaries, *sub* 5 Feb. 1802. 75 For example, Henry Agar, Calcutta, to Agar, 19 July 1802, T/3719/C/36/16. 76 Welby to Agar, 28 Mar. 1800, T/3719/C/34/11. 77 I am grateful for this information to Terence Finley. 78 21 M 57/T285. 79 Diana Agar to Agar, 5 July 1799, T/3719/C/33/20. 80 Diana Agar to Agar, 13 June 1804, T/3719/C/38/33. 81 See 116n.

Dr Moncrieffe, who had a great character and seems to be a very sensible man. He says everything that is comfortable to me, but so they all do. I ride double[82] every day that will answer for it, which he lays great stress upon. He says, if I have patience for this place, I shall get well. ... I am become a great porter drinker. I don't like it, but Dr M. insists on it; so I am tormented with porter at dinner, and riding double or thinking of it, all the rest of my time. Thus much for Scotch doctors.[83]

Like many intelligent women of her day and class, she was inclined to take a man's view of her fellow-females. Commenting in July 1799 on Agar's report of the dislocated state of his household in St Stephen's Green, Dublin, she remarked: 'Your cook in the gout and housekeeper ready to lie in, must be very inconvenient. She [the housekeeper] is frequently in that disorder, which is troublesome; but the world can't go on without it.'[84]

The value of her letters lies in the fact that, in common with those from Agar's wife, they serve as a plain woman's guide to Agar. Also like Mrs Agar's letters, they come close to that most impenetrable of areas, Agar's personal religious conviction. Writing to him in March 1807, following a death in the family, Diana Agar declared: 'It would be presumption in me to attempt to say more to you than that your own great religion and great sense must give you such advantages and resources as I trust and hope will enable you to bear this and all other misfortunes as well as we are capable of doing in this world.'[85] When Agar himself died in July 1809, Diana wrote with simple certainty that he was now in heaven, for which he would not want to exchange the many 'good things of life' which he had 'most deservedly ... possessed. ... I am thoroughly sensible of and thankful for all his kindness and affection for me and his very affectionate mention of me in his will. I have often prayed and wished that he might outlive me.'[86] If Agar was not a man of some religious faith, he had successfully fooled someone who was very close to him.

Apart from his siblings, Agar's other contemporaries within his immediate family were his cousins, the two sons of James Agar of Ringwood (d.1769), George Agar, later Lord Callan, and the Rev. Charles Agar. Because of his proprietorship of Callan borough, George Agar is best discussed in the context of Chapter Three. His younger brother, Charles, successively archdeacon of Emly and rector of Galbally (near Tipperary town), was beneficed and twice promoted by the Archbishop, and proved to be – not as dangerously embarrassing as Henry Agar – but certainly a thorn in the archiepiscopal side. In July 1788, the prebend of Killenelick, which incorporated the union of Galbally, alias Duntrileague, Co. Limerick ('the best ... in my gift', according

---

82 I am assured by one who rides side-saddle that 'riding double' cannot mean riding astride, as I had conjectured, but may mean riding pillion. However, equestrians of long experience are a bit baffled by the expression. I am grateful to Mrs James Villiers-Stuart for her help with this conundrum. 83 Diana Agar to Agar, 15 May 1796, T/3719/C/30/16. 84 Diana Agar to Agar, 5 July 1799, T/3719/C/33/20. 85 Diana Agar to Agar, 14 Mar. 1807, T/3719/C/41/12. 86 Diana Agar to 2nd earl of Normanton, 23 July 1809, 21 M 57, 2nd earl's unreferenced correspondence.

to Agar), fell vacant. It was worth more than £600 a year at this time, and £1,400 ten years later. Agar conferred it on his cousin, Charles, provided the latter gave up his existing preferments (including the archdeaconry of Emly) and undertook to build a glebe-house at Galbally. The latter stipulation was in line with Agar's standard practice in cases of institution to parishes where glebe-houses were wanting. Charles Agar, it soon transpired, was in acute financial difficulties, and then fell seriously ill. In December 1788, Agar wrote urgently to George Agar, then in England, reporting that Charles' 'conduct, situation and circumstances for a long time past have been such as have kept me in a state of continued anxiety, and at seven o'clock on Tuesday last he came to me in the actual custody of the sub-sheriff of this county and attended by him on his way to Clonmel gaol'. His debts at present stood at £432, and he was about to be turned out of his house. 'To save him from irreparable ruin, your assistance will be indispensably necessary. I wish therefore to know what time you propose to return to Ireland.'[87] No sooner had Agar averted the scandal of his cousin, and a leading clergyman of his diocese, being lodged in Clonmel gaol, than he was faced with another scandal – that of Charles Agar reneging on his commitment to build Galbally glebe-house. Charles' wife appealed to Agar's on this subject, but met with a stony response: the Archbishop's 'answer was ... that, were he to permit his own cousin to decline building upon one of the very best benefices in his gift, he could not with any propriety oblige any other man to build upon a benefice of inferior value, and that such an act of partiality would be justly censured and attended by very bad consequences.'[88] The problem was soon afterwards solved by Charles Agar's death in April 1789.

Worse was to follow. Archbishop Agar's nephew, the new Lord Clifden's younger brother, John, was intended for the Church. Welbore Ellis, who not long ago had reported to Agar that John Agar 'is so much in debt that I suspect he has run away from [college to escape] his creditors', now urged that 'this opportunity of providing for John should not be missed. He is to take deacon's orders on Trinity Sunday with the full approbation of the Dean [of Christ Church] ... . The only difficulty is the getting into priest's orders so soon.'[89] Probably with considerable reluctance – in view of the value of the living and the youthfulness and dubious character of John Agar – Agar agreed to present him to Duntrileague, on the same conditions as he had imposed on the late Charles Agar. Lord Clifden promised £1,000 to build Galbally glebe-house, and Welbore Ellis praised Agar's 'bountiful act to your nephew, John ... . I hope that he and the rest of his family will always testify to you a due sense of the obligation.'[90] Only John Agar himself was ungrateful, as the following extraordinary and impertinent letter to Agar makes clear:

87 Agar to George Agar, 20 Dec. 1788, T/3719/C/22/54.   88 Mrs Agar to Rev. Charles Agar's wife, 9 Feb. 1789, T/3719/C/23/16. A 'Plan, elevation and notes re Galbally glebe-house by William Cleary' will be found at 21 M 57/B14/30–31. For Duntrileague church, see p. 209.   89 Ellis to Agar, 26 May 1788 and 4 May 1789, T/3719/C/22/20 and C/23/22.   90 Clifden to Agar, 12 June 1789, and Ellis to Agar, 23 July 1789, T/3719/C/23/24 and 29.

Lord Clifden has desired me to inform you that in a little more than a month he will have £100 ready to pay for what may have been done towards building my house. But I hope and trust you will not be so hard upon me as to expect that any more of my paternal fortune should be sunk in this business, but leave the living to build it, particularly as I have contracted a considerable debt at Oxford for which I fear it will be necessary to sink at least £300 or £400. This being the situation of my affairs, I flatter myself you will not require what the world would think very unreasonable and hard in any bishop, but particularly so in a relation.[91]

This, not surprisingly, evoked a long and thunderous reply, in which Agar emphasised that the £1,000 promised by Clifden for the glebe-house was a condition of John Agar's preferment, and that Agar had no intention of treating John Agar differently from the late Charles Agar or from every other clergyman in his diocese. He pointed out that the living would very soon repay the outlay on the house, that John Agar was not being asked to spend more than two years' income of the living on it, and that therefore the entire cost of the building would be reimbursed by John Agar's successor.[92] 'I deem it', he concluded, 'to be conducive to your honour and interest as a clergyman and to the general well-being of the Established Church, to the advancement of morality and the extension of true religion.'[93] John Agar replied, with some attempt at contrition: 'I am very sorry some expressions that dropped from me in my letter should have offended you. ... All I wished was sufficient time, in order that the living should bear the greater part of the expense, the unreasonableness of which desire I confess I cannot see.' Agar was far from mollified by this half-hearted recantation, and in reply reiterated his demand that John Agar proceed immediately with the building and find the means to pay for it.[94]

In consequence of this exchange, Galbally glebe-house began to rise, but so slowly that it was clear that John Agar was still determined to pay for it out of the income of the living. In May 1791, Agar 'with much reluctance and some pain' appealed to Clifden.[95] But all he got was a shuffling answer. It now transpired that the £1,000 which the latter had promised was part of John Agar's own fortune, which Clifden held only as a trustee. He therefore claimed that, when he promised the £1,000, he did not mean to say that he would make any payment without his brother's consent. In another letter,

91 John Agar to Agar, 5 Oct. 1789, T/3719/C/23/32. 92 *10 William III, cap. 6.*, authorised bishops, clergymen, etc., to charge their successors with two-thirds of their outlay on building and improving their palaces, glebe-houses, etc.; *12 George I, cap. 10, sec. 2* (passed in 1726), increased the proportion to three-quarters; and *11 and 12 George III, cap. 17, sec. 3* (1772) increased it to full reimbursement in the case of a brand-new building. Under this 1772 Act (as explained by another of 1774), the successor was repaid three-quarters by his successor, who received two-thirds of that sum from the next incumbent, who received one-third from the next. So, the cost of the building was spread over five incumbents. For a discussion of this legislation and its effects, see pp 338–47. 93 Agar to John Agar, 25 Oct. 1789, T/3719/C/23/33. 94 John Agar to Agar, 13 Nov. 1789, and Agar to John Agar, 20 Nov. 1789, T/3719/C/23/36–7. 95 Agar to Clifden, 22 May 1791, T/3719/ C/25/13.

he added: 'I know not what I can do more for the accommodation of each party.'[96] In January 1792, Welbore Ellis, who had started all this trouble, was insensitive enough to crack a little joke with Agar on the subject: 'John is about to furnish his house with a wife. The scorners will ask whether that will promote *residence*.'[97] Eventually, the matter was resolved. By July 1792, John Agar had spent £790 on Galbally, and settled accounts with Agar for that amount.[98] In November 1795, he wrote to his uncle explaining why he was still not 'settled in my parish'. He lamented that the builder had exceeded his estimate, and sought permission, 'as the value of the living will admit of it', to increase the sum named in his memorial to the board of first fruits from £1,200 to £1,392, which – with the £100 expected from the board – would cover his whole expenditure of £1,492.[99] On 31 August 1796, Agar certified formally that John Agar had 'completely finished his glebe-house and improvements at Galbally' and was entitled to the grant of £100.[100] Then, in January 1797, John Agar very suddenly died. He was dining with friends in Co. Kilkenny, and expired 'before he had drank [*sic*] a pint of port' after dinner. 'The apothecary' continued this quaint report to Agar 'seems to think it was merely nature exhausted. It was not by any intemperance ... certainly; for he has lived remarkably regular and temperate for this some time.'[101] Following his early death, his widow, with help from the Archbishop, obtained full reimbursement of John Agar's expenditure on Galbally from his successor, the Rev. Joseph Preston.[102]

This protracted correspondence over Galbally shows how badly Agar was let down by members of his own family, and also shows their incomprehension of the standards he sought to uphold as a churchman. It was not the clerical Agars alone who were at fault: Welbore Ellis, a great stickler for the rights of the clergy, showed himself less than exacting where their duties were concerned, and Clifden's role in the saga was unhelpful and ambivalent. In general, Clifden's succession to the title in January 1789 heralded a shift in the balance of power within the family and a reduction in the influence of Archbishop Agar. The 1st Lord Clifden, to whom Agar naturally looked up as an elder brother, had in practice deferred to and depended on Agar. But when the 37–year-old 2nd viscount succeeded, the situation altered. At the beginning of February, he wrote fulsomely to Agar: 'I trust you will believe me when I say that ... whatever of weight or influence I possess shall invariably be directed and employed for your service at all times and in all ways that you judge advantageous. I trust, therefore, that ... you will consider yourself first and me afterwards, as I must think your objects of more consequence than my own.'[103] But the background to these assurances was his recent, unilateral decision to desert the government on the regency issue – a decision which necessarily implicated Agar, even though the latter had not

96 Clifden to Agar, 22 and 23 May 1791, T/3719/C/25/14–15. **97** Ellis to Agar, 11 Jan. 1792, T/3719/C/26/1. **98** Account between Agar and John Agar, 26 July 1792, 21 M 57/B7/1. **99** John Agar to Agar, 11 Nov. 1795, 21 M 57/B23/25. For the role of the board, see pp. 220–30. **100** Agar's 'state' of the diocese of Cashel, 1779–1801, 21 M 57/B6/1. **101** Robert Langrishe to Agar, 23 Jan. 1797, T/3719/C/31/3. **102** The Hon. Mrs Harriet Agar, widow of John, to Agar, 17 Feb. 1797 and 24 Apr. 1798, T/3719/ C/31/8 and C/32/49. **103** Clifden to Agar, 2 Feb. 1789, T/3719/C/23/14.

been consulted, and which spoke louder than these words (see pp 164–5). In more general terms, it was easier for a man of Agar's ability, experience and prominence to accept as the head of his family an elder brother than a much younger nephew. Nevertheless, there was never a breach, nor anything more marked than a tension, between uncle and nephew. In a letter to Archbishop Moore, written in February 1792, Agar said proudly: 'a young man of more honour, better principles or more amiable manners than Lord Clifden, I have never known. He is well informed, perfectly well bred and free from all the fashionable vices of the times.'[104]

CHARLES AGAR'S AESTHETIC INTERESTS AND INTELLECTUAL FRIENDSHIPS

If Agar was increasingly distanced from his family by differences of generation and of attitude to the Church, it is also fair to say that there had always been an intellectual barrier between him and them. With the possible exception of Welbore Ellis, none of them was Agar's intellectual equal. The 1st Lord Clifden was an Agar through-and-through, unrefined by the intellectual strain introduced by the Ellises. Agar's son, the 2nd earl of Normanton, once described a letter from the 2nd Lord Clifden as 'A neat letter in Lord Orford's [i.e. Horace Walpole's] style'.[105] But the letter in question hardly lives up to that description, and no one, certainly, would have so described the hurried and confused compositions of the 1st Lord Clifden. By contrast, Agar's correspondence with the principal members of his personal and political circle, while it is characterised by a slightly *risqué* sense of humour granted that the recipient was a churchman, bespeaks a genuine sense of culture and good taste and sometimes attains to an almost literary quality.

A number of examples of Agar's intellectual interests have been cited or quoted from in the discussion on pp 37–8 of that side of his correspondence with Welbore Ellis. Others to be found elsewhere in Agar's papers include his notes on numerous books (in addition to the statute book), one of them *The Aeneid,* and catalogues of his private library, which from 1779 was split between Cashel and Dublin.[106] Even at the deanery, Kilmore, he had a library which was either large enough or good enough to merit 'classing' – as will be seen. In 1784, he built himself a study in a secluded and almost detached addendum to the Cashel palace (see pp 349 and 354–5). It is proof, not only of the new study's seclusion, but of Agar's determination to spend a long time there, that he equipped it with a water-closet.[107] The main catalogue of his

104 Agar to Archbishop Moore, 7 Feb. 1792, Lambeth Palace Library, Moore papers, vol. 6, ff. 211–12. I am indebted for this reference to Terence Finley.   105 Endorsement by the 2nd earl on a letter of 28 Dec. 1826, 21 M 57, 2nd earl's unreferenced correspondence.   106 Hampshire RO list of 21 M 57/D28–42.   107 Plans and estimate by Agar's architect, Oliver Grace, 1784 and N.D., 21 M 57/B14/1(a), (b) and (c). I am grateful to Professor Anne Crookshank for drawing my attention to the water-closet, and to Mr Aidan O'Boyle (formerly of the Buildings of Ireland Project, UCD) for reminding me that a water-closet was technologically newsworthy in Ireland at that date.

private library, which seems to have been compiled between 1791 and 1801, shows that it comprised some 3,250 titles (as opposed to volumes) and, since numerous purchase prices are recorded, that it was constantly being augmented. Most important of all, it is entirely in Agar's own handwriting.[108] As has already been noted, Agar read as well as catalogued his books. The Rev. Edward Ryan, prebendary of Donoughmore in St Patrick's Cathedral, Dublin, 1790–1819, who dedicated two books to Agar, observed in the dedication of one of them, *A short but comprehensive view of the evidences of the Mosaic and Christian codes* ... (Dublin, 1795), that Agar had 'improved the author's works by his ingenious remarks'.[109] On a number of occasions, because Agar's fluency in both English and Latin composition was well known, he was asked to devise 'expressive, simple and elegant' inscriptions for pictures, monuments, etc.[110] One of the most expressive is the inscription on the drinking fountain erected in memory of a lord lieutenant who had actually died of drink, and still to be seen in Merrion Square, Dublin (though the inscription cannot because of weathering):

> To the memory of Charles Manners, duke of Rutland, whose heart was as susceptible of the wants of his fellow-creatures as his purse was open to relieve them, this fountain for the use of the poor is with all humility dedicated. At his command it was undertaken, and at his sole expense it would have been erected had not premature death [in 1787] suddenly deprived the poor of their best benefactor and the rich of their brightest example. 'Large was his bounty and his soul sincere'.[111]

Agar's own obituary in the *Morning Post* for 14 July 1809 stated that he stood 'pre-eminently high' as (in this order) 'a scholar, a prelate and a statesman'; his great friend, John Scott, described him in 1773 as 'uniting poetry and music to politics and religion'; and one of his clergy in the diocese of Dublin wrote of him in 1806, 'Conceiving clerical exertions as bound to society in every possible point, that enlightened prelate has not only permitted, but encouraged, his clergy to promote the interests of Ireland in every walk of literature, from abstrusest science to the humblest compilation.'[112]

Agar seems, generally speaking, to have chosen for his friends people who were intellectual equals and good fun, and who shared his literary and musical interests and his gregarious instincts, rather than people who were likely to advance his career. Some of these friends were politicians on the make, like himself – rivals as well as kindred spirits. Some were women, because he married late, when he was over forty, and was

---

108 21 M 57/D38.   109 I am grateful to Dr Raymond Refaussé, librarian and archivist of the RCB Library, Dublin, for drawing this dedication to my attention.   110 1st earl of Milltown and William Dunn to Agar, 12 Apr. 1781, T/3719/C/15/7; Lord Clifden to Agar, 12 May 1781, 21 M 57/B23/8; Sir John Blaquiere to Agar, 25 Aug. 1791, T/3719/C/25/23.   111 Draft by Agar for the inscription, 31 July 1791, 21 M 57/D71 (part).   112 *The Farington diary*, v. 207 (quoting the *Morning Post*); Scott to Agar, 27 Feb. 1773, T/3719/C/7/2; Rev. Matthew Sleater, *Introductory essay to a new system of civil and ecclesiastical topography* ... (Dublin, 1806), p. v.

clearly a great hit with the opposite sex – there is one reference in *c.*1775 to his 'amorous complexion'.[113] Some, of both sexes, were people who had no advantages of birth, wealth or position, and with whom he could therefore relax and be himself. In 1776 he married one such, Jane Benson. The most obvious examples from his earlier life were Richard and Elizabeth Griffith of Maidenhall, Bennetsbridge, Co. Kilkenny. Although there was a small Agar of Gowran estate at Bennetsbridge,[114] Richard Griffith was in fact a tenant of the Agars' cousins, the Wemyses of Danesfort. He was 'an unsuccessful [flax]mill owner with a bare 600 acres', and his wife and he were both authors. Indeed, they published, very soon after the event, their letters to each other, under the disguise of *A series of genuine letters between Henry and Frances*. Fanny Burney extolled these letters as 'so elegantly natural, so unassumingly rational', and thought them much superior in good taste and good feeling to Goldsmith's near-contemporary *Vicar of Wakefield*.[115] They throw light on Agar's circle and lifestyle both in Ireland and in London in the period 1766–9 – a period which is not well documented in Agar's own correspondence.

Mr and Mrs Griffith moved to London in August 1764, living at first in lodgings and then, two years later, taking a house at 2 Hyde Street, Bloomsbury, where Elizabeth Griffith opened a modest salon.[116] This she called her 'coterie', and Agar was jokingly appointed its chaplain. In his more serious role as chaplain to the lord lieutenant, Lord Northumberland, Agar followed him to London at the end of February 1765 (presumably to press his own suit for the deanery of Kilmore). It was then that he became the star and focal point of the 'coterie'. Mrs Griffith was lively, full of high spirits, sensible comment and sensibility, but not, like the celebrated Elizabeth Montagu, a wit or a blue-stocking. She wrote to Agar in November 1767: 'my feelings have been all my life too strong for my reason, and I am now determined not to love you, or anybody but my Henry, half so well as I have done.' Members of her 'coterie' were selected for their feeling hearts rather than their wit, for their domestic virtues and commitment to marriage, and perhaps – quite simply – for their proximity as neighbours in London. They included a Capt. John Cooke, impatiently awaiting the command of an East India Company ship, and 'his lady'; Mrs Griffith's apothecary, Mr Spooner, and his wife (the latter an old acquaintance of Dr Johnson

113 Scott to Agar, [*c.*1775], T/3719/C/9/5.   114 Leases of the Agar estate at Bennetsbridge, 1741, 1781, 1839, 1844, 1846 and 1857, Annaly/Clifden papers, F/3/1. For the acquisition of the Agar estate there, see p. 16.   115 Hubert Butler, *Escape from the anthill* (Mullingar, 1985), pp 15–23. Hubert Butler became interested in the Griffiths because he was a subsequent owner of their house at Bennetsbridge.   116 This and the next two paragraphs are based, almost entirely and sometimes *verbatim*, on the draft text of a forthcoming biography of Mrs Griffith by Professor Emeritus Betty Rizzo, formerly of the City University of New York, supplemented by extracts from letters which Professor Rizzo wrote to me on 15 June, 30 July, 16 August and 21 November 1999. The quotations from the correspondence between the Griffiths were made by Professor Rizzo from the 1770, four-volume edition of *A series of genuine letters between Henry and Frances*. The orthography has been slightly modernised by me. I am more than grateful to her for her most generous help in placing all this at my disposal and allowing me to use it in this way. For the Griffiths, see also Hubert Butler, *Escape from the anthill*, pp 15–23.

and 'a near acquaintance of the Muses'); and other members of the professional class – the class among whom Mrs Griffith usually found her friends, most of whom were without a university education. This was certainly a contrast to the world into which Agar had been born: his prominence in the coterie shows that he was not only the man of real sentiment whom Mrs Griffith admired but also no stickler for rank. It was also a contrast to the world of Richard Griffith, who was most at home with the Irish gentry and aristocracy and strove for acceptance among the literary *élite*. Mrs Griffith herself was acquainted with Thomas Sheridan and Garrick, and was a friend of the actress, Kitty Clive, who introduced her to Horace Walpole (on whom she made no particular impression). Prior to this encounter, Walpole had written patronisingly that, apart from his own *Castle of Otranto*, 'There is nothing else new [in January 1765] but a play called "The Platonic wife", written by an Irish Mrs Griffiths [*sic*], which in charity to her was suffered to run three nights.'[117] The near-failure of her play must have been a great disappointment to her. She had hoped that her husband and she could make a better living in the literary world of London; also that Richard Griffith, through his family connections, might obtain some government office.

In the meantime, he was at least out of range of his Irish creditors, although he returned to Ireland for several months once or twice a year and probably spent more time there than in London. One complication in the Agar-Griffith relationship was that Richard Griffith had a vote in Callan borough, then in dispute between Agar's uncle, James Agar of Ringwood, and Henry Flood (see pp 100–2). Aware of Griffith's financial difficulties, Charles Agar tried to win, or rather bribe, him over to the Agar side in May 1768 – without success. This did not impair the relationship. In the spring of 1766, when Griffith was in Ireland, Mrs Griffith wrote to him from London: 'Our coterie is dispersed – ... our chaplain in Hampshire [presumably staying at Welbore Ellis' then house in the country, Tylney Hall], and the rest scattered in sundry places.' In December 1767, Griffith, then in Dublin, was proposing to spend Christmas with Agar at the deanery, Kilmore, and Mrs Griffith wrote to him that, 'though I love the good Dean extremely, I shall grudge him the pleasure of your company'. Griffith found Kilmore 'no pleasant country, nor is this spot [the deanery] any situation'. He reported that yesterday he was 'classing the library here', and found 'a certain fine edition of *Pastor Fido* that I had seen before in a certain bookcase. "Cadenus and Vanessa redivivus!" I cried. They mingled love and books together. These *deans* are dangerous people, I find.' In reply, Mrs Griffith assured him that he 'need have no jealousy about his *Amaryllis*'. In the following year, 1768, after Agar's appointment as bishop of Cloyne, Griffith visited him there twice, in July and, apparently, August. In July or early August he wrote: 'I have been to see the Bishop and have the pleasure to acquaint you that he appears to be in perfect health. He was often ill in London, and has been a good deal so since he came over, particularly when I was with him at his deanery.' Later, probably in August, he wrote from Cloyne: 'Our friend is the same

117 Walpole to 1st earl of Hertford, 27 Jan. 1765, printed in Peter Cunningham (ed.), *The letters of Horace Walpole, earl of Orford* (9 vols., London, 1857–9), iv. 319.

kind of good-humoured, affable person he was in Craven Street. He is extremely hospitable and affable, and I dare say will be much liked and respected in this country. ... I never was in an easier house in my life, for such a pilgrim as I am: neither drink, play, suppers nor constraint on one's time.'

There are disappointingly few letters from Mrs Griffith among Agar's papers. But two, written in April and June of the following year, 1769, are of interest. Both make it clear that he was in great social demand, especially among women, because of his conversation and manners 'of a perfect courtier'. In April she scolds him 'for staying so long from [his London] friends who truly love you; but I have reason to believe that you find such, wherever you are known'; and in June: 'You say that the *Fathers* have dulled the liveliness of your imagination and rendered you unfit for conversation. If your Lordship will but please to talk as you write, I say let the *daughters* take care of their hearts.'[118] Towards the end of July, still in London, she wrote to her husband in Ireland that their once cheerful coterie 'is dwindled into a small and sorrowful party at present. O! return to us soon [from Ireland], and kidnap our dear chaplain over with you.' Soon afterwards, Griffith wrote to her that he had been at Cloyne for two days, where her novel, *The delicate distress,* was much in demand. 'The Bishop speaks of it. A very pretty Miss Berkley sat up reading it all night, and her attention was so great that she suffered her cap to take fire, but said that she *quenched it with her tears.*' Later, when Mrs Griffith's letter had reached him, Griffith replied: 'I read your paragraph to your chaplain, as you style him; and he says that the kidnapping of him would be catching a Tartar'. These references to Agar, inconsequential though in most respects they are, are of interest, partly because they illuminate a time of his life which is little documented in his own correspondence, and partly because they depict him in the unexpected environment of a non-political, platonically flirtatious, literary circle of friends.

This discussion of his aesthetic interests has so far been focussed on literature and music. In Scott's already-quoted tribute of 1773, the visual arts are not mentioned; but, from other evidence, it is clear that they were important to Agar. His forays into architecture are the principal theme of Chapters Seven and Eight, which show that he was not simply contemporary and fashionable in his taste, but had some appreciation of the architecture of previous generations and centuries. In the case of painting, his taste was perhaps fashionable – and derivative. His family and he were painted by predictable, big-name artists – John Hoppner(?), George Romney,[119] and

118 Mrs Griffith to Agar, 2 Apr. and 17 June 1769, T/3719/C/3/1–2.   119 There is some confusion about the identity of sitters and the attribution to artists in some of the family portraits at Somerley. The putative Hoppner is a very neo-classical portrait of a young woman who is supposed to be Mrs Agar in 1776 (the year of her wedding), but on grounds of style and costume is much more likely to be the Agars' only daughter, perhaps in the year of *her* wedding in 1798 (fig. 10). The painter, it has been tentatively suggested, is not Hoppner but Frederick Prussia Plowman (1773–1820), a follower of Hugh Douglas Hamilton (1739–1808). In the hall at Somerley is a portrait, supposedly of Mrs Agar, by one 'Paull'. But the sitter seems to be a different person from the Mrs Agar whom Stuart painted *c.*1790. More probably, it is 'Miss Agar', Agar's adored sister, Diana. On stylistic grounds, this portrait could be by Hoppner. I am

Gilbert Stuart. It was almost certainly Welby who suggested Romney as the painter of Agar's portrait for the Christ Church Hall in 1782 (see the front cover). Ellis, too, was full of advice about painters, as about most things.[120] But the painter with whom Agar is most strongly associated, the American-born Gilbert Stuart, was not recommended to him by either Welby or Ellis. There are no less than five Stuarts at Somerley, all of them commissioned by Agar: Sir George Macartney, Earl Macartney (1737–1806); John Scott, 1st earl of Clonmell (1739–98); Hugh Carleton, Viscount Carleton (1739–1826); Mrs Agar; and Agar himself (see figs. 5–8). Four of the five (the omission is Clonmell) were recorded by Strickland in 1913.[121] But none seems, until now, to have been reproduced, and no writer on Stuart appears to have looked at them. For this reason, Agar's importance in the Irish phase of Stuart's career has not hitherto been appreciated.

Stuart fled to Ireland to escape his English creditors in early October 1787, and from Ireland back to the United States to escape his Irish creditors in March 1793.[122] The intervening period was his Irish phase. In mid-June 1787, shortly before it began, Mrs Agar wrote to Lord Macartney, who was her cousin as well as a close friend of the Agars, asking him to oblige them by sitting for a portrait. The portrait, now at Somerley (fig. 5), is dated 1787, so it was probably painted in London before Stuart left.[123] At this time, Stuart's leading patron in London society was Macartney's brother-in-law, the 2nd duke of Northumberland, whose children Stuart also painted in 1787.[124] So, Northumberland is likely to have recommended Stuart to Macartney. Furthermore, there was a direct and close connection between Northumberland and Agar (see p. 139), and Northumberland is bound to have given Stuart a letter of introduction to Agar before Stuart set out for Dublin. Stuart's most promising introduction in Dublin was to the lord lieutenant, the already-mentioned duke of Rutland;[125] but Rutland died very soon after Stuart's arrival. This gave vicarious and surrogate consequence to the introduction to Agar.

Agar's ensuing patronage led directly, not only to the four Somerley portraits painted in Ireland, but also to commissions from Lord Clonmell for portraits of himself and Lady Clonmell (the former presumably a variant of the Somerley portrait) and for a double portrait of the Clonmells' children.[126] 'During his stay in Ireland, Stuart painted at least six bishops of the Established Church [Agar

grateful to the Knight of Glin for his help with these problems.   **120** Ellis to Agar, 19 Mar. 1788, T/3719/C/22/4.   **121** Walter George Strickland, *A dictionary of Irish artists* (2 vols., Dublin and London, 1913), ii, pp. 414–16.   **122** Charles Merrill Mount, 'The Irish career of Gilbert Stuart', in the *Quarterly Bulletin of the Irish Georgian Society*, vi, no. 1 (Jan.–Mar. 1963), pp 6 and 25. For help with reference material relating to Stuart, I am grateful to the Knight of Glin, Dr Sighle Bhreathnach-Lynch and Mr Brendan Rooney of the National Gallery of Ireland, and Mrs Anne Stewart of the Ulster Museum.   **123** Mrs Agar to Macartney, 16 June 1787, Macartney papers, PRONI, D/572/9/9; catalogue of the Somerley picture collection, 1884, 21 M 57, general boxes, no. 5.   **124** Richard McLanathan, *Gilbert Stuart* (New York, 1986), pp 58–61.   **125** Ibid., p. 63.   **126** Mount, *Gilbert Stuart: a biography* (New York, 1964), p. 358; Dorinda Evans, *The genius of Gilbert Stuart* (New York, 1999), p. 49.

included]', plus two deans who later became bishops.[127] Not all of them were friends of Agar. But, on the other hand, it would be very surprising if Agar was not responsible for setting a Stuart trend among senior clergymen of fashion. Finally, there is the question of Stuart's famous full-length portraits of Lord Chancellor FitzGibbon/Clare and Speaker Foster, both painted *c.*1790 and to an almost matching size. The portraits are said to have been commissioned to mark the two men's joint term of office as lords justices of Ireland, 1789–90.[128] But as this was not an institutional commission, and as FitzGibbon and Foster had 'always hated each other',[129] it seems likely that they became united in their choice of Stuart because of the recommendation of someone who was a common friend to both of them, as well as a patron of Stuart. Agar certainly fits that bill. All told, it would appear that, if not a connoisseur of painting, he certainly acted as a catalyst where one major painter was concerned.

CLONMELL, CARLETON AND CLARE: AGAR'S POLITICAL CIRCLE

Apart from the Griffiths, their coterie and his other female admirers, most of Agar's friends were politicians, and not necessarily with a strong literary bent like Welbore Ellis. But they, too, were chosen on the basis of intellectual sympathy and equality: in 1797 one of them paid tribute to Agar's 'steady and sincere attachment, ... independent mind and distinguishing understanding'.[130] Most of them were self-made or partly self-made men, distinguished (like himself) as men of business and/or parliamentary performers. Five of them were painted by Stuart. Nearly all of them were lawyers, practising or otherwise. They included, pre-eminently: John Hely-Hutchinson, prime serjeant, 1761–74, and provost of Trinity College, Dublin, 1774–94;[131] Macartney, who had been chief secretary, 1768–72; John Scott, Lord Clonmell, successively solicitor- and attorney-general, 1774–82, and lord chief justice of the king's bench, 1784–98; Hugh Carleton, Lord Carleton, solicitor-general, 1779–87, and lord chief justice of the common pleas, 1787–1800); and, to a lesser extent, Speaker Foster, Lord Chancellor FitzGibbon/Clare, who had been attorney-general, 1783–9, and John Toler, 1st earl of Norbury, successively solicitor- and attorney-general, 1789–1800, and lord chief justice of the common pleas, 1800–27.

Two others who must be included in Agar's inner circle were in a different category. They were Richard Boyle, 2nd Earl of Shannon (1728–1807), and Charles Tottenham Loftus, 1st Baron and Viscount Loftus and 1st earl and marquess of Ely (1738–1806). Both were great borough-owning magnates, not careerists and/or younger sons. Lord Shannon was the leading political magnate in Co. Cork, Agar's

127 Hugh R. Crean, 'Gilbert Stuart and the politics of fine arts patronage in Ireland, 1787–93 ...' (unpublished postgraduate dissertation, City University of New York, 1990), p. 194.   128 Ibid., pp 260–61. But cf. Mount, *Gilbert Stuart: a biography*, pp. 149–50.   129 2nd earl of Shannon to his son, Lord Boyle, 15 Feb. 1791, quoted in Malcomson, *John Foster*, p. 393.   130 Lord Carleton to Agar, 27 Nov. 1797, T/3719/C/31/96.   131 Ellis to Agar, 11 Oct. 1778, Hely-Hutchinson to Agar, 18 Oct. 1778, and Scott to Agar, 11 Nov. 1778, T/3718/C/12/15–16 and 18.

nearest neighbour at Cloyne (see p. 198) and a relation-by-marriage of Lady Clifden; he was intelligent, high-minded and possessed of a boyish sense of humour which he preserved into old age.[132] Agar was even friendlier with Loftus, who rose through all the ranks of the peerage to become marquess of Ely in 1800; he was of coarser fibre than Shannon (or Agar), somewhat 'shifty' and opportunistic in his politics, but also very good company.[133] So the two political magnates had most of the personal qualities of Agar's friends with their way to make in the world. Moreover, because Shannon and Ely had inherited borough-based political interests which were much more extensive than their landed properties, they both had to live – like Agar and the others – by their political wits. Agar had no wish to see himself mixed up with and perhaps subsumed into the Shannon and Ely interests; he saw it as his business to advise the 1st and 2nd Lords Clifden and to steer clear of other political connections. So, his friendship with Shannon and Ely is to be regarded as personal rather than political: exchanges of courtesies and visits with the Shannons, efforts to keep the choleric Ely safely clear of an election duel over Co. Fermanagh in 1797,[134] and preferment and advice to Ely's second son, Lord Robert Tottenham Loftus who, like Agar himself, entered the Church on the strength of family influence and, yet, became a creditable bishop.[135] Nevertheless, there was community of political sentiment among them on Catholic Relief legislation. In a letter to Ellis of late June 1778 on the bill recently transmitted to the British privy council, Agar explained: 'Lord Shannon and Lord Ely [this was Ely's uncle and predecessor], who have the best interests in this country [he presumably means the House of Commons], ... thought the present concessions destructive of the civil and ecclesiastical constitution of this kingdom and are determined to oppose this bill in every stage.'[136] His collusion with them on this occasion ended when Shannon and Ely espoused the unsuccessful wrecking tactic of inserting in the bill a clause repealing the Sacramental Test against protestant dissenters;[137] Agar was not prepared to play politics with the Test. In addition to Shannon and Ely, he was on good, though not so close, terms with two other political magnates. One was George de la Poer Beresford, 2nd earl of Tyrone and 1st marquess of Waterford (1735–1800), and the other Arthur Hill, 2nd marquess of Downshire (1753–1801) – 'our worthy friend, Lord Downshire', whom both Agar and his wife 'liked and esteemed'.[138]

132 Malcomson, 'Lord Shannon', in Esther Hewitt (ed.), *Lord Shannon's letters to his son ...*, *1790–1802* (Belfast, 1982), pp xxiii–lxxix.   **133** G.C. Bolton, *The passing of the Irish Act of Union: a study in parliamentary politics* (Oxford, 1966), pp. 95–6; Malcomson, 'The Irish peerage and the Act of Union, 1800–1971', in *Transactions of the Royal Historical Society, sixth series*, x (2000), pp. 306–7. **134** Ely to Agar, 15 Aug. and 19 Oct. 1797, T/3719/C/31/87–90 and 93, and Judge Tankerville Chamberlain to Agar, 26 Aug. 1797, T/3719/C/31/91.   **135** Agar's 'state' of the diocese of Cashel, 1779–1801, 21 M 57/B6/1, entry *sub* 8 May 1798 (when Agar made Ely's son precentor of Cashel and rector of Bansha, worth *c.*£500 per annum); Acheson, *Church of Ireland*, p. 76.   **136** Agar to Ellis, 24 June 1778, T/3719/C/12/10B.   **137** 2nd earl of Buckinghamshire (the lord lieutenant) to Lord George Germain, 24 June 1778, NLI, Heron papers (Heron was Buckinghamshire's chief secretary), Ms. 13036/12.   **138** Agar to Lady Somerton, 12 Sep. 1801, T/3719/C/35/20.

Nevertheless, even when in political accord or actual concert with him, all these 'friends' had their own fish to fry, and were never going to promote his objects and wishes at significant cost to themselves. The main difference lay in sentiment and tone. When Agar was disappointed of the primacy for the last time, in 1800, Lord Shannon expressed what was obviously sincere regret, while Agar's supposed friend and col-league, Lord Clare, expressed undissimulated glee (see p. 596).[139] Where the political magnates had a certain dignity and detachment about them, bred of generations of political influence, Agar's careerist friends were uninhibited in their jealousies and rivalries. Of the latter, the only one who actually (though unintentionally) damaged Agar's career was Provost Hely-Hutchinson in 1778 (see pp 151–2). He stands out in all political companies in the second half of the eighteenth century because of his insatiable pursuit of power and personal gain, and soon fades from Agar's circle and largely from his correspondence.[140] The rest of Agar's circle had a more benign influ-ence on his career and even made common cause with him, when their own interests coincided with his. Scott's, for example, did so in 1778–80, when Agar and he both laboured to oust Buckinghamshire's 'Patriot' advisers and, when that failed, Bucking-hamshire himself. But, since most of them had been chosen as friends by Agar because they were on or near an intellectual par with him, it was inevitable that they, as well as he, should be ambitious, rising men with their own names and fortunes to make, and that this should be their first priority.

The closest to Agar of them all, at least for a considerable length of time, was John Scott, 1st Lord Earlsfort and 1st Viscount and earl of Clonmell. Scott has not – to say the least – had a good press. If half of what has been written to his disparagement were true, Agar's friendship with him would cast doubt, not just on Agar's judgement, but on his character. Scott has been represented as callous, bullying, cheating, unscrupu-lous, avaricious, meretricious, buffoonish, ignorant, low-born and fat. A near-contem-porary character sketch softens the picture with some insights plainly based on personal knowledge. It begins with an account of how Scott was taken up by the lord lieutenant, the 4th Viscount Townshend, in 1769, and

> not only answered, but even exceeded, the most sanguine expectations ... . Without much encumbrance of argument ..., all the light artillery ... of jests and *bons mots*, pointed sarcasms, popular stories and popular allusions were entirely his own. ... [As attorney-general from 1777 onwards], the positions which Mr Scott often advanced were the offspring of the moment, of a mind hurried and driven beyond its sphere – in short, of a political combatant who was obliged at any rate to defend administration. In this situation, he was often ungenerously left almost alone ... . [As prime serjeant in 1784], he was listened to with evident satisfaction in that House where a year or two before ... "he had made himself marvellously ungracious". ... He had many social virtues and, in

139 Shannon to Agar, 26 July 1800, T/3719/C/34/30; Clare to Auckland, 24 July [1800], printed in Arthur Aspinall (ed.), *The later correspondence of George III* (5 vols., Cambridge, 1962–70), iii, pp 380–81. 140 But see p. 444*n*.

convivial hours, much unaffected wit and pleasantry, with a cordial civility of manners. To his great honour be it recorded, he never forgot an obligation, [and] ... his gratitude to persons who had assisted him in the mediocrity of his fortune was ... marked by real generosity and munificence.[141]

Surprisingly, the 'political recollections' of Sir Laurence Parsons, 5th Bt, the disciple of Scott's great adversary, Henry Flood, also speak indulgently of Scott. Parsons recounts how Scott made his House of Commons *début* as a runner or whipper-in on behalf of Dublin Castle. He 'was not a man of eloquence, but had great felicity in telling a story. He was a very entertaining companion and an admirable mimic.' In one parliamentary exchange, probably in 1779,

> Flood ... drew a ludicrous picture of Scott and of a recent attack on his house by the mob, insinuating that he represented this as much more serious to government than it really was, in order to enhance his merits. He described him as going to the Castle to the lord lieutenant to state his sufferings, weeping in the ante-chamber, blubbering in the presence chamber, etc., and getting his windows repaired again with *crown* glass.

The revealing postscript to this anecdote is that, shortly afterwards, Scott bumped into Flood outside the Commons' chamber, and spoke to him in Scott's usual, 'good-humoured way'.[142] This latter quality in Scott also struck the lord lieutenant of the day, another political enemy: '[He is] a good-humoured, pleasant man, with strong nerves, some imagination and information, but indiscreet in debate and without a follower'.[143]

Scott's letters to Agar, a hitherto unknown source, also throw new light on the man. For example, the charge of callousness is to a considerable extent answered by a letter of 1780 containing his very plausible justification for pronouncing the death sentence, and resisting the clamour for its commutation, in the *cause célèbre* of the abduction and rape of the Misses Catherine and Ann Kennedy of Rathmaiden, Co. Waterford.[144] In general, his letters show why, to anyone with a sense of fun, Scott must have been a treasured companion. They are not perhaps so suitably charitable or so morally proper as to be addressed to a churchman: for example, writing of their common political opponents in September 1778, Scott rejoiced that 'We are both very

---

141 Francis Hardy, *Memoirs of the political and private life of James Caulfeild, [1st] earl of Charlemont* (2nd ed., 2 vols., London, 1812). Hardy did not enter parliament until 1783. This passage is quoted, without attribution, in Stephen Barlow, *The history of Ireland from the earliest period to the present time* ... (2 vols., London, 1814), i, pp 393–6.   142 Rosse papers (Parsons succeed in 1807 as 2nd earl of Rosse), Birr Castle, Co. Offaly, F/13.   143 Buckinghamshire to Hotham Thompson, 3 June 1780, Hotham papers, PRONI, T/3429/1/60.   144 Scott to Agar, [late Oct.–early Nov. 1780], T/3719/C/14/33. For a sentimental and unconvincing expression of the contrary view, see Margery Weiner, *Matters of felony: a true tale of eighteenth-century Ireland* (New York, 1967). See also draft address of thanks, in Agar's hand, from the sheriff and grand jury of Co. Kilkenny to Scott, 7 Apr. 1787, T/3719/C/15/6, and Lord Clifden to Agar, 12 May 1781, 21 M 57/B23/8.

young, thank God, and with the blessing of the Almighty and the assistance of an archbishop, you shall see some of those folks in a way of salvation, if repentance conduceth to it.'[145] But the great majority of his letters show that their writer was a man of wit and education, and not the brutal and unlettered careerist of legend.

All, however, is not revisionism. One fairly early letter, written in cheerful and bawdy middle age, tends to confirm the extravagances of behaviour attributed to him by the mid-nineteenth century, nationalist writer, W.J. Fitzpatrick.[146] In December 1776, Scott wrote Agar the following amusing account of his private, or not-so-private, life:

> I wish to inform your Lordship that I am neither married nor settled, but as much in love and as ignorant with whom as ever schoolboy or simple girl was. ... Finding myself given in marriage to a lady with whom I never once spoke *tête-à-tête* nor never most assuredly mean to, I thought the most effectual way to prevent any mischief to her and to cry down the report was to go to the green boxes of the playhouse, where I had the honour of appearing at the side of two common wenches. I sat very demurely until my friends of the upper gallery, struck with the modesty and bashfulness of my appearance, cried out with one voice, Ah, Mr Copperface [a term of abuse applied to Scott in the House of Commons because of his brazenness], are *you* there? Having received the charge, I retired in good *order*, but not without some apparent confusion, and since that I have not been saluted *au Benedict*, nor have I spoiled a lady's market whose mutton I certainly never meant or intend to stick a fork in.[147]

Agar clearly enjoyed jokes about his friend's unsavoury reputation. Preserved among his papers is a printed squib of 1775 protesting at the rumoured appointment as solicitor-general of this 'most profligate and notorious upstart',

> Whose front, all o'er bronz'd, mark'd with gibbets and halters,
> In defence of injustice, ne'er winces nor alters.[148]

Physically, the two friends were a gift to the caricaturist (though there is no known example of a caricaturist's having accepted the gift), with Agar small and spare and Scott increasingly corpulent. The latter's embarrassingly frank diary, gleefully gobbetted by Fitzpatrick,[149] abounds in confessions like: 'My size is so much increased that I have

---

145 Scott to Agar, 2 Sep. 1778, T/3719/C/12/12. Agar was not yet an archbishop, which is the point of the joke. 146 W.J. Fitzpatrick, *Ireland before the Union, with revelations from the unpublished diary of Lord Clonmell ...* (London, 1867), and the already-cited *Sham Squire*. These two repetitious jumbles of material both quote from Clonmell's diary, although Fitzpatrick states that he had not seen the original, but worked from a privately printed version run off by one of Clonmell's executors 'about 1810' for the perusal of a few of his friends. There is a copy of a subsequent privately printed version in the TCD Library (OLS B.4.11), which dates from the 1850s or early 1860s and at all events from no later than 1864. 147 Scott to Agar, [29 Dec. 1776?], T/3719/C/10/7. 148 T/3719/C/9/6. 149 Fitzpatrick, *Ireland before the Union*, pp 34–5, and *Sham Squire*, p. 103.

broken two carriage springs'. It also abounds in good resolutions, such as 'a complete reform from snuff, sleep, swearing, sloth, gross eating, malt liquor and indolence' and an acknowledgement that it was a 'disgrace if you are caught in bed by anybody – so said Demosthenes'.[150] Their frequency, however, only testifies to their ineffectiveness. In March 1788, he actually began a letter to Agar with an apology 'that your Grace should have caught me in bed'! A later and more earnest diary entry of April 1796 runs: 'I have made many enemies by my levity and unguardedness in mimicry ... . From this day, then, ... no buffoonery, no mimicry, no ridicule.'[151] Scott's most memorable aphorism, obviously deemed by Fitzpatrick to be too explicit for the Victorian public, was: 'Man has very few such enemies as his tongue, his palate and his penis.'[152]

The most recent study of Scott concludes that he was much more than the buffoon depicted by Fitzpatrick.[153] The quick combativeness of which he had made himself a perfect master in the House of Commons might have seemed a near-dis-qualification for the judicial bench. But in May 1784, at the very outset of his career as a lord chief justice, the new Lord Earlsfort strongly impressed one by no means sympathetic member of the House of Lords, Thomas Barnard, bishop of Killaloe. Addressing that House in its judicial capacity, Earlsfort defended his own judgement in the king's bench in the long-running *cause célèbre* of Loftus v. Hume (over the Ely estate in Co. Fermanagh), and refuted the counter-arguments of the lord chancellor, the 1st Viscount Lifford, 'with great facility and clearness ... . He was great indeed, not only beyond what the world expected from him, but even above anything I have ever heard anywhere', and spoke 'to the admiration of everyone that heard him and to the conviction of some ... who came into the House prepared to vote for the reversal of his judgment.'[154] Earlsfort did not sustain this achievement. By August 1787, it was his superficiality as a judge which was the subject of comment.

> In the course of last sessions, a bill was brought in and passed in the House of Commons for fixing forever and uniformly throughout the kingdom, the time of the assizes. However, by the eloquence of that great luminary of the law, Lord Earlsfort, who assured the House of Lords that it was a positive violation of Magna Charta, they were prevailed upon to throw it out. ... This regulation was so unanswerably beneficial to the whole kingdom and to everyone concerned with circuits, that the judges ... have unanimously acknowledged the propriety [of it]. I hope Lord Earlsfort will be left to bewail this infringement on the Great Charter.[155]

Another, much more serious criticism of him in his judicial capacity was made in the following year by Henry Flood, with whom his relations had clearly deteriorated:

150 *Clonmell Diary (TCD)*, p. 297.   151 Ibid., p. 439.   152 Ibid., p. 175.   153 Draft new *DNB* entry for Clonmell by Professor S.J. Connolly, of which he kindly made me a photocopy.   154 Barnard to his patron, Buckinghamshire (an enemy of Earlsfort), 10 May 1785, NLI, Heron papers, Ms. 13047/4.   155 William Disney to Christopher Henry Earbery, 4 Aug. 1787, Crofton (Earbery) papers, TCD, Mss. 3575–3587a/142.

Lord Earlsfort's charge [to the jury in a politically motivated case of alleged riot] was such as might be expected from a man who waded to the Bench through every sink of corruption. It was not law, it was not justice, it was not truth; but a cunning, insidious, perplexed suppression of every fact that was in ... [the accused's] favour, and an exaggeration of whatever was likely to make against him.[156]

These comments, in conjunction with diary entries like 'I observe my memory much impaired' (November 1791),[157] suggest that Clonmell suffered from dramatically declining powers. But there is every reason to suppose that, in his prime, he was Agar's intellectual equal as well as boon companion.

If W.J. Fitzpatrick's version of events were to be believed, Agar should never have become Scott's boon companion because of Scott's alleged double-dealing with Agar's relations, the Mathew family of Thomastown, Co. Tipperary. Scott was a Tipperary man himself. He was a younger son of Thomas Scott of Mohudder, a substantial squire with a 1,400-acre estate, and by 1778 he had built himself a country house called Dovehill, between Carrick-on-Suir and Clonmel.[158] In 1768, he had married Catherine Roe, a widow, the daughter of Thomas Mathew of Annfield, later of Thomastown (d.1777), and sister of Francis Mathew of Thomastown, later 1st earl of Landaff (d.1806). Agar, too, was closely connected by marriage with the Mathews; his first cousin, Ellis, or Ellisha, Smyth, who died young in 1781, was Francis Mathew's first wife. Scott is accused by Fitzpatrick of having defrauded the Mathew family in two different instances: first, he had 'intruded himself as a trustee for lands [Boulyduff] which [Thomas] Mathew had settled on his mistress [one Celia Robinson] and in 1771 obtained its possession ...; [and he] eventually laid claim to moneys in right of his wife following her death in 1771'. The former dispute allegedly involved sleight of hand by Scott under the Penal Laws, because Thomas Mathew had been born and brought up a catholic, though he had conformed in 1755.[159] The latter is lost in the mists of Mathew family settlements. Scott is 'said to have claimed two separate sums of £6,000 cash as due to him, through his late wife, ... and in 1776 to have accepted 2,000 acres of land, worth £1,000 a year, in settlement of his claim.'[160] Before his claim was settled, he is supposed to have fought a duel with his brother-in-law, Francis Mathew, later 1st earl of Landaff, Thomas Mathew's son and successor.

There was definitely a quarrel between Scott and a Mathew; but it does not seem to have been with Francis Mathew (whom Scott described to Agar in a letter of 1781 as 'our friend and cousin'),[161] but with his father, Thomas, and it was over the

---

156 Flood to Laurence Parsons, [May–July 1788?], Rosse papers, C/8/45.   157 *Clonmell diary (TCD)*, p. 370.   158 Thomas P. Power, *Land, politics and society in eighteenth-century Tipperary* (Oxford, 1993), p. 105.   159 Fitzpatrick, *Ireland before the Union*, pp 13–14; Power, *Eighteenth-century Tipperary*, p. 105. For a subsequent instance of Clonmell's alleged chicanery towards a connection of the Mathew family, see Fitzpatrick, *Sham Squire*, p. 104.   160 Connolly, 'Clonmell'.   161 Scott to Agar, 24 [Jan. 1781] and 7 July 1781, T/3719/C/15/8. In the context, the words cannot have been satirical.

Co. Tipperary election of 1776. Thomas Mathew had actually brought Scott forward as the running-mate to Francis Mathew in this election.[162] There was then some dispute between them, about which Scott wrote obscurely to Agar: 'In consequence of Mr [Thomas] Mathew's outrageous conduct to you, I have declared in Clonmel for Mr [Henry] Prittie', one of the opposing candidates.[163] In the end, Scott withdrew from the election contest, and Prittie and Francis Mathew were narrowly victorious. Scott was a well known duellist and – unusually for a crown lawyer and judge – publicly defended the practice.[164] He may have fought a duel with a Mathew. If so, it is more likely to have been over the election than over Mrs Scott's fortune, and he probably had the sympathy and support of Agar. In the election and local politics of the county, the Mathews, though converts, were at the head of what Agar described in August 1787 as 'the popish interest', which were 'much the most numerous, and having by various means for many years been gratified by the appointment of sheriffs friendly to them and their party, ... are said to have misused that indulgence'.[165] In October 1796, Agar's wife wrote Agar a couple of letters containing sardonic criticism of the Mathews and their Emancipationist politics. She concluded: 'I only lend my ears, but not my belief, to any of that family, knowing that not one of them ever open their mouth but to deceive.'[166] In family politics, too, Agar was at odds with them. In 1786, his first cousin, Sir Skeffington Smyth, 1st Bt, the brother of Ellis, or Ellisha, Mathew (d.1781), wrote to Agar complaining bitterly of Francis Mathew's 'very unjust demands' of Smyth; he also complained of Mathew's 'very dishonourable' conduct towards the comte de Jarnac (1740–1813), a French Huguenot nobleman who had married another of Smyth's sisters in 1777.[167] It may be that Fitzpatrick, knowing something of these various family quarrels involving the Mathews, jumped delightedly to the conclusion that the villain of the piece was Scott. The clearest indication of Scott's innocence is the compliment which Agar paid him in 1781 of making him godfather to Agar's third son.[168] Scott was the only godfather or godmother to any of Agar's children who was not a family member; and it would be utterly out of character for Agar to have made this exception in favour of a man who had defrauded Agar's cousins-by-marriage.

162 Power, *Eighteenth-century Tipperary*, p. 276.   163 Scott to Agar, [May? 1776?], T/3719/C/10/5.   164 Kelly, *Duelling in* Ireland, pp 149 and 163. Dr Kelly computes the number of duels fought by Scott as four. In the most sensational of these, Scott's duel with James Cuffe, later Lord Tyrawly, Scott was the entirely innocent and unoffending party – Scott to Agar, [pre-25 Oct. 1774], T/3719/C/8/5–6.   165 Agar to Thomas Orde (the chief secretary), 11 Aug. 1787, T/3719/C/21/32. See also Kevin Whelan, 'The Catholic Church in Co. Tipperary, 1700–1900', in William Nolan (ed.), *Tipperary history and society* (Dublin, 1985), p. 216.   166 Lady Somerton to Agar, [16] and 19 Oct. 1796, T/3719/C/30/36 and 40. The same sardonic tone is evident in a later letter to their son, the 2nd earl of Normanton, from his Irish agent about the extravagant expenditure of the 2nd earl of Landaff on Tipperary electioneering and entertaining – John Hare to Normanton, 3 Dec. 1812, 21 M 57, 2nd earl's unreferenced correspondence.   167 Smyth to Agar, [?9 or 19] May 1786 and Oct. 1786, T/3719/C/20/8 and 33. For Jarnac, see: *Almanach de Gotha ... 1872* (Gotha, [1871?], p. 191; L.M. Cullen, *The Irish brandy houses of eighteenth-century France* (Dublin, 2000), pp 65 and 167.   168 Notebook, 1761–1827, mainly used by Agar to record family information, 21 M 57/D47.

For reasons unconnected with the Mathew family, Agar's relations with Scott had their ups and downs (and went steadily down from *c.*1790): this was because Agar and Scott, and Agar, Scott and their other careerist cronies, were a highly competitive crew, most members of whom delighted in backbiting jokes at each other's aspirations and limitations. Late in 1786, John Toler wrote brutally about the dying lord chief justice of the common pleas: 'Paterson is not yet dead, except in law, but it is not possible he should ever come into the Hall before he goes to the Abbey.'[169] Nor did he. Scott, now Lord Earlsfort, recorded in his diary: 'Wednesday, 25th April, 1798. ... Lord Chief Justice Paterson, my sincere friend, dead; his intended successor, Carleton, a worthless wretch, though I was his maker; Lord Chancellor Lifford, a declining, insincere trickster.'[170] In June 1788, Carleton discussed the probability that Lifford would resign his office and never return to Ireland, and the departure of Lord Earlsfort, Attorney-General FitzGibbon and Provost Hely-Hutchinson for England, all ostensibly because of their wives' health, and all really for the purpose of pressing their claims to the chancellorship. In October Carleton reported: 'Lord and Lady Earlsfort are well, and she as fine as £10,000 or £12,000 expended in [*sic*] diamonds can make her.'[171]

FitzGibbon was of course the successful candidate for the chancellorship, and went on to be created earl of Clare in 1795. In that year, through no fault of Clare, the legal element in the House of Lords had to be strengthened by the conferring of a peerage on the chief baron of the exchequer. In recommending this peerage, the lord lieutenant remarked censoriously of the two chief justices: 'Lord Clonmell is no lawyer, and Lord Carleton is so often ill that he cannot be reckoned upon.'[172] Most of Carleton's illnesses were the product of valetudinarianism; he was, besides, timid and old-womanish.[173] In November 1797, Lord Ely amusingly described the reluctance of Carleton and the attorney-general, Arthur Wolfe, to attend a cabinet meeting where Co. Carlow was to be placed under the Insurrection Act, and how both came eventually, looking 'like fellows going to be hanged'.[174] In the same month, November 1797, Carleton reported to Agar that Clonmell, too, had been 'very alarmingly ill. ... The Attorney[-General, Wolfe] has been in great expectations [of succeeding Clonmell], but probably will for the present be baffled.'[175] It was also reported that 'Toler is at present much in confidence, and ... will soon be preferred, as Lord Clonmell is declining fast. He cannot sit this term.'[176] When Clonmell at last died, there was a series of changes and promotions, as a result of which Wolfe succeeded him as chief justice, and Toler was promoted from solicitor- to attorney-general. In

169 John Toler to Agar, 7 Nov. 1786, T/3719/C/20/35.   170 *Clonmell diary (TCD)*, p. 332. 171 Carleton to Agar, 15 June and 15 Oct. 1788, T/3719/C/22/26 and 36.   172 Camden to Pitt, 4 May 1795, Pratt papers, Centre for Kentish Studies, Maidstone: photocopy in PRONI, T/2627/ 4/14.   173 For an excellent specimen of all these failings, see Carleton to 1st Lord Redesdale, 28 June 1804, Hardwicke papers, Add. Ms. 35750, f. 242. On the other hand, Carleton had moments of robust decisiveness – see Carleton to Orde, 5 Oct. 1784, Bolton papers, NLI, Ms. 16350, ff. 28–30, and Cornwallis to Portland, 20 July 1798, Home Office papers, HO 100/66, ff. 350–52.   174 Ely to Agar, 16 Nov. 1797, T/3719/C/31/95.   175 Carleton to Agar, 27 Nov. 1797, T/3719/C/31/96. 176 John Stewart to 1st marquess of Abercorn, 7 Nov. 1797, Abercorn papers, PRONI, T/2541/ IB2/30.

August 1798, the House of Commons was busy 'trying whether men have been *guilty of high treason who have been already hanged for the same*. Toler ... talks nonsense incessantly ... . If our former Attorney [Wolfe] was a bad politician, our present one is a bad lawyer; so that the leap from political imbecility to legal ignorance has not mended our situation much.'[177] It deteriorated further in July 1800, when 'Our friend, Carleton ...', as Clare put it, 'very foolishly resigned his office of chief justice ... under a foolish impression that his health suffers by the labours of his court. I feel annoyed at losing him as a judge, and much more annoyed at the apprehension that he will be succeeded by Toler.'[178]

In an early, but undated, entry in his diary, Clonmell wrote: 'connect yourself with as few in intimacy as you can, but never with a man in the same line or profession with yourself.'[179] Because Agar was not in the same profession as his lawyer-cronies, he was not in direct competition with them for office. When writing to him, Clare – for example – was always friendly and even deferential. In a letter of August 1793, he declared: 'in ... every ... instance in which the Church is interested, I shall always take the liberty to communicate privately with your Grace before I take any step which may become the topic of public discussion.'[180] However, as Agar must have known perfectly well, Clare did not always live up to these professions. Even under the stressful conditions of his interrogation by the Irish privy council early in 1798, Thomas Reynolds of Kilkea Castle, Co. Kildare, a United Irishman (and informer), sensed the tension between the two men; he noted that Clare 'rather petulantly [cut Agar short with] "My Lord, you interrupt the business" '.[181] Agar was probably unaware of the extent of Clare's jealousy of and treachery towards him; and, on Agar's side, there is no recorded instance of treachery or even backbiting in relation to Clare – beyond the fact that he did disloyally harbour among his papers three anti-Clare squibs or poems.[182] But it takes little imagination to see that Agar was a threat and rival to Clare and other senior lawyers: though by profession a churchman, he was alarmingly well travelled in the statute book, a master (under Ellis' tutorship)[183] of legal and parliamentary precedent (see p. 35), and often referred to and deferred to for his opinion on such matters.

In February 1782, for example, he promoted a bill which had no connection whatever with the Church – a very technical measure 'for making the recovery of debts secured by judgement, statute staple or recognizance more effectual'.[184] The isolated record of the debates in the House of Lords during the session of 1783–4 which is printed among *The proceedings and debates of the House of Commons ..., 1781–97*, gives two examples of Agar's quoting 'with great ability The mirror [of

---

177 Robert Johnson to 2nd marquess of Downshire, 18 [Aug. 1798], Downshire papers, PRONI, D/607/F/351. **178** Clare to Auckland, 24 July 1800, *Later correspondence of George III*, iii, pp 380–81. **179** *Clonmell diary (TCD)*, p. 65. **180** FitzGibbon to Agar, 27 Aug. 1793, T/3719/C/27/7. **181** Thomas Reynolds Junior, *The life of Thomas Reynolds ... by his son ...* (2 vols., London, 1838), pp 269–70. I am indebted for this reference to Sir Richard Aylmer, Bt. **182** T/3719/C/29/45/1–3. **183** Agar to Ellis, 21 and [pre-21] Mar. 1787, and Ellis to Agar, 23–4 Mar. 1787, T/3719/C/21/13–15. **184** Printed copy of Agar's bill, 1781, and his speech notes on it, 14 Feb. 1782, 21 M 57/A17/4 and A17/1.

parliament] and several ancient law books, ... [and] displaying much legal and parliamentary knowledge'.[185] On the appeal to the House of Lords in Loftus v. Hume in
March 1784, Agar 'took a leading part in the debate ... in favour of the king's bench
[i.e. in support of his friend, Loftus/Ely]'. '[He] was truly powerful in his chain of
reasoning and correct in his law quotations', and did not hesitate to differ from Lord
Chancellor Lifford.[186] In June 1784, just after the promotion of Scott to the lord chief
justiceship and a peerage, and five years before the promotion of FitzGibbon, it was
noted by a Dublin Castle official: 'The Archbishop of Cashel has been leading in the
House of Lords, both as politician and judge. No confidence at all in the Chancellor.'[187] In March 1792, on another technical measure relating to the small-debt
jurisdiction of manor courts, Agar recorded that he 'spoke for the bill against the
Chancellor [now FitzGibbon] and Lord Carleton, but would not vote out of respect
to them'.[188] In 1795, on a bill 'to explain the Summary Tithe Act of the 3rd and 4th of
George III' which 'was particularly offensive to Lord Clonmell and not approved by
other law lords', Agar agreed with the objections of the lawyers, but took obvious
pleasure in showing that he had no need of their assistance. He 'therefore struck out
in the committee all such parts as were objected to, and substituted other provisions
which gave general satisfaction'.[189] In the same year, 1795, he did not hesitate to pit his
own interpretation of the English Coronation Oath Act against that of the Lord
Chancellor of England (see pp 517–19). At a humbler and more practical level, he
busied himself during the 1790s in codifying the scattered statute law in the following
three subject areas – glebe-house building, the improvement of barren lands, and
special powers possessed by magistrates (see pp 347, 483 and 524.).

     Within Ireland, Agar was in competition with the 'law lords', and with other peers,
for the unofficial roles of leading member of the lord lieutenant's cabinet and leading
spokesman for the administration in the House of Lords. Preserved among his papers
is a considerable rarity, an account of what passed at a council or cabinet meeting held
by Buckinghamshire at the Castle in May 1780 to consider an opposition motion for a
separate Irish Mutiny Act. The intended recipients of the account were Ellis and,
through him, Lord North; so it is not so much a minute of the proceedings as the first
of a number of examples of Agar's gift, and awareness of the need, for self-publicity.
Since Agar was at variance with most of Buckinghamshire's other advisers, he naturally
gives himself the longest, ablest and toughest speech, and the only one containing all

185 *The Parliamentary register or history of the proceedings ... [etc.]* (17 vols., Dublin, 1782–1801), iii
[part 2], pp 31 and 117. The source of this record appears to have been the 2nd Viscount
Mountmorres, a Co. Kilkenny peer but in the opposite camp to Agar on most issues recorded; so his
seems to be a genuinely independent tribute. For Mountmorres, see Malcomson and D.J. Jackson,
'Sir Henry Cavendish and the proceedings of the Irish House of Commons, 1776–1800', in D.W.
Hayton (ed.), *The Irish Parliament in the eighteenth century: the long apprenticeship* (Edinburgh, 2001),
p. 143.   186 Bishop Barnard to Buckinghamshire, 25 Mar. 1784, NLI, Ms. 13047/3.   187 Edward
Cooke to William Eden, 1 June 1784, Auckland papers, BL, Add. Ms. 34419, ff. 396–7.   188 Note
by Agar on the Manor Courts Bill, 16 Mar. 1792, 21 M 57/A32/11. *The journals of the House of Lords
of the kingdom of Ireland* (8 vols., Dublin, 1780–1800), vii. 57, show that the bill was dropped on
17 March.   189 Agar's 'state' of the diocese of Cashel, 1779–1801, 21 M 57/B6/1.

the things which North would be glad to hear.[190] Within the subsequent and usually less heterogeneous and divided 'Irish cabinets' of the 1780s and 1790s, Agar also seems to have preferred to be an isolated figure and solo performer. He was out on his own in another respect: his anxiety to stand well with an extra-parliamentary audience. It was his practice to provide newspaper editors with 'copy' in the form of the text of his speeches, possibly before they were given. In one instance, a famous speech he made in February 1789 (see p. 168), his autograph draft, which is word-for-word the same as the newspaper version, runs: 'In this part of his argument his Grace showed a perfect knowledge of the subject [!] ... [His] reasoning ... was delivered in a most forcible, striking and spirited manner, and appeared to meet the general concurrence of as crowded an assembly as was ever seen in any House of Parliament. We lament that we can give only so imperfect a sketch of some parts of it.'[191]

Before FitzGibbon succeeded the unsatisfactory Lord Lifford, the leadership of the House of Lords to a considerable extent revolved among Agar, Earlsfort and others, and there was often 'No confidence at all in the Chancellor'. Earlsfort complained that Lifford, as well as being an indifferent lawyer, was 'a miserable speaker'.[192] Indeed, Earlsfort owed his peerage to that circumstance: the chief secretary, Thomas Orde, remarked in March 1784 that, 'as the happy day of trying the apellant jurisdiction is arrived, the Chancellor must not be left the only law lord in the House of Peers'.[193] Lord Buckingham, during whose lord lieutenancy (1787–9) Lifford at last died, went much further. He maintained that for the twenty-two years that Lifford had held the great seal, he had been charged with 'constant misconduct and inefficiency as a political character, reprobated by almost every lord lieutenant who has been in Ireland, who all felt, not only the want of assistance from him, but the actual mischiefs of his language and conduct ... [as] the minister of the House of Lords.'[194] In December 1786, when Agar was temporarily out of favour with the Castle because of his vehement opposition to any species of tithe or Church reform, Thomas Orde agonised 'about the conduct of business in the House of Lords in the next session. The situation does not admit of entire confidence in the Archbishop of Cashel. Lord Earlsfort in his wantonness threw away his consideration and consequence. The Chancellor is not well circumstanced for directing the business of government.'[195] In January 1788, with Lifford almost eighty and sinking fast, Orde's successor, Alleyne Fitzherbert, had even greater reason for anxiety, and besought assistance from Agar over a 'motion which had been made the preceding day in the House of Lords'. With tongue in cheek, Agar recorded:

> Mr Fitzherbert appeared to the Archbishop to have a greater reliance on the
> Archbishop's attention to such subjects than could be warranted by anything

190 Minute by Agar, 8 May 1780, T/3719/C/14/22A.   191 Text of, and gloss on, Agar's speech on the Pension Bill (both in Agar's hand), [30 Mar. 1789], 21 M 57/A16/4.   192 *Clonmell diary (TCD)*, p. 347.   193 Orde to 2nd earl of Shelburne, 8 Mar. 1784, Jupp/Aspinall transcript from the Bowood papers.   194 Buckingham to his brother, Hon. W.W. Grenville, 13 May 1789, *H.M.C. Dropmore Mss.*, i, pp 467–71.   195 Orde to Rutland, 11 Dec. 1786, *H.M.C. Rutland Mss.*, iii. 361.

said to him either by the lord lieutenant [Buckingham] or Mr F. The
Archbishop therefore told Mr F. that the persons to whom he had entrusted
the conduct of business on the part of government in the House of Lords were
alone, he conceived, responsible for such matters. Mr F. instantly added that
the lord lieutenant and himself considered the Archbishop as the first feather
in their wing, and if he would accept that trust, it was their wish to confide in
the Lord Chancellor, the Archbishop and Lord Earlsfort and to depend upon
them jointly for the direction and management of all matters in the House of
Lords.[196]

It may be suspected that, where Agar could see the funny side of the Castle's unco-
ordinated blundering, Earlsfort would have interpreted it as a slight. It may also be
suspected that Earlsfort's friendship with Agar was closer in the years up to 1784,
when Earlsfort joined Agar in the upper house. It was easier for earlsfort to hail Agar
as 'the most active, decided and useful supporter of administration in the House of
Lords'[197] when Earlsfort was still in the House of Commons.

The gap between Earlsfort's public comments about Agar (and others) and the
private views he confided to his amazing diary, widens with the passage of time.
'[Bishops are] composed of very bad materials indeed – hypocrisy, insolence, avarice
and cruelty. An ecclesiastical despot is the most absolute of all tyrants. You should
never risk any familiarity with a bishop, especially in company. They are all proud, and
jealous of their sacred functions, and look for as much respect as a kept mistress.'
'Never, if you can, connect yourself with a very ambitious man. ... He has no real
friendship, and his pride makes him hate those to whom he is obliged – *viz.* ... Provost
Hutchinson; ... Agar, archbishop of Cashel, etc., etc.'[198] As Fitzpatrick comments
(aptly, for once): 'The later entries in his diary [from 1789 onwards], and evidence
derived from other sources, show that his once active mental powers eventually sank.
... His nerves were shattered by the reaction of convivial indulgence; and the dyspepsia
under which he suffered conjured up the dreadful mental torments of self-distrust.'
In other words, he was succumbing to paranoia and, almost certainly, drinking to
excess. These later diary entries include: 'September 20, 1789. ... FitzGibbon made
chancellor and Carleton a peer; these, with the Archbishop of Cashel, are likely to
unite to lessen me in the king's bench and House of Lords. *Quere*: how to prevent
them? ... [May/June 1791:] ... By neglect of yourself, you are now an helpless,
ignorant, unpopular, accused individual, forsaken by government, persecuted by
parliament [in May 1791 on the issue of *fiats*], hated by the Bar, unaided by the Bench,
betrayed and deserted by your oldest friends. Reform, and all will be well. Guard
against treachery in others and passions in yourself.'[199] Clonmell's last surviving letter
to Agar is dated 1794,[200] and is the first to survive since 1789. Granted the random and

---

196 Notebook containing 'political memoranda' by Agar, 1782–95, 21 M 57/A18, entry *sub* 18 Jan.
1788. 197 Scott to Ellis, 4 Dec. 1778, T/3719/C/12/29. 198 Fitzpatrick, *Ireland before the
Union*, pp 24 and 26–7. 199 Ibid., pp 33–4 and 38–40. 200 Clonmell to Agar, 13 June 1794,
T/3719/C/28/10.

widespread destruction perpetrated by Henry Carter, there is not necessarily any significance in this. Yet, it is hard to believe that random destruction would have reduced to nothing a once so prolific source of letters to Agar.

From 1789 onwards, there was also a divergence in Clonmell's and Agar's political paths – although they had been politically at variance in earlier years without any obvious strain on the friendship. Clonmell was hostile to the 'detested administration'[201] of Lord Westmorland, with which Agar was on close terms. Moreover, he had better reason than paranoia for feeling himself eclipsed by Agar and others: from having been on level pegging with Agar in the late 1780s in the role of leader of the House of Lords, he found himself so reduced in influence by January 1793 that he 'had very serious thoughts of resigning [as lord chief justice], if I can make a good bargain'.[202] He was in this period deputy speaker of the House of Lords, and also a commissioner of the great seal when Lord Chancellor FitzGibbon was absent.[203] But, in February 1793, he came nearly last of the peers elected by ballot to serve on the secret committee to investigate the activities of the United Irishmen. On this ballot, Agar came second with 41 votes, and Clonmell eighth with 23.[204] This was a committee of which the lord chief justice of the king's bench was a more appropriate member than an archbishop; so the outcome may be regarded as a judgement on Clonmell passed by his peers. He did not seek to serve on the secret committee of 1797, when Agar came top in the ballot with 46 votes.[205] In late March 1793, by-passing the lord lieutenant, Clonmell appealed direct to the home secretary, Henry Dundas, whom he rightly regarded as the main author of the policy of Catholic Relief which Westmorland had been reluctantly implementing. Clonmell's object was an earldom, and he described himself – with the hyperbole characteristic of his private diary – as 'constantly worried [by the Westmorland administration], not once gratified, often consulted, never considered' during the last three sessions of parliament. In the present session, he had supported, 'in direct opposition to the opinions and conduct of some of their most confidential advisers ..., the relaxation of the Popery Laws and ... an universal Militia Bill, unweakened by any clause of religious exclusion'.[206] This was a veiled attack on Agar. Four nights previously, Agar (and FitzGibbon) had been in a minority of 10 to 23 in the debate in the House of Lords on the clause admitting catholics to serve in the militia.[207] Two years later, in 1795, Agar and Clonmell clashed very publicly in the House of Lords over a bill to extend the leasing powers of bishops, which Agar opposed and Clonmell supported (see pp 397–9).

Clearly, Clonmell had become an isolated, disgruntled and perhaps maverick figure. Because of this, rather than from any change of heart on Catholic Relief (which he had opposed as recently as 1792),[208] he espoused the 'liberal' line in 1793, and later

201 *Clonmell diary (TCD)*, p. 367. 202 Ibid., pp 376 and 386. 203 Ibid., pp 357 and 378. 204 Printed list of members of the House of Lords, with Ms. annotations recording the number of votes cast for each of them, 12 Feb. 1793, 21 M 57/A36/1. 205 Ibid., 5 May 1797, 21 M 57/A36/2. 206 Clonmell to Dundas, 30 Mar. 1793, Home Office papers, PRO, HO 100/46, ff. 53–4. 207 John Thomas Troy, Roman catholic archbishop of Dublin, to his opposite number at Cashel, Thomas Bray, 26 Mar. 1793, Dublin Diocesan archives, Troy correspondence, 116/5/134. 208 1st marquess of

proclaimed his disinclination to extreme counter-insurrectionary measures.[209] Almost
at the end of his life, on 12 March 1798, he confided to his diary: 'This day near
twenty of the U[nited] I[rishmen] have been arrested. ... I see to a demonstration that
I am not in the confidence of the administration. The papers seized were examined by
the Chancellor, Speaker, Archbishop of Cashel ... [etc., etc.]. Perhaps it is intended as
a slight to me, though the other chief judges also were omitted. ... My best course is
to affect indifference and contempt, with guarded cheerfulness and dumb silence upon
political subjects.'[210] Agar, on his side, continued to have a regard for Clonmell.
Following the latter's death in May 1798, he ordered plaques for his companion Stuart
portraits of Clonmell and Carleton (figs. 6–7).[211] The fact that the portrait of
Clonmell, commissioned in 1790, was still a prized possession in 1798, speaks for itself.
However much they may have differed politically in the 1790s, and however much
Clonmell may have declined in every way, Agar still valued the friendship.

LORD MACARTNEY, MRS AGAR AND THE AGARS' FAMILY LIFE

If Clonmell was the most colourful and, at least during the 1770s and 1780s, the
closest of Agar's friends, Macartney became as time went on not just a friend but an
integral part of Agar's family. Agar had got to know Macartney when the latter was
chief secretary in 1768–72. Though he gave himself airs, owned a smallish north
Antrim estate at Lisanoure, near Ballymoney, and had married one of the plain and
poorly portioned daughters of the short-lived prime minister, Lord Bute, Macartney
came from a Belfast mercantile background. Like most of Agar's intimates, he was a
careerist and bent on making his fortune. But, unlike them, he was ambitious of a
diplomatic or proconsular career away from Ireland. Commenting in January 1781 on
Macartney's election as governor of Madras, Scott wrote: 'Poor fellow! I hope he will
bring himself *home* in every sense, but that is so infernal a climate that he, I fear, will
have a diabolical time out [there]. He seems to laugh at the terror of it, which to be
sure will make him a nabob.'[212]

The other big difference between Macartney and Agar's other bright and ambi-
tious friends was that Macartney was a cousin-by-marriage; it was not until after
Agar's marriage in November 1776 that Macartney became a really close friend. In
August 1780, Agar asked him (as well as Scott) to be godfather to the Agars' third son,
George Charles (who was called 'George' after Macartney).[213] In 1793, Macartney

Downshire to Clonmell, Mar. 1792, Downshire papers, Down County Museum, Downpatrick, DB
505, Env. 4. **209** *Memoirs of the life and times of the Rt Hon. Henry Grattan* (5 vols., London,
1839–46), iii. 376; Tony Gaynor, 'The politics of law and order in Ireland, 1794–8' (unpublished
University of Dublin Ph.D. thesis, 1999), p. 44; and Bolton, *Union*, p. 52. **210** *Clonmell diary
(TCD)*, pp 449–50. This reference was kindly sent to me by Sir Richard Aylmer. **211** Miscellaneous memorandum book kept by Agar, [1790s], 21 M 57/D56. The entry is undated, but must
be post May 1798, since the plaque to be put on Clonmell's portrait includes the year of his death.
212 Scott to Agar, 24 [Jan. 1781], T/3719/C/15/1B; Peter Roebuck (ed.), *Macartney of Lisanoure,
1737–1806: essays in biography* (Belfast, 1983), *passim*. **213** Agar to Macartney, 4 Aug. 1780, printed

took Mrs Agar's brother, Colonel George Benson ('a smart, correct and active officer, well known to ... and selected by him'),[214] with him on his celebrated embassy to China.[215] He also did his best for the needy son and namesake of the Rev. Henry Agar when Henry Junior was packed off to Bombay as an East India Company writer in 1798.[216] Welby said of Macartney in 1804: 'A more amiable gentleman does not exist, nor a more attached man to his friends.'[217] In that year, Macartney was the means of obtaining a commission in the third regiment of Guards for George Charles Agar, who acknowledged that Macartney had behaved to him in this affair like a father rather than a godfather.[218] A letter from Lady Somerton (as Mrs Agar now was) to Macartney shows that the latter was also a peace-maker within the Agar family. 'What does not Welbore [the eldest son, later 2nd earl of Normanton] owe you for what by your interest and intercessions you accomplished for him with his father, deaf and inexorable to every voice but yours! And what everlasting advantages have you now procured for George, left as he was to himself and as it were cast off!' She concluded by calling Macartney 'the best of friends and kindest of relations'.[219] Many years later, when she was countess dowager of Normanton and Macartney was long dead, she referred to him in her will as 'our dear, respected friend and valuable relation'.[220]

Macartney may or may not have introduced the Agars. His cousin, Jane Benson/Agar, had been born in 1751, and so was some fifteen years Macartney's and Agar's junior. Jane Benson's father, William Benson of Downpatrick, sometime a merchant in Abbey Street, Dublin, was dead by 1776, the year of her marriage. But, essentially, she came from a clerical, not a mercantile, background: her father's father was the Rev. Edward Benson (d.1741), prebendary of St Andrew's, diocese of Down, and her father's two brothers had been dean of Connor and archdeacon of Down respectively. Her mother was Frances Macartney-Porteous, and her paternal grandmother (Mrs Edward Benson) had been Jane Winder, another cousin of the Macartneys and another northern clergyman's daughter.[221] Those of the Bensons who were not clerical were as impecunious as those who were. Jane Benson's father, William, cannot have been much of a merchant; and another Benson, who wrote to Macartney in 1789 soliciting a small loan, detailed how he had dissipated an estate of £3,000 per annum in electioneering for the borough of Newry, Co. Down.[222] Agar's was therefore an

in *Macartney in Ireland*, p. 332. **214** Quoted in Helen H. Robbins (*née* Macartney), *Our first ambassador to China: an account of the life of George, Earl Macartney* ... (London, 1908), p. 203*n*. **215** Ellis to Agar, 18 Aug. 1792, T/3719/C/26/11. **216** Mendip to Agar, 11 Sep. 1799, T/3719/C/33/46. **217** Welby to Agar, 30 Jan. 1804, T/3719/C/38/5. **218** Hon. G.C. Agar to Agar, 21 Jan. 1804, T/3719/C/38/2; Agar to Macartney, 4 Feb. 1804, Macartney papers, PRONI, D/572/8/191. **219** Viscountess Somerton to Macartney, 25 Jan. 1804, D/572/8/190. **220** Will of Jane, countess of Normanton, 4 Sep. 1810, with numerous codicils up to 25 June 1825, 21 M 57/T278. **221** Canon James B. Leslie and Dean Henry B. Swanzy, *Biographical succession lists of the clergy of [the] diocese of Down* (Enniskillen, 1936), pp 58, 125 and 148; Leslie et al., *Clergy of Connor from Patrician times to the present day* (Belfast, 1993), p. 219; General George Benson to Agar, 2 Apr. 1806, T/3719/C/40/27; Rev. Richard Wynne to Charles Brodrick, coadjutor archbishop of Dublin, 10 Sep. 1814, Midleton papers, NLI, Ms. 8871/7. **222** J. Bowes Benson to Macartney, 27 June 1789, D/572/9/47.

imprudent marriage, except in the sense that he was wise to marry someone fully prepared for the role of a churchman's wife.

The marriage settlement[223] is an extraordinary document, in that it refers to the portion which Agar *will* receive with his wife, but does not state the amount. This suggests that it cannot have been much, and possibly was nothing. One reason for the omission of the amount might have been to prevent its embarrassing smallness from being recorded in the Registry of Deeds, Dublin. Agar himself had little jointuring power at this stage of his career: he settled on Jane Benson, should she outlive him, £100 per annum plus the nett income from his townland of Ballynaboley, Co. Kilkenny. The parties to the settlement, in addition to the couple themselves, were Jane Benson's mother, Frances (her father being dead), Welbore Ellis, and Macartney (*in absentia*). Macartney, the only politically useful connection whom Jane Benson brought in her train, was of no foreseeable use to Agar for years to come. In 1776, he was governor of the defenceless West Indian island of Grenada and became in 1779 a prisoner-of-war in France. In fact, it was Agar who was subsequently to prove a useful connection for numbers of importunate Bensons seeking to obtain through him preferment or promotion in the Church or the army. Of the clerical Bensons, he made William Benson chancellor of Cashel in 1791 and precentor in 1795, and Francis Benson rector of Fethard, Co. Tipperary, in 1791; and it was probably he (as opposed to his predecessor as archbishop of Dublin) who made Hill Benson prebend of Tipper in St Patrick's Cathedral and vicar of Blessington, Co. Wicklow, in 1801. The military Bensons fared equally well.[224] In other words, it looks very much as if Agar, the supposedly mercenary worldling, married for love. This was certainly the view of his sister, Diana: 'I well know that money never weighed with you, and undoubtedly happiness is the only rational pursuit. To complete yours, there was only wanting what you have now found, I trust. All the other goods of life you possess sufficiently and have a very fair prospect of having them considerably increased.'[225]

Granted Agar's reputation for 'love of lucre', the suggestion that he married for love is startling. But it is borne out by his attitude to two other disadvantageous marriages in his family. The first was that of his only and much-loved daughter, Frances ('Fanny'), who married in 1798 the Hon. Thomas Ralph Maude, son and heir of Agar's already-mentioned neighbour in Co. Tipperary, Sir Cornwallis Maude of Dundrum, near Cashel, now 1st Viscount Hawarden. Fanny was a paragon (fig. 10), being variously described as 'sweet', 'pleasant', 'pretty' and 'lively' by two successive chief secretaries for Ireland.[226] Her marriage portion was the considerable sum of

223 Of 22 Nov. 1776, 21 M 57/T358.   224 Agar's 'state' of the diocese of Cashel, 1779–1801, 21 M 57/B6/1; Canon James B. Leslie, *Clergy of Derry and Raphoe* (reprint, Belfast, 1999), p. 83; 'Copies of the Archbishop's letters to Lord Temple [the new lord lieutenant] and General Burgoyne for the majority of the 12th Dragoons for Capt. [George] Benson', 8 Apr. 1783, T/3719/C/17/11; an indecipherable Benson to Miss Mary Benson, Mrs Agar's sister and constant companion, 13 July 1784, T/3719/C/18/19; Lieutenant Henry Benson to Macartney, 1 Jan. 1788, D/572/9/27; and Colonel Arthur Benson to Agar, 20 Dec. 1807, and reply, 22 Dec. 1807, T/3719/C/41/44–5.   225 Diana Agar to Agar, 17 Oct. 1776, T/3719/C/10/4.   226 William Wickham to Agar, 1 Mar. 1806, T/3719/C/40/18; Sir Evan Nepean to Agar, 23 Sep. 1805, C/39/16.

£15,000; and Lord Hawarden's estate was so burdened with debts and family charges – he had sixteen children and a young (third) wife – that he was not in a position to make a proportionate settlement on the young couple. Their courtship had been carried on in Bath while Agar was in Dublin, and he had some reason for chagrin at being the last to be told about it. Lord Hawarden, 'not being a man of business' (as Lady Hawarden put it mildly in a letter of apology),[227] also gave Agar ground for offence in the course of the marriage negotiations. However, Agar forbore and the marriage went ahead. His brother-in-law, Colonel George Benson, referred 'to the noble part you have acted throughout the whole of this delicate affair, and great must be the gratification of the self-approving mind, the reward in part of so much disinterestedness'.[228] In the event, things went much awry. Fanny Agar's husband succeeded as 2nd Viscount Hawarden in 1803, but died young in 1807.[229] He had marked 'in the fullest and strongest manner his love and respect for her' by the dispositions he made in his will[230] but, from then until her death in 1839, Fanny and her trustees had the greatest difficulty extracting what was due to her from the next viscount, and she was in constant 'pecuniary embarrassment'.[231] Agar may indeed have been blameably soft at the time of the marriage negotiations in 1798.[232] The other marriage in the family which seems to disclose a romantic streak in him was that of his distant cousin on the Mathew side, the vicomte de Chabot; in 1809, de Chabot married a childhood sweetheart, Lady Isabella Fitzgerald, the poorly portioned sister of the 3rd duke of Leinster.[233] De Chabot's father, the already-mentioned comte de Jarnac, a penniless *émigré* and pensioner on the Irish establishment, philosophised to

227 Isabella, Viscountess Hawarden, to Agar, 8 June 1798, T/3719/C/32/77.   228 Benson to Agar, 16 Oct. 1798, T/3719/C/32/147.   229 Entries in the account books, 1788–92 and 1803–7, of Austin Cooper (who was agent for the Hawarden as well as the Cashel see estate) for Oct. 1790, 29 June 1804 and July–Dec. 1806 (PRONI, MIC/251/1–2) provide evidence of major financial strain.   230 Diana Agar to Agar, 14 Mar. 1807, T/3719/C/41/12.   231 Will and codicils of Jane, countess of Normanton, 4 Sep. 1801–20 June 1825, 21 M 57/T278.   232 For the Hawarden marriage negotiations and some of the sequel, see (in addition to the above): 1st Viscount Hawarden to Agar, 13 May, 7 and 18 June and 5 Nov. 1798, T/3719/C/32/54, 75, 89 and 157; Agar to Hawarden or Lady Hawarden, 19 May, 11 June and 15 Oct. 1798, C/32/59, 79 and 145; Agar to Hawarden, Apr. 1799, and reply, 2 May 1799, C/33/9–10; Hon. T.R. Maude, 2nd Viscount Hawarden, to Agar, 3 Jan. 1801 and 6 Sep. and 28 Dec. 1803, C/35/1 and C/37/24 and 49; Agar's correspondence with and about the Hawardens, 6 Feb.–2 Mar. and 5 and 11 May 1804, C/38/7–11 and 23–7; ibid., 9–15 Aug. 1808, C/42/52–7; and Frances, Viscountess Hawarden, to 2nd earl of Normanton (her brother), postmarked 6 Oct. 1809, 21 M 57, 2nd earl's unreferenced correspondence.   233 Bill from Dr [Joseph?] Stock [later bishop of Killala during the '98 Rebellion?] to Agar for tuition, board, etc., during the vicomte de Chabot's residence with the Leinster children at Carton, Co. Kildare, May 1794, 21 M 57/D27/2; note by Agar in a memorandum book of the 1790s of the 'Count de Jarnac's income, Feb. 1796, received from Sir S[keffington] Smyth', 21 M 57/D56; proposals from Jarnac to the lord lieutenant, Lord Cornwallis, for raising a corps in Ireland, 17 June–12 July 1798, with a letter to Agar from the Irish treasury, 18 July [1798] about Jarnac's pension, T/3719/C/32/85–8; Sir Arthur Wellesley (the chief secretary) to General the Hon. W. [*sic* – Charles] Stewart about a pension for Jarnac, 1 June 1807, *Civil correspondence and memoranda of Field-Marshal Arthur, duke of Wellington ...: Ireland, from March 30th, 1807, to April 12th, 1809* (London, 1860), p. 70; Louis Philippe, duc d'Orléans, to the Prince Regent about Chabot's military

Agar about the importance of high birth, numerous connections and personal merit, and the comparative unimportance of money. He concluded with the significant comment: 'I am certain that you, who are so wise, will be of the same opinion.'[234]

Agar's own marriage to Jane Benson was outstandingly successful. Her principal fault was that she looked up to him with almost embarrassing admiration, starting her few surviving letters to him with 'My dear Lord', 'My dearest Archbishop', 'Dearest A.B.', 'Dear A.B.', or something else which, even by late eighteenth-century standards, fell far short of the endearments to be expected between husband and wife. Her concern for his wellbeing sometimes verged on the ludicrous. At the beginning of January 1789, for example, when Lord Clifden was, as it turned out, dying at Gowran, and Lady Clifden too was ill, Agar had rushed over to be with them. At this more than anxious time, Mrs Agar wrote to 'My dear Lord': 'I am afraid you have a very heavy cold. ... I hope you were put into a well-aired bed, for that was what I dreaded the most, fearing that out of respect the servants would place you in the state bedroom, which perhaps had not been lain in for weeks before.'[235] However, she was tender-hearted and solicitous about things of much greater importance than Agar's possibly unaired bed. Following Lord Clifden's death, Agar told the widowed Lady Clifden that Mrs Agar's 'nerves are too weak and her sensibility too great for such occasions, and I really believe that the present impression will hardly be effaced while she lives'.[236] Her surviving letters to Agar are few because the Agars were inseparable. She even accompanied Agar on visitation, in spite of the pompous, male-chauvinist strictures of Welbore Ellis, who had 'always ... been of the opinion that a lady is not quite a becoming part of the suite of an archbishop in the exercise of his highest archiepiscopal functions'.[237]

On the other hand, Mrs Agar, if too uncritical of and, literally, too attached to her husband, was no fool and no cypher. She was often called upon to make copies of his most important letters, and did so faultlessly. She would have been the last to appreciate her own efficiency. Her own letters, all too few of which survive, reveal wit, humour and a trenchant turn of phrase. One such, addressed to Macartney in 1787, refers to the surprising change which has come over one of the Agars' friends: 'I hear Lord Tyrone, whom one was always accustomed to pass over as dull and insensible (to the fair sex, I mean), did all he could to flirt and flaunt away in London, that he made love and eyes and sighs to every pretty woman he met. Indeed, he began last year to practise these little gallantries *envers notre belle duchesse* [of Rutland, the beautiful but coquettish vicereine].'[238] Her letters to Agar are similarly gossipy. On another of the

services since 1793, 10 Jan. 1815, *HMC Bathurst Mss.*, p. 325. Because of the Smyth-Mathew marriage connection, the Chabots' son, the next vicomte de Chabot, succeeded in 1841 to the wreckage of the Mathew of Thomastown estate, under the will of Lady Elizabeth Mathew, sister of the 2nd earl of Landaff and, effectively, the last of the Mathews – Power, *Eighteenth-century Tipperary*, p. 333.   234 Jarnac to Agar, 20 May 1809, T/3719/C/43/98.   235 Mrs Agar to Agar, 1 Jan. 1789, T/3719/C/23/1.   236 Agar to Lady Clifden, 4 Jan. 1789, 21 M 57/D53/14.   237 Ellis to Agar, 28 May 1787, T/3719/C/21/21.   238 Mrs Agar to Macartney, 16 June 1787, D/572/9/9.

rare occasions when they were apart, in October 1796, she wrote amusingly about social life and local politics in the Cashel area.[239] The tone of these letters, and of the relationship, is established by the following: 'We have been very dismal since you left us ... . The [Dublin] Evening Post presumes to say that you parliament folks are to stay a month. This will appear a long time to the sisterhood of this palace. ... We shall all be so learned and accomplished *pendant notre solitude* that we shall put all you idle and dissipated town folks to the blush.' Nevertheless, this same series of letters also demonstrates that she knew her own mind (see pp 365–6). Much later, in April 1808, the comte de Jarnac was put to flight by her strongly held, conventionally conservative views. A follower of the guillotined duc d'Orléans ('Philippe Egalité'), Jarnac admitted that he had done something to assist Orléans' natural daughter, Pamela, Lady Edward Fitzgerald, the widow of the United Irish leader; for which transgression Lady Somerton, now countess of Normanton, made it clear to him that he was *persona non grata* in the Agars' London house. Agar was reduced to carrying on a clandestine correspondence with Jarnac, but – at least in the short term – was unable to effect his rehabilitation.[240] More usually, however, Lady Normanton lived up to the amiable and gracious image presented in Stuart's portrait of her, painted *c.*1790 (fig. 8), when she was approximately forty. It shows a stylish woman, of mature good looks, dignified bearing and serene expression. It also suggests character and intelligence.

The few epistolary proofs of the Agars' relationship are revealing of aspects of Agar's character which are otherwise hard to penetrate. For example, a hint of the seriousness of Agar's personal religious commitment comes in a letter to him from Lady Somerton, written in October 1801. The occasion was Agar's translation to the archbishopric of Dublin. News of this promotion reached her first, because she was staying with Lord and Lady Mendip at Pope's Villa, while Agar was at Cashel with their sons. The party at Pope's Villa 'were assembled round the dinner table' when a letter from the prime minister, Henry Addington, arrived. 'Lord M. read this letter aloud, and immediately (good man) filling a bumper of Burgundy, he drank to our new A.B.'s health; "And also let us drink", say[s] he, "[to] the crown and Addington ... . But, above all, let us not forget to be grateful to the Author of all this good to us. Let us thank God", said he – which fervently some of us did.'[241] A little earlier in this same period of separation in the autumn of 1801, Agar wrote from Cashel to Lady Somerton about family and domestic matters. This is almost the only letter from him to her which survives, and it reveals an Agar who was a good father in an almost modern sense of that term. He begins by describing how he passes the time with young Welbore, George and James (then at university or in their upper teens) and the horses he has bought for them:

239 Lady Somerton to Agar, 13 Oct. 1796, T/3719/C/30/34.   240 Jarnac to Agar, 11 Apr. and 24 Oct. 1805, T/3719/C/42/20 and 72.   241 Lady Somerton to Agar, 26 Oct. 1801, T/3719/C/35/21. On this question of the seriousness of his personal religious commitment, see Agar to Lord Westmorland, the lord lieutenant, 18 Nov. 1793 (T/3719/C/27/12), on the death of Westmorland's wife.

[The horses are] free from every vice, have no tricks and are in all respects safe. This is a great comfort to me when I can't accompany them [the boys]. I shall be glad to know the nature of George's last letter to you. I should suppose it was a proper one, as he seems to be in better spirits since he wrote it than he was before, and therefore has probably unburdened his mind and got rid of the load that oppressed him. I fear he has not as much amiable sensibility as has fallen to the share of his two brothers. But I really don't discover in him any bad disposition of any sort, and he seems to be perfectly good-humoured.[242]

As Lady Somerton's already-quoted letter of 1804 to Macartney makes plain, it sometimes required the intervention of a third-party to keep father-son relations on this intimate footing. (The letter also makes plain that she knew how to manage her husband!) On this occasion, Macartney had intervened to break to Agar the news that George's heart was set on the army and that he had an 'irrepressible repugnance'[243] to going up to Christ Church. Agar's letter to George on this subject is a model of paternal tenderness:

My choice for you was directed by my judgement and by my wishes to promote your happiness and your welfare. My displeasure (while it lasted) arose, not from your rejection of that choice, but from your declining to make one for yourself. You have now done so, and God grant that it may answer your expectation. You have my hearty concurrence, since you told me that your happiness depended upon the accomplishment of this object. Let me know when your appointment takes place, that I may write to Lord Macartney and thank him for this most kind instance of his friendship for us all.... It is my intention to make you a present of your regimentals and all things necessary for your outfit, and to continue to you your annual allowance of £200 in addition to your pay. Your mother and aunt are well and send their love to you, as does, my dear George, your affectionate father. C[harles] D[ublin].[244]

Brought up in this way, the Agars' sons, and their daughter, Fanny, were devoted to their parents and, for the rest of their lives, to each other.[245]

One of the imponderables of Agar's relationship with his wife was whether he was conscious of having married beneath him or – more to the point – felt that she was self-conscious about his having done so. Does this help to explain 'his passion for ... [temporal] titles', which would give her the rank and status which his spiritual titles did not? In general, there was a widely recognised anomaly about 'the unadorned state of a bishop's wife. Although her husband sat in the House of Lords and was entitled to be addressed as "My Lord", she remained a humble "Mrs", below the most vulgar

242 Agar to Lady Somerton, 12 Sep. 1801, T/3719/C/35/20.   243 Hon. G.C. Agar to Agar, 21 Jan. 1804, T/3719/C/38/2.   244 Agar to Hon. G.C. Agar, 26 Jan. 1804, T/3719/C/38/4.   245 Hon. Welbore Agar to Agar, 18 Mar. 1801, T/3719/C/35/9.

wife of the most ludicrous City knight. Since bishops' wives were sometimes known for their fashionable lifestyle and pretentious manners, this gave rise to anguish in episcopal palaces and mirth elsewhere.'[246] Mrs Agar was no Mrs Proudie. But perhaps she was a Mrs Pontifex, who thought to herself in Samuel Butler's novel that her

> influence as plain Mrs Pontifex, wife, we will say, of the bishop of Winchester, would no doubt be considerable ...; but as Lady Winchester – or the bishopess – which would sound quite nicely – who could doubt that her power for good would be enhanced. ... The fact that a bishop's wife does not take the rank of her husband ... had been the doing of Elizabeth, who had been a bad woman, of exceeding doubtful moral character, and at heart a papist to the last.[247]

When Agar first applied for a peerage, in 1789, it was for Mrs Agar (see p. 167). On the next (recorded) occasion, in 1794–5, the application was for Agar himself; but his go-between with Dublin Castle described 'that mark of royal favour' as very 'gratifying to ... [Mrs Agar] and, on that ... account only, so desirable to his Grace'.[248]

Is it, however, credible that it was only on Mrs Agar's account that Agar desired a peerage? Might this not more plausibly be seen as a put-up job concerted between them? It was quite common for politicians to use their wives as an *alibi* (as those in quest of the lord chancellorship in 1788 had done), or as an excuse for actions of their own which were unpleasing to the government[249] or as the pretext for requests which smacked of vanity, immodesty or immoderacy. Mrs Agar, now safely ensconced among the viscountesses, was later sent into battle to obtain Agar's promotion to the earldom of Normanton. In February 1805, she wrote a much-quoted but still startling letter to a Dublin Castle under-secretary, Alexander Marsden:

> There is nothing that the Archbishop and I have so near at heart as the adorning our dear son [Welbore], now on his travels, with a little feather to make him more presentable, etc., etc., wherever he goes. On the Continent, rank is inestimable, and even at home it is no small addition to a young man whom [*sic*], in our partiality, we think wants nothing else to recommend him *partout*, having the advantages of the best education, the first alliances, and possessing all fortune's goods, if an income of £10,000 per annum [actually it was nearly £18,000] can be so considered, and which his father would leave him tomorrow. ... [This] cannot be had in any other way than by that of his father's advancing a step in the peerage – a step, certainly, of no use or consequence to the A.B. himself, who is a *flight of stairs* above it in his own person already.[250]

246 Paul Langford, *Public life and the propertied Englishman, 1689–1798* (Oxford, 1991), p. 519. 247 Samuel Butler, *The way of all flesh* (Penguin ed., 1995), p. 70. 248 John Lees to Mrs Agar, 22 Nov. 1794, T/3719/C/28/17. 249 Malcomson, *Lord Shannon*, pp xxxix–xliv. 250 Michael MacDonagh (ed.), *The viceroy's post-bag: correspondence hitherto unpublished of the earl of Hardwicke, the first lord lieutenant of Ireland after the Union* (London, 1904), pp 207–8.

It has been asserted that Agar's promotion to an earldom in 1806 was the (somewhat delayed) fulfilment of a Union engagement to him.[251] But this was not the case.[252] Nevertheless, since the fees on the earldom came to over £600,[253] it cannot have been solicited on such light and whimsical grounds as Lady Somerton's, and there must have been more serious and higher-level communication over this promotion than her letter to the Castle under-secretary. Whatever it was, it has not transpired.[254] So the impression remains that the application for the barony of Somerton was for the benefit of Mrs Agar, and the application for the earldom of Normanton was for the benefit of the incipient Lord Somerton. Neither can possibly be true. Good family man though Agar was, he thought in terms of dynasty as well as family; and good churchman though he was (according to his lights and by the standards of his day), his strongest though unspoken ambition was for permanent, hereditary, temporal rank. All three steps in the peerage are probably best seen as the progressive fulfilment of his ambition to found what Lady Normanton called '*the second house* (Lord Clifden being the first)'.[255]

AGAR'S PHYSIOGNOMY AND PERSONALITY

Many passages in the already-quoted letters from Agar's friends and family throw light on Agar the man. It remains, however, to highlight those aspects of his personality which most struck those who knew him well and which are emphasised in their correspondence with him and with each other. His most prominent physiognomical feature was his nose, and Scott was an *aficionado* of noses. He recorded in his diary· 'talents appear as often in the shape or point of the nose as in any other feature. A long nose, very sharp at the end, marks superiority, whether it turns up or down, viz. Edmund Burke, [William] Gerard Hamilton, William Pitt, all turn up. The acquillines are generally more sagacious.'[256] Agar was presumably flattered when Scott described him in 1773 as 'a man who ... can combine the utmost discretion with the longest nose, [and who therefore] need not be much afraid of the difficulties of this life or the dangers of the next', or when Scott coupled this physical feature with the rumoured gallantries of Agar's private life by calling him *c.*1775 'a young bishop with the longest nose and the most amorous complexion I ever saw ..., [and] the most prudent and discreet Christian prelate I ever knew or read of'.[257] But his feelings must

251 D.H. Akenson, *The Church of Ireland: ecclesiastical reform and revolution, 1800–1885* (New Haven, 1971), p. 75.   252 For example, it is not mentioned in a letter about such promotions written by Hardwicke to Addington on 26 Apr. 1804 – Hardwicke papers, BL, Add. Ms. 35705, f. 273. 253 Receipt from Peter Le Bas to Agar, 3 Feb. 1806, T/3719/C/40/8.   254 The nearest to it is Nicholas Vansittart [chief secretary, Mar.–Sep. 1805] to Agar, 10 Mar. 1806, T/3719/C/40/20. 255 Lady Normanton to 2nd earl of Normanton, 25 Apr. 1816, 21 M 57, 2nd earl's unreferenced correspondence. When the earldom was conferred, Lord Clifden barely concealed his displeasure at being out-ranked by '*the second house*' – Clifden to Agar, 14 Feb. 1806, T/3719/C/40/13. 256 Fitzpatrick, *Ireland before the Union*, p. 26.   257 Scott to Agar, 27 Feb. 1773 and [c.1775], T/3719/C/7/2 and C/9/5.

have been more mixed when, in March 1809, at the end of his life, he received a letter from the artist, George Dance, who sought permission to reproduce, in a series of profile portraits which have come to be called 'George Dance's nose portraits', the portrait of Agar 'which you may recollect having permitted me to draw' (fig. 19).[258] The publication of this engraving must have had Agar's 'sanction and approbation', and yet of all the portraits in the series his is probably the one which most nearly approaches a caricature.

The most distasteful part of Watty Cox's obituary attack on Agar is his comments on Agar's personal appearance: 'His Lordship's person was offensive, as his mind was vicious – about five feet four inches in height, [and] so ill-featured that, were he not usually disguised under a large wig, he might be mistaken for an overgrown baboon.' There is nothing 'offensive' about smallness of stature; and Agar's portrait by Stuart (who worked on the basis that 'a painter may give up his art if he attempts to alter to please'),[259] gives the lie to the other vituperations. Agar is not wearing a large wig; his nose is, of course, too large, and his mouth too small; there is a certain foxiness about his expression; but the overriding impression is that this is the face of a highly intelligent man. In unlikely company with Watty Cox, Lord Clare also made fun of Agar's size. Writing in July 1800 to their mutual friend, Lord Auckland, Clare referred to it twice in the same letter, calling Agar 'little Cashel' and 'the aforesaid little prelate'.[260] Clare, it should be noted, was himself a small man; so, this was not a battle of the giants. Smallness is popularly associated with pugnacity. Certainly, both Agar and Clare were pugnacious – and hot-tempered. In March 1774, Macartney was informed that Agar had had 'a violent altercation' in the House of Lords with the 1st Viscount Irnham. At the end of it, Agar declared

> that Lord Irnham would not have dared to use him as he did but for his profession, upon which Irnham drily asked him why he did not, as the bishops of old did, send his champion to him; to which the Bishop, enraged, replied: 'Send my champion! I will send my chairman.' ... Lord Irnham ... told the House he would complain of the ill-language the Bishop gave him, and appointed a day for the purpose. All persons were engaged, either in endeav-ouring to reconcile matters, or in hopes the breach would continue open and afford one day of fun. However, with much difficulty, it was adjusted.[261]

Later, in December 1778, Agar had what Lord Clifden called an 'intemperate quarrel' with General Sir John Irwine, commander-in-chief in Ireland,[262] a particular aversion of Agar's.[263] 'Violent' and 'hot-headed' were among the epithets which Bishop Hotham applied to him c.1785.[264] Scott, now Clonmell, affected reluctance to make an

---

258 Dance to Agar, 13 Mar. 1809, T/3719/C/43/150.   259 Quoted in Mount, *Irish career of Gilbert Stuart*, p. 15.   260 Clare to Auckland, 24 July [1800], *Later correspondence of George III*, iii, pp 380–1.   261 Robert Waller to Macartney, 19 Mar. 1774, printed in *Macartney in Ireland*, pp 187–8.   262 Clifden to Agar, 5 Dec. 1779, T/3719/C/12/35.   263 Agar to General Lord Percy, 14 Aug. 1779, T/3719/C/13/33.   264 Hotham to Sir Charles Hotham Thompson, 13 June

'ecclesiastical request from [sic] his Grace', because Agar was 'very quick and jealous and apt to take fire'.[265] According to a Mrs Dunn of Bickley in Kent, whose family had been intimate with Agar and who spoke of him in July 1810 to the painter-cum-diarist, Joseph Farington, Agar 'was of a nervous habit, and was subject to violent headaches, which he relieved by drinking the essence of coffee, and would rise in the night for that purpose; but Mrs Dunn thought it injured his constitution. In the last six or seven years of his life, his temper changed. He was always of a warm temper, but now became irritable and peevish.'[266] Agar's wife confirmed the diagnosis that he was 'of a nervous habit'. 'Don't forget', she adjured him while he was absent from Cashel in October 1796, 'to eat something between breakfast and the late dinners every day. You know nothing is more pernicious than long fasting for nervous people.'[267] Agar was not only of a warm and nervous temper, but obsessive. In February 1781 Scott wrote him a revealing letter on this subject. Scott counselled that there was no need for Agar to be 'as much alive ... as you seem' about the 'possibility of some juggling' at the forthcoming Co. Tipperary assizes, but added: 'as you will while you live be very much alive about something or other, this might as well be for an instant the object of anxiety as anything else of the same size'.[268]

    As with Agar's outsize nose, so with his activity: the important thing is not the physical or personality defect, but Agar's good-humoured willingness to be ribbed about it, whether by a social equal like Scott or a social inferior like George Dance. Indeed – although this impression is completely at variance with Agar's popular reputation – good humour and good fun are a leading characteristic of his corres-pondence and of his relationship both with his circle of friends and with many people outside it. In 1787, when the two men were in or around fifty years of age, Scott, now Lord Earlsfort, wrote in almost schoolboyish terms to arrange a meeting at the circuit judges' lodgings in Clonmel. 'If I do not catch your Grace in the courthouse or at our house, I shall certainly go to the tavern, as I find that is the most likely place to meet with the head of the Church. If you can mortify with us, endeavour to reconcile yourself to some Clonmel salmon and a bad beef steake [sic].'[269] 'The head of the Church' used his ecclesiastical patronage to advance at least one kindred spirit. The Rev. Patrick Hare, master of Cashel school, who 'got the vicar-generalship of Cashel [in 1779] when ... Agar became archbishop there, besides other good windfalls', was clearly good company, and no toady or yes-man. 'He was ... amazingly clever and sensible, but very severe and satirical where he took a dislike. Many were his oddities,

[c.1785], Hotham papers, PRONI, T/3429/2/12. **265** Clonmell to 1st Marquess Townshend [the former lord lieutenant], 1 Sep. 1789, Townshend papers, Osborn collection, Beinecke Library, University of Yale, box 14. I am grateful for this reference to Dr James Kelly. **266** *The Farington diary*, vi. 98. A William Dunn of Dublin wrote two (surviving) letters to Agar in the early 1780s (T/3719/C/15/7 and C/17/5), and Agar one letter to 'My dear Dunn' (C/17/2), who was probably the same man. These letters are all three couched in very friendly terms. This Mrs Dunn may have been his widow. **267** Lady Somerton to Agar, [16] Oct. 1796, T/3719/C/35/36. **268** Scott to Agar, 2 Feb. 1781, T/3719/C/15/2. **269** Earlsfort to Agar, 12 [Aug.] 1787, T/3719/C/21/36.

and his *bons mots* and eccentricities were every day repeated. ... Smart at repartee and clever in his opinions, he made his own way amongst the great.'[270] Hare seems to have lived up to this description. Writing to Agar in early April 1795 to report his failure to neutralise the resolutions of an Emancipationist Co. Tipperary meeting, he concluded: 'The defeat, the disappointment and vexation (or perhaps my preceding ailment) brought on me a severe *cholera morbus*, and I was very near giving your Grace an opportunity of bestowing my ample preferments to [*sic*] another.'[271]

As the proposal to meet in a tavern would suggest, Agar did not stand on ceremony and his sense of what was due to his rank was not disfigured by pomposity. Earlier, Scott had written: 'you showed us that lawn sleeves may be very well plated [*sic* – pleated] without the starch of pride, and virtue piously practised without austerity or dissimulation'.[272] In another part of Mrs Dunn's already-quoted description, Agar is characterised as 'a remarkably agreeable man, calculated for conversation with any description of society'. In 1799, a clergyman who asked Lady Shannon to intercede for him with Agar, said that Agar was 'both good-natured and liberal, ... and he is a gentleman as well as an archbishop'; and this had been Sir Joshua Reynolds first impression – 'his appearance and [polite] manner prejudice one ... in his favour as much as his character does.'[273] In a farewell address to him in 1801, the gentlemen of the city of Cashel and its neighbourhood remarked tellingly: 'It does not always happen ... that easy manners are the accompaniment of power.'[274] At his first visitation of his new diocese in June of the following year, a Dublin newspaper report (which, of course, Agar might have written!) noted how, 'in a manner peculiar to himself, [he] conciliates the authority of the superior by the politeness and urbanity of the gentleman'.[275] Precisely this point had been made by a non-Anglican in 1796. At that time, the town of Cashel had a parish priest, the Rev. Dr Edmund Cormac, who was the late eighteenth-century equivalent of the excruciatingly ingratiating Father Healy of Little Bray, Co. Wicklow. Dr Cormac had a nephew (presumably a real nephew) called Anthony Costello, who took after him and on whose behalf Cormac was always pestering Agar about promotion in the revenue service. In April 1796, Costello discovered that there were sixty-four people ahead of him in the waiting-list for appointment as gaugers of excise, and was told by his uncle

> to apply to your Grace. He desired I should ... place unlimited confidence in you, [and] ... speak to you as an affectionate father ... . [He] told me your friendship was steadfast and sincere, and that your Grace's constant, uniform and regular manner of acting would not permit you to neglect a person whom you were graciously pleased to take under your protection.[276]

270 *Retrospections of Dorothea Herbert, 1770–1806,* [*with*] *accompanying commentary by L.M. Cullen* (new ed., Dublin 1988), pp 39–41. **271** Hare to Agar, 8 Apr. 1795, T/3719/C/29/20. **272** Scott to Agar, 27 Feb. 1773, T/3719/C/7/2. **273** [Rev.] Thomas May to Lady Shannon, 17 Apr. 1799, T/3719/C/33/7; Reynolds to Rev. Joseph Palmer, 7 Dec. 1787, printed in John Ingamells and John Edgumbe (eds.), *The letters of Sir Joshua Reynolds* (Yale, 2000), p. 188. **274** Address, 14 Dec. 1801, 21 M 57/B8/24. See p. 295. **275** *Faulkner's Dublin Journal,* 19 June 1802, 21 M 57/A2/21. **276** Anthony Costello to Agar, 7 Apr. 1796, T/3719/ C/30/13.

Agar's almost flamboyant affability, coupled with dignity of demeanour and a patrician sense of display, were already a little old-fashioned at this date: by the 1790s, it has been argued, the new type of statesman was 'discreet in manner, unpretentious in appearance, reserved if not cold, ... disdainful of men and their wants'. In this revolution in manners, Dublin lagged behind London.[277] But, even in post-Union London, Agar was a definite social success. Perhaps this was because of the now rarity of his style: certainly, it was because of his virtuosity as a wit and *raconteur*.[278]

He was still at his most successful with members of the opposite sex – 'the *daughters*' rather than 'the *Fathers*': his wife, his sister, Mrs Griffith and Mrs Dunn, were simply symptomatic of a widespread admiration which he evoked among women. In one of Lady Somerton's letters of October 1796, she quotes the sentiments of a young woman called Miss Lockhart in a way which provides one of those very rare glimpses of the domestic life of a public man. Miss Lockhart, she says,

> would like to repose comfortably for the winter in the bosom of the old lion in the tower [Agar], whom she says she loves exceedingly, as he is a noble and generous animal, of which she gave us an instance in the care he took of a little dog that some wicked person threw into his den, hoping to see him devour it, instead of which he fondled it, kept it closely to his bosom, would not let anyone molest it, and now it eats and drinks with him quite *en famille*.[279]

Other tributes, some of which will be repeated in their respective contexts, came from: his aunt, the countess of Brandon, who had 'an almost implicit faith in him'; his sister-in-law, Lady Clifden, who praised his kind disposition and his deep interest 'in the welfare of every branch of his family';[280] Mrs Ann Lidwell, a distressed gentlewoman who had 'long experienced your clemency and consideration ... [and] your indulgence in not calling for your money';[281] the formidable countess of Clanwilliam, who declared that his 'most flattering and unremitting kindness has absolutely spoiled me';[282] and the flirtatious countess of Clare, who hoped she would 'always deserve such goodness as I have now experienced from you. To be allowed by you to

277 Langford, 'Politics and manners from Sir Robert Walpole to Sir Robert Peel', in *Proceedings of the British Academy*, xliv (1997), pp 118 and 116 and *passim*. One Irishman, the short-lived prime minister of 1783, Lord Shelburne, went to the opposite extreme and was far too cold and reserved; his career was 'wrecked ... [by his] unfortunate personal manner, attributed by some to a backwoods Irish upbringing which even two years at Christ Church could not correct' (p. 120).   278 1st Lord Arden to Redesdale, 14 June 1804, Jupp/Aspinall transcript from the Redesdale papers, Gloucestershire RO. The able and long-serving chairman of committees in the Lords, the 2nd Lord Walsingham, described Agar as 'so amiable a private and so distinguished a public character' – Walsingham to 2nd earl of Normanton, 18 July 1809, 21 M 57, 2nd earl's unreferenced correspondence.   279 Lady Somerton to Agar, [12] Oct. 1796, T/3719/C/30/33.   280 Lady Clifden to Agar, 30 Dec. 1780, T/3719/C/14/44.   281 Mrs Lidwell to Agar, 27 Sep. 1808, T/3719/C/42/70.   282 Lady Clanwilliam to Agar, 12 Jan. 1796, T/3719/C/30/1. For the authority for the adjective 'formidable', see Malcomson, 'A woman scorned?: Theodosia, countess of Clanwilliam (1743–1817)', in *Familia: the Ulster Genealogical Review*, no. 15 (1999), pp 1–25.

call you my friend, raises me in my own opinion, and I hope never to forfeit such friendship.'[283]

Recorded instances of Agar's sense of humour are few. But this is because of the accidents of survival in other people's papers and because, generally speaking, he himself retained copies only of his most important letters, and seldom even of these. One exception is a letter of August 1779 to General Lord Percy, later 2nd duke of Northumberland, whom he assures with mock seriousness that, in spite of the unprotected state of Ireland and its vulnerability to Franco-Spanish invasion,

> my confidence in the powers of our troops and the abilities of our commander-in-chief [the already-mentioned Sir John Irwine], don't permit me to despair ..., [though] my security would not be lessened if I could persuade myself to believe that the business of a general could be learnt at St James', or that as much knowledge was to be acquired by attending a review in Hyde Park as by serving a campaign in America. ... These considerations, and the defenceless state of this island, make me often wish that, to our polite knight's theory, we could add your Lordship's practical knowledge.[284]

This is a rather strained and stilted effort – perhaps because Agar was writing to a 'grand' English acquaintance whom he was trying to impress. Agar's humour is best inferred from that of his correspondents and from the general tone of the correspondence – for example, from Scott's nonsensical description of King James I as 'a very learned, classical, stately, perpendicular prince, ... [of whom] Sir Anthony Weldon, who wrote the history of his court, says [that he] generally wore his hand on his codpiece'.[285] In 1788, Scott, now Earlsfort, described a letter from Agar as not only 'the best proof of your being in health but in the cheerful exercise of the best style of manly composition and communication of friendly sentiment I ever remember either you or any other of my epistolary correspondents to enjoy'.[286] In her well known *Retrospections ..., 1770–1806*, Dorothea Herbert, the daughter of one of Agar's clergymen and a poetess and woman of sensibility (*à la* Griffith), records an occasion in 1793 when she was persuaded to read her poems 'to a *levée* of Roscommon officers and all the *literati'* of Cashel (a rather incongruous assemblage, it might be supposed). After this reading, 'Mrs Agar, the Archbishop's lady, sent for them. His Grace himself was much entertained with them, and some parts of them made him laugh heartily.'[287] Unless the impression given of Agar is very misleading, it is that of a man who, into middle life and beyond, was as much an *enfant terrible* as an *eminence grise*.

283 Countess dowager of Clare to Agar, postmarked 15 Mar. 1802, T/3719/C/36/8.   284 Agar to Percy, 14 Aug. 1779, T/3719/C/13/33.   285 Scott to Agar, [spring or summer? 1778], T/3719/C/12/9.   286 Earlsfort to Agar, 7 Oct. 1788, T/3719/C/22/34.   287 Dorothea Herbert, *Retrospections*, p. 324.

3

The Agar power-base in Kilkenny, 1715–1800

The Agar power-base in Co. Kilkenny derived from the size and location of the family estate. To that extent, it was an early eighteenth-century phenomenon, and part-and-parcel of the inheritance of Agar's eldest brother, James Agar, 1st Viscount Clifden. But things were not as straightforward as that. While the Agars of Gowran dominated the borough of that name from at least 1713, they did not gain control of their other borough, Thomastown, until the early 1740s; and their power in both was then challenged in a family feud which was not resolved (in their favour) until the second half of the 1750s. Nor did they become a 'county family', in the sense of representing their county in parliament, until as late as 1761. Meanwhile, their cousins, the Agars of Ringwood, were still embattled over the borough of Callan, and Charles Agar's uncle, James Agar of Ringwood, was shot dead in the sensational election duel over Callan in 1769, when Charles Agar was already bishop of Cloyne. Violent and venal electioneering had been characteristic of Co. Kilkenny earlier in the century, but the Agars prolonged such practices, or rather malpractices, into the more decorous 1760s. This was not the ideal background or image for a bishop. Moreover, even after the county seat was won and the two boroughs of Gowran and Thomastown were safely subjugated, the Agars of Gowran – partly because of the 1st Lord Clifden's already-mentioned financial difficulties – were not as strong in terms of votes in the House of Commons as in theory they ought to have been. The upshot was that Charles Agar incurred much odium from his membership of a borough-owning family, and derived less advantage from it than might be imagined.

POWER VACUUM AND POWER STRUGGLES, 1715–27

The flight of the 2nd duke of Ormonde into Jacobite exile in 1715 created a power vacuum in Kilkenny and either originated or exacerbated power struggles over the various constituencies within the county. Watty Cox for once caught something of the truth when he quipped in his obituary of Agar: 'At this time, the county of Kilkenny was remarkable for three [actually, there were rather more!] families, whose respective vices were objects of common animadversion, the Floods, Agars and Bushes, which the wits of the time lampooned ... [as] Floods of iniquity, Eager for pelf and every Bushe harbouring a rogue.' The leading politically active families who operated in early-to-mid-eighteenth century Kilkenny, were the Agars, Bushes, Cuffes, Deanes,

Floods, Fownesses, Langrishes, Ponsonbys and Wemyses, most of them mid-seventeenth century in their Irish origins. Between and among themselves, they jostled, bargained, manoeuvred, competed and occasionally fought over the numerous (seven) boroughs in Co. Kilkenny and over the county representation as well. In this last pursuit – the representation of Co. Kilkenny – they were joined by other families, including two surviving, protestant, cadet branches of the Anglo-Norman house of Butler, the Viscounts Ikerrin (later earls of Carrick) and the Viscounts Mountgarret. Another very major county family (since the second half of the 1630s) were the Wandesfords, represented in the period 1751–84 by John Wandesford, 5th Viscount Castlecomer and only Earl Wandesford. This pattern of political instability in the county and its component boroughs roughly coincided with the submergence of the Ormonde Butlers between 1715 and *c.*1775. After the 2nd duke's departure in 1715, 'many of ... [his] followers in his own counties of Kilkenny and Tipperary either dropped into decent obscurity or began to arrange a new set of political relationships for themselves. Even in the 1715 general election, Sir Henry Wemys [of Danesfort, MP for Co. Kilkenny, 1703–14, and an Ormondite Tory] was willing to compromise with his opponents in Co. Kilkenny ...; [and] it was not long before *quondam* Tories like ... [James Agar of Gowran (1671?–1733), Wemys' son-in-law] were happy to call themselves Whigs.'[1]

James Agar was therefore typical of the recently rich and politically ambitious and versatile families who emerged to fill the power vacuum. He had been high sheriff of Co. Kilkenny in 1702–3, had entered parliament in 1703 (see p. 18), and was to sit there continuously, though for a variety of Kilkenny and nearby constituencies, until his death in 1733.

> In 1715 he was appointed mayor of Kilkenny [city], having previously been an alderman. Burtchaell has the following to say of his election: 'A scheme was introduced into the corporation by which all authority was entrusted to the mayor and the aldermen, the effect of which was that the Tory aldermen managed to keep themselves in power and excluded the Whigs. The feud lasted for some time but, in 1715, a kind of compromise was come to, known as the "Kilkenny Peace", when by consent of all parties Alderman Agar was chosen mayor.'[2]

As mayor, James Agar was, at least overtly, non-partisan, and tried in vain to restore harmony and end litigation by persuading the corporation of the wisdom 'of being unanimous in their elections'.[3]

1 Hayton, 'The political following of the 2nd Duke of Ormonde', p. 233.   2 Moran, 'The Agars of Gowran', p. 112.   3 James Agar to [?], 6 Oct. 1716, transcripts of the State Papers (Ireland), PRONI, T/448; Thomas P. Power, 'Parliamentary representation in Co. Kilkenny in the eighteenth century', in *Kilkenny history and society*, pp 313–14.

At the general election held in that year [1715, the Whigs] succeeded in ousting Sir Richard Levinge, Bt, and ... Darby Egan, the [Tory sitting] members for the city, and returning Alderman ... Ebenezer Warren, the leader of the Whig aldermen, and ... Maurice Cuffe ... . [They also succeeded in] bringing the affairs of the corporation before parliament. At the enquiry which followed, it appeared among other matters that, whereas the salary of the mayor had been reduced to £100 per annum, ... Agar while mayor had a bye-law passed raising it to £260. [In addition,] he had the whole income of the customs given him, which amounted to £260.) Also 'the said Mr Agar held over his year two months, for which the corporation gave him £40, and to him, more, to procure his picture, £32.[4]

James Agar, though a peace-maker, was clearly determined that peace should be at a price payable to him. By 1717, his political rehabilitation was complete. The act passed in that year 'for the better regulating the corporation of the city of Kilkenny, and strengthening the protestant interest therein' (*4 George I, cap. 16*), which named the local leaders of 'the Jacobite interest' ('Jacobite' being the usual pejorative term for 'Tory'), did not mention James Agar in that context.

The 'Kilkenny Act' did not bring peace to Kilkenny city. For one thing, it glanced at but did not resolve the question of who had the right to vote in the annual elections for mayor – the mayor and aldermen only, or the freemen as well – and the related question of whether the mayor had a vote except in the case of an equality of votes for two candidates.[5] The other reason for continuing disputes and petitions over Kilkenny city is that the Whigs, having eliminated any real Tories who remained, fell out among themselves. James Agar ceased to be active in city politics except as an aldermanic ally of his patron, the politically active local bishop, Sir Thomas Vesey, 1st Bt, bishop of Ossory, 1714–30, and like Agar himself an erstwhile Ormondite Tory.[6] Vesey, as bishop, had the principal interest in the borough of St Canice or Irishtown, a distinct corporation and parliamentary borough from the adjoining Kilkenny city, which was unsuccessfully challenging in the courts this very point of St Canice's distinctness in the period 1718–21.[7] In November 1720, Vesey received the formal thanks of the corporation of St Canice for his 'paternal care and great expense in so seasonably defending and thoroughly asserting the liberties of this your Lordship's burrow [*sic*]'[8] against the city corporation in a dispute over the regulation of trade and the billeting of soldiers. Because of the relative importance of clergymen in the small electorates of the first third of the eighteenth century,[9] the bishop of Ossory had great influence in both the city and county of Kilkenny. At a by-election for the city due to take place in 1721, it was expected that one candidate would 'carry it, if your Lordship gives him

4 Moran, 'The Agars of Gowran', p. 112. 5 [Rev. Dr] James Doggarell [Ossory diocesan school-master] to Bishop Vesey of Ossory, 5 July 1720 (two letters), De Vesci papers, NLI, J/1. 6 Vesey to Thomas Medlicott, 26 Oct. 1714, ibid. 7 Opinion of Francis Bernard on the jurisdictional dispute, 2 Mar. 1718/19, and Daniel Sulevan to Vesey, 4 Feb. 1720/21, ibid. 8 Doggarell to Vesey, 14 Nov. 1720, J/24. 9 Rev. Dr William Andrews [diocesan registrar of Ossory], to Vesey, 5 Nov. 1720, J/24.

your interest'.[10] But, in the same year, Bishop Vesey's influence there received a permanent set-back when his cousin, either Maurice Cuffe, city MP from 1715 to 1727, or Cuffe's younger brother, Capt. John Cuffe, 'most strangely gave up his allies', as James Agar put it. 'Had he kept to his promise, the corporation would have been entirely in his power.'[11]

At the time of the 1727 general election, Co. Kilkenny (to say nothing of St Canice) was 'known to be ... at your Lordship's devotion',[12] and in that constituency Vesey supported, and possibly constructed, the victorious alliance between James Agar's brother-in-law, Patrick Wemys senior (1679–1747), also a client of Vesey, and the Hon. William Ponsonby, son and heir of the 2nd Viscount Duncannon (later 1st earl of Bessborough).[13] Wemys was the son and successor of Sir Henry. He had sat for Gowran, 1703–14, had been sitting for Co. Kilkenny since 1721, and continued to do so until his death. The unsuccessful candidate in 1727 was Warden Flood of Burnchurch, Co. Kilkenny, who had appealed in vain for an understanding with Vesey. In other words, James Agar had chosen a powerful, albeit an impermanent and *ex officio*, patron.

THE AGAR BOROUGHS OF GOWRAN, THOMASTOWN AND CALLAN, 1727–*c.*1770

The state of play in these other constituencies, and the fact that James Agar was a political dependant of Bishop Vesey, are important to an understanding of what was going on in the constituency of particular concern to James Agar, Gowran. As has been seen, Gowran had been the Agars' place of abode since the time of James' father, Charles, the putative 'livery-stable ostler in Dublin'. Charles Agar had served as portrieve of Gowran from 1690 to his death in 1696, and had attempted to become one of its MPs in 1692. James Agar was MP for Gowran, 1713–14, and was returned for Gowran in 1715 but chose to sit for Callan; and his elder son, Henry, represented Gowran from 1727 to 1746. Two letters in Bishop Vesey's papers establish fairly clearly the extent of James Agar's influence in Gowran by 1727. The first is from an Ossory clergyman writing to Vesey (then at Bath) from Kilkenny in September 1727:

> Though I have been this fortnight in your Lordship's citadel overlooking our affairs, I forbore writing till I could assure you of our security in your faithful borough [St Canice]. Mr Agar and [Richard] Dawson [the Bishop's brother-in-law] have been this day elected our representatives unanimously, notwithstanding the threats by some envious and sorry people. There was the vastest appearance of your friends of all conditions that I ever saw ... . We used all the

10 Daniel Sulevan to Vesey, 3 Nov. 1720, J/1.   11 Agar to Vesey, 21 Mar. 1720/21, J/19.
12 Warden Flood to Vesey, 5 Aug. 1727, J/1.   13 Rev. Dr Philip Ridgate to Vesey, 28 Jan. 1720/21, joint letter from Patrick Wemys and James Agar to Vesey, 17 Dec. 1728, and [Rev Dr] Edward Maurice to Vesey, 20 Sep. [1727], J/19, J/23 and J/1.

precautions necessary to guard against malcontents that might have been on the lurch [*sic*] for matter for a petition, and shall carry the same with us to Gowran, so that my friend, John [Denny Vesey, the Bishop's son], shall have a sure seat in spite of his minority.[14]

The second letter is dated mid–October and unfolds a complicated proposal for the purchase of a seat, if necessary, for Vesey's son at the 'medium or reasonable price' of £300. None of this actually came to pass, so the key sentence, which comes early in the rigmarole, is: 'Upon an intimation [to the writer] from Mr Agar and Mr Wemys, ... Mr Agar keeps open his borough of Gowran till he can know your Lordship's pleasure on this proposal.'[15]

Between them, these letters prove a number of things. First, James Agar was returned for St Canice in 1727 (and sat for it until his death in 1733), not because his influence over both seats for Gowran was doubtful, but as part of a wider-ranging agreement with his patron, Vesey. Second, Gowran was so secure that the return of a minor for it could be risked (which it could not in St Canice); the return of a minor, if objected to in a petition to the House of Commons, was bound to be declared invalid. Third, James Agar was in a position to keep both seats for Gowran open (which he did until 6 November by various delaying tactics in regard to the election writ), which means that his son, Henry, and David Chaigneau of Corkagh, Co. Dublin, who were returned on that date, can both be regarded as nominees of James Agar. It might otherwise be assumed that Chaigneau, as a major landowner in the borough, was at this stage co-proprietor or co-patron with James Agar. In fact, Chaigneau was returned only because the second seat for Gowran was not needed for John Denny Vesey.[16]

In other respects, too, James Agar took the lead among the different proprietary interests in Gowran – David Chaigneau, Lewis Bayly, the corporation and himself. It was James Agar who initiated (and probably helped to finance) the rebuilding of Gowran church in 1721.[17] Then, shortly before his death, he founded an almshouse in the town. It is still there today, 'a square building ornamented with black marble', and 'situated near the gate of the demesne'. It used to bear the inscription: 'The foundation of this poor house and a perpetual annuity of £21 was begun and instituted by James Agar Esq., deceased in the year 1733, finished and completed by his wife, Mary, in the year 1735'. Four widows were to be maintained in the almshouse, each receiving £5 per annum, with the remaining £1 used for the repair of windows (as opposed to widows!).[18]

Following his death in 1733, James Agar's sons, Henry of Gowran and James of Ringwood, soon showed that they had inherited his 'avaricious appetite for land' and his 'political ambition to control the boroughs of south Kilkenny ... . Differences emerged within the family which led ... [to a] struggle ... [between the brothers] for

14 Maurice to Vesey, 20 Sep. [1727], J/1.   15 Richard Nutley, to Vesey, 14 Oct. 1727, J/1.   16 Maurice to Vesey, 20 Sep. [1727], J/1.   17 Agar to Vesey, 21 Mar. 1720/21, J/19.   18 Moran, 'The Agars of Gowran', p. 114.

control of Gowran. ... The corporation of the borough was vested in a portrieve, twelve burgesses and an unlimited number of freemen, who [enjoyed the vote in parliamentary elections, but were nominated and, ultimately controlled] by the burgesses. It was tailor-made for control by' one patron or another,[19] and Henry Agar was determined that he would be the one. He was firmly in the saddle by mid-1736. 'The surviving corporation book for Gowran begins in ... [that year], when Henry Agar, MP, was portrieve, and was apparently his gift'. The occasion of the gift was the successful outcome of a legal dispute between the brothers, which had been submitted to the prominent lawyer, Henry Singleton, either for counsel's opinion or for arbitration. It had been objected against Henry 'that by the charter Henry cannot be portrieve two years successively, and that one of the burgesses, who is to make up the six at his being sworn in, is married to a Popish wife, though such marriage was had before the Popery Act [of 1728]'.[20] On the most material points, Singleton upheld Henry Agar's claims. So, Henry continued to serve as portrieve until his death in 1746, 'and for the remainder of the century the office was held by the Agars [of Gowran] themselves ... or their nominees'.[21]

James Agar of Ringwood had been worsted in the legal proceedings of 1736.[22] But, following Henry's premature death, and the minority of Henry's eldest son, James Agar junior (the future Lord Clifden), James of Ringwood was returned to parliament for Gowran at the by-election which took place on 26 October 1747, and made a second take-over bid for the borough. The corporation book shows that he was abetted by, among others, a member of the Flood family, Francis, and two members of the Wemys family, Henry and Patrick. (These latter were probably Henry Wemys, MP for Callan from 1727 until his death in 1750, and Patrick Wemys junior, MP for Co. Kilkenny, 1747–60, who were the first and second sons, respectively, of Patrick Wemys senior.) On 27 June 1748, there was a contested election for portrieve, which the Agar of Gowran side won by 25 votes to 14, and on 5 August there was another contest, this time for the recordership, when the voting was 23 to 9. The next year's election for portrieve was uncontested and, thanks to a considerable infusion of new freemen, all species of election for Gowran, whether municipal or parliamentary, were unanimous from 1749 onwards.[23] When David Chaigneau, the other MP for Gowran (since 1715), died in 1753, James Agar junior, though a year and a half short of twenty-one, was elected in his place. (Primate Stone had hoped that Welbore Ellis could be persuaded to bring in a full-age government supporter whose vote would be immediately operative,[24] but Ellis must have thought that the opportunity to return the young head of the family was not to be missed.) Forced prematurely to the forefront by his father's early death, James Agar junior soon showed that he had a mind and will of his own. In his relations with the borough of Gowran, he was facilitated by the fact that the corporation had been heavily in debt to his father and,

19 Kelly, *Henry Flood*, pp 35–61.   20 'A state of the case relative to the borough of Gowran', 23 June 1736, NA, M 3239; Moran, 'The Agars of Gowran', p. 117.   21 Power, *Kilkenny representation*, p. 322.   22 NA, M 3239.   23 Gowran corporation book, 1736–1800, RSAI, C7A5.   24 Stone to Lord George Sackville, 30 Jan. 1753, *H.M.C. Stopford-Sackville Mss.*, i. 189.

consequently, now to him. 'In December 1755 this [debt] stood at £1,935, and ... [to satisfy it] all corporation lands were conveyed to [James] Agar [junior] at a fee farm rent of £10 per annum in 1756.'²⁵ In 1766, as if in token of submission, James Agar of Ringwood sold to James Agar Junior the former's property in Gowran for £466.²⁶ This made the Agars, not the sole but the main landowners in Gowran, whereas in Thomastown, which was on the edge of the Agar estate, their landownership was minimal.²⁷

In Thomastown, 'the electorate consisted of the sovereign and the burgesses ... [i.e. the freemen, though they existed, did not vote in parliamentary elections. The burgesses] usually numbered twelve, although the governing charter had no restriction in this respect (in September 1755 there were twenty ...). As the borough came under the predominant control of the Agar family, the electorate was reduced, so that by 1790 it consisted of six burgesses. In the period up to 1727, a number of families shared the representation of the borough. These included ... Arthur Bushe (1695–... [17]15) and [Capt.] John Cuffe (1715–27).'²⁸ The Cromwellian Hewetson family of Thomastown were the ground landlords of much of the borough until they sold their estate in 1791. Christopher Hewetson was MP for Thomastown, 1695–1703, and recorder from at least 1707 until his death, c.1740; and in the years 1690–1730, a Hewetson held the office of sovereign almost continuously.²⁹ 'During this period the election of freemen and burgesses was entered in the corporation books in a rather haphazard manner', which suggests that the families with the predominant influence in Thomastown 'had become careless in maintaining their control of the borough'.³⁰

The Agars feature, in a subsidiary capacity, in the corporation records from c.1695 onwards. On 3 September 1698, James Agar senior was sworn a burgess and freeman. His younger brother, Peter (who died young), was a freeman from c.1704.³¹ But serious Agar intervention in the borough did not take place until the early 1740s. In the intervening years (1710–33), James Agar and his wife, Mary, were active in lending money to prominent local families (including the Hewetsons), the loans being secured on lands in the neighbourhood of Thomastown.³² In 1738, the widowed Mary Agar lent £2,000 on mortgage to one Worsop Bushe of Derrynahinch, Co. Kilkenny,³³ a son of the Arthur Bushe who had sat for Thomastown earlier in the century. This loan, and its predecessors, may have been politically motivated, and designed to hold the recipients in thrall. On 27 June 1743, James and Mary Agar's elder son, Henry Agar

25 Power, 'Kilkenny representation', p. 322.   26 Conveyance from James of Ringwood to James of Gowran, 14 May 1766, NA, D 20109a.   27 'Falkland' [Rev. John Scott], *The parliamentary representation of Ireland* (Dublin, 1790), quoted in The history of the Irish Parliament database, *sub* 'Thomastown'; Joe Doyle, 'The Hewetsons of Thomastown', *In the shadow of the steeple*, no. 2 (1990), pp 12–27.   28 Power, 'Kilkenny representation', p. 320.   29 Information from vol. i of the Thomastown corporation book, RSAI, C7A1, kindly given me by John Kirwan.   30 Moran, 'The Agars of Gowran', p. 118.   31 Information from John Kirwan.   32 ROD, memorials no. 2065, 30000, 36882, 42680, 43883, 50551, 62891, 90041 and 132095. Again, I am indebted for these references to John Kirwan, and through him, to Mr Liam Hoyne of Thomastown.   33 Deed of mortgage, 25 Feb. 1738, Annaly/Clifden papers, F/4/2.

of Gowran, was elected a freeman, a burgess and sovereign of Thomastown, all on the same day (and that, moreover, not the charteral day for the election of a sovereign). Two other Agarites were made freemen and burgesses on that day, eight more (including 'Welbore Ellis Esq. of London') on 1 July, seventeen on 26 July and so on. On 29 September, the correct day for electing a sovereign, Henry Agar was 'newly elected, admitted and sworn'. Thirty-eight burgesses and freemen voted for him, and thirteen against, including Amyas Bushe (of Kilfane, Co. Kilkenny) and Henry and Patrick Wemys. Sixteen more people were admitted freemen and burgesses on 3 September 1744, including Henry Agar's brother, 'James Agar of The Roar [i.e. Ringwood]'.[34]

> Once the Agars had gained control, they were very vigilant in maintaining their interest. Henry Agar held the position of sovereign until his death in 1746. After his death his opponents, hoping to take advantage of the weakness of his family (his eldest son was only thirteen years old), tried to wrest control back from them. In 1747 Amyas Bushe of Kilfane stood against George Forster, the Agar nominee [for the sovereignty], but was defeated. He afterwards contested the result, right up to the king's bench in England, where he lost his suit [in 1751].[35]

'This victory represented the displacement of the older Bushe interest in the corporation by that of Agar.'[36]

The second volume of the corporation book was a present from 'James Agar Esq., eldest son of Henry Agar, to the corporation. In April 1752, James Agar was chosen as a burgess, and a further entry for that month records the thanks of the corporation to Mrs Anne Agar, widow of Henry Agar, for "her unwearied and successful endeavours in procuring peace and liberty to the said corporation and in defeating the powerful attempts made on the franchises and privileges thereof".'[37] This, incidentally, is a surprisingly overt acknowledgement (for the mid-eighteenth century) of the political role of a woman. 'In 1764, the corporation ordered a survey of its lands, so that the woods could be sold to reimburse James Agar ... [for] his large disbursements in defence of [its] liberties and privileges".'[38] These 'powerful attempts' so expensively resisted had not been made by the Bushes, or at least by the Bushes alone. James Agar junior's real adversary was Sir William Fownes, 2nd Bt, of Woodstock, Inistioge, Co. Kilkenny, representative of an English speculator in Irish land, Stephen Sweet, who had come second to James Agar of Gowran (d.1733) as a purchaser of land in

34 Vol. i of the Thomastown corporation book, RSAI, C7A1.   35 Moran, 'The Agars of Gowran', p. 118.   36 Power, 'Kilkenny representation', p. 320. In November 1746, the Rt Hon. Luke Gardiner, who sat for Thomastown on the Bushe interest, engaged in somewhat mysterious lobbying of the lords justices (who were in charge in the absence of the lord lieutenant), over the choice of a sheriff for Co. Kilkenny for the forthcoming year. This was probably to do with the picking of a jury to try the case being brought by Amyas Bushe. See 1st earl of Bessborough to Gardiner, 19 and 26 Nov. 1746, and [Gardiner] to [Bessborough, c.20 Nov. 1746], Domvile papers, NLI, Mss. 9399 and 11848.   37 Power, 'Kilkenny representation', p. 320.   38 Ibid.

Kilkenny from the trustees of the forfeited estates.[39] Fownes had already made a take-over bid for the borough of Inistioge. More important, he was married into the great Co. Kilkenny family and Irish political dynasty, the already-mentioned Ponsonbys of Bessborough, near Pilltown, in the southernmost part of the county, who had co-operated with him in Inistioge.[40] It was therefore a considerable achievement for the young James Agar to have 'recovered ... [Thomastown] from ... Fownes'.[41] Since the crucial testing-time in both Gowran and Thomastown had come in the second half of the 1740s, when he was only a teenager, it must strongly be suspected that his maternal uncle and guardian, Welbore Ellis, was the successful manager of his interests in both boroughs. Ellis' election as a freeman and burgess of Thomastown in 1743, his presence at Gowran following the death of Henry Agar in 1746,[42] and the tribute paid by the corporation of Thomastown to Anne Agar, Ellis' sister, in 1752 – all tend to confirm this suspicion.

The Agar interest in Thomastown continued to be based exclusively on control of the corporation, not ownership of land in the borough. Corporation land as well as woods were sold post-1764, but James Agar was not the purchaser. In 1773, he was offered first refusal of some woods and the residue of a lease under the corporation, but appears not to have bitten.[43] In 1779, the Hewetson heiress, Jane, married Eland Mossom of Mount Eland, Ballyragget, Co. Kilkenny, MP for Kilkenny City, 1777–83. The Mossoms seem soon to have run into financial difficulties, because in the mid-1780s they mortgaged their Thomastown estate for £9,500 to none other than Archbishop Charles Agar. Mortgagees often ended up as the purchasers of the property on which they held a mortgage, and the Archbishop may have had thoughts of gaining a firmer foothold for the Agars in the borough. If so, nothing came of them. In 1791, the Hewetson/Mossom estate (of over 2,000 statute acres) was sold for *c.*£19,250; and the purchaser was neither Archbishop Agar nor the 2nd Lord Clifden (the latter of whom was in no financial state to buy it at that time – see pp 44 and 129 30).[44]

Callan, the most contentious borough in eighteenth-century Kilkenny and, with the possible exception of Swords, Co. Dublin, in eighteenth-century Ireland, was an unprepossessing spot. In 1755, it was described as 'a poor, dirty town, interspersed with the numerous ruins of old castles and religious houses'.[45] Like Gowran and Thomastown, it had been left stranded by the receding tide of Ormonde power and prosperity. Its complex politics have been exhaustively explored elsewhere in recent

39 Brennan, 'Co. Kilkenny landowners, 1641–1700', p. 184.   40 Edward Maurice to Bishop Vesey, 20 Sep. [1727], and [Sir] John Staples, [5th Bt], to Vesey, 22 Jan. 1727/8, De Vesci papers, J/1 and J/23.   41 Ellis to the marquess of Hartington, 7 Oct. 1755, Chatsworth papers, Chatsworth, Derbyshire: photocopies in PRONI, T/3158/923.   42 Some of the agent's letters from November 1746 onwards to Ellis in PRONI, T/3403/1, are addressed to him at Gowran.   43 Michael Vicary, Wexford, to Rev. Dr Thomas Hewetson, 19 Apr. 1773, Annaly/ Clifden papers, F/4/7; Doyle, 'Hewetsons of Thomastown', pp 23–5.   44 Doyle, 'Hewetsons of Thomastown', pp 16, 23 and 26–7.   45 Quoted in J.L. McCracken, 'Central and local administration in Ireland under George II' (unpublished QUB Ph.D. thesis, 1941), p. 81.

years.[46] By 1761, Callan was the only one of the three boroughs where the Agars had been active which had not yet fallen decisively under the control of one patron. It was also the only sphere of action left to James Agar of Ringwood. At first it was disputed between and among: both branches of the Agar family; their cousins, the Wemyses of Danesfort and Delville;[47] the Cuffes of Castle Inch (seven miles from Kilkenny City) and of nearby Desart Court, Callan; and, most important of all (in the light of future events), the Floods of Burnchurch (between Kilkenny City and Callan), later renamed Farmley. One Callan voter, torn between and among these contending interests, later complained of 'the fatigue both of body and mind, the hazard of my liberty, the danger of life and the utter ruin of my fortunes'.[48] In *c*.1762, James Wemys of Danesfort, who had just succeeded to that estate, transferred his interest in Callan to James Agar of Ringwood. He was followed, or perhaps accompanied, by James Agar of Gowran – as if as a *quid pro quo* for James Ringwood's decision to bow out of Gowran. At a by-election for Callan in August 1765, it was noted 'that Jemmy Agar of Gowran does not interfere on this occasion'.[49] Ellis Agar, countess of Brandon, went far beyond mere neutrality and was a warm partisan of her brother, James of Ringwood; in 1762, in conscious or unconscious imitation of Mary Tudor, she had declared dramatically that Callan 'was engraved deeply on her heart'.[50] Perhaps she felt so strongly because she was a woman scorned. Many years and two husbands earlier, in *c*.1725, she had been offered in marriage to Warden Flood, eldest son of the Agars' rivals over Callan, the Floods of Burnchurch.[51] The young Warden Flood had rebelled and made a love match for himself in London (though not fast enough to legitimise his son and heir, and his other children). This son and heir, the celebrated Henry Flood, was now James Agar's most formidable rival for control of Callan. Flood 'repeatedly offered' to divide the patronage of the borough, so that each would return a member. But 'Mr Agar's answer was, all or none'.[52]

In 1765–6, James Agar obtained an important psychological advantage by buying the Callan estate and the lordship of the manor of Callan from the war-weary John Cuffe, 2nd Lord Desart, at a cost of £17,120.[53] But he was impatient, or perhaps

46 Kelly, *Henry Flood*, pp 40–61.   47 Patrick Wemys Junior, MP for Co. Kilkenny, 1747–60, is described as 'of Delville, Co. Kilkenny', in a deed of 11 July 1749 – Annaly/Clifden papers, F/4/2. There are genealogies of the Wemyses in a footnote to the entry for 'Clifden', in John Lodge (ed. Mervyn Archdall), *The peerage of Ireland ...* (8 vols., Dublin, 1789), vi, pp 74–5, and in John Burke and John Bernard Burke, *A genealogical and heraldic dictionary of the landed gentry of Great Britain and Ireland* (3 vols., London, 1846–8), ii. 1549.   48 Richard Griffith (see p. 61) to Agar, 2 May 1768, T/3719/C/2/4.   49 Talbot to Flood, 27 Aug. 1765, Flood papers, BL, Add. Ms. 22930, f. 7, printed (with the date and other things wrong) in T[homas] R[odd] (ed.), *Original letters to the Rt Hon. Henry Flood ...* (London, 1820), p. 35.   50 Theodosia, Lady Branden, to her husband, the 1st Lord Branden, 17 Sep. [1762?], Talbot-Crosbie papers, NLI. It is a confusing coincidence that Lady Branden was writing about Lady Brandon.   51 Kelly, *Henry Flood*, p. 25. Ellis Agar married her first husband, the 7th Viscount Mayo, in 1726.   52 Griffith to Agar, 2 May 1768, T/3719/C/2/4. 53 Kelly, *Henry Flood*, p. 52 (which states, on the evidence of ROD, that the purchase was made in 1765); deed of conveyance from Desart to James Agar of Ringwood, 12 June 1766, Annaly/Clifden papers, F/6/1. Both 1765 and 1766 are correct. James Agar bought the estate at an auction held

fearful of what Flood's parliamentary weight and the nuisance value of his oratory might induce the government to do on his behalf. For whatever reason, in August 1769 he provoked Flood into a duel, which was fought at Dunmore, Co. Kilkenny, and in which Flood shot him dead. This was the culmination of a series of fights and affrays over Callan.[54] On the field of honour, as during the preliminaries to the duel, James Agar's behaviour was violent and offensive. As Flood's second wrote afterwards: 'In justice to the living, no man could have sought his own death more than Mr Agar. Indeed, nothing could equal his infatuation, for the cause of challenging which he alleged, was wonderfully frivolous; and if it were an offence, it was precisely as much an offence any day these ten months as it was at the moment of resenting it.'[55] So James Agar came badly out of the affair: for one thing, he was dead; for another, gentlemanly public opinion was against him; for a third, the court of king's bench completely cleared Flood following a murder trial at the spring assizes of 1770.[56] James Agar was succeeded by his elder surviving son, George (1751–1815), later 1st Lord Callan, who was then a minor. By 1776, George Agar had fulfilled his late father's ambition, and was firmly in control of Callan,[57] though Flood made one final, unavailing attempt to win it back at the general election of 1783. This victory in Callan brought little or no advantage to his cousin, James Agar junior and the latter's brother, the bishop, though both shared in the notoriety of all these excesses.

JAMES AGAR AND THE REPRESENTATION OF CO. KILKENNY, 1755–61

James Agar junior, now the undisputed patron of both Gowran and Thomastown, was not content with four seats in parliament. He next capped the ambitions of both his father and grandfather by aspiring to represent the county of Kilkenny. In this aspiration, he was again seconded by Welbore Ellis, who of course was happy enough to use a nephew with Irish political clout as a makeweight to his own faltering career in British politics. Not for the only time, it was a moot point whether the Agars were under an obligation to him, or he under an obligation to the Agars. Ellis, as has been seen, was politically connected with Henry Fox, and so was the lord lieutenant of Ireland, the marquess of Hartington, soon (December 1755) to succeed as 4th duke of Devonshire. Two of Hartington's sisters were married to sons of the 1st earl of Bessborough: William Ponsonby, now Viscount Duncannon, MP for Co. Kilkenny (1727–58), and John Ponsonby, speaker of the House of Commons (1756–71) and MP for Co. Kilkenny (1761–83). Against this literally Anglo-Irish background, Ellis opened his campaign on behalf of Agar (and himself).

under a decree of the court of exchequer on 8 May 1765; but he did not come into full legal possession of it until the date of the conveyance.   **54** Kelly, *Henry Flood*, pp 52–60.   **55** G.P. Bushe to 1st earl of Charlemont, 26 August 1769, *H.M.C. Charlemont Mss*, i, 294.   **56** Kelly, *Duelling in Ireland*, pp 101–3.   **57** Ellis to Agar, 28 Nov. 1775 and 5 Dec. 1778, T/3719/C/9/3 and C/12/33.

In early October 1755, he reported to Hartington that Agar was willing to return a nominee of Hartington's for a seat then vacant for Thomastown, but asked 'you to give him someone entirely attached to yourself because ... a recommendation from the Ponsonbys might hurt his interest there. The price he talked of was £900.' (In other words, the price of seats had trebled since 1727, in spite of the advancing years of George II.) The negotiation over Thomastown proved abortive – not through any fault of Agar's, but because Hartington's nominee changed his mind. This, however, was a side-issue in comparison to the representation of Co. Kilkenny. To Ellis in Whitehall and Hartington in Dublin Castle, this seemed a simpler matter to arrange than was the reality on the ground. Clear indications of a hiccough presented themselves in December 1755. In that month Hartington, now duke of Devonshire, heard that Agar was 'engaged with the other side' in county politics. This he regretted, because he thought he could guarantee that Agar 'shall come in for the county without any trouble or expense, and by joining with Wemys, it will be both hazardous and expensive.' ('Wemys' was Patrick Wemys junior, the other sitting member, who had succeeded at Danesfort following the death of his eldest brother, Henry, in 1750.) Ellis, meanwhile, had 'received a letter from my nephew which greatly surprised and vexed me. He tells me in it that he has joined Mr Wemys' interest in the county [of Kilkenny], and the Speaker [Henry Boyle] and Lord Kildare in parliament. ... This strange transaction ... shall be a lesson to me, and I shall not for the future answer for a son of my own.'[58] The reference to 'a son of my own' suggests some degree of emotional as well as political dependence on his nephew, which was subsequently transferred to James Agar's younger brother, Charles.

In March 1756, Ellis' initial optimism returned. James Agar, he reported, was 'truly out of countenance about his Irish politics, in which I find he had been grossly misled, but ... was unshook in his attachment to your Grace and the measures of government'.[59] From the Ponsonby side, Devonshire was assured that an Agar-Ponsonby junction of interests would be 'the certain way of making everything easy in that country [sic]'.[60] But by December 1756, nothing had happened. In that month Ellis complained to Devonshire that no overture had been received from Lord Bessborough, which was necessary if Agar were 'to disengage himself with honour' from the 'rash' commitments he had previously made. Meanwhile, a rumour had spread 'that Lord Bessborough's and Mr Agar's interests were joined', which would undoubtedly cause Patrick Wemys junior to demand from Agar an explicit denial or otherwise of the report.[61] Presumably Agar, who must have had a grudge against Wemys on account of the latter's opposition in Thomastown elections in the 1740s, would have been glad to be off with the old love, but wanted first to be sure that he was on with the new. The nub of the matter was that the Agar-Ponsonby alliance 'was

58 Ellis to Hartington/Devonshire, 7 Oct. and 23 Dec. 1755, and Devonshire to Ellis, 30 Dec. 1755, Chatsworth papers, PRONI, T/3158/923, 1038 and 1049. 59 Ellis to Devonshire, 9 Mar. 1756, T/3158/1153. 60 Ponsonby to Devonshire, 1 July 1756, T/3158/1275. 61 Ellis to Devonshire, 5 Dec. 1756, T/3158/1344.

not yet *ripe*', as Lord Bessborough put it in conversation with Agar. Though Bessborough himself was well disposed towards Agar, some of his leading friends on the spot were not, and opposed Agar in matters of county business. The friends of the powerful Lord Castlecomer, by contrast, seconded him in such business, and Castlecomer himself, in mid-1756, had offered Agar his support, amounting to no less than 100 voters, at the next election. Since Ellis computed Agar's own strength at 80 votes or nearly so, and the total electorate at only 400, Castlecomer's offer of an alliance was very tempting and, after about a two-year delay, Agar closed with it.[62]

These leisurely negotiations, whether for an Agar-Ponsonby or an Agar-Wandesford alliance, had been directed towards the next general election, which seemed imminent in view of the age of the King. But they were suddenly up-staged by the by-election thrust on to Co. Kilkenny by the death of Lord Bessborough at the beginning of August 1758 and his succession by Lord Duncannon, the county MP For that by-election, neither side had a candidate, since both Agar and John Ponsonby, younger brother of the new Lord Bessborough, already sat in parliament for other seats which, as the law then stood, they had no means of vacating. Because the by-election could not be held until parliament next assembled, in October 1759, the sheriff appointed for the following year would be the returning officer. The new Lord Bessborough was therefore alarmed to receive a report in the second half of August 1758 that Agar and Castlecomer had made a joint request to the lord lieutenant for the nomination of the sheriff.[63] Whether this was true or false, Castlecomer certainly had applied to succeed the late Lord Bessborough as governor of the county. He was well warranted in so doing, as his uncle, the 2nd viscount Castlecomer, and his father, the 4th, had both been governors. He received an evasive reply,[64] but almost immediately afterwards, on 15 August, was promoted to the earldom of Wandesford. A month later, Agar's aunt, Ellis, Lady Athenry, was created countess of Brandon for life.

Ellis Agar's elevation has always been something of a mystery. She was in no financial state to support an earldom – indeed, it was reported in December of that very year that 'All Lady Brandon's furniture and her [Dublin] house is [*sic*] to be sold by auction next Tuesday'.[65] As late as 1807, nearly twenty years after her death, her residuary legatee was still struggling to extract from the representatives of Lord Athenry a debt due to her which had stood at £1,000 in 1787.[66] A family tradition holds that she was 'a friend of George II, who created her countess of Brandon'.[67] There is no other reference to her having some kind of special relationship with George II (who was an old man in 1758); but earldoms for life were the standard reward for female royal

62 Ellis to Devonshire, 20 Aug. 1758, T/3158/1592.   63 2nd earl of Bessborough to Devonshire, 18 Aug. 1758, T/3158/1591.   64 4th duke of Bedford, Devonshire's successor as lord lieutenant, to Castlecomer, 16 July 1758, *Irish official papers*, ii. 194.   65 Jane Lehunte to Mrs Clothilda Tickell, 9 Dec. 1758, Tickell papers, A/78 (private collection in the possession of Major-General M.E. Tickell). By the time of her death in 1789, she had a house in Merrion Square.   66 George Agar, Lord Callan, to Archbishop Agar, 8 Jan. 1807, T/3719/C/41/1.   67 E.M.S. Casey (Lady Casey), *An Australian story, 1837–1907* (London, 1962), pp 102–3. The author had a collateral, female descent from Lord Callan. I am indebted to the Knight of Glin for this obscure reference.

favourites, usually mistresses. In 1751, the two nieces of her first husband, Lord Mayo, the beautiful Gunning sisters, had taken London by storm. So, she would have had easy access to the court from then on, if not earlier. In her second portrait by Philip Hussey, probably painted to mark her earldom in 1758 (fig. 12), she is shown holding the rolled, parchment charters of Gowran and Thomastown.[68] These were boroughs which she herself never controlled, and which when the portrait was painted, were controlled by her nephew, James Agar. Could it be that the visual allusion to the boroughs was a veil thrown over the real reason for her peerage? Or is the George II connection a myth, and was the earldom connected with a tripartite Agar-Wandesford-Ponsonby alliance in Co. Kilkenny, brokered by Dublin Castle and aimed at getting two supporters returned for Co. Kilkenny at the general election? James Agar was himself too young for a peerage, and had had no opportunity to win the county seat and establish his family politically; so the earldom and the portrait may have been an expression and recognition of the importance of the Agars of Gowran.

To address the more immediate problem of the by-election, a compromise candidate acceptable to James Agar, the new Lord Wandesford and John Ponsonby (now speaker of the House of Commons, in succession to Henry Boyle) was found. This was Henry Flood, who was unanimously elected in October 1759. Flood expected that this would be the start of a long innings in the county representation, and did little to improve his standing in the constituency in the short time available to him between then and the general election. Others, more prescient, recognised that he was only a stopgap until that event, when more powerful candidates in the persons of Agar and Ponsonby would be able to take the field, and when the other sitting member, Patrick Wemys junior, might also be fighting for re-election.[69] The manoeuvrings which ensued in county politics between the death of George II in October 1760 and the general election in April 1761 were complicated, and have been misunderstood.[70] The determining factor was that the Agar-Ponsonby alliance held firm, so that Patrick Wemys junior found himself 'deserted by one of his most powerful associates'[71] – Agar himself. In mid-September 1760, some weeks before the death of George II, the 1st earl of Carrick 'was informed by Mr Wemys that the union between him and Mr Agar for this county was dissolved. ... At this crisis' wrote Carrick to Lord Wandesford, 'the eyes of every independent gentleman in the county are fixed on your Lordship. They know your great property and interest ... [and] the zeal you have ever shown for the cause of ... the independent interest [and] liberty ... . I doubt not but that if the Bessborough family engage with any new friends, they must break their promises to old ones who then will join the opposite party.'[72]

A nebulous 'independent interest' existed in most counties for most of the time. In essence, it was composed of middling landowners – squires, not peers; and it

68 I am grateful to the Knight of Glin for a blown-up photograph of this part of the canvas.
69 Kelly, *Henry Flood*, pp 38–9 and 79.   70 Power, op. cit., p. 307.   71 Earl Wandesford to 1st earl of Carrick, 1 Dec. 1760, Shannon papers, PRONI, D/2707/A1/5/29. These copies of important Co. Kilkenny election letters come to be there because Carrick was Henry Boyle, 1st earl of Shannon's, son-in-law and political follower.   72 Carrick to Wandesford, 14 Sep. 1760, ibid.

inclined towards opposition to the government, but not in any concerted or systematic way. The Wemys family, hitherto supported by their cousins, the Agars, were clearly at the heart of the independent interest, as hitherto constituted, in Co. Kilkenny. Henry Flood had superficial affinities to it. But he was obviously a career politician, who hoped to use local politics to strengthen his power base at the centre. The independent interest had therefore fielded a medium-sized landowner, John Hely of Foulkscourt, near Johnstown, Co. Kilkenny,[73] in brief and unsuccessful opposition to him at the 1759 by-election. More genuinely affiliated to the independent interest in Co. Kilkenny were the titled magnates, Wandesford, Carrick and Mountgarret. This was theoretically a contradiction in terms; but in practice nearly all independent interests depended on the support of one or more disgruntled or maverick grandees, for otherwise they would have been made up of too many small and volatile components to have been capable of effective group action. This of course made it possible for grandees to affect membership of the independent interest, as a means of advancing themselves and their own families. But such was not the case in Co. Kilkenny in 1758–61, when the sons of Lords Wandesford, Carrick and Mountgarret were not of age, and Wandesford's, in particular, was a sickly infant who died young. By the same token, the independent interest had no good candidate in 1761, just as it had had none in 1759. Carrick later made it plain that he had not had Wemys in mind as a candidate for the general election. Soon after it, in 1762, Wemys died, closely followed by his youngest brother and successor, James Wemys, in 1765. By 1761, the influence and probably the estates of the Wemys family seem to have been receding rapidly.[74]

The only person to come forward in opposition to the Agar-Ponsonby junction was Flood, who soon withdrew his pretensions. His withdrawal from the county was not unconnected with Callan. In 1759, he had hailed Speaker Ponsonby as 'a thorough friend', not just in the by-election for the county, but in 'a thing of much greater consequence to me ..., the corporation of Callan'.[75] Quite apart from whatever influence Ponsonby possessed in the borough itself, his influence in the House of Commons when, for example, it came to the trying of election petitions relating to Callan, was important to Flood. Wemys was at this stage united with Flood in maintaining a joint interest in Callan; so Wemys, too, had good reason to abandon the county. As Wandesford (anxious of course to justify his desertion of the independent interest in Co. Kilkenny) remarked of Wemys: 'He saw the management of a county and a corporation election, both stiffly to be contested, in his hands at the same time,

---

73 For a character sketch of Hely in later life, see C.T. Bowden, *A tour through Ireland in 1790* (Dublin, 1791), p. 138.   74 James Wemys of Danesfort (*c.*1750–1820), only son and successor of the James who died in 1765, re-surfaces as MP for Kilkenny City, 1793–1800. But he sat as a nominee of his kinsman, the 1st earl of Desart, who by then controlled one seat for the city. In 1801, Desart referred to James Wemys' financial 'distresses' and need of a government employment – Desart to Alexander Marsden, Dublin Castle, 6 and 14 Aug. 1801, and Wemys to Marsden, 8 Jan. 1802, NA, Official Papers, 518/108/1 and 520/131/1. For the reduced circumstances of other members of the Wemys family, whom Archbishop Agar later assisted, see Mrs Ann Frances Wemys to Agar, 9 Apr. 1794, and her daughter, Anna Maria Wemys, to Agar, 22 July 1806, T/3719/C/28/4 and C/40/36. 75 Flood to Robert Langrishe, 7 Apr. 1759, printed in Burtchaell, op. cit., pp 145–6.

and ... it was much to be apprehended that his pursuit of both object[s] must be the cause of his miscarrying with each.'[76] (He miscarried in Callan anyway because, although returned in 1761, he was unseated on petition.) As for Wandesford himself, he not only had no near relation to espouse as a candidate, but was also under obligations to Devonshire and to the current lord lieutenant, the 4th duke of Bedford, for his earldom.[77] Moreover, the British prime minister, the duke of Newcastle, was his connection by marriage (Newcastle's sister having been the wife of Wandesford's uncle, the 2nd Viscount Castlecomer). Under these circumstances, he was unlikely to oppose an Agar-Ponsonby union blessed by Dublin Castle. He also, by mid-November 1760, had the minor inducement that 'a compliment ... will be paid any friend of his of a seat in a borough in the county of Kilkenny upon much easier terms than seats are now generally disposed of'.[78] This compliment, of which in the end he seems not to have availed himself, must have been paid him by Agar. Faced with this Agar-Ponsonby-Wandesford alliance, Agar's uncle, James of Ringwood, the Wemys family and Lords Carrick and Mountgarret could do nothing except make plain their impotent displeasure at the uncontested return of Ponsonby and James of Gowran.[79]

JAMES AGAR'S INTEREST IN KILKENNY, 1761–78

James Agar of Gowran sat for the county from 1761 until his elevation to the peerage in 1776. He flourished politically on the strength of his two boroughs and the four members they returned, and also because he had a very good estate in Kilkenny. As has been remarked, contemporary acreage and/or rental figures for the estate do not seem to exist: Tighe's *c.*20,000 statute acres of 1802 is the nearest guesstimate available, and is valid (roughly) for the period 1733–1815. A contemporary comparator does, perhaps, exist in the form of the Wandesford estate. This could field 100 freeholder votes in 1758 as opposed to James Agar's *c.*80, had a rental of £2,395 in 1773 rising to £7,339 in 1821, and comprised 11,128 Irish acres in 1746 and 19,920 statute acres in 1850. These figures for rental exclude the proceeds from the famous Castlecomer collieries (which were popularly supposed to reach £10,000 per annum in the late eighteenth century). There are many complaints in the Wandesford estate records, and elsewhere, about the transgressions of the colliers: in late May 1798, for example, just before the rebellion, the 2nd Viscount Clifden expressed the view that 'the only bad point in this county is in the collieries', and the colliers lived up to his ill opinion by joining the rebels and 'totally destroying' the Wandesford seat, Castlecomer

---

76 Wandesford to Carrick, 1 Dec. 1760, D/2707/A1/5/29.   77 Wandesford to Bedford, 4 July 1758, T/2915/5/3. Wandesford must, however, have considered that his principal obligation was to Devonshire (which helps to explain his adhesion to the Agar-Ponsonby coalition): to this day, a principal street in Castlecomer is called Chatsworth Street, after Devonshire's seat in Derbyshire. 78 William Talbot, a great friend of Wandesford's, to William Forward, 20 Nov. 1760, volume of typescript copies of some of the Wicklow papers in NLI, PRONI, MIC/246.   79 See, for example, Carrick to Wandesford, 6 Dec. 1760, D/2707/A1/5/29.

House.[80] So it may be assumed that not too many of them would have been trusted far enough to be made freeholders, and that the existence of collieries and colliers does not invalidate this very crude comparison between the Agar and Wandesford interests. There were certainly no colliers among the few and very substantial head tenants of the Wandesford estate in 1746.[81] By 1773, the number of head tenants who actually had freeholds was only 54, a clear indication that colliers were still excluded.

Deliberate multiplication of freeholders may actually have been more marked on the Agar side. The Agars were alleged to have 'encourage[d] protestant tenants' and 'protestant manufacturers'.[82] In view of James Agar's willingness to act as a protestant trustee for a catholic neighbour (p. 43), this is likely to have proceeded from motives of electioneering, not bigotry (catholics were excluded from the parliamentary franchise in county elections between 1728 and 1793). In any case, the allegation may have been partly based on a confusion between Gowran and Ringwood: soon after his acquisition of the manor of Callan, in 1766, James of Ringwood established a weaving industry there, based probably on Huguenot labour,[83] but there seems to be no evidence that James of Gowran did likewise. Where the latter's electoral interest did benefit was from the number of small towns and villages (Gowran itself, Goresbridge, Graiguenamanagh, Dungarvan, etc.), on his estate, which meant that the number of freeholder votes which he could field in county elections was even greater than his acreage would suggest. (The inhabitants of even a parliamentary borough like Gowran, if they had a freehold of appropriate value, were not excluded from the county franchise.) Only the enfranchised tenants on his property in Kilkenny city – a county borough and a geographical and electoral enclave – were precluded from voting in the county. His electoral interest was also the stronger because of the compactness of his estate and its concentration on the Gowran and Graiguenamanagh area. Some major borough magnates, for example Lords Ely and Shannon, and many minor ones, were stronger in borough patronage than they were in landed wealth. Others controlled boroughs in parts of the country, or of a county, in which they had no property. James Agar of Gowran was not like one of these. He was an example of the 'good species of interest' in the Irish House of Commons: as the lord of the soil, he possessed the 'natural interest' in Gowran (though not quite in Thomastown), and his borough and county interest went hand-in-hand.[84]

80 Rental and valuation of the Wandesford estate, 1773, Prior-Wandesforde [*sic*] papers, NLI, Ms. 35480/1 (Wandesford was spelt without the final 'e' in the eighteenth century); William Nolan, [*The barony of*] *Fassadinin* [*Co. Kilkenny*]: *settlement and society in southeast Ireland, 1600–1850* (Dublin, 1979), pp 96, 98 and 115, and pp 77–215 *passim*; Clifden to Agar, 24 May and 27 June 1798, T/3719/C/32/61 and 96; a female member of the Kavanagh family of Borris, Co. Carlow, to her sister, 31 May 1801, Kavanagh papers, Borris House, Co. Carlow: photocopy in PRONI, T/3331/23.   81 Report by Lullum Batwell of Dublin to the 4th Viscount Castlecomer on the Wandesford estate, 6 Jan. 1746, Ms. 35479/17.   82 J.S. Donnelly junior, 'Irish agrarian rebellion: the Whiteboys of 1769–72', in *Proceedings of the Royal Irish Academy* (hereafter *Proc. RIA*, vol. 83, sec. C, no. 12 (1983), p. 304, quoted in Kelly, *Henry Flood*, p. 171.   83 Joe Kennedy, 'Callan: a corporate town, 1700–1800', in *Kilkenny history and society*, p. 291.   84 For a discussion of the qualitative distinctions between different types of electoral interest in the Irish parliament, see

He was, however, beginning to feel the pinch of supporting an unpopular administration 'by his own vote and by the utmost of his influence, when threatened with an opposition and with the loss of his county interest for so doing'; these 'menaces' he complained, 'proved but too true and caused him great expense at the ensuing [1768] election'.[85] Even in his boroughs, constant nursing and attention were necessary. In Gowran, this extended to the unenfranchised inhabitants: there, Agar 'endowed a poor-house [or, more probably, augmented his grandfather's endowment] with £20 a year, ... [plus] eight guineas at Christmas and 3s 6d a week for bread'.[86] Perhaps this was pure charity. What clearly was not was the provision he made in his will of *c.*1770 that his trustees might, if necessary, raise and charge on his estates up to £10,000 to maintain his interest in Gowran and Thomastown.[87] This was an ample, but not excessive, provision: in 1771 or 1772, Flood lamented that 'The borough of Callan cost me ten years' waste of health and time [actually it was longer], the repeated hazard of life, and £12,000.'[88] Nor, at this stage, was his expenditure on Callan at an end. The reason for Agar's complaint about the increased difficulty and expense of maintaining his county interest was a near-revolution in national politics which took place in 1767–9. The ostensible issue was the 'Augmentation' of the proportion of the peacetime army which Ireland paid for, although personal animosity towards the lord lieutenant, Lord Townshend, and Townshend's refusal to be blackmailed into conceding the exorbitant patronage demands of Speaker Ponsonby and his allies, were the real issues. As a result of these contentions, Ponsonby and some other major connections went into opposition. Ponsonby was dismissed as chief commissioner of the revenue in 1770 and, quite needlessly, resigned as speaker in 1771. In the same period Agar, the *quondam* member of the independent interest in Co. Kilkenny, continued to support the government, and was rewarded in February 1772 by appointment as one of the commissioners of the revenue, in this respect visibly rising from the ashes of Ponsonby.

Although this was how things must have looked from a Co. Kilkenny perspective, there was a general tendency for hitherto 'secondary' interest like the Agar connection to be fostered and promoted during the Townshend viceroyalty, as a counterweight to the great interests like the Ponsonbys who had gone into opposition. Moreover, even in the narrow context of Co. Kilkenny, there was no inconsistency in Agar's abandoning Ponsonby (as there had been in his abandoning the independent interest in 1755–61), because the Agar-Ponsonby junction had been based purely on the political

Malcomson, 'The Newtown Act: revision and reconstruction', in *Irish Historical Studies*, xviii (1973), 'The politics of "natural right": the Abercorn family and Strabane borough, 1692–1800', in *Historical Studies*, x (Galway, 1976), and 'The parliamentary traffic of this country', in Thomas Bartlett and D.W. Hayton (eds.), *Penal era and golden age: essays in Irish history, 1690–1800* (Belfast, 1979).   85 Welbore Ellis to the lord lieutenant, Lord Townshend, 12 May 1770, Clifden papers, Cornwall RO: photocopy in PRONI, T/2930/10. PRONI's calendar of these few letters was published in *Irish official papers*, i, pp 103–5. The originals were in the late and last Viscount Clifden's house, Lanhydrock, in Cornwall, which for some time has been a National Trust property. 86 Phillips, *Church of Ireland*, iii. 283.   87 Will, pre-1771, of James Agar, 21 M 57/D51/3. 88 Flood to his cousin, Warden Flood, [dated by Kelly as post-Nov. 1771], Burrowes papers, RIA, Ms. 23 K 53, f. 10.

arithmetic of the constituency, not on harmony of political sentiment or unity of parliamentary purpose. This was a point strongly argued by Charles Agar, the episcopal
pamphleteer, *c.*May 1772:

> Mr A. never had any other connection with Mr P. than as a colleague in the
> county of Kilkenny, where they mutually served each other with equal honour.
> In what instance, then, ... did Mr A. forsake Mr P.? ... Mr A. has often voted in
> parliament on a different side of the question from Mr P. ..., [and] why should
> he not? Was Mr A. under any kind of engagement to Mr P. that should induce
> a man of honour to do otherwise? I again repeat that it is well known ... to every
> gentleman in the county that these gentlemen were not otherwise connected
> than as joint candidates and representatives for that county.[89]

To a modern way of thinking, this is an odd form of political alliance or connection.
But it was widespread in county and other open constituencies under the unreformed
electoral system.

For this reason, Ponsonby's going into opposition did not break up the Agar-
Ponsonby alliance and did not reduce its effectiveness at the general election of 1768,
even though on this occasion there was a contest. Agar's and Ponsonby's opponents
were Flood and the Hon. Edmund Butler of Ballyconra, Co. Kilkenny, son and heir
of the 10th viscount Mountgarret, and of age since 1767. It is not absolutely clear that
Flood and Butler were 'joint runners'. But the voting figures suggest that they were:
Ponsonby, 494; Agar, 438; Butler, 331; and Flood, 323.[90] Because each voter at a
general election had two votes, it was advisable for individual candidates who were
faced by a junction to unite, and so ensure that their second votes did not go to the
enemy (another interesting quirk of eighteenth-century political connection).
Ponsonby's and Agar's polling was particularly strong among the more affluent voters,
and – in spite of the fact that the sheriff and returning officer, Gervase Parker Bushe
of Kilfane, near Thomastown, was an ally of Flood – their majority was 'so respectable' that 'no scrutiny was demanded'.[91] The cost of the election does not bear out
Agar's later assertion that he had been put to 'great expense' by his support of an
unpopular administration. 'The Speaker told me', reported a well-informed Dublin
Castle official, Thomas Waite, 'his election for Kilkenny had cost him £3,000, besides
immense expense of health, and that Mr Agar's had amounted to £2,000 at least.'[92] So
it would seem that Agar spent less than Ponsonby. This is not surprising. As has been
noted, Agar was an excellent country gentleman, whereas Ponsonby was an absentee from Co. Kilkenny. His brother's seat, Bessborough, was always empty,[93] and
Ponsonby himself lived at Bishopscourt, Co. Kildare. If he injured his health, as he

89 21 M 57/A4/3 and 5–6.   **90** Kelly, *Henry Flood*, pp 129–30.   **91** [Rev. Dr] Thomas Hewetson
to 2nd Lord Branden, 18 July 1768, Talbot-Crosbie papers, TCD, Ms. 260.   **92** Waite to Sir Robert
Wilmot, 27 Aug. 1768, Wilmot papers, Derbyshire RO: photocopy in PRONI, T/3019/6128.
93 John Gore (ed.), *Creevy: selected and re-edited from the Creevy papers (1903) ... and Creevy's life
and times (1934)* ... (London, 1948), pp 297–8.

claimed, it was through pre-election drinking, not unwearied attention to grand jury business. Even Flood, who was no country gentleman either, at least had a seat in Kilkenny, where he frequently resided and occupied himself with gentleman-farming and, late in life, the re-building of his house.[94] Moreover, the expense of nursing Co. Kilkenny probably decreased for Agar thereafter. From 1768, he had some call on Charles Agar's episcopal patronage; and from 1772 a major call on what Ponsonby had previously monopolised in and near the county, the patronage of the revenue board. In 1775, the 2nd earl of Shannon grumbled at the extent to which revenue patronage was mortgaged to 'Agar and his damned Kilkenny interest'.[95]

Other significant developments occurred in and around 1768 besides Ponsonby's going into opposition and Agar's obtaining government office. The main one was that Lord Wandesford, under the influence of Flood's political ally, the 1st earl of Charlemont, broke with the Agar-Ponsonby coalition, and went over to Flood in advance of the 1768 general election. At that election, Wandesford gave Flood 'all my weight', which was interpreted as meaning 'both his voices'.[96] But, although this seems sufficiently explicit, it left room for misunderstanding, and a quarrel broke out between them. Flood was later accused (in Bishop Charles Agar's pamphlet of *c.*May 1772) of taking advantage of 'the duped weakness of a noble peer', of demanding, 'under pretence of a factitious promise, the second votes also of those freeholders', and of allowing 'his benefactor this grateful alternative either to hazard his life in an immediate duel or to pay the expenses of the present [i.e. the 1768] election and bind himself to give his utmost assistance on the next vacancy for the county to this honourable, independent gentleman'.[97] Wandesford had shown weakness in advance of the 1761 election and given contradictory undertakings to different people.[98] Probably he had done the same in 1768. Years later, in 1784, the 'trick' which Flood had played on 'the late Lord Wandesford' was still a talking-point.[99]

Just before the election and the quarrel, Wandesford had asked Flood what he had done about 'old Agar' (James of Ringwood). 'I fear he will go against you. But he will give all his interest to Mr Butler. I would have you consult Lord Mountgarret upon that head; he has great influence over him.'[100] This 'great influence' derived from the fact that James of Ringwood and Lady Mountgarret were first cousins; she had been born Charlotte Bradstreet, and was a granddaughter of Charles Agar of Gowran, whose daughter had married Samuel Bradstreet of Tinnescolly, Co. Kilkenny, in 1692.[101] In 1754, James of Ringwood had made Lord Mountgarret one of the godparents of his youngest son.[102] How James of Ringwood used his interest in

94 Kelly, *Henry Flood*, pp 151, 231–2 and *passim*; Flood to Parsons, 23 Sep. [1791], Rosse papers, C/8/85.   95 Shannon to James Dennis, 17 Nov. 1775, D/2707/A2/3/36.   96 Wandesford to Flood and Charlemont to Flood, [both written in spring? 1768?], BL, Add. Ms. 22930, ff. 9 and 8. 97 21 M 57/A4/3 and 5–6.   98 D/2707/A1/5/29.   99 3rd earl Temple to 4th duke of Rutland, 12 Apr. 1784, *H.M.C. Rutland Mss.*, iii. 87. For the context, see Rosse papers, C/8/2–4 and 19. 100 Wandesford to Flood, [spring? 1768?]. BL, Add. Ms. 22930, f. 9.   101 Burtchaell, op. cit., pp 114 and 167.   102 Notes on events in recent family history by the Hon. Mrs Rebecca Agar, James of Ringwood's wife, [*c.*1760], 21 M 57/D48.

Co. Kilkenny at the 1768 general election is unknown. He certainly, as Wandesford somewhat naïvely feared, must have given it against Flood. Undoubtedly, he would have supported Edmund Butler, and then either sunk his second votes or given them to Ponsonby or James of Gowran. It is not impossible that he gave them to James of Gowran. With Wandesford now in the camp of Flood, James of Gowran had no reason to withhold support in Callan from James of Ringwood. In January 1769, James of Gowran used all his influence as a governor of, and as MP for, Co. Kilkenny to induce Lord Townshend to set aside the Flood-biased return of sheriffs for the coming year. He argued that it was not usual to accord the nomination of the sheriff to a steady opponent of government, against the wishes and interests of its steady supporters. He also pointed out that a jury picked by whomever was appointed sheriff was likely to be trying Flood for an attempt to assassinate an Agar supporter in Callan.[103] Clearly, therefore, some degree of reconciliation between Gowran and Ringwood had taken place even before Flood killed 'old Agar' in the duel later in that year.

That fatal event removed the greatest obstacle to reconciliation – James of Ringwood himself. His elder surviving son, and successor, George Agar (1751–1815), was not quite eighteen at the time, and had not been born in the late 1740s when James of Ringwood had played the part of wicked uncle in the borough of Gowran. Of this, George Agar was not guilty by association. Nor does he seem to have gone on living at Ringwood itself after his coming-of-age in 1772. Quite apart from its dark associations for the Agars of Gowran and (following the duel) George Agar himself, Ringwood was inconveniently situated from the point of view of running an estate which, since 1766, had comprised Callan as well as the Rower. A deed of 1774 describes George Agar as 'of Kilmurry' and he wrote from that address in 1781.[104] Kilmurry, which is near Thomastown, was roughly equidistant from Callan and the Rower. It belonged to his father's ally in Callan borough affairs, the Rev. Thomas Bushe, rector of Gowran, 1761–95. Bushe's eldest son, the celebrated and 'incorruptible' Charles Kendal Bushe, who later sat for Callan, 1796–9, under George Agar's auspices, was born at Kilmurry in 1767. The Rev. Thomas Bushe already possessed two other houses (which had been left to him in the 1730s by a benefactor called Charles Kendal of Sutton, Co. Dublin). He also had an official residence at Kingston College, Mitchelstown, north Cork (to which he was unanimously elected chaplain by 'the four trustee bishops', presumably headed by Charles Agar as archbishop of Cashel, in 1780).[105] So Kilmurry became available for renting, and Ringwood became a herdbook name only. At about the same time, in 1774, and for the same geographical reason, George Agar established his agent at Castlefield, between Gowran and Thomastown, and near Kilmurry.[106]

103 Agar to Townshend, 9 Jan. 1769, Townshend papers, NLI, Ms. 8009/3   104 Deed involving George Agar 'of Kilmurry', 29 Nov. 1774, NA, D20074; George Agar, Kilmurry, to Archbishop Agar, 8 May 1781, 21 M 57/B23/7.   105 E.O. Somerville and Martin Ross, *An incorruptible Irishman: ... Chief Justice Charles Kendal Bushe* ... (London, 1932), pp 1, 6–8 and 28–31; John Kirwan, 'Mount Juliet [Thomastown]', in *Old Kilkenny Review, 1998*, pp 118–19; Rev. Thomas Bushe to Shannon, 28 Feb. 1780, D/2707/A2/2/75. For Kingston College, see pp 296–300.   106 Caroline Corballis,

A vivid glimpse of George Agar at about this time is provided by a remarkable *cache* of his personal effects which has survived in, of all places, Australia.

> His miniature, painted by Jeremiah Meyer,[107] shows an extremely handsome, bewigged young man; his [court] suits are of vivid beauty ..., [one of them made] of cocoa-coloured brocade embroidered with sapphire and pearl beads. This type of long-waisted coat, worn over knee breeches, was cut at the back to droop like the tail of a bird; the sleeves were curved like boomerangs. ... [All] these brilliant garments [were] ... tailored for a tall, narrow man. ... [It is tempting to imagine] the dashing, unmarried Callan dying young, from tuberculosis perhaps. But not at all; he lived to be sixty-one. Recently, a copy of an early will of his has turned up. ... [To his] beloved aunt, Ellis ... Agar, countess of Brandon, he leaves £5,000; to his dear mother £1,000; and to his mixed brood of reputed children, sums for their education and to their various mothers. One was Rosetta Clarke, daughter of a comedian at Covent Garden theatre, by whom he had three children.'[108]

When he came to make his operative will, in 1809, he had sixteen surviving 'reputed' (i.e. illegitimate) children by two different mistresses, Rosetta Clarke and one Mary Sanguiser. To all of them he had given the surname Agar. He left to be shared equally among them the interest deriving from a trust fund of £70,000, plus lump sums of £1,000 each on their coming-of-age or marriage.[109] In short, he was just the sort of young man-about-town, dandy and rake who would have appealed to an ageing, childless aunt like the countess of Brandon, who had buried two husbands and perhaps had 'a past' herself. In any case, his father, James Agar of Ringwood, had been her favourite brother and she had Callan 'deeply engraved on her heart'. In the end, she not surprisingly made George Agar her principal heir.[110]

From the summer of 1775 on, there were negotiations and canvassing in anticipation of the next general election for Co. Kilkenny, which did not take place until June of the following year. One of the reasons for this early start was that James Agar of Gowran was hankering after a peerage. He consulted Welbore Ellis about his aspiration, who

> gave no great encouragement ..., unless he [Agar] was apprehensive for his health, which might be injured by maintaining his country interest, and his *pocket* also, if there should be an opposition ... . I never heard more on the subject till he informed me that he was resolved to stand for the county, and he thought he had great probability of success on his own legs only [i.e. without

'Castlefield House', in *In the shadow of the steeple*, no. 5 (1996), pp 107–10.   **107** Could this be one of two 'pictures' which were delivered to Welbore Ellis' London house in 1787, in spite of 'Mr Meyer's obstinacy'? – Ellis to Agar, 10 Mar. 1787, T/3719/C/21/12.   **108** Lady Casey, *An Australian story*, pp 102–3.   **109** Probate (1815) of the will (1809) of George Agar, Lord Callan, NA, T10997.   **110** 'Substance of Lady Brandon's will', 2 May 1787, 21 M 57/D51/5.

Ponsonby[111]]; after which I understood that upon the canvass he had been so well received as to consider his election to be in a manner sure, and then I supposed the present thoughts of a peerage suspended.[112]

They were not. In the same month, November 1775, James Agar announced (somewhat prematurely) his forthcoming elevation to the peerage, and urged his supporters to transfer their suffrages to his cousin, George Agar.[113] Ellis disapproved. The proposed transfer of votes to George Agar would, in Ellis' view, effect 'the revival of that interest [presumably the old independent interest] ... which, if properly managed, will beat you all out of that county. ... I fear [James Agar] ... will find some of the gentlemen not well pleased with his turning so short upon his heel after they had acted so handsomely towards him.'[114] As Ellis had implied, George Agar enjoyed support independent of and additional to that which James Agar sought to transfer. For example, on his mother's side he was a first cousin of William Flower, 2nd Viscount Ashbrook, whose family owned some 7,000 statute acres in the county and had represented it in the 1715–27 parliament. However, his connection with Lord Mountgarret had probably been weakened, because it was on Lady Mountgarret's side and she was estranged from her husband by 1775.[115] Moreover, George Agar – though tough and determined in his resistance to Flood in the borough of Callan – was probably too dandified and *dilettante* to be a serious candidate for a popular constituency. This suggestion is supported by his later failure to return from England for the important parliamentary session of 1777–8, though urged by the chief secretary 'to come home' in early January 1778.[116] For whatever reason, George Agar was not taken up by the Hon. Edmund Butler; and nor was he acceptable to a number of James Agar's supporters. Accordingly, he withdrew from the campaign.

The three remaining contestants were Ponsonby, Butler and Flood. Each stood 'on his own legs only', Ponsonby having taken steps to avert a junction between Butler and Flood. Ponsonby headed the poll, and Butler came second. Flood then petitioned against Butler's return, but his petition was rejected by the House of Commons in November 1777.[117] Flood's defeat was decisive and irreversible, because in 1776 he enjoyed for the only time the full weight of the government's influence in Co. Kilkenny. In October 1775, after three years of tortuous negotiation, he had finally accepted office as one of three vice-treasurers for Ireland. Eventually, one of the existing vice-treasurers had been tempted to exchange his office for a better one, and so make room for Flood. The other two had, previously and in turn, been tempted in vain. One of them, of course, was Ellis, and with the Agar interest in mind he had not only refused but put every possible obstacle in the way of a government *rapprochement* with

111 The frequently cited canvassing list of Co. Kilkenny landowners, 1775 (*Analecta Hibernica*, xii), was probably compiled in order to enable Ponsonby to determine whether or not to preserve the alliance.   112 Ellis to Agar, 28 Nov. 1775, T/3719/C/9/3.   113 Kelly, *Henry Flood*, pp 232–3. 114 Ellis to Agar, 28 Nov. 1775, T/3719/C/9/3.   115 Canvassing list of Co. Kilkenny landowners, 1775, *Analecta Hibernica*, xii. 144.   116 Buckinghamshire to Heron, 7 Jan. 1778, NLI, Ms. 13036/2. 117 Kelly, *Henry Flood*, pp 241–3.

Flood.[118] Among other terms exacted from the lord lieutenant, the 1st Earl Harcourt, Flood claimed to have obtained 'the exclusive patronage' of Co. Kilkenny, 'including the nomination of sheriffs' and a promise that the lord lieutenant would 'influence the Agar family to give up the borough of Callan'.[119] No wonder Harcourt, an experienced diplomat, exclaimed privately: 'Since I was born, I never had to deal with so difficult a man, owing principally to his high-strained ideas of his own great importance and popularity.'[120] Flood was allowed to nominate the sheriff for 1776, a known election year, although he later complained that his nominee, Francis Flood, a cousin, had let him down. Ponsonby's daughter thought differently. She had 'no doubt of his [Ponsonby's] having a legal majority', but she feared that 'with so partial a sheriff, and one so devoid of principle, there is no saying who may be returned'. In spite of this advantage, and 'an impressive haul' of local patronage, Flood still polled third in the county election.[121] He fared no better in Callan. There was a double return for that constituency at the general election of 1776, so the result was left to the decision of an election committee of the House of Commons. In November 1777, it declared Flood and his colleague not duly elected, and seated George Agar and George Agar's colleague, the Hon. Pierce Butler, younger brother of the 2nd earl of Carrick. So, for the first time since 1727, no member of the Flood family sat in parliament for Callan.

Meanwhile, trouble over the nomination to the Co. Kilkenny shrievalty persisted. This still mattered, even though the general election was over, because of the selection of juries to try the various lawsuits raging over Callan. Harcourt's successor as lord lieutenant, the 2nd earl of Buckinghamshire, felt that he had been manoeuvred into a position where 'I should either have been obliged to have offended the Agars by appointing ... [someone] attached to Mr Flood, or exasperated that already dissatisfied gentleman by taking some other person'.[122] In the end, Buckinghamshire wriggled out of the difficulty. But he was not disposed to concede to Flood more than 'an equal share of the patronage of the county'.[123] He did not confide in Flood when it came to planning and conducting parliamentary business, and Flood, partly because of this and partly because of the alleged breach of Lord Harcourt's promises, gave only fitful support to the government and was frequently absent from the House.[124] For some time it was rumoured that he was to be dismissed, Lord Shannon promoted to the vacant vice-treasurership and Clifden appointed to succeed Shannon as muster-master general for Ireland. Shannon himself wrote in January 1778: 'I have no doubt but that Lord Clifden has been applying for my office so long ago as the time of my illness, and I am certain that the friends and connections of that family on this and the other side of the water would, for many reasons, wish to get ... [Flood] dismissed.'[125] In the end,

---

118 *Ibid.*, p. 208 and pp 171–218 *passim*.   119 Buckinghamshire to the prime minister, Lord North, 25 Oct. 1779, Macintosh collection, BL, Add. Ms. 34523, f. 266.   120 Quoted in Kelly, *Henry Flood*, p. 215.   121 Lady Shannon to James Dennis, 28 May 1776, D/2707/A2/3/40; Kelly, *Henry Flood*, pp 231–6 and 242–3.   122 Buckinghamshire to Lord George Germain, 20 Feb. 1777, and William Power Keating Trench to Buckinghamshire, 26 Feb. 1777, Heron papers, NLI, Ms. 13035/3. 123 Note [from Buckinghamshire to Heron], Nov. 1779, *ibid.*, Ms. 13038/16.   124 Kelly, *Henry Flood*, pp 219–82.

Flood became so 'exasperated' and 'dissatisfied' that his sense of reality left him. In May 1780, he actually wrote to an English mentor: 'My elections are a point which a certain person [Lord Buckinghamshire] ought surely to decide in my favour without delay. ... A peerage to Mr George Agar would free me from him in Callan, and the county [of Kilkenny] could be settled for me with Lord Clifden and the Archbishop of Cashel ... [text defective].'[126] Long before November 1781, when he was dismissed from the vice-treasurership and went back into opposition, Flood was in effect out of office; and long before his last attempts on Co. Kilkenny and Callan at the general election of 1783, his cause in both constituencies was lost.

KILKENNY POLITICS, 1778–90

At the very time that Flood's influence was declining, the potentially much more formidable influence of the Ormonde Butlers was reasserting itself. The Ormonde come-back began in Kilkenny city, the family's historic stronghold. Between 1727 and *c.*1765, Kilkenny city politics had dissolved into a kaleidoscopic factionalism[127] which was intensified by the absence of a Kilkenny Castle interest. Then, in 1766, the Ormonde estates and (although this did not become clear until 1791) the Irish peerage honours of the Ormondes, passed to a local member of the family, Walter Butler of Garryricken, Co. Kilkenny. Kilkenny Castle had been occupied only intermittently, and mainly by agents, since 1715; but in 1768, Walter Butler, now *de jure* 16th earl of Ormonde, moved into it,[128] thus providing a focus for the revival of the Ormonde interest in Kilkenny City.[129] Later in the century, the castle, 'though only a portion of the old duke's, was still such as to remind the spectator of its former magnificence. ... [In] a spacious court ... were preserved two sides of the original edifice, and a third was ... rebuilding.'[130] Walter Butler was a catholic, and so remained until his death in 1783,[131] but his son and heir, John Butler of Kilkenny Castle (1740–95), had conformed to the Church of Ireland in 1764.

Walter Butler's persistent catholicism may have been a liability from the point of view of the designs which John had on the very protestant constituency of Kilkenny city. For whatever reason, John Butler had not stood for the city at the general election of 1776, but had been returned by Lord Clifden for Gowran. So, had he wanted to, he was not available to contest either of the two city by-elections which took place soon after the general election. At the first of these, which was held in November 1777, he formed an alliance with Otway Cuffe, 3rd Lord Desart. The latter was the son of the

125 Lord Shannon to James Dennis, 'received 9 January 1778', D/2707/A2/3/48.   126 Flood to William Markham, archbishop of York, 4 May 1780, Rosse papers, C/2/40.   127 Power, 'Kilkenny representation', pp 314–15; Neely, *Kilkenny*, pp 144–9.   128 Walter Butler to Thomas Kavanagh, 24 May 1768, Kavanagh papers, PRONI, T/3331/3. Kavanagh was Walter Butler's son-in-law. 129 Neely, *Kilkenny*, pp 111–13.   130 Sir Jonah Barrington, *Personal sketches of his own times* (new ed., Dublin, 1917), pp 140–1.   131 John Butler to Lord Townshend, 28 Sep. 1768, Townshend letter-book, Representative Church Body (hereafter RCB) Library, Dublin, Ms. 20/100.

Lord Desart who had sold the manor of Callan to James Agar of Ringwood in 1765–6, and the grandson of one of the Cuffe brothers who had failed to seize their opportunity to gain control of the corporation of Kilkenny in 1720. This alliance was to last until after the Union. It was victorious in 1777, when the Butler/Cuffe side 'out-polled [Gervase Parker] Bushe by forty, exactly the number of gentlemen from Kerry'.[132] The 'gentlemen from Kerry' were non-resident voters created and imported specially for the purpose of winning Kilkenny City elections for the Butlers. At the next by-election, which took place in April 1778, George Agar's younger and only surviving brother, Charles (not to be confused with the Archbishop, though he sometimes is) was the successful candidate. The background to Charles Agar's candidature is unknown. It cannot have been unrelated to the struggle over Callan, because Charles Agar's opponent was Gervase Parker Bushe of Kilfane, a close friend and ally of Flood, and Flood's second in the duel with Charles Agar's father. But this only provides a motive for Charles Agar's candidature: it does not explain who set him up as a candidate. As far as is known, the Agars had not been active in Kilkenny city since the mayoralty of James Agar of Gowran in 1715–16; and by 1778, neither branch of the family, again as far as is known, had any significant interest of its own in the constituency, though both owned some house property there and probably influenced a few votes in right of that. So, Charles Agar must have been the representative of some other interest in city politics, and this can only have been John Butler. Butler must have been glad to find a candidate who had local standing (and was of protestant, indeed Cromwellian, stock), but who had no rival influence or ambitions in the constituency. The fact that Butler owed his current seat to Charles Agar's cousin would have been an additional motive.

Making an ill-timed visit to the city in April 1778, John Wesley found that 'the election for parliament-men had put all Kilkenny in an uproar'.[133] From 1783 onwards, the constituency fell decisively under the control of the Butlers and the Cuffes;[134] but the 1778 by-election proved to be a setback for them. Initially, all went well. The result of the poll 'was 377 votes to 354 in favour of Agar. After this victory, he was "chaired through the town to the Castle Square where a fireworks display celebrated his victory". The victors were entertained to dinner in the Wheat Sheaf inn. [But] shortly after the election, a petition of several freemen and freeholders of the city of Kilkenny was presented [to the House of Commons] ... alleging bribery and corrupt practices.'[135] The election committee found that, among other irregularities committed by the sheriffs (one of whom was the Hon. Edmund Butler) and by Charles Agar himself, the latter had 'opened houses for the entertainment and seduction of the freemen and freeholders' who had promised to vote for Bushe.[136] 'The result was reversed and

132 Description, including some passages of quotation, of the Herbert papers then [c.1975] in the possession of T.M. Hickey Esq., Le Mont Billet, Trinity, Jersey, PRONI, ENV 5/HP/14/2.
133 Entry for 21 Apr. 1778 in *The journal of the Rev. John Wesley* (4 vols., London, 1827), iv. 115.
134 Power, 'Kilkenny representation', pp 315–16.   135 Moran, 'The Agars of Gowran', p. 124.
136 Burtchaell, op. cit., p. 173.

Bushe elected instead.'¹³⁷ Following his very short tenure of a seat in parliament, Charles Agar took holy orders and, as has been seen (pp 54–5), featured significantly and discreditably in the ecclesiastical career of his cousin and namesake. His election campaign for Kilkenny city was hardly a suitable preparation for the Church.

The Butlers were slower to re-establish themselves in the county of Kilkenny. This was partly because they made the city their first priority, partly because they also suffered in the county from the stigma of 'popery', and partly because their inheritance, though very large, was not free of complications. In 1760, it was reckoned that 'the wreck and skeleton' of the once immense Ormonde estate was still worth 'more than £14,000 per annum'.¹³⁸ But, in 1769, £62,000 of the rents from previous years was still in the hands of a former agent, who was refusing to disgorge.¹³⁹ In the end, the Butlers re-entered county politics on the back of the wayward Lord Wandesford, whose only surviving child and heiress presumptive married John Butler in February 1769.¹⁴⁰ Reporting this event, John Butler's father, Walter, announced with paternal and dynastic pride: 'Notwithstanding the base and malicious misrepresentations and insinuations ... to Lord Wandesford's family about my son, ..., [he] was married last Monday ... to Lady Anne Wandesford'.¹⁴¹ This marriage alliance immediately put the wind up Ponsonby, who said publicly later in 1769 that he heard he was 'to be turned out entirely'.¹⁴² His fears were premature and, ultimately, proved groundless. At the 1776 general election, Wandesford and John Butler, acting for the moment in concert,¹⁴³ supported Edmund Butler and Ponsonby (whom they disliked less than they did Flood). This explains why Edmund Butler later abused his position as sheriff of Kilkenny City to aid Charles Agar. In county politics, John Butler, like all before him who had tried to maintain an alliance with Wandesford, soon had to declare his independence of his father-in-law. This was probably what a relation of Walter Butler had in mind when he assured him in 1777: 'You will give law to the county by gradually increasing your interest ... [until you become] on your own [i.e. independent of Wandesford] account the first power in your country.'¹⁴⁴ In 1784 Wandesford died, having almost certainly taken a different part from John Butler at the general election in the previous year. From this time on, it was inevitable that the Ormonde, now incorporating the Wandesford, interest would command a seat for the county. It first

137 Moran, 'The Agars of Gowran', p. 124.   138 Willes to Lord Warwick, 1760, *Willes letters*, p. 41. 139 St[ephe?]n Creagh Butler to Thomas Kavanagh, 29 Nov. 1769, PRONI, T/3331/8.   140 There is a draft of the marriage settlement, with counsel's opinion dated 31 December 1768, in the Prior-Wandesforde papers, NLI, MS. 35457/4. The draft specifies a portion of £10,000 for Lady Anne, with a further £10,000 if her father, who then had no children besides her, died without issue male. However, in that event, it was obvious that Lady Anne would succeed to the whole Wandesford estate. The Prior-Wandesforde papers are Mss. 14171–14214, 32726–32829 and 35457–35681. Unfortunately, they are an almost exclusively nineteenth- and twentieth-century archive, and include virtually no eighteenth-century correspondence. For this reason, Lord Wandesford's manoeuvrings must remain something of a mystery.   141 Walter Butler to Thomas Kavanagh, 15 Feb. 1769, T/3331/7.   142 G.P. Bushe to Flood, 31 Nov. [1769], Rosse papers, C/1/3.   143 Power, 'Kilkenny representation', p. 310.   144 Lodge Morres to [Walter Butler], 20 Aug. 1777, Ormonde papers, NLI, Ms. 2480, p. 269.

did so in 1789. In 1792, a susceptible admirer of the newly recognised 17th earl of Ormonde (John Butler), exclaimed 'What an immense fortune will Lord Ormond[e]'s be! ... Some German princes are obliged to support standing armies with less'.[145] It was presumably with an eye to these future developments that Lord Clifden had returned him for Gowran in 1776.

During the heady 'Patriot' years 1778–83, economic and constitutional concessions were wrested from successive British governments by the Irish parliament, backed in the country at large by the Volunteers. The Volunteers had begun as an unpaid, self-sufficient local police force, and Clifden did his duty as a country gentleman in raising corps in Co. Kilkenny. 'In 1779 when a battalion of four companies of the Volunteers was formed in Gowran barony, he became their commander.'[146] But, while Clifden was diplomatically silent amid the political out-pourings of the Volunteers, George Agar was vociferous. As colonel of the Callan Union Volunteers, he supported the demand for legislative independence in a published address of 10 April 1782, and did the same as a member of the Co. Kilkenny grand jury at the Lent assizes, where his co-signatories included John Butler, the Hon. Pierce Butler (MP for Callan), G.P. Bushe, James Wemys[147] and two cousins of Henry Flood.[148] John Ponsonby's son and heir, William Brabazon Ponsonby, was also active in political Volunteering. In Kilkenny City, the situation was so charged that, following the government's unsuccessful scheme to draw the sting of Volunteering by raising fencible regiments commanded by pliant country gentlemen, there was a 'disturbance at Kilkenny between the fencibles and the townspeople', during which a bullet lodged in a pillar just above John Butler's head. 'It threatened [so] much mischief ... that a regiment with some field pieces and Colonel Luttrell was sent thither to suppress it.'[149]

During this period, and acting as a kind of sub-plot to its main events, another row within the Agar family was coming to a head. It was between the countess of Brandon, supported by George Agar, on the one hand, and Lord Clifden on the other. It originated in some provision of the will of her mother and his grandmother, Mary Agar (*née* Wemys), who had died in 1771. Next after George Agar, the charming and amusing Archbishop was Lady Brandon's favourite, and he stepped in as peace-maker between Clifden and her in October 1779. In response to this overture, Lady Brandon concurred with his

> strong, wise and affectionate advice in recommending family union, [which] coincides with my own wishes. I have almost an implicit faith in you, and am satisfied you would not advise me to act improperly. No doubt Lord Clifden

145 Mrs O'Connell of Cranary, Co. Longford, to Miss Sarah Ponsonby [who, with Miss Eleanor Butler, constituted 'the Ladies of Llangollen'], 27 Apr. 1792, PRONI, Register of Irish Archives: Hamilton of Hamwood papers, B/16/1. 146 Moran, 'The Agars of Gowran', p. 119; Neely, *Kilkenny*, p. 161. 147 See p. 106, 74*n*. 148 C.H. Wilson (ed.), *A complete collection of the resolutions of the Volunteers, grand juries, etc., of Ireland which followed the ... first Dungannon diet ...*(Dublin, 1782), pp 201 and 141–2. 149 Bishop Barnard to Buckinghamshire, 13 Apr. 1783, Heron papers, NLI, Ms. 13047/3.

has treated me most unkindly, and as far as he could endeavoured to lower me in the opinion of as many people as he could influence. But it hurt me not, and as the law dispute between us is I think the bone of contention, let him withdraw it out of the courts and say to me 'Dear aunty, I am sorry I ever vexed you', and I will kiss and [be] friends, and so sure as I do, he may rely, I shall not do things by halves. As soon as I receive Lord Clifden's answer, I shall write to George Agar that I accept the compliment he made me of the disposal of his interest on the ensuing election for the county of Kilkenny.[150]

Clifden grudgingly consented to stop the legal proceedings, though he clearly did not do so out of any regard for Lady Brandon.[151] Towards George Agar his feelings were much warmer. When the Archbishop collated George's newly ordained brother, Charles (the short-lived MP for Kilkenny city), to the union of Tipperary, Clifden thanked the Archbishop for doing what 'will highly serve me in this country [Co. Kilkenny]; and what serves me ... will equally serve you and all our family. This promotion ... has made G.A., I think, quite cordial towards us. He and Charles dined here a few days ago and I never saw him in such spirits and so happy.'[152] George Agar himself expressed to the Archbishop his 'warmest acknowledgements for this repeated mark [sic] of your friendship for me and my brother'.[153] Later in the year, Lady Brandon and George Agar acted as godparents to the Archbishop's third son, James, born on 10 July 1781.[154]

In the event, Clifden did not obtain from Lady Brandon 'the disposal of' George Agar's 'interest at the ensuing election for the county of Kilkenny'. This was the general election which took place in 1783, when the Agar-Ponsonby coalition reappeared in the persons of William Brabazon Ponsonby and Clifden's son and heir, the Hon. Henry Welbore Agar. Shortly before the poll, Clifden complained that George Agar had declined to commit himself.

> Very fortunately, the event of the day does not depend upon him, but if he takes a turn against us, it will make the poll longer and more expensive. I am at a loss what to do or how to act as to P[onsonby]. In honour, I think I should let him know how matters stand with respect to G.A., and if I do, I apprehend he will treat with F[lood] immediately. ... Although I think G.A. will in the end declare for us, think how he encourages the opposition to go on by this conduct.[155]

George Agar probably behaved in this way, partly (as usual) to assert his independence, and partly because the main opposition came from his former associate and MP for Callan, Pierce Butler. 'The event of the day' did 'not depend upon him' because

150 Countess of Brandon to Agar, 19 Oct. 1779, T/3719/C/13/39.   151 Clifden to Agar, 21 Oct. 1779, T/3719/C/13/40.   152 Clifden to Agar, 12 May 1781, 21 M 57/B23/8.   153 George Agar to Agar, 8 May 1781, 21 M 57/B23/7.   154 Notebook, 1761–1827, mainly used by Agar to record family details, 21 M 57/D47.   155 Clifden to Agar, 30 July 1783, T/3719/C/17/23.

Clifden enjoyed the crucial support of John Butler (though Butler's father-in-law, Wandesford, was 'not to be come at'[156]). The result was: W.B. Ponsonby, 430; H.W. Agar, 430 (proof of a very well disciplined junction); and Pierce Butler, 209.[157] At the same general election, George Agar returned himself for Callan, along with John Bourke O'Flaherty of Castlefield, the son of his former agent, a *protégé* of Lady Brandon and a great-nephew of her first husband, Lord Mayo.[158] Shortly afterwards, George Agar tired of opposition politics, and went over to the government. This caused some initial confusion – which Clifden probably did nothing to dispel. A Dublin Castle list of the Irish House of Commons said of Callan: 'This borough belongs to Mr George Agar who returns Mr O'Flaherty together with himself. At present they go with Lord Clifden, whose cousin Mr Agar is, and they are in support.'[159] Having presumably got wind of this, George Agar made it clear, in April 1784, that 'the two members for Callan' were 'a distinct company' and 'not to be considered as part of Lord Clifden's force'.[160] So, a later Dublin Castle survey of the Irish parliament, this one dated 1785, contained the *caveat*: 'The two last members [George Agar and J.B. O'Flaherty] on his [Clifden's] list are very precarious.'[161] They were so 'precarious' that in 1789 they deserted the Archbishop and H.W. Agar, now 2nd Lord Clifden, during the Regency Crisis.

For the moment, the two branches of the Agar family were at least united in supporting the government. So were Clifden and Ponsonby, who from 1784 were joined in the same government office. What was now awkward about Clifden's situation in Co. Kilkenny was that John Butler, his most powerful backer (especially since Wandesford's death in 1784), was in opposition. This was a re-enactment of the scene in the period 1769–82, when Clifden and John Ponsonby had been united in county politics, but on opposite sides in College Green. In the present instance, it mattered more, because national politics impinged considerably on local politics in the summer of 1784. In 1783, radical elements in the now dwindling Volunteers, partly under the leadership of Flood, had moved on to demand parliamentary reform. In 1784, they adopted the legally and constitutionally doubtful tactic of electing delegates on a county basis to a congress in Dublin. Clifden and Ponsonby's father, as governors of the county, were unable to stay neutral; also – because their parliamentary interest was based on close boroughs where they were not necessarily the ground landlord – they were likely to react differently to parliamentary reform than Flood, who had no borough interest left, or John Butler, whose power base was his own city of Kilkenny. In mid-August 1784, Clifden wrote to the chief secretary, Thomas Orde, warning him

156 Clifden to Agar, [pre-17 Feb. 1783], T/3719/C/17/4. 157 Burtchaell, op. cit., p. 175. 158 Ibid., p. 177; substance of Lady Brandon's will, 21 M 57/D51/5; and Caroline Corballis, 'Castlefield House', pp 109–13. These O'Flahertys were a junior branch of the O'Flahertys of Lemonfield, near Oughterard, in east Galway. The father, Thomas, had clearly been brought to Co. Kilkenny and made George Agar's agent *c.*1772–4 through the influence of Lady Brandon. 159 Quoted in Moran, 'The Agars of Gowran', p. 126. 160 Beresford to Robinson, 11 Apr. 1784, *Beresford correspondence*, i, pp 253–5; Moran, 'The Agars of Gowran', p. 126. 161 Quoted in Malcomson, *John Foster*, p. 201.

that Flood was endeavouring to get five delegates of his nomination chosen to represent Co. Kilkenny at the Volunteer congress, and was being abetted by Butler. The
sheriff had shown constitutional propriety by refusing to call a county meeting for the
purpose at their requisition, and Clifden now urged Orde to use the Castle's influence
with various Co. Kilkenny gentlemen to induce them to be present at the assizes, so
that a respectable grand jury could be empanelled and vote addresses which would
carry weight.[162] To Archbishop Agar he wrote on the same day to the same effect,
adding: 'I wish you would send me the heads of what you may think a proper address
as matters are circumstanced.'[163] The fact that this initiative came from Clifden, not
the Castle, would seem to bear out a contemporary criticism that there was not 'to be
found anywhere the smallest trace of a system on the part of government' to capitalise
on the better dispositions 'of persons of property in this country ... or to call them
forth to public notice. ... In Kilkenny, [W.B.] Ponsonby declares that the whole was
mere accident.'[164]

For whatever reason, the anti-reformers did not have things all their own way.
Flood, John Butler and sundry freeholders convened a county meeting of their own
for later in the same day (23 August) as the grand jury meeting. At this county
meeting,

> a vote of censure was passed on the grand jury address, which ... [had] thanked
> the sheriff for his conduct and disapproved of Congress as 'highly dangerous'.
> Five delegates were elected at the meeting, all 'except three or four', Orde
> maintained, '... persons of the lowest rank'. The grand jury in response tried
> to remove their credentials as authorised representatives by declaring the
> election was the result of 'a partial meeting held ... without any legal summons,
> attended by not a tenth part of the freeholders and out of the jurisdiction of
> the magistracy'. But the reformers were not so fastidious and the delegates
> stood.[165]

It is likely that these reformers included the relics – or, rather, the sons – of the old,
pre-1760 'independent interest', who had been kept going by the Carrick and
Mountgarret Butlers, had captured a county seat at the general election of 1776, and
now looked for leadership to the Butlers of Kilkenny Castle. In Kilkenny city, the
result of the 1784 trial of strength was less favourable to government and the anti-
reformers than it was in the county. In his letter to Agar, Clifden had reported
optimistically: 'Jack Butler has changed his mind and now wishes he had never signed
the order to call the [county] meeting, and means to stop this proceeding or adjourn

162 Clifden to Orde, 17 Aug. 1784, Bolton papers, NLI, Ms. 16350/5.   163 Clifden to Agar,
17 Aug. 1784, T/3719/C/18/25.   164 2nd earl of Mornington to W.W. Grenville, 10 Sep. 1784,
H.M.C. Dropmore Mss., i. 237. Mornington had his own selfish motives for wanting to discredit the
Irish administration, so his strictures need to be taken at a discount.   165 James Kelly, 'The Irish
parliamentary reform movement: the administration and popular politics, 1783–5' (unpublished
UCD MA thesis, 1981), p. 243. I am also grateful to Dr Kelly for guidance on these points.

the meeting, if possible.' But this supposed change of mind had not manifested itself in Butler's actions in either the county or the city. In the city, 'the Ponsonbys were completely routed when, on 18 August, five delegates, including Henry Flood ..., were nominated, and their election approved by the city grand jury'.[166] The implication of Clifden's remark is that Butler was at heart a moderate, seeking an honourable retreat from a too-advanced position. But this was not the experience of the lord lieutenant, Rutland, on a tour of the south-west a year and a half later, in December 1785: 'Every great town through which I passed paid every respect ... . Kilkenny alone refused a compliment ..., [because] the influence of Mr Butler interposed to prevent any mark of attention being paid to me.'[167]

Nevertheless, the Clifden-Butler friendship and political alliance held firm. Even when Clifden died suddenly and unexpectedly at the very beginning of 1789, precipitating a by-election and providing 'Jack' Butler with a golden opportunity, Butler remained true to the Agars. On 5 January, the Dowager Lady Clifden reported to the Archbishop that Butler had stated his determination 'not to oppose any candidate offered by your nephew [Lord Clifden] on the present occasion, [and] that the wishes of the people were unanimous for one of my sons to be the person offered'.[168] Lady Clifden, however, did not trust Butler. This was 'because the Butlers think he [Clifden] is not under any engagement to Ponsonby, and that by their suffering him to elect any candidate he pleases, they having none at present to offer, they might hereafter ... make a junction with him and throw out Mr Ponsonby, which would in my opinion be base and dishonourable.'[169] She later discovered that Ponsonby was undeserving of her loyalty, because he had declared as soon as the vacancy took place that 'he was not engaged to any person for this county'.[170]

The 1789 by-election resembled the 1776 general election in that the Agars of Gowran really had no relation closer than George Agar to offer as a candidate.[171] It could not have come at a worse time or caught the Agars more unprepared. The situation was further complicated by the fact that the 2nd Lord Clifden was abroad when his father died and was then delayed in getting back to Ireland. Archbishop Agar wrote pressingly to him urging him, as soon as he reached Ireland, not to 'lose one moment before you see Mr P[onsonby] ... and settle with him what is to be done about the county. John [Agar, Lord Clifden's next brother] is the only person of your own family qualified to be a candidate. You are therefore to determine whether you will set him up, or any other person, or have nothing more to do with the county at present.'[172] John Agar had long been intended for the Church (see pp 55–7), and Clifden's youngest brother, Charles Bagenal Agar, was not quite of age. So Clifden turned

---

166 Ibid.; Neely, *Kilkenny*, pp 163–4.   167 Rutland to 1st Lord Sydney (the home secretary), 6 Dec. 1785, *H.M.C. Rutland Mss.*, iii. 265.   168 Lady Clifden to Agar, 5 Jan. 1789, 21 M 57/D53/16.   169 Lady Clifden to Agar, 25 Jan. 1789, 21 M 57/D53/24.   170 Lady Clifden to Agar, [4] Feb. [1789], 21 M 57/D53/28. Worse, Ponsonby made an unsuccessful take-over bid for her late husband's valuable office in the administration at the very time when Agar was trying, also unsuccessfully, to secure it for her son, the 2nd viscount. See p. 164.   171 Agar to George Agar, 2 Jan. 1789, 21 M 57/D53/8.   172 Agar to 2nd Viscount Clifden, 2 Jan 1789, T/3719/C/23/7.

to my cousin, George Agar, to whom I am sorry to say ... [Ponsonby] did not
express any good inclination. He talked more of general politics than on that
particular subject, [and] therefore of course did not propose any engagements
or promises on my part towards him. I saw George Agar yesterday, who seemed
much pleased with my proposal and offer, but, as was reasonable, desired to have
a little time to consider on the subject, and said he would set out for Dublin to
see and talk with you upon the matter. It is not possible for me to put an advertisement in the paper until he is determined upon the subject, and I shall then
be obliged to you for a few lines which you may think proper to address [to] the
county.[173]

Ponsonby probably did not take Lady Brandon's indulgent view of George Agar's
private life. In any case, there was a problem about money. Neither Clifden nor George
Agar was willing to incur election expenditure. So Walter Butler Junior (his father,
John, already being in parliament as MP for Kilkenny City) was elected unopposed
and then re-elected, in conjunction and alliance with Ponsonby, at the general election
in April 1790. Between 1789 and the Great Reform Act, the representation was
invariably shared between the Ponsonby family, headed by the earls of Bessborough,
and the Butler family, headed by the earls, later marquesses, of Ormonde – a remarkable record of continuity, and one which spelt the exclusion of all other county
families, including the Agars. So, a later list of the members of the Irish parliament,
this one dated 1791,[174] comments on the 'Clifden interest' that it was then reduced to
only the four members for the boroughs of Gowran and Thomastown.

Callan, for obvious reasons, was excluded. George Agar's reward for supporting
Dublin Castle throughout the Regency Crisis and its aftermath in 1789, and for giving
the Castle, free of charge, the nomination to his two borough seats at the 1790 general
election, was a peerage, conferred on him later that year. Flood had been informed in
July 1789 that this and the other new peerages were being held back 'till those they are
intended for give security to bring in each two friends to government in the new
approaching parliament'.[175] Shamelessly, George Agar took as his title 'Callan', the
borough whence it derived. The new Lord Callan was now more explicitly associated
with the borough in another respect: from at least 1789, he leased Westcourt Castle,[176]
the old manor house of Callan, from the catholic branch of the Ormonde Butlers who
had been lords of the manor until 1735. Then, in 1794, he bought the castle, which he
demolished and replaced with a new mansion on the same site, Westcourt House, thus
giving visual expression to his lordship of the manor and control of the borough.[177]

---

173 Clifden to Agar, 19 Jan. and 2 Feb. 1789, T/3719/C/23/12 and 14.   174 E.M. Johnston[-Liik]
(ed.), 'The state of the Irish House of Commons in 1791', *Proc. RIA*, vol. 59, sec. C, no. 1 (1957),
p. 48.   175 2nd earl of Aldborough to Flood, post-marked 4 July 1789, Rosse papers, C/8/61. In
addition to his peerage, George Agar probably obtained at this time the collectorship of the revenue
at Kilkenny for his connection and former MP, John Bourke O'Flaherty.   176 Caroline Corballis,
'Castlefield House', p. 113.   177 Kennedy, 'Callan', p. 291.

Over time, good relations between Ringwood, now Westcourt, and Gowran were re-established. In September 1798, Archbishop Agar asked Lord Callan (as well as Lord Clifden) to be a trustee of the marriage settlement of Agar's daughter, Fanny, the future Viscountess Hawarden.[178] When, in March 1800, the entire Agar connection waited on the lord lieutenant to urge him to promote Archbishop Agar to the primacy, Lord Callan, backed by his two votes in the House of Commons, was part of the deputation.[179] Moreover, when the junior branch became extinct in the male line with the death of Lord Callan in 1815, Callan, the Rower and the rest of Lord Callan's estates passed under his will to Lord Clifden.[180] But for most of the period between Lord Callan's coming-of-age in 1772 and the disfranchisement of Callan under the terms of the Act of Union, the members for Callan were 'a distinct company'. Although it only became obvious at times like the Regency Crisis, the jealousy between the senior and junior branches of the Agar family, dating from at least the mid-1730s rivalry over Gowran and Callan, was not easily assuaged.

THE DISPOSAL OF THE GOWRAN AND THOMASTOWN SEATS, 1761–1800

Even within the Agar connection narrowly defined as the Agars of Gowran, there were differences of view, emphasis and policy, and good-natured but discernible jockeyings for position. The Agars were an 'affective' family[181] – i.e. they got on remarkably well together – parents with children, siblings with siblings, cousins and even second cousins with each other – and were to continue to do so well into the nineteenth century. The Hely-Hutchinsons, earls of Donoughmore, are similar as a political connection in this respect and in this period (c.1795–1830); but their criticisms of each other are more cutting than those which were bandied about between and among the 1st Lord Clifden and his two important brothers (i.e. setting aside the 'incapable' Rev. Henry).[182]

Clifden, though the head of the Agars of Gowran and the possessor of the family estate and electoral interest, was clearly much the intellectual inferior of Welby and the Archbishop; so, the already much-quoted Dublin Castle lists of the Irish parliament usually assume – probably correctly (granted Clifden's frequent deference to his views)[183] – that the Archbishop directed the political conduct of his eldest brother. But

---

178 Clifden to Agar, 28 Sep. 1798, T/3719/C/32/127.   179 Marquess Cornwallis to duke of Portland, 24 Mar. 1800, *Cornwallis correspondence*, iii, pp 217–18.   180 Probate (1815) of Lord Callan's will (1809), NA, T/10997. Deeds and leases relating to Lord Callan's estates in Callan and Waterford City will be found in the Annaly/Clifden papers, F/6/1 and F/8/2.   181 This is to extend a concept formulated by Lawrence Stone in *The family, sex and marriage in England, 1500–1800* (New York, 1977), *passim.* For a masterly discussion of the broad issues, see Eileen Spring, *Law, land and family: aristocratic inheritance in England, 1300–1800* (Chapel Hill, 1993), pp 151–79. 182 See, for example, Lord Hutchinson to Francis Hely-Hutchinson about their brother, the 1st earl of Donoughmore, 3 Nov. 1822, Donoughmore papers, TCD: photocopy in PRONI, T/3459/ F/10/56.   183 For an example of Lord Clifden's deferring to and dependence on the Archbishop,

Clifden sometimes slipped his lead. Welby warned the Archbishop in May 1784 that their brother would 'make use of your interest, and probably has made use of it already, to obtain a considerable living ..., and will vainly boast afterwards with Lady C. & Co. what ascendancy he has over the Archbishop'.[184] One of the many sub-plots of Agar's correspondence is the way in which the different members of the Agar family interacted and how they settled among themselves the optimum way in which to mobilise their electoral and political interest, and the division of the ensuing spoils. In most situations, it was facile and optimistic for Clifden to write as he did in 1781: 'What serves me ... will equally serve you [the Archbishop] and all our family'. This was mainly because his acute, if short-term, financial difficulties (see pp 42–4) put him under constant pressure to make money, but forfeit influence, by selling seats for his boroughs. It was all very well for Welby to exhort him to play a waiting game, as befitted the fourth or fifth-largest electoral interest in Ireland, to hold out for increasingly remunerative and prestigious offices for himself and his son, and never again to sell seats:[185] Clifden had the greatest difficulty in making ends meet if he acted on this undoubtedly sensible advice. A Castle list of 1785 noted (with a mixture of accuracy and inaccuracy): 'This is the first time Lord Clifden ever pretended to a following in parliament, as he constantly sold his five [*sic* – four] seats .... His fortune is not equal to such an exertion as he has now made, and therefore it is impossible for him to continue it.'[186] Welby was probably ignorant of the reality of Clifden's financial situation: Archbishop Agar was fully informed of it, as a result of the already-mentioned distress signals from Lady Clifden, to which he responded by advancing money from his own increasing resources in order to keep Clifden afloat. This, it should be noted, shows a pleasing and perhaps unexpected strain of gratitude and open-handedness in the Archbishop, and demonstrates the closeness of relations within the family.

Welby was right in principle to emphasise the harm which the selling of seats did to the standing of the Agar connection: 'As he [Clifden] sold his seats in parliament [at the 1776 general election]', wrote Buckinghamshire in January 1779, 'he has no influence in the House of Commons.'[187] But Buckinghamshire did not fully understand (or, more likely, was deliberately misrepresenting) the basis on which Clifden sold at least some of his seats; and Welby may not have fully understood it either. As has been suggested, some of Clifden's sales were more in the nature of barter – barter of a seat for one of his boroughs in return for support for himself or his eldest son in elections for the county of Kilkenny. It was all too easy for an aspirant to a county seat who had borough seats in the same locality at his command, to become involved in such barter. On this basis, Clifden may have returned Redmond Morres, younger brother of Hervey Morres of Castlemorres, Co. Kilkenny, 1st Viscount Mountmorres, for Thomastown, 1755–60; on this basis, he also appears to have offered Wandesford

---

see the already-quoted Clifden to Agar, 30 July 1783, T/3719/C/17/23.   184 [Welby] to Agar, 19 May 1784, T/3719/C/18/8.   185 Welby to Lord Clifden, 22 Nov. 1780, T/3719/C/14/41. 186 Quoted in Malcomson, *John Foster*, p. 201.   187 Buckinghamshire to Lord George Germain, 14 Jan. 1779, *H.M.C. Lothian Mss*, p. 343.

a seat, at a reduced price, in November 1760. This latter offer it seems was not accepted. But William Burton, who did sit for Gowran, 1761–8, was a nephew of Speaker Ponsonby, and may have been returned, perhaps at a reduced price, in token of the new-found Agar-Ponsonby friendship. Nothing of the kind can have happened in the 1768 parliament: apart from anything else, Bishop Charles Agar in his *c.*May 1772 pamphlet piously scouted the idea of 'trafficking and bartering a seat for this county for a seat in one of Mr A.'s boroughs'.[188] However, John Butler's return for Gowran in 1776 is unlikely, as has been seen, to have been a straight market transaction. In 1786, when there was a by-election for Thomastown, Clifden attempted another piece of barter. He offered the seat to Thomas Boyse of Bishopswell, who had been 'one of the steady friends to this House [the Agars] upwards of thirty years ... [and] has £4,000 a year in this county' (the inaccurate canvassing list of 1775 had said £2,000). But Boyse declined 'on account of his age and not being able to give attendance'.[189] The other MP for Gowran in the 1776 parliament (besides John Butler) was Sir Boyle Roche, a 'worthy knight ... [and] a known servant of the crown'[190] – actually, a burlesque government hack. His return, free of charge, was a *quid pro quo* for Clifden's peerage,[191] as possibly was the return of one of the members for Thomastown. Only the second seat for Thomastown seems to have been sold on the open market.

The House of Agar was not unanimous in thinking that the boroughs should be made accessory to the county, or indeed in thinking that the county seat was worth pursuing. Echoing Welbore Ellis' own sentiments, Diana Agar wrote to him in January 1777: 'I feel most sensibly the correctness of everything that you say about Lord C. ... The county of Kilkenny has been his destruction, and ... I shall lament very much the seeing his son placed in the very same situation'.[192] On Clifden's death in January 1789, his widow wrote Archbishop Agar a revealing and very sensible letter on this subject:

> I think, if Henry [her son, the new Lord Clifden] could have one member now and forever without a contest, I could not wish him to engage in it. ... I am convinced it would ... embitter every moment of his life; for, even supposing he succeeded on every vacancy, the numberless solicitations for favours from those friends who should support him in such a business, it would be impossible for him to satisfy. This was a source of endless torment to his poor, dear father, and I will now say to your Grace was (in my poor opinion) very injurious to himself and his family; for, I am sure you know that every trifling favour

188 21 M 57/A4/3 and 5–6.   189 Lady Clifden to Agar, 27 Jan. 1789, 21 M 57/D53/25. 190 Dominick Trant to Agar, 21 Mar. 1780, T/3719/C/14/16. Trant is describing an anti-government meeting in Roche's native county of Kerry. He goes on to give a derisive account of how Roche 'made some long speeches, not well received, and was at length by many hisses, etc., obliged to retreat precipitately.' Roche was also famous for his 'Irish bulls'.   191 Lord Harcourt to Buckinghamshire, 11 Apr. 1777, Heron papers, NLI, Ms. 13035/5.   192 Diana Agar to Ellis, 7 Jan. 1777, T/3719/ C/11/1.

asked of government is set down at double the value to the person that asks it. With four members in the House of Commons, *which whilst I live I shall always recommend to Henry to have at his command*, his own voice in the other House, and above all your Grace's advice and assistance as he shall deserve it, I think he may for himself and his family obtain anything in reason.[193]

Lady Clifden also used her new-found and short-lived freedom to criticise her late lord's choice of members for his boroughs. In her view, 'men of ability' were wanted, and this meant '*four other men* than the present representatives'; 'that they are to be found, I have no doubt', she added. Ellis had expressed the same view five years previously: 'I am confident he [Clifden] would soon find men of talents who would be glad to attach themselves to him and to act by concert and on principle'.[194]

The four representatives in 1789 were certainly a rum, dumb lot. They were headed by Clifden's stepfather, George Dunbar (1719?–1803) of Green Bank, Ballitore, Co. Kildare, who had married Clifden's widowed mother in 1753. She died in 1765 and he remarried two years later. He sat for one of the Agar boroughs from 1761 to 1776 and from 1783 to 1800. (To his 'disgrace and dishonour', in Ellis's view,[195] Clifden left Dunbar out of the 1776 parliament.) Dunbar was described, unflatteringly, as 'a steady little man and a dead voice on all occasions'. From 1773, he was in receipt of a pension of £300 per annum during pleasure, which at least prevented him from becoming a burden on Lord Clifden and meant that returning him was of some financial benefit to the family.[196] Years later, in 1798, when the 2nd Lord Clifden got the pension converted to a grant for life, it was apparently the only thing which was keeping Dunbar out of gaol for debt.[197] So he was hardly a creditable MP. Moreover, the Dowager Lady Clifden did not subscribe to the received view of his steadiness, describing him in 1789 as a man 'for whom nobody can answer'. She also had a low opinion of George Burdett (*c.*1730–1818) of Heath House, Maryborough, Co. Laois, MP for Gowran or Thomastown, 1783–1800. She explained to Agar that it had been 'your poor dear brother's thought and liking [to return him], knowing him to be a man of exceeding good family with the fairest character'. She acknowledged that he had 'fulfilled his trust hitherto in the most perfect manner', but found him 'of a ceremonious disposition', and in the absence of her son, the 2nd Lord Clifden, sought Agar's help in dealing with him.[198] The other MPs for Gowran and Thomastown in the last third of the eighteenth century were similarly undistinguished – with the notable exception of John Butler. He was not only a great county magnate and the representative of the oldest family in Kilkenny but, as Barrington rather endearingly described him, 'well read and friendly, *a hard goer*, as it was called, and an incessant talker'.[199]

193 Lady Clifden to Agar, 25 Jan. 1789, 21 M 57/D53/24.   194 Ellis to Agar, 6 May 1784, T/3719/C/18/6.   195 Ellis to Agar, 28 Nov. 1775, T/3719/C/9/3.   196 History of the Irish Parliament database, *sub* 'Dunbar'.   197 Clifden to Agar, 14 Feb. 1798, T/3719/C/32/5.   198 Lady Clifden to Agar, 22 Jan. 1789, 21 M 57/D53/23/1.   199 Barrington, *Personal sketches*, p. 141.

Lady Clifden was, however, wrong in assuming that her late husband had not tried to improve the breed. He had. But, as he pithily observed, 'it is not easy to find people so circumstanced as to fortune and situation as to be willing to reside in Dublin and attend to p[arliament] for other people's views or pursuits'.²⁰⁰ This was written in advance of the 1783 general election, and at the same time Clifden had entered into a negotiation with John Philpot Curran, then a young opposition lawyer on the make, over one of his seats. The negotiation foundered because of Curran's 'paltry conduct',²⁰¹ which presumably consisted of an avowal of his intention to advance his own 'views or pursuits', and not those of the Agars. Curran's was a special case. But even the mediocrities whom Clifden did return were generally speaking not 'so circumstanced as to fortune and situation' that they could be expected to attend parliament for nothing (it goes without saying that payment of MPs was undreamt-of until the twentieth century). They were not as voracious as Lord Downshire's 'hungry Greeks',²⁰² but they needed feeding. Thus, George Dunbar obtained his pension, George Roth, MP for Thomastown, 1783–6, was appointed clerk of the report office in 1784, and Patrick Welch, MP for Thomastown, 1783–90, and for Gowran, 1790–8, became collector of excise at Naas.²⁰³ Poor George Burdett was entitled to be treated 'ceremoniously' by the Agars, because he sat and voted for them from 1783 to the end of the Irish parliament, receiving nothing in return until 1798, when he became a commissioner of appeals at *c*.£500 per annum.²⁰⁴ In settling for such untalented, unenterprising and therefore undemanding MPs, Clifden was probably bowing to the inevitable. He may have been the intellectual inferior of Ellis, Welby and the Archbishop, but he was clearly not deficient in blunt reasoning. He was only articulating what was true, by implication, of just about all the great electoral interests – namely, that they did not attract to their ranks 'men of ability' and ambition, because such people wanted to enter parliament on a footing of independence.²⁰⁵

'THE ENORMOUS FOLLY' OF CONTESTING CO. KILKENNY, 1789–1801

A commentator on the Irish parliamentary scene in 1790 thought very ill of the 2nd Lord Clifden: 'as he is known to entertain a marked dislike to this country [Ireland], which he has too openly and incautiously expressed, he will most probably become an absentee, and then the borough[s of Gowran and Thomastown] will of course go to market to enlarge the supplies for foreign expenditure'.²⁰⁶ The prediction was crude and inaccurate. Lord Clifden's pattern of residence was peripatetic, at least until after

---

200 Clifden to Agar, [pre-17 Feb. 1783], T/3719/C/17/4. **201** Ellis to Agar, 6 May 1784, T/3719/C/18/6. **202** Quoted in Malcomson, 'The gentle Leviathan: Arthur Hill, 2nd marquess of Downshire, 1753–1801', in *Plantation to Partition* ... (Belfast, 1981), p. 111. **203** Burtchaell, op. cit., pp 177–8. **204** History of the Irish Parliament database, *sub* 'Burdett'. **205** Malcomson, *John Foster*, p. 206. **206** 'Falkland', *Parliamentary representation*, quoted in the History of the Irish Parliament database, *sub* 'Dunbar'.

the Union; he did not become an absentee; and he did not sell seats. What he did was withdraw, slowly and never completely, from Co. Kilkenny politics. In other words, he followed or coincided in the views expressed by his mother to Agar, except that he did not make any attempt to change, in 1790 or thereafter, the members or type of member whom his father had returned for the two boroughs.

From 1789 until his death in 1836, he acquiesced in, or at any rate did not challenge, the Ponsonby and Butler monopoly of the representation of Co. Kilkenny. He wrote to Agar in October 1795 that he had 'no intention ... of falling into the enormous folly of embarking in [*sic*] a contest for the county of Kilkenny. ... Could a person of fortune be found in the county, willing to stand at his own cost and for his own benefit, it might then become worth our consideration how far our family should support him. ... [But], for myself, I think it more wise to pay the debts affecting my estate.'[207] However, he continued to assert a claim to his share of 'the patronage of the county'. Two months earlier, for example, Lord Camden, the lord lieutenant, had complained of having received 'the most impertinent letter' from Clifden, who was offended that the nomination of the next sheriff for Co. Kilkenny had been promised to the 17th earl of Ormonde.[208] Camden seems to have forgotten his indignation at this letter and indeed the entire episode; for, after his departure from Ireland in the summer of 1798, he informed his successor that Clifden's family had usually nominated the Kilkenny sheriff, but that in 1797, in Clifden's absence in England, Camden had given the nomination to Ormonde's son, Walter, the 18th earl,[209] which had vexed Clifden greatly. 'From the other county favours having been shown to Lord Ormonde, it seems reasonable that so strong a parliamentary interest and so large a property [as Clifden's] ought to be attended to there.' Camden therefore advised, not at all consistently, that the nomination be given to Clifden in future.[210] Between 1798 and at least 1801, Ormonde and Clifden nominated jointly – which, as Clifden acknowledged, meant in practice that Ormonde did so singly, as Clifden was 'usually' absent.[211] However, as late as 1802 Clifden regarded himself as entitled to recommend to the collectorship of the revenue for Kilkenny city (in succession to Lady Brandon's great-nephew, Thomas Bourke O'Flaherty, who had in effect gone bankrupt).[212]

The persistence of Clifden's county influence is a little surprising. Because of Gowran and Thomastown, he was still a force in Co. Kilkenny in 1795; but by 1801 his boroughs were disfranchised and his 'strong ... parliamentary interest' was largely gone. What worked to his advantage was that one of the county members, whichever Ponsonby it was who was returned, was in opposition from 1789 to 1806 and then again from 1807 onwards. So the Ponsonbys had no claim to government patronage.

207 Clifden to Agar, 9 Oct. 1795, T/3719/C/29/37.   208 2nd Earl Camden to his chief secretary, Thomas Pelham, 22 Aug. 1795, Pelham papers, BL, Add. Ms. 33101, f. 222.   209 Camden to Agar, 17 Feb. 1797, T/3719/C/31/7.   210 Camden to the acting chief secretary, Lord Castlereagh, 16 Sep. 1798, Castlereagh papers, PRONI, D/3030/277.   211 Clifden to the chief secretary, Charles Abbot (with whom he was on good terms from pre-Union days), 14 Dec. 1801, Colchester papers, PRO, 30/9/1, part 2/1.   212 Clifden to Abbot, 15 Jan. 1802, ibid.; Caroline Corballis, 'Castlefield House', p. 117.

Dublin Castle, it is true, did try to woo W.B. Ponsonby on non-political and law-and-order matters – the county governorship up to 1796 and the forming of the county militia in 1792–3.[213] But law and order became a political issue in its own right, and Ponsonby was not to be wooed. Another point in Clifden's favour was, as Camden mentioned, 'the other county favours' heaped upon Lord Ormonde. The 17th earl was appointed governor of Co. Kilkenny in 1793, his son, Lord Thurles, colonel of the county militia in the same year, and Lord Thurles then succeeded as governor when his father died at the end of 1795 and he became 18th earl of Ormonde. The 18th earl, though a government supporter, was not a favourite at Dublin Castle. He created embarrassment all round by being 'found ... abed' with Lady Clare, the chancellor's wife, although the incident was later represented as 'a business on the sofa at worst'.[214] The Kilkenny militia had a poor record of service – unruly in peace and unreliable in war.[215] Moreover, Lord Ormonde, though a powerful influence in favour of the Union in both Kilkenny City and County, especially among the local catholics, blotted his copybook in December 1799 by haggling over the price of his support. The Castle felt 'much deceived in the opinion' they had formed of him, and his ill-behaviour was reported to the home secretary. It was deemed preferable that he go into opposition (which he did not) than that his 'grievances' be listened to.[216] So, thanks to Ormonde's importunity and Ponsonby's inflexibility, Clifden must have been regarded as, comparatively speaking, an easy man to deal with.

Not that he lacked pertinacity himself. He pointed out to the Castle that the 1802 general election for Co. Kilkenny would be uncontested because he, the only person capable of setting up an effective opposition to the sitting members, did not intend to do so. He grandly claimed in a letter to Pitt that he had 'risked his life and spent his money to suppress the Irish rebellion. ... [Later, he] claimed that "no man in England" supported the Union "more earnestly", in token of which he turned out three hostile members sitting for his two Irish boroughs.'[217] (The fact that by this time he saw himself in an English, not an Irish context, is revealing of his outlook.) The first of

213 Robert Hobart (the chief secretary) to Ponsonby, 18 Dec. 1792, and reply, 19 Dec. 1792, Grey/Ponsonby papers: photocopies in PRONI, T/3393/16–17; Camden to Shannon, 16 Jan. 1796, and Ponsonby to Shannon, 20 Jan. 1796, Pratt papers, PRONI, T/2627/4/197–8. 214 Lord Wycombe to Lady Holland, [20 May 1798], Holland House papers, BL, Add. Ms. 51682, f. 153; Ann C. Kavanaugh, *John FitzGibbon, Earl of Clare* ... (Dublin, 1997), p. 103. I am grateful to Dr C.J. Wright of BL for providing me with the up-to-date reference for the letter from Lord Wycombe. 215 Henry Clements to the Rt Hon. H.T. Clements, 21 Oct. 1785, Clements papers, TCD, Ms. 7308/73; Thomas Pakenham, *The year of liberty: the story of the great Irish rebellion of 1798* (revised ed., London, 1997), p. 311. The Kilkenny militia led the flight at the infamous 'Races of Castlebar'. Lord Ormonde 'first ... "begged and beseeched them [to stand]"; then he "upbraided and swore at them"; finally, he burst into tears.' 216 Ormonde to Cornwallis, 14 July 1799, and 1st earl of Desart to Cornwallis, 19 Aug. 1799, PRONI, D/3030/871 and 934; Cornwallis to Portland, 14 Aug. 1799, and Castlereagh to Portland, 11 Dec. 1799, *Cornwallis correspondence*, iii, pp 125 and 152; and Portland to Castlereagh, 18 Dec. 1799, Portland papers, Nottingham UL, PWF 111. 217 R.G. Thorne (ed.), *The History of Parliament: the House of Commons, 1790–1820* (5 vols., London, 1986), iii. 52.

these claims, though it might have been more becoming in Clifden not to have made it, was fairly well founded. He had spent the period between mid-April and early October 1798 on active service at the head of his yeomanry corps. He wrote on 27 June: 'I have not been in bed for three nights and was on horseback for eighteen hours yesterday.'[218] Because these were yeomen, not militia, they served in their county of origin, Kilkenny, which was far from being as undisturbed in 1798 as has been imagined,[219] and where Clifden's local influence and standing were of value. A couple of weeks after the Kilkenny militia's flight from the French at Castlebar, Co. Mayo, Clifden wrote from Gowran: 'During the invasion, every effort was made in Carlow and Kilkenny to excite the people to rise, ... and certainly the greatest care and vigilance are necessary. I feel this so strongly that, though extremely pressed to return to England and very anxious to do so, I shall remain a fortnight or three weeks longer in the country.'[220]

He would have had more difficulty in establishing his claim to have been an exceptionally useful Unionist. He has been credited with 'Unionist sentiments' in November 1798, and according to a Castle list of very late 1798 or very early 1799 which tended to be optimistic in its guesses, was 'understood to be decidedly favourable'.[221] But the truth is that he was slow to make up his mind about the Union, and that his new Unionist members were not available for voting until March–April 1800, which was rather late in the day. Of the four Clifden members in 1799, only two – George Burdett and James Kearney – were present at the critical divisions on 22 and 24 January. They voted with the government, but may have done so without prompting from Clifden. The other two, who unusually or uniquely for them had formed an opinion of their own on the issue, stayed away – again, quite possibly without prompting from Clifden. Kearney must either have changed his mind and become an anti-Unionist, or else have treated his late January votes as what they literally were – his consent to *consider* measures for consolidating the strength of the Empire. Either way, he eventually had to be removed, along with the two Clifden members who had been hostile from the start. By contrast, Lord Callan took very prompt action. He had returned Charles Kendal Bushe, the son of his father's old friend, for Callan in 1797, but Bushe proved to be a leading anti-Unionist pamphleteer and orator, and was removed before he could speak or vote. He was replaced by a Unionist in April 1799.[222]

Clifden was hesitant about the line he would take on the Union, as – much more importantly – was Agar (see Chapter Twelve). But Clifden did not hesitate in acting on the view he (and his mother) had formed of the Agar interest in Kilkenny. *Pace* his uncle, Welby, he begged leave to doubt if the Agars of Gowran were one of the great electoral interests in Ireland. Most of these 'great' interests, when subjected to the

218 Clifden to Agar, 27 June 1798, T/3719/C/32/96.   219 See pp 521–3, and Rev. Patrick Comerford, 'The Church of Ireland in Co. Kilkenny and the diocese of Ossory during the 1798 rising', in *Old Kilkenny Review, 1998*, pp 146–8.   220 Clifden to Agar, 13 Sep. 1798, T/3719/C/32/121.   221 Bolton, *Union*, p. 76; canvassing list, [post-16 Dec. 1798], Stanhope/Pitt papers, Centre for Kentish Studies, U1590/C.67/8.   222 Burtchaell, op. cit., pp 17–18.

same degree of scrutiny, turn out to be much smaller than at first sight appears, and at least one, Lord Tyrone/Waterford's, was – in terms of 'his real influence in the House of Commons'[223] – as small, problematical and precarious as the Clifden. The Clifden was the fourth or fifth-largest electoral interest in Ireland only when it succeeded in extending itself beyond the four seats for Gowran and Thomastown. Much of its importance derived from the fact that it was able, when an Agar of Gowran was available to fill it, to hold one seat for Co. Kilkenny in the period 1761–89. Some of its importance derived also – vicariously and misleadingly – from the fact that George Agar, Lord Callan, was almost undisputed master of Callan from 1777 onwards. The 1st and 2nd Lords Clifden were unable to make a lasting impression on either Co. Kilkenny or Lord Callan: on the latter, because he made it his business to maintain his independence; on the former because a Ponsonby and Ormonde/Wandesford alliance was too strong for them. The 2nd Lord Clifden might have responded to the overtures made to him in 1789 by John Butler and, using George Agar or someone more co-operative as his candidate, have formed an anti-Ponsonby alliance. But that would have required unremitting concentration on Co. Kilkenny and the sacrifice of all other considerations to it. Even in the period 1789–94 and 1794–1806, when the Ponsonbys were in opposition, the Irish administration was usually anxious at least to soften them; and, had he been trying to hold on to one of the county seats, Clifden's demands on county patronage would undoubtedly have been such as would have antagonised Ormonde. So, Clifden would have found himself being as much of a nuisance to, and as much disliked by, the government he supported as Flood had been in 1775–81.

Bowing out of the representation of the county may therefore be reasonably regarded as the most sensible course open to him, just as the contrary course followed by his father in the period 1761–89 had been sensible enough under the circumstances of that time. Nevertheless, the two courses had it in common that they left the Agar political interest mustering and performing well below its potential maximum. This is an important conclusion, because it provides a corrective to the oft-repeated assertion that Archbishop Agar rose in the Church of Ireland on the back of his family's political interest. The next Chapter will take the argument one stage further by considering the ways in which his family's political interest were an actual obstacle to Agar's rise.

223 Buckinghamshire's instructions to his chief secretary, Heron, for the latter's negotiations with the British government, 26 Dec. 1777, Heron papers, NLI, Ms. 13035/16.

4

The Agar political connection, 1763–1800

To be a political prelate in eighteenth-century Ireland, particularly during the first two-thirds of the century, was nothing out of the ordinary (see pp 475–83). 'Between ... [1702 and 1764], ecclesiastical statesmen were almost as prominent in the government of Ireland as they had been in that of France during the seventeenth century.[1] The lords lieutenant were largely non-resident, and during their absence the country was governed by two or three lords justices, one of whom was almost invariably the primate or an archbishop.'[2] As has recently been demonstrated, the dominant 'High Church' party in the early eighteenth-century Church of Ireland were 'primarily political operators'; it was mainly because their politics were Tory – rather than for theological reasons – that their 'Low Church' opponents gravitated to Whiggery.[3] Such was the factionalism of this period, and such the interference of Tory clergymen in the general election campaign of 1713, that a lasting anti-clerical prejudice was created among the Irish landed class and its representatives in the House of Commons.[4] After the triumph of Whiggery in 1714, a new political battle developed between the 'English' and the 'Irish' interests on the episcopal bench. This was initially a battle for control of the House of Lords, where the bishops were mostly Tory and anti-government and where they sometimes constituted a majority of those present. The practice of promoting Englishmen to the eighteenth-century Irish bench accelerated because of the need, from 1714 onwards, for an infusion of Whigs into the upper house. It is exemplified by, and particularly associated, with the English-born Hugh Boulter, archbishop of Armagh, 1724–42, who saw himself, and was seen, as the watchdog of the 'English interest' in Ireland, and who carefully kept open a hot line to the British prime minister, Sir Robert Walpole.[5] Boulter's main antagonists within the Church of Ireland were the Irish-born William King, archbishop of Dublin, 1703–29, and Theophilus Bolton, archbishop of Cashel, 1730–44. When it was wittily

---

1 As L.M. Cullen has pointed out, the comparison with France could be extended into the late eighteenth century – 'The politics of clerical radicalism in the 1790s', in Liam Swords (ed.), *Protestant, catholic and dissenter: the clergy and 1798* (Dublin, 1997), p. 279. 2 Phillips, *History of the Church of Ireland*, iii. 17. See also Falvey, 'Church of Ireland episcopate', pp 107–9. 3 Hayton, 'The High Church party', p. 139. See also: John Walsh and Stephen Taylor, 'The Church and Anglicanism in the "long" eighteenth century', in Walsh, Taylor and Colin Haydon (eds.), *The Church of England, c.1689–c.1833 ...* (Cambridge, 1993), pp 33–5; and Peter Nockles, 'Church parties in the pre-Tractarian Church of England, 1750–1833 ...', ibid., pp 335–7. 4 McNally, *Early Hanoverian Ireland*, pp 151–2. 5 Ibid., p. 53; Phillips, *History of the Church of Ireland* , iii, pp 201–6; Swift to the Rev. James Stopford, 26 Nov. 1725, NLI reports on private collections, no. 97.

remarked in 1733 that Boulter and Bolton were 'as great enemies as Christianity will permit', this was an allusion to political, not theological, disagreement.[6] Boulter's not-quite-immediate successor, the English-born George Stone (archbishop of Armagh, 1747–64), was also a political primate, but of a different and far from Olympian kind. Stone was a 'noxious and troublesome' party man,[7] and brought the primacy into more than passing disrepute, partly because of this and partly because of the storm of politically inspired squibs to which his private life gave rise.[8]

What made Agar highly unusual, and probably unique, among eighteenth-century Irish bishops is that he was a political prelate who had been born into a major Irish political connection. None of the eighteenth-century primates (or, more precisely, none of the primates of the period 1702–1822) came from such a background, because all of them were English.[9] If they, or any other Englishmen on the Irish bench, sought to put themselves at the head of an Irish political connection, as Stone was probably the only one who did, they had to fashion it by artificial means. Of the Irishmen on that bench, a few belonged to minor Irish political connections (those returning no more than one or at most two members to the House of Commons): the Hon. Joseph Deane Bourke, archbishop of Tuam, 1782–94, and (from 1792) 3rd earl of Mayo; the Hon. Charles Brodrick, later Agar's successor as archbishop of Cashel; the Hon. William Knox, bishop of Killaloe, 1794–1803; and William Cecil Pery, bishop of Limerick, 1784–94, and 1st Lord Glentworth (1790). However, apart from Agar himself, only Agar's younger contemporary, the Hon William Beresford (bishop of Ossory, 1782–94, and archbishop of Tuam, 1794–1819), belonged to a major Irish political connection; and he was not politically important in his own right. There had been a Boyle archbishop of Armagh until 1702 (when he died), and there were to be Beresford (in addition to William Beresford), Ponsonby and Tottenham Loftus bishops from the early nineteenth century onwards. But, for some reason, these and the other major political connections, for example the Fitzgeralds, earls of Kildare and dukes of Leinster, and the Hills, earls of Hillsborough and marquesses of Downshire, did not produce bishops in the eighteenth century (with the exception of William Beresford). They all had clients in the Church (for example, the 2nd earl of Shannon had the Rev. George Chinnery, and Thomas Conolly of Castletown, Co. Kildare, had the already-mentioned Rev. Richard Woodward), for whom they solicited and usually obtained bishoprics; but such men were satellites, not members, of these family-based political connections. Perversely – because in general terms Church history in the eighteenth and nineteenth centuries has as one of its themes a process of de-secularisation – the most extreme case of a prelate at the head of a political connection was Lord John George Beresford (archbishop of Armagh, 1822–62), in the period 1826–32. In those years, as well as

---

6 McNally, op. cit., p. 111.   7 Quoted in G.O. Simms, archbishop of Armagh, 'The founder of Armagh's public library: Primate Robinson among his books', in *Irish Booklore*, vol. 1, no. 1 (1971), pp 142 and 145.   8 James Walton (ed.), *'The King's business': letters on the administration of Ireland, 1740–1761, from the papers of Sir Robert Wilmot* (New York, 1996), pp xxxvii–xliv.   9 Phillips, op. cit., iii. 176.

being primate, he was guardian of his nephew, the 3rd marquess of Waterford, during the latter's minority, and controversial custodian of the Beresford family's political interest in Ireland at an extraordinarily difficult time.[10]

The politically important bishops of Irish background on the eighteenth-century Irish bench (again with the exception of Agar) seem to have been men without constituency influence and without a House of Commons connection at their back. The most obvious example is Archbishop King. Of King it was said by the Chief Secretary in 1709 – and in spite of greatly changed times the same could have been said of Agar from *c.*1775 – that he was 'the oracle of the Church party ..., a great speaker both in the House of Lords and at the council table ..., [and] a very high figure among the laity as well as the clergy for his hospitable way of living and exact care of his diocese'.[11] King's political *protégé,* Theophilus Bolton (*c.*1678–1744), had no inherited constituency influence either and, as will be seen (p. 290), made himself very unpopular in Co. Tipperary by his unsuccessful attempts to acquire such influence on the strength of his position as archbishop. Of Edward Synge, bishop of Elphin, 1740–62, the lord lieutenant, the 4th earl of Chesterfield, said in 1745 (again in terms similar to those which would later be applied to Agar) that Synge was 'without dispute equal, if not superior, in abilities to any on the bench, and ... is also the Speaker and the efficient man in the House of Lords'.[12] But Synge had no constituency influence and belonged to a distinguished family of churchmen, not to a political connection. In this respect, Agar and the Agar political connection stand virtually alone. This may not have been entirely accidental. Lord Buckinghamshire – the lord lieutenant who had reluctantly recommended Agar for Cashel – expressed the view in October 1780 that any member of a leading political connection who was promoted in the Church would always feel that he owed the favour to family influence and not to the crown:

> Dr [William] Beresford, my last bishop, ... declines giving a living, when one
> in his gift becomes vacant, to the son of one of his own friends at my recom-
> mendation. The Archbishop of Cashel, when his nomination was fixed,
> refused giving me some preferment which became vacant in Cloyne. This
> proves the expediency of English ministers interfering in Irish patronage!
> The Beresfords and the Agars bask in the sunshine of cabinet favour. The
> two prelates of those families promoted by me have declined making any
> return: the others, who stand in the same degree of obligation, have uni-
> formly offered every piece of preferment which fell.[13]

This suggests, and so it will be argued in this Chapter, that Agar's membership of a major family and political connection was not an unmixed blessing to him.

10 Malcomson, *John Foster*, p. 289n.   11 Joseph Addison to 1st Earl of Godolphin, 26 May 1709, quoted in Robert S. Matteson, 'Archbishop William King and the conception of his library', in *The Library, sixth series,* vol. 13, no. 3 (Sep. 1991), p. 253.   12 Quoted in Marie-Louise Legg (ed.), *The Synge letters: Bishop Edward Synge to his daughter, Alicia, Roscommon to Dublin, 1746–1752* (Dublin, 1996), p. xi.   13 Buckinghamshire to Hotham Thompson, 11 Oct. 1780, Hotham papers, PRONI, T/3429/1/68.

Undoubtedly, it helped him to rise in the Church when he was young and personally untried. But it is arguable that he might have reached the top (for example, the archbishopric of Dublin in 1778 and the primacy in 1794) if he had stood on his own merits alone. Dublin Castle lists of the members of the Irish parliament and the major parliamentary connections during the period 1784–7, almost make this point. They record that he was 'one of the ablest men of business in the House. [His object is] to be primate, but in that event his power would be very great, Lord Clifden commending [*sic*] five members in the House of Commons and [there being] a borough annexed to the primacy.'[14] The other three archbishoprics, Cashel included, had no borough attached – or at any rate no borough controlled by the archbishop (see pp 287–92). Moreover, Agar's membership, and assumed direction, of an Irish political connection made him seem too powerful already, and also too Irish. Ideally, he should have stood on his own pretensions as a churchman, backed only by the English influence of Welbore Ellis. (A more fundamental obstacle to Agar's translation to the primacy was that it already had 'a very tough incumbent in fine preservation', Richard Robinson.)[15]

Agar was compromised by his membership of a family and political connection in another respect: a churchman with patronage at his command was under particular pressure, when family influence had contributed to his rise, to use it on behalf of his family. Agar's troubles with three of the family members whom he preferred in the Church, and the disrepute which one of them brought upon him, have been discussed on pp 54–7. Other members of the Agar connection to whom he gave preferment included Welbore Ellis Agar (second son of the infamous Rev. Henry), whom he successively made prebendary of Fennor in 1799 and chancellor of Cashel in 1800, and his more distant cousin (on the distaff side), the politically well-connected Joseph Preston, whom he successively made rector of Ballintemple in 1795 and prebendary of Killenelick in 1797. (Among his wife's relations, he made William Benson chancellor of Emly in 1791 and precentor in 1795, and Francis Benson rector of Fethard in 1791.)[16] All these, it should be said – in marked contrast to the Revs. Henry, Charles and John Agar – seem to have done credit to his recommendation. Yet even they, simply because they were relations, contributed – however factitiously – to his reputation for nepotism (see pp 47–55, 80, 120 and 244–5).

In other words, it was impossible for a churchman who belonged to a family-based political connection to be viewed in isolation from that connection. For this reason, the present Chapter is devoted to a discussion of the Agar connection, the ways in which it operated, the objects which it pursued, the prejudices which it engendered and the likelihood that it hindered as well as helped Agar's ecclesiastical career.

---

14 Ed. E.M. Johnston[-Liik], *Proc. RIA*, vol. 71, sec. C, no. 5 (1971), p. 166.   15 Scott to Agar, 19 May 1783, T/3719/C/17/15.   16 Rev. St John D. Seymour, *The succession of parochial clergy in the united diocese of Cashel and Emly* (Dublin, 1908), pp 24, 28, 33, 36, 52 and 63–6; Agar's 'state' of the diocese of Cashel, 1779–1801, 21 M 57/B6/1.

AGAR'S RISE IN THE CHURCH OF IRELAND, 1763–78

Because he was an Irishman, Agar's family's political influence was important in setting him on course for a bishopric at a time when Englishmen dominated the Church
of Ireland episcopate. 'By 1760, the 22 bishops were divided equally between those
born in Ireland and those introduced from England, with three of the four
archbishops in the latter category. A more exhaustive analysis of the later eighteenth-
century Irish bishops finds 67 sent from England and 56 supplied by Ireland.'[17] One
imported English bishop, Timothy Godwin, later (1727–9) archbishop of Cashel, had
written brazenly to a clergyman friend in Warwickshire in 1717: 'I wish I knew how to
bring you over amongst us. We should get a numerous plantation of English.'[18] Agar's
own grandfather, Bishop Welbore Ellis, an English Tory, 'pursued a campaign of
political rehabilitation from 1717 at least, [and] was eventually rewarded for his
services to the English interest in Ireland'; he was Primate Boulter's first choice for the
archbishopric of Cashel in 1727, was described by Boulter on that occasion as 'an
hearty Englishman'.[19] Agar must have known perfectly well that he was entering a
profession in which he would have to swim upstream for his mitre. Hence, perhaps,
his unusual (for an Irishman) career decision in 1763 to seek appointment as a
viceregal chaplain.[20] Hence also – a century and a half later – the outrage of a
'collateral descendant of this great Irish churchman', when the nationalist MP and
polemicist, J.G. Swift MacNeill, wrote a letter to a newspaper in 1911 in which he
referred to Agar as 'an English ecclesiastical adventurer'.[21]

In 1763, the lord lieutenant was the 2nd earl, subsequently 1st duke, of
Northumberland. How Agar came to know him or to be recommended to him is
unclear, although it is perfectly clear that Northumberland's appointment of him as

17 T.C. Barnard, 'Improving clergymen, 1660–1760', in Alan Ford, James McGuire and
Kenneth Milne (eds.), *As by law established: the Church of Ireland since the Reformation* (Dublin,
1995), p. 141. However, it has been pointed out that this was nothing new: 'in the seventeenth
century, the ratio was 85 non-Irish to 37 Irish bishops' – Falvey, 'Church of Ireland episcopate',
p. 109. For a study of the situation in 1750–1800, see Akenson, *Church of Ireland*, pp 12–28 and 35–7.
Professor Akenson also makes the point (p. 37) that, in relation to the episcopate of the Church of
England, that of the Church of Ireland was well paid, at least in this period. By 1830–31, the English
bishops seem to have forged ahead (pp 82–3). 18 Godwin, then bishop of Kilmore, to Rev. Mr
Welchman, 10 Oct. 1717, part of a collection of miscellaneous 'autographs' among the papers
formerly at Holloden, Bagenalstown, Co. Carlow. These were listed by PRONI *c.* 1970 by courtesy
of the late Miss Faith O'Grady. 19 Quoted in Philip O'Regan, *Archbishop William King of Dublin
(1750–1729)* ... (Dublin, 2000), p. 326. 20 Other Irish examples were Agar's predecessor at Cashel,
Michael Cox, who had been a chaplain to the 2nd duke of Ormonde, 1711–13, and Edward Synge,
who had been a chaplain to the 1st duke of Bolton, 1717–19; they had to wait 20 and 11 years
respectively for bishoprics. On this question of viceregal chaplaincies, see pp 138–40, 188–9, 485–9
and 601–2, and also Akenson, *Church of Ireland*, pp 13–14. 21 Typescript copy of a letter to an
editor from S.A. Quan-Smith, Bullock Castle, Dalkey, Co. Dublin, in a box of documents deriving
from Robert Wyse-Jackson, dean of Cashel, 1945–61, now in the Bolton Library, Cashel. I am
grateful to Mr Norman Lund, library assistant in that library, for sending me copies of this and other
relevant items in his care.

second chaplain in that year was the making of Agar. An already-quoted (p. 91) letter of August 1779 from Agar to General Lord Percy, later 2nd duke, the son of his 'old patron',[22] shows that Agar was on friendly terms with Percy, although from what date is unclear. They were both Christ Church men, but Percy was seven years younger than Agar. He went into the army and was stationed in Limerick in the late 1760s;[23] so Agar may only have got to know him when bishop of the adjoining diocese of Cloyne. Percy's father, the lord lieutenant, must have known Welbore Ellis. They were almost exact contemporaries, Northumberland having been born in 1714 and Ellis in 1713. They were also fairly close neighbours in their Middlesex second homes; Northumberland lived for part of the year at Syon, Brentford, and Ellis (as has been seen) from 1761 lived for part of the year at Twickenham, in Pope's former villa. However, the catalyst actually seems to have been Agar's forceful and sometimes embarrassing 'aunty', the countess of Brandon. In July 1763, she wrote to Northumberland asking for a peerage for her brother, James Agar of Ringwood, on the grounds of his parliamentary interest (a doubtful claim, granted the then parlous state of Callan) and the regard which Northumberland had always borne Lady Brandon.[24] Lady Brandon was never overcome by bashfulness, but it is incredible that she would have claimed a friendship with Northumberland, to his face, if it did not exist. This Northumberland, it should be noted, though married to the Percy heiress, was the son of a Yorkshire baronet of fairly humble origins called Smithson;[25] so it is perfectly possible that the Smithsons were friends or connections of their fellow-Yorkshiremen, the Ellises. Equally, Lady Brandon's asserted friendship with Northumberland may be a further indication that she really had occupied a position at court and/or in London society. Whatever the basis of her claims on Northumberland, no peerage was forthcoming for James Agar of Ringwood. Could the chaplaincy for Lady Brandon's nephew have been a consolation prize?

Unless they were exceptionally unlucky, the first – and sometimes the first two – in the team of chaplains who attended each lord lieutenant, in due course became bishops. In 1751, when approving the elevation of Robinson to his first bishopric, George II commented sensibly: 'all the bishoprics must not be given to chaplains'.[26] But nothing was done to curtail the practice. All told, forty eighteenth-century bishops – nearly all of them Englishmen – started off as 'chaplain to the lord lieutenant or some other powerful lay lord'.[27] Northumberland's lord lieutenancy saw out the most important political prelate of the mid-eighteenth century, and saw in the most important of the late eighteenth century (though Stone and Agar were, in political

22 Ellis to Agar, 8 June 1786, and 2nd duke of Northumberland (formerly Lord Percy) to Agar, 2 July 1786, T/3719/C/20/11 and 16.   23 Judith Hill, 'Davis Ducart and Christopher Colles: architects associated with the custom house in Limerick', in *Irish Architectural and Decorative Studies (the Journal of the Irish Georgian Society)*, ii (1999), pp 127–8.   24 Lady Brandon to Northumberland, 15 July 1763, Northumberland papers, Alnwick, Northumberland: photocopy in PRONI, T/2872/6.   25 Roebuck, *Yorkshire baronets*, pp 23 and 297–8.   26 Quoted in Rev. Christopher Mohan, 'Archbishop Richard Robinson: builder of Armagh', in *Seanchas Ard Mhacha*, vi, no. 1 (1971), p. 96.   27 Falvey, 'Church of Ireland episcopate', p. 110

type and style, as different as the times in which they operated).[28] There is heavy irony in this. Northumberland did not mourn the passing of Stone and had no wish to see anything like his like again. Indeed, he spoke 'of the Primate's death rather with pleasure than regret, and ... [has] found him out in a thousand tricks ... . The conversation of my Lord Lieutenant's family is ... that business will go on much better when the Primate is dead and when my Lord Lieutenant takes everything under his own management.'[29] The comparison between Stone and Agar is also of value in demonstrating that Agar was far from being a fast-stream, political promotee. Stone's 'advancement' had been 'dazzling ... . [He] was consecrated bishop of Ferns in 1740, translated to Kildare in 1743, to Derry in 1745, and became primate in 1747 at the exceptionally early age of thirty-nine. He owed everything to the patronage of his brother, Andrew, who as well as being the under-secretary to the English ecclesiastical minister, the duke of Newcastle, was also the governor of the future King George III.'[30] The rise of Stone's *protégé* and successor, Richard Robinson, was almost as rapid: bishop of Killala, 1751 (the year of his arrival from England as a viceregal chaplain), bishop of Ferns, 1759, bishop of Kildare, 1761, and primate, 1765. And it, too, was accelerated by connections at court (see pp 439–41). Agar, as an Irishman, needed exceptional advantages if he were to hold his own against such English competition.

From 1763 onwards, there is no difficulty in documenting Agar's next upward moves in the Church of Ireland. In general terms, he owed his successive promotions to the growing importance of his family's electoral weight in Ireland, to the influence in England of Welbore Ellis, and to his own ability, personality and good standing as a churchman. Specifically, he owed the deanery of Kilmore, to which he was preferred in March 1765, to his 'intimate'[31] relations with the Northumberland family, to Ellis' new political connection with Lord Bute, and to the marriage of Bute's daughter to Northumberland's son, Lord Percy, in July 1764. It was later remarked – not specifically about Agar – that 'When ... Lord Bute became the rising sun, the clergy, like Persians, paid their adoration to this luminary.'[32] Bute urged Northumberland to do something more for Agar, and Northumberland (who needed little urging) made him dean of Kilmore.[33] Agar was now twenty-nine and had to wait three years for a bishopric. The delay was in part to do with English competition and in part to do with his youth. During the lord lieutenancy of Northumberland's successor, the 1st earl of Hertford (1765–6), Agar was promised the second bishopric to fall vacant. However, when the vacancy occurred, he was not of episcopal age (i.e. thirty). This canonical requirement had been regularly waived in the past, but Primate Robinson was (rightly) insistent that it be adhered to. Then, in the 2nd earl of Bristol's time (1766–7), Agar

28 At the time, of course, Northumberland's most important ecclesiastical appointment was that of Robinson as primate in succession to Stone. For the political roles, and rivalries, of Robinson and Agar, see pp 149–57 and 445–61.   29 William Gerard Hamilton (Northumberland's chief secretary) to John Hely-Hutchinson, 2 Dec. 1764 [misprinted as 1769], *HMC Emly/Pery* Mss. [part 1], p. 191. 30 Falvey, 'Church of Ireland episcopate', p. 111.   31 Diana Agar to Agar, 20 Jan. 1809, T/3719/ C/43/15.   32 *The British Mercury ..., by J.W. von Archenholtz, vol. iii for 1787* (Hamburg, [1787?]), p. 148.   33 Welbore Ellis to Lord Townshend, 2 Aug. 1767, *Irish official papers*, i. 103.

passed over in favour of the lord lieutenant's brother, Frederick Hervey (in spite of Ellis' already-quoted attempt to ingratiate himself with Bristol and with Bristol's patron, Chatham, the new prime minister). In August 1767, Ellis wrote to the new lord lieutenant, Townshend, expressing his concern lest Agar be passed over again. He pointed out that Agar's eldest brother was MP for Co. Kilkenny, and 'has two boroughs in that county ..., in one of which there is now a vacancy ...; and as from particular events a greater number of Englishmen have successively been promoted to bishoprics in that kingdom, without the intervention of one native, than hath been usual, it may appear both popular and prudent to make a bishop of that country'. Ellis' playing of the Irish card is significant, and must have paid off. In March 1768, not long after his representations were made, Frederick Hervey, most fortunate of viceregal chaplains and of imported Englishmen, was translated after only two years at Cloyne to the very senior and valuable bishopric of Derry, and Agar, a 'native', succeeded him at Cloyne.

It is important to give due weight to the contribution made by Agar's personal attributes to this outcome: good connections did not on their own guarantee prefer-ment, or at any rate speedy preferment – otherwise, the already-mentioned Irishmen who became prominent ecclesiastics in Ireland with little or no political influence at their back would never have reached the episcopal bench. In Ireland, as in England, 'the Church remained a career open to the talent of the humbly born'[34] – for example, Archbishop King. If Agar's promotion to the bench was slower than that of his English-born comparators, it was faster than that of the better-connected Irishman, William Beresford. Born in 1743, Beresford reached the episcopal age in 1773, but did not become a bishop until 1780. His brother, Lord Tyrone, grumbled in 1776 that William Beresford had been made a viceregal chaplain in 1766 (i.e. only three years after Agar), that his current preferments totalled £1,500 per annum (i.e. they were about equivalent to the worst bishoprics), and that still no bishopric had been found for him. Nor was this for want of vacancies. At the end of 1777, Tyrone complained to Buckinghamshire that there had already been 'three promotions to that bench' since Buckinghamshire's appointment, and still no reward, in episcopal form, had been given for the Beresfords' 'constant, steady support of his Majesty's government through successive administrations'.[35] The difference between Agar and Beresford can only have been that Agar was the abler man and better churchman,[36] and was pro-moted accordingly. As bishop of Cloyne, he lived up to these expectations and acquitted himself with distinction. But Cloyne was a bishopric of middling seniority and a generous promotion for a young man and first-time bishop. Agar could therefore expect to remain there for some time acquiring the experience and length of service to

---

34 Walsh and Taylor, 'The Church and Anglicanism', p. 4. 35 Tyrone to Buckinghamshire, 1 Sep. 1776, 31 Dec. 1777 and 28 Apr. 1779, Heron papers, NLI, Ms. 13034/1, Ms. 13035/16 and Ms. 13037/10. 36 For example, when promoted to Ossory, where he remained from 1782 to 1794, Beresford proved to be a less than energetic diocesan – Comerford, 'The Church of Ireland in Co. Kilkenny', pp 154–62 and 168. On the other hand, when sitting to Stuart for his portrait, Beresford annoyed the peppery painter by talking religion to him! – Mount, *Irish career of Gilbert Stuart*, p. 21.

qualify him for one of the limited number of dioceses which would be an advance on Cloyne, or for one of the four archbishoprics. Years later, in 1790, it was alleged by a Whig, opposition polemicist that the influence deriving from the Agar boroughs had 'accelerated ... the creation of peers and archbishops'.[37] Though this was true of Lord Clifden's peerage, it was manifestly untrue of Agar's archbishopric; for, there is abundant evidence to show that Agar earned the latter by his own endeavours, political and ecclesiastical.

In the political sphere, he used the seat in the House of Lords which Cloyne brought with it to establish a reputation as 'a constant attender and good speaker'.[38] At this time, as John Scott remarked, the *ex officio* speaker of the Lords, Lord Chancellor Lifford, only 'kept himself up by persuading the public that government was riveted to him, when they would have wished to remove him'.[39] In March 1774, Ellis 'was informed that the Castle trusted the management of affairs in that H[ouse] principally to you. If that be so', Ellis warned Agar, Lord Lifford 'will never forgive you, as having supplanted him; and yet, by what you hint, he must have been very unfit for it. I shall not feel much for him if he should get a broken pate. Depend upon it, you will lose but a hollow friend.'[40] There is precisely contemporary corroboration of Agar's new role in the House of Lords: 'Lord Bellamont ... and the Bishop [of Cloyne] are the managers in the Lords. The Chancellor is a cypher.'[41] From this point on, as has been seen (pp 74–6), jostling for the position of leader of the Lords was to be a theme of Agar's political career. At the end of 1774, he was vexed that his services to the administration of Lord Harcourt, and the good wishes expressed by Harcourt to him, had not resulted in an offer of the vacant archbishopric of Tuam. Scott, however, counselled forbearance: 'I believe your wiser part, considering what your essential wishes are, is to make a merit of not pressing, and keep your eyes steadily on Cashel.'[42] Perhaps the Castle had not offered him Tuam because they knew his eyes were on Cashel. In the following year, a Castle-compiled list of the members of the House of Lords recorded that the 'expectation' of succeeding to Cashel or something as good or better had been held out to him. When Harcourt's administration came to an end in July 1776, Agar was assured that, 'had the archbishopric of Cashel become vacant, it was his Excellency's design to have recommended your Lordship to his Majesty for that preferment'; and at the end of the year, the prime minister, Lord North, when discussing other Irish ecclesiastical arrangements, made the assumption that the bishopric of Cloyne was about to fall vacant.[43]

Two years later, in December 1778, with Agar still bishop of Cloyne, and Dublin the archbishopric which looked likeliest to come a-begging, Scott wrote the following

37 'Falkland', *Parliamentary representation*, quoted in the History of the Irish Parliament database *sub* 'Thomastown'.   38 William Hunt (ed.), *The Irish parliament, 1775 ...* (London, 1907), p. 75. 39 *Clonmell Diary (TCD)*, p. 40.   40 Ellis to Agar, 18 Mar. 1774, T/3719/C/8/2.   41 Robert Waller to Macartney, 19 Mar. 1774, *Macartney in Ireland*, pp 187–8.   42 Scott to Agar, 19 Dec., and Agar to Scott, 25 Dec., 1774, T/3719/C/8/8–9.   43 Hunt, *Irish parliament, 1775*, p. 75; Sir John Blaquiere (Harcourt's chief secretary) to Agar, 2 July 1776, T/3719/C/10/3; North to Bucking-hamshire, 4 Dec. 1776, Heron papers, NLI, Ms. 13034/3.

assessment of Agar's pretensions, clearly with the intention that it should be laid before Lord North:

> The Bishop of Cloyne has been for [the] ten years that I have narrowly attended to parliamentary concerns here, the most active, decided and useful supporter of administration in the House of Lords, infinitely the first ecclesiastic if not in all respects the first man of business in that assembly. Lord Townshend confided in him, Lord Harcourt rested upon him, and if one might have judged from his services or connections, Lord Buckingham[shire] might have been supposed sincere in those sanguine assurances which I know his Excellency and his Secretary had given him of protection and support.[44]

Although Scott mentioned Agar's 'connections', and elsewhere in the same document described the Agars as 'an ancient family with some talents and estate amongst them' (had he never heard of the Dublin livery-stable ostler?), the whole emphasis of his recommendation of Agar lay upon Agar's personal merits as a politician and spiritual peer. These were matched by his achievements as a churchman (see pp 198–9 and 295–302).

THE PROPOSED 'REMOVAL OF THE DUBLIN CUSTOM HOUSE', 1773–8

The other, and very simple, reason for playing down the influence of the Agar boroughs and connection on the rise of Agar during the 1770s, is that that influence had been directed to objects other than his advancement during those years. His eldest brother had not been residing in Dublin and attending to parliament 'for other people's views or pursuits', but for his own. James Agar's first pursuit had been office for himself, which he had obtained when appointed a commissioner of the revenue in 1771, and his next a better office and/or a peerage. He had obtained his peerage in 1776, although in return he had had to give the government the disposal of at least one of his seats. Consequently (since neither he nor any other Agar now sat for Co. Kilkenny), he found his influence at a very low ebb in the 1776 parliament, when the archbishopric of Dublin did in fact fall vacant. These pursuits of Lord Clifden's had been sensible and legitimate. Unfortunately for Charles Agar, however, the private interests of Ellis as an owner of Dublin real estate, coupled with Clifden's adventitious ability as a commissioner of the revenue to promote them, had tempted the Agar connection early in the 1770s into a pursuit which was neither sensible nor perhaps legitimate. This was a Canute-like attempt to stem the eastward development of Dublin and to prevent the bridging of the River Liffey at points which made clear geographical sense.

The then most westerly bridge over the Liffey, Essex bridge, had been completed in 1753. On the south bank of the river, to the west of Essex bridge, lay

44 Scott to Ellis, 4 Dec. 1778, T/3719/C/12/29.

the symbolic and commercial heart of the city – its cathedrals, tholsel, law courts, guild halls. To the east of ... the line joining the bridge with the Castle ... lay an unbridged river, and two areas of recent development, one on the north bank, and one on the south. On the north lay the Gardiner estates, the most conspicuous focal point of which was the residential [Gardiner's] Mall ... . On the south, also to the east of the old city and of Essex bridge, lay the College, the Parliament House, Stephen's Green and Leinster House ... . The most strategically interesting of these developments was Gardiner's Mall. ... From one end of the mall ... an avenue [might be opened] leading – [via Sackville (now O'Connell) Street and] a new bridge – to College Green. With interest thus diverted from the Capel Street-Essex Bridge axis, the centre of gravity of the entire city plan [would be] ... altered.[45]

The first moves in parliament to facilitate this easterly development by building 'an additional bridge at the ferry boat slip, a considerable way below the custom house', had been made in 1752, even before the completion of Essex Bridge, and had been defeated, 'to the great joy of the citizens of Dublin'[46] and, of course, of Ellis. As far as Ellis was concerned, the key issue was the custom house. It was located on his property on the south bank of the river (most of the Ellis estate was actually on the other bank, and further to the west), and was a vital source of animation to that part of the old city. It had been built as long ago as 1707, and increasingly was a source of complaint, partly because the accommodation it offered was now so inadequate 'that the revenue suffers daily for want of room for the storage of goods', and partly because its location, 'besides great inconvenience to trade, loses many thousand pounds to the revenue'.[47] Essex Bridge had had to be sited just upstream from the custom house, so that it did not cut off access to the latter by seaborne traffic. But to get this far upriver the seaborne traffic had to be of fairly shallow draught, and the distance between the custom house and ships of deep draught facilitated smuggling. 'Easterly development depended on the building of a new bridge, and ... a new bridge depended on the building of a new custom house downstream'. Accordingly, in 1773 the revenue commissioners, by a majority decision, recommended to Lord Harcourt the removal of the custom house to a new, easterly site. This proposal was put to the House of Commons in 1774, when it was opposed by, among others, the corporation of Dublin and the merchants and inhabitants of the old city.[48] Meanwhile, the structural problems of the custom house were such that it was thought 'the old building cannot stand'.[49] It looked likely to fall down before the dispute over its future came to a resolution.

Within the revenue board, the minority opposing the change of site was, of course, headed by James Agar, Lord Clifden. In his own right, and not just as Ellis'

45 Edward McParland, *James Gandon: Vitruvius Hibernicus* (London, 1985), pp 35–6 and 41–4. See also Maurice Craig, *Dublin, 1660–1860* (London, 1952), pp 239–45.   46 Waite to Wilmot, 22 and 29 Feb. 1752, Wilmot papers, PRONI, T/3019/1851 and 1859.   47 Buckinghamshire to Heron, 9 Jan. 1778, NLI, Ms. 13036/2; Buckinghamshire to Lord George Germain, 14 Jan. 1779, *HMC Lothian Mss.*, p. 343.   48 McParland, loc. cit.   49 Buckinghamshire to Heron, 9 Jan. 1778, NLI, Ms. 13036/2.

nephew, he had some vested interest in the prosperity of the Ellis estate. In 1744, Ellis had let in fee farm to Clifden's father, Henry Agar, premises on Arran Quay.[50] Much more important, it must have been known within the Agar family, or at any rate been regarded as highly probable, that Clifden and his issue were Ellis' heirs. The majority on the revenue board who favoured the change was headed by John Beresford, Lord Tyrone's younger brother and an able and prominent public servant, particularly in the sphere of revenue administration. Beresford and James Agar were both made founding members of the new Dublin paving board set up in 1773 under *13 and 14 George II, cap. 22*; so they probably crossed swords there as well. While Beresford undoubtedly had sound administrative reasons for wanting a change of site for the custom house, Ellis and James Agar were not alone in arguing their case from a position of vested interest: Beresford's 'property interests and [those] of his family' lay in the neighbourhood of the new custom house site,[51] just as Ellis' and James Agar's lay in the neighbourhood of the old. Moreover, in 1774 Beresford married, as his second wife, Barbara Montgomery, a noted beauty, whose sister and fellow-beauty, Elizabeth, had married Luke Gardiner in the previous year. Gardiner owned the north Dublin residential development which bore his name and which stood to benefit enormously from the abandonment of the old custom house.

From the point of view of Bishop Charles Agar, who personally had no vested interest in the custom house issue, a dispute between his family connection and Beresford must have been exceedingly unwelcome. Scott, who was appointed attorney-general in 1777, was on close political and personal terms with Beresford.[52] Beresford's already-mentioned younger brother, William, was so much junior to Agar in their profession that there was for many years to come no possibility of rivalry between them. So, Agar had every reason to be on good terms with the Beresford connection in the second half of the 1770s. There is no direct evidence for the line he took on the custom house, and nothing about it in his papers. However, a letter which Clifden wrote to Agar a few years later, in 1783, seems to show that Lord Tyrone was on terms of 'intimacy' with Agar and 'rather light and indifferent as to' Clifden.[53] Writing to Agar in 1786, Lord Shannon referred to 'our friend Tyrone'.[54] Tyrone himself wrote in deferential tones to Agar in 1788.[55] They paid family visits to each other and co-operated on local law-and-order matters.[56] When Tyrone, now 1st marquess of Waterford, died at the end of 1800, Agar was regarded by his family as one of their 'best friends', and the clerical member of the family, Lord John George Beresford, who wrote to Agar to that effect, added that he personally had derived from that 'friendship ... the most solid advantage and the most sincere satisfaction.'[57] This is an

50 Lease from Ellis to Henry Agar, 31 Oct. 1744, Clifden estate papers, NLI, D 10685–10692; conveyance from the Dowager Viscountess and the 2nd Viscount Clifden, 16 May 1789, NA, D 20141. In 1773, Bishop Charles Agar's Dublin house was on Arran Quay (T/3719/C/7/1). 51 McParland, *Gandon*, p. 43. 52 Heron to Buckinghamshire, 9 Apr. 1779, NLI, Ms. 13037/8. 53 Clifden to Agar, [pre-17 Feb. 1783], T/3719/C/17/4. 54 Shannon to Agar, 20 Aug. 1786, T/3719/C/20/25. 55 Tyrone to Agar, 5 July 1788, T/3719/C/22/29. 56 Tyrone to Agar, 15 June 1789, T/3719/C/23/25. 57 Rev. Lord John George Beresford to Agar, 16 Dec. 1800,

interesting tribute from the first Irishman to become primate since 1702 to the Irishman who twice failed in that attempt.

However, the most telling – and relevant – indication of Agar's attitude to the Beresfords was the part he subsequently played in a House of Lords committee which sat between 1793 and 1795 and which had been set up to inquire into financial irregularities allegedly committed by John Beresford and his fellow-commissioners – not, this time, of the revenue, but of the Dublin Wide Streets – in opening up a new road and building a new bridge to the south and east of the old city.[58] The terms of reference of the committee did not say as much, but basically the focus of its inquiry was the 'heavy and universal suspicion ... [of] much imputed malversation' under which Beresford laboured.[59] A finished draft of the committee report, presented on 9 May 1795, is to be found in Agar's handwriting among Agar's papers.[60] This is a hitherto unknown document and is an important source in its own right. For present purposes, suffice it to say that its wording, and the subsequent act sponsored by the Lords for regulating the work of the wide streets commissioners,[61] evinced a disposition to deal leniently with Beresford and avoid any retrospective censure of his activities. As the lord lieutenant, Camden, reported to London in late March 1796: 'the business which has so long troubled the parliament and has caused such unpleasant and personal reflections upon the characters of individuals ..., is now fortunately brought to a conclusion ..., to the satisfaction of all reasonable persons'.[62] Taken in conjunction with all the other indications, this outcome suggests strongly that Agar was determined to steer clear of the custom house dispute and the animosities it engendered.

The custom house rapidly became a *cause célèbre*, and probably did as little for the reputation and standing of the Agar family as James Agar of Ringwood's duel with Henry Flood. Early in 1774, a well informed observer reported to a friend in England: 'as to politics: violent contentions about a new bridge and custom house, and that's all I know of them.'[63] Later in the year, 'after the Commons had recommended an easterly site for the custom house, heads of a bill to enable the revenue board to buy land for the building fell foul of the privy council in London and failed to become law. In 1775 the same thing happened again'[64] and also in 1776. On the latter occasion, Ellis wrote triumphantly: 'The Custom House Bill is not returned'[65] – i.e. the British privy council had suppressed it. It was later alleged that 'Ellis and the attorney-general of England [James Wallace, were the influence] by whose means the scheme of a new

T/3719/C/34/39. **58** *Irish Lords' journals*, vii, pp 163, 183, 201, 238 and 310–11. **59** Auckland to Agar, 23 June 1795, T/3719/C/29/33; E.A. Smith, *Whig principles and party politics: Earl Fitzwilliam (1748–1833) and the Whig party* (Manchester, 1975), pp 191–3 and 210–12; Fitzwilliam to Portland, 3 Feb. 1795, Home Office papers, HO/100/56, f. 271; *Beresford correspondence*, ii, pp 49–120. **60** Draft report, [early summer 1795?], 21 M 57/A38. **61** *Irish Lords' journals*, vii, pp 361–2 and 467. **62** Camden to Portland, 31 Mar. [1796], HO/100/62, ff. 101–2. **63** Rev. Dr Thomas Foster to John Baker Holroyd, later 1st Lord Sheffield, 26 Feb. 1774, Stanley of Alderley/Sheffield papers, Cheshire RO: photocopy in PRONI, T/3725/2. **64** McParland, *Gandon*, p. 71. **65** Ellis to Pery, 23 Mar. 1776, Emly/Pery papers, Huntington Library, San Marino, California: photocopy in PRONI, T/3087/1/80.

bridge ... has so often miscarried'.[66] The fact that English influence at this level, and the power of the British privy council, had been invoked on one side of the dispute inevitably caused the proponents of a re-located custom house to try to trump this move. Harcourt's successor, Lord Buckinghamshire, who favoured re-location and was hostile to the Agar connection, thought it would 'not be amiss to talk to Lord North upon the subject'.[67] As first lord of the British treasury, North had departmental responsibility for the Irish revenue; as a prime minister waging a ruinously expensive war overseas and faced with a financial and economic crisis at home, he had the strongest motives for reforming the collection of that revenue and increasing its nett yield.[68] He is therefore likely to have been attracted by the idea of re-location and unsympathetic to the vested interests which stood in its way.

Within Ireland, Ellis and James Agar had a powerful supporter in Edmond Sexten Pery, speaker of the House of Commons (1771–85): years later, in December 1784, Ellis wrote to Pery referring to 'your friendship for me' and 'the many obligations I am proud to acknowledge myself under to you'.[69] Pery was not a member of the Agar connection. He was a heavyweight politician and a loner (as speaker he was, in any case, an *ex officio* loner); a modern authority has aptly called him 'a sort of litmus test of Irish parliamentary opinion'.[70] But it looks as if he must have been related by marriage to the Agar family. His first wife had been the daughter of one John Martin of Dublin, and Clifden's wife, Lucinda, was also (as has been seen) the daughter of a John Martin of Dublin. The connection is a little tenuous, in that Pery's first wife died in 1757, a year after their marriage, and Clifden did not marry her putative sister until 1760. But it was close enough to make Pery a periodic protagonist of the Agars, and *vice versa*, in spite of there being little politically in common between them – particularly between Pery and Bishop Charles Agar. (Agar privately considered him 'an enemy to every interference of the British legislature with regard to this country'; and Portland, the lord lieutenant who reluctantly conceded the constitution of 1782, called him 'the hollowest, most cunning, intriguing and hitherto successful knave in this kingdom'.[71]) In *c.*1776, Pery stated his 'willingness to do anything' to obtain a better bishopric, or an archbishopric, for Charles Agar;[72] and, reciprocally, James Agar delayed his acceptance of his peerage for several days in May–June 1776 in order to return himself for Gowran purely to vote for Pery's re-election as speaker. Later, in November 1780, Charles Agar, during an administration on which his influence was unusually strong, was to use his good offices to obtain a conditional promise of the next vacant bishopric for Pery's younger brother, then dean of inconveniently distant Derry.[73] On the custom house issue, Pery had the means to be, and was, an important

66 McParland, *Gandon*, p. 71.   67 Buckinghamshire to Heron, 1 Jan. 1778, NLI, Ms. 13036/1.   68 Germain to Buckinghamshire, 5 Oct. 1777, NLI, Ms. 13035/12.   69 Ellis to Pery, 31 Dec. 1784, *H.M.C Emly/Pery Mss.*, [*part 2*], p. 184.   70 Agar to Macartney, 26 Mar. 1780, *Macartney in Ireland*, p. 332.   71 Quoted in Malcomson, 'Speaker Pery and the Pery papers', in the *North Munster Antiquarian Journal*, vol. xvi (1973–4), p.39; James Kelly, *Prelude to Union: Anglo-Irish politics in the 1780s* (Cork, 1992), p. 100.   72 Clifden to Pery, [1776?], Emly/Pery papers, PRONI, T/3087/1/49.   73 Harcourt to Sir Archibald Acheson, 6th Bt, 29 May 1776, PRONI, Gosford papers, D/1606/

ally. The speakership, in spite of its nominal neutrality, gave him tactical and procedural opportunities to help or hinder a measure. Moreover, the views of Pery, as an individual, on matters of town planning would have carried great weight because he was renowned for his initiative in adding a grid-plan new town, Newtown Pery, to his native city of Limerick.[74]

In December 1778, when the archbishopric of Dublin fell vacant, Ellis and Clifden were still doggedly holding the line of Essex Bridge; but they were beginning to look like an entrenched vested interest, and an unpopular and, what was worse, a losing cause. This may well have been the view which Pery had begun to take of the matter – to judge from his reaction to Agar's candidature for the vacant archbishopric. At the beginning of December, Scott itemised – probably for the benefit of Lord North – all the prominent and influential people who would be soured if Agar were not promoted to fill the vacancy, and warned of 'a squeeze of lemon from the Speaker and Lord Clifden'.[75] A 'squeeze of lemon' does not suggest serious dissatisfaction – though the coupling of Pery with Clifden is odd, since Clifden certainly did exert himself heart and soul on Agar's behalf. He wrote to Agar: 'You must bury me if we fail, for I shall hardly survive it. ... Pery I shall see tomorrow and will make him, if possible, take an active part.'[76] There is no evidence that Pery did 'take an active part'. He was approaching the peak of his influence at this time: in 1779–80, to the private disapprobation of Agar,[77] he came near to being the arbiter of British policy towards Ireland. Had he exerted himself over the archbishopric, he would very probably have done so with effect. He may have been disinclined to Agar politically. But, more probably, he felt that, because of the custom house, he had for the time being done plenty for the Agar connection.

THE CONTEST FOR THE ARCHBISHOPRIC OF DUBLIN IN 1778

It has been argued, in general terms, that Irish electoral interest and the backing of an Irish political connection were unnecessary and even inappropriate to the making of an archbishop, especially when the aspirant concerned had personal claims as strong as Agar's. In the particular circumstances of December 1778, when the archbishopric of Dublin fell vacant, Agar's claims were undermined by his presumed association with Ellis and Clifden in a pursuit which was actually contrary to his wishes as well as his interests, and when the influence which the Agar connection normally possessed was heavily mortgaged to Clifden's peerage. In January 1779, following Agar's disappointment of the archbishopric, the lord lieutenant, Buckinghamshire, wrote as follows to his main, indeed sole, ally in the British cabinet, Lord George Germain:

1/85; Agar to Pery, 8 Nov. 1780, and reply, 18 Nov. 1780, T/3719/C/14/36 and 38. While archbishop of Cashel, Agar also used his influence in Limerick City and County on behalf of the Perys. **74** Judith Hill, *The building of Limerick* (new ed., Cork, 1997), pp 71–134.   **75** Scott to Ellis, 4 Dec. 1778, T/3719/C/12/29.   **76** Clifden to Agar, 5 Dec. 1778, T/3719/C/12/35.   **77** Agar to Macartney, 26 Mar. 1780, *Macartney in Ireland*, pp 331–2.

It is said that the friends of the Agar family express their dissatisfaction ... with a warmth bordering upon resentment. Yet, it appears to me that the favours of government have rather been lavished upon them. The Bishop of Cloyne, discontented as he may be, is morally sure of being recommended to the archbishopric of Cashel. Lord Clifden has just [1776] been created a peer and is a commissioner of the revenue ..., and I should suppose that Mr Ellys [*sic*], holding a capital office in England [the joint vice-treasurership for Ireland], is not entitled to advance claims here. Yet he had weight sufficient at Westminster to prevent the removal of the Dublin custom house ... . In this and in some other instances, English ministers are most amazingly mistaken with respect to the consequence of individuals here.[78]

Buckinghamshire's hostility to the Agars is of interest in itself. Paradoxically (and the paradox is a warning against applying the Namierite approach to political connection less subtly than Namier did), he was the only lord lieutenant of the period 1761–1801 with whom they had family and/or personal links, however distant: his sister was married to a Hotham, who was a first cousin of Gertrude Hotham, Welby's wife; and one of his closest friends was the Rt Hon. Hans Stanley of Paultons, whose sister and co-heiress was married to Ellis.[79] Lord George Germain, the recipient of Buckinghamshire's complaints, was a great protagonist of Agar's rival in the contest over the archbishopric of Dublin. And here, too, there is a paradox; for, George Agar was Germain's godson and had been called after him.[80]

Scott, who laboured most zealously on Agar's behalf at this time, saw it all as a Germain take-over bid for Ireland – though Germain was not the secretary of state with responsibility for that kingdom, but for the colonies (including North America), which it might be thought would have kept him sufficiently occupied. At the beginning of December 1778, Scott – in his already much-quoted letter written with a view to onward transmission to Lord North – declared that he had

great respect for Lord G.G. as a very civil gentleman and a man of abilities, but I have worked in another shop, have been substantially indebted to Lord North, and ... must be a damned scoundrel indeed if I have not some feeling of gratitude, or preference and attachment to that nobleman. Lord G.G. has already placed here an amiable dependant of his [Sir John Irwine] at the head of the army. The Primate is of the Dorset House. Another dependant in Dublin ... will give Lord G.G. almost every stronghold in this nation; and yet Lord North is the minister of England.[81]

---

78 Buckinghamshire to Germain, 14 Jan. 1779, *HMC Lothian Mss.*, p. 343. 79 Stanley to Buckinghamshire, 20 Mar. 1777, 3rd Lord Cadogan to Buckinghamshire, 15 Jan. 1780, and Ellis to Buckinghamshire, 15 and 27 Jan. 1780, *HMC Lothian Mss.*, pp 299–301 and 360–1. Stanley was at this time MP for Southampton and cofferer of the household to George III. 80 21 M 57/D48. 81 Scott to Ellis, 4 Dec. 1778, T/3719/C/12/29.

To Agar, Scott wrote more succinctly: 'The Primate and Lord G.G. have damned you'.[82] These are revealing comments. Agar's 'intemperate quarrel' with Sir John Irwine has already been mentioned (p. 87). It now begins to look, not like a sudden outburst, but one incident in a wider struggle for advantage.[83] Germain, who had changed his patronymic from 'Sackville', the family name of the dukes of Dorset, on inheriting an estate in Northamptonshire, had been chief secretary to his father, the 1st duke of Dorset, when the latter had been lord lieutenant, 1750–5. At that time both had fallen under the baneful influence of Primate Stone, who led them to defeat and discredit in a quite unnecessary power struggle with 'the Irish interest', then represented by Speaker Boyle. Robinson had come to Ireland in 1751 as Dorset's chaplain and had prospered subsequently under the patronage of Stone; so, in a non-genealogical sense, he was 'of the Dorset House'. The implication, however, is that 'the Dorset House' stood for 'the English interest' and Agar for the contrary. Agar, almost by the force of gravity, later (from December 1779) aligned himself with the only Irishman in the cabinet, the 1st earl of Hillsborough, who was the secretary of state with responsibility for Ireland, and on notoriously bad terms with Buckinghamshire.[84]

This opposition of the English to the Irish interest was fatal to Agar in 1778 and, later, in 1794 and 1800. In 1778, assuming that Robinson remained 'in fine preservation', three archbishoprics were imminently likely to fall vacant by reason of the age and infirmities of their incumbents – Dublin, Cashel and Tuam (in order of seniority, not infirmity). There was a loose convention in this period that the archbishoprics of Armagh and Dublin were reserved to Englishmen, and that mere Irishmen could aspire no higher than the archbishoprics of Cashel and Tuam.[85] This, at any rate, was the explanation, or rather excuse, offered to Agar and his backers when Robert Fowler, bishop of Killaloe, an Englishman, was leap-frogged over Agar to Dublin. It carried no conviction. Fowler had been bishop of Killaloe only since 1771, and therefore was somewhat junior to Agar in seniority as a bishop; Killaloe was a junior bishopric to Cloyne; and Fowler, a 'paltry, pragmatical man of straw'[86] (according to an Agar partisan), in no way came up to Scott's *résumé* of Agar as 'infinitely the first ecclesiastic' in the House of Lords. The 'reserved to Englishmen' rule had not been invariably applied to the archbishopric of Dublin: even since the death of William King in 1729, one incumbent, Arthur Smyth, archbishop, 1766–71, had been Irish. If ever there was

---

82 Scott to Agar, 3 Dec. 1778, T/3719/ C/12/27. Scott was correct in the leading part he assigned to Germain; see Buckinghamshire to Germain, 8 Dec. 1778, *HMC Stopford-Sackville Mss.*, i. 253. 83 For indications of an alliance between Irwine and Primate Robinson, see Irwine to Germain, 8 Dec. 1779, ibid., i. 263. It is interesting to note that, privately, Buckinghamshire concurred with Agar's view of Irwine's insufficiency and ridiculed it in similar language – Buckinghamshire to Hotham Thompson, 18 Apr. 1779, Hotham papers, PRONI, T/3429/1/44. 84 Agar to Hillsborough and, on the same date, to Ellis, 27 Dec. 1779, T/3719/C/13/49–50. 85 John Ryder, bishop of Down and Connor, to Wilmot, 25 Jan. 1752, Wilmot papers, PRONI, T/3019/1846; John Hotham, bishop of Clogher, to Germain, now 1st Viscount Sackville, 9 July 1782, *HMC Stopford-Sackville Mss.*, i. 279; Akenson, *Church of Ireland*, pp 24–5. 86 John Hamilton (the partisan and indiscreet military under-secretary in Dublin Castle) to Agar, 8 Dec. 1778, T/3719/C/12/43.

an occasion to set the rule aside, it was the present, not only because of Agar's infinite superiority to Fowler, but because Agar's brother, Welby, was a commissioner of customs in England, and Agar's uncle and principal backer, Ellis, was a member of the British government, and had considerable influence with the British prime minister. In the latter stages of Lord North's ministry, Ellis' influence, such as it was, was stronger than it had ever been before or ever would be again, until it culminated and terminated in his very short possession of Germain's office of secretary of state for the colonies. Actually, Ellis' lack of success on Agar's behalf derived partly from the fact that he persisted in behaving like an Irish politician and stating Agar's claims on Irish grounds. Meeting Buckinghamshire's chief secretary, Sir Richard Heron, in London, he reminded him of Clifden's 'five' (!) seats, and formed the impression that Heron was ignorant of the existence of the two Agar boroughs.[87] Heron was a notably incompetent chief secretary. But he obviously knew more about Clifden's current voting strength than, apparently, did Ellis.

Ellis also threw himself into a peculiarly Irish *imbroglio* over the governance of Trinity College, Dublin, warmly taking up the cause of the provost, Agar's friend, John Hely-Hutchinson. Hely-Hutchinson had been appointed provost of TCD on dubious political grounds, in July 1774. At that time, Ellis had expressed his anxiety 'that the government here should fill that place with a proper person. It concerns their own credit and the education and welfare of the youth of that country.'[88] Hely-Hutchinson hardly came up to Ellis' idea of 'a proper person'. His changes to the curriculum, his shifting of its emphasis to a more secular form of education, his favouritism towards some fellows and persecution of others, and his efforts to turn the university constituency into a Hely-Hutchinson borough, soon involved the college and himself in legal and pamphlet warfare. The attorney-general, Philip Tisdall, and Primate Robinson, who was both vice-chancellor and visitor of TCD, together led the counter-attack against him. One of Robinson's *protégés*, Dr Patrick Duigenan, a junior fellow who became regius professor of feudal and English law in 1776, supported them with scurrilous anti-Provost compilations, the first of them entitled *Pranceriana* – an allusion to Hely-Hutchinson's introduction of dancing lessons into the curriculum and to his 'prancing' – i.e. displays of oratory and independence – in the House of Commons,[89] and the second entitled *Lachrymae academicae*. At the end of April 1777, Hely-Hutchinson and Tisdall had a set-to in the law courts, during which the former called the latter an 'old scoundrel and a rascal' – words which Tisdall interpreted as a deliberate attempt to provoke him to a duel. He responded by initiating in June 1777 a crown prosecution of Hely-Hutchinson for incitement to a breach of the peace.[90] Buckinghamshire – out of his depth as usual – had decided to

87 Ellis to Agar, 5 Dec. 1778, T/3719/C/12/33.   88 Ellis to Agar, 23 June 1774, T/3719/C/8/4.
89 Hely-Hutchinson to Agar, 24 Nov. 1778, T/3719/C/12/21; Kelly, *Duelling in Ireland*, pp 131–2; Constantia Maxwell, *A history of Trinity College, Dublin, 1591–1892* (Dublin, 1946), pp 122–8; R.B. McDowell and D.A. Webb, *Trinity College, Dublin, 1592–1952: an academic history* (Cambridge, 1982), pp 51–8, 66 and 520–1; Richard Cumberland to Heron, 26 Apr. 1777, Ms. 13035/5.   90 Kelly, *Duelling in Ireland*, pp 167–8.

let the law take its course. Hely-Hutchinson, he wrote, 'has not many friends ... . The Primate, the Attorney-General and all the clergy [!] have determined his ruin. Should government interfere, they will not easily forgive it.'⁹¹ By the autumn of 1778, the prosecution of Hely-Hutchinson had reached the court of king's bench in England on appeal. Ellis, though fully aware that there were major faults on Hely-Hutchinson's side, now busied himself in getting it stopped. Early in November 1778, he reported smugly to Agar that he had carried this point, but 'under the condition of his [Hely-Hutchinson's] asking it as a favour of the Castle. This I think is no more than fair, and I intimated to him in my first letter that I should solicit it, but on the foot of its passing through the proper medium.'⁹²

At first sight, it might appear that TCD was as wasteful a side-issue for the Agar connection as the Dublin custom house; and, certainly, there was an element of officiousness in Ellis' intervention. However, there was good reason for Agar to make common cause with Hely-Hutchinson, since both were under attack from Primate Robinson and his allies. The archbishop of Dublin was an *ex officio* visitor of the university and therefore a potential counterpoise to Robinson. The dying Archbishop Cradock had been censured by Duigenan in *Lachrymae academicae* for allegedly favouring Hely-Hutchinson;⁹³ and Hely-Hutchinson wrote to Agar in late November declaring his 'official interest in being placed under your Lordship's immediate protection'. (He added: 'There is a valuable lease of this see near expiring'.)⁹⁴ Scott saw Agar's and Hely-Hutchinson's interests as inextricably intertwined; according to Scott, it was vital to both of them to prevent the appointment of 'an humble slave of the Primate's' as archbishop of Dublin. If Robinson carried this point, he would,

> as a visitor of our university, ... again throw everything there into tumult and confusion and actually rout the Provost, as well as by religious faction ruin the college to restore it to the arms of the Church. ... The Provost, from the deadly hatred which subsists between the Primate and him, will do all manner of mischief ... . That evil would be prevented by putting the Bishop of Cloyne to Dublin, whose abilities will keep the Primate quiet as they have hitherto diminished his Grace's infallibility and absolute sway.⁹⁵

The centrality of the Robinson-Agar antagonism is repeatedly emphasised. Shortly afterwards, a Dublin Castle official wrote privately to Agar: 'you have talents which the Pri[mate] does not possess. He hates you for it and will endeavour to prevent your standing in his way.'⁹⁶ Writing in February 1779, Lord Shannon commented: 'I am satisfied that, had my neighbour [at Cloyne] succeeded in Dublin, there would have been a strong junta against the Primate, and so there will when he goes to Cashel.'⁹⁷

---

91 Buckinghamshire to Germain, 14 May 1777, NLI, Ms. 13035/6.   92 Ellis to Agar, 9 Nov. 1778, T/3719/C/12/17.   93 Kennedy, 'Dublin and Glendalough', p. 205.   94 Hely-Hutchinson to Agar, 27 Nov. 1778, T/3719/C/12/23.   95 Scott to Ellis, 4 Dec. 1778, T/3719/C/12/29.   96 John Hamilton to Agar, 8 Dec. 1778, T/3719/C/12/43.   97 Shannon to James Dennis, 28 Feb. 1779, Shannon papers, PRONI, D/2707/A/2/3/56.

Independently of the Agar-Robinson antagonism, Agar also had reason to be hostile to Robinson's ally in the battle over TCD, Attorney-General Tisdall. Tisdall was the keystone of the ministerial arrangements which had been made at the beginning of Buckinghamshire's administration and which tended towards the exclusion of the Agars and their allies. These arrangements involved extruding some of the old Castle gang (particularly Hely-Hutchinson), reducing the influence of others (Scott, John Beresford and Agar) and introducing some new blood. The new blood came from Buckinghamshire's family connections in Ireland, which over- lapped with Tisdall's political connections. Thomas Conolly of Castletown, Co. Kildare, Buckinghamshire's brother-in-law, and Conolly's brother-in-law, the 2nd duke of Leinster, became Buckinghamshire's most important advisers from the sidelines; Walter Hussey Burgh, a satellite of Leinster, was made prime serjeant; and John Foster (the future speaker), who was Tisdall's *protégé* and Burgh's brother-in-law, was made chancellor of the exchequer in all but name. Because of Burgh's, Conolly's and Leinster's previous politics, this group of advisers gave the administration a popular and 'Patriot' look. But there was nothing popular or 'Patriot' about Tisdall, who was intended to give direction, cohesion and ballast to what was otherwise a high-risk combination.[98] One of its riskiest features was his advanced age (he was seventy-five). He died suddenly in September 1777 (to be succeeded by Scott), and his disappearance from the scene made the composition of the Buckinghamshire administration appear more tessellated than it originally had been, and exposed its 'Patriot' bias to damaging attack.

Foremost among the attackers was Agar, who in a succession of letters addressed to Ellis, but intended for North, reiterated the view that every plan was abortive

> that can be suggested for forming an administration under our present chief governor. First, he himself is a man of neither abilities or [*sic*] resolution. Secondly, his secretary [Heron] is inferior in both respects to himself, if that be possible. Thirdly, he is so attached to Mr C[onoll]y ... and to Mr B[ur]gh, our late prime serjeant, who is himself a worshipper of popular applause and the principal director of the duke of L[einster], ... that I consider him both as unwilling and unable to act spiritedly and decidedly in favour of Lord North. He received from his predecessor a very respectable and sufficient majority. [But] in compliance with his own prejudices and predilections, the favours of government were engrossed, its means diminished and its influence so reduced that at this moment a majority must depend altogether upon the popularity of the measure and not upon the support it receives from the Castle. ... I often expressed a wish that Lord North could send to us a man of spirit and ability whom he knows to be his friend. Until this shall be done, you must expect frequent and unpleasant disappointments. Lord North's friends here see with pain too often what they condemn but cannot correct.[99]

98 Malcomson, *John Foster*, pp 33–4; Buckinghamshire to Germain, 31 Oct. 1777 and 28 Oct. 1779, *HMC Stopford-Sackville Mss.*, i, pp 246 and 259.   99 Agar to Ellis, 27 Dec. 1779, T/3719/C/13/50.

Although written a year after the adverse decision on the archbishopric of Dublin, this is the best surviving version of sentiments he had 'often expressed' before that event, always with the intention that Ellis would pass them on to North. Ellis, it would seem, fulfilled this intention rather feebly. In November 1778, he reported – as if this was a big break-through – that 'in conversation with L[ord] N[orth], I happened in speaking of the Irish affairs to quote your name, upon which he said, "The Bishop of Cloyne is a very sincere and hearty friend of ours". I thought that you would not be sorry to receive that anecdote.'[100] The 'anecdote' actually suggests that Ellis, in his role of intermediary and negotiator, was easily fobbed off with meaningless pleasantries, of which the weary, indolent and much-harassed North was a past master.

Measures as well as men made Agar antagonistic to the Buckinghamshire admin- istration – in particular, the measures of concession to Irish catholics and dissenters favoured by Buckinghamshire and his advisers, and anathema to nearly all churchmen. In Great Britain, North's government had combined 'a more sympathetic catholic policy with a softening of legal restrictions on dissenters', and from late 1777 had become convinced that a measure of relief for Irish catholics was 'essential for security reasons during the war'.[101] Agar knew that an Irish Catholic Relief Act was unavoid- able: his concern was to prevent Buckinghamshire from making much greater, and political, concessions to Irish non-Anglicans in order to counter the threefold threat of invasion, mass emigration from Ireland and a shortfall in recruitment for the British forces. Deftly, Agar expressed his sentiments in terms which gave them applicability to English circumstances. Arguing in late June 1778 against the return of the Catholic Relief Bill (which by now had the clause repealing the Sacramental Test tacked on to it), Agar asked Ellis rhetorically: 'If the bill be sent back to us as it now is, what will the dissenters of England say, to whom a similar indulgence has been repeatedly refused? ... Were I to advise, you should suppress the *whole bill at present*, and in the next session of parliament all proper and reasonable concessions will I am sure be made to the papists.'[102] Agar's ideas for 'proper and reasonable concessions ... to the papists' included the sensible one that the 'absurd and disgraceful' penalties still attaching to the practice of their religion should be removed as a higher priority than 'granting indulgences ... in respect to their *property*'.[103] (English catholics had been granted a legal toleration earlier in 1778, but Irish catholics not until 1782.) As a churchman, he urged that some inducements to conformity on the part of propertied

---

100 Ellis to Agar, 9 Nov. 1778, T/3719/C/12/17.   101 G.M. Ditchfield, 'Ecclesiastical policy under Lord North', in Walsh, Taylor and Haydon (eds.), *The Church of England, c.1689–c.1833*, p. 240; Maureen Wall, 'The quest for Catholic equality, 1745–78', in Gerard O'Brien (ed.), *Catholic Ireland in the eighteenth century: the collected essays of Maureen Wall* (Dublin, 1989), pp 125–33.   102 Agar to Ellis, 24 June 1778, T/3719/C/12/10B.   103 This view was shared by the catholics' strong advocate, Frederick Hervey, bishop of Derry (Wall, op. cit., p. 132). The only possible explanation is a purely pragmatic one: 'While the religious provisions of the penal laws had been for many years dead letters on the face of the statutes, the property provisions had continued alive and threatening and requiring only the greed of men to put them into operation' – Patrick Fagan, *Divided loyalties: the question of the oath for Irish catholics in the eighteenth century* (Dublin, 1997), p. 162.

catholics should be retained. As a practical man, knowledgeable of human nature, he thought that the bill should not 'lavish everything at once on' the catholics; they should be allowed to become '*tenants* on the very best terms', not given the opportunity to become owners by collusion. Indeed, rather than leave an opening for ownership by collusion, he thought it would be wiser to let them own land outright, but 'subject to gavel' (i.e. equal division among their children). The weakness of these arguments, as he acknowledged, was that the bill as it then stood 'allow[ed] the papists here the same privileges [in regard to property] which have been granted to them in England by your late acts of parliament'.[104]

The proposed repeal of the Test, however, stood on a quite different footing. This continued to be 'repeatedly refused' in England until 1828. In 1778, the British privy council suppressed that clause of the Irish Relief Bill, and North was still most reluctant to concede the repeal in 1780, when pressed even more strongly to do so by Buckinghamshire and his advisers.[105] (Thomas Conolly, for one, sat for the northern constituency of Co. Londonderry, where the influence of the dissenters was strong.) North must have approved Agar's speech on the bill in the House of Lords, made (with some political courage) after it had unanimously passed the House of Commons:

> He was, he said, a friend to toleration when it did not interfere with the principles of the constitution in Church and State, but the removal of the Sacramental Test left the first offices of the state open to Turk, Jew, infidel and papist. Every country, he continued, had some established religion, and it was the custom for a state, however tolerant, to confine its positions of honour and trust to those of the established religion. Should the Irish parliament, added the Archbishop, set itself against the wisdom of the ages and enlightened nations?[106]

North, however, did not feel strong enough in 1780, as he had in 1778, to suppress the bill in the British privy council. So, it became law as *19 and 20 George III, cap. 6*.

This is to anticipate. In the summer of 1778, Agar's representations, and Scott's earlier-quoted letter about Lord George Germain's gaining 'every stronghold in this nation', were penned not only for the purpose of defeating or modifying particular measures, but also with the general aim of rousing North to recall and replace Buckinghamshire. In late November 1778, not long before the archbishop of Dublin died, Agar had good grounds for thinking that there was about to be a change of lord lieutenant.[107] Buckinghamshire, for his part, was always aware of the threat to his position from 'a paltry faction inimical to me'[108] and their machinations behind his back in England: hence his complaint, quoted at the beginning of this Chapter, that

104 Ibid. For the 'gavel' clause and, more generally, the best modern discussion of the Penal Laws, see Conolly, *Religion, law and power*, Chapter Seven. 105 Maurice R. O'Connell, *Irish politics and social conflict in the age of the American Revolution* (Philadelphia, 1965), p. 207. 106 Ibid., pp 208–9. 107 Scott to Agar, 11 Nov. 1778, and John Hamilton to Agar, 28 Nov. 1778, T/3719/ C/12/18 and 24. 108 Quoted in Malcomson, *John Foster*, p. 36.

'The Beresfords and the Agars bask in the sunshine of cabinet favour'. He was in correspondence with Ellis' brother-in-law, Hans Stanley, and through him may have sought to soften Ellis' hostility by explaining at great length (as he did to many people) the difficulties of his situation.[109] But his more usual response was to invoke the aid of his own friends in British government circles, notably Germain. Two other factors favoured him. One was the characteristic inertia of North, who on this occasion had the good excuse that it would be extraordinarily difficult to find anyone willing to succeed Buckinghamshire at a time of such risk and responsibility. The other was the Agar-Beresford feud over the custom house. Buckinghamshire was actually facing, not one inimical faction, but two, who were not united in their opposition to him. The 'sunshine of cabinet favour' in which the Beresfords basked was reflected from North's joint secretary to the treasury and parliamentary manager, John Robinson (no relation of the Primate), who was an intimate of John Beresford (and also a friend of Scott).[110] John Robinson was much subtler and more successful than Ellis in bringing North to decisions (for example, the decision of early 1780 that Buckinghamshire should be called upon to accept Beresford as his chief secretary in lieu of Heron).[111] Although there is no direct evidence of this, he is likely, because of his regard for Beresford and concern for the interests of the British treasury and the Irish revenue, to have taken a poor view of the Agar connection. Since Bishop Charles Agar was guilty by association with Ellis and Clifden, John Robinson may well have encouraged North to stay out of the disputed succession to the archbishopric of Dublin.

In early December 1778, a still-optimistic Agarite mole in Dublin Castle thought that 'the Fowler' had 'overshot his mark'.[112] It was actually the Agars who had over-shot theirs. They had brought influence to bear at too high and inappropriate a level, and had by passed 'the proper medium' for such applications. They had also turned the filling of an Irish archbishopric – not normally a matter of very serious concern unless it was Armagh – into an issue of confidence in the lord lieutenant and a source of division within the British cabinet in the middle of a world war. As Primate Robinson smugly reassured Chief Secretary Heron in mid-December, on the eve of the *dénouement*, 'The English ministry have sometimes interposed when they wished to promote a bishop from the English bench, but in cases of translations, the lord lieutenant has always been understood as the sole judge. ... The Bishop of Cloyne's friends in England will soon see that the lord lieutenant's recommendation must finally

109 Buckinghamshire to Stanley, 9 Apr. 1779, Macintosh collection, BL., Add. Ms. 34523, f. 193. **110** Scott to Robinson, 21 and 26 Nov. 1779, and Beresford to Robinson, 22 and 26 Nov. 1779, *Beresford correspondence*, i, pp 81–95. **111** North to Buckinghamshire, 18 Feb. 1780, NLI, Ms. 13039/3; Agar to Macartney, 26 Mar. 1780, *Macartney in Ireland*, p. 331. In this letter, Agar reports how Buckinghamshire 'resisted manfully the recommendation of Beresford' and that 'Sir Richard Heron is to return to us to finish the session with the same splendid abilities which have hitherto produced such extraordinary effects'. See also Malcomson, *John Foster*, pp 41–2. **112** John Butler to Agar, 5 Dec. 1778, T/3719/C/12/34. Butler was first clerk in the military department of Dublin Castle, 1777–82. The more important mole was his superior, John Hamilton, the military under-secretary. Hamilton had the additional advantage of being a cousin of North – North to Buckinghamshire, 6 Feb. 1780, Ms. 13039/3.

prevail.'[113] However understandable the decision of 'the Bishop of Cloyne's friends in England' to take up the cause of Hely-Hutchinson with the British government, this had been a tactical error. It had given Robinson the opportunity to call in Germain, and to bring what Scott called Robinson's 'Machiavellian cunning and hypocrisy'[114] to bear on the filling of the archbishopric. The primate had actually no formal role, even a consultative one, in Irish episcopal appointments; his influence over such things varied from primate to primate and according to the circumstances of the time. In the circumstances of late 1778, Buckinghamshire and Germain were only too happy to have the authority of the head of the Church to back their purely political decision. Buckinghamshire then raised the stakes still higher by announcing that he would resign if Fowler were not made archbishop of Dublin.[115] Heron, who was in London at the time, communicated this threat to North. Often, the prime minister could not be brought to give attention to really serious business, but on 12 December he had submitted to a meeting with Heron on the sole subject of 'the succession to Dublin'.[116] When Fowler's appointment was announced, Agar seems – unwisely – to have written to Buckinghamshire complaining about the way in which Agar had been passed over. He received the tart rejoinder that, if 'there have been any solicitations urged in an unaccustomed mode and pressed with particular energy, they did not proceed from a lord lieutenant'.[117] In the same letter Buckinghamshire did at least refer guardedly to the failure of the archbishop of Cashel to die and thus give Buckinghamshire an opportunity to oblige Agar. In this he was disregarding the advice of the implacable primate, who had warned that 'A promise of Cashel ... will give a security that may prove inconvenient to the lord lieutenant'.[118]

The Agar connection's greatest mistake had been to intrigue prematurely for the recall of Buckinghamshire. They were understandably alienated by Buckingham-shire's preference for other and less orthodox advisers; and Agar, as the churchman of the family, would have been a time-server if he had not championed the cause of the Established Church. But self-interest required that they temporise until he was safely translated to Dublin. As matters stood in December 1778, Agar was fatally vulnerable to the charge that he belonged to a family connection which was too powerful already, too well rewarded, too pushy and too Irish. The outcome would probably have been different if the vacancy in Dublin had come a year or more later. Towards the end of 1779, with Agar now promoted to Cashel, North sent an unofficial envoy to Ireland to assess the situation (and sound out the possibilities for a union); and his choice of envoy may have been Ellis- and Agar-inspired, because it was Lord Macartney, who had the good pretext of his north Antrim estate for paying a visit to Ireland.[119] Agar's forthright and forceful letters to Macartney about the imbecility of the Buckingham-shire administration and the virtual collapse of English government in Ireland,[120] must

---

113 Robinson to Heron, 19 Dec. 1778, Ms. 13036/13. 114 Scott to Agar, 21 Dec. 1778, T/3719/C/12/61. 115 14 Dec. 1778, Ms. 13061. 116 Heron to Buckinghamshire, 12 Dec. 1778, *ibid.* 117 Buckinghamshire to Agar, 3 Jan. 1779, T/3719/C/12/1. 118 Robinson to Heron, 19 Dec. 1779, Ms. 13036/13. 119 North to Buckinghamshire, 19 Dec. 1779, Ms. 13038/18. 120 Correspondence between Macartney and Agar, 21 Jan.–26 Mar. 1780, T/3719/C/14/4–17, and

have made an impression on North. Another disastrous session of the Irish parliament ensued, during which the repeal of the Test was not the bitterest of the many pills which North had to swallow. These events seemed to bear out all the criticisms made by Agar. Buckinghamshire was at last recalled in October 1780. The success then achieved by his able replacement, the 5th earl of Carlisle, and the latter's astute chief secretary, William Eden,[121] whose task was made the more difficult by all that Buckinghamshire had conceded before their arrival, gave retrospective support to the Agar view of 1778–80 that the main reason for the Castle's loss of control of the Irish parliament was Buckinghamshire. There is little doubt that, if the archbishopric of Dublin had fallen vacant in 1780, Agar would have got it. More to the point, he would probably have got it in 1778 if he had not been part of an over-ambitious political connection which had over-shot their mark.

COMPROMISE OVER THE CUSTOM HOUSE, 1780–86

At about the same time as the change of Irish administration in 1780, the struggle over the custom house came to an issue. In spite of Ellis' success up to 1776, and a respite in the intervening years, it was clear that in the long term, nothing could

> prevail over the inevitability of a new bridge, or the might of the ruling party among the revenue commissioners ... . In 1780 the pace of events quickened, thanks partly to the condition of the old custom house ..., [which was so bad that it was feared] that 'the first violent storm may damage it very materially'. [John] Beresford was appointed chief commissioner ... and in December 1780 returned to Dublin with [his chosen architect, the Englishman, James] Gandon's, first hasty sketches for the building. ... [On 8 August 1781], the foundation stone of the new custom house on its new site was laid by ... Beresford.[122]

The building of a new bridge and the re-location of the custom house, made it possible to build or complete two grand avenues linking the Gardiner estate with the south side of the city – one down Gardiner's Mall and Sackville Street over the new bridge (ingratiatingly named Carlisle Bridge) to the Parliament House, the other from Mountjoy Square down Gardiner Street to the new custom house itself, which it reached at the more appropriately named Beresford Place (begun in 1790).[123] So, thanks mainly to geography and considerations of town-planning, Beresford, Gardiner and the wide streets commissioners were at last victorious in the struggle with the merchants and the property-owners in the old city, led by Ellis and Clifden.

But Ellis and Clifden, though defeated, were successful in exacting a price for their eventual complaisance ... by securing a site upstream for the law courts. The decision to build the law courts on the Inns Quay in the neighbourhood of the Ellis property was taken in 1781, thus ... [prompting the satirical suggestion] of *The Dublin Evening Post* for 17 April 1781 ... '[that those] by whose means the scheme of a new bridge ... has so often miscarried, have been *convinced* how much such a measure must prove beneficial to Dublin'.[124]

Ellis himself acknowledged that 'The plan which was adopted in Mr Eden's administration of building the public offices and the Four Courts on the Inns Quay, being in the neighbourhood of my property, ... [will] be of great advantage to me.'[125] In December 1784, there was a last blip (apparently resolved through the intervention, at Ellis' entreaty, of Speaker Pery). Matters thereafter proceeded according to Ellis' wishes. The earliest known drawing for the Four Courts, more-or-less as built, is dated 1785. On 13 March 1786, the foundation stone was laid. The architect, as in the case of the custom house, was James Gandon who, however, did not have as free a hand with the Four Courts because of the constricted nature of the site and the false starts already made. In order to improve the approach to and vista of the Four Courts (and of course to improve the Ellis estate), Clifden proposed in April 1786 'the building of a bridge opposite the portico and the opening of approaches to it from High Street ... . As late as 1813 Gandon ... [expressed] the opinion that such a bridge could, if carefully handled, be "a very great improvement".'[126] The custom house, begun in 1781, was completed in 1791, and the Four Courts, begun in 1786, was completed in 1796. So, with a short limbo period, Ellis' estate was compensated for the loss of one public building by the erection of another.

Since nearly all the estate lay on the north bank of the Liffey (the opposite side from the old custom house), stretching from Arran Quay to the gates of Phoenix Park, the exchange was actually to Ellis' advantage. The short-term effect was dramatic. One holding currently let for £12 per annum, was revalued in 1796 as being worth no less than £710 per annum, and was expected by Agar to be worth more than that when the lease expired in 22 years time, because of 'the improvements made in that part of the town by the building of the Four Courts, etc.' (The entire Dublin City estate had had a rental of only £803 in the 1770s.) These calculations, however, proved highly optimistic.[127] Sooner rather than later, the Ellis estate fell into decline with the drift of fashionable Dublin to the south and east and the depreciating impact of the Union on Dublin City property.[128] In other words, the somewhat discreditable campaign fought

124 Ibid., pp 150–4.   125 Ellis to Pery, 31 Dec. 1784, *HMC Various*, p. 184.   126 McParland, *Gandon*, pp 149, 159 and 198.   127 Mendip to Agar, 22 Feb. 1796, T/3719/C/30/4; calculations by Agar 'on Mr Groom's holding', 1802, 21 M 57/D26/3; rental of Ellis' various Irish estates, [*c.*1770s], 21 M 57/D26/2.   128 Report on the Ellis estate in Dublin city, [*c.*1870?], NLI, Ms. 8796/2; leases of Dublin City premises, 1882, 1886, 1891 and 1947, NLI, D 10685–10692; Annaly/ Clifden papers, F/8/2; Charles William Hamilton's report, [*c.*1870], Hamwood papers, A/25/3. For other evidence of this trend, see pp 257 and 413–14.

by Ellis and Clifden was a waste of effort in the long term, while in the short it damaged the reputation of the Agar connection and with it, however undeservedly, the reputation of Archbishop Charles Agar.

THE AGAR CONNECTION DIVIDED BETWEEN PITT AND FOX, 1783–8

Following Agar's disappointment of Dublin in December 1778 and his acceptance of the consolation prize of Cashel in August 1779, further opportunities for his advancement did not actually arise until, first, 1794, when Primate Robinson died, next, 1800, when Primate Newcome did likewise, and finally, 1801, when Archbishop Fowler at last followed them. With hindsight, therefore, a fifteen-year waiting period lay ahead. But that was not apparent at the time, when Agar's ambition for the primacy was as well known as were Robinson's advancing years and ill-health. What Agar failed to do during those fifteen years was establish at least a moral claim to the primacy – in the way that FitzGibbon did to the lord chancellorship (which did not fall vacant until 1789) during the duke of Rutland's lord lieutenancy in 1784–7.[129] The comparison is valid, because FitzGibbon was much the younger and junior man, and the lord chancellorship, like the primacy, was a post which had long been reserved to Englishmen. In 1781, Lord Carlisle had opened the campaign for an Irish lord chancellor of Ireland in a sensible and indeed eloquent letter which was wasted on its curmudgeonly addressee, the lord chancellor of England, Lord Thurlow. If, Carlisle argued, there were good reasons for thinking

> that the being born and connected here [Ireland] would give a bias and inclination unfavourable to ... the superintending power [of England], such a recommendation ought to be without ceremony dismissed and rejected. [However, if another Englishman is] ... raised to this situation, he enters upon an honourable banishment for life: new connections must be found to repair the loss of those he had abandoned, new friendships are to be acquired, new admirers, if his abilities are splendid, are to be attracted; and in the anxious endeavour to show that there is no remnant about him of partial inclination for any other air or soil, the very mischief and danger may be incurred, to guard against which was the motive of the choice.[130]

The same reasoning applied, of course, to the primacy, and had been exemplified by Primate Stone.

One major reason (apart from the most important – English prejudice) for Agar's failure to establish a claim to the primacy in the period 1779, was that, following the Rightboy disturbances in Munster in 1785–7, the government attempted in 1786 and

129 Ashbourne, *Pitt*, pp 255–6.   130 Carlisle to Thurlow, 1 July 1781, *HMC Carlisle Mss.*, p. 513.

again in 1788 to devise and impose plans for the reform of the Church of Ireland, to which he gave dogged and effective opposition (see pp 230–40). This – like his opposition to the religious policies of Buckinghamshire in 1778–80 – was high-principled, but imprudent. As Clonmell cynically put it, 'Irish political advancement, humiliating as it is, can be attained but by cultivating Englishmen and being well with the secretaries and dependents of English government.'[131] Another major reason for Agar's failure was that, for most of the fifteen years, Ellis had no influence in British government circles because, having led the Agars a merry dance round Dublin city and obtained next-to-nothing for them from Lord North, he had followed North into opposition. Ellis' going into opposition is perhaps the most deafening 'not said' of Agar's correspondence. Though never alluded to, there was between 1783 and 1794 a tug of war between the Agar connection's affiliations to Ellis in British politics and its aims and objectives as an Irish parliamentary group. Ellis was almost seventy when North fell from power in 1782, had plenty of money (his own and that of both his wives) and, as things turned out, should have retired from politics. However, he hankered after a British peerage. This would be of limited advantage to himself, because he had no children; but it would be of advantage to Clifden, assuming that Ellis could obtain the already-mentioned special remainder to the issue male of his sister, Anne Agar. As a result, having joined North in opposition to the Rockingham and Shelburne administrations (1782–3), Ellis then joined him in his alliance with the Foxite Whigs, and almost obtained the coveted peerage from the Fox–North Coalition in May 1783.[132] Following the Coalition's dismissal, he was described by Wraxall as 'occupying during several years a distinguished place in the opposition under Lord North and Fox'; with North's increasing decrepitude and loss of interest in politics, Ellis was given the less flattering description of 'Fox's jackal'.[133]

Meanwhile, during this period of almost invariable opposition on Ellis' part, the Agar connection in Ireland as invariably supported the Irish branch of the British government of the day – with one exception – until the Regency Crisis of 1788–9. The one exception was the administration of the 3rd duke of Portland, lord lieutenant, April–July 1782. Agar had formed a close political and personal relationship with the outgoing chief secretary, William Eden, whose 'hasty'[134] supersession, in Agar's view, undid all Eden's skilful work of parliamentary management and encouraged those very motions for legislative independence which Portland was anxious to avert.[135] Portland, however, had his own agenda, and the mouths of many Irish Whigs and fellow-travellers to feed. He therefore carried out a 'general sweep'[136] which removed, not only Eden, but Agar and many long-tried and experienced Irish advisers of previous Dublin Castle administrations. Agar, though he was excluded from confidence,[137] held no office from which it was possible to dismiss him. Scott was

131 *Clonmell diary (TCD)*, p. 220.   132 Scott to Agar, 19 May 1783, T/3719/C/17/15.   133 *The complete peerage*, sub 'Mendip'; Malcomson, *John Foster*, p. 401.   134 Agar's political memoranda, 1782–95, 21 M 57/A18, *sub* 14 Apr. 1782.   135 Kavanaugh, *Lord Clare*, pp 53–5; Agar to his brother, Welby, 11 July 1782, T/3719/C/16/4.   136 Malcomson, *John Foster*, p. 375.   137 Agar to

dismissed as attorney-general, allegedly because of 'the extreme profligacy and want of principle which he publicly avowed and boasted of'. Scott now described himself humorously as a 'poor, degraded, dowagered attorney-general', while Portland soon found to his cost that Scott had 'it in his power to do ... much mischief' and was 'formidable' in 'opposition'.[138]

When North, with Ellis in tow, entered into the coalition with Fox, the nominal head of the government they formed in April 1783 was none other than Portland. But, because this was a coalition, it did not pursue in Ireland the exclusively Whig agenda of April–July 1782: Agar was received back into confidence, and office was about to be found for even Scott when the Coalition was ousted in December 1783. Nevertheless, there was at this stage no love lost between the Agar connection in Ireland and Ellis' new party chief in England. In September 1783, it was reported: 'Several powerful individuals are dissatisfied, amongst others, Lord Clifden ... . [But] Clifden is not stout-hearted enough to oppose; he will growl, but he dares not bite.'[139] The Coalition were aware of Clifden's dissatisfaction, and hoped to mollify him with the special remainder. Their lord lieutenant, the 2nd earl of Northington, wrote to Portland that, if Ellis were made a British peer, the remainder should be represented as a favour emanating from the Irish administration. Clifden, Northington added, was going to return his son for Co. Kilkenny and four friends for his two boroughs at the forthcoming general election.[140] North was then appealed to to use his influence with Ellis to persuade the 'Archbishop of Cashel and the numerous dependencys [*sic*] and connections of Lord Clifden' to support the Irish administration.[141] Clifden's growling was not so much over the non-delivery of the British peerage, as over the inadequacy of his current office to his (and his brothers') notion of his own political consequence. He had been a commissioner of the revenue at £1,000 a year since 1772 and, following the compromise on the custom house in 1781, had no ulterior motive for staying in that post. Yet, in the short time at its disposal, the Coalition did nothing to better his condition. Its time was short because of the hostility of George III. It fell from power at the end of 1783, to be succeeded by the King's choice, William Pitt the younger, who headed an initially weak and precarious ministry.

The ensuing reverberations and negotiations in Ireland were graphically reported to the fallen Coalition's parliamentary manager, John Robinson, by his friend, John Beresford, in April 1784:

10th earl of Westmorland, 2 Mar. 1795, T/3719/C/29/7. **138** Portland (writing as prime minister during the Fox-North Coalition) to Thomas Pelham (the chief secretary), 27 Oct. 1783, and undated reply, PRONI transcripts of the Pelham papers in BL, T/755/1, pp 255–9; Scott to Agar, 19 May 1783, T/3719/C/17/15. I am grateful for the first two references to his Honour, Judge A.R. Hart, who kindly lent me, prior to its publication, the part of the text of his book, *A history of the king's serjeants at law in Ireland: honour rather than advantage?* (Dublin, 2000) which relates to Scott. The relevant pages are pp 98–101. **139** 2nd earl of Mornington to W.W. Grenville, 15 Sep 1783, *HMC Dropmore Mss, i. 220.* **140** Northington to Portland, 4 July 1783, Northington letter-book, BL, Add. Ms. 38716, ff. 41–2; North to Northington, 11 July 1783, Pelham papers, BL, Add. Ms. 33118, ff. 193–5. **141** Quoted in James Kelly, *Prelude to Union*, p. 67.

On the arrival of our present government [Rutland and his chief secretary, Thomas Orde], things turned out precisely as I stated them in London. The duke of Leinster declared himself totally attached to Mr Fox ...; Lord Clifden and the Archbishop had heard from Ellis, but did not choose to work for nothing. Thus things stood, and the parties threatened opposition. However, negotiation took place. Conolly professed support; Clifden and his brother demanded *quid pro quo*, and were rather stout; but I encouraged Orde and spoke to both of them myself strongly, and brought them to reason. Luckily, the duke of Leinster had got scent of a new office, president of the council, demanded it, and resigned his pretensions to the post office, which just suited Clifden and secured him. His brother, however, being told that his demand [for a promise of the primacy] could not be complied with, they struck.[142] But the two members for Callan have declared to Orde that they are a distinct company, which lowered his numbers to five,[143]

and brought Clifden and Agar back to heel. The primacy – like the other top positions in the Church of Ireland, only more so – was never going to be promised or filled on the basis of voting strength in the Irish House of Commons. The Agars' other '*quid pro quo*', the joint postmastership-general for Clifden, was a different matter. It was a new, prestigious office, deriving from the separation of the Irish postal service from that of Great Britain; and with a salary of £1,500 per annum, it was exactly the level of office Clifden's siblings and he had had in mind.[144] The colleague he was given as joint postmaster-general was W.B. Ponsonby, a prominent Portlandite, who 'was left to himself [by Portland] and ... closed with government'.[145] He was also Henry Welbore Agar's colleague as MP for Co. Kilkenny, which gave the new Irish post office a parish-pump appearance. In August 1784, Clifden and Ponsonby were both made privy councillors.[146] In September of the following year, 1785, H.W. Agar himself received an office, the clerkship to the privy council, worth *c.*£950 per annum (made vacant by the death of the 1st Viscount Sackville, formerly Lord George Germain). His father, Clifden, did not long enjoy the *otium cum dignitate* of the post office, because he died at the very beginning of 1789. This at least relieved him from the perplexity of deciding what part to take, or which party to adhere to, in the looming crisis created by 'the madness of King George'.

---

142 This must be a misreading, possibly of 'stuck'. In the later eighteenth-century, 'struck' did not mean 'went on strike', but 'struck one's colours', i.e. surrendered; which is the opposite of Beresford's meaning. The point cannot be checked, as the whereabouts of the original of the letter are unknown.   143 Beresford to Robinson, 11 Apr. 1784, *Beresford correspondence*, i, pp 253–5.   144 Clifden to Agar, [pre-2 July 1784], T/3719/C/18/11; Bishop Barnard to Buckinghamshire, 7 July 1784, Heron papers, NLI, Ms. 13047/3.   145 Beresford to Robinson, 11 Apr. 1784, *Beresford correspondence*, i, pp 253–5.   146 Sydney to Rutland, 12 Aug. 1784, *HMC Rutland Mss.*, iii. 131.

THE REGENCY CRISIS OF 1788–9

The Regency Crisis was a traumatic event for many Irish political connections, for example that of W.B. Ponsonby and, through him, that of his brother-in-law, Lord Shannon.[147] They, and the Agars, are examples of how the interaction of British and Irish politics was of extreme importance to the latter. But, while Ponsonby's family connections with English Whiggery went back a long way, the Agars were perhaps the most important Irish victims of the Fox-North Coalition. Though the Regency Crisis broke suddenly, it brought to the surface differences within the Agar connection which had existed latently since 1783. In January–February 1789, the 2nd Lord Clifden and Archbishop Agar allowed the evenly weighted scales of Irish politics to be tipped by Ellis' British party affiliations. As a result, they took a course of action which exposed – as has been seen – the precariousness of the alliance between George Agar and them, suggested some degree of divergence between Archbishop Agar, on the one hand, and Ellis and Clifden, on the other, and damaged Agar in the estimation of Pitt and the King.

Agar found himself at a great disadvantage, and indeed caught on the hop, when the crisis was at its height in England. He was detained in the country, first, by the near-scandal created by George Agar of Ringwood's younger brother, the Rev. Charles Agar (see pp 54–5), and then by the serious, and as it turned out terminal, illness of his own brother, the 1st Lord Clifden. He therefore had to form a judgement on the basis of second-hand information. In mid-December 1788, Lord Earlsfort wrote to him from Dublin expressing the view that 'The King's recovery ... is the only cobweb for any of the present ministers to catch at or hope to hold by', and mentioning that Lord Carlisle (with whom Agar had worked closely in 1780–2) was one of the people spoken of as a possible Whig lord lieutenant of Ireland.[148] Agar was still detained in the country by Clifden's sudden death and other domestic complications, when the time came, in January–February 1789, for the leading Irish political connections to make their choice between Pitt and Fox. From Gowran he wrote in early January to Pitt's lord lieutenant, Lord Buckingham, with whom he had already clashed over Buckingham's plans for Church reform (see pp 230–40), asking him to appoint the new Lord Clifden to succeed his father at the post office. But this request was turned down. Buckingham proffered his condolences, but pretended[149] that the joint post-mastership-general was bespoke, following an engagement entered into by Buckingham's predecessor, Rutland.[150] Ponsonby had also made a request – to be appointed sole postmaster-general (signal proof of his readiness to quarrel with the Agars in Co. Kilkenny elections). Buckingham refused this too, and gave the late Lord Clifden's half of the office to Agar's friend, Lord Loftus.[151] By this action, Buckingham

147 Malcomson, *Lord Shannon*, pp xxxvii–xliv.   148 Earlsfort to Agar, 17 Dec. 1788, T/3719/C/22/52.   149 Hon. and Rev. Charles Brodrick to his brother, the 4th viscount Midleton, 1 Feb. 1789, Midleton papers, Surrey History Centre, Woking, Ms. 1248, vol. 14, f. 146. The Midleton papers are split between NLI and the Surrey History Centre.   150 Buckingham to Agar, 3 Jan. 1789, T/3719/C/23/8.   151 Buckingham to W.W. Grenville, 15 Jan. 1789, *HMC Dropmore*

offended both the Agars and the Ponsonbys and failed to secure Loftus, who went into opposition on the Regency.

On 15 January, Buckingham wrote: 'I doubt whether the Archbishop of Cashel will support; I rather think not, as I refused him Lord Clifden's office for his nephew.'[152] Unknown to Buckingham, the decision was at this very moment being taken out of Agar's hands. Because the new Lord Clifden was abroad when his father died, and because he passed through London on his way home to Ireland, he was captured by Ellis before Agar could get his hands on him. Between them, Ellis and Clifden in effect pre-empted Agar, because they asked, and obtained, from Portland a virtual promise of the joint postmastership-general. As Clifden wrote emolliently on 20 January, 'the one party having refused what the other has granted, it seems almost impossible for me, when I arrive in Ireland, to support Lord B[uckingham] after having gone so far with the duke. ... [But] I acknowledge I feel embarrassed at having taken any step without your knowledge and concurrence'.[153] Possibly Clifden had merely anticipated the line which Agar would have taken anyway: in mid-November 1788, for example, Agar had not expected that Buckingham would 'eat his Christmas dinner in Ireland'.[154] Buckingham's personal obnoxiousness (see pp 230–31), and his deliberate provocation into opposition of people whom he disliked and who might have supported or stayed neutral, were also major factors in Agar's decision. As John Foster, Pery's successor as speaker of the House of Commons, wrote in mid-February 1789: 'the Marquess['s] ... want of friends and his extreme unpopularity would have precluded all hope of success ... [in forming] a party for Mr Pitt in this kingdom ...; for, I believe there never was a lord lieutenant who received so strong and ... [created] so weak a government.'[155] At the end of the month, William Preston, bishop of Ferns (a great friend of Earlsfort), put the point much more strongly in a letter to one of the members of the British government who was closest to Pitt:

> The news ... of the King's convalescence without interruption, and in consequence the suspension of the [British] Regency Bill, ... will not be likely to give a decisive advantage, if any, to the M. of B. in the present struggle ... . If ... any other of rank and character suited to the situation [of lord lieutenant] ... could be sent amongst us, ... this formidable combination would ... break to pieces and dissolve almost at his approach.[156]

This sensible advice was ignored, presumably because Buckingham was Pitt's first cousin and the elder brother of W.W. Grenville, home secretary, 1789–90; and as a result the personal jealousies and hatreds of one very insecure man were allowed to bring about a defeat of the government in both houses of the Irish parliament and, still worse, to shape Irish politics well into the 1790s.

Mss., i. 400. **152** Ibid. **153** 2nd Lord Clifden to Agar, 20 January 1789, T/3719/C/23/13. **154** Earlsfort to Agar, 12–13 Nov. 1788, T/3719/C/22/44. **155** Foster to 1st Lord Sheffield, 12 Feb. [1789], Stanley of Alderley/Sheffield papers, PRONI, T/3725/4. **156** Preston to [Henry Dundas], 27 Feb. [1789], Pitt/Pretyman papers, PRONI, T/3319/1.

From the beginning of February 1789, events moved very fast. By the 4th, Clifden (still in London) had instructed three of his members 'to oppose the restrictions so improperly forced on the regent in England', and asked Agar to seek out George Dunbar, who (characteristically) had gone missing, and give him the same instructions.[157] On the 6th, Buckingham picked a quarrel with Agar and gave him effectively no option but to go into opposition.[158] If left to himself, he would probably have temporised further, from motives of self-interest and of what Bishop Preston called 'duty to the king's government ..., personal attachment to Mr Pitt and real concern for the ease and success of his administration here and elsewhere'. The clearest indication of what Agar's real attitude was is his response to a letter he must have received on the fatal 6 February. Charles Dodgson, bishop of Elphin, had written to him from London asking him directly 'whether you mean to vote for a regency with restrictions, similar to those passed in England, as far as the states of the two kingdoms will admit, or without any. If the latter, I hope I shall not be suspected of having any disrespect for your Grace if I desire another friend, whose opinion coincides with my own, to be my proxy till the affair of the regency be settled.' Agar replied on 6 February – whether before or after he received Buckingham's declaration of war, will never be known: 'As my conduct on the question, or perhaps (to speak more properly) on the many questions, which may arise out of the subject mentioned by your Lordship will depend upon the nature of the questions and a variety of circumstances altogether unknown to me at this moment, your Lordship will not only not offend, but certainly oblige, me by applying to some other person to be your Lordship's proxy till the business you mention be settled.'[159] This was not the language of eager opposition.

Agar's defection gave his leading competitor for the primacy, Archbishop Fowler of Dublin, his chance to steal a march on him. On 18 February, Fowler 'concurred with fourteen other peers in protesting against the ... address of the Irish House of Lords to the Prince of Wales ... . He also joined [on 20 February] in protesting against the resolution of the Lords that the answer of the lord lieutenant, refusing to transmit the address, was disrespectful to his Royal Highness and conveyed an unwarrantable censure on both houses of parliament.'[160] Fowler was not part of any political connection, and so was at liberty to do what he always did – consult nothing but his own self-interest. Meanwhile, the Agar connection – rapidly, but too late – recovered its balance following the recovery of George III's sanity. On 4 March 1789 'everything which could be mustered' by Clifden against the government was so mustered, but in vain; on 9 March it was thought that he had 'writ to press for leave from Welbore Ellis' to desert the opposition and make his peace; on 22 March it was reported that Clifden was very likely to surrender unconditionally; and by 31 March he was 'very stout' (in

157 Lady Clifden to Agar, [4] Feb. [1789], 21 M 57/D53/28.   158 Alleyne Fitzherbert (the chief secretary) to Agar, and reply, 6 Feb. 1789, T/3719/C/23/40–1.   159 Dodgson to Agar, 4 Feb. 1789, with a copy of Agar's undated reply, T/3719/C/23/15. Dodgson has the vicarious distinction of having been the great-grandfather of Lewis Carroll.   160 D'Alton, *Archbishops of Dublin*, pp 348–9.

support of the government) and Agar 'very warm, and spoke wonderfully with us last night'.[161] This was on 'a bill then depending in parliament to limit the powers of the crown to grant pensions'. Bishop Woodward of Cloyne expected that it would 'be the great trial of strength in the Lords. Those who tell noses think that it will be determined by a majority not exceeding two or three, perhaps by a single vote.'[162]

Agar's support of the government on this critical occasion followed a characteristic piece of 'canvassing and closeting'[163] on the part of Buckingham. Panic-stricken at the solidity of the opposition, in spite of the king's recovery, Buckingham was now trying to undo the effects of his own vindictiveness and provocativeness (and not just in Agar's case).

> His Excellency [so Agar minuted their conversation on 25 March] condescended to solicit very earnestly a return of the Archbishop's accustomed support [on the Pension Bill], ... and added that, if the Archbishop had any object, he wished to know it. The Archbishop answered that he would certainly use his best endeavours to defeat this and every other attempt to lessen the powers of the crown; that it had not been his intention to embarrass his Excellency with any application for favour for himself, but that, as his Excellency had a desire to know whether he had any object, he should not conceal from him that he should be gratified by having the peerage which had become vacant within the last fortnight by the death of his aunt, Lady Brandon, revived in his wife, Mrs Agar, with reversion to his children. His Excellency said that he thought the application reasonable and fair,

and promised to recommend it shortly.[164] On 28 March, Agar furnished Buckingham, at Buckingham's request, with a statement of what Agar had said in the House of Lords on 16 February on the question of the regency. The statement began:

> I was of the opinion his Royal Highness the Prince of Wales, our gracious sovereign's eldest son and the rightful heir to his crown, was the properest person to be appointed regent during his Majesty's indisposition and *no longer*, ... that, if I could conceive it to be intended to appoint the Prince of Wales regent by the sole authority of an address of the two houses of parliament, I should oppose the address, not only as an unconstitutional measure, but as a vain and nugatory attempt to convey powers by the resolutions of two branches of the legislature which could alone be granted by an act of a complete parliament; ... and that, should his Royal Highness condescend to signify his pleasure to accept our offer, the address must necessarily be followed by an act of parliament to render it effectual; that, considering the address in this light,

161 Letters of those dates from Buckingham to Grenville, *H.M.C Dropmore Mss*, i, pp 425, 427, 435 and 441.   162 Woodward to Brodrick, 14 Mar. 1789, Midleton papers, NLI, Ms. 8870/1.   163 Brodrick to Midleton, 1 Feb. 1789, Surrey History Centre, Ms. 1248/14, f. 146.   164 Memos. by Agar of his conversation with Buckingham on 25 March 1789, T/3719/C/23/18–19.

I saw no reason for opposing it, nor for giving it any delay, because the same question had been asked already by the two British houses of parliament, and his Royal Highness had already answered that he would accept the regency of the British dominions.[165]

After two month's delay, Buckingham forwarded this paper to London, describing it as 'a very singular letter from the Archbishop of Cashel. He drew it as a *mémoire justificatif* of his conduct, and wishes it to be shown to the King, as preparative to an application for a peerage. The letter requires no answer, but I wish to be able to say that it was laid before the King.'[166] This is proof positive of Buckingham's mis-representations and duplicity: it was he, at the time he needed Agar's support against the Pension Bill, who had offered Agar a peerage and invited him to draw up the '*mémoire justificatif*'.

In his speech of 30 March on the Pension Bill, when even Buckingham acknowl-edged that he 'spoke wonderfully', Agar managed to turn his previous anti-government vote to tactical advantage. He began with a discussion of the general questions of the size of the pension list and the legality of pensions, arguing that 'The several bills brought into parliament from time to time in Ireland, and those passed into laws in England, for limiting, restraining and regulating this branch of the king's prerogative, were ... so many admissions of the right: otherwise, the laws would have declared the practice to be illegal, and not have admitted the right by regulating the exercise of it.' He then explicitly cited the recent address to the Prince of Wales, and used its terms as a justification for the existence of the pension list in its present extent and on its present unfettered footing:

> when it had been declared from the throne by the lord lieutenant that our gracious sovereign was incapable to govern his kingdoms and that provision must be made for that lamentable defect, ... the parliament of Ireland had not deemed it necessary to impose on a regent any restrictions ... . Confidence in the son was the natural effect which flowed from allegiance to the father. But were we to vote for this bill, should we not virtually say that ... we were willing to permit a regent to grant a pension not only of £300 but of £3,000 per annum, as often as he should think fit, without depriving the grantee of any privilege whatsoever, but we will not permit our sovereign to reward distinguished merit, recompense faithful services or relieve the distresses of the unfortunate, by a pension exceeding £300 per annum.[167]

In spite of Agar's best endeavours as a self-publicist (see pp 74–5), it is impossible, particularly because his text is couched largely in reported speech, to recapture the 'wonderful' effect which the oration is said to have had. But the ingenuity of the

165 Agar to Buckingham, 28 Mar. 1789, T/3719/C/23/42.   **166** Buckingham to Grenville, 28 May 1789, *HMC Dropmore Mss.*, i. 471.   **167** Text in Agar's hand of his speech on the Pension Bill, [30 Mar. 1789], 21 M 57/A16/4.

argument is impressive. The speech sounds as if it comes from a politician fully in command of the situation, not from one who is dodging and weaving in order to retrieve an error.

These and other[168] attempts at self-justification and damage-limitation having produced no results, on 29 October he wrote to Buckingham, of whose integrity he was rightly suspicious, asking him what the outcome of Buckingham's representations to the King had been. Buckingham replied promptly, but evasively: 'I have not been able to receive his Majesty's commands in person since my return from Ireland, and I have not been informed of his pleasure ... . Your Grace may be assured that I have done justice to the zeal and abilities with which you opposed the Pension Bill.'[169] Distrustful of this response, Agar (probably showing for once a lack of judgement, but no lack of political courage) determined to go straight to Pitt and then the King. He saw Pitt on 3 December and went over all the old arguments, concluding his minute of the interview: 'N.B. Mr P. heard the Archbishop for about an hour with great attention, and from his manner the Archbishop thought he collected that the marquess of B. had not stated his recommendation of the Archbishop or of his conduct to government.'[170] On 9 December, Agar was received in audience by the King, and confined himself 'to a single subject' (possibly the King's health), eschewing matters which 'related principally to myself'. These he addressed subsequently in a letter to the king of 17 December, in which he enclosed a copy of the statement he had given to Buckingham on 28 March. Cuttingly, he apologised for doing so if Buckingham had submitted the original.[171]

All this probably served only to make a bad business worse. It was literally true that Buckingham had quarrelled with Agar, not Agar with Buckingham. But the breach had taken place on 6 February, *after* Ellis' and Clifden's negotiation with Portland must have become widely known. The sentiments of Agar's speech on 16 February, to which he directed the attention of Buckingham, Pitt and the King, were actually the merest common form. Speaking on 20 February on Grattan's motion of censure on Buckingham for refusing to transmit to the Prince of Wales the addresses of both houses of the Irish parliament, FitzGibbon declared:

> There is not a lawyer in this kingdom, and I am confident I may say in England, who will assert that an address of the Lords and Commons of Ireland can convey regal powers; ... the first law authorities in this kingdom have protested against such a principle, and indeed every member of the upper house who supported this address, asserted that it was only a form of compliment or respect, calling upon the Prince to accept of powers to be hereafter bestowed upon him by act of parliament; ... every sober man deserted it on the ground of conferring power.[172]

168 Text in Agar's hand of a prayer of thanksgiving for the King's recovery composed by Agar, 14 Apr. 1789, 21 M 57/B33/1; Agar's 'state' of the diocese of Cashel, 1779–1801, 21 M 57/B6/1. 169 Memo. by Agar, post 25 Mar. 1789, and Agar to Buckingham, 29 Oct. 1789, T/3719/C/23/18 and 34. 170 Memo. by Agar, 3 Dec. 1789, T/3719/C/23/38. 171 Agar to the King, 17 Dec. 1789, T/3719/C/23/43. 172 *Irish parliamentary register*, ix. 135.

Grattan himself stated that such an address must be followed by a bill; and he, too, used the phrase 'and no longer'[173] to emphasise that the existence of a regency was limited to the duration of the royal malady. The line which FitzGibbon tutored government supporters to follow was that the Irish parliament must wait until an act of the British parliament had conferred the regency, on whatever terms it did, on the Prince of Wales; it was then the duty of the Irish parliament to pass a bill of exactly the same tenor, which would become law only after the regent had affixed to it the great seal, not of Ireland, but of England. Agar's sentiments had fallen very far short of these, and consequently – however briefly – he had been in opposition. In any case, the votes of Clifden's members in the House of Commons spoke louder than any words of Agar's in the House of Lords.

THE LONGER-TERM CONSEQUENCES OF THE REGENCY CRISIS, 1789–94

His brief moment of opposition almost certainly had adverse consequences for Agar, though not for the rest of the Agar connection. Ellis, in an audience he had sought with George III in July 1779, just after Agar's promotion to Cashel, had assured the King that, 'next to your duty to God, you would make it the study of your life to exert your talents in his service and to show in every instance your loyalty, zeal and gratitude to him; [and] that all your family had been so much distinguished by his favour that I should think you all the basest and most unworthy of mankind if you should fail in exerting your joint endeavours to show your sense of his goodness.'[174] Agar unwittingly struck the same note in his statement of 28 March 1789, when he called upon Buckingham 'to state fully ... what my conduct has been ..., and what your Excellency believes both mine and that of my family to have invariably been during a series of above twenty years, in which time I have in no instance failed to give proof of the gratitude that I bear to my sovereign for repeated instances of his royal favour'. Both these professions are reminiscent of the much better-known declaration of two-faced Lord Chancellor Thurlow in December 1788: 'When I forget my King, may my God forget me!'[175] No doubt the King received Thurlow's and Agar's professions with the same degree of scepticism. He knew that, whatever the Agars had been doing in Ireland, Ellis had been in opposition in England – and in what the King regarded as factious opposition to boot – since 1784, and was still in opposition in March 1789, when Agar wrote to Buckingham, and in December 1789, when Agar spoke and wrote to the King.

Of Agar's political circle, the two tooth-and-nail supporters of Buckingham on the Regency were FitzGibbon and Lord Tyrone, who were rewarded with the lord

---

173 *Ibid.*, p. 128; Kavanaugh, *Lord Clare*, p. 144. For the Regency Crisis generally, the roles of Shannon, Ponsonby, Loftus, etc., see Kavanaugh, pp 136–55.   174 Ellis to Agar, 25 July 1779, T/3719/C/13/18.   175 John Ehrman, *The younger Pitt: the years of acclaim* (London, 1969), p. 355.

chancellorship and the marquessate of Waterford respectively. FitzGibbon's promotion, which broke through an anti-Irish taboo, ought to have facilitated Agar's ascent to Armagh, but did not – for reasons which will be suggested later in this Chapter. Of Agar's circle, the only other sufferer (besides himself) by opposition on the regency was Lord Shannon, whom Buckingham detested quite as much as he did Agar. Shannon remained in the wilderness until 1793, when he was restored to favour and given the best office he ever held, the newly created first lordship of the treasury. Agar's friend and ally, Earlsfort, who had advised Agar in mid-December 1788 that Pitt's situation was desperate, in the end did not act on his own advice. He enjoyed a flexibility in negotiation which was denied to Agar, because he was independent of political connection ('a single lord', as he himself put it).[176] He amazed and disgusted Buckingham on 8 January 1789 by declaring 'that his attachments are to Lord North', but immediately allowed himself to be won back to his former allegiance by the gift of a better office to a dependant and the promise of promotion in the peerage for himself.[177] Unlike Agar, Earlsfort could afford to push his luck; he knew that he already held the highest office to which he could aspire. When the crisis was past and the pay-off took place, Buckingham recommended Earlsfort for an earldom, as requested, but privately advised that a viscountcy would be plenty. He also recommended a barony for Agar's friend, Carleton, 'for the sake of the law of the House of Lords, and [for the sake] of the government, to which he has been ever steady; and because his presence would materially check the conduct of Lord Earlsfort, whom you know to be slippery'.[178] Lord Loftus, who had been given the post office in preference to Clifden, and then had 'ratted', was amnestied. He not only held on to the office but, adducing a previous and ambiguous promise of a viscountcy when next a promotion to that rank was made, succeeded in piggy-backing on Earlsfort to the viscountcy of Loftus.[179]

Of the Agar connection, Lord Clifden – its new head – remained infuriatingly unscathed. In *c.*1785, Agar had calculated that the average nett produce of the fees of Clifden's office, the clerkship to the council, was £521 per annum, 'exclusive of a salary of £400 and £40 yearly allowed for stationery, etc., etc.' He later recorded that Buckingham, probably as part of his post-Regency Crisis amnesty and as a consolation prize for the post office, doubled Clifden's salary, and that in 1790 the next lord lieutenant, Lord Westmorland, added another £200 to it, thus bringing the total nett emoluments of the clerkship to over £1,500 per annum.[180] Moreover, by 1791 Clifden's mother, the Dowager Lady Clifden, was in receipt of a pension.[181] In other words, Clifden, in spite of having gone into opposition in the meantime, was considerably better-off than he would have been if appointed joint postmaster-general in succession to his father in January 1789. In September 1794, he heard that there was

176 *Clonmell diary (TCD)*, p. 301.   177 Buckingham to Grenville, 8 and 10 Jan. 1789, and Robart Hobart to Grenville, 22 June 1789, *HMC Dropmore Mss.*, i, pp 396–7 and 481.   178 Buckingham to Grenville, 17 May 1789, *ibid.*, p. 469.   179 Buckingham to Grenville, 22 Mar., 22 Apr. and 19 Aug. 1789, *ibid.*, pp 435, 458 and 491–3.   180 Calculations and notes by Agar, *c.*1785 and *c.*1790, 21 M 57/D53/33 and 36.   181 *Proc. RIA*, vol. 59, sec. C, no. 1, p. 48.

some threat to his office, but viewed it with equanimity: 'I have some force in myself, I have Lord Mendip at Burlington House [the duke of Portland's London house] and the duke of Marlborough in Downing Street [Pitt's official residence]; so that, under all the circumstances of the case, if hostility is intended, I defy it.'[182] The duke of Marlborough, a new prop of the Agar connection, was Clifden's father-in-law (Clifden had married his daughter in 1792); and though not an actual Pittite, was a 'King's Friend' who supported Pitt with a number of votes at Westminster because Pitt had been the choice of the king. 'Under all the circumstances of the case', Clifden was therefore right to be confident of success. He was still clerk of the council at the time of the Union, following which (and in reward for his support of that measure), the office was granted to him for life instead of during pleasure; so the possibility of his being dismissed ceased to exist. At the Union and thereafter he was vigilant in reporting, and in obtaining compensation for, reductions in his fees consequent on changes in the business of the privy council. When the clerkship itself was abolished in 1817, he received compensation in full.[183] In 1833, the hostile *Kilkenny Journal* put the post-Union emoluments of the office, whether in the form of salary and fees or the equivalent in annual compensation, at £1,670 per annum, and calculated that up to that date Clifden had 'robbed the Irish people of £55,138 17s. 6d.'[184]

Ellis waited for his rehabilitation until 1794. In that year, his friend and leader, Portland, led the majority of the Whigs and the dwindling band of Northites into wartime coalition with Pitt, and Ellis received as his reward the long-awaited British barony complete with the long-coveted special remainder (the latter being, for the foreseeable future, of huge benefit to Clifden and none to Agar). From 1794 onwards, with the Agars in Ireland and the new Lord Mendip in England all supporting government, there were no divided loyalties within the Agar connection. Conveniently forgetting that the Fox-North Coalition and the Regency Crisis had ever happened, Mendip observed disapprovingly in March 1797: 'It appears that there is a concerted coalition between the two oppositions of G.B. and I.'[185]

Meanwhile, at about the same time as Ellis' elevation to the peerage in the autumn of 1794, the 'dreadful dilemma'[186] of whom to make primate *vice* Robinson at last arose. Irishness of itself ought no longer to have been a disqualification: the lord chancellorship was only one, though the highest, in a series of high offices which had been 'brought back to Ireland' (i.e. conferred on Irishmen instead of Englishmen) in the last quarter of the eighteenth century. In an undated letter of *c.*1785–8, Bishop Hotham, who was English and a potential candidate for the primacy himself, had foretold that 'a most ambitious, violent, hot-headed Irishman' (Agar) would 'certainly' be

182 Clifden to Agar, 30 Sep. 1794, 21 M 57/B23/22.   183 Thorne, *House of Commons, 1790–1820*, iii. 52; undated list in Edward Cooke's handwriting of rewards promised to Unionist peers, Castlereagh papers, PRONI, D/3030/1356; Moran, 'The Agars of Gowran', p. 126; Clifden to William Wickham (the chief secretary), 23 Nov. and 3 Dec. 1802, Wickham papers, Hampshire RO: photocopies in PRONI, T/2627/5/Q/93 and 101.   184 Quoted in Neely, *Kilkenny*, p. 246.   185 Mendip to Agar, 18 Mar. 1797, T/3719/C/31/26.   186 Westmorland to Pitt, [pre-5 Sep. 1794], Chatham papers, PRO, 30/8/331, ff. 310–15.

appointed.[187] It is possible that, had he supported Buckingham unswervingly on the regency, Agar would have been the man. The regency notwithstanding, the well informed and well connected Lord Auckland thought in late October 1794 that Agar would still 'carry his point'.[188] But the out-going lord lieutenant, Westmorland, the abject Pittite who had succeeded Buckingham in 1789, did not recommend Agar, in spite of the political intimacy which to outward appearances subsisted between Agar and him. In a private letter to Pitt, Westmorland had warned that 'Cashel, who is certainly a very able man, excellent government principles and strongly attached to England, ... [is] of a most violent temper, busy, and would probably be very trouble-some'.[189] Westmorland favoured some Englishman already on the Irish bench: Pitt, however, favoured an English bishop. His confidant in ecclesiastical matters and future first biographer, George Pretyman (later Tomline), bishop of Lincoln, declared: 'There is no one upon the Irish bench fit for it.'[190] In mid-November 1794, Pitt blithely informed Westmorland that 'all opinions here will concur clearly in the propriety of appointing the Bishop of Norwich [Charles Manners Sutton], so that no difficulty can arise on that head'.[191] But Sutton refused the offer and, in the meantime, Fitzwilliam's appointment as lord lieutenant was declared. This was thought to make no difference to the basic policy decision that 'The primate is certainly to come from this side of the water [England]. It is understood to be Cleaver of Chester, and ... [that] Lord W. gives way to the administration here in taking their primate.'[192] Meanwhile, Bishop Pretyman had written to Pitt 'in my own name to sound him' as to the pos-sibility of Pretyman himself being appointed (an aspiration which may have been influenced his judgement that 'there is no one upon the Irish bench fit for it'!).[193] But Pitt presumably thought that Pretyman was too closely identified with himself to be acceptable to his new coalition partners: William Cleaver, bishop of Chester (and his brother, Euseby, bishop of Ferns), had the merit of association with Lord Egremont, a Whig (see p. 1912). It looks, therefore, as if Cleaver was offered the primacy, and refused. The only thing which is certain is that Pitt had not favoured Agar, for reasons which may or may not have been connected with the Regency Crisis, so that the Pitt-Portland coalition did not affect the outcome as far as Agar was concerned, except to the extent that it gave him a second chance.

In view of the fact that Ireland was about to be a Whig sphere of influence, had been given a Whig lord lieutenant (the 4th Earl Fitzwilliam), and had become part of Portland's new responsibilities as home secretary, Westmorland's position was increas-ingly anomalous. Portland was reported as speaking about him 'with some asperity'.

---

187 Hotham to Hotham Thompson, 13 June [c.1785], PRONI, T/3429/2/12.   188 Auckland to Beresford, 23 Oct. 1794, *Auckland correspondence*, iii. 253.   189 Westmorland to Pitt, [pre-5 Sep. 1794], loc. cit.   190 Pretyman to his wife, 15 Oct. 1794, Stanhope/Pitt papers, Centre for Kentish Studies, U1590/S5 C.67/6.   191 Pitt to Westmorland, 19 Nov. 1794, printed in 5th Earl Stanhope, *Miscellanies* (London, 1863), pp 12–16, and reprinted in *Later correspondence of George III*, ii, pp 268–71; Westmorland to Portland (officially recommending Sutton), 28 Nov. 1794, Home Office papers, HO 100/46, f. 229.   192 Hon. William Brodrick to his brother, Charles, [post-19 Nov.] 1794, Midleton papers, NLI, Ms. 8883.   193 Pretyman to his wife, 15 Oct. 1794, loc. cit.

'He says that Lord W. has had (exclusive of the primacy ..., the nomination of one archbishop [Tuam] and two bishops [Cloyne and Clonfert] since the duke has been in office'.[194] Portland, however, in spite of his association with Mendip and the 'friendship' which he later professed had 'existed between' Agar and himself 'for near half a century',[195] was not favourable to Agar's claims in late 1794 to early 1795. Portland was notorious for his inability to give a decisive 'no' to any patronage application, and was to bequeath to the home office when he left it in 1801 a legacy of muddle and raised expectations. But to Mendip, after some preliminary beating about the bush, he made it very clear in late November 1794 'that I ought not to give you any encouragement to hope for success on the vacancy respecting which you were pleased to ask for my support'.[196] It would have been a remarkable irony if Agar, the High Protestant churchman *par excellence,* had been promoted to the archbishopric of Armagh by the Whig and Emancipationist lord lieutenant, Fitzwilliam.[197] But it was an even greater irony that the intimation of his disappointment was conveyed by Portland, the man who had tempted Clifden with the post office, and who would have become prime minister, in 1789; also that William Newcome, bishop of Waterford, the man promoted to the archbishopric of Armagh in 1795, was the friend and former mentor of Charles James Fox, who had vowed in 1785 to make his harvest in Ireland and who had done so with even greater success in 1789.[198]

The primacy having gone to Newcome, there remained the question of the temporal peerage which had been as good as promised to Agar by Buckingham and which Agar had 'so long had in view'. In spite of strained relations between them over the primacy,[199] Westmorland assured him that 'My recommendation of you for a peerage was transmitted in the course of the last summer to Mr Pitt, whose concurrence in that recommendation was signified to me.'[200] But, once Westmorland was replaced by Fitzwilliam, there was a hitch. Pitt did nothing to press the matter and Portland was hostile. It was as if Agar had done just enough at the time of the regency to offend the former, and not enough to oblige the latter. In the end it was actually the King – the one person most entitled to be offended with both Agar and Mendip – who took Agar's part. Following the arrival of Fitzwilliam's recommendation of a peerage for someone else, the King wrote to Portland (and at the same time to Pitt) stating firmly that 'It would be unjust to forget the uniform support of the Archbishop of Cashel, who has for some time requested the same favour, which I have no doubt the duke of Portland must have heard from Lord Westmorland as well as from Lord Mendip.'[201] This intervention on the part of the King forced Portland's hand. To

---

194 Albinia, Dowager Viscountess Midleton, to Brodrick (her son), 18 Dec. 1794, Ms. 8885/11. 195 Portland to Agar, 30 Oct. 1801, T/3719/C/35/23. 196 Portland to Mendip, 28 Nov. 1794, Portland papers, Nottingham UL: photocopy in PRONI, T/2905/22/26. 197 Malcomson, *John Foster,* p. 391. 198 Ibid., p. 400. For Newcome, see pp 467–74. 199 John Lees to Agar, 20 Oct. 1794, and to Mrs Agar, 22 Nov. 1794, T/3719/C/28/16–17. 200 Westmorland to Agar, 31 Dec. 1794, T/3719/C/28/23–4. The recommendation made 'last summer' must have been a private one: the official recommendation is Westmorland to Portland, 27 Nov. 1794, HO 100/46, f. 215. 201 The King to Portland and to Pitt, 13 Jan. 1795 (both letters), *Later correspondence of George III,* ii,

Fitzwilliam he wrote, with shabby cynicism, that it would now be difficult to resist Agar's promotion, particularly if 'we want a job or two ourselves'.[202] Against this background, Fitzwilliam's official recommendation of Agar was amazingly fulsome: 'His Majesty may be assured that the fortunes, family, rank in life and character of the Archbishop point him out for such a mark of his Majesty's consideration.'[203] Accordingly, Agar was created Baron Somerton on 12 June 1795. The six-year delay can reasonably be attributed to the Regency Crisis.

THE 'BOROUGH ANNEXED TO THE PRIMACY'

To Agar, the peerage was of less importance than the primacy; and the main objection to him as a candidate for the primacy was, not that his family connection and he had gone into opposition on the regency (which could hardly be held against him by a new coalition government including Portland), but that he belonged to a borough-owning, Irish political connection in the first place. This was the only objection made to his pretensions in the already-quoted Castle list of 1784–7. It was also the theme of Westmorland's private letter to Pitt:

> I consider it at all times a decided principle that the bishoprics with the boroughs should be kept from persons connected with the Irish party. To this principle, therefore, we should strongly look in the disposal of the primacy. The candidates here would be the Archbishops of Dublin and Cashel and [William] Beresford. The latter is a respectable man and firmly attached to the king's government, but certainly attached to a party in Ireland, and his appointment would throw too much weight to that scale. [His comments on Agar have already been quoted, and those on Archbishop Fowler of Dublin are quoted on p. 466.] I have understood the King had some thoughts of Newcome ... . He is a very respectable man, but played [?deceiving] foul at the regency ... and, though a general supporter of government, owes his fortunes to that party [the Whigs], and would certainly upon an opportunity follow it. ...
>
> Clogher is certainly going likewise [i.e. Bishop Hotham was dying]. That bishopric is worth £6,000 a year and the borough. ... I think we ought to stick to Englishmen and those particularly attached to you, ... and we should then have secured all the boroughs for the crown; and, if we do not, I hardly know how we shall bring in the [chief and under-]secretaries at the next parliament. Every Irish bishop will have his own connections, and even Beresford would bring [i.e. insisted on bringing] in his own son last parliament [for St Canice].[204]

pp 291–3. **202** Portland to Fitzwilliam, 14 Jan. 1795, ibid., p. 293. **203** Fitzwilliam to Portland, 24 Jan. 1795, HO 100/56, ff. 117–18. **204** Westmorland to Pitt, [pre-5 Sep. 1794], Chatham papers, PRO, 30/8/331, ff. 310–15.

One of the sub-texts of this letter was Westmorland's wish to get his already very rapidly promoted nephew, William Bennet, bishop of Cloyne (see pp 487–9), advanced to the bishopric of Clogher; so, some allowance for that piece of English jobbery needs to be made. But, basically, Westmorland was only voicing an obsessive governmental concern of the 1780s and 1790s with 'resisting applications [from Irish political connections] for bishoprics with boroughs'.[205] In March 1795, Fitzwilliam was accused (falsely, as things turned out) of giving the Ponsonby party 'the disposal of the two seats of Ossory' by making the Irish Whig, Thomas Lewis O'Beirne, bishop of that diocese.[206] In November of the same year, Fitzwilliam's successor, Camden, acknowledged to Portland 'that it is not desirable to entrust the borough [of Clogher] into the hands of a zealous and active Irishman'. And two years later he wrote, again to Portland: 'I believe I do not overstate your Grace's opinion when I say that ... you think a preferment with a borough attached to it *ought* to be given to an Englishman'.[207] Westmorland's analysis was actually more subtle, in that he – like Carlisle before him – allowed for the possibility of Englishmen becoming mixed up in Irish political connection.

Because Ireland had neither treasury nor admiralty boroughs, the government had some reason to attach importance to the four so-called 'bishops' boroughs', Armagh, Clogher, Old Leighlin and St Canice, since they alone provided a way of bringing government nominees into parliament free of charge and free of obligation to private borough patrons. Yet, the convention much invoked in the 1780s and 1790s – that the four bishops with boroughs were 'understood to be bound to take the nomination of government'[208] – was in fact relatively new. Arguably, it could not have come into being until the Octennial Act of 1768 made Irish elections a frequent and fairly regular occurrence, thus inflating the price of seats and acting as a forcing-house for conventions concerning the relationship of patron to member. In the first third of the eighteenth century, there clearly was not much rhyme or reason to what the bishops did with their seats. In 1727, the politically active Bishop Vesey of Ossory (see pp 94–6) had returned for St Canice Agar's grandfather, James Agar (d.1733), a political client of Vesey's, and Vesey's brother-in-law, Richard Dawson; both these members, though supporters of the government, were nominees not of the government but of himself.[209] Successive archbishops of Cashel behaved in the same way with regard to Cashel borough in the same period (see pp 288–91). The mid-century evidence, too, suggests that at that stage there was still no convention that the bishops should return the nominees of the government of the day. For example, the future Primate

205 Westmorland to Grenville, 20 Mar. 1790, *HMC Dropmore Mss.*, i. 568.   206 Brodrick to Midleton, 11 Mar. 1795, Midleton papers, Ms. 1248, vol. 16, ff. 25–6.   207 Camden to Portland, 19 Nov. [1795] and 9 Nov. 1797, HO 100/46, ff. 333–7, and 70, ff. 289–93.   208 Francis Bickley (ed.), *The diaries of Sylvester Douglas, [1st] Lord Glenbervie* (2 vols., London, 1928), i. 41. Douglas was chief secretary, 1793–4.   209 It looks as if, following Vesey's death in 1730, his son, Sir John Denny Vesey, possibly aided by Patrick Wemys (and James Agar?), tried to wrest the borough from the see and bring it under the private patronage of the Vesey family – entry for 11 Oct. 1731 in the St Canice corporation book, 1692–1799, NLI, microfilm p. 5143.

Robinson, when bishop of Ferns and about to become bishop of Kildare, had a row with the outgoing lord lieutenant, Bedford, over the disposal of the seats for Old Leighlin, Co. Carlow, at the general election of 1761. Bedford asserted that Robinson was honour-bound to return the candidates nominated by 'him who had obtained from the crown your two last promotions, especially as at that time he was honoured with his Majesty's commission of chief governor of Ireland':[210] Robinson, by contrast, had regarded himself as being at liberty to oblige his original patron, the duke of Dorset, and through him, Primate Stone and Speaker Ponsonby (see pp 439–40). Very significantly, Bedford viewed the fact that he was lord lieutenant as only a contributory element in his claims upon Robinson.

Robinson was forced to climb down in this instance, but adhered to his interpretation of the obligations which bound a bishop who had cure of a borough. In 1768, when he was primate, he returned the chief secretary of the day, Agar's friend, Macartney, for the borough of Armagh. But this was a coincidence. He had originally promised to return Macartney at the request of the 1st duke of Northumberland,[211] who had helped Robinson to obtain the primacy, and long before Macartney was even under consideration for the post of chief secretary. Similarly, one of Robinson's predecessor at Ferns, John Garnett, who was bishop, 1752–8, had been allowed to behave as if he had the sole disposal of a seat for Old Leighlin which was vacant in 1757. 'My little vacant borough' he wrote 'filled my apartments for ten days with full as much and as good company as I saw ... at the Castle.'[212] His successor at Ferns, the Hon. William Carmichael, acted on the same assumption in 1758.[213] Meanwhile, Garnett had been translated to Clogher, for which he returned at the 1761 general election his brother-in-law, Sir Capel Molyneux, 3rd Bt, with whom he had a great 'private friendship'.[214] Like Robinson, Garnett owed his introduction to Ireland (as a viceregal chaplain) and his first bishopric (Ferns) to the then lord lieutenant, Dorset. He also attributed his promotion to Clogher to Dorset influence and, as late as the general election of 1768, was pledged to Dorset's son, the 2nd duke, to return two nominees of his for Clogher. They turned out to be Ponsonby nominees, and so joined the opposition. Not in the least abashed, Garnett wrote to the hard-pressed lord lieutenant, Townshend, in November 1769, asking him to find a seat for Mrs Garnett's 'near relation', Thomas St George (1738–95), whom Garnett had made agent for the Clogher see estate. Townshend scouted this 'impertinent address', which he angrily endorsed: 'To be shown to the King, as an instance of the weakness of his government in this country and [of] the prelates' ingratitude.' Notwithstanding Garnett's display of ingratitude, the next lord lieutenant, Harcourt, allowed him to return St George for Clogher at the general election of 1776.[215]

210 Bedford to Robinson, 4 Apr. 1761, *Irish official papers*, ii. 265.   211 Thomas Waite to Wilmot, [*c*.1766?], Wilmot papers, PRONI, T/3019/6069.   212 Garnett to [Richard?] Burgh, 6 Jan. 1757, Burgh papers, NLI, Ms. 8606.   213 Charles O'Hara to his wife, Lady Mary [*née* Carmichael], 1 Apr. [1758], O'Hara papers, NLI: photocopy in PRONI, T2812/10/26.   214 Molyneux to Bedford, 7 Dec. 1760, Bedford papers, Woburn Abbey, Bedfordshire: photocopy in PRONI, T/2915/10/63. 215 Garnett to Townshend, 15 and 16 Nov. 1769, Townshend letter-book, RCB Library, Ms.

All the same, it is clear from Townshend's indignation, and his reference of the matter to the King, that the Octennial Act of 1768 had made a difference and had led to an assertion of the Castle's control over the bishops' boroughs and to the unconscious formulation of a new convention. One explanation for the failure to enforce the new convention uniformly is that two of the bishops' boroughs were insecure. This gave the bishops concerned the justification or perhaps pretext for declining to accept the nomination of the government, at least for both seats. In St Canice, opposition to the bishop's control was endemic, and the freeman body sufficiently numerous to be a constant source of anxiety. In 1779, Ossory was described by one lord lieutenant as 'a preferment which is understood to be attended with many agreeable circumstances, though possibly you may not deem the having the management of a borough to be one of them'.²¹⁶ Hugh Hamilton, bishop of Ossory, 1799–1805 (see p. 570), acknowledged that it was 'impossible to ascertain exactly how many electors might claim a right to vote in case of a contested election'.²¹⁷ In order to avoid a contest, successive bishops made compromises with the potential opposition, which in turn created the impression that the borough was more secure than was actually the case. Between 1756 and his death in 1774, Eland Mossom of Mount Eland, Ballyragget, a popular local barrister, who was recorder of Kilkenny City, 1750–74, and a supporter of the Ponsonbys rather than of the government, was thrice returned for St Canice, without enthusiasm on the bishop's part and for the sake of peace.²¹⁸ William Newcome, when bishop of Ossory, was subjected to 'a great expense ... [and] the greatest obloquy and newspaper abuse' at the general election of 1776, when he returned two government candidates in the teeth of 'a most contested opposition headed by Mr [John] Ponsonby in favour of Mr [Eland] Mossom [the previous member's son], a popular candidate and a native of this place'.²¹⁹ (This was the Eland Mossom who married the Hewetson heiress in 1779 – see p. 100.) Significantly, one of the government candidates was also a local, John Monck Mason, 'the chairman of accounts, a commissioner of revenue, a person strongly connected with the interests of the borough in question, and a gentleman of course to be brought in somewhere by government'.²²⁰ These somewhat defensive remarks were made at the time of the general election of 1783, when the government was trying to get the then bishop, William Beresford, to return someone else, and Beresford refused on the ground that dropping Monck Mason would

20/5–6. It was also alleged that Harcourt's choice of bishop of Ferns in 1772 put Old Leighlin in jeopardy (Godfrey Lill to Macartney, 28 Sep. 1772, *Macartney in Ireland*, p. 227). **216** Buckinghamshire to Hotham Thompson, 12 Oct. 1779, T/3429/1/49. **217** *Report of the commissioners of compensation for boroughs disfranchised by the Act of Union, Session 1805 (89)*, viii, pp 29–31. **218** Burtchaell, *Kilkenny MPs*, p. 144; Canon James B. Leslie, *Ossory clergy and parishes ...* (Enniskillen, 1933), pp 64–5; *Cork Chronicle*, 14 July 1768; St Canice corporation book, NLI, p. 5143; Charles Dodgson, bishop of Ossory, to Townshend, 2 June 1772, RCB Library, Ms. 20/52. **219** Newcome to John Hely-Hutchinson, 8 Sep. 1779, *HMC Donoughmore Mss.*, p. 293; *Journals of the House of Commons of the kingdom of Ireland, 1613–1800* (19 vols., Dublin, 1796–1800), ix. 298. **220** William Eden (later 1st Lord Auckland) to Northington, 20 Aug. 1783, Pelham papers, BL, Add. Ms. 33100, ff. 298–9.

jeopardise the seat. There was no such justification for the other member he returned, who was his nephew, the Hon. Richard Annesley; and in 1790, he returned his son, Marcus Beresford. The return of the latter had angered Westmorland (see p. 175); but, when called upon early in 1794, Bishop Beresford accommodated the government by vacating his son's seat to make room for Westmorland's new chief secretary, Sylvester Douglas.[221]

In Clogher, the electorate was, from small beginnings, increasingly widened, and by the early 1780s the once biddable borough was becoming insecure. The opposition which manifested itself at the time of the 1783 general election, was fanned by the Volunteer movement,[222] just as a later opposition in 1800 would be fanned by the opposition to the Union (see p. 571). In advance of the 1783 election, Bishop Hotham claimed that the politically volatile state of the borough made it unsafe for him to set up either of the candidates nominated to him by the government. Under very strong pressure, he 'squeaked' (as the lord lieutenant unceremoniously put it). But he still insisted that the late Bishop Garnett's *protégé*, Thomas St George, the episcopal agent, who was one of the sitting members and popular among the locals, should again be set up: otherwise, he prophesied, one or both seats might be lost to the bishop and the government.[223] In the event, there was an opposition, followed by a petition against what Hotham called 'the most constitutional ... [return] in the kingdom'. The outcome was that the election of St George and the Castle's nominee, Under-Secretary Sackville Hamilton, was confirmed.[224] In 1783, as in 1800, the matter at issue was the extent of the borough boundaries;[225] and it was very remiss of Hotham not to get this sorted out between 1783 and his death in 1795.

The nominees of government were unwelcome to the locals for two good reasons. The first was that, because they were often Castle officials, they were complete outsiders to the borough concerned – Sylvester Douglas thought that he was being returned for St Eunice![226] Such carpet-bagging was a positive danger in an insecure borough. But even in secure Old Leighlin, with its small electorate comprising the thirteen burgesses of the corporation, all of them dutiful clergy of the united dioceses of Ferns and Leighlin, Bishop Garnett was relieved in 1757 to find that the government was willing 'to make some disposition more favourable to me than putting a person plump upon me that I might either not like, or perhaps not know'.[227] At the general election of 1797, Under-Secretary William Elliott was so little-known in St

221 Burtchaell, *Kilkenny MPs*, pp 179 and 183.   222 Hotham to Sackville, 9 July 1782, *HMC Stopford-Sackville Mss.*, i. 279.   223 Northington to William Windham (his chief secretary), 11 May and 18 [July?] 1783, Windham papers, BL, Add. Ms. 37873, ff. 11–13 and 23; Hotham to Windham, 4 July 1783, HO 100/9, ff. 211–12; Hotham to Windham, 8 July 1783, Northington letter-book, BL, Add. Ms. 38716, f. 53.   224 Hotham to Buckinghamshire, 7 Nov. 1783, *HMC Lothian Mss.*, pp 421–2; *Irish Commons' journals*, xi, pp 27–8 and 185; copy extracts, 1783–98, from the Clogher corporation book, PRONI, T/1566.   225 *Irish Commons' journals*, xix, pp 34, 54, 73–4 and 122; John Porter, bishop of Clogher, to Castlereagh, 21 Apr. 1800, NA, Official Papers, 515/85/5.   226 *Glenbervie diaries*, i. 41.   227 Garnett to [Richard?] Burgh, 6 Jan. 1757, Burgh papers, NLI, Ms. 8606.

Canice (for which he had been sitting since 1796), that he was returned by the wrong christian name, and the validity of the return had to be confirmed by an election committee of the House of Commons.[228] In order to mitigate the foreignness of such representatives, the bishops rightly insisted that they should pay all the expenses which local traditions and sensitivities required. At Old Leighlin in 1790, these expenses amounted to £30 7s. 6d. each,[229] and at Clogher in 1797 to something similar plus a donation of £50 each towards local improvements.[230] The other reason for carpet-baggers from the Castle to be unpopular locally was that their election often meant that the borough was unrepresented for years, particularly in the absence of a Place Act until 1793.[231] This applied particularly to chief secretaries, because there was more rapid turnover among them than among the under-secretaries and smaller fry. Even after 1793, the chief secretaries continued – needlessly – to be a blight, simply because old habits died hard. In May 1796, Camden noted: 'Lord Milton, [Sylvester] Douglas and ... [Lord Hobart] are all members of the Irish parliament and have all kept their seats. ... It would be desirable that these gentlemen should vacate by accepting the escheatorship of Munster, etc., ... as I do not suppose that any of them are desirous of retaining their situations.'[232] Hobart, who was MP for Armagh, had been Westmorland's first chief secretary, but had been in India since 1793! In view of this negligence, it was ridiculous for Westmorland to claim that he did not 'know how we shall bring in the secretaries at the next parliament'.

The best justification there was for the government's jitteriness about the bishops' boroughs was the behaviour of Walter Cope of Drumilly, Co. Armagh, who was bishop of Ferns, 1782–7. In 1772, Cope's brother-in-law, Sir Archibald Acheson, later 1st Viscount Gosford, another Co. Armagh landowner, had urged Townshend to promote Cope to Ferns, so that Cope would be able to return Acheson's two sons for old Leighlin at the next general election. Townshend was hard-pressed for votes and did not want to offend Acheson. So he did not point out the impropriety of this proposal.[233] Cope was promoted to Ferns ten years later, and entered into some kind of understanding with the lord lieutenant at that time, Portland, about the future return of the Hon. Arthur Acheson. However, following Portland's resignation later in 1782, Portland punctiliously pointed out that he had 'transacted that business as lord lieutenant, and it consequently belongs to the present lord lieutenant to recommend, or to whomsoever may be the lord lieutenant at the time of the dissolution of the parliament, the condition being made for government.'[234] Fortunately for Cope,

228 Opinion of Viscount Pery, [2 Aug. 1797–15 Jan. 1798], Foster/Massereene papers, PRONI, D/567/7594; *Irish Commons' journals*, xvii, pp 196, 216, 218 and 222.   229 Copy statement of election expenses, 4 May 1790, Gosford papers, PRONI, D/1606/1/146B.   230 Bishop Porter to Castlereagh, 24 Jan. 1800, Castlereagh papers, PRONI, D/3030/1193.   231 Charles O'Hara to Edmund Burke, 9 July 1768, printed in Ross J.S. Hoffman, *Edmund Burke: New York agent* (Philadelphia, 1965), p. 435.   232 Camden to Pelham, 23 May 1796, Pelham papers, BL, Add. Ms. 33102, ff. 16–18.   233 Acheson to Townshend, 2 Sep. 1772, Townshend papers, NA, M 655; Townshend to Acheson, 7 Sep. 1772, Gosford papers, PRONI, D/1606/1/75B.   234 Lord Edward Bentinck (writing on behalf of his brother, Portland) to [the Hon. Arthur Acheson], 28 Feb. 1783, D/1606/1/101.

the lord lieutenant at the time of the 1783 general election, Northington, was 'a good friend' of Arthur Acheson, who accordingly was returned.[235] In the following February, Northington – now in his turn out of office – wrote to his successor recommending Lord Gosford for a viscountcy and pointing out that, at the previous election, Cope had been the only bishop with a borough who had given both seats to the government.[236] This was strictly speaking true, but only because the government approved of the relation whom Cope wanted, and probably intended, to return anyway.

At the beginning of 1787, when the other seat for Old Leighlin fell vacant because the sitting member, Lord Luttrell, succeeded to his father's earldom of Carhampton, Cope appeared in his true colours. He was now over seventy-five[237] and evidently took the view that he was too old to be in line for further promotion in the Church. He therefore resolved to flout the wishes of the government and consult the interests of his own family again, this time by returning Nicholas Archdale of Castle Archdale, Co. Fermanagh, who was married to his niece and heiress (Cope himself being childless). The government had other plans for the seat. It also had a candidate likely to appeal to an electorate of thirteen clergymen (assuming that they were all clergymen in 1787, as they certainly were in 1800). This was Edward Leslie of Tarbert, Co. Kerry, who was described in a discreetly worded canvassing letter from Dublin Castle as 'the son of the late bishop of Limerick [James Leslie (d.1770)] ..., [who] has showed himself very zealous in support of the Church against the Whiteboys, by which he has suffered in his property.'[238] Cope and the government were still at loggerheads when parliament re-assembled on 19 January 1787 after the Christmas recess, and a procedural wrangle ensued in the House of Commons. An opposition member moved for the writ to issue for the Old Leighlin by-election, but Attorney-General FitzGibbon opposed this on the ground that Lord Luttrell had not yet taken his seat in the House of Lords and his right to the peerage might be disputed or even rejected. Speaker Foster, though a prominent government supporter, saw it as his first duty to support the independence of the House. He ruled that the House was bound to keep its numbers full, and that its writ should not 'depend either on the will of the other House, of the crown or of the peer himself'. Normally, the speaker's ruling on a matter of this kind would have been final. But tempers were so inflamed over Cope's behaviour, that the government forced a division, which it carried by 80 to 26.[239] Meanwhile, the will of the House of Lords could not be ascertained, because

235 Endorsement by Acheson on a letter to him from the portrieve of Old Leighlin, 30 July 1783, D/1606/1/104. 236 Northington to Rutland, 27 Feb. 1784, *HMC Rutland Mss.*, iii. 76. 237 Canon James B. Leslie, *Armagh clergy and parishes ...* (Dundalk, 1911), p. 354. Leslie states that Cope was born c.1711. 238 Thomas Orde (the chief secretary) to Speaker Foster, 23 Jan. 1787, Foster/Massereene papers, PRONI, MIC/680/L/2/30. 239 Speaker Foster's account of the proceedings in the House of Commons on 19 Jan. 1787, Foster/Massereene papers, PRONI, D/562/7564. This is also the source of the information that Cope wanted to return Archdale. The outcome of a debate on 12 Oct. 1773 about precisely this procedural point, recorded in the *Clonmell diary* (TCD), p. 272, had anticipated Foster's view.

it had been adjourned, 'principally to give time to influence the Bishop of Ferns to return a friend of government in the room of Lord Carhampton'.[240] By 23 January, either Cope was won round or the electors looked like deserting him, because on that date the writ issued. Edward Leslie was in due course elected, but Cope must have secured a *quid quo pro*: Arthur Acheson, the other member, was re-elected at the general election of 1790 and sat until he succeeded as 2nd Viscount Gosford later in the year. Meanwhile, Cope – as if to demonstrate that this had been his last throw – had died soon after the *furore* of January 1787.[241]

Cope's was an extreme case. No bishop with anything to gain or lose at the hands of government (certainly no heavyweight political prelate like Agar) would have stooped to the small-time advantage of sneaking a return for a bishop's borough. What is also significant about the Cope case is that the government had over-indulged Cope in 1783 and was ultimately successful in bringing him to heel in 1787. The general election of 1783, when for the first time it was stated as an ancient custom and usage that the bishops returned none but the nominees of the government of the day, took place under decidedly exceptional circumstances. It was preceded by three rapid changes of British, and therefore of Irish, administration; and 'the government of the country for the time being' suspected that in 1782–3 Bishops Hotham of Clogher and Beresford of Ossory were being swayed by promises to one or other previous administration, rather than by genuine fears of local opposition.[242] As has been seen, Cope was really a worse offender than either of them, and so indeed was Primate Robinson. Robinson faced no local opposition in Armagh borough, and yet suited himself rather than the government of the day in his choice of MPs for Armagh in 1783 (see p. 459).

There was not much the government could do about a real opposition in one of the boroughs (except urge the bishop to deal with it more effectively than Hotham did in Clogher). But, in other respects, the prevention and cure of episcopal recalcitrance lay in the government's own hands. In the case of William Foster, who was the younger brother of the politically very active speaker, and whom Camden reluctantly made bishop of Clogher in 1795, Camden took the sensible and obvious course of extracting a written pledge that William Foster would accord to 'the government of the country for the time being ... the privilege of recommending exclusively the members who may be to serve in parliament for that borough'. 'I do not suppose' Camden added 'it will weaken his good intention to know that [such a document] ... exists in the secretary of state's office in England.'[243] No such pledge had been extracted by Fitzwilliam from Newcome. But just after Fitzwilliam's recall it was stated with confidence: 'as to Armagh, those seats will go with the government of the

240 E.H. Pery to Lady Hunt, 23 Jan. 1787, Sir Vere Hunt letter-books, no. 3, Limerick Regional Archives. 241 *BLGI*, followed by Canon Leslie in the three *Clergy and parishes* volumes in which Cope appears, gives the date of Cope's death as 31 July 1787: *Musgrave's Obituary* gives 2 August. 242 2nd earl of Shelburne to Portland, 18 May 1782, and Northington to North, 4 July 1783, HO 100/1, f. 225, and HO 100/9, ff. 211–12; North to Northington, 11 July 1783, Pelham papers, BL., Add. Ms. 33100, ff. 193–5. 243 Camden to Portland, 'received' 15 Dec. 1795, HO 100/46, ff. 348–52.

country'.[244] In 1797, Newcome, unmindful of what he owed the Emancipationist Fitzwilliam, toadyingly 'made a particular request' that the anti-Emancipationist Camden's chief secretary be returned for Armagh.[245] In mid-April 1800, when the primacy was still vacant following the death of Newcome, it looked as if a by-election for Armagh was going to become necessary, and the Castle feared for the consequences in view of the then state of public feeling on the Union. However, the Very Rev. Charles Mongan Warburton, who was one of the burgesses (and was most anxious to be made a bishop)[246] wrote reassuringly that the sovereign (or mayor) and twelve burgesses considered themselves as trustees for the government and would return anyone recommended by the government to the sovereign.[247]

For all the confusion and hype over the bishops' boroughs, the reality was rela-tively simple: allowance had to be made by the Castle for the endemic shakiness of episcopal control in St Canice and its new and growing shakiness in Clogher; but, otherwise, any administration of reasonable competence was well able to control the bishops and any bishop of reasonable competence was well able to control his borough in the interests of government. This reality was obscured by the coincidence that the 1783 general election came in the middle of a period of rapid turnover of adminis-trations, and by the fact that some administrations – notably those of Northington and Westmorland – were at once feeble and alarmist in their handling of the bishops' boroughs. The consequences of the Castle's muddled obsessiveness fell dispropor-tionately upon the Irishmen on the Irish episcopal bench, since they were inherently more likely than the Englishmen to belong to Irish political connections. In this respect, Cope, the electoral-bishop of Ferns, did his compatriots a great disservice. Because he was Irish, his insubordination towards the government quite effaced from memory the recollection that three of the previous or current delinquents in this respect, Garnett, Robinson and Hotham, were English. Robinson was also implicated in Cope's delinquency, since Cope was a *protégé* of Robinson. Indeed, it was asserted in August 1782 that 'the Primate got Cope to Ferns' and 'most probably they have taken care of the two seats for next general election'.[248] In spite of all this recent experience to the contrary, unreliability in the management of bishops' boroughs was deemed (except by Westmorland) to be an exclusively Irish failing.

The consequences for Agar were profound. No Irish bishop was more obviously a member (many would have said the leader) of an Irish, borough-based political connection than was he. The primacy fell vacant in 1794, during the period between 1787 (Cope) and 1795 (William Foster), when the government's alarmism about the bishops' boroughs was at its peak. In 1794 there was also, in effect, a viceregal interregnum, complicated by all the tensions and difficulties inherent in forming a

244 Brodrick to Midleton, 11 Mar. 1795, Ms. 1248, vol. 16, ff. 25–6. 245 Brodrick to Midleton, 21 July 1797, Ms. 1248, vol. 17, f. 30. 246 The King to Portland, 12 Mar. 1795, *Later correspondence of George III*, ii. 320. 247 Warburton to Colonel Littlehales, 13 Apr. 1800, NA, Official Papers, 515/85/4. Warburton had to wait for his bishopric until 1806 (see p. 507). 248 General John Pomeroy to his brother, Arthur, later 1st Lord Harberton, 11 Aug. 1782, Pomeroy papers, PRONI, T/2954/4/8.

coalition government; so, clear thinking about the disposal of the office was not to be expected. Against this background, it is not over-dramatic to suggest that Lord Clifden's boroughs and 'the borough annexed to the primacy' were the rocks on which Agar's pre-eminent pretensions foundered. They were extraordinary and indeed frivolous grounds for disqualifying him, granted that he was far and away the strongest candidate on the Irish bench, and granted that much more was at stake in selecting a head of the Church of Ireland than the security of 'the borough annexed to the primacy'. The consequences for the Church were also profound. It failed to get an energetic and efficient leader. It also failed to shake off English dominance of its highest positions at a time when every other major Irish institution – the judiciary, the revenue, the exchequer and the treasury (everything except the Dublin Castle adminis-tration itself) – had already done so, some of them many years previously. Even the chief secretaryship went Irish in 1798, and Castlereagh was not the first Irish appointee to that office. In 1822, when Lord John George Beresford became the first Irishman to attain the primacy in 120 years, the same objection might have been made to him as had been made to his uncle, William Beresford, or to Agar, in 1794; he was 'certainly attached to a party in Ireland, and his appointment would throw too much weight to that scale'. The difference in 1822 was that there was no longer an Irish parliament to manage, the bishops' boroughs in Ireland were no longer an obsession of government because only Armagh had survived the Union, and the Anglo-Irish ruling class no longer had the power to be 'busy' and 'troublesome' – in other words to defend its interests against English encroachment or betrayal.

5

Agar as improving and reforming churchman, 1768–1801

Agar was by profession a churchman, and because he took his profession seriously, it was his most important role in life. This may sound a little simplistic. However, the fact is that he has generally been thought of as a politician and judged, usually harshly, from that perspective; and insofar as his role as a churchman has been considered at all, it has been for the purpose of demonstrating his self-aggrandisement, his nepotism and his general worldliness. The same slanted view was until recently[1] taken of FitzGibbon. Though FitzGibbon was a lawyer by profession and for most of his comparatively short life a law officer or lord chancellor, little attempt was previously made to assess him in that professional role, which apart from anything else consumed most of his time and made him at best a part-time politician. What follows, in this and the succeeding Chapters, is an attempt to provide a proper focus in Agar's case by considering the leading features of his churchmanship – administration, legislation, building, music, clerical standards and organised defence of the Established Church. These are likely to have been the achievements by which Agar himself expected to be judged. The inscription on his fine funeral monument in the north choir aisle of Westminster Abbey, sculpted by John Bacon junior in 1815 (fig. 17), runs as follows:

> In the course of his episcopal labours, not less than seventeen churches, and twenty-two glebe houses for the residence of the clergy, were built under his direction and assistance;[2] and he erected, principally at his own charge, the cathedral church of Cashel. As a statesman and prelate, he was an able and zealous supporter of the religion which he professed and taught, and of the country whose councils he assisted. His care for the welfare of the Church is testified by the numerous acts of parliament he framed for her permanent regulation and support. The perfect state in which his diocese was left, and the veneration impressed by his talents and virtue[s][3] on the hearts of those over whom he presided, are nobler monuments than any which can be erected to his memory.[4]

1 Kavanaugh, *Lord Clare*, especially Chapter Eight.   2 These figures may be Lady Normanton's misreading of a passage in Agar's 'state' of the diocese of Cashel, 1779–1801 (21 M 57/B6/1), because they overestimate his record of building at Cashel. If they relate to Cloyne and Dublin as well as Cashel, they are an underestimate.   3 In autograph drafts of the inscription by Lady Normanton, the word is the less immodest 'virtues' – 21 M 57, 2nd Earl's unreferenced correspondence.   4 Transcription made by Dean Wyse-Jackson and preserved among his papers in the

This was the inscription which later provoked the misplaced indignation of Lecky (see p. 5). In addition to the inscription, Agar's monument includes a full-length representation of Agar in archiepiscopal robes, a scaled-down model of Cashel cathedral, and a figure of a young clergyman who holds a book open at the text from St Paul's *Letter to the Galatians*, 'Let us not be weary in welldoing'. According to a family tradition, the young clergyman is Agar's nephew, the Rev. Welbore Ellis Agar (1774–1810), although this is likely to be a mistake for Agar's third, and only clerical, son, the Hon. and Ven. James Agar (1781–1866).[5] The introduction of a 'nephew' into a monument to a prelate widely accused of nepotism was perhaps unfortunate: was Agar never weary of welldoing, or was he never weary of doing well for himself and family?

However, the essential point which the inscription grasps, and most subsequent comments on Agar, including Lecky's, miss, is that Agar was first and foremost a churchman, and that by the standards of churchmen of the last third of the eighteenth century, his record of welldoing is impressive. In considering his 17 churches and 22 glebe-houses built in the time he was at Cashel (or perhaps at Cloyne and Cashel), it is important to remember that he died just a year after the big bonanza in ecclesiastical building in Ireland began to happen (see pp 276–80), financed by the parliament of the United Kingdom under the liberal and indulgent terms of a key act of 1808 (*48 George III, cap. 65*). On figures alone, Thomas Lewis O'Beirne, bishop of Ossory, 1795–8, and of Meath, 1798–1823, seems a more improving churchman than Agar, because O'Beirne lived until the year when the bonanza ended, and so could claim, in Meath alone, 72 glebe-houses and 57 churches on his funeral monument.[6] But this is not to compare like with like and Agar with approximately contemporary bishops of the period *c.*1760–1810.

IMPROVING OR INACTIVE?: THE IRISH EPISCOPATE

Agar became a bishop in what was in many respects an age of episcopal improvement, in the values and civilising aspirations of which he warmly participated. 'Improving ... leaders of the Church of Ireland' of the period 1660–1760

> rationalised parochial organisation, facilitated clerical residence, set or supplemented minimum salaries and assisted in the building of churches and

---

Bolton Library, Cashel. 5 S.A. Quan-Smith to a newspaper editor, 29 Sep. 1911, Wyse-Jackson papers, Bolton Library; information kindly provided by Mr Terence Finley. For the careers in the Church of these two young Agars, see pp 137 and 244–5. The young clergyman in the background is likely to be Agar's nephew. The older man beside him, who has been identified in family tradition as Lord Mendip (whom he in no way resembles), is probably Agar's vicar-general in Cashel, the Rev. Patrick Hare (see pp 88–9). 6 Rev. John Healy, *History of the diocese of Meath* (2 vols, Dublin, 1908), ii. 163.

... [glebe-houses] and the provision of glebes where they were wanting. Concurrently, most bishops and affluent clergymen set a better example, passing at least the summer in distant dioceses, chivvying, chiding and leading the parish incumbents, [and] endowing and ornamenting churches, libraries and charities ... . Clergymen keen to improve themselves and others took up building and architecture. ... Bishops and the wealthier clergy exerted a disproportionate influence over the reception of classical archi-tecture into Ireland in the later seventeenth and early eighteenth centuries, because they had trained and travelled outside Ireland ..., at Christ Church ..., [and in] London, France, Italy or Holland, ... and returned ... confident that building bestowed larger cultural, ideological and practical benefits.[7]

Edward Synge, bishop of Elphin, 1740–62, was one of the ornaments of this slightly self-indulgent age of improvement (in which the episcopal palaces and 'private palazzi' built by the bishops were much more splendid than their churches and cathedrals): 'He built the present palace [at Elphin] himself, and all the offices. 'Tis an extreme[ly] good gentleman's house of six rooms on a floor, with colonnades and the offices at each end of them. His demesne, which he has finely improved, is about 300 Irish acres. He lives in great plenty and hospitality, and keeps an exceedingly good and genteel table. The demesne ... furnishes his house'.[8] For Synge, Elphin represented 'house, improvements, everything now the comfort and joy of my life'.[9] Higher clergy like him were important trend-setters and fashioners of fashion for the further, very practical reason that they, unlike lay landowners, were able to build and landscape their palaces and ex officio residences largely at the expense of their ecclesiastical successors (see pp 337–47).

This pleasing prospect of an age of episcopal improvement in the Church of Ireland has been portrayed in darker colours by Jeremiah Falvey in a recent 'over-view' of eighteenth-century Irish bishops and bishoprics:

> With twenty-two bishops to maintain ordination levels among 600 lower clergy, to administer confirmation to one person in twenty of the Irish population, to hold a cursory annual diocesan visitation [and for archbishops a triennial provincial visitation] and to attend parliamentary sessions every other year for practically the whole century (annual parliaments were from 1784 onwards), the prelates had plenty of time on their hands to enjoy and, at times, selfishly to defend, their benefits and privileges ... . On numerical evidence alone, it is obvious that there were too many Irish bishops for the discharge of the light episcopal duties which they were obliged to perform. ... In England, the twenty-six bishops were required to attend at *annual*

---

7 Barnard, 'Improving clergymen', pp 138 and 146.   8 Edward McParland, *Public architecture in Ireland, 1680–1760* (Yale, 2001), p. 49; Willes to Lord Warwick, 1761, *Willes letters*, p. 86. For the question of palace-building, see Chapter Eight.   9 Synge to Owen Wynne, 18 Aug. 1757, Wynne papers, PRONI, MIC/666/D/7.

parliaments in London for up to nine months of the year. As well, confirmations in England were often huge affairs, very often involving thousands
of confirmands. This is why Irish bishoprics were sometimes very attractive
propositions to ... English clergy, especially those whose inclination tended
towards the cultivation of improvement and leisure.[10]

These comments are extremely useful in establishing a context in which the light-
ness or heaviness of the episcopal load may be considered. But Falvey's contrast is
overdrawn and introduces some distortions.

For one thing, much the same has been said of the twenty-six English bishops.
Professor Plumb, for example, concluded (somewhat sweepingly): 'There is a
worldliness, almost a venality, about eighteenth-century prelates which no amount
of apologetics can conceal. The clerical duties of visitation, ordination and confirmation were done only as political duties allowed.'[11] More tellingly, the prime
minister, George Grenville, observed in late 1764 or early 1765 that the bishoprics
of the Church of England were 'of two kinds: bishoprics of business for men of
abilities and learning, and bishoprics of ease for men of family and fashion. Of the
former sort he reckoned Canterbury and York and London and Ely ...; of the latter
sort, Durham and Winchester and Salisbury and Worcester.'[12] It was said of one
bishop of Winchester, the Hon. Brownlow North (Lord North's younger brother),
that 'as a bishop, he belonged rather to the ornamental order ..., absent for years in
Continental travel'. Brownlow North was briefly (1770–1) dean of Canterbury; and
the *Lives of the deans of Canterbury* of the period 1760–1809, some of whom
became bishops or in one instance an archbishop, reveal that only one dean out of
nine was distinguished as a clergyman, the rest being conspicuous for nepotism,
favouritism, pluralism and neglect.[13] So, there was no need for a well connected
clergyman of the Church of England to come to Ireland for a life of leisure.

Falvey's strictures are also more applicable to the first two-thirds of the century
than to most of Agar's time on the Irish bench. There is a general tendency to
transpose evidence from the first third of the century – particularly the many
complaints which came from the busy pen of Archbishop King – to a later period,
with distorting effect. In 1718, King lamented that there were under 200 good
benefices in the country, 'one-half of which are in the crown; and, our chief governors
changing in a year or two, they complain that there are not avoidances enough during
their time to prefer their chaplains they bring along with them', each of whom 'must
have a bishopric or at least £400 per annum'.[14] King later complained that 'the bishops
sent to us from England follow the same track in many instances. The Bishop of Derry
[William Nicolson] since his translation to that see [in 1718] has given about £2,000

10 Falvey, 'Church of Ireland episcopate', pp 105–6.   11 J.H. Plumb, *England in the eighteenth
century* ... (Harmondsworth, 1970), p. 43.   12 Autobiography of Thomas Newton, bishop of
Bristol, printed in Adam Clarke (ed.), [*Compendium edition of*] *the lives of ... Newton ..., [etc.], and
of the Rev. Philip Skelton by Mr [Samuel] Burdy* (2 vols., London, 1816), ii. 154.   13 J. Meadows
Cowper, *Deans of Canterbury, 1541 to 1900* ... (Canterbury, 1900), pp 174–207.

[per annum] to his English friends and relations.'[15] ... King's views were probably overstated at the time; and the situation changed greatly in a number of respects – for example the absolute and relative value of the bishops' patronage (see pp 193–4 and 213–17) – in the course of the century.

One factor was the disuniting of geographically inappropriate or financially overlucrative unions of parishes which, together with some modest progress made in augmenting the value of small livings, meant that there was a tendency towards the levelling of clerical incomes. The lower clergy numbered 600 in the 1720s; but Grattan reckoned them at 900 in 1788, and the figure had climbed to 1,625 by 1830.[16] This, too, had some effect in spreading income more evenly. Nor did it conduce to greater leisure. This was because the growth of the Anglican population outstripped the increase in clerical numbers (and the growth of the population as a whole even more so). Thus, in the diocese of Dublin, there were *c.*140 clergymen (including 47 curates) in 1801, as compared to 87 in 1700; but the Anglican population of the diocese, and with it the workload of the clergy, increased still more strikingly over the same period. The ratio of clergy to flock was 1:856 in 1700 and 1:1308 in 1800.[17]

Another change was that the Church of Ireland became progressively less open and less attractive to English interlopers. The growing influence and unmanageability of the Irish House of Commons meant that, from the 1750s onwards, an increasing proportion of livings in the Church of Ireland (though not of bishoprics until the end of the century – see pp 489–90 and 600–6) had to be given to Irishmen and often with an eye to parliamentary management. The rise of the Catholic Question from the early 1770s onwards, and the explosion of the tithe question in the mid-1780s, made Ireland additionally unattractive to English clergymen, including those like Primate Robinson who were already serving there (see pp 448 and 461). Even before then, at the time of Robinson's appointment in 1765, it had proved impossible to induce bishops on the English bench to accept the exceedingly lucrative archbishopric of Armagh (p. 441), 'the first and richest in Ireland, and perhaps richer than any in England'.[18] The same happened again when Robinson died in 1794 (p. 173), and it very nearly happened again in 1800 (pp 592–8). In 1768, John Green, bishop of Lincoln, tried to get himself made bishop of Derry (without success, because of the more powerful influence of Frederick Hervey). Green's aspiration is understandable: Derry was the richest bishopric in Ireland, and Lincoln, as Green himself put it, was the bishopric with the largest jurisdiction and the least revenue in England.[19] Green's was therefore an extreme case. More typical of the English clergyman surveying the Irish scene in the

---

14 Quoted in Kennedy, 'Dublin and Glendalough', pp 75–6, and in O'Regan, *Archbishop William King*, p. 325.   15 Quoted in Johnston[-Liik], 'Problems common to both protestant and catholic Churches in eighteenth-century Ireland', in Oliver MacDonagh, W.F. Mandle and Pauric Travers (eds.), *Irish culture and nationalism, 1750–1950* (London, 1983), pp 15–16.   16 Johnston-Liik, 'Common problems', p. 15; John C. Erck, *An account of the ecclesiastical establishment ... in Ireland, as also an ecclesiastical register of the ... dignitaries and parochial clergy and of the parishes ...* (Dublin, 1830), p. xxv.   17 Kennedy, 'Dublin and Glendalough', p. 224.   18 *Autobiography of Bishop Newtown*, loc. cit., ii. 156.   19 Green to Townshend, 15 June 1768 and 24 May 1771, Townshend letter-book,

last third of the eighteenth century was Euseby Cleaver, who became bishop of Ferns in 1789 and archbishop of Dublin, in succession to Agar, in 1809. In 1784, Cleaver declared categorically: 'No prebend[ary] of Westminster will accept Killala'.[20] As recently as 1771, Fowler, then a prebendary of Westminster, dean of Norwich and a chaplain to the king, had accepted the less desirable bishopric of Killaloe; so the explanation which Cleaver gave a couple of years later, in 1787, for the diminished appeal of Ireland is of great interest:

> The Church is [not] an inviting profession in Ireland. The parochial clergy
> have ... many difficulties respecting their income and their residence, even
> in times which are not tumultuous ... . The dignities are but few in number,
> and those you will say too much occupied by English. But in some degree
> from ill-founded prejudice and in some degree from the influence of your
> [the Irish] parliament, that evil will decrease daily.[21]

Not only did the members of the Irish parliament absorb Church patronage; they were hostile to English carpet-baggers, and a great many of them were anti-clerical.

In June 1786, a frightening picture of the gentry's indisposition to the clergy was painted by Charles Brodrick, who was serving as a clergyman and as representative of his absentee brother, the 4th Viscount Midleton, in the east Cork parish of Midleton, and therefore in the eye of the Rightboy storm. 'There is not in the whole country [Co. Cork] one gentleman out of twenty that is not ..., as far as the paying of tithe goes, a perfect Whiteboy, and they seem to carry their prejudices so far that no person has as yet shown the smallest disposition to stop the dreadful outrages that we hear of every day'.[22] Primate Robinson concurred. In May 1788 he observed to Agar 'that the real cause [of clamour against the clergy] is to be found in the persevering purpose of the landowners for half a century to transfer the property of the clergy and the impropriators to their own uses.' To this Agar replied: 'The landowners (as your Grace observes very truly) are certainly the originators and promoters of the various attempts to deprive the clergy of their property.'[23]

Such accusations and lamentations from churchmen are commonplace in this period: what is harder to find is an expression of the reasoned views of the gentry. A good example of the latter is a letter of March 1788 from Robert Day, M.P. for Ardfert, Co. Kerry, to the patron of that borough and of Day himself, the 2nd Earl of Glandore, who lived at nearby Ardfert Abbey. Day was a friend of Grattan, who

RCB Library, Ms. 20/157 and 163; William Law Mathieson, *English Church reform, 1815–1840* (London, 1923), p. 75; Akenson, *Church of Ireland*, p. 82. In general, bishops of the Church of Ireland had responsibility for smaller dioceses, comprising fewer benefices, than bishops of the Church of England. So, the case for reducing the number of Irish bishops was strong – see p. 506.   20 Cleaver to his Irish friend, Charles O'Hara, 19 June [1784], O'Hara papers, PRONI, T/2812/18/8.   21 Cleaver to O'Hara, 16 Sep. [1787], ibid., T/2812/18/14.   22 Brodrick to Midleton, 20 June 1786, Ms. 1248, vol. 14, f. 94.   23 Robinson to Agar, 23 May 1788, and Agar to Robinson, 2 June 1788, T/3719/C/22/19 and 22.

at this time was taking a lead with proposals for tithe reform,[24] and whose 'present scheme', as reported by Day,

> is to make a run at the bishops by introducing a number of reasonable bills for limiting the tithes of the three staple articles of flax, hemp and rape to 5 per cent per acre, for exempting reclaimed bog and mountain from all tithe for seven years [Grattan's so-called Barren Lands Bill], ... etc. These it is expected will be rejected by the bishops, or through their influence, and then when some scandal and indignation are excited, he will introduce his great [tithe] bill and circulate it through the kingdom, and by next session he is sanguine enough to hope that the whole south, clergy as well as laity, will press forward to demand it, and so they ought; for nothing can be more simple, practicable or just.[25]

Agar, too, had a correspondent from this part of Co. Kerry. This was Thomas Graves, dean of Ardfert (a diocese united to that of Limerick since 1661). He wrote in the same month to Agar (his metropolitan), whom he hailed as 'the most zealous and the most able advocate for the character, the property and the rights of the clergy that I can with any propriety resort to', stating the view that in Kerry, where 'very large tracts' of land 'in all parts' of the county 'are likely to come under the description of "barren" ..., the effect of such a law ... will be the reduction of the income of the clergy ... by one *full third* in the space of a very few years, and the engaging 'em in endless perplexity, expense and litigation in endeavours to disprove the allegations of their parishioners that such and such lands are "barren lands" ' .[26]

What is interesting about these very conflicting views of Grattan's tithe reform proposals is that they not only came from the same neck of the woods, Ardfert, but from two men who on other issues had a great deal in common. Day was no radical (he was appointed a judge in 1798); Lord Glandore and he generally speaking supported the Dublin Castle administration; and Graves had been made dean of Ardfert through Lord Glandore's influence with the Castle. So, there can be no doubt that this correspondence of March 1788 illustrates how widespread, even among men of conservative views in the Irish parliament, were attitudes 'hostile to the rights of the clergy'.[27] A month earlier, Cleaver's patron, the lord lieutenant, Lord Buckingham, had written: 'the temptation which parliament feel to bribe themselves by a share of ... tithe plunder will operate very unfavourably for the clergy [of the Church of Ireland], who certainly depend only on the support of the crown for their existence.'[28]

Cleaver's own career move to Ireland, which took place *after* this anti-tithe agitation of 1785–7, seems superficially to be a contradiction of his argument that the Irish Church had ceased to be 'inviting' to Englishmen. Like Agar, he was an old

---

24 *A full report of the speech of the Rt Hon. Henry Grattan ... on Thursday the 14th of February 1788 in the debate on tithes, taken in shorthand by Mr Franklin* (Dublin, 1788), *passim.*   **25** Day to Glandore, 11 Mar. 1788, PRONI, MIC/639/16/38.   **26** Graves to Agar, 27 Mar. 1788, T/3719/C/22/7.   **27** Robinson to Agar, 8 July 1780, T/3719/C/14/23.   **28** Buckingham to Grenville, 18 Feb. 1788, *H.M.C. Dropmore Mss.*, i. 305.

boy of Westminster school, where he had been a contemporary and friend of George Wyndham, 3rd earl of Egremont (1751–1837). In due course, Egremont presented him to the living of Spofforth in Yorkshire and then, in 1783, to that of Petworth-cum-Tillington in Sussex, where Egremont's seat, Petworth House, was situated. Cleaver thought that there were 'very few gentlemen of £2,000 per annum better accommodated' than himself, and that Egremont had been 'uncommonly kind'.[29] In 1787, Egremont successfully recommended Cleaver as a viceregal chaplain to Buckingham, who was Egremont's cousin. Cleaver's father had been rector of Twyford, beside Buckingham's seat, Stowe, so Buckingham already knew Cleaver. In 1789, he made Cleaver bishop of Cork and then, a couple of months later, bishop of Ferns.[30] There were, however, special circumstances attending Cleaver's initial career move to Ireland in 1787. First, Cleaver was under pressure from his Irish wife, Catherine, daughter of the Rt Hon. Owen Wynne of Hazelwood, Co. Sligo, to make their home in Ireland.[31] Second, Egremont most indulgently kept Cleaver's Petworth living open for him, in case he did not fare well in Ireland. Third, Cleaver had the additional financial incentive to go to Ireland that he had been offered the position of head agent, or 'general supervisor', of Egremont's huge estate in Cos Clare and Limerick. This was an unseemly but not unheard-of sideline for a bishop of the Church of Ireland.[32] Cleaver was particularly well qualified for it. 'Finance happened to be the Bishop's hobby', remarks the historian of the Wyndham family with some surprise, obviously writing under the misapprehension that Cleaver was a man of God. 'No one was better informed on the terms of a government loan nor on bankers' and merchants' rates of exchange.'[33] Cleaver is also significant for the adventitious reason that he is probably the only Irish bishop who actually said that he had 'a great deal of leisure' (and so gives implicit support to the view that English clergymen were attracted to Ireland for that reason). In fact, he seems to have been a diligent diocesan (see p. 588), and probably made the remark simply because he was anxious at the time to confirm his suitability for the agency. Cleaver is therefore, on all these counts, no exception to his own rule that the Church of Ireland was increasingly uninviting to English clergymen.

29 Cleaver to O'Hara, [Mar.–May 1783] and 13 Aug. [1784], T/2812/18/7 and 9.   30 Rev. Henry Cotton, *Fasti Ecclesiae Hibernicae: the succession of the prelates and members of the cathedral bodies in Ireland* (6 vols., Dublin, 1845–79), i, pp 233–4; Hon. Joseph Deane Bourke, archbishop of Tuam, to Agar, 17 Dec. 1788, T/3719/C/22/53.   31 Cleaver to O'Hara, 13 Aug. [1784] and 24 [Nov.] 1788, T/2819/18/9 and 15.   32 The Hon. H.A. Wyndham, *A family history, 1688–1837: the Wyndhams of Somerset, Sussex and Wiltshire* (Oxford, 1950), pp 259–60. Other bishops who acted as agents for estates were Bishop Woodward of Cloyne (see p. 494), William Cecil Pery, bishop of Limerick (see Malcomson, *Speaker Pery and the Pery papers*, p. 38), Charles Brodrick, and the Hon. Power Le Poer Trench, archbishop of Tuam (1819–39) – the last two *before* they became bishops in 1795 and 1802 respectively. Of Trench's role as agent, his mid-nineteenth century biographer remarks: this was 'a course the law, happily, would not now permit, though in his case it proved of much benefit to all parties' – Rev. J.D. Sirr, *A memoir of ... [the] last archbishop of Tuam* (Dublin, 1845), p. 11. In all these cases, the bishop concerned was not acting in a purely commercial capacity, but on behalf of patrons or relations.   33 Wyndham, *A family history*, pp 259–60.

The life of an Irish bishop was so far from being more leisured than that of an English that, in important respects, Irish bishops – 'even in times which are not tumultuous' – had more than English bishops to do. Their annual visitations may in some instances have been 'cursory'; but at least they were annual. This was rarely the case in England.[34] When it was proposed in 1799 that they should be, the already-mentioned English expert, Sir William Scott, protested that such a duty would be 'new ..., incessant and painful, and productive of expense for which no fund whatever is provided'.[35] The four Irish archbishops were kept especially busy for, as the Hon. William Stuart, archbishop of Armagh, 1800–22, explained to the lord lieutenant in 1806,

> The archbishops in this country exercise a more extensive jurisdiction than is exercised by the archbishops in England. An English archbishop has little connection with his suffragan bishops and no connection with the clergy under those bishops. But in Ireland an archbishop not only visits his diocese regularly every year, but each diocese in his province once in three years, during which visit the functions and powers of suffragan bishops are entirely suspended [see pp 29 and 50]. He examines personally and publicly every individual clergyman, and puts what questions he thinks proper to the bishops, who are obliged to answer them in the presence of all the clergy.[36]

As well as having more frequent visitations to conduct, Irish archbishops and bishops had a more comprehensive patronage to administer. In Ireland, most of the patronage of each diocese (with the exception of Dublin – see pp 244–5) lay in the hands of the diocesan, which was a completely different situation from that obtaining in England.[37] In Ireland, 922 of the 1,396 benefices in existence in 1830 (or almost two-thirds) were in the gift of the diocesan, 64 were in some form of shared or alternate patronage involving the diocesan, and 410 were in the gift of the crown, lay corporations and individual laymen. In *c.*1810, Wakefield put the figure for crown patronage (by which he presumably meant exclusive, not shared, crown patronage) at 249, leaving only some 160 benefices in the exclusive patronage of lay corporations and individual laymen.[38] These country-wide statistics concealed some diocesan aberrations. For example, Bishop O'Beirne of Meath complained in 1803 that the 'numerous non-cures ... under the patronage of the crown and Lord Drogheda are the great nuisance of this diocese and are altogether useless to any purpose of religion or civilisation'.[39] But these non-cures, though a 'nuisance', did not alter the fact that the

34 Akenson, *Church of Ireland*, p. 28.   **35** Scott to Lord Grenville, 27 Dec. 1799, *H.M.C. Dropmore Mss.*, vi. 88.   **36** Stuart to 6th duke of Bedford, 27 Apr. 1806, Stuart papers, Bedfordshire and Luton RO, WY 993/12: *H.M.C. Dropmore Mss.* viii, pp 130–31. For his help with the Stuart papers, I am most grateful to Mr James Collett-White of the Bedfordshire RO. Copies of them have been available in the Armagh Public Library (founded by Primate Robinson) since 1999, and I am also most grateful to the librarian, the Very Rev. Herbert Cassidy, for the kindness he showed me while I was working on the copies.   **37** Akenson, *Church of Ireland*, p. 63.   **38** Erck, *Ecclesiastical register*, pp xxxiii and xliii; Wakefield, *Account of Ireland*, ii. 472.   **39** O'Beirne to Stuart, 2 Nov. 1803, Stuart

bishop of Meath presented to the majority of the livings in the diocese. Such patronage was not simply a matter of emolument and *largesse*. To an improving bishop it provided the wherewithal to encourage and reward deserving clergy, in a situation where bishops of both the Churches of England and Ireland were alleged to be 'destitute of power' to coerce and discipline the peccant (as Bishop Watson of Llandaff put it in 1803, and Primate Stuart in 1806, with reference to clerical residence).[40] In contrast to his English counterpart, a bishop of the Church of Ireland could make purposeful use of the system of annual visitations to identify clergy who were fit objects for 'the very extensive patronage'[41] in his gift.

Again, the statistic given in Falvey's 'overview' that only one member of the population in twenty was an Anglican requires comment. 'Eighteenth-century popula-tion statistics are notoriously unreliable and subject to continuous revision. However, it has been estimated that ... the Anglican population was probably about 1:8 of the population at the beginning of the century and 1:10 at its close.'[42] Whatever the statis-tics may be, they obscure the important fact that the maintenance of an extensive Establishment, without the presence and support of large numbers of Church of Ireland laymen, presented major difficulties of its own – and major obstacles to a life of leisure. The shortage of laity was graphically described in 1808 by Charles Brodrick, Agar's successor as archbishop of Cashel; Brodrick told his brother in England 'that in most instances in Ireland, we are obliged to elect churchwardens of the Romish persuasion, many of whom cannot read or write, and all of whom consider themselves, and are considered by others, as only the legal instruments for collecting parish rates. In all matters more immediately connected with church services, they do not interfere, nor are desired to interfere.'[43] So people to deal with 'all matters more immediately connected with church services' had, as a separate exercise, still to be found. Under the canons of the Church of Ireland, the bishops had certain powers of intervention when parishes failed to elected churchwardens, and in other cases of a like nature.[44] Statute law was also operative in this sphere. Under *33 George II, cap. 11*, churchwardens, whether of 'the Romish persuasion' or otherwise, were elected by and answerable to a select vestry composed of the protestant ratepayers of the parish. However, 'doubts' about these provisions (i.e. opposition to them) had been raised, 'which greatly tend[ed] to preventing the repair of parish churches'.[45] So Agar in 1785 sponsored an act (*25 George III, cap. 58*), which he called, more informatively than the official title, an act for ensuring that 'churchwardens ... [are] chosen by protestants

papers, Bedfordshire RO, WY 994/26.   40 Watson to George Hardinge, 19 Feb. 1803, *Anecdotes of the life of Richard Watson* ... (London, 1817), pp 361–4; Stuart to Brodrick, 24 Mar. 1806, NLI, Ms. 8869/5. The two churchmen used this phrase independently of each other. The reasons for the alleged powerlessness were different in the two Churches (see pp 232–7 and 270–74).   41 Camden to Portland, 9 May 1797, Home Office papers, HO/100/70, ff. 289–93. Camden was speaking of the patronage of the bishop of Clogher.   42 Johnston-Liik, 'Common problems', pp 14–15. For the most recent discussion of these problems, see Connolly, *Religion, law and power*, pp 144–9.   43 Brodrick to Midleton, post-marked 19 Aug. 1808, Ms. 1248, vol. 19, f. 21.   44 William Wickham (the chief secretary), to Agar, 6 July 1803, T/3719/ C/37/11.   45 *25 George III, cap. 58, sec. 3*.

only, and for the easy recovery of the salary of parish clerks',[46] should the select vestry fail to raise the latter or the churchwardens fail to pay it. He was also the initiator of three other pieces of legislation relating in whole or in part to church-repair and churchwardens – *11 and 12 George III, cap. 16, sec. 17, 21 and 22 George III, cap. 52,* and *29 George III, cap. 27.*

The exclusively protestant composition of select vestries, as confirmed by his act of 1785, was not overturned by the Catholic Relief Act of 1793, sweeping though that measure was. It made catholic ratepayers eligible for service on the general vestry, which was responsible for the local government duties of the parish, but stipulated that they should continue to be excluded from the select vestry and from the 'right to vote for levying of money to rebuild or repair any parish church, or respecting the demising or disposal of the income of any estate belonging to any church or parish, or for the salary of the parish clerk, or at the election of any churchwarden' (*33 George II, cap. 21, sec. 6*). However, major obstacles to the work of an improving bishop, which Agar's act had not even endeavoured to address, still remained. One was that protestant dissenters were eligible for service on both species of vestry (except for a short-lived incapacitation, 1774–6, which the pressure they applied to the northern members of the House of Commons swiftly terminated).[47] They were therefore in a position to block the raising of cesses for church repairs and other Anglican purposes, particularly where they were numerically and economically strongest, in Ulster. In 1795, Frederick Hervey, now 'earl-bishop' of Derry (who posed as the dissenters' friend and had supported the repeal of the Test in 1780), complained to Agar: 'I am overrun and run over with presbyterians'.[48] Another obstacle to the improving bishop may be inferred from a chance comment made by an English clergyman, the Rev. J. Burrows, who was on a visit to Ireland in the summer of 1773 in his capacity as tutor to the son of the Co. Monaghan magnate, the 1st Lord Dartrey. Burrows, struck by what he believed to be a contrast to the Church of England practice, remarked that an Irish bishop failed 'generally ... to attend [to] the state of the churches of his diocese, or rather, I suppose, is afraid of putting the law in execution, which is to bear hard upon the laity, for the parson repairs [i.e. pays for the repair] no part, not the chancel, of his church'.[49] This, if correct, was an important difference between the two Churches, and an unfortunate tradition in the Church of Ireland.

Another huge problem for an Irish bishop of any degree of conscientiousness was the extremely uneven size and apparently illogical distribution of parochial and clerical income. These anomalies dated from mediaeval times – or, rather, from the way in which mediaeval arrangements had been disturbed and distorted by the Dissolution of the Monasteries.

---

46 Agar's 'state' of the diocese of Cashel, 1779–1801, 21 M 57/B6/1. For his autograph draft of this act, see 21 M 57/B26/4.   47 Acheson, *Church of Ireland*, p. 111; B. Trainor and W.H. Crawford (eds.), *Aspects of Irish social history, 1750–1800* (Belfast, 1969), pp 153–65.   48 Agar to Macartney, 17 Feb. 1780, *Macartney in Ireland*, p. 330; Hervey to Agar, 22 Nov. 1795, T/3719/C/29/39. Hervey had succeeded his brother as 4th earl of Bristol in 1779.   49 Burrows' tour journal, 3 June–12 Aug. 1773, NLI: photocopy in PRONI, T/3551/1.

The income of the parish [since mediaeval times] was derived from the tithes, which amounted to one tenth of the income of the agricultural produce of the parish [see pp 536–9]. The tithes were subdivided into rectorial tithes, or greater part (two thirds of the total), and vicarial or lesser tithes (one third the total). Either all the tithe or one of the subdivisions could be allocated to a monastery or to the cathedral officers, who then provided the parish with a temporary curate. By this practice, the duties and finances of the parish were intertwined with those of the monasteries. Paradoxically, parishes were poorest and had the least share of the tithes in the wealthiest parts of the country, where the monasteries had been established. ... It was common practice that the rectorial tithe, or perhaps all the tithe, was annexed to the cathedral chapter or a monastery.

Tithes which were paid to other churchmen were described as 'appropriate'. A parish could have tithes which were appropriate (partly annexed) or wholly appropriate (the entire sum was paid elsewhere). ... When the monasteries were suppressed, the tithes which had been appropriated by them passed largely into lay hands. If the tithe was paid to individuals or corporations outside the church, the tithe was described as 'impropriate' or 'wholly impropriate', depending on how much was assigned away. In the case of a wholly appropriate or wholly impropriate parish, the parish clergyman faced the unhappy situation of being assigned a parish with almost no revenue, one probably unable to support either the church therein or a resident clergyman. ... *The fourth report of the ecclesiastical commissioners*, which dates from 1833, ... [after] three centuries had passed since the Dissolution, and some [intervening] reform and improvements had taken place, ... shows how these allocations of tithe income endured into modern times.[50]

Euseby Cleaver roundly declared in 1807 that the origin of the pluralities and non-residence in the Church of Ireland was 'that at the Reformation the tithes of near 700 parishes [out of 2,450] were granted [in whole or in part] to laymen, and that from want of maintenance these parishes were *necessarily united* to others'. This was an underestimate: in 1830, the number of lay impropriators was stated, more officially, to be 718. The proportion of tithe income in lay hands was about one-sixth. (However, the situation in England, where 'laymen owned approximately a third of all tithes', was even less favourable to the Church.)[51] The frequent mismatch by the last third of the eighteenth century between churches and clerical residences, on the one hand, and centres of Church of Ireland population density, on the other, constituted another organisational problem. So did the quantity and importance of the historic buildings for which the Church of Ireland had inherited (or arrogated to itself) responsibility.

---

50 Dolan, *Large mediaeval churches*, pp 38–41.   51 Cleaver to 3rd earl of Egremont, 24 Mar. [1807], Petworth House papers, West Sussex RO, Chichester, PHA/57/52; Erck, *Ecclesiastical register*, pp xliv and lvi–lvii; Connolly, *Religion, law and power*, p. 180; Evans, *The contentious tithe*, p. 17.

The response of the bishops to this heritage varied from reverence to indifference and from restoration to replacement (see pp 304–7, 331–2 and 365–70). Either way, the problem added to their workload.

In some other respects, too, Falvey's assumptions and assertions need to be reconsidered. It is hardly fair to couple 'improvement' and 'leisure', since improvement in the main had a serious purpose. The equation of parliamentary attendance with time usefully spent is equally dubious: 'parliament winter' in Dublin was the season of leisure, pleasure and dissipation as well as of senatorial activity, and at Primate Stone's dinner parties in Henrietta Street, 'the rake took the place of the archbishop'.⁵² It may also be suggested that the number of ordinations and confirmations performed is an odd measure of episcopal activity. Such tasks, though of great importance in a sacramental sense, were in practical terms mechanistic. The archbishop of Dublin performed more of them than any other Irish bishop, because the resident and transient Church of Ireland population of Dublin was larger than that of any other place in Ireland, and the transients, in particular, were of high social class and wanted an archbishop to officiate at major events in their families.⁵³ Yet Agar's period of maximum episcopal activity was not his years at Dublin, but his preceding years at Cashel. In other words, 'numerical evidence alone', is in most respects misleading.

AGAR AS BISHOP OF CLOYNE, 1768–79

Agar was made a bishop when still in the full vigour of youth, and was destined to stay at Cloyne for the perhaps optimum period of ten years. He was fortunate in not starting at the very bottom of the episcopal ladder in what was quaintly, but aptly, called one of the 'climbing sees',⁵⁴ and then having to make a series of short-lived career moves from one rung to the next. In late 1795, one sardonic commentator described such moves as the 'usual ... general change of quarters among the black coats. There seems to be some jealous policy that a bishop shall no more get familiar with his diocese and clergy than the redcoats with the citizens or inhabitants of any particular quarter.'⁵⁵ The duration of Agar's tenure of Cashel – twenty-two years – though longer than he initially expected or hoped, was also long enough to enable him to make a tangible and creditable impact on that backward diocese. Some bishops and archbishops stayed longer in the one diocese than that: Agar's predecessor at Cashel was there for twenty-five years (and died there aged eighty-eight); and Primate Robinson was in Armagh for nearly thirty. The effect of such lengthy sojourns was usually that the incumbent lost his health, his faculties or, more simply, interest.

---

52 *The Georgian Society records of eighteenth-century domestic architecture and decoration in Dublin*, ii (reprint, Dublin, 1969), p. 12, quoting George Montagu (Horace Walpole's friend) when on a visit to Ireland in 1761–3.   53 For example, 10th earl of Meath to Agar, 26 Nov. 1803, T/3719/ C/37/44.   54 Quoted in Acheson, *Church of Ireland*, p. 73. See also Akenson, *Church of Ireland*, pp 17–24.   55 Day to Glandore, 12 Dec. [1795], FitzGerald papers, PRONI, MIC/639/5/82.

Cloyne, as befitted a bishopric of middling seniority and importance, was worth
£2,500 per annum at the time of Agar's appointment in 1768, which rose to £4,300
per annum by 1794.[56] Nor was it one of the 'distant dioceses' already referred to, or a
backwater. It covered the northern and eastern half (or more than half) of Co. Cork,
amounting to an area of 539,700 statute acres. It comprised 125 parishes (in 1837), 'of
which 22 are unions, ... [divided among] 91 benefices, of which 13 are in the patronage
of the crown, 69 in that of the bishop, 2 in that of the incumbents, 6 in lay patronage,
and one in the alternate patronage of the bishop and a layman.'[57] Its most noteworthy
inhabitant, and Agar's immediate neighbour, was Lord Shannon. One of the minor
perks enjoyed by Agar while at Cloyne was his own key giving him privileged access
to Lord Shannon's demesne at Castlemartyr.[58] The proximity of Lord Shannon meant
that Cloyne, during the parliamentary recess, was as near to being the hub of affairs as
anywhere else in provincial Ireland. Lord Shannon affected the contrary. He had
written to a friend in 1765: 'I lead a domestic life in this remote corner, and seldom
know anything but what G[eorge] Faulkner [proprietor and editor of *Faulkner's Dublin
Journal*] is pleased twice a week to give [me] the pleasure of deciphering'; and many
years later, in 1796, he reverted to this theme when he wrote to Agar: 'We live here in
an elbow out of the direct line of intelligence'.[59] However, the Cloyne postmaster knew
better. At various points in 1778–9, for example, his post office must have been
buzzing with letters to Agar about Agar's expectations of succeeding either to Dublin
or Cashel, and to Lord Shannon about Shannon's expectations that his *protégé*, Dr
George Chinnery, would succeed Agar at Cloyne (see pp 148–58 and 509).

Cloyne in 1768 was a challenging appointment for an improving and architecturally minded bishop, as the Christ Church-educated Agar naturally was. His
architectural activities while there (and at Cashel) will be discussed in Chapters Seven
and Eight; they comprise his work on his cathedrals, his palaces and their demesnes
and, in the case of Cloyne, his contribution to the completion of Kingston College,
Mitchelstown, north Cork. His other improvements, including his building of parish
churches, will be discussed in the present Chapter. This is because his churches are of
little architectural interest, and also because church-building is inextricably bound up
with the issue of clerical residence, which this chapter addresses (see pp 211–20).
While at Cloyne, he applied successfully to the board of first fruits (see pp 220–30),
and raised other funds from church cess and private subscriptions, for the building of
new churches at Ballyhooly, Blarney, Clonrohid, Curryglass, Dongourney and Whitechurch, Co. Cork, in 1770–7, at least three of them to the designs of John Morrison,[60]
the architect of Kingston College (pp 295–300) and one much favoured by Agar. At
this time, the board's resources were limited, and church-building a hand-to-mouth
enterprise. To its *ex officio* treasurer, Primate Robinson, Agar explained in June 1771

56 Lord Townshend's patronage list, [1768?], NLI, Ms. 14299; Richard Marlay, bishop of Clonfert,
to 1st earl of Charlemont, 18 Oct. 1794, *H.M.C. Charlemont Mss.*, ii. 250.   57 Samuel Lewis, *A
topographical dictionary of Ireland* ... (2 vols., London, 1837), i. 382.   58 Agar to Shannon, Sep. 1779,
T/3719/C/13/36.   59 Shannon to Robert FitzGerald, 16 Sep. 1765, MIC/639/1/94; Shannon to
Agar, 13 Dec. 1796, T/3719/C/30/52.   60 21 M 57/B2/2–8 and B6/1.

that he had 'made every necessary preparation for building my churches, but am loath to begin them until I can be sure of getting in time the money that is granted, as the work would suffer greatly were it to lie exposed to the moisture and frost of a winter. But if your Grace should give me good hopes of getting it in two months, I would instantly expend the money levied by cess and subscription, and I think I could contrive to roof my churches before winter.'[61] When the board's resources were for the first time swelled by a parliamentary grant (the session of 1777–8), Agar was the first man in with an application – £400 for his new church at Dongourney – and not surprisingly was successful.[62]

Moreover, the period 1768–79 furnishes other, non-architectural examples of Agar's acting energetically and successfully as diocesan. These include his initiative in getting a 'state of the diocese of Cloyne with respect to the several parishes thereof' compiled in 1771 from visitation and other records in the diocesan registry. They also include his attention to the poor of Youghal, Co. Cork, and his success in recovering a legacy to them of £100, both of which were acknowledged in a letter to him from the corporation of the town in May 1777.[63] For the future, however, one of the most significant features of Agar's time at Cloyne was the experience it gave him of the utility of the office of rural dean. Rural deans were

> beneficed clergymen of the diocese who served as a channel of communication between the bishop and the parish clergy. Normally, the diocese would be broken into several rural deaneries, each served by a rural dean chosen from the clergy of the deanery. The office in Ireland, however, had almost completely died out [by the eighteenth century] ... until Bishop Berkeley's ... revival of ... rural deans. ... Agar [followed suit and, when] ... translated to Cashel ..., created rural deaneries in his new diocese. His example was followed [in 1795–1800] by Archbishop Newcome of Armagh [who had previously served, with Agar as his metropolitan, as bishop of Waterford].[64]

In consequence of his good and innovative performance as a bishop (quite as much as his political influence and standing), Agar was clearly destined for higher things in the Church of Ireland. In the event, they took the form of the archbishopric of Cashel, to which he was translated in August 1779.

'APPROACHING DESOLATION': CASHEL IN 1779

The deplorable state of the diocese of Cashel in 1779, and the amount of effort required to bring it up to scratch, were so self-evident that they produced temporary unanimity between Agar and Primate Robinson. In mid-August, Robinson wrote with

61 Agar to Robinson, 6 June 1771, T/3719/C/5/1.   62 Minute of the board's proceedings, 20 Mar. 1778, Armagh diocesan registry papers, PRONI, DIO 4/11/12/45.   63 Hampshire RO list of 21 M 57/B1–3.   64 Akenson, *Church of Ireland*, pp 6–8 and 131–2.

some disingenuousness to congratulate him on his promotion, and observed that he would have 'employment which will not be disagreeable to a man actuated by such clear ideas of order and regularity as you had manifested in the diocese you have left.'[65] In reply, Agar described the existing state of Cashel as

> very discouraging. I am told that the churches are few and ruinous, that the protestant gentry do not support the clergy in assessing, much less in levying, taxes for the repairing of the parish churches, so that in some parishes money has not been assessed for this purpose for many years, and in others, where it has been assessed, the popish interest is so prevalent that churchwardens cannot apply for the payment of it but at the hazard of their lives, and very few indeed are found so hardy as to attempt to *enforce* the payment of it. Under these circumstances, a diocese can afford no other prospect than that of approaching desolation. But it shall be my endeavour to prevent an evil whose progress has not I fear been even retarded for some years past.[66]

This 'approaching desolation' was largely due to the inertia of previous archbishops, particularly of Agar's long-lived and self-indulgent predecessor, Michael Cox, archbishop, 1754–79.

Cox was the sixth son of Sir Richard Cox, 1st Bt, of Dunmanway, Co. Cork, lord chief justice and lord chancellor of Ireland in the period 1701–7. Michael Cox became an archbishop on somewhat adventitious grounds: his seniority on the bench and his Irishness. He had been appointed 'bishop of Ossory [in 1743], and ... owed his promotion [to Cashel] to the good offices of the duke of Dorset [lord lieutenant, 1750–5], who insisted that, as the three other archbishops were Englishmen, an Irishman should now be appointed. ... In 1755, he was sworn a member of the privy council, but he did not take an active part in political life. ... [He was] distinguished more for his amiable character and refined tastes than for active piety.'[67] That Cox possessed 'refined tastes' is beyond dispute: that he had an 'amiable character' is more questionable. According to Dorothea Herbert, he was best-known for his gluttony and foul temper. She records how, at a dinner he gave to, among others, the master of Cashel school, the Rev. Patrick Hare (later vicar-general of the diocese under Agar), the Archbishop had reserved a whole turkey 'dressed with [a] remarkable celery sauce for his Grace's own eating, he being a great epicure.' The rest of the company were supposed to content themselves with beef, but Hare – presumably for badness – 'freely told him he could get beef and mutton enough at home amongst his boys, but when he dined with his Grace he preferred turkey and high sauce.' She proceeds: 'The archbishop was ... an odd character. He was very close [i.e. mean] and often blew out the wax lights before half his company dispersed. The clergy [except, obviously, for

65 Robinson to Agar, 14 Aug. 1779, T/3719/C/13/34.   66 Agar to Robinson, 24 Aug. 1779, T/3719/C/13/35.   67 Thomas U. Sadleir and Page L. Dickinson, *Georgian mansions in Ireland ...* (Dublin, 1915), p. 40.

Mr Hare] trembled at his nod, and few of them escaped a severe stricture at his visitations. He was excessively fond of cards, but so cross at them that few would venture to be his partner.'[68]

It might be imagined that residence on the part of a diocesan was a *sine qua non*. But this was not the case. Writing after the Union, when there was more excuse for absenteeism, but referring also to the pre-Union period, Wakefield criticised the 'absentees among the Irish bishops, some of whom think it sufficient to visit Ireland and reside there for a month or six weeks in the summer; while others, preferring the enjoyment of society to a dull residence at the diocesan palace, fly from the uncultivated wilds and cheerless bogs by which they are surrounded, ... [and] participate for years in the pleasures of Bath or London, without ever seeing Ireland'.[69] Among contemporary bishops, Cox was a striking example of an 'internal absentee'.[70] Though he seldom attended parliament, he kept up a Dublin townhouse and came infrequently to Cashel. This was particularly true after 1767, when he started to build himself a most distinguished house, Castletown Cox, near Pilltown, Co. Kilkenny (scene of the episode of the 'turkey and high sauce'). This had originally been part of the Cox of Dunmanway estate, but had been sold or let in perpetuity by the Archbishop's father, Sir Richard, to the Cooke family of Cookestown, Co. Kilkenny. The Archbishop's third wife, by coincidence, became the Cooke heiress, and through her he inherited it in 1751. It lay just outside the diocese.[71] As a visitor to Cashel observed in 1775: 'The present Archbishop has a house upon his own estate, where he lives.'[72] A much more extreme (and famous) case of episcopal absenteeism was Frederick Hervey, who was abroad for the last twelve years of his episcopate (1791–1803) and generally absent from Derry before 1791. When he wrote to Agar about his troubles at the hands of the Derry presbyterians, he was actually in Berlin! Not surprisingly, his successor found that 'the churches in the diocese of Derry were mostly in a ruinous state'.[73] Primate Robinson, too, was a notable absentee (see pp 443 and 448–54): during the last eight years of his primacy and his life, the period 1786–94, he resided in London, Bath, Clifton or 'some other English pool of Bethesda'.[74] Cox devoted his time to Castletown Cox and his family estate partly because he wanted to emulate Robinson in another respect. Following the conferring of a temporal peerage on Robinson (as Baron Rokeby in the peerage of Ireland) in 1777, Cox wrote a fatuous letter to the lord lieutenant claiming that his own 'pretensions to a peerage are not common. Many of the principals of the ministry are my intimate friends, and I kissed the King's hand since [I was made an] archbishop, so that I could have obtained from the King the

68 *Restrospections*, pp 39–40. 69 Wakefield, *Account of Ireland*, ii, pp 473–4. 70 Malcomson, 'Absenteeism in eighteenth-century Ireland', in *Irish Economic and Social History*, vol. i (1974), pp 22–7. 71 Hunt, *Irish parliament, 1775*, p. 62; Mark Bence-Jones, *A guide to Irish country houses* (revised ed., London, 1988), pp 76–7; *Georgian Society records*, v (Dublin, 1913), pp 74 and 79–80. 72 [John Campbell, LL.D.], *A philosophical survey of the south of Ireland, in a series of letters to John Watkinson, M.D.* (Dublin, 1778), p. 128. 73 Stuart to Brodrick, 12 Mar. 1804, NLI, Ms. 8869/2. 74 Quoted in R.B. McDowell, *Ireland in the age of imperialism and revolution, 1760–1801* (Oxford, 1979), p. 161.

honour, but I chose to owe it to your Excellency.'[75] Needless to say, his application met with no success. His career is best summed up in the famous lines attributed to Edmond Malone. Observing some years after Cox's death the still uncarved inscription on his funeral monument in St Canice's Cathedral, Kilkenny, Malone quipped that it was

> A truth, by friends and foes alike confess'd,
> That by this *blank* thy life is best express'd.[76]

With such a predecessor as Cox, Agar had need of the organisational and administrative skills to which Robinson paid tribute. What is interesting about Agar's tenure of the diocese of Cashel is that, in spite of frequent entreaties from Dublin Castle and from political associates of Agar's in the capital, he was very hard to shift from Cashel to Dublin.[77] There would seem to have been strong archiepiscopal reasons for this surprising 'Cincinnatus' streak in him, although domestic reasons, too, must have played their part. It has to be remembered that he married comparatively late in life, that his eldest child, Fanny, was born in 1777, and that Mrs Agar suffered miscarriages and general difficulty in child-bearing, to which allusion is frequently made in the correspondence.[78] All the same, as his record as bishop of Cloyne in 1768–79 (during most of which time he was still a bachelor) had demonstrated, he was a conscientious diocesan, and he became, effectively, the first resident archbishop of Cashel since Theophilus Bolton (1730–44). He was in Dublin for the parliamentary session, and he seems to have spent up to four or five months in England every second year, networking and lobbying among British politicians quite as much as holidaying in Hampshire. Otherwise, he was at Cashel, because the exigencies of the diocese required that he be on the spot. They also required that his vicar-general be resident;[79] which is why Agar immediately appointed Patrick Hare. With Hare's predecessor, Dr Patrick Duigenan, Agar remained on good and confidential terms, and Duigenan was to be his vicar-general in the diocese of Dublin, 1801–9; but Duigenan had spent much of the time since 1774 away from the diocese of Cashel making life miserable for Provost Hely-Hutchinson in TCD (see p. 151), and was also vicar-general of Armagh and at this time very much a *protégé* of Robinson.

The diocese of Cashel covered roughly two-thirds of the county of Tipperary – one of the largest and richest counties in Ireland – and, because since 1569 it had incorporated the once separate diocese of Emly, it extended a considerable way into Co. Limerick. In 1837, it was calculated that Cashel (excluding Emly) comprised an estimated 278,000 statute acres, of which 600 were in Agar's native Co. Kilkenny, 850 in Co. Limerick and the remainder in Tipperary; and that Emly comprised an

75 Cox to Buckinghamshire, 13 May 1778, Heron papers, NLI, Ms. 13036/9.   76 Quoted in *Georgian Society records*, v (Dublin, 1913), p. 75. See also Smithwick, *Georgian Kilkenny*, pp 91–2. 77 See, for example, Thomas Orde to Agar, 8 Jan. 1785 and 3 Jan. 1786, T/3719/C/19/2 and C/20/1.   78 See, for example, Ellis to Agar, 15 Aug. 1784, T/3719/C/18/23.   79 For the duties and importance of the office of vicar-general, see Akenson, *Church of Ireland*, p. 30.

estimated 138,050 statute acres, of which 86,150 were in Co. Limerick and 51,900 in Tipperary.[80] Dr Beaufort, in his celebrated work of ecclesiastical and general topography, published in 1792, noted that 'the united sees', as well as covering a large area, 'are very compact, extending 32 miles one way and 30 the other'.[81] This would not have been obvious in 1779. In his third-person 'state' of the diocese, Agar later wrote:

> The Archbishop's predecessors either were not possessed of a map of their dioceses or did not consult it when disposing of vacant preferments; in consequence of which, the livings had been, with respect to their situation, disposed of so injudiciously that hardly one clergyman in the two dioceses held contiguous parishes – nay, almost every man who had two parishes found them at as great distances as the limits of the dioceses would permit. In a variety of cases two valuable livings, and sometimes more, where churches were not wanted but where there were good glebes, were given to one man, while smaller parishes, contiguous to these, where there were churches but no glebes, were given separately to different incumbents. ... The Archbishop could ... [never have] in any respect established residence, without which religion would soon be little more than a name, if he had not first obtained a map of his dioceses.[82]

In addition to his (neglected) diocesan responsibilities, the archbishop of Cashel was metropolitan of the ecclesiastical province of Cashel, comprising in Agar's day the bishoprics of Cloyne, Cork, Killaloe, Limerick and Waterford.

Agar was starting from a low base, in that Cashel was almost the most backward diocese (and was the most backward province) in Ireland in most infrastructural respects. The diocesan part of the problem was not solely attributable to archiepiscopal neglect since Bolton's death in 1744. It had deeper roots in Cashel's location in a wealthy part of the country where there had been important monastic foundations and consequent appropriations of the tithe incomes of Cashel's parishes. Dr Beaufort's calculations of 1792 reveal that, of the 155 parishes in Cashel (and Emly), the rectorial tithes of 28 were (since the Dissolution) in lay impropriation, as were the vicarial tithes of another three. In per centage terms, this placed Cashel below the national diocesan average for impropriations and therefore in a comparatively healthy position in regard to the proportion of its parochial income available for parochial purposes. But the national diocesan average was distorted by two dioceses in the province of Tuam – Elphin and Killala – which had a very high proportion of impropriations, so Cashel's position was not as advantageous as at first sight appears. Moreover, the parochial income of Cashel (£31,206 per annum in 1832) was low in relation to Cashel's seniority in the hierarchy: eight dioceses had a higher income, and of the four presided over by an archbishop, only one (Tuam) had a lower.[83]

80 Lewis, *Topographical dictionary*, i, pp 287 and 599. **81** Rev. Daniel Augustus Beaufort, LL.D., *Memoir of a map of Ireland, illustrating the topography of that kingdom, and containing a short account of its present state, civil and ecclesiastical* (London, 1792), p. 123. **82** Agar's 'state' of the diocese of Cashel, 1779–1801, 21 M 57/B6/1. The map of which he speaks is presumably B9/3. **83** Beaufort,

AGAR'S IMPROVEMENTS AND REFORMS IN CASHEL, 1779–1801

Agar repeated in the diocese of Cashel the improvements and improved administration for which he had been remarkable at Cloyne. One of his first initiatives was the
introduction of his Cloyne rural deaneries. In his 'state' of the diocese, sections of
which relate to the metropolitan province as well, he recorded that, in 1781,

> the Archbishop established the ancient and most useful office of rural deans in
> every diocese in the province of Munster, that of Cloyne excepted, where, and
> where alone in Ireland, they have always existed. But the Archbishop new-
> modelled the commission and thereby rendered the office what it is at this day.
> The Archbishop also formed that plan of a visitation book which by his
> recommendation has been adopted and used by every diocese in Munster from
> the year 1781.

He also quotes from the new commission, which empowered the rural deans of the
province

> to inspect into the state and condition of the ... churches and of the church-
> yards, the communion tables, pulpits, desks, pews, vestments, books and all
> things necessary for the decent celebration of divine serve, as also to examine
> the several glebe-houses and the glebes thereunto belonging ... and also to
> certify unto us [the archbishop or bishop] which rectors, vicars and curates are
> resident within their respective parishes and which are not.

Finally, he quotes his reply to a letter received in June 1791 from Thomas Percy,
bishop of Dromore, 1783–1811, requesting more detailed information about Agar's
operation of the institution of rural deans:

> Some of the powers of the ancient rural deans would, if now exercised, be
> resisted, and perhaps do more mischief than good. I therefore included in the
> present commission nothing that could in my opinion be disputed, and I am
> happy to say that it has been unanimously approved of and adopted by the
> clergy of this great and respectable province, and though no oath is adminis-
> tered to the rural deans, their annual returns to their respective bishops and
> their triennial returns to me are made as honestly and conscientiously as if they
> acted under the impression of an oath. These returns are annually made to the
> registrar of the diocese by the respective rural deans, each dated and signed by
> the rural dean who sends it, one month before the day of visitation, which
> enables the registrar to enter in the bishop's visitation book the rural dean's
> remarks in the exact place to which they refer ... I change my rural deans ...

Memoir of a map, pp 104–37, especially 122–4; Akenson, *Church of Ireland*, pp 92–4. See also pp
229–30.

every three years. I also take care always to appoint each to the deanery which, from his situation, he can visit with the least trouble to himself. ... It may not be amiss at the first revival of this office to select the most respectable of your clergy to fill these offices. The exemplary mode in which such men will execute the trust will not only recommend the officers, but the office also, to the rest of their brethren. ... At each visitation, I require the incumbent of every parish chargeable with quit or crown rent to exhibit his last receipt for the payment thereof. For want of attention to this, I have myself known poor clergymen who were obliged to discharge the crown or quit rent of twenty years which had become due in the time of their predecessors.

Some such reform was necessary in the Church of Ireland, where the visiting Rev. Burrows had noted with surprise in 1773 'that no archdeacon ... has any jurisdiction. The bishop has everywhere swallowed it up all'.[84] But Agar's initiative was innovative in Church of England as well as Church of Ireland terms. Late in 1799, when the former lord lieutenant, Lord Buckingham, his brother, Lord Grenville, their cousin, Pitt, and a small group of English clergy and civilians were laboriously planning a new Clerical Residence Bill and other measures to improve the performance of the Church of England, Buckingham pointed out, as if this was a discovery: 'The idea of constant parochial visitation, independent of that of the bishop or archdeacon, exists in the ancient establishment of rural deans – an appointment now hardly known, but spoken of in the highest terms by our ecclesiastical writers.'[85] 'The ancient establishment of rural deans' was actually somewhat better-known in the Church of England than Buckingham realised. In 1799, and probably long before, rural deans were well known and well developed in the diocese of Exeter.[86] In Wales, too, in the successive dioceses held by Bishop Horsley, St David's (1788–93) and St Asaph (1802–6), there seems to have been 'an intensification of ruridecanal activity', and in both dioceses the office existed long before Horsley. However, the use of rural deans did not become general in the Church of England until the two decades up to 1835, so the Church of Ireland, thanks largely to Agar, was well ahead. It is interesting that Buckingham, a hostile critic and would-be reformer of the Church of Ireland, seems to have been unaware that the office of rural dean was widely known, and in the process of being widely extended, in that Church at the time of his two viceroyalties during the 1780s. The main difference between the two Churches in respect of rural deaneries, apart from chronology, was that in the Church of Ireland they in effect superseded the diocesan functions of the archdiaconate, whereas in the Church of England, where 'archdeaconries had not generally fallen into disuse, but at the end of the eighteenth century ... [were] rarely fully efficient', the two were used in conjunction to effect a

84 PRONI, T/2551/1. 85 Buckingham to Grenville, 9 Nov. 1799, *H.M.C. Dropmore Mss.*, vi, pp 14–16. 86 The rest of this paragraph is based on R. Arthur Burns, 'A Hanoverian legacy?: diocesan reform in the Church of England, *c.*1800–1833', in Walsh, Haydon and Taylor (eds.), *The Church of England, c.1689–c.1833*, pp 267–72.

'diocesan revival'. Rural deans were used for multifarious purposes in the Church of England: in the Church of Ireland their purpose was to inform and strengthen the visitorial process. This had 'stagnated' in the Church of England by 1820, whereas it was healthy and vigorous in Ireland, at both annual episcopal and triennial archiepiscopal level.

The benefits of the reintroduction of rural deans would obviously be felt only gradually: Agar also, immediately after his promotion to Cashel, took steps which would lead to more immediate results. In 1779, he called for statistical information about the rentroll of the see, the see lands, the beneficed clergy and curates, the parishes which had churches in them, the distances of churches from the principal towns, etc., etc. In the following year, 1780, he got a valuation made of the estates of the see, and from then on was extremely active in getting maps and surveys of the see lands carried out. This was to establish just what the see owned, and to assist him in his efforts to recover lands alienated from it. In 1781 he obtained from a clergyman called John Armstrong (there were two or three different clergymen of that name in the diocese at the time) a brief view of the several unions and parishes in the diocese. He also began to keep a record of the improvements to its infrastructure which were effected in his period as archbishop, including a list of 'churches and glebe-houses built and glebes procured'.[87]

Plans and estimates for some of the churches he built, as also for completing the new Cashel cathedral and making good the old cathedral of Emly, are present among his papers. At least one of the proposed churches – Doon, Co. Tipperary – was not built according to these plans. In 1790 Richard Morrison produced designs for it comprising 'Alternative gothic and classical schemes ... for a small church ... with a tower and spire at the west end, a shallow recess at the east end and two windows in each of the side walls. The church which was actually built a few years later [by Agar in 1798] does not correspond with Morrison's drawings. This church was subsequently rebuilt ..., and later demolished.'[88] (Actually, it was not demolished, but deconsecrated and converted into a restaurant.)[89] Agar's contribution to both Cashel cathedrals will be discussed separately in Chapter Seven. His work on his other cathedral, that of Emly, which he planned with Richard Morrison in August–September 1790 and presumably paid for out of his own pocket, was on a very modest scale, estimated by Morrison to cost only £96. Agar noted:

> Emly cathedral for many years past had been merely secured against the effects of the weather. The inside never seems to have been furnished but on one side

---

87 21 M 57/B6/2. See also 21 M 57/D4–19 and B37–69. For the destruction of what should have been the main source of information about Agar's diocesan administration, the Cashel diocesan registry archive, see p. 338n.   88 21 M 57/B14/4; Edward McParland, Alistair Rowan and Ann Martha Rowan, *The architecture of Richard Morrison (1767–1849) and William Vitruvius Morrison (1794–1838)* (Dublin, 1989), p. 175.   89 Oral information from Mr David Butler, who as well as being a Ph.D. student in geography at University College, Cork, lives at Carrigeen Castle (the former bridewell), Cahir, and is a fount of local knowledge, particularly about churches.

with pews, and the other side was neither paved nor flagged. This church ...
was in such a condition that it was necessary to reduce it nearly to its bare walls
and to furnish it with every requisite of every kind, plate excepted. ... [It] is
now receiving a complete repair, and the inside is to be entirely fitted upon a
plan of the Archbishop's, in a style he hopes suited to the place.[90]

It was 'completely repaired, gutted and new furnished in 1791', and thereafter was
usable in a rough-and-ready way as a parish church. Plate, as Agar mentioned, was the
only requisite which Emly possessed before he got going; and plate was something to
which he was as attentive as he was to the state of the churches themselves. In 1790,
for example, 'Cahir parish [Co. Tipperary] was censured at the triennial visitation of
the Archbishop ... for only having a block tin chalice and paten'.[91] Agar was correct in
his censure, because the parish owned a silver paten assayed in 1731; this presumably
had been overlooked or mislaid in 1790. Such was his obsessive attention to detail, that
a visitation conducted by him must have been a stressful occasion for his clergy.

　　D'Alton, the chronicler of the archbishops of Dublin, who is in other connections
critical of Agar, records that, while at Cashel, 'he completed the new cathedral, caused
the old churches to be restored and eleven new ones to be built and provided new
glebe-houses and glebes'.[92] This is in fact rather more than Agar claimed for himself
in his already-mentioned statement of 'churches and glebe-houses built and glebes
procured'. Of the 11 churches built, at least a couple were a case of re-building, not
new building, and Agar's statement does not give information about restoration of
churches, except in the already-mentioned case of Emly cathedral. He seems personally to have paid for the building of three of the new churches, and at least to have
contributed to the cost of a fourth. In the other cases, either the parish or a local
landlord, such as Sir William Barker, 4th Bt, of Kilcooly Abbey, paid. In some or most
cases, the board of first fruits must have given its standard and maximum grant of
£500 per church. It is not possible to be precise about the number, because of the
board's 'requirement that the benefices must have been bereft of churches for at least
twenty years before the board ... would make the £500 grant'[93] – a stringent stipulation, which disqualified or pre-empted many applications (see pp 221–3). The 21 new
glebe-houses are a simpler matter. On them, a staggering sum of £17,097 was spent,
including a contribution of £100 each from the board. In general, the rest was paid by
the incumbent, who was entitled to claim the expenditure back from his successor,
provided it did not exceed two years' income of the living (see pp 56–7 and 344–6). In
most instances, the incumbent presumably acted under duress from Agar, but in a
couple cheerfully spent more than two years of his income. The cost of the new
houses ranged from £381 to £1,631. Of the 14 'glebes procured', 9 were 'procured' or

90 Agar's 'state' of the diocese of Cashel, 1779–1801, 21 M 57/B6/1; Morrison's estimate, 15 Sep.
1790, *ibid.*, B14/6a.　91 [Very Rev.] R.B. MacCarthy, 'Cahir Church and Parish', in *The Church
yearbook for the united dioceses of Cashel and Emly, Waterford and Lismore* (Waterford, 1963). I am
indebted for a xerox of this leaflet to Rev. and Mrs Arthur Carter, Suir Villa, Cahir.　92 D'Alton,
Archbishops of Dublin, p. 350.　93 Akenson, *Church of Ireland*, p. 116.

'obtained' by Agar himself. But this seems not to have involved a financial contribution from him (or perhaps it did?): rather, he negotiated leases with local landowners and the governors of the Erasmus Smith schools (a charity which owned a good deal of land in Co. Tipperary[94] and of which he himself was a governor) and the rent was paid by the incumbent. Sometimes the glebes were a gift or an exchange, and sometimes the board of first fruits gave a maximum of £100 towards the acquisition. In all these arrangements, even where there was no financial cost to Agar, there was plainly a cost in effort, planning and negotiation.

A topographical as opposed to statistical view of his near-transformation of the diocese can be obtained from the Rev. Matthew Sleater's *Introductory essay to a new system of civil and ecclesiastical topography, and [an] itinerary of [the] counties of Ireland ...* (Dublin, 1806). This book is dedicated to Agar's wife and is to some extent a piece of pro-Agar propaganda (though not necessarily a put-up job because, as has been seen, Agar's own valedictory statement of his practical achievements at Cashel is modest enough). In pursuing his itinerary through Cos Tipperary and Limerick, which he does in that order, Sleater pays frequent tribute to Agar:

> Newport [Co. Tipperary]. ... Parsonage built 1790 by ... direction of his Grace the earl of Normanton, then archbishop of Cashel. ... Kilmastulla church and steeple [on the Tipperary-Clare boundary] built 1790 ... by his Grace ... . Borrisoleigh church built by the earl of Normanton [in 1784–92, to the design of Oliver Grace and at an estimate by him of £428[95]] ...; glebe-house built 1791 on glebe procured by his Grace. ... Templenoe parsonage built [1794] under the direction of his Grace ... . Clonbeg parsonage built 1789 by direction of his Grace ... Emly parsonage built [1782–4] with the approbation of his Grace ... . Knockgraffon ...: glebe of 40 acres joining the churchyard procured by exchange by his Grace ... . Parsonage built under his Grace's direction in 1784[–6 and] cost £1,300. ... Fethard ... parsonage built [*c.*1796] with the approbation of his Grace ... from a plan of Mr Richard Morrison, architect. ... Newchapel parsonage [near Clonmel] built under the direction of his Grace ... . Bansha [i.e. Templeneiry] ... parsonage [near Tipperary town] built 1793 under the direction of his Grace ... . Clonoulty church and parsonage [near Holycross] built by his Grace ... on a glebe procured from Lord Viscount Hawarden, 1784[–6]. ... Glankeen parsonage built 1780 by direction of his Grace ... . Kilfithimon[e] ... parsonage built 1793[–4] by direction of his Grace ... on a new glebe procured. ... Church and parsonage in Kilvemnon parish built [1789–]1793 by direction of his Grace [the parsonage in 1786, and the church to the design of Oliver Grace, dated 1791, and at an estimate by him of £548[96] ... . Templetuohy church, steeple and parsonage built [1786] under the

---

94 The rental of its Tipperary estate stood at £1,387 per annum in 1794 – statement of the charity's funds, 2 Mar. 1795, Armagh diocesan registry papers, PRONI, DIO 4/8/9/1/17.   95 Plans, estimate and accounts for Borrisoleigh church, 1784–92, 21 M 57/B14/18–19 and B7/2.   96 Estimate for Templetuohy, 5 Jan. 1791, 21 M 57/B14/7.

auspices of his Grace ... . Mealiffe church and spire of hewn stone [1791–3], and parsonage, built [1800] on a glebe procured 1791, all effected by his Grace.

The *Itinerary* then proceeds to Co. Limerick. Here the influence of Agar was less marked. Whereas in Co. Tipperary, 96 of the parishes were in the diocese of Cashel and 20 in the diocese of Emly and only 41 and 32 in Killaloe and Lismore respectively, in Co. Limerick it was the other way round. There, 85 of the parishes were in the diocese of Limerick, 38 in Emly and only 1 in Cashel (there were also 2 in Killaloe). So, all that Sleater has to record is: 'At Doon is a church built 1794[–8] by his Grace ... . Aney parsonage built 1794 by direction of his Grace ... . Cahirconlish ... parsonage built 1794[–6] by direction of his Grace ... . Palicegrean [*sic* – Pallas Grean] ... glebe obtained 1781 by his Grace'.[97]

In spite of these exertions, much remained to be done, particularly in respect of the churches in Emly. 'Before the close of the century, some of them were in very bad repair. Cullen is described in 1793 as being very much stripped, and the pews in bad repair, while by 1803 the ceiling of Duntrileague had become so dangerous that the parishioners were afraid to attend service, all the pews except four were rotten, and the canopy over the pulpit had fallen down and lay on the floor. Other, similar instances could be given ..., [although allowance must be made for] the disturbed state of the district at this period.'[98] Duntrileague/Galbally was, as has been seen, the most valuable union in Agar's gift, and in the period 1788–1803 (and beyond) was held by relations of his. So it is hard not to regard the state of Duntrileague church as a reflection upon him. On the credit side, the state of Abington, Clonbeg and Doon churches, all in Emly, was warmly commended in rural deans' reports of 1801.[99] Sleater does not record the edifying work of any other archbishop or bishop, which betrays a pro-Agar bias. On the other hand, a quite independent observer had paid tribute in 1790 to Agar's

> unremitting attention to the convenience of his clergy as well as to the improvement of his diocese. I am informed [that] before his translation, his see was destitute of glebe-houses[100] and almost as destitute of churches. ... The traveller's eye is [now] struck in different places with the neat appearance of the rising spires of the churches he has built, the architecture of which, though simple yet elegant, strongly illustrates the taste of their founder.[101]

97 Sleater, op. cit., pp 119–35 and 285–7. Sleater has been modified in square brackets in the text, in the light of evidence from 21 M 57 and from rural deans' reports cited by Seymour in his *Succession of clergy in Cashel and Emly.* There remain a couple of major discrepancies. Sleater states that Kilvemnon church was built in 1793, and Seymour in 1771. Sleater states that Templetuohy glebe-house was not built at the same time as the church, but in 1807. Agar's valedictory statement is silent about Kilvemnon church, but says that Templetuohy glebe-house was being built in 1801. Again, I am grateful for the help of Mr David Butler. 98 Rev. St John D. Seymour, *A history of the diocese of Emly* (Dublin, 1913), p. 254. 99 Ibid., pp 260–61. 100 In his 'state' of the diocese of Cashel, 1779–1801 (21 M 57/B6/1), Agar recorded: 'In the year 1779, when Dr Agar was translated from Cloyne to Cashel, there was in the diocese of Cashel only one glebe-house and in the diocese of Emly only two'. 101 Bowden, *Tour through Ireland in 1790,* pp 150–51.

The evidence is overwhelming – and even the blatantly hostile Primate Robinson contributes to it – that Agar was outstanding as a resident, active and efficient archbishop, the more so because his diocese was Cashel, which was located in a very disturbed part of the country during the 1780s and in a part of the country not less disturbed, except during the '98 Rebellion itself, than the rest of Ireland in the 1790s.

Although there were no pitched battles in the diocese during '98, the experiences of individual clergymen were harrowing enough. 'The rector of Clonbeg, William Massy, never left his house during the rebellion ... . The inference to be drawn from this is not that all the other clergy did, but that the glen of Aherlow, being always a disturbed district and a refuge for persons endeavouring to evade the arm of the law, was a place which the rector might well be excused for ... [avoiding].'[102] In the absence of Dorothea Herbert and the rest of the family from one of her father's rectories, her 'nurse had been riddled with bullets by the rebels and the sexton had been hacked to pieces with a chopper'.[103] A year and a half later, another clergyman had been inside when his house came under attack:

> In 1796 the Rev. William Galwey became rector of Abington but, as the glebe-house had not yet been built, he was compelled to reside in a pretty cottage between two and three miles from his church, called 'Liliput' on account of its diminutive size, but in recent years known as Clonshavoy. Here he resided for some time with his wife, seven young children, a tutor and the servants, while a young sailor brother-in-law, Robert Webb, providentially happened to be staying with them at the time that the following events occurred. Mr Galwey was a magistrate, and as such had been instrumental in bringing several evil-doers to justice. In consequence he knew that he was marked out for vengeance, and therefore took the precaution of barricading all the windows, and also kept guns and pistols ready loaded for instant use. One evening in December 1799, ... shots were heard, ... the windows were broken by blows of heavy clubs ..., [and] Mrs Galwey discovered her husband badly wounded and bleeding to death ... . The attack went on all night, but ... when the day broke, and when the news of the siege spread, several parishioners hastened to the house and with their assistance the wounded man and his family were taken to Limerick. ... [He recovered, but] on another occasion ... was shot at when walking to church, but fortunately his assailant missed him.[104]

---

102 Seymour, *Diocese of Emly*, p. 256.   103 Hubert Butler, *Escape from the anthill*, p. 49.   104 Seymour, *Diocese of Emly*, pp 256–8. Galwey recovered from his wounds and died archdeacon of Cashel. He was not, as might be suspected from the degree of hostility which he had aroused, an officious or sanguinary magistrate. In 1813, the Rev. John Jebb, one of his successors at Abington and later (1823–33) a notable bishop of Limerick, described Galwey as 'a man, unpopular indeed with some from his exertions in the cause of justice, but of good report with multitudes in this parish from his unaffected benevolence' – Rev. Charles Forster, *The life of John Jebb ... with a selection from his letters* (2 vols., London, 1836), ii. 192.

These examples[105] are a reminder of the reality and imminence of danger to clerical life. They are also a reminder that strong nerve and faith in the future must have characterised the diocesan who persevered with an ambitious building programme against such a background (although the contrasting experiences of the Revs. Massy and Galwey may indicate that there were practical security advantages in building a good, defensible, two-storey rectory). It is remarkable that Agar did not suspend building and other improvements in order to give top priority to the preservation of clerical life and property and to the suppression of disorder.

AGAR'S PROMOTION OF CLERICAL RESIDENCE, 1777–1801

The fact that the clergy of Cashel and Emly stuck to their posts in dangerous times, is one of many proofs of the emphasis Agar placed on clerical residence ('without which religion would soon be little more than a name'). He himself, as has been seen, set a good example of episcopal residence. He also showed neither fear nor favour in requiring residence of his clergy, particularly those whom he introduced or promoted in the diocese and for whom he was particularly responsible. There are a number of well documented examples. When asked in March 1777 to oblige Chief Secretary Heron with a living in the diocese of Cloyne for Heron's nephew, he had complied only on condition that the nephew undertook to reside constantly.[106] This was clearly Agar's consistent policy. In February 1784, he accepted the recommendation of the lord lieutenant, the 2nd earl of Northington, of a clergyman for the living of 'Lis-mullin' (Lismalin, near Callan, but in Co. Tipperary). However, he stipulated that the clergyman must reside – otherwise, he would 'be equally ready to accept your Lordship's recommendation of any other person ... who will reside in the parish'.[107] In the same year, 1784, he required Dorothea Herbert's father, the Rev. Nicholas Herbert, a well and widely beneficed clergyman in the diocese, to spend £1,000 building a rectory in one of his parishes, Knockgrafton, now Knockgraffon, near New Inn, Co. Tipperary, in order to entitle himself to £350 available from other sources for the same purpose; Agar also required Herbert to spend three months of the year living in it.[108] Earlier, in 1782, the Rev. Anthony Armstrong, vicar of Emly, had been so

---

105 For other examples of intimidation, etc., of the Cashel clergy in 1798–9, see pp 549 and 577. **106** Agar to Heron and Heron to Agar, [pre-26] and 26 Mar. 1777, T/3719/C/11/5–6.   **107** Agar to Northington, 28 Feb. 1784, 21 M 57/B23/10.   **108** Bond, 15 July 1785, and receipt, 13 Feb. 1791, both relating to Knockgraffon, 21 M 57/B7; Agar's 'state' of the diocese of Cashel, 1779–1801, *sub* 12 June 1786, 21 M 57/B6/1; *Retrospections of Dorothea Herbert, 1770–1806* ... p. 171; Seymour, *Succession of the clergy of Cashel and Emly*, p. 85. Under *1 George II, cap. 15, sec. 5*, a bishop had the power (under certain specified conditions as to the value of the living, etc.) to compel a clergyman of his diocese to build a glebe-house in any parish where there was none and none adjacent, and to reside in it; and under *31 George II, cap. 11, sec. 1*, this provision was extended to a second parochial benefice, if the clergyman had more than one and they were not adjacent. By this second act, the bishop was also empowered to stipulate for what length of time per annum the clergyman should reside in the second glebe-house.

anxious to please Agar and to hasten the work of building Emly glebe-house in 1782–4 (see p. 208), that 'he actually lived in a tent which he had pitched near the scene of operations. ... The rural dean arrived, found him shaving in his tent, and reported at the next visitation that Mr Armstrong was *intent* on residence. When this phrase was explained to the Archbishop, he was so pleased that he gave him [presumably Mr Armstrong] a vacant sinecure.'[109] It would seem that between 1784 and 1819 'the majority of the present [1913] residences [in Emly] came into being'.[110] In 1790, Agar introduced a new rule of residence for the united diocese (presumably requiring that his clergy reside unless authorised by him to do otherwise). Welbore Ellis commented approvingly: 'The rule you have adopted and pursue seems so well calculated to intro-duce and maintain good order in your province that it is not unlikely to be pursued by your successors, and thus the good you do will be entailed upon posterity.'[111]

Ellis must have been premature in assuming that the rule initially applied to the metropolitan province as well as the diocese. It was certainly extended to the former in 1793. One of its first casualties was the Rev. Charles Brodrick, who lived just outside his Cloyne parish, in the agent's house attached to the Midleton estate. Brodrick and Bishop Woodward (who was his father-in-law) seem to have thought that the dis-ciplining of Brodrick was Agar's retaliation for the attempted prosecution of the Rev. Henry Agar (see pp 48–51). But Agar wrote soothingly to both of them explaining that the vicar general, Patrick Hare, had been right to treat Brodrick's residence elsewhere than in the glebe-house of his parish, as non-residence, and undertaking to solicit Hare to suspend the execution of the rule.[112] Another victim was 'a clergyman of exemplary good character', the Rev. John[113] Bennett, whose parish was in the diocese of Limerick. Bennett does indeed seem to have been victimised, but by his diocesan (see p. 499), not by Agar. FitzGibbon wrote to Agar on Bennett's behalf:

This gentleman serves the cure of Athlacca and has resided constantly on the verge of his parish, in which he has most regularly and conscientiously discharged the duties of it. ... Yesterday, on calling over Mr Bennett's name at the visitation, ... [the Bishop] thought fit to order his name to be struck off the roll, and inhibited him from officiating in his diocese. Mr Bennett asked him whether any imputation lay to his character and conduct, and he was pleased to acknowledge that it [*sic*] was exemplary, but he accused him of non-residence. Mr Bennett told him, as the fact was, that he resided within a walk of five minutes to his parish, and that he had actually got a house within the parish in which it was his determination to reside; to which the Bis-hop's answer was in so many words, 'You lie'; and, notwithstanding the

---

109 Seymour, *Diocese of Emly*, p. 252, and *Succession of clergy of Cashel and Emly*, p. 96. 110 Seymour, *Diocese of Emly*, p. 251. 111 Ellis to Agar, 20 Sep. 1790, T/3719/C/24/8. 112 Agar to Brodrick and to Woodward, 13 Aug. 1793, NLI, Ms. 8861/2. 113 This identification assumes that the clergyman was the same man as the John Bennett who was vicar of Cahircorney and Rochestown (both in the diocese of Emly), 1800–7.

remonstrances of Mr Bennett, he persisted in his inhibition. If I do not mistake the civil law, residence within the precincts of the parish is not essential. If the clergyman's residence is *bona fide* contiguous to his parish, so as to enable the parishioners who may have occasion to call upon him for the discharge of parochial duties at all times conveniently to have access to him, I do believe that non-residence cannot be objected to him.[114]

The cases of Brodrick and Bennett are of significance because they support the argument advanced by Agar (pp 233–4 and 273) and most bishops that, in any plan devised for the better enforcement of clerical residence, a discretion must be left to the diocesan. Agar himself seems to have exercised that discretion wisely.

The diocesan's area of discretion extended much more widely than cases of the above kind – where the non-residence was technical and was not obstructing any of the practical objects of residence. The diocesan, at his own discretion, could in effect divide a parish by creating within it a perpetual curacy. Alternatively, he could unite parishes 'episcopally' into one benefice, and such an 'episcopal union' would last until the incumbent concerned either died or moved on, at which time it could be dissolved or re-made as the diocesan should determine. If it was desired to make a permanent union of parishes, or to dissolve a permanent union previously made, the diocesan had first to obtain the consent of the incumbent, and then make the case for a 'privy council union' to the lord lieutenant and privy council.[115] When asked formally about these provisions in 1806–7, Agar responded that they were fully sufficient for 'parochial reformation'.[116] The other main area of diocesan discretion was the already-mentioned one of patronage (see pp 193–4). Because of the comprehensive patronage within their respective dioceses which bishops of the Church of Ireland enjoyed, they were in a position to offer very practical incentives to reside.

In view of this, it is frustrating that statistics for the volume and/or value of the preferments in a bishop's gift during Agar's time in the Church of Ireland are comparatively hard to come by. They exist for the diocese of Dublin (see p. 244), but not for Cashel, or indeed for most dioceses. In 1837, Cashel comprised '49 benefices, of which 22 are unions, and 27 single parishes or portions of parishes; 3 are in the gift of the crown, 3 in lay patronage, and the remainder in the patronage of the archbishop'; and the diocese of Emly comprised '17 benefices, of which 9 are unions of 2 or more parishes and 8 are single parishes; of these, 4 are in the patronage of the crown and 13 in that of the archbishop of Cashel.'[117] The number of benefices might have risen by perhaps ten per cent since Agar's day, but these figures are unlikely to be significantly misleading. Agar presented to all eight of the Cashel cathedral dignities (below the level of dean). Wakefield estimated, *c.*1810, that all the 'livings in the gift of

114 FitzGibbon to Agar, 27 Aug. 1793, T/3719/C/27/7.   115 Akenson, *Church of Ireland*, p. 58. The need to obtain the consent of the incumbent before a privy council union or disunion could be made was a potential problem for diocesans, but an attempt to dispense with this requirement was defeated by the House of Commons in 1732 (see p. 223).   116 Agar's 'state' of the diocese of Dublin, early 1807, 21 M 57/B2/1b.   117 Lewis, *Topographical dictionary*, i, pp 287 and 599.

the archbishop of Cashel are worth £35,000 per annum'. If Cashel was probably richer in the value of its patronage than Dublin, it was poorer than some other, even junior, sees: Wakefield estimated the patronage of the bishop of Cloyne as £40,000–£50,000 and that of the bishops of Cork and Ferns as £30,000 each.[118] Some other comments on, or figures for, episcopal patronage may usefully be quoted at this point. In 1772, William Gore, the newly appointed bishop of Limerick, claimed that nearly all the livings of value in his diocese were in the gift of the crown or of lay patrons; but as he was fighting off a patronage request from the lord lieutenant at the time, this assertion should probably be taken at a discount.[119] It is known, on good authority, that the patronage of the bishop of Ossory (a see considerably junior to Limerick) amounted to £8,000 per annum in 1794.[120] Earlier, in 1759, it was noted that 'there are six prebends [belonging to Armagh cathedral]; the worst of them is £500 per annum, and the rectory of Armagh above £1,000'.[121] All these were in the gift of the archbishop, whose patronage of course extended far beyond the cathedral and parish of Armagh.

The other cathedrals (always excepting Christ Church, Dublin – see p. 245) resembled Armagh in that their dignities below the level of dean were, with less than twenty exceptions, in the gift of the diocesan. Most of these dignities – and this included the deaneries – were 'of but small value'. In May 1788, Agar patronisingly reminded Primate Robinson (who had been in Ireland since 1751!): 'Remember that in this country the Church Establishment differs much from that of England. We have few deaneries and still fewer prebends ... [of sufficient value to] induce our nobility and gentry to educate their children for the Church'.[122] Most cathedral dignitaries (for example, the dean of Cashel) depended for their income on benefices annexed to their dignities *ex officio* or held *in commendam* by them as individuals. Deaneries, with two exceptions and one unclear case – St Patrick's, Dublin (see pp 465–6) – were in the gift of the crown. If they were not in the gift of the crown, they were not in that of the bishop, but elective by the cathedral chapter (over whom the bishop was of course likely to have influence).[123] They were in demand, not usually because of their remuneration, but because they conferred rank, status and the title 'Very Rev'. For example, the lord lieutenant remarked in December 1802 that 'The deanery of Kilmacduagh is ... only of the annual value of £250, but it is a dignity in the Church and therefore the object of ... [great] solicitation.'[124] Accordingly, he used it to gratify a borough-owning family. The dean foisted by the then lord lieutenant upon Agar and

118 Wakefield, *Account of Ireland*, ii. 472. See also Akenson, *Church of Ireland*, p. 94.　　119 Gore to Townshend, 12 Nov. 1772, Townshend letter-book, RCB Library, Ms. 20/48.　　120 Brodrick to Midleton, 10 Dec. 1794, Ms. 1248, vol. 15, f. 171.　　121 Willes to Lord Warwick, 25 Apr. 1759, *Willes letters*, p. 31.　　122 Sir Joshua Reynolds to Buckingham, 2 Dec. 1787, *Reynolds letters*, p. 187; Agar to Robinson, 8 May 1788, T/3719/C/22/15. Figures for 1776–9 quoted by Akenson (*Church of Ireland*, p. 45) show that there were only three deaneries (Down, Derry and Raphoe, in that order) which were well remunerated in their own right. On this point, see p. 392.　　123 Akenson, *Church of Ireland*, p. 52; McNally, *Early Hanoverian Ireland*, p. 47.　　124 Hardwicke to Addington, 19 Dec. 1802, BL, Add. Ms. 35772, f. 63.

upon Cashel in 1787 was preferred on more singular grounds. Joseph Palmer was an Englishman, a sinecurist and pluralist in the Church of Ireland, and a frequent absentee.[125] He was a nephew of Sir Joshua Reynolds, and owed the deanery of Cashel to Reynolds' influence with the art-loving duke of Rutland, and at least some of his previous preferments to Reynolds' influence with Primate Robinson (of whom Reynolds had painted eight versions of three different portraits).[126] Palmer remained dean until his death in 1829, which not surprisingly took place in his native Devon. Agar was on good terms with him, and had no organisational reason, as his archbishop, to be otherwise. In Ireland deans (and other cathedral or diocesan functionaries, especially archdeacons) had virtually no role; which was why Agar attached great importance to, and developed, the office of rural dean.[127] A letter of 1728 to Bishop Vesey of Ossory demonstrates that even a resident and active dean could effect next-to-nothing in his cathedral without the interposition of the bishop.[128] During 1797–9, a two-year period at the other end of the century, the same dean and cathedral chapter (Ossory/St Canice) did not meet once as a body – an omission which derived much more from the non-residence of its members and the want of corporate business, than from the disturbed state of the country.[129] So the crown's right of appointment to deaneries constituted no great in-road into the diocesan's patronage and power in his cathedral.

The normal patronage of the diocesan, in his cathedral and in his diocese as a whole, was liable to temporary invasion by the crown under three sets of circumstances. Theoretically, if a see were vacant, the crown could present to vacant livings normally in the diocesan's gift. However, the sharpness of Frederick Hervey's protest that this had happened in Derry just before his translation in 1768, and the tone of outraged rectitude adopted by the lord lieutenant in his denial, suggest that this right of presentation, *sede vacante*, was a dead letter.[130] Secondly, it was 'usual' for the crown 'to request that a parson or two may be provided for' out of the patronage of a newly promoted or translated bishop, and for the bishop to 'assist government as much as he can'.[131] This – as it sounds – was a pretty loose convention, and was not observed, for example, by William Gore in 1772 or by Agar and Bishop Beresford in 1779–80 (see pp 214 and 136). The third circumstance under which the crown could, and this time almost always did, supersede the rights of other patrons, including the diocesan, was when it promoted a clergyman to a bishopric, deanery, living or some other piece of

125 Comerford, 'Church of Ireland clergy and the 1798 rising', pp 223 and 226; Dean Palmer to Agar, 30 Dec. 1804, T/3719/C/38/54.   126 Reynolds to Rutland, 24 Sep. 1784, and 20 Feb., 21 Mar. and 29 Aug. 1786, *H.M.C. Rutland Mss.*, iii, pp 138, 283, 289 and 340; Simms, 'Primate Robinson', pp 139–40; and John Coleman, 'Sir Joshua Reynolds and Richard Robinson, archbishop of Armagh', in *Irish Arts Review* (1995), pp 131–6.   127 Akenson, *Church of Ireland*, pp 39–52.   128 Robert Mossom, dean of Ossory, to Vesey, 1 May 1728, De Vesci papers, NLI, J/23.   129 Comerford, 'Church of Ireland in Co. Kilkenny', p. 160.   130 Hervey to Townshend, 16 Feb. 1768, with endorsed denial, Townshend letter-book, RCB Library Ms. 20/30. Charles Jackson, bishop of Kildare, later assumed the contrary, but may have been misinformed – Jackson to Townshend, 20 Jan. 1772, Ms. 20/38.   131 Sir Arthur Wellesley (the chief secretary) to 4th duke of Richmond (the lord lieutenant), 2 July 1807, Jupp/Aspinall transcript from the Richmond papers, NLI.

patronage in its gift; on such an occasion, it had the right, for that turn only, to present
to the benefice/s vacated by the promoted clergyman – 'his leavings', as Reynolds
inartistically put it in 1786 – and 'through [the] many [ensuing] gradations'. This right
of presentation was definitely in full operation in Agar's day, although Agar himself
took the view that the diocesan retained a say in the succession.[132] In the case of his
own presentation by the crown to the deanery of Kilmore in March 1765, the crown
presented in April to the rectory of Skreen, Co. Meath, which his promotion had
vacated.[133] In August 1787, the death of just one bishop gave the crown the opportunity, at a stroke, to fill that vacancy, make another bishop, promote one dean and
make another, and present to two humbler 'leavings'.[134] This was often a valuable form
of windfall patronage to the crown. A well-beneficed clergyman – like William Beresford with his already-mentioned £1,500 per annum in 1776 or his nephew, Lord John
George Beresford, with his £2,400 in 1803[135] – could be as well off as a junior bishop.
But all the livings were unlikely to be in the one diocese, so any one diocesan was
unlikely to find his usual patronage greatly invaded by the practice.

Agar's papers include a number of examples of a diocesan's patronage being used
to good and purposeful effect within his diocese, of which the following is the most
telling. Giving Agar (as metropolitan) an account of the improved state of Killaloe in
July 1801, the Bishop of that diocese cryptically observed: 'Mr Palmer [not the dean
of Cashel] has built [a glebe-house] at Tulloh [near Nenagh]; and for having done so,
I have given him a much better living.'[136] In 1797, Agar himself had recognised the
merits of 'an impoverished curate' of Cashel by preferring him to the valuable rectory
of Ballintemple (see p. 578). Moreover, because of the comparative unimportance of
lay presentation in most dioceses (apart perhaps from Dublin), the diocesan was
actually in a position, if he were energetic, to influence lay patrons for the better and
so set the standard for the diocese as a whole. In 1776, the lay patron of the living of
Ballymote, Co. Sligo, explained to the clerical *protégé* whom he wanted to present to
Ballymote that the Bishop of Killala (Samuel Hutchinson) was 'conscientious and
strict ... to a very great degree' and made it a rule that the residence of all his clergy
was 'indispensably requisite'.[137] In other words, the lay patron was in this instance
endorsing the bishop's rule by, in effect, making residence a condition of presentation.
The crown, too, seems generally speaking to have been willing to co-operate with the
bishop – over the disposal of windfall patronage,[138] and more generally. In 1808,
Bishop O'Beirne of Meath referred nostalgically to the communication which had

132 Jackson to Townshend, 20 Jan. 1772, Ms. 20/38; Lord Chancellor Lifford to Buckinghamshire,
18 [Feb.] 1779, *H.M.C. Lothian Mss.*, pp 345–6; Reynolds to Rutland, 29 Aug. 1786, *H.M.C. Rutland
Mss.*, iii. 340; Dr Patrick Duigenan to Brodrick, 18 Dec. 1811, Midleton papers, NLI, Ms. 8861/6;
Agar to Clifden, 10 Aug. 1794, 21 M 57/B23/20.   133 *Faulkner's Dublin Journal*, 12 Mar. and
16 Apr. 1765. I am indebted for these references to Professor Betty Rizzo.   134 Orde to Rutland,
1 Aug. 1787, loc. cit., iii. 402.   135 2nd marquess of Waterford to Hardwicke, 23 Dec. 1803, printed
in *The viceroy's post-bag*, pp 126–7.   136 Bishop Knox to Agar, 26 July 1801, T/3719/C/35/19;
Erck, *Ecclesiastical register*, p. 206.   137 Hon. Thomas Fitzmaurice to Rev. Samuel Riall, 19 July
1776, Riall papers, NLI, Ms. 8395.   138 Bedford to Stuart, 3 July 1806, Stuart papers, Bedfordshire
RO, WY 993/15.

'always' taken place in the 1780s and 1790s (and in fact much earlier) between the lord lieutenant, via his first chaplain, and the bishops over 'the disposal of the crown patronage in the several dioceses on vacancies and exchanges'.[139] So the wishes and practices of energetic bishops were likely to be taken into account by the crown as well as by ordinary lay patrons. The cumulative effect of all this was to place in the hands of the bishops of the Church of Ireland, if they chose to exercise it, a formidable power of persuasion; and granted the continuity of tenure which Agar enjoyed in both Cloyne and Cashel, especially the latter, he in particular was in a position to use his patronage to effect a major reformation of those dioceses.

In the exercise of his various powers and discretions, even Agar met with occasional setbacks and actual defeats. One such defeat was inflicted on him by the Rev. Henry Newman, vicar of Aney in the diocese of Emly. Agar induced him to start building a rectory in 1791, but failed (for once) to oblige him to complete and/or live in it between then and Newman's death in 1800.[140] Newman was a difficult problem for Agar, not least because he was a cousin of Agar's friend, Lord Chief Justice Carleton. Agar, while at Cloyne, had presented Newman to livings in that diocese with which Newman had a family connection. But this was at the strong solicitation of Lord Townshend (by whom Agar had been promoted to Cloyne), at a time when Agar did not know Newman and probably knew Carleton only slightly. It was from Aney, not from the Cloyne livings, that Newman was a persistent absentee; and it was not Agar, but Cox, who in 1777 had presented him to Aney.[141] Characteristically, Agar proceeded against him as rigorously as he could, disregarding his connection with Carleton, just as he had disregarded the appeals made to him by peccant members of his own family (with the possible exception of his brother, Henry). The contrary has been asserted by one historian of the Church of Ireland.

> Shocking cases of pluralism are easy enough to find … . For example, in 1782 Charles Agar, archdeacon of Emly and vicar of Tipperary, decided to reside in the latter benefice where he would be assisted by a curate. To take care of the few souls under his charge in the corps of the archdeaconry, he hired a Rev. Garrett Wall as curate for £4 a year and another curate, a Rev. A[nthony] Armstrong, at £3 a year. But Wall and Armstrong were not downtrodden clerical serfs, for they themselves were pluralists. Wall was vicar of a comfortable living that adjoined the corps of the archdeaconry, while Armstrong was simultaneously vicar of Emly and prebendary of Killardry.[142]

The index to this work assumes that this Charles Agar was Agar himself, while of course he was Agar's cousin, the younger brother of George Agar of Ringwood.

---

139 O'Beirne to John Foster, chancellor of the Irish exchequer at Westminster, 28 Mar. 1808, Foster/Massereene papers, PRONI, D/207/50/4.   140 Seymour, *Diocese of Emly*, p. 252.   141 Agar to Townshend, 27 Sep. 1772, RCB Library, Ms. 20/19; Brady, *Records of Cork, Cloyne and Ross*, ii, pp 60 and 287–8. I am indebted for this latter reference to Dr Raymond Refaussé.   142 Akenson, *Church of Ireland*, p. 59. This account is based on Seymour, *Diocese of Emly*, p. 253.

Moreover, the cathedral of Emly was only some five miles distant from the parish of Tipperary; so that this particular piece of pluralism made geographical sense. The Ven. Charles Agar's punctiliousness in employing and paying for two curates is perhaps the surprising feature of the case.

If the Ven. Charles Agar was in the clear on this issue, he was soon to put himself in the wrong over the building, or rather not-building, of Galbally glebe-house (see pp 54–5), and his successor, John Agar, was to offend in the same way and much more contumaciously. (Agar seems to have had no such difficulty with his wife's cousin, the Rev. Francis Benson; collated to the rectory of Fethard in 1791, Benson had his glebe-house built by 1797.)[143] The protracted recriminations over Galbally glebe-house show that Agar was in earnest when he stipulated for clerical residence. There was no difference in tone and language between his public utterances on this subject and his private communications with close relations. It was almost certainly a waste of paper to write to John Agar about 'the general well-being of the Established Church, ... the advancement of morality and the extension of true religion'; but this choice of words is in itself significant. More generally, Agar emerges from the correspondence over Galbally glebe-house as a churchman who is some distance along the path of reform. He practises nepotism as a matter of course; but he is perhaps ahead of his times in his insistence that cousins and nephews must do at least their public duty, and in his willingness to quarrel with them if they do not.

His insistence on clerical residence derived from his conviction, not just of the good it did and the example it set, but of the danger that, if the bishops did not set their house in order, government or parliament might, on this or any other subject, intervene and legislate for the internal affairs of the Church of Ireland. Shortly after the Union, and shortly before his departure from Cashel, he had an impromptu opportunity to pay tribute in parliament to the residence record of the clergy of his diocese. The occasion was a House of Lords debate of 29 June 1801 on a bill for enforcing clerical residence in England, in the course of which an irrelevant attack was made on the Irish clergy.

> The Archbishop of Cashel rose ... to state ..., from his own actual residence in Ireland, that there was no district in the United Kingdom where the clergy were more in the habits of residing among their parishioners than where his Lordship's diocese was situated, and he could answer there were other parts of that kingdom where the same practice was equally prevalent. He could not answer for every particular parish, but he could avow and solemnly declare in duty that no want of attention on the part of the clergy could be imputed to them as contributing to the unhappy situation to which that country was lately reduced by the effects of civil confusion and its consequent evils.[144]

---

143 Agar's 'state' of the diocese of Cashel, 1779–1801, 21 M 57/B6/1.   144 Report of the debate in *The Porcupine*, 30 June 1801, 21 M 57/B30/4.

He was particularly thanked for this speech in a farewell address from the clergy of Cashel.[145] Meanwhile, in October 1801, when recommending Agar to the King for translation to the archbishopric of Dublin, the home secretary, Lord Pelham, stated that he was 'well acquainted [as a previous chief secretary] with the merits of the present Archbishop of Cashel in his diocese, where he has enforced residence and established a discipline amongst his clergy that reflects the highest honour upon his character'.[146]

Once translated to Dublin, Agar gave at his first visitation of his new diocese, in June 1802, a charge to his clergy which forcefully set forth his conception of the importance of residence, particularly in revolutionary times like the 1790s. Where, he demanded rhetorically,

> was good example to be found, where were objects of virtuous imitation to be sought, if not among the ministers of religion? ... If the rector of a parish, instead of residing upon and discharging the duties of it, gave himself up to the pleasures of the town or to other pursuits, and became a stranger and alien to his parishioners, could it be matter of wonder that they should be led to consider the sacred office of a priest but as a mere source of emolument to the individual – a matter to him of pecuniary profit, without any reciprocity or exchange of moral advantage to them? It was such conduct as this, added to a relaxed example in many cases where residence was observed, that had aided the destructive arts and strengthened the delusive arguments of those fanatical and deceptious theorists in religion and politics ... who sought their own distinct profit and aggrandisement in the turbulence of the times and the overthrow of social order and fixed establishments.
>
> This overthrow they never could have hoped to effect while Christianity maintained its influence over the public mind. ... When these disturbers of human happiness ... excited discontent and envious rage in the bosoms of the poor by falsely contrasting their situation with that of the rich, it was the business of the benficed pastor to pen his fold from the political wolf and recover the strayed sheep of his flock, to pour into the diseased mind the healing doctrines of religion, and reconcile the poor and lowly to the inevitable distinctions and inequalities of all human associations ... . He should have made himself familiarly acquainted with the condition of all his parishioners of every description and of every sect, by which means he would have been enabled to represent, as was his duty, the wants of the sick and poor to his more wealthy parishioners, thus soliciting and becoming the active medium of that benevolence and charity so strongly recommended by the Christian religion. ...
>
> It was not enough that the rector might conceive the pastoral duties of his parish sufficiently discharged by a resident curate. However exemplary and

145 Address, 4 Dec. 1801, 21 M 57/B8/24.   146 Pelham to the King, 26 Oct. 1801, *Later correspondence of George III*, iii, pp 619–20.

virtuous that curate might be, he could not possibly possess an influence so
efficacious as that of his superior. To one class of parishioners he too nearly
approximated, and from another he was too far removed in situation, to excite
for his representations or admonitions a necessary respect ... . And here,
observed his Grace, was seen the wisdom and the necessity of a respectable and
independent provision for the clergy, which not only enabled them to assist
their poor parishioners out of their own means, but by placing them on a
degree of equality with the rich and rendering them independent of those
sacrifices of character and conduct into which poverty too often betrays men,
imparted a weight to their representations and an efficacy to their instructions
which they would not otherwise possess.[147]

From all this, it is clear that Agar's achievements as a promoter of clerical residence
and, more generally, as an ecclesiastical improver and reformer, were not simply the
effects of a busy and tidy mind. They were inspired by a clear, if limited, vision. To a
modern way of thinking, his vision is repellent as well as limited, because it was firmly
focused on outward example and appearances; also, because it saw religion as an agent
of social control, as a means of making the poor man sit contentedly at the gate of the
rich. It is true that Agar adjures his clergy not to regard their spiritual office as 'a mere
source of emolument'; but in another passage he stresses the importance of having that
office filled by men of superior social class enjoying 'a respectable and independent
provision'. This is an altogether too convenient way of looking at things, from the point
of view of the beneficed clergy. On the other hand, the viewpoint shifts if Agar's vision
is set against Falvey's bleak *résumé* of how the eighteenth-century episcopate in Ireland
saw its own role. 'Prelates conceived of themselves as promoting and upholding an
existing system of Church order and Establishment ... . The fact that in Ireland the
majority of the inhabitants did not profess ... allegiance to the State Church was
irrelevant to the ecclesiological and theological outlook of the majority of Anglican
bishops. For them, the primary consideration was the nature and extent of those temporal rewards of wealth, status and influence which accrued from episcopal office.'[148]
Agar's emphasis on the effect of good example, on Anglicans and non-Anglicans alike,
while it is not redolent of missionary zeal, at least softens this harsh image of the
eighteenth-century prelates of the Church of Ireland.

THE BOARD OF FIRST FRUITS, 1763–1801

Agar's instrument foer the building of clerical residences and of 'decent and
comfortable places of public worship' (p. 280) was the board of first fruits, of which

147 Page from *Faulkner's Dublin Journal*, 30 June 1802, recording Agar's visitation charge, 21 M
57/A2/22. The *Dublin Evening Post* also recorded this charge, but Agar complained to the editor that
the *DEP* version did not report a single 'sentence uttered by me' – Agar to H.B. Coke, 23 June 1802,
T/3719/C/36/14.   148 Falvey, 'Church of Ireland episcopate', p. 104.

Agar became treasurer *c.*1787; and his promotion to Cashel in 1779 roughly coincided with a major upturn in the fortunes and finances of the board, which helped him greatly in counteracting the backwardness and long neglect of his new diocese.

> The first fruits, also known as the 'annates', represented the first year's revenue of a benefice, dignity or bishopric. Before the Reformation, this tax was remitted to Rome, but after 1534, the payment was transferred to the English crown. Because of the difficulties faced by the Irish Church due to lack of proper churches and glebes, the clergy resisted the payment of the first fruits. In 1711 they successfully negotiated the setting up of the board of first fruits [which was incorporated by an act of 1723], composed ... of members of the hierarchy, who had the use of the first fruits for buying up impropriations, the building and repairing of parish churches, and to aid in the purchase of glebes and glebe-houses. ... By 1780, the board had purchased glebe lands for 16 benefices at a cost of £3,543, had assisted the building of 45 glebe-houses at a cost of £4,080, and had bought impropriate tithes for 14 incumbents at a cost of £5,855 – a useful but not expensive philanthropy.[149]

They also on occasion received 'voluntary contributions' and windfalls from government sources, such as a king's letter in February 1758 granting £6,000 for the building of churches.[150]

In allocating their resources, the board were careful to uphold the already-mentioned principle that 'the parishes were by law bound to repair their respective churches'. Under a regulatory act of 1755 (*29 George II, cap. 18, sec. 25*), the board were empowered, subject to the approbation of the lord lieutenant, to formulate rules for the management of their funds; and one of the earliest of these was the already-mentioned rule never to grant-aid the building of a church unless there already was none in the parish concerned or, if there were, unless divine service had not been performed in it for the previous twenty years. The 'twenty-year rule' existed to discourage deliberate neglect; 'for, if vestries once suppose they can obtain from the board money for the repair of churches, they will never again be induced to vote a penny for that purpose, and we [the board] have no permanent fund to supply such an expense.'[151] But the rule also created difficulties for the board – and for the parishes. 'Obviously, in a parish where the Anglican church had been in ruins for twenty years, many of the parishioners would have abandoned the Anglican communion altogether.'[152] Conversely, if the incumbent and parishioners struggled to keep the church

---

149 Ana Dolan, 'The large mediaeval churches of the dioceses of Leighlin, Ferns and Ossory', in *Irish Architectural and Decorative Studies*, ii (1999), pp 52–3. Her account is based on Akenson, *Church of Ireland*, pp 113–15. See also T.J. Kiernan, *History of the financial administration of Ireland to 1817* (London, 1930), pp 249–50.   **150** Richard Rigby to Sir Robert Wilmot, 19 Feb. 1758, Wilmot papers, PRONI, T/3019/3324.   **151** Stuart to Brodrick, 12 Mar. 1804 and 16 June 1810, NLI, Ms. 8869/2 and 6.   **152** Akenson, *Church of Ireland*, p. 116.

in use, in spite of grave defects in its fabric, their reward was disqualification from the grant. The upshot was that, at times, the board actually had trouble finding objects on which to expend their resources! By 1763, an embarrassing surplus had built up. The royal windfall of 1758 was one contributory factor, but the main problem seems to have been the incompetence – or worse – of Primate Stone as *ex officio* treasurer to the board. It was later alleged that he 'wasted' a surplus of £60,000 'to £12,000 ..., [and] was obliged to apologise to the House of Lords'.[153] Granted the smallness of the board's then resources, the £60,000 sounds fantastical. But, clearly, there was a crisis in the affairs of the board in 1763.[154]

This, and the problem of potential surpluses, was solved by a shift of emphasis towards glebe-house building. Years later, a leading member of the board stated that 'From the year 1763 to the year 1802 about 270 glebe-houses have been built, which is about seven in each year'.[155] The shift of emphasis was also, no doubt, a response to other pressures being brought to bear on the board at about this time: in August 1765, *Faulkner's Dublin Journal* reported 'that inquiry will be made next session of parlia- ment into the causes of the non-residence of the clergy'.[156] It was possibly in response to this threat that the newly promoted Primate Robinson 'laudably laid down for himself'[157] a rule never to grant any one clergyman a faculty to hold more than two benefices at the one time, though sometimes the two pieces of preferment had to be impossibly far apart,[158] because of the then low value of many livings and the need to combine them in order to provide adequate remuneration for clergymen (see pp 229–30). The discretion to authorise or forbid pluralities lay exclusively with the primate – the other three archbishops did not exercise it within their respective provinces, nor the bishops within their respective dioceses[159] – so it gave Robinson the possibility of effecting a country wide improvement based on fairly consistent criteria and subject only to the already-mentioned financial constraints.

These various developments suggest that the mid-1760s mark something of a turning-point: from then on, the board – led by Robinson as its treasurer – began a more concerted and a sustained attack on pluralism and non-residence, with the result that Primate Stuart found in 1800, at any rate in his own immediate diocese of Armagh, that 'residence ... [was] as perfect as any English diocese with which I am

153 Tour journal of Rev. Dr D.A. Beaufort, Aug.–Dec. 1787, TCD Library: microfilm in PRONI, MIC/250, p. 63.   154 Stuart to Brodrick, 7 Mar. 1802, Ms. 8869/1.   155 Euseby Cleaver, bishop of Ferns, to Stuart, [22] Mar. 1802, Wickham papers, PRONI, T/2627/5/S/14.   156 *Faulkner's Dublin Journal*, 17 Aug. 1765. I am indebted for this reference to Professor Betty Rizzo. 157 Buckingham to Archbishop Fowler, 10 Apr. 1788, Stowe papers, Huntington Library, San Marino, California, STG, box 29; Akenson, *Church of Ireland*, p. 59; John Garnett, bishop of Clogher, to Townshend, 6 Feb. 1772, Ms. 20/9. See pp 233–5 below.   158 Hon. Thomas Fitzmaurice to Rev. Samuel Riall, 19 July 1776, Riall papers, NLI, Ms. 8395.   159 Brodrick to Stuart, 29 Aug. 1804, Stuart papers, Bedfordshire RO, WY 994/42; Hon. and Ven. James St Leger to Agar, 20 Sep. 1808, T/3719/C/42/69; Robinson's faculty authorising Agar to hold Belturbet along with the deanery of Kilmore, 4 May 1765, 21 M 57/D74; Isaac Mann, bishop of Cork, to Shannon, 31 Jan. 1786, Shannon papers, PRONI, D/2707/A2/2/100.

acquainted' (see p. 271). To be fair to the previous generation of bishops, this was not a new departure. Boulter had been moving in the same direction from 1724, the year of his appointment as primate, until blown off-course, first, by a successful opposition stirred up in the House of Commons by Swift in 1732 to an extension of the bishops' powers to enforce residence and, next, by the famous resolution of the House of Commons in 1736 that the so-called 'tithe of agistment' (see p. 575) should cease to be levied on pasture.[160] This resolution, obviously, produced a fall in clerical incomes in parts of the country where pasture was prominent, and made it financially impossible to disunite unions and thereby reduce pluralism and promote residence. From the 1760s, however, agricultural prices were in general rising, and rents and tithes rose with them. Then, in the mid-1780s, an increasingly appreciable swing from pasture to arable took place,[161] accentuated from 1793 by war and British wartime dependence on Irish corn. These developments spelt a rise, uneven no doubt but still very marked, in clerical incomes (see pp 261–2). This in turn re-opened the possibility of disuniting unions and stepping up the glebe-house building programme. The latter continued, until 1808 (*48 George III, cap. 65, sec. 9*), to be financed very largely by the incumbents themselves, because prior to 1808 the board of first fruits generally speaking contributed no more than £100 per glebe-house. They were limited to that maximum by the act of 1723 (*8 George I, cap. 12*), which had been designed to ensure that their bounty would be spread widely, fairly and of necessity thinly.

The 'twenty-year rule' restricting grants towards the building of churches was also removed in 1808 (*48 George III, cap. 65, sec. 2*). Up to that time, church-building proceeded as fast as resources and eligible applications permitted. 1778 marked another turning-point, because in that year (as has been mentioned) the board's church-building programme was additionally financed, under *17 and 18 George III, cap. 1, sec. 17*, by a grant from parliament. This grant fluctuated from £6,000 to £1,500 between 1778 and 1785, and then settled down at £5,000 a year until 1808 (when it began to rise dramatically).[162] 'By these means, 102 churches were built wholly by gift between 1787 and 1805, while another 41 received gifts of £100 towards their building costs.'[163] The parliamentary grant was a sum so large in relation to the small income which the first fruits yielded, that the name of the board became a misnomer. The original impost was still being calculated according to a partial and piecemeal valuation carried out between 1538 and 1624 and never adjusted in line with inflation.[164] On the basis of this valuation, Agar himself – to give one example – paid the receiver of the first fruits £25 in respect of Cashel and £13 in respect of Emly in 1779.[165] (The same problem existed in the Church of England, where Bishop Watson

---

160 Connolly, *Religion, law and power*, pp 181–92; Bric, 'The tithe system in eighteenth-century Ireland', in *Proc. RIA*, vol. 86, sec. C, no. 7 (1986), pp 275–6, 279 and 283–4; Acheson, *Church of Ireland*, p. 73; Akenson, *Church of Ireland*, p. 58; McNally, *Early Hanoveran Ireland*, pp 151–2.   **161** J.S. Donnelly junior, 'The Rightboy movement, 1785–8', in *Studia Hibernica*, nos. 17–18 (1977–8), pp 152–3.   **162** Akenson, *Church of Ireland*, pp 115 and 117.   **163** Acheson, *Church of Ireland*, p. 111.   **164** Akenson, *Church of Ireland*, p. 113.   **165** Payment of 11 Dec. 1779, recorded in a first fruits office composition bond book, 1737–1805, TCD, Ms. 1744.

urged vainly in 1800 that the first fruits, and the livings exempt from paying them by reason of alleged poverty, should be re-assessed 'on a real valuation'.)[166] In 1755, the first fruits were yielding less than £300 per annum (*29 George II, cap. 18, sec. 1*). In 1789, Agar sponsored[167] an act for the better enforcement of payments of first fruits (*29 George III, cap. 26*), but even with this back-up, the yield was only £346 in 1792 and £433 in 1794 (to pick two dates at random).[168] In 1811, it was £3,000;[169] so perhaps Agar's act effected some improvement in the longer term. However, it was the parliamentary grant which was critical to the success and expansion of the board's work: what was also critical was that no watchdogs of the interests of parliament were imposed upon the board. Instead, its membership continued to comprise the archbishops and bishops of the Church of Ireland, plus the lord chancellor, the chief judges and the law officers of the crown (one of whom was necessary to the constitution of a quorum under *29 George III, cap. 18, sec. 1*).

Remarkably, nothing is known about the background to the first parliamentary grant; and, on the face of things, the timing could not have been more extraordinary. 'The miserable state of his Majesty's treasury' in Ireland in April–May 1778 made it necessary to defer the payment of pensions and official salaries and to borrow £50,000 from the Bank of England. Yet, at this very time (May or early June), a new expenditure of £6,000 was authorised.[170] The explanation must be that the grant to the board of first fruits was a bribe to the bishops to refrain from opposing or amending the Catholic Relief Bill when it came before the Irish House of Lords in the second week of August (having by that stage passed the Irish and British privy councils and the House of Commons). If this explanation is correct, the credit for obtaining such a sop must go to Agar, as leader of the potential opposition in the Lords (see pp 154–5 and 446): Primate Robinson, for reasons of his own (see p. 446), had been 'liberal and temperate'[171] in his attitude to the bill. An 'abstract' of the correspondence which passed between Buckinghamshire and Heron at this time refers tantalisingly to a letter of 5 December 1778 containing 'Lord Shannon's anecdote of the bishops' conduct on the R. Catholic Bill'.[172] What this anecdote was will never be known, as the letter is no longer extant. Indeed, there is a gap in Heron's usually voluminous correspondence between June 1778 and January 1779. John Scott, who as attorney-general was required to lead for the bill in the Commons, had publicly 'taken great pains in support of' it.[173] But his private sentiments were as hostile as Agar's. To Agar, he wrote some months after the passing of the measure: 'Damn the Popery Bill to hell a thousand times. I wish you had stayed and opposed it like a dragon.'[174] Agar, who had been present when the Lords had debated the bill on 10 August, was absent when it

166 Watson to Pitt, 16, and to Grenville, 22, Apr. 1800, *Anecdotes of Watson*, pp 350–57.   167 Agar's 'state' of the diocese of Cashel, 1779–1801, 21 M 57/B6/1.   168 TCD, Ms. 1744.   169 Wakefield, *Account of Ireland*, ii. 476.   170 Buckinghamshire to North, 30 Apr. 1778, NLI, Ms. 13036/7; North to Buckinghamshire, 1 June 1778, and Sir Stephen Cottrell (clerk to the British privy council) to Heron, 2 June 1778, Ms. 13036/11.   171 Buckinghamshire to Germain, 5 May 1778, Ms. 13036/8.   172 Ms. 13061.   173 Buckinghamshire to North, 21 June 1778, Ms. 13036/12.   174 Scott to Agar, 9 Dec. 1778, T/3719/C/12/44.

next came before the House two days later. 'Since no protest was entered in the Lords' *Journal* [following these debates and votes], it is difficult to identify which bishops opposed the bill.'[175] They would surely have been headed by Agar unless some substantial concession had been made to the Church of Ireland?

In a wider Established Church context, the timing of the grant was also extraordinary. In England, with the exception of a one-off grant in 1711 which was used to build ten magnificent churches in suburban London, there was no legislation authorising parliamentary assistance for church-building until as late as 1818[176] – forty years after the precedent had been set in Ireland. In 1818, one million pounds was granted for the purpose, followed by half a million in 1824. This was belated generosity, because industrialisation and urbanisation had created a crying need for more Church of England churches long before 1818. In *c.*1812, 'Manchester and Salford, comprising thirty townships and a population of 136,000, were [still] "one immense parish"; and in both Lancashire and Middlesex, the deficiency of church accommodation was estimated at a million seats. ... In 1810, there were said to be more meeting-houses than churches', and it began to look as if 'the religion of the Established Church would [soon] not be the religion of the majority of the people'.[177] In Ireland, parliamentary grants for church-building had preceded by a decade or so parliamentary grants for alternative modes of strengthening the Established Church at parochial level: in England it was the other way round. 'For the eleven years beginning in 1809, parliament voted £100,000 annually towards endowing and augmenting benefices in populous districts' of England and Wales.[178] This included a programme of glebe-house building, for which public funds had been available in Ireland (see pp 227–8), admittedly on a much smaller scale, since 1789, and on a comparable scale since 1803 (see p. 263). Writing to his patron, the lord lieutenant, Rutland, in January 1787, Bishop Watson pointed out somewhat tartly that, if 'in many parts of Ireland there are no parsonage houses, this is true also of England'.[179]

At about this time, Agar – to whom more than to any other individual the increasing parliamentary support of the board of first fruits was due – was appointed its treasurer. This was, in effect, a formalisation of his leadership role, on the board and in the Church, because the treasurership had hitherto been held *ex officio* by the primate. As treasurer, Agar had the authority to convene meetings of the board (a matter of great tactical importance), although it is possible that this was only when the primate was unavailable.[180] The date of Agar's appointment to it is unknown,[181] and – incongruously – has to be inferred from what was said at the time he resigned from it

---

175 Francis G. James, *Lords of the Ascendancy: the Irish House of Lords and its members, 1600–1800* (Dublin, 1995), pp 139–40.   176 Walsh and Taylor, 'The Church and Anglicanism', p. 10.   177 Mathieson, *English Church reform*, pp 17–19; Walsh and Taylor, op. cit., p. 19.   178 Mathieson, loc. cit.   179 *Anecdotes of Watson*, pp 155–9.   180 Brodrick to Stuart, 10 Mar. 1802, Bedfordshire RO, WY 994/22.   181 The board's archive was destroyed in the Four Courts fire in 1922. The surrogate fragments (TCD, Mss. 1743–4, and PRONI, DIO 4/19/7) do not throw light upon the problem, and the board – for some extraordinary reason – is not covered by the *Almanacks* until well after the Union.

in 1803. In May 1803, the then lord chancellor of Ireland, the 1st Lord Redesdale (who had been in Ireland for only a year and therefore may have been wrong), mentioned in a letter that Agar had held the treasurership for 'many years'.[182] Agar himself, at the time of his resignation, recalled that Primate Robinson 'held the office till he went to Bath, previous to his death, at which time he resigned it, and the late Archbishop of Dublin [Fowler] succeeded him, but kept the office for a short time only, and on his resignation the board prevailed on me to accept it.'[183] Robinson left Ireland for Bath and for good in October 1786, so – allowing for the short Fowler interregnum – it is reasonable to assume that Agar was treasurer by the beginning of 1787.

This assumption accords with his strong reaction at that very time to what he saw as a threat to the board's parliamentary grant. In February 1787, one of his suffragans, Thomas Barnard, bishop of Killaloe, reported: 'In our House, we are likely to have a disagreeable debate ... about a bill sent up from the Commons consolidating the usual parliamentary grants to the charter schools, Hibernian school, ... etc., into one act, which had usually been separated'; Lord Hillsborough was going to oppose this consolidation, as contrary to the standing orders of the Irish House of Lords, and would be supported by Agar. But Barnard, 'with due submission to such authority and parliamentary experience as theirs', doubted if the order applied to this particular case.[184] In a Lords debate in December 1783, Hillsborough and Agar had joined forces to assert the rights of the upper house in regard to money bills, Agar describing himself as 'no great admirer of jumbling a mass of extraneous matter with the supplies to his Majesty; it had been the mode of late, but he wished to see it at an end.'[185] In 1787, the point of principle was sharpened by the practical consideration that the grant to the board of first fruits was part of the jumble – something which Barnard may not have realised at the time he wrote his letter. In Agar's view, as expressed in a series of memoranda in February/March, if what was known as 'the great Bill of Supply' came up to the House of Lords with 'several grants for distinct and different purposes' lumped together in the one bill, this would 'tend to deprive the Lords of a separate consideration of each grant and oblige them either to adopt or reject the whole'. This mode of proceeding, he pointed out, was even more objectionable than that adopted in the years 1783–6, when 'all the grants' had at least been 'in separate bills' – £10,000 for the foundling hospital, £9,000 for the charter schools, £8,600 for the Dublin house of industry, £1,000 for the Hibernian school, £5,000 for first fruits, etc. In 1787, a global sum of £29,719 6s. 7d. was being voted for all of these.[186] Through Welbore Ellis, Agar consulted English experts in parliamentary procedure. Their opinion was that it was parliamentary to proceed by one bill, but only if it included 'specific clauses assigning particular parts of a gross grant to

182 Redesdale to Spencer Perceval, 17 May 1803, *Irish official papers*, ii. 378. For the context, see p. 432.   183 Agar to Stuart, 24 Jan. 1803, NLI, Ms. 8861/4. Stuart must have passed the letter to Brodrick, who succeeded Agar as treasurer.   184 Barnard to Buckinghamshire, 22 Feb. 1787, NLI, Ms. 13047/5. Buckinghamshire was on the worst possible terms with both Hillsborough and Agar, which makes it likely that the *caveat* is satirical.   185 *Irish parliamentary register*, iii [part 2], pp 66–7. 186 Draft queries by Agar, [pre-21 Mar. 1787], T/3719/C/21/14.

specific services'. The new Irish mode of proceeding was therefore un-parliamentary in British terms, as well as being 'directly in contradiction to' the standing orders of the Irish House of Lords (whatever Barnard might say to the contrary).[187] Agar's concern for the privileges of the House of Lords was of course more practical than constitutional: that was the House where he and his fellow-bishops sat. Nevertheless, his efforts seem to have met with no success, as 'the great Bill of Supply' in 1787, 1788 and 1789 contained just such a lumping-together of grants as he had endeavoured to prevent.[188] In March 1788, the hostile lord lieutenant, Lord Buckingham, reported that there would be little further 'business in the House of Lords, except to resist a silly claim of separating every matter in the money and other bills'.[189]

Defeated in his attempt at ring-fencing the parliamentary grant, Agar next endeavoured (this time successfully) to ensure that it became more flexible in its application. Originally, it was not applicable to the full range of the board's activities, but was 'confined to the purpose of building and rebuilding churches' (as Agar put it),[190] which in turn was confined by the board's own 'twenty-year rule'. These restrictions had resulted in another embarrassing surplus. Accordingly, Agar proposed, late in 1787, that the board should apply to parliament for authority to use part of the grant for the purchase of glebes. In this he was opposed by the absent Primate. Robinson wrote to him from Bath in December 1787 repeating that he

> was not quite satisfied with any alteration of the appropriation of money granted by parliament for building churches, nor indeed was I satisfied that an application to parliament for money to purchase glebes was in itself proper. A grant of the public money for this purpose is new and unprecedented, and in these times will certainly be opposed. It is impossible to conjecture what course of inquiry the committee will take to whom this matter must be referred. After a careful review of the subject, I must acquaint you that, was I able to attend the opening of the sessions, I should make no application to the Castle for any further sum of money for building of churches at this time, when the board of first fruits is in possession of a large sum of money unappropriated to the purposes for which it was granted by parliament, much less would I apply for a grant of the public money to purchase glebes.[191]

In Agar's view, however, the board was 'in possession of a large sum' of unspent money, precisely because the objects and conditions on which the parliamentary grant could be spent were too restricted.

At the beginning of 1789, he returned to the attack, this time placing the emphasis on glebe-houses rather than glebes.

---

187 Ellis to Agar, 23–4 Mar. and 17 Apr. 1787, T/3719/C/21/15–16.   188 *27 George III, cap. 1, sec. 24; 28 George III, cap. 1, sec. 30; 29 George III, cap. 1, sec. 20.*   189 Buckingham to Grenville, 2 Mar. 1788, *H.M.C. Dropmore Mss.*, i. 306.   190 Entry for 11 Feb. 1790 in Agar's political memoranda, 1782–95, 21 M 57/A18.   191 Robinson to Agar, 9 Dec. 1787, T/3719/C/21/41.

The Archbishop of Cashel, foreseeing that this accumulation of unemployed money [now amounting to £20,000] might prevent the parliament from making any grants in future, and knowing that the fund for encouraging the building of glebe-houses was in debt above £3,000, proposed to the Primate and the rest of the archbishops and bishops to try to obtain a power from parliament to pay the said debt out of the money granted for building of churches, and to enable the board of first fruits to appropriate to the same purposes such parts of the remaining sum as they should judge to be expedient.[192]

The result was a clause sponsored and carried by Agar in 1789 (*29 George III, cap. 18, sec. 17*). It accomplished the desired widening of the objects of the parliamentary grant, without conceding to parliament an undesirable involvement in the running of the board. (As Primate Robinson had put it in late January 1788: 'could the money be granted in the same manner [as that for church-building], without an inquiry [by parliament] into the expenditure, my objection is removed.')[193] Indeed, Agar's clause permitted considerable latitude to the board, and evidently comprehended the purchase of glebes (presumably as sites for or adjuncts to glebe-houses). In 1830, it was reported that 'within the last fifty years' 177 glebes had been purchased, 'partly by means of the supplies voted by parliament ..., at a total expense of £61,484'.[194] Most of this expenditure must have taken place in the years after the Union, and particularly from 1808 onwards (*48 George III, cap. 65, sec. 9*); but, clearly, the process had been inaugurated by Agar. Likewise, the board's expenditure of £100 on each of 116 glebe-houses (a total of £11,600) in the period 1791–1803, was almost entirely due to his success in widening the scope of the parliamentary grant, and the £500 spent on each of 88 churches (a total of £44,000) over the same period, was largely due to his success in establishing the principle of parliamentary subvention in 1778 and in lobbying for the grant to be kept going thereafter.[195] In all these respects, his achievements in the diocese of Cashel are attributable, not to fortunate timing, but to his own perseverance and influence as a member of the board of first fruits and of the House of Lords.

This is not to say that his development of the role of the board went as far as he would have wished – granted the anti-clerical temper of the House of Commons, this was not to be expected. Obviously, the financial resources of the board remained inadequate. The ability of incumbents to raise money for the building of their own glebe-houses also needed enhancement, and to that end Agar did in fact project, *c.*1790, a Benefice Mortgage Bill. (He resurrected this proposal after the Union, and it is more usefully considered in that later context – see pp 259–62.) Above all, there remained the problem of 'small livings' – that is, livings whose incomes were too small to provide a decent wage for their incumbents, far less to enable them to build glebe-houses with the aid of a grant from the board which could not exceed £100. The

192 Entry for 11 Feb. 1790, 21 M 57/A18.   **193** Robinson to Agar, 30 Jan. 1788, T/3719/C/22/3.
194 Erck, *Ecclesiastical register*, p. xl.   **195** These figures are taken from Akenson, *Church of Ireland*, p. 116.

principal resource for 'the augmentation of small livings' was 'Primate Boulter's fund', set up under Boulter's will in 1742, and increased by a legacy from Primate Robinson in 1794. Although the fund was distinct, it was administered by the board, subject to the provisions of an act of 1758 (*29 George II, cap. 18*). In 1758, a small living had been defined (sec. 8) as one worth less than £60 per annum, which was unrealistically and restrictively low by the 1790s. There were three methods of augmenting small livings: by buying glebes for them, by buying impropriate tithes in their neighbourhood and, where neither option was available, by annexing for as long as was necessary an additional allowance to the incumbent's stipend. The board could assist with the first two of these methods, but only out of the small first fruits fund (not out of its parliamentary grant), and only to a limit of £100 per glebe or impropriation (which would not go very far towards such purchases). For example, it was reckoned in 1808 that the maximum size for a glebe was twenty acres and that the purchase of a glebe of that size would cost anything up to £800.[196]

There were 147 livings of under £100 per annum in 1808,[197] and £100 in 1808 corresponds very roughly to the £60 of 1742. These *c.*150 small livings were so poor in income 'as not to admit of a charge sufficient for building a tolerable house';[198] many of them had no glebe either, or no conveniently situated glebe, to provide a site for a glebe-house. The number of small livings would have been greater if that problem had not been mitigated at the cost of creating another – the problem of over-large unions. In 1803, Nathaniel Alexander, bishop of Clonfert in the province of Tuam, explained that,

> to supply even a very bare subsistence to the parochial clergy, a number of parishes are united, so that throughout the diocese, there is near 20,000 acres, Irish measure, to each union, an extent of country over which it would be impossible for any clergyman to do his duty, if any considerable number of the inhabitants were protestants. There are in [the united dioceses of] Clonfert and Kilmacduagh 60 parishes, which at present make up 14 benefices ... . Mr John Hacket, vicar of Clonfert, [for instance], has in his union seven vicarages, very inconvenient to each other, but if all [were] united by [act of] council, they would not ... allow him to expend more than £160 (two years' income) [on building a glebe-house].[199]

From Westport, Co. Mayo, in the diocese and province of Tuam, Agar's friend, the 1st marquess of Sligo, wrote to him in the following year, 1804: 'In this union, where one protestant clergyman can just exist, there are eleven popish priests ... . The district is not wanting in cultivation, but the fund arising from tithes is too small ... [to maintain another clergyman], even if collected at its real value ..., [and] I do think

---

196 [John Foster's] 'Scheme for building glebe-houses and churches and purchasing glebes', [Jan. 1808], *Wellington civil correspondence, 1807–9*, pp 434–7.   197 Ibid.   198 Brodrick to Stuart, [early Dec. 1802], Stuart papers, Bedfordshire RO, WY 994/51A.   199 Alexander to William Wickham, 19 Aug. 1803, Wickham papers, PRONI, T/2627/5/S/32.

some means for adding to the Protestant Establishment' must be found.[200] There was one historical eccentricity (as Alexander mentioned elsewhere in his letter) about the tithes of the province of Tuam.[201] But eccentricities of one sort or another were to be found in the other three provinces as well (see pp 538–9). Because of vagaries and variations in the incidence of tithe all over Ireland, Charles Brodrick reckoned in 1800 that those clergymen 'who have a competency [of income] are compelled to draw their resources from quarters so distant from each other as to give rise to an egregious deformity in our Church Establishment'.[202]

To overcome the problem of small livings, what obviously was needed was, first, much more money and, second, much greater flexibility in the application of Primate Boulter's Fund, of the first fruits fund and of the parliamentary grant made to the board of first fruits.[203] In fact, it was not until the passing of two acts of 1806 and 1808 respectively (see pp 276–80) that these desiderata were achieved. But in the late 1780s, Agar's hopes must have been high that better provision would soon be made for the augmentation of small livings, as for the enlargement of the borrowing power of incumbents.

REFORM BY A 'CRITICAL STRANGER':[204] LORD BUCKINGHAM'S PROPOSALS OF 1788

With the reappointment of Lord Buckingham to the lord lieutenancy of Ireland in November 1787, these hopes were blasted and, instead of an extension of the policy of promoting clerical residence by what was later called 'a wise liberality' (see p. 274), the Church was threatened, among other new and unwelcome policies, with the rigid enforcement of clerical residence by means which excluded episcopal discretion and indeed authority. Before considering these policies and their appropriateness, it is important to make the point that they were tainted from the outset by association with the 'insufferable'[205] Buckingham. Buckingham was a man of considerable ability. But he 'had more ambition than his abilities eventually could sustain',[206] and it was his tragedy that they were not matched by personal equilibrium, self-control and discretion of language. His weaknesses were exacerbated by his proximity to Pitt and Grenville, on whom he constantly sought to impress the view that the accident of primogeniture entitled him to office or at least confidence.[207] In Ireland, as has been seen (p. 165), there was properly speaking no Regency Crisis: rather, there was a run against an almost universally obnoxious lord lieutenant. Meanwhile, in England, the

200 Sligo to Agar, 30 July 1804, T/3719/C/38/37.   201 Erck, *Ecclesiastical register*, pp lii–liii.   202 Brodrick to Midleton, 23 Oct. 1800, Ms. 1248, vol. 17, ff. 136–7.   203 Agar's 'state' of the diocese of Dublin, early 1807, 21 M 57/B2/1b.   204 For the significance of this term, see p. 240.   205 Richard Pares, *King George III and the politicians* (revised ed. Oxford, 1963), p. 144.   206 P.J. Jupp, 'Genevese exiles in Co. Waterford', in *Cork Historical and Archaeological Journal* (1970), p. 30. See also Jupp, *Lord Grenville, 1759–1834* (Oxford, 1985), pp 16–17, 105–6 and 302.   207 Pares, op. cit., pp 37–9.

mad George III had allegedly said 'in one of his soliloquies ..., "I hate nobody, why should anybody hate me?" – recollecting a little, he added, "I beg pardon, I do hate the marquess of Buckingham".'[208] Such was his unpopularity and the conspiracy-theories woven round him, that a politically *naive*, Whiggish lady, closely connected with the Conolly and Leinster families, made the absurd suggestion in 1795 that, 'during Lord Westmorland's administration ... every dispatch sent to and from London called at *Stowe* and was opened by Lord Buckingham; so that, in fact, it is ... [he who has] so long and so ill governed Ireland ... by back-stair influence, ... and Mr Pitt, the duke of Portland and others all give way to him ... to please a very great *villain*'.[209]

In religious terms, Buckingham was compromised by the fact that his wife was an 'Old English' Nugent from Westmeath. She was the daughter of Robert, Earl Nugent, who had made his career in England and been a nominal protestant,[210] but she herself counted as an Irish catholic. The supposed influence of Lady Buckingham made Buckingham's policies additionally suspect. In January 1793, Brodrick's brother, Lord Midleton, a pro-war, middle-of-the-road English Whig, reported to Brodrick: 'Lord Buckingham says it is the same to England whether Ireland is protestant or catholic, and thinks England not pledged to support the protestants'. Later, in March, he added: 'If the catholics in Ireland were to be disaffected to the Establishments, all England but Lord Buckingham would support' those Establishments.[211] In September 1792, it was reported that

> the conversations ... publicly held at Stowe may well encourage ... [the Irish catholics] in any extravagance. Lord Buckingham says it is absurd not to grant them at once the whole extent of their demands, as it will be impossible to withhold anything from them which they may unite to claim; that it is folly to think that both *Constitution* and *Establishment* must not mould themselves to their desires. And he seriously dissuaded a clergyman, who repeated these conversations to me, from building his glebe-house, as most probably he should only build it for some Father O'Mooney.[212]

By 1792–3 the Irish Catholic Question was alive and to the fore in a way that it certainly had not been in 1788, and Buckingham's opinions and language were also the more extreme for the reverses he had suffered in the latter year. So, it is dangerous to use evidence drawn from 1792–3 in the context of 1788. Nevertheless, it does give some indication of the indiscretion of Buckingham's pronouncements, particularly on his chosen subject of clerical residence. On that or any other subject, his ideas were fated never to be considered on their merits alone, but in light of the dislike and distrust he increasingly aroused.[213]

208 Quoted in *ibid.*, p. 145*n*.   209 Lady Sarah Napier to Dr John Ferguson of Derry, 20 Mar. 1795, Montgomery of Benvarden papers, PRONI, T/1638/5/9.   210 Malcomson, *Pursuit of the heiress*, pp x and 22.   211 Midleton to Brodrick, 27 Jan. 1793 and 20 Mar. [1793], Ms. 8889/7 and 9. 212 The future Bishop O'Beirne to W.B. Ponsonby, 15 Sep. 1792, Grey/Ponsonby papers, PRONI, T/3393/15. See also Sir Richard Musgrave, 1st Bt, to Agar, 25 Feb. 1809, T/3719/C/43/32. 213 This by no means applied to Agar alone or was exclusive to Irish churchmen and protestants: see,

Animated solely by the problems which the now suppressed Rightboy disturbances had exposed, and disregarding – or more probably ignorant of – the 'parochial
reformation' currently being effected on the basis of 'a wise liberality', Buckingham
made it clear in 1788 that he was planning a programme of bracing reform for the
Church of Ireland. For him, that Church was an inferior and corrupted offshoot of
the Church of England, not 'the Church of England in Ireland' which it regarded
itself as being. He at once announced his intention of curbing non-residence by
imposing British-style clerical residence legislation on the Church of Ireland. He also
proposed a further reduction in the tithe income of the clergy – a move which could
not fail to remind Irish churchmen of the exemption obtained from the tithe of agistment in 1736 and the blow which that had dealt Boulter's programme of glebe-house
building. He arrived in Dublin in mid-December 1787. Within a month he summoned
Agar to the Castle and unfolded a comprehensive scheme for enforcing residence,
subsidising parish schools at the expense of the clergy, and encouraging the linen
industry by reducing the tithes payable on the crops mentioned in Day's letter to Lord
Glandore (see p. 190–1). Buckingham made the excuse that one of these crops, hemp,
was vital to the manufacture of sailcloth for the British navy.[214] From the recentness of
his arrival in Ireland, it was evident that his whole plan of reform was of British
manufacture! As if to prove this point, he complained in late January 1788 to his
brother, Grenville, that the resistance of the Irish bishops was likely to 'put off till next
year a plan which I have digested, and which you will discuss with Moore, for carrying
into execution the ideas of reforming the points which we discussed together'.[215] It is
also indicative of the arrogance of the thirty-four-year-old Buckingham that he
referred to the archbishop of Canterbury as 'Moore'; he obviously expected to make
even shorter work of 'little Cashel'.

Instead, he found himself faced with a battery of local knowledge about the
Church of England as well as the Church of Ireland. With his Christ Church background, his regular visits to England, especially Hampshire,[216] and his contacts, via
Ellis, with leading English Anglicans, Agar soon demonstrated that he knew more
about the Church of England than did Buckingham. Here is part of Agar's lengthy
account to Robinson in Bath of what passed during his audience with the lord
lieutenant:

> He [Buckingham] began by professing an intention to secure to the clergy their
> legal maintenance and rights, and added that he wished at the same time to do
> something to convince the people that he meant to remove whatever was
> objectionable on the part of the clergy. For this purpose, his first proposition

for example, Stuart to Brodrick, 29 Oct. 1805, Ms. 8869/3.   214 Ellis to Agar, 19 Mar. 1788,
T/3719/C/22/4. Ellis concludes, pithily and sensibly: 'I do not like the taking commercial bounties
out of the pockets of the Established clergy.'   215 Buckingham to Grenville, 26 Jan. 1788, *H.M.C.
Dropmore Mss.*, i. 299.   216 Notes by Agar in a commonplace book on the levels of tithe payable in
Hampshire, 13 Mar. 1792, including 'A tenth for agistment tithes of barren cattle', 21 M 57/A1,
p. 80.

was to introduce a law similar to the English act of 28 H[enry] VIII, cap. 13, by which clergymen wilfully absenting themselves from their benefices for one month together, or two months' division in the year, incur a penalty of £5 to the king and £5 to any person that shall sue for the same. But instead of enabling *any person* to sue for this, he proposed to vest that power in the board of first fruits, and on their failing to sue, then in the attorney-general for the time being. The reasons he assigned for introducing this law were, first, to meet the expectations of the people, and, secondly, to supply a method of enforcing residence, the bishops not having any power at present of doing so.

In answer to this, it was said [by Agar] that such a law for very obvious reasons ought not to be introduced into this country (though it existed in England), especially at this time, unless it should be found to be indispensably necessary, as it would carry upon the face of it a sort of exculpation or at least an apology for the combinations and violences of Whiteboys and Rightboys, and a declaration that the clergy of the Established Church had provoked and merited the persecution they had suffered for the last two or three years. Secondly, because it evidently charged the clergy of Ireland with being so generally non-resident as to require an additional legal restraint, whereas upon inquiry it would probably be found that they are as generally resident as the circumstances of the [?times] and their situations will admit. Thirdly, because such a law would con[v]ey to the world an idea ... that the bishops either had not already power to enforce residence (which is not true) or that, having it, they had abused the trust reposed in them and omitted to do their duty. ... By the canon law [they] have a power to deprive for non-residence, and ... it should be first ascertained that ... [they] would not use their present powers before a law should be passed which would tend to take out of their hands the government of the Church.

His Excellency said his next object was to restrain the clergy by a law from holding more than two benefices, and those at an ascertained distance from each other, as in England [where the ascertained distance was thirty miles]. To this it was answered that such a law is not necessary in Ireland, because we have no statute law enabling our clergy to hold church preferment of any kind with a living having a cure of souls, without a faculty; but by the ecclesiastical law (which in this case is the only law of Ireland), no two pieces of church preferment of any kind whatsoever could be held by the same person without a faculty, and that your Grace would not grant a faculty for more than two;[217] that in this case, therefore, there was no cause for complaint, and of course for no law of this kind; that in England, by a special act of parliament, deaneries, treasurerships, chancellorships, archdeaconries, prebends and canonries might

---

217 This regulatory power, unique to the primate and without Church of England equivalent, was of great potential significance, though in practice it was not purposefully exercised until the 1820s (see 222 and 276).

be held with one or more livings having cure of souls, without a faculty, and therefore it was not a very uncommon thing in that country to see one man very improperly beneficed with four or five distinct preferments, of who [*sic* – which] two might be livings with cure of souls, but that we had no such act in this country, and of course no such instances could be found here.

With respect to his Excellency's intention of ascertaining a distance beyond which no man could hold a second living, it was said that, if the law which prescribed this in England could be justified (which seemed very doubtful), still, the situation and circumstances of the Church of Ireland rendered such a law very unfit for this country; that in England the number of livings afforded each clergyman a tolerable chance of getting two parishes within the statutable distance of thirty miles, but if he could not do this, one living in general would afford a tolerable maintenance in that country, where the clergy actually receive tithe, or a compensation for the tithe, of every article which is by law titheable; that in Ireland the number of livings is much smaller, the country not half peopled or improved, and that the clergy do not receive tithe of above six or seven different articles;[218] that even this is obtained at great expense and trouble, and if the clergy were restrained from holding two livings unless at given distances, their incomes would be inadequate to their support, the churches would be filled by mean and illiterate men, and a dirty traffic for the exchange of benefices among the clergy would be the result; that the only object of such an act was to enable a clergyman to visit occasionally his second parish; that he could do this, whether his journey was to be performed in one day or two days; that the canon law already requires every man who has two benefices, though he must reside principally upon one of them, to visit the other every year, and to execute certain functions of his office therein; [and] that he who does this answers every sensible and rational purpose, whether his parishes be thirty, sixty or an hundred miles asunder.[219]

This lengthy defence of Irish arrangements for enforcing clerical residence has been given in full, because it is a sample of Agar's forceful reasoning, and also because it is packed with detailed information about the discipline and government of the two Churches and about how they differed from each other historically, legally and practically. These differences were again to be of great importance at the time of the Union (see pp 564–8 and 584–7). Robinson, in his reply, took a different line about the politics of the matter. He was more flexible and subservient than Agar in his attitude to the government. It may also be suspected that, as an Englishman, he found the English practice less alien than did Agar. Robinson's reaction was that Buckingham

---

218 For a discussion of the differences between the Churches of Ireland and England in respect of tithes, see pp 534–41 and 556–8.   219 Agar to Robinson, 15 Jan. 1788, T/3719/C/22/1.

will not be satisfied unless something in the way of reform is done. Under this persuasion, I will recommend to your consideration the introduction of a bill to regulate faculties [i.e. restrict pluralities] with his approbation. If this is not done by the bishops, some hard bill and oppressive to the clergy will probably receive the assent of both Houses. ... You may remember that I recommended to you formerly a bill for the regulation of faculties ... [which provided] that no person should have a faculty to hold a second benefice that had not resided on his first. Subsequent to this clause, I would recommend ... one declaratory of what shall be considered as *legal residence* ... . If any rector should be absent more than *ninety days* in any one year, conjunctive or divisive (a term in England considered as a short residence), the bishop should be directed and required to sequester the benefice, unless the bishop should grant him a licence of further absence, specifying the reasons for it, under his seal; and in case the rector should not reside within six months subsequent to the sequestration of his benefice, the bishop should be directed and required to proceed to a deprivation, unless the bishop should think proper to grant a further licence in a case of necessity. Effectual residence will be better secured in this manner than by any pecuniary penalty to be recovered by the attorney-general, and the jurisdiction of the bishop, with a discretionary power, will be preserved.[220]

In other words, Robinson was for bowing to governmental and parliamentary pressure, while Agar's strategy was at all costs to keep these sacred subjects out of the parliamentary arena, even if the object of the intended legislation was to preserve 'the jurisdiction of the bishop'. To a considerable extent, this was a case of 'principle or pragmatism'.[221]

Agar's objections were not just to the principle of legislation, but to the imposition upon the Church of Ireland of 'many ... ideas ... very ill-suited to this country'.[222] Moreover, he was not taken in by what Buckingham claimed was the English paradigm. At this date, the English act of 28 Henry VIII was 'practically, if not quite, inoperative'. The penalty of £10 a month for non-residence was enormous in relation to the average value of livings in Henry VIII's reign, but 'the law ... declined in severity with the purchasing power of money', and the incentive to sue for the penalty declined correspondingly.[223] In practice, therefore, clerical residence was enforced (or otherwise) in England by episcopal authority, as it was in Ireland. The effect of Buckingham's proposed legislation on Ireland would, however, have been not only real but dramatic. It would, as Agar argued in another letter to Robinson, take 'the government of the clergy out of the hands of the diocesan ..., [and] arm the attorney-general with the whole influence of the clergy, for the papists in the south and the dissenters in the north will not fail to give him notice as often as any clergyman absents himself a day longer than his legal allowance'.[224] Ironically, something of the kind later

220 Robinson to Agar, 30 Jan. 1788, T/3719/C/22/3.   221 For the significance of this quotation, see p. 498.   222 Agar to Robinson, 8 May 1788, T/3719/C/22/15.   223 Mathieson, *English Church reform*, p. 23.   224 Agar to Robinson, 8 May 1788, T/3719/C/22/15.

happened in England. From 'about 1798 ... informers, inspired by or taking advantage of the Evangelical revival, began to institute prosecutions' under the act of 28 Henry VIII.[225] The response of the British government to this new situation was, not to enforce the law, but to suspend and amend it. From late 1798 onwards (see pp 275–6), the already-mentioned team of Grenvilles, Pitt, and selected churchmen and Civilians, notably Sir William Scott, laboured to prepare a more satisfactory Clerical Residence Bill. In the interim, a series of temporary measures (for example, *41 George III, cap. 102*) was passed to protect the clergy of the Church of England from what even the reforming Bishop Watson called 'illiberal and oppressive prosecutions, to which they were liable for non-residence'.[226]

Significantly, the comments which this group of draftsmen made, and the views they encountered, bore a striking resemblance to the things which Buckingham had complained about in the Church of Ireland in 1788. Buckingham himself wrote to Grenville in November 1799:

> I ... have very long groaned over the many abuses which I am willing to sup-
> pose the bishops cannot correct, because most certainly they do not wish to
> grapple with them. ... I contend most strenuously that the bishops have shown
> themselves not, as a body, fit to be trusted with the uncontrolled liberty of
> allowing non-residence, in the cases in which you seem inclined to give them
> this discretion. Such a licence ought to be controlled certainly by the metro-
> politan and, if given for more than twelve months, by the crown. ... You ...
> [should] limit in future the dispensation for two livings to a shorter line [than
> a distance of thirty miles], and to one more distinctly ascertained than the
> present, which is most fraudulently uncertain.[227]

An English ecclesiastic much consulted by the Grenvilles described the power of the bishops of the Church of England as 'not inconsiderable', but added that 'their authority is weakened by the delays of the courts ... . The truth is, the connection between the bishops and the clergy is not much considered ... . It has not been unusual to reside, or leave residence, indifferently, without notice to the bishop.'[228] Another great abuse pointed out to Grenville was that 'dispensations for pluralities are founded upon the most irregular principles' – generally the plea that a living was worth less than £8 per annum in Henry VIII's reign, when this either was not so or had long ceased to be so. 'Even the present mode of giving dispensations by the archbishop is founded upon positive falsehood. The pluralist gives a bond to the archbishop that he will perform certain duties in his second parish, which ... very rarely occurs, and the bond is never acted upon.'[229]

225 Mathieson, loc. cit.   226 *Anecdotes of Watson*, pp 360–61.   227 Buckingham to Grenville, 9 Nov. 1799, *H.M.C. Dropmore Mss.*, vi, pp 14–16.   228 William Cleaver, bishop of Chester (brother of Euseby Cleaver, bishop of Ferns, and a potential primate in 1794 and again in 1800), to Grenville, 13 Nov. 1799, ibid., pp 20–21.   229 Thomas Langley to Grenville, 17 Feb. 1800, *ibid.*, pp 135–6.

Moreover, the reaction of Sir William Scott in December 1799 to an ambitious and later abandoned Grenville plan for enforcing residence was very like Agar's to Buckingham's proposals of 1788:

> I object to it that it does most materially alter the constitution of the Church [of England] by taking the care of it in a great degree out of the hands of the bishops and putting it into the hands of a set of trustees, who are to have an unlimited power of dividing large livings and uniting small ones, as they think fit, and compelling the patron as well as the bishop to submit to those alterations, however they may disapprove them. ... The effect of this in time will be to introduce a presbyterian equality ... very incompatible with the peculiar nature of our ... Establishment of Church and State. ... I object to ... the ... laying down as an inflexible rule for plurality that no man shall hold more than two benefices, when the fact is notorious that in many parts of the kingdom a man may hold two benefices, and even three, without receiving £40 a year from them. I object to ... certain fixed legal rules for residence, which no discretion is to relax under any circumstances whatsoever. In my opinion, this is a matter which *must* be left to the proper constitutional discretion – that of the bishops.[230]

As Buckingham's reform plan for the Church of Ireland had unfolded, it too had been found to contain a provision which tended towards 'a presbyterian equality', *viz.* that unions were 'to be so divided ... [by] the lord lieutenant and privy council ... that they shall, after being disunited, yield £160 or £200 per annum'.[231] In theory, incumbents with incomes of only £100 per annum and upwards were supposed to be financially capable of building glebe-houses;[232] but, in practice, something like a minimum of £200 per annum was appropriate to the late 1780s. So, Buckingham's division of unions would have prolonged non-residence by impeding the building of additional residences. It is likely that he was not fully *au fait* with the Irish legislation governing the building of glebe-houses. This was not well understood in England: for example, Agar had to explain it to Archbishop Moore, at Moore's request, in 1792 (see p. 260). Buckingham's proposed equalisation of incomes, thirty-mile-limit and system of fines were instruments too blunt to solve the problem of non-residence in Ireland, or at least in many parts of Ireland, arising as it did from the 'egregious deformity in our Church Establishment'.

Not only was the intended assimilation of Irish to British practice crude; it also presupposed that the Church of Ireland had everything to learn from the Church of England, whereas the contrary was often the case. When Agar warned Buckingham of the danger of creating in Ireland 'a dirty traffic for the exchange' – and he could have added 'sale' – 'of benefices among the clergy', he was alluding to current English

230 Scott to Grenville, 27 Dec. 1799, *ibid.*, pp 86–9.   231 Agar to Robinson, 8 May 1788, T/3719/C/22/15.   232 *1 George II, cap. 15, sec. 5.* One hundred pounds was worth a great deal more at the start of George II's reign than it was in the late 1780s.

practice, and was also implying that the clerical residence legislation and the thirty-mile limit which existed in Britain, encouraged that 'dirty traffic'. In the Church of England of 1788, advowsons 'were advertised, bargained for and conveyed exactly like other forms of property. Their value partly depended on the age of the existing incumbent. ... Purchasers had the assistance of elaborate actuarial calculations in valuing potential purchases. ... It was common to install caretaking clergy who undertook to resign as soon as the intended beneficiary, usually a relation of the patron, was of age and ordained. The resignation bond required of such clergy was legally enforceable'.[233] In May 1783, Bishop Watson, in his maiden speech in the British House of Lords, inveighed against such arrangements as an 'unholy traffic in holy things ..., [not] practised in any protestant Church in Christendom, at least not in the same degree in which it is practised in our own'.[234] The decision of the House in its appellate capacity on this occasion placed the legality of resignation bonds in some doubt, and the practice was disallowed by the Lords in 1827. But 'it was legalised next year'.[235] 'In the 1870s, hundreds of advowsons were on the open market and the *Ecclesiastical Gazette* carried advertisements from agents offering livings with light duties in sporting country.'[236] (By that date, most lay patrons in Ireland had voluntarily surrendered their advowsons to the post-Disestablishment Church authorities.) So it was not literary licence when Samuel Butler, referring to the situation in the Church of England in the mid-1850s, wrote that Ernest Pontifex would be able to buy, for £5,000, a very good living of £600 or £700 a year, 'the rector of which was now old ..., with a house and not too many parishioners'.[237] This is not to say that sales of Church of Ireland advowsons were not a regular occurrence.[238] A visitation notebook relating to the diocese of Ossory in 1731–2, 'reported that a house in Callan and the advowson for three turns were sold to Mr Cuff[e]'s family for £800 by Mr Dean[e], who had a grant of these turns from the sovereign and burgesses of Callan'.[239] But the hearsay nature of this entry of itself suggests that the transaction had not been flagrant or even public. The fact that only some 160 livings in Ireland were in the exclusive patronage of the laity (other than the crown) set limits to the scale of such sales or exchanges; the

---

233 Langford, *Public Life and the propertied Englishman*, pp 18–19. 234 *Anecdotes of Watson*, pp 111–23. 235 Mathieson, *English Church reform*, p. 82. See also pp 6–7. 236 Walsh and Taylor, 'The Church and Anglicanism', p. 63. 237 Butler, *The way of all flesh*, p. 183. 238 The following are some random examples of sales of advowsons: in 1769–70, the 4th (titular) Viscount Kenmare, a Roman catholic, sold or at any rate negotiated the sale of the advowsons of Aney, Ulla, etc., Co. Limerick, for £1,200 – Rev. Richard Lloyd and Lord Kenmare to Lord Townshend, 15 Aug. 1769 and 25 Feb. 1770, Ms. 20/146 and 145; in 1771 (according to an unreliable family history in *The Weekly Irish Times* of 2 Sep. 1939), Sir Robert Deane, 6th Bt, bought from the 6th earl of Barrymore the advowson of St Mary's Shandon, in Cork city – PRONI's Register of Irish Archives, Springfield Castle papers, Drumcollogher, Co. Limerick section G; and in 1785, John McClintock of Drumcar, Co. Louth, bought the advowson of nearly Kilsaran – ibid., Rathdonnell papers, Lisnavagh, Co. Carlow, D/1 and 4. For case papers, etc., 1633–1818, relating to the advowson of Carrigaline, near Cork City and in the diocese of Cork, and its successive owners, the 2nd Viscount Shannon, the earl of Middlesex and the 2nd and 3rd earls of Shannon, see Shannon papers, PRONI, D/2707/B/2. 239 NA, M 2462.

presence of a large, hostile non-Anglican majority in the population of the country, must also have imposed restraints.

Finally, Buckingham adopted a high-handed and inquisitorial mode of collecting information about the existing state of the Church of Ireland. In April 1788, he wrote a lengthy 'public' letter to the Archbishop of Dublin (in the absence of Primate Robinson), which the latter was to circulate round all the Irish bishops and which informed them of Buckingham's legislative programme for Church reform. On one subject, 'the faculties by law unlimited', he made a small concession: 'the limitation of the distance within which the two cures can be held by law in England should ..., allowing for the particular circumstances ... [of Ireland, be extended] to fifty Irish miles'.[240] The letter also required each bishop to furnish direct to the chief secretary's office in Dublin Castle a signed return of the churches and glebe-houses, the unions and benefices, and the clergy and their places of residence, in their respective dioceses. This gave immediate umbrage, even to the complaisant Robinson. Buckingham had made patronising reference in the letter to Robinson's 'piety and discretion'. But Robinson, unmollified, wrote to Agar:

> I am very unwilling, as you know, to introduce a precedent that seems to acknowledge a visitatorial power in the Secretary's office. If a requisition such as the present is [? quietly] acquiesced in, it may establish all the powers of visitation in all cases which are foreign to the business of the Secretary's office. However, I wish very much in this to avoid giving offence, especially as the House of Commons may in a degree be considered as a party in [the] requisition. ... The requisition is made to the bishops, but it is desired the return may be signed, with a view I suppose, if the return is not full and satisfactory, that some person may be produced and examined at the Bar of the House of Commons.[241]

This was certainly not the way the Church of England would have been treated in a similar situation. Indeed, Bishop Watson complained that the new British Clerical Residence Act which was eventually passed in 1803 was a failure because no information about clerical residence and the value of benefices had been collected prior to its drafting.[242] The information required by Buckingham in 1788 did not exist in respect of the Church of England until returns were furnished pursuant to the 1803 Act. Watson's proposed mode of obtaining the information was also significant. He considered that the laws respecting the residence of the clergy should be investigated in conjunction with 'the laws respecting ... [their] maintenance', and that this task should be entrusted to a commission of six temporal and six spiritual members of the British/UK House of Lords, who would proceed *in camera* and be empowered to

---

240 Buckingham to Fowler, 10 Apr. 1788, Stowe papers, Huntington Library, STG, box 29. For Buckingham's letter, see also Akenson, *Church of Ireland*, pp 58–60.   241 Robinson to Agar, 30 Jan. 1788, T/3719/C/22/3.   242 *Anecdotes of Watson*, p. 370.

examine witnesses on oath.[243] What was also provocative about Buckingham's approach in 1788 was the lofty and hectoring tone of his letter to Archbishop Fowler, and his affectation that he was speaking in the King's name. As Dr Stephen Radcliff, judge of the prerogative court, 1777–95, remarked pointedly to Agar in early May, Primate Robinson, who was in London at the time, 'might properly discover what were royal commands and what not'.[244]

The fast-moving events of the 1788 session of parliament are discussed in greater detail on pp 450–54. Broadly speaking, Agar succeeded in parrying almost all the blows aimed at the Church by what Bishop Woodward of Cloyne called the 'confederacy between the minister and the demagogues'[245] – i.e. Buckingham and Grattan. (In fact, there was no 'confederacy': in his proposed alterations to the tithe system, all of them to the detriment of the clergy, Buckingham was seeking to gain popularity in the House of Commons and steal Grattan's thunder.[246]) Agar expected a renewed onslaught in the next session. But the Church was reprieved by the Regency Crisis, which broke in October 1788. Nevertheless, the clash between Buckingham and Agar is of great importance, not only in the longer term (because the issues were recurrent), but from the point of view of establishing where the Church of Ireland stood in relation to the contemporary Church of England. From such comparison between them as is reasonable and possible, the Church of Ireland does not necessarily emerge as the more backward, somnolent and flagitious of the two. The clash is also of importance because it throws into high relief Agar's ideas for the governance of the Church of Ireland – for example, his insistence that clerical residence was to be achieved exclusively by episcopal administration, exhortation, reward and example, backed up by an increase in the resources and a widening of the role of the board of first fruits. This was not a tactical response to Buckingham's threat of legislation: it was Agar's sincerely held view which he had acted upon, and continued to act upon, in the three dioceses over which he successively presided. Basically, it has been the main theme of the present Chapter.

In 1971, Professor Akenson coined, and used as chapter headings, the two phrases, 'The era of graceful reform, 1800–1830', and 'Reform by critical strangers, 1830–1867'.[247] Thirty years on, these are still vibrant and useful concepts. 'Graceful reform' beautifully sums up what Agar and others stood for – reform of the Church of Ireland by churchmen, in their own time and on their own terms. It was put into contemporary language by Bishop O'Beirne in a letter to Primate Stuart of December 1805: 'If we want reform, let it be by ourselves and under the sole authority which we can recognise.'[248] There might now be disagreement as to when 'The era of graceful reform' began: Dr Barnard would date it to the 1690s, when a 'dynamic and largely Irish-born and [Irish-]educated group ... came to prominence';[249] Professor Connolly,

243 Ibid., pp 355–7 and 361–4.   244 Radcliff to Agar, 6 May 1788, T/3719/C/22/13.   245 Woodward to Agar, 6 May 1788, T/3719/C/22/14.   246 Buckingham to Grenville, 18 Feb. 1788, *H.M.C. Dropmore Mss.*, i. 305.   247 Akenson, *Church of Ireland*, p. vii.   248 O'Beirne to Stuart, 24 Dec. 1805, Stuart papers, Bedfordshire RO, WY 994/47.   249 Letter from Barnard to Malcolmson, 8 Aug. 2001.

while allowing for the High Church fervour of the 1690s and early 1700s, thinks it 'possible that the general level of interest in reform and improvement grew rather than diminished in the years after 1714';[250] on the impressionistic evidence presented earlier in this chapter, the 1760s might be thought a more appropriate date. At all events, 1800 must surely be far too late. Perhaps it would be reasonable to suggest that, whereas the improvers and reformers were an influential group within the Church of Ireland hierarchy in 1750, by the end of the century they were the norm. There would be less, or no, disagreement over the date at which reform was externally imposed by critical strangers. Rather, the problem here is that ecclesiastical historians who have had their sense of shock absorbed by the events of the 1830s find it hard to realise how shocking were the short-lived and abortive reforms proposed by Buckingham in 1788. Churchmen at the time were not in a position to console themselves that they were getting off more lightly than their successors would forty years later: instead, they saw the threatened measures of 1788 as a re-run of the reverses of 1732–6, when the interventions of critical strangers frustrated the graceful reforms of Boulter.

250 *Religion, law and power*, pp 171–3 and 189.

6

Agar as improving and reforming churchman, 1801–9

On 19 June 1802, *Faulkner's Dublin Journal* carried the following eulogistic report (possibly communicated by Agar himself) of Agar's first visitation of his new diocese of Dublin:

> On Wednesday and Thursday last the visitation of these dioceses [Dublin and Glendalough] was held at the cathedral of St Patrick by his Grace the Archbishop of Dublin, and never was there a more excellent charge than he delivered to his clergy on the occasion [see pp 219–20], who may well indeed be congratulated on the acquisition of so invaluable a pastor ... . Clear in his conceptions, wise in his regulations and firm in enforcing them, these dioceses will experience the happiest effects under his pastoral care ... . The highly respectable and admirably regulated state to which the diocese of Cashel, and indeed the whole province of Munster, attained under his wise and salutary discipline, is a standing memorial of that zeal and attention with which he regards the cause of religion.[1]

This was the public image of the new archbishop. Privately, Agar can only have regarded Dublin with a sense of *déjà vu*. It had almost been his in 1778, twenty-three years previously, and in the interim he had been carrying most of the burdens of the Church of Ireland, while others reaped its richest rewards (see Chapter Ten). What would have been a glittering prize to a young bishop just under forty, now came as a consolation prize to an elderly archbishop in his mid-sixties. With a man twenty-five years his junior ensconced in Armagh, Agar now knew that he had reached the peak of his ecclesiastical career. Moreover, he had somewhat run out of steam (and health) by the time he was translated to Dublin; and during his years there – as things turned out – he ceased to be the dominant figure in the Church of Ireland which he had been in *c.*1780–1801. However, in spite of all these discouraging circumstances, he proved on the whole to be an effective diocesan in a diocese famed for its unmanageability. He also remained – mainly because he held a seat for life (see pp 560 and 598–9) in the new House of Lords of the United Kingdom – an important influence on the wider politics of the Church.

1 21 M 57/A2/21.

'IN SUCH A SEE AS DUBLIN'![2]

Dublin was a difficult and thankless diocese because it had a patronage too small for its responsibilities, a clergy who tended to be too fashionable and well connected for archiepiscopal comfort, and an infrastructure which combined the extremes of a populous metropolis with the remote fastnesses of the Wicklow mountains.

> In 1214 the bishoprics of Dublin and Glendalough had been united and toget-her extend over a surface of about fifty Irish miles in length from north to south by thirty-six in the greatest breadth. ... [The diocese] comprises the whole of the county of Dublin, the most of Wicklow, a great part of Kildare and part of Wexford and Queen's County. This is an estimated area of 477,950 acres, of which 142,050 acres are in the county of Dublin, 257,400 acres in Wicklow, 75,000 acres in Kildare, 2,900 acres in Wexford and 600 in Queen's County.[3]

Within the walls of the old city of Dublin, the population amounted to an estimated 15,633 inhabitants in 1798. One of the administrative problems of the diocese was that the inhabitants of old, ruinous houses in the old city paid much more towards the income of the clergy than inhabitants of newer houses outside the walls.[4] Another was the need for the archbishop to achieve 'a greater accuracy in the compilation of bills of mortality' – a reform initiated by Agar's predecessor, Fowler.[5] Such was the popu-lation density of the old city that the pluralist rector of St Werburgh's, the Rev. Richard Bourne (who was also beneficed in the diocese of Armagh) replied as follows to a series of queries addressed to him by Agar in December 1808:

> I beg leave to inform your Grace that I do not reside within the parish, and in excuse for my non-residence that there is neither glebe-house nor a possibility of procuring a fit and convenient residence therein, inasmuch as every part thereof is closely built on and occupied by shops, except about one-third of the same, which is occupied by his Majesty's Castle. I beg leave to add that for twenty-eight years, during which I have been the incumbent of said parish, I have resided in Holles Street within fifteen minutes' walk of the church; that I have constantly and regularly attended the duties thereof, and never in all that time heard any complaint of any neglect; that I have always had a curate assis-tant and a reader to aid me in the duties thereof, who have been generally resident within the same (the former always) and that the present curate assistant resides within ten yards of the church.[6]

Bourne's impertinent reply is indicative, not just of the built-up state of the old city, but of the difficulty of dealing with Dublin's fashionable and well connected

---

2 Primate Stuart to Brodrick, 23 July 1811, NLI, Ms. 8886. For the context, see p. 503.   3 Kennedy, 'Dublin and Glendalough', pp 3–4.   4 Ibid., pp 213–14.   5 Ibid., p. 211.   6 Rev. Richard Bourne to Agar, 12 Dec. 1808, T/3719/C/42/86b; Kennedy, 'Dublin and Glendalough', pp 225–6.

clergymen. Bourne's principal connection was with the now deceased 2nd duke of Leinster. It was thanks to Leinster (p. 463) that Bourne had been instituted in 1781 as chancellor of St Patrick's and rector of St Werburgh's and Finglas (which were annexed to the chancellorship); and it was thanks to Bourne that Leinster's brother, Lord Edward Fitzgerald, had been decently interred in St Werburgh's in 1798. Bourne's preferments were actually in the gift of the archbishop: the reason that Agar had so little control over him was that they had been conferred on him by Agar's predecessor. In more general terms, the weakness of the archbishop's position *vis-à-vis* his clergy derived from the fact that the archbishop's patronage was limited. Information about this is unusually full (see p. 213) because the diocese of Dublin is (or, rather, used to be) blessed with good, surviving records, and because its administration has been the subject of doctoral research.[7] In 1725, the archbishop claimed that he had 'not seven [livings in his gift] ... worth £100 per annum'. In 1772, his patronage amounted to 51 benefices (12 of them valued at £200 per annum or more) and 23 dignities, including the chancellorship of St Patrick's and the rectories of St Werburgh's and Finglas (which together were valued at £400). More precise information is available for the slightly altered circumstances of 1801, when Agar became archbishop. The archbishop was then the sole patron of 48 benefices, joint patron of four with the dean and chapter of St Patrick's, joint patron of two with the lord chancellor and the chief justices, and joint patron of one with a layman, William Bryan. 'Of the dignities, he was patron of the precentorship of St Patrick's, the archdeaconries of Dublin and Glendalough, and 18 of the prebends [of St Patrick's] were also in his gift.' (He himself held one of those prebends, Cullen, *ex officio*.) Though this was an ample patronage for a diocesan by English standards, it was poor by Irish – particularly in view of the fact that Dublin was the Church of Ireland's second see in seniority.

Agar experienced personally as well as officially the limited nature of his patronage. Only one of his three sons, James, the youngest, went into the Church. In 1805, Agar induced the dean and chapter of St Patrick's to appoint him perpetual curate of St Nicholas Without[-the-Walls], and to elect him prebendary of Tymothan.[8] The latter sounds a good preferment, but in fact did 'not produce one shilling per annum. The duty ... is to preach at St Patrick's in turn. His Grace is the patron of it. ... [For] a curate in the city, it would be a respectable situation, although not a productive one.'[9] In the following year, Agar grumbled: 'So bad is my patronage that I have not been able to give ... [James] more than about £200 per annum. His progress must depend upon events not controllable by me.'[10] Agar's outspoken sister, Diana, thought that

7 The thesis concerned is Kennedy, 'Dublin and Glendalough'. Since its presentation in 1968, the diocesan records on which it was based (and post-1801 records as well) have been seriously damaged by negligent storage. Currently, they are accessible only via the selective microfilming previously carried out by NLI.   8 Agar's 'acts' as archbishop of Dublin, 1801–9, 21 M 57/B21a, *sub* 19 Nov. 1805.   9 Rev. Charles Cobbe Beresford (the previous prebendary) to John Hare (son of Rev. Patrick Hare, and agent for Agar's archiepiscopal and private estates), 11 Apr. 1805, T/3719/C/39/8. 10 Agar to Viscount Somerton, 23 Sep. 1806, 21 M 57, 2nd earl's unreferenced correspondence.

'Mr James Agar is out of luck very much to be an archbishop's son and in such a length of time not to have better preferment'; and a couple of months before Agar's death, a fellow-bishop commented that James Agar was 'not by any means competently beneficed'.[11] Then, at the beginning of July 1809, Agar, 'becoming sensible of the approach of death' (as D'Alton snidely put it), presented James Agar 'to the valuable prebendal stall of St Michael [he meant St Michan's] in Christ Church Cathedral'.[12] Even this belated promotion proved illusory, because the prebend was not actually in the archbishop's gift, and Agar's presentation was invalid. In the end, after Agar's death, the lord lieutenant, the 4th duke of Richmond, and his successor, Earl Whitworth, made James Agar vicar of Carrigallen, Co. Leitrim, in 1809, rector and vicar of Hollywood, Co. Dublin, in 1814, and archdeacon of Kilmore in 1816. This they did because his own conduct had been 'excellent',[13] and because of who his father had been.[14] In other words, James Agar's progress in the Church of Ireland actually owed almost nothing to his father's patronage as archbishop of Dublin.

What particularly weakened the position of the archbishop was that in the diocese of Dublin, unusually and probably uniquely, the other patrons of dignities and livings, if their patronage were combined, enjoyed considerably more than he did. In Christ Church Cathedral, he enjoyed no patronage at all.[15] This helps to explain the great difficulty which Archbishop King and some of his successors experienced in dealing with the dean and chapter of Christ Church. (Agar seems to have had no difficulties with the chapter; but he did have difficulties – see pp 256–7 and 282 with the second of the deans who held office in his day, the Hon. Charles Lindsay, bishop of Kildare and dean of Christ Church, 1804–46.) It also underlines the importance of patronage as a buttress to archiepiscopal and episcopal authority. Because for long years King could not assert any authority over Christ Church (see pp 28–9), he was also thwarted in his reformation of considerable parts of the diocese of Dublin. This was because the tithes of twenty-seven parishes constituted part of the income of the chapter, who 'either failed to supply the cures or did so badly. ... [Nor would they] agree to rebuild ruined churches, as they would then be obliged to supply curates.'[16]

Within the cathedrals themselves, the special – indeed unique – positions of the two deans meant that the archbishop enjoyed nothing of the direct authority to which Agar had been accustomed in Cashel and, before then, in Cloyne. This applied even to St Patrick's, where the dean was not of episcopal rank, where the archbishop enjoyed most of the patronage in the chapter, where he conducted his annual, diocesan visitations and where, historically, he was enthroned.[17] To Agar, the archbishop's

11 Diana Agar to Agar, 22 Dec. 1807, T/3719/C/41/48; Christopher Butson, bishop of Clonfert, to Agar, 17 Apr. 1809, T/3719/C/43/74.   12 *Archbishops of Dublin*, p. 351; John Hare to Agar, 22 June 1809, T/3719/C/43/111.   13 Diana Agar to the 2nd earl of Normanton (her nephew), 12 Jan. 1810, 21 M 57, 2nd earl's unreferenced correspondence.   14 Sir Edward Newenham to Robert Peel (the chief secretary), 24 Aug. 1815, Peel papers, BL, Add. Ms. 40229, f. 214. I am grateful for this reference to Dr James Kelly.   15 Kennedy, 'Dublin and Glendalough', pp 11, 204, 215–16 and xxxv.   16 Dolan, *The large mediaeval churches of Leighlin, Ferns and Ossory*, p. 49; Phillips, *Church of Ireland*, iii, pp 176 and 182–4.   17 In his quarrel with the dean and chapter of

irrelevance must have mattered most in the sphere of cathedral music. He loved music and had made a major contribution to the musical life of Cloyne and, especially, Cashel (see pp 302 and 318–23). He had also been for a long time a well known figure in Dublin musical circles. When the charitable music society in Dublin was incorporated under an act of 1778 (*17 and 18 George III, cap. 12*), Agar had been one of the founder directors, specifically mentioned by name in the act. In April 1788, two charity concerts in 'commemoration of Handel' had been held in Christ Church 'under the direction of the Archbishop of Cashel', with part of the proceeds earmarked for 'the fund for decayed musicians' administered by the charitable music society.[18] To an arch- bishop with this background, and an ardent Handelian, it must have been frustrating to have little or no part to play in the work of the two cathedral choirs which had combined (under the auspices of the then unincorporated charitable music society) to give the first performance of *Messiah* on 13 April 1742. Since the Restoration, the two choirs had in effect been combined for purposes of cathedral music too (with St Patrick's losing out as a result of this arrangement, since weekday services were no longer held there by 1800 nor again until 1865).[19] Fortunately, the artistic standards and finances of the choirs were in a flourishing state in Agar's day,[20] and had no need of the reforming energy he had had to bring to bear on both when archbishop of Cashel. The bell-ringers, however, were in need of reformation. They, too, were a combined facility, but had become financially dependent on the city corporation, which paid them to ring the bells on civic and protestant triumphalist occasions.[21] They also ran a successful business on the side. In 1782, a wealthy visiting Scot with an Irish earldom (who had decided to come to Dublin to take his seat in the House of Lords and inspect the Irish capital) had been surprised to receive the following letter: 'Knowing of your safe arrival in this kingdom, we, the ringers of his Majesty's Chapel Royal, known by [the] name of Christ Church and St Patrick[s'] Cathedral[s], made bold to ring many joyous peals on said bells, not doubting the usual bounty on such [a] great occasion.'[22] Agar, with his tidy-mindedness and sense of decorum, would certainly have stopped this scam, if he had been in a position to do so.

Though silent about the cathedral choirs and bell-ringers, the Dublin visitation records provide in other respects a good picture of the infrastructure of the diocese at that time of Agar's succession to Fowler. At the 1801 visitation, which had been held some months prior to that event, it was reported that there were at least 33 glebe-houses and 'probably 71 churches in good repair ... . Over the [previous] century, the number of churches in good repair had more than doubled', reflecting a country-wide increase. In 1801, 'six churches were mentioned for their poor or ruinous state. These were: St

---

Christ Church, Archbishop King asserted the archbishop's alleged right to be enthroned in Christ Church as well, and this second enthronement was held between 1703 and 1864 – Very Rev. H.J. Lawlor, *The fasti of St Patrick's Cathedral, Dublin* (Dundalk, 1930), pp 36–7.   **18** *Dublin Evening Chronicle*, 8 Apr. 1788; Milne, *Christ Church Cathedral*, pp 298–301.   **19** Milne, *Christ Church Cathedral*, p. 314.   **20** Ibid., pp 311–14 and 339–45.   **21** Ibid., pp 189 and 304–5.   **22** Quoted in Alistair and Henrietta Tayler (eds.), *Lord Fife and his factor: being the correspondence of James, 2nd Lord Fife (1729–1809)* (London, 1925), p. 142.

Michael and St Nicholas Without, which were in ruins; Hollywood, 'a barrack; Fonts-town, "destroyed" during the 1798 rebellion; ... Arklow, ... "out of repair"; and ... Ballymore, "in bad order". ... Castledermot was under repair in 1801.'[23] In Dublin City, one of the great problems was the collapsing state of St Patrick's, which will be discussed on pp 314–16. In general, church provision in Dublin was continually being out-run by population growth, in spite of church-building and the creation of new parishes in the course of the eighteenth century. St Stephen's, Upper Mount Street, was one of three chapels of ease built within St Peter's parish; it was the 'elegant church in Merrion Square' to which Fowler had subscribed in or before 1792,[24] but it was not completed until 1824. North of the Liffey, St George's parish was formed in 1793, and the new church, where the future duke of Wellington was married in 1806, was built by Francis Johnston (1760–1829) between 1802 and 1813. St Andrew's church, Westland Row, was rebuilt between 1793 and 1807, also by Johnston. Outside the city, Monkstown was built, 1785–9, Rathfarnham, 1786–95, and at Howth in 1793, where 'there was no church ... [and there had been] no service for forty years past, ... £500 [was] granted for a church by [the board of] first fruits] in or before 1801'.[25]

Agar was only ten years younger than his predecessor; so, on grounds of age alone, he was not ideally qualified to devote to the diocese of Dublin all the attention required – for example, to undo the ill-effects of Fowler's absence during his last four years or so as archbishop (see p. 464). Moreover, Agar had good reason – much better than Fowler – for being himself an absentee. Having taken great pains to secure for himself a seat at Westminster, he made attendance in the House of Lords a priority and in practice was away from his diocese for up to half the year during half the period 1801–9. William Cobbett's *Parliamentary history* and *Parliamentary debates* record only three speeches made by Agar: one in favour of the Irish Martial Law Bill (*41 George III, cap. 61*) – a post-Union renewal of an act of the Irish parliament – in 1801; one on a procedural matter concerning the basis on which Luke Fox, an Irish judge whose conduct was under investigation, should appear before the House of Lords in 1805; and one in favour of an Irish Churches and Glebe-Houses Bill (*47 George III, cap. 23 [sess. 2]*) in 1807.[26] This was certainly not an exhaustive list (see, for example, p. 218). However, it is not altogether surprising that his speeches were not more numerous. Though capable of speaking 'wonderfully', he had always been a debater and a man of business rather an orator. So, a paucity of set speeches has no bearing on his record of attendance and on his role behind the scenes. It may possibly reflect a difference in the style of debate characteristic of the two Houses of Lords, and the difficulty which an elderly man experienced in adapting himself to a new environment. Adapt himself he did, as there is no doubt that he made his mark – both on the House and on the

---

23 Ibid., pp 216–18 and 246. 24 Fowler to 1st marquess of Downshire, 12 Mar. 1792, Downshire papers, PRONI, D/607/B/338. 25 Kennedy, 'Dublin and Glendalough', pp 218–19; Lewis, *Topographical dictionary*, ii, pp 353–7; Craig, *Dublin*, pp 282 and 294; Milne, *Christ Church Cathedral*, p. 292. 26 [William Cobbett (ed.)], *The parliamentary history of England from the earliest period to the year 1803* ..., vol. xxxv (London, 1819), pp 1242–3, and *Cobbett's parliamentary debates* ..., vol. v (London, 1805), p. 142, and *vol. ix* (London, 1807), p. 907.

political dinner-parties of London. He was also supposed to be a frequenter of the court and a favourite with the King.[27]

Many of his initial contacts in British politics and London society were members of Lord Mendip's circle or of former Dublin Castle administrations. When Henry Addington succeeded Pitt as prime minister early in 1801, his administration included Lord Westmorland, the lord lieutenant of 1789–94, and (from July 1801) Thomas Pelham, now Lord Pelham, who had been chief secretary, 1795–8.[28] Lord Auckland, too, was in the government, though not in the cabinet, and was to be in the government for the rest of Agar's life, with an intermission in 1804–6. When Pitt returned to the premiership in May 1804, replacing Addington, Pelham was dropped from the cabinet, but Westmorland remained, Camden (the lord lieutenant of 1795–8) was a member of the new cabinet,[29] and Robert Hobart, Westmorland's chief secretary, 1789–93, and now 4th earl of Buckinghamshire, joined it in January 1805. Mendip's friend, Portland (with whom Agar usually left his proxy[30]), was in the cabinet from 1801 until 1806 and was prime minister, 1807–9. Moreover, Agar made new, post-Union contacts of his own, and favourably impressed some former antagonists. Among these latter was the 1st Lord St Helens,[31] who was appointed to the minor political office of a lord of the bedchamber by Pitt in 1804; as Alleyne Fitzherbert, St Helens had been Buckingham's chief secretary, 1787–9, and had come into conflict with Agar. In 1806–7, Agar struck up a perhaps surprising friendship with the Foxite Whig lord lieutenant, the 6th duke of Bedford, whom he described as 'a very respectable and worthy man, and likely to give satisfaction wherever he goes'.[32] The friendship ripened in London, after the close of Bedford's short period of office in Ireland: in July 1808 Agar officiated at the marriage of Bedford's son and heir, Lord Tavistock, and Lady Anne Maria Stanhope (who was given away by that bright, but misplaced, hope of the Whigs, the Prince of Wales).[33]

Agar was to survive the Union by only eight and a half years. But at least he did not die or retire immediately or soon after its passing, like three other members of the former Irish cabinet, Sir John Parnell, Lord Clare and John Beresford. Clare had expected to become, in England, a kind of secretary of state for Ireland without portfolio, and was cruelly disappointed.[34] Agar had no such exalted expectations, and adjusted himself to the new world of the United Kingdom surprisingly well (granted his age). Indeed, it is a fair guess that, post-1801, he was more influential in London

27 *Farington diary*, vi. 98; Sir A.H. Giffard and Edward Giffard, *Who was my grandfather: a biographical sketch [of John Giffard]* (London, 1865), p. 85. I am indebted for this latter reference to Dr Jacqueline Hill. Both pieces of evidence are anecdotal and derive from impressionable people. 28 Pelham to Agar, 28 Nov. 1803, T/3719/C/37/45. 29 Camden to Agar, 26 May 1804, T/3719/C/38/30. 30 Portland to Agar, 18 Jan. 1806 and 13 Feb. 1809, T/3719/C/40/2 and 43/24. 31 St Helens to Agar, 14 Nov. 1808, 21 M 57, 2nd earl's unreferenced correspondence. 32 Agar to Viscount Somerton, 23 Sep. 1806, 21 M 57, 2nd earl's unreferenced correspondence. 33 Agar's 'acts' as archbishop of Dublin, 1801–9, 21 M 57/B21a; Hampshire RO list of 21 M 57/B22/6. 34 His enemies said 'he expected to have been king of Ireland after the Union, and was vexed to find he continued to be only chancellor' – *Glenbervie diaries*, i. 313.

than he was in Dublin (see below). In April 1809, an Irish bishop observed: 'It is well known what attention is paid in Downing Street to your Grace's opinions and recommendations, especially in Irish ecclesiastical affairs.'[35] This was possibly true during the premiership of Portland. The only other survivor of the former Irish cabinet was the ex-speaker, John Foster (b.1740), who served as chancellor of the Irish exchequer at Westminster, 1804–6 and 1807–11. But, where Foster remained rooted in the particular politics and economic concerns of Ireland,[36] Agar – in spite of his age and his seniority as an Irish statesman – seems to have been interested in and capable of genuine assimilation to the new United Kingdom.

Even when Agar was in Dublin (which he was for the majority of the time in 1801–9), his diocese did not and could not receive his undivided attention. This was because he was involved in memberships, trusteeships, etc., of numerous institutions not specifically or at all diocesan in character. These included: the board of first fruits (of which he remained treasurer until 1803); TCD (of which he was a visitor);[37] the order of St Patrick (of which the archbishop of Dublin was chancellor); the incorporated society for promoting English protestant schools – the charter schools – and the already-mentioned charitable musical society (of both of which he was vice-president); the foundling hospital, the lying-in hospital, the Royal Hospital, Kilmainham, the house of industry, the Erasmus Smith foundation, the association for discountenancing vice, Dr Stevens' hospital, Sir Patrick Dun's hospital, etc. (of all of which Agar, either personally or *ex officio*, was a governor); the school at Swords 'for the purpose of educating and apprenticing the children of the humbler classes, without any religious distinctions' (see p. 574*n*)[38] and 'Mrs Bonnell's charity'[39] (of both of which the archbishop of Dublin was a trustee); the Dublin paving board, the board of charitable donations and bequests (of both of which Agar was a member); the commission for the relief of suffering loyalists, of which he was the senior member (see pp 527–8 and 544–7) and which sat on until 1807; and so on. In 1807, Agar was also appointed by the out-going lord lieutenant, Bedford, first 'perpetual president' of the newly founded humane society of Dublin, and – almost at the end of his life – a vice-president of the Richmond institution for the industrious blind.[40] As Bishop O'Beirne had pointed out in 1800 (p. 562), 'There is scarcely a great institution to which ... [the archbishops of Armagh and Dublin] are not acting trustees, nor a charitable board at which their attendance is not essentially necessary.' In Agar's case, some of these avocations (notably the treasurership to the board of first fruits) long ante-dated his translation to Dublin; but his presence in Dublin instead of Cashel when parliament was not sitting, meant that he became more actively involved in them.

35 Bishop Butson to Agar, 17 Apr. 1809, T/3719/C/43/74.   36 Malcomson, *John Foster*, pp 443–8. 37 Address of compliment from TCD to its visitors, Agar and Arthur Wolfe, 1st Viscount Kilwarden, 24 July 1802, 21 M 57/B20/5. Primate Stuart succeeded Kilwarden after the latter's assassination in 1803.   38 John Malone to Agar, 26 May 1809 (applying for the situation of master of the new school at Swords for himself and for that of mistress for his wife), T/3719/C/43/100. 39 Copy minutes of a meeting of the trustees of Mrs Bonnell's charity, 6 Apr. 1809, T/3719/C/43/67.   40 Bedford to Agar, 8 Apr. 1807, and reply, 9 Apr. 1807, T/3719/C/41/17–18;

Others happened to require attention and consume time during the period
1801–9. In 1802, for example, as a visitor of TCD and a governor of the Erasmus
Smith foundation, he was doubly involved in the decision to spend £8,000 of a surplus
in the Erasmus Smith funds on the purchase for TCD of the 20,000–volume library
of Henry Fagel (1765–1838), the exiled chief minister of Holland. Initially, Agar
opposed the purchase.[41] He probably shared Primate Stuart's (and Archbishop
Brodrick's) view that 'the education of the people is a matter of ... much more
importance than an additional library for Trinity College'.[42] The cataloguing and, in
the longer term, the space implications were a further worry, the more so as TCD was
just beginning to feel the effects of having been made a copyright library under the
Copyright Act of 1801 (*41 George III, cap. 107*).[43] Finally, the Fagel books not only
represented a 40% increase in TCD's holdings, but also – and disquietingly to a
churchman – tilted the balance of the TCD library in a secular direction. Another preoccupation of Agar's in the educational sphere was the commission set up in
September 1806 under the Irish act of *28 George III, cap. 15*, as up-dated and
amended by *46 George III, cap. 122*, 'to enquire into the state of schools and public
education in Ireland'. Five of the eleven commissioners, Agar among them, were
chosen by, and from the ranks of, the commissioners of charitable donations and
bequests, and the archbishop of Dublin chaired their meetings when the primate was
absent.[44] The government-nominated members, predictably (granted the complexion
of the government in September 1806), were mostly Whiggish and reforming, but on
the whole 'the conservative, clerical members on the board dominated its proceedings,
thereby limiting criticism of the Established Church'.[45] The board did not make its
final, and misleadingly 'liberal', report until 1812, three years after Agar's death, so his
work as a commissioner is mainly noteworthy – particularly in the present context –
as a distraction from his purely diocesan responsibilities. In 1808, he drafted most of
a report to the board on the state of 20 of the 36 charter schools;[46] perhaps these were

Hugh Ferguson to Agar, 13 June 1809, T/3719/C/43/110.   **41** Pelham (the home secretary) to
Agar, 26 Feb. 1802, T/3719/C/36/7; G. Waterhouse, 'The family of Fagel', in *Hermathena*, no. xlvi
(Dublin, 1931), pp 80–86; R.B. McDowell, 'The acquisition of the Fagel library', in *Annual Bulletin
of the Friends of the Library of Trinity College, Dublin* (1947), pp 5–6; Vincent Kinane, 'The Fagel
collection', in Peter Fox (ed.), *Treasures of the [TCD] library ...* (Dublin, 1986), pp 158–69. I am
grateful to Dr Charles Benson, keeper of early printed books, TCD, for referring me to all these
printed sources, and for help much beyond the call of duty.   **42** Stuart to Brodrick, 7 Mar. 1802,
quoted in Kenneth Milne, 'Principle or pragmatism: Archbishop Brodrick and Church education
policy', in Ford, McGuire and Milne (eds.), *As by law established ...*, pp 188–9; Brodrick to Stuart,
8 Mar. 1802, Bedfordshire RO, WY 994/21.   **43** For the Copyright Act and TCD, see Charles
Abbot (the chief secretary) to Sir George Shee, 1st Bt (under-secretary at the Home Office), 25 Sep.
1801, and Hardwicke to Pelham, 19 Oct. 1801, HO 100/104, ff. 125–6 and 205–6.   **44** Rev. Philip
Hunt (Bedford's private secretary) and Bedford himself to Agar, 1 and 5 Sep. 1806, T/3719/C/
40/40 and 42; Milne, 'Principle or pragmatism', pp 188–9; Milne, *The Irish charter schools,
1730–1830* (Dublin, 1997), pp 227–8; Akenson, *Church of Ireland*, p. 140. I am grateful to Dr Milne
for help on this tricky subject of education.   **45** Harold Hislop, 'The bishops and the schools,
1806–12', in *Search: a Church of Ireland journal*, xiii, no. 2 (winter 1990), pp 36–43. Again, my thanks
to Dr Milne for this reference.   **46** Report [mainly in Agar's hand] by John Corneille, secretary to

the top twenty, because his comments were much more laudatory than the general state of the institution (of which, as its vice-president, he was of course protective) would have warranted.[47] On the other hand, he had already shown an interest in Joseph Lancaster's system of education[48] which, among other things, was avowedly non-denominational and which did not find favour with most Irish churchmen (Archbishop Brodrick for one), and particularly with those actively involved in the management of the charter schools.[49]

In addition to these important, but extra-diocesan avocations, his career as archbishop of Dublin was interrupted by illnesses which were exacerbated by old age. In September 1806, he wrote that he was now enjoying 'as good health as I could reasonably expect at my time of life.'[50] But this was not true to previous, and subsequent, form. In October 1800, he was reputed to be 'in bad health, possibly in danger'. He was laid up between December 1801 and January 1802,[51] and had again been ill later in 1802. Of this latter illness the 2nd Viscount Clifden had written to Agar's son: 'I very truly lament the state of your father's health, which does not appear to mend, though I have not exactly heard what his last attack was.'[52] In September 1805, he was again ill – this time at Cheltenham; and his visitation of the diocese had to be carried out by his vicar-general.[53] All told, he was prevented by ill-health from going over to London to attend the parliamentary sessions of 1801–2, 1803–4, 1805–6 and 1806–7. In mid-January 1807, when in Dublin, he had a fairly serious fall. This elicited from his old, 'sincerely attached friend', John Toler, now Lord Norbury and, as Clare had feared (p. 73), chief justice of the common pleas, a letter expressing the hope 'that you do not feel as much pain in your bones as I did in my nerves from your tumble. However, you have the pleasure to recollect that you have made but very few false steps in your life, and few men have been more seldom found tripping'.[54] In late September 1808, after returning to Dublin from the 1807–8 session, Agar wrote to his son:

> I am at present so engaged in business that I can hardly find time to write these few lines to you. I hold the visitations of my own dioceses on the 27th and 28th

the board of charitable donations and bequests, endorsed by Agar 'Mr Corneille's report of the charter schools to the board of education', 1808, T/3719/C/42/95. For a subsequent attack on the charter schools and Agar, see Corneille to Agar, 20 Feb. 1809, T/3719/C/43/27. **47** For the charter schools, see: Milne, *Charter schools, passim*; Oliver MacDonagh, *The inspector general: Sir Jeremiah Fitzpatrick and the politics of social reform, 1783–1802* (London, 1981), pp 88–104; and Connolly, *Religion, law and power*, pp 304–5. **48** Agar to John Foster, 16 Mar. 1805, Gratz autograph collection, Historical Society of Pennsylvania, case 12, box 29. I am indebted for this reference to Dr James Kelly. See also Lancaster to Foster, 9 Oct. 1806 and 11 Aug. 1807, Foster/ Massereene papers, PRONI, D/207/60/1 and 3. The lord lieutenant, Bedford, was an enthusiastic Lancasterian. **49** Milne, 'Principle or pragmatism', p. 192; Akenson, *Church of Ireland*, pp 140–41; Mathieson, *English Church reform*, p. 14. **50** Agar to Somerton, 23 Sep. 1806, 21 M 57, 2nd earl's unreferenced correspondence. **51** 3rd earl of Altamont to 2nd Viscount Gosford, 10 Oct. 1800, Gosford papers, PRONI, D/1606/1/1/232C. Agar to Cornwallis, 8 Jan. 1802, T/3719/C/36/1. **52** Clifden to Somerton (then Hon. Welbore Agar), 25 Oct. 1802, 21 M 57, 2nd earl's unreferenced correspondence. **53** Agar's 'acts' as archbishop of Dublin, 1801–9, 21 M 57/B21a. **54** Norbury to Agar, 14 Jan. 1807, T/3719/C/41/3.

of this month, and my triennial visitations of this whole province begin on the 4th of October. I doubt whether I shall have strength enough to go through this laborious but necessary business, which will not end till the 20th of October or perhaps later.[55]

Between 25 October and 1 June 1809, there is a gap in Agar's record of his official 'acts' as archbishop of Dublin. He went back to London for the next parliamentary session, but spent most of the first half of 1809 laid up in his town house in Great Cumberland Place. There he received lengthy instructions from William Wilberforce on a new method of relieving his 'very, very severe pain'.[56] The Chabot marriage which he solemnised on 1 June 1809 (see pp 81–2) was an isolated as well as final 'act'. He died in London on 14 July.

AGAR'S ACHIEVEMENTS AS A DIOCESAN, 1801–9

At first sight, his own papers, and other sources and indications, confirm the impression that his activity while he was archbishop of Dublin was limited. D'Alton comments, with unaccustomed euphemism: 'in truth, the principal events of this prelate's life are more legitimately connected with the Church history of Cashel'.[57] Agar's papers relating to the archbishopric of Dublin are relatively few in number.[58] One of them is a notebook recording, as already mentioned, his official 'acts' as arch-bishop.[59] In contrast to his 'acts' at Cashel, these relate almost entirely to the licensing, instituting, etc., of clergy of all ranks, and to the baptising and marrying of lay people. In 1804 there is a record of three payments of £500 each from the board of first fruits towards the rebuilding of the churches of St Nicholas Without, St Michael's and St George's, and in 1807 there is a reference to the building of a glebe-house. (Of St Nicholas Without and St George's, Fowler had written in 1792 that they had 'been in ruins for many years; and as no aid can be procured from government, they are likely to continue in that deplorable state';[60] so Agar had clearly done a great deal better than Fowler in getting them rebuilt so soon.) Otherwise, the 'acts' are not infrastructural. Another of the papers relating to Dublin is the familiar 'state' of the diocese, giving particulars of the benefices, clergy, the number and condition of churches and glebe-houses, the number and names of curates, etc. This 'state', however, unlike its pre-decessors, was not initiated by Agar and was drawn up late in his incumbency, at the beginning of 1807. It was compiled in response to the 'queries' addressed to the four archbishops and, through them, to the bishops on 16 July 1806.[61] Even the admiring

55 Agar to Somerton, 23 Sep. 1808, 21 M 57, 2nd earl's unreferenced correspondence.   56 Agar to Hon. Cecil Jenkinson, 17 Apr. 1809, and Wilberforce to Agar, 5 June 1809, T/3719/C/43/76 and 109.   57 D'Alton, *Archbishops of Dublin*, pp 351–2.   58 Hampshire RO list of 21 M 57/B20–22. 59 21 M 57/B21a.   60 Fowler to Downshire, 12 Mar. 1792, PRONI, D/607/B/338.   61 21 M 57/B21b; Stuart to Brodrick, 1 July, [late July] and 31 July 1806, NLI, Ms. 8869/4; Bedford to Stuart (acknowledging receipt of the return for the province of Dublin), 24 Mar. 1807, WY 993/24;

Sleater makes no mention of building work or other improvements carried out by Agar while archbishop of Dublin, although in most respects Sleater's book is up-to-date with its year of publication, 1806.

Nevertheless, Agar's record as a diocesan is not as blank as all this might suggest. His 'acts' and 'state' may be less full and purposeful than the equivalent documents relating to Cashel, his earlier drive and many initiatives may have been wanting, but – as his general and not specifically diocesan correspondence testifies – he was swiftly responsive to the initiatives of others, whether beneficial or baneful to the diocese. Among the baneful initiatives were an act of 1807 for paving and lighting the city of Dublin and a Dublin Police Act of 1808, both of which threatened the archbishop's jurisdiction in his liberties and/or manors of St Sepulchre, etc., 'which include[d], not only the entire of the parishes of St Kevin's and St Nicholas Without, with a considerable part of St Peter's parish, in Dublin, but also a very considerable and wealthy tract of the country containing the villages of Rathmines, Rathfarnham, Tallaght, Milltown, Dundrum, Williamstown, Merrion, etc., all in the neighbourhood of Dublin'.[62] Agar obtained a clause of exemption from the 1807 Act,[63] but not from the 1808. In the case of the latter, his position was fatally weakened by Fowler's earlier failure to notice the passing of the first Dublin Police Act in 1786, and by the simple fact that the archbishop's jurisdiction in criminal matters had in effect lapsed.[64] However, Agar did prevail on the Irish administration to appoint his seneschal as the assistant barrister who, under the 1808 Act, had responsibility for the district comprising most of the archiepiscopal manors. This in practice achieved something of the object of a legal exemption, and probably gave the seneschal greater authority than had of recent years been recognised.[65]

The initiatives beneficial to the diocese to which Agar gave a ready and facilitating response lay in the areas of church and glebe-house building and the rationalisation of pluralities. When memorialised – according to the procedure set out in *48 George III, cap. 65, sec. 3* – by clergymen, churchwardens or parishioners who had raised money for church-building by a mixture of parochial cess and private subscription, Agar lost no time in pressing their claims to financial support on the board of first fruits. He sometimes threw in tactical or legal advice of his own for good measure. Examples drawn from his general correspondence for 1809 are: Castleknock church, Co. Dublin (a grant of £1,000 from the board); St George's church, Dublin (further assistance, in the form of a £5,000 loan); Foyran church and glebe-house, Co. Meath (this parish was not in the diocese, but its rectorial tithes were appropriate to the vicars choral of Christ Church and St Patrick's); Ballymore Eustace church and glebe-house,

abstracts of the archbishops' and bishops' answers, 30 Jan. 1808, Foster/Massereene papers, PRONI, D/207/50/21; Akenson, *Church of Ireland*, pp 124–5.   **62** Mark Hare (John Hare's brother and the seneschal of Agar's manors) to Agar, 13 Mar. 1808, T/3719/C/42/14.   **63** John Hare to Agar, 12 Apr. 1808, T/3719/C/42/21.   **64** Mark Hare to Agar, 22 Apr. 1808, T/3719/C/42/25. **65** Agar to Sir Arthur Wellesley (the chief secretary), 11 Apr. 1808, Mark Hare to Agar, 16 and 29 Apr. and 27 July 1808, and Dr Patrick Duigenan (Mark Hare's predecessor as seneschal) to Agar, 1 Oct. 1808, T/3719/C/42/18, 22, 27, 45 and 71.

Co. Kildare (unspecified financial assistance from the board); Taney church, Co. Dublin (a loan of £5,000); and Arklow church, Co. Wicklow (a loan of £500).[66] This is a far from exhaustive list, mainly because much of Agar's correspondence has not survived, but it serves to demonstrate the even greater incompleteness of the diocesan 'acts' and 'state'. Not all of this parochial endeavour was inspired by pure piety. Writing of the new church at Taney, the Dublin Orangeman and corporation activist, John Giffard (1745–1819), assured Agar that 'there is not in our parish a protestant who does not venerate the prelate and love the man [Agar]. Recollect, my Lord, this is the parish in which I raised a corps of 200 yeomen in one day by hoisting an Orange-coloured flag on one of my towers – this in the midst of rebellion.'[67]

The provisions and procedures in regard to loans for church-building under *48 George III, cap. 65, secs. 3–5*, create the impression that the initiative came from the parish every time and that the diocesan's role was reactive. But this may be misleading. In the case of Ballymore Eustace church, and possibly in that of some other of these building ventures, the initiative had actually come from Agar, not the parish. At his visitation in June 1803, it had been minuted that the Ballymore Eustace church-wardens should 'be compelled to repair their church'; three years later, at the visitation in June 1806, the church was reported as being 'in ruins'.[68] So, the proposed new church of 1809 was plainly a belated response to this earlier pressure from Agar (and an immediate response to the new availability of funds – see pp 279–80) and not a spontaneous move on the part of the parishioners. However initiated, there was plainly a good deal of building activity in the diocese of Dublin while he was archbishop. One of the surviving records of the board itself shows that, between 1804 and 1809, Dublin received £3,372 in loans and £1,350 in gifts towards glebe-house building, £9,300 and £2,000 respectively towards church building, and gifts of £600 towards the purchase of glebes. This makes a grand total of £14,822, which is more than the dioceses of each of the three other archbishops received during the same period.[69]

The rationalisation of pluralities in the diocese was an equally important, though less well documented, initiative. In this process, Agar was assisted by the determination of Irish administrations from Bedford's onwards to discountenance non-residence. Hardwicke had been slipshod in this respect (even when not acting under the duress of so-called 'Union engagements'). He was aware of the problem that too many privy council unions had been made on what he called 'loose and insufficient evidence of expediency', contrary to the tight requirements of the order in council made in 1726, which still governed this matter.[70] But his actions spoke louder than,

---

66 Rev. Dr John Connor to Agar, 20 Feb. 1809, Rev. William Bushe to Agar, 27 Mar., 18 Apr. and 15 May 1809, Rev. Dr W. Vavasour to Agar, 29 Mar. 1809, Rev. Gerald FitzGerald Junior to Agar, 10 Apr. 1809, John Giffard to Agar, 13 May 1809, and Rev. H.L. Bayly to Agar, 15 May 1809, T/3719/C/43/28, 60, 77, 95, 61, 70–72, 92 and 96.   **67** Giffard to Agar, 13 May 1809, T/3719/C/43/92.   **68** Visitations of Dublin and Glendalough, 9 June 1803 and 6 June 1806, RCB Library, MIC 20. MIC 20 also contains another copy of Agar's 'state' of the diocese (21 M 57/B21b). **69** Armagh diocesan registry papers, PRONI, DIO 4/11/2/75.   **70** Hardwicke to Stuart, 23 Sep. 1804, WY 994/44.

and in the opposite sense to, these words. In 1805, for example, he had recommended Agar's most troublesome clergyman, the Rev. Richard Bourne, to Primate Stuart for the living of Kildress in the diocese of Armagh, well over a hundred miles from Bourne's Dublin parishes, and Stuart had (very improperly) complied.[71] As a diocesan, Stuart should not have accepted a clergyman who was already beneficed so far away; and as primate, he should not have exercised his unique discretion in the matter of faculties (see p. 222) to permit Bourne to hold a third benefice. From 1806 on, standards were raised. The question of 'unions of livings was one chief object of' the Bedford administration's 'attention' from the outset.[72] This explains why, from this point on, Agar's general correspondence provides examples of his being consulted by Dublin Castle about a number of ecclesiastical patronage proposals, mainly exchanges of livings. The Castle became involved when one or both of the livings concerned was in the patronage of the crown, or when one or both formed part of a union of parishes which had been or which it was proposed should be effected by act of the privy council. By the early nineteenth century, the most common reason for proposing a privy council union was that a clergyman with more than one living could not charge both or all his livings with the cost of a new glebe-house (up to the usual maximum of 'two years' income of the whole'), unless the livings were united by act of council. But he ought not to be allowed to get them so united unless they were 'contiguous'.[73] Bedford also adopted, and his successor, the duke of Richmond, continued, 'a rule of rigid investigation into improper unions' made in former times,[74] often under circumstances of financial exigency which no longer obtained.

Agar, because of his good relations with Bedford, may have had some bearing on the development of this desirable policy, and certainly was a party to its implementation in his capacity as either diocesan or metropolitan.[75] In a mixture of these capacities, for example, he was asked in September 1806 to advise on a request for an exchange which came from the late Lord Clonmell's nephew, John Scott, dean of Lismore and rector of Clonenagh, Co. Laois. Dean Scott wanted 'to exchange the living of Clonenagh [the right of presentation to which was shared between the crown and the bishop of Ferns] for that of Carrick in the county of Waterford. Carrick is not twenty miles from Lismore: Clonenagh is above sixty, and without either glebe or residence.' Agar's prompt and succinct reply was: 'Carrick being so much nearer ..., is a very canonical reason for the exchange.'[76] In another instance, he was assured that 'the lord lieutenant [Richmond] has determined to withhold his consent to any exchange that may be proposed to him unless the

71 Hardwicke to Stuart, 5 May 1805, WY 993/3.   72 Stuart to Bedford, 27 Apr. 1806, *HMC Dropmore Mss.*, viii, pp 130–32.   73 Bishop Alexander of Clonfert to Wickham, 14 Aug. 1803, PRONI, T/2627/5/S/32; case of Rev. Thomas Wilson, late rector of the union of Mulrankin, diocese of Ferns, [22 Aug. 1806], T/3719/C/40/38.   74 Bedford to Agar, 22 Aug. 1806, T/3719/C/40/37.   75 Ibid.; William Elliot (the chief secretary) to Agar, 29 Aug. 1806, and Sir Arthur Wellesley to Agar, 9 June 1807, T/3719/C/40/39 and 41/24. Wellesley's letter is also printed in *Wellington civil correspondence, 1807–9*, pp 78–9.   76 Case put to Agar, and Agar's reply, 8 Sep. 1806, T/3719/C/40/45–6.

archbishops and bishops in whose diocese the livings may be situated should give their assent'; in response, he both approved the exchange and acknowledged Richmond's 'attention to the true interests of the Established Church'.[77] The rationalisation of pluralities on geographical grounds was in many instances necessary before the location, scale and cost of churches and, particularly, of glebe-houses could be determined upon. It may therefore be assumed that Agar, as diocesan, metropolitan or both, quietly negotiated other rationalising exchanges for which evidence does not survive because there was no prominent third party like Dublin Castle involved in the negotiation. It was in the nature of such arrange-ments that they should be quiet because, unlike most species of reform, they actually suited the convenience of interested parties – the financial as well as geo-graphical convenience, since they might well remove the need to pay a curate. As Charles James Fox (who was thinking purely of patronage and not at all of pastoral efficiency) wrote to Bedford, his friend and *protégé*: 'There is a clergyman of the name of Radcliff at Enniscorthy [Co. Wexford], who has a living at 140 miles' distance at Portaferry in the diocese of Down. What he wants is to exchange that living for one nearer to Enniscorthy, and as he was protected by the late bishop of Down [William Dickson – a lifelong friend of Fox (see p. 470)], I should be glad if this favour, apparently not unreasonable, could be managed for him.'[78]

In some other, more miscellaneous respects, too, Agar made a permanent con-tribution to the diocese of Dublin. In 1808, he was 'the promoter of a bill for securing the estates and funds devised by the Rev. Richard Daniel in trust to apply the profits for the relief of the poor of St Luke's parish in the city of Dublin, the support of the hospital of incurables and other charitable institutions, etc.'[79] Earlier, in 1804, he had taken the controversial, but in financial and administrative terms sensible, decision to sell off the archbishop's expensive and impractical town palace (see pp 365–8). Conversely, he seems to have prevented Charles Lindsay, bishop of Kildare and dean of Christ Church, from saddling Lindsay's successors and the oeconomy fund of the cathedral with the cost of building a new deanery.

The existing deanery in Fishamble Street, near the cathedral, built on the initia-tive of Agar's grandfather, Bishop Ellis (see pp 379–80), had been let since the mid-1740s, but was not irrecoverable (and, eventually, was recovered).[80] In 1792, Lindsay's predecessor, George Lewis Jones, had obtained Fowler's consent to pass an act of the Irish parliament authorising the letting (presumably for villa-development) of most of the dean and chapter's 'considerable demesne about eight miles south-east of Dublin', and the building of a new deanery, either on the unlet part of the demesne (amounting to 126 out of 526 acres), or – as Lindsay proposed – 'in an open area' to be created by demolishing 'streets' and avenues west of the Castle'.[81] Lindsay in fact envisaged a square made up of deanery, 'prebendal houses' and houses for other cathedral

77 Agar to Wellesley, 13 June 1807, T/3719/C/41/25.   78 Fox to Bedford, 3 May [1806], Holland House papers, BL, Add. Ms. 27569, ff. 280–83.   79 D'Alton, op. cit., p. 351.   80 Milne, *Christ Church Cathedral*, p. 291.   81 Lindsay to Agar, 21 Jan. 1806, T/3719/C/40/3, and to Stuart,

dignitaries.) The 1792 Act had been imperfectly drafted, and Lindsay now wanted a new one remedying the defects. Some of these were purely technical, but one was fundamental: the act had been 'wholly concealed from' the chapter, though the demesne belonged to the dean and chapter, and not exclusively to the dean. If, however, the chapter did not ratify the act *ex post facto*, the leases of the 400 acres would be invalid and the dean would presumably have to compensate the tenants and refund the £3,500 received so far in entry fines (and, presumably, earmarked for the new deanery fund). If this sum had to be refunded or, as was probable, was inadequate to the cost of the deanery, it was hard to see where alternative or additional resources were to come from. The times were not propitious. In consequence of the southward and westward drift of fashionable Dublin (see pp 159 and 413–14), and particularly in consequence of the Union, rental values in the old city were falling,[82] and property in that location constituted the remainder of the dean and chapter's and the oeconomy fund's assets. Altogether, this was a most complicated situation, created by a fraudulent transaction on the part of Bishop Jones and, if he knew about the concealment, Archbishop Fowler.

How Agar responded to the representations which Lindsay made to him, first orally and then by letter, is unclear, except that the response was unsatisfactory to Lindsay. A week later, Lindsay tried his luck with the primate. The response is, again, unclear. Whatever happened about the act and the dean and chapter's demesne, no new deanery was built, and Lindsay continued to reside in and rent, as a private individual, Glasnevin House, Co. Dublin. Two months after his approaches to Agar and Stuart, he made what Stuart called an 'unprovoked attack upon' Agar at a meeting of the board of first fruits;[83] whatever the pretext for this row, the cause was probably the abortive deanery scheme. In his 1807 'state' of the diocese, Agar recorded firmly that the dean's residence was in Fishamble Street.[84]

CHURCH AND GLEBE-HOUSE BUILDING IN IRELAND, 1802–6

If Agar was not a 'great' archbishop of Dublin, like King, he just about sustained in Dublin his high reputation as a diocesan administrator, improver and reformer. In these last years, however, he did not sustain the role of effective headship of the Church of Ireland which he had played since *c.*1780. At first, it looked as if, in spite of the appointment of Stuart in 1800, Agar would still be virtual primate, particularly after his position was further strengthened by his translation to Dublin (see p. 599).

28 Jan. 1806, Bedfordshire RO, WY 994/48.   82 Milne, *Christ Church Cathedral*, pp 291–7. This recent history is silent about the saga of the dean and chapter's demesne and the deanery.   83 Stuart to Brodrick, 31 Mar. 1806, Ms. 8869/4. This was only one of many rows in which Lindsay was involved – see Milne, op. cit., pp 287–90. His relations with Agar were further soured because Lindsay's *bête noir* within the cathedral chapter, Rev. Dr Richard Graves – was a *protégé* of Agar – Graves to Agar, 6 Dec. 1796, T/3719/C/30/49.   84 21 M 57/B21b.

He had the great moral advantage that it had been he who had steered the Church through the final negotiations over the relevant provisions of the Act of Union. In particular, it had been he who had given the Church its post-Union nest-egg by successfully arguing that the £45,000 compensation payable with effect from 1 January 1801 for the disfranchisement of the three bishops' boroughs of Clogher, Old Leighlin and St Canice should go to the board of first fruits (see pp 568–9 and 573–4). But all these portents of post-Union Agarite hegemony proved to be misleading. Stuart did not turn for advice and local knowledge to the elder ecclesiastical statesman who had been the strongest internal candidate in opposition to him in 1800, but to Stuart's own contemporary, Charles Brodrick, whom Stuart regarded as one of the two 'most exemplary characters on the bench'.[85] When Brodrick was promoted in December 1801 to the archbishopric of Cashel in succession to Agar, he became third in the Church of Ireland episcopate in seniority; he was also second only to Agar in ability. Moreover, he was becoming increasingly hostile to Agar (see pp 364 and 416–17), and therefore was ripe for an alliance with Stuart. From Stuart's point of view, such an alliance was to be welcomed; he could lean on Brodrick without weakening his own position, whereas he would be regarded as a cypher if he leant on Agar. In March 1802, Stuart wrote to Brodrick lamenting the latter's absence in London, 'as your assistance in the settlement of this business [the accounts of the board of first fruits] will be very essential, and I put little confidence on [*sic*] our brethren, who seem easily frightened.'[86] In the context, this meant frightened of Agar.

At just this time – March 1802 – Euseby Cleaver, bishop of Ferns, addressed a memo. to Stuart suggesting that the £45,000 and the other resources of the board of first fruits should be employed to set up a revolving, interest-free loan fund on which clergymen might draw for the purpose of building glebe-houses.[87] This idea of a loan fund has been particularly associated with Stuart and Brodrick.[88] But Cleaver had mooted it, in the individual case of his own diocese, as early as January 1801 (see p. 569), so it is reasonable to regard him as the originator of the idea. Stuart took it up enthusiastically. He wrote to Brodrick in November:

> Two different schemes have been proposed to me. The one is to fund a part of the surplus ... and, adding the interest of that to the interest of the compensation money, to apply the whole annually as a bounty for building glebe-houses, giving to each clergyman willing to build £500. The other scheme is to lend the principal of the compensation money, interest-free (in certain proportions), to every clergyman willing to build, the clergyman repaying the money so borrowed by yearly instalments of 15% or 20%.
>
> With regard to the first scheme, I conceive it would be doing little for the public, how much soever it might ease individuals; for the average number of houses built during the last ten years, though years of war and rebellion, is

85 Abbot to Stuart, 23 Dec. 1801, WY 994/10.   86 Stuart to Brodrick, 14 Mar. 1802, Ms. 8869/1.
87 Cleaver to Stuart, [22] Mar. 1802, Wickham papers, PRONI, T/2627/5/S/14.   88 Akenson, *Church of Ireland*, pp 116–17.

nine, of the preceding ten years the average number is eleven. We may therefore confidently fix the future average at ten, although no bounty were given;
and, unless the bounty can be extended beyond ten houses, I see not how the
public would be materially benefited by such an application of the money.
Upon the whole, therefore, I prefer the second scheme; for were £45,000, the
amount of the compensation money, to be lent to clergymen to enable them to
build, it must in a short time produce a considerable effect. In 1803 70 houses
might be begun, in 1805 15 houses, in 1805 18 houses, etc., etc. In short, by this
method a greater number of houses would be built in ten years than could be
built by merely employing the interest of the money in forty years, the principal would remain entire, and might afterward be applied to augmenting small
livings or to any other useful purpose.

   If this scheme should be adopted, it will be necessary to procure an act of
parliament to give us security for the money thus lent, and to enable us to
recover it with facility. But whether we adopt or reject this scheme, it is
absolutely necessary that some specific application should immediately be
made of this money.

Brodrick enthusiastically endorsed the second scheme.[89]

   It is not clear to what extent, if any, Agar was involved in the discussion of these
proposals. At the beginning of January 1803 he submitted, not to Stuart but to the
chief secretary, William Wickham (of Binsted Wyck, Alton, Hampshire, who may well
have been a Paultons acquaintance)[90] 'a sketch of the act which, with your
approbation, I mean to offer to parliament this session, and with it I send you three
English acts which served as precedents for drawing the present act. ... Dr Duigenan
has revised and amended it.'[91] Wickham was asked to do the same and to comment
generally. Unfortunately, he was also asked to return the enclosures, which do not
survive either in his or Agar's papers. However, it is obvious that Agar was re-running
the Benefice Mortgage Bill which he had drafted *c.*1790. This was a measure
empowering (and, where necessary, compelling) all incumbents whose livings were
worth £100 or more per annum to build or buy glebe-houses and/or to buy glebes 'by
enabling them to borrow money at interest for that purpose on the security of their
respective benefices'. As matters stood *c.*1790, and in 1803, 'when a clergyman
undertakes to build a glebe-houses, ... no money-lenders choose to advance money on
the security of a certificate to be granted [by the diocesan] against the [clergyman's]
successor, not so much from any defect in the title, ... but from the uncertainty of the
time of repayment, as the certificate cannot operate till the death or removal of the
borrower from his benefice.'[92] The legal and practical position in England and Wales
was more conducive to Agar's purpose. His papers include a printed pamphlet of 1785

---

89 Stuart to Brodrick, 11 Nov. 1802, Ms. 8869/1; Brodrick to Stuart, [early Dec. 1802], WY
994/51A. 90 Wickham to Agar, 1 Mar. 1806, T/3719/C/40/18. 91 Agar to Wickham, 4 Jan.
1803, T/2627/5/S/15. 92 Cleaver to Stuart, [22] Mar. 1802, T/2627/5/S/14.

which he endorsed: 'On the English acts to encourage the building of glebe-houses by enabling the clergy to borrow money by mortgaging their benefices, by Dr [John] Warren, bishop of Bangor'.[93] However, Agar's bill went far beyond the English precedents on which it was founded; so much so, that Archbishop Moore of Canterbury wrote to him at the beginning of 1792 requesting a copy. This is a fortunate circumstance, as the copy sent to Moore[94] seems to be the only one which survives: the bill never got the length of being presented to the Irish parliament and therefore was not printed; nor was it ever 'laid before any lawyer'[95] – further proof of Agar's grasp of the technicalities of legislation (see pp 73–4), since it is long and complicated.

In essence, it extended to the mortgagor-builder of a glebe-house or the mortgagor-purchaser of a glebe-house or glebe, the benefits of the existing legislative code regarding expenditure for those purposes. He was to be eligible for the board's respective grants of £100, and for full reimbursement by his successor on the usual basis (so that the repayment of the principal would be shared among the four successors of the original mortgagor, each of them paying all the interest which fell due during his incumbency). The money borrowed was to be paid into the hands of the diocesan, who was made a necessary party to every stage of the business. This meant that the loan ceased to be a private arrangement between incumbent and lender, but was given the additional security of the diocesan's authority, which guaranteed the payment of interest and the repayment of principal. Presumably, a mortgage so secured could be assigned and re-assigned, like any other mortgage, on the open market. Finally – and this was probably the provision which militated most against the enactment of the bill (because of the number and influence of the vested interests it threatened) – any incumbent who, after he had held his living for a year and still had taken no steps towards building a glebe-house, was liable to be compelled by the diocesan to mortgage the living for that purpose. Admittedly, the diocesan already had the power under existing legislation to compel an incumbent to build. But in practice this must generally have been evaded on a plea of poverty. Under Agar's proposal, no such plea would be admissible.[96]

This was a measure which was characteristic of him and of the path of prudence which he consistently recommended that the Church should follow. It was characteristic in that it strengthened episcopal authority and widened episcopal discretion; also in that it was founded on the principle that the Church should maximise its existing resources and not run the gauntlet of parliament except under very favourable

93 21 M 57/B30/1.　94 Dated 7 Feb. 1792, Lambeth Palace Library, Moore papers, vol. 6, ff. 213–22. I am indebted for this reference to Terence Finley, and for a painstaking transcript to Sir Adrian FitzGerald, Bt, Knight of Kerry.　95 Agar to Moore, 7 Feb. 1792, ibid., ff. 211–12.　96 In January 1787, Bishop Watson proposed to his patron, Rutland, then lord lieutenant of Ireland, a scheme which would not have affected the incumbent's nett income, but would temporarily have deprived the parish of pastoral care. Where there were no glebe-houses, he recommended that 'the livings, when they become vacant, should be *sequestered* for two or three years and the moneys thence arising should be applied to the erection of houses ..., and residence should then be *enforced*' – *Anecdotes of Watson*, pp 155–9.

circumstances. Apart from the obvious effect of a great increase in the number of glebe-houses being built, it would have benefited the Church in a variety of more indirect ways. One of the weaknesses of the Church of Ireland was that almost all of its considerable wealth was tied up in the remuneration of its clergy (at all levels – from primate to curate): Agar's bill would have released a portion of this wealth and re-deployed it to a common Church purpose – the promotion of clerical residence. Second, the earmarking of a considerable proportion of the incomes of many livings for the repayment of glebe-house mortgages would have provided a justification and defence for the size of some of those incomes, the more so as it would be the richer clergy – the John Agars of the Church – who would be the first whom their diocesan would compel to build by borrowing. Finally, glebe-house mortgages would have given numerous lay lenders a vested interest in the preservation of the clergy's rights to tithe and to the other sources of clerical income, and so would have broadened the base of the Established Church's defence.

In spite of these promising features, the bill made no headway in the 1790s, nor in 1803 when Agar made his final effort to have it enacted. And yet, the circumstances of the late eighteenth and very early nineteenth century would seem to have been propitious to it. The most obvious change in these decades was the dramatic, albeit uneven, rise in clerical incomes. Brodrick, though a leading advocate of the rival scheme to Agar's, was strongly influenced by this rise. He saw the period of wartime prosperity which Ireland was enjoying as the 'critical' opportunity to undo the many unions of livings which the 'general poverty' of an earlier age had necessitated, to divide 'the very extensive and lucrative benefices' which now existed in various parts of the country (for example, the diocese of Cloyne), and 'to restore the Church to its originally intended strength in point of numbers'.[97] Unless the critical opportunity was seized, there was a great danger that the increasing wealth of the clergy would become a reproach to the Church. The visiting Church of England clergyman, Burrows, had thought it a reproach as long ago as 1773:

> The parochial clergy are rather too well provided for in Ireland, as their incomes commonly enable them, and their inclinations almost always carry them, to take up their abode in more amusing places than a country parish. ... As far as I can observe, the clergy in general have a greater share of outward respect than their brethren in England, because their revenues are greater; but I do not think them even so well beloved, as clergymen, and I think that they have even less spiritual influence over their flocks. ... The scheme which the chief governor and council have a power to enact, and which they have lately executed, of dividing large benefices into two and even three parishes, will in time diminish the riches of the parochial clergy.[98]

---

97 Brodrick to [William Bennet], bishop of Cloyne, 9 Sep. 1802, Ms. 8892. Part of the letter is quoted in Akenson, *Church of Ireland*, p. 71.   **98** PRONI, T/2551/1.

By the early nineteenth century, political economists were still noting a rise, not a diminution, in 'the riches of the parish clergy' of Ireland. Wakefield, writing in 1808, commented that 'A living of £500 is but a middling one in Ireland, and anything beneath is considered as very low.'[99] (It may be recalled that in 1831, the Rev. Theobald Pontifex was offered, and accepted, 'one of the best livings in the gift of ... [Emmanuel] College ..., being in value not less than £500 a year with a suitable house and garden'.)[100] Another commentator, following in Wakefield's wake, argued:

> The extension of tillage in Ireland was stated in 1805 as having been sixfold within the preceding 21 years ... The gross aggregate revenues of the Established Church in Ireland amount ... probably at this time [1815] to about £676,000 per annum and have increased full 50 per cent since 1779. And if the aggregate income of the parochial clergy was equally apportioned to each benefice or union, every incumbent would enjoy an average income of £420 per annum, notwithstanding the abolition of agistment tithes ..., the non-payment of small tithes ..., [etc.]. And an income of £420 per annum in Ireland, allowing one-third for the difference of living, etc., etc., in England and Ireland ..., is an income double in value to the equalised average incomes of the parochial clergy in England.[101]

The precise figures for Ireland in 1808 were stated to be as follows: 147 incumbents of parishes drew less than £100 per annum from their benefices, 165 drew between £100 and £200, 214 between £200 and £500, and 116 more than £500.[102] This shows that a great many incumbents in Ireland did not need the indulgence of an interest-free loan; it also suggests that Stuart had been unjustifiably pessimistic in his expectation that under the existing legislative code, only ten glebe-houses per annum (or much the same number as had been built in the 1780s) would be built in 1801–10. Furthermore, from the point of view of encouraging clergymen to build glebe-houses, Agar's proposal was more effective than Stuart's: Agar required the builder to do no more than pay interest on the sum borrowed, leaving the principal to be repaid by his three successors (who had to pay the interest as well), while Stuart required that the builder repay the principal at the savage rate of 15% or 20% per annum. This actually suggests (and so it will be argued in another context (see pp 430–2) that Stuart was not strong on finance. There can be no doubt about Agar's understanding of the money market and therefore of the practicality of his scheme. On that assumption, it was surely foolish of Stuart not to proceed on the basis of open-market mortgages in respect of the richer livings, so that the old and any new resources of the board could be concentrated on the poorer ones.

99 Wakefield, *Account of Ireland*, ii. 469.   100 Samuel Butler, *The way of all flesh*, p. 55.   101 Rev. Morgan Cove, *An essay on the revenues of the Church of England* ... (third ed., London, 1816), pp 166–70. Professor Connolly argues (*Religion, law and power*, pp 180–1) that, pre-1760, the Church of Ireland clergy were only modestly well-off in comparison to other groups within Ireland – e.g. lay landowners.   102 [John Foster's] 'Scheme for building glebe-houses and churches and purchasing glebes', [Jan. 1808], *Wellington civil correspondence, 1807–9*, p. 434.

Foolishly or otherwise, Stuart persisted in the interest-free loan scheme. In late January 1803, Agar resigned as treasurer to the board, ostensibly on the ground of ill-health,[103] but presumably in protest against the rejection of his alternative proposal. Later in the year, two Board of First Fruits Acts were passed, the first on 27 July and the second on 12 August. Both came very late in the session – an early warning of the difficulty the Church of Ireland was going to experience in obtaining parliamentary time at Westminster for the legislation it sought. It may also have been an early warning of what Lord Auckland was to describe in the following session as the 'real public grievance of the first magnitude that bills of a most important and disputable nature are permitted to be brought forward in July, to be decided by 45 members in the House of Commons and 4 or 5 in the House of Lords.'[104] The first of the Board of First Fruits Acts of 1803 (*43 George III, cap. 106*), 'gave the board ... the power to lend money [out of its existing resources, including the £45,000] for glebe[-house] construction, not merely to provide grants upon house completion as it had in the past. These loans were to be made interest-free to the incumbents'. They were to be repaid, not at Stuart's proposed 15% or 20% per annum, but at the much gentler and more realistic rate of 6% per annum – the rate proposed by Brodrick, who equated it with the rent an incumbent would have to pay for a hired glebe-house.[105] 'Further, [under 43 *George III, cap. 158*,] the Irish treasury was given the power to lend up to £50,000 interest-free to the board ... for the purpose of increasing the number of glebe loans. Ironically, after all the attention the matter was given, the board continued its old policy of grants rather than loans, approving only eight glebe-houses loans by the year 1808',[106] all of them advanced out of existing resources under the terms of *43 George III, cap. 106*. This was not in fact an irony. The board did not take up the large additional sum held out to it by *43 George III, cap. 158*, partly or perhaps mainly because of the strings attached to the loan. Under sec. 1, the lord lieutenant was authorised to grant to the board, interest-free, 'any sum or sums of money not exceeding £50,000 Irish money ... as he ... shall think fit from time to time' for glebe-house loans as prescribed in the previous act. Under sec. 2, the securities and the other arrangements for repayment were to be such as the Irish treasury, with the approbation of the lord lieutenant, 'shall direct and appoint'. Plainly, these conditions for the first time subjected the work of the board to external scrutiny, and indeed control. This was Agar's, and Primate Robinson's, old nightmare, and the very thing which Agar's mortgage scheme had been designed to avoid, because it would not have raised the difficult issue of accountability for loans of public money.

The first act (*43 George III, cap. 106*) had been largely the work of Brodrick – and, short though it was, its drafting had exposed his inexperience (at this stage in his career) of such business.[107] The second act (*43 George III, cap. 106*) was drafted in

103 Agar to Stuart, 24 Jan. 1803, Ms. 8861/4.   104 Auckland to 1st Lord Sheffield, 25 July 1804, Jupp/Aspinall transcript from the Auckland papers, BL.   105 Brodrick to Stuart, [early Dec. 1802], WY 994/51.   106 Akenson, *Church of Ireland*, p. 117. See also Forster, *Life of Jebb*, ii, pp 185–7. 107 Brodrick to Wickham, 20 June 1803, T/2627/5/S/18.

London and had a more mixed paternity. In mid-May 1803, the solicitor to the board of first fruits reported to Brodrick that the first draft of *43 George III, cap. 158*, which had been the work of Dr Arthur Browne, MP for TCD, 1783–1805, had been subjected to 'many alterations' by Dr Duigenan, who expressed his disapprobation 'of the whole plan in general'. (This was, presumably, because Duigenan had been associated with Agar in the rival mortgage scheme.) Duigenan's amendments made the bill 'quite inadmissible to the Bishop of Killaloe', William Knox, who called in Lord Redesdale, the overbearing and unpleasant Englishman who had succeeded Clare as lord chancellor of Ireland early in 1802. Redesdale 'almost new-modelled it', making it much simpler.[108] At first, Brodrick and Stuart did not realise how sinister this simplicity was. Wickham assured Brodrick in early July 'that the attainment of the object which the act has in view will alone regulate the lord lieutenant's discretion as to the mode and time of repayment'; and when Wickham wrote to Stuart in mid-August to inform him of the passing of the act, Stuart responded with a letter of fulsome gratitude.[109] In mid-October, Brodrick still seems to have been unsuspecting, because he wrote to Wickham asking 'to be informed at what periods they [the bishops] may draw for the sum set apart for their use by the legislature'.[110] It is not clear how long it took Stuart and him to realise that there were strings attached to the government loan. By May 1804, Brodrick was writing reproachfully to Wickham's successor that the bishops had 'expected that the £50,000 to be lent to them would be left in their hands to be kept in perpetual circulation for the purposes of the act of 43 George III, cap. 106, and not to be repaid to the treasury', and especially not to be repaid piecemeal as instalments were received back by the board from individual clergymen.[111] But he could obtain no assurance from the Irish administration that this latter, 'injurious' interpretation would not be put on the clause.

Matters were made worse by the explanation offered by Redesdale, who with transparent duplicity tried to pin the blame for the 'obnoxious clauses' on Agar – of all people! But Stuart was not deceived, and reported to Brodrick that,

> when I pressed him for proof, he shuffled, and at last could only say that he was told it by a friend of a friend of Wickham. If these strange clauses were introduced by the Archbishop of Dublin, whom they [Redesdale and the Irish government] oppose and hate, why should they not abandon them? How happens it that they cling to them so violently? At this moment they are the only matter in dispute, and ... [vest a power in] the lord lieutenant never vested in any of his predecessors, and the use of which they have not to this moment condescended to explain. They mean to deceive us, my Lord, when they assert that this innovation was introduced without their knowledge. It was entirely their own contrivance, and they well know the effects it might be made to produce.[112]

108 Richard Martin to Brodrick, 17 May 1803, Ms. 8861/4.　109 Wickham to Brodrick, 9 July 1803, T/2627/5/S/28; Wickham to Stuart, 15, and Stuart to Wickham, 18, Aug. 1803, WY 994/25. 110 Brodrick to Wickham, 17 Oct. 1803, T/2627/5/S/37.　111 Brodrick to Sir Evan Nepean, 11 May 1804, Ms. 8888.　112 Stuart to Brodrick, 19 Apr. 1805, Ms. 8869/3.

So, Stuart, Brodrick, Agar and all or most members of the board regarded the introduction of the principle of Castle and treasury directions and approbation as a very dangerous precedent, resented the fact that it had been done without the knowledge or consent of the board, and were determined not to touch the money until the 'obnoxious clauses' had been removed. Though the 'fabricators' of the clauses, plainly, were Hardwicke and Redesdale, the fault to a considerable extent lay with Stuart himself, who had had a major and unavailing row with Hardwicke in late 1801–early 1802 over an episcopal appointment (see pp 609–12), and since then had become an object of dislike and suspicion to him.

Not only did the board hesitate to take up the proffered government loan, it also did almost nothing to implement the previous act, which related only to its own, existing resources. The initial (or perhaps ostensible) reason given by Brodrick to Wickham was that the board could not dispose of its holdings 'in government securities ... at the present low rate of public funds ... [without] a very considerable loss ... and a very large diminution ... in their annual income'.[113] Possibly, Stuart and Brodrick were also reluctant to make a start with the board's existing resources alone, lest this give a damaging appearance of self-sufficiency; more probably, they could come to no estimate of the board's immediate financial requirements because of divisions of opinion within it over what scheme of glebe-house building was to be adopted. In April 1804, Stuart lamented to Brodrick:

> It appears to me that instead of advancing we are receding, and at the last board were still employed in debating first principles. In truth, I misunderstood the object of that board, which I thought was to ascertain the number of houses which each bishop would undertake immediately to build: whereas I found, from the Archbishop of Dublin and the Bishop of Meath [O'Beirne], that it was to ascertain the number of houses wanted in each diocese. I know not the use of such an inquiry; for, though we certainly want a house on each benefice, the difficulty of procuring glebes and many other circumstances must prevent this want [from] being supplied for many years, even though the fund were sufficient to defray the expenses of building. In my own opinion, we should confine our inquiries to the demand that will be made upon the fund this year, or in other words the number of houses that clergymen will instantly commence building.[114]

A similar picture is conjured up by a letter written in May by O'Beirne to Stuart. 'We have many meetings, but we get on but a very little way.'[115]

Brodrick's next letter to Stuart described a more fundamental policy difference. (It also shows that Agar was still a power within the board, and suggests that he was manoeuvring to sabotage the glebe-house loan scheme.)

113 Brodrick to Wickham, 17 Oct. 1803, T/2627/5/S/37.   114 Stuart to Brodrick, 21 Apr. 1804, Ms. 8869/3.   115 O'Beirne to Stuart, 21 May 1804, WY 994/36.

The question [was] whether we should expand, out of our own funds and in
addition to the sum [of £50,000] granted to us last session of parliament, the
[further] £50,000 which we gave the public to understand last year we were
prepared to appropriate ... . The Bishops of Meath, Derry and Kilmore ...
[contended that the board was pledged to do so. But] it was urged by the Archbishop of Dublin that it would be highly [in]expedient to draw upon our
capital ... [because of] the present aspect of public affairs and the strong tendency which had been shown by many persons who may come into power to
injure the Church ... . The Archbishop's reasoning ... carried conviction to the
Bishop of Meath's mind.[116]

The other problem was that, if the board put up a matching sum of £50,000 out of its
own resources to get the glebe-house loan scheme going, it would be left with
insufficient income to meet its other objectives and commitments unless it could be
sure that the current parliamentary grant of £5,000 per annum would be continued.[117]
Then, in May 1804, the deliberations of the board, and Stuart's and Brodrick's
negotiations to get the government loan of £50,000 freed from the restrictions under
which 'all our proceedings must be clogged',[118] were interrupted by the fall of the
administration of Henry Addington and the return to power of Pitt.

Hardwicke, though an Addington appointee, was retained in office by Pitt; but his
authority, inevitably, was weakened by the change of government in London. Moreover, in consequence of the Union, the survival of the lord lieutenancy as an
institution was itself an issue[119] – so far, largely unresolved. The period 1801–4 had
also seen a series of clashes of authority, jurisdiction and rights of patronage between
the lord lieutenant, on the one hand, and on the other the home secretary, the
commander of the forces in Ireland, the commander-in-chief at the Horse Guards and
the chancellor of the Irish exchequer. This last office-holder was, during Pitt's weak
ministry of 1804–6, John Foster, whom Pitt appointed first lord of the Irish treasury
as well as chancellor of the Irish exchequer. This implied prime ministerial powers,
which Pitt almost certainly intended and Foster promptly assumed.[120] He took it upon
himself to approve or reject warrants for the issue of money signed by Hardwicke,
with the result that the dispute between Hardwicke and the board was subsumed into
a more important power struggle between Hardwicke and Foster. In 1805, when
matters came to a head, Stuart was in London taking his turn as representative of the
Church of Ireland in the House of Lords. In London, he had discussions with Foster,
whom he found well disposed to co-operate with the board. In fact, Foster had always
been friendly to the Church, except on the one issue of tithes on articles necessary for

116 Brodrick to Stuart, 26 Apr. 1804, WY 994/32.   117 Ibid.   118 Brodrick to Stuart, 28 Apr.
1804, WY 994/34.   119 Edward Cooke to Camden, 18 July 1800, and memo. by Camden, 1 Aug.
1800, Pratt papers, PRONI, T/2627/4/119 and 122; paper about 'the situation of the lord lieutenant
and his secretary', 24 Oct. 1801, and memo. by Portland, 5 Dec. 1801, PRO, HO 100/104, ff. 269–79
and 298.   120 Malcomson, *John Foster*, pp 88–103; T.R. McCavery, 'Finance and politics in Ireland,
1801–17' (unpublished QUB Ph.D. thesis, 1981), pp 70–85.

his first love, the linen industry; and his late brother had been a bishop (see p. 182). The view which Stuart formed on the basis of these discussions he transmitted in a series of letters to Brodrick about

> the need to amend 43 George III, cap. 158, in order to give authority to the treasury to advance money for glebe-house loans out of the £50,000 on receipt of [nothing more than] a certificate from the board of first fruits. ... With this Mr Foster assures me he shall be contented, and by this the Treasury will be merely the bank of the commissioners of first fruits ... . In truth, all that we want is the money, and if we can procure it without any restraint and without any application to the lord lieutenant or his secretary, I think it will be better and we shall avoid great inconvenience. ... It is in vain to struggle against Mr Pitt and Mr Foster, and I have good reason to think that Mr Foster's opinions in all matters relating to money are adopted by Mr Pitt. Though I would on no account whatever interfere in the differences which subsist between Lord H[ardwicke] and Mr F[oster] ..., [and] I think of him [Foster], ... I believe, as you do, ... he is I am persuaded no less powerful than enterprising and may do us great mischief in many different ways ... . We must either adopt his plan or relinquish all hope of the £50,000.[121]

The part Agar played in all this is not explicit. Almost no Foster-Agar correspondence survives. The little there is comprises four letters, all dating from 1805. They none of them relate explicitly to board business, but they suggest a degree of personal and political cordiality, and one of them requests an urgent meeting in July.[122] Moreover, as Agar and Foster, like Stuart, were together in London for the parliamentary session, lack of letter-writing does not betoken the absence of collusion. Agar had known Foster, who was an approximate contemporary, since the 1760s. They had been colleagues in the Irish cabinets of the 1780s and 1790s, and by 1805 (as has been seen) were unique survivors of that forum. Agar had some years earlier, in 1798, gone to trouble and expense to assist Foster's candidate in a parliamentary election.[123] At the beginning of February 1801, following a very premature report that Foster was to be appointed to the chancellorship of the Irish exchequer, Agar had 'expatiated on Foster's abilities and the weight he would give to the new administration'.[124] In June 1804, Diana Agar commented somewhat naively: 'I should suppose it must be a most desirable thing Mr Foster's being the Irish minister. ... It is a most universal opinion in this country that Mr P. is not a friend to Ireland, but his making Mr Foster minister looks well.'[125] Much more revealingly, Agar's brother, Welby, wrote in September: 'Your friend, Mr Foster, is at last arrived at the summit of his ambition, for he will in a great measure govern Ireland. I take for granted that your intimacy and good opinion

---

121 Stuart to Brodrick, 21 and 25 Mar. and 2 Apr. 1805, Ms. 8869/3.   122 Foster to Agar, 29 Jan. and 25 Mar. 1805 and 2 July [1805?], D/207/63/1–3; Agar to Foster, 16 Mar. 1805, Gratz autograph collection (loc. cit.).   123 Rev. Patrick Hare to Agar, 8 Mar. 1798, T/3719/C/32/20.   124 Jupp/Aspinall transcript from the Glenbervie diaries, *sub* 1 Feb. 1801.   125 Diana Agar to Agar,

still subsist.'[126] Agar preserved among his papers two copies of a printed address of December 1805 from 'Black Bean' (Agar's *protégé*, John Giffard) making numerous critical and abusive comments about Hardwicke, and concluding: 'He has failed in a contest with the great patron of Irish constitution and Irish prosperity; he has been unable to humble the good and honest spirit of the Patriot Foster.' Agar endorsed one of the copies: 'Very good on Lord Hardwicke'.[127] Since Hardwicke and Redesdale 'hated' Agar, as Stuart put it with un-Christian bluntness, and hated Foster even more vehemently, Agar and Foster had good political reasons for making common cause.

They also shared a common ambition to advance the interests of the Church of Ireland by promoting clerical residence, even though Foster had in mind a level of parliamentary *largesse* which must have struck Agar as imprudent, not to say danger-ous. Two years after Agar's death, Foster acknowledged that it was his hope that the then annual grant of £60,000 'may be continued ... until every parish wherein a glebe, glebe-house or church is wanting shall be amply provided with each, and that the repayments of the loans which you [the board] have given or shall give for the purpose may be permitted to accumulate and rest in your hands for putting the cathedral churches of Ireland on such a dignified and respectable footing as they ought to be and as they generally are in England'.[128] This was going far further than Agar, and was a far cry from Agar's cautious mortgage scheme. Nevertheless, the 1803 Acts having passed and the policy they represented having been adopted in broad outline, it was obviously necessary to make the most of them and break the deadlock which had arisen over *43 George III, cap. 158.*

Such ought to have been Brodrick's view, too; the more so as Brodrick had every reason to dislike Hardwicke. (Years before the great deception of 1803, Brodrick had been warned by his brother, Lord Midleton, that Hardwicke was 'a very petulant, conceited blockhead'[129]). In September 1804, Brodrick had urged on Stuart the necessity 'that we should be informed how the new chancellor of the exchequer stands affected towards us, and whether he will be disposed to forward the scheme which we wish to carry into effect'.[130] In the spring of 1805, however, Brodrick – isolated as he was in Dublin – seems to have been primarily concerned with maintaining his ascen-dancy over Stuart and with counteracting the influence which Foster and, almost certainly, Agar were bringing to bear on Stuart in London. Brodrick's hostility to Agar

23 June 1804, T/3719/C/38/35. **126** Welby to Agar, 6 Sep. 1804, T/3719/C/38/46. **127** Printed address (2 copies), 18 Dec. 1805, 21 M 57/A2/24–24A. Hardwicke had dismissed Giffard from his post in the customs (to which he was restored in 1807) for publishing in his government-subsidised newspaper, *Faulkner's Dublin Journal*, an attack on the Roman catholic petition to parliament for Emancipation. Hardwicke's own chief secretary and, more important, Pitt thought Hardwicke's action extreme and ill-judged. See: Hardwicke to Hawkesbury (the home secretary), 23 Mar. 1805, to Marsden, 26 Apr. 1803, and to Charles Yorke, 4 May 1805, and Nicholas Vansittart (the chief secretary) and Hawkesbury to Hardwicke, 2–3 and 15 May 1805, Hardwicke papers, BL, Add. Ms. 35710, f. 46, 35706, ff. 232 and 220, 35716, ff. 55 and 57 and 35759, f. 57. Agar was also involved – Giffard, *Who was my grandfather*, p. 85. **128** Foster to Brodrick, 14 Mar. 1811, Foster/Massereene papers, PRONI, D/207/50/56. The original is WY 994/58. **129** Midleton to Brodrick, 2 Dec. 1793, Ms. 8889/8. **130** Brodrick to Stuart, 9 Sep. 1804, WY 994/43.

has been noted. Since pre-Union days, he had never held 'John Foster, *ci-devant* Speaker, in very high estimation', and they had clashed more recently over the Erasmus Smith foundation's application or misapplication of its funds to buy the Fagel library in 1802.[131] Brodrick may also have feared that the glebe-house loan scheme which Stuart and he 'wish[ed] to carry into effect' was in danger of being fundamentally redefined. More than a hint of this is to be found in a letter written a year earlier by O'Beirne, another ally of Foster. O'Beirne had argued in favour of accepting the government loan of £50,000 (probably on the existing terms), adding to it '£50,000 out of our own funds', and requiring the incumbent to contribute one year's income to the building costs. As he reckoned that the average cost of a glebe-house was £500, this meant that the total sum available for building would be £20,000, which would pay for 400 glebe-houses.[132] In one sense, this represented an ingenious compromise between Stuart's and Brodrick's notions of liberality (wise or otherwise) and Agar's of stern self-help: in another, it was a rejection of the principle of the interest-free loan scheme. These various considerations probably explain Brodrick's hostile reaction to Stuart's wavering. In effect, Brodrick threatened an open breach with him in order to bring him back to his allegiance. In any case, nothing came of Foster's promise and intended bill to free up the workings of the board and make the treasury merely its 'bank' – that is, until 1808. By October 1805, it was clear that the special relationship between Foster and Pitt had collapsed. Then, in late January 1806, Pitt himself and his ministry collapsed.

CLERICAL RESIDENCE LEGISLATION FOR IRELAND, 1806–8

He was succeeded as prime minister by Lord Grenville, who formed a coalition 'Ministry of All the Talents' with the Whigs. Following this change of government, the issue of loans to the board of first fruits fell into abeyance, and the emphasis of government policy towards the Irish Church shifted from measures to ease and encourage clerical residence to measures to enforce it, backed by an enquiry into the extent of non-residence. Foster's successor as chancellor of the Irish exchequer was Sir John Newport, 2nd Bt, MP for Waterford City, a friend of the Grenvilles (in spite of his provincial, mercantile and comparatively humble origins). According to Agar's ally, the Dean of Waterford, Newport had been 'a partner in a [Waterford] bank with his father and brother. He was created a baronet by the marquess of Buckingham, who knew him at Eton. He and his family are dissenters, ... very warm and slashing reformists in Church and State [and] champion[s] of Roman Catholic Emancipation to its utmost extent.'[133] Of Newport, Stuart had recently written:

---

131 Brodrick to Midleton, 31 Oct. 1800, Ms. 1248, vol. 17, f. 138, and to Stuart, 8 Mar. 1802, WY 994/21. **132** O'Beirne to Stuart, 21 May 1804, WY 994/36. **133** Christopher Butson to Henry Addington, 17 Mar. 1795, Jupp/Aspinall transcript from the Sidmouth papers, Devon RO.

[His] real object is to subvert the Establishment by making it apparent, not only that the grossest abuses prevail, but that in the greatest part of Ireland, the clergy are paid for doing nothing, while the catholic priests, who alone perform the pastoral office, receive no emolument from the state. This is the language of the marquess of B[uckingham], and this I believe to be the object of Sir John Newport, who is certainly his instrument.[134]

With Newport appointed to office in February 1806, and Buckingham an adviser from the sidelines, a re-run of the events of 1788 looked imminent.

In order to provide a statistical basis for clerical residence legislation, a regal visitation of the Church of Ireland was proposed, to which Stuart said he would not have objected under Pitt, but which he much feared now, granted the character of the Irish advisers of Lord Grenville (especially Newport, and the new lord chancellor of Ireland, George Ponsonby). 'In the long conversations I have had with Lord Grenville' wrote Stuart in July 1806, 'I found him inclined to two measures, one respecting residence, the other respecting tithe, which appear to me fatal to the Establishment.'[135] Amusingly, Stuart was not impressed by Agar's proposed guidelines for the replies which the bishops should make to the government's inquisition. 'In truth, ... [they] are not only unsatisfactory, but plainly evasive, and every way unworthy of men in our situation.'[136] Brodrick seriously expected (or so he said to Stuart) that the two old-stagers, Agar and William Beresford, archbishop of Tuam, would decline to co-operate, so that replies would be forthcoming from only two of the four metropolitan provinces.[137] He acknowledged that the 'fingers' of most members of the administration 'itched to ... undermine and piecemeal to overturn the Church Establishment'; but he made an exception of the lord lieutenant, Bedford, 'an honest-minded and I believe truly religious man, and highly favourable to the Established Church'.[138] Stuart concurred with this view and appealed to Bedford, who prevailed on Grenville to accept a compromise. This was that the necessary information should be obtained, not by a regal visitation, but by means of diocesan returns forwarded to and co-ordinated by each of the four archbishops on a provincial basis.[139] This mode of proceeding, Stuart argued, would provide no pretext for evasion. Bedford, for his part (who at this stage was only slightly acquainted with Agar), hoped that the archbishops of Dublin and Tuam would be mollified, 'though the one is somewhat too impracticable, and the other too indolent, to hope for much essential service from either'.[140]

The fact was that, unless the government behaved inquisitorially and provocatively, it was pushing an almost open door. The issue of clerical residence legislation

134 Stuart to Brodrick, 29 Oct. 1805, Ms. 8869/3.   135 Stuart to Brodrick, 24 Apr. and 1 July 1806, Ms. 8869/4.   136 Stuart to Brodrick, 30 July 1806, ibid.   137 Brodrick to Stuart, 19 Apr. 1806, WY 994/51B.   138 Brodrick to Midleton, 16 Apr. 1807, Ms. 1248, vol. 19, f. 146.   139 Akenson, *Church of Ireland*, pp 124–5; copies of letters from 2nd Earl Spencer (the home secretary) to Bedford and from Bedford to Stuart, with queries to be submitted to the Church of Ireland bishops, 18 June and 16 July 1806, Wickham papers, T/2627/5/T/10.   140 Bedford to Grenville, 2 May 1806, *HMC Dropmore Mss.*, viii, pp 128–30.

for Ireland had moved on considerably since 1788. Stuart, for one, favoured it. To Brodrick he wrote:

> There being no statute law to compel the residence of clergymen, and the ecclesiastical law being so ridiculed and ill-understood by judges and masters in chancery, on whom the decision depends, ... no bishop will in time to come venture to institute a suit against a clergyman who is able to contend against him. To be harassed with law proceedings for seven years, as has been the case of the Bishop of Ferns [Euseby Cleaver], or for four years, as has been your case, and this at the expense of £300, is so little desirable that I am persuaded few bishops will hereafter endeavour to compel any refractory clergyman to reside upon his benefice. If government do not wish the Irish clergy to reside, no new law is necessary; but if they do wish them to reside, they must in some way or another give power to enforce residence. ...
>
> In common justice, they should either declare that we have no power to enforce residence, and relieve us of the odium of neglecting our duty as to that matter, or give us the power without exposing us to the anxiety of a lawsuit or the penalty of £500 when we are required to exercise it.[141]

To Bedford's chief secretary he argued the point even more strongly. Two recent decisions of courts of delegates, on appeal from a bishop's consistorial court, had put

> an end to the canon law for any practicable purpose. For it is wild to suppose that bishops will henceforward act upon the canon law, which may involve them in a chancery suit of long duration, productive of all the trouble, vexation and expense which are incidental to such legal contests. ... Even in my own diocese, ... I have received letters from several clergymen, since the decision of these causes, stating that they mean to live for a time in England, some of them on pretence of educating their children, others on pretence of ill health; nor shall I be much surprised to find, at my next visitation, that many more have abandoned their livings without even the formality of a letter. ... If a Roman catholic priest or a dissenting minister neglects his duty, he is instantly punished or removed, and this even in cases ... where their congregation is extremely small, and their salary extremely scanty. Whereas, if a clergyman of the Established Church, possessed of a large protestant parish, an excellent house and ... income ..., thinks it fit to desert his charge, he may do so with impunity.[142]

Bishop O'Beirne had a similar experience. He complained that, out of the 92 benefices in the diocese of Meath, 47 were held by non-residents. 'There are at present' he noted 'instances of great encouragement to refractoriness in this essential point of discipline, taken from some late decisions of the court of delegates'.[143]

141 Stuart to Brodrick, 24 and 31 Mar. 1806, Ms. 8869/5 and 4. 142 Stuart to William Elliot, 8 Apr. 1806, *HMC Dropmore Mss.*, viii, pp 90–3. Stuart's retained, but undated, draft or copy is WY 993/11. 143 Healy, *Diocese of Meath*, ii. 132.

This is a complex issue. 'By the canon law, every clergyman having cure of souls is bound to residence, without any limitation or exception, in respect of time or place.'[144] If his bishop considered him guilty of non-residence and could not persuade him to residence, the bishop or some third party would bring a charge against him in the bishop's consistorial court. If the charge was upheld, the clergyman had a right of appeal against the ecclesiastical censure imposed on him to a court of delegates. Courts of delegates were set up on an *ad hoc* basis whenever they were required; the party seeking to have the decision of a consistorial court set aside would ask the lord chancellor to issue a commission naming delegates to hear the appeal. By the nineteenth century, it seems to have become common practice for the commission to be made up of a number of superior court judges and masters in chancery: at an earlier date, ecclesiastical lawyers and even clergymen would regularly have been included. This shift in the composition of courts of delegates may have had a bearing on their decisions. Another factor may have been a general tightening-up of the administration of ecclesiastical law in the first couple of decades of the nineteenth century – part of the process of graceful reform – as a result of which bishops were now refusing to license clerical absences on grounds which would have been accepted some years or decades previously. Something of this sort may have multiplied the number of appeals; but, in general, there had always been much scope for argument about what exactly constituted non-residence – for example, what happened if the clergyman lived close to but not in his parish, or was absent, but only intermittently. 'The great point on which' the appeal rested in the case brought by Cleaver against a non-resident clergyman, was 'whether articles should have been exhibited against the delinquent. Sir William Scott is of opinion they were not necessary'.[145]

The final factor was changes since the Union in the personalities at the head of the Law in Ireland. Lord Clare had had a good knowledge of canon law, an interest in the issue of clerical residence, and at least one run-in with a court of delegates:[146] Lord Redesdale, as an Englishman, may not have given a proper lead in an area of chancery appeal jurisdiction which had no English equivalent (because in England clerical residence was a matter of statute law). Besides, a number of the new judges and masters of the immediate post-Union period were poor lawyers, promoted because of the parliamentary support they had given to the Union. As Redesdale put it, with characteristic trenchancy: 'Government is now suffering from the profligacy with which Lord Castlereagh [chief secretary at the time of the Union] braved public opinion in the nomination of judges. The bench and the bar must be redeemed from their present disgraceful situation, or the country must suffer and the government be under continual embarrassments.'[147] This confirms the impression created by Stuart's

144 Edward A. Stopford, *A hand-book of ecclesiastical law and duty for the use of the Irish clergy* (Dublin, 1861), p. 266. I am indebted to Professor W.N. Osborough for this reference, as for the content and much of the wording of the present paragraph. In the main, I am paraphrasing a letter of 13 June 2001 from him, in characteristically helpful response to a letter from me seeking guidance. 145 Cleaver to Stuart, 6 Apr. 1804, WY 994/30. 146 Clare, then FitzGibbon, to Agar, 27 Aug. 1793, T/3719/C/27/7; Kavanaugh, *Lord Clare*, pp 182–4. 147 Redesdale to Hardwicke, 16 Jan.

letters – that wayward decisions on the part of 'judges and masters in chancery' were a recent phenomenon.

In early 1807, Agar continued to urge that canon law was the appropriate way to deal with non-residence, though recently 'obstructed by appeals', and that the outcome of a test case currently before commissioners of review should be awaited before recourse was had to a Clerical Residence Act.[148] A commission of review was the rarely utilised procedure[149] adopted in the case of an appeal against the decision of a court of delegates. No machinery for setting one up 'was provided by statute, and persons seeking a review made use of the usual means whereby an exercise of the royal prerogative was sought – a petition to the king in council'.[150] It is not clear how the commission of review which heard the test case was constituted and what its decision was.[151] Nor is it clear whether, if that decision was unfavourable to episcopal authority, it satisfied Agar of the unavoidability of the act by the time it was passed in June 1808 (*48 George III, cap. 66*).[152] O'Beirne, for one, was not an admirer of the 1808 Act. Giving evidence in 1820 about its deficiencies, he argued:

> The powers vested by the canon law and the primitive discipline of the Church in the archbishops and bishops to enforce residence, when duly exercised, and no longer checked by appeals to a court of delegates, constituted as of late years it has been in Ireland, would have been amply sufficient to remedy the abuses arising from non-residence ... In carrying the provisions of this act into practice, it has been seen how ineffectual all substitutions for the operation and influence of the primitive discipline of the Church must prove, and that when, in the place of the obligations to canonical obedience and a professional feeling, a clergy are required to look for the great rule of their conduct in the discharge of their spiritual duties to the enactments of parliamentary statutes and the mere letter of the law, there can be but little hope of forming an exemplary and useful parochial ministry. There is no way of evading the regulations of such statutes, and of the temporal penalties that they provide, of which they will not avail themselves.[153]

This was presumably Agar's view, too; and certainly Agar had bitter experience, during the last year of his life (p. 243), of the evasiveness of clergy when threatened with the penalties provided by the act.[154] What is hard to understand is why the old procedure for enforcing residence by the authority of canon law was not strengthened in the first instance – before recourse was had to statute law. Since the composition of

1805, BL., Add. Ms. 35718, f. 571. For other strictures on post-Union common lawyers, with particular reference to their lack of knowledge of civil law, see p. 364.   **148** 21 M 57/21b.   **149** Again, I am indebted to Professor Osborough.   **150** G.I.O. Duncan, *The high court of delegates* (Cambridge, 1971), p. 75.   **151** Apart from some chance survivals elsewhere, the records of courts of delegates and commissions of review were destroyed in the Four Courts in 1922.   **152** For a summary of the provisions of this act, and of its 1824 successor (*5 George IV, cap. 91*), see Akenson, *Church of Ireland*, pp 125–6.   **153** Healy, *Diocese of Meath*, ii, pp 133–4.   **154** Rev. Richard Bourne

a court of delegates was a matter for the lord chancellor, there seems no good reason why it should have continued as it had been 'of late years ... in Ireland'. This omission is the more striking in that canon law went on coexisting with statute law as a means of enforcing residence. An ecclesiastical law text-book of 1861 affirms: 'The bishop has full power to enforce that law [ie. the canon law on clerical residence] in the ecclesiastical court, by ecclesiastical censure.'[155]

The explanation may be that Stuart and Brodrick – but almost certainly not Agar – were panicked into clerical residence legislation because the recent failures to enforce residence by canon law threatened their cherished glebe-house building programme. In one of his letters, Stuart specifically linked the two:

> How can we hope that any house will be built in time to come, or that any clergyman will be induced to subscribe the papers which he must subscribe before we can commence building? Where a man knows he must reside, he will put himself to some inconvenience to procure a comfortable residence, and had rather submit to the trouble of superintending the building of a house and the expense of fitting it up and furnishing it when built, than pay a yearly rent for a miserable lodging. But, if he knows that residence is optional, he will most assuredly decline such trouble and expense.[156]

Because Stuart and Brodrick were in a hurry to get the 1803 Board of First Fruits Acts amended to their satisfaction and put into belated operation, they were probably reluctant to be sidetracked into reforming the system of appeals from decisions of the consistorial courts. This linkage between clerical residence legislation and glebe-house building becomes more obvious still when it is noted that 1808 was not only the date of the Clerical Residence Act for Ireland, but also of the act (*48 George III, cap. 65*) which at last freed the board of first fruits from the trammels of 1803. This is not to say that Stuart's and Brodrick's line on clerical residence was wise. Writing in 1808, a young acolyte of Brodrick's was more struck by the contrast than by the connection between the two acts. 'I look far more to the gradual results of a wise liberality, than to any compulsory acts of parliament, for an efficiently resident clergy. Provide comfortable accommodation, at a small expense to the incumbent, and you will soon have the clergy at their posts. Here and there, there may, and will be, instances of neglect; but ... it is the genius of our establishment rather to be won by kindness than driven by terror.'[157] These sentiments were Agar's entirely. And, as Agar had found to his cost, driving clergymen of the Church of Ireland 'by terror' was easier said than done.

to Agar, 12 Dec. 1808 and 13 Jan. 1809, Rev. Sir Thomas Forster, 1st Bt, to Agar, 17 and 19 Jan. 1809, and Agar to Forster, 16 Feb. 1809, T/3719/C/42/86B and 43/6 and 12–14; Wellesley to Sir Charles Saxton, Bt [under-secretary, Dublin Castle], 22 Mar. 1809, *Wellington civil correspondence, 1807–9*, pp 615–16.   155 Stopford, *Hand-book*, p. 266. Professor Osborough points out that the continuing jurisdiction of canon law in this field is confirmed by *5 George IV, cap. 91, sec. 82*. 156 Stuart to Elliot, 8 Apr. 1806, *HMC Dropmore Mss.*, viii, pp 90–93.   157 Rev. John Jebb to Rev. Jos. McCormick, 24 Dec. 1808, printed in Forster, *Life of Jebb*, ii, pp 146–7.

To most churchmen – certainly to Agar and O'Beirne – the principle of canonical obedience was of paramount importance. The best that could be said for the 1808 Clerical Residence Act was that it was a quick, short-term palliative; also, that the visitorial fact-finding exercise which had preceded it, benefited the Church of Ireland by giving it good propaganda. The comparison now possible between the Churches of England and Ireland redounded to the advantage of the latter. This was partly because of the ineffectiveness of the British Clerical Residence Act which had eventually materialised in 1803. When Grenville and Pitt had become preoccupied with other things and then, in February 1801, had resigned from office, the tortuous drafting of the new legislation for England and Wales fell to Sir William Scott, who had been (pp 236–7) strongly critical of the ambitious Grenville plan of November 1799–March 1800. Scott produced what he acknowledged was an unsatisfactory cobble, designed to reconcile 'the comfort and the conscience of the Church [of England] ... . After two ineffectual attempts, the bill became law on July 7, 1803, and ... could be described with equal accuracy as an act to prevent and an act to authorise non-residence.'[158] Bishop Watson was of the opinion that it 'rather increased than lessened the evil'.[159] From the return furnished to parliament in 1808, under the provisions of the 1803 Act, 'it appeared that 3,699 clergymen [of the Church of England] were non-resident legally, and no fewer than 2,446 illegally – that is "without notification, licence or exemption".'[160] From the returns furnished to the four archbishops of the Church of Ireland in 1806–7, in preparation for the Irish Clerical Residence Act, Wakefield concluded: 'It is but just to the Irish clergy to observe that, on counting the number of residents and absentees in each diocese respectively, as reported to parliament by [the] several bishops, it appears on a comparison with the clergy in England that there is a greater proportion of residents in Ireland.'[161]

The main problem for the future governance of the Church of England[162] was the discretion left to the diocesan under British clerical residence legislation, and the

---

158 Mathieson, *English Church reform*, pp 23–4.   159 *Anecdotes of Watson*, p. 370.   160 *Mathieson*, loc. cit.   161 Wakefield, *Account of Ireland*, ii, pp 474–5.   162 A subsidiary problem, which seems to have had little or no Irish equivalent, was 'the right of a peer or peeress ... to appoint a number of chaplains, *pro rata* according to rank, for his (or her) private household. These "scarves" entitled their holders to partial exemption from the rules against pluralities ... . [They were] generally reserved by peers to reward their clerical friends and dependants ... . But some were sold for cash' – Langford, *Public life and the propertied Englishman*, pp 23–4. The practice long survived the 1803 Act. Irish peers enjoyed the same right, but their domestic chaplaincies were 'a qualification for other purposes' in the Church of England, not in the Church of Ireland – Rev. T.G. Roberts to 2nd earl of Leitrim, 13 Apr. 1825, Killadoon papers, NLI, Ms 36062/2. In Ireland, the only chaplaincies which conferred some degree of 'legal covering' were viceregal chaplaincies. In 1801, Brodrick – who, as bishop of Kilmore, had been 'engaged in a process to deprive a clergyman of a living for non-residence ... [and had] no doubt of ultimately succeeding' – reported that the clergyman 'had obtained from Lord Hardwicke an appointment of chaplain, hoping to foil me. But I have had an understanding and explanation on that point' – Brodrick to Midleton, 25 June 1801, Ms. 1248, vol. 18, f. 32. The Irish Clerical Residence Act of 1808 closed the loophole of the viceregal chaplaincies – Wellesley to O'Beirne, 25 May 1808, *Wellington civil correspondence, 1807–9*, p. 432. In this respect (as in some others), the Church of England had something to learn from Irish precedent and practice.

frequency with which exemptions were granted for no good reason. This is why
Stuart had insisted that the Irish Clerical Residence Act should be 'Sir William Scott's
act, without the exceptions, many of which are not applicable to the state of Ireland'.[163]
They were not applicable to the state of Britain either. Years later, in 1831, Archbishop
Howley of Canterbury acknowledged in the House of Lords that two-thirds of the
pluralities in the Church of England at that time were due to exemptions from the
Henrician thirty-mile limit of which Buckingham had made so much.[164] Even this
assumed that a clergyman could reasonably be regarded as resident in a parish thirty
miles distant from where he actually lived – the point which Agar had made in 1788.
In Ireland, by contrast, where the power of exemption remained, after 1808 as before,
exclusively with the primate, the situation was much more satisfactory in 1831 than it
was in England and Wales. This was mainly because Lord John George Beresford,
who became archbishop of Armagh in 1822, not only tightened up on Robinson's rule
of not granting any clergyman a faculty to hold more than two benefices, but
voluntarily introduced the thirty-mile limit into the Church of Ireland, and – in
marked contrast to the English practice – rigorously adhered to it.[165] In fairness to
Stuart, it should be noted that he had tried to move in the same direction in 1810. He
did not propose a thirty-mile-limit. But he did anticipate Beresford in proposing that
no clergyman should be allowed to hold more than two livings, and that he should not
be allowed to hold as many as two if one of them was already a union. Stuart's
proposal was cautiously received by the prime minister and the lord chancellor of
England, who were concerned about the inevitable read-across to the Church of
England, and also about the restriction which the proposal would place on the royal
prerogative (presumably to fill crown livings as the king thought fit).[166] While ways
round these difficulties were being considered, George III became irrevocably insane
and ministers preoccupied with other things. As a result, Stuart's proposal must have
been shelved.

THE CHURCH AND GLEBE-HOUSE BONANZA, 1808–23

The Ministry of All the Talents had concentrated on 'compulsory acts of parliament
for an efficiently resident clergy' during its short term of office between February
1806 and March 1807. But one small step towards the augmentation of small livings,
and hence towards the building of glebe-houses for them, had been taken during this
time. In March–June 1806, Dr Duigenan (possibly at Agar's instigation, but also with
Brodrick's support) presented and carried a bill (*46 George III, cap. 60*) under which
a 'small living' was redefined as one worth £100 per annum instead of the 1758
maximum of £60.[167] This meant that the resources of Primate Boulter's fund could

163 Wellesley to Spencer Perceval, 27 Oct. 1807, *Wellington civil correspondence, 1807–9*, p. 150.   164
Mathieson, *English Church reform*, p. 61.   165 Akenson, *Church of Ireland*, p. 130.   166 Spencer
Perceval (the prime minister) to Stuart, 4 June 1810, WY 995/22.   167 Duigenan to Brodrick,
5 Mar. 1806, Ms. 8861/4; Brodrick to Stuart, 7 June 1806, WY 994/50.

now be more widely deployed. But they were still too limited to make much impression on the problem, and the old restrictions (see p. 229) on the size and applicability of the board's other resources still applied.[168] Most of these obstacles were in the end removed, though Agar had to wait until the First Fruits Act of 1808 (*48 George III, cap. 65*). Under sec. 7 of that act, the parliamentary grant was made applicable to the purchase of glebes and impropriations, and under sec. 9 a sliding-scale of non-refundable grants for glebe-house building was set down, whereby livings worth less than £100 per annum were eligible to receive the maximum grant of £450. (At the other end of the sliding-scale, livings worth between £350 and £400 per annum were eligible for only £200, and livings worth more than £400 per annum for no grant at all.) This extension of the board's powers was of the first importance. For example, it addressed 'the Clonfert problem' (see p. 229) – which was that, in Clonfert and similar dioceses, it was impossible to build glebe-houses by means of loans, because the incumbent would not have the means of building a decent house or of repaying the loan unless huge and impractical unions of parishes were made or confirmed. Although there is no evidence for this, it must be assumed that Agar had intended some such special treatment of small livings as an accompaniment to his mortgage scheme.

In March 1807, the Grenville ministry fell from power. It was succeeded by a 'No Popery' government whose nominal head was Agar's friend, the now decrepit and almost senile duke of Portland. John Foster returned to office, this time as chancellor of the Irish exchequer but not as first lord of the Irish treasury, and soon showed (in the words of O'Beirne) 'that you have not forgotten or deferred your motion on the First Fruits Loan Bill. ... Lord Hardwicke and Mr Wickham made us expect a further loan of £50,000'[169] over and above the original £50,000 which had been sitting, untouched, since 1803. In presenting what he called the Irish Churches and Glebe-Houses Bill, Foster stated that 'the money directed to be applied for the benefit of the Church by the acts in 1803 had never been properly applied', and that 'the residence of the clergy ... could not be aimed at in Ireland till such times as they had parsonage houses to reside in'. In the Lords, an unlikely configuration manifested itself. Hardwicke opposed the bill, contending (predictably) that the existing legislation of 1803 made it superfluous: Redesdale and Agar (of all surprising allies) supported it, the latter declaring that it was a matter of 'the most urgent necessity', mainly because 'it made it imperative on the Irish treasury to advance the money'.[170] The bill passed on 1 August 1807 (*47 George III, cap. 23* [*sess. 2*]). It repealed the conditions attached to the loans under secs. 1 and 2 of *43 George III, cap. 158*. However, it then re-enacted (sec. 3) the previous, very restrictive regulation (p. 264) that, once the full £50,000 had been applied, all the loan repayments were to go back to the treasury and stay there, instead of forming part of a board of first fruits revolving fund. As a result of this stipulation, the 1807 Act, too, remained inoperative.

---

168 21 M 57/21b.   **169** O'Beirne to Foster, 3 July 1807, D/207/50/33.   **170** *Cobett's Parliamentary debates*, ix, pp 498 and 906–7.

Not until the following session was a liberating measure finally enacted. All the running was, once more, made by Foster, possibly with the help and advice of Agar (who was again in London). In early January 1808, Foster submitted to Spencer Perceval, the 'Evangelical' chancellor of the British exchequer (who was to succeed Portland as prime minister in the following year), Foster's 'scheme for building glebe-houses and churches and purchasing glebes', of which he sent a copy to O'Beirne for consideration by the board and/or the bishops then in Dublin.[171] This was a comprehensive scheme, the cost of which was to be phased over several years, for meeting all the infrastructural requirements of the Church; Foster stated (O'Beirne thought rather over-stated) these requirements as 642 new glebe-houses ('to complete one for each benefice'), 346 new glebes, and 230 new churches ('to give a church to every benefice'). The gross start-up cost to the state would be just over a million pounds, most of which would ultimately be repaid. Perceval agreed enthusiastically, and actually suggested that the government should give more towards the building of new churches.[172] The board of first fruits was also enthusiastic. In mid-February, O'Beirne (in a letter to Foster) quoted Brodrick as saying that the board 'not only highly approved of, but felt very grateful for, the plan as communicated to us, and that with some few exceptions which might be easily removed, nothing had ever been suggested or proposed so effectually calculated to remove all our difficulties'.[173] Granted Brodrick's past hostility to Foster, this was a handsome tribute.[174]

However, this unwonted unanimity did not last. Brodrick set off for London, where Stuart and Agar already were, and they and the other bishops then in London entered into detailed discussion of Foster's new Irish Churches and Glebe-Houses Bill with the chief secretary, Sir Arthur Wellesley. Wellesley afterwards reported that he had had

> two meetings with the Primate [and] the Archbishops of Dublin and of Cashel, and I saw the two latter frequently ... . My original plan was to grant an additional £50,000 for the purposes of the Glebe-House and Church Bill, and I altered it at the suggestion of the Primate and the Archbishop of Cashel, ... [so that] the additional grant will be confined to £5,000 per annum, making the whole parliamentary grant £10,000. ... Mr Foster's plan was a very able one, and founded upon very enlarged principles, but the Primate objected to it.[175]

In late March, O'Beirne expressed to Foster his astonishment 'at the disinclination you experience in the bishops to consult with you on the interests of the Church, knowing as they do the exertions you are making in its favour'.[176] A month later, Stuart

---

171 D/207/50/22–3. There are two more copies of Foster's plan in Agar's papers (21 M 57/B30/7–8), one of them in Brodrick's handwriting. It is printed in *Wellington civil correspondence, 1807–9*, pp 434–7.   172 Perceval to Wellesley, [Jan–May? 1808], *Wellington civil correspondence, 1807–9*, p. 433.   173 O'Beirne to Foster, 18 Feb. [1808], D/207/50/26.   174 Years later, Brodrick acknowledged that Foster had 'always been our strenuous advocate' – Brodrick to Foster, 27 Feb. 1811, D/207/50/55.   175 Wellesley to O'Beirne, 25 May 1808, *Wellington civil correspondence, 1807–9*, pp 432–3.   176 O'Beirne to Foster, 28 Mar. 1808, D/207/50/4.

wrote to Foster: 'I heard from the Bishop of Meath, with equal astonishment and pain, that you had written to him complaining of me and other archbishops and bishops then in London, for having obstructed a scheme which you were meditating for the improvement of the Irish Church.'[177] Stuart went on to allege that O'Beirne had failed to explain the scheme properly to the board in Dublin, or even to give a copy of it to the bishops then present; which is wholly at variance with O'Beirne's account of events and of the enthusiastic reception given to Foster's proposals.

For all these misunderstandings and recriminations, the Board of First Fruits Act (*48 George III, cap. 65*), in the form in which it passed into law on 18 June 1808, was a huge stride in the right direction. It recited (sec. 6) that no part of the £50,000 authorised to be advanced to the board under *43 George III, cap. 158*, as amended by *47 George III, cap. 23*, had in fact been paid over, and that accordingly 'the manner of issuing the said sum ... and the conditions of advancing the same' were hereby repealed: in other words, the idea of Castle and treasury superintendence was at last abandoned. The acts of 1803 and 1807 had stuck obsessively to the principle of loans. The crucial change made by the 1808 Act was the already-mentioned extension of the board's powers to grant-aid the augmentation of small livings (sec. 7), together with the sliding scale established for the grant-aiding of glebe-house building in livings worth less than £400 per annum (sec. 9). This not only targeted the areas of greatest need, but made it unnecessary to assist on a loan basis those incumbents whose security was most precarious. In this way, the problem of guaranteeing the repayment of loans of public money was largely avoided. Other features of the act were (in the words of Professor Akenson), that 'it consolidated all the board's funds [including the borough compensation money] into a single account and removed most of the restrictions on its freedom of operation. The board was now allowed to lend money or give grants ... for either church building [and re-building] or glebe[-house] construction. Further, it could now spend its funds on parish churches without having to wait for twenty years for them to be in ruins.'[178] Essentially, the difference between Foster and O'Beirne, at the one extreme, and Stuart and Brodrick at the other, was over tactics and timing. The former wanted to obtain a grant of £50,000 in 1808 on top of the untouched loan of £50,000 dating from 1803, and apply both to building projects in the year 1808–9: the latter, probably fearful of wrangles within the board of first fruits and a consequent under-spend, thought that the board should not start off with more than it could usefully and safely expend in the first year, and defined that as a loan of £50,000 and a grant of £10,000.

In the end, something very much resembling Foster's 'very enlarged' ideas was put into practice, and at a total cost of just over one million pounds, as estimated by him in 1808.[179] Parliament dramatically increased its financial support for the board; and, while the board proceeded mainly on the basis of loans to incumbents and parishioners, parliament proceeded mainly on the basis of grants to the board. The

177 Stuart to Foster, 26 Apr. 1808, D/207/64/1.   178 *Church of Ireland*, pp 117–19. See also Acheson, *Church of Ireland*, p. 112.   179 Foster/Massereene papers, D/207/50/37–9.

annual grant remained at £10,000 in 1809, but rose to £60,000 from then to 1816, dropping to £30,000 in 1817 and thence back to £10,000 in 1822 and 1823, when it ceased. The only restriction on the application of these resources was that no part of the parliamentary grant could be devoted to the augmentation of small livings. The small livings could be augmented indirectly by the purchase of glebes for their benefit; but an actual increase of stipend to the incumbent of a small living had still to come from Primate Boulter's fund or from the board's extra-parliamentary resources.[180]

Where Agar stood in all this is not clear. Wellesley's account of the negotiations of *c.*March 1808 suggests that the changes to the bill came from Stuart and Brodrick, and for the first half of 1809 Agar was, in effect, dying. On the precise issue of tactics and timing which was to the fore in March–May 1808, he was probably in the Stuart/Brodrick rather than the Foster/O'Beirne camp. But the 1808 Act itself was much more acceptable to Agar, and more nearly in line with his policy, than Stuart's and Brodrick's original loan scheme of 1803. Agar would particularly have welcomed all the 1808 Act's provisions for the benefit of livings worth less than £400 per annum. No doubt he would have contended that it was neither necessary nor expedient to give interest-free loans for glebe-house building to incumbents with incomes above the £400 mark; such people could well afford open-market mortgages, as he had unsuc-cessfully proposed in 1803. Even Brodrick, from the spring of 1804 onwards, had begun to wonder if the original glebe-house loan scheme had not been indiscrim-inately lavish. He thought that the board ought perhaps to 'class the benefices and allow a larger proportion – perhaps two-thirds – to the smaller benefices, and one-half only to those above £500 or £600 [per annum]'. He also accepted in principle the desirability 'of engaging the interest of the builder in the regularity of his expenditure of the money ... by making him undertake a proportion of the risk'.[181] But this still begged the question, did clergymen of £500 or £600 per annum deserve or require any element of interest-free loan?

Interest-free loans for church-building were a different matter. But, here, Agar had misgivings on two counts. First, it is clear that he valued parochial self-help as a good thing in its own right. In his 1802 visitation charge to the clergy of Dublin (delivered before the idea of interest-free loans for churches had made much, if any, progress), he had

> urged ... the absolute necessity of a sufficient number of decent and comfortable places of public worship, in order to uphold and promote the influence of religion. ... It was not sufficient excuse that parliamentary aids were not granted: it was the rector's duty to awaken the slumbering piety of his parishioners and to promote contributions for the repairs or erection of a church, and his Grace was confident that there was no parish so poor or so destitute of piety as not to afford the means of a decent and commodious place of public worship.[182]

180 Brodrick to Stuart, 30 Apr. 1816, WY 994/94.   181 Brodrick to Stuart, 26 Apr. 1804, WY 994/32.   182 21 M 57/A2/22/2. See also p. 569.

Second, Agar had misgivings about what would now be called 'sustainability'. *48 George III, cap. 65, secs. 4 and 5*, provided that loans were to be repaid at the rate of 6% per annum, that the repayments were to be applotted on the parish, and that the parish, as heretofore, was to be responsible for future maintenance and repair. But, as one Cashel clergyman and landowner, the Rev. Samuel Riall, wrote to Agar in February 1809,

> Where a parish is so unhappily circumstanced as to have no protestants in it, or but two or three at most, and that the parish is situated so near another parish in which there is a church that the protestants can resort to it without much inconvenience, I should think it more advisable to defer building a church there until it shall please God in his good time to dispel in some degree this almost impenetrable cloud of superstition and idolatry with which this country is enveloped, and not to suffer us to appear ridiculous in coming out of a church with two or three people or perhaps with Dean Swift's dearly beloved Roger and finding ourselves on the outside with perhaps 200 or 300 people laughing at us.[183]

Riall also wondered where the money was going to be found to pay for the upkeep of all these new churches, even supposing that they had been built by grant, not loan, and that loan repayments were not an issue.

Even O'Beirne, the most forward of the Irish bishops in seeking financial assistance from parliament, was concerned that some of the churches currently being built or rebuilt were in such remote spots that access to them was problematic.[184] Writing to Foster in April 1809, he reminded him

> of a promise you made to get a clause inserted in the first [Road] Bill ... for empowering grand juries to present roads to churches, as well as to market or seaport towns. We are now in numberless places building churches on the ruins of old churches, the lands about which are possessed by persons who in general graze the churchyard, after levelling its enclosures, and who allow no access to them but to foot people carrying corpses to the grave. The parishioners must, therefore, be shut out from these churches, unless such a power as I suggest be granted to the grand juries, on the application of the minister and church-wardens. I have four new churches at this moment in that predicament.[185]

---

183 Riall to Agar, 28 Feb. 1809, T/3719/C/43/37.   184 The same point was made about the glebe-house which Brodrick required a *protégé* of Agar's, James St Leger, archdeacon of Emly, to build 'at the archdeaconry. ... The site is dreadful – on the top of a bleak mountain, almost inaccessible,[and] without water. It would take a man and horse every day to supply a house with that necessary article' – St Leger to Agar, 20 Sep. 1808, T/3719/C/42/69. This, however, may not have been an instance of a diocesan taking the provisions of the 1808 Act to extremes, but of Brodrick taking an opportunity to smite an Agarite (see p. 417).   185 O'Beirne to Foster, 10 Apr. 1809, D/207/50/8.
186 Memorial from Beaufort and Foster to Stuart, 26 Oct. 1810, and letter from Stuart to Foster,

Another church adjoining but not in O'Beirne's diocese which was soon to be in a predicament of a different nature was Collon church, Co. Louth. Situated near Dublin, in Stuart's own diocese and at Foster's gates (he was the ground landlord of Collon), Collon church ought to have been a model of the 1808 Act in operation. However, it was rebuilt to an over-ambitious design (based on King's College Chapel, Cambridge) by its incumbent, Dr Beaufort, and though financed by an unspecified donation from Foster and a grant of £800 and a loan of £1,700 from the board of first fruits,[186] its costs rapidly outran these resources. In 1813, through the influence of Stuart and O'Beirne, a further loan of £2,000 was made by the board. When the rebuilding was completed, the final cost was £6,500. The responsibility for this overshoot was Beaufort's, and neither Foster nor the parish was prepared to bale him out. So, at the time of his death in 1821, he was being threatened with the sequestration of his livings, and with debtor's prison, because of his failure to repay a loan which should not have been authorised in the first place.[187]

Agar, of course, was long dead when this cautionary tale came to its unsatisfactory conclusion. Had he lived longer, he might have restrained the board from some of these excesses, particularly in the sphere of loans. However, the simple fact remains that the policy pursued from 1803 onwards was not Agar's, and indeed was in opposition to Agar's. After 1803, though he never ceased to exercise some influence on Church affairs, his role was essentially that of a limiter of damage. Brodrick regularly consulted him, but did not necessarily heed his views, and was personally hostile to him;[188] Stuart, after his initial wariness of Agar, seems from perhaps 1805 onwards to have developed a sneaking regard for him. This shows, for example, in the account he gave Brodrick of the row which took place between Agar and Charles Lindsay, bishop of Kildare, at the board of first fruits meeting in late March 1806:

> The Archbishop of Dublin promised to me the night before our meeting to keep his temper and lend his best assistance to advance the business of the board, and though a very rude and intemperate and unprovoked attack made upon him by the Bishop [of] Kildare excited his passion and produced a warm and indecent altercation, he shortly recovered his good humour and seemed to me extremely desirous of assisting us without affecting superiority or contempt, and without uttering a word that could fairly give offence.[189]

This condescending tribute shows that Agar's standing with Stuart (though hardly with Brodrick) was by this stage higher than it had been in, say, 1803. But he was still very far from being virtual primate himself, as he had been in the years up to 1801.

In spite of the alliance early formed between Stuart and Brodrick, the two of them certainly did not have things entirely their own way within the board of first

3 Nov. 1810, D/207/50/47–9.   187 Canon C.C. Ellison, *The hopeful traveller: the life and times of Daniel Augustus Beaufort, LL.D., 1739–1821* (Kilkenny, 1987), pp 85–7 and 114–15.   188 Brodrick to Wickham, 11 June 1803, T/2627/5/S/16.   189 Stuart to Brodrick, 31 Mar. 1806, Ms. 8869/4.

fruits, at least for the first decade of Stuart's primacy. This was partly because their leadership was discredited by the impasse into which they led the Church in 1803. Moreover, in the years immediately following the Union, there was an unusually large number of able and energetic bishops to contest Stuart's and Brodrick's leadership role – Agar, Alexander, Cleaver, Knox, Lindsay, O'Beirne and others. At the time of the passing of the Act of Union, it had been feared that attendance in the House of Lords of the United Kingdom would lure more bishops away from the meetings of the board in Dublin than could be spared under the existing *quorum*. Accordingly, an act of the Irish parliament (*40 George III, cap. 46*) had been passed, probably by Agar (though he did not say so – see p. 444), reducing the board's *quorum* from seven to four.[190] The precaution proved unnecessary. In the first decade after the Union, there was greater difficulty in imposing a common purpose, and even order and seemliness, on the board's proceedings than in obtaining a *quorum*. At times, indeed, it was like a congested bishops board. The rota arrangements for archiepiscopal and episcopal representation in the post-Union House of Lords (to which Agar had vainly objected – see pp 559–63), did, however, contribute to diffuse influence among the bishops, rather than concentrate it in the hands of one or two. Agar's permanent presence in the House of Lords as an Irish representative peer (see pp 598–9) was another important factor. So was Duigenan's presence in the House of Commons as MP for Armagh City until his death in 1816; though he owed his return to Stuart, he was something of a law unto himself.[191] Much more important was the presence of a 'strenuous [lay] advocate' of the Church in the person of John Foster. Foster was probably the dominant figure in the history of the board of first fruits in 1805 and again in 1807–11 (he retired from office in the latter year, at the age of seventy-two). Agar may have been closely associated with him in 1805 and again in 1807–8 – the evidence is inconclusive; but from 1808 onwards, Foster's main ally and spokesman on the Irish bench was O'Beirne. It was not until Foster quitted the stage in 1811, that Stuart and Brodrick came into their own and became, for the next decade, undisputed leaders of the Church.

This is not to say that their policy of bonanza went unchallenged. In 1808, O'Beirne had written to Wellesley: 'I allow that it is a matter of great delicacy to bring the state of the Church in this part of the United Kingdom into public discussion. ... The British ministry seem to be so nervous upon all questions that affect us that, with increasing difficulties such as they have reason to apprehend, ... [we] despair of that strong and vigorous support that our situation requires.'[192] In April 1816, Brodrick

---

190 Interestingly, *40 George III, cap. 46*, not only reduced the *quorum*, but made it unnecessary for a legal luminary to be one of the four commissioners present, thus silently repealing that provision of *29 George II, cap. 18, sec. 1* (see p. 224). It would be just like Agar to have seized an opportunity of minimising lay influence on the board. Confusingly, *43 George III, cap. 106, sec. 3*, and *46 George III, cap. 60*, added two additional and different *quora* (one of them partially reinstating the legal luminaries), so that three *quora* existed at the one time, varying according to what business was before the board.   191 Akenson, *Church of Ireland*, pp 124–5.   192 O'Beirne to Wellesley, 16 May 1808, *Wellington civil correspondence, 1807–9*, pp 438–9.

reported to Stuart the upshot of his discussion in London with the chief secretary, Robert Peel, a firm Anglican and anti-Emancipationist, about the renewal of the annual grant of £50,000 (to which Peel made no demur), and about Stuart's wish for 'an extension of our powers in the disposal of it for the purpose of aiding Boulter's fund.

> He admitted the expediency of giving every facility to the residence of the clergy on small livings ... and of increasing their incomes ...; but then he said that the H. of Commons would object to this being done out of government funds, and he himself thought that the Church as a corporation was most richly endowed in Ireland, and that it might be expected to be urged in parliament that this very desirable object should be provided out of the larger benefices of the kingdom as they shall become vacant. In fact, he looks I believe to a new valuation of benefices and an increased charge upon them as [*sic* – for] first fruits.[193]

Plainly, Peel was being influenced by the prejudice against the rich endowments of the Church of Ireland which Agar had always been anxious to allay. Agar's policy derived from his long-held view that the clergy must avoid the imputation of greed or ostentation – a view in which Stuart concurred when he argued that, though the clergy needed money for glebe-houses, what was of supreme importance to them was, not money, but 'character'.[194]

Would it have made much difference if, in 1803, Agar's policy of financing glebe-house building largely out of current clerical incomes, with special measures to augment the value of small livings and outright glebe-house grants for the poorer clergy, had been adopted? The answer is that it almost certainly would – at any rate in the short term, before the situation was transformed and the position of the Church of Ireland irretrievably weakened by the advent to power of Whigs, radicals and O'Connellites in the early 1830s. What was really advantageous, in practical terms, about Agar's alternative policy was that it avoided the more-than-difficult problem of accountability for loans of public money. By contrast, Stuart's and Brodrick's poorly conceived scheme ran into head-on collision with this problem. As a result, church and glebe-house building was stalled for five, if not seven, years, from 1803 until 1808 or possibly 1810. This was not just because of the delay in getting the glebe-house loan scheme into operation; it was also because the very mention of interest-free loans did the Church what Brodrick acknowledged was 'the real injury ... of stopping the operation of the old laws' whereby clergymen financed the building of glebe-houses out of income or from their private credit.[195] The lull might have had more serious consequences, because the political difficulty of getting measures for the financial support of the Church of Ireland through the House of Commons at Westminster

---

193 Brodrick to Stuart, 30 Apr. 1816, WY 994/94.   194 Stuart to Elliot, 8 Apr. 1806, *HMC Dropmore Mss.*, viii, 90–93.   195 Brodrick to Stuart, 28 Apr. 1804, WY 994/34.

was increasing all the time. In view of this, it is possible that parliamentary resources, if they had been applied on Agar's terms with effect from 1803, would simply have dried up five or seven years sooner. But it is more likely that they would have continued to flow until 1823 or thereabouts, simply because Agar's scheme was better thought-out, more frugal and more effective from the point of view of targeting need. Indeed, if the board of first fruits had followed his advice, there might have been enough money, and enough parliamentary goodwill, still left to make it possible to tackle the problem of Ireland's cathedrals. It was in respect of cathedral-restoration that the Church of Ireland really did lag behind the Church of England: in church and glebe-house provision the Church of Ireland arguably did not. It would be unfair to regard Collon church as anything but a travesty of Stuart's and Brodrick's scheme (though Stuart's personal complicity in the *débâcle* is far from creditable to him). Nevertheless, the fact remains that the £6,500 poured into Collon church would have restored a small (ie. similarly sized) Irish cathedral. Cathedrals, mainly those with which Agar was concerned, are the main subject of the next Chapter.

7

Cashel city and cathedral, 1694–1801

'Cashel is a good town, but a poor city', wrote a visitor in 1775. 'It consists, as I guess, of between five and six hundred houses, some of which are very decent and look as if inhabited by persons of condition. It must have formerly been a place of the first consequence in Ireland.' Now it was sadly sunk, particularly as an ecclesiastical capital. 'How differently is the state of the diocese of Armagh represented! It is said that the archbishop of that see has not only decorated his cathedral, given it an organ and fixed a choir there, but that he has built one of the best houses in the kingdom, a real palace suited to his elevated rank'[1] A description of Armagh City just before Robinson's coming to it in 1765, confirms the extent of Robinson's achievement. It was 'an ugly, scattered town. [The] cathedral ... is a sorry old building and is used as a parish church. ... The lord primate has no palace here,... [just] an apartment for ... when he comes'[2]. Cashel was better-served than Armagh at this time and for another decade, in that it had a palace. But it was worse-served in that it had no cathedral. However, the real difference between Armagh and Cashel lay outside the respective cities and was that Armagh had a higher parochial and glebe income and was more amply endowed with churches and glebe-houses than any other diocese in Ireland.[3] Robinson was therefore at comparative liberty to concentrate his building and patronage on his cathedral city (not that he neglected the rest of his diocese): Agar, by contrast, had to do everything at the one time. In spite of starting at this great disadvantage, he was successful in combining improvements to the infrastructure of his diocese as a whole (pp 204–20) with signal achievements in respect of the cathedral, choir, organ and palace of Cashel itself. He was also successful in winning the regard and even affection of most of the inhabitants of Cashel and its neighbourhood – sentiments which Robinson's cold and formal personality (see pp 352 and 458–9) failed to inspire in Armagh or anywhere else.

1 [John Campbell], *Philosophical survey*, pp 121 and 132.   2 Willes to Lord Warwick, 25 Apr. 1754, *Willes Letters*, p. 31.   3 Erck, *Ecclesiastical register*, pp xxxviii and xlviii; Akenson, *Church of Ireland*, pp 56 and 111–14; Acheson, *Church of Ireland*, pp 116–19. The part of the diocese which covered the whole county of Armagh needed to be, since Armagh was by the late eighteenth century the most densely populated county in Ireland, and the proportion of its population which was Church of Ireland was, compared to other counties, very high.

CASHEL BOROUGH, 1694–1779

As well as an ecclesiastical capital and an ancient ecclesiastical site, Cashel (like Armagh) was a parliamentary borough. It had been incorporated in 1233 for the benefit of the then archbishop, Marianus O'Brien, and its next charter, confirming the first, had been granted to Archbishop Roland Bacon in 1557.[4] By Agar's time – indeed, by the 1750s – the archbishop had ceased to control the return for either of the borough's two seats, following conflicts which had, in the first third of the eighteenth century, disturbed relations between the corporation and the palace, the town and the clerical gown. At the centre of these conflicts had been William Palliser, archbishop of Cashel, 1694–1727, Theophilus Bolton, archbishop, 1730–44, and, the Pennefather family of New Park, near Cashel. It is by no means clear who had the controlling interest in Cashel borough at the outset of Archbishop Palliser's episcopate – the archbishop, the Pennefathers or a confused form of power-sharing between the archbishop and a number of local men with influence in the corporation. Among the latter, the Pennefathers may not have been the most important at this early date. Lists of tenants of land and urban property owned by the corporation, which are respectively dated 1677, 1692 and *c.*1730, do not include the Pennefathers, though the corporation estate was fairly valuable (its rental in *c.*1730 was over £200) and the Pennefathers were later to do very well out of it. Instead, the estate was parcelled out among a number of local families, nearly all of them represented on the corporation – Buckworths, Butterfields, Chadwicks, Cookes, Harrisons, Irbys, Melshams, Prices, Robinsons, Russells and Stevenses.[5]

Of these, the Buckworths looked at least as prominent as the Pennefathers. Richard Buckworth (1675–1738), who was probably 'of Ballycormuck', Co. Tipperary, sat in parliament for Cashel, 1715–39, and was succeeded by his son, William, who sat for Cashel, 1739–53. The Buckworths were related to Archbishop Bolton, whose mother was Anne, daughter of the Rev. Anthony Buckworth, vicar of Magheradroll, diocese of Dromore, Co. Down, and niece of Theophilus Buckworth, bishop of Dromore, 1613–52 (from whom Bolton presumably derived his christian name). This explains why Bolton, having bought from Richard Buckworth for £5,000 the latter's lease of Cashel corporation lands, was empowered to retain the purchase money and use it for the payment of Buckworth's creditors.[6] In 1732, the corporation had granted Buckworth a lease (or, more probably, a renewal) of one-third of its estate, for an unspecified down payment and an annual rent of only £87;[7] this, presumably, was the lease conveyed to Bolton. Buckworth's son and successor (in property and parliamentary seat), William Buckworth, assumed the additional surname of 'Carr', because

---

4 Typescript notes on the early municipal and parliamentary history of Cashel, N.D., NLI, Ms. 17978. 5 Cashel common council minute books, 1672–1825, NLI, Mss. 5575–8. 6 William Buckworth Carr to Anthony Foster (Bolton's executor), 30 June 1744, Foster/Massereene papers, PRONI, D/562/1382. 7 Typescript copy of a master in chancery's plan of 1844 for applying to local improvements a fine of £6,000 imposed on William Pennefather on account of the illegality of his former lease of Cashel corporation lands, NLI, Ms. 17978.

he had married the daughter and heiress of a man called William Carr. William Buckworth Carr was a barrister, and seems to have acted as Bolton's legal adviser.[8] So, it is clear that, although Richard Buckworth had long been MP for Cashel by the time Bolton became archbishop, Bolton took advantage of the relationship, and of Richard Buckworth's financial difficulties, to strengthen his own political interest in the borough; also, that William Buckworth Carr may be regarded as the archiepiscopal nominee when elected for Cashel in 1739. It is significant that, once in parliament, he echoed Bolton's 'liberal' (by the standards of the day) views on the Penal Laws.[9]

As for the Pennefathers, they appear comparatively late in the common council books of Cashel. The first Pennefather to feature is Kingsmill Pennefather of New Park, who is mentioned as being an alderman on 29 June 1696. He served as mayor in 1708–9. No other Pennefathers are mentioned as being members of the corporation until as late as 1727. By 1733, the now elderly Kingsmill Pennefather had been joined as an alderman by his sons, Richard and William.[10] The Pennefathers were more prominent in the parliamentary representation of Cashel then they were on the common council. Kingsmill Pennefather was MP, 1703–14, and then sat for the county of Tipperary, 1715–35 (in which year he died); his younger brother, Capt. Matthew Pennefather, was MP for Cashel from 1710 until his death in 1733; and Kingsmill Pennefather's son and heir, Richard, who stood at the by-election in 1734 occasioned by Capt. Matthew's death, acted for the family in corporation politics from at least 1727. Although the Pennefathers dominated the returns for Cashel between 1703 and 1727, they were joined by Richard Buckworth in 1715, and Archbishop Palliser clearly continued to enjoy a considerable interest in the borough. Palliser was none-too-squeamish in his methods of cultivating it: in c.1715, for example, he got his coachman elected a freeman.[11]

The key period from the point of view of determining who was going to control the borough for the future was the years between Palliser's death at the beginning of 1727, and the decision of an election committee of the whole House of Commons in March 1734. At the first opportunity after the Archbishop's death, on 29 June 1727, Richard Pennefather began a process of excluding the freemen of the borough from its common council, which met annually on that date.[12] He could not exclude them from voting in parliamentary elections because the charter of the borough entitled them to do so. But by excluding them from the common council, where he seems already to have commanded a majority, he obtained control over the future intake to the freeman body. Archbishop Timothy Godwin (1727–9) seems to have been politically inactive and to have done nothing to resist Richard Pennefather's narrowing of the composition of the corporate body. It was left to Bolton, who succeeded Godwin in 1730, to take up the Pennefather challenge. He began by contesting the exclusion

---

8 History of the Irish Parliament database entries for the Buckworths; D/562/1382.   9 Fagan, *The oath for Irish catholics*, pp 79 and 84.   10 NLI, Mss. 5575–8.   11 *Irish Commons' journals*, iv, pp 124–32. Unless otherwise stated, information about Cashel borough up to and including 1734 is taken from this source.   12 *Municipal Corporations (Ireland): appendix to the first report of the commissioners* (1835 [28]), i, pp 463–4.

of freemen from the common council and other alleged irregularities in municipal elections. According to the involved and rambling evidence heard by the election committee in March 1734, 'His Grace the Archbishop of Cashel had an ordination in Dr Burgess' mayoralty, when there was [*sic*] about eighteen young gentlemen ordained, and ... they were ... all admitted freemen of said corporation.' The common council book contains an entry for 10 August 1732 which mentions that John Burgess was mayor on that date; this means that he must have been elected on 29 June 1732, clearly with the support or at the instigation of Bolton. On 14 August, a by-law was passed, this time at Pennefather instigation and in retaliation for the admission of the eighteen clergymen, providing that for the future the mayor could admit only two freemen per annum without the consent of the majority of the common council or unless the candidates for the freedom were men who had served an apprenticeship in the borough. On 14 November 1732, an alderman called John Cooke was sworn in as mayor, which means that Bolton's mayor, Dr Burgess, must have been ousted.[13] By June of the following year, the Pennefather candidate for the mayoralty was Kingsmill Pennefather himself. On 11 June, he wrote – with affected pathos – to Henry Boyle, speaker of the House of Commons: 'I ... hope with your assistance to battle the sinister and ambitious views of my potent adversary, who seems determined on the destruction of me and my family. No doubt he'll cause his creatures to apply to the government and [privy] council [which since 1672 had been charged with confirming or rejecting mayoral elections], by the extraordinary steps he has taken of late, upon the return of a magistrate for this town.' However, only a week later it was reported that Archbishop Bolton had 'met with a devilish rebuff in his power at Cashel. Tomorrow there is to be a grand dispute there.'[14] The 29th of June was the real testing-time, and on that day Kingsmill Pennefather was elected mayor. He was sworn into office on 29 September, having received the approbation of the privy council.[15]

Municipal elections were ultimately decisive of parliamentary elections. But, when a parliamentary by-election became necessary following the death of Capt. Matthew Pennefather late in 1733, Kingsmill Pennefather's prevailing influence in the common council of Cashel was not yet reflected in the freeman body and in the parliamentary constituency. The by-election took place on 3 January 1734, and Bolton's candidate, Stephen Moore of Barne, outside Clonmel, was returned. But the defeated candidate, Richard Pennefather, petitioned the House of Commons against this outcome. During the ensuing proceedings, Bolton was heavily censured for his allegedly high-handed actions, a fellow-bishop, Josiah Hort, bishop of Kilmore, commenting that 'he was treated very freely, and indeed too roughly, as all sides will allow'.[16] Most of the evidence heard by the House consisted of rigmaroles about secret admissions of freemen by both sides in irregular places at irregular hours, and the usual charges and counter-charges about voters being 'papists' or being 'married to

13 NLI, Ms. 5577.   14 Kingsmill Pennefather to Henry Boyle, and William Moore to Boyle, 11 and 19 June 1733, Shannon papers, PRONI, D/2707/A/1/2/104 and 106.   15 NLI, Ms. 5578.   16 Sadleir and Dickinson, *Georgian mansions*, p. 37.

popish wives'. But one significant piece of evidence which emerges from the voluminous proceedings of the Cashel election committee was given by a witness who was
'asked in whom the interest was before the archbishop of Cashel. [He] said in Mr
Pennefather, and said there was [*sic*] but 80 legal voters in the corporation, of which
he believed your member [Stephen Moore, Bolton's candidate] had but about nine.'
This does not make it clear whether the interest had been 'in Mr Pennefather' only
since 1727 or for far longer – for instance, from 1703, when a Pennefather was first
returned for Cashel. Perhaps there was a corporation interest, which was 'in Mr
Pennefather', and a popular interest among the freemen, which looked for leadership
to the archbishop because he was the principal resident, dispenser of patronage and
employer of labour in the town. These two interests may have coexisted without overt
hostility until 1727, when the Pennefathers endeavoured to strengthen themselves at
the expense of a newly appointed English archbishop bereft of local connections,
which in turn provoked a counter-attack by Bolton from 1730 onwards.

In the immediate circumstances of the 1734 by-election, it was the Archbishop
who was the aggressor and the Pennefathers who were on the defensive, because it was
the Pennefather seat which was under attack. The other seat, as has been seen, was
held by Richard Buckworth. This made it easy, and possibly not unfair, for the
Pennefathers to accuse Bolton of seeking to monopolise the representation and of stir-
ring up un-Christian strife. In December 1733, just before the by-election for Cashel,
one Co. Limerick gentleman remarked that Bolton was obnoxious to many people 'on
account of the great hand he has in all popular disputes and the flame that he has
put the county of Tipperary in' – a 'flame' which had spread from Cashel to the
Tipperary borough of Clonmel and to county politics as well.[17] Many years later it was
said of Bolton that 'all his virtues were sullied by ambition, which was his reigning
passion, and to gratify which he used such methods as brought him under great
contempt'.[18] He clearly did not act on the widely held principle that an archbishop or
bishop should give way to those 'holding hereditary rank in the county' (in the words
of a subsequent archbishop of Cashel, Brodrick).[19] Nor did he share Edward Synge,
bishop of Elphin's, philosophy that a bishop should be a promoter of harmony in the
localities where his see gave him influence. Writing to a prospective candidate for Co.
Sligo in 1757, Synge stated:

> I have been a bishop going on twenty-eight years and I set out with the resolu-
> tion to keep clear, wherever I was, of county interests and elections. This rule
> I have hitherto constantly observed, except when one side appeared to me not
> protestant, or when, by my interposition, I hoped to preserve peace and pre-
> vent divisions in a county. ... Nothing I have in more detestation than the
> divisions and animosities which contested elections in counties always produce.

17 William Taylor to Lord Perceval, 11 Dec. 1733, Egmont papers, BL, Add. Ms. 46984, pp 214–16.
18 Richard Mant, bishop of Down, *History of the Church of Ireland ... [to 1810]* (2 vols., London,
1840), ii, pp 580–82; McNally, *Early Hanoverian Ireland*, p. 111.   19 Archbishop Brodrick to 1st
earl of Donoughmore, 26 Dec. 1818, Donoughmore papers, T/3459/D/31/6.

They destroy neighbourhood, friendship, everything pleasing; and the baneful effects are sometimes worse even than these. The course of justice is perverted. He who is with me cannot be wrong: the man against me cannot be right.[20]

In this spirit, the election committee of 1734 not only treated Bolton's conduct 'freely' and 'roughly', but declared his candidate, Stephen Moore, unduly elected and seated Richard Pennefather in Moore's place.

This did not immediately put control of Cashel into the hands of the Pennefathers,[21] since William Buckworth Carr, Bolton's nominee, succeeded Richard Buckworth at the already-mentioned by-election of 1739. William Buckworth Carr sat for Cashel until his death in 1753. But, from then on, both seats were filled by Pennefathers, Richard Pennefather, for example, representing the borough without interruption or contest from 1734 until his death in 1777. During these years, the strategy of reducing the number of the freemen and bringing them firmly under the control of the common council was persevered in with complete success. By Agar's time, there was no possibility of an archiepiscopal come-back. Had there been, the government would presumably have thought twice about translating him to Cashel, as they later did about translating him to Armagh (see pp 137 and 175–84). Cashel, like Armagh, survived the Union without disfranchisement, though both became single-member constituencies. But, as one seat in Westminster was the equivalent in value of two in the Irish parliament, the Pennefathers did well out of going to market with the return for Cashel,[22] which is what they generally did during the next thirty years. On the eve of the Great Reform Act, which finally wrested Cashel borough from the Pennefathers, all sixteen members of the common council were members or relations of that family and Pennefather control was more entrenched than ever. Yet, from the vantage point of a hundred years later, it certainly looked as if the town would have prospered more under the affluent archbishop than the fairly impecunious Pennefathers. In the 1830s, it was reported that

> The estates entrusted to the corporation for the benefit of the city consist of nearly 4,000 statute acres of arable land, worth at least 20s. per Irish acre per annum, ... yet the rents at present ... amount to no more than £219 18s. 10?d. per annum. From the *Report of the commissioners on municipal corporations in Ireland* [of 1833] ... it would appear that this very inadequate return has been caused by the disposal of large holdings to members of the corporation at rents which may be termed nominal ... . In consequence of this alienation of the public property, and from the mayor and aldermen having converted to their own uses the tolls and customs of the city, the public works of Cashel have

20 Synge to Owen Wynne, 18 Aug. 1757, Wynne papers, PRONI, MIC/666/D/7,   21 For an anti-Pennefather – and I now think over-simplified – interpretation of the events of 1727–34, see Malcomson, 'The parliamentary traffic of this country', pp 145–6.   22 See, for example: William Elliot to Lord Grenville, 14 July 1806, *HMC Dropmore Mss.*, viii. 235; and George Canning to George Rose, 15 Aug. 1806, Rose papers, BL, Add. Ms. 42773, ff. 131–3.

fallen into a state of ruin almost unexampled in the kingdom. ... The water-works (which Dr [Charles] Smith described as 'truly noble, [and] which must perpetuate the name of the donor ...') created in ... [1732] by Archbishop Bolton, have gone completely to decay; the underground conduits upward of two miles in length, are choked up or obliterated and the stream is diverted to alleys that branch from it; and the whole of the suburbs are mean and wretched.[23]

AGAR AND THE TOWN AND NEIGHBOURHOOD OF CASHEL, 1779–1801

Since – for good or ill – there was nothing which Agar could have done to set the clock back and re-build archiepiscopal influence in the borough, he had the grace and sense to cultivate friendly relations with the Pennefathers and the corporation. He provided well for the clerical member of the family, the Rev. John Pennefather, whom he collated to the treasurership of Cashel, 'worth above £200 [per annum, on 10 May 1787. Subsequently, on] ... February 27, 1789, the Archbishop collated ... [him] to the union of Newport, worth about £600 per annum, in exchange for the treasurership'.[24] Agar also conferred benefits, great and small, on the town/city of Cashel. For a start, his presence there and the lavishly hospitable life-style he introduced into the palace (see pp 350–53), made Cashel a regular recipient of viceregal visits, for example from Lord Westmorland in late October 1790,[25] with all the bustle and additional business which such visits entailed. Even more practically, he obtained in July 1794 'four additional posts in the week to Cashel from Clonmel, and also an additional mail weekly from Dublin to Cashel'.[26] No doubt his friend, Lord Ely, then Lord Loftus, who had succeeded Lord Clifden as joint postmaster general in 1789 (see pp 164–5), was instrumental in making these post office arrangements.

Agrarian outrage, and law and order generally, were always live issues in Co. Tipperary. Agar was prominent in drafting, and defending in parliament, the Magistracy Act of 1787 (see p. 444), which empowered county grand juries to increase the local constabulary as necessity required and to appoint a paid and legally qualified 'assistant to the justices at sessions'.[27] However, when it came to implementing the act in Co. Tipperary, Agar's influence with Dublin Castle had to be exerted forcefully to obtain in practice the benefits which the act held out in theory, particularly in respect of the barony of Middlethird, where Cashel is situated. To the chief secretary, Thomas Orde, he wrote at the beginning of August:

23 Mr and Mrs S.C. Hall, *Ireland, its scenery, character, etc.* (3 vols., London, 1841–3), ii. 101. See also NLI, Ms. 17978. The illegal lease discussed in this latter source dated only from 1830, and had not been in Pennefather possession before then.   24 Agar's 'state' of the diocese of Cashel, 1779–1800, 21 M 57/B6/1.   25 Westmorland to Agar, 22 Oct. 1790, T/3719/C/24/9.   26 21 M 57/B6/1.   27 Agar to Thomas Orde, 1 Aug. 1787, T/3719/C/21/29.

The act directs that there shall be sixteen constables in each district, and certainly a smaller number would not be effectual. Now at this moment, as well as for many years past, there have been eighty constables in each of the baronies of Clanwilliam and Middlethird; so that, if these two baronies are to constitute one district, the number of constables will not be increased by that union, and ... [is clearly insufficient] to preserve the peace and execute the law in those baronies, where forcible possessions, violence and outrage of every kind have prevailed and will I believe continue should not the means of preventing them be increased. ... You have by this time, I hope, signified to Mr [Dominick] Trant your intention of appointing him assistant to the justices of this county. On the appointment of an able man to that office will I am persuaded depend in a very great measure the good effects which may be expected from this very necessary law.[28]

Orde replied with a rather woolly 'opinion of those learned in the law [that] ... the baronies of Clanwilliam and Middlethird cannot now be made separate districts. Yet as the justices have a power in case of a riot or tumultuous or unlawful assembly to collect all the constables of the county, I hope the peace will be sufficiently secured upon all great occasions, and that upon common ones the number of constables for the district may be found sufficient.'[29] He also queried whether Agar's *protégé*, Dominick Trant, was sufficiently resident in the county to be an appropriate appointee as assistant barrister.

This drew from Agar a strong and informative rejoinder, in which he explained why 'The administration of justice has been ... defective in this county for many years', and re-stated the case for appointing Trant.[30] Agar also urged that the government use its influence with a number of Co. Tipperary gentlemen likely to be serving on the grand jury, to induce them to pass presentments for the money necessary for the implementation of the act; these likely grand jurors included 'William Pennefather Esq., collector [of the revenue at] Clonmel'.[31] In the end, Agar's views, and his recommendation of Trant,[32] prevailed. In mid-August, John Scott, Lord Earlsfort, then on circuit and presiding over the Tipperary assizes, assured him that

> a respectable and decisive majority ... of the grand jury ... [were resolved] to do what they have been explicitly informed by the bench they ought to do. All your friends justify the pains you have taken upon this subject, and are steady to their duty to the public and the peace of the country, as I have very faithfully stated to Mr Orde. A variety of little arts have been played off to mislead and misrepresent, but they prove abortive, and on Monday evening I trust that Tipperary will be as well disciplined as Cork, so far at least as the Magistracy Act can tend to quiet it.[33]

28 Ibid.   29 Orde to Agar, 6 Aug. 1787, T/3719/C/21/30.   30 Agar to Orde, 11 Aug. 1787, T/3719/C/21/32.   31 Agar to Orde, 8 Aug. 1787, and Sackville Hamilton to Agar, 11 Aug. 1787, T/3719/C/21/33 and 35.   32 Trant to Agar, 16 Aug. 1787, T/3719/C/21/37; Kavanaugh, *Lord Clare*, p. 210.   33 Earlsfort to Agar, [*c*.15] Aug. 1787, T/3719/C/21/39.

The arguments over the implementation of the Magistracy Act are a well documented example of Agar's influence being exerted for the benefit of the neighbourhood of Cashel. But in some respects it is a bad example. As has been seen (pp 190–91), many country gentlemen had varying degrees of sympathy with the anti-tithe protests of the Rightboys. Many were also suspicious of the act, which could be seen as an engine of patronage and of despotism.[34] The escalation of Rightboy violence in the summer of 1786 and the publication of Bishop Woodward's and other highly effective pro-Church pamphlets in late 1786 (see pp 328 and 480–1), brought about a change in the mood among the country gentlemen and the members of the House of Commons.[35] Even so, Agar was still an object of some hostility in such quarters, since he was prominent as an out-and-out upholder of the rights of the clergy. Above all, there was the issue of money, which always played an important part in 'The politics of law and order'.[36] Implementing the Magistracy Act cost the Tipperary gentry money, and therefore, as Earlsfort reported, was unpopular with a minority of the county grand jury. On the other hand, some of the disturbances – notably the 'forcible possessions' mentioned by Agar – were directed solely against lay landlords and had nothing to do with the clergy. They were, literally, sieges, in which the besieged were former tenants whose leases had expired but who refused to give up possession of their farms. Recently, from the autumn of 1784 to that of 1785, there had been a notorious and protracted 'forcible possession' at Ballinulta, near Cullen, on the estate of Joseph Damer, later 1st earl of Dorchester.[37] Under all these complicated circumstances, Agar's line on the Magistracy Act was probably such as enhanced his standing among the Tipperary nobility and gentry, particularly those resident or with property in the barony of Middlethird/neighbourhood of Cashel.

In other, more conventionally political terms, Agar – even when at variance with his Cashel neighbours – went out of his way to be gracious towards them. On 23 May 1782, for example, a meeting of 'the Cashel Volunteers' under the chairmanship of one John Power, had sent Agar an address of thanks 'for his obliging readiness to communicate the glorious news of this day'.[38] This actually referred to Admiral Rodney's defeat of the French off Dominica on 12 April.[39] But it followed hard on the concession of the constitution of 1782, which Agar privately attributed to a woeful failure of parliamentary management and to an inglorious surrender to the extra-parliamentary pressure of the Volunteers. Under these circumstances, the civilities exchanged between the local Volunteers and him suggest a mutual determination to be friends. As time went on, Agar and the corporation and town of Cashel found

34 Bric, 'Rightboy protest in Co. Cork', pp 120–21.   35 James Kelly, 'The genesis of "Protestant Ascendancy": the Rightboy disturbances of the 1780s and their impact upon protestant opinion', in Gerard O'Brien (ed.), *Parliament, politics and people: essays in eighteenth-century Irish history* (Dublin, 1989), pp 104–22. For other explanations of the change of mood, see Bric, op. cit., pp 116–20.   36 The title of Dr Gaynor's already-cited thesis.   37 Orde to Agar, 18 Oct. 1784, T/3719/C/18/36; Agar to Orde, 8 Nov. 1784, Bolton papers, NLI, Ms. 16350, ff. 59–60; Power, *Eighteenth-century Tipperary*, p. 745.   38 Address from the Cashel Volunteers to Agar, 23 May 1782, 21 M 57/A15/3. 39 Donald Macintyre, *Admiral Rodney* (London, 1962), pp 206–52.

themselves increasingly in political accord, notably over the Catholic Question and the Union. In February 1792, Agar was assured by his vicar-general, the Rev. Patrick Hare, that the mayor 'will convene the corporation of Cashel' to petition parliament against the Catholic Relief Bill then before it.[40] This meeting and petition took place. Then, on 19 December 1792, a public meeting was held in Cashel, with the secret approval of the Irish administration, to pass resolutions drafted by Agar against the next and more radical instalment of Catholic Relief.[41] Among Agar's papers is a draft, in Agar's hand, of a Unionist address from the corporation of Cashel dated 29 July 1799[42] – the first public manifestation, or perhaps manifesto, of Agar's enrolment as a campaigner for the Union (see pp 551–4). The address was peppered with Pennefather signatures. But in fact the role of prime mover in the town had for some time past devolved on Agar because, as the head of the Pennefather family, Colonel Richard, put it in a letter to him, 'my mind has been so disturbed of late that I could not bring myself to go into company'.[43] At the time of the Union address and of a visit paid to Cashel by the lord lieutenant (when on a Unionist missionary tour of Munster), Agar took the lead and on 30 July hosted in the palace the local dinner in honour of the viceroy.

What is perhaps most expressive of Agar's relationship with 'the gentlemen of the city and neighbourhood of Cashel' is the farewell address they presented to him in mid-December 1801, on his translation to Dublin:

> It does not always happen, my Lord, that rank and abilities are united, or that easy manners are the accompaniment of power. In the ready and spirited exercise of your talents on every public concern, this neighbourhood has experienced the many benefits of your presence, and in our more private intercourse we have found you, my Lord, the zealous, faithful friend, the polished gentleman.[44]

The address was signed by Colonel Richard Pennefather, who chaired the meeting (and whose mental faculties had presumably been restored), Lord Mathew, Thomas and Hugh Barton, John Palliser, Samuel Alleyn (who had been mayor in 1792), Samuel and William Cooper (the former of whom was Agar's registrar and agent for the see lands – see p. 349*n*) and thirty-two others.

KINGSTON COLLEGE, MITCHELSTOWN, 1768–1801

The 'many benefits' deriving to Cashel from Agar's 'presence' included – perhaps top of the list – his completion of the new Cashel cathedral. For this and his other

---

40 Hare to Agar, 9 Feb. 1792, 21 M 57/A33/1.   41 Notice of the meeting and resolutions passed at the meeting, 19 Dec. 1792, 21 M 57/A33/11–12; Robert Hobart (the chief secretary), to Agar, 25 Dec. 1792, T/3719/C/26/17.   42 Draft address, 29 July 1799, 21 M 57/A45/2.   43 Robert Marshall (private secretary to the acting chief secretary, Lord Castlereagh), to Agar, 31 Mar. 1798, T/3719/C/32/36; Pennefather to Agar, 29 July 1799, T/3719/C/33/28.   44 Address, 14 Dec. 1801, 21 M 57/B8/24.

architectural achievements in Cashel, his apprenticeship had been served in Cloyne. It was perhaps more of a baptism of fire than an apprenticeship. This was because of the bickering which attended a project which was under way when Agar arrived at Cloyne in 1768 – the building of Kingston College, Mitchelstown, a charitable foundation being set up out of an endowment of £25,000 provided for that purpose by the will of the 4th Lord Kingston (d.1761). It was to comprise accommodation for 'poor decayed gentlemen and ... gentlewomen', a chapel and a library.[45] The bishop of Cloyne, in whose diocese Mitchelstown is situated, along with the bishops of the neighbouring dioceses of Limerick and Waterford, and the metropolitan, the archbishop of Cashel, whose diocese also adjoined, were *ex officio* trustees of Kingston College.[46] Agar took a keen interest in this part of his duties. He was also consulted in July 1777 by the young Viscount Kingsborough, who was married to the Mitchelstown heiress, about the layout of his new, planned town of Mitchelstown.[47]

The architect in charge of the building of the college was the already-mentioned John Morrison (p. 198). Morrison had been appointed prior to Agar's promotion to Cloyne. He must have been chosen by, among others, Agar's predecessor, Frederick Hervey, because in 1767 Morrison asked Hervey, and Lord Shannon, to be godparents to his son. This was the future Sir Richard Morrison (who evidently was called Richard after Lord Shannon). But Agar clearly endorsed the selection of John Morrison and became his enthusiastic patron.

> John [Morrison] was prominent in the south of Ireland in the 1760s and 1770s. ... He ... designed three small churches for ... Agar [when] bishop of Cloyne, and [in the diocese of Cloyne] ... he designed ... [Kingston] College, an attractive range of almshouses, [library] and chapel in vernacular-classical idiom. In 1775, with building of the college in progress, Morrison ran into trouble. A dispute arose over a payment of £600. Morrison eventually accepted responsibility for a mistake; the Bishop of Waterford and Lismore [Richard Chenevix] complained, privately, that no mistake was involved, but misconduct, and that Bishop Agar's prejudice in favour of Morrison in the affair was 'very extraordinary'.[48]

So, according to Bishop Chenevix, was a letter which Agar wrote on the subject. A copy of what appears to be this letter survives, and its content seems sensible rather than 'extraordinary':

> He [Morrison] requests the trustees to appoint some skilful person to examine and value such works as were not included in his estimate [of £5,350], but were

45 Bill Power, *White Knights, dark earls: the rise and fall of an Anglo-Irish dynasty* (Cork, 2000), pp 7–9, and pp 1–27 *passim*. 46 A.L. King-Harman, *The Kings of King House* (Bedford, 1996), pp 22–6; printed extract from the will of the 4th Lord Kingston, 1761, establishing almshouses, a library, etc., in Mitchelstown, King-Harman papers, PRONI, D/4168/A/1/2. 47 Kingsborough to Agar, 6 July 1779, T/3719/C/13/15. 48 McParland, Rowan and Rowan, *The Morrisons*, pp 1, 2, 11nn., 54 and 175.

agreed to be paid for by valuation; and ... I confess I do not at present see any objection to complying with this request, though it might be very unadvisable to advance Mr Morrison £600 before this be done; and should it appear by the report of the person whom we shall nominate to examine the extra works that Mr Morrison has (as he says) expended £1,400 on those works, that the money has been fairly and honestly laid out, that he can fully prove the expenditure of it, and that he was by his contract with the trustees warranted to lay out this money for articles exclusive of those contained in his estimate, I shall in that case, but not otherwise, be of opinion that Mr Morrison has a fair demand on the trustees for £600.[49]

Chenevix, in fact, took the same view. He was opposed to paying the £600 on account until Morrison's estimate and accounts had been compared, and his 'extra works' inspected by another architect, 'because I fear he may have charged as extra ... what is already allowed in the estimate'. He also complained that Morrison had been 'very imprudently suffered in a manner to draw ... up [his contract] himself'.[50] But this last criticism did not lie at Agar's door, because he had not been a trustee at the time (though Chenevix had).

In the event, and following the inspection (which was carried out by a Mr Stokes, whom Chenevix thought Morrison had unduly influenced), Morrison seems to have been reimbursed, not the full £1,400 which he claimed to have spent on extra works, but £650. So he does not seem to have been greatly indulged. However, a dispute over, by coincidence, another sum of £600, broke out three months later. Morrison had been paid a total of £6,000, but until Chevenix checked with the trustees' bankers, acknowledged 'only the receipt of £5,400 ... . Now he allows the mistake was on his side. It was very happy I thought of writing to our bankers, otherwise the difference, £600, might have been lost. ... Your Lordship will see by the Bishop's [Agar] last letter [not present] that there is no demand now for £600 ..., but Mr Morrison will engage to finish the college next May without any conditions.'[51] Chevenix, who enjoyed a contemporary reputation for 'his vigilance and industry' in uncovering fraud,[52] may have been over-eager to enhance that reputation. Alternatively, since he was seventy-seven at the time, he may genuinely have got the two sums of £600 mixed up, and thought that Agar had sought to justify Morrison's claim that he had received £5,400 when in fact he had received £6,000. Another possible explanation is that Chenevix, so far from being in his dotage, was secretly trying to get Morrison supplanted by another architect, John Roberts (whom he does not actually name), with whose

49 Agar to William Gore, bishop of Limerick, 9 May 1775, Limerick papers (i.e. the papers of William Cecil Pery, a later bishop of Limerick and the father of the 1st earl of Limerick), NLI, PC 875, bundle 15/24.   50 Chenevix to Gore, 16 May 1775, ibid., bundle 19/7.   51 Chenevix to Gore, 15 Aug. 1775, ibid., bundle 22/4.   52 [Richard Chenevix Trench, archbishop of Dublin, 1864–85], *The remains of Mrs Richard Trench* ... [his mother, who was Bishop Chenevix's granddaughter and heiress] (London, 1862), p. 10.

integrity, skill and experience I have been long acquainted ..., he having finished the episcopal house, and he has built two houses for me, and on whose report the trustees I am certain may safely rely. He is well known to the Archbishop of Cashel, Lord Tyrone (whose fine offices [at Curraghmore, Portlaw, Co. Waterford] he built) and the chief gentlemen of this county, having been employed by most of them in considerable buildings and to their entire satisfaction, and he has now undertaken the rebuilding of the cathedral of Waterford, his plan having been approved of by the corporation and the clergy.

The fact that Roberts did not in the end act in this minor capacity may suggest that hopes of a more extended remit for him had been the ulterior motive and were dashed. Agar was a great patron of Morrison. But it would have been out of character for him to betray a charitable trust or act with anything other than the rigour he was soon to exercise against Lord Kingsborough.

Perhaps because of his 'mistake' or 'misconduct' over the second sum of £600, '[Morrison's] practice seems to have declined ... at about this time. ... He charged professional fees of five per cent and, where trouble was involved, six per cent, an unusual step in the ambiguous world of contracting and building in provincial Ireland in the 1770s. ... [But he] certainly retained the powerful patronage of Agar.'[53] Agar's patronage of him, however, was very far from exclusive: he employed a little-known Dublin architect, Oliver Grace, on Cashel cathedral and palace in 1780–4 and on an extension to Kingston College itself in 1786; and in September 1780 and again in September 1783, Thomas Cooley (1740–84), Primate Robinson's preferred architect, furnished plans for glebe-houses and offices in the diocese of Cashel.[54] In 1793 Richard Morrison dedicated to Agar Morrison's '*Useful and ornamental designs in architecture composed in the manner of the antique and most approved taste of the present day* ..., [which he] could reasonably claim in his advertisement ... was "the first work of the kind that has been attempted in Ireland". His *Useful and ornamental designs* had penetrated as far as Philadelphia by 1795.'[55] In the first half of the nineteenth century, Morrison and his son, William Vitruvius (who pre-deceased him) were to make a contribution to architecture, particularly to country-house architecture, which was unique in British as well as Irish terms. Agar's early and discerning patronage of the Morrison family, so far from being matter of reproach to him, constitutes one of his claims to fame. He also profited from his troubled experience over the Kingston College accounts: Cashel cathedral was built on the basis of a precise estimate and a tight budget, and the architect was not responsible to a committee.

The next row over the college was not architectural in character and was with Lord Kingsborough. Agar, as has been seen, had been on good terms with Kingsborough up to at least July 1777. But Kingsborough had been augmenting his income out of the £25,000 left by his kinsman in 1761, instead of paying all of it over to the

53 McParland, Rowan and Rowan, *The Morrisons*, p. 2.   54 Power, *White Knights, dark earls*, p. 8; Hampshire RO list of 21 M 57/B14/26–9 and 38. Cooley died in 1784.   55 McParland, Rowan and Rowan, *The Morrisons*, p. 2.

trustees or at least allowing the interest to accumulate. This issue simmered during Agar's last years at Cloyne and boiled over soon after his translation to Cashel. On 26 February 1780 Kingsborough was compelled to enter into an agreement with the trustees, whereby he obliged himself to pay £8,000, the outstanding amount, on a specified time-scale. He then reneged on this obligation and, in a letter to the trustees, pleaded poverty:

> In order to expedite the discharge of all arrears, I reduced the expenses of my family into as narrow a compass as possible, and at the same time wrote to the Archbishop enclosing him my proposal for paying off the entire arrears as well as the growing interest after November 1783, which I am sorry to find has neither been approved of or [*sic*] understood. I shall return to Ireland at the beginning of April, ... in order to attend your Lordships at any meeting with the [Lord] Chancellor, or to defend myself at law in case that should be your mode of proceeding.

He next had the effrontery to add: 'Lady Kingsborough requests your Lordships will be so good [as] to include Mrs Turvin's name in your list. She is her first cousin and her circumstances are such as entitle her to a place in the Mitchelstown Charity' – i.e. in the almshouses.[56] As Lord and Lady Kingsborough were young, giddy and extravagant, and known to be moving in the most fashionable circles in London, the plea of retrenchment did not carry much conviction. Agar, writing from Cashel, urged a fellow-trustee then in Dublin to explain to the Chancellor that Kingsborough was £3,547 short of the sum he agreed to pay in 1780, and

> that the trustees have been so often disappointed by Lord Kingsborough, who has not observed any one engagement with them, that they do not think it prudent to elect persons into the college ... . Therefore, the trustees humbly request the Lord Chancellor to say whether he can in this case afford them any relief, without obliging them to have recourse to law, which would both retard the appointment of persons to fill the college (thereby defeating in some measure the testator's intentions) and would also exhaust a part and perhaps a considerable one of the fund appropriated to a great and excellent charity.[57]

When Kingsborough chose this untimely moment to renew his request in favour of Lady Kingsborough's poor relation, Mrs Turvin, Agar replied witheringly that the trustees had 'been hitherto prevented from appointing any persons to occupy the college for want of the money which is due to them by Lord Kingsborough'.[58] Eventually, the matter was settled to the satisfaction of the trustees. Ironically, this outcome was later attributed – by implication – to Chenevix (who had died in 1779!):

56 Kingsborough to the trustees, 16 Mar. 1781, Limerick papers, NLI, PC 875, bundle 22/5.
57 Agar to [Bishop Gore], 1 Apr. 1781, ibid., bundle 8/37.   58 Agar to Kingsborough, 18 Apr. 1781, and Agar to Gore, 18 Apr. 1781, ibid., bundle 15/5 and bundle 15/8.

'In more instances than one, he wrested from the strong grasp of power and affluence the portion of those who had none to help them, and saved from rapacious heirs the revenues of the establishments ... for the comfort of the widow and the fatherless.'[59] It has been Agar's misfortune that, while his doubtful actions have always been magnified to his discredit, his good deeds have usually been ascribed to others.[60]

After 1781, his role as an *ex officio* trustee of the college became less active: the buildings had been built and Kingsborough had been brought to book. In 1794, the 1st marquess of Lansdowne (who, as Lord Shelburne, had been prime minister in 1782–3) wrote to him recommending 'an object of very great pity', Elinor Deane, the widow of Hugh Primrose Deane, 'a very promising artist at Rome, who did not use Lord Lansdowne very well about a picture ..., [and was] a very immoral character', for a place in 'the college of Mitchelstown ... for the support of decayed gentlemen and women'.[61] Presumably Agar got her in. He certainly obtained the admission of another deserving widow, his sister-in-law, Mary Agar (*née* Tyrrell), following the death of the Rev. Henry Agar in May 1798.[62] He continued to supervise the investment of the Kingston College trust money until January 1802, a couple of months after his translation to the archbishopric of Dublin. At that time, his co-trustee was the bishop of Cloyne, and presumably that bishop and his metropolitan had always acted in this capacity. In January 1801, the trust fund stood at £8,702, invested in 3 per cent consols.[63]

Another sequel to Kingston College which did not occur until 1782, after Agar had been translated to Cashel, was 'New Geneva'. This was a scheme for building a university town at Passage, between Waterford City and Dunmore East, Co. Waterford, and settling there a colony of protestant watchmakers and other craftsmen from Geneva. The hidden agenda of the lord lieutenant who adopted the scheme, was to keep them well away 'from the northern republicans and to place them where they might make an essential reform in the religion, industry and manners of the south.'[64] In November 1783, Agar (along with John Beresford and several of the Dublin wide streets commissioners) was named 'one of the commissioners ... for the settlement in Ireland of a colony of emigrants from the city of Geneva.'[65] As metropolitan of the province of Cashel, his appointment could hardly have been avoided. But, more

59 *The remains of Mrs Richard Trench*, p. 10.   60 For examples of the former, see pp 4–6, 305–10 and 406–34, and for other examples of the latter, pp 443–54 and 568–74.   61 Mrs Deane to Lansdowne, 17 Dec. 1793, and Lansdowne to Agar, 6 Jan. 1794, T/3719/C/28/1–2.   62 Clifden to Agar, 7 Mar. 1798, and Mendip to Agar, 23 May 1798, T/3719/C/32/14 and 60; Mrs Mary Agar, Kingston College, to Agar (acknowledging receipt of £20), 17 Sep. 1808, T/3719/C/42/89; notes on family history by Mr Terence Finley.   63 Kingston College trust account between Agar and Willis, Wood, Percival & Co., Lombard Street, his London stockbrokers, 29 Jan. 1801, 21 M 57/B17/8; *précis* of letter from Agar to Willis & Co. transferring the account to Archbishop Brodrick under the power of attorney previously granted to Agar and the Bishop of Cloyne, 9 Jan. 1802, 21 M 57/D55; and Brodrick to Agar, 23 Aug. 1802, T/3719/C/36/18.   64 Quoted in Jupp, *Genevese exiles in Co. Waterford*, p. 31. For New Geneva, see Jupp, *Genevese exiles, passim*, Butler, *Escape from the anthill*, pp 25–31, and McParland, *James Gandon*, pp 175–7 and 199.   65 The Hon. Thomas Pelham (then chief secretary), to Agar, 17 Nov. 1783, T/3719/C/17/29.

important, his architectural experience at Mitchelstown, which had involved an element of town-planning as well as the design and construction of a prestigious range of high-quality buildings, made him an excellent choice on practical grounds. The plans for Passage, drawn up by Beresford's architect for the Dublin custom house, James Gandon, were much more extensive and ambitious than those for Mitchelstown.[66] But, in the end, the scheme was abandoned. In the main, this was because the Genevans and the Irish government had always been politically and ideologically at cross purposes. The forty or so houses which 'were erected are remembered now only as a military barracks featuring in the rebel songs of 1798.'[67] So, Agar was never called upon to perform a role which would have been highly congenial to him in architectural terms, and in which he would almost certainly have co-operated fruitfully with Ellis' and Clifden's antagonist, John Beresford.

AGAR AND CLOYNE CATHEDRAL, 1768–79

This discussion of Kingston College and its sequel has left far behind, in chronological terms, Agar's 'restoration' of the ancient cathedral of Cloyne (dating from 1250). This was carried out in the mid-1770s, and seems principally to have comprised a re-roofing of the whole building and the enlargement and conversion of the Choir into a self-contained church-within-a-church.[68] The only authority who does not attribute all this work to Agar is Samuel Lewis. Writing in or before 1837, Lewis commented: 'The Choir is tastefully fitted up and is used as the parish church; but, being found too small for that purpose, the organ was removed in 1780 to the junction of the nave and transepts, by which the Choir has been lengthened 21 feet.'[69] The other evidence accords with this account, except for the (suspiciously round) date '1780.' The 2nd earl of Normanton noted on one of Agar's papers: 'My father ... [when] at Cloyne ..., enlarged the body of the cathedral and founded a choir.'[70] Thomas Crofton Croker stated that the erection of 'the present cross wall at the entrance of the Choir ... was done by Bishop Agar in 1776.'[71] More recently, the Rev. Peter Galloway has attributed the work to Agar 'in 1774.'

> [It] was effected in the classical style which was typical of the age but ludicrous in this gothic cathedral. The chancel was lengthened westwards to incorporate the crossing. Most of the chancel arch was walled up and the rest was blocked by a classical-style wooden screen to divide the chancel from the nave. The arches leading from the crossing into the north and south transepts were similarly blocked to allow the erection of galleries on the west, north and south

66 Butler, op. cit., pp 25–31.   67 McParland, *James Gandon*, p. 177.   68 Terence Finley's notes on a locally printed or duplicated local history called *The book of Cloyne*, which he encountered on a visit to Cloyne in August 1995.   69 Lewis, *Topographical dictionary*, i. 183.   70 Marginal note added to Agar's 'state' of the diocese of Cashel, 1779–1801, 21 M 57/B6/1.   71 Croker, *Researches in the south of Ireland ...* (Dublin, 1824), p. 241.

walls of the chancel. The west gallery contained the organ ... . 'The whole
structure, in fact, has been ... often and bunglingly patched, daubed, and played
with by empiricism and stupidity ...'. The late eighteenth-century work mostly
disappeared in further alterations in 1894.[72]

Much the same verdict was passed on, and fate befell, the 'restoration' carried out
*c.*1760 on St Canice's Cathedral, Kilkenny, by Richard Pococke, bishop of Ossory,
1756–65. Pococke 'replaced the roof and saved the fabric of the cathedral.' But most
of his other 'work was most unfortunate and has been removed since.'[73]

    Whatever the verdict on his architecture, and more generally on Georgian
restorations, Agar's work on Cloyne cathedral typifies his approach to the infrastructural problems of the Church: practical, economical and governed by the
principle that the Church should make the best of what it had. His work also made it
possible for him to raise 'the standard of the music to the highest level in the
cathedral's history' (as he was to do at Cashel). He improved the organ in 1771. He
augmented the cathedral's music library by 'purchases of volumes of anthems by
Blow, Purcell, Croft, Greene and Woodward, as well as Boyce's collection of cathedral
music and Handel's overtures.' He brought boys from Dublin to stiffen the choir, and
saw that all the choirboys were instructed in instrumental music as well as singing.[74] It
became a 'choir of surpassing excellence ... . His Lordship's interest in the ... [music
of Cloyne cathedral] may be estimated by some of his purchases ..., [for example] a
goatskin to mend the [organ] bellows.'[75] In September 1778, he obtained from the 1st
earl of Mornington, professor of music at TCD, a copy of some music which had
been performed in St George's Chapel, Windsor; 'It is an unusually affecting
composition. Its simplicity is one of its greatest merits.'[76] Agar's papers include lists
of music, some manuscript music, and indexes to canons, catches and glees, 1771–93.
These are all indications that, as Dorothea Herbert later put it in her *Retrospections,* he
was 'music mad.'[77] In *c.*1830, it was noteworthy that, in spite of some neglect and
temporary regression between 1801 and then, the metropolitan province of 'Cashel ...
had more choral foundations than the other provinces put together.'[78] The foundations
at Cloyne and Cashel, or at any rate their revival,[79] are directly attributable to Agar;
those in the other dioceses of the province are probably attributable to his example.

72 Rev. Peter Galloway, *The cathedrals of Ireland* (Belfast, 1992), pp 52–3. The sources of Mr
Galloway's two quotations are, respectively, T.M. Fallow, *The cathedral churches of Ireland* (London,
1894), p. 43; and *The parliamentary gazetteer of Ireland* (Dublin, 1844–6), i. 470. What looks like
Agar's 1770s pulpit is still to be seen, abandoned, in a corner of the disused nave.   73 Smithwick,
Georgian Kilkenny, pp 87–90.   74 W.H. Grindle, *Irish cathedral music: a history of music at the
cathedrals of the church of Ireland* (Belfast, 1989), p. 53.   75 Terence Finley's notes on *The book of
Cloyne.*   76 Mornington to Agar, 6 Sep. 1778, T/3719/C/12/13.   77 Hampshire RO list of 21 M
57/D28–43; *Retrospections,* p. 98.   78 Akenson, *Church of Ireland,* p. 50.   79 In Cloyne, there had
existed since 1464 a college comprising a warden, fellows and eight singing men, founded in Youghal

AGAR AND CASHEL CATHEDRAL, 1779–1801

In February 1783, a Dublin friend of Agar's (and someone who clearly did not know Cashel) heard that 'you have not omitted to render unto a Superior Being the things that are His, for that you have built an excellent church.'[80] This must refer to the new Cashel cathedral, which was Agar's greatest architectural achievement, and in more than one sense became a monument to him. 'Cathedrals [re-built or] built during the Georgian era included Cork (1735), Clogher (1745), Waterford (*c.*1773), with its delicate rococo [*sic* – neo-classical] interior, Cashel (1778 [*sic*]), Down (1790) and Achonry (1823). They were usually single-room buildings [as is Cashel], with the stalls at the west end, the choir and organ in a west gallery ..., and the reading desk and pulpit near the altar. ... The people were between the chapter and the officiating minister, and not "strained spectators in the nave". The new cathedrals were also no larger than good-sized parish churches, and most served as such.'[81] This question of size particularly struck those accustomed to the Church of England. In July 1782, the newly translated John Hotham wrote to a fellow-Englishman: 'Since your Lordship was at Clogher things are greatly changed. My cathedral is now no longer a miserable but very neat and respectable parish church. It was rebuilt by Bishop Ste[a]rne and substantially repaired and beautified by the late Bishop [Garnett].'[82] (Curiously, what he failed to mention was the obvious fact that Clogher cathedral is on such a commanding site that, though small, it is visible for miles in most directions.) Agar's initiative in the building of the new Cashel cathedral owed much to his own obsessive energy and his sense of the Church's role. But a diocesan's close involvement with the fabric of his cathedral, and also with its day-to-day functioning as a place of worship, had its origins in the constitution of the Church of Ireland, where

> the relation of bishop to his cathedral and to the cathedral chapter was extremely close, and in this respect contrasted with the situation in the Church of England. Bishops were often benefactors of the cathedrals, and some bishops, such as the archbishop of Cashel [and of Dublin] ..., held ranks within their cathedral as well as being the ordinary of the diocese. ... The bishop possessed considerably more power over the chapter and patronage in the chapter than in England ...; [and] the Irish cathedrals were generally less well endowed, both in revenue and in fabric, than their English counterparts.[83]

To say that Cashel is an ancient ecclesiastical site, if anything understates the point. In 1101, Muirchertach O Briain of Thomond gave it to the Church, and in

by the 8th earl of Desmond. This was alienated in 1641, but was re-possessed by Edward Synge, bishop of Cloyne, 1663–78. See records relating to Cloyne, RCB Library, D.16/8/1. 80 William Dunn to Agar, 19 Feb. 1783, T/3719/C/17/5. 81 Acheson, *Church of Ireland*, p. 95. 82 Hotham to Viscount Sackville, 9 July 1782, *HMC Stopford-Sackville Mss.*, i. 279. 83 Akenson, *Church of Ireland*, pp 40 and 42.

IIII the first great reforming synod to be convened in Ireland, the synod of Rath Bresail, was held nearby. In 1127, after Cormac MacCarthaigh had become king of Cashel, he began the oldest part of the famous cathedral on the Rock of Cashel, Cormac's Chapel, which was consecrated in 1134. Although essentially a building of foreign inspiration, it marks 'the beginnings of Irish Romanesque.'[84] The main part of the cathedral on the Rock continued to be used for Anglican worship from the Reformation until the mid-1740s. The English traveller in Ireland, John Loveday, had commented in 1732: 'at present the Choir only is roofed and in repair ... . There is not above twice a year any use made of it.'[85] But Archbishop Bolton had set matters to rights. He 'was unusual among his contemporaries in appreciating mediaeval architecture. Writing in 1735 to his friend, Dean Swift, he described the cathedral as "a very venerable old fabric that was built here in the time of our ignorant, as we are pleased to call them, ancestors".'[86] In the same letter, he announces that he has 'laid aside all my county politics, sheriffs, elections, feasts, etc.';[87] so, it may be conjectured that, frustrated in his political designs on Cashel borough and other Tipperary constituencies, he diverted his restless energies to the cathedral on the Rock. He told Swift that he intended ' "to lay out a thousand pounds to preserve this old church", ... [but] in fact spent three thousand of his own money on repairing the cathedral and improving the way up to it.'[88] He was justly proud of this achievement. A 'copperplate' of the cathedral (fig. 13), fully re-roofed and shown from the south (with some artistic licence), appeared in the 1739 Dublin edition of the *Works* of Sir James Ware, and was one of the illustrations specially commissioned for that publication.[89] A different and more realistic engraving of the cathedral (fig. 14), seen from the south-east, and with the re-roofing of the crossing-tower still under way, was published in 1790 in the first edition of the Rev. Edward Ledwich's *Antiquities of Ireland* and re-published in the second edition in 1804. It corresponds broadly to that of 1739,

84 Liam de Paor, 'Cormac's Chapel ...', in Etienne Rynne (ed.), *North Munster Studies: Essays in commemoration of Monsignor Michael Moloney* (Limerick, 1967), pp 133–145.   85 I am grateful for this reference to the ever-generous Dr Edward McParland of the Department of the History of Art, TCD. Loveday, described by Constantia Maxwell as 'an intelligent Oxfordshire squire' – *Country and town in Ireland under the Georges* (revised ed., Dundalk, 1949), p.73 – wrote a *Diary of a tour in 1732 through parts of England, Wales, Ireland and Scotland*, which was first published by the Roxburghe Club in 1890.   86 Mark Bence-Jones, *Country Life*, 24 August 1972. This is the first of a two-part article in *Country Life*, respectively dated 24 and 31 August 1972 and entitled 'An acropolis in Tipperary' and 'An archbishop's Palladian palace'.   87 Quoted in Mant, *Church of Ireland*, ii. 582.   88 Bence-Jones, *Country Life*, 24 Aug. 1972.   89 NLI, prints and single drawings, 1757TC. The artistic licence principally consists of: (a) the removal of the vicars' choral building to provide a clear view of the south transept; (b) the elongation of the lancets in the south transept; and (c) a general heightening of what in fact is a fairly stocky building. The engraving looks as if it is giving an idealised impression of what the cathedral will, or ought to, look like when restored. It appears that the artist, Jonas Blaymires, had wanted to depict it 'before the alterations be made', but had been told by Bolton to wait and incorporate (or, more probably, anticipate) them. I am most grateful to Joanna Finegan of the Prints and Drawings Department for spotting the relationship with the 1739 edition of Ware, to Dr T.C. Barnard for the information about Blaymires, and to Professor B.M.S. Campbell for valuable guidance.

though taking less artistic licence. The draughtsman of the original was A[nthony] Chearnley of Burnt Court, Co. Tipperary (*c.*1718–1785).[90] So, although published much later, it too must relate to the Bolton restoration and date from *c.*1740.

These two images cast great doubt on the received wisdom that the building 'was still in a poor state ... at [Bolton's] ... death in 1744.'[91] His successor, 'that barbarian Archbishop [Arthur] Price',[92] who was archbishop, 1744–52, decided to abandon it in favour of the mediaeval St John's Church, down in the city of Cashel, allegedly because he found the climb up to the Rock from his palace too stiff. This story may be true: in 1747 an ambitious bishop was eyeing Cashel hopefully because Price was 'seventy and very corpulent.'[93]

> Accordingly, in 1749 ... [the cathedral] was dismantled and unroofed, the work being carried out by soldiers from the 22nd regiment of foot quartered in the town. Price has gone down in history as a monster of vandalism, but he merely had the practical outlook of his time, regarding the old cathedral as 'incommodiously situated' and impossible to repair and maintain properly, since it lacked an adequate endowment. ... [The foundations of the new cathedral were not laid until] ... 1763, ... and it was not roofed until 1781. From the demolition of the old St John's in 1758 or soon afterwards until the opening of the new cathedral ... [on christmas day] 1783, the protestants of Cashel were obliged to hold their services in the courthouse. Lack of funds and inertia on the part of the chapter ... combined to cause this slowness. Price and his short-lived immediate successor did nothing; it was ... Cox ... who got things started. By 1767, £900 had been spent on the walls. This was clearly the limit to which the Archbishop and chapter were prepared to go, for [unsuccessful] attempts were now made to obtain a parliamentary grant. ...
>
> We can only speculate as to who designed the main body of the church. An obscure Mr Howgan, described as an architect, is reported as having given evidence before the parliamentary committee which considered Cox's petition for a grant. Assuming that the design was not his, the most likely architects would be John Roberts of Waterford, the Sardinian Davis Duckart, who at that time was engaged on Cox's own country house, Castletown in Co. Kilkenny, or John Morrison ... [of Kingston College fame or infamy]. Richard Morrison's name appears on a design for the steeple adopted in 1791, so he was clearly its author. He was then a very young man [who had just set up in practice in Clonmel, Co. Tipperary], which suggests that he obtained the commission on the strength of his father having been the architect of the main body of the church. ... Nothing more seems to have been done until after 1779, when Cox died.[94]

90 Ibid., 1658TA. There appears not to have been a subscription list for the 1790 edition of Ledwich's *Antiquities*: Agar was a subscriber to the 1804.   **91** Bence-Jones, *Country Life*, 24 Aug. 1972.   **92** As Dr Beaufort called him; see Ellison, *The hopeful traveller*, p. 90.   **93** John Ryder, bishop of Down and Connor, to Sir Robert Wilmot, 31 Jan. 1746/7, T/3019/831.   **94** Bence-Jones, *Country Life*, 24 Aug. 1972.

A contemporary impression, written in 1775, of the situation shortly before Cox's death, runs as follows: 'There is not even a roofed church in this metropolis ... . In a sorry room where country courts are held, ... I found a thin congregation, composed of some well dressed women, some half-dozen boys and perhaps a half a score of foot-soldiers; for there is a charter school and a barrack in the town. ... A new church [i.e. cathedral] of ninety feet by forty-five was ... begun and raised as high as the wall-plates. But in that state it has stood for near twenty years.'95

Agar's first thought following his translation to Cashel was to return to and restore the cathedral on the Rock. This is in flat contradiction to Colonel Chester's charge of a hundred years later that 'there is no evidence ... that he made a vain attempt' to do so (see p. 5), and to the usually temperate and judicious Lecky's still wilder claim that 'Archbishop Agar was ... remarkable ... for having allowed the fine old church at Cashel to fall into ruins' (p. 5). Sleater states that Agar 'wished to restore' the cathedral on the Rock, 'but, the walls being in a dangerous state, [he] relinquished the design.'96 This is borne out by Agar's own account of events:

> The Archbishop was enthroned and installed on the 19th day of August [1779] ... within the unfinished walls of the present cathedral ...: a circumstance which necessarily suggested to his mind the propriety, or rather the necessity, of rebuilding the cathedral where it now stands or refitting the old cathedral upon the Rock; for, upon inquiry, the Archbishop found that there had not been a church of any kind in the city of Cashel ... in which divine service had been performed for above twenty-five years, ... the congregation having during ... [that time] assembled every Sunday in one end of a wretched room immediately over the common gaol, ... and which in the year 1779 had hardly any covering except at the end where the congregation met, the other parts being stripped of the slates and exposed to the effects of the weather. ...
>
> In compliance with the wishes of many antiquarians, men of taste and literature, and friends to religion and the Church, the Archbishop would have refitted and repaired the old cathedral on the Rock, had not the walls thereof upon examination been declared by ... Mr Oliver Grace of Dublin,97 a very skilful and honest architect whom the Archbishop brought to Cashel, ... to be in ... [a dangerous] state ... . Such quantities of the stones had been picked out of the buildings in various parts, that some of the oldest and most curious, such as Cormack's [*sic*] Chapel, etc., must have soon fallen to the ground, if considerable additions had not been made to them. All that was necessary to secure the outside from ruin and to render the inside as neat as such a place perhaps can or need be kept, has been done. A good gate was put to the churchyard and another to the church, a house built for John Butterfield, who has the care of

95 Campbell, *Philosophical survey*, pp 129 and 132.   96 Sleater, *op. cit.*, p. 120.   97 Best-known for his later work of *c*.1797 for the 1st Lord Cloncurry on Lyons, near Newcastle, Co. Kildare. I am grateful for this point to Mr Aidan O'Boyle.

the place, and a quarterly salary paid to him in addition to the perquisites arising from burials and showing these ancient and curious buildings to strangers.[98]

It has not hitherto been known that Agar was the rescuer of Cormac's Chapel. Moreover, it is interesting to note that, child of the eighteenth century though he was, he would have been prepared to allow the work which had already been done on the new cathedral to go for nothing.

How much work had actually been done on it by 1779 has until now been conjectural. In his famous *Fasti Ecclesiae Hibernicae*, the Rev. Henry Cotton (who, as the son-in-law and right-hand-man of Richard Laurence, the last archbishop of Cashel, ought to have been well-informed) stated that Agar's contribution was to build the tower and spire.[99] These, in fact, were the only things he did not get round to building! Colonel Chester went to the opposite extreme and implied that Agar had built the whole of the new cathedral; but this was of course because he wanted to saddle Agar with the blame for 'supplanting' the old one. Mr Mark Bence-Jones, in his already-quoted article, states that 'Agar ... completed the cathedral largely at his own expense. Having roofed and furnished the main body of the church between 1781 and 1783, he turned his attention to the steeple in 1791.' This is substantially correct, as far as it goes. Agar's most informative comment on the matter comes in his valedictory statement of 1801 and is cryptic and imprecise; he says that 'the outward walls only were built', that he 'finished and furnished' the building, 'and [that] a steeple is also building.'[100] If 'outward walls' means not only the rubble-stone structure but the cut-stone facing which is superimposed upon it and which is done to a very high standard, then his predecessor had got very good value indeed for £900 (or £900 was not the full amount spent up to 1779): the grandest of the glebe-houses built in Agar's day, that at Thurles, cost £1,631, and Kingston College cost *c.* £6,000. A possible explanation is that one side of the cathedral was finished before Agar and the other by him, since the two sides do not match exactly. They are both, as Bence-Jones notes, encased in 'crisp, grey stone, with arched windows and a cushion frieze, but on the side visible from the street the frieze is supported by ionic pilasters, which are omitted on the other, less conspicuous, side.'[101] On close inspection, this difference seems to derive from economy, not from any time-lag in the building. A change can, however, be seen in both the shape of the frieze and the colour of the stone once a comparison is made between the main block and the porch. So it really does look as if only the latter is attributable to 1779–83 and to Agar. This is confirmed by a very detailed and precise estimate furnished to Agar by Oliver Grace in *c.* 1779–80 for the cost of 'finishing the cathedral.' The following items plainly relate to exterior stonework:

---

98 Agar's 'state' of the diocese of Cashel, 1779–1801, 21 M 57/B6/1.   99 Cotton, *Fasti*, i. 27.   100 21 M 57/B6/2.   101 Bence-Jones, *Country Life*, 24 Aug. 1972.

	£	s	d
109 feet of cutt [*sic*] stone in the ashlar work in the part unbuilt at 12*d*. per [foot]	5	9	6
97½ feet of stone cornice and bed mould for ditto at 21d. per [foot]	8	10	7
85 feet in the frieze and architrave for ditto at 15d. per [foot]	5	6	3
To quarrying the stone and carriage of the cutt work to the building	5	0	0
309 [?feet] in the cutt stone for setting at 1?d. per [foot]	1	18	7
54 perches of stone wall in the breach and blocking course at 6*s*. per [perch]	16	4	0[102]

Materials and workmanship to the value of some £45 seem barely sufficient to build the porch and the lower part of the tower (which Agar definitely did), so there can be no possibility that he completed the main block.

Mysteriously, there is one section of the main block, to the right of, and largely hidden by, the porch, which – apart from one piece of cut-stone facing attached to its top right-hand corner – is still in its unfinished, rubble state. Local tradition has it that this is a surviving portion of the wall of the mediaeval church of St John the Baptist.[103] But the stone looks too modern and too like coursed rubble to be of mediaeval derivation (though it is of course possible that the old parish church had been heavily restored). And there is another mystery. Just round this corner of the main block, on the 'less conspicuous side', there is a moulding at roughly eye-level which, though now shorn off, originally led outwards from the building, as if in continuation of the entrance front. Could it be that some appendage to the old church survived until Agar's day and beyond, that the Georgian cathedral was built alongside it, and that, while it remained, the part of the facade to the right of the porch was hidden from view? Whatever it was, it was gone by the late 1830s. The first Ordnance Survey shows nothing on that side and corner of the building – except trees, planted very close and obviously camouflaging the unfinished bit of cathedral. If it can safely be assumed that little or nothing of the mediaeval St John's remained, then Cashel cathedral qualifies for the distinction hitherto accorded to the Church of Ireland cathedral in Waterford that it is 'the first new cathedral (not incorporating parts of an older building) created in either England or Ireland since Wren's St Paul's'.[104]

The next building-phase at Cashel dates from 1791 at earliest, since that is the date of

> [Richard] Morrison's elevation [of the tower and steeple], ..., a ... composition that was a good deal more vigorous than the cheaper version completed about

---

102 21 M 57/B14/12.   103 Oral information from the Very Rev. Philip Knowles, dean of Cashel.   104 L.M. Cullen et al., *St Mary and St Michael parish church, New Ross, 1902–2002: a centenary history* (Dublin, 2001), p. 3.

1807, after Agar's – and Morrison's – translation to Dublin. ... The lower part of the tower, up to the pediment, was built according to this design, but the second stage of the tower and the steeple, completed in 1807, are different, perhaps following a modification devised by Morrison himself. Morrison reworked his original idea for the spire in his competition entry for St George's Church in Dublin in 1800. Stepping forward from the west front of the cathedral, the tower and spire with their superimposed geometrical forms derive from [James] Gibbs in concept. The pulvinated frieze of the body of the cathedral, which would have seemed old-fashioned by the 1790s, is omitted from the tower[105]

As completed, Cashel cathedral is a successful solution to the perennial problem of adding a steeple to a classical building.[106]

Oliver Grace's estimate of c.1779–80 comes to a total of £1515 1s. 11½d., and mostly relates to the cost of the roof, plasterwork, woodwork and furniture (excluding the organ). It would not be surprising if more in the end had to be spent: on the other hand, he would be a brave man who exceeded an estimate submitted to and agreed with Agar – and, plainly, Grace retained Agar's favour after the work on the cathedral was done. Agar's record of how it was financed is of great interest:

> The funds [for the new cathedral] were few and small. It was therefore impossible to adopt a plan of much ornament. Correct proportions, chasteness and simplicity of design, goodness of materials and neatness in execution, without any prouder objects, greatly exceeded all apparent means provided by public or private liberality for completing this building. The Archbishop's predecessor, Dr Michael Cox, left by his will £500 to his successor for this purpose, provided the successor should by bond oblige himself to *finish and complete* it. This proviso ... afforded little encouragement to his successor to accept his donation unless ... he was determined, independently of that consideration, to build the church. Dr Agar, being determined to do so, accepted the donation with gratitude ... . In addition to this sum, the Archbishop obtained from the board of first fruits £500, Richard Pennefather Esq. subscribed for himself and the corporation of Cashel £40, the Countess of Clanwilliam gave £50 without any solicitation and in a manner that rendered the donation doubly acceptable, the parish of Cashel raised £250 by cess as the condition on which the board of first fruits gave their aid, the clergy of the two dioceses of Cashel and Emly subscribed towards this pious work as much as their respective means would enable them, and the deficiencies (if any there were) the Archbishop thought himself bound to supply.[107]

---

105 McParland, Rowan and Rowan, *The Morrisons*, p. 54. **106** The story of the steeple, however, continues into very recent years. In 1995, Dean Knowles raised the remarkable sum of £120,000 for essential restoration work on the steeple and on stonework elsewhere. **107** 21 M 57/B6/1.

Assuming that Grace stuck to his estimate, and that 'the clergy of the two dioceses' did their bit, the 'deficiencies ... [which Agar] thought himself bound to supply' must have amounted to nothing (or to an absolute maximum of £165), plus the cost of the organ – a separate item which will be dealt with separately; so neither Bence-Jones nor Agar's funeral monument[108] is strictly speaking warranted in saying that Agar built the new cathedral 'largely' or 'principally' at his own expense. On the other hand, he did incur considerable risk and responsibility, and entail them on his family, by accepting the conditions of Cox's bequest of £500.

In addition to the £1,500–plus spent on completing the main block of the cathedral, Agar raised between 1789 and 1792 a further £466 towards the erecting of the steeple (and may have raised more by the time he left Cashel in 1801). This was made up of a subscription (voluntary or otherwise!) of £138 from the clergy of Cashel and Emly, £228 raised by parish cess and a donation of £100 from Agar himself.[109] The size of the 'steeple fund' invites the question: since Agar had got so far, why he did not finish the job? Colonel Chester, referring of course to the restoration of the old cathedral, considered (erroneously) that this could have been accomplished by the 'devotion to this purpose of a comparatively small portion of the immense fortune which he acquired ..., the loss of which he could scarcely have felt.' Agar's fortune was certainly 'immense' by the time of his death thirty years later. But it was built up gradually out of income and investment (see pp 426–8) and, particularly in relation to the other calls upon him which the run-down state of the diocese of Cashel made, was not 'immense' in the 1780s. Nor was the income of the archbishopric of Cashel in Agar's time at all commensurate with its seniority in the hierarchy (see p. 391). There is also the simple fact that cathedrals were then a luxury rather than a first priority. In 1830, Primate Beresford was warned by his right-hand man in the diocese of Armagh that Beresford's intended rebuilding of Armagh cathedral should be on a modest scale, so as 'not to excite envy at the wealth of "*the richest Church in the world*".'[110]

THE ECONOMICS OF CATHEDRAL RESTORATION, 1766–1809

This remark was made only semi-seriously. But the need to proceed warily with cathedral-building was emphasised, in all seriousness and with deep regret, in 1809, the year of Agar's death, by his friend and ally, John Foster (see pp 267–8). Foster lamented that, at a time when the board of first fruits had 'agreed to applications to the amount of £134,000 for glebes, glebe-houses and churches', all to be paid for out of money voted by parliament, it would still be imprudent for him

> to add an estimate of what sums would be necessary to erect or repair cathe-
> drals in every diocese in such a style of proper architectural ornament as is
> suited to the dignity and appearance which an Established Church requires,

108 Transcript of the inscription, Wyse-Jackson papers, Bolton Library, Cashel.   109 Notebook kept by Agar, 1780–1801, 21 M 57/B7/2.   110 Quoted in Akenson, *Church of Ireland*, p. 163.

and which has been so useful here in impressing the public with a respectful awe and reverence. ... This must wait till the more essential object of parochial churches is accomplished, and then I think we shall all concur in keeping the public purse open for that purpose.[111]

Irish cathedrals stood in need of help from the public purse because, as has been seen (p. 303), they were very poorly endowed. It was no coincidence that most of them 'were no larger than good-sized parish churches', because that was the basis on which their re-building or building was financed – by parish cess and, if the right conditions were fulfilled and if funds permitted, by grant from the board of first fruits. The £500 from the latter was the maximum payable in respect of a parish church so ruinous that divine service had not been celebrated in it for at least twenty years. Agar, with his insider's knowledge of the affairs of the board, would have known that there was an embarrassing under-spend on the parliamentary grant of £1,500 in the session of 1779–80, and that his application could not have been better timed.[112] The only extra resource which a cathedral could draw upon was a contribution from the diocese (in this case the dioceses of Cashel and Emly) of which it was the centre. As for the diocesan himself, he had no financial incentive to generosity: while expenditure on palaces was reimbursed, largely or entirely, to one bishop by his successor, expenditure on cathedrals – inconsistently and illogically – was not (see p. 187). The same distinction applied to glebe-houses and churches. So cathedral-building was an act of pure beneficence.

Why, then, did Agar not use his considerable powers of persuasion to raise the money by subscription among the laity: he did, after all, accept the £50 offered 'without any solicitation' by the countess of Clanwilliam. The answer may lie in the phrase 'without any solicitation.' The Church of Ireland, as Lord Hardwicke astutely observed in 1803, 'requires every support and encouragement, notwithstanding its supposed and apparent opulence.'[113] It was rich, but almost all its riches were ear-marked for its bishops and clergy in their individual capacities. Institutionally, it was poor. In particular, the so-called 'oeconomy' estates which had 'anciently' been pro-vided for the up-keep of cathedrals and their functionaries, had been 'so shamefully ... reduced' and even alienated in former centuries that they were almost all of them 'inadequate for the discharge of the uses for which they had originally been appro-priated.'[114] This was the opposite of the situation in the Church of England (a cir-cumstance likely to promote mutual misunderstanding). 'In England [and Wales], the episcopal revenues were comparatively small, whilst the capitular revenues were large' – £157,737 for the bishops and £284,141 for chapters or their individual members in the first half of the 1830s – 'but in Ireland these conditions were reversed, the four

---

111 Foster to O'Beirne, 12 Apr. 1809, Foster/Massereene papers, PRONI, D/207/50/37. 112 Account of the expenditure of the 1779–80 grant, PRONI, DIO 4/11/12/55. 113 Hardwicke to his half-brother, Hon. Charles Yorke (shortly to be appointed home secretary), 13 Aug. 1803, *The viceroy's post-bag*, p. 124. 114 Erck, *Ecclesiastical register*, p. xxxiv.

archbishops and eighteen bishops having a net revenue of £130,000, and the deans and chapters in their official and corporate capacities ... of little more than £2,000.' (The £2,000 does not include livings and other emoluments held by members of chapters as individuals.)[115] The perception of many of the laity of the Church of Ireland was, in the graphic words of Bishop O'Beirne in 1798, that 'the revenue set apart for our [the clergy's] support [w]as a robbery on the public.'[116] To set up a subscription among the laity for an ecclesiastical purpose was therefore only to invite comment on the size of the revenue already set apart for the support of the clergy. Agar, with his first-hand experience of fighting the battles of the clergy in the Irish parliament, is certainly likely to have taken that view.

The only remotely contemporary example of a general subscription to defray the cost of a cathedral is that got up by the 1st, 2nd and 3rd marquesses of Downshire to rebuild Down cathedral, Downpatrick, which raised some £5,000 between 1789 and 1792, and ultimately amounted to some £13,000 before the cathedral was finished in the early nineteenth century.[117] The considerable correspondence generated by this huge fund-raising effort, directed towards a larger and much more architecturally ambitious structure than Cashel cathedral, throws light on the latter project in a number of respects. For a start, Agar – though pressingly solicited – did not subscribe to Down cathedral. The 1st marquess of Downshire, as earl of Hillsborough, had been secretary of state for the southern department, 1779–82, and an ally of Agar's against Buckinghamshire (p. 150). He wrote to Agar in March 1792 referring flatteringly to 'the generous and becoming part your Grace has taken in the completion of the cathedral church of Cashel', mentioning that two bishops of Agar's province, Cloyne and Waterford, had subscribed £50 each without solicitation, and expressing confidence that Agar would not 'make me unhappy by refusal.'[118] Agar's answer does not survive. This is a major misfortune, because his grounds for refusal were probably revealing of his attitude to a subscription which went beyond the clergy of the diocese concerned. A number of other bishops replied excusing their refusal, or the paucity of their subscriptions, on the ground that charity began and ended within their own dioceses. John Law, bishop of Killala, stated that he had just given £50 towards mending the roof of Killala cathedral, which had no other support to look to than its dean, chapter and bishop; William Cecil Pery, bishop of Limerick, said that he had just spent £400 building a church in his own diocese and had other outstanding commitments there; and Charles Dodgson, bishop of Elphin, complained that he was frequently called upon to contribute 'towards the building of churches and steeples'

115 Mathieson, *English Church reform*, pp 76 and 111–12. See pp 214 and 392.   116 Quoted in Acheson, *Church of Ireland*, p. 106.   117 J. Frederick Rankin, *Down cathedral: the church of St Patrick of Down* (Belfast, 1997), pp 107–14. I am indebted to Mr Rankin for the figure of £13,000 (the best guess he can make) and for help in other respects.   118 Downshire to Agar, Mar. 1792, Downshire papers (incorporated in 1911 in the Down diocesan archive), Down County Museum, DB 505, Env. 4. Downshire's good relations with Agar are obvious from the letter, and are also referred to in Ellis to Agar, 2 Sep. 1784, T/3719/C/18/39. Agar's refusal may be inferred from Downshire to Bishop of Kildare, 3 May 1792, DB 505, Env. 4.

in Elphin.[119] Bishop Percy of Dromore and Bishop Bennet of Cloyne both stated the view that legislation should be passed empowering the board of first fruits to grant-aid the rebuilding of cathedrals; but Primate Robinson, characteristically and for once rightly cautious, did not 'wish to have the present restraints on the first fruits fund to be relaxed.'[120] Agar had not needed legislation to authorise grant-aid from the fund for Cashel cathedral. This was partly because Cashel cathedral (unusually for a cathedral) met the criterion that divine service had not been celebrated in it for at least twenty years, and partly because Agar had so trimmed the 'ornament' and 'design' that the standard grant of £500 was enough to make his new cathedral possible.

It has been regarded as a remarkable circumstance that the Down cathedral subscription was spearheaded by a layman. However, this is likely to have been the secret of its success. Lord Downshire was no ordinary layman. He was an exceptionally rich, if increasingly indebted, grandee. In the 1789–92 fund-raising phase, he individually subscribed £600 towards the building of the cathedral and pledged £300 more for the organ, and his son and heir subscribed 300 guineas.[121] As a former cabinet minister and a thick-and-thin supporter of Dublin Castle at the time of the Regency Crisis, Downshire had been able to secure a donation of £1,000 from George III, provided he obtained the equivalent from other subscribers. In his circular letter to potential subscribers, he stated that he was acting at the request of the dean and chapter of Down, and he skilfully added that the Dean had granted 'a generous deduction ... [of £300 per annum] to arise out of his deanery to constitute an oeconomy [i.e. a cathedral fund] during his incumbency and that of his successors.'[122] This latter gesture, which was indeed generous, helped to allay the scepticism of the laity, as did the identity of the Dean. He was the Hon. William Annesley, younger brother of the 1st Earl Annesley of Castlewellan, Co. Down (who subscribed 100 guineas), an ally of Downshire's in county politics. (William Annesley, incidentally, had been treasurer of Cashel in 1786, the year in which the Agar-donated organ was installed (see pp 318–23); so, Cashel cathedral may have provided some degree of inspiration for Down.)[123] Moreover, Downshire's political importance transcended county boundaries, for he was a great borough-owning magnate, with boroughs and/or estates in Cos Louth, Offaly, Westmeath and Wicklow as well as Down.

He was therefore well placed to solicit subscriptions from prominent laymen, as well as churchmen, all over Ireland. One such was Lord Earlsfort, now Lord Clonmell. Clonmell replied, with what can only be called extreme unction, hailing the Down cathedral project as 'a matter that so highly redounds to your magnificence and zeal for the splendour of the Church and the ornament of that part of the kingdom

119 Bishops of Killala, Limerick and Elphin to Downshire, 22, 12 and 26 Mar. 1792, ibid. 120 Bishop Percy to Downshire, 20 Feb. 1792, *ibid*. Percy later disgraced himself by subscribing only 20 guineas, which a bishop of Agar's province thought insufficient granted that Percy's diocese was in Co. Down – Bishop of Killaloe to Downshire, 20 Mar. 1792, ibid. Percy was notoriously mean – see p. 346*n* and 491. 121 Printed subscription list enclosed in Downshire's circular, [[pre-12 Mar.] 1792, ibid., and reproduced in facsimile in Rankin, *Down cathedral*, p. 109. 122 Downshire's circular, [pre-12] Mar. 1792, ibid., and printed in Rankin, *Down cathedral*, pp 107–8. 123 Cotton, *Fasti*, i. 63.

which owes so much of its civilisation to your exemplary residence and spirited exertions', and promising a 'minikin subscription.'[124] Clearly, if Agar had thought it appropriate to get up a subscription for Cashel among the laity, he would have been able to count on, or at any rate to blackmail, Clonmell. Clonmell owned no land in the north and a great deal in the diocese of Cashel; he also held land on bishops' leases;[125] and Agar had made Clonmell's nephew, John, a prebendary in 1786.[126] But, then, Clonmell was by no means a figure of the stature of Downshire – indeed, his heading a subscription list for any pious purpose would have raised a laugh – and Tipperary, unlike Down, was a county where 'the popish interest' was 'by much the most numerous.'[127] Even if it had been otherwise, Agar would almost certainly have rejected the idea of lay subscription on principle.

Significantly, he made no attempt to raise a lay subscription under the much more propitious circumstances attaching to the diocese of Dublin when he was archbishop of it between 1801 and 1809. Lord Downshire's circular had elicited informative, if not strictly relevant, comments on the sorry state of the two ancient cathedrals of Dublin, Christ Church and St Patrick's, in 1792. Bishop Welbore Ellis' then successor as dean of Christ Church, Bishop Jones of Kildare, wrote to Downshire in March:

> To support a repair and additional improvements, the chapter has engaged in a plan which, on an estimate, amounts to upwards of £7,000, and without other aid or support than the slender one directed to this purpose from its [the chapter's] annual oeconomy and the private benefactions of its members, we entered upon this work last year and have expended already upwards of £2,000. Here we pause, but ... we flatter ourselves that we shall be able to resume our work in the course of a year or two.[128]

The next bishop and dean gave a much less optimistic account of the situation in a letter written to Agar (as archbishop of Dublin) in 1806: 'The oeconomy of the dean and chapter of Christ Church is ... [by] a series of misfortunes and of wretched management ... reduced ... so low that it is not at present adequate to support the cathedral, to which purpose, indeed, it is not strictly applicable, but it is the duty of the chapter nevertheless to keep the church, if possible, from ruin.'[129] In 1792, Archbishop Fowler had likewise declined making any contribution to Down cathedral, in his case because of the state of St Patrick's:

> I should be very happy should a sum equal to ... [£2,047, the current amount of the subscription towards Down cathedral] be procured for my cathedral of

124 Downshire to Clonmell, Mar. 1792, DB 505, Env. 4; Clonmell to Downshire, 13 and 24 Mar. 1792, Downshire papers, PRONI, D/607/B/339 and 343. For other significant letters in the Downshire papers proper, see also D/607/B/342, 344–5, 348 and 368. 125 See pp 397–8. 126 Cotton, *Fasti*, i. 63; Clonmell (then Lord Earlsfort) to Agar, June 1787, 21 M 57/B23/12. 127 Agar to Orde, 11 Aug. 1787, T/3719/C/21/32. 128 Quoted in Rankin, *Down cathedral*, pp 110–11. 129 Bishop Charles Lindsay to Agar, 21 Jan. 1806, T/3719/C/40/3.

St Patrick; but although repeated applications have been made to different administrations, not a shilling has been granted to save it from destruction. The consequence therefore must be, that venerable fabric in a very few years, to the disgrace of the kingdom, will be an entire ruin. ... As I never had either estate or patronage in the very wealthy county of Down, and as my diocese wants every assistance I can give it, your Lordship must excuse me from complying with your request.[130]

This might be interpreted as just another excuse from Fowler, who was notoriously mercenary (see pp 413–15), for concentrating his resources on himself and his family. But a letter from the 2nd duke of Leinster, also in response to the Down cathedral appeal, confirms what Fowler said about the state of St Patrick's: 'I know that [if] something is not done soon ... St Patrick's ... will be down. Should a subscription be set on foot for that, I should think myself, as a knight of St Patrick, bound to pay something toward it.'[131] The duke's letter was prophetic, as the north transept of St Patrick's did fall down in 1794.

But the main significance of his letter is that it points out a way in which a subscription for the restoration of St Patrick's could have been started on a uniquely favourable basis – the basis of St Patrick's being the mother cathedral of the order of St Patrick, of which Fowler and Agar were *ex officio* chancellors as archbishops of Dublin. Agar, in particular, would have been well placed to set such a subscription on foot, because he was socially, personally and politically connected with many of the knights, who included – for example – his old cronies Ely and Shannon. George III, who had given a conditional £1,000 to the Down cathedral fund, was sovereign of the order of St Patrick, and could not have done less for that cathedral. Yet Agar took no initiative on behalf of St Patrick's, leaving matters in the hands of the 'amiable and excellent' James Verschoyle, dean from 1794 to 1810, who had made the restoration of the cathedral his 'favourite object' and 'anxious wish.'[132] It remained a 'wish' for want of more influential support. Thus, for the duration of Agar's time in Dublin, and indeed until the advent of another Lord Downshire, Sir Benjamin Lee Guinness, 1st Bt, in 1860, St Patrick's continued 'tottering to its fall, without an effort to restore it.'[133] On 25 September 1805 Lord Hardwicke visited St Patrick's and invited 'Mr Park [*sic*], the architect' (this was Edward Parke, architect to the Dublin Society and designer of the near-contemporary Royal College of Surgeons), 'to make a plan and estimate for building a cathedral on the same site and in the same style of architecture.' In the duke of Bedford's time as lord lieutenant (1806–7), it was estimated that £16,000 was needed to repair the existing structure, and four and a half times that sum to build a new cathedral on the site. When leaving office, Bedford stated – as politicians so

130 Fowler to Downshire, 12 Mar. 1792, Downshire papers, PRONI, D/607/B/338.   131 Leinster to Downshire, 20 June 1792, *ibid.*, 366.   132 J. Warburton, Rev. J. Whitelaw and Rev. Robert Walsh, *History of the city of Dublin from the earliest accounts to the present time* ... (2 vols., London, 1818), i, pp 484–8.

circumstanced are wont to do – that, had he remained, St Patrick's was one of the
things which would have engaged his most serious attention! On 2 March 1808, the
dean and chapter petitioned his successor, the duke of Richmond, 'representing to
him the decayed and dangerous state of the edifice.' Again, nothing happened.[134] In
all of these representations and negotiations, Agar's name is not mentioned. He was
not, when archbishop of Dublin, the fit, energetic and ambitious man he had been at
Cashel (see pp 251–2). Nevertheless, it is much more likely that his failure to seize the
fund-raising opportunities presented by St Patrick's was due to indisposition to lay
subscription, not to indisposition *per se*.

In Armagh, the newly promoted Primate Robinson had proceeded in the second
half of the 1760s on the same basis as Agar in Cashel in 1779–83 – that is, by drawing
exclusively on the resources of the cathedral dignitaries and himself.

> Robinson appropriated a considerable sum towards the task and ... this was
> further augmented by subscriptions from the dean and chapter. Stuart[135] says
> that the dean and each member of the chapter 'subscribed, we believe, £50,
> about the 28th of August 1766 ....' When ... Robinson had collected his funds,
> he began his improvements on the cathedral by slating the western aisle which
> had been previously shingled by Margetson [archbishop, 1663–78] ... [and
> fitting] the interior in a manner which he considered more suitable for divine
> service.

Following this 1760s building phase, Robinson in 1782–3 made a famous attempt to
erect a 100–foot tower 'in imitation of that of Magdalen College, Oxford', in place of
the existing one on the cathedral In spite of Thomas Cooley's best endeavours to
support the structure with strengthened internal arches and additional external
buttresses, Stuart records a panic among the local Anglicans

> that the entire fabric would tumble and bury the congregation in its ruins.
> Their fears spread and the church was in danger of being deserted. Primate
> Robinson then [1783] ordered the new tower to be pulled down, even to the
> roof of the building from whence it sprang, that is, to the very spot from which
> the old one, carrying its spire, cross and weather-cock had been removed. Thus
> ended the Magdalen steeple. In the year 1784, ... Cooley died and [the young,
> Armagh-born] Francis Johnston became architect to his Grace, and by his
> express directions made a plan as near as possible to that of the original steeple,
> with the exception of having two windows, on each side of the tower, instead
> of one. This plan, Mr Johnston put into execution by raising the tower on the
> old piers and arches, about 38 feet above the roof of the church to the top of
> the battlements with a spire of about 40 feet more.

133 Ibid.   134 William Monck Mason, *History of St Patrick's*, pp 463–4.   135 James Stuart, author
of *Historical memoirs of the city of Armagh for a period of 1373 years ...* (Newry, 1819).

'This' concludes Mohan ' is the best account of the final work done by Primate Robinson on the cathedral. The cathedral remained untouched until the primacy of Lord John George Beresford, who between the years 1834 and 1840 is estimated to have spent £34,463 18s. 7½d. on repairs (£24,000 of which was donated by the Primate himself).'[136] Even Robinson's last and least ambitious spire had eventually to be taken down.[137] It is a curious coincidence that Robinson, Hervey[138] and Agar were all three defeated by their cathedral spires, the first two because their spires had to come down, and the last because his never went up. In the diocese of Dublin, too, Archbishop Arthur Smyth offered in 1771 to donate £1,000 to the adding of a spire to Christ Church Cathedral, but architects advised that the walls would not bear the weight.[139]

THE CASHEL CATHEDRAL ORGAN AND CHOIR, 1783–1801

The example set by Robinson in respect of the organ and choir at Armagh was much more relevant to Agar's contribution to Cashel cathedral than to the very different task of construction which faced Agar. Immediately on his promotion to Armagh in 1765, Robinson had turned his attention to the long-neglected music of the cathedral.[140] Although the existing organ had been 'repaired twice in the 1750s', in other respects the music had been neglected since the death of Primate Lindsay in 1724. In particular, Primate Stone had compounded his own absenteeism by 'giving vicar choralships in Armagh to men resident in Dublin.' Robinson already owned 'a small, seven-stop, portable chest organ built ... in 1742' by John Snetzler (1710–85), a Swiss who had settled in London *c.*1740 and 'was very much the leading [organ] builder of the day.' Accordingly, in 1765, Robinson commissioned from Snetzler and presented to the cathedral 'a new organ possessed of many stops and of most pleasing and powerful tones.' The existing organ was retained, apparently for choir practice, and the new one installed in a loft or gallery (and subsequently moved about in the wake of Robinson's 'Magdalen tower' experiments). There already was one full-scale Snetzler organ in Ireland, in the Rotunda rooms, Dublin, and a couple more were to follow as a result of Robinson's trend-setting. But the late nineteenth-century architect and organ buff, Sir Thomas Drew, pronounced the Armagh instrument 'Snetzler's finest Irish organ.' It was removed at the time of the rebuilding of the cathedral in the 1830s, sold, and destroyed by fire in 1849.

Because Agar inherited a half-built and roofless cathedral at Cashel, he was not in a position to give the immediate priority to music which Robinson had done in

136 Mohan, 'Archbishop Richard Robinson', pp 107–8, quoting from Stuart, *Armagh*, pp 449–50, and from an unspecified issue of *The Newry Magazine*. 137 C.E.B. Brett, *Buildings of Co. Armagh* (Belfast, 1999), p. 47 and, for the cathedral in general, pp 47–50. 138 Peter Rankin, *Irish building ventures of the earl-bishop of Derry (1730–1803)* (Belfast, 1972), pp 9–10. 139 Kennedy, 'Dublin and Glendalough', p. 200. 140 The whole of this paragraph is taken from A.G. McCartney's admirable, recent study, *The organs and organists of the cathedral Church of St Patrick, Armagh, 1482–1998* (Armagh, 1999), pp 5–16.

Armagh. Indeed, in 1783, when Cashel cathedral was newly completed, Agar was as good as accused of dragging his feet! The rural dean reporting on the St John the Baptist union praised the work so far done on the cathedral, but pithily lamented that it had 'an organ loft and no organ; a Choir and no choir; a noble church and no steeple.'[141] (Agar's rural deans must have felt free to make remarks critical of Agar – a pleasing indication that he did not hold himself exempt from the processes of reformation and renovation which he had initiated at Cashel, and certainly not a freedom which Robinson would have permitted.) By 1801, however, as part of the valedictory statement which Agar compiled, he was able to record that 'a choir [had been] established, consisting of an organist, six singing men and six choristers, [and] a house and office built for the master of said choristers ..., in which the master for the time being and [the] six choristers reside.'[142]

In his much longer and more detailed 'state' of the diocese, he explained the intricate administrative background to his re-creation of the choir:

> He [Agar] did not forget that he was building a cathedral church in which divine service ought to have the usual assistance and embellishments of an organ and a choir of singing men and boys. ... By the ancient constitution of the cathedral, there were belonging to it five vicars choral, but it does not appear that these vicars did ever chaunt [*sic*] or sing the service, and for many years certainly their offices were considered as mere sinecure places and given to persons who not only did not understand church music, but were not even required to reside at the cathedral or officiate therein in any way. ... These five vicarages were in the gift of the dean and four dignitaries, ... [who] assured the Archbishop that they would accept his recommendation as soon as there should be vacancies in these offices. In a reasonable or indeed a short time, four of the five vicars died or resigned, the Archbishop having provided for two of them, and gentlemen perfectly qualified to execute the business of singing men were appointed to succeed them.
>
> An organist and singing boys were then to be provided, for which purpose funds were to be created, there being none appropriated to those ends in the constitution of the cathedral, and certainly there never was before in this cathedral an organ, organist or singing boys. But at some ancient period now unknown, some person bequeathed certain portions of land in and about the city of Cashel for the maintenance of a parish clerk, of which the present parish clerk (and perhaps his predecessors) made leases of 31 years, though himself liable to be removed at any time from his office. ... [Agar paid the then parish clerk 30 guineas to resign, compensated two of the tenants (one of them with 60 guineas) and re-let the lands at realistic rents.] After this, the amount of the parish clerk's lands and holdings was £48. 1s. 3d per annum, independent of ground on which the Archbishop built a house, which cost above £150,

141 Seymour, *Succession of clergy in Cashel and Emly*, p. 90.   142 21 M 57/B6/2.

adjoining the churchyard, which is appropriated to the vicar choral (at present Mr C. Sweeny) who has the care of the six choir children, and also of a piece of ground next to it, on which the Archbishop means to build another house, which he proposes to set to one of the vicars choral for an adequate rent, to go in aid of the general fund. ...

The dean and chapter of Emly liberally gave towards the support of the choir of Cashel out of their oeconomy £45 per annum, and the Archbishop having undertaken the management of the oeconomy of Cashel, which had always been set before his time at £15 per annum, has raised it to £120 or thereabout [*sic*] communibus annis. Out of these several funds, the organist, Mr [John] Matthews, is paid £40 yearly, and Mr C. Sweeny receives £84 for lodging, boarding, clothing and teaching six boys to sing and play upon the harpsichord at the rate £14 each boy, and [?Mr] Michael Owens is paid 12 shillings per annum for each boy for their instruction in reading, writing and arithmetic, besides the expense of paper, pens, etc.[143]

All this was characteristic of Agar's insistence – manifest, for example, in his Benefice Mortgage Bill (see pp 259–61) – that the Church must as far as possible live within its existing resources, maximising them where possible and reclaiming them where necessary. His re-creation of the Cashel cathedral choir was hugely costly in administrative effort. But he obtained no new resources for it, and paid what was needful out of his own pocket – at least £250, plus (no doubt) inducements to various people to resign or accommodate themselves to his plans, plus the cost of building the house to be let to one of the vicars choral.

The good effects were soon apparent. In her well-known *Retrospections ..., 1770–1806*, Dorothea Herbert, daughter of the compulsorily part-resident rector of Knockgraffon, recorded in 1784 that at Cashel 'there was a new Archbishop, a new and elegant cathedral and the first choir in the kingdom, appointed by the Archbishop (Doctor Agar) who was a great amateur and music-mad.' The Herbert family accordingly set off to hear a performance in the cathedral.

I had never heard any powerful music before – but the oratorios no sooner began than I felt myself quite overpowered ... and I found myself fainting away and just on the wing to heaven, as it were. I knew not what passed till I found ... a smelling bottle [held] to my nose, which the Archbishop's lady, Mrs Agar, had humanely handed over the pew. ... The Archbishop's throne was just over our pew. He noticed all that passed, and seemed delighted at the effect his music had on a novice. After service, Mrs Agar asked my mother if I was her daughter, declaring herself much pleased with my sensibility. 'Comfort ye my people', 'Every valley shall be exalted', and 'The trumpet shall sound' were the

143 Ibid. The figures in the last paragraph do not square with those in an archdiocesan account book, 1780–1801, kept by Agar (21 M 57/B7/2), which states that salaries in respect of the organist and choir totalled £875 over the period 1791–1801.

principal oratorios, and I do believe there was never a more capital performance, as the Archbishop spared no cost or pains on it.[144]

In 1787, Agar used his position as a member of 'the committee of fifteen' who ran the
Irish charter schools, to turn the Cashel charter school founded by Archbishop Price
into a nursery for the choir. At his request, it was ordered 'that the charter school of
Cashel should from henceforth be for boys only, and the school of Newport
[Co. Tipperary] for girls only, and that all the girls now in Cashel school be removed
to Newport, and all the boys in Newport removed to Cashel, ... which boys might, if
duly qualified, be instructed in music and introduced in the choir.'[145] (This is a good
example of Agar's policy of rationalising existing resources instead of incurring new
expenditure.) A visitor to Cashel in 1797, who attended 'divine service at the
cathedral ..., [was] highly delighted with the music. The singers are numerous and well
chosen, and under the fostering care of the present archbishop, the choir has risen to
a pitch of excellence well befitting a metropolis.'[146]

Agar also 'spared no cost or pains' to obtain a 'befitting' organ, though his account
of the steps he took is understated enough:

> There was no other difficulty than to supply the price of it and employ the best
> maker of the present time. This created no delay, and an organ which will
> probably do honour to the abilities of Mr William [*sic* – Samuel] Green of
> London as long as a pipe of it shall remain to bear testimony to his skill as an
> artist, was provided; and such was the honourable anxiety of Mr Green for his
> reputation that he came himself from London to put up his own organ, lest he
> should be deprived of any part of the praise which he expected justly to derive
> from this specimen of his skill and industry, by the negligence or misconduct
> of another artist.[147]

The unavoidable delay between 1779 and 1786 in obtaining an organ for Cashel had
deprived Agar of the possibility of commissioning Snetzler, who died in 1785 at the
age of seventy-five. But Samuel Green (1740–96), who had been building organs since
1768, was the Snetzler of the next generation. He had

> succeeded ... Snetzler as organ-builder to King George III, and thus was
> assured of widespread patronage from the Church and the nobility. His ideas
> influenced considerably the development of English organ design during the
> half-century following his death. Green is important historically because he
> may be described as the innovator of that trend in English organ history which
> sought to Romanticize the instrument, to modify it into a substitute for an
> orchestra or band and make it suitable for playing any music other than genuine
> organ music.[148]

144 *Retrospections*, pp 98–100.   145 Quoted in Kenneth Milne, *Irish charter schools*, p. 139.
146 George Holmes, *Sketches of some of the southern counties of Ireland collected during a tour in the
autumn of 1797* ... (London, 1801), p. 35.   147 21 M 57/B6/1.   148 David C. Wickens, *The*

The Cashel cathedral organ was Green's first Irish commission. (He later built an organ for TCD which he was working on at the time of his death in 1796.)[149] Agar's intermediary with Green was, not surprisingly, Welbore Ellis.[150] Ellis may have known him because of Green's work on the Winchester College organ in 1779–80.[151] But Green's position as organist to the king would have been sufficient in itself to bring him to Ellis' attention. Nevertheless, Ellis sought a second opinion, probably from the organist, Joah (or Josiah) Bates; this proved to be that Green was 'incomparably the best organ-builder in the kingdom.'[152] In mid-August 1784, Ellis wrote to Agar reporting that he had come to an arrangement with Green and providing the details.[153]

There was then an almost two-year delay on Green's part. In June 1786 he wrote to Agar apologising, but strongly implying that Cashel cathedral was rather small beer to him. He loftily explained that the delay was due to urgent orders for 'a very large organ' for a musical festival in Westminster Abbey, a new organ for St George's Chapel, Windsor, and the rebuilding of the chamber organ at the Queen's House (i.e. Buckingham House, later Buckingham Palace).[154] Green had built an organ for the Handel commemoration held in Westminster Abbey in 1784, but it was immediately moved to Canterbury cathedral, so it is presumed that Green had then to provide a replacement organ for the Handel commemoration of 1785. The two prestigious royal commissions, however, do not seem to have interfered unduly with Cashel, since neither was completed until 1790. Green regarded the St George's Chapel organ 'as his *chef d'oeuvre*. ... George III ... took a personal interest in it, appointing "a day to hear its powers" before it was officially inaugurated. Green ... admitted ... [that, because of it], he had "been obliged to lay by several other large orders".'[155] So Cashel did not fare too badly. Moreover, as Agar noted with admiration, Green showed an 'honourable anxiety' to install the Cashel organ in person. The total cost of Green's work was £536 (inclusive of case),[156] which freight and other expenses seem to have rounded up to roughly £600. This seems to have been at the lower end of Green's price-scale for church or chapel organs: the St George's Chapel organ cost £1,010 and Rochester cathedral (1791) 600 guineas, both without the case.[157] Green's detailed specification for the Cashel organ and the tricks and tropes of which it was capable, shows that it was typical of its time and, at seventeen stops over three manuals, would have been one of the larger in Ireland and would have been comparable to many English cathedral organs of the day.[158]

instruments of Samuel Green (London, 1987), p. 1. **149** Ibid., pp 156–7. **150** Agar's letters and papers about the organ, which were not known to Dr Wickens, will be found at 21 M 57/B12. **151** Wickens, *Samuel Green*, p. 116. **152** Third-person note from Mr Bates, Victualling Office, London, to Ellis, 16 July 1784, 21 M 57/B12/1. Perhaps this was a different 'Mr Bates'? **153** Ellis to Agar, 14 July 1784, 21 M 57/B12/3. **154** Green to Agar, 7 June 1786, 21 M 57/B12/4. Although the last-named organ ended up in Buckingham Palace years later, it looks as if it was not installed there in the first instance, but at Windsor. **155** Wickens, *Samuel Green*, pp 8, 120–21, 137–8 and 160. **156** Receipt from Green to Agar, 14 Oct. 1786, 21 M 57/B12/10. **157** Wickens, *Samuel Green*, pp 133–4. For other figures for the cost of organs, organists, choristers, etc., see Jonathan Barry, 'Cultural patronage and the Anglican crisis: Bristol, *c*.1689–1775', in Walsh, Taylor and Haydon (eds.), *The Church of England, c.1689–c.1833*, pp 206–7. **158** 21 M 57/B12/13; letter to Malcomson from

The new organ was first played in late September or early October 1786.[159] Responding to Agar's account of the inaugural concert, Ellis wrote (somewhat mysteriously): 'I really think that it was a fortunate disappointment of your organist, for I verily believe his place was better filled, both for the instrument and the audience, and I am confident that the success of the performance must have given you great pleasure. I am very glad that Mr Green has given you satisfaction.'[160] Does this mean that Green himself played at the inaugural concert? On 6 November, the inhabitants of Cashel presented an address of thanks to Agar for completing the cathedral and for his gift of this 'admirable organ, which must long remain a monument of your Grace's taste and liberality.'[161] Contemporary expert opinion soon confirmed the excellence of the Cashel instrument. In December 1786, the bibliophile and musicologist, the 7th Viscount Fitzwilliam of Merrion (later the founder of the Fitzwilliam Museum, Cambridge), wrote to Agar thanking him for his hospitality in Cashel to Fitzwilliam and a Mr Nicholls, and promising to send

> the volume of Mr [John] Keeble's *Voluntaries.* I shall not hesitate to recommend them to Mr [John] Matthew's [*sic* – Matthews', the organist] study and practice. He will find his account in both, and so would the most skilful professor. They would be found of great use, not only in voluntaries and thus calculated for the service of the church, but in the fugues, particularly, will display the powers of your Grace's organ, an instrument as complete as any I ever heard.[162]

More *Voluntaries* followed: an entry in one of Agar's account books under the date, 28 September 1788, runs: 'To a volume of Volantaries [*sic*] for the organ by Handel, Stanley and others, £1 1s. 8d.; binding, 2s. 8½d.'[163] In 1797, the Cashel organ was described as 'a fine new instrument, ... admirably performed on by Mr Mat[t]hews.'[164]

Church organs have a notoriously short life – at least in their original and unmodi- fied state. The Cashel organ lasted far longer than most. In 1873, after architectural devastation had fallen upon the cathedral as a whole (see p. 330), Samuel Green's instrument was moved 'from the gallery to the chancel, with little alteration to the stop-list. The unwanted case ..., a typical three-tower Renaissance design ..., orna- mented with festoons ..., was moved to Wicklow parish church. ... In 1913, the organ was reduced to two manuals [by Messrs Magahy of Cork] ... and the stop-list con-

A.G. McCartney and A.R. McLaughlin of the Pipe Organ Preservation Company of Ireland, 30 Aug. 2000. Messrs McCartney and McLaughlin are organ-builders as well as organists and scholars of the organ. I am very grateful to them for their expert advice. **159** Seymour, *Succession of clergy in Cashel and Emly*, p. 115. **160** Ellis to Agar, 29 Oct. 1786, T/3719/C/20/34. **161** 21 M 57/B8/56. **162** Fitzwilliam to Agar, 1 Dec. 1786, T/3719/C/20/35. Matthews was organist from 1786 to 1798. In February of the latter year, he took himself and his family off to Dublin, without leave or notice, and in breach of 'the orders for the regulation of the choir' – Rev. Patrick Hare to Agar, 22 Feb. 1798, T/3719/C/32/6. He was replaced by one Robert Linton – archdiocesan account book kept by Agar, 1780–1801, 21 M 57/B7/2. **163** 21 M 57/B7/1. **164** George Holmes, *Sketches of some of the southern counties*, p. 35.

siderably altered.' Later documentation of 1948 describes what was done in 1913: 'Woodworm having attacked the old soundboards, we rebuilt the organ, incorporating the old pipework. ... The old Green pipes were in very bad condition; a number had to be scrapped.'[165] It seems that further major alterations were made to the organ in the 1970s and again in the 1980s.[166]

These unwelcome developments lay far in the future. The last word about the situation in Agar's own day may be taken from the farewell address he received from the vicars choral of Cashel at the end of 1801:

> We lost upon the occasion a powerful patron and (we hope we are not arrogant) a *kind friend*. ... From your Grace we derive our establishment as a choir and the enjoyment of our incomes, which (after a just compromise) you reclaimed from the parties who possessed them as sinecures; for, when your Grace came to this diocese, you found a cathedral whose dome [actually, there never was a dome, and when Agar came, no roof!] had never resounded to the solemn peal of the organ, nor to the sublime anthems of the immortal Handel. But your Grace's piety restored the service to its ancient pomp, and your private generosity contributed liberally to defray the expense. As individuals we have to thank your Grace for your steady and constant assertion of our respective rights before the tribunal of public justice, and for your friendly counsel and assistance upon various occasions. Whilst kind to our merits and indulgent to our faults, we have at all times experienced from your Grace the politeness of the gentleman and the condescension of the peer.[167]

Long after his translation from Cashel, Agar continued to take an interest in the state of the cathedral's oeconomy fund.[168] He also corresponded in 1807 with one of the barons of the exchequer about a judgement of that court in relation to the leasing powers of the Cashel vicars choral, which ran counter to a legal opinion obtained by Agar in 1793, and which was bound to reduce the income from the vicars choral estate.[169] This was probably the 'assertion' of the vicars' choral 'rights before the tribunal of public justice' referred to in their address. In general, that document suggests that he had spent more on the cathedral choir out of 'private generosity' than is recorded in his own statements and accounts.

ARCHITECTURAL EMULATION BY THE CATHOLIC CHURCH IN
MUNSTER, 1782–96

Present-day Cashel has the agreeably incongruous feeling of a small Georgian cathedral city superimposed on a mediaeval ecclesiastical site. Although Cashel's

165 Wickens, *Samuel Green*, pp 102, 122–3 and 154.   **166** Rev. Barbara Fryday, *A tale of two cathedrals* (N.P., c.1975), pp 9–10.   **167** Address, *c*.Dec. 1801, T/3719/C/35/39.   **168** Timothy Sullivan to Agar, postmarked 23 Feb. 1805, T/3719/C/39/6.   **169** Baron Smith to Agar, 15 Jan.

growth and prosperity stultified under the dead, or rather the 'griping', hand of the
Pennefathers, some building went on in the last third of the eighteenth century. A
good example is the 'dignified houses with fanlights'[170] in John Street, an obviously-
genteel thoroughfare which leads at right angles up to the cathedral from the main
street, on the far side of the street from the palace. Some of these houses appear to
post-date Agar's time and to have been built – or, almost certainly, re-modelled – in
the *c.*1810s–1830s. But John Street looks as if it was up-graded under Agar's influence
to act as an appropriate approach to his new cathedral. The street-line itself is
probably mediaeval. It is narrow and crooked, and is not directly opposite the palace
gates; so its pre-existence made it impossible for the front door of the palace to be
aligned with the porch of the cathedral and for an elegant mall to be built leading from
the one to the other. In the absence of such a vista, the best to be had in the town of
Cashel is from the early fourteenth-century Hacket effigies, now set into the wall of
the cathedral close, over the house-tops and the (invisible) palace up to the Rock, with
Agar's cathedral on the right and the old cathedral straight ahead. The cathedral close
itself seems not to have been completed until long after the opening of the new
cathedral. A rural dean's report of 1785 describes the cathedral as surrounded by
'spacious, elegant walks adorned with antique statues in niches' (the Hacket effigies?);
but it would seem that the fine, cut-stone gate piers leading into the cathedral close
were not erected, or rather begun, until 1786. Samuel Cooper, Agar's agent and
diocesan registrar, must have been referring to them when he wrote to Agar from
Cashel in April of that year: 'I have not been able to get the stone-cutter to put up the
churchyard gate, but he will soon begin to lay the work.'[171]

   The walling of the close cannot have been finished until the mid-1790s, because
it was then that Agar used the wall to cut off a very narrow passage running at a right
angle to John Street. This is the only thoroughfare in Cashel which was called after
him; it is still called 'Agar's Lane.'[172] The purpose of this concession of ground was
to give access from the top of John Street to a new Roman catholic church, built in
1795, on a nearby site as elevated as that of the cathedral. The site was historic as well
as elevated; it had previously been occupied by a ruined thirteenth-century Francis-
can friary known, after its founder, Sir William Hacket, as 'Hacket's Abbey' (and the
original resting-place of the effigies). The ruins belonged to Joseph Damer, 1st earl
of Dorchester (1718–98), whose heir, George Damer, Viscount Milton (1746–1808),
was chief secretary to the Emancipationist Lord Fitzwilliam in 1794–5. Lord Dorchester readily granted a lease on moderate terms, and the remaining stones of the
old friary were incorporated in the new church.[173] The parish priest of Cashel, the
already-mentioned Dr Edmund Cormac (see p. 89), approached Agar in late

1807, T/3719/C/41/4–5.   **170** Bence-Jones, *Country Life*, 24 Aug. 1972.   **171** Seymour, op. cit.,
p. 90; Cooper to Agar, 16 Apr. 1786, 21 M 57/B10/15.   **172** I am indebted to Mr Martin O'Dwyer
of the Cashel folk village for drawing my attention to this.   **173** I am indebted for this information
to Mr David Butler. See also *An Irish antiquary: the sketches, notes and diaries of Austin Cooper
(1759–1830), ... edited by Liam Price* (Dublin, 1942), p. 34.

May 1794 asking him if a 'deputation of the catholics of this city' might wait upon him to solicit his 'interest and support towards building a chapel.' Agar replied that there was no need for a deputation to take the trouble of waiting upon him, and arranged for Dr Cormac to call on his own, when Agar would be happy to 'attend to any application he shall be pleased to make.' Agar presumably made a donation, because in early July Cormac asked for another meeting and in his usual ingratiating manner acknowledged 'the many favours already conferred on him.'[174] Actually, Agar was being generous in all senses over this Damer-abetted project. Politically and personally, he was at extreme variance with the Fitzwilliam (and Milton) administration, under which he was passed over for the primacy, and under which a Catholic Emancipation Bill was introduced which he was prominent in wrecking (see pp 517–20). At this particular juncture, an anti-Emancipationist churchman might have been expected to oppose the building of a catholic church in visible competition with his own Church of Ireland cathedral.

Although there had been almost no restriction on the building of catholic churches since the passing of the Catholic Relief Act of 1782 (except that steeples and bells were not formally legalised until 1829), it was not usual until the early nineteenth-century for catholic, or dissenting, churches in the south of Ireland to be built on prominent sites.[175] Exceptions were 'the magnificent new cathedral erected in Waterford, ... natural capital [of the Roman catholic diocese of Cashel], in 1792', and the 'major chapel' built in Cashel. These heralded the transition from 'the simple chapels or "mass-houses" ..., symbols of poverty and backwardness' and of the Penal Era, to the 'more grandiose chapels' whose construction marked 'the arrival of the Catholic Church as a potent force in the landscape.'[176] Against this background, it is significant that Agar helped instead of hindered the re-siting of the catholic church in Cashel and its transformation into a 'major chapel.' The attitude of his successor, Brodrick, another anti-Emancipationist but a much younger man, when confronted with a similar building-proposal a decade later, confirms the generosity of Agar's response. The proposal made to Brodrick related, obviously not to Cashel, but to his brother's town of Midleton, near Cloyne, where, as he related to Lord Midleton

> the Roman catholic priest and inhabitants of the parish... [had sought] liberty to build a chapel on the Rock of Midleton. ... I am very desirous that they should have decent edifices wherein to perform the duties of public worship,

---

174 Cormac to Agar, 28? May and 9 July 1794, and Agar to Cormac, 28? May 1784, T/3719/C/28/8–9 and 12. One of the letters of 28 May is misdated, since they cannot both have been written on the same day.   175 David Butler, 'The meeting-house of the protestant dissenter: a study of design, layout and location in southern Ireland [mainly Cork and South Tipperary]', in *Chimera: The UCC Geographical Journal*, no. 14 (1999), pp 118–24.   176 Kevin Whelan, *Catholic Church in Tipperary*, p. 227. The catholic cathedral in Waterford was supposed to be capable of seating between 3,000 and 4,000 people – Dean Butson of Waterford to Agar, 14 Apr. 1797, T/3719/C/31/36. Aidan O'Boyle has made the interesting point that it may not have been as prominent at the time it was built as it is today.

and every necessary accommodation and comfort. But ... I object strongly to bringing them forward to occupy the most conspicuous station ..., in the prospect ... of entering into rivalship with the Established Church. That this is the object with them, is obvious from the magnificence of the edifices which they are erecting in many parts of Ireland, and from their building steeples and putting up bells, very generally in the very teeth of the statutes.[177]

In the same year, 1804, a fellow of TCD wrote from his college living in Co. Cavan to Agar complaining at length about the local priest of his neighbourhood, who had presumed 'to build the walls of a popish chapel upon my glebe land, not only without my knowledge but against my consent. ... I now think it my duty to apprise your Grace, as visitor of the university of Dublin, of this extraordinary procedure, which is evidently designed to insult me, to injure the patronage of the college and trample upon the Established Church.'[178] Granted Agar's own record of forbearance and helpfulness in such matters, he is unlikely to have shared this dramatic view of the priest's designs.

Agar was also conspicuous for his neighbourly relations with his Roman catholic opposite numbers. The case of Dr Cormac has already been considered, and was not isolated. Two years after Cormac approached him about the new chapel in Cashel, in 1796, the catholics of Cloyne petitioned him 'for assistance to build a chapel at Cloyne ..., the chapel which they built when your Grace resided among them having fallen to the ground, [and] they ... [being] now under the necessity of attempting to build one (from the increased population of the parish) on so large a scale as will exceed their ability to finish, though honoured with liberal donations from many protestant noblemen and gentlemen.' In this case, though the scale of the church is again a significant development, what is even more interesting are the expressions of the petitioners' 'profound respect, esteem and gratitude to your Grace for your paternal kindness during a long residence among them, and the marked attention you pay every application made by any of them ever since their misfortune removed your Grace to a distance from them'[179] – an implied contrast, perhaps, to Agar's successor at Cloyne for most of these years, Brodrick's father-in-law, Bishop Woodward.

Agar was on particularly good terms with the aristocratic and conservative James Butler, catholic archbishop of Cashel and Emly, 1774–91 (and the third member of the

---

177 Brodrick to Midleton, 8 and 21 Oct. 1804, Midleton papers, Ms. 1248, vol. 18, ff. 102–4. The second letter shows that Lord Midleton agreed with his brother. In 1805, the new chapel in Tralee, Co. Kerry, was stated by the local catholic bishop to have cost over £3,000, 'though not near being finished' – Bishop Sughrue to Francis Moylan, bishop of Cork, printed in Evelyn Bolster (ed.), 'The Moylan correspondence in Bishop's House, Killarney, part 2', *Collectanea Hibernica*, no. 15 (1972), p. 72. This, surely, was more than any board of first fruits church of the period, except the over-ambitious Collon (see p. 282)? 178 Rev. William Hales to Agar, 15 Aug. 1804, T/3719/C/38/41, and on the same date to Stuart, who was the other visitor and also Hales' metropolitan, Stuart papers, WY 994/42. 179 Petition from William O'Flinn, M.D., and the catholics of Cloyne, 30 July 1796, T/3719/C/30/23.

catholic side of the Co. Kilkenny Butlers to hold that dignity in the eighteenth century).[180] Educated at St Omer, Butler was the spearhead of Gallicanism within the Irish catholic hierarchy, and was indifferent if not hostile to the survival of the regular clergy in Ireland. In 1776, he failed to block the promotion of the Ultramontane Dr Troy, himself a Dominican, to the catholic bishopric of Ossory, and from that point on Troy became Butler's increasingly influential rival. In February 1782, Butler listened sympathetically to an abortive plan of Agar's, with which Speaker Pery and Primate Robinson were also associated, to allow the king a limited veto over appointments to Irish catholic bishoprics[181] – possibly the first round in what was to culminate in the celebrated 'Veto Controversy' of 1808–13. At about the same time, Agar and Butler entered into negotiations over the second of Luke Gardiner's Catholic Relief Bills, the Education Bill. This provided, among other things, that catholic schoolmasters should be permitted to teach catholic schoolchildren under licence from the Church of Ireland diocesan. Agar had been 'clamorous' against the first version of the bill, 'evidently on the grounds that the bishops' superintending power over education was not sufficiently underlined.' But, after its defeat, he helped to draft the second version, which he supported in the Lords and which became law on 27 July. Following this, he showed his goodwill by promising Butler 'that he would license no schoolmaster who had not received "a certificate of approbation" from' Butler.[182] In April 1784, he presented to the House of Lords a measure proposed to him by Butler for making usurious interest illegal; he hoped that it would 'answer all your wishes and expectations', and thought that, with the assistance of Pery in the Commons, it would pass without amendment – which it did (*23 and 24 George III, cap. 55*).[183] This act may be described, without too much grandiloquence, as an inter-denominational reassertion of Christian values. Agar's friend, Scott, also went out of his way to demonstrate goodwill towards Butler: as attorney-general, he helped to protect him against the unpleasant consequences of a trumped-up charge of disloyalty brought against him in October 1780 by a parish priest with a grudge.[184]

This inter-denominational goodwill manifested itself at a more social and personal level; Butler visited the Cashel palace, and the Agars were invited to spend a day with him in his much humbler archiepiscopal residence at Thurles.[185] (In spite of Butler's personal wealth – in 1788, for example, it was reported, improbably, that he had inherited an estate of £7,000 per annum from his only brother, Robert Butler of Ballyragget, Co. Kilkenny[186] – he continued to live in the 'two-storeyed, thatched

---

180 Whelan, *Catholic Church in Tipperary*, pp 245–6. In his *Tour through Ireland in 1790* (p. 33), C.T. Bowden reports, somewhat improbably, that Archbishop Fowler of Dublin 'and Dr Troy, the titular archbishop, are ... constantly together [and] inseparable friends'. 181 Eamon O'Flaherty, 'Ecclesiastical politics and the dismantling of the Penal Laws in Ireland, 1774–82', in *IHS*, xxvi, no. 101 (May 1988), pp 34–7, 39–42, 44 and 46–9. 182 Wall, 'The making of Gardiner's Relief Act[s], 1781–2', in O'Brien (ed.), *Collected essays of Maureen Wall*, pp 44–5. 183 Agar to Butler, 23 Apr. 1784, printed in Very Rev. Dr Laurence F. Renehan, *Collections on Irish Church history ...* (Dublin, 1861), p. 345. 184 Renehan, *Collections*, pp 338–43. 185 Butler to Agar, 15 July 1781 and 1 Jan. 1785, T/3719/C/15/9 and C/19/2. 186 *The Gentleman's and London Magazine*, June 1788.

house on the site of the present archiepiscopal residence' which the previous Butler archbishop had built.)[187] The Agars were also in the habit 'of dining with your brother and Mrs Butler' at Ballyragget. Dr Renehan, the historian of the Irish catholic Church, comments that, 'in the midst of religious and political strife, we ... seldom meet with the least trace of such kindly intercourse between opposite parties.'[188] But Agar's good personal relations with Archbishop James Butler are not very surprising, granted their Kilkenny links and, more important, the fact that Agar's great-uncle, Philip Ellis, had been a catholic bishop.

Their good personal relations survived the 'Paper War' initiated in 1786 by Bishop Woodward's *Present state of the Church of Ireland*. Woodward, among other things, accused the catholic clergy in his pamphlet of 'sedition and disloyalty' and questioned the sincerity of catholics who took the oath of allegiance prescribed in an act of 1774 of which Butler had been the leading promoter among the catholic hierarchy.[189] Butler 'was so annoyed by this that, as well as preparing a refutation of the main allegations in Woodward's tract for publication ..., he also protested in person to ... Agar ..., who, he claimed, shared his unease. Evidently taken aback by this, Woodward quickly assured Butler that "no personal reflections were intended".'[190] By an amusing coincidence, Butler's ally, the leading catholic layman, Lord Kenmare, wrote of Butler at this time, in terms and tones remarkably similar to those later applied to Agar by Lord Clare (see pp 87 and 596): 'Our little friend, the Archbishop, has been indefatigable ..., [but] is assailed by a whole hive of pamphleteers.'[191]

Butler's successor was Thomas Bray, catholic archbishop of Cashel, 1792–1820. Bray had been parish priest of Cashel since before Agar's translation, and was the predecessor of Dr Cormac. So, Agar must have been well acquainted with him. However, Bray was in the Troy camp, and was discreetly active in the catholic agitation for the Catholic Relief Acts of 1792–3.[192] Another reason for Agar – and Brodrick – to have been on less easy terms with Bray than Agar had been with Butler was purely social. Bray was not an aristocrat or even a gentleman: he was the son of a wine merchant in the small town of Fethard, Co. Tipperary.[193] However, Bray's coadjutor (from 1814) and successor (in 1820) was a different story. He was the well-born Dr Patrick Everard, president of Maynooth, 1810–13, and Brodrick invited him to stay at the palace in 1811. Reporting on this visit, Brodrick declared enthusiastically:

> If his Reverend Brethren were all like him, you would probably never hear more of rebellion in Ireland, and this country might then offer a pattern which

187 Whelan, *Catholic Church in Tipperary*, p. 246.   188 Renchan, *Collections*, p. 345.   189 Fagan, *The oath for Irish catholics*, pp 146–54.   190 Kelly, 'The "Paper War" of 1786–8', pp 47 and 57–60. 191 Kenmare to Moylan, 23 Feb. 1787, printed in Bolster (ed.), 'The Moylan correspondence ...', part 1', *Collectanea Hibernica*, no. 14 (1971), p. 93. Butler's 'work' was *A justification of the tenets of the Roman catholic religion* (Dublin, 1787). For Butler's politics, see also his address to Lord Westmorland on behalf of the catholics of Cashel and Emly in 1790, 21 M 57/B13/11–12. 192 Bray to Moylan, 26 Dec. 1792 and 27 Apr. 1793, ibid., pp 113–15; Troy to Bray, 16 Mar. and 9 Apr. 1793, Dublin diocesan archives, Troy correspondence, 116/5/133–4.   193 Whelan, *Catholic*

England itself would not be ashamed to imitate. He has resided a long time in France and Spain [Bordeaux and Salamanca respectively], in the former of which he held high ecclesiastical offices. He emigrated with the rest of the clergy, and with great difficulty made his escape. ... I do not feel a necessity even to bolt my bedroom door at night; the Doctor has given me no reason to apprehend that in leaving the house he will make a bonfire of the palace of an heretical archbishop.[194]

Everard died in 1821, the year following his succession to Bray and the year before Brodrick himself died.

AGAR'S CASHEL AND ROBINSON'S ARMAGH, *c.*1770–*c.*1820

All told, Agar must have spent at least £1,000 on Cashel cathedral, plus whatever he spent shoring up the cathedral on the Rock and contributed to the cost of the new cathedral close, plus his donation of £100 to the un-built (in his day) spire, plus the £100 he spent on the cathedral at Emly. This was a significant sum for a younger son with four young children, and gives the lie to the charge of avarice frequently levelled at him (for example, the 'love of lucre' imputed to him by Watty Cox). The money, however, was as naught compared to the administrative labour required of, and lovingly detailed by, Agar. This in itself demonstrates how far from leisured was the life of an improving bishop of the late eighteenth century (see pp 187–97). Agar would have been pleased with two tributes paid to his cathedral in the same year, 1797, but independently of each other. 'One visitor ... thought it "a new, plain, but very well furnished building internally" and "the music and singing delightful". Another ... thought it was "a magnificent structure of Grecian architecture; yet, notwithstanding its beauty and freshness, I cannot reflect on the venerable Rock, without commiserating in its forlorn and neglected situation." '[195] Agar would have joined in that commiseration. But, clearly, he regarded the new cathedral as his single, most important achievement – and rightly so because, as Dr McParland observes, it vies with John Roberts' Church of Ireland and Roman catholic cathedrals in Waterford for the palm of the finest eighteenth-century cathedral in Ireland.[196] The comparison with the almost exactly contemporary Church of Ireland cathedral in Waterford is particularly flattering to Cashel because Waterford, while it did not cost the £13,000 which Down eventually did, cost the very sizeable sum of £5,397.[197] But for Agar's

Church in Tipperary, pp 243–4.   **194** Brodrick to Midleton, 18 July 1811, Ms. 1248, vol. 19, f. 67. **195** Galloway, *The cathedrals of Ireland*, p. 39, quoting from Michael Quane (ed.), 'Tour in Ireland by John Harden in 1797' in *C.H.A.J.*, lviii, no. 187 (1953), p. 30, and from George Holmes, *Sketches of some of the southern counties*, p. 21.   **196** McParland, *Gandon*, p. 146.   **197** Lewis, *Topographical dictionary*, ii. 690. In Waterford, one of the moving spirits was Cutts Harman of Newcastle, Ballymahon, Co. Longford, dean of Waterford, 1759–84. Dean Harman, a rich country gentleman, donated the Waterford cathedral organ and was an amateur architect of distinction.

tight control over both design and budget and his emphasis on a 'sober cast of architecture',[198] Cashel would have got no cathedral at all. His funeral monument in Westminster Abbey (pp 185–6) depicts him at about the age he was when translated to Cashel in 1779, with his nose borne proudly as a mark of distinction, not obliquely as a disfigurement, and with his right hand resting on a plinth on which is depicted a representation of the porch, tower and spire of the cathedral. Close inspection of this monument reveals, interestingly, that the steeple is not that designed for him by Morrison in 1791, but that erected to the inferior design after Agar's departure from Cashel. The monument dates from 1815. But it is incredible that the design for it or, at least the broad outline, was not Agar's idea and a reflection of what he thought was the highpoint of his career.

Alas, the cathedral itself proved a less durable monument. Agar's successor, Charles Brodrick, at some point between 1802 and 1814 made unspecified 'improvements in the church' in Cashel (which, from the context, must mean the cathedral). Some further, minor improvements were recommended to him in January 1815: 'the communion rails were of the commonest kind and not at all corresponding with the other works of the church. ... The Gloria should have been placed as if descending instead of ascending. ... The flooring of the aisles and matting the centre part of them would be of use.'[199] Draconian alterations followed in the second half of the nineteenth century. 'The interior was entirely remodelled in 1867',[200] at the instigation of J.C. MacDonnell, dean of Cashel, 1862–73.

> During Dean MacDonnell's reorganisation, most of the eighteenth-century interior ... [was swept away], including the carved stalls [for the vicars choral] which lined the nave, the |carved and| canopied pulpit ['one of the church's glories'[201]] and the box pews ... . The body of the cathedral ... [had originally been] arranged in the style of a Choir with return stalls for the dean and chapter below the front of the west gallery; the rest of the area forming the narthex. These... eighteenth-century chapter stalls, ... [in] classical style, [with] Ionic columns divid[ing] the seats, ... [were left at] the west end of the nave ... [in 1867], when a bishop's throne and new stalls of pine were erected in the chancel. Cashel therefore enjoys the distinction of being a cathedral church with two sets of chapter stalls. ... The walls [of the interior now] have painted wooden panelling, and the nave ceiling is also panelled in pine, the panels being laid in a chevron pattern; in fact the ceiling resembles a parquet floor. ... The two-bay chancel has Romanesque arches resting on marble piers, and a polychromatic tiled floor. The ceiling has stencilled decoration. ... The work was a disaster.[202]

198 Bowden, *Tour through Ireland in 1790*, p. 155.   199 William Welland to Brodrick, 21 Jan. 1815, NLI, Ms. 8871/18. For the significance of Welland, see pp 370–76.   200 Bence-Jones, *Country Life*, 24 Aug. 1972.   201 Charles Wolfe, dean of Cashel, *Cashel, its cathedral and library* [c.1965], Irish Architectural Archive (hereafter IAA), Cashel press cuttings file.   202 Galloway, *The cathedrals of Ireland*, p. 39.

It is ironical, after Agar's Georgianising of the Gothic cathedral at Cloyne, that his Georgian cathedral at Cashel should later have been Romanesqued.

This chapter began with some comparisons between Agar's Cashel and Robinson's Armagh, and will end on the same theme. Whereas Agar's building initiatives have received little and mostly hostile notice, Robinson's have had a good press, particularly among Armagh-based writers.[203] More general histories have also, on the whole, been kind to him.

> The primacy [writes Chart] gave him an opportunity to indulge in the princely benefactions in which he delighted. It is no exaggeration to say that he transformed his primatial city of Armagh, which had since the middle ages been a byword for its poverty, barbarism and ignorance. ... It became a city of stone dwellings, its many hills crowned with stately public buildings. Robinson ... inserted in leases of see property a condition requiring that any building erected should be of a substantial type. ... [He] was a bachelor and devoted his savings to his projects. He repaired and, in the view of that time, embellished his cathedral, ... but with little sympathy for its original characteristics.[204] Most unfortunately, he removed the [*c.* 1613–25?] tracery of the west windows and replaced it by a commonplace, modern window opening. ... [He] built beside it houses for its officers reproducing something of that effect of seclusion and peace which their closes give to some English cathedrals. He was the chief mover in the erection of a public infirmary and barracks [1773–4]. He built and endowed a public school [1774], an excellent library [1771] (containing even now the finest collection of manuscripts and rare books to be found in Ireland outside Dublin), and somewhat of a novelty in the country, an observatory [1789–91]. It was his ambition, never realised, to make Armagh the centre of a university for the north of Ireland, and certainly he had provided beforehand several of the institutions that it would have required.[205]

Constantia Maxwell echoes these sentiments (minus the criticism of Robinson's lack of respect for earlier architecture). But she adds that he was ostentatious and over-fond of veneration.[206]

The verdicts of most of Robinson's contemporaries and near-contemporaries on his buildings and improvements were also favourable, some to the point of adulation.

203 Mohan and Simms, ops. cit.; Stuart, *Armagh*, pp 444–57. 204 Mohan, op. cit., pp 99–100, quotes from Edward Rogers, deputy-keeper of the Robinson Library in Armagh, 1838–94, who in his *Topographical sketches of Armagh and Tyrone* (Armagh, 1874), lamented that 'the liberality and munificence of Primate Robinson was not guided by good taste or by any respect for the ancient remains of the country to which he had been removed. When bishop of Ferns, he had part of the venerable old cathedral pulled down in order to build the walls of the churchyard, and he surrounded the walls of the ancient abbey of Armagh with the farm offices [for his new palace].' In these instances, Robinson compares unfavourably with Agar in Cashel, though perhaps not with Agar in Cloyne. 205 Phillips, *Church of Ireland*, iii, pp 244–5 and 277. 206 *Country and town*, pp 335–6.

Lord Hillsborough, who later, as 1st marquess of Downshire, initiated the re-building of Down cathedral, expressed the view at the beginning of 1777 that Robinson had already 'effected more for the civilisation and improvement of Ireland than any ten men for these hundred years' and was a man of 'most distinguished and remarkable merits.'[207] John Hotham, who had been invited to Armagh by Robinson when still only a viceregal chaplain and taken into the latter's confidence, was more back-handed in his praise. Writing to his elder brother in England, Hotham pointed out that Robinson could well afford to be generous, and that his generosity was more than tinged with vanity:

> I must insist (if you please) on finishing my career with the primacy, the income being only between £8,000 and £9,000 per annum at present. I am just [October 1778] returned from Armagh, which is indeed a magnificent thing, and will be more and more so every year. ... The Primate is going to England, and after he has used the Bath waters awhile, means to pass most of the winter in London. As soon as you meet him there, 'if you value your life, this remember to do': take your watch in your hand and flatter him in my name by the hour about his creations at Armagh, his munificence, magnificence, noble public-spiritedness, foresight, taste, wisdom and astonishing success as to improvements, in so short a term of years. You may safely do so, for he really deserves it all; and as it is his hobby-horse, he will bite like any gudgeon. I am not holding him cheap in what I say, for upon my honour I think him by very far the greatest man in this country, though he does not like women so well as you and I have formerly done.[208]

Ironically, in view of these comments, Stuart described Robinson as 'inaccessible to flatterers.'[209] Two years before Hotham's letter, an arch-flatterer of Robinson's 'creations at Armagh', Arthur Young, had written his famous account of them, which was soon to be published. Entertained and patronised by the Primate (who was careful to subscribe for three copies of Young's forthcoming book), Young bit 'like any gudgeon.' Thus was born, among other things, the legend that, before the coming of Robinson, Armagh consisted of 'a nest of mud cabins' (a favourite term of Young's), and that, following the coming of Robinson, it was 'rising out of its ruins into a large and prosperous city.'[210] In reality, Armagh in 1765 consisted of at least as many 'decent houses' as Cashel before Agar's time, and was a substantial and reasonably well built, if 'straggling', town.[211]

207 Hillsborough to the newly arrived lord lieutenant, Buckinghamshire, 20 Jan. 1777, *HMC Lothian Mss.*, p. 298. It may have been on the advice of Robinson that Hillsborough commissioned a Snetzler organ for Hillsborough parish church, Co. Down.   208 Hotham to Hotham Thompson, 19 Oct. 1778, T/3429/2/3.   209 Stuart, *Armagh*, p. 453.   210 Young, *A tour in Ireland* ... (London, 1780), subscription list and pp 103–4. The subscription list is highly significant, and is a unique feature of this London first edition.   211 For a more detailed discussion of Armagh pre-Robinson, see Malcomson, 'Primate Robinson (1709–94): "a very tough incumbent in fine preservation" ' (in preparation).

In two other respects, too, Robinson's personal role in the development of his archiepiscopal capital has been over-emphasised. First, though he encouraged the building boom in Armagh which began soon after he became primate, the boom was based broadly on economic prosperity (the fact that the city had the biggest brown linen market in Ulster in the period *c.*1770–*c.*1820), not narrowly on Robinson's patronage.[212] Cashel, by contrast, experienced no wave of economic prosperity to diffuse more widely Agar's architectural example. Second, Robinson controlled the Armagh corporation and its revenues and was the ground landlord of Armagh; this placed him – in comparison to other bishops and indeed lay landlords – in an unusual and very favourable position of local monopoly. Agar, for one, did not occupy the same position in Cashel, and so was powerless to counteract the Pennefathers' selfish engrossing of corporation resources. In short, Armagh and Cashel were as different in their economic situations as were Robinson and Agar in their personal and financial circumstances. The most which could be said for Cashel (even in its Agarite heyday in 1797) was that it was conspicuous for 'neatness and cleanliness' and 'an apparent ease and comfort in the inhabitants, ... notwithstanding little or no appearance of trade.'[213] In 1834, on the eve of the transfer of the archiepiscopal residence to Waterford City, Cashel was still 'rather a pretty town', with a 'wide and well built ... principal street ...; but the place is far from being in a flourishing condition. It was formerly a place of much resort and consequent prosperity, but it is now almost entirely an absentee town. ... The population ... is at present about 7,000, and the number of protestant communicants about 150.'[214] Cashel depended 'for its apparent ease and comfort' on its two archbishops of the period 1779–1822, Agar and Brodrick, whereas Armagh did not even falter when its greatest archiepiscopal patron died in 1794. To the city and diocese of Cashel, Agar single-handedly left – and in part paid for out of his own resources – a significant architectural and musical inheritance. If his buildings were 'simple', 'elegant' and architecturally 'sober', then much the same can be said of Robinson's, notwithstanding the latter's greater resources and opportunities. Robinson, in Dr McParland's deflating assessment, 'provided buildings for the practical purpose of worship. [He] neither invoked ([n]or was alert to) the symbolical value of great architecture ..., [and] frustrated Thomass Cooley's great potential by feeding him fat commissions for dull buildings.'[215]

---

212 I am indebted for this point to Professor B.M.S. Campbell.   213 George Holmes, *Sketches of some of the southern Counties*, p. 16.   214 Henry D. Inglis, *Ireland in 1834 ...* (second ed., 2 vols., London, 1835), i, pp 110–12.   215 McParland, *Public architecture*, p. 49.

8

The Cashel and other palaces, 1728–1833

When he was made archbishop of Cashel in 1779, Agar became responsible for two architectural treasures. The first, the cathedral on the Rock, was by then widely recognised as a venerable ancient monument: the second, the archbishop's palace, was in danger of being regarded as merely old-fashioned. Agar's first impression of it was as follows: 'The present palace of Cashel appears to have been built by Archbishop Theo[philus] Bolton ... . [It] certainly had undergone no alterations, and probably received but few repairs, from the time it was built [until 1779] ...; and, as the house is wainscotted [i.e. panelled] throughout the parlour and bedchamber stories, and much of the former had been originally painted of a dark brown colour, it made at this time but a dismal appearance.'[1] The palace, to judge simply from its present appearance, looks as if it was 'modernised', particularly on the inside, at some time or in stages between c.1780 and c.1820. Agar's part in this process has not hitherto been precisely defined. But it has been assumed that, because he was a man of taste, fashion and ambition, he must have made extensive changes or, alternatively, that he was forced to make extensive changes following damage allegedly done to the building by a militia regiment quartered in it during the '98 Rebellion. The Cashel palace is one of the most important pieces of domestic architecture in Ireland; so it is an end in itself to establish the whens and wherefores of its building history. It is also important, in a book based round Agar, to try to define his personal contribution to that history – did he, for example, wilfully impose late eighteenth-century notions of taste on an earlier building conceived in an idiom of its own day? Finally, it is important to set the Cashel palace in the context of eighteenth- and early nineteenth-century palace building, altering and demolishing. Such things were regulated by an over-complex legislative code which governed 'improvements' and 'dilapidations' to all forms of clerical residence, and which was the cause of a good deal of friction, and therefore of disunity and inefficiency, in the upper reaches of the Church of Ireland.

PEARCE'S PALACE, 1728–44

Sir Edward Lovett Pearce (1699?–1733), the short-lived apostle of Palladianism in Ireland, architect of the new Parliament House, 1729–39, and surveyor-general of

1 21 M 57/B6/1.

buildings, 1731–3, designed the Cashel Palace. This last fact, along with the facts about some other of Pearce's generally undocumented Irish commissions, re-emerged only in 1964, with the publication of a series of drawings by Pearce and his uncle and mentor, Sir John Vanbrugh, which had turned up in the library of the descendant of one of Pearce's principal Irish patrons.[2] Pearce's accepted design for the palace is reproduced in this book to a scale which makes the detail impossible to read.[3] But, actual-size, photostat copies of both the rejected and the accepted designs are on display in the palace (which, since 1962, has been a hotel). They are festooned with comments and measurements in Pearce's crabbed and intractable hand.

Although the identity of the architect had long been submerged, much was still known about the palace – for example, that it was completed in or by 1732. In that year, John Loveday described it as a 'large and handsome new house ..., not built in the same place as the old palace.'[4] From the early twentieth century, its architectural importance (though not yet its architect) was recognised, and it was one of the select band of buildings outside Dublin to be extolled in publications inspired by the newly founded Irish Georgian Society:

> [The palace] ... is a large, two-storeyed house, with dormer windows, built of red brick with limestone dressings, and situated in its own grounds on the edge of the town. It has a spacious hall, panelled in red pine, with an entablature supported by Corinthian columns of carved wood. To the right of the hall is the library [*sic* – it was the dining room until *c.*1780, and in the eighteenth-century was never a library], an almost square room devoid of decoration. Behind it, approached from another door in the hall, lies the grand staircase, of red pine, following the early Georgian type, with twisted balusters and ramps at the newel posts, which are treated as Corinthian columns. Note particularly the graceful detail of the *fascia*, in style reminding us of Santry Court [Co. Dublin], Saunders Grove [Co. Wicklow] and Mount Ievers [Co. Clare].[5]

Writing in more recent times (1972), but continuing in the same vein, Bence-Jones describes the palace as

> of rose-coloured brick with stone facings ..., the lower-storey windows ... firmly set on a string course above the plinth, the bases of those above being likewise tied together. ... Pearce produced designs for a house of either two or three storeys over a basement. ... In the event, it was the two-storeyed version which was carried out, with attic rooms lit by dormers in the high-pitched roof.

2 Howard Colvin and Maurice Craig (eds.), *Architectural drawings in the library at Elton Hall* [*Peterborough*] *by Sir John Vanbrugh and Sir Edward Lovett Pearce* (Oxford, 1964), *passim*. The drawings were acquired by the Victoria and Albert Museum, London, in 1992.   3 Colvin and Craig, *Elton Hall drawings*, no. 172 and plate lxvi.   4 I am indebted for this reference to Dr Edward McParland. The 'old palace' was at Camus, about two miles from Cashel, according to Rev. John Gleeson, *Cashel of the kings ...* (Dublin, 1927), p. 283.   5 Sadleir and Dickinson, *Georgian mansions*, pp 36 and 41.

... The hall is a noble room, with a screen of fluted Corinthian columns and
pilasters ... . The carving of the capitals is of splendid quality, but surpassed as
an example of the woodcarver's art by the staircase, which is approached
through a door to the right of the hall. ... Colvin and ... Craig suggest that the
latter may have been inspired by the Maison Carrée at Nimes, which Pearce
drew in 1723.[6]

These twentieth-century descriptions require modification in two respects. First,
the palace is not made of brick, but of coursed rubble (incorporating some remains of
mediaeval masonry). This stone is at present visible on the garden front, where it
contrasts insufficiently with the dressed ashlar mouldings round the windows and
elsewhere, and also with the rougher stone of the basement. Originally, however, the
coursed rubble may have been rendered,[7] as the two sides of the house are at the
present time. (This is the likliest interpretation of an ambiguous reference to the matter made in a letter[8] to Agar from Lady Somerton.) Brick appears only on the entrance
front, and is skin-deep, not structural. It was used by Pearce for the striking effect of
its colour-contrast with the dressed ashlar. It is inherently unlikely that a *c.*1730
structure in Cashel would have been built of brick, since limestone is the indigenous
building-material of the area and the common denominator between Cormac's chapel
and Pearce's palace.[9] The second respect in which the twentieth-century descriptions
require modification is the matter of the prominent dormers. They do not appear in
either of Pearce's alternative designs, and their attribution to him is based, plausibly
enough, on stylistic grounds only. As will be shown on pp 271–2, there is fairly strong
documentary evidence to suggest that the dormers are a harmonious afterthought
dating from seventy years after Pearce and two years after Agar.

A long-established tradition, accepted by Agar, associates the decision to build a
new palace and the commissioning of Pearce with Archbishop Bolton, who was
translated to Cashel in 1730: 'The presence of a first edition of *Palladio* [printed in
Venice in 1616] in the Cashel library poses the question ... whether Bolton – assuming
the book was his and not a later archbishop's – was versed in the current English
architectural fashions before embarking on the palace and chose Pearce for this reason,
or whether it was through Pearce that he became interested in *Palladio*.'[10] However, an
account presented to Bolton, presumably on his translation in 1730, and endorsed by
him 'relating to the buildings at Cashel', seems to show that the palace was begun in
October 1728, when Bolton's fleeting predecessor, Timothy Godwin, was arch-

6 Bence-Jones, *Country Life*, 31 Aug. 1972.   7 The earliest photograph of the garden front seems
to be one of 1880–1900, which does not show how the coursed rubble was treated, because that side
of the house was then smothered in ivy – National Photographic Archive, Dublin, Lawrence, Cab
7964 (fig. 16). I am grateful to Ms Grainne MacLochlainn for drawing this photograph to my
attention.   8 Of 15 Oct. 1796, T/3719/C/30/35.   9 I am indebted for these observations to
Professor B.M.S. Campbell.   10 Bence-Jones, *Country Life*, 31 Aug. 1972. The book is dated 1616
and is lavishly illustrated with woodcuts.

1 Thomas Burgh's Dublin custom house of 1704–7: detail of the illustration in Walter Harris's *The history and antiquities of the city of Dublin* (Dublin, 1766). Photograph: Dr James Kelly.　2 Welbore Ellis, 1st Lord Mendip: mezzotint after the portrait by Gainsborough painted in 1763 and later presented by Ellis to Christ Church (author's collection).　3 Bust of James Agar, 1st Viscount Clifden, by Edward Smyth, 1789?, in Leighlin cathedral, Co. Carlow (photograph: Mr P.L. Cavan).　4 Engraving of Henry Welbore, 2nd Viscount Clifden and 2nd Lord Mendip, from a portrait of *c.*1815 (author's collection).

THE RIGHT HONORABLE
GEORGE MACARTNEY
LORD MACARTNEY
OF LISSANOURE
1787

5 George Macartney, Earl Macartney, painted for Archbishop and Mrs Agar by Gilbert
Stuart in 1787, and now in the collection at Somerley. It is reproduced by kind
permission of the earl of Normanton.

6 John Scott, 1st earl of Clonmell, painted for Agar by Gilbert Stuart in 1790
(courtesy of Lord Normanton).

7 Hugh Carleton, Viscount Carleton, by Stuart, *c.*1790 (courtesy of Lord Normanton).

8 Mrs Agar by Stuart, *c.* 1790 (courtesy of Lord Normanton).

9 Agar, after Stuart, *c.*1790: mezzotint by William Say, 1803 (author's collection). The original is at Somerley, but was over-mounted into an oval, *c.*1870s?, to fit it into a marble over-mantel in the library.

10 Agar's daughter, Frances?, *c.*1798?, possibly by Frederick Prussia Plowman
(courtesy of Lord Normanton).

11 Agar's unmarried sister, Diana?, *c.*1790?, possibly by Hoppner
(courtesy of Lord Normanton).

12 Ellis Agar, countess of Brandon, by Philip Hussey, 1758?
(courtesy of the Knight of Glin).

The South Prospect of the Cathedral Church of St Patrick and the Rock in Cashell.

13 'Copperplate' of the cathedral on the Rock of Cashel, after a drawing by Jonas Blaymires, 1739 (see p. 304), reproduced by courtesy of NLI (prints and single drawings, 1757TC).   14 Engraving of the cathedral on the Rock after a drawing by Anthony Chearnley, *c.*1740 (see p. 304); NLI, 1658TA.

15 Sketch by 'R. Gibbs', 1813, of Gowran Castle as it looked after its re-modelling or
rebuilding of c.1715 (courtesy of the Knight of Glin and the Irish Architectural Archive).
16 Lawrence photograph of the garden front of the Cashel palace, 1880–1900
(National Photographic Archive, Dublin, Lawrence, Cab. 7964).

17 Agar's funeral monument in
Westminster Abbey, by John Bacon
junior, 1815 (photographs: the Very
Rev. Philip Knowles, dean of Cashel).

18 Archbishop Charles Brodrick by Hugh Douglas Hamilton, possibly painted in 1795 at the time of Brodrick's elevation to the bishopric of Kilmore. The portrait is reproduced by kind permission of the Viscount Midleton.

Archbishop of Dublin

19 Archbishop Charles Agar: 'nose portrait' by George Dance; engraved and
published by Dance, 1809 (author's collection).

20 Agar's son and successor, Welbore Agar, Viscount Somerton and 2nd earl of Normanton, by Sir Thomas Lawrence, begun 1815 (courtesy of Lord Normanton).

21 'The Union fishery': caricature of January-July 1800 mainly about the vacant primacy; the caricaturist is Alexander McDonald and the publisher W. McCleary. Apart from Castlereagh and Grattan on the left and Pitt and a devil on the far right, the figures are Agar, an unknown ecclesiastic, and either Archbishop Beresford or Euseby Cleaver. The unknown ecclesiastic, who looks as if he is a Roman catholic, may be O'Beirne (see p. 476n), but is more likely to be Dr Troy (p. 470n).

bishop.[11] The papers of the Physico-Historial Society in Armagh Public Library (K1 II 14) include a comment of *c.*1740–4 that it was begun by Godwin and that Bolton added to it by creating 'a stately library.' Moreover, Richard Pococke, later (1756–65) bishop of Ossory, who toured Ireland in 1752, also mentioned that this 'very fine house' was begun by Godwin and 'finished by Bolton, with offices for registry and library, and [that] he left the best part of his books to it.'[12] So, while tradition ascribes the choice of architect and design to Bolton, perhaps because he was Irish and a major figure in the history of the diocese and of the eighteenth-century Church of Ireland, the evidence points to Godwin, 'an accidental person from England.'[13]

Bolton completed the palace with the same rather careless generosity which he showed towards the cathedral on the Rock; for, when he died in 1744, his executor had difficulty finding evidence for Bolton's expenditure which was sufficiently detailed to obtain the usual level of reimbursement from Bolton's successor. Bolton's law agent thought 'it would be a very difficult and perplexed account, but believed that he would be able in some time to prove and vouch to a trifle most of the disbursements. ... I know the Archbishop about three years ago talked of ... [this], so that it is probable he made an entry of the several articles of expense; but the matter of difficulty will be in the proof.'[14] Meanwhile, Bolton's successor, the barbarian Price (who surely does not deserve Bence-Jones' extenuating comments – see p. 305), was making difficulties of his own. 'Though of Irish birth', as Chart indignantly emphasises,[15] he not only failed to comprehend the importance of the old cathedral, but also failed to comprehend the importance, certainly in Irish architectural terms, of the new palace. Indeed, he complained to Bolton's executor

---

11 It may be more than a coincidence that Pearce is supposed to have designed Palliser House, Rathfarnham, for William Palliser, son of Godwin's predecessor, *c.*1725. Archbishop Palliser was far too old for palace-building in 1727, but William Palliser might have mentioned Pearce to Godwin. See William Laffan (ed.), *The Sublime and the Beautiful: Irish art, 1700–1830* (London, 2001), p. 44. 12 Again, I am indebted for these three references to Dr McParland. Pococke says that Archbishop Price carried on this architectural tradition to the extent of contributing to build 'a sumptuous charter school for sixty children', completed in 1751 – George T. Stokes (ed.), *Pococke's tour in Ireland in 1752* (Dublin, 1891), p. 127. (This was the school later made subservient by Agar to the interests of his cathedral choir.) The account (of 1730?) presented to Bolton, is in the Foster/ Massereene papers, PRONI, D/562/458. It must refer to the palace. It may have been endorsed by Bolton 'buildings', in the plural, because it included the cost of pulling down 'the old house' (i.e. palace?) and clearing its site. 13 Bishop Percy of Dromore to Downshire, 20 Feb. 1792, Down County Museum, DB 505, Env. 4. The words were used in another context and the description was not applied to Godwin in particular. Nevertheless, it is apt. For Godwin's missionary Englishness, see p. 138. 14 William [Buckworth] Carr to Anthony Foster, 30 June 1744, Foster/Massereene papers, PRONI, D/526/1382. Anthony Foster, a well-known Dublin barrister and, later, chief baron of the exchequer, came to be Bolton's executor because Foster's sister, Alice, had been married to Bolton's nephew and heir presumptive, Thomas Bolton of Knock, Co. Louth (d.1741). Thomas and Alice Bolton's son was now the Archbishop's heir. Anthony Foster began, and his more famous son, John, the speaker, continued, a magnificent collection of pamphlets, mainly on economic subjects, now in the Henry collection, QUB. The earliest volumes of these pamphlets have Ms. tables of contents in Archbishop Bolton's hand and clearly come from his library. 15 *History of the Church of Ireland*, iii. 222.

of the very bad condition many things are in ... . Some of the wainscoat is downright rotten, and the rest of it all out of order. The roof the house [is] in a bad way, the doors, gates, sashes and widows of[f], the offices very bad. I think the right way will be for you to send a carpenter and I will have another, besides a measurer. If these matters be not adjusted, there must be a commission of dilapidations obtained, which greatly increases the expense and trouble.[16]

Could the palace have possibly got into this state in the space of only twelve years? Almost certainly, Price was trying to reduce the nett cost of his translation by making a pre-emptive strike on the issue of 'dilapidations.' According to Agar, who was always accurate in matters of this kind, the no-longer-extant 'register book in the registrar's office at Cashel' contained a certificate issued to Bolton's widow on 11 July 1746 stating that Bolton's approved expenditure on the palace amounted to the huge sum of £3,240.[17] As the law governing the proportion of such certified expenditure which an incumbent was entitled to recover from his successor stood in 1744 (see below), Price was liable for three-quarters of this, so the temptation to attempt a counter-claim was strong. Although architecturally aware,[18] he had no interest in an expensive palace in Cashel, since he intended to reside there only fitfully and to continue to base himself on the large and handsome mansion, subsequently called Oakly Park, which he had built in 1724 at Celbridge (of which he was then vicar) in his native Co. Kildare. Castletown, the seat of his friend and patron, Speaker Conolly,[19] is also located at Celbridge; and, through Conolly, Price must have known that Pearce was the architect of the Cashel palace, since Conolly, as speaker, had been Pearce's patron over the Parliament House commission.[20] So, his indifference to Pearce's work is as surprising as his exploitation of the issue of dilapidations is discreditable.

IMPROVEMENTS AND DILAPIDATIONS: THE ECONOMICS OF THE EPISCOPAL PALACE, 1713–1819

Disputes over improvements and dilapidations are a perennial feature of Church history in the eighteenth century and indeed until Disestablishment. By a series of acts, starting with *10 William III, cap. 6, sec. 1*, bishops and archbishops were reimbursed by their successors on the same basis as rectors building new glebe-houses (see p. 56n) – at first two-thirds of the certified and approved outlay, then three-quarters and finally, from 1772, the lot. As Dr Barnard remarks, apropos the period 1660–1760, this legislation 'could provoke unedifying squabbles over what was owed, and

---

16 Archbishop Price to Foster, 20 Aug. 1744, *ibid.*, D/567/1375.   17 21 M 57/B6/1. For the extent of the destruction (in 1922) of Cashel diocesan registry material, 1437–1873, see Herbert Wood, *A Guide to the records deposited in the Public Record Office of Ireland* (Dublin, 1919), pp 246–7. I am grateful to Dr Raymond Refaussé for pointing this out to me.   18 Healy, *Diocese of Meath*, ii, pp 92–3.   19 Sadleir and Dickinson, *Georgian mansions*, pp 38–9; Bence-Jones, *Irish country houses*, p. 227.   20 Colvin and Craig, *Elton Hall drawings*, p. xlvii.

sometimes threatened to saddle successors with the extravagance of the showy.'[21] Conversely, *10 William III, cap. 6, sec. 6*, empowered successors to reclaim from outgoing archbishops and bishops the cost of making good all or any dilapidations to the palace which had occurred during the previous incumbency. This legislation also tended to 'provoke unedifying squabbles' in which the roles of the parties were reversed – as in the case of Price and Bolton's executors.

The papers of a bishop of the first third of the eighteenth century, the already-mentioned Sir Thomas Vesey, bishop of Killaloe, 1713–14, and of Ossory, 1714–30, provide examples of the system in slow and contentious operation. In August 1713, the then bishop of Ossory, John Hartstonge, obtained from his metropolitan (Archbishop King of Dublin) a certificate that he had spent £240 on 'certain buildings and reparations ... builded and made in and about his episcopal palace and .. fit and necessary for his more convenient residence.'[22] The law provided for a period of grace before even a straightforward and undisputed claim for reimbursement was settled. So, in April 1715, Vesey paid his predecessor £210 for the latter's work on the palace at Killaloe,[23] a diocese from which both of them were long departed. The lapse of the same two-year period meant that Hartstonge's claim against Vesey for work on the palace in St Canice did not fall due until November 1716. In that month Hartstonge wrote from his new diocese asking for payment of 'the two-thirds due to me by act of parliament for the improvements, etc. ... [and for] all the pictures, big and little, that are in the room upon the stair head, with all other things for which your Lordship has not paid for [*sic*]. The hangings in your bedchamber I shall discourse with your Lordship [about] when we meet.'[24] Hartstonge and Vesey were still meeting, and speaking, at this stage. But their negotiations over Hartstonge's two-thirds, possibly complicated by the extraneous issue of a lease of land behind the palace,[25] eventually led to a breakdown in their relations. In November 1721, Hartstonge wrote briefly and frostily to point out that, five years on (and seven years after Hartstonge's translation from Ossory), he still had not received a penny.[26]

Barnard suggests (optimistically) that 'Soon enough, the admissible improvements were more strictly defined';[27] but this stricter definition certainly did not eliminate disputes. In Agar's case, there seems to have been none with Cox's executors when Agar was translated to Cashel in 1779. This was presumably because by then the palace was quite demonstrably in a neglected state; writing to congratulate Agar, Sir Cornwallis Maude, later 1st Viscount Hawarden, invited him to stay at nearby Dundrum, 'when you come to look at your palace and to order the repairs I believe necessary before it can be fit for your accommodation.'[28] Agar's own comment on the lack of repairs has already been quoted. However, there was to be an acrimonious dispute over the palace between Agar and his successor, Brodrick, in 1801–6 (see

21 Barnard, 'Improving clergymen', p. 139.   22 Certificate, 26 Aug. 1713, De Vesci papers, NLI, J/19.   23 Receipt from Vesey to Thomas Lindsay, now archbishop of Armagh, 2 Apr. 1715, ibid. 24 Hartstonge, now bishop of Derry, to Vesey, 10 Nov. [1716], ibid.   25 Hartstonge to Vesey, 10 Nov. [1718], ibid.   26 Hartstonge to Vesey, 7 Nov. 1721, ibid.   27 Barnard, 'Improving clergymen', p. 139.   28 Maude to Agar, 10 Aug. 1779, T/3719/C/13/31.

pp 363–4). In *c.*1798, the recent building and financial history of the Meath palace, Ardbraccan House, near Navan, proved so bewildering that Bishop O'Beirne and the son and executor of his predecessor, the Hon. Henry Maxwell, bishop of Meath, 1766–98, 'compromised the dilapidations' and obtained a special, private act of parliament to define their respective liabilities. Thereafter, the terms of this compromise and act impeded O'Beirne in getting his metropolitan's sanction 'for the alterations and improvements which I am anxious to make in the offices and farmyards of this place.'[29] In 1819, another metropolitan – Brodrick as archbishop of Cashel – had to intervene to head off a potential dispute over the palace in Waterford. Writing to the Bishop, the Hon. Richard Bourke, in July of that year, Brodrick pointed out that he had approved and certified an expenditure by Bourke of £1,342 'over and above the sum awarded as dilapidations against your predecessor', but that the commissioners appointed to view and report on Bourke's improvements stated that they had exceeded that sum and cost £3,076.[30]

The laws relating to improvements and dilapidations were important in a number of respects. First, they tended (with other aspects of the system) to turn even the most unworldly churchmen into businessmen. Second, they gave rise to disputes which marred good personal relations within the hierarchy of the Church of Ireland and hampered collective action in other spheres. Third, they generated claims and counter-claims and a good deal of documentation which – granted the poor survival-rate of diocesan registry archives – provides key information about these financial, administrative and architectural aspects of Church history. (In the case of the architecturally important Cashel palace, they make possible the following calculation. It looks as if Bolton's predecessor, Godwin, had spent £1,484 by the time of his death at the end of 1729. Assuming that this expenditure was certified and approved, Bolton would have been liable for three-quarters of it. So, adding the remaining quarter to the £3,240 for which Bolton in turn was liable, we are able to suggest a figure of £3,611 for the total cost of Pearce's palace in Cashel.[31]) Fourth, the laws relating to improvements and dilapidations caused certain bishoprics to become temporarily undesirable, thus deranging the episcopal *cursus honorum*. A successor who paid three-quarters of the cost of his predecessor's outlay was himself entitled to receive two-thirds of the same sum from *his* successor, who in turn was entitled to receive one half, and so on. Wakefield, who made his enquiries about these matters *c.*1810, reported: 'I have known gentlemen reduced to great inconvenience by being obliged to pay this money on their appointment to a bishopric.'[32] Fairly often, they avoided the inconvenience by declining the appointment. In December 1745, for example, it was noted that 'there is a great deal to

29 Ellison, *The hopeful traveller*, p. 90; O'Beirne to Primate Stuart, 21 May and 21 June 1804, Bedfordshire RO, WY 994/36–7.   30 Brodrick to Bourke, 15 July 1819, Midleton papers, NLI, Ms. 8888.   31 In his *Fasti*, v. 4, Rev. Henry Cotton, who like Agar would have had access to the now destroyed Cashel registers, put the figure at £3,730. This is so close to my own extrapolation as to make no matter.   32 Wakefield, *Account of Ireland*, ii. 472. For the 'great inconvenience' suffered by Joseph Stock on his translation from Killala to Waterford in 1810, see Akenson, *Church of Ireland*, p. 39.

be paid for Waterford' (because the late bishop had built a brand new palace, to the design of Pearce's pupil, Richard Castle), with the result that that bishopric was regarded as a doubtful promotion for anyone. In 1747, Cashel itself was rated above the unusually rich bishopric of Derry in terms of rental income, but overall was regarded as perhaps less attractive, 'as there are large demands for the house at Cashel',[33] amounting to two-thirds of whatever sum Price had eventually paid Bolton's executors.

Sometimes, it was not 'demands for the house' alone, but in conjunction with other things, which made a bishopric desirable or undesirable. In 1758, a translation from Clonfert to Ferns was thought desirable, in spite of their rough equality of income and an expense of £320 in entering upon Ferns, because Ferns had 'a noble patronage, ... a borough ... [and] no demesne', and Clonfert had 'a country house which was very expensive' and which any bishop would be glad to 'get rid of.'[34] In 1759, Ferns, though a poorer diocese than Killala, was thought a preferable place to reside; but this was not because of the Killala palace but the risk of 'being carried off by a privateer' (Killala being the episcopal seat located nearest to the coast).[35] In 1794–5, Brodrick thought the bishopric of Killala so undesirable that he had rather not become a bishop at all than accept it. He pointed out to an emissary from Dublin Castle 'that there was a large sum to be paid down for the house, which it is not in the present state of affairs so certain will ever be repaid me; that the country is so disturbed there [north Mayo] that sometimes the present bishop's [John Law] family have been detained there from fear of coming to town, and once his harness was cut to pieces on the road ...; that, in short, every circumstance occurred to pronounce Killala to be one of the very worst situations in Ireland.'[36] The next bishop of Killala but one, Joseph Stock, was to find it the very worst when the French sailed into Killala Bay in late August 1798. By contrast, Brodrick's enquiries in 1794–5 elicited from the out-going bishop of Ossory the opinion that that bishopric (which others had at other times decried) was currently well worth having: it was 'worth £2,000 per annum. There is only £100 to be paid on coming in ... . The patronage amounts to about £8,000 per annum; one very good living likely to be soon vacant. The place is expensive as to living, but on the whole the situation is comfortable and gentlemanlike.'[37] A 'comfortable and gentlemanlike' place of residence might, of course, have the opposite effect, by inducing the current incumbent to decline promotion. This was particularly likely if he had gone to Agar's trouble and expense to make 'everything here [Cashel] so much to our minds in our house, gardens, etc., that ... [only] a *very tempting thing* ... should induce us to relinquish them.'[38] Such inducements to stay put were simply the obverse of the same coin – that considerations attaching to a palace could derange the episcopal *cursus honorum*.

33 John Ryder, bishop of Down and Connor, to Sir Robert Wilmot, 3 Dec. 1745 and 31 Jan. 1746/7, T/3019/706 and 831.   34 Charles O'Hara to his wife, 28 [Feb?] and 4 Mar. 1758, O'Hara papers, PRONI, T/2812/10/17–18.   35 Samuel Hutchinson (the newly appointed bishop of Killala, where he remained – unkidnapped – until his death in 1780) to Wilmot, 17 Apr. 1759, T/3019/3573.   36 Brodrick to Midleton, 18 Feb. 1795, Ms. 1248, vol. 16, f. 16.   37 Brodrick to Midleton, 10 Dec. 1794, Ms. 1248, vol. 15, f. 171.   38 Lady Somerton to Agar, 13 Oct. 1796, T/3719/C/30/34.

In 1778, following the passing of the legislation to permit of full reimbursement by his successor to a bishop who had built a brand new palace on a new site (*11 and 12 George III, cap. 17, sec. 3,* as explained by *13 and 14 George III, cap. 27, sec. 6*), John Hotham, still a viceregal chaplain, was studying the form among the junior Irish bishoprics, and reported the (disappointing) results to his elder brother:

> Supposing me to be appointed to succeed the Bishop of Killaloe [Fowler] tomorrow, ... I must begin by paying him £5,000 for the new house he has built; and of that money, I should lose, upon any translation of my own, ... a fourth part, besides paying interest for the whole sum all the time I continued in the see at six if not seven per cent, the income of the bishopric being by his own account £2,500 per annum, but by the account of those who know it better than he himself does, a bare £2,000, and even that wretchedly paid, as in truth in these times they all are. The expense of getting oneself dubbed a bishop, in patent fees, fees of office, fees of parliament, etc., etc., is not less than £700, and I believe you will allow that £300 more will not fit up and furnish my palace at Killaloe very gorgeously. But, besides all this, I must inevitably have an house in Dublin of at least two rooms on a floor, and for this, according to the uncouth tenures prevalent in this country, I must pay a small actual rent, it is true, of £60, £70 or £80, but I must also pay down a fine at setting out of at least £2,000 more, which whole money is lost at the expiration of my lease. Having, however, gotten happy possession of my town house, I must furnish that as well as my country one, and I fancy you will not grudge me another £500 at least for that pleasant purpose. ... Wherever there are any houses, something is to be paid, according to the yearly value of the preferment; and where there are not, the successors are for the future not only expected but even engaged in honour previous to their consecration, to build.

Two months later, his researches into episcopal economics produced more welcome results:

> I have visited some bishops in their sees, and have made pretty minute enquiries after others, the result of all which is that people who see Dublin only, know nothing of Ireland, and that an Irish bishopric (one or two of them excepted) is a preferment not to be wantonly refused. I know but of two, and I believe only one, that is not upwards of £2,000 per annum, and a man may live much more as he pleases at his see than he can in England, which with me I own is a great matter. I should not be much averse to beginning with Clonfert, where I have been. It is full £2,200 per annum with only £600 to pay, and though the house is but bad even now, yet I really think I could make the place a pretty place at little or no expense. I advised the Bishop to burn his clipped yew hedges and let his house stand (as it wishes to do) in an elegant, sloping lawn of about 50 Irish acres, i.e. above 60 English ones. ... From thence my

translation might be made to Elphin, where I have also been, because the house is a good house with excellent offices, standing nobly in a demesne of 300 acres, with nothing to pay at setting out, and the annual income is full £3,700 even now. ... To say the truth, ... [the Primate] has set my mind considerably at ease with regard to the raising and recovering of the sums necessary to be paid on coming to a see or on building a new house, if there should be none upon it. The matter, as he has explained it, is neither difficult, distressing nor cruel, though I had thought it all three. But what signifies this palaver? It is no affair of mine, for not a soul [on the episcopal bench] will got to heaven or anywhere else![39]

Fortune smiled on the shameless Hotham. The following year, 1779, he was made bishop of Ossory by his brother-in-law, Lord Buckinghamshire. Ossory was not usually – *pace* Brodrick – regarded as a desirable preferment. A subsequent bishop complained over fifteen years later that it was worth about £2,200 per annum and was capable of being increased only to about £2,500; also that it was 'the most expensive residence of any of ... [the bishops' palaces], not excepting Dublin.'[40] For Hotham, however, it was only a short-lived purgatory, through which he passed in 1782 to the very desirable bishopric of Clogher. Clogher was very desirable, partly because of its income, and partly because in 1782 it was an almost idyllic place of residence. It took Agar years of effort and expenditure to bring Cashel, *mutatis mutandis*, to the pitch of perfection in which Hotham was lucky enough to find Clogher:

> Bishop Ste[a]rne ... built the present palace,[41] ... which though not so well contrived as it might have been, is far from a despicable place of residence, especially as my predecessor added two wings, the one an eating room of thirty feet by twenty, the other a library of thirty-two feet by twenty-two, exclusive of the bow window in each. The demesne is sufficiently planted, and from that circumstance, and the uncommon irregularity of the ground, in my opinion extremely beautiful. It measures 560 English acres, and the whole is surrounded by a stone wall ... . The country is healthy and fine and the roads about me very good. ... Finally, the income of the see is not less, as I am informed, than £4,000 per annum, which in my judgement is no trifling emolument.[42]

39 Hotham to Hotham Thompson, 17 Aug. and 19 Oct. 1778, Hotham papers, PRONI, T/3429/2/2–3. 40 O'Beirne, then bishop of Ossory, to Portland, 4 Nov. 1795, *Irish official papers*, i. 145. 41 According to Lewis (*Topographical dictionary*, i. 343), 'Between 1690 and 1697, Bishop [Richard] Tenison repaired and beautified the episcopal palace, and his successor, Bishop St George Ashe, expended £900 in repairing and improving the palace and [demesne] lands, two-thirds of which was repaid by his successor. Bishop [John] Stearne [who succeeded Ashe in 1717 and died in 1745] in 1720 laid out £3,000 in building and other improvements of the episcopal residence, two-thirds of which was charged on the revenues of the see [*sic* – actually, reimbursed by his successor].' 42 Hotham to Viscount Sackville, 9 July 1782, *HMC Stopford-Sackville Mss.*, i, pp 279–80.

It was probably rather more than Cashel was worth at the time. Though he hankered, partly in jest, after the primacy, Hotham remained among the earthly felicities of Clogher until his death in 1795, having a year previously – like his role model and fellow-Yorkshireman, Primate Robinson – succeeded to the family baronetcy.

This success story should not, however, distract attention from the very real expenses incurred and risks run by an aspirant to an Irish bishopric – those which Hotham himself had forcibly described in his first letter of 1778. In 1792, the newly appointed bishop of Cork, William Bennet, a brand-new bishop, lamented 'the expenses of my late preferment (including near £5,000 for my see house).'[43] In 1800, the second primate after Robinson – faced with what was still a huge bill for the Armagh palace (see pp 382–3) – tried to evade appointment to the primacy on the ground, among other things, that 'the great expense of taking possession of Armagh would utterly ruin my children.'[44] Under *9 George III, cap. 13, sec. 2*, a bishop's liability to his predecessor, or to his predecessor's executors, was cancelled if the bishop died or was translated within a year of coming to the see (on the principle that it was unreasonable for him to have to pay for improvements which he did not live long to enjoy). But the 'patent fees, fees of office, fees of parliament, etc., etc.', payable on promotion or translation to a bishopric were not refundable. Nor did Hotham exaggerate their magnitude. Four translations of the period 1771–5, two from bishoprics to archbishoprics and two from one bishopric to a better, cost £474 and £581 (the archbishoprics) and £459 and £203 (the bishoprics) respectively.[45] The discrepancies in the amounts probably derived from the custom that an office-bearer waived his fee when the person appointed was a friend or potential benefactor. Since none of these churchmen was becoming a bishop for the first time, the House of Lords fees in their case would be minimal. Hotham's figure of £700 for a brand-new bishop was therefore not unreasonable – assuming that none of the fees was waived.

Among Agar's contemporaries or near contemporaries on the Irish bench, Hotham was one of the most calculating and one of the luckiest. Even more calculating, but in most respects very unlucky, was another Englishman, the already-mentioned Euseby Cleaver, bishop of Ferns. For all his financial acumen, Cleaver allowed himself to be sucked into a vortex of expenditure on the palace at Ferns. In March 1792, when excusing himself to Lord Downshire (whose circular, as has been seen, elicited a good deal of incidental and important information about the state of *other* cathedrals and ecclesiastical buildings), Cleaver pleaded that he had been a bishop for only three years and had been

> placed in a diocese in which there had been no establishment for a bishop since the Reformation. I found a see house begun by a predecessor on so large a scale that, in my endeavours to complete it, exclusive of furniture, I have already

43 Bishop Bennet to Downshire, 21 Mar. 1792, D/607/B/341.   44 Stuart, then bishop of St David's, to the King, 16 July 1800, *Later correspondence of George III*, iii. 377.   45 Fees on Irish patents, 1752–83, BL, Add. Ms. 23711, ff. 64 and 95. In late 1800 or early 1801, Primate Stuart paid £495 for fees in connection with his patents as archbishop alone – Bedfordshire RO, WY 994/5.

been under the necessity of expending three years' income and have yet much to do. Under the weight of this burthen, which perhaps too liberal an attention to my successors has increased beyond my duty to my children, I am sorry to say that it is not in my power to become a subscriber to a plan which, under different circumstances, I should have been proud to have promoted.[46]

As has been seen in the case of Galbally glebe-house, only expenditure up to a maximum of *two years' income* was recoverable from a successor. This was a deliberate and salutary restraint on 'the showy' or on clergymen with ample private means, such as the earl-bishop of Derry or the 'predecessor' referred to by Cleaver, who was Walter Cope of Drumilly, Co. Armagh, a substantial and childless landowner from the north (see pp 180–2).[47] It was certainly not in character for Cleaver to have shown 'too liberal an attention to my successors', or liberality of any kind; so presumably his problem was that the scale of the palace was 'so large' that he could not reimburse his predecessor and make it comfortable for himself for less than three years' income, which was one year more than he was entitled to recoup under the act of 1772.

The building history of the Ferns palace is complicated, and so therefore is the question of reimbursement. The palace was begun in 1785 by Cope, who was bishop from 1782 until his death in 1787. In building it, he was able to draw on the income of the see, the income of the Drumilly estate, and legacies of £300 and £700 respectively made for that purpose by two previous bishops of Ferns, Bartholomew Vigors (d.1722) and Edward Young (d.1772).[48] Cope's executors would have received full reimbursement of his expenditure on the palace (minus, presumably, the value of the two legacies) from his successor, William Preston, who died in April 1789 and was succeeded by Cleaver. Assuming (though this is not known) that Preston incurred no expenditure of his own on the palace, Cleaver would then have been required to reimburse to Preston's executors three-quarters of Preston's payment, and Cleaver in turn could expect to receive two-thirds of that sum (or half Cope's original outlay on the palace) from Cleaver's successor. In May 1798, he claimed that he had 'expended £10,000 in establishing a residence for my successors in a see that had no reception for its bishop since Charles I's time', but expected 'that my successor will repay me above £7,000.'[49] The £7,000 probably represented two years' income of the see – a likely enough figure for Ferns in 1798 (though not of course collectable in that particular year, because the heaviest fighting in the rebellion took place in the diocese of Ferns). The inconsistency in Cleaver's claims that the palace was the first 'since the

---

46 Quoted in Rankin, *Down cathedral*, pp 112–13.   47 Of course, bishops with private means did not necessarily want to spend them on palaces: Cox, as has been seen, did not (unless he spent something on the bishop of Ossory's palace in Kilkenny); nor did Richard Marlay, bishop of Waterford, 1795–1802, who had £5,000 a year of his own and spent as little of it as possible and none on the Waterford palace – see Brodrick to Midleton, 31 Jan. 1795, Ms. 1248, vol. 16, f. 10, and Sirr, *Archbishop Trench of Tuam*, p. 25. The point is that not all bishops were, or remained, impecunious younger sons.   48 Canon James B. Leslie, *Ferns clergy and parishes ...* (Dublin, 1936), p. 17.   49 Cleaver to Egremont, 8 May [1798?], PHA/57/7A; McParland, *James Gandon*, p. 197.

Reformation' and the first 'since Charles I's time' is typical: neither, in fact, was true. But he probably did not exaggerate the grandness of Cope's design. *Walker's Hibernian Magazine* for November 1790 remarked of the Ferns palace: 'The house and offices are the completest and best-finished of any episcopal building in Ireland, and – what is singular – the house is covered with copper, the first attempt of this kind in this kingdom.'[50] Cope must have been trying to outdo Primate Robinson, his patron and Co. Armagh neighbour.

Agar, not surprisingly, was a past master at interpreting the law in relation to improvements and dilapidations. His papers include a closely written page of notes on the complicated instalment system by which the cost of improvements was reimbursed by a successor, with one tariff for residences on new sites and another for residences on old, under *10 William III, cap. 6, 12 George I, cap. 10, sec. 2, 11 and 12 George III, cap. 17, sec. 3, 13 and 14 George III, cap. 27, sec. 6,* and *31 George III, cap. 19.*[51] Agar did not need to interpret these acts on his own behalf until 1801 – when, as will shortly be seen, he really had to employ his knowledge of the system in the diocese of Dublin. But, prior to then, his brains were frequently picked by others. In March 1783, for example, Thomas Percy, bishop of Dromore (and like Agar a *protégé* of the 1st duke of Northumberland, with whom he claimed kinship[52]), turned to Agar for an expert opinion on the knotty subject of a half-finished palace. Percy wanted to know whether Percy or Percy's predecessor, William Beresford, was liable for the cost of making 'a proper and easy communication between the house and stables [at Dromore], which at present are almost inaccessible to each other, from the sudden removal of my predecessor, who had but time to finish the shell of the house.'[53] Agar directed him to the relevant *Statutes* which embodied the law relating to unfinished palaces, etc., as it then stood; but the law needed codification and clarification, which it received under *31 George III, cap. 19.* (Agar did not claim responsibility for this act – see p. 444 – but it would be surprising if he had not made a major contribution to it.) Twenty years later, Percy, having completed the palace and out-buildings and had his necessary improvements valued by a commission, turned again to Agar for advice on a quite different matter. This was what he was to do about a detached 55 acres of demesne at Magheralin, Co. Down, which had been annexed to the see by *10 William III, cap. 6, sec. 5,* and on which a now ruined palace had been built. As the 55 acres was demesne land, Percy was not empowered to lease it. Yet, if he were so empowered for even 21 years, the tenant would demolish the ruins of the palace and build a decent house, like those adjoining the site in the village of

50 Quoted in Leslie, op. cit. 51 21 M 57/A1, p. 79. 52 Writing to Egremont, a connection of the Northumberland family, Cleaver described Percy, with heavy sarcasm and underlining, as '*your cousin of Dromore*' – Cleaver to Egremont, 14 Dec. 1797, PHA/57/5. Percy was, in fact, of humble origins. 53 Percy to Agar, 18 Mar. 1783, T/3719/C/17/8. According to Dr Beaufort, the palace was 'a good, plain house, built by Beresford' (in 1780–82), and Percy was simply fabricating pretexts for extracting money from Beresford: 'The Bishop [Beresford] told me the whole of the Bishop of Dromore's dispute and anger with him, and how he pacified him by £25' – Beaufort's journal, 1787, PRONI, MIC/250, p. 19.

Magheralin. Agar was therefore asked to advise whether it would be sufficient to repeal the former act of parliament, or whether it was necessary to pass a new one.[54]

A more flattering acknowledgement of his expertise in these matters was made by Archbishop Moore of Canterbury, who asked him in February 1792 'to collect for your Grace [Moore] the several acts passed in this country [Ireland] to encourage the building of glebe-houses [palaces, etc.] from the 10th year of King William to the present time.' Agar dispatched his codification two months later, explaining that, 'as each of them contains something not to be found in the others, it is much to be wished that the substance of them all should be formed by some skilful person into one act.'[55] Bishop Newton's short account of the palace-building activities of Edmund Keene, bishop of Ely, 1771–81, suggests that the Irish system of reimbursement for improvements had no English counterpart.[56] So, there clearly were facets of the Irish legislation which were deemed worthy of English consideration and perhaps emulation and, clearly, Agar was deemed the expert on the Irish legislation.

THE BOLTON LIBRARY, 1732–1836

If the Ferns palace was 'the completest and best-finished of any episcopal building in Ireland', the Cashel palace had the distinction, not only of having been designed by Pearce, but of having annexed to it that 'great and useful appendage',[57] the Bolton library, which Archbishop Bolton had built and to which he had left his collection of *c.*8,000 volumes. It seems to have been his intention to found such a library from as early in his episcopate as 1732. But the opportunity to turn it into a collection of major importance did not come until *c.*1735, when Bolton bought privately 'perhaps the great bulk' of the library of his late friend and patron, Archbishop King. It looks as if almost all the *c.*8,000 volumes had once been King's. Bolton's intentions were formalised and given perpetual legal effect under the terms of his will, proved in 1744.[58] In making this generous bequest, he was continuing 'a tradition popularised earlier by [Bishop] Foy at Waterford, [Bishop] Maule and [Archdeacon] Pomeroy in Cork, and [Archbishop] Marsh ... in Dublin.'[59] Unfortunately, Bolton's not-quite-immediate predecessor at Cashel, Archbishop Palliser, had also favoured Dublin; at his death in 1727, he had left his library to TCD.[60] But Bolton's example was followed by,

---

54 Percy to Agar, 20 Apr. 1802, T/3719/C/36/10.   55 Agar to Moore, 7 Feb. and 2 Apr. 1792, Lambeth Palace Library, Moore papers, vol. 6, ff. 211–12 and 228.   56 Adam Clarke (ed.), *Compendium edition of the lives of Newton, Rev. Philip Skelton, etc.*, ii. 156.   57 21 M 57/B6/1. 58 The late G.M.D. Woodworth, dean of Cashel, *Cashel's museum of printing and early books: a short history of the GPA-Bolton library* (Clonmel, 1994), pp 4 and 6; Matteson, 'King and his library', *passim*; Woodworth, 'In Cashel forever' (an unpublished history of the Bolton library, left almost ready for publication by Dean Woodworth at the time of his sudden and early death in 1994). I am very grateful to his son, Simon, for making this unpublished history available to me and for allowing me to draw upon it. There are some discrepancies between the three sources here cited; I have preferred 'In Cashel forever', as being Dean Woodworth's last word on the subject, in cases of doubt. 59 Phillips, *Church of Ireland*, iii. 221; Barnard, 'Improving clergymen', p. 147.   60 King, *A great archbishop of Dublin*, p. 85*n*. For some discussion of Palliser's (fairly predictable) taste in books, see

for instance, Charles Este, bishop of Waterford, 1740–45, and Edward Maurice, bishop of Ossory, 1754–6, who both left their books to their respective diocesan libraries.[61]

The Bolton library is principally noteworthy as 'a magnificent collection of fifteenth, sixteenth and seventeenth-century books, including an illustrated *Nuremberg Chronicle* of 1493 and a Caxton *Chaucer*.'[62] It also contains a Rouen *Missal* of 1515 (of which there is no other recorded copy) and a Tyndale *Bible* of 1537.[63] It was already 'esteemed valuable' in Agar's day – in 1797, to be precise – for its 'many curious manuscripts, amongst which is said to be ... the *Psalter of Cashel*, written by Cormac McCulenan [*sic* – MacCuilennain], ... king of Munster and bishop of Cashel, anno 901.'[64] The oldest manuscript in the library is in fact English and was begun in 1168 and finished *c.*1220.[65] The library's 'theological works left a life-long impression on the scholarship of ... John Jebb [the future bishop of Limerick] ..., a copious theological writer ... [and] the father of the Oxford Movement in the Anglican Church.'[66] However, 'the topics covered are by no means exclusively ecclesiastical. There are substantial elements on mathematics, astronomy, architecture, the natural sciences, medicine, literature, travel, geography, history, heraldry ... [etc.]. This reflects the character of the early collectors as scholarly gentlemen who were also churchmen ... . The great bulk of the material dates from before Bolton's death in 1744.' In spite of highly regrettable losses and sales over the years, the latter including works by Galileo and Spinoza, the library contains 12,000 volumes today.[67]

The building in which Bolton housed it is located to the left of the entrance front of the palace – initially detached from it, but by 1779 connected to it by a passage and a gallery.[68] The library building ran backwards like an arm of the entrance front and at right angles to it. It was 'a two-storey structure, the first floor of which was modelled [very roughly] on the Long Room in Trinity College, Dublin',[69] and the ground floor of which presumably housed the registry which Bishop Pococke mentions that Bolton had built. By 1779, this 'Long Room' was partially divided by a wall in the middle, into each side of which a fireplace had been inserted. This wall has long gone, and the 'Long Room' is now one of the show-pieces of the Cashel Palace Hotel and is used for weddings and other functions.[70] It was certainly not something to be proud of at the outset of Agar's episcopate. Agar

> found the ... books so completely covered with an uniform coat of bluemould
> when he first saw the room in 1779, that he walked to the end of the second

Palliser to Rev. William Perceval (soon to become archdeacon of Cashel), 8 Feb. 1700/01, and Perceval to Palliser, 4 May 1703, Perceval papers, PRONI, D/906/57 and 66.   61 Leslie, *Ossory clergy and parishes*, pp 22, 26 and 29.   62 Bence-Jones, *Country Life*, 31 Aug. 1972.   63 Charles Wolfe, dean of Cashel, *Cashel, its cathedral and library*.   64 George Holmes, *Sketches of some of the southern counties*, pp 20 and 17.   65 Woodworth, *A bishop, bogs and books*, N.P., N.D. [c.1985?] (article, without provenance, in IAA's Cashel Palace press cuttings file).   66 Robert Wyse Jackson, dean of Cashel, untitled article of c.1960, IAA, Cashel Palace press cuttings file.   67 Woodworth, *Cashel's museum of printing*, pp 20, 22, 24 and 26.   68 21 M 57/B6/1.   69 *A short history of the library* (Dunmurry, Belfast, 1991), p. 2.   70 I am grateful to its proprietor, Mr Patrick Murphy, for showing me round in February 1999, August 2000 and February 2001.

room without knowing that there was a book in either room, for not one was visible. This he perceived to arise principally from the windows being all on the north-east side of the room, and none on the south-west side. He therefore made windows instantly on the S.W. side, which with the common care of supplying the rooms with fresh air by opening the windows, has rendered the rooms dry and will probably preserve the books in as good state for many years as they were in when he received them.[71]

This was a modest, but sensible, conservation measure. Oliver Grace's plan for the alterations survives, and an estimate presented by him for this and other work on the palace and its gardens, shows that 'opening the wall and fixing the four new frames' in the library was going to cost only £30.[72] The plan suggests that book-space lost by the opening of the windows was regained by building 'bays' of full-height bookcases at right-angles to the walls. Agar also interested himself in the contents of the library. In what was apparently 'his only recorded activity in Cashel', Archbishop Cox had commissioned a catalogue. This was compiled by his diocesan registrar and agent, William Cooper (1721–69) of Killenure Castle, Co. Tipperary.[73] Completed in 1757, it recorded the number of volumes as 8,230, and – *mutatis mutandis* – remained the library's standard finding-aid for the next seventy-five years.[74] 'Together with the original listing of all William King's books, ... [it is an] invaluable source for estimating the original size and scope of the collection, before it began to sustain losses.'[75] Agar had his own personal copy of the 1757 catalogue made, and this copy records that the library contained 6,156 titles (as opposed to volumes) in his day. Some of the books are entered in Agar's own hand, suggesting that they were either presented by him or recovered as a result of his efforts. This catalogue is to be distinguished from that of Agar's private library, which at this stage was split between Cashel and Dublin,[76] and the Cashel part of which was housed in the study which he added to the palace (see p. 58 and 354–5) in 1784.

71 21 M 57/B6/1.   72 21 M 57/B23/3 and B/14/23.   73 William Cooper was the first of three generations and four members of the Cooper family to be employed by successive archbishops of Cashel. He was succeeded as registrar and agent by his elder son, Samuel Cooper of Killenure (1750–1831), who has already featured in connection with the Cashel cathedral close and the farewell address to Agar from Cashel (see pp 295 and 324). Samuel Cooper seems to have retired from the archbishop's service when Agar left Cashel in 1801. His younger brother, Austin Cooper (1759–1830) of Merrion Square, Dublin, then succeeded, probably as agent only; he was agent for numerous estates, including that of Lord Hawarden at nearby Dundrum, and was also a treasury official and well known antiquary (whose comments on various ancient structures have been or will be quoted). By 1816, Austin Cooper had been succeeded as agent by his nephew (Samuel Cooper's only son), William Cooper of Killenure (1772–1850), who in turn was succeeded in or before 1819 by Brodrick's nephew, Major Richard Woodward. A pastel portrait recently acquired by the Bolton library purports to be of William the cataloguer; but, on the evidence of costume and age, it must be of the William who was born in 1772. Killenure Castle is on the road from Cashel to Dundrum. 74 Woodworth, 'In Cashel forever'.   75 Woodworth, *Cashel's museum of printing*, p. 8.   76 Agar's copy of the 1757 catalogue bears reference 21 M 57/B38; the catalogue of his personal library bears

Militiamen quartered in the palace in 1798 are supposed to have damaged the
Bolton library and vandalised the books.[77] This, however (as will be seen), is almost
certainly a myth. Under Agar's successor, Brodrick, a librarian was appointed at a very
modest salary. But there may also have been neglect: Brodrick's particular *protégé*, John
Jebb, makes an alarming reference in 1808 to 'hunt[ing] through the worm-eaten folios
of the Cashel library.'[78] Of Brodrick's successor, in 1822, Chart writes: 'Richard
Laurence, the last archbishop, ... [was] an eminent chemist and orientalist [and had
been regius professor of Hebrew at Oxford]. As Bampton Lecturer he had essayed to
prove that the Thirty-Nine Articles were not Calvinistic. He was also the first English
writer to translate the Ethiopic version of the Book of Enoch.'[79] To Cashel (and to the
Church of Ireland), Laurence brought the Rev. Henry Cotton, author over a lengthy
period (1845–78) of the six-volume *Fasti*. Cotton's ample preferments (which created
something of a scandal), and his limited parochial and cathedral duties, enabled him
to devote himself to scholarly and occasionally polemical pursuits.[80] He had been sub-
librarian at the Bodleian, and so was well qualified to take charge of the Bolton library.
Going to the root of the problem, he pointed out that Bolton had 'left no funds for the
enlargement or even the preservation of the collection.' He 'began by recovering some
of the lost works – 160 were found in the Archbishop's own study! He put together a
shelf catalogue ... and bought books from Marsh's Library [Dublin] in the 1830s.'[81]
Following the transfer of the archbishop's seat from Cashel to Waterford, the library
was re-located in 1836 to another purpose-built two-storey structure in the cathedral
close (in which it remains and which was restored in 1986).[82] Cotton reorganised the
books 'within this space', assigned new shelf numbers and began a new catalogue.
'The mark of his patient and painstaking work can be seen everywhere.'[83]

AGAR'S 'IMPROVEMENTS' TO THE CASHEL PALACE, 1779–97

Agar's alterations to the library wing of the palace were dictated purely by considerations of conservation: the reasons for his 'improvements' to the main building of the
palace were that 'it bore ... but a dismal appearance' and was ill-suited to some of the
purposes he had in mind:

> Though the house was substantially built and the plan originally a good one in
> most respects, in some it stood in great need of amendment. The eating

reference 21 M 57/D38. The fact that both are numbered 38 in their respective sections of the
archive is just a confusing coincidence. It does not appear that bibliographers interested in The
history of the Bolton library have yet looked at/heard of 21 M 57/B38.   77 Woodworth, *A bishop,
bogs and books*, and idem, *Cashel's museum of printing*, p. 8.   78 Jebb to Rev. Jos. McCormick, 24 Dec.
1808, printed in Forster, *Life of Jebb*, ii. 145.   79 Phillips, *Church of Ireland*, iii. 290.   80 Acheson,
Church of Ireland, pp 142 and 272n.; Milne, *Christ Church Cathedral*, pp 286–7.   81 Woodworth,
Cashel's museum of printing, pp 8 and 10.   82 Galloway, *The cathedrals of Ireland*, p. 39.   83
Woodworth, *Cashel's museum of printing*, pp 10–11; Acheson, *Church of Ireland*, p. 138.

parlour was only 19 feet 6 inches by 17 feet [actually, it was 19 feet 6 inches by 18 feet 9 inches], a room certainly altogether too small for such a purpose in such a house. This room was on the east side of the great hall of entrance and could not be enlarged. On the west side of the hall was a room of the same dimensions, at the north end of which, and between it and the breakfast parlour, was a dark passage from the hall to the gallery leading to the library, in which there was a staircase, which communicated by a trap door with the north end of the corridor in the bedchamber storey. Dr Agar removed this staircase entirely, took down the wall of partition and threw the passage into the eating room, which made it 30 feet long by 19 feet 6 inches broad, and placed a window over the door leading to the library, in order to render that part of the eating room more light.

By an interesting coincidence, Agar had to go to this trouble to create at Cashel an 'eating room' just a little smaller than the one Hotham simply walked into at Clogher in 1782 (which was thirty feet by twenty, excluding a bow which the Cashel room lacked). Today, Agar's eating room is thrown together with the 'breakfast parlour' in the south-west corner of the main block, to form one room over 47½ feet long, which is now – appropriately enough – the main dining room of the hotel.

Agar was not intending to open a hotel, but he did mean to entertain in a style and on a scale appropriate to his new archiepiscopal station. His papers include a bundle of menus, written in his own hand, dated 1782, and showing his table layout, with a 'frame' (usually a looking glass intended to magnify the effect of flowers or silver) in the middle, and the position of each dish precisely marked.[84] Clearly, his minute attention to detail extended into the domestic domain. Bence-Jones comments that 'There had been a tradition of lavish hospitality at the palace ... [in the] time of Bolton, but it was under the Agars that it came closest to the Great World.'[85] (Frederick Hervey was so lost in 'the Great World', and to all sense of religion, that when inviting an acquaintance to 'share some claret which is truly *episcopal*', he adjured him: 'Do not therefore *Dissent* from my *Communion*.')[86] Dr Barnard has rightly emphasised the importance of hospitality in the agenda of the improving churchman. 'A bishop residing in his diocese during the summer months, in a substantial house with a good table, entertaining visiting [and diocesan] clergy, officers, judges on assize, ... made up for deficiencies in the local gentry.' 'The expectation that ... bishops should entertain, formally enjoined on them by James II, offered a chance ... to ingratiate themselves with local society and perhaps to check the anti-clericalism latent among the laity. Largesse could also appease the lower clergy and even assist in the creation of a sense of clerical cohesion',[87] though – overdone – it could as easily create jealousy and

84 21 M 57/D68. I am most grateful to Mrs Nuala Cullen for her expert advice on these menus, which she considers a rare and valuable source. D66–7 comprise *recipés* and culinary instructions, a few of them in Agar's hand, and most of them of a more humdrum character. 85 Bence-Jones, *Country Life*, 31 Aug. 1972. 86 Hervey to Dr John Ferguson of Derry, [c.1780, Montgomery of Benvarden papers, PRONI, T/1638/5/1. 87 Legg, *The Synge letters*, p. xvi; Barnard, 'Improving

promote division. These two passages relate to the pre-1760 period. But granted the
neglect of his clergy and diocese of which Archbishop Cox had been guilty, and the
anti-clericalism displayed by the gentry of the metropolitan province of Cashel during
the Rightboy disturbances of 1785–7, they are entirely appropriate to Agar's day. It
may be assumed that, when Agar entertained, he did not place second class viands
before his clergy (as Cox had done), or plunge them into darkness before they had
finished. But Cox had at least fed them something. A visitor to Primate Robinson in
Armagh in *c.*1772–4 recorded, in a famous passage: 'After divine service, the officiating
clergy presented themselves in the hall of his palace to pay their court. I asked him
how many were to dine with us. He answered, "Not one"; he did them kindness[es],
but he gave them no entertainments; they were in excellent discipline.'[88]

Against this background, an accusation of abject meanness brought against Agar
by Watty Cox is particularly inapt:

> He on some occasions allowed the travelling paupers, when his dogs were
> absent, to take away ... broths or waters in which meat had been boiled, but
> under the strictest commands that no solid food should be allowed to be added.
> One day, [when] some poor people were departing with their pitchers from his
> house, he pursued them and with his walking cane searched every vessel to
> discover had any broken meat been given away ...; on which, one of the poor
> creatures abruptly applied the following words to the *man of God*:

> 'Agar the Negar,[89] to show he was great
> Put his stick in my pitcher to fish up some meat.'

Agar ran a very efficient household, paying his bills weekly and in cash, and expecting
corresponding punctiliousness from his tradesmen.[90] But he also believed in and
practised episcopal 'largesse.' Even if he had been heartless (which there is no good
reason to think that he was), the man who caused three beggars, in attitudes of
thankfulness, to be featured in the foreground of his funeral monument (fig. 17),
would not have been caught in an act of petty parsimony. It is possible that the
allegation of meanness derived from a misunderstanding or misrepresentation of the
more sophisticated bill of fare which he seems to have introduced into his households
and which was not dominated by heavy, Hibernian helpings of meat. The model for
this was what he saw for himself at Paultons, possibly at Pope's Villa, and at the
Mendips' town house in Little Brook Street. Along with the autograph menus dated
1782 are preserved similar but more numerous menus and table layouts for
October–November 1791 and October–December 1797, headed 'Paultons' or
'London' and obviously recording the light, French-style *cuisine* which he sampled at

clergymen', pp 146–7.   **88** Quoted in Mohan, 'Archbishop Richard Robinson', p. 123.   **89** i.e.
'niggard'; Dr Roger Blaney tells me that the word, usually spelt 'neager', is of Old
English/Scandanavian, not Irish, derivation.   **90** Bill from, and correspondence of Agar's steward
with, one Gartland, 'tea man', Portman Square, London, *c.*30 Nov. 1801, T/3719/C/35/30–32.

his uncle's houses. These again show his attention to detail – and his command of culinary French. What is also remarkable about them is that it was Agar himself who wrote them up, even though his wife must have accompanied him on these visits.[91]

His alterations to other aspects of the palace besides the dining room were likewise motivated by a mixture of practicality and fashion:

> The door from the hall into the salon [i.e. the drawing room] was exactly opposite the hall door, and there was in the salon a door into the garden exactly opposite to the door of the room; which not only cut the room, as it were, in two, but rendered it so cold that, as often as any one of the three doors was opened, the room was not habitable with comfort, for no company could be so situated as not to feel the wind. The Archbishop, ... therefore, stopped up the door in the centre of the room and took away entirely that which opened into the garden [and which has since been reinstated in the form of a French window]. He placed the door in the hall at the end of the south side, let all the windows of the salon down to the ground, and put double doors to this and every other room on the parlour storey and new-sashed the parlour and bedchamber stories in front and rear. He ... put the best species of register grates in the hall, salon and eating parlour and in all the other rooms of the house ... . He also ...painted the whole house once, and some parts twice since he has inhabited it.[92]

A letter from Lady Somerton to Agar, written in mid-October 1796, confirms that the Agars were assiduous about painting and whitewashing, both outside and in. She also suggested that 'It would be a good thing to have the grate in the hall, which both smokes and consumes a great deal of coals, Rumfordized;[93] likewise that in the housekeeper's room.'[94] Agar's account mentions almost as an aside that he 'let all the windows of the salon down to the ground.' Yet this – a very common late Georgian practice – was his most sweeping, single alteration. From inside, it greatly enhanced the view of the garden as it sweeps up through trees to the Rock, which now became, in Bence-Jones' striking phrase, 'a stupendous eye-catcher.' This was Agar's intention. Many years later, his widow mentioned in a codicil to her will 'two drawings of the justly celebrated *Rock of Cashel* taken from a window in the palace, when on a visit to us, by Lord Doneraile's nephew, Mr R[edmond] Barry, justly admired for his correct pencil.'[95] These two drawings feature in a list of the Somerley pictures made by the

---

91 A careful trawl of Agar's account books and memorandum books might turn up the name/s of his cook/s in this period, and perhaps throw light on the nationality, salary and proficiency of the person/s for whose instruction these menus were intended. In 1808, Agar's (new?) cook in London was one Thomas Cregan, who sounds Irish, was paid the substantial salary of 40 guineas per annum, and worked for Agar in Dublin as well as London – Cregan to Agar, 11 Aug. 1808, T/3719/C/42/51. 92 21 M 57/B6/1. 93 The inventor, Count Rumford, had paid his first visit to Ireland between the spring and autumn of that year and had been rapturously received by the Dublin Society and prominent parliamentarians. 94 Lady Somerton to Agar, 15 Oct. 1796, T/3719/C/30/35. 95 Will and codicils of Jane, countess of Normanton, 4 Sep. 1810–20 June

2nd earl of Normanton in 1845,[96] and are at Somerley to this day. Externally, the lowering of the windows has a less happy effect. It punctures Pearce's string course, muddles his taut and consistent design, and breaks the symmetry between the garden and the entrance fronts. However, the bases of the windows do at least rest on another horizontal band. Surprisingly, the already-quoted early twentieth-century description of the palace does not note this change, though it does note that on the garden and the entrance fronts, 'the original heavy sashes [i.e. glazing bars] have been replaced by those of a late eighteenth-century type.'[97]

Nearly all this work on the palace and the Bolton library took place early in Agar's time at Cashel. Oliver Grace's estimate for the new library windows is thrown in with other things – mainly estimates for garden buildings – one of which dates from 1780.[98] Grace's separate plan and estimate for Agar's new study, with its previously mentioned water-closet, are dated 6 January 1784.[99] By 1793, Agar had spent £842 on the palace[100] and, since the total of Grace's estimates comes to £1,177,[101] this constituted the lion's share. Probably, the lion's share had already been spent by 1785. The purpose of the expenditure was twofold: to introduce light and alleviate the 'dismal appearance' of the building which had struck him forcibly in 1779; and to make it habitable by a resident archbishop, who needed the defence of a porter's lodge and the self-sufficiency in produce provided by Agar's garden buildings and his reorganisation of the gardens.

Grace's estimate for the cost of the study was £245. It was Agar's only piece of new-build in connection (literally) with the palace – all his other new buildings were in the grounds. The study, which was built over offices to the rear and right of the entrance front, was reached via a door off the half-landing on Pearce's staircase. Presumably, it was 'the tower' where Miss Lockhart's 'old lion' had his den (see p. 90). In addition to its comparative remoteness and privacy, it gave Agar a unique view of the ruins of St Dominick's Abbey (founded in 1243 but rebuilt in the late fifteenth century) and which must then have been invisible from the other rooms of the palace. Otherwise, the new study had little to recommend it. It was all outside wall; even its floor was partially exposed to the elements, because it overhung the offices below and was supported on stilts sunk into the palace yard. In February 1813, Agar's successor, Brodrick, was considering how to remedy the dampness of the room – whether by 'staunching' from without or 'studding' from within. The latter method was recommended, although it could not be made a good job unless 'the bookcase' (presumably a series of cases running round the room?) were removed and then put back again.[102] By mid-May 1813, 'the chimney piece ... [had been] taken out of your Grace's study', and in mid-May 1818 'the covering of the yard' was under

1825, 21 M 57/T278.   **96** List dated 16 May 1845, 21 M 57/T264.   **97** Sadleir and Dickinson, *Georgian mansions*, p. 41.   **98** 21 M 57/B14/23.   **99** 21 M 57/B14/1(a), (b) and (c).   **100** Small, miscellaneous notebook kept by Agar, 1793, 21 M 57, general boxes, no. 2.   **101** See also Brodrick to the agent for the Cashel see estate, Austin Cooper, 30 May and 3 June 1806, Clements papers, Ms. 7309/24–5.   **102** William Welland (agent to Brodrick's brother, Lord Midleton) to Brodrick, 13 Feb. 1813, NLI, Ms. 8871/17.   **103** Welland to Brodrick, 17 May 1813 and 1 May 1818, Ms.

discussion.[103] This suggests that Agar's study-cum-watercloset had a very short life – from *c.*1785 to *c.*1815 – because of its situation and construction. It was probably not until its demolition that the room to the right of the front door became a library (as noted in the early twentieth-century description) for the accommodation of the archbishop's personal collection of books. Agar must have kept his own books in the study, and is likely to have used the room to the right of the front door for the purpose which its location implied – that of office or business room.

AGAR'S IMPROVEMENTS TO THE PALACE GARDENS, 1779–1801

When Agar came to Cashel in 1779, he was already well versed, by observation and experience, in the improvement of gardens and grounds. By 1772, he had spent 'a great deal of money on the [bishop's] house, gardens and demesne' at Cloyne.[104] The house, where Agar dispensed the hospitality remarked upon by Richard Griffith, was 'a large edifice, built by Bishop Crow [Charles Crow, bishop of Cloyne, 1702–26] in 1718, and enlarged by several of the succeeding prelates.'[105] It was described in Agar's day as a 'comfortable and handsome residence', though Thomas Crofton Croker thought it 'an old-fashioned and clumsy building, without any claims to architectural beauty.'[106] Infinitely more important than the palace at Cloyne was the garden, with which Agar's most famous predecessor, George Berkeley (bishop of Cloyne, 1734–53), had taken particular pains. Berkeley had reserved for his own enjoyment and use a garden of about four acres, a demesne of fifty and a farm of four hundred.

> In a rocky dell he planted shrubberies and laid out gravelled walks, one of which was lined with myrtles, whose roots he personally covered with large balls of tar, as he believed in its horticultural efficacy. ... In 1796, a later bishop of Cloyne wrote ...: 'at the end of the garden in what we call the rock shrubbery, [there is] a walk leading under young trees among sequestered crags of limestone, which hang many feet above our heads, and ending at the mouth of a cave of unknown length and depth.' Dr Beaufort ... [had] described ... [this cave] in September 1788 ... [as] 'broken and divided into numerous chambers, high, low, broad, [and] narrow, by the most fancifully perforated rocks that imagination can conceive, full of small spars and stalactical exudations petrified in the most grotesque forms ....' [In 1735, Berkeley had written] *The querist,* ... and his estate at Cloyne was the practical exemplification of his theories [expounded in that work]. One such query was no. 121: 'Whether an expense in gardens and plantations would not be ... a domestic magnificence employing many hands within, and drawing nothing from abroad?'[107]

8871/17 and 20.   **104** Agar to Macartney 5 Jan. 1772, *Macartney in Ireland*, p. 303.   **105** Lewis, *Topographical dictionary*, i. 381.   **106** Terence Finley's notes on *The book of Cloyne*; Croker, *Researches in the south of Ireland*, p. 244. What survives today seems to justify Croker's description, and does not suggest that the palace was ever 'a large edifice'.   **107** Edward Malins and the Knight of Glin, *Lost Demesnes: Irish landscape gardening, 1660–1845* (London, 1976), p. 129.

Another episcopal horticulturist whose attitude and activities anticipated the cult of 'the Romantick' and 'the Sublime', and who may have influenced Agar, was Robert Clayton, bishop of Clogher, 1745–58. According to the 5th earl of Orrery (a good judge), Bishop Clayton ate, drank and slept in taste. He succeeded at Clogher to a palace and demesne which had cost £3,000 and which were adorned with a basin and canal and with forts as eye-catchers, and as well as reimbursing his predecessor, proceeded to

> go on with more vigour ... . I have finished one of my cascades, and tomorrow morning shall lay the foundation stone of my grotto, the shell of which I hope to finish before I leave this, and the inside will be the employment of next summer for Mrs Clayton's fancy to embellish. [Actually, it was Mrs Delany who finished the embellishment, which she did with shells. In] ... this country, which is beautifully wild, ... you would have an opportunity of seeing nature in almost its original state. I have walked in the beds of rivers, where I have found some very amazing petrifications that will make a figure in the grotto. I have gone where human footsteps never trod before, under craggy rocks and tremendous precipices, in mountain brooks that were deserted by their streams.[108]

Clayton is not directly relevant to Agar or the bishoprics which Agar occupied. But since Clayton died, still bishop of Clogher, in 1758, and Agar was appointed dean in the next-door diocese of Kilmore in 1765, it is impossible that Agar should not have been familiar with Clayton's 'Romantick' improvements. Agar's specific contribution to the garden and demesne at Cloyne is not recorded, so Cloyne must simply be regarded as his training-ground for Cashel, where he was certainly to be distinguished for 'expense in gardens and plantations.'

Agar's work on the gardens, like his work on the palace, was a mixture of practicality and aesthetics. Pearce's palace occupied a site which was basically *urbs in rure*. Although set back from the main street and its building line by some 150 yards, it still looks as if it was built on an original, long and narrow burgage plot. At the front of this plot and right on the street would have stood the burgage building which was subsequently demolished to make way for the palace fore-court; to the rear was an area of garden, farm or pasture rising up to the Rock without the interruption of other buildings, but cut in half by the old town wall of 1317, which at this point runs parallel with the main street. To the left of the entrance front, and starting level with it, is a walled-in area which today serves as a municipal car park. Some of the walls derive from ancient structures, including a stretch of town wall.[109] The probability is that this

108 Bishop Clayton to Edward Weston (the chief secretary), 4 Sep. 1748, T/3019/1128. For Clayton more generally, see Phillips, *Church of Ireland*, iii, pp 230–31.   109 This impression, from present-day appearances, is confirmed by Welland to Brodrick, 12 Feb. 1803, Ms. 8871/9. The rest of this paragraph is largely based on suggestions made by Professor B.M.S. Campbell on a joint visit to the palace in August 2000 and on the evidence of the first OS map of Cashel.

was Agar's walled garden, where he grew the wide variety of produce which would not have been available for purchase in late eighteenth-century Cashel; and, pre- sumably, some of his new garden buildings were located there. But the ice-house was situated in the north-west corner of the gardens, surprisingly far from the house; and a huge greenhouse, or perhaps two adjoining greenhouses, was situated just to the north-east of the house, in the ornamental garden immediately behind it. 'The ... 28 acres of garden ... were originally an integral part of the cathedral grounds ... [and are] older than the house itself, with two charming mulberry trees planted in 1702 to commemorate the coronation of Queen Anne.'[110] Partly thanks to Agar, the gardens spread wider than the rear of the palace site, particularly to the west and north-west. 'By the handrail leading into the gardens from the house ... stands a diminutive [hop-] plant ..., set there [*c*.1745] by one Richard Guinness' (*c*.1690–*c*.1770), butler to Archbishop Arthur Price, after whom he called his son, Arthur. This Arthur Guinness (1725–1803) was the founder of Guinness' brewery.[111]

The palace, the gardens and the Rock were clearly, in Agar's thinking, one *ensemble*. It is therefore entirely appropriate that Grace's already-mentioned estimate should cover, in the one document, an alteration to the palace, an addition to the palace and a series of garden, demesne and farm buildings. This unified approach is belied by Agar's own account of his (in effect) creation of the gardens, which is as usual matter- of-fact and understated:

> [The Archbishop] laid out the garden next to the house (which was before a kitchen garden) in its present form, built all the forcing houses, melon pits, etc., made a new garden at the end of the vicars' gardens on the piece of ground belonging to the Archbishop, built therein an ice-house, and planted every wall in the three gardens with fruit trees which he brought from Holland, England, Dublin, etc., as also put a great many trees into the quarters of each garden. ... Dr Agar, finding that the nearest part of his demesne was a mile from his house, which rendered it almost useless to keep a cow, and highly inconvenient to turn out any horses that were in use, did by dint of much trouble and considerable expense procure the field at the back of his upper kitchen garden from a variety of persons who had interest therein, and which field he means to leave to his successor, provided he will pay to his heir or representatives the money which Dr Agar paid for the same and for enclosing it with a wall. This field has been planted by Dr Agar, and it is his desire that the trees may never be cut down, but remain a shelter and ornament to the habitation of his successors.[112]

His papers show that he was an enthusiastic and a knowledgeable gardener, and brought to gardening, as he did to everything which interested him, his enormous command of detail. They include a notebook entitled 'Cashel garden' containing

110 *Cashel Palace hotel prospectus for 2001*, p. 15.   111 Ibid.; untitled article by Joan Tighe, [c.1965], IAA, Cashel Palace press cuttings file.   112 21 M 57/B6/1.

planting lists, 1779–1784, and other material running from 1772 to 1794 about the planting and management of young fruit-trees, the management and cultivation of melons, cucumbers and pineapples, plans of fruit houses, hot houses, frames, etc.[113]

The outdoor structures comprised in Grace's estimate, which comes to a total of £932, are a porter's lodge and, on the other side of the building, a cow house, a grape house, a greenhouse, pineries, a pigeon house and a peach house (in addition to the already-mentioned ice house and greenhouse).[114] Grace's porter's lodge, which was a small and simple structure,[115] was replaced – probably in 1806 – by the one which stands today, and his other 'houses' have since disappeared. The peach house can be dated to 1780, because the model for it was one 'now building in the [Phoenix] Park by Sir John Blaquier[e]', an ex-chief secretary who had granted himself the sinecure of bailiff of the Park; Blaquiere sold his lodge in Phoenix Park in 1782. In 1791, he sent Agar a plan of a peach house which seems to have been located at Portlemon, Blaquiere's house near Mullingar, Co. Westmeath.[116] But this was presumably his Phoenix Park peach house reassembled, or a replica of it, and it may have been sent because a peach house at Cashel erected *c.*1780 to the design of Blaquiere's peach house in the Park was not functioning properly. The pineries can be firmly dated to 1780. In July of that year Grace reported back to Agar the results of a kind of study tour on which he had been sent: at Bishopscourt, John Ponsonby's seat in Co. Kildare, 'all their pineries and forcing-houses [are] heated by lime kilns ..., [and] the gardener ... gives the preference to this manner of heating the flues to any other that had been practised before'; 'the lime kiln in Gowran kitchen was beyond my imagination'; and 'the gardener at that place had a particular method of forwarding roses to bloom in the winter months ... [by] putting a common brick on the top of the first flue in the pinery ..., and on that flue the pot with the usual compost and rose tree is to be placed and watered at the proper times.'[117] In July 1783 Agar, 'induced by my gardener's earnest request', wrote to that great panjandrum of the pineapple, William Speechly, the duke of Portland's pioneering gardener at Welbeck Abbey, Nottinghamshire:

> Last year ... [Agar's gardener] perceived that his plants were infested, in the leaves and at the roots, by the white mealy crimson-tinged insect described by you in page 110 of your *Treatise on the culture of the pineapple*.[118] To free them from these insects, he treated them exactly in all respects according to your directions contained in your *Treatise*. But I am sorry to tell you that I now find both my fruiting and succession plants again greatly infested by the same vermin in their leaves and roots. My gardener is almost in despair.[119]

113 21 M 57/D59–64. See also letters referring respectively to melon seeds and fruit trees, from Scott to Agar, [late 1778–early 1779], and from Ellis to Agar, 8 June 1786, T/3719/C/12/63 and C/20/11. 114 21 M 57/B14/1. See also B23–25 and 43–44 and D/62/6. 115 21 M 57/B23/3. 116 Blaquiere to Agar, 4 July 1791, T/3719/C/25/21. 117 Grace to Agar, 2 July 1780, 21 M 57/D59/3(a). 118 York, 1779. Strangely, Agar did not subscribe for Speechly's next work, a *Treatise on the cultivation of the vine* (York, 1790), though Archbishop Fowler of Dublin subscribed for two copies. 119 Agar to Speechly, 6 July 1783, 21 M 57/D59/3(b). See also Sir William Gleadowe

It is not clear what became of Agar's pineapples, or of his gardener, who was called Bannerman. In the case of the latter, Agar may have decided that he wanted, if not a Speechly who would write books, at least a gardener who could conduct his own correspondence. In May 1792, a letter to Agar from Mrs Ellis' nephew, Hans Sloane, dated May 1792, reveals that Agar was willing to import from England an experienced gardener called Roberts and pay him £40 per annum. 'I thought this an high demand, but ... Mr Ellis ... did not think so, for a gardener which [*sic*], in my real belief, is perfectly qualified in every point respecting hothouses and all other productions of a garden.'[120]

Agar was interested in the aesthetics of garden landscape as well as in the 'productions of a garden', his interest in the former being focused on the Rock. 1779, the year of his translation to Cashel, marked the founding by Colonel William Burton Conyngham of Slane Castle, Co. Meath, of 'the Hibernian Society, which reflected a growing pride among the Ascendancy in the heritage of Ireland's past that had been gathering momentum since the 1750s.'[121] Agar's papers include a manuscript history, *c.*1780, of the old cathedral, together with some contemporary engravings of it,[122] all of them possibly related to his abortive scheme of restoring that building and transferring the Church of Ireland cathedral back to it. He had what would have been regarded by the hazy standards of the day as a scholarly interest in antiquities. The view he gave himself – hardly by accident – of St Dominick's Abbey, has already been mentioned. In the same year, 1784, when he heard that a marble 'stone' (presumably slab) had been removed from Holycross Abbey, Co. Tipperary, he took prompt action to ensure that it was returned to its rightful place;[123] and he took a great interest in a solid gold ring found in the palace garden in 1793.[124] He was an early, and perhaps founder (1786), member of the Royal Irish Academy. However, his attitude to the Rock must have been influenced by 'the Romantick' and 'the Sublime' quite as much as by a serious sense of history and antiquity. There is no explicit expression by Agar of this outlook, but it may be inferred from what he had seen, approved and probably improved upon at Cloyne. The Cashel palace garden was of course tame in comparison to the 'stalactical exudations' in the cave at Cloyne, to say nothing of Bishop Clayton's 'craggy rocks' and 'tremendous precipes' at Clogher. But, then, Agar had no need to construct a 'rock shrubbery' or a shell-decorated grotto because he already had a 'stupendous eye-catcher', to exploit which he landscaped the palace garden and demesne and lowered the palace windows. This exploitation of the Rock can be dismissed as Ascendancy arrogance. But a more flattering and probably fairer explanation

Newcomen, 1st Bt, to Agar, 8 July 1783, 21 M 57/D59/4. **120** Sloane to Agar, 21 May 1792, T/3719/C/26/5. Ellis' own gardener at Pope's was as uncommunicative as Bannerman, so perhaps this was a breed characteristic. Following Ellis' death, Lady Mendip wrote: 'Smallcorn is ... in search of a more permanent service. He is a good gardener in every branch and has a bad manner of expressing himself' – Lady Mendip to Agar, 23 Mar. 1802, T/3719/C/36/9. **121** Note provided by Professor Peter Harbison on item 15 in Irish Art Associates' *Catalogue* for summer 2000. **122** 21 M 57/B11. **123** Archbishop James Butler to Agar, 6 Sep. 1778, T/3719/C/18/51. **124** 21 M 57/D70/2.

is that Agar was still the man of sensibility whom Elizabeth Griffith had admired in his younger days.

THE PALACE'S 'RUINOUS CONDITION', 1798–1801

It has been incorrectly assumed that Agar's improvements came late rather than early in his episcopate, and that he was not a free agent in the making of them, because damage is supposed to have been done to the palace by the putative militiamen quartered in it in 1798. The early twentieth-century account states: 'Much of the woodwork in the palace was put in by him to replace [*sic*] damage caused by the soldiers who had been in occupation during the Irish rebellion'; the 2nd Lord Brocket, who bought the palace in 1960, wrote later that, in the aftermath of '98, the rooms 'were re-decorated with Regency cornices and dados by Archbishop Agar'; and Bence-Jones, presumably following suit, states that 'The three main reception rooms in the garden front ... were re-decorated in a simple manner at the beginning of the nineteenth century by ... Agar ..., the palace having suffered damage [in] 1798.'[125] Even on the face of things, this is slightly improbable. Is it likely that government troops, supposing that they had been billeted on the palace, would have occupied the principal reception rooms of one of the most important and influential advisers and supporters of the government? And if they did, surely the pair of carved Corinthian columns and matching pair of pilasters in the entrance hall ('the columnar screen which is ... typical of Pearce's planning'[126]) would have been among the first things to be damaged? Yet they survive intact, as does Pearce's original, magnificently carved staircase.

However, setting aside appearances and probabilities, and turning to harder evidence, we find nothing in the (admittedly incomplete) manuscript and printed records of the commissioners for the relief of suffering loyalists which refers to damage to the Cashel palace.[127] The same applies to the one episcopal palace which definitely suffered major damage in 1798, that of the unlucky Cleaver at Ferns. This means that no particular significance need be attached to the absence of any reference to Cashel; it also invests Cleaver's hard-luck stories, which survive in letters to Lord Egremont, about 'the desolation of my property in the county of Wexford'[128] with unique if vicarious interest. Cleaver's new and very expensive palace was occupied, not by government troops, but by rebels, who drank the cellar dry and deliberately vandalised the building and its contents under the direction of some of his own servants, who he hoped – uncharitably –

125 Letter from Brocket to the editor, *Country Life*, 10 Jan. 1963; Bence-Jones, *Guide to Irish country houses*, p. 61. See also Galloway, *The cathedrals of Ireland*, p. 39.   126 Colvin and Craig, *Elton Hall drawings*, p. lxvii.   127 Neither Agar nor Brodrick is listed as a claimant in the suffering loyalists appendix to *The Commons' journals (Ireland)*, vol. xix (Dublin, 1800), which lists claims entered up to February 1800, and in NA, Official Papers, 61/4, 80/5, 103/2, 126/4, 150/2, 172/5 and 196/1.   128 Cleaver to Agar, 19 June 1798, T/3719/C/32/92.

have fallen in this rebellion. I find the villains have visited my house since June 4th, and have wantonly destroyed chimney pieces, wainscoats, etc., etc., but that the walls and roof remain uninjured. Independent of expense, the trouble of such a repair in the interior of the country is an Herculean labour. I felt that originally. The desolation of the country will increase it.

I see that it is proposed by parliament to repay the losses of the sufferers in this rebellion. This will take off the great weight of my loss. But in a large house, offices and gardens there are many things which cannot be ascertained. It will depend, indeed, upon the proof required, how far I can avail myself of this bounty. My books, cellars, furniture and livestock I value at near £4,000. ... The priest of the parish twice interfered and prevented the house from being burnt to the ground.[129] ... You would be puzzled to conjecture the use my folio books were of to the rebels. They tore out the leaves and made *saddles* of them for their *cavalry*.[130]

It was remarked, after the compensation claim made by Lord Bantry and paid by the government following the French descent on Bantry Bay in 1796–7, that Lord Bantry would 'wish to be invaded again.'[131] Cleaver was unlikely to be a sufferer by his losses if the commissioners set up by parliament to 'repay the losses of the sufferers in this rebellion' (see pp 544–7) accepted his valuation of 'near £4,000': in *c.*1795, Agar had insured the Cashel palace and its contents for only £4,300 (which must have covered the Bolton library, since the contemporary insurance on his very grand Dublin house and its contents was £2,700).[132] More relevant to the case of the Cashel palace was Cleaver's next assertion: 'the king's troops are now in my house and do me as much mischief nearly as the rebels ... . They have torn down the fences of all my plantations, and are very disorderly.'[133] This example – the only one he gives – clearly does not support his assertion. Nothing short of the damage which the palace at Ferns suffered at the hands of rebels on the rampage would have necessitated the kind of alterations which were made at Cashel.

Agar was himself a commissioner for the relief of suffering loyalists (see pp 527–8); so it might be expected that his own papers would have supplied the blank in the official record, especially as they are very full for the year 1798. But they do not. Nor do they contain anything else to substantiate the story of a disorderly militia regiment more formidable to the Cashel palace than to the enemy. They do, however, contain a number of indications tending to refute the story. For a start, because Cashel

---

129 The intervention of the priest was later, uncharitably and improbably, ascribed to the idea that the palace 'would make a good home for Father John Murphy [of Boolavogue, one of the rebel leaders] after the rising.' See Patrick Comerford, 'Church of Ireland clergy and the 1798 rising', in *The clergy and 1798*, p. 233.   130 Cleaver to Egremont, 6 and 24 July 1798, T/3719/C/32/92. 131 Shannon to Boyle, 27 June 1799, *Lord Shannon's letters to his son*, p. 196. Though regarded by Shannon (who was first lord of the treasury) as exorbitant, Bantry's claim was for only £1,200. 132 Miscellaneous notebook, 1761–1827, kept mainly by Agar, 21 M 57/D47.   133 Cleaver to Egremont, 24 July 1798, PHA/57/10.

was a barracks town, it had purpose-built accommodation for officers and 147 infantrymen, and stabling for 3 horses.[134] This barracks was a few houses away from the palace, with its entrance off the main street, and its garden and 'ordnance ground' to the rear abutted the palace gardens. It was Agar who on a number of occasions in the second half of the 1790s requested troops for Cashel, not the authorities who forced them upon the town. In September 1796, for example, he wrote to the lord lieutenant, Lord Camden, referring to the company of foot which at Agar's request had been stationed in the barracks, to the great relief of the inhabitants; and in late March 1798, on the eve (as things turned out) of the rebellion, he wrote to Camden begging 'that some troops may be quartered in the barracks of Cashel to prevent a continuance of these horrid outrages.'[135] This was not mere alarmism. A document of later date reveals that Agar's 'old verger at Cashel' had discovered 'that the city of Cashel was to be attacked on a certain night [in 1798] by a body of 3,000 rebels, which he instantly communicated to the officer then commanding there. In consequence of this, a body of the army was sent out without delay, who made prisoners of, and brought into Cashel, fifteen of the ringleaders, five of whom were hanged and one shot, and thus was prevented a very great carnage which would in all probability have taken place.' The truth of all this was attested by Pat. Hare.[136]

The 'body of the army ... sent out without delay' on this occasion was, by the sound of things, already stationed in Cashel. Had the accommodation in the barracks, then or at some other time in 1798, been inadequate for the number of troops required, Agar had more than enough influence to prevent the overspill from being quartered on the palace. In May 1800, for example (and though it is a later example, it is still pertinent), the lord lieutenant's private secretary wrote 'to assure you most unequivocally that ... Dundrum House [Lord Hawarden's seat] is upon no consideration to be occupied by the king's troops, and I shall this day convey his Excellency's further commands ... not to station any detachment of soldiers at ... Ballinard or the glebe-house belonging to Lord Ely's son ..., unless with the perfect acquiescence of the proprietors.'[137] Had any soldiers ever been accommodated in the palace (and there is no evidence that any were), this would have been just such a small detachment, and it would have been with Agar's 'perfect acquiescence' and for the purpose of defending his house and its contents. Although Agar himself was in Dublin for most of 1798, he had a steward called Timothy Sullivan who lived in the palace, certainly in Agar's absence. The energetic and efficient Pat. Hare was also at hand, and he would

---

134 Gleeson, *Cashel*, p. 283.   135 Agar to Camden, 3 Sep. 1796 and 23 Mar. 1798, T/3719/ C/30/23 and C/32/30; Camden to Agar (with enclosure), 27 Mar. 1798, and Samuel Alleyn to Agar, 28 Mar. 1798, T/3719/C/32/31–2 and 34.   136 Rev. Francis Benson to Agar (his brother-in-law), 24 June 1808, covering a memorial from John Matthews to the duke of York seeking an employment, T/3719/C/42/38–9. This John Matthews, the former verger, was different from John Matthews, the organist. There was also yet another John 'Mathews' (spelt thus), a Dublin musicologist associated with St Patrick's Cathedral; he lived in Dublin from 1776 to 1799, and was famous or infamous for the 'improvements' he made to music which he was copying.   137 Colonel E[dward] B[aker] Littlehales to Agar, 12 May 1800, T/3719/C/34/20.

undoubtedly have intervened at the first sign of licentiousness, and subsequently reported his proceedings to Agar. There is no trace of any such report. Instead, in early March 1798 Hare wrote: 'The officers and privates of the Waterford Militia quartered here [in Cashel, and presumably in the barracks] are very sober, regular, well-behaved men ..., zealous and indefatigable.'[138] They were followed by the Meath Militia, who must have behaved equally well, because when two companies of them were ordered away from Cashel, the officer commanding in the town wrote to Agar urging him to use his influence to get them replaced.[139] In the following month, October 1798, there comes at last a report of soldiers being quartered in at least the precincts of the palace and of their misbehaving. This was not a militia regiment, but men of the Princess of Wales' light dragoons. 'Fifteen of the officers' horses were in your Lordship's stables and the men billeted in the storerooms. ... The servants that attended the stables found means of breaking into the room where I had the apples and pears stored and took a quantity of each', to the value of 14s., which was reimbursed by the colonel.[140] The offending cavalrymen were in Cashel for only a couple of days, and the barracks was not designed for their accommodation, since it was 'by *infantry* chiefly that, from the nature of the country, this place [Cashel] is to be defended.'[141] The fact that the billeted men got no nearer to the palace than the storerooms, and the fact that a trifling and immediately restituted loss of 14s. was thought worthy of Agar's immediate attention, strongly suggest that nothing much more serious had happened before or during the rebellion.

What, then, is the origin of the myth of the militiamen? The first mention of it seems to be that made by Henry Cotton in volume one of his *Fasti* (p. 95), published in 1845. The myth was probably at least twenty years old by then. Since there is some evidence that the library had been neglected in Brodrick's time, perhaps an apologist for Brodrick, or a negligent librarian seeking to justify himself, spun the innocent Cotton, newly arrived in Cashel in the early 1820s, a plausible yarn. But there may be more to the story than that. In June 1797, Lord Hawarden (who was living in Bath at that time), had written to Agar: 'It gives me great satisfaction to hear that you have traced out the *reporter* of your Grace having been inhospitable to the army. A detection of that kind is always a great satisfaction to the injured.'[142] This casual reference suggests that there had been some reputed and well-publicised falling-out between Agar and the army. It occurred a year before the rebellion, and it may have been a fabrication. But it was perhaps sufficient to gain credence in popular mythology and to provide some foundation for the story which Cotton heard and to which he gave substance in his monumental *Fasti*.

Moreover, the exaggerated complaints of dilapidations to the palace which Brodrick made on taking possession of it at the end of 1801, may have given further

---

138 Thomas Kemmis (Agar's attorney) to Timothy Sullivan, 'Palace, Cashel', 8 Nov. 1795, 21 M 57/T358; Hare to Agar, 4 Mar. 1798, T/3719/C/32/10.   139 Colonel Sir Alexander Don to Agar, 11 Sep. 1798, T/3719/C/32/120.   140 Christopher Sturdy (a servant or employee of Agar's), to Agar, 27 Oct. 1798, T/3719/C/32/153.   141 Don to Agar, 11 Sep. 1798, T/3719/C/32/120.   142 Hawarden to Agar, 12 June 1797, T/3719/C/31/73.

credence to the idea that serious damage had been done in Agar's time. Like Price in 1744–6, Brodrick now started an unedifying wrangle which was to last until 1806 and which helped to preclude co-operation between Brodrick and Agar on matters of real importance to the Church (see pp 258–85). Writing to his brother in January 1802, he lamented that, 'when I come to examine the house and offices, I find them to be in a most ruinous condition, and the roof of the house in danger of falling in; whereas my full expectation, in consequence of the discourse he [Agar] held to me, was that not a nail was out of its place. ... I have the prospect of having no house to cover me next summer at Cashel. But, besides this, from my knowledge of the man I have to deal with, I am confident I cannot bring matters to any settlement without an open breach, and probably receiving much unpleasant language.'[143] Primate Stuart, as usual, echoed Brodrick's sentiments: 'I am extremely sorry that you are likely to be engaged in a dispute concerning dilapidations in a country where dilapidations are ill-understood, and with a man disposed to take every illiberal advantage.'[144] Eight months later, with his 'difference with the Archbishop of Dublin' unresolved and a commission of dilapidations appointed or on the point of being appointed, Brodrick inveighed against the inadequacy 'of our laws on dilapidations, particularly the 10th of William III ... . It is very much to be lamented that either ... [they] are so confused in themselves, or else so little understood by the gentlemen of that profession, that opinions the most contradictory to each other are given by the same person, a lawyer of the first eminence.'[145]

In the case of the Cashel palace, as in many other things, the perception of Agar was far worse than the reality. In 1806, the commission of dilapidations to whom Brodrick's 'difference with the Archbishop of Dublin' had been referred, found against Brodrick, ordered that he was 'not to be allowed the costs of suit or the dilapidations' and valued the latter at only £200.[146] Brodrick no doubt (although there is no evidence of this) attributed the decision to ignorance of, or confusion in, the law: he can hardly have attributed it to Agar's disposition 'to take every illiberal advantage', since Agar and he would have had an equal say in the composition of the commission. Granted that Agar had been in occupation of the palace for twenty-two years and that his 'improvements' to it had affected only parts of it and in any case appear to have been completed by 1785, dilapidations valued at only £200 seem to betoken a very high level of stewardship. The commission of dilapidations then went on to value these 'improvements.' They confirmed Agar's figure of £1,123 for the cost of his work on the palace and garden, and ordered Brodrick to pay two-thirds of it, with interest back to 1802. The proportion of two-thirds requires comment. In general, the act of 1726 (*12 George I, cap. 10*) which still regulated the rebuilding and improvement (as opposed to the new building) of palaces, glebe-houses, etc., provided that three-quarters of the cost of all duly certified improvements should be reimbursed by the

143 Brodrick to Midleton, 5 Jan. 1802, Ms. 1248, vol. 18, ff. 44–5.   144 Stuart to Brodrick, 7 Mar. 1802, NLI, Ms. 8869/1.   145 Brodrick to Stuart, 23 Nov. 1802, ibid. For other strictures on the low calibre of the bar and bench in Ireland in the wake of the Union, see pp 271–2.   146 Brodrick to Austin Cooper, 30 May and 3 June 1806, TCD, Ms. 7309/24–5.

successor. But sec. 4 made an exception of 'any repairs, additions or improvements which shall be made to any buildings or other improvements which have been formerly made.' This is a fairly faithful, if inelegant, description of the largely cosmetic nature of some of Agar's alterations. The figure of £1,123, it should be noted, was certainly not inflated: Grace's two sets of estimates, the first dateable to 1780 and the second dated 1784, come (as has been seen) to a grand total of £1,177. The discrepancy of £54 can probably be attributed to the cost of lowering the windows on the garden front, which would have been inadmissible because the change served no structural or remedial purpose. Ultimately, much depended on what Agar's ecclesiastical superior, in this case Primate Robinson, had been prepared to certify as 'fit and necessary for ... [Agar's] more convenient residence.' It looks as if Robinson had taken the view that pineapples were a necessary part of the diet of an Irish archbishop!

THE ARCHBISHOP OF DUBLIN'S 'OLD AND MISERABLE MANSIONS', 1778–1821

While this dispute was raging between Agar and Brodrick, Agar had a more momentous decision to take in regard to the two palaces appertaining to the archbishopric of Dublin, the town palace of St Sepulchre, in Kevin Street, near St Patrick's Cathedral, and the country palace at Tallaght, Co. Dublin. When Agar had been in the running for Dublin in 1778, the archiepiscopal agent, George Gamble, had mentioned the two palaces and the Tallaght demesne as assets and attractions of the archbishopric; and a diocesan clergyman who was probably Mrs Fowler's nephew, later claimed that Archbishop Fowler had put the two palaces 'in perfect repair ... [and] maintained in both ... [a] liberal and unvaried hospitality.'[147] But Agar had had since 1775 a fine Dublin house of his own in St Stephen's Green (where he continued to reside), had no need of St Sepulchre and had practical and plausible reasons for considering it to be no longer suitable as a residence. In 1796, when the state of Fowler's health opened the possibility that Agar would be translated to Dublin, his wife, Lady Somerton, had written him a spirited letter on the subject of the Dublin palaces:

> I confess I am of your mind and should not think it worthwhile to exchange from where you are at this present time; for, in the first place, you would remove from two very comfortable houses [Cashel palace and St Stephen's Green] in excellent repair with everything to your mind and agreeably situated, to two horrible old, cold, smoky and disagreeable dungeons, sadly out of repair and tumbling about your ears, for which you would have to pay £3,000 or £4,000 *hard cash*. ... You would be uncomfortable for two years at least, if you were to take either of these old and miserable mansions into your hands, and

147 Gamble to Agar, 12 Dec. 1778, T/3719/C/12/54; Kennedy, 'Dublin and Glendalough' (quoting the Rev. Dr Robert Dealtry [1755–1830]), p. 208.

after all you would never make them what this house [Cashel palace] really now is, most commodious and agreeable. Besides, I don't like to part with *cash* in these hard times. ... Nothing can be more horrible than ... that desolate and uninhabited Siberian country about T[allaght] Castle. We should all die of the vapours, and both residences would take us out of the way of everything and everybody we love and like ... to go and live in the alehouses and buttermilk cellars of Kevin Street ...; and as to Tallagh[t] C[astle], except two rooms which are habitable *to look at*, all the interior and exterior are dreadful, and uncomfortable to the last degree. ... [In addition to the £3,000 or £4,000] we should be obliged to lay out a good sum in order to be able to live in any comfort in either of the houses.[148]

An act of 1742 (*15 George II, cap. 5, sec. 5*) authorised 'archbishops and bishops ... to change the sites of their mansion houses.'[149] But this applied only when the existing palace was in an inconvenient situation – which could not possibly be said of St Sepulchre, in view of its proximity, not only to St Patrick's but to Christ Church Cathedral as well. (Admittedly, it was also near the dangerous and intermittently riotous Liberties.[150]) In the case of St Sepulchre, it was the building itself which was inconvenient. Fowler had made one attempt, probably in 1793, to replace it with an alternative house (belonging to his son-in-law, the 12th Viscount Mountgarret,[151] so some form of financial sharp practice is to be suspected). Presumably, he had been deterred by all the legal and other complications. Agar, more purposeful than Fowler, obtained a valuation of St Sepulchre in 1803 and applied to parliament in 1804 for authority to sell it to the government and earmark the proceeds for the purchase of a more suitable archiepiscopal residence. Primate Stuart was displeased: 'the Archbishop of Dublin's bill ... has in its present form ... no precedent.'[152] Agar did not attend the 1803–4 session of parliament; but, clearly, he wrote to relations and friends to ask them to support his bill. To Macartney, a British as well as an Irish peer, he explained at the beginning of February 1804 that the bill authorising the sale of St Sepulchre had been 'drawn under the direction of government ... . [The] old palace ... in the Liberties ... will be very useful to them, although altogether unfit in every respect for the residence of the archbishop of Dublin.'[153] In response to a similar letter, Lord Clifden replied in mid-March expressing the view that 'it will meet with no opposition, having the assistance of government and being in itself so very right and proper.'[154] Lords Callan and Carleton also agreed to 'pay every attention to the business you have mentioned.'[155] (Lord Clifden, it should be remembered, had a seat in

---

148 Lady Somerton to Agar, 13 Oct. 1796, T/3719/C/30/34.   149 D'Alton, *Archbishops of Dublin*, p. 336.   150 Legg, *The Synge letters*, pp xvi and xxxi–xxxii. These refer to a much more unruly period fifty years previously. However, 'a number of villains' invaded the palace, in Fowler's absence, in November 1787, murdered the porter and a housemaid and set fire to the building in several places – *The British Mercury ...*, vol. iii for 1787, pp 358–9.   151 Lady Somerton to Agar, 13 Oct. 1796, T/3719/C/30/34.   152 Stuart to Brodrick, 21 Apr. 1804, Ms. 8869/3.   153 Agar to Macartney, 4 Feb. 1804, PRONI, D/572/B/191.   154 Clifden to Agar, 14 Mar. 1804, T/3719/C/38/12. 155 Callan to Agar, 14 Mar. 1804, T/3719/C/38/14.

the Lords as 2nd Lord Mendip, and Lords Callan and Carleton were, like Agar himself, Irish representative peers.)

Meanwhile, the bishop of Derry, the Hon. William Knox, was in the process of making a similar application, in his case so that he could replace the palace built *c.*1760 in Bishop Street, within the walls of Derry City, with a palace situated in the episcopal demesne on the outskirts. Both the unsecluded situation and the general inconvenience of this town palace had been remarked upon by Dr Beaufort in 1787. It was 'very large', but had 'no good room, being very ill-contrived.' In *c.*1770, Frederick Hervey had addressed this latter problem by building, and then re-building, a banqueting house in the garden. This and other 'improvements' would saddle his successor, by Beaufort's reckoning, with a bill for £2,000.[156] However, Hervey then abandoned, neglected and let the palace, so that when he died in 1803 his executors had to pay Knox £4,000 for dilapidations.[157] Since the previous year, it had been let to the government as a barracks,[158] and Knox decided to sell it for the same object, and to use the proceeds (plus the supposed difference of £2,000 between the value of the improvements and that of the dilapidations) to build a more suitable replacement. Although this all seemed sound and sensible, Stuart considered that 'the sale of episcopal houses at this moment, and circumstanced as we are [seeking to get the controls imposed by *43 George III, cap. 158*, removed (see pp 263–5)], is scarcely a prudent measure.'[159] Stuart may also have suspected that Agar and Knox were acting in concert, since they had been on friendly, metropolitical terms in their previous dioceses, Cashel and Killaloe.[160] Neither, evidently, consulted Stuart. The next he heard was 'that the Bishop of Derry has sold his house to government without obtaining a special act of parliament for that purpose. ... This transaction, ... if it has taken place, may be productive of very important consequences.'[161] The circumstances of the two transactions were different, in that the sale of the Derry palace possibly came within the terms of the act of 1742. For whatever reason, Agar did not follow the Derry precedent and obtained his special act of parliament (*44 George III, cap. 63*), which received the royal assent on 29 June 1804. The price realised was £7,000.[162]

Stuart was also concerned about the familiar issue of dilapidations. 'If the Archbishop of Dublin received money for dilapidations, that money should be vested, with the purchase money of the house, in the hands of trustees, and be applied to the same use, as in fact it makes a part of the value of the house.'[163] He need not have fretted, as this was provided for in the act. Agar had received from Fowler's executors £923 12*s.* 7*d.* for dilapidations, which was added to the £7,000 to constitute an interest-bearing fund to go towards the purchase of the new town palace which would be required by a successor who, unlike Agar, did not already possess a suitable Dublin

156 Beaufort's journal, 1787, PRONI, MIC/250, pp 25–6.   **157** Stuart to Brodrick, 3 June 1804, Ms. 8869/3.   **158** Peter Rankin, *Irish building ventures of the earl-bishop of Derry*, pp 8–9. **159** Stuart to Brodrick, 3 June 1804, Ms. 8869/3.   **160** Knox to Agar, 26 July 1801, T/3719/ C/35/19.   **161** Stuart to Brodrick, 21 Mar. 1805, Ms. 8869/3.   **162** Samuel A. Ossory Fitzpatrick, *Dublin: a historical and topographical account of the city* (London, 1907), p. 57.   **163** Stuart to Brodrick, 12 Mar. 1804, Ms. 8869/2.

house. It also had to cover the cost of a site or a building to be used as the courthouse for the archbishop's manorial court of St Sepulchre (hitherto a part of the palace).[164] In October 1806, the fund stood at £9,873,[165] and by 1810, when Agar's successor bought No. 16 St Stephen's Green as a see house (but with no provision for a courthouse), it stood at £11,763 10s. 2d., all invested in government 5 per cent stock. The new town palace cost some £8,600, so the archbishop was (in valuation terms) more amply provided-for; and, as Francis Johnston reckoned that a new courthouse could be bought for £1,200, the diocese had made a profit – all thanks to Agar's decision to relieve himself and his successors of St Sepulchre. Agar personally was some hundreds of pounds out of pocket as a result. This was because he had paid Fowler's executors £885 7s. 10d., representing three-quarters of the amount which Fowler had spent c.1781–3 on improvements to St Sepulchre. Agar never received any value for that sum, because he never lived in that palace; and at his death, his executors received only £590 5s. 2½d. (i.e. half Fowler's expenditure) from Agar's successor (who also received no value for his money).[166] Once again, Agar's reputation for sharp dealing had given rise, in Stuart's mind, to a suspicion which was not only unfounded but the reverse of the truth. Agar's motivation was, simply, to bring the expenditure of the archbishopric of Dublin more nearly into line with its resources. If anything about the transaction was reprehensible, it was the long-term architectural consequences to St Sepulchre. From an army barracks it was eventually converted into the Kevin Street police barracks, and today little of it remains except a mediaeval vault, a sixteenth-century window, a Mannerist Jacobean doorcase and an eighteenth-century staircase.[167]

Watty Cox claimed that Agar had 'converted the ancient and venerable episcopal palace in Kevin Street into a barrack, and the palace at Tallagh[t] into a deserted wilderness.' In fact, Agar took no such radical decision in regard to Tallaght, though the country palace did not have the antiquity and venerability of St Sepulchre to recommend and protect it. In the quaint language of D'Alton, John Hoadly, archbishop of Dublin, 1729–42, had 'committed great havoc on the antique remains here, in the progress of what antiquarians would not deem improvements.'[168] Elsewhere, D'Alton commented, more indulgently, that Hoadly had 'expended about £2,500 in overturning the ancient remains of the castle of Tallaght, and constructed from the materials a convenient and elegant episcopal palace.'[169] Other authorities, however, agreed with Lady Somerton that it was neither convenient nor elegant.

> The extensive ruins of the ancient castle of Tallaght ... stood on the site of an
> earlier monastic establishment ... . [The] large episcopal mansion [built by

---

164 Case paper relating to dilapidations, [1822?], Armagh diocesan registry papers, PRONI, DIO 4/19/7/3. 165 'The state of Earl Normanton's property, 1806', 21 M 57/D23. 166 DIO 4/19/7/3. 167 Craig, *Dublin, 1660–1860*, p. 6; oral information from the Knight of Glin and the Very Rev. R.B. McCarthy, dean of St Patrick's. 168 D'Alton, *The history of the county of Dublin* (Dublin, 1838), p. 768. (D'Alton's *County of Dublin* and *Archbishops of Dublin* were companion volumes, published in the same year and financed by the same subscription list.) 169 D'Alton, *Archbishops of Dublin*, p. 336.

Hoadly was] thus described by Austin Cooper, the antiquary, in 1779: 'For a thing of the kind it is the poorest ever I saw. It is a large piece of patchwork ... devoid of either order or regularity ....' Brewer in his *Beauties of Ireland* (1826) gives the following account of it as it existed shortly before its demolition: 'The present structure is a spacious, but long and narrow, building ..., destitute of pretensions to architectural beauty. The interior contains many apartments of ample proportions, but none that are highly embellished ... . From all the windows of the reception rooms, fine views are obtained.'

Although these were unremarked by Austin Cooper a year later, 'Archbishop Fowler [had] enclosed the garden and made other improvements in the palace' in 1778.[170] Between then and 1787, Fowler spent some £3,800 on improvements to Tallaght, of which Agar reimbursed Fowler's executors three-quarters, or some £2,850. (Lady Somerton had been correct in her calculation of 1796 that Agar 'would have to pay £3,000 or £4,000' for both palaces: the actual sum was £3,735.) This was offset by the £1,493 15s. 2d. which Fowler's executors paid Agar for dilapidations, so that the nett cost to Agar of taking possession of Tallaght was some £1,356.[171]

To judge from a letter written to him by Lady Mendip, Agar initially welcomed the fact that 'your summer residence is so near Dublin [that] you will be able to overlook yourself your garden and be well supplied from thence.'[172] He set about applying the dilapidations money for Tallaght, once he received it, to the refurbishment of the building. In late April 1803, he urged Alderman Thorpe (the builder he was employing) to have everything done by the end of June; towards the end of June, he wrote to his agent, John Hare, 'about having the slating, gutters and roof of Tallaght palace and offices perfectly staunched'; and at the beginning of July he wrote again to Hare 'to say I hope Tallaght is ready for me in all respects.'[173] This again shows that Primate Stuart's suspicions about the use to which Agar put dilapidations money were unfounded. For all this initial expenditure, and for all Agar's tidy-mindedness and interest in architecture, he concerned himself no further with Tallaght and simply contributed to its decay by neglect. He maintained the gardens and a home farm, employing a steward, Robert Parker, to look after them, keep vandals and robbers at bay, and send him fresh fruit and vegetables to Stephen's Green. But he let the demesne, and 'had the hearths at Tallaght stopped, and gave notice thereof to the [hearthmoney] collector';[174] so he can never have lived in the palace. Presumably, he took the view that finding a radical solution to one palace was quite enough for any one archbishop. As will be seen (pp 503–4), there was in effect an *interregnum* in the archbishopric between 1811 and 1820, so that the time for a radical solution to the problem of Tallaght did not come until the latter year. 'The palace

170 D'Alton, *History of Co. Dublin*, p. 768.   171 DIO 4/19/7/3; 'Admeasurement of dilapidations at the palace, offices and demesne at Tallaght', Mar. 1802, DIO 4/19/7/1.   172 Lady Mendip to Agar, 3 Nov. 1801, T/3719/C/35/27.   173 Notebook containing *précis* by Agar of the substance of his out-letters, 1800–03, in this instance out-letters of 27 Apr., 22 June and 1 July 1803, 21 M 57/D55.   174 21 M 57/D23; John Hare to Agar, 2 Apr. 1808, T/3719/C/42/15.

having fallen into ruinous condition, ... and there being no funds wherewith to repair it, an act of parliament was passed in 1821 divesting the see of the responsibility for its maintenance.'[175] The act stated 'that the buildings and offices ... were then in such a state of decay as to be unfit for habitation, that a country residence for the archbishop of Dublin was unnecessary, and that the income of the see was inadequate to support the expense of the two establishments [i.e. Tallaght and the see house in Dublin which by then had been bought to replace St Sepulchre].'[176] This last point was valid (and would have been warmly endorsed by Agar), even though the income of the see had revived very considerably by 1821 from its drooping state of £4,208 nett per annum in 1806 (p. 412). As for Tallaght, by 1838, 'only one tower' of the palace remained, 'while, immediately beneath, lie the lawn and extensive gardens, preserving in the Friar's Walk, as one particular avenue is termed, and in the ancient yews, cypresses, laurels and above all some magnificent walnut trees, the reminiscences of the olden time.'[177]

BRODRICK'S ALTERATIONS TO THE CASHEL PALACE, 1803–14

In contrast to Agar's experience in Dublin, Brodrick clearly admired the palace he found awaiting him at Cashel. He was, however, much more of a 'moderniser' than Agar, and embarked on an extensive, and expensive (although details do not survive), programme of works on both palace and gardens. If there is a dearth of accounts for these improvements, there is no dearth of correspondence. Brodrick's brother, Lord Midleton, employed as his head agent one William Welland, who was plainly an architect *manqué*.[178] He had scope for this talent in the management of Lord Midleton's estate, which included all or part of Cobh harbour, where a great deal of building and town-planning was afoot in the early nineteenth century. Brodrick relied on Welland, not Austin Cooper (the agent for the Cashel see estate), to supervise the work on Cashel palace, to which Welland paid frequent visits when Brodrick was absent in Dublin or London. From Cashel (or from Midleton or Cobh), he wrote numerous letters during the period 1802–21 describing what was going on, reporting difficulties and requesting instructions. These letters are of great architectural interest in their own right; they also establish precisely what Agar did *not* do to the palace, and provide corroboration that the militiamen are a myth.

175 Weston St John Joyce, *The neighbourhood of Dublin, its topography, antiquities and historical associations* ... (Dublin, 1939), p 200.   176 D'Alton, *History of Co. Dublin*, p. 769.   177 Ibid., p. 759. 178 One of his sons, Joseph (1798–1860), became a professional architect. Through Brodrick's influence, Joseph Welland was apprenticed to John Bowden, the architect to the board of first fruits, c.1817. When Bowden died in 1821, William Welland asked Brodrick to secure the succession to Joseph (Welland to Brodrick, 26 Dec. 1821, Ms. 8871/21). There followed a *hiatus*, at the end of which the booming architectural work of the board was divided, and c.1826 Joseph was appointed architect to the metropolitan province, not of Cashel, but of Tuam. He was appointed sole architect to the board's successor body, the ecclesiastical commission, in 1843, at a salary of c.£700 per annum, and died in post in 1860. I am indebted for much of this information to Mr David Griffin, Director of IAA.

The earliest of them confirm that the palace roof was, as might have been expected from Brodrick's alarmist description of it, Brodrick's first concern. In late January 1803, Welland commented: 'With respect to the lead gutters of the palace, I think myself they can be repaired. ... The stone-cutter is settled with about the eaves'; and in early April, he advised Brodrick 'to agree for the slates, even if they should be something higher than usual.'[179] However, the offices at least cannot have been as 'ruinous' as Brodrick had alleged, since 'the entire new roof' for the stables was not undertaken until 1812.[180] The work carried out on the palace roof in 1803 amounted to much more than the repairs and re-slating necessitated by Agar's dilapidations and suggested by Welland's first letter. In the end, the roofline was dramatically altered, with a view to making the top floor rooms habitable by guests as well as, or instead of, servants. In late April, Welland wrote:

> I foresee there will be some difficulty in making the skylights for the use of the upper rooms from the interior part of the roof, and I fear, along with the increase of expense, that it will cause some delay also. If they were made on the front, they would be seen, unless something by way of ornament could be contrived on the parapet opposite to them, to hide them from view.[181]

A later reference to re-using the glass from 'the old attic storey sashes'[182] shows that there already were windows admitting light to the top floor, while Welland's concern that the proposed new 'skylights' would be seen, suggests that the existing windows were invisible. By 'sashes' he seems to mean what we would call 'skylights', and by 'skylights' what we would call dormers. The roof has a central valley, and the original idea in late April may have been to insert invisible dormers into the facing slopes of the *inside* of the roof.[183] In just over a week, the whole plan had been changed and a much bolder one adopted, presumably on Brodrick's instructions. On 6 May, Welland reported: 'The carpenters are all employed in splicing the beams and principals in front of the palace.'[184] This must have been preparatory to the insertion of the four present dormers into the front of the roof. There is no mention in Welland's letters of the four matching dormers on the garden front and the two on the side of the house facing St Dominick's Abbey, but presumably they date from the same time. No attempt was made to conceal the dormers. Rather, they were built as a deliberately prominent feature, which not only does not detract from Pearce's design, but could be (and has been) mistaken for an integral part of it. By creating 'three best garrets' – i.e.

---

179 William Welland to Brodrick, 30 Jan. and 6 Apr. 1803, Ms. 8871/9.   180 Welland to Brodrick, 27 Apr. and 16 July 1812, Ms. 8871/16.   181 Welland to Brodrick, 28 Apr. 1803, Ms. 8871/9.   182 Welland to Brodrick, 8 Mar. 1804, Ms. 8871/11.   183 I am grateful to Mr David Sheehan of Sheehan & Barry, architects, who worked on the palace in the mid-1990s, for pointing out that this would not have admitted much light. This is because a relatively high-ceilinged, axial corridor runs the whole way along the underside of the central valley. Today, one of the rooms on the top floor is lit – ineffectively – by a skylight set into the inside of the roof.   184 Welland to Brodrick, 6 Apr. [*sic* – he means May] 1803, Ms. 8871/9.

good rooms on the attic storey – and later by creating or extending 'the servants' apartments ... below' in the basement[185] and by building a detached, two–storey mews to the right of the entrance front and running between it and the porter's lodge, Brodrick 'gained in accommodation',[186] while at the same time preserving the essentials of Pearce's design.

The next phase of Brodrick's work related to the entrance and approach to the palace (and perhaps included the building of the mews, for the dating of which there is no documentary evidence). The 'steps at the hall door' were re-made, and 'the iron railing' on either side of them installed, late in 1806. At the same time, 'the enormous sum of £1 12s. 6d. [was paid] for liberty to quarry the stones for your Grace's piers' – presumably the gate piers at the main entrance from the street.[187] Grace's elevation of *c.*1780 showing his proposed porter's lodge and the then gates, establishes that in Agar's time the piers were low and insignificant and the gates wooden and narrow.[188] So the present inviting and yet dignified gates, gate piers and approach to the palace, can be dated to *c.*1806. The same must apply to the present porter's lodge, a pleasing, two-storey, 'Gothique' building, with matching bows on either side of its front door. The first O.S. (which dates from nearly twenty years after Brodrick's death) shows a 'sweep' in the forecourt of the palace, instead of the formal, axial approach which must have been there originally and which is there again today. It was probably Brodrick who made this change to the approach.

The re-modelling of the interior of the palace did not begin until 1812, although there is one isolated reference in a letter from Welland of late September 1803 to his having 'altered the cornices of [the] drawing room windows.'[189] The early twentieth-century description concludes perceptively (granted that it was based on only the visual evidence) that 'The reception rooms, opening off one another, contain no Georgian features of interest, ... [because they were] denuded of the original panelling and mantels apparently about 1810, when some so-called improvements were carried out.' From Welland's letters, it is certain that Agar had preserved 'the original panelling' in the business room to the right of the front door and in the eating rooms he created on the left side of the hall, and almost certain that he had preserved the drawing room panelling as well.[190] The letters also show that Brodrick was hesitant about sweeping away the panelling in these rooms and upstairs, and that it was Welland who egged him on or presented him with a *fait accompli*. In February 1812, he wrote:

> I have taken down all the wainscot of the dining parlour and breakfast room here, as I totally despaired of making a good and permanent job by letting any part of it remain up. I now wish to be informed whether your Grace would wish to have the stoco [*sic* – stucco] frieze and cornice plain or ornamental. The

185 Welland to Brodrick, 17 May 1813 and 16 July 1812, Ms. 8871/17 and 16.   186 Welland to Brodrick, 25 May 1813, Ms. 8871/17.   187 Welland to Brodrick, 17 Nov. 1806, Ms. 8871/14. 188 21 M 57/B23/3.   189 Welland to Brodrick, 28 Sep. 1803, Ms. 8871/10. Aidan O'Boyle points out that the plasterwork of the drawing-room cornice is early nineteenth-century in style and almost certainly post-Agar.   190 Welland to Brodrick, 16 July 1812, Ms. 8871/16.

difference between the latter and former will be something about forty guineas. But as they are principal rooms, my own opinion is that they should be finished well.[191]

Presumably, Brodrick had wanted to leave the panelling up to dado height? In mid-July, Welland asked him 'to consider whether you would have the drawing room stocoed [*sic* – stuccoed] and new trimmed now or not … . The necessity of doing it is more obvious than ever.'[192] In the end, the only panelling on the *piano nobile* to survive Welland's purge was that in the entrance and staircase halls. What is now to be seen in Agar's business room/Brodrick's library to the right of the front door, is mostly original to Pearce and the palace, but has been re-cycled round the house until reaching its present location only in the mid-1990s.[193]

Welland then moved up to the main bedroom floor. The early twentieth-account notes with relief that 'successive archbishops did not think it necessary for appearance sake to transform the upper part of the house, so the bedrooms retain the original window seats, broken architraves and fireplaces; the corridors communicating are panelled in the same manner as the hall, and both rooms and doors are very high.' However, both the woodwork in the bedrooms and the panelling in the corridors had narrow escapes. In January 1813, Welland wrote:

> What your Grace proposes with respect to letting the timber work about the windows and doors in the bedrooms remain in its present form, can of course be adopted. … But the frames, mouldings and every part of the work is [*sic*] so different from anything made in the present day, and will I conceive project so much into the rooms, that it certainly will do but little credit to your Grace's taste, and – what is still worse – will deprive you of self-approbation every time you see it.[194]

Having lost this argument, he urged that 'the wainscot in the corridor should be taken down and the walls plastered, leaving none of it remaining above stairs except what is in the staircase'[195]. Austin Cooper (surprisingly for an 'antiquary') and 'several gentlemen who have visited the palace' agreed with Welland. But Brodrick stood firm.

The original chimneypieces, with Agar's grates set into them, must have seemed too small and plain for the 'principal rooms' on the *piano nobile*, now that their panelling had been removed. Accordingly, Welland went to town on new ones, which cost a surprisingly large amount of money. For the dining room, he bought a chimneypiece 'of Limerick black marble. … The price of all together [chimneypiece and grate] is £43 5s. 0d. – too much, I fear, but I could not meet with what pleased me cheaper, or indeed at any price.'[196] In order to give pride of place to this insertion, he had changed 'the fireplace so as to have it in the centre of the dining room.'[197] (Clearly,

191 Welland to Brodrick, 17 Feb. 1812, ibid.   **192** Welland to Brodrick, 16 July 1812, ibid.   **193** Oral information from David Sheehan.   **194** Welland to Brodrick, 9 Jan. 1813, Ms. 8871/17.   **195** Welland to Brodrick, 25 May 1813, ibid.   **196** Welland to Brodrick, 16 July 1813, ibid.   **197** Welland to

Agar had left it off-centre when he created his new, enlarged room.) Another new chimneypiece, costing £18, was ordered from Mr Hargrave of Cork City. It was 'of the same pattern of that in your Grace's [i.e. Agar's soon-to-be-demolished] study. The fluted parts, shelf and returned slips are white and the slabs that fill up the space between the fluted parts and the returned slips is [*sic*] mottled with dark blue and white.'[198] Then the supply of chimneypieces in Cork City dried up. In April 1814, Welland wrote that there was 'no alternative but to get one of the Midleton marble [chimneypieces from Mr Shanahan], because there is not more than two or three drawing room chimneypieces in Cork and they are not what your Grace would approve of, either in shape or price.'[199] Following the insertion of new and more fashionable chimneypieces in most of the *piano nobile* rooms, those which they replaced were moved to the main bedroom floor, and those which they in turn replaced were moved to 'the best garrets.' There was also 'the chimneypiece which was taken out of your Grace's study ... [and which Welland] put up in the middle bedroom on the south side of the house.'[200] This means that the 'original ... fireplaces' in the rooms on the main bedroom floor and in some of those in the attic storey were not original to the rooms concerned, and were grander than those installed *c*.1730. Even with all this shuffling around, three new chimneypieces were needed for the main bedroom floor, 'one for the best bedroom and one for each of the middle dressing rooms.'[201]

Along with the moving and inserting of chimneypieces went something similar in respect of communicating doors and 'sham doors', particularly on both sides of the dining room, and between the dining room and the breakfast parlour.[202] But in the north-east corner of the house, a major structural change was made. In Pearce's palace, the space behind where the main staircase rose was occupied by a one-bay room overlooking the garden and by the backstairs. The former must have been 'the house-keeper's room' in Agar's day.[203] Brodrick caused the two spaces to be knocked together to form 'the little drawing room', which has two windows overlooking the garden and which, to judge from present-day appearances, must have made a charming *boudoir* for Mrs Brodrick. Shanahan's Midleton-marble chimneypiece was installed there. The

Brodrick, 17 Feb. 1812, Ms. 8871/16.   **198** Welland to Brodrick, 25 Nov. 1812, ibid.   **199** Welland to Brodrick, 23 and 28 Apr. 1814, Ms. 8871/18. Aidan O'Boyle informs me that this was the Michael Shanahan who built Downhill for the Earl-Bishop of Derry in the 1770s and 1780s.   **200** Welland to Brodrick, 17 May 1813, Ms. 8871/17.   **201** Ibid. In the intervening two hundred years (almost), there has been a good deal more shuffling. All Welland's grand Regency chimneypieces have gone from the *piano nobile* (Archbishop Laurence was probably too mean or uninterested to buy them!). The dining-room chimneypiece of today matches the one in the best bedroom, and both look as if they date from *c*.1730, but were beefed-up with *c*.1780 columnar additions to their sides. The drawing-room chimneypiece is a modern replica, and the skirting and dado on both sides of it have been cleverly spliced to fill the gaps left by the removal of a larger predecessor.   **202** See, for example, Welland to Brodrick, 17 Feb., 4 Mar. and 16 July 1812, Ms. 8871/16.   **203** For the evidence on which this conjecture is based – the existence of hobs on the grate in that room – see Lady Somerton to Agar, 15 Oct. 1796 (T/3719/C/30/35), and Welland to Brodrick, 25 May 1813 (Ms. 8871/17).

creation of this new room made it necessary to build an addition to the main block in which the new backstairs were located, along with a 'lobby' or landing on the main bedroom floor and a new 'passage to the garden' from the *piano nobile*.[204] Referring to the latter, Welland wrote in mid-July 1812: 'I hope ... [it] will be more convenient than your Grace expected, as it opens from the hall under the grand stairs, and has no communication with the backstairs.' He added: 'The small drawing room is nearly plastered and all the trimmings ready to put up.'[205]

All these changes to the exterior and interior of the palace were accompanied, and in the main preceded, by alterations to the garden. Welland's letters of 1802–4 are full of the latter: indeed, he at one point justifies the 'backward' appearance of the garden on the ground that everything in it 'is begun anew.' Not suprisingly, the gardener – presumably an inheritance from Agar – was 'disheartened.' The letters of these early years mention the planting of 'two beautiful red cedars', building a 'grapery' or 'grape-house', building a 'long peach-house' (which was additional to the peach-house built by Agar), building new 'hot-houses' or 'forcing-houses', buying and planting twenty new pine plants, building a wall to support the ice-house, and so on.[206] As is usual in such situations, no credit is given to Brodrick's predecessor for the latter's formative work on the gardens. Instead, Welland reported, as if this were a new development, that 'the vegetable and fruit gardens are clean and cropped'; also that 'the fruit trees in general are more judiciously pruned than heretofore.'[207] He found fault with the layout of 'the pleasure ground', and in particular with Agar's positioning of 'a necessary', which created 'an awkwardness in the walk running east and west parallel with the palace.'[208] The general tendency of his letters, whether about house or garden, is to egg Brodrick on to fresh expenditure, while the doctrine which he is always preaching is economy. Thus, he proposed taking on as gardener one Nick. Flood, who had been working under Pedlie, the royal gardener at Hampton Court; and when Brodrick queried the financial implications of this proposal, Welland warned him sagely of the danger of employing an unskilled man: 'It may be the work of years to recover the mischief of a day.'[209] In fact, Welland answered his own description of his pet aversion, 'the Dublin tradesmen'; they, he complained, were 'more destructive than even the dry rot, often penetrating to the bottom of a gentleman's pocket before he is aware of their devouring influence.'[210] When the work on the palace was well advanced, its cost considerably inflated by Welland's determination to make do with as little as possible of the original fabric, he lamented to Brodrick: 'It is hard that such heavy expenses should fall on one individual. Your Grace knows best whether there be any means of bringing a share of those expenses on your succes-

---

204 The addition and the new access to the garden are shown very clearly in the Lawrence photograph of 1880–1900 – NPA, Lawrence, Cab 7964 (fig. 16). 205 Welland to Brodrick, 16 July 1812 and 23 Feb. 1813, Ms. 8871/16 and 17. 206 Welland to Brodrick, 4 Mar. 1802, 17 Jan., 6 Apr. and 13 Dec. 1803, and 19 and 23 Jan. and 8 Mar. 1804, Ms. 8871/8–11. 207 Welland to Brodrick, 6 Apr. 1803, Ms. 8871/9. 208 Welland to Brodrick, 12 Feb. 1803, ibid. 209 Welland to Brodrick, 2 and 18 June 1804, Ms. 8871/12. 210 Welland to Brodrick, 12 May and 13 Oct. 1821, Ms. 8871/21.

sors.'[211] Since Brodrick's alterations had been generally speaking much more cosmetic than even Agar's, Welland must have known perfectly well that a share of only a small proportion of them could possibly be brought on Brodrick's successor.

Brodrick's successor, the last archbishop of Cashel, was Richard Laurence. He was archbishop of Cashel, 1822–38, and bishop of Waterford, 1832–8. Brodrick, though a teetotaller himself, maintained Agar's tradition of hospitality; he well knew how to live in the style and with the 'domestic magnificence' becoming an archbishop[212] and, as Agar had done, he entertained his own clergy with an open hand, and extended his open-handedness to his Roman catholic opposite numbers (pp 328–9). However, under Laurence, the diocese and the city of Cashel experienced an abrupt change of style. This was hardly surprising. Laurence was sixty-three when, at the earnest solicitation of the prime minister, the 2nd earl of Liverpool,[213] he was plucked from his donnish unsociability in Oxford to become an Irish archbishop. One visitor to Cashel in 1834

> was sorry to hear bad accounts of the protestant Archbishop. I found him universally disliked, even by those dependent upon him and of the same religious persuasion. He does no good, and by all accounts is a close, hard man, in every sense far overpaid by £7,000 or £8,000 a year, which he enjoys. He has the disadvantage, indeed, of being compared with his predecessor, whom all, protestant and catholic, unite in praising. .... [However,] I spent a charming morning ... [in] his Lordship's gardens ... . All that can delight the senses is here. Parterres of lovely flowers and rare shrubs; velvet lawns; secluded walks rich in odours; and, above the fine screen of holly and laburnum, and lilac, and copper-beech, and laurel, towers the Rock and the magnificent ruin that covers it. There is a private way [up which Archbishop Price had painfully and puffingly climbed] through his Lordship's grounds communicating with the Rock, ... [so that] he may retire to this solemn spot and meditate on the insufficiency of earthly enjoyments. The Archbishop has a palace as well as a garden; but it is reported that he means to reside in Waterford in future [Cashel having been united to Waterford at the end of 1832].[214]

Agar had perhaps been over-fond of 'earthly enjoyments', but at least he had brought bustle and a superficial sort of prosperity to a town which derived its energy from the archbishop, the archiepiscopal palace and the archiepiscopal building projects. Brodrick, a fellow-aristocrat, had followed suit. Laurence, by contrast, an academic and not an aristocrat, did not appreciate the attractions and amenities of the Cashel palace – apart from the Bolton library. As predicted, he lost no time in transferring his residence to Waterford, the main centre of population density in his combined

211 Welland to Brodrick, 9 Jan. 1813, Ms. 8871/17.   212 Seymour, *Diocese of Emly*, pp 262–3. 213 Cotton, *Fasti*, i, pp 27–8.   214 Henry D. Inglis, *Ireland in 1834*, i, pp 110–12. The copper beeches mentioned by Inglis still flourish.

diocese: whereas Agar and even Brodrick (who was roughly Laurence's contemporary) had wanted to live somewhere which gave them some privacy. Brodrick had specifically expressed this preference when threatened with promotion to Waterford in 1795; Waterford, he claimed, was less 'retired' than any other bishopric, and its bishop 'moves from the great city of Dublin to the great city of Waterford to spend his summer, where he has not an acre of ground to feed a cow or a horse, and spends the whole twelve months in eating and noise.'[215]

THE SURVIVAL OF PEARCE'S PALACE

Following Laurence's dutiful departure to this far from appealing place of residence, the Cashel palace was downgraded in status. It was divided in two. One side became the deanery, and the other was occupied by one or more of the canons of the cathedral. In the absence of the archbishop, a deanery was much needed, and was lacking. (The present, late-Georgian deanery was acquired for the diocese only in 1960 and is the house called 'Maryville' on the first O.S.) The original deanery was located in the main street, and was described in 1783 as 'a strong, high, stone building, decorated with a profusion of hewn stone over doors and windows, with battlements, all in the Gothic style ..., [with a roof which was] then to be thatched.'[216] This seems to be the building mentioned by Austin Cooper, who recalled *c.*1800 that 'the deanery house, as well as I can recollect, was pulled down about ten years ago [*c.*1790?].'[217] This fact and date are borne out by the excuse later made by the Dean, Joseph Palmer, for his absenteeism – that there was 'not a proper residence' in Cashel for the accommodation of his large family.[218] The last dean to live in the palace-cum-deanery was Robert Wyse Jackson, 'who became bishop of Limerick in 1960. Fearing its demolition or destruction ..., [he] persuaded Lord Brocket ... to take over the palace and convert it into a first-class hotel';[219] this he did, using E.A. Newenham as his architect. Lord Brocket, clearly, was a great admirer of the building: 'The ... pine-panelled ... staircase' he wrote in 1963, 'with three balusters on each tread, is as good an example of an early Georgian or Queen Anne staircase as I have seen.'[220] He made only one major mistake: the reduction of the height of the chimney stacks by one-third.[221] Since the palace opened as a hotel in May 1962, it has had a whole succession of owners, but has survived and is now in as good hands as it was in Lord Brocket's time. Its danger period, paradoxically, was not the years of (salutary) neglect between 1822 and 1960, or the vicissitudes of the hotel business between 1962 and the present day: it suffered most, and was in greatest danger of suffering far more, during its occupancy by the only two archbishops after Bolton who were resident, architecturally aware and energetic.

215 Brodrick to Midleton, 31 Jan. 1795, Ms. 1248, vol. 16, f. 10.   216 Seymour, *Succession of clergy in Cashel and Emly*, p. 90.   217 *An eighteenth-century antiquary: Austin Cooper*, p. 34.   218 Palmer to Agar, 30 Dec,. 1804, T/3719/C/38/54. Agar, of course, had left Cashel by then. But Palmer was seeking Agar's recommendation to government for something better than the deanery of Cashel.   219 *Cashel Palace hotel brochure*, [c.1965], IAA, RP. D.23.5.   220 Brocket's letter to the editor, *Country Life*, 10 Jan. 1963.   221 Oral information from the Knight of Glin.

To a modern way of thinking, any tinkering with Pearce which was not absolutely necessary is reprehensible – and nothing was absolutely necessary, because the episode of the militiamen seems never to have happened. However, it would have been out of character for men like Agar and Brodrick not to have altered the palace in line with the most approved, late eighteenth- and early nineteenth-century taste. More drastic alterations, and inappropriate enlargement in particular, were the common fate of early eighteenth-century Irish houses which, from the late eighteenth-century onwards, were owned by rich and powerful individuals or families. Some escaped enlargement because they were originally built on a large scale (Russborough, Co. Kildare) or on an actually palatial scale (Castletown, Co. Kildare, and Summerhill, Co. Meath). Others, though small, escaped enlargement because their owners either did not prosper or actually declined economically – Beaulieu, Co. Louth, Mount Ievers, Co. Clare, and Bellamont Forest, Co. Cavan (also Pearce's unaided handiwork); or because their owners acquired another house as their principal place of residence and so left their original house unaltered – the Damer House, Roscrea, and Shannongrove, Co. Limerick. But the majority of early houses underwent alterations which varied in their impact from obtrusiveness to obliteration.

Castle Durrow, Co. Laois, the seat of the Agars' cousins, the Flowers, Viscounts Ashbrook, suffered waves of invasion from the late eighteenth century onwards as, less disastrously, did Westport House, Co. Mayo. Westport House, and Carton, Co. Kildare, both lost their original character without becoming the grand houses which the descendants of their builders hoped to achieve. The eighteenth-century 'doll's house' at Adare, Co. Limerick, disappeared altogether under the huge, nineteenth-century Adare Manor; and Gowran Castle and Castle Hume, Co. Fermanagh, were simply knocked down and replaced with new houses on nearby sites in the 1810s and 1830s respectively. Other houses were compromised less dramatically, but still compromised, by the addition of wings and extensions which 'throw' their original scale – Hazelwood, Co. Sligo, Mountainstown, Co. Meath, Newcastle, Co. Longford, Strokestown, Co. Roscommon, and Woodstock, Co. Kilkenny. In most of these cases, the enlargement of windows and the breaking of existing window-rhythms, are one among a number of regrettable features, whereas at Cashel they are the worst things which Agar did. Granted that bishops (and other clergymen) received legislative encouragement to spend money on building, and granted that the legislation encouraged bishops to add rather than to modify, to flatten rather than to improve, the survival of the Cashel palace to the present day in something resembling its original state, is actually remarkable. The Clogher palace, for example, which had struck Hotham in 1782 as a 'far from ... despicable place of residence', was described in 1812 by the then bishop of Clogher as 'old, dark and inconvenient' and was totally replaced in the early 1820s.[222]

Since 'it was under the Agars that ... [the Cashel palace] came closest to the Great World', it is at first sight surprising that they did not modernise the building accordingly. A number of explanations may be suggested. Perhaps Agar had decided

222 Malcomson, 'Belleisle [Co. Fermanagh] and its owners', in *Clogher Record: 1998*, p. 33.

that he had better things to do with his money than tie it up in a way which, at best, would yield nothing but full reimbursement without interest, and quite certainly would be of no advantage to his descendants. Some such decision may have been of contributory importance. But there remains the simple fact that the Agars were well content with the palace as it was after their minor alterations in the first half of the 1780s. In another of her informative letters of October 1796, Lady Somerton – coupling the palace with the Agars' town house in Dublin – described them to her husband as 'two very comfortable houses in excellent repair, with everything to your mind and agreeably situated.'[223] This was not the language of someone who was conscious of having stitched, mended and economised where the palace was concerned. Agar, brought up in an earlier and very bumkin version of the palace – Gowran Castle – may have been unusually tolerant of old-fashioned panelled rooms, provided they gave him the accommodation he wanted and were not painted a 'dismal' colour.[224] Agar may also have regarded the palace as a link in the chain of his succession from that 'great Irish churchman', Archbishop Bolton, to whom he attributed its building, and for whose name and handiwork he would have had great respect.

And what of Pearce? Clearly, the memory of Pearce had faded considerably by the late eighteenth century; Dr Beaufort, in spite of being an (over-enthusiastic) amateur architect (see p. 282), brusquely described the palace in 1792 as 'a plain, large house, to which a public library is annexed'[225] – which suggests that he, for one, attached no architectural significance to the building. Agar probably took a different view. As a member of the House of Lords, he spoke in defence of and took an interest in Gandon's sensitive and respectful enlargement of the Lords' accommodation in Pearce's Parliament House, which was going on in the period 1784–9.[226] This re-working of Pearce's most important public building is bound to have reminded the grandsons of Pearce's private clients of his numerous essays into domestic architecture. Agar was a case in point. In 1731–3, Pearce had built the long-forsaken deanery in Fishamble Street, Dublin (see p. 256), for Agar's maternal grandfather, Bishop Welbore Ellis. Ellis, in fact, never occupied the deanery he had commissioned, because he was translated to Meath the year before, and died the year after, it was completed. A payment of £50 to Pearce in November 1733 was recorded in the 'acts' of the dean and chapter,[227] and must have reappeared in Ellis' executorship accounts when his son,

---

223 Lady Somerton to Agar, 13 Oct. 1796, T/3719/C/30/34.   224 He was not being uniquely old-fashioned in this attitude. Primate Robinson, surprisingly, retained the original panelling in Belvedere, Drumcondra, a small, probably *c.*1730, brick villa on the outskirts of Dublin which he leased and lived in from *c.*1770 to the 1780s (*Georgian Society records*, ii. 13). The panelling is there to this day. I am grateful to Dr James Kelly for showing me Belvedere, which now constitutes the nucleus of St Patrick's College, Drumcondra.   225 Beaufort, *Memoir of a map*, pp 123–4. He was less prosaic about the cathedral, which he called 'a large and handsome edifice completed by the present archbishop'.   226 *Irish parliamentary register*, iii [part 2], pp 80–82; McParland, *Gandon*, pp 76 *et seq.*   227 McParland, 'Edward Lovett Pearce and the deanery of Christ Church, Dublin', in Agnes Bernelle (ed.), *Decantations* (Dublin, 1992), pp 130–33. I am grateful to the present dean of Christ Church, the Very Rev. John Paterson, for drawing my attention to the existence of this source and sending me a photocopy.

the future Lord Mendip, came to wind up his father's estate and obtain reimbursement for part of the cost of the deanery. Since Mendip knew about Pearce, Agar must
have known about Pearce, and that knowledge must have influenced Agar's decision
not to allow the deanery to be replaced in 1806 (see pp 256–7) and, more importantly,
his attitude to the Cashel palace. Equally important, and reinforcing these aesthetic
and sentimental considerations, was Agar's belief that churchmen should not spend
money unnecessarily and ostentatiously.

There was a further, and practical, explanation for Agar's preservationist approach
to the palace. Lady Somerton's letter, with its coupling of the Cashel and the Dublin
houses, provides the clue. It was the Dublin house, No. 40 (now 47) St Stephen's
Green, which was the Agars' point of entry into 'the Great World': the palace was a foil
or contrast to it, a place in the country (or almost), and the focus of family life when
their children were young. Agar had bought No. 40, on the east side of the Green, on
a long (probably 99-year) lease in 1775, the year before his marriage. It had been built
as recently as 1769 by the Dublin architect, John Ensor. 'Some of the finest houses in
Dublin are to be found on ... [this] side of St Stephen's Green', including No. 52 and
its 'sister house', No. 53 (where Agar's friend, Lord Carleton, came to live), sump-
tuously decorated by Michael Stapleton *c.*1770, and the somewhat earlier Meath
House, No. 56, decorated by Robert and John West in 1760.[228] Agar's house, by contrast, though 'large', with 'good, well proportioned rooms', had 'little decoration.'[229]
Agar added to its grandeur by upgrading 'all the chimneypieces, mahogany doors, etc.',
which remained Agar family property when the house was eventually sold by the 2nd
earl of Normanton *c.*1866.[230] The rent was only £100 per annum;[231] but, in view of
what Hotham called 'the uncouth tenures prevalent in this country', this belied the size
and desirability of the house. No doubt Agar had paid an entry fine of £2,500 or
£3,000 when he bought the lease.

The purchase of the lease was followed, not only by the already-mentioned
upgrading of the key fixtures, but by the acquisition of a magnificent service of plate
to set the tone of Agar's grand political entertaining in 40 St Stephen's Green. This
was bought from 'Mrs Tisdall' in November 1779, and cost the very large sum of
£856 (representing 6s. per ounce on a weight of silver calculated by 'Mr D'Olier of
Dame Street', Dublin, as 2,854 ounces 12 pounds).[232] Welbore Ellis wrote to 'congratulate you on the opportunity you have had to furnish yourself with a handsome

228 Frances Gerard, *Picturesque Dublin, old and new* (London, 1898), pp 160–62; C.P. Curran, *Dublin decorative plasterwork of the seventeenth and eighteenth centuries* (London, 1967), pp 61 and 84 and plates 108–10. 229 *Georgian Society records*, vol. iii (Dublin, 1909), pp 66 and 75. The house has disappeared, and is now represented by a *pastiche* building occupied by Barclay's Bank. 230 Note by the 2nd earl of Normanton dated 25 Apr. 1832 on an earlier inventory of the contents of the house, 21 M 57, 2nd earl's unreferenced correspondence. 231 Note of a payment on 24 June 1779 to Agar's Co. Kilkenny associate, Redmond Morres, from whom he sub-leased the house, recorded in an account book of 1765–1807, 21 M 57/D15. Agar's landlord was later Morres' son and successor, Lodge Morres, who had himself ennobled (absurdly) as Viscount Frankfort de Montmorency and even changed his surname to 'de Montmorency'. He appears as Lord Frankfort in subsequent account books. 232 Calculations by [Isaac] D'Olier, 16 Nov. 1779, 21 M 57, miscellaneous boxes, no. 6.

service of plate upon the most easy terms. You would have been to be blamed if you had missed the occasion.'[233] It was a symbolic purchase as well as a good buy: 'Mrs Tisdall' must have been the widow of the recently deceased attorney-general, and Agar must have been thinking of Philip Tisdall's place in the counsels of government and role in Irish politics generally (p. 153), when he bought Tisdall's service of plate. The Stephen's Green house was Agar's first priority, partly because it was the show-piece for his political entertaining, and partly because it was a possession which, unlike the Cashel palace, would be hereditary in his family.

In Brodrick's case, the relationship between Dublin house and Cashel palace was in effect inverted, but the one still had a major bearing on the other. In his first decade as archbishop of Cashel, Brodrick continued to live in a leasehold house of his own in Merrion Square. However, when he became coadjutor-archbishop of Dublin, follow-ing Archbishop Cleaver's descent into mental illness in 1811, Brodrick moved into the recently purchased Dublin see house or town palace at 16 St Stephen's Green, which Cleaver had just bought out of Agar's carefully husbanded proceeds from the sale of St Sepulchre.[234] This was another house with fine Stapleton plasterwork, built in 1776.[235] In June 1812 the architect to the board of first fruits, John Bowden, reported that it was ready for occupation by Brodrick.[236] From then until Cleaver's death at the end of 1819, Brodrick lived in Dublin at Cleaver's expense (see pp 503–4).[237] It can be no coincidence that Brodrick's major remodelling of the interior of the Cashel palace took place from 1812 onwards. For all Welland's real or feigned anxiety over expense, Brodrick was probably spending on Cashel only what he was saving on Dublin.

THE 'EDIFYING'[238] ARCHBISHOPS

The varying importance which different archbishops attached to the Cashel palace is one of the themes of its history and explanations for its survival. Archbishop Laurence and the bishops of Cashel who came after him attached none. Archbishops Price and Cox had attached little, in their case not because of their Dublin houses but because of

---

233 Ellis to Agar, 25 Dec. 1779, T/3719/C/13/48. The terms may not have been all that 'easy', since the service was still valued at the same amount in 1793 (Agar's will, 17 Apr. 1806, and probate, 16 Nov. 1809, 21 M 57/T285). By the time of his death, he had added to the service c.£80 worth of new purchases.   234 Agar to Thomas Williams, July 1808, T/3719/C/42/43; Rev. Richard Wynne (Mrs Cleaver's brother) to Brodrick, 1 Jan. 1812, NLI, Ms. 8861/6.   235 Curran, *Dublin decorative plasterwork*, pp 82 and 84.   236 Bowden to Brodrick, 16 June 1812, *ibid.*   237 In view of the absence of any precedents for a coadjutorship in the Church of Ireland, it was inevitable that there should later be a lengthy wrangle over dilapidations. This was still raging between and among Cleaver's and Brodrick's executors and Lord John George Beresford, Cleaver's successor at Dublin, after Beresford had been promoted to the primacy in 1822 – case about the liability for the dilapidations, [1822?], Armagh diocesan registry papers, PRONI, DIO 4/19/7/3.   238 This is Magdalen King-Hall's well-worn pun; she called her biography of Agar's *bête noire*, Frederick Hervey, *The edifying bishop* (London, 1951). Stuart, *Armagh*, p. 445, attributes the act of 1772 to Robinson, but gives a very misleading *résumé* of its provisions.

Oakly Park and Castletown Cox respectively. For Archbishop Bolton, the palace had been of pre-eminent importance, even though it is now clear that the credit for its building has to be more than shared between Bolton and his predecessor, Archbishop Godwin, and that Bolton's only unique contribution to the palace was the Bolton library. In light of the evidence presented in this and the preceding chapter, it becomes apparent that Agar was a not-unworthy successor of Bolton: apart from his achievement in completing the new cathedral, he followed Bolton's example of shoring up the cathedral on the Rock, and he preserved the Bolton library from physical deterioration. But his and Bolton's positions were essentially different. Agar never intended, if he could help it, to die as archbishop of Cashel; and in the decade between 1784 and 1794 his hopes of better things were justifiably high (see pp 137 and 160–3), even if – in the event – they did not materialise. Bolton, by contrast, had no such hopes. As a representative of 'the Irish interest', and a successor to Archbishop King's political tradition as well as the purchaser of most of King's books, Bolton had known that Cashel was the apogee of his ecclesiastical career, and had built and endowed accordingly. Moreover, the heir to Bolton's property was a distant relation (a very young great-nephew), whereas Agar had three sons and every intention of founding a dynasty.

Similar considerations need to be borne in mind when comparing Agar with his more obvious and more nearly contemporary rival as an edifying archbishop, Primate Robinson. Robinson had reached the apogee of an Irish ecclesiastical career when he was promoted to Armagh in 1765: he certainly had nowhere higher to go. Moreover, he resembled Bolton, and differed from Agar, in that he was childless (Robinson was in fact a bachelor). Robinson's 'munificence, magnificence, noble public-spiritedness, etc.', as Hotham satirically called them, have been referred to on p. 332 and will be discussed more fully on pp 455–61.[239] It suffices for present purposes to point out that they were not much in evidence in Robinson's palace-building in Armagh. Writing in 1778 to his elder brother in England, Hotham explained that the 'late act of parliament [of 1772, by which] every bishop who built a new house in his see is authorised to charge his immediate successor with the *whole* money so laid out by him, and that whole money is by law allowed to be two full years' income of the bishopric', had been passed 'under the auspices of the Primate.'[240] The effect of this legislation, and of a certificate obtained by Robinson in December 1775 in accordance with it, was that the full cost of the handsome new palace in Armagh which he had built between 1766 and 1775 to the design of Thomas Cooley, fell upon Robinson's successor. The certificate states that the cost had been £15,081 14s. 5¾d., that this had been approved by a commission of valuation, and that it did not exceed the clear yearly value of the see over a two-year period (the income of Armagh then being £8,163 17s. 4⅜d. per annum, exclusive of fees and proxies).[241] The £15,000–odd excludes the cost of the nearby archiepiscopal chapel, built c.1781–6 to the design of, first, Cooley and then, after

239 For a fuller discussion, see Malcomson, 'Primate Robinson' (in preparation).   240 Hotham to Hotham Thompson, 17 Aug. [1778], PRONI, T/3429/2/2.   241 Copies of a memorial from Robinson to the lords justices, 4 Aug. 1766, of a warrant from them to Robinson, 12 Aug. 1766, and of a certificate from the lord lieutenant to Robinson, 23 Dec. 1775, DIO 4/40/5/1, 2 and 8.

Cooley's death, to that of Francis Johnston.[242] It is an architectural gem and must have been very costly in relation to its small size. No documentary evidence for the cost seems to have survived, nor does any contemporary or near-contemporary commentator appear to have recorded a good guess. In the absence of such information, it is reasonable to suggest that such a building must have cost something like £3,000. By 1786, the Armagh see rental must have been easily £9,000 a year; so Robinson would have been entitled to charge the full £18,000 (i.e. not more than two years' rental income) on his successor. The only apparently conflicting evidence is the fact that Robinson's successor, 'Primate Newcome ..., bound himself to pay to Robinson's heirs a sum of between £15,000 and £16,000.'[243] This might suggest that the chapel cost less than £1,000 (an impossibility) or that it was treated as a separate church and therefore not included in the cost of the palace at all. But it is much more likely to suggest that Newcome made as large a down payment as he could afford to Robinson's executors and gave an interest-bearing bond or I.O.U. for the rest.

On this last assumption, Robinson's 'magnificence' must have entailed upon Newcome an expenditure of *c*.£18,000, and Newcome must be the clearest example of a successor saddled 'with the extravagance of the showy.' No wonder he 'did nothing to promote'[244] Robinson's last wish, which was for a university to be established in Armagh (see pp 455–6) – another instance of the hostilities created by the system of reimbursement. Robinson's executors did not in fact receive full reimbursement, since the *c*.£18,000 made no allowance for interest. Even so, the surprising upshot is that Robinson's major operations on the Armagh palace cost him personally little more than Agar's tinkering with the Cashel palace cost Agar. What was defining about Robinson's palace-building in Armagh was the simple but extraordinary fact that he was the first primate of modern times to fix Armagh as his official place of residence. Before Robinson, that designation still applied to the long-ruinous archiepiscopal palace at Termonfeckin, outside Drogheda, or to the early seventeenth-century palace in Drogheda itself;[245] and his immediate predecessor, Archbishop Stone, had maintained lodgings in Armagh suitable for merely temporary periods of residence, and had lived for most of the year – and in 'Polish magnificence'[246] – in one of the two grandest houses in Dublin's highly fashionable Henrietta Street.[247] In this respect, there was no such scope for fundamental change in Cashel, which had always been the seat of the archbishop, even if the archbishops immediately preceding Agar had been personally non-resident.

---

242 For the architectural merits of the palace and chapel, see Brett, *Buildings of Co. Armagh*, pp 32–3 and 122–3.   243 Joseph R. Fisher and John H. Robb, *Royal Belfast Academical Institution: centenary volume, 1810–1910* (Belfast, 1913), p. 24. Fisher is here quoting or paraphrasing Reid's *History of the Presbyterian Church*, but neither Reid nor he realised that the £15,000–£16,000 was connected with the palace. I am grateful to Sir Peter Froggatt for drawing my attention to this source.   244 Ibid. 245 The warrant of 12 Aug. 1766 from the lords justices to Robinson (DIO 4/40/5/2) specifically authorises the change of primatial residence from Drogheda to Armagh.   246 Richard Cumberland, *Memoirs* (London, 1806), p. 172.   247 Robinson bought the long leasehold of this house from Stone's executors, and retained it until his death. Since the house had been built for Primate Boulter and was occupied by the next three primates – Hoadly, Stone and Robinson – Henrietta Street in their day was sometimes called 'Primate's Hill'. See *Georgian Society records*, ii, pp 12–13 and 63–4.

9

See estates and Agar's 'love of lucre', *c.*1750–1833

Robinson did nothing illegal when he threw the entire cost of his new palace on his successors, the first two of whom were family men who lacked his resources. But he certainly exploited a system intended to help ordinary clergymen and poorer bishops, and it was a further reflection on him that he derived great financial benefit from an act of his own passing. Agar, too, exploited the system. However, in his case it was not the system regulating the building and improvement of clerical residences, but that which regulated the remuneration of bishops by means of estates annexed to their sees. In 1792, he acquired for himself a leasehold interest in a major part of the see lands of Cashel. This is the most controversial, perplexing and apparently discreditable episode in his career. It seems inexplicable that a man with a strong sense of the responsibilities as well as the privileges of churchmen, and with an ambition to become the head of the Church of Ireland in name as well as in fact, should have compromised himself by trafficking in see lands. Though what precisely he did, or how and when he did it, has not until now been ascertained, the widespread awareness that he did something has influenced most of the judgements passed upon him.[1] The purpose of this Chapter is, first, to examine the management of see estates in Agar's day, the complex legal and practical arrangements which were in place, and Agar's role as a legislator in both defending and redefining them. Second, the Chapter tells, with as much precision as the evidence permits, the story of Agar's see lands leases. Third, it considers the origins and build-up of his personal fortune and the validity of the charges of financial sharp practice made against him in other connections besides the see leases. Fourth, it compares his standards of behaviour with those of his predecessor in the archbishopric of Dublin and his successor in the archbishopric of Cashel

THE 'ODIUM' INCURRED BY THE BISHOPS AS LANDLORDS

The episode of the Cashel see leases occurred at a time when the darkest possible interpretation was likely to be placed on any such action on the part of a bishop. Moreover, Agar's own papers at first sight confirm that interpretation: they include two damning lists of townlands in Co. Tipperary, dated 1802 and *c.*1805 respectively, with endorsements in his handwriting on the back of each that these had been see lands and were now 'my own.'[2] This suggests, and has been taken as meaning, outright

1 For example, Akenson, *Church of Ireland*, p. 74.   2 21 M 57/18/243.

alienation of Church property.[3] However, it is hardly credible that in the late eighteenth century any ecclesiastic could have got away with a violation of the statutory restriction on ecclesiastical and other such leases, which was that they should run for no longer than 21 years in the case of agricultural land. Agar, in particular, would not have got away with it, because he had distinguished himself as the champion of the Church's proprietary as well as its other rights, and if he himself had infringed, or endeavoured to infringe, them in so flagrant a way, his behaviour would have been eagerly seized upon by his own and/or the Church's enemies. As it was, hostile mention of Agar and the Cashel see lands was made in a memo. of *c.*1798 in the papers of Lord Castlereagh, chief secretary, 1798–1801: 'From the shortness of the leases, bishops are often tempted not to renew with their tenants, in order, at the expiration of the leases, to make beneficial leases to their families. This practice is growing common. The Bishop of Derry and the Archbishop of Cashel have made great estates to their families by this mode. These circumstances throw an odium on the Church possessions.'[4] Obviously, this memo., highly critical of Agar, would have said so if he had done worse than grant 21–year leases to himself and/or his family, and had expropriated see lands outright.

It is ironic that Frederick Hervey, earl-bishop of Derry, Agar's predecessor at Cloyne and a churchman of whom he strongly disapproved,[5] should have been singled out as Agar's contemporary comparator in these malpractices. Frederick Hervey had been born a younger son, but following the deaths of both his elder brothers had succeeded in 1779 to the earldom of Bristol, an alleged 30,000 statute acres, mainly in Suffolk, and an alleged rental of £20,000 per annum. He therefore did not have Agar's excuse that he trafficked in see leases in order to overcome the disadvantages to which he had been subjected by the harsh laws of primogeniture. He was also in the enjoyment of a much richer see, Derry being worth nearly twice as much as Cashel in 1779 (although, thirty years earlier, Cashel had been more valuable than Derry – see p. 341). Actually, he was motivated by his hatred of his sons, and his wish to set up a favourite second cousin, the Rev. Henry Bruce, as a landed gentleman and the heir to virtually all the property within Hervey's disposable power. In September 1784, the lord lieutenant, Rutland, reported that 'the Bishop of Derry has ... has turned his son, Lord Harvey [*sic*], out of his house.'[6] Years later, in 1803, following the earl-bishop's death, Lady Mendip heard that 'Lord Bristol has left all his Irish property to some person in Ireland [i.e. the Rev. Henry Bruce] and not a sixpence to his daughters. The present Lord succeeds to £16,000 [per annum, the English settled estates].'[7]

It was not in the earl-bishop's nature to do anything without boasting about it. Moreover, he was absent, usually abroad, for so much of the time (including, as has been seen, the last twelve years of his episcopate) that it was unavoidable that he should commit more to paper than the cagey Agar. Writing to his daughter, Lady

3 Malcomson, *John Foster*, p. 284.   4 Printed in 3rd marquess of Londonderry (ed.), *Memoirs and correspondence of Viscount Castlereagh ...* (first ser., 4 vols., London, 1848–9), ii, pp 70–71.   5 Agar to Macartney, 17 Feb. 1780, *Macartney in Ireland*, p. 330.   6 Rutland to Pitt, 13 Sep. 1784, *HMC Rutland Mss.*, iii. 137.   7 Lady Mendip to Agar, 14 Nov. 1803, T/3719/C/37/42.

Erne, on 8 March 1787, Hervey reported, without the least tincture of embarrassment: 'I have begun a new villa [actually a large mansion, Ballyscullion] upon that
leasehold estate ... which fell in to me on the first day of last month. The rents amount
to £593 a year. The situation is beautiful and salubrious beyond all description'. On 5
October 1791, he wrote to the Rev. Henry Bruce informing him that he had 'left you
all my property in Ireland of every denomination whatever', and explaining that it
took the form of leases under the see 'held in trust by Sir Charles Davers [his brother-
in-law] and others; most of these nominal lessees had not 'yet made a declaration of
trust, which [omission] might involve you in great difficulties. The first thing, then,
to be done is get ... [one] from all these gentlemen.' Hervey's will – a public document
once it was probated – refers openly to leases held under the see of Derry 'for the joint
use of me and my wife' or 'in trust for me', and Wakefield reported it as 'certain' that
Hervey 'realised above £4,000 a year by [these] leases'.[8] In any case, having erected
very large houses, Downhill and Ballyscullion, on the two major concentrations of see
lands held in trust for him (Dunboe, Magilligan, etc., in respect of Downhill, and
Ballyscullion, etc., in respect of Ballyscullion), he had already advertised his activities
much more widely than by his will, and many years before his death in 1803.
Downhill, the first of his great Irish houses, was built from 1775 onwards on the north
coast of Co. Londonderry, fifteen miles from the Giant's Causeway. Ballyscullion was
near Bellaghy and, as has been seen, was begun in 1787. He did not seek, nor (since
the palace in the city of Derry was the bishop's official residence – see p. 367) would
he have been granted, certificates for the building of his other houses. Besides, no
subsequent bishop of Derry would have wanted to take on responsibility for the cost
and up-keep of a very large house like Downhill, on one of the most exposed sites in
western Europe; the more so as the Rev. Henry Bruce already held leases under the see
of the site of the house and the outlying land. Bruce, however, could not afford to keep
up Ballyscullion as well, and it was abandoned and dismantled in 1813. No doubt this
enabled him to do a deal with the then bishop of Derry whereby Bruce surrendered
the Ballyscullion lands in return for renewals, on reasonable terms, of the lands round
Downhill.

   Since long before Hervey's death and the publication of his all-too-explicit
will, the leasing power of bishops of the Church of Ireland had been a public issue,
from which a great deal of adverse publicity had accrued to the bishops. The
visiting English clergyman, the Rev. J. Burrows, commented in 1773:

> The bishops, who considering the extent of this island have an amazing
> property in it, are every day losing ground in the affections of the landed
> gentry ... . A very considerable part of the estate of almost every gentleman
> I have seen consists of a bishop's lease. While they held these leases on the

8 William S. Childe-Pemberton, *The earl-bishop* ... (2 vols., London, *c.*1925), ii, pp 399–400, 427–8 and
654–6; Wakefield, *Account of Ireland*, ii. 470. For Hervey, see Childe-Pemberton, *passim*, and Peter
Rankin, *Irish building ventures of the earl-bishop of Derry, passim*.

old, easy terms, which all over the king's dominions did not amount to much above half of their real value, the interests of the Church were the natural interests of the gentry, and the bishops screened the envy of their large incomes under the private advantage of their leaseholders; and thus, beside their own numerous body, they had always a strong party in both Houses of Parliament. Within these last twenty years, on seeing every gentleman raise the value of his land, ... the bishops have put in for a share of the profits ..., [and] every bishop has improved upon his predecessor, either in the fine he demands on a renewal, or the annual rent he insists on receiving ... .

To some extent, this was just a standard gentry-grouse, reiterated in every era. Under the very different circumstances of 1821, for example, the 2nd earl of Leitrim, a large leaseholder under the archbishop of Tuam, grumbled: 'These reverend prelates seem lately to have established it as a sort of matter of course that, whenever they succeed to a new bishopric, all rents and fines are to be raised.' Burrows, rightly, saw the bishops' attempts to 'put in for a share of the profits' in the context of a general, overall rise in landed incomes in the 1770s.[9] However, the gentlemen-tenants of the bishops did not take this view and sought to make further gains at the expense of the bishops. There were full-scale debates on the issue in both Houses of Parliament, followed by legislation in 1795 (see pp 397–9), and in 1803 there was talk of further legislation. Primate Stuart reacted sharply: 'A law to enable bishops to lease their see lands for three lives would ruin the Irish Church. I cannot, therefore, believe that his Majesty's ministers countenance such a measure, and unless they do countenance it, I am well persuaded it will not pass both Houses of Parliament.'[10] Among Agar's papers, there is a manuscript copy of an extract, dated 17 November 1804, from what seems to be a letter to a newspaper editor. The anonymous writer advocates an extension of the bishops' leasing power (this time to 41 years), and for reasons very unflattering to the bishops:

The eighth part ... of the lands of this kingdom are held under the Church by tenants of every denomination – protestants, dissenters and catholics. ... This large body of tenants [should be given] a more permanent security for their lands than they now possess by an act not only authorising but obliging the bishops, for the good of the community at large, to grant leases for 41 years instead of 21. ... To prevent any diminution of income to the present bishops, let a clause be inserted obliging the tenants under forfeiture of such leases to renew as frequently as they now do, and on the same terms, during the incumbency of the present bishops. ... The income of their successors in their respective sees would in a great degree remain at a stand, but surely from £3,000–£12,000 a year is fully adequate to their stations? ... In former

9 PRONI, T/3551/1 Leitrim to Cooper, 9–10 Mar. 1821, Killadoon papers, NLI, Ms. 36,064/12.
10 Stuart to Brodrick, 23 Jan. 1803, NLI, Ms. 8869/1.

days, ... [leases of see] lands were considered as little less valuable than
patrimonial estates. But the case is much altered of late. The income of two
sees has within these three years been advanced from £8,000 to £12,000 a year,
and in some instances a positive refusal has been given to renew on any terms,
the leases have been permitted to expire, and have been then renewed to the
children or relations of the bishop ... . [The measure proposed would therefore
conduce to the permanency of the Established Church] by interesting in that
permanency such numbers who hold valuable leases under the respective sees.
It would tend also in a very high degree to the improvement of the external
appearance of the country in building and agriculture.[11]

Armagh and Derry must have been the two sees whose rentals were supposed to
have been advanced within the previous three years from £8,000 to £12,000 per
annum. The allegation is not fantastic, since £9,000 per annum was the figure mentioned for Armagh and £8,000 for Derry in the late eighteenth century, and their gross
rentals stood at £17,669 and £14,193 respectively in 1831.[12] In other respects, however,
this polemic was unreasonably hostile to the bishops, and was particularly misleading
in the impression it gave that the head tenants of see estates were all occupiers and
farmers. In fact, there were usually tiers of middlemen between the bishop and the
occupying tenants, and by the time their cuts had been taken, the occupying tenants
were left paying a rack rent and felt no obligation to the Church or anybody else. The
head tenants, while clamouring for longer leases for themselves, did not necessarily
pass on to the next tier of tenants the full extent of the 21–year tenures which they
themselves currently enjoyed. Years later, the interesting point was made that
'see lands in the north of Ireland are so much more improved than in the south ...
[because] the tenants holding immediately under the bishop give to their under-
tenants the same term they have themselves, and in many cases *toties quoties* covenants.'[13] Again, the political allegiance of even the most pampered head tenant of the
Church, could by no means be guaranteed. Of those who held leases of the greatly
underlet lands in which Agar acquired an interest, one – Edward Scully of Kilfeakle
– was so far from being attached zealously to 'the government in Church and State'
by this circumstance, that Agar's wife was convinced in 1796 that he was a United
Irishman.[14] Finally, a recent act of 1795 (for which, as will be seen, Agar was responsible) had left bishops with very little incentive to run their lives against existing leases,
because if they successfully pursued this strategy, the new lease was required by the

11 21 M 57/B18/18.   12 For league tables giving, from two different sources, rough figures for the
incomes of the Irish archbishoprics and bishoprics in the second half of the 1770s, see Akenson,
Church of Ireland, pp 35–7, and for acreages and rentals in 1831, see pp 80–84. It is not clear what
account these figures took of renewal fines, a complicated and crucial issue which will be discussed
below.   13 John Hare (agent for the Normanton estates in Ireland and son of Rev. Patrick Hare,
former vicar-general of Cashel) to 2nd earl of Normanton, 15 Apr. 1829, 21 M 57, 2nd earl's
unreferenced correspondence.   14 Lady Somerton to Agar, 15 Oct. 1796, T/3719/C/30/35.

act to reserve to the see 'one full moiety of the highest improved [annual] value' of the land.[15]

Paying the bishops by means of see estates was actually a bit like paying the parochial clergy by means of tithes:[16] the method was very visible, opprobrious and inefficient, and the gap between perception and reality was wide. The reality, as calculated by Wakefield 'from the conjecture of well informed persons', was that if a sample of four see estates 'were now out of lease' (by which he presumably meant if they could be re-let for 21 years to the occupying tenants, without regard to the intermediate tenants' tenant right), they would let for staggeringly large annual sums. Armagh, which according to Wakefield currently had a rental of £12,000 per annum, would let for £140,000; Derry (£12,500) for £120,000; Clogher (£7,000) for £100,000; Kilmore (£5,000) for £100,000; and Waterford (£6,000) for £70,000.[17] The same point had been made about Armagh fifty years earlier. 'The value of the primacy is not what we consider it worth ... . I know from very good authority it is not more, *communibus annis*, than £7,000 per annum; and yet ..., since ... [Stone] has been primate, he might have raised it to be double that value without any oppression upon the tenants, but he lays it down as a rule not to raise the fines.'[18] Such moderation was not in fact peculiar to Stone, but characteristic of the management of the Armagh see estate and of Irish see estates generally. In October 1794, when it was rumoured that Lord Buckingham was likely to obtain the primacy for William Cleaver, bishop of Chester, elder brother of Euseby, and like Euseby 'rather sordid', John Beresford expressed his dismay: 'If an avaricious man be sent to Armagh who will attempt to screw the tenants, he will cause a rebellion in Ulster and overturn the Church.'[19] Another good example of moderation was the management of the estate of the archbishop of Dublin. This comprised over 12,000 statute acres, but was located in scattered units throughout the counties of Dublin and Wicklow, in Dublin City and, in the case of one unit, in Co. Cork. In view of these geographical considerations, successive archbishops chose to let the several units at moderate rents to reliable local gentlemen, and so obviate the necessity for expensive management arrangements and/or regular visits of inspection by the archbishops themselves. 'The ... estate in Cork was tenanted by the powerful local figure, Sir Richard Cox [of Dunmanway]; [and] according to the 1714 [see] rental ... about 40% of the tenants were of the rank of esquire or above.'[20] Such a tenurial profile was typical of see estates. Moreover, moderate rents were characteristic even of see estates which were fairly compact. In 1787, the Dromore see estate in and around Dromore, Co. Down, comprised '16,000

15 Archdeacon James Agar to 2nd earl of Normanton, 20 Oct. 1819, 21 M 57, 2nd earl's unreferenced correspondence. 16 Akenson, *Church of Ireland*, pp 87–95. 17 Wakefield, *Account of Ireland*, ii, pp 469–70. 18 Willes to Lord Warwick, 25 Apr. 1759, *Willes letters*, p. 32. 19 Beresford (who knew about Ulster because he held a long-leasehold estate in Co. Londonderry) to Auckland, 22 Oct. 1794, Auckland papers, BL, Add. Ms. 34453, f. 62. I am grateful for this reference to Terence Finley. 20 Raymond Refaussé and Mary Clark (eds.), *A catalogue of the maps of the estates of the archbishops of Dublin, 1654–1850, with an historical introduction by Raymond Gillespie* (Dublin, 2001), pp 22 and 34.

acres, worth a pound round.' Yet, its rental was only £2,500 per annum.²¹ In other words, the supposedly rapacious bishops in fact enjoyed a relatively small proportion of the rents derived from their lands.

Furthermore, the rentals of see estates were fluctuating and unpredictable, and over time²² ceased to reflect the seniority of the sees to which they were attached or the level of responsibility borne by the bishops concerned. In the short term, the unscrupulousness of a bishop's predecessor, the misdeeds of 'a knavish agent'²³ or the inefficiency of a tenant, might contribute to this imbalance; but ultimately it was economic forces which were decisive of the directions in which change went. 'Directions', in the plural, is the right word: well informed contemporaries, notably the bishops (who naturally were the sharpest students of form), could see that the relativities were always in flux. In 1729, Primate Boulter pointed out that the archbishopric of Dublin, though second only to Boulter's own archbishopric of Armagh in seniority, was not as desirable as the archbishopric of Cashel and the bishoprics of Derry and Kilmore from the point of view of 'providing for a family.'²⁴ (Kilmore soon afterwards fell in relative value and was relegated to the second division.) A bishop without a family might of course think differently. In 1755, Arthur Smyth, bishop of Down and Connor, expected to be offered Limerick, 'worth about £2,200 a year, no house, but a fine demesne for building upon'; but he thought that, 'to one who has no children, the patronage of Down was more desirable than the difference in the value of the bishoprics.'²⁵ So, family circumstances, and circumstances attaching to patronage and the palace (see pp 340–41), all combined with economic forces to add to the state of flux.

In 1751, John Ryder, bishop of Down and Connor, who was carefully contemplating his next move, declared that he would gladly accept Dublin or Cashel, but was advised that Tuam, though an archbishopric, was not as attractive a prospect as any of the bishoprics of Meath, Derry and Clogher: Meath was worth £2,700 per annum plus a tithe income of £1,500; Clogher used to be reckoned at £2,200 per annum, but was now nearly as good as Derry; and Derry was £3,000 per annum.²⁶ Sixty years

21 Dr Beaufort's journal, 1787, PRONI, MIC/250, pp 69–70.   22 Professor Connolly has assembled, on the evidence of contemporary correspondence, figures for 'some gross episcopal revenues' in the period 1717–45 (*Religion, law and power*, p. 181). For other estimates of the incomes of Irish sees in the period c.1715–c.1750, some of them hard to interpret, see Lambeth Palace Library, Ms. 2168, ff. 127–8. I am grateful to Dr D.W. Hayton for drawing this latter source to my attention.   23 Richard Marlay, bishop of Clonfert, to Charlemont, 18 Oct. 1794, *HMC Charlemont Mss.* ii, pp 250–51.   24 Quoted in Kennedy, 'Dublin and Glendalough', p. 175.   25 Smyth to marquess of Hartington, 8 Apr. 1755, Chatsworth papers, PRONI, T/3158/644. I am grateful to Mr Peter Day, keeper of collections at Chatsworth, for reminding me of the existence of this letter. 26 Wilmot to Ryder, 19 Feb. 1750/51, and Ryder to Wilmot, 4 Mar. 1750/51, T/3019/1694–5. By 1772, Clogher must have been better even than the archbishopric of Dublin. In that year, John Garnett, bishop of Clogher, asked to be offered Dublin, 'but upon a previous assurance that he would not accept it'; presumably, he wanted his seniority and his suitability to be recognised, but preferred the superior emoluments of Clogher. The bishop who was in the end promoted to Dublin, John Cradock, bishop of Kilmore, was later described as 'seldom choaked [*sic*] with gratitude' – though this perhaps was an allusion to his personality rather than his dissatisfaction with Dublin. See Hunt, *The Irish parliament, 1775*, pp 71–2 and 62.

later, Wakefield sought to document the same phenomenon on an all-Ireland basis and over a longer time-span. He produced a table of see incomes as they stood *c.*1810, 'as correct, in all probability, as any estimate of property can be, which is so variable in its nature', and set beside them the equivalent figures collected by Arthur Young in the late 1770s. Overall, see incomes had almost doubled; but this statistic concealed a number of aberrant individual cases. The biggest surprise was Elphin. Young reckoned its income at £3,700, which placed it seventh in the episcopal league-table: Wakefield gave a figure of £10,000, which placed it fourth (above two of the archbishoprics, Cashel and Tuam).[27] Young may, in fact, have understated Elphin: its bishop in 1765, William Gore, had declined a translation to Meath.[28] Agar was himself the victim of one major fluctuation in income, because in the fifteen or so years after 1779, when he left Cloyne on promotion to Cashel, the gap in the income of the two sees narrowed until Cloyne came level with Cashel at c.£4,300 per annum.[29] The income of Cashel was being artificially lowered by one inefficient tenant, whose removal by Agar is, basically, the subject of much of this Chapter. But even Agar could not restore Cashel to the income which befitted the third most senior diocese in Ireland. If a long-term comparison is made between the incomes of the archbishoprics and bishoprics which had come within Bishop Ryder's purview in 1751 and their incomes in 1831, what is obvious is that Clogher had fallen back in relation to Derry (or Derry had again surged ahead), and both had become more desirable financially, not just than Tuam, but than any archbishopric except Armagh. Either Elphin's glory-days were over by 1831, or Wakefield's figure for 1810 was wrong. However, the most dramatic decline by 1831 was that of Meath, which (although in rank and precedence the senior bishopric), had sunk well below both Derry and Clogher in income, and even below Tuam.[30] Agar was never bishop of Meath. But as archbishop of Cashel and then of Dublin, he held sees which in his day were on the way down, relatively and perhaps absolutely, in terms of estate income.

The only thing to be said for the Irish system was that it was less inefficient and opprobrious than the system of remunerating bishops of the Church of England. In that Church, 'The bishoprics ascended in value from Llandaff [the poorest] with about £1,000 [per annum – far lower than any Irish bishopric – in 1831] to Canterbury and Durham with £17,000.'[31] Most bishops of the Church of England could not support themselves on the incomes from their see estates alone. Thus, the reforming Bishop Watson of Llandaff 'held nine livings' and a professorship in Cambridge in his individual capacity, plus a further seven livings which were annexed *ex officio* to his see.[32] In 1787, John Hinchcliffe, bishop of Peterborough, 1769–94, was master of Trinity College, Cambridge. The bishop of London was 'dean to the archbishop of Canterbury, an office of great dignity and trust', and the dean of St Paul's was 'always

27 Wakefield, op. cit., ii. 469; Akenson, *Church of Ireland*, pp 35–7.   28 *DNB*, *sub* 'Richard Pococke', who accepted Meath in 1765 and then died.   29 Marlay to Charlemont, 18 Oct. 1794, loc. cit.   30 Akenson, *Church of Ireland*, pp 80–84. The second-senior was Kildare, which was well ahead of Meath by 1831. Both entitled their holders to an *ex officio* place on the Irish privy council and the title of 'Rt Hon.'   31 Mathieson, *English Church reform*, p. 113.   32 Ibid., p. 26.

the bishop of another diocese.'[33] In 1794, Dr Henry Courtenay, then newly promoted to the bishopric of Bristol, maintained that 'the almost exhausted revenues of the bishopric would not admit of my resigning any of my preferment[s].'[34] In 1815, the Hon. Henry Ryder, the first Evangelical to be made a bishop, retained the deanery of Wells after his appointment as bishop of Gloucester, 'this being one of the poorest sees ... . He held the deanery for seven years after he had been translated to the better-endowed see of Lichfield, and even then exchanged it for a prebend – not so valuable – at Westminster. But even Lichfield ... must have been more expensive than lucrative.'[35] In the 1830s, a bishop of Llandaff subsequent to Watson 'was also dean of St Paul's, an office which carried about £5,000 ... – more than five times the value of the see itself. The bishop of Rochester was also dean of Worcester, which post doubled his income.'[36] One bishop, Edward Venables Vernon, bishop of Carlisle, 1791–1808, took a principled stand by resigning preferments which he could have held in commendam with his bishopric.[37] But, as a general rule, it was a major weakness of the Church of England that the system of remunerating its bishops actually promoted non-residence and compelled most of the bishops to set a bad example to their parochial clergy.

As some of these examples imply, deans and other cathedral dignitaries in the Church of England were well remunerated *qua* dignitaries; which, again, was the opposite of the situation in the Church of Ireland, where 'The incomes of a very large portion of the dignified clergy chiefly arise ... from the incomes of livings generally annexed to their respective dignities.'[38] There were some exceptions to this general rule in Ireland, but they cannot have numbered more than a dozen, if so many. One of the few really valuable deaneries was Derry. In 1739, its fame reached the ears of the duke of Newcastle, ever alert to the rustle of patronage; Newcastle exclaimed that the deanery estate 'is actually let to farmers for £1,260 per annum.'[39] In 1787, Down was £1,500 per annum and Raphoe almost as much.[40] This was better than some bishoprics, although the poorest bishoprics were pulling ahead of the richest deaneries at about this time. But, apart from these three rich northern deaneries, most cathedral dignities in the Church of Ireland were in the same situation as the bishoprics of the Church of England – dependent on auxiliary, and mainly parochial, income.

Bishops were more conspicuous than 'dignified clergy'; and at episcopal level, there were few examples in the Church of Ireland of income being derived from sources other than see estates. The most glaring was that of the bishop of Kildare; 'of Bishop Charles Lindsay's gross revenue of £6,507 [in 1833], practically everything came from rents or renewal fines from his property as dean [of Christ Church].'[41] The other examples were comparatively minor as well as few. As has been seen (p. 390), the

---

33 *The British Mercury, vol. iii for 1787*, pp 298 and 246–7. For other deaneries held *in commendam* with bishoprics, see Cowper, *Deans of Canterbury*, p. 189.   34 Courtenay to Agar, 16 Apr. 1794, T/3719/C/28/7.   35 Mathieson, op. cit., p. 112.   36 Evans, *The contentious Tithe*, p. 5. See also p. 2.   37 Vernon to Pitt, 29 Jan. 1805, Jupp/Aspinall transcript from the W.D. Adams papers. 38 Cove, *Essay on the revenue of the Church of England*, p. 168. See also p. 214.   39 Newcastle to 3rd duke of Devonshire (the lord lieutenant), 7 July 1739, Chatsworth papers, PRONI, T/3158/87. 40 Beaufort's journal, 1787, PRONI, MIC/250, pp 55 and 14.   41 Milne, *Christ Church Cathedral*,

bishop of Meath enjoyed a tithe income of £1,500 per annum in 1751, on top of his see lands rental of £2,700. The income from the rectory and rectorial glebe of Athboy, Co. Meath, was appropriated to the primate by a papal bull of 1399, and so remained until disappropriation in 1852–4.[42] Likewise, the rectorial tithes and advowson of Blackabbey [i.e. Donaghadee and Carrowdore], Co. Down, were appropriate to the primacy. But this appropriation was the subject of acrimonious litigation in the period 1730–75, and the rectorial tithes were voluntarily surrendered by Primate Beresford in 1837.[43] Another such appropriation, this time to the bishopric of Cloyne, was the advowson and rectorial tithes of St Mary's, Youghal; the latter added £1,600 per annum to a see lands rental of £5,000 in 1831, but were surrendered by John Brinkley, bishop of Cloyne, at about that time.[44] An act passed on the initiative of Primate Robinson in 1784 (see p. 445) encouraged bishops who were the beneficiaries of such appropriations to mitigate their ill-effect on the parishes concerned by endowing perpetual curacies, and Robinson himself took the lead in this respect. But episcopal appropriations were 'but few' in Ireland, and except in Cloyne and Meath constituted only a 'trifling' addition to episcopal income.[45] Only Kildare was an exception to the general rule that bishops of the Church of Ireland were in a position to support themselves comfortably, and in some cases opulently, on the incomes from their see estates.

THE TENANTRY ACT OF 1780 AND 'THE ARCHBISHOP OF CASHEL'S ACT' OF 1795

In spite of never occupying a particularly lucrative see, Agar was pre-eminent as a defender in parliament of the property rights of the bishops and the Church. The first demonstration of this came in 1780, the year after his translation to Cashel. In May–June and August 1780, there were heated debates in the Irish parliament over what was called the Tenantry Bill (*19 and 20 George III, cap. 30*), which sought to define and very much narrow the circumstances under which a head landlord could evict a perpetuity tenant. Such a tenant held a lease for the lives of named individuals, with a covenant for perpetual renewal, provided he inserted a new life in the place of each life which dropped, and on each insertion of a new life paid a renewal fine (which, like the annual rent, was stipulated and fixed by the original perpetuity lease).[46] Perpetuity leases of Church lands originated in the years before 1635, when an act had been passed 'for the preservation of the inheritance, rights and profits of lands belonging to the Church and persons ecclesiastical' (*10 and 11 Charles I, cap. 3*);

pp 315–16.   **42** Papers about Athboy, 1399–1862, Armagh diocesan registry papers, PRONI, DIO 4/2/3/1–12.   **43** Papers documenting the appropriation and the litigation, 1569–1852, ibid., DIO 4/26/3/1–7; Susan E. Pack-Beresford, *Christ Church, Carrowdore* (Belfast, 1994), pp 3–12.   **44** Lewis, *Topographical dictionary*, i. 382, and ii. 728.   **45** Erck, *Ecclesiastical Register*, p. lv.   **46** The first and best discussion of the Tenantry Bill, in all its political and economic bearings, will be found in O'Connell, *Irish politics and social conflict*, pp 266–81.

this act restricted such persons to granting terminable leases for no longer than 21 or
at most 40 years. There seem only to have been a couple of perpetuity leases of the see
lands of Cashel (Agar was to encounter many more in the diocese of Dublin). Nevertheless, Agar was a warm opponent of the bill. Lord Buckinghamshire reported in
October 1780, with his usual *animus* against Agar:

> The uncontrolled fury expressed by the Archbishop of Cashel in a debate
> upon a bill for regulating leases, has sunk him in the opinion of all temperate
> men. The measure was not of a nature to call for the interference of govern-
> ment. Yet, without proof, he was pleased to suspect me of having influenced
> some votes; and at a dinner at the Chancellor's the day after, he behaved to me
> with such marked impropriety that you would have given great credit to my
> forbearance in not manifesting a marked degree of resentment. His Grace, if I
> divine aright, will hereafter be materially inconvenient to every Irish govern-
> ment whom he is not admitted to govern, and should he once obtain the reins,
> Phaeton comparatively would be a careful driver.[47]

The passions of more parliamentarians than Agar were inflamed by the Tenantry
Bill. Many great landlords were perpetuity tenants of other landlords in respect of
parts of their estates; and those whose vested interests on balance placed them on the
side of the tenants did not scruple to court popularity and pose as underdogs and
champions of an oppressed under-class. As it happened, most of the prominent
supporters of Dublin Castle were also supporters of the bill, while many members of
the so-called 'Patriot' opposition, particularly in the Lords, were its opponents. The
government was, as Buckinghamshire asserted, officially neutral. But it was delighted
at the opportunity thus given to its supporters to appear in a popular cause, and at the
wrong-footing of its opponents. The man who introduced the bill was the Attorney-
General, Agar's old friend, Scott. Scott called it his 'favourite bill', and justified it on
the ground that 'property, by some late determinations of the British House of Lords
[on appeals from Ireland] upon covenants for perpetual renewals of leases, ... [had
been] very much set at sea.'[48] (The confusion of English law lords on the subject was
understandable, since perpetuities were a form of lease peculiar to Ireland.) Scott also
professed that his own estate was so circumstanced that he had no vested interest in
the matter. Part of Agar's Co. Kilkenny property seems to have been held by him
under a perpetuity lease, and another part was apparently lost to him through the
failure of his brother, Welby, to renew perpetuity leases in time.[49] But this vested
interest did not cause him to deviate from his opposition to a bill which professed to
be 'for the relief' of perpetuity tenants who through inadvertence or for technical
reasons had failed to stick rigidly to the terms of their covenants for perpetual renewal.
His concern must have been that the Church should not be deprived of the chance it

---

47 Buckinghamshire to Hotham Thompson, 11 Oct. 1789, PRONI, T/3429/1/68.   48 Both
quotations occur in O'Connell, op. cit., pp 266 and 270.   49 Agar's marriage settlement, 22 Nov.

still had of repossessing any land which had been in effect alienated through perpetuity-leasing.

Primate Robinson shared Agar's hostility to the bill. Writing from England, he thanked Agar, with his usual hypocrisy, for the 'account you give me of your employment in the [Irish privy] council ... . My attention has been employed in the same manner for some years without a coadjutor, and I cannot refrain to express my concern when I perceive that the temper of the rising generation in the House of Commons is equally hostile to the rights of the clergy as I have ever found it.'[50] On 19 August, the opposition to the bill in the Lords, headed by Agar, was defeated by only one vote. On the same day, a dissentient minority of twenty-one lords entered a protest in the Lords' *Journals*, which is word-for-word the same as a draft in Agar's handwriting among Agar's papers.[51] Contrary to Buckinghamshire's description of Agar's intemperance on the subject, the tone of the protest is reasonable and the argument highly effective:

> In most instances, the lessors have, by another covenant, provided that they shall *not* be obliged to renew any life which drops, unless the tenant shall tender the stipulated fine within the said given time, but shall be discharged from the covenant in that respect. Therefore, this bill is altogether unjust, for it discharges one of the contracting parties from the literal obligations of his covenants, and leaves them obligatory on the other. ... It, is an *ex post facto* act, construing the intentions of the parties differently from the evident meaning of the covenants.
>
> ... The lessee names the lives, and probably of persons unknown to the lessor, and therefore ought to be obliged by this bill to discover the death of each life to the lessor, and the time when it happened, which is not the case. ... [This bill] ... applies one rule to all cases. It makes no difference where there is a remedy for recovering the fine, and where there is none. It makes no difference where there has been a neglect for a few days, and one life only lapsed, and where all the lives are dropped and perhaps twenty years lapsed. It makes no difference, where the fine payable for each life amounts to a large sum of money, or where it is only a peppercorn.
>
> For these and a variety of other reasons mentioned in debate, we wished to set aside this bill, and being sincerely anxious to procure for the tenants to such leases every relief which a just, fair and equitable bill could give to them, we earnestly, strenuously and repeatedly urged that the judges should be directed to draw such a bill as should answer this most desirable purpose and which, instead of doing injury to one man under the pretence of relieving another, should do equal and impartial justice to all men.

1776, 21 M 57/T358; James Agar of the Temple to Agar, 28 Dec. 1805, T/3719/C/39/28. **50** Robinson to Agar, 8 July 1780, T/3719/C/14/23. **51** Agar's draft for, and a printed version of, the Lords' protest, 19 Aug. 1780, 21 M 57/A14/15–16.

Primate Robinson, now returned from England, headed the signatories to Agar's protest.

The nub of the matter was the failure of the Tenantry Act to protect the landlord against fraud, particularly the tenant's concealment from him of the fact that a life or lives had dropped. The act purported to relate to cases of 'mere neglect', where 'no circumstance of fraud be proved against such tenants.' But Agar was almost certainly correct in his judgement that the existence of fraud was going to be hard to establish. Nevertheless, it seems that, notwithstanding the Tenantry Act, he took proceedings against a major perpetuity leaseholder under the see of Cashel, Wray Palliser of Derryluskan, near Fethard, Co. Tipperary. Wray Palliser was the great-grandson of Archbishop Palliser of Cashel (d.1727), and Archbishop Palliser is popularly supposed to have converted see leases to perpetuities for the benefit of his own family.[52] In 1779, half of the see lands, or 7,325 Irish acres, were in the hands of two branches of the Palliser family, though only a fraction of them – 2,500 Irish acres at most – were held in perpetuity. Provokingly, the Palliser holdings included Ballypadeen, parish of the Rock of Cashel, right under Agar's proverbially long nose.[53] In February 1781, Scott – who was as usual 'going' the Munster circuit – wrote to Agar: 'it never before appeared to me that ... you, a living archbishop of Cashel, could be denied justice in the country of Tipperary against such an opponent as yours is, the son of a dead archbishop.'[54] Wray Palliser was *not* the son of the dead archbishop, but it would be an extraordinary coincidence if Scott was not referring to the Palliser case. It seems, however, that Agar was 'discouraged from going to trial' in 1781, and that the issue was amicably resolved. This is not surprising. In spite of first appearances, Archbishop Palliser was almost certainly not guilty of abusing his trust and illegally granting himself and his family a perpetuity or perpetuities. What is likelier to have happened is that Palliser, using inside information from the see rentals and from his dealings with the see tenants, bought out a perpetuity tenant whose lease derived from a long-antecedent archbishop. By 1796 the Agars and the Pallisers of Derryluskan (now represented by Wray Palliser's son and successor, John) were on friendly, visiting terms,[55] which they would hardly have been if the Palliser perpetuity had really been a 'steal' from the diocese and if there had been a bitter and protracted lawsuit over it. Agar's successor, Brodrick, also thought well of John Palliser.[56]

Between 1780 and 1795 there were various attempts to better the position of the generality of tenants of Church lands – those who held 21–year leases only. Actually, these attempts were a continuation of a much older House of Commons tradition.

---

52 Power, *Eighteenth-century Tipperary*, p. 144.   53 For Agar's surveys and valuations of lands held by members of the Palliser family, principally the non-perpetuity lands held by Dr John Palliser, see Hampshire RO list of 21 M/57/B45–69, MP49 and 139, B9/103 and 61 and D17. It is impossible to be precise about acreage, because the surveys of the see lands were far from precise until Agar's day. Moreover, there was no point in a survey's being precise about the acreage of a perpetuity, since the rent and renewal fine were both fixed where that species of tenure was concerned.   54 Scott to Agar, 2 Feb. and 25 July 1781, T/3719/C/15/2 and 10.   55 Lady Somerton to Agar, 13 Oct. 1796, T/3719/C/30/34.   56 Brodrick to Midleton, 17 Mar. 1804, Ms. 1248, vol. 18, ff. 88–9.

Bills extending the leasing powers of the bishops beyond 21 years and/or empowering them to grant leases for lives were introduced in 1735, 1751, 1758, 1769, 1771, 1774, 1781, 1782, 1785, 1786, 1789 and 1793.[57] In 1788, though no actual bill materialised, Henry Grattan threatened to bring in a number of 'reasonable bills' hostile to the bishops, including one for 'enabling ... [them] to make leases for three lives, as in England, etc.'[58] The closest shaves, from the point of view of the bishops, came in 1782 and 1795. On 8 June 1782, W.B. Ponsonby, the Co. Kilkenny MP, introduced a bill extending the leasing powers of bishops and other ecclesiastical persons to 61 years or three lives. This measure passed the Commons on 20 July and went up to the Lords on the same day (this being the brand-new procedure under the constitution of 1782). It was still in committee in the Lords when the session ended.[59] Immediately afterwards, on 27 July, Primate Robinson sent to the Archbishop of Canterbury a representation unanimously signed by the Irish bench declaratory of their opposition to this proposal.[60] Since the bill had the innocent appearance of bringing the leasing of Irish see estates more nearly into line with English law and practice, it is hard to see how the Archbishop could have been expected, in consistency, to give opposition to a revival of it in a subsequent session of the Irish parliament.

The great attack on the Irish bishops as landlords did not in fact come until 1795. Agar himself described what happened as follows:

> [In] May [1795] ... a bill was sent from the House of Commons to the Lords 'for the further and immediate improvement of this kingdom by enabling archbishops and bishops and other ecclesiastical persons to make leases for lives or years.' The object of this bill was to enable archbishops, etc., to let their see land for 21 years or three lives, whichever should last the longest, reserving a rent greater than the present reserved rent on each lease of a moiety of the present rent [i.e. one-and-a-half times the present rent]. The direct tendency of the bill was to mend the situation of the immediate lessees, without any benefit to the terre-tenants, and [to] the injury of all succeeding archbishops and bishops, etc., and to the destruction of the patronage of the crown. In the House of Commons this bill was introduced and supported by the lessees of ecclesiastical persons, and particularly by the Primate's tenants, amongst whom Mr James Stewart [of Killymoon, Cookstown], and Mr [John] Staples [of nearby Lissan, both in Co. Tyrone] were the most active. Application was made to the Lord Lieutenant (Lord Camden) and to his Secretary, Mr Pelham, by the Primate and by the Archbishop of Cashel to have this bill rejected in the H. of C., and Mr P. did seem to give it opposition. However, his endeavours were ineffectual.
>
> In the House of Lords it was most strenuously supported by Lord Clon-

57 This information is drawn from the *General index to the journals of the House of Commons of the kingdom of Ireland, 1613–1800* (2 vols., Dublin, 1802), *sub* 'Bills'. 58 Robert Day to Lord Glandore, 11 Mar. 1788, MIC/639/5/16 (pp 190–91). 59 *Commons' journals*, x, pp 241, 364 and 376; *Lords' journals*, v, pp 357 and 364. 60 Lambeth Palace Library, Moore papers, vol. 6, ff. 194–7.

mell, chief justice of the king's bench, who holds most valuable possessions under ... [the Church]. In the debate on this bill, Lord Clonmell, alluding to the act of the 10th and 11th Charles I, cap. 3, said that at present no tenant to any archbishop or bishop had a legal lease, and their only security depended on the perjury of juries. In answer to this the Archbishop of Cashel admitted that the foregoing act did create very alarming doubts about the validity of ecclesi-astical leases made contrary to the tenor of that act, and that such doubts ought to be instantly removed. He accordingly on the following day drew a bill to remove all such doubts, entitled 'An act to explain and amend an act passed in the 10th and 11th of Charles I entitled an Act for [the] preservation of the inheritance, rights and profits of lands belonging to the Church and persons ecclesiastical.' This bill passed unanimously through the two Houses of Parliament.[61]

Elsewhere, Agar described its object as being 'not only to confirm all leases heretofore made contrary to said statute, but to authorise the present practice of renewing leases'[62] without re-calculating the rent in light of the value added by the sitting tenants' improvements. He might also have said that the object was also to discourage bishops from the opprobrious practice of running their lives against see leases.

This account of the events leading up to 'the Archbishop of Cashel's Act' is endorsed by the independent testimony of Brodrick. Writing to Lord Midleton in the second half of May 1795, he described the defeat in the House of Lords of the Commons' bill

> empowering ecclesiastical persons to grant long leases ... . Our government here exerted themselves to throw it out. Without their assistance, we could not have done it, although the bench of bishops, a powerful phalanx, were unani-mous against it. Of 22 archbishops and bishops, 18 voted in person, one by proxy, the Bishops of Derry and Clogher were absent, and there is as yet no bishop of Killala. I hope it will not escape you that the bishops now alive would have realised to their families a very considerable sum, if the bill had passed. Of the lay Lords, we had 16 on our side to 8, which composed the minority against us. Mr Pelham spoke against it in the H. of C. at the second reading, but was beat by a majority of four. They [the government] made no further exertion there, and I am told afterwards began to be alarmed lest the bill should make its way through our House. The lay Lords who voted in our favour are not usually very friendly to the Church.[63]

Years later, Agar's son, the 2nd earl of Normanton, received a similar account of how the Commons' bill

61 Agar's 'state' of the diocese of Cashel, 1779–1801, 21 M 57/B6/1.   62 Agar's 'political memoranda', 1782–95, 21 M 57/A18.   63 Brodrick to Midleton, 19 May 1795, Ms. 1248, vol. 16, ff. 50–51.

was so ably and eloquently and disinterestedly opposed by your Lordship's father ... that ... [it] was thrown out, many Lords (particularly the late Lord Dillon) declaring that, though they came down to the House for the purpose of supporting the measure, yet they were so persuaded by what fell from the Archbishop of Cashel (your father) that they felt called upon to oppose it, which they did, to the great discomfiture of Lord Clonmell, who got no credit for disinterested feelings on the occasion.[64]

So 'the Archbishop of Cashel's Act' was rightly so-called; and a draft of it, more-or-less conforming to the enacted version, is to be found in Agar's handwriting among Agar's papers.[65] It became law on 5 June 1795.[66]

THE LEASING STRATEGIES OF BISHOPS, *c.*1740–1809

The system which Agar successfully defended and strategically re-defined in 1795 was ramshackle in the extreme, and depended on a number of conventions and unspoken rules without which it would have been unworkable in practice. The already mentioned act 'for the preservation of the inheritance, rights and profits of lands belonging to the Church and persons ecclesiastical' (*10 and 11 Charles I, cap. 3*), not only restricted bishops to leases for not more than 21 years (or 40 in respect of property in a corporate or market town), but also required that the land be let for not less than half its annual value at the time of making the lease. It was the almost universal departure from this latter requirement which had caused Clonmell to assert 'that ... no tenant to any archbishop or bishop had a legal lease.' The 1635 Act was the Irish counterpart of legislation passed in England in 1559 and 1571.[67] The act was not retrospective. So, its effect, as Dr Barnard has shown, was that, 'belatedly, the systematic loss of the Church's wealth to the families, neighbours and patrons of the clergy ... was stopped. But what had been lost already could not now be retrieved. ... Since some ... new leases continued the old, it may be that a right to automatic renewal negated the intention of the act. ... The suspicion grows that advantageous terms were still granted as part of the complex of social and economic relationships with which any shrewd clergyman established himself in his neighbourhood.'[68]

Moreover, the restriction to 21 (or 40) years was not an absolute. By *15 George II, cap. 5*, the 40–year dispensation was extended to demesne land in a town or up to half a mile from a town. The theory was that 40–year leases would encourage tenants to build, though in practice the term was rather too short to give such encouragement. By *17 and 18 Charles 11, cap. 2*, 'Augmentation' lands could be let for three lives at their value in the reign of Charles II, or at the same rent as had been paid for the previous twenty years. 'Augmentation' lands were impropriate church lands which had

---

64 John Hare to 2nd earl of Normanton, 22 Feb. 1827, 21 M 57, 2nd earl's unreferenced correspondence. 65 21 M 57/B19/6. 66 Ibid. 67 Gillespie's historical introduction to Refaussé and Clark, *Dublin see maps*, p. 24. 68 Barnard, 'Improving clergymen', p. 139.

been forfeited by their lay owners in the 1640s or 1650s, and had been granted at the Restoration to eight southern bishoprics (of which, in practice, only five – including Cashel – actually came into possession of the 'Augmentation' lands intended for them).[69] Finally, an act of 1726 (*12 George I, cap. 10, secs. 13 and 16*) empowered bishops to let 'bog or fenny land' for 60 years, at a very low rent (to encourage the tenant to undertake reclamation), at the expiration of which term the land was to be re-let at three-quarters of its then value.[70]

Even within the 21–year norm, there was ample scope for negotiation and variation. This centred round renewals and renewal fines – matters of quite as much importance as the basic reserved rent. 'In 1718, the Bishop of Derry [William Nicolson] said that the rents of the see for six months, without one shilling in fines, had brought him in £1,213; and three years later, when a good many of his leases were due for renewal, he estimated that the fines would amount to about £2,000.'[71] Sixty years later, in 1787, the rents from the Dromore see estate amounted to £1,500 per annum, while the annual average of the renewal fines was no less than £1,000.[72] Among Agar's papers is an 'Abstract ... of the method practised by Dr Bolton, late archbishop of Cashel, who was a notably ingenious man in renewing leases.'

> When two or three years lapsed, he expected half a year's rent for the renewal, without raising the rent except some small matter. For renewing upon a lapse of five years, he raised the rent a twentieth part, and took one year's rent, including the rise, as a fine, as for example – if a lease paid £100 rent per annum, he raised it to £105 and took £105 fine. If seven years were expired, he raised the rent a tenth part and took two years' rent as a fine; for example – a lease of £100 per annum he raised to £110 and took £220 fine. His further rule was to take a year's rent for every two years lapsed after seven and to raise the rent considerably, but can't be certain what he raised the rent to when more than seven years lapsed. His reason for not raising the rent when two or three years only lapsed, was to encourage the tenants to renew often. Note: Archbishop Bolton computed these fines by the reserved rent.

An alternative method was to calculate the 'fines ... according to the profit rent of the lands, or their value after deduction of the reserved rent; and as the value of the lands in Ireland ... has of late years risen one-quarter part, and ... the interest and value

69 Notes by Agar for his speech on 'the Archbishop of Cashel's Act' of 1795, 21 M 57/B18/22; provisional lease for three lives or 31 years from the bishop of Ossory of Augmentation lands in Co. Limerick intended for the estate of that see as soon as the bishop passed a patent for them, 12 Apr. 1676, and survey of the 565 Irish acres in Co. Limerick and 1,844 in Co. Cork granted as Augmentation lands to Ossory, 26 Apr. 1676, De Vesci papers, NLI, J/20.   70 Case, with the opinion of Beresford Burston, 2 July 1799, 21 M 57/B18/16.   71 J.L. McCracken, 'The ecclesiastical structure, 1714–60', in T.W. Moody and W.E. Vaughan (eds.), *A new history of Ireland, iv: eighteenth-century Ireland, 1691–1800* (Oxford, 1986), p. 85.   72 Beaufort's journal, 1787, MIC/250, pp 69–70.

of money has decreased in proportion, ... bishops' fines should advance accordingly.' According to this method, the fine on renewing a 21–year lease after the expiration of four years was the equivalent of six months' rent, after the expiration of ten years was two years' rent, after the expiration of seventeen years was six years and nine months' rent, etc., etc.[73] The problem was that the bishop did not necessarily know what the tenant's profit rent actually was, or even the quantity of the land comprised in the lease, and the tenant and the tenant's sub-tenants had every motive for keeping the bishop in the dark. Agar, shrewd though he was, is a good example of a bishop kept in the dark – as will be seen. Most bishops were either in the dark or chose not to jeopardise their relations with influential gentry-tenants by seeking enlightenment. The legal rate of interest in Ireland was 10% in 1660, 8% by 1703, 6% by 1731 and 5% by 1788. 'To compensate for this change, fining rates should have risen, but they do not seem to have done so [at any rate on the see estate of Dublin, where] ... tenants on the archbishop's lands were taking large gains.'[74] What seems to have happened over much of that estate from the late seventeenth or early eighteenth century onwards is that leases were renewed after five years on payment of a fine which equated to twice the reserved (not the profit) rent. Practice varied from see to see, but it is unlikely that renewal fines were anywhere raised to reflect in full the lowering of interest rates.

Because of this disparity, renewal fines did not adequately compensate for the undervalue at which see lands were almost always let. However, the practice became very general of maximising income to each incumbent by 'topping up' bishops' leases every year or couple of years, so that they always had 20 or 21 years to run. 'When I was made bishop of Cloyne', wrote Agar in January 1772,

> I found that my predecessor [Frederick Hervey] had renewed every lease of consequence in the diocese immediately previous to his quitting it, many of the leases bearing date on 2 February 1768, and the king's letter appointing him bishop of Derry arrived in Dublin on the following day ... . I have never had an opportunity of renewing more than two of them since I have been there, which is now four years, and I shall be a very considerable loser were I to quit that see without receiving some of the fines.[75]

This letter was written in the context of Agar's possible translation to the bishopric of Elphin. The situation of that bishop, William Gore, was the reverse of Agar's: as Gore explained to the lord lieutenant, he needed to move to another bishopric in order to make a killing on fines:

> I have a wife, three children and one coming, all depending on my uncertain life ..., and since I was bishop have not had it in my power to save much for the

---

73 21 M 57/B10/7.   **74** Gillespie's historical introduction, p. 34; information kindly given me by Dr Gillespie, who gleaned it from the *First report of the commissioners on ecclesiastical revenue and patronage* (1833), pp 14 and 215.   **75** Agar to Macartney, 5 Jan. 1772, *Macartney in Ireland*, p. 303.

provision of my family. On this account, I would take it as the greatest obligation and favour if your Excellency would be so kind as to recommend me to succeed to the bishopric of Limerick, now vacant. I confess honestly my motive for desiring this favour is to get the money which may be received from the tenants on the renewals of their leases. I may venture to say the bishopric of Elphin is a better income than Limerick.[76]

At Elphin, the fines were in effect part of the annual income, which Gore reckoned was at least £3,352 per annum. He explained that 'most of the tenants would gladly renew on my terms ... every year. ... The mode I have followed in renewing these leases is to take three-quarters of a year's rent as a renewal fine at the expiration of every two years.'[77] At Cashel, too, Agar found a system or practice of annual or biennial renewals: almost all the terminable see leases (36 out of 42) had 21 years to run in 1779.[78] The Dublin practice of five-yearly renewals cannot have applied across the board: just before Agar's death in 1809, his agent sent him 'six sets of *annual* [my emphasis] renewals for the 24th of this month [June – i.e. midsummer day], ... [and] my accountable vouchers for the fines due upon said renewals.'[79] By such means, the fines became a one, two or at most five-yearly addition to the rent. This process was called 'fining down the rents.'

Against this background, Agar had good reason to maintain in the House of Lords debate in 1795:

> Twenty-one years is the term equally beneficial to lessor and lessee – witness that bishops are satisfied and the profits of the tenants are notorious. ... Augmentation lands [are] let for three lives and [are] not better improved than those at 21 years. ... The law [of 1635] acted on principles of justice, and while it allowed churchmen to let their lands for the benefit of the laity at half value, it likewise obliged them to let but for 21 years, thereby enabling them to make up in some measure the deficiency of their rents by frequent renewals.[80]

He could have pressed the point about Augmentation lands further, because they made it difficult for the bishops who had them 'to make up in some measure the deficiency of their rents by frequent renewals.' In this respect, the bishop of Ossory was alleged to be at a particular disadvantage, 'on account of the number of leases for three lives which have been made of the Augmentation lands that compose a great part of the property. These are of very little value but as the lives drop in ...; [and] it is impossible to say what the income may be in any one year.'[81] In 1804, Lord Macartney – writing, not about Augmentation lands, but about parts of his own north Antrim estate at

76 William [Gore, bishop of] Elphin, to Townshend, 21 Sep. 1771, Townshend letter-book, RCB Library, Ms. 20/42.   77 Gore to Macartney, [early] Jan. 1772, *Macartney in Ireland*, pp 302–3. 78 Power, *Eighteenth-century Tipperary*, pp 138–9.   79 John Hare to Agar, 22 June 1809, T/3719/C/43/111.   80 Notes by Agar for his speech on 'the Archbishop of Cashel's Act', 21 M 57/B18/22.   81 Bishop O'Beirne to Portland, 4 Nov. 1795, *Irish official papers*, i. 145.

Lisanoure, near Ballymoney – confirmed this gloomy view of the uncertain duration of leases for lives: 'There is certainly something uncommonly healthy in the climate of Lisanoure, for I observe that very few people die in its neighbourhood, especially if their lives happen to be connected with a good lease.'[82]

The English practice of letting bishops' lands for lives, though warmly recommended for Ireland by those with interested motives for so doing, was liable to similar objections. In England, 'The system of Church leases, normally let to laymen on lives, ... ensured that individual churchmen had no interest beyond fat renewal fines and the realisation of immediate profits.' It meant that Church of England clergy were preoccupied 'not merely [with] the prospective mortality of superiors occupying desirable preferments, but also that of laymen on whose "lives" beneficial leases depended. It also tended to prevent the Church as a whole from benefiting from agricultural improvement at a time [the 1770s onwards] when lay landlords were abandoning beneficial leases in favour of tenancies-at-will and frequent rent reviews.'[83] In a sense, the Irish system of renewing 21–year leases of church lands every year or two, which gave churchmen the opportunity to try to reflect their tenants' rising rents in increased renewal fines, was a rough equivalent of the 'tenancies-at-will and frequent rent reviews' which were becoming prevalent on lay estates in England. According to Wakefield, such a system of renewals would be illegal in England, because it was 'contrary to the decision of the English court of chancery. ... [In England], a life holder cannot annihilate a lease by which his estate is let and grant a new one upon receiving a fine ..., because this would keep his successor out of his income when he came to his estate.'[84] Wakefield may not have been right about this. In the period 1803–6, the tenant of a lease of tithes under the see of St David's of which about seven years had lapsed, sought to top it up on payment of a renewal fine. The Bishop, Thomas Burgess, acquiesced and asked for a fine representing two and a half years' rent. However, he calculated the rent at an exorbitant figure, and negotiations were broken off. When the tenant tried again, he found that the Bishop had 'granted a concurrent lease of the tithes to Mrs Burgess, his wife.'[85] Obviously, neither the proposed renewal within the term of the existing lease, nor the 'concurrent lease', would have been legal on Wakefield's reading of the situation.

In Ireland, these practices were legal and uncontroversial; and many bishops and senior churchmen in Ireland made fortunes by these and other means. Robert Maxwell, dean of Armagh, 1610–22, and his son, Robert Maxwell, bishop of Kilmore, 1643–73, founded the Maxwell family of Farnham, Co. Cavan, later earls of Farnham, and another Scot, John Leslie, bishop of Raphoe, 1633–61, and of Clogher, 1661–71 (known as 'the Fighting Bishop') that of the Leslies of Castle Leslie, Glaslough, Co. Monaghan. Richard Tenison, an Englishman who was successively bishop of Killala, Clogher and Meath, 1682–1705, founded three Irish gentry families of

82 Macartney to Agar, 8 Aug. 1804, T/3719/C/38/39.   83 Paul Langford, *Public life and the propertied Englishman*, p. 14.   84 Wakefield, *Account of Ireland*, ii, pp 469–70.   85 Bishop of Chester (who happened in his private capacity to be a St David's see tenant) to Primate Stuart (a former bishop of St David's), 20 Apr. 1806, Bedfordshire RO, WY 994/49.

Tenison; and subsequent Irish bishops of English birth who founded Irish gentry families included Charles Cobbe, archbishop of Dublin, 1743–65, and one of his successors, Archbishop Fowler (see pp 461–7). John Vesey, archbishop of Tuam, 1679– 1716, the son of a humble archdeacon, and his son, the already-mentioned Sir Thomas Vesey, bishop of Ossory, founded the Vesey family of Abbeyleix, Co. Laois, who were created Barons Knapton in 1750 and viscounts de Vesci in 1776. The Veseys were also helped by the fact that Bishop Vesey's wife was a granddaughter and co-heiress of another very rich churchman, Michael Boyle, archbishop of Armagh, 1678–1702. Edward Maurice, a *protégé* of Sir Thomas Vesey and a subsequent (1754–6) bishop of Ossory, acquired the Dunmore estate, Co. Laois, and other lands which together were worth £4,000 per annum by 1830.[86] The already-mentioned Edward Synge, bishop of Elphin, a member of another clerical dynasty like the Veseys, might like them have founded a peerage family if his sons had not died young. His only surviving child and heiress, Alicia, was supposed to be worth £50,000 at the time of her marriage; and Synge, when he died four years later, in 1762, was supposed to be worth £100,000, 'all of the acquisition of the Church' – i.e. wealth amassed by his father, his uncle and Synge himself, each of whom was a senior churchman.[87]

In 1795, an aspirant to a bishopric commented: 'Elphin is I understand £4,000 per annum and, besides, a lease under the see will expire on the 25th of March next, value £700 per annum. This would be the means of providing comfortably for a young family without injustice to anyone.'[88] As far as is known, the foregoing examples were mainly of money being made 'without injustice to anyone.' In spite of its geographical proximity to the archiepiscopal manor of Swords, the Cobbe estate at Newbridge, and the rest of the Cobbe lands in Co. Dublin, do not seem to have had an ecclesiastical origin. Perhaps the Leslies of Glaslough might have had difficulty explaining how they first came into their large Pettigo estate, straddling the boundary of Co. Donegal and Co. Fermanagh, held by them under the see of Clogher for some two hundred and fifty years?[89] Frederick Hervey as outgoing bishop of Cloyne in 1768 was certainly guilty of sharp practice. So was Charles Dodgson as outgoing bishop of Ossory in 1775; Dodgson's successor complained four years later that Dodgson had 'exhausted' the see 'on his removal by taking fines to the amount of more than £2,600 a fortnight after his name was in the *Gazette* for Elphin.'[90] Yet another case, which will be

86 Copy of Bishop Maurice's will, 1756, and epitome of the property of Sir Robert Staples, 8th Bt, of Dunmore, c.1828, Staples papers, PRONI, D/1567/B/10 and D/2/4. Dunmore had been bought by Jonas Wheeler, bishop of Ossory, 1613–40, and Maurice acquired it by marriage with the Wheeler heiress (Leslie, *Ossory clergy and parishes*, pp 16 and 29). The rest of the estates were probably purchases of Maurice's own. 87 Legg, *The Synge letters*, pp xv and xxxi. 88 Brodrick to Midleton, 18 Feb. 1795, Ms. 1248, vol. 16, f. 16. 89 Introduction to the Leslie archive, PRONI, Register of Irish Archives. It is not clear if Bishop Leslie granted the lease in trust for himself. In the first three-quarters of the eighteenth century it served as a provision for a cadet branch of the family, but in 1780 reverted to Charles Powell Leslie of Glaslough. In the early nineteenth century, it became an object of family ambition to get the then bishop in the family translated to Clogher, but the government saw the danger and did not comply. 90 William Newcome, then bishop of Ossory, to Lord [Chancellor Lifford], 16 Mar. 1779, Heron papers, NLI, Ms. 13037/3.

discussed on pp 413–15, was that of Archbishop Fowler, who pushed the maximising of income to the extreme of asset-stripping.

Bishop Woodward, in his explicit and uninhibited letters to his son-in-law, Brodrick, provides some interesting examples of what a reasonably conscientious bishop regarded as either permissible or sharp practice in the matter of see leases – and this in the period just before a bishop's discretion was narrowed by 'the Archbishop of Cashel's Act', which was passed a year after Woodward's death. Woodward had no qualms about trafficking in leases under another see. In January 1792, he announced with triumph that he had acquired a 'pretty considerable ... lease ... under the see of Armagh ... . Mr Whaley is the seller.'[91] Woodward had bought the tenant's interest, and the tenant was the notorious Thomas ('Buck') Whaley (1766–1800) of Whaley Abbey, Co. Wicklow, who was in acute financial difficulties at the time.[92] The lease had been held by generations of the Chappell family, whose heiress had been Whaley's great-grandmother; and, like most see leases, it would have gone on being renewed to future generations of the same family,[93] and never come on the open market, but for the near-bankruptcy of Whaley. When Woodward's son, whom Woodward called 'lucky Dick', made a good marriage in the following year, Woodward gave 'him up my primate's leases, which have a clear profit [rent] of £719 after paying the annual fine. This last will be higher under the next primate, but the land will rise infinitely more.'[94] When it came to the administration of his own see estate, however, Woodward was more scrupulous – or perhaps more concerned to appear in a good light. At the very time he bought out Buck Whaley, he was considering the sum offered by a Capt. Drury as a renewal fine for a Cloyne see lease. Woodward disliked 'suffering leases to run out', but thought Drury was not offering 'quite enough' for a fine which Brodrick had valued at over £1,000. 'If he [Drury] does not renew with me, there is no chance of a successor thinking of renewal. ... [But] I had rather accept the sum offered than stand out, as in case of my death before the lease expires, I shall suffer a loss, or if I survive, shall incur the censure of being too rapacious.'[95]

Whether for conscientious or practical reasons, or from sensitivity to adverse publicity, 'Most bishops were more interested in annual income', supplemented by regular and large renewal fines, 'than in becoming themselves, by their trustees, tenants of church lands on 21–year leases.'[96] If a bishop wanted to let see lands to himself, he had, first, to be prepared to incur contemporary odium and, second, to run the risk that legal means would be found, probably after his death, to 'break' his leases.

---

91 Woodward to Brodrick, 15 Jan. 1792, NLI, Ms. 8870/2.   92 Sir Edward Sullivan, Bt (ed.), *Buck Whaley's memoirs* ... (London, 1906), pp xii–xxx.   93 For example, the Dawson family, later Lords Dartrey, who were cousins of the Chappells and had a female descent from Henry Ussher, archbishop of Armagh, 1595–1613 (Stuart, *Armagh*, p. 346; Lodge, ed. Archdall, *Peerage of Ireland*, vi. 78). The Dawsons derived their Blackwatertown and other Armagh properties (worth, according to Rev. J. Burrows, 'not less than £800 a year' in 1772) from that Ussher connection. They went on renewing with the archbishop until, in the middle of the nineteenth century, new legislation (see p. 420) enabled the 1st earl of Dartrey to buy the fee simple.   94 Woodward to Brodrick, 27 Apr. 1793, Ms. 8870/4. 95 Woodward to Brodrick, 18 Feb. 1792, Ms. 8870/2.   96 Peter Rankin, *Irish building ventures of the earl-bishop of Derry*, p. 14.

Good examples of both experiences are two successive provosts of TCD (who, in regard to the college estate, were legally in much the same position as bishops). In September 1774, following the death of Francis Andrews (provost, 1758–74), it was reported

> that the present provost [Hely-Hutchinson] means to contest the legality of some college leases which Andrews granted. ... The story is told here with some unpleasant circumstances, but they are so improbable, I can't believe them to be true. It is said that old Provost Baldwin [Richard Baldwin, provost, 1717–58] had granted some beneficial leases to himself or his family, which Andrews broke when he became provost, and afterwards granted others of a similar nature for his own advantage. This seems as contradictory to poor Andrews' good sense as to every other part of his character.[97]

There were other risks, too. A provost or bishop who wanted to let college or see lands to himself or his relatives, had to 'run his life' against the leases, take a chance on his living long enough and staying long enough at his post to benefit from this strategy, and forego present for the sake of future advantage. He might of course try to buy out sitting tenants. But this might be an expensive business, although at least it would obviate the risk that he would die or be translated before the leases fell in. The strategy of running one's life against the leases was all very well for a bishop situated as Frederick Hervey was: the bishopric of Derry was probably the second most lucrative in Ireland (see pp 388–91), he had been appointed to it at the early age of thirty-eight, and he was quite certainly not going to be translated to higher things. Indeed, he was lucky not to be tried for sedition, and deposed.[98]

AGAR'S ACQUISITION OF CASHEL SEE LEASES, 1792–1804

Agar, as an extremely ambitious man, had every intention of being translated to higher things. 'He does not lose sight of the primacy or the see of Dublin', wrote the lord lieutenant officially in March 1784;[99] and he probably did not expect to remain in Cashel for the twenty-two years he did – in other words, for just a little longer than would have been necessary to run his life against the leases.[100] D'Alton, in his zeal to

97 Richard Rigby to Robert FitzGerald, 20 Sep. 1774, MIC/639/4/14. See also a petition from the provost, fellows and scholars of TCD to the Irish parliament, 25 Jan. 1780, in which they object to a bill which has been introduced to confirm Andrews' 'leases ... in trust ... for himself' and recite the proceedings and events of the period 1774–80 – Foster/Massereene papers, PRONI, D/207/25/4. 98 Rutland to Pitt, 13 Sep. 1784, and to Lord Sydney, 7 Oct. 1784, *HMC Rutland Mss.*, iii, pp 137 and 141. 99 Rutland to Sydney, 24 Mar. 1784, *ibid.*, pp 82–3. 100 In fact, it would take a bishop only twenty years to run his life against a 21–year lease, because once the lease had no more than a year to run, the bishop had the power 'to make a concurrent lease of the premises' – John Hare to 2nd earl of Normanton, 13 Sep. 1813, 21 M 57, 2nd earl's unreferenced correspondence. This

denigrate Agar, showed complete incomprehension of what was involved in running your life against a lease, and did not consider the alternative strategy of buying out sitting tenants (which was in the main what Agar did). D'Alton asserted that Agar 'acquired £40,000 on a single fine ... by running his own life against that of the existing lessee.'[101] This is nonsense. £40,000 was almost three times what in fact he did pay. Moreover, if he had gone to the trouble and loss of running his life against the lease, he would have taken the land and not the fine. It was not deliberate planning on Agar's part, but the failure of a tenant to observe the mutually advantageous practice of 'frequent renewals' which led, ultimately, to Agar's acquisition of his first and most important lease of Cashel and Emly see lands.

The tenant concerned was another member of the Palliser family, Dr John Palliser. Dr Palliser was a nephew of Archbishop Palliser. He was rector of Rathfarnham, Co. Dublin, and chancellor of Agar's former diocese of Cloyne. He was also the biggest, single tenant of the Cashel see estate. The lease to Dr Palliser which gave rise to contention between Agar and him, was a 21–year renewal granted earlier in the year of Agar's succession by his predecessor, Archbishop Cox, on 1 February 1779. It encompassed three groups of townlands, some of them unfindable in a modern *Topographical index* because the spellings are taken from seventeenth-century patents, but apparently scattered and in overlapping locations. The three groups were: the Augmentation lands of Ballypadeen, Ballinvreena, Duncummin, Ballynoe, Ballynagrana, Clonomolontin and Ballynefehorin, comprising a little over 1,000 Irish acres, and mainly in the baronies of Kilnamanagh and Middlethird, Co. Tipperary; the lands of Freighduff, Kilmore, Ballymorris, Ballygarrane, Bishop's Wood, Gortroame, Clonleigh and Gortskegratt, baronies of Clanwilliam, Kilnamanagh and Middlethird, Co. Tipperary; and the lands known as the west division of the manor of Emly, comprising Ballyholohan, Drumcomoge, Ballynaveen, Bartoose, Ballyvistea, Ballycarrane, Ballyhone and Kildromin, baronies of Clanwilliam, Cos. Limerick and Tipperary, Kilnamanagh, Co. Tipperary, and elsewhere in those counties.

Although Archbishop Cox had been entitled to let the Augmentation lands for three lives, he had lumped everything together in the one 21–year lease. (As a former bishop of Ossory, he may have been leery of the uncertainties of three-life leases.) This omnibus renewal replicated the terms of previous leases granted to Dr Palliser and his father before him, and its terms probably reflected the difficulty, experienced early in the century and no longer applicable, of attracting solvent tenants. Palliser's rent was only £990 per annum, and his annual renewal fine (assuming that the archbishop and he agreed to renew annually) was only £30 less, £959. What his acreage was, was unclear – probably even to himself. The figure of 1,000–plus for the Augmentation lands was taken from the patent of 1665 granting them to the see; and, on similarly dated and inaccurate evidence, the west division of Emly lands were reckoned as 3,500 acres. Archbishop Cox had calculated in 1771 that all the lands comprised in the lease

'concurrent' lease would not come into effect until the existing one fell in, but it would be good in law even if the bishop died in the interim.　**101** D'Alton, *Archbishops of Dublin*, p. 350.

totalled 5,000 acres: in 1787 Agar was informed by the surveyor, Richard Frizzell, that the reality was 6,500; and in 1789, when Agar had them properly surveyed for the first time, the west division of Emly lands alone were computed at 5,077 acres[102] – i.e. more than Archbishop Cox had thought was comprised in the entire lease, and nearly one-third of the total acreage of the see estate.

In August 1781, when two and a half years of the lease granted by Cox in February 1779 had lapsed, Agar opened the customary *pas de deux* over a 21–year renewal. He asked for a renewal fine of £2,540 (i.e. roughly two-and-a-half times the hitherto unpaid annual fine of £959), but did not seek to increase the rent of £990. Palliser proved evasive[103] and remained so until 1789. In that year, when ten years had lapsed, he offered a renewal fine of 'about £9,245 ..., provided his tenants co-operated.' To Agar, who had been thinking in terms of *c.*£12,000, in 1787, £9,245 was far below even a conservative valuation, and the proviso relating to Palliser's tenants (which meant that the deal was off unless they agreed to pay a proportion of the entry fine) was understandably unacceptable.[104] It is too machiavellian to conclude, on the basis of what happened in the end, that Agar had deliberately set out to run his life against the lease and, if possible, frighten Palliser out of it. For one thing, the terms he proposed were extremely moderate, and took no account of the real value of the lease. For another, his eyes were set throughout the 1780s on the archbishopric of Armagh, so it made sense that he should prefer regular renewal fines to any long-term commitment to Cashel. From 1789 onwards, he may have despaired of getting Palliser to renew. But he was probably taken aback when, in November 1792, Palliser expressed willingness to surrender the unexpired term of the lease in return for a payment by Agar of £14,000 sterling.[105]

What actually seems to have happened is that Agar completely misjudged the economics of Palliser's situation. He calculated that Palliser was paying annually, in rent and fine, 4s. per acre for lands which were worth 30s. – a calculation borne out by subsequent valuations but, in the period 1781–9, incapable of exactitude because of the uncertainty about the number of acres comprised in the lease. From this Agar deduced, quite incorrectly, that Palliser enjoyed a profit rent of *c.*£4,500 per annum and was therefore well able to meet the renewal terms offered to him. Palliser, on the other hand, stated in February 1783 to Agar's agent, Samuel Cooper, that his profit rent was only £1,000, 'which he says is the least he can have on such a lease', and that

102 Cases, with the opinions of Dr Patrick Duigenan and Michael Smith, about the re-letting of the Palliser lands, 21 Dec. 1792 and 25 Mar. 1793, 21 M 5 7/B18/1 and 3; calculations by Agar on the terms and profit to Dr Palliser of the Palliser lease, [c. 1780], 21 M 57/B10/4; calculation by Archbishop Cox of the acreage of Dr Palliser's holdings, 18 Nov. 1771, 21 M 57/B10/1; calculations by Agar of the renewal fine Palliser ought to pay, together with a note of Frizzell's computation of the acreage, c. Aug. 1787, 21 M 57/B10/18; copy of Frizzell's survey of the West Division of Emly, 1789, 21 M 57/B61.   103 Calculation of Palliser's renewal and annual fine, 1 Aug. 1781, and letter from Samuel Cooper to Agar, Cashel, 20 Feb. 1783, 21 M 57/B10/8 and 12/1.   104 Calculation by Agar of Palliser's renewal and annual fine, 1 Aug. 1787, letter from Samuel Cooper to Agar, 18 Jan. 1789, and reply, 22 Jan. 1789, 21 M 57/B10/18 and 20.   105 Memo. by Thomas Kemmis of the sum agreed to be paid to Palliser for his interest in the lease, 25 Nov. 1792, 21 M 57/B18/4.

even this had in the past only been achieved by passing on part of the annual fine to his tenants.[106] This might seem to be simply a bargaining ploy, and obviously must have been regarded in that light by Agar. But when Agar acquired the unexpired term of the lease in November 1792, Palliser handed over to him a rental which seemed to prove the truth of Palliser's previous assertion. The gross rental stood at £2,595,[107] which rent to the archbishop and other outgoings could well have reduced to £1,500 nett. Thus, if Palliser had been paying an annual renewal fine, and had been receiving half of it from his tenants, his profit rent would indeed have been only £1,000 per annum. The explanation is that the profit from the lease was enjoyed by Palliser's tenants. As his rental showed, most of these were, like Palliser himself, Tipperary squires, who in turn sub-let the lands they held from Palliser – Caleb Powell, Thomas Lloyd, Austin Cooper (Samuel Cooper's brother and successor in the archiepiscopal agency), Edward Scully (the alleged United Irishman), Samuel Alleyn, etc., etc.. These were the sort of acquaintances and social equals on whom Palliser, who was clearly no businessman and was elderly (he died, probably in his eighties, in 1795), would have found it difficult to lean. In consequence, both Palliser and, because of Palliser's unassertiveness, the archbishop, were locked out of the profits of c.6,500 Irish acres of good land.

Even if £14,000 sterling was a lot for the unexpired term of Palliser's lease, Agar had no real option but to pay it. By November 1792, thanks to Palliser's failure to renew annually and pay his annual renewal fine of £959, Agar had lost something like £13,250 plus interest: put another way, any tenant but Palliser would by then have been willing to pay £18,000 or more (according to Dr Bolton's first 'method') for a 21–year renewal. If Palliser pottered on, paying his rent and not renewing, Agar might be dead or translated before the lease expired. (Actually, he was neither; but he was not to know that in 1792.) Since Agar calculated his total income from the see lands of Cashel at this time as only £3,107 per annum (which proxies, fees, etc., brought up to £4,312),[108] the loss of the £959 per annum was a serious consideration; this sum was nearly equivalent to all the annual fines which he did receive, and which totalled £997 of the £3,107. Indeed, it may be conjectured that 'the Palliser factor' was the main reason for the striking phenomenon already-mentioned – the way in which the income of the see of Cloyne temporarily overtook that of Cashel in the period between the late 1770s and the early 1790s. This, surely, would not otherwise have happened? According to Lewis, the see estate of Cashel amounted to 20,046½ statute acres, and that of Cloyne to '12,482 ..., much of which is rough, unprofitable mountain.' Young had reckoned Cashel at £4,000 per annum and Cloyne at £2,500; and Wakefield's estimates were £7,000 and £5,000 respectively. The differential had been restored by Wakefield's time because Agar had taken the plunge and accepted Palliser's terms for surrendering the lease. Agar now had two options: to let the lands for 21 years to

106 Cooper to Agar, 20 Feb. 1783, 21 M 57/B10/12/1.   107 Rental of his see lands, received from Palliser, 12 Dec. 1792, 21 M 57/B10/25.   108 Small, red notebook kept by Agar, c.1790s, in which he recorded (uniquely) his income as archbishop of Cashel, 1793, 21 M 57, general boxes, no. 2.

another tenant, or to let them in trust for himself. He would not recoup his loss by letting to another tenant unless that tenant came up with an entry fine of *c.£*28,000 Irish. This was an impossible expectation granted the then rental; even if obtained, it would have left the tenant incapable of renewing and paying a renewal fine for years to come. Realistically, there was no alternative to letting the lands in trust for himself and seeking to recoup his loss of *c.£*28,000, and perhaps in the end making a profit, by better management of the estate than Palliser had practised.

Agar proceeded with secrecy and caution in his dealings with the Palliser lands. To avoid the odium of acquiring see lands in his own name, he used the name of his attorney, Thomas Kemmis, in the conveyance from Palliser. There was not much danger of this cover being blown. Palliser was under obligations to Agar who, long ago, in 1771, had made him chancellor of Cloyne. The Agars, as has been seen, were on friendly terms with the Pallisers of Derryluskan. The sum Agar paid Palliser in 1792 was generous; it amounted to a payment in advance of much more than Palliser would have made out of his lease if it had run its full 21–year course. On grounds both of friendship and self-interest Agar could therefore expect discretion from Palliser. His choice of the trustee in whom nominally to vest the lease was also clever. The trustee was the Hon. and Ven. James St Leger (1757–1834), third son of the 1st Viscount Doneraile, whom Agar had made archdeacon of Emly in 1788. St Leger was a choice of trustee which would have excited no suspicion: not only was he archdeacon of Emly, he also came from a titled and monied background, and was just the sort of person who might have been interested in leases of church lands, and who was in a good position to obtain them. Like Agar, St Leger came from an adjoining county (his family's seat was Doneraile Court in north Cork) and was not a Tipperary man with connections among the Tipperary squires who constituted the majority of the tenants. His official situation in the diocese gave him status and independence, and also placed him geographically in a good position to keep an eye on an estate which was mostly concentrated on the west division of Emly.

Agar also proceeded with caution in the letting of the trust lands – and not only by keeping his own name out of the transaction. It was his wish to divide the Palliser lease into three separate leases which would take account of both geography and tenure. He wanted to let the Augmentation lands for the three lives which the law warranted, and to divide the rest geographically into two distinct 21–year leases. To confirm the legality of this procedure, he took the opinion of two eminent counsel, Dr Patrick Duigenan (see pp 202 and 283), who became judge of the prerogative court in 1795, and Michael Smith, who became master of the rolls in 1801. Duigenan advised separating the Augmentation lands, but keeping the others together in the one 21–year lease: Smith advised that the three leases proposed by Agar would be legal.[109] In the event, Agar seems to have followed Smith's advice (although he did a good deal of chopping and changing in his leases during the period 1792–*c.*1796). This still meant that the leases were strictly speaking invalid under the act of 1635, because they did

109 Cases with counsels' opinions, 21 Dec. 1792 and 25 Mar. 1793, 21 M 57/B10/1 and 3.

not reserve a rent equivalent to half the 1792 value of the lands. But on that basis, nearly all bishop's leases would have been invalid (as Clonmell had argued), and Agar's could not have been overturned without upsetting the title to between an estimated sixth and an estimated eighth of the lands of Ireland.[110]

Any doubt on this point was removed by 'the Archbishop of Cashel's Act' of 1795. Under its provisions, church lands, if surrendered to the bishop or other ecclesiastical person or body, need not be let to the new tenant for the half-value specified in the act of 1635, provided they were let for the same rent as had been received for them during the previous twenty years (the same alternative as the act of 17 and 18 Charles II relating to Augmentation lands had first introduced). This proviso applied to lands surrendered for the purpose of being re-let to the same tenant before his existing lease had expired. Furthermore, when next let, or re-let, such lands need not be let in the same units as in the previous demise, but could be divided into a number of different lettings – a dispensation which precisely fitted Agar's situation. Surprisingly, this circumstance, 'the benefit and protection in time to come'[111] which was extended to all church tenants by the 'Archbishop of Cashel's Act', and indeed the existence of such an act, escaped the notice of hostile contemporaries and subsequent historians: otherwise, the act would have been interpreted as an artful dodge on Agar's part to safeguard his recent investment (the more so as it discouraged his successors from running their lives against the Agar leases). Such an interpretation may be dismissed on three counts. First, the act, as already discussed, was made politically necessary by the success of a bill hostile to the interests of the Church and absolutely not of Agar's initiation. Second, in major respects the act ran counter to Agar's private interests as a tenant of see lands. From that point of view, it would have been to his advantage to have paid for the Palliser lands three-quarters of their annual value in 1635 rather than the same rent as Palliser had been paying over the last twenty years. It would also have been highly advantageous to have held all the Palliser lands for lives (which is why he was anxious to restore the Augmentation lands to their original tenurial footing), and yet he made this impossible for himself by the terms of the act.

The final reason for concluding that the act was not designed by him to safeguard his investment in Cashel see lands, is that it did not apply to two other leases which he then or subsequently granted in trust for himself. The first was a lease (originally two leases, which he consolidated into one in 1795 or early in 1796) of the Augmentation lands of Palmershill, Ballypadeen (both in the parish of the Rock of Cashel) and Coolgorth (parish of Kilfithmone), and the second was a lease of the former bog or fenny townland of Monagee (parish of Ardmayle). The two new leases were granted by Agar, in trust for himself, to his kinsman, John Preston of Bellinter, near Navan,

---

110 In his notes for his speech on the 1795 Act (21 M 5 7/B18/22) Agar gives the figure of one-sixth. The already-quoted letter to a newspaper editor of 17 Nov. 1804 (21 M 57/B18/18), gives the figure of one-eighth. An even higher figure of one-fourth was also bandied about (Malcomson, *John Foster*, p. 283). Possibly these different estimates derived from counting different combinations of things – church lands, charity lands (including TCD), corporation lands, etc.   111 Bishop of Kildare to Agar, 21 Jan. 1806, T/3719/C/40/3.

Co. Meath, who was created Lord Tara in 1800.[112] Two of the three Augmentation townlands, Palmershill and Coolgorth, did not qualify for the dispensation under the 1795 Act (that they could be let for the same rent as had been received for the previous twenty years), because Agar had allowed the previous lease of them to expire, and the dispensation applied only to leases surrendered or re-negotiated within the term of the previous lease. The lease of Monagee, which dated from 1739, was still governed by the provisions of the 1726 Act (*12 George I, cap. 10*) relating to bog or fenny land.[113]

In rental terms, of course, the three townlands which did not come under the protection of the 1795 Act were unimportant in comparison to all those which did.[114] By 1806, the gross rental of the three, plus that of Ballypadeen, which was also let in trust to Lord Tara, was £322 per annum.[115] Four years earlier, in 1802, the lands let in trust to St Leger had a gross rental of £6,690 (as compared to £2,595 in 1792).[116] Since 1792, the St Leger lands had been managed with a new assertiveness and a new determination to maximise profits. Agar renewed annually to St Leger, so that there would always be 21 years to run when Agar left Cashel by either translation or death. While he remained at Cashel, what he paid to himself in rent and annual renewal fine was merely a book-keeping exercise; so, the entire proceeds from the St Leger lands during the nine years between 1792 and 1801 could be devoted to recouping the loss of *c.*£28,000 inflicted on him by Palliser.

THE SEE LANDS OF DUBLIN, 1778–1806

Following this reconstruction of events, Agar's motives for granting himself trust leases of between one-third and one-half of the see lands of Cashel, and the circumstances which led to this controversial action, become reasonably clear. A revealing perspective on what he had done in Cashel is provided by what he found in Dublin in 1801. There the see estate was plainly in a more 'exhausted' state than that of Cashel. As has been seen, the archbishop of Cashel's income from all sources had been £4,312 in 1793: in 1803, it was reckoned by Lord Hardwicke at '£6,000 per annum.'[117] Moreover, it was due to rise further. As soon as the Agar trust leases were renewed, whether to the Agars or to new and different tenants, the rent would be ripe for an increase and the renewal fine ought to be calculated on the basis of a gross rental which had been nearly trebled between 1792 and 1802. In Dublin, by contrast, Agar came into possession of a total see income which he reckoned in 1806 as £4,208 per annum nett.[118] This figure is surprisingly low. Over half a century earlier, in 1742, it

---

112 'Calculations [by Agar] of annual fines on the leases held under the see of Cashel', [1799–1800?], 21 M 57/B19/8.   113 Cases, with counsels' opinions, 7 Mar. and 6 Apr. 1796, 22 Mar. 1798 and N.D., 21 M 57/B18/8–11 and 14; observations on the leases of the lands of the archbishop of Cashel, 20 Aug. 1779, and cases, with counsels' opinions, 9 Apr. 1798, 26 June 1799 and 21 Jan. 1800, 21 M 57/B10/6 and B18/12–13 and 15–17.   114 Two sets of calculations by Agar, [1799–1800?] and 1804, 21 M 57/B19/6–8 and 10.   115 'The state of earl Normanton's property, 1806', 21 M 57/D23.   116 Calculations by Agar of the profit rent, [1802?], 21 M 57/B19/9.   117 Hardwicke to Hon. Charles Yorke, 13 Aug. 1803, *The viceroy's post-bag*, p. 124.   118 21 M 57/D23.

had been £2,940, and twenty-five years later, in 1831, it was over £9,000 (rents, £2,340; fines, £4,746; and fees, proxies, etc., making up the rest).[119] In 1778, when it looked as if Agar might be promoted to Dublin, the already-mentioned archiepiscopal agent, George Gamble, had informed him that the income was 'a fair £6,000 per annum, besides ... fines now [due] ... worth £5,000.'[120] An income of £6,000–plus in 1778 ought to have gone up, not down, by 1801. It is just possible that 1806 was a lean year for renewal fines. But, then, the object of a system mainly based on five-yearly renewals would surely have been as far as possible to equalise annual receipts from the estate?

On the whole, the likeliest explanation for the (temporary) fall in see income is the money-making activities of Archbishop Fowler between 1778 and 1801. As if to justify the description of himself as 'a paltry, pragmatical man of straw', Fowler was guilty of some squalid and short-sighted asset-stripping. He 'felled, three times in twenty-four years, nearly 200 acres of oak on see lands near Glendalough, Co. Wicklow. This was both wanton and foolish, as each sale realised only £100 ... [and] the timber, would have ... [fetched] at least £6,000 in fifty years.'[121] (Fowler was also the innocent and involuntary recipient of at least one other windfall: in 1790, he received a one-off payment of £754 for see land taken from him to make part of the line of the Grand Canal.[122]) Nothing much is known about his leasing practices as archbishop of Dublin. In 1779, his successor at Killaloe (see p. 509) had been described as going 'to Ciberia [*sic*], to an house not yet inhabited and leases let to run out and letten [*sic*] in trust by' Fowler.[123] One Dublin see lease which had 'run out' – a lease of the lands of Clondalkin, part of the manor of Tallaght, Co. Dublin[124]– became the subject of a dispute, and possibly of litigation, between Agar and Fowler's son and heir, Archdeacon Robert Fowler.[125] The details are obscure (except that Agar received no rent from this part of the see estate up to and probably beyond 1808); but perhaps this was some form of covert trust lease which Agar had to 'break.'

Moreover, the progressive urbanisation of the part of the see estate to the south of the old city, particularly what was called 'the farm of St Sepulchre', offered great potential for the enrichment of the archbishop for the time being. In August 1778, a controversial act was passed, at the instigation of John Scott, 'for the further improvement of the city of Dublin' (*17 and 18 George III, cap. 46*). This actually meant the enlargement of the term of Scott's lease of the site of his house in Harcourt Street, later called Clonmell House,[126] from 21 years to 40. The site measured only one

119 Kennedy, 'Dublin and Glendalough', p. 183; Gillespie's historical introduction to Refaussé and Clark, *Dublin see maps*, pp 22 and 33. 120 George Gamble to Agar, 12 Dec. 1778, T/3719/ C/12/54. Gamble must have known what he was talking about, as he had been agent since 1772 – Archbishop Cradock to Townshend, 2 and 3 Oct. 1772, Townshend letter-book, Ms. 20/40 and 39. 121 Malins and the Knight of Glin, *Lost demesnes*, p. 131. 122 Kennedy, 'Dublin and Glendalough', p. 196. 123 Scott to Ellis, 4 Dec. 1778, T/3719/C/12/29. 124 William Monck Mason's notes on the rules, boundaries, etc., of the archbishop of Dublin's liberties, *c.*1810, NA, M 2545. 125 John Hare to Archdeacon Fowler, 29 Apr. 1808, and reply, 30 Apr. 1808, T/3719/ C/42/29–30. 126 Craig, *Dublin*, pp 228–9; Curran, *Dublin decorative plasterwork*, pp 84–5.

acre and thirty perches, so it is hard to see what the controversy was about. Nevertheless, Scott complained to Agar that Scott had been subjected, in Agar's absence, to

> a great, great deal of very wanton and unnecessary as well as ill-judged sarcasm
> and abuse from that ruffian, Lord Irnham, who wasted two days [10–11
> August 1778] in worrying me through the House of Lords. I had the honour
> to be opposed by Lords Irnham, Charlemont, Eyre, Aldborough, Bishop of
> Meath and Lord Louth. Everybody else were [*sic*] with me except a few who,
> following the Primate's example, went to dinner.[127]

The bill had in fact been concerted between Scott and Fowler's predecessor,
Archbishop Cradock. Cradock fell ill and died before a new lease could be executed –
Scott commenting brutally 'Though I should lose my house by it, I cannot say it
would grieve me to mourn for his Grace.'[128] But Fowler acted on the powers given to
the archbishop by the act, and on 5 November 1778 Scott noted in his diary that he
was 'settled in my house in Harcourt Street.'[129]

Presumably, what was important was the precedent of 'empowering the
archbishop of Dublin to make building leases'[130] and of enabling him to raise large
sums in fines. Years later, in 1814, a tenant of 'part of the farm of St Sepulchre's
containing about forty acres' urged that an act be obtained empowering the archbishop
to lease it to him for 40 instead of 21 years, and offered an addition of £560 per annum
in rent. He stated that his proposal was 'founded on an act obtained by Lord Clonmell
in the Irish parliament to enable Archbishop Fowler to grant a 40–year lease of part of
the same farm of St Sepulchre's, on which Harcourt Street now stands. ... In England
the archbishop of Canterbury and the bishop of London added considerably to the
value of their respective sees by building acts.'[131] This was all very well in England,
where long leases of see lands were the norm. But it would have been highly dangerous in Ireland, where the Church was under parliamentary pressure in this very
period to relax the restrictions on the leasing powers of the bishops. So, there were no
more acts after 1778 to extend the leasing powers of the archbishop of Dublin, and it
had been no accident that the Clonmell House Act was disguised under the title of an
act 'for the further improvement of the city of Dublin.' Fowler had some surveying
done of see tenants' holdings in the farm of St Sepulchre, particularly in 1789,[132] and
this may have been in response to a demand for what would nowadays be called
development land. Perhaps the demand was strong enough to enable him to raise large
sums by fining down leases for only 21 years.

By 1793, Fowler had become so rich that he was in a position to settle £90,000 on
Archdeacon Fowler, who reputedly spent £12,000 of it building himself a townhouse

---

127 Scott to Agar, 2 Sep. 1778, T/3719/C/12/12.   128 Scott to Agar, 26 Nov. 1778,
T/3719/C/12/22.   129 *Clonmell diary (TCD)*, p. 237.   130 Scott to Heron, [pre-26 May] 1778,
and Sir Stephen Cottrell to Scott, 26 May 1778, NLI, Ms. 13036/1.   131 Rev. Richard Wynne
[brother-in-law to Archbishop Cleaver] to Brodrick [Cleaver's coadjutor], 23 Nov. 1814, Ms. 8871/7.
132 Refaussé and Clark, *Dublin see maps*, pp 77–80.

in Dublin. This still left Archbishop Fowler with the wherewithal to portion his two daughters, who both married into the Irish aristocracy, and later to buy himself a country seat and estate in Essex, where he spent at least the last two years of his episcopate.[133] Archbishop Fowler did not have private means. His father had been 'a grazier in Lincolnshire'[134] and he himself had started off in Ireland as a 'mendicant bishop' (see p. 462). So it looks as if Fowler's capital must have derived, at least in part, from asset-stripping the see estate. It is ironical that Agar's manipulations of see leases in Cashel, which were unplanned and raised the income of his successors, should have achieved greater notoriety than those of Fowler in Dublin, which were deliberate and may have reduced the income of his successors for years to come. Moreover, allowing for what Palliser had cost Agar and what renewals and other transactions over the leases cost Agar's heirs, the 2nd and 3rd earls of Normanton, it was a long time before the Agar family netted from their Cashel lands Fowler's fortune of very much more than £90,000. It is also ironical that one of Agar's ploys for augmenting the depleted emoluments of Dublin served mainly to confirm his own reputation for 'love of lucre.' This was his dogged campaign, fought between November 1804 and November 1808, to assert the archbishop's entitlement, as chancellor of the order of St Patrick, to the perquisite of the collar of each knight who died during his incumbency.[135] As the collars were worth £200 apiece, this would have been a significant addition to an income of £4,208.[136] But it was unlikely to benefit Agar himself very much, since he was older when he became archbishop of Dublin than all but one of the knights.[137]

133 Hubert Butler, *Escape from the anthill*, p. 42; Diana Agar to Agar, 22 Dec. 1807, T/3719/C/41/46; and D'Alton, *Archbishops of Dublin*, p. 349.   134 Bishop of Clogher to Hotham Thompson, 5 Oct. 1785, Hotham papers, PRONI, T/3429/2/9.   135 Peter Galloway, *The most illustrious order of St Patrick, 1783–1983* (Chichester, 1983), pp 90–2; copy letter from Francis Townsend, College of Arms, London, to Sir Chichester Fortescue, Ulster king-of-arms, 17 Nov. 1804 (confirming that the chancellor of the order of the Garter enjoyed this perquisite), T/3719/C/38/51; Agar to Hardwicke, 24 Mar. 1806, and Hardwicke to Agar, 27 Mar. 1806, T/3719/C/40/25; Agar to Hawkesbury (the home secretary), 2 Nov. 1808, T/3719/C/42/80. This is a small selection, including the earliest and the latest letter, from a much larger correspondence on this subject.   136 Galloway, loc. cit. This is confirmed by the reward notice issued by the Dublin Metropolitan Police on 10 July 1907 following the theft of the so-called 'Irish crown jewels' (strictly speaking, the king's insignia as sovereign of the order, plus some other bits and pieces). The stolen items included five collars of knights, which were valued at a total of £1,050. I am grateful for this information to George Mealy & Sons Ltd, auctioneers, Castlecomer, Co. Kilkenny, who have a framed copy of the notice hanging in their office.   137 Although Agar could not have foreseen this, no less than four knights died while he was chancellor, as compared to seven between the founding of the order in 1783 and Fowler's death in 1801. When the 1st marquess of Sligo died in 1809, his widow sent Lord Sligo's collar to Agar, and this collar is still preserved among the Normanton papers (21 M 57/D10–11). Galloway writes (loc. cit.): 'After further delay, a compromise was reached whereby the chancellor was assigned the duty of reclaiming collars and badges of deceased knights, returning them to the grand master, and receiving a fee of £100 for every set so returned.' In 1822, the matter was finally laid to rest when William Magee, newly appointed as archbishop of Dublin, waived all claim to either the collar or the £100.

THE CASHEL SEE LANDS ESTATE AFTER AGAR, 1809–90

Writing of the trust leases granted by Frederick Hervey to himself and his heirs, Wakefield indulgently observed that they made 'no more difference to his successor [in the see of Derry] than if these leases had been purchased by any other person.'[138] This was certainly true of Agar's trust leases, which had also been much more innocent in their origins than Hervey's. Agar's intention, as the terms of his will made clear, was that the leases should be renewed, the lands remain in Normanton occupation, and the profits be shared with successive archbishops through the usual mechanism of renewal fines. In other words, he never had any intention of milking the see. However, the question of renewal became complicated by deteriorating relations between Brodrick and him on other fronts. In the same letter of January 1802 in which Brodrick complained bitterly to Lord Midleton about the alleged dilapidations to the palace (see pp 364), he also expressed his resentment that Agar 'would not suffer me to have his furniture by valuation but, after taking all his best things to Dublin [where they might well have been taken prior to the rebellion], he put up to auction all the refuse, and all that I *must* buy; and in the most scandalous manner he employed the clergy of his diocese, who were connected by blood to him, to act as puffers.'[139] This marked the beginning of a continuing combat between an Agarite and a Brodrickite faction in the diocese which lasted until at least 1805.[140]

Brodrick does not seem to have complained about the trust leases in his letters to Lord Midleton, and he certainly did not in his less voluminous letters to Primate Stuart or to Austin Cooper, now the archiepiscopal agent, though to all of them he unburdened himself about the issue, or non-issue, of the dilapidations. Yet, it is impossible that Brodrick, or anyone intimately acquainted with the diocese, could have failed to penetrate the disguise of the trust. St Leger, as has been argued, made a fairly convincing tenant: Lord Tara was a different matter. He was a second cousin of Agar's and connected with him in politics, certainly at the time of the Union. He had no connection with the diocese of Cashel or the province of Munster except that his brother, Joseph, was an opulently beneficed clergyman of Emly, again on the strength of the relationship to Agar. So, Lord Tara was as transparent a trustee as St Leger was convincing. In October 1802, Lord Tara wrote to Brodrick (at Agar's dictation) requesting what he called his annual renewal on the usual terms.[141] Brodrick took avoiding action by declaring in reply 'that it is against the rule I have in all cases laid down to myself, to lay myself under any obligation of renewals during incumbency.'[142] After Lord Tara wrote again, Brodrick replied firmly in January 1803: 'I have now to state to your Lordship that at present I am not satisfied that the demises under which your Lordship appears as lessee to the see of Cashel, are such as the law authorises.'[143] This legal doubt, however, related more probably to the level of rent due from the

138 Wakefield, *Account of Ireland*, ii. 470.   139 Midleton papers, Ms. 1248, vol. 18, ff. 44–5.   140 Forster, *Life of Jebb*, i, pp 71–3.   141 Tara to Brodrick, 14 Oct. 1802, 21 M 57/B19/1.   142 Brodrick to Tara, 21 Oct. 1802, 21 M 57/B19/3.   143 Tara to Brodrick (draft in Agar's handwriting), 25 Dec. 1802, and Brodrick to Tara, 4 Jan. 1803, 21 M 57/B19/4–5.

three townlands which lay outside the dispensation of the 1795 Act, than to the principle of leases in trust. The level of rent was certainly re-negotiated to Brodrick's advantage, either by the mutual consent of Lord Tara and him or as a result of arbitration. Nevertheless, the tone adopted by Brodrick strongly suggests that he knew that the real tenant was Agar.

Brodrick's penetration of the disguise would have been of less consequence to Agar and his heirs, if Brodrick had also understood the unplanned exigency of the case and the need to get rid of Dr Palliser. Brodrick himself had ambitions for his family, which he deliberately underplayed when he told his brother in 1800 that he had 'but one object in this world, *viz.* to put my children into *reasonable* competence of comforts ... . I have no desire of expense or of parade for myself or for them.'[144] However, Agar's actions – and particularly his secrecy – made it look as if he had aimed at more than a '*reasonable* competence of comforts' and had deliberately run his life against the leases in order to make a great estate to himself and his family. Bishop Woodward's already-quoted fears of 'the censure of being thought too rapacious' had no doubt made a due impression on his son-in-law. Years later, in 1811, when it was suggested that Brodrick was planning to run *his* life against the Agar leases, Brodrick, in denying this, complained that the report was 'prejudicial to his character.'[145] Presumably, he thought that the trust leases were 'prejudicial' to Agar's. Moreover, a letter written by St Leger to Agar in 1808 suggests that Brodrick was victimising St Leger because of St Leger's association with Agar; 'His Grace of Cashel is inclined to be disagreeable to several of the clergy',[146] concluded St Leger guardedly. Agar presumably decided that Brodrick was likely to be 'disagreeable' to him, too, and that Agar's son would stand a better chance than Agar of obtaining a renewal on reasonable terms. For whatever reason, following the rebuff Brodrick gave Lord Tara in 1802–3, no further attempt was made in Agar's lifetime to obtain a renewal of any of the leases.

Agar died on 14 July 1809, and in the second half of October his son and successor, the 2nd earl of Normanton (fig. 20), obtained – for confidentiality's sake – a London legal opinion on the status of the trust leases. This is important in its own right, and also for its implication that, *pace* English detractors of Agar, such leases were not out of line with English practice:

> If this was the case of an English bishop, I should think his right to purchase an existing lease of the estates of his own see and to have them [*sic*] assigned to others in trust for himself, unquestionable, and his right to grant renewals to the same persons with a trust for himself, equally so. Nor am I aware of there being any difference in this respect between the case of an English bishop and an Irish one. Therefore, unless there be some statute or other peculiar law on

144 Brodrick to Midleton, 3 Feb. 1800, *ibid.*, vol. 17, f. 116. **145** John Hare to 2nd earl of Normanton, 9 May 1811, 21 M 57, 2nd earl's unreferenced correspondence. **146** St Leger to Agar, 20 Sep. 1808, T/3719/C/42/69.

the subject in Ireland, I think that the son or other person, being legal representative of the late archbishop ..., will not incur any risk from avowing the trust of the leases or from taking an assignment of them from the trustee, and that the present archbishop's not having granted renewals will not alter the law of the case.[147]

At the beginning of 1810, pursuant to this advice, the 2nd earl's agent, John Hare of Dublin, son of Patrick Hare, the former vicar-general, notified Brodrick that the leases formerly held by St Leger and Lord Tara were now vested in Lord Normanton.[148] There then began a ten-year dialogue, or rather duel, over the renewal. This began with Lord Normanton offering a renewal fine of £18,000 in September 1810, and ended with his agreeing to pay a renewal fine of £55,000 in January 1820.[149] Over roughly the same period, his profit rent from the see lands rose from c.£5,500 to c.£8,350.[150]

For present purposes, the important aspect of this negotiation is the further light it sheds on Agar's intentions in regard to the see lands. Queries put to counsel in February 1814 recited that Agar had, by his will, left to the 2nd earl 'all his real and freehold estates and lands in Ireland or elsewhere' and 'all my chattel leases and lands held by lease ..., whether in my own name or in the name of any person or persons in trust for me', with the same remainders as his real and freehold estates, 'or as near thereto as the nature of chattel leases and lands will by law admit and allow of.' Agar had further directed that 'his personal estate and fortune' should be earmarked for the purchase of additional lands or beneficial interests in lands in Great Britain and/or Ireland, these too 'to be settled to the same uses as ... the real and freehold estates.'

At the time of the testator's death he derived a considerable interest in chattel lands which were held ... in trust for him, under a bishop. ... [The 2nd earl] has from time to time endeavoured to obtain from the bishop a renewal of said leases, but has been precluded from renewing in consequence of the very great fines demanded. There are now nearly thirteen years lapsed in the term of said leases, and the fines required, or for which a renewal can be obtained, exceed the rents which accrued due out of said lands since the testator's death [by] nearly £20,000. ...

Presented with this statement of case, counsel opined that the 2nd earl,

147 Opinion of Francis Hargrave, New Boswell Court, [London], 21 Oct. 1809, communicated in a letter of the same date from Stephen Moore to the 2nd earl of Normanton, Stephen's Green, Dublin, 21 M 57, 2nd earl's unreferenced correspondence. Since English bishops had more extended leasing powers than Irish, the *potential* for expropriation was greater in England. 148 Hare to 2nd Viscount Clifden (who had been called in to act as intermediary with Brodrick), 5 Sep. 1812, ibid. 149 Ibid.; Hare to Normanton, 30 and 31 Jan. 1820, and Normanton to Hare, 3 Feb. 1820, ibid. 150 Hare to Normanton, 23 Oct. 1819, *ibid.*

having accepted the bequests and devises made to him by his father, is bound to renew the leases in due course and to pay, himself, the fines and expenses attendant upon such renewal. I do not think, however, that this obligation extends so far as to compel him to comply with extravagant and unreasonable terms on the part of the lessor. But if for any such reason he could justify in a court of equity his not having renewed the leases, it must be upon the terms of securing for the benefit of those in remainder what would have been during his life the amount of reasonable fines. It is clear that ... [the 2nd earl] cannot be entitled to apply any part of the testator's residuary personal property in the payment of these fines.[151]

It is impossible that wily old Agar had been unaware that the terms of his will would so constrain his successor. In his Oxford youth, the 2nd earl had shown very mild symptoms of extravagance (never, however, to reappear after his succession in 1809),[152] and Agar may well have thought it a salutary discipline that the 2nd earl be required to keep up the Cashel see lands estate out of income. He clearly intended that the leases should be renewed, except in the event of Brodrick or a subsequent archbishop insisting on 'extravagant or unreasonable terms.'

Unfortunately, the fact of Agar's having died extremely rich was almost universally known, whereas the restrictions placed by his will on the application of those riches were not. When the 2nd earl's brother, Archdeacon James Agar, took up the role of negotiator, he took care to disabuse Brodrick's nephew, agent and spokesman, Major Richard Woodward, of the idea that the 2nd earl was 'very largely provided to meet any extraordinary demand for a renewal by the money left by the late Lord Normanton.'[153] Various other arguments were used by the 2nd earl's side to reduce Brodrick's demands.[154] In October 1819, when the leases had only three years to run, and the 2nd earl was offering £40,000 as an entry fine and Brodrick demanding a minimum of £60,000, Archdeacon Agar urged 'the advantage to the see of Cashel in having a tenant like Lord N. responsible for so large a yearly rent for such a set of tenants and in such a county as *Tipperary*, and that in all calculations, great allowances should be made to him for (what I called) his *agency* under the see, etc., etc.' Taking advantage of the terms of 'the Archbishop of Cashel's Act', he pointed out 'that on the expiration of the lease, there must be one full moiety of the highest improved value reserved to the see; that it was for him to consider what would be the situation of ... Mr Brodrick [the Archbishop's son], subject to a rent payable to the see of from £2,000 to £3,000 annually from so many tenants in such precarious times ...; that the Archbishop's receiving £40,000 would be a better bargain both for himself and for his family.'[155] Privately, Major Woodward shared the view that 'in such precarious times,

151 Opinion of John Leach, Lincoln's Inn, on the terms of Agar's will, particularly as regards the see lands lease, 26 [?Feb.] 1814, *ibid.*   152 Hon. Welbore Agar (later 2nd earl of Normanton) to his cousin, Lord Clifden, [pre-25 Oct. 1802], ibid.   153 Archdeacon James Agar to Normanton, 20 Oct. 1819, *ibid.*   154 Brodrick to Normanton, 29 Nov. 1816, ibid.   155 Archdeacon Agar to Normanton, 20 Oct. 1819, *ibid.*

when property is so uncertain and [rents] so ill-paid, to exchange such an estate for money is surely most desirable.'156

The question, of course, was how much money. Lord Normanton, who had a keen eye for the stockmarket (inherited, as will be seen, from his father), calculated that, if the see lands yielded £8,000 per annum nett, in ten years he would make only £20,000 on an investment of £60,000 in the entry fine, whereas an investment of £60,000 in the Funds, or in something similar, ought to yield £3,000 per annum forever.157 In short, he was inclined to let the lease expire. Hare, however, worked out in late 1819 that, according to the usual 'method' (which must have been Archbishop Bolton's 'alternative' of calculating the fine as a multiple of the profit rent), 'The fine for 18 years lapsed in 21 years is 7 years 5 months [and] 10 days, or £62,133.' So Brodrick was actually within his rights to ask £60,000. Even at £60,000, it was Hare's view that Lord Normanton would make 8% on his investment and could obtain so high a return in no other way.158 If this was an unusually favourable (from the lessor's point of view) basis of calculation, it was offset by the fact that, even by the standards of see estates, the Agars' rent from 1801 to 1819 (£920 per annum) had been very low.

Lord Normanton not only paid £55,000 for a 21–year renewal in 1820, but continued to renew on this time-honoured, complex basis until 1868 (though, after Brodrick's death in 1822, no subsequent archbishop or bishop of Cashel proved as 'tough' an 'incumbent' in such negotiations). In the intervening period, new legislation was passed crucially affecting the situation of tenants of church lands. The Church Temporalities Act of 1833, as well as providing for a reduction in the number of archbishoprics and bishoprics, enacted that a sitting tenant of see lands might obtain a perpetuity of them on tender of a sum equivalent to roughly six years' purchase, and thereafter would pay a rent which was the same as his former rent plus an annual average of the renewal fines he had been in the habit of paying.159 In August 1849, this facility was further extended – and not just in respect of church lands – by 'Lord Campbell's Act' (*12 and 13 Victoria, cap. 104*), the full title of which was 'An act for converting the renewable leasehold tenure of lands in Ireland into a tenure in fee.' These changes were widely regarded as highly disadvantageous to the bishops and highly advantageous to their tenants. But Lord Normanton was not so sure. He jibbed at the very much larger expenditure required to purchase the perpetuity of the Cashel see lands, because he was convinced (as he noted in 1857) that 'All the property of

---

156 Woodward to Brodrick, 17 Jan. [1820], Midleton papers, NLI, Ms. 8865/2. The only comparator for these enormous fines, in either the Church of Ireland or of England, are those raised by the coal-rich bishop and dignitaries of Durham. In the same year, 1819, the dean and chapter asked £56,000 for the renewal of a lease of Rainton colliery, but settled for £40,000 – see A.J. Heesom, *The founding of the university of Durham: the Durham cathedral lecture for 1982* (Durham, 1982), pp 11–12.   157 Normanton to Hare, 12 Dec. 1819, 2nd earl's unreferenced correspondence. 158 Hare to Normanton, 23 Oct. and 21 Dec. 1819, *ibid.*   159 [Very Rev.] R.B. MacCarthy, *The Trinity College estates, 1800–1923* ... (Dundalk, 1992), p. 16. Normanton bought the perpetuity of Ballynaboley, his Co. Kilkenny townland held under a bishop's lease, for 7½ years' purchase in 1840 – Charles Knox to James Fitzgerald, 9 May 1840, 21 M 57, 2nd earl's unreferenced correspondence.

[the] protestant Church in Ireland is unstable.'[160] He did not want to be caught with a longer interest in an unstable property than his current 21–year lease.[161] Eventually, in 1868, his hand possibly forced by the probability that the Church of Ireland would be disestablished and its assets in land converted to cash, he decided to buy both the perpetuity and the fee in the one transaction.[162] His son, the 3rd earl of Normanton, then sold the entire estate *c.*1890.[163]

These developments lay far in the future and are barely relevant to Agar, who had died as long ago as 1809. They do, however, establish that a crude balance sheet of the cost and profit of the see lands estate over the period 1810–56, which was drawn up for the 2nd earl in March 1856,[164] is relevant to the state of play at Agar's death. For the whole of this period, the tenure remained the same and the pre-1833 system of regular haggling with a succession of archbishops and bishops still obtained. In other words, Agar himself would have felt quite at home. Between 1810 and 1856, the 2nd earl received £338,798 in rents out of the estate, and paid £140,090 in renewal fines, annual fines and head rent. Allowing for 'poor rate, income tax, quit rent and [tithe] rentcharge', he actually received £198,708. This should be further reduced to allow for the agent's salary, which was overlooked in the calculation. In the 1840s, John Hare was being paid £400 a year (for managing Agar's much smaller Kilkenny estate as well as the see lands estate),[165] of which perhaps £300 is reasonably attributable to the see lands. This reduces the receipts from the estate to *c.*£184,600.

Clearly, this represented a reasonably good investment. How it compared with the Funds or with a purchase of fee simple land, is problematical (apart from anything else, interest rates and the return on the Funds fluctuated over time). But, as the 2nd earl had remarked in 1819, investment in stock was for ever, while investment in a bishop's lease was for 21 years. The bishop's lease was also an expensive, troublesome, risky and, while Brodrick was archbishop of Cashel, cliff-hanging, sort of investment, which looked better with mid-century hindsight than it had done at various times between 1810 and 1856. For example, it seems highly probable that the 2nd earl would have surrendered the lease (as Palliser had done), or allowed it to expire in 1822, if the legal opinion he obtained in 1814 about the interpretation of Agar's will had not revealed the obstacles to so doing. So, in spite of his sharp eye to the Funds, the lease was persevered with not solely for economic reasons, and partly because it was already there. It entailed trouble and risk, because 'Lord N. [was] responsible for so large a

160 Irish estate accounts, 1835–55, settled 16 Aug. 1856, and endorsed by the 2nd earl in April 1857, 21 M 57, general boxes, no. 3. **161** By remaining a 21–year leaseholder, he was also in a position to obtain very good terms from the bishop: if he took out the perpetuity or bought the fee simple, the down payment he had to make would go to the ecclesiastical commission set up by the 1833 Act, whereas his renewal fines on a 21–year lease continued to go to the bishop personally. See Akenson, *Church of Ireland*, p. 173. **162** Statement of the position of the see lands estate, 1880, 21 M 57, General Boxes, no. 3. **163** T.T. Mecredy & Sons, solicitors, Westmoreland Street, Dublin, to 3rd earl, 9 June 1890, enclosing particulars of sales to date, 21 M 57, general boxes, no. 40. **164** Calculations of the total receipts from the see lands estate from 1810 to March 1856, set against the outgoings on renewal fines, etc., Mar. 1856, 21 M 57, 2nd earl's unreferenced correspondence. **165** Irish estate accounts, 1835–55, settled 16 Aug. 1856, 21 M 57, general boxes, no. 3.

yearly rent for such a set of tenants and in such a county as *Tipperary*', and because the estate was by any standards very large. In 1883, it was reckoned at 7,625 statute acres in Co. Tipperary and 1,003 in Co. Limerick.[166] A near-contemporary valuation of 1885 in the Normanton papers bears this out, putting the total acreage figure only slightly lower, at 8,594.[167] An estate of this size required careful management, the more so as it was 'unstable' Church property. Few people could have been found in 1820 with the means to pay £55,000 for a renewal, and fewer still, perhaps, would have invested that kind of money in a see lands lease. There really was 'advantage to the see of Cashel in having a tenant like Lord N.', and Agar's successors in the see gained greatly, because the renewal fines paid by Agar's heirs, the 2nd and 3rd earls of Normanton, were (or ought to have been) calculated on the basis of a greatly increased profit rent.

In effect – and not from altruistic motives or as the outcome of any deliberate plan, but from sheer desperation – Agar had relieved the archbishopric of an incubus. He was not, as Castlereagh alleged, one of the bishops who 'made great estates to their families' at the expense of their sees. Apart from anything else, Agar's motivation was different from that of the others. He acted out of self-defence, not from motives of self-aggrandisement; he acquired the lease as his only means of limiting the damage done by Palliser to his relatively modest income. Moreover, it was only when Agar's son bought the perpetuity and fee that a Lord Normanton was able to call the see lands estate 'my own.' This came about, not just as a result of the cash payment, but of a series of radical and secularising reforms, unthinkable in 1792, and contrary to Agar's most deeply held convictions. Had he lived to see them, he would have opposed them, contrary to his own self-interest, with even greater vigour than he had the comparatively mild, anti-clerical proposal of 1795 to extend the leasing powers of bishops. Even the perpetuity which was available for purchase by Lord Normanton from 1833 onwards, would not have been the preferential tenure it then was if Agar's views on the Tenantry Bill of 1780 had prevailed.

AGAR'S MAKING OF A GREAT ESTATE TO HIS FAMILY, 1762–1809

Agar died as rich (partly in land and mainly in money) as his detractors supposed: what is at issue is the part which the Cashel see lands and the other resources of the archbishopric played in the build-up of his fortune. Before addressing this issue, it is first necessary to establish how rich he was at the time of his death. The earliest full statement of his financial situation comes in 1806.[168] It is in his own hand and, clearly, it relates to his ability to support the rank of earl which he was about to attain. His

166 The acreage figures are taken from *Bateman*. For comparative figures for other estates in the area, see D.G. Marnane, 'Landownership in south Tipperary, 1849–1903' (unpublished UCC Ph.D. thesis, 1991). I am grateful for this reference to Mr David Butler.   167 Summary of the rental of the Irish estates, 1878, and valuation of the see lands estate, [29 Dec. 1885?], 21 M 57, general boxes, no. 3.   168 'The state of earl Normanton's property, 1806', 21 M 57/D23.

principal asset was a huge sum of money bearing interest or yielding dividends of £9,324 annually, of which the largest component was '£181,502 19s. 9d. in the 3 per cent consols in the Bank of England.' This money in the Funds or out at interest produced in 1806 half the income of £17,832 which he was in a position to bequeath to his heir (i.e. excluding his *ex officio* income from the diocese of Dublin). The landed component of it comprised £2,492 per annum from his estate in Co. Kilkenny and £5,924 'nett profit rent' from the Cashel see lands leases.

The capital value of his assets at the time of his death over three years later is not set out so conveniently. According to the terms of the 2nd earl of Normanton's marriage settlement of 1816, Agar had left £90,208 Irish in stock and investments in Ireland, and £225,690 British in 3% consols.[169] This would seem to be an under-estimate, in that it omits cash and money owed to Agar. According to John Hare's calculations of July 1809 and the eventual probate valuation of November 1812,[170] Agar's assets in Ireland amounted to *c.*£107,000 Irish, mainly comprising £52,028 in 5% government stock, £26,213 in 3½% government stock and £16,667 in Bank of Ireland stock ('very valuable'). This excluded arrears of rent, books and plate (£1,400) and the value of the Stephen's Green house, and was nett of testamentary expenses and other liabilities. The English assets were as stated in the 2nd earl's marriage settlement, though it looks as if they should be increased by a further £7,564 British in 3% consols standing in the 2nd earl's name and clearly a gift from his father.[171] As to land, the capital value of the freehold estate in Kilkenny might have been £50,000 to £55,000 in 1809,[172] and of the unexpired term of the Cashel see lands lease something like £75,000. These figures show that, in the context of Agar's overall financial situation at the time of his death, his 'chattel leases' under the see did not constitute the great estate which Castlereagh supposed. In 1809, the see lands produced (in round figures) considerably less than one-third of the income which he was in a position to leave the 2nd earl of Normanton, and in terms of capital value they constituted (because of the nature of the tenure) a much smaller proportion of Agar's fortune. The figures also suggest that Farington, and D'Alton, understated Agar's wealth when they postulated a figure of £400,000:[173] £500,000 would be nearer the mark.

Of this colossal amount, a fraction had been inherited. Under his father's will, Agar was left Henry Agar's 'estate and interest in the lands of Lisnafunshin [near Castlecomer] in the county of Kilkenny, and also the lands and houses in and about the city of Kilkenny ... in the possession of his sister, the Lady Mayo [Ellis Agar, later countess of Brandon], and also the lands of Ballynaboley in the barony of Gowran and Co. Kilkenny.' In 1762, Agar had a nett income of £353, made up of the interest on his portion of £4,000, and the rents of the townlands of Ballynaboley and

Lisnafunshin and the Kilkenny City property left him in 1746. In 1770, he bought out the life interest of Lady Brandon in the last, paying her in lieu an annuity of £100 which fell in at her death in 1789. Ballynaboley certainly, and possibly some of the Kilkenny property, were held under the see of Ossory.[174] Bishops' leases were a not uncommon form of provision for younger sons, because – since they were non-freehold and therefore produced no votes in parliamentary elections – they did not contribute to the political interest over which the head of the family presided. As a delayed-action consequence of his father's will, Agar also succeeded to the lands of Lower Grange, barony of Gowran, on the death of his elder brother, Welby, in 1805.[175] This was a not ungenerous provision for a younger son, which is what it is always important to remember that Agar was. To all outward seeming, particularly from 1779 onwards, he was a man of wealth and rank, sufficiently possessed (as his sister, Diana, had said) of all the material good things of life. He occupied, not the largest, but the most architecturally distinguished house in Co. Tipperary; he enjoyed a rental income higher than that of all but the greatest county magnates; and in terms of precedence he outranked everybody in Ireland except the royal dukes with Irish titles (who never came to Ireland), the lord chancellor and the archbishops of Armagh and Dublin. Yet, all these worldly felicities were held by him *ex officio* and would die with him. Unless Agar took positive measures to improve the prospects of his eldest son, the 'hereditary rank'[176] which would fall to the latter would be that of a commoner and very minor landed gentleman. Hence Agar's dynastic urge to found a 'second house.'

It was not uncommon for a younger son to be fortunate enough to pick up some windfall inheritance from a collateral relation (or indeed to become the eldest son through the death of a brother or brothers). But this was not to be Agar's lot. Indeed, he experienced a series of testamentary disappointments at the hands of relations who respected primogeniture to the exclusion of him. The first of these was Lady Brandon in 1789. In spite of the reciprocal regard subsisting between Agar and her (see pp 19 and 119–20), she favoured the Ringwood over the Gowran branch of the family, and George Agar over his younger brother, the Rev. Charles.[177] She left George Agar several thousand pounds and her house in Merrion Square – just the size of inheritance for which a younger son might have hoped. The Rev. Charles Agar, having provided for his widow, also favoured his elder brother, George, though he did leave his books to Archbishop

174 'A sketch of the estate of the Rev. Mr Charles Agar in the county of Kilkenny ...', 29th June 1761', 21 M 57/D/13; Hampshire RO list of 21 M 57/B44, B49–B53, B55–B56, B58, B64 and B66; deed whereby Henry Agar purchased Lisnafunshin (for £1,850), 10 Aug. 1736, list of deeds relating to Lisnafunshin, 1741, and settlement on Bishop Charles Agar's marriage, 22 Nov. 1776, 21 M 57/T358; sale advertisement for Agar's lease of the 400 Irish acres of Ballynaboley, *Faulkner's Dublin Journal*, 23 July 1765; deeds of lease and release, 27–8 Feb. 1770, ROD 179910. 175 Bundle of deeds relating to Lower Grange, 1691–1749, Annaly/Clifden papers, F/4/2; renewals of Lower Grange granted by Welby, 16 Mar. 1771 and 17 Feb. 1790, 21 M 57/T358; proposals for the 2nd earl's marriage settlement, 1816, and rental of the Irish estates, 1878, 21 M 57, general boxes, no. 3. 176 Brodrick to 1st earl of Donoughmore, 26 Dec. 1818, PRONI, T/3459/D/31/6. 177 'Substance of Lady Brandon's will' of 2 May 1787, in Agar's handwriting, 21 M 57/D51/5.

Agar.[178] Considering Archbishop Agar's generosity to the Rev. Charles, who had owed his livelihood to him since 1781 and had only recently been bailed, not just baled, out by his timely intervention, this was surprising. It was also surprising that his uncle, Lord Mendip, left him nothing but a derisory £300, and virtually everything else to the 2nd Viscount Clifden.[179] Welby, as has been seen (pp 45–7), ignored his brothers and their children in his will, and when he died in 1805 left everything to his two illegitimate sons. George Agar, now Lord Callan, struck a balance between the claims of his natural children and those of his collateral relations. But, having provided handsomely for the former, he left everything else (the Rower and Callan estates and over £160,000) to the already much-blessed Lord Clifden.[180] In any case, Lord Callan outlived Agar by six years. Only Agar's devoted sister, Diana, remembered him, and she too outlived him, dying in 1814. By her will, she left the Kilkenny property with which she had been endowed (pp 25 and 42) to Agar's sons in succession, beginning with the youngest; it had a rental of c.£620 in the 1880s, and had merged with the Normanton estate in Ireland in 1866.[181] Clearly, she took the view that her family had carried primogeniture too far. Of Lord Clifden she remarked coldly in 1804: he 'is a rich man indeed, and if he lives some time, will be much richer in all probability, as it will roll on rapidly.'[182]

Marriage was another possible source of wealth for a younger son. Agar's friend, Clonmell, another younger son (and of a much lesser gentry family than the Agars), made sure that he did well financially out of both his marriages. But not even Clonmell could have calculated that his second wife, the daughter of 'an eminent banker in the city of Dublin ..., [would inherit] a fortune of £68,000', when her only brother died, young and unmarried, in 1787.[183] Agar, as has been seen (pp 79–80), had married very badly from the financial point of view. Here again, fortune favoured the senior branch of the Agar family. In 1804, Lord Clifden's youngest brother, the Hon. Charles Bagenal Agar, married the heiress to the Lanhydrock and other estates in Cornwall. Welby exulted: 'he will get £10,000 per annum by his wife, and what is more, an improveable property ..., and with address and some little expense will recover two boroughs which were in her family.'[184] In 1806, Lord Clifden wrote to Agar, in a letter packed with insensitivity and smugness, 'our family, taken in all its branches, possesses a considerable property and interest' in the Empire. But, where Clifden's and C.B. Agar's had come to them effortlessly through inheritance and marriage respectively, Agar's had been hard-earned.

---

178 Copy of the Rev. Charles Agar's will, 25 Nov. 1788, 21 M 57/D51/7; Archbishop Agar to George Agar, 20 Dec. 1788, T/3719/C/22/54.   179 Probate (1802) of Lord Mendip's will (1799) and codicils (1799 and 1801), PRO, Prob. 11/1370.   180 Probate (1815) of Lord Callan's will (21 Dec. 1809), NA, T10997 (1809); release in respect of Callan's personal assets in Ireland from Clifden to Callan's executors, 22 May 1834, NA, D 20149. This latter mentions a similar release of 8 January 1817 detailing the disposal of the English assets, but the 1817 document has not so far come to light.   181 Probate (1814) of Diana Agar's will (1811), 21 M 57/T366; rental and valuation of the estate inherited from her, 29 Dec. 1885, 21 M 57, general boxes, no. 3.   182 Diana Agar to Agar, 5 Feb. 1804, T/3719/C/39/6.   183 *The Gentleman's and London Magazine* for Feb. 1787. 184 Welby to Agar, 6 Sep. 1804, T/3719/C/39/46.

Against this background, it is significant that Agar practised rigid male primogeniture in his own will: 'to his daughter ..., he had given £15,000, but to his two
younger sons, a clergyman and an officer, he left only about £5,000 each, and to his
widow about £1,200 a year only', which left her 'in circumstances comparatively too
limited for her situation in life and for his fortune ..., his opinion being that women
should not have much.'[185] This was Farington's version of Agar's actions and intentions. It was wrong to the extent that the bequests to his younger sons were actually
£10,000 each, on top of the money spent buying George Charles commissions in the
army and the (so far inadequate) Church preferment found for James; also to the
extent that Lady Normanton was left the Stephen's Green house for life in addition
to her jointure of £1,200.[186] Agar had changed his will to allow for the increase in his
family's rank consequent on the earldom conferred on him in 1806. The family of the
recently deceased Lord Clare was similarly situated: Clare had married when a
commoner and died an earl. However, where Lady Normanton had brought with her
a marriage portion of next-to-nothing, Lady Clare had brought one of £11,000. Yet,
Lady Clare's 'slender settlement' (as it was satirically described) was a jointure of only
'£1,100 per annum, that is £100 per annum for each thousand she brought in fortune
to her deceased Lord' – the usual tariff in marriage settlements.[187] (Perhaps Clare
remembered his wife's infidelities in his will.) Compared to this, Lady Normanton was
generously treated. In fact, during the seventeen years of her widowhood, she seems
to have been in comfortable circumstances, with small amounts of capital at her
disposal. It may be that Agar took the view 'that women should not have much'; but it
is more likely that he feared for Lady Normanton's soft-heartedness towards others in
pecuniary need, particularly her spinster sister, Mary Benson, who lived with and off
her.[188] Nevertheless, even when all these correctives have been applied to Farington's
assertions, it still looks as if Agar upheld and maintained in his will the system of male
primogeniture under which he had been a loser all his life.

Since there is no evidence that he was the beneficiary of any form of windfall at
any stage in his career,[189] it has to be assumed that he made his fortune on the stock
market, and that, from small beginnings, it 'rolled on rapidly.' Clearly, it was his
income as a bishop and archbishop which provided him with start-up capital. One of
his account books[190] shows that the £6,247 he received for proxies, visitation fees, etc.,
between 14 October 1779 and 17 January 1793 was all spent on the purchase of
treasury debentures, as was the £28,000 he received from 'chief rents of Cashel'
between 13 May 1791 and 18 January 1793. But as Cashel was not a particularly rich
see, and as no allegation was ever made, even by his enemies, that he asset-stripped it
in the way in which Fowler seems to have asset-stripped Dublin,[191] this source of

185 *Farington diary*, vi. 98.   186 Probate (1809) of Agar's will (as far as it relates to Ireland), 21 M
57/T285.   187 *The Dublin Journal*, 30 June 1802, 21 M 57/A2/22; Malcomson, *Pursuit of the
heiress*, pp 5–15.   188 Will and codicils of Jane, countess of Normanton, 4 Sep. 1810–20 June 1825,
21 M 57/T278.   189 Primate Robinson was reputed to have been 'the last survivor of a tontine in
France, from which he derived considerable property' – Stuart, *Armagh*, p. 456.   190 21 M 57/D15.
191 For example, the same account book shows that between 9 Apr. 1781 and 27 June 1788, he

investment capital can never have yielded him any one large sum at any one time. The difficulty and danger of this form of speculation from small beginnings, particularly on the part of aristocratic amateurs, was graphically outlined to Brodrick by Lord Midleton in 1793:

> Whatever you do, never think of speculating in [the] Funds. Our stocks are now on such a footing of universal interest that no chance of rise or fall can be foreseen but it must be paid for. ... The only tolerably prudent mode is to take the price of the day in whatever stock you choose, provided it bears the proper proportion to the consols which, as being the great bulk, is [*sic*] not liable to fluctuation from trivial or accidental causes. But, depend upon it, if money is to be made in the Funds on speculation, it will be made by brokers, by bankers, by merchants (and these, by the bye, [are] often mistaken), but not by persons like you or me. ... The Funds are ... only to be meddled with on the price they bear at the moment, and not on speculation.[192]

Agar certainly learnt to hold his own with brokers, bankers and merchants, and flourished by speculation. In the words of Farington: 'He originally had but a moderate fortune, but he used it with great management; had shares in the first national Irish bank [the Bank of Ireland, founded in 1783]; and changed and chopped his money about.'[193] Just after Agar's death, John Hare also testified, in a letter to the 2nd earl of Normanton, to Agar's 'great management'; his business affairs, wrote Hare, 'were conducted with so much judgement, talent and attention ... that I think you will have little difficulty in the regulation of them.'[194]

There is insufficient evidence to permit more than an impressionistic account of the accumulation of Agar's fortune. In the mid-1780s, he had £9,500 in hand to lend to Eland Mossom Junior on the security of Mrs Mossom's Thomastown estate (see p. 100). In January and February 1788, he spent £1,815 on tickets in the Irish lottery (with what outcome is not known).[195] In lists of investors with £2,000 or more in Bank (of England) stock published by *The Gentleman's and London Magazine* in March 1788 and again in April 1790, he is set down on both occasions for £4,000. In 1789, when he first solicited a peerage, he was asked by the lord lieutenant what hereditary property he had to support one, and replied that he had £3,000 per annum with the prospect of more soon to come.[196] In *c*.May 1791, he had £20,000 in readiness for the purchase of land.[197] A year or so later, he recorded: 'The Archbishop [had] to pay his subscription to the Bank of Ireland of 40% on £4,000 – thus on 20 Sep. and 20 Dec. '91 and on 20 Mar. and 20 June '92, £400 each day, making £1,600.'[198] In the period

received only £4,088 in Cashel renewal fines.   **192** Midleton to Brodrick, 20 Mar. [1793], NLI, Ms. 8889/9.   **193** *Farington diary*, vi. 98.   **194** Hare to Normanton, 19 July 1809, 21 M 57, 2nd earl's unreferenced correspondence.   **195** Agar's account book, 1765–1807, 21 M 57/D15.   **196** Memo by Agar of what passed during his audience with Lord Buckingham on 25 Mar. 1789, T/3719/C/23/18.   **197** Very miscellaneous memorandum book kept by Agar, [1790s], 21 M 57/D56.   **198** 21 M 57/D15.

1791–3, he was in a position to buy the lands of Brownstown, etc., Co. Kilkenny, with a rental of £260 per annum, followed by the lands of Kilmanagh, near Callan, followed by an addition to his inherited property at Lisnafunshin.[199] Then or thereafter, a townland which he described as 'Newtown otherwise Normanton', adjoining Lisnafunshin, and fairly near Castlecomer, was added to the Kilkenny estate.[200] The estate had a nett rental of £2,492 by 1806, and comprised 4,794 statute acres. In addition to these purchases of land, he managed over the period January 1794 to January 1807 to purchase, via his London stockbrokers alone, £183,926 worth of stock, mainly in 3% consols.[201] The measure of his success on the stock market, in broad terms and making no allowance for inflation, is the already-mentioned rise in his private income from £353 per annum in 1762 to £3,000 in 1789 to £17,832 in 1806.

This was a dazzling, though not unprecedented, success story. Arthur Smyth, archbishop of Dublin, 1766–77, 'amassed during [*sic*] his preferments property to the amount of £50,000.'[202] In the Church of England, Charles Moss, bishop of St David's, 1766–74, and of Bath and Wells, 1774–1802, 'amassed a private fortune of £140,000 (certainly too much for a bishop) ...; he ought to have done something for the Church', but instead divided his entire fortune between his children[203]. A later bishop of the Church of England, George Pretyman-Tomline, left £200,000 at his death in 1827. However, this figure – though oft-quoted – is difficult to interpret, because Pretyman-Tomline held a rich bishopric (Winchester) for only the last seven years of his episcopal career, and was a sizeable lay proprietor in his private capacity. He had inherited a small estate at Bacton in Suffolk, and in 1803 a Lincolnshire benefactor called Tomline, 'with whom I had very little acquaintance' except as the local bishop, left him the Riby estate in north Lincolnshire, 'now let for £1,300 a year and I am assured ... worth much more ..., [and] said to contain 3,000 acres with a good mansion house, newly built.'[204] So, Pretyman-Tomline's £200,000 may not have been too much for a bishop.

In the Law, even more commonly than in the Church, great fortunes were made. When he committed suicide in 1794, Richard Power, a baron of the Irish exchequer and usher to the court of chancery (the latter a sinecure worth £900 per annum), was 'said to have amassed a large fortune – 'tis alleged near £80,000 – which is [in]vested in [the] British Funds.'[205] Lord Clonmell confided to his diary that he was worth

199 Rentals and other papers relating to Brownstown, 1791–2, 21 M 57/T356–7; renewal of Kilmanagh to W.P.K. Trench, 11 Dec. 1790, 21 M 57/T358; Agar to W.P.K. Trench, 30 Sep. 1792, T/3719/C/26/12; assignment from Agar to Rev. Francis Benson in relation to the additional part of Lisnafunshin, 29 June 1793, 21 M 57/T358.   200 'The state of earl Normanton's property, 1806', 21 M 57/D23. This was a place name of importance for the future (see p. 16), and Agar's subsidiary barony and viscountcy of Somerton also derived from a place name, or more probably some elaboration of a place name, on his Kilkenny estate.   201 21 M 57/D15.   202 D'Alton, *Archbishops of Dublin*, p. 343.   203 Cassan, *Lives of the bishops of Bath and Wells*, pp 175–6. 204 Evans, *The contentious tithe*, p. 5; Pretyman-Tomline to 'My dear Sir', 29 June 1803 (author's collection); oral information from Mark Bence-Jones, whose wife is a descendant of Pretyman-Tomline.   205 *The Gentleman's and London Magazine* for Feb. 1794; Temple to Grenville, 28 Mar. 1783, *HMC Dropmore Mss.*, i, pp 205–6.

£15,000 per annum in the second half of the 1790s. (He also confided to Sir Laurence Parsons, *c.*1785, 'that the subjects debated in the Irish parliament had so little to do with the rest of the world, that no fame could be acquired by any display of abilities there; that he had early formed the decision that there no passion could be gratified but avarice; and that he had made the most he could of the situation.'[206]) The £15,000 comprised the income from his estates and investments (including his second wife's £68,000), his salary of £4,500 as the highest-paid of the three chief judges, and the proceeds (*c.*£2,500 per annum) from a lucrative sinecure in the courts which was given him for life in 1783.[208] The 'sordidly avaricious'[207] Lord Lifford, lord chancellor of Ireland, 1768–89, arrived from England with a personal fortune of only £20,000, had a salary of £3,000 per annum and a sessional allowance (when parliament was in session) of £1,000 as speaker of the House of Lords, and died worth £130,000 or £140,000, 'which he made by savings out of the emoluments of his office.'[209] This was roughly the same as the figure of £130,000 quoted (p. 500) for Primate Stuart's fortune at the time of his death, over thirty years later, in 1822.

Agar was associated in one piece of demonography – not with Stuart – but with two other near-contemporary churchmen, Fowler and John Porter, bishop of Clogher, 1798–1819: 'Three archbishops [*sic*] who have died since the Union – Agar, Porter and Fowler – have left behind them, though originally possessing nothing, £800,000.'[210] The total amount is believable: after Armagh and Derry, Clogher was the richest see in Ireland, worth by an informed guess made in 1797 no less than £7,000 per annum.[211] In terms of the proportion of the £800,000 attributable to him, the greatest of these three was Agar. Yet, where Fowler and Porter made their money, as far as is known, mainly out of their see incomes and assets, Agar – who occupied the poorest see of the three – made his more innocently on the stock market. William Beresford, a bishop from 1780 and archbishop of Tuam, 1794–1819, left £250,000 at his death and, like Agar, obtained a temporal peerage, the barony of Decies (in 1813); it is not known how he made his fortune, but Tuam was a significantly richer diocese than Cashel. At the time of William Beresford's promotion to it, his brother John remarked: 'I hear it is £5,000 per annum and an excellent patronage, so ... the Bishop has fallen on his legs at last.'[212] As for Frederick Hervey and the bishopric of Derry, nobody has as yet put a figure on the immense fortune made by him during a thirty-five year tenure of that very lucrative see.

206 Parsons' 'Political recollections', [post-1816], Rosse papers, Birr Castle, F/13.   **207** Fitzpatrick, *Ireland before the Union*, p. 29; *Clonmell diary (TCD)*, p. 386; Buckingham to Grenville, 26 Mar. and 26 Apr. 1788, *HMC Dropmore Mss.*, i, pp 313 and 325.; Camden to Portland, 31 Mar. 1796, HO 100/63, ff. 272–5.   **208** *Clonmell diary (TCD)*, p. 347.   **209** 'Most private' memorandum by Lifford, 11 Apr. 1789, and Robert Hobart (the chief secretary) to Pitt, 31 Jan. 1792, Pitt/Pretyman papers, PRONI, T/3319/2 and 10; Buckingham to Grenville, 13 May 1789, *HMC Dropmore Mss.*, i. 470.   **210** Quoted in Moran, 'The Agars of Gowran', p. 119.   **211** Robert Day to Lord Glandore, 18 Nov. 1797, MIC/639/6/5/1; Malcomson, 'Belleisle and its owners', pp 31–5.   **212** Phillips, *Church of Ireland*, iii. 307; John Beresford to Lord Auckland, 23 Aug. 1794, Auckland papers, BL, Add. Ms. 34453, f. 12; Charles Abbot to Stuart, 30 Oct. 1801, Bedfordshire RO, WY 994/8; Brodrick to Midleton, 8 Nov. 1801, Ms. 1248, vol. 18, ff. 44–5. Abbot's and Brodrick's letters show

The very fact that holders of particular forms of stock, purchasers of lottery tickets, subscribers to certain government loans, etc., were listed in newspapers and magazines alongside figures for the extent of their stakes, ought to have provided contemporaries with a clue to where Agar's money was being made. Instead, it seems merely to have added to his reputation for 'love of lucre' and to have increased suspicions about the Cashel see leases. If Castlereagh took the view, either in 1798 or at least before Agar left Cashel in 1801, that Agar had made a great estate to his family out of the see lands, the Irish government must have been under the same misapprehension, and the British government and, almost certainly, the King. And if the King did so, his disapproval must have had a bearing on the elimination of Agar as a candidate for the primacy in 1800. Nor did the adverse consequences of this misapprehension end in 1800.

AGAR'S ACCOUNTS AS TREASURER TO THE BOARD OF FIRST FRUITS, 1787–1803

The passing of the Act of Union was accompanied by a good deal of English wishful thinking and hypocrisy about its purifying effects on Irish public life (see pp 591–8); and one of the objects all sublime of the post-Union administration of Lord Hardwicke was to rescue 'the care of the public charities' from 'the boards which are supposed to have mismanaged them for years.'[213] The board of first fruits was a case in point. Indoctrinated by Brodrick, Primate Stuart looked with a suspicious eye at Agar's accounts as treasurer to that body, and in particular at the £43,000 allegedly in Agar's hands in early January 1802 and the £30,000 still allegedly in his hands in early March. Writing to Brodrick in early March, Stuart acknowledged that it was not 'manifest that interest had been made [for Agar's personal gain] out of the surplus money', but then went on to jump to that very conclusion:

> I am of your opinion as to the propriety of proceeding with coolness and deliberation. There is no occasion to irritate the Archbishop of Dublin with harsh language, or to pass any harsh censure upon his conduct. All that can be said is that he has availed himself of the supine neglect of the board. ... Perhaps the best mode of proceeding will to be to follow the example of our predecessors in the year 1763 and, at a proper time, appoint a committee to examine the balances in the hands of the treasurer, to report how those balances may be best employed, and if any abuse exists in the management, what remedies shall appear to them best and most effectual. ... [Then] there can be no reasonable cause for offence, though the loss of a large annual income will

that William Beresford had first refusal of Cashel in 1801; since he refused it, in spite of its proximity to the Beresford power base in Co. Waterford, Tuam must still have been richer than Cashel at that time. In 1831, it had a gross rental of £8,206 as compared to Cashel's £7,354 (Akenson, *Church of Ireland*, p. 84).   213 Hardwicke to Addington, 5 Jan. 1802, *The viceroy's post-bag*, p. 112.

not please the Archbishop of Dublin. In short, something must be done, for by this management the Church loses a considerable sum, the money arising from the boroughs is flung into the pockets of an individual, but [*sic*] all of us are exposed to very dishonourable imputations.[214]

This was plainly a prejudiced and alarmist view of the situation, based on Brodrick's animus against Agar and Agar's popular reputation rather than on a proper examination of Agar's accounts. It is significant that Stuart's figures do not tally with Agar's own. According to Agar, at 1 May 1801 £31,949 of the board's funds had been in his hands as treasurer, £9,830 in the hands of the board's Dublin bankers, Latouche & Co., and £1,538 in the hands of the board's agent, Thomas Burgh. This made a total of £43,319, which corresponds roughly to the £43,000 mentioned by Stuart as *all* being in Agar's hands 'three months' before March 1802. However, according to Agar's figures, the surplus funds stood on 2 January 1802 at £31,623: £21,797 with Agar, £8,309 with Latouches and £1,516 with Burgh.[215] Moreover, the involvement of the Latouches and Burgh is significant from more than an arithmetical point of view. They to some extent shared responsibility with Agar for the funds of the board, and to that extent were in a position to act as a brake and check upon him. The Rt. Hon. David Latouche was still animated by some of the zeal of his Huguenot ancestors, and is unlikely to have condoned any misuse of the funds of a Church of Ireland institution; Thomas Burgh was probably the same Thomas Burgh who was secretary to the treasury, and though that body was not of spotless purity or exemplary efficiency, at least he would have understood public accountability.

Besides, it is possible from Agar's accounts to establish just what became of 'the money arising from the boroughs', which Stuart suspected was 'flung into the pockets of an individual.' Agar received the first instalment of the compensation money for the disfranchisement of the three bishops' boroughs on 12 January 1802. It amounted to £18,086. On 12 February he lodged with Latouches £3,998 worth of 5 per cent government debentures which he had just bought, and the balance of the £18,086 in cash. This procedure he followed with the further instalments, always lodging fairly promptly the cash and/or securities. The third instalment, which was probably the last, was received by Agar on 14 July 1802 and amounted to £9,374.[216] The dates on which the commissioners of compensation made these payments do not matter, as interest was payable on the whole £45,000 from 1 January 1801.[217] What does matter, from the point of view of establishing whether or not Agar misused the money while he was treasurer, is that it was definitely 'left to accumulate, and ... now [1808] amounts to £60,000.'[218] This is a very satisfactory return on £45,000 notionally received just over seven years previously, and surely exculpates Agar from Stuart's charge?

214 Stuart to Brodrick, 7 Mar. 1802, Ms. 8869/1. Brodrick replied at considerable length on 10 March (Bedfordshire RO, WY 994/22) putting as unfavourable a construction as possible on Agar's activities as treasurer.   215 Agar's account book, 1778–1808, 21 M 57/D16.   216 Ibid.   217 Cleaver to Stuart, [22] Mar. 1802, Wickham papers, PRONI, T/2627/5/S/14.   218 Bishop O'Beirne to John Foster, 13 Feb. 1808, D/207/50/24.

In any case, by January 1803, Stuart was reporting a state of affairs which he considered much improved, although this was possibly his way of avoiding the admission that he had been wrong the first time. 'I rejoice to find that the balance in the treasurer's hands has been so much reduced. It amounts indeed to a less sum than has been left in his hands at any time during the last ten years.'[219] Considering that £45,000 plus interest had passed through Agar's hands since Stuart had last seen the accounts, and that none of it had stayed there, this was tantamount to an exoneration of Agar. Unwilling to admit as much, Stuart was unconcealed in his satisfaction when Agar resigned as treasurer a couple of days later and Stuart was able to pass the office on to Brodrick.[220] To Brodrick he wrote: 'I was not much surprised to hear from the Archbishop of Dublin that the state of his health made it quite necessary for him to resign the office of treasurer to the board of first fruits.' The implication of these remarks is that Agar had resigned, either out of pique at having his accounts queried or because he saw no further scope for irregular profit-making. Actually, the plea of ill-health was not without justification, and the rejection of his policy on glebe-house building (see pp 258–65) was the likeliest reason for his resignation. Agar was not one for hanging around in the ante-rooms of power when he felt that real confidence had been withdrawn from him (see pp 530–3). Significantly, once he had held the treasurership for a few months, Brodrick found a satisfactory explanation for the extent of the balances in the treasurer's hands: 'there are demands to a very considerable amount (of grants agreed to by the board) outstanding, and ... part of the balance now in [the] Bank [of Ireland] would have been funded if the board had not thought it probable that the scheme for encouraging the building [of] glebe-houses would go on this year.'[221] The danger of funding money which might soon be needed was that the price of the Funds would fall in the interim.

Even after Agar's resignation as treasurer, the allegation that he had invested the money for his private profit rumbled on. In May 1803, Lord Chancellor Redesdale mentioned to his brother-in-law, the British attorney general, Spencer Perceval: 'For many years the sum of £50,000 ... accumulated in ... [Agar's] hands as ... treasurer, and he is afraid lest there should be some observation on this awkward circumstance.'[222] Redesdale had no first-hand knowledge of what had happened 'many years' ago. Furthermore, he was animated by much more than the usual English prejudice against Irishmen and their alleged disposition to jobbery and other things.[223] (In 1804 he wrote tactlessly to Agar that he was 'very unwilling' to employ an Irish coachman, 'knowing their disposition to drink spirits and general carelessness of horses'![224]) Before the Union, as after, the surplus had never amounted to as much as £50,000 (in May 1797 – for example – it had stood at £30,000[225]), and it had never been solely in the hands of the treasurer. Moreover, Stuart himself provides the authority for ignoring Redesdale's strictures. He later complained to Brodrick that Redesdale was in the habit of writing intemperate (and sometimes mendacious) letters

219 Stuart to Brodrick, 23 Jan. 1803, Ms 8869/1.   220 Stuart to Brodrick, 27 Jan. 1803, ibid.   221 Brodrick to Wickham, 21 June and 17 Oct. 1803, T/2627/5/S/34 and 37.   222 Redesdale to Perceval, 17 May 1803, *Irish official papers*, ii. 378.   223 Malcomson, *John Foster*, pp 236–41 and 338–40.   224 Redesdale to Agar, 30 June 1804, T/3719/C/38/36.   225 21 M 57/D16.

ill-calculated to excite favourable sentiments of our Establishment. ... [In one] he enters into a detail of neglects [by Agar] in the diocese of Dublin, and he concludes by saying that the Irish bishops make false representations of the state and discipline of their dioceses ... . Such language as this, written by the Chancellor, who all the English suppose is well acquainted with the ecclesi-astical state of Ireland and suppose a bigoted admirer of our Establishment, cannot fail to make a deep impression.[226]

There is in fact evidence, going back 'many years', for Agar's attitude to interest-bearing trust funds. In June 1786, he had thought it worthy of critical comment that 'no interest was allowed' by Archbishop Cox and Cox's son on a legacy to the diocese of Cashel which had been in their respective hands for the previous twenty years.[227] At the beginning of 1789, he had pointed to the danger of leaving a large balance (it was then £20,000) in the hands of the treasurer to the board of first fruits – *viz.* 'that this accumulation of unemployed money might prevent the parliament from making any grants in future' (see p. 228). There was therefore no reason for Stuart to imagine that Agar would be touchy on this issue and that the much earlier precedent of 1763 would have to be appealed to. The Kingston College trust fund, of which Brodrick became an *ex-officio* trustee in succession to Agar in 1802, also bore witness to Agar's business ethics. On 6 December 1797, that fund had been described, in the books of Agar's London stockbrokers, Willis, Wood, Percival & Co., as 'standing in the Archbishop of Cashel's name, but the property of the college at Mitchelstown.'[228] Similarly, Agar's personal holding in Bank of Ireland stock was distinguishable from the Bank stock held by the trust fund for the purchase of a new palace by the archbishop of Dublin. This caused a difficulty in July 1808, when Agar wrote to the secretary to the Bank:

> I find ... that my Bank stock standing in my name as earl [of] Normanton (it being my own private property) has been increased pursuant to the act of parliament for renewing the Bank charter. But I have also £500 Bank stock belonging to me as archbishop of Dublin for the time being, which stands in the Bank book in the name of Charles Dublin. I know of no fund out of which I could pay the necessary subscription as archbishop of Dublin for the renewal of this £500. Nevertheless, if it cannot be contrived better, I am willing to pay it out of my own purse for the benefit of my successors.[229]

These examples show that Agar appreciated and observed the distinction between *meum* and *tuum*. The supposition of his making 'a large annual income' out of the funds of the board of first fruits was as far-fetched as the suspicion that he had misapplied the money he had received for dilapidations on the palace of St Sepulchre,

226 Stuart to Brodrick, 29 Oct. 1805, Ms 8869/3. 227 Agar's 'state' of the diocese of Cashel, 1779–1801, 21 M 57/B6/1, *sub* 12 June [1786]. 228 Account between Agar and Willis, Wood, Percival & Co., 6 Dec. 1797, 21 M 57/B17/2. 229 Agar to Thomas Williams, *c.*10 July 1808, T/3719/C/42/43.

or that he had made false claims over dilapidations and improvements to the Cashel palace, or that he had misappropriated part of the Cashel see lands.

THE 'LOVE OF LUCRE'

Ironically – in view of the fact that Brodrick had prejudiced Stuart and others against Agar on this account – 'love of lucre' characterised Brodrick's own handling of the Cashel see lands, particularly the Agar leases, in the period 1810–20. John Hare, who was biased, decided in 1812 that Brodrick was 'a cunning, crafty, avaricious man' and a dissembler (see p. 497). The *dénouement* over Lord Normanton's renewal in December 1819–January 1820 seemed to corroborate this view. Hare had earlier remarked that Brodrick was being 'a great enemy to himself in holding out.'[230] So it proved. In December 1819, Archbishop Cleaver, whose coadjutor Brodrick had been since 1811, at last died. It was assumed that Brodrick would succeed to Dublin,[231] and the offer was made to him – and refused. From the timing of events, it is clear that the determining factor was Lord Normanton's renewal fine, which Brodrick would receive only if he stayed at Cashel. The lord lieutenant who had offered the arch-bishopric of Dublin to Brodrick, the 3rd Earl Talbot, was at this stage on leave in England, and following discussion with the Prime Minister and Home Secretary, he reported to Dublin Castle on 23 January 1820 that a churchman from England was likely to be sent over to fill the vacancy.[232] (It is, incidentally, a moot point whether Brodrick counted as English or Irish by 1820.) At the end of the month, Lord Normanton offered £52,000 for the renewal, and Brodrick, who had stipulated for £60,000 as recently as October 1819, refused it. Major Woodward wrote, in obvious perplexity, to his uncle: 'I certainly would act ... as if the archbishopric was not vacant ..., it being your Grace's intention to remain at Cashel ... . I think it likely that, if your Grace's mind is made up about Dublin, it will be vacant for some time. Government don't know on whom to fix.'[233] Immediately after this, Lord Normanton increased his offer to £55,000, payable by instalments, and Brodrick accepted that sum.[234]

From Brodrick's point of view, £55,000 payable by instalments was a considerable climb-down from the straight £60,000 for which he had stipulated in the previous October, when the lease had a little longer to run, but when Cleaver was still assumed to be in good physical health. Like his refusal of Lord Normanton's previous offer, Brodrick's acceptance of the new one must have been inspired by thoughts of Dublin. There had been no success in finding an English bishop or churchman to fill it.

---

230 Hare to Normanton, 14 Jan. 1814, 21 M 57, 2nd earl's unreferenced correspondence. 231 Archdeacon James Agar to Normanton, 29 Dec. 1819, ibid.   232 Talbot to William Gregory, under-secretary in Dublin Castle, 23 Jan. 1820, Talbot-Gregory correspondence, PRONI, D/4100/2. I am grateful for references from this source to Dr Ann McVeigh of PRONI.   233 Woodward to Brodrick, 29 Jan. [1820], Ms. 8865/2.   234 Hare to Normanton, 30 and 31 Jan. 1820, 21 M 57, 2nd earl's unreferenced correspondence.

Brodrick therefore had good reason to expect that he would be given another chance, and intimated to the chief secretary, Charles Grant, that he might 'change his mind.' But it was too late. Absent from Ireland and from immediate information about this development, Lord Talbot had got himself into 'a sad bother about the A.B. of Dublin.' By 1 February he had written 'to the Bishop of Clogher [Lord John George Beresford] offering him the dignity. Should he refuse (which I expect) ..., the situation will be well filled' by Brodrick.²³⁵ Very improperly, Chief Secretary Grant leaked to Woodward, 'in strict confidence, that the archbishopric of Dublin is offered to the Bishop of Clogher, that he is very ill and it is thought will decline, and then it would be disposable to your Grace [Brodrick]. ... Perhaps [added Woodward], if I cannot bring Agar to reason, I might yield something to get rid of them [the Agars]. Dick Wynne [the late Archbishop Cleaver's brother-in-law] says the fines to be now got in Dublin are £8,000.'²³⁶ Illness apart, Bishop Beresford had good reason to hesitate: because of the mismatch which had grown up between episcopal seniority and episcopal income, Clogher was worth considerably more than Dublin, and a translation to Dublin could be justified only on the ground that it was a career move leading to Armagh (which, famously, it was to do in Beresford's case). For whatever reason, Beresford did not decide and/or inform Dublin Castle of his decision until *c.*20 February.

Meanwhile, a new wrangle had broken out between Brodrick and Lord Normanton, this time over the details of the instalment scheme.²³⁷ A Brodrick supporter suggested that 'The report here of your translation is (I am sure) the cause of their [the Agars'] keeping back, and as usual they show every disposition to take advantage.'²³⁸ William Gregory, under-secretary at the Castle, wrote to the still-absent Lord Talbot on 16 February: 'I find the Archbishop of Cashel has not finally concluded with Lord Normanton, as there is some twopenny dispute about interest which his Grace, from scruples of conscience no doubt, cannot relinquish.'²³⁹ Gregory, clearly, was of Hare's opinion that there was much humbug and hypocrisy about Brodrick. However, by the time Beresford's acceptance of Dublin was declared, Brodrick had committed himself too far to Lord Normanton to recede. So, he had lost something in excess of £5,000 for the Cashel renewal without gaining the £8,000 in 'fines to be now got in Dublin.' The episode is significant, not just as showing Brodrick in his true colours, but as a final and signal demonstration of the inefficiency and invidiousness of paying bishops through the medium of see estates. In Brodrick's case, this mode of payment clearly prevented his natural progression to Dublin. In Agar's case, it may have contributed to his being baulked of Armagh and it certainly contributed very largely to his unsavoury and on the whole undeserved reputation for sharp pecuniary practices. Equally important, it fuelled the hostility and the non-cooperation between these two notable churchmen.

235 Talbot to Gregory, 1 and 4 Feb. 1820, D/4100/2 and 3. It is significant that Talbot expected Beresford to refuse: in 1831, the gross rental of Clogher was £10,371 and that of Dublin £9,320. **236** Woodward to Brodrick, post-marked 11 Feb. 1820, Ms. 8865/1.   **237** Ibid.; agreement signed by Woodward and Archdeacon Agar, 16 Feb. 1820, Ms. 8865/1.   **238** Cooper to Brodrick, 12 Feb. 1820, Ms. 8861/11.   **239** Gregory to Talbot, 16 Feb. 1820, D/4100/2.

In more general terms, the very complexity of managing see estates gave rise to much misunderstanding and misrepresentation of the bishops' actions: although most of them were generous landlords – or at any rate reluctant to depart from the tenurial practices and even the levels of rent which prevailed on their see estates – they were blamed for rapacity by both their successors and the local gentry. A different system of remuneration, which made episcopal incomes less controversial, unequal and uncertain and perhaps was based on a sliding scale proportioned to seniority and responsibility, would have made for greater harmony and efficiency in the upper reaches of the Church of Ireland. It would also have addressed the major image-problem which bedevilled the Church's relations with its natural supporters, the gentry. The extent of this problem is revealed by a letter written in 1789 (significantly, soon after Fredrick Hervey had granted his first Derry see lands lease in trust for himself) by Sir Edward Newenham, M.P. for Co. Dublin. The writer was a radical; but he was also a High Protestant and, later, a great admirer of Agar (see p. 245*n*). Newenham's verdict on the higher clergy of the Church of Ireland in the late 1780s was that

> we cannot boast of virtuous a[rch]bishops or bishops or any high Church dignitaries; they worship mammon ... . The parson leaves his flock to the parish clerk and attends the court *levées*; gaming houses are increasing and churches deserted; scarce a bishop resides more than one month in a year in his diocese, and some of them are running their lives against their leases.[240]

240 Newenham to Benjamin Franklin, 26–28 July 1789, quoted in James Kelly, 'Sir Edward Newenham, M.P., 1734–1814: the life and politics of a radical protestant' (forthcoming, Dublin, 2002). I am grateful to Dr Kelly for this reference. As has been seen (p. 413), Fowler at Killaloe had preceded Hervey in the practice or malpractice of leases in trust.

Three 'accidental' archbishops from England: Robinson, Fowler and Newcome, c.1760–1800

The preceding Chapters (Five to Nine) have inquired into what might be called the political economy of the Church of Ireland in Agar's day – diocesan and metropolitan administration, the building and rebuilding of churches, cathedrals, glebe-houses and palaces, and the management of episcopal estates. This has involved considerable discussion of Agar's administrative and political effectiveness and of his (much questioned) personal probity. It has also demonstrated that Agar was, in fact but not in name, the leading figure in the Church in most of these respects, as well as 'infinitely the first ecclesiastic' in the House of Lords. The present Chapter is devoted to a discussion of those ecclesiastics who out-ranked him and who ought to have fulfilled the leadership role which devolved on him by default. Foremost among these is Robinson. But the comparison needs to be broadened to take in the three principal figures – Fowler and Newcome as well as Robinson – who were senior to Agar in the Church during the period between his elevation to the episcopal bench and the Union. This selection disregards the unimportant Arthur Smyth and John Cradock, who between them were archbishops of Dublin, 1766–78, Archbishop Cox of Cashel, and the elderly John Ryder and Jemmett Browne, who were archbishops of Tuam, 1752–75 and 1775–82 respectively. It also disregards Primate Stuart, who has been or will be discussed on pp 257–85 and 593–614.

PRIMATE ROBINSON (1709–94)

By the late 1770s, when Agar – in spite of Robinson's best endeavours – joined him on the archiepiscopal bench, Robinson was already in his late sixties and to outward seeming was a largely ornamental, detached, elder-statesmanlike figure. In a letter of January 1777, which has been partially quoted already, Lord Hillsborough described him to the new lord lieutenant, Buckinghamshire, 'as one of the best men living. He is a man of very sound judgement and what is better of a very sound heart, a true friend to the dignity and interest of government, and has effected more for the civilisation and improvement of Ireland than any ten men for these hundred years. He hates and despises a job, and whatever information he gives you I will venture to say you may depend upon.'[1] Buckinghamshire, who was on at best uneasy terms with Hillsborough, soon arrived independently at a similar conclusion:

1 Hillsborough to Buckinghamshire, 20 Jan. 1777, *HMC Lothian Mss.*, p. 298.

> The Primate of Ireland, of all the churchman I ever knew in any country, does the most honour to his profession, happy in the talents of reconciling ease with dignity, and of blending the strictest attention to the respectable duties of the situation with the amiable qualities of society, and no otherwise interfering in the tumultuous politics of this country than to give a decent support to the interests of England, and to testify a becoming gratitude to that government from whence he derived the consequence of those emoluments which he so respectably enjoys.[2]

This image of Robinson was essentially a self-image.[3] He had not always been thus, nor in reality was he thus even in the late 1770s.

Robinson, as has been seen (pp 149–50), was a *protégé* of the Sackville/Dorset family. Through them, he became a follower of their ally in Irish politics, Primate Stone, who in any case had been Robinson's contemporary and friend at Christ Church. Dorset was recalled in 1755. In 1759, Stone successfully recommended Robinson to the then lord lieutenant, Bedford, for Robinson's next bishopric, that of Ferns.[4] As bishop of Ferns, 1759–61, Robinson endeavoured to testify to his continuing political allegiance to 'the Dorset House' by returning two Sackville nominees for his bishop's borough of Old Leighlin at the general election of 1761. He claimed that he had made his arrangements for the disposal of the seats before he learned early in 1761 of his promotion, at Bedford's recommendation, to the bishopric of Kildare. It was, however, a suspicious circumstance that Bedford had just resigned the lord lieutenancy, and so could be of no further use to Robinson. With considerable effrontery, Robinson wrote to him in late March 1761 expressing the hope

> that my engagements ... for filling the borough... will appear to your Grace to be agreeable to the strictest principles of probity and equity. Accounts have been received in Ireland, perhaps destitute of all foundation, that two gentle- men different from those to whom I stand engaged, will be recommended by Dr Jackson [his successor at Ferns] as candidates for Leighlin. ... If it is ... expected that my engagements with persons of the first rank, honour and influence in this kingdom should be annihilated by the acceptance of the bis- hopric of Kildare, I do not see that I can at this time accept that bishopric thus conditioned, unless I would relinquish the comfort and credit of being esteemed an honest man the remainder of my life.[5]

That Bedford by no means esteemed Robinson an honest man in this transaction, has already been seen (pp 176–7). Bedford's chief secretary, Richard Rigby, who currently sat for Old Leighlin, also inveighed against Robinson and called what he had written to Bedford

2 Buckinghamshire to Hotham Thompson, 11 Mar. 1777, Hotham papers, PRONI, T/3429/1/8. 3 For Robinson's adeptness at publicising a self-image, see Coleman, 'Reynolds and Robinson', pp 133–4. 4 Stone to Bedford, 27 Mar. 1759, *Irish official papers*, ii. 218. 5 Robinson to Bedford, 28 Mar. 1761, ibid., p. 264.

the most Jesuitical, shuffling letter I ever read in my life. Was there ever a greater rascal than this bishop! I hope your Grace will be of opinion with me that the sooner Jackson goes to Ireland, the better, for it will be horrid provoking to have this villain get this additional preferment from you, at the very instant when he is flying in your face in the last see to which you promoted him. ... I think, if Jackson is upon the spot, and gives the people to understand that they must never expect any future favours from him, if they do not obey him in this most material circumstance, that the new bishop must prevail over the old one.[6]

The new bishop, Charles Jackson, who was a Bedfordshire *protégé* of the duke and one of his chaplains, naturally endorsed the ducal sentiments, and resented the attempt to deprive himself of this important part of the patronage of his see. He called Robinson's letter 'such an ungrateful one ... as I could not have expected to have come from any man, much less one of his rank and order'[7]. Robinson now realised that he had over-stepped the mark, and was fearful of incurring the displeasure of the King. He therefore wrote to his younger brother, General Sir Septimus Robinson, who had been governor of two of George III's younger brothers, the dukes of Gloucester and Cumberland, 1751–60, and was now gentleman usher of the Black Rod[8] (circumstances of considerable importance for the future), in an effort to rehabilitate himself. 'The letter from Bishop Robinson to his brother, Sep.' wrote Rigby 'was no other than a copy of his elaborate epistle to the duke of Bedford. Sep. showed it to Lord Waldegrave [governor of George III, as prince of Wales, 1752–6] and others, who all abused the performance and its author as much as I have done, but not so much as I will do when the election at Leighlin is over.'[9] Finally, Robinson read his 'recantation'[10] and Bedford's two nominees were returned for Old Leighlin. In fact, there seems to have been no great quarrel, except about the principle of who did the nominating, over one of Robinson's candidates. The real quarrel was over the other. Robinson had engaged to return Speaker Ponsonby's brother, Richard, and Bedford to return the provost of TCD, Francis Andrews, an important supporter of the government. (As vice-chancellor and a visitor of TCD from 1765 onwards, Robinson was hostile to Andrews, so perhaps their antagonism originated in Old Leighlin.[11]) Speaker Ponsonby and Primate Stone, the 'persons of the first rank, honour and influence in this kingdom' referred to in Robinson's 'elaborate epistle', were at this time using their position as lords justices in Bedford's absence to thwart his wishes and curry popularity in Ireland.[12] So Richard Ponsonby was, under the circumstances, a highly

6 Rigby to Bedford, 30 Mar. 1761, ibid., pp 264–5.   7 Jackson to Bedford, 2 Apr. 1761, ibid., p. 265.
8 Adam Clarke (ed.), *Compendium edition of the lives of Bishop Newton, Rev. Philip Skelton, etc.*, ii. 157.
9 Rigby to Wilmot, 13 Apr. 1761, T/3019/4358.   10 Rigby to Wilmot, 16 Apr. 1761, T/3019/4361.
11 John William Stubbs, The history *of the university of Dublin from its foundation to the end of the eighteenth century* ... (Dublin, 1889), pp 227–9. Robinson and Andrews also clashed over the disposal of the bishopric of Limerick in 1770–71 – Robinson to Townshend, 23 and 30 Nov. 1770, Townshend letter-book, RCB Library, Ms. 20/3 and 2.   12 Robert E. Burns, *Irish parliamentary*

objectionable choice. Clearly, Robinson, contrary to his later reputation, was involving himself in 'the tumultuous politics of this country' and following the factious lead of 'that man of bustle and noisy name', Primate Stone.[13]

Between 1761 and Stone's death in December 1764, Robinson continued to court and follow him, turning a blind eye to Stone's vices, of which addiction to political intrigue was not the greatest.

> The Primate of Ireland ... had every vice but hypocrisy, [and] took every shape but that of a man of virtue and religion: polite, insinuating, generous, the pimp of pleasure and the spy of state, a slave to one vice, but the other vices, especially the most natural one, he made to serve his purposes. Had he been galant [*sic*], he could have obliged but one lady at a time, but from his own seraglio he obtained many. He governed private families by providing the ladies with lovers of his own educating. They were taught by his Lordship to spell the love letters they wrote. This prelate was much such a successor to St Patrick as Pope Sixtus to St Peter.[14]

The writer of these withering words, the famous Blue Stocking, Mrs Elizabeth Montagu (*née* Robinson), was Robinson's favourite cousin, who went to see him every year at Bath or Bristol, where he spent much of the long Irish parliamentary recess.[15] So there can be no doubt about the source of her information. According to another, less reliable source, Horace Walpole, Stone's constant political entertaining had made him 'a sacrifice to drunkenness, which, however, was but a libation to ambition.'[16] In spite of all this, Robinson stuck to Stone (and, in 1765, perpetuated the association by taking on the lease of Stone's house in Henrietta Street, scene and symbol of the latter's Dublin debaucheries). It was through Stone's – and other political – influence that he rose in the Church and eventually was made primate. As has been drily observed: 'Robinson, it would seem, achieved little of any real importance in the three bishoprics which he held before the primacy.'[17] Something similar was said, in a more convoluted way, at the time of his promotion to Armagh. His appointment 'was not owing to any interest that ought to have contributed to it. The qualities of the successor [to Stone] are ... in all points (except ability) the same as those of his predecessor, who is suggested to have established this extraordinary succession before he departed.'[18]

politics in the eighteenth century [*1714–60*] (2 vols., Washington DC, 1989–90), ii, pp 298–314. 13 Horace Walpole to Sir Horace Mann, 20 Dec. 1764, printed in Cunningham (ed.), *The letters of Horace Walpole*, iv. 303.   14 Mrs Montagu to her husband, Edward, 20 Dec. 1764, printed in Reginald Blunt (ed.), *Mrs Montagu, 'Queen of the Blues': her letters and friendships from 1762 to 1800* (2 vols., London, 1923), i, pp 120–21. For a similar indictment, see Rev. James Gordon, *A history of Ireland from the earliest times to ... 1801* (2 vols., London, 1806), ii. 222.   15 Mohan, 'Archbishop Richard Robinson', p. 127. Father Mohan's source for this pattern of meetings relates to 1783, but Mrs Montagu states that Robinson had been doing it 'always'.   16 Walpole to Mann, 20 Dec. 1764, op. cit., pp 303–4. Walpole's information in this instance came first-hand from his friend, George Montagu – *Georgian Society records*, ii. 12.   17 Mohan, 'Archbishop Richard Robinson', p. 99.   18 Edward Sedgwick to Edward Weston (who had been chief secretary at the time of Stone's promotion

There was, in fact, much more to Robinson's elevation than the recommendation of the dying Stone: apart from anything else, the lord lieutenant who made the appointment, Northumberland, was on such bad terms with Stone (see pp 139–40) that he would never have acted on Stone's advice unless there were other circumstances favouring Robinson. The most important of these was Sir Septimus Robinson's position in the royal household, the Princess Dowager's attachment to him, Lord Bute's attachment to the Princess Dowager, and Northumberland's attachment to Lord Bute. Another important circumstance was George III's bad relations with the ministry of the day, headed by George Grenville.[19] Grenville favoured candidates other than Robinson, and a primate in the Boulter not the Stone mould. To Thomas Newton, bishop of Bristol, he wrote asking him to accept the primacy, 'always to be one of the lords justices, constantly to correspond with him [Grenville, and] to give him certain intelligence of everything material.'[20] Newton was actually his second choice, his first having been Edmund Keene, bishop of Chester; but both declined. Bedford, the lord president of the council in the Grenville administration, and on close terms with the Prime Minister, was understandably anxious to keep out Robinson; he favoured a Scotsman on the Irish bench, who was much senior to Robinson and a perfectly creditable candidate.[21] Grenville recorded in his diary: 'The King pauses upon appointing anyone to it as yet, and in that and some other instances of delays ... and averseness to what Mr Grenville proposes ..., he feels the effects of some inferior persons who get about his Majesty, and seemingly indispose him to his principal servants.'[22]

This was of course what happened. Robinson's 'extraordinary succession' was as much a 'Bedchamber Plot' as his patron, Stone's, had been in 1747, with the aggravation in Robinson's case it also owed something to his condoning of Stone's vices. One Irish MP who had belonged to Stone's political following quipped in January 1765 that 'part of the ministry were for having a good politician, part for a good churchman, and in the end they have chosen neither.'[23] This was a harsh verdict, particularly in relation to the good things which Robinson was to do for the Church in the early years of his primacy. But, in relation to Robinson's previous record and to the events of December 1764–January 1765, it is hard to accept the view 'that his appointment marked a deliberate move to have a primate who would concentrate on Church rather than political affairs.'[24] Moreover, the circumstances of his appointment

to the primacy), 8 Jan. 1765, ibid., p. 98.   **19** Grenville 'irritated George III more than any other prime minister he ever had' – Pares, *George III and the politicians*, p. 145. See also *idem*, pp 147*n* and 152*n*, and. Jupp, *Lord Grenville*, pp 7–8.   **20** Quoted in Simms, 'Primate Robinson', p. 142. **21** Walpole to Mann, 13 Jan. 1765, op. cit., pp 310–11.   **22** William James Smith (ed.), *The Grenville papers: being the correspondence of Richard Grenville, Earl Temple, K.G., and the Rt Hon. George Grenville, their friends and contemporaries* (4 vols., London, 1852), ii, pp 533–5. I am indebted for this reference to Mr Peter MacDonagh.   **23** Edmond Sexten Pery to Robert FitzGerald, 31 Jan. 1765, printed in M.A. Hickson (ed.), *Old Kerry records ..., second series* (2 vols., London, 1874), ii, 279. This is an appendix printing a small selection of the early letters in the already-cited MIC/639.   **24** Peter MacDonagh, '"Hostile, indigested innovations": official pressures for reform of the Church of Ireland in the 1780s' (forthcoming article). I am most grateful to Mr MacDonagh for his generosity

invite comparison with the circumstances of Agar's rejection in 1794. It was feared, without proof or even probability, that Agar might be an unreliable custodian of a bishop's borough, whereas Robinson had a proven record of trickiness in this regard; Agar was an object of suspicion because of his extensive political connections in both Ireland and England, although these were solid and honourable in comparison to Robinson's; and Agar's pretensions were supported by a distinguished record of achievement as a diocesan, while Robinson as yet had achieved nothing in this line.

Nevertheless, from these inauspicious, even suspicious, beginnings, Robinson made a considerable mark in his first twelve or so years in the primacy, and in spite of his 'Jesuitical' past, proved to be the antithesis of his patron, Stone – a contrast which greatly enhanced his standing. It could, however, be argued that he had little choice but to abjure politics and concentrate on his ecclesiastical concerns. His influence at court declined rapidly, with the death of his brother, Sir Septimus, later in 1765, the waning of the influence of Lord Bute, and the death of the Princess Dowager in 1772. He tried in 1776–8 to invoke the aid of 'Sep.'s' former charge, the duke of Gloucester, who had been made chancellor of TCD in 1771, in the battle with Hely-Hutchinson. But the duke, having in an unguarded moment 'very graciously received ... [Dr Duigenan] and promised him a visitation', took avoiding action and declined to be involved.[25] The only development in court and cabinet which was of potential advantage to Robinson was the appointment of Stone's and his old patron, Lord George Sackville/Germain, as secretary of state for the colonies in 1775. In more general terms, Robinson's first decade in the primacy coincided with a conscious change of government policy, whereby authority was 'brought back to the Castle' (as the contemporary phrase ran), the lord lieutenant became full-time resident from 1767 onwards, and the need to appoint the primate or any other prominent figure as a lord justice ceased to exist unless under exceptional circumstances. These, in fact, arose only twice between Robinson's enthronement as primate and his death[26] – in 1787 and in 1789. On both occasions, Robinson was one of three *ex officio* lords justices appointed (the others being the lord chancellor and the speaker of the House of Commons); on both, he was – and remained – in England. This was a striking contrast to the behaviour of Stone, who would have embraced Islam sooner than forgo service on the commission of lords justices. Otherwise, Robinson was a stranger to even quasi-political office – so much so that, when appointed a trustee of the linen manufacture (a numerous body and a by no means rare distinction) in 1777, he could state without conscious irony that membership of that board was 'out of the line of my profession.'[27] Because he

in sending me this important and persuasive piece in draft. There are only a couple of points (such as this interpretation of Robinson's appointment) about which I have any reservations. **25** Hely-Hutchinson to Agar, 24 Nov. 1778, T/3719/C/12/21; Stubbs, *History of Dublin university*, pp 239–40. Gloucester's elder brother, Cumberland, had been chancellor, 1751–65, had appointed Robinson vice-chancellor in the latter year, and had then died, only to be succeeded by Robinson's old enemy, Bedford. Bedford died in 1771, when Gloucester succeeded. **26** Lords justices, excluding Robinson, were appointed on 22 Feb. 1765, but this was before his enthronement. **27** Robinson to Buckinghamshire, 11 June 1777, Heron papers, NLI, Ms. 13035/7. Lord Hillsborough's letter to Buckinghamshire, quoted earlier and possibly written at Robinson's prompting, toed such a line (at least ostensibly), his 'political conduct' deserved, in the tribute paid him by the out-going lord lieutenant, Harcourt, in 1776, 'the highest encomium that can be given to it. He is an enemy to all intrigue and faction. His only object is the king's service and the honourable support of his government.'[28]

Moreover, in his first dozen years of 'graceful reform', he had many positive achievements to his credit as a builder and improver, an administrator at diocesan, metropolitan and primatial level, a legislator, and an enforcer of lapsed ecclesiastical standards. Examples of this last have been given (pp 140 and 222); and something has also been said (pp 286, 316–17 and 382–3) of his architectural achievements and other diocesan work. In his day, he was credited with the maxim 'that the first step towards civilisation is a resident clergy' – although one resident clergyman of Robinson's province, Philip Skelton, quipped that Robinson 'was very careful to build churches, but did not care what sort of clergymen he put in them.'[29] Bishop Richard Mant asserted: 'No primate ever sat in the see of Armagh, who watched more carefully over the interest of the Church of Ireland, as the statute book evinces'; and Chart, taking up this theme, wrote: 'to his general church administration the statute book of the Irish parliament during his twenty-nine years of office (1765–94) bears witness'.[30] In fact, three-quarters of the sixteen acts of parliament which Robinson sponsored over the period 1758–84 were concentrated on the period 1768–76, during those fruitful first twelve years of his primacy. He claimed that he had been present at the start of every session of parliament between 1751 and 1785.[31] But he did not set foot in the House of Lords after September 1785 and left Ireland, never to return, in October 1786; so the last nine years of his primacy may be deducted from the twenty-nine mentioned by Chart. During his first twenty years he 'attended very regularly', being present for 'approximately 545' meetings of the House.[32] But attendance was measured on the basis of who was present for prayers (a very episcopal function) at the beginning of each day's sitting, not on the basis of who was there for all or most of the day. Moreover, attendance in this period was not unduly onerous, since parliament met, generally speaking, for only six months in every two years until 1784. In the intervening periods of a year and a half, Robinson was free to attend to his diocese and metropolitan province and, more to the point, go to London, Bath or 'some other English pool of Bethesda'. These prolonged absences in England should not be regarded as a matter of course: in 1765, Thomas Newton, one of the two English bishops who had been offered the primacy ahead of Robinson and had declined it, stated that, 'if he had accepted ..., it was his firm resolution to become a perfect Irishman ..., never to entertain a thought of returning even upon a visit to England, but ... there [Ireland] to have passed and ended his days.'[33]

had urged Buckinghamshire to appoint Robinson to the board. **28** Quoted in MacDonagh, op. cit., p. 4. **29** Euseby Cleaver to Charles O'Hara, 3 Oct. [1786], PRONI, T/2812/18/21; Adam Clarke (ed.), *Compendium edition of the lives of Bishop Newton, Rev. Philip Skelton, etc*, ii. 429. **30** Mohan, 'Archbishop Richard Robinson', p. 120; Phillips, *Church of Ireland*, iii. 245. **31** Robinson to Orde, 19 Jan. 1785, Bolton papers, NLI, Ms. 16350, ff. 71–2. **32** Mohan, op. cit., pp 121–2 and 124.

The question now arises: who, if not Robinson, was responsible for much of the ecclesiastical legislation of the period *c.*1780 onwards which 'the statute book evinces'. The answer, in the main, is Agar. Very conveniently, both Robinson and Agar have left lists of the legislative enactments for which they were respectively responsible.[34] Of the sixteen acts which Robinson sponsored, one made its predecessor perpetual and one amended another. In addition, one of Robinson's acts (*7 George III, cap. 21*) had to be amended by Agar's *35 George III, cap. 32*, which was an act 'to explain 3 George III, *cap.* 25, and 7 George III, *cap.* 21, *viz.* the summary tithe law'. Up to the Union, Agar credited himself with fourteen acts and two clauses, the earlier of the two clauses being sec. 17 of Robinson's act of 1772 for the 'erecting of new chapels of ease in parishes of large extent' in the diocese of Armagh and elsewhere (*11 and 12 George III, cap. 16*). The slight overlap between Robinson's and Agar's legislation may have caused historians to attribute a number of pre-1794 measures to Robinson when in fact they were the handiwork of Agar. The list of Robinson's acts is almost certainly exhaustive: the list of Agar's is not, because Agar erred on the side of under-statement. He seems to have excluded some ten acts to which he was a major contributor, but of which he was not the sole author – for example, two of the anti-Rightboy measures of 1787 in favour of the clergy (*27 George III, caps. 36 and 40*).[35] Robinson may not have been the sole author of any of the acts listed as his, for the good reason that he enjoyed, for almost the whole of his primacy, the expert assistance of two veteran ecclesiastical administrators and diocesan officials, Henry Upton, the diocesan and provincial registrar of Armagh, and Henry Meredyth, the agent for the archiepiscopal estate, a former Dublin Castle official and an M.P. for Armagh borough, 1776–89.[36] Agar

---

33 Adam Clarke (ed.), op. cit., ii. 155.   34 'Titles of the several acts of parliament passed at the instance of the late Primate Robinson', [1794?], Armagh diocesan registry papers, PRONI, DIO 4/11/5/1; 'A list [made in 1800] of the acts of parliament for ecclesiastical purposes prepared by Dr Charles Agar, Archbishop of Cashel', in Agar's 'state' of the diocese of Cashel, 1779–1801, 21 M 57/B6/1. The list of Robinson's acts given by Mohan (p. 124) is seriously incomplete.   35 Between 10 and 30 March of the previous year, Agar had drafted, with the assistance of Dr Stephen Radcliff, the judge of the prerogative court, a Clergy Compensation Bill (his autograph draft of this is possibly 21 M 57/B31/20). This was then set aside to make way for Hely-Hutchinson's alternative measure, which was introduced on 30 March, was much less satisfactory to the clergy and was eventually postponed to a distant day (Agar's account of these events is at 21 M 57/B31/20; see also Hely-Hutchinson to his son, 7 Apr. 1786, PRONI, Register of Irish Archives, Donoughmore papers, D/4, and Robinson to Agar, 1 July 1786, T/3719/C/20/15). In the following year, 1787, a Clergy Compensation Bill divested of the objectionable provisions of Hely-Hutchinson's, became law (*27 George III, cap. 36*), and Agar seems to have contributed to its drafting ('Scheme of indemnification given to Mr Orde', 19 Feb. 1787, 21 M 57/B31/21). In mid-February 1787, he had been invited to contribute to the Magistracy Bill (Orde to Agar, 14 Feb. 1787, T/3719/C/21/10), and the speech he made in support of it in the House of Lords in April suggests that he had been prominently involved (his *précis* of the speech is at 21 M 57/A42/31/2). It became law as *27 George III, cap. 40*. Moreover, a letter from Ellis to Agar of 10 Mar. 1787 (T/3719/C/21/12) suggests that Agar played a part in both measures. See also pp 548 and 577–8. For references to *all* the legislation in which Agar had or may have had a major hand, see under 'Agar' in the index.   36 History of the Irish Parliament database, *sub* 'Henry Meredyth'; Thomas Waite to Heron, 22 Dec. 1776, and Sackville Hamilton to Buckinghamshire, 12 Jan. 1778, Heron papers, NLI, Mss. 13034/5 and 13036/6.

enjoyed no such back-up. Significantly, the list of Robinson's acts is in Upton's handwriting, while the list of Agar's is in Agar's own.

However, the most important difference between Robinson's and Agar's acts is that the former were almost all local to the diocese of Armagh and/or uncontroversial, while the latter were general and almost always involved a high level of political difficulty, particularly when it came to getting them through the House of Commons. Even Robinson's ostensibly general acts had a strong local imperative. His last measure, passed in 1784 (*23 and 24 George III, cap. 49*), 'An act for making appropriate parishes belonging to archbishops and bishops perpetual cures, and the better to enable such archbishops and bishops to endow and augment the endowments of vicarages and curacies [therein]', was partly inspired by his generous intentions in regard to the Co. Louth part of his diocese (see below). Likewise, his previously discussed and misleadingly entitled act of 1772 'for rendering more effectual the several laws for the better enabling of the clergy, having cure of souls, to reside upon their benefices, and to build upon their respective glebes, and to prevent dilapidations' (*11 and 12 George III, cap. 17*), was partly passed for the decidedly less generous purpose of throwing the whole cost of his new palace upon his unfortunate successor (see pp 382–3). Typical of Robinson's legislative programme was his act of 1772 'to prevent burying dead bodies in churches' (*11 and 12 George III, cap. 22*) – a useful, uncontroversial, health-and-safety measure.

Although only one of Agar's measures, the clause which he contributed to one of Robinson's acts of 1772, fell within the twelve-year period which has been characterised as Robinson's prime, for part of that period Agar was in other respects establishing his credentials as 'infinitely the first ecclesiastic, if not the first man of business, in the House of Lords.' During one of the first attempted in-roads into the Penal Laws, the bill of 1772 allowing catholics to lend money to protestants on mortgage, Agar's speech in opposition to it on 22 May seems to have been decisive of its defeat by the narrow margin of two votes. In this speech, he not only took the line which might have been expected of a bishop, but also showed a grasp of the economics of the issue. Among other things, he argued that 'papists' did not invest in the linen manufacture, that they could not lend money in England on any different terms than in Ireland, and that it did not appear that they sent money to foreign countries; so what, he asked, was the authority for claiming that they were a 'monied people' at all?[37] 'The Popish Mortgage Bill' was reintroduced in the next session and (though in the end it was lost in the House of Lords in April 1774[38]) scraped through the Lords, after a strenuous debate, on 17 December 1773. Robinson headed the list of the Lords who entered a protest against the bill in the *Journals* of their House. The first paragraph of this protest raised the whole principle of the Penal Code and argued that 'every actual or virtual repeal of any part of those laws will encourage the spirit of popery, and in proportion ... lay a foundation for just apprehensions in the breasts of protestants,

37 Notes containing the substance of Agar's speech, 22 May 1772, 21 M 57/A5/5. 38 I am indebted for this information to Dr James Kelly.

especially as arguments were offered in support of this bill by some of the advocates of it, which may be considered as levelled against the whole system of Popery Laws.'[39] However, Robinson's primacy among the protestors was simply a matter of rank: Agar's papers include an autograph draft of the protest,[40] roughly but essentially corresponding to the printed version, and thus establishing that Agar was the author of the latter.

In view of Robinson's opposition to the 'Popish Mortgage Bill', a comparative side-issue, it is surprising to find that, when a radical dismemberment of the Penal Code as it restricted catholic landholding was mooted in the spring of 1778, his language was 'liberal and temperate.'[41] What was to become the Catholic Relief Act of 1778 (*17 and 18 George III, cap. 49*) was not a government measure, but was favoured by Dublin Castle with increasing overtness.[42] Robinson had already been showing a self-abasing amenability to the wishes of Buckinghamshire and his obscure and lightweight chief secretary, Heron (whom Robinson described as 'a man of so respectable a character'[43]). Plainly, Robinson had ulterior motives. For one thing, he wanted Buckinghamshire's backing in the power-struggle with Hely-Hutchinson over TCD (see pp 151–2) – though he disingenuously professed to seek and advise no more than official neutrality.[44] However, it must be suspected that his principal motive was the vacancies looming in both Cashel and Dublin, and that he was being 'liberal and temperate' about the Relief Bill with a view to dishing Agar, the strongest and, from Robinson's point of view, the most threatening candidate for either archbishopric. The politics of the Catholic Relief Bill of 1778 were extraordinarily complicated, particularly after the clause had been tacked on to it repealing the Sacramental Test against protestant dissenters.[45] So it would be over-simple to attribute the absence of formal protest from the bishops to Robinson's leadership or lack of leadership, the more so as other considerations, notably the parliamentary grant to the board of first fruits (see pp 224–5), had their due weight. But Robinson's current subservience to the administration and his intrigues against Agar must have played their part.

After Dublin had been filled to Robinson's liking in December 1778, his self-confidence as a politician soared and carried him far 'out of the line of my profession.' It was reported in April 1779 that 'The Primate has a very high opinion of Mr [Thomas] Kelly's fitness in all respects for the office of solicitor-general';[46] and later

39 Quoted in Mohan, op. cit., p. 125.   40 21 M 57/A5/3/1.   41 Buckinghamshire to Lord George Germain, 5 May 1778, NLI, Ms. 13036/8.   42 Buckinghamshire to Germain, 3 June 1778, and to North, 21 June 1778, NLI, Ms. 13036/11 and 12.   43 Robinson to Heron, 16 Dec. 1776, Ms. 13034/4; Richard Cumberland to Heron, 26 Apr. and 6 June 1777, Ms. 13035/5 and 7; Germain to Buckinghamshire, 5 Oct. 1777, Ms. 13035/12; and Buckinghamshire to North, 13 Oct. 1777, ibid. 44 Robinson to Buckinghamshire, 11 June 1777, Ms. 13035/7.   45 See pp 65 and 154–5. See also a series of letters from the Agarite under-secretary at the Castle, John Hamilton, to Heron, 20 June and 6, 14, [pre-15] and 23 July 1778, Ms. 13042. Hamilton was reporting back from a mission to London on which he had been sent in connection with the bill. The proposals he makes which involve Agar may be assumed to have been concerted with Agar in advance.   46 Heron to Buckinghamshire, 7 Apr. 1779, Ms. 13037/7. In light of subsequent events (*Clonmell diary, TCD*, p. 317), it looks as if Robinson was grooming Kelly as a rival to Agar's friend and ally, Scott.

in the year Robinson, in response to soundings from Lord Hillsborough, declared himself 'entirely for' the latter's pet project of a union.[47] But this period of political resurgence was short-lived. With Agar's promotion to Cashel against Robinson's wishes and intrigues, the predictions that Robinson would be eclipsed by Agar in both ability and influence were fulfilled. Robinson's own behaviour acknowledged the fact. At the cabinet or council meeting of 8 May 1780 held to consider the very difficult issue of the Irish Mutiny Bill, Agar's already-mentioned minute of the proceedings records that Robinson was present, but remained silent.[48] Earlier, at the beginning of February 1780, when the Church of Ireland bishops were mustering their forces for a last (and unavailing) attempt to defeat the second bill repealing the Test (*19 and 20 George III, cap. 6*), it was again Agar who took the lead – and tried to put some fight into Robinson. In a letter intended to be seen by Lord North, he wrote:

> I waited upon the Primate (who I knew to be an enemy upon principle to this bill), [and] stated to him the fatal consequences which seemed likely to me to arise out of it to this kingdom and the obvious embarrassment which it must occasion to the king's affairs in England [where the dissenters had for some time been agitating for the same relaxation]. I must here do his Grace the justice to say that his ardour to prevent the evil effects ... to this country did not exceed his anxious efforts to relieve English administration. ... We therefore determined to try whether we could not prevail on the bishops now in Dublin to apply by a joint letter to the Archbishop of Canterbury to use his endeavours in the privy council of England to suppress the bill, if that be possible ..., [or] to have it altered by the addition to the end of the bill of a clause which substitutes a declaration to be made by every person in lieu of the Sacramental Test.[49]

On 2 May, Agar, the Archbishop of Tuam and two bishops (one of them Robinson's old antagonist, Charles Jackson) – alone among the members of the House of Lords – recorded themselves as 'dissentient' when the bill passed the Lords, and Agar entered a solitary, additional protest.[50] Robinson held back. On other measures relating to the Church where Robinson co-operated with him – the protest of 19 August 1780 against the Tenantry Act (see pp 395–6) and of 3 May 1782 against the 'Act to permit marriages by dissenting teachers' – Robinson took precedence over him, but Agar's papers again show that Agar had taken the lead by drafting the protests.[51] On the issue of Gardiner's contemporary Catholic Relief Acts, which the bishops modified but did not oppose *in limine*, Agar was reported to be directing Robinson's conduct, and to be

47 Hillsborough to Buckinghamshire, 4 Oct. 1779, Ms. 13038/14. Hillsborough's conversation with Robinson had taken place earlier in the year. 48 Minute by Agar, 8 May 1780, T/3719/C/14/22A. 49 Agar to Macartney, 1 Feb. 1780, *Macartney in Ireland*, p. 327. Archbishop Fowler seconded these efforts – Fowler to Germain, 5 Feb. 1780, *HMC Stopford-Sackville Mss.*, i, pp 267–8; D'Alton, *Archbishops of Dublin*, p. 348. The Archbishop of Canterbury proposed this, or some such amendment, in the British privy council, but was out-voted – Heron to Buckinghamshire, 10 Mar. 1780, Ms. 13039/4. 50 *Lords' journals*, v. 171. 51 Ibid., pp 216–17 and 320–21; 21 M 57/A14/1 and B28/2.

stimulating him, and others, to (successful) opposition to the first version of the Education Bill (see p. 327).[52]

Robinson's renunciation of his leadership role as primate – in fact, his cession of it to Agar – certainly did not derive from any spirit of toleration. His attitude to the Irish catholics – notwithstanding the 'liberal and temperate' sentiments he had affected in 1778 – actually became increasingly hardline. In January 1765, it had been alleged – a little fancifully – that his appointment was 'highly acceptable by the commonality who, being mostly Roman catholics, naturally preferred the moderate principles of an Englishman to the early Protestant bigotry a Scotchman or an Irishman imbibes.'[53] But, over the years, Robinson's supposedly 'moderate principles' gave way to something approaching alarmist extremism. From the early 1780s, he spent an increasing amount of time, and from 1786 all of his time, in possibly hypochondriacal retreat in England, spreading more gloom and despondency than even the Irish situation merited – or, as John Scott put it in 1784, 'croaking all manner of discontent.'[54] At about the same time, the then lord lieutenant, Rutland (who was himself fairly inventive of popish plots), remarked impatiently: 'The Primate, with the utmost zeal for the good of the two kingdoms, is too apt to despond; [and] his prejudices against the Roman catholics increase his apprehensions.'[55] The hostile reaction of British ministers to Robinson's 'croaking' was stronger. In the years when the policy of Catholic Relief gathered momentum in British governmental circles, the views of the Primate of All Ireland on the subject could, with a facility dangerous to the Church, be dismissed as those of a crank.

Robinson's departure from Ireland for good (as it turned out) in 1786, could not have been worse-timed. The period 1785–8 was that of the Rightboy disturbances and their aftermath, and the aftermath included the mild and vague proposals by government in 1786 for the improvement of clerical performance and the reform of the tithe system (see pp 480–1 and 536–9), and the substantive and more sweeping proposals of the same nature in 1788.[56] Robinson's jealousy of and uneasy relations with Agar told against united episcopal action. So did his highly regrettable choice of Fowler as his second-in-command. Fowler's shortcomings, which had commended him to Robinson because they meant that Fowler was no threat to him, made Fowler a malleable instrument in the hands of a forceful lord lieutenant like Lord Buckingham. This meant that the role of champion of the interests of the Church of Ireland devolved on Agar. Though he has been represented as a time-server by subsequent detractors, Agar was not afraid to quarrel with Dublin Castle and even with the British government when the wellbeing (as he conceived it) of the Church seemed to him to be at stake. Writing later and in another context, in May 1797, an admirer of Agar remarked that, 'however *other great ecclesiastics* might adjust their politics to those of their patrons

52 Wall, 'The making of Gardiner's Relief Act[s], 1781–2', pp 140 and 144; James, *Lords of the Ascendancy*, pp 139–40.   53 Mohan, 'Archbishop Richard Robinson', pp 97–8, quoting a letter of 26 January from the countess of Moira.   54 Scott, now Lord Earlsfort, to Agar, 1 Nov. 1784, T/3719/C/18/40; Malcomson, *John Foster*, p. 440.   55 Rutland to Sydney, 7 Oct. 1784, *HMC Rutland Mss.*, iii. 141.   56 See pp 230–40 and MacDonagh, op. cit., pp 9–42.

[possibly a reference to Primate Newcome and Lord Fitzwilliam], the *Rock of Cashel* was not to be moved by any such considerations.'[57] It is possible that, consciously or sub-consciously, Robinson absented himself in part because he felt overshadowed by 'the Rock of Cashel.' Agar, however, needed Robinson, because of Robinson's rank and authority and the independence of government which they gave him, and because of the impossibility of looking for leadership to Fowler. Everything in Agar's correspondence, and not just in his letters to Robinson, suggests that he was scrupulous in giving Robinson his place as primate, looked to Robinson for the exercise of his primatial authority, and only became highly irritated when Robinson failed to give directions or assistance to those on the spot.

Part of a long letter which Agar wrote in mid-January 1788 to Robinson (who at this stage had already been absent for over a year[58]) has been quoted *in extenso* (pp 232–4). That part related to Buckingham's ideas for legislation to enforce clerical residence by means other than episcopal authority. This was only one of a quiverful of proposals from Dublin Castle.[59] From the letters which Robinson wrote to Agar from Bath during 1787, it soon became clear how much help Robinson was going to be in a situation which he admitted was 'alarming.' In late January, he declined to be involved in the drafting of measures to compensate the clergy for their losses of tithe income in 1786 and to restore order in Munster, making the excuse 'that my opinion might be misapprehended and of course not truly represented', and that the matter should be 'left ... to the wisdom and prudence of government.'[60] Accordingly, the Clergy Compensation, the Whiteboy and the Magistracy Acts were passed with a considerable contribution from Agar (see p. 444) and none from Robinson. In December, Agar submitted to him Agar's proposal (see p. 227) that the purposes of the parliamentary grant to the board of first fruits should be broadened. Rejecting this proposal for 'prudential reasons', Robinson concluded: 'This is my decided opinion ... . But I mention it to you only at present, as I shall not interpose in the business unless I find it necessary to give my opinion.'[61] This of course was a subject on which the Primate of All Ireland's opinion should not have been a secret; nor should such an important initiative have had to come from the archbishop who was only third in seniority within the Church of Ireland. In his next letter (acknowledging Agar's detailed report of Agar's audience with Buckingham), Robinson – instead of praising Agar's political courage – actually had the nerve to suggest that Agar should have said more! 'It would not have been improper, before you quitted the room, if you had desired him to inform you what were the measures he proposed to adopt to check the violent and oppressive spirit which is the evil of the present hour and which [?threatneth] the being of the Established Church.'[62]

In spite of the crass insensitivity of this remark, and the contrast between the course which Robinson recommended to Agar and that which he pursued himself,

57 'H.G.M.', Templemore, Co. Tipperary, to Agar, 21 May 1797, T/3719/C/31/58.   58 Robinson to Agar, 27 Jan. 1787, T/3719/C/21/9.   59 Agar to Robinson, 15 Jan. 1788, T/3719/C/22/1.   60 Robinson to Agar, 27 Jan. 1787, T/3719/C/21/9.   61 Robinson to Agar, 9 Dec. 1787, T/3719/C/21/41.   62 Robinson to Agar, 30 Jan. 1788, T/3719/C/22/3.

Agar continued to seek guidance from Robinson. One of the next issues to be discussed was the visitorial, or rather inquisitorial, demand for a return to be made to the chief secretary's office of the state of each diocese (see p. 239). Responding to Agar's call for leadership and action, Robinson wrote at the end of January 1788: 'I have strong objections to a compliance with this article. ... But, as I am absent, I believe I shall do nothing, unless upon a fresh application. Was I in Dublin, I would frame such a return as I understood would be satisfactory to the L[ord] L[ieutenant] and deliver it to him.'[63] Events then moved too fast for reference to Robinson to be possible. Two separate bills were introduced, one after the other, into the House of Commons – the first fixing the tithe on hemp at 5s. per acre (and threatening a similar modus on flax and other items), and the second exempting from tithe for seven years 'barren lands' which were in the process of being improved. Agar, who had agreed to accept the first bill if it were confined to hemp only and were couched in such terms as precluded its being used as a precedent for other commutations, was eventually successful in persuading Buckingham to adhere to this compromise. On the second bill, however, over which there had been no previous negotiation between the bishops and the Castle, and which was brought forward by Henry Grattan without warning, Agar led a successful opposition in the House of Lords. He carried an amendment giving to the ecclesiastical courts sole jurisdiction in disputes over what constituted barrenness and improvement. This was, in effect, a wrecking amendment, and the Commons sulkily dropped the bill on its return to that House.[64]

Writing to Welbore Ellis in mid-April, Agar commented:

> I am not without serious apprehensions for what may happen in another session of parliament. The Primate's absence and the part which the Archbishop of D[ublin] has taken in all these matters, together with the desertion of two or three more of the b[isho]ps [William Beresford and Richard Marlay], must give our enemies such encouragement as cannot fail to produce various attempts to invade the property of the Church. Hitherto, we have, I thank God, defended ourselves, though with great difficulty. But to me it seems very doubtful how long we may be able to do so.[65]

Predictably, Buckingham reacted to the modification or loss of these measures by pressing on with preparations for the Clerical Residence Bill which he had already adumbrated to Agar (see pp 232–4) and which he intended to introduce in the next session of parliament.[66] Robinson acknowledged that this 'critical situation of ... affairs in Ireland requires my fullest exertions', but pleaded that he was 'disabled from undertaking a journey to Ireland and am directed to return to the hot wells at Bristol.' As has been seen (pp 235), he advised Agar to prepare two forestalling measures, a

63 Ibid.   64 [Rev.] Horace Townsend to Agar, 22 Mar. 1788, Dean Thomas Graves to Agar, 27 Mar. 1788, and the Bishop of Killala to Agar, 30 Mar. 1788, T/3719/C/22/5, 7 and 8; MacDonagh, op. cit., pp 27–30.   65 Agar to Ellis, 13 Apr. 1788, T/3719/C/22/11.   66 Agar to Robinson, 8 May 1788, T/3719/C/22/15.

Barren Lands Bill containing proper safeguards for tithes, and a bill to regulate faculties (i.e. restrain non-residence), and seek to obtain Buckingham's approbation of them before worse befell.[67] On this as on other occasions, Robinson showed that, even in his old age, he was a flexible and resourceful political tactician. However, he declined to take a lead and make himself unpopular in any influential quarter.

To what extent his illness was genuine and to what extent assumed, is hard to establish. A myth has gained currency that he had been seriously ill in 1769. But this is based on a misreading by Sir John Gilbert of the date of a letter which he published in 1881 in an *H.M.C. Report*: the illness referred to was in fact the last illness of Primate Stone in December 1764.[68] The 'regimen', 'diet' and course of 'physic' attributed to Robinson in the early 1770s by Richard Cumberland, which included numerous 'rhubarb pills' and fighting off 'the bile with raw eggs and mutton broth mixed up with muscovado sugar',[69] suggest that he was a hypochondriac. Robinson may have taken after his elder brother, William, who succeeded to the family baronetcy in 1777 and whom Cumberland described as 'a feeble, infirm man and a real valetudinarian.' In October 1785, Robinson's fellow-Yorkshireman, Bishop Hotham, feared the effects on Robinson of the death of 'Sir William Robinson, ... [his] only surviving brother. This, from the extreme regard subsisting all their lives between them, I fear will shock *my friend* fundamentally, ... [who may] droop and exchange this life for a better.'[70] Others took Robinson's drooping state less seriously. John Scott, as has been mentioned (p. 137), thought that the 74-year-old Robinson was 'a very tough incumbent, in fine preservation'; and it was noteworthy that, in the years of Robinson's absence from Ireland, he always 'kept a hospitable table.'[71] In late November 1786, Chief Secretary Orde, who had 'had much conversation ... to no great purpose' with Robinson in Bath during Robinson's first weeks away from Ireland, saw no reason why Robinson should not return to London for a discussion with the prime minister, Pitt, on the Rightboys and Church reform, and then to Ireland to do his duty there. Rutland felt the same, and Pitt intended to 'make a point of it.'[72] All three were, of course, to be disappointed.

Thereafter, the major source of information about Robinson's health is Welbore Ellis' letters to Agar which, since Ellis was himself inclined to be a *malade imaginaire*, ought perhaps to be taken at a discount. In mid-May 1787, Ellis wrote: 'I am very sorry to understand that my old friend, the Primate, has had an unpleasant attack of either gravel or stone. This is indeed a lamentable event, as it will make the reminder of his life probably very painful, and he has been induced to try a quack medicine which has made his case worse. He is, as I am informed, at present at Clifton, near

67 Robinson to Agar, 23 May 1788, and Agar to Robinson, 2 June 1788, T/3719/C/22/19 and 22.
68 W.G. Hamilton to Hely-Hutchinson, 2 Dec. 1769 [*sic* – 1764], *HMC Emly/Pery Mss.*, p. 191. Mohan, 'Archbishop Richard Robinson', p. 104, and Simms, 'Primate Robinson', p. 145, follow Gilbert into error. 69 Quoted in Mohan, 'Archbishop Richard Robinson', p. 129. 70 Hotham to Hotham Thompson, 5 Oct. 1785, PRONI, T/3429/2/9. 71 Scott to Agar, 19 May 1783, T/3719/C/17/15; *DNB, sub* 'Robinson'. 72 Orde to Rutland, 28 Nov. 1786, *HMC Rutland Mss.*, iii, pp 358–9.

Bristol Wells.'73 In March 1788, he returned to London, 'as I understand, in good health', but has not as yet fixed any time for his departure.'74 By late May, however, Robinson was 'firmly convinced of the impossibility of performing the journey [to Ireland]. To say the truth, he is much altered ..., is grown pale and languid, can't bear going about the streets in a carriage, declines very much the dining from home, and when in company has not his usual spirits.'75 Then, in late August:

> The reason he [Robinson] alleges why he cannot go to Ireland, though he might reach Holyhead by easy journeys, is that the sea always brought on convulsive spasms, and he is fully persuaded that it would now revive those dreadful spasms in his bladder, which he thinks of with horror. Besides, whether he moves from Bristol to London or back again, he never is far from skilful advice and assistance, if he should be stopped on the road by one of the paroxysms of his complaint, but if that happened in Wales he thinks he might perish in tortures. But the less able he may think himself for going there, the more strongly is he called upon for exerting himself here, where I think he might do most essential service.76

While Ellis tried to prevail on Robinson to render 'essential service' by speaking to Pitt and/or the King, Agar continued to endeavour to induce him to write to Buckingham or to make some public declaration for Irish consumption. He argued at the beginning of June:

> I entirely agree with your Grace that, if a proper [Barren Lands] Bill of this kind ... should be drawn and submitted to the lord lieutenant, it would probably be accepted and supported, and prevent many crude and improper plans from being obtruded upon us. ... [But] why should you not *yourself* transmit it to his Excellency for his consideration? He would probably accept such a bill coming from you and to be supported by your brethren, much rather than hazard the success of one not sanctioned by such authority.77

Robinson, though he talked big, was not willing to take any step so decisive. However, when referring in July 1788 to the Barren Lands Bill which Agar had succeeded in fatally amending, Robinson boasted (again with crass insensitivity) that 'if *he* had been on the spot, he should not have attempted to have only amended or qualified it, but would have opposed it directly and done his utmost to have it thrown out.'78 To Ellis, Robinson reported that

> he had two long conferences with his brother of L[ambe]th, who ... suggested, after he had perused the circular and plan of reform whether, as [the]

73 Ellis to Agar, 19 May 1787, T/3719/C/21/19.   74 Ellis to Agar, 19 Mar. 1788, and Dr Stephen Radcliff [judge of the prerogative court] to Agar, 6 May 1788, T/3719/C/22/4 and 13.   75 Ellis to Agar, 26 May 1788, T/3719/C/22/20.   76 Ellis to Agar, 25 Aug. 1788, T/3719/C/22/32.   77 Agar to Robinson, 2 June 1788, T/3719/C/22/22.   78 Ellis to Agar, 12 June and 25 July 1788,

P[rimate]'s health would not permit him to go over, he would not do the next-best service in his power by explaining fully to the M[inister, Pitt] the importance of the subject and prevent him from being misled by other representations and induced to adopt measures from which it might be difficult to recede. [The] P[rimate] replied that *he* had a great difficulty in his way, for hitherto the L[ord] L[ieutenant] had acted towards him with the appearance of some confidence and of some consideration, which he should endeavour to make use of to dissuade or divert him from the most objectionable parts of his plan ..., but ... if he should go to the M[inister] ..., he should lose all means of doing good in one quarter and perhaps in both.[79]

Ellis subsequently ascertained from Archbishop Moore of Canterbury that the latter did not agree with Robinson in this delicacy.

At this point Agar lost his temper, and wrote Robinson a letter which began with the following (by late eighteenth-century standards) strong language:

> To the three last letters which I wrote to your Grace I have not had the honour of receiving any answer: a circumstance which would certainly prevent me from troubling you again on any subject but that of the Church of Ireland, over which your Grace presides and which in the first instance is committed to your care. Personal respect for your Grace and for your station has hitherto determined me to solicit your opinion on all matters of importance, and not to commit myself in any measure of consequence to the welfare or government of the Church without first knowing your sentiments. ... I wish much to know your Grace's final opinion on this subject, that I may regulate my conduct accordingly, on which probably that of some others may depend.[80]

Robinson replied huffily: 'My means of information in every respect, particularly as to the temper of the Castle, in my present situation, [were] very imperfect. ... If you cannot make allowance for these and many other similar circumstances arising from my absence and the fluctuating state of my health, our correspondence will no longer be confidential or satisfactory to either of us.'[81] He persisted in his already exploded view that it was better for the Church that he preserve his flimsy relationship with Buckingham and communicate privately with the latter to the exclusion of the rest of the bishops. Agar, perforce, had to content himself with this final evasion. He continued to correspond with Robinson over tactics and measures for the next session of parliament, and even wrote to him at the end of October:

> As I have reason to suspect that much pains have been taken [by Buckingham] to misrepresent my conduct where I most wish to have it rightly understood

T/3719/C/22/24 and 31.   **79** Ellis to Agar, 25 July 1788, T/3719/C/22/31.   **80** Agar to Robinson, 11 Oct. 1788, T/3719/C/22/35.   **81** Robinson to Agar, 18 Oct. 1788, T/3719/C/22/37.

[in the eyes of the King], I place a full confidence in your Grace's wisdom and justice ... for a fair and impartial statement of my conduct ..., [which] has been productive of many serious inconveniences to me, which I might have escaped as easily as others, had I been equally indifferent to the true interests of the Church of Ireland.[82]

It is unlikely that Agar expected Robinson to do anything of the sort: rather, the passage must surely be interpreted as implying that Robinson was one of those who had 'escaped ... many serious inconveniences' through being 'indifferent to the true interests of the Church of Ireland.'

The danger to the Church in the next session of parliament which Agar had foretold, and to which Robinson's pusillanimity materially contributed, evaporated for the time being because of the Regency Crisis of 1788–9. Between 1790 and 1794 (the year of Robinson's death), the danger took a new form. Now it was the British government's Catholic Relief measures, first enacted for Britain in 1791 and then, more radically, for Ireland in 1792–3. A letter to Agar of early February 1792 about the Catholic Relief Bill of that year, shows that Robinson was still up to his old tricks. The writer was Bishop Woodward of Cloyne, who was at Bath at the same time as Robinson:

The moment is an awful one, beyond any I ever saw. ... I urged [on Robinson], as far as I could with propriety, the great importance that it would be of ... that his opinions, expressed to me repeatedly, should be known in Ireland. I even went so far as to urge that he would authorise some person to declare them, as *commissioned* by him. This he declined, as not wishing to assume so much, but said that he thought, and *did not desire to keep his opinion secret*, that the [proposed] concessions to the Roman catholics ... *would endanger the protestant interest in Ireland.* Being determined to know how far I had his permission to go, I asked whether I was at liberty to mention so much to a friend by letter. He said I was at liberty. The best use I can make of this liberty is to inform your Grace.[83]

To his son-in-law, Woodward wrote more freely. 'The Primate croaks if possible more than I do.'[84] 'I have sent my proxy to the Archbishop of Cashel, on whom I depend for a strenuous opposition to it [the bill]. The Primate thinks it will have been thrown out.'[85] In other words, Robinson 'croaked' but was not prepared to do anything except hope for the best. By September 1792, both Woodward and he feared that there would be disturbances in Ireland and consequent non-payment of rent, and the public-spirited resolution which both adopted was to instruct their respective agents to send over to Bath as much spare cash as possible.[86]

82 Agar to Robinson, 30 Oct. 1788, T/3719/C/22/39.   83 Woodward to Agar, 2 Feb. 1792, T/3719/C/26/2.   84 Woodward to Brodrick, 15 Jan. 1792, Midleton papers, NLI, Ms. 8870/2. 85 Woodward to Brodrick, 18 Feb. 1792, ibid.   86 Woodward to Brodrick, 30 Sep. 1792, Ms.

This demonstration of mercenariness, which it will be argued (pp 490–91) was characteristic of the Englishmen on the Irish bench, provides the clue to a better understanding of Robinson. Robinson's fabled (in all senses) expenditure on Armagh City and the diocese of Armagh was smaller than has hitherto been realised. The best source of information about his buildings, benefactions and will is still Stuart's *Armagh*. According to Stuart's figures, and subject to the deduction of the *c.*£18,000 reimbursed by Newcome for the palace (which Stuart did not know about), Robinson in his lifetime and by the terms of his will spent no more than *c.*£18,000 on Armagh.[87] This was of course a large sum; and of course Robinson had not been under any obligation to spend anything. But it should be weighed in the balance against the *c.*£75,000 (at least) in income which Robinson drew between 1786 and 1794 from the diocese he never saw. The accuracy of the nett figure of *c.*£18,000 depends upon the accuracy of the gross figure of £41,000 given by Stuart for Robinson's benefactions to Armagh. This was certainly a complex calculation, and it would be interesting to know how Stuart handled various problem items.[88] However, it is reasonable to assume that, since Stuart was very favourable to Robinson and was writing at a time when there were still plenty of Robinson *protégés* about whom he could consult and whose information would also be favourable, Stuart is likely to have erred on the side of over-statement.

A special problem of interpretation attaches to the £5,000 which Robinson, famously, left for the establishment of a university in Armagh. During life, he had often maintained that 'The establishment of another university is the only permanent provision for the preservation of the Established Religion and indeed of the protestant interest in Ireland' and that, without such a foundation, 'the teachers of the Established Religion will be the most illiterate teachers of the people in the kingdom.'[89] Yet, the £5,000 which he actually provided for its endowment, was obviously inadequate to the purpose, and Robinson must have known that nothing would happen unless far more than matching finance were found elsewhere. A detailed scheme of endowment and incorporation which was drawn up (by Chief Secretary Pelham in 1795–8) depended for its viability on a number of extremely doubtful expedients: the probably illegal raiding of the funds of other educational charities; the appropriation of the incomes of one living in each of the dioceses in the metropolitan province of Armagh; and the distortion (again probably illegal) of Robinson's intentions by opening the university, its scholarships, fellowships and professorships, to dissenters.[90] Not surprisingly, these various expedients raised as many enemies to the scheme (including

8870/3. **87** Stuart, *Armagh*, pp 444–57. **88** For a full discussion of this point, see Malcomson, 'Primate Robinson' (in preparation). **89** Robinson to Agar, 29 Apr. 1787, T/3719/C/21/17. For the background to this declaration, see James Kelly, 'The context and course of Thomas Orde's plan of education of 1787', in *The Irish Journal of Education*, xx, no. 1 (1986), p. 19. **90** Rev. Thomas Carpendale, master of Armagh royal school, 1786–1817, came up with a scheme which, though blatantly self-interested, was more practical and less controversial than Pelham's – Carpendale to Newcome, 26 Mar. and 10 Apr. 1799, Stuart papers, Bedfordshire RO, WY 994/2–4.

Newcome) as they did funds. Under the terms of Robinson's will, the bequest was due to lapse in five years if the university had not been incorporated within that time. The Irish government remained sympathetic to Pelham's revamping of the proposal. The British government, however, thought it 'utterly impracticable' and rejected it in late August 1799, when there was just a month to go.[91] In a long letter of rejection, the home secretary, Portland, raised the fundamental objection (which he may have got from Agar) that 'the Primate would [never] have contributed in any manner whatever to the establishment of an institution for the encouragement of schismatics and separatists from the Church.'[92] The £5,000 thus reverted to Robinson's family, and therefore has not been included in the figure of c.£18,000 at which Robinson's benefactions to the diocese of Armagh have been tentatively set. Stuart, whose purpose was to establish the extent of Robinson's generosity, almost certainly included the £5,000 in his total.

As a childless man, Robinson was in the same category as those other great benefactors of the Church in the eighteenth century, Archbishops King, Boulter and Bolton, John Stearne, bishop of Clogher, 1717–45, and Richard Pococke, bishop of Ossory, 1756–65. While bishop of Derry, King bought for the diocese the library of his predecessor, Ezekiel Hopkins, and contributed to the cost of a building in which to accommodate it. While archbishop of Dublin, he founded and endowed a chair of divinity at TCD, and in the course of his 'parochial reformation' of the diocese of Dublin, sometimes purchased land for glebes himself and in general set 'a good example to the wealthy by generous contributions from his own purse.' In addition to these benefactions during his lifetime, he left all his property, to the value of nearly £17,000, to public charities when he died in 1729.[93] According to Stuart, Boulter's 'charitable donations amounted, in the kingdom of Ireland alone, to above £40,000.'[94] Bolton's benefactions have been discussed (pp 292, 304, 337, 347–8 and 382). Stearne, among other acts of remarkable generosity, 'financed the completion of Clogher cathedral ..., provided capital to the ... [board of] first fruits to purchase glebes and impropriations for resident incumbents ..., [paid for] a printing-house and ten annual exhibitions [at TCD]' and left his books to Marsh's Library, Dublin. By his will, 'he disposed of about £50,000 in charity.' This computation almost certainly excluded the capital value of the Middletown estate, Co. Armagh, which he left as an endowment to the Stearne charity, Middletown, and which had a rental of £1,226 per annum in 1820.[95]

91 Fisher and Robb, *Belfast Academical Institution*, pp 24–9. **92** Portland to Cornwallis, 31 Aug. 1799, *Castlereagh correspondence*, ii, pp 381–6. **93** Matteson, *King and his library*, p. 253; Phillips, *Church of Ireland*, iii, pp 176 and 182–4; Kennedy, 'Dublin and Glendalough', p. 125. **94** Stuart, *Armagh*, p. 427; papers about Boulter's (and Primate Marsh's) bequests of money to augment small livings and provide houses and pensions for the widows of deserving clergymen, 1711–1808, DIO 4/9/1 and DIO/4/11/2; *29 George II, cap. 18, sec. 5*; Acheson, *Church of Ireland*, p. 75. **95** Copies of the will of Bishop Stearne and of the act giving effect to his charitable bequests, 1744 and 1773, with tenants' petitions, correspondence, rentals, accounts, leases, etc., 1776–1822, DIO 4/9/5/1–9; Acheson, *Church of Ireland*, p. 82 (which includes the unfortunate misprint that Stearne left '£50,000' to St Werburgh's Church, Dublin, when in fact the sum was £50); Leslie, *Clogher Clergy and parishes* ... (Enniskillen, 1929), p. 17; Phillips, *Church of Ireland*, iii, pp 191, 219–20 and 222.

Pococke, in addition to restoring St Canice's Cathedral in his lifetime, 'left his whole estate to the incorporated society at Lintown', Co. Kilkenny, an industrial school with an essentially proselytising agenda.[96] If the comparison is extended into the nineteenth century, it must bring into the reckoning Primate Beresford, the most munificent childless prelate in Church of Ireland history, who is supposed to have given during the forty years of his primacy 'in excess of £280,000 to religious and charitable objects.'[97]

Compared to these other childless benefactors, Robinson gave 'a widow's mite, ... [not] a bachelor's bounty'.[98] This was because he went out of his way to finance and endow two not-very-close relations and their respective dynasties of Robinson. He himself was the last survivor of the eight Robinson brothers, not one of whom had produced a son. The eldest brother, Sir Thomas Robinson, 1st Bt, an uncontrollable amateur architect and spendthrift, had eventually succeeded in alienating the family estate. Placed under trusteeship by his brothers in 1742, and packed off to be governor of Barbados from then until 1747, he had committed fresh extravagances on his return, until it became necessary in 1769 to sell Rokeby Park. Robinson 'was much chagrined and displeased.'[99] This was because that estate would no longer be available for the support of the family baronetcy and of Robinson's Irish barony of Rokeby, when both titles passed by special remainders at Robinson's death to his second cousin, Matthew. Accordingly, Robinson left Matthew Robinson £10,000 to purchase a replacement estate in Yorkshire, and a total of £9,000–plus in legacies to other members and connections of the Robinson family in England.[100] This was not really necessary. The next Lord Rokeby already had a Yorkshire estate called West Layton (near Rokeby Park), and a house and estate at Mount Norris, Kent; and he or a subsequent lord was also almost certain to succeed to the large estates, in Yorkshire and elsewhere, which Mrs Elizabeth Montagu had been left by her husband in 1775.[101] So, there already were replacements for the loss of Rokeby Park. In any case, none of the English Robinsons was Robinson's principal heir and residuary legatee. This was the Rev. John Freind (1754–1832), the son of Robinson's sister, Grace. Robinson had already provided well for this nephew out of Robinson's patronage as primate, making him prebendary of Tynan (diocese of Armagh) in 1778, archdeacon of Armagh in 1786, registrar of the prerogative court, etc. But he also settled on Freind (possibly in 1793, when Freind changed his name to Robinson) his long-leasehold estate in Co. Louth. He had spent an estimated £30,000–plus in the mid-1780s acquiring it, and a definite £30,000 in the late 1780s building on it Rokeby Hall, near Dunleer, and a series of model farmhouses. This outlay was over three times his nett benefactions

---

96 *DNB*, *sub* 'Pococke'; Neely, *Kilkenny*, p. 154. 97 Canon. W.E.C. Fleming, *Armagh clergy, 1800– 2000* ... (Dundalk, 2001), p. 37. 98 Quoted in Cowper, *Deans of Canterbury*, p. 63. 99 Draft deeds of trust from Sir Thomas Robinson to his brothers, 1742, Barrington & Son papers, PRONI, D/3805/2A/1–2; Stuart, *Armagh*, p. 452. 100 Abstract of part of Robinson's will, printed in Stuart, *Armagh*, pp 454–6nn. 101 Betty Rizzo, *Companions without vows: relationships among eighteenth-century British women* (Athens, Georgia, 1994), p. 117. Professor Rizzo's study of Mrs Montagu reveals that she was a hard, cold, adulation-seeking woman; so perhaps this was a Robinson characteristic.

to Armagh. Equally telling, the rental of the Louth estate stood at £2,264 per annum in 1839[102] – an income fully adequate to support the baronetcy conferred on the nephew in 1819. In short, Chart was quite mistaken in his view that Robinson, because he was 'a bachelor ..., devoted all his savings to his projects.'

For this and other reasons, it is clear that Robinson's 'most distinguished and remarkable merits'[103] have been over-rated. Flattery set in early – partly at Robinson's own instigation. Stuart, as well as Young, is a case in point. Stuart involves himself in the following euphemisms about Robinson: 'Lord Rokeby, has not, we believe, enriched the republic of letters by any important works of his own composition. The sermons which he sometimes preached were, both in style and in doctrine most excellent, but his voice was low and indistinctly heard.'[104] In plain English, he wrote nothing, and his few sermons were inaudible! In his prime, he was 'a colossal man', tall and stately, with a magnificent bearing and 'a penetrating eye.'[105] He knew how to deploy these attributes to the best effect, and it may well be that people like Lords Hillsborough and Buckinghamshire who praised his judgement, *gravitas* and statesmanship, mistook appearance for reality. The mistake was easily made, because – as has recently been argued – Robinson seems to have deliberately cultivated his image. He was painted three times by Reynolds (setting aside a number of variants of the second and third portraits). The first, painted in 1758, when Robinson was still in his first bishopric, Killala, shows a cold, proud, inscrutable and calculating man. Not until the second (1763) and, particularly, the third (1775) is the expression softened by benignity, real or affected. The second shows the benign scholar among his books – the image of Robinson for which the late Primate Simms fell; the third shows the benign improver in his landscape.[106] But was Robinson benign at all? Richard Cumberland, who struggled to think the best of his host during his visit to Armagh *c.*1772–4, clearly thought not – as his famous and already-quoted (p. 352) description of Robinson's arrogant and inhospitable behaviour to his clergy amply demonstrates. Horace Walpole called Robinson 'proud and superficial', and a modern commentator 'distant ..., somewhat proud and a little dull.'[107] The distantness and formality may

---

102 Robinson estate account, 1839, PRONI, D/3805/2C/10; Malcomson, *John Foster*, p. 18; Bence-Jones, *Irish country houses*, p. 245; and Stuart, *Armagh*, pp 452–3. From the mid-1780s on, Robinson's church-building and parochial endowing were focussed on the neighbourhood of the Rokeby Hall estate. So it might be appropriate to regard these benefactions as reflecting his role as a landowner and founder of an Irish family rather than as a diocesan. **103** Hillsborough to Buckinghamshire, 20 Jan. 1777, *HMC Lothian Mss.*, p. 298. **104** Stuart, *Armagh*, p. 454. **105** Mohan, 'Archbishop Richard Robinson', p. 130; Simms, 'Primate Robinson', p. 139. **106** Coleman, 'Reynolds and Robinson', pp 131–6; Mrs Reginald Lane Poole, *Catalogue of portraits in the possession of the university, colleges, city and county of Oxford*, iii (Oxford, 1926), pp 74–5 (I am indebted for this reference to Dr T.C. Barnard); Nicholas Penny (ed.), *Reynolds* [R.A. exhibition catalogue] (London, 1986), p. 57. In suggesting that the 1763 Reynolds portrait of Robinson may have been intended as a kind of advertisement of Robinson for the primacy, Coleman perhaps forgets that Stone and Robinson were contemporaries. Could Stone's death at the end of 1764 have been foreseen early in 1763? **107** Simms, 'Primate Robinson', pp 140–1; Mohan, 'Archbishop Richard Robinson', p. 129.

also have masked insecurity: Robinson ordered all his personal papers and correspondence to be destroyed[108] – an action which surely betrays a want of confidence in his own views and actions. The distantness and formality certainly denoted a lack of any sense of humour. There does not appear to be any recorded instance of Robinson's cracking a joke. In June 1787, when contradicting a rumour that he was dying at Bath, Mrs Agar said that he was reputedly 'alive and *merry*',[109] and the fact that she underlined 'merry' speaks for itself.

Robinson, plainly, did not deserve Primate Simms' often-quoted tribute that, as primate, he 'was a public rather than a political figure', or Mant's conclusion that he did not take 'a prominent part in the political administration of affairs.'[110] It is true that, because of changed political circumstances, he was not formally involved in the government of the country, as his predecessors had been; nor did he personally follow the bad example of his immediate predecessor, Stone, by setting himself up as a party leader. It was not in him to be a party leader. He was probably bad at thinking on his feet; and, where Stone had shown the most amazing resilience, Robinson disliked opposition, confrontation and getting hard knocks. When confronted, he tended to back off, as he did with Bedford in 1761, with Hely-Hutchinson (after Robinson's ally and activist, Attorney-General Tisdall, died in 1777), and with Agar (once Robinson had failed to block Agar's promotion to an archbishopric in 1779). He resembled Stone, however, in his 'Machiavellian cunning and hypocrisy'; and many examples of his practising of these arts have been given.

He was also far from being above the lowest political manoeuvres – as witness his passion for exploiting bishops' boroughs. The cases of Old Leighlin in 1761 and Armagh in 1768 have been cited. But Robinson's weakness for parliamentary patronage did not end there. The suspicion that he was implicated in Bishop Cope's electioneering in Old Leighlin in 1783 and 1787, has already been mentioned (p. 183). Of the MPs whom Robinson himself chose for Armagh borough in 1783, one, Colonel George Rawson, later 'gave several votes against' the Castle on the Regency in February–March 1789; the other, Henry Meredyth, either absented himself deliberately or, more probably, was too old and ill to attend (either way, he was no help to the government).[111] Robinson was at this time understandably incensed at Buckingham's assault on the Church. But he wrote most disingenuously from Bath in mid-March 1789, in response to Buckingham's request that he assist with his proxy to defeat the

> strong party ... formed in opposition to the administration of the king's government in Ireland ... . My disposition to resist such a mischievous combination by every means in my power cannot be doubted. I will not therefore attempt to describe the great anxiety of my mind, when I acquaint

108 Simms, 'Primate Robinson', pp 140–41. 109 Mrs Agar to Lord Macartney, 16 June 1787, Macartney papers, PRONI, D/572/9/9. 110 Simms, 'Primate Robinson', p. 143; Mant, *Church of Ireland*, ii. 747. 111 General John Pomeroy to Lord Harberton, 25 July 1789, PRONI, T/2954/4/19. For Robinson's MPs of 1783, see the History of the Irish Parliament database, *sub* 'George Rawson' and 'Henry Meredyth'.

you that I cannot give the assistance that is desired by proxy, consistently with my constant practice on former applications. I must rely on your Excellency's favourable construction of the reasons that have induced me frequently to avow my decided indisposition to sign a proxy on any occasion.[112]

Buckingham by no means put a 'favourable construction' on this refusal, particularly in view of the record of Robinson's two MPs, and shortly afterwards urged in vain that Robinson should not be paid the 'compliment' of being appointed one of the lords justices.[113] None of this was the behaviour of 'a public rather than a political figure', far less that of a venerable elder statesman.

Robinson was 'publicly ambitious of great deeds'[114] and, as Hotham noted, insatiable in his desire for praise on that account. To a man of his temperament, building was a softer path to celebrity than politics, and Armagh City, where he encountered none but admirers and yes-men, was the ideal theatre for his building operations. Yet, even in Armagh, he was not the great builder and benefactor he has been cracked up to be. His importance as a builder lies in the force of his example, his planning and encouragement and the covenants in his building leases, not so much in the amount of his own money which he spent. Unlike the other great childless benefactors in Church of Ireland history, his biggest beneficiary was his own family, not the Church or charities. As a Church leader he was unexceptional. He achieved much as a 'graceful' administrative reformer in the first twelve years of his primacy; and as an adviser from the sidelines in the critical year of 1788, when he was almost eighty, he showed tactical and political skill. But his feebleness and evasiveness as a political leader are indefensible. They are also hard to explain. Retaining the favour of the government for a variety of self-interested reasons – including the advancement of his nephew – may have been one motive from the mid-1770s onwards. From then on, Robinson may also have welcomed opportunities of wrong-footing Agar, particularly if he really thought his own illnesses of the late 1780s serious enough to make a vacancy in the primacy imminent. However, Robinson's reluctance to act or speak out on the subject of the Catholic Relief Act of 1792 is not explicable on grounds of 'jealousy and perhaps envy'[115] of Agar, since many besides Agar were opposed to it, and since it was not a measure for which the King had any enthusiasm. Moreover, the alarmist fears of Irish catholic conspiracy which had been the theme of Robinson's 'croaking' in the mid-1780s, had hardly diminished with the passage of time and the approach of a new world war. A man who, after thirty-seven years' membership of the House of Lords, could say that he had never given his proxy, must have been reluctant to take a decisive part. Something of this is also evident in his aloofness from the turbulent and increasingly sectarian politics of Co. Armagh from the late 1770s onwards.[116] All-in-

112 Robinson to Buckingham, 15 Mar. 1789, part of the collection of miscellaneous 'autographs' among the papers formerly at Holloden, Bagenalstown, Co. Carlow.   113 Buckingham to Grenville, 21 June 1789, *HMC Dropmore Mss.*, i, pp 480–81.   114 Mohan, 'Archbishop Richard Robinson', p. 130 (quoting Richard Cumberland).   115 Ellis to Agar, 16 May 1788, T/3719/C/22/16.   116 Robert Livingston to 1st earl of Charlemont, 23 Oct. 1779, and Rev. Edward Hudson to Charlemont,

all, it is hard to account for Robinson's abnegation of his political leadership of the Church except on the basis of a psychological reluctance to stand up and be counted.

In September 1793, it was claimed that 'the Primate's age and infirmities' precluded him from attending to serious Church business.[117] Nevertheless, it would not be surprising if Robinson for most of the latter years of his primacy, was just old, tired and anxious to be allowed to enjoy his 'emoluments' and his ill-health in peace. He was, after all, eighty-four in 1793. Age, indeed, is a factor which needs to be borne in mind throughout his time at Armagh. He was fifty-six when he attained the primacy. Reynolds' second portrait of him, painted in 1763, when he was still bishop of Kildare, shows a seated man who would nowadays be called old. Robinson's third portrait of him, painted in 1775 (when 'age', according to Walpole, had 'softened [him] into a beauty'), actually makes him look younger, because he is standing up and something of his imposing physical stature comes out from the canvas.[118] Robinson may have been old, or at any rate valetudinarian, before his time. In any case, no man who had learnt the trade of Irish politics in the early 1750s could possibly have felt at home in a world dominated by the Catholic Question and in which the British government espoused the catholic cause. Nor could any primate have felt at home in a Church dominated by a much junior archbishop, whose promotion he had notoriously endeavoured to prevent. It is likely that his permanent retreat from Ireland was a reaction, conscious or sub-conscious, to the ascendancy of Agar. More generally, Robinson in his last decade was one of a number of senior churchmen of that era whose incumbency out-lasted their utility because they held office in a Church which had made no provision for coadjutorships (see pp 499–504).

Nowadays, Robinson is a cult figure in Armagh. This is mainly because of the importance of his building ventures to a city currently as dependent for its prosperity on tourism as it once was on linen and archiepiscopal patronage. But when his jealous refusal to make what would now be called 'succession-planning' for the Church of Ireland, and his abandonment of its headship during his latter years, are weighed in the balance with his buildings, there is little doubt that he is found wanting. Like King Ludwig II of Bavaria his good points are mainly visible in retrospect and in light of subsequent touristic developments.

ARCHBISHOP FOWLER (1726–1801)

The senior aspirant to the archbishopric of Armagh when Robinson at last died was Fowler. Something has already been said of his time-serving. Ellis wrote scathingly in late May 1788 that Fowler seemed 'ready to carry his complaisance to any lengths, as hoping thereby' to succeed to the primacy.[119] Time-serving was never a disqualification

8 July 1794, *HMC Charlemont Mss.*, i. 361, and ii. 244; Mohan, 'Archbishop Richard Robinson', pp 128–9. **117** Woodward to John Moore, Archbishop of Canterbury, 14 Sep. 1793, Moore papers, Lambeth Palace Library, vol. 6, f. 233. I am indebted for this reference to Mr Terence Finley. **118** Quoted in Simms, 'Primate Robinson', p. 139. **119** Ellis to Agar, 26 May 1788, T/3719/C/22/20.

for an appointment which was 'absolutely reserved for England'.[120] What militated more seriously against Fowler was his advanced age, his low reputation and, perhaps, the realisation that he had been over-promoted already – and all for the purpose of keeping out Agar. Fowler really was an 'accidental person from England'. Scott used this very adjective in 1778 when he described him as 'an accidental, mendicant bishop, coming hither [to the bishopric of Killaloe] merely to gratify a Dr Young, a friend of Lord Townshend's, who declined it'.[121]

At Killaloe, he proved an undistinguished diocesan, although he was 'highly commended by John Wesley for the solemnity and devotion with which he read the services of our Church'.[122] In Dublin, his record was more praiseworthy. The already-mentioned Rev. Dr Robert Dealtry (p. 365), to whom he gave a succession of preferments in the diocese between 1782 and 1795,[123] described him as 'invariably ... a zealous and watchful prelate' (although it would be legitimate to ask, watchful for what?).[124] Skelton, the model parish clergyman of the age (who cannot have had much first-hand experience of Fowler), 'spoke of the Archbishop's great regard for religion as well as of his kindness and affability, "not, however, unattended by warmth of temper" '.[125] 'Warmth of temper' was clearly his leading characteristic. Gilbert Stuart, who exhibited the same shortcoming, found Fowler 'arbitrary, [and] therefore he was resolved not to yield to his rude and overbearing temper'; they had a celebrated run-in, c.1789, over a portrait of one of Fowler's daughters, when Fowler (according to Stuart) retired hurt from the encounter.[126] The author of *A tour through Ireland in 1790* had

> heard many anecdotes of his [Fowler's] servants laying plans to irritate him to passion. His generosity on reflection assuredly compensates, and that very amply, the objects of his resentment. ... He was never known to prefer ... a clergyman, however high in connection, who had not more than ordination to recommend him. He is a great admirer of learning and learned men.[127]

His patronage and promotion in 1789 of the Rev. Walter Blake Kirwan, a convert from Roman catholicism and the leading pulpit orator and fund-raiser of the late eighteenth-century Church, is a good example of his ability to spot talent.[128] It is

120 Robert Hobart to Grenville, 17 Feb. 1790, *HMC Dropmore Mss.*, i, pp 561–2. 121 Scott to Ellis, 4 Dec. 1778, T/3719/C/12/29. Dr Young was a viceregal chaplain to Townshend, and employed by him (as was usual) in confidential patronage business relating to the Church. Prior to his appointment to Killaloe, Fowler was dean of Norwich and a prebendary of Westminster Abbey. It was from Westminster that he wrote to Townshend accepting Killaloe, so presumably he never served, however briefly, as a viceregal chaplain, but was rewarded for Dr Young's services. See Bishop Garnett to Townshend, 16 Nov. 1769, and Fowler to Townshend, 14 June 1771, Townshend letter-book, RCB Library, Ms. 20/6 and 130. 122 Cotton, *Fasti*, i. 467. 123 Canon James B. Leslie's notes on the dioceses of Dublin and Kildare, [c.1920?], NA, M 2818. 124 Quoted in Kennedy, 'Dublin and Glendalough', p. 207. 125 Ibid., p. 208. 126 Mount, *Irish career of Gilbert Stuart*, pp 13–15; McLanathan, *Gilbert Stuart*, p. 53. 127 C.T. Bowden, *Tour*, pp 32–3. 128 Ibid.; Kennedy, 'Dublin and Glendalough', p. 223.

also to Fowler's credit that he did not forget his maker,[129] Buckinghamshire, who had raised him two or three steps at the one time, from the bishopric of Killaloe to the archbishopric of Dublin. Fowler continued to provide for Buckinghamshire's nominees, including the Rev. Richard Bourne (pp 243–4 and 255), 'the duke of Leinster's friend',[130] in his new diocese for at least a year and a half after Buckinghamshire's recall from Ireland, in disgrace, in September 1780.

However, Fowler drew the line in 1783 at supporting Luke Gardiner, the principal sponsor of the Catholic Relief Acts of 1778 and 1782, in the forthcoming general election for Co. Dublin. To Buckinghamshire's application on Gardiner's behalf, Fowler replied that Gardiner had 'repeatedly' insulted him and was guilty of 'Irish effrontery' in making such a request, being 'considered by many of the clergy as the avowed promoter of every project which can injure the rights of our Established Church, or advance those of any [other] religious persuasion.'[131] Fowler then proceeded to carry his principled opposition to Gardiner well beyond the bounds of prudence (in contrast to Agar's circumspect intervention in the Co. Limerick election of the same year); he wrote letters to the freeholder-clergy of Co. Dublin directing how they should exercise their franchise – which constituted undue influence and was also an unconstitutional interference by a member of the upper house in an election to the lower.[132] His behaviour was not formally complained of to the House of Commons, as it well might have been. But it unwisely reawakened the old prejudice against clerical interference in elections. The opposition press complained that 'the cloven hoof too clearly showed itself' and satirically hailed Fowler as 'a paragon of excellence in the public estimation ... for meekness, piety and purity of morals.'[133] Worse, Fowler's interdict had little or no effect on his clergy.[134]

In the administration of his diocese, as in his parliamentary and public defence of the Church in the period 1778–82, Fowler merely followed the example of Robinson and, to a still greater extent, Agar. The historian of the diocese of Dublin suggests, on the evidence of the (now unavailable) visitation books (see p. 244*n*), that there was a new 'administrative vigour' following Fowler's appointment. Visitation 'queries' addressed to each incumbent seem to have been introduced from at least 1780. 'The main emphasis in the visitation books ... [up to] 1786 was on the provision of parochial schoolmasters and parish clerks ... . [Although there was] considerable dilatoriness in carrying out the Archbishop's injunctions ..., with persistence [on his part, not unattended with warmth of temper!], his wishes were obeyed. From 1782, there was

---

129 'Professor Sykes has shown ... that Newcastle's joke about the bishops forgetting their maker was not wholly justified, since nearly half of his nominees stuck to him for some years after he lost power' – Pares, *George III and the politicians*, p. 42. 130 Fowler to Buckinghamshire, 19 Mar. 1781 and 18 Jan. 1782, *HMC Lothian Mss.*, pp 386 and 408-9. 131 Fowler to Buckinghamshire, [post-5] May 1783, ibid., p. 418. See also Gardiner to Buckinghamshire, 27 Apr. 1783, and Buckinghamshire to Gardiner and to Fowler, 5 May 1783, ibid., p. 417. 132 Agar to FitzGibbon, 8 Sep. 1783, T/3719/C/17/26. For the rest of the information in this paragraph, I am indebted to Mr Eugene A. Coyle and his M.Litt. research in progress at TCD into '... Politics and society in Co. Dublin, 1760–97'. 133 *The Freeman's Journal*, 18 Sep. 1783. 134 Ironically, Fowler's son later married Gardiner's daughter, though in the teeth of Fowler's opposition – Rev. Robert Fowler to Archbishop

a certain emphasis on residence, which became a strong feature of successive visitations. ... The Archbishop ... required at the 1782 visitation "All clergymen three years in possession of a benefice who have a glebe and no glebe-house to give in a memorial for building on or before Michaelmas next, otherwise their livings to be sequestered".' At his 1786 visitation, Fowler ordered that no city church hereafter be shut up without his permission.[135] In 1790, he risked a quarrel with the influential Latouche family of Bellevue, Delgany, Co. Wicklow, by insisting that the internal layout of the new church in Delgany which they had just paid for, should be altered to reduce the ecclesiological prominence of their family monument.[136] From 1793 on, and particularly after the damage done in 1798, attention at the visitations was focussed on the state of churches. 'In 1793, in Cloghran [near Swords] ... the churchwardens were "to be cited for not repairing the church" '.[137] By 1798, however, Fowler had ceased to be personally involved. His last appearance in the House of Lords was made in April 1797,[138] and he died in England in October 1801.

Either because of Fowler's decline and eventual absenteeism or because archiepiscopal 'vigour' was more apparent in the visitation books than in reality, Bishop O'Beirne, when writing to congratulate Agar on his succession to Fowler, deplored 'the neglected state from which providence has rescued the see'.[139] Moreover, at Fowler's coming to the see, in 1778, he had found it well documented from previous visitations and ready-divided up into rural deaneries: not for him the '*blank*' which Agar found at Cashel in the following year, and which Agar had to fill in by getting a 'state' of the diocese specially drawn up. It may also be suggested – perhaps a little cynically – that the spirit of 'graceful reform' was by this stage so much in the ascendant that any ambitious prelate was bound at least to pay lip-service to it.[140] There can be no doubt that Fowler was inordinately ambitious – and also shamelessly self-seeking. This probably explains the contempt in which he was held by Gardiner and by many others. As soon as he had acquired the requisite seniority as archbishop of Dublin, he was ripe in his own estimation for translation to Armagh. This aspiration, as has been seen, caused him to depart from his earlier adherence to the interests of the Church and to show marked subservience to the wishes of the government in the period 1787–9. Robinson had assured the Irish administration in December 1778 that Fowler's 'character in all respects is unexceptionable, and in my opinion his public conduct will be always clear and consistent'. If this was Robinson's sincere opinion, which is unlikely, it was a sad reflection on his judgement; and it certainly did not survive a 'dispute ... conducted with great heat' between them in 1783 over their relative precedence in the newly constituted order of St Patrick.[141] In the end, even Robinson

Fowler, 19 Sep. 1795, Domvile papers, NLI, Ms. 9399.   135 Kennedy, 'Dublin and Glendalough', pp 222, 234–6, 238, 240 and 243.   136 Judith Flannery, *Between the mountains and the sea: the story of Delgany* (Delgany, 1990), p. 70.   137 Kennedy, op. cit., pp 244–5.   138 Ibid., p. 210.   139 O'Beirne to Agar, 9 Nov. 1801, T/3719/C/35/28.   140 'State' of the diocese of Dublin, 1777–8, up-dated to 1788, Fowler papers, in the possession of John Fowler Esq., Rahinstown, Rathmolyon, Co. Meath. Mr Fowler also has the portrait of Fowler's daughter which was the subject of the row between Fowler and Gilbert Stuart, together with a magnificent Romney of Fowler himself, *c.*1783, in his robes as chancellor of the order of St Patrick.   141 Robinson to Heron, 19 Dec. 1778, NLI, Ms. 13036/13;

was sickened by Fowler's time-serving. In May 1788, he expressed dismay (and this was tough talking by Robinson's standards) 'that we cannot much depend on the natural and principal resources in difficulties such as exist at present'.[142] Following his political support of Dublin Castle during the Regency Crisis (see p. 166), Fowler claimed 'a promise from Lord Buckingham of a peerage at the next creation of peers', and in February 1790, 'after many attempts to prevail on Lord Westmorland [Buckingham's successor] to recommend him for the primacy and a peerage, ... [he] determined to go to England with a view ... of laying his services in person before his Majesty and making his own representation of the engagements of Lord Buckingham.'[143] Whether or not he saw the King, he certainly saw the home secretary, who was then Buckingham's brother, Grenville. On Grenville, he made no impression.[144] Westmorland, too, was of the blunt opinion that Fowler could 'plead no service but in the House of Lords – a service I should think very fairly to be expected from an archbishop of Dublin'.[145]

Other instances of Fowler's self-seeking are his self-enrichment at the expense of the archiepiscopal estate (pp 413–15) and his unprincipled promotion of his only son, another Robert, who was also a clergyman of the Church of Ireland. There is some doubt about Fowler Junior's date of birth, whether it was 1766 or 1768. Either way, 'He must have been ordained long before the canonical age'.[146] In 1789, his father collated him precentor of St Patrick's and vicar of St Ann's, Dawson Street, both in the diocese of Dublin, when he was either twenty-one or twenty-three and, what was worse, when he was absent from Ireland and off womanising on the Continent.[147] St Ann's, built *c.*1720, was then the most fashionable church in Dublin (St George's was not built until early in the nineteenth century – see p. 247), and the vicarage was worth £1,200 per annum. Not satisfied with this, or in the least embarrassed by his son's youth and absenteeism, Fowler next tried, in 1793, to get him elected dean of St Patrick's, then – as now – the most important deanery in Ireland, though not then in the undisputed gift of the cathedral chapter. There had been a famous legal battle between the chapter and the crown over the right of presentation following Dean Swift's death in 1745, on which occasion the right of the chapter had been upheld. Since then, the issue had not again been tried because the intervening deans had all been promoted to bishoprics, which meant that the disposal of their 'leavings' fell to the crown (see pp 215–16). In 1793, however, the then dean had died; so both crown and chapter prepared to renew the contest of 1745.[148] Browbeaten by Fowler, the chapter elected Fowler Junior on 15 October 1793. He was installed on 21 February 1794, following a hurried and enforced return to Ireland, and then – somewhat mysteriously – resigned on 4 April. Canon Leslie states that this was because Lord Chancellor FitzGibbon refused to allow a faculty enabling Fowler Junior to hold his

Galloway, *Order of St Patrick*, p. 13.   **142** Robinson to Agar, 23 May 1788, T/3719/C/22/19.   **143** Hobart to Grenville, 17 Feb. 1790, *HMC Dropmore Mss.*, i, pp 561–2.   **144** Grenville to Hobart, 26 Feb. 1790, ibid., pp 564–5.   **145** Westmorland to Grenville, 9 Mar. 1790, ibid., pp 566–7.   **146** Leslie, *Ossory clergy and parishes*, pp 38–9.   **147** Butler, *Escape from the anthill*, pp 32–45.   **148** Akenson, *Church of Ireland*, p. 51; Erck, *Ecclesiastical register*, pp 274–5.

precentorship and the deanery *in commendam* to pass the great seal.[149] However, since
he could always have resigned the precentorship, it seems more probable that he was
induced to resign the deanery because a candidate unanimously acceptable to the
chapter and entirely suited to the dignity was deemed to be necessary if the chapter
were to see off the threat from the crown. On 8 April, the Rev. James Verschoyle, who
was to prove an excellent and universally respected dean, was elected in place of
Fowler Junior; and, eventually, the court of king's bench confirmed the election and
the chapter's right to elect.[150] In the meantime, Archbishop Fowler had been obliged
to content himself with making his son archdeacon of Dublin (worth at least £900 per
annum) instead of dean of St Patrick's.

Coming, as it did, so soon before the death of Robinson and the vacancy at
Armagh, this piece of barefaced nepotism over the deanery of St Patrick's ought to
have eliminated any chance of the primacy which Archbishop Fowler still had. But it
did not. There followed a disgraceful episode worthy of all the fulminations of Froude
about the shallow and short-sighted policies of 'The English in Ireland in the
eighteenth century'. In Lord Westmorland's already-quoted letter of very early
September 1794, in which he warned Pitt against appointing Agar, William Beresford,
Newcome or anyone with Irish political connections, he actually recommended
Fowler, and for every cynical, wrong reason:

> [The Archbishop of] Dublin is a man of very violent temper, extremely disliked
> and, though he might by his influence [as primate] assist government, would
> never be troublesome to it. ... He has always acted coldly and distantly to me on
> account of the peerage he says Lord Buckingham promised. However, ... I think
> he would be the best [of the contenders from the Irish bench]. *Imprimis*, he is
> sixty-five years of age at least, has had fainting fits and would therefore keep the
> other expectants in suspense. Secondly, it would be a regular move – nobody
> could complain of being passed over. And, lastly, he is an Englishman and
> unconnected. ... [His] age is a great recommendation for the primacy.[151]

Fortunately for the Church, these considerations and this recommendation did not
prevail. In any selection for the primacy in which merit was allowed to play a part,
Fowler's most serious disqualification was that, if an incident recorded with relish by
Agar is anything to go by, he was not a man of any resourcefulness or ability:

> The Archbishop of Dublin having received an order of council (in the absence
> of the Primate) directing him and the other archbishops and bishops to prepare
> a form of prayer as a thanksgiving for the recovery of the King, kept it by some

149 Leslie, *Ossory clergy and parishes*, p. 38.   150 William Monck Mason, *History of St Patrick's*, pp 456–7
and 462.   151 Westmorland to Pitt, [pre-5 Sep. 1794], PRO, 30/8/331, ff. 311–12. Westmorland was
incorrigible. Long after he left Ireland, he continued to interfere in Irish patronage, ecclesiastical patronage
included. In May 1807, he recommended for the bishopric of Cork a former Roman catholic priest, whose
wife was a catholic and whose 'character is not good. ... You might as well make Horne Tooke a bishop' –
Richmond to Hawkesbury, 30 May 1807, Jupp/Aspinall transcript from the Liverpool papers, BL.

means for five days in his own possession, *viz.* from the 8th to the 13th of April [1789], on which day for the first time he communicated it to his brethren, though ... [it was necessary that] it should be prepared, printed and put into the post office by the 15th. ... This necessarily threw the burthen upon the Archbishop of Cashel, he being next in rank to the Archbishop of Dublin, who did prepare by 12 o'clock on the following day [with assistance from the Bishop of Waterford] the form which was used.[152]

PRIMATE NEWCOME (1729–1800)

It may be suspected that Agar in this account of events paid tribute to Newcome because he did not regard him as a competitor and rival. Nor, probably, did anyone else until Newcome beat Agar to the primacy in January 1795; for, up to then, Newcome was known primarily as a Hebrew scholar and the author of a number of theological works (ultimately numbering seven, one of them published posthumously). One of his first acts as primate was to send to Lady Fitzwilliam a thank-you present of a finely bound copy of one of them, his *Observations on Our Lord's conduct as a divine instructor and on the excellence of His moral character* (Dublin, 1782).[153] His publications, however, had a mixed reception; and in his last two, both of them about biblical translation, his 'zeal outran his judgement'.[154] He himself did not adduce them among his claims to promotion. Writing to Portland, the newly appointed home secretary following Pitt's coalition with the pro-war Whigs, in September 1794, Newcome if anything understated his pretensions:

> I have had a seat on the episcopal bench for 28 years; I have only three seniors on that bench, the Primate [Robinson], and the Bishops of Meath and Elphin; and I can plead the *jus liberorum* more strongly than most men, as I have twelve children now living. It gives me great concern to hear that the Bishop of Clogher's health is precarious. That see recommends itself peculiarly to my wishes.[155]

This suggests that Newcome, too, had no thought of the primacy – until, that is, the thought was put into his head by others.

As he stated, Newcome was Agar's senior in some respects, having been born in 1729 and made bishop of Dromore in 1766. In 1768, he had tried to nip into Cloyne ahead of Agar (reasonably enough, as Cloyne was senior to Dromore), but was unsuccessful in his application.[156] Then, with Agar's translation to Cashel and Newcome's to Waterford, both of which took place in 1779, Agar forged ahead and

---

152 Agar's 'state' of the diocese of Cashel, 1779–1801, 21 M 57/B6/1.   153 Author's collection. In the fly-leaves is an accompanying letter of 24 Feb. 1795.   154 Mant, *Church of Ireland*, ii, pp 745–7.   155 Newcome to [Portland], 10 Sep. 1794, Fitzwilliam papers, PRONI, T/3302/2/75.   156 Newcome to Townshend, 20 Jan. 1768, Townshend letter-book, RCB Library, Ms. 20/23.

became Newcome's metropolitan. Between the years 1775 and 1779, and the sees of Dromore and Waterford, Newcome held the troublesome bishopric of Ossory, to which was annexed responsibility for managing St Canice (see pp 178–80). In 1795, a subsequent bishop of Ossory, the very politically minded O'Beirne, observed that 'the borough, instead of an advantage, is an additional source of expense to me.'[157] Managing it involved Newcome in 'a style of living ill-suited to my disposition and circumstances', or, as his friend, Shute Barrington, bishop of Durham, remarked in 1777, involved him in the sort of work which was foreign to his nature.[158] Newcome himself grounded his pretensions to promotion from Ossory on his 'services to government in this borough, and ... [the] trouble, expense and obloquy I sustained.'[159] Immediately following his translation to Waterford in 1779, he took a political stand which both marked his gratitude to Buckinghamshire for promoting him and was true to his English Whig form: almost alone among the bishops he supported in the House of Lords the bill for the repeal of the Test. He argued, among other things, that the Test politicised a sacrament and, in any case, was no barrier to the unscrupulous office-seeker, since it had to be tendered to anyone willing to take it.[160] Later, as Westmorland vainly warned Pitt (see p. 175), he appeared in Whig party-political colours at the time of the Regency Crisis. Hence his eagerness to assist Agar in drawing up prayers of thanksgiving for the King's recovery.

In other words, and in spite of Newcome's unworldly traits and scholarly avocations, his promotion to the primacy in 1795, like his promotion to Waterford in 1779, owed a good deal to political considerations. The most important of these was Pitt's coalition with the Portland Whigs. Once Fitzwilliam had been appointed to the lord lieutenancy, and the attempts to find a politically bland English bishop for the primacy had failed (see p. 173), it probably suited Pitt very well to cede to his new Whig allies a top job in Ireland to which he attached no particular importance. Prominent among these new allies was the 1st marquess of Hertford, the very man who as lord lieutenant in 1765–6 had brought Newcome to Ireland as his chaplain and raised him to the episcopal bench. Newcome had maintained his association with Hertford[161] and Hertford now pressed for Newcome's promotion to Armagh. The association derived from Newcome's time as vice-principal of Hertford College, Oxford,[162] where he had been much in demand as an academic tutor, and where his pupils had included Hertford's second son, Henry Seymour-Conway, and also, as has been mentioned, the opposition Whig leader, Charles James Fox. Fox and Newcome had remained on friendly terms. 'The friends', writes Chart with his characteristic gift of understatement, 'were quite dissimilar in character, and to the casual observer there can have

---

157 O'Beirne to Portland, 4 Nov. 1795, *Irish official papers*, i. 145.   158 Barrington to his brother, 2nd Viscount Barrington, 18 Feb. 1777, Mackintosh collection, BL, Add. Ms. 34523, f. 180. 159 Newcome to Lord [Chancellor Lifford], 16 Mar. 1779, Heron papers, NLI, Ms. 13037/5. 160 O'Connell, *Irish politics and social conflict*, p. 209.   161 Newcome to Hertford, 7 Apr. 1768, Egerton Mss., BL, Eg. 3260, ff. 47–8: photocopy in PRONI, T/3076/2/22.   162 The college had nothing to do with the marquess: it had been founded by an obscure mediaeval clergyman called Elias de Hertford. I am grateful for this information to Dr T.C. Barnard, a fellow of the college.

seemed to be little in common between the serious and earnest ecclesiastic and the rather wild-living politician.'[163] 'The rather wild-living politician' was constantly criticised for his indolence; so he took delight in later life in carrying about with him and producing as evidence in his defence a letter written to him by Newcome in 1765 which included the remark: 'Application like yours requires some intermission.'[164] Less amusingly, Fox may have been responsible for Newcome's loss of his left hand: 'We believe but are not certain, that this misfortune was occasioned by the sudden closing of a door, in a sportive mood, by his pupil, Fox.'[165] If so, Fox's debt to Newcome was great indeed.

Fox was not directly in a position to repay it in 1794, as he remained in opposition when the Portland Whigs joined Pitt. But the recently appointed Fitzwilliam, in spite of the new political divide between them, was still Fox's 'warmest and most affectionate friend.'[166] The Irish Whig figurehead, the 1st earl of Charlemont, certainly thought that Fox's influence lay behind Newcome's appointment (Lord Hertford, whose influence on the occasion was probably as important as Fox's, was of doubtful purity in the eyes of mainstream Whigs). Writing to his old friend, the Belfast Whig, Dr Alexander Haliday, in January 1795, Charlemont enthused: 'Already we have a foretaste, an earnest of his [Fitzwilliam's] administration. Regardless of ministerial convenience and of that darling of all vicious governments, court influence, he has ... placed at the head of the Church a prelate, not from recommendation, but from character, and whose unassuming virtue, conduct, principles and erudition have alone recommended him to that high office. ... Public utility alone has been considered ...: Newcome had no English patron but Charles Fox.'[167] If, as Charlemont seems to have known, Fox had the means (Fitzwilliam) of advancing Newcome's cause, he almost certainly had the will to do so. Because he was in office so little, it is necessary to extrapolate from sentiments he expressed during those short periods in order to make a guess about his attitude to Newcome in 1794–5. In April–June 1806, in particular, he wrote a series of letters about Irish episcopal patronage, particularly the claims of Newcome's brother-in-law, Joseph Stock, bishop of Killala, 1797–1810. These include the comments: 'He is, I know, a very moderate man respecting the catholics [and, he might have added the dissenters], but is more a man of learning than a politician.' 'If I had my own way, except in very particular cases, I never would make a man a bishop who was not eminent in some branch of learning. ... Besides, ... it is our duty to recompense ... those who have been oppressed on account of their moderation.' Fox set no great store by good diocesan performance, for which Newcome was not conspicuous. Nor, in spite of affected sympathy with the 'Patriot' cause in Ireland, was he at all averse to placing important Irish offices, archbishoprics included, in English hands. Writing specifically of Irishmen on the Irish bench, he quipped: 'you may as well look for an Irishman free from the brogue as one free from job.'[168]

163 Phillips, *Church of Ireland*, iii. 268.   **164** Lord John Russell and others (eds.), *Memorials and correspondence of Charles James Fox* (4 vols., London, 1853–7), i, pp 14 and 22; L.G. Mitchell, *Charles James Fox* (paperback ed., London, 1997), p. 8.   **165** Stuart, *Armagh*, p. 458.   **166** E.A. Smith, *Earl Fitzwilliam and the Whig party*, pp 168–70.   **167** Charlemont to Haliday, 10 Jan. 1795, *HMC Charlemont Mss.*, ii. 257.   **168** Fox to Bedford, 13 and 26 Apr., 3 and 13 May, and 9 and 16 June 1806,

Other circumstances also favoured Newcome. First, he was much the most senior and the best-qualified Whig on the Irish bench.[169] Indeed, apart from William
Dickson, bishop of Down, 1783–1804, and Richard Marlay, bishop of Clonfert,
1787–95, and of Waterford (in succession to Newcome), 1795–1802, he was in effect
the only one. Dickson was an Eton and Hertford friend of Fox and had been
appointed first chaplain to the Fox-North Coalition's lord lieutenant in 1783 (the year
he became a bishop); Marlay was the uncle of Grattan. Both were junior bishops in
junior bishoprics, and neither was an efficient diocesan. Dickson's lack of merit is
obvious from a bid for the primacy which his wife had made to a friend of Fox at the
height of the Regency Crisis (when Robinson, be it noted, was no iller than usual):

> I beseech you to see Charles Fox by himself, and set this matter of the primacy
> in the true light to him. Tell him ... that he can make no man primate that
> would be such a friend to him and his party as Mr Dickson. Others will, for
> court favour, soon betray him: with Mr Dickson at the head of the Church of
> Ireland, he will ever have a great weight to add to ... [that of] his other friends
> there. ... If you could bring Charles Fox to speak to the Bishop [Dickson] on
> the matter, I know it would soon be settled in our favour. ... I shall struggle hard
> for what I know will be so fine a provision for my family, so great a thing for my
> husband and myself, and what will give us such a charming residence for life,
> and ... enable us to provide so amply for many of our friends.[170]

Besides lack of credible Whig competition, the other point in Newcome's favour was
– *pace* Lord Charlemont – 'court influence.' The King would no doubt have preferred
a bishop from the English bench, if one could have been found who was willing to go.
But he must have known Newcome by scholarly and theological repute, because
Westmorland had been aware in early September that 'the King had some thoughts of
Newcome' (see p. 175). A candidate favoured by both George III and Charles James
Fox must have seemed heaven-sent to the primacy!

Nor was Newcome so politically unsophisticated that he failed to brighten his own
prospects. At what stage he signalled his acquiescence in the favourite policy of
Fitzwilliam and the latter's Irish advisers, Catholic Emancipation, is unclear. Probably,
it was prior to his appointment, and therefore contributed to that outcome.[171] If his
motives were mainly self-interested, at least he remained loyal to Fitzwilliam after the
latter's disavowal and recall. 'Strongly impelled' by his fear of the consequences of 'an
abrupt disappointment of well founded expectations as to relaxing the Popery Laws',
he wrote to Portland at the beginning of March 1795 warning him against

Holland House papers, BL, Add. Ms. 47569, ff. 270–2, 275–8, 280–8 and 293–9.
169 Archbishop Bourke of Tuam, a Portland Whig, was dying.   **170** Mrs Dickson to the Irish Whig,
John Forbes, [late 1788–early 1789], Forbes papers, NLI: photocopy in PRONI, T/3391/68.
171 On 31 December 1794, Lord Ely joked to George Ogle, the ultra-protestant MP for Co.
Wexford: 'Report says Dr Troy is to be primate' (Ogle papers, NLI, Ms. 8148/13). Troy was the
Roman catholic archbishop of Dublin (see p. 327 and fig. 21).

the rapid overturning of so popular an administration ... . While Lord Fitzwilliam continues with us, we are secure from general commotions. The very waving of his hand would compose a tumult. ... The plan which the prelates intended to pursue, as soon as the bill for emancipating the Romanists reached the House of Lords, was to frame another bill tending to fence the ecclesiastical establishment by a continuance of such disabilities and restraints as ... [excluded catholics from any involvement in the religious or adminis- trative affairs of the Church of Ireland]. This point having been obtained, many of the prelates would have been well-disposed to the general measure, ... and in a tranquil state of the Empire experience would have instructed the legislature how the Church of Ireland might have been occasionally guarded and strengthened.[172]

The conversion of the Head of the Established Church to Catholic Emancipation was a very remarkable occurrence. Yet, it appears to have escaped comment, then or since.[173] The explanation must be that, in his endeavours to reconcile 'the prelates ... to the general measure', Newcome represented himself as acting under duress and in response to an initiative which had the sanction of the British as well as the Irish government.

Had Fitzwilliam remained, and had his Emancipation Bill been countenanced by London, it is improbable that Newcome would have been successful in silencing the opposition of 'the prelates' – certainly of Agar. On issues of a good deal less delicacy and moment than this, Newcome soon proved to be woefully inadequate as a political leader of the Church. Closely following his appointment, his two influential see tenants, Stewart of Killymoon (a close friend and ally of Charlemont), and Staples of Lissan, promoted their bill to relax the restrictions on the leasing powers of bishops (see pp 397–9). Although the proximate cause of this trouble was the see lands of Armagh, it was Agar, not Newcome, who persuaded the House of Lords to throw out the bill, and pass 'the Archbishop of Cashel's Act' instead. The want of judgement which Newcome had earlier shown in his assessment of Fox did not desert him in later life. Called upon early in 1798 to decide on a legal question – probably a bill (*38 George III, cap. 49*) to enable the dean and chapter of Christ Church to convey grounds in Dublin city to King's Inns – Newcome declared that he 'wished to be guided in this nice matter by your [Agar's] superior judgement.' But, not finding Agar at home when he visited him for that purpose, he threw himself upon 'the Archbishop of Tuam and the Bishop of Elphin, who are both of opinion that the measure may be conceded with prudence.'[174] Another decision which had to be made was scholarly, not legal. 'Primate Robinson ... had bequeathed £10,000 [*sic* – £5,000] ... to found a new college ...; the

---

172 Newcome to [Portland], 2 Mar. 1795, HO 100/56, ff. 351–4.   173 For example, on the day Fitzwilliam's successor, Camden, arrived, Newcome – by a nasty irony – was attacked by a Dublin mob, although its main quarry was Newcome's fellow-lord justice, FitzGibbon – Camden to Portland, 1 Apr. 1795, HO 100/57, ff. 41–4.   174 Newcome to Agar, 8 Mar. 1798 (two letters), T/3719/C/32/16–17.

choice of the first three fellows on the establishment was entrusted to ... Newcome ....
[who ducked it and] delegated ... [it] to his brother-in-law, Dr [Joseph] Stock, bishop
of Killala.'[175] (This might be regarded as Newcome's way of dissociating himself from
a foundation to which he was hostile,[176] in which case it would surely have been wiser
not to fill the fellowships in the first place?) In another instance, when Newcome at
least took a decision, it was a wrong one which entailed adverse publicity on the board
of first fruits and served as an unhappy precedent for Primate Stuart's glebe-house
loan scheme; Stuart lamented in 1804 that 'the board at the suggestion of Primate
Newcome, lent a Mr Murphy of this diocese £200 from Primate Robinson's fund to
build a house, the plan of which was approved of. With this money he has built a barn
and stables, but no house, and is now so involved in debt that I question whether the
board will ever recover the money lent.'[177]

On the important issue of an increase of pay to curates of the Church of Ireland,
which gathered momentum in the period 1796–1800, and was resolved by an act
sponsored by Agar in the latter year (see pp 578–81), Newcome's conduct was feeble
and inept. In early September 1799, a curate of the diocese of Armagh

> waited on the Primate to inquire whether our co-operating with our brethren
> of ... [the other dioceses] would meet his Grace's approbation. He told me
> there had been a meeting of the bishops during the last session of parliament,
> in order to adopt a plan to augment the salaries of curates, but that it was post-
> poned on account of the disturbed situation of the south. He recommended
> that I should write a circular letter to the curates of this diocese requesting
> them to meet at Armagh; and that we should draw up a memorial to him, and
> that he would convene a meeting of the bishops early in the next session, and
> lay our memorial before them, which he thought would considerably serve our
> cause. He also said he wished every diocese in the kingdom would adopt the
> same mode, each diocese presenting a memorial to its own bishop. The curates
> of Ireland must feel themselves much obliged to our much respected Primate
> for his good intentions in our behalf, and I make no doubt that, if the matter
> entirely rested with him, we should soon find ourselves comfortable and happy.
> His Grace's countenance must indeed materially serve our cause, but we think
> that we should be prepared for every event. It may please providence to rob us
> and the Church of our worthy Primate, or the bishops may not unanimously
> concur in his sentiments ... . It is therefore the opinion of our committee that
> in addition to a memorial of each diocese to its respective bishop, they should
> at least have a petition prepared to present to parliament at its meeting.[178]

175 Forster, *Life of Jebb*, i, 56; Mohan, 'Archbishop Richard Robinson', p. 112.   176 Cornwallis to
Portland, 29 July 1799, *Castlereagh correspondence*, ii, pp 364–5.   177 Stuart to Brodrick, 21 Apr.
1804, Midleton papers, NLI, Ms. 8869/3.   178 Printed circular letter from Rev. Thomas E.
Higginson, chairman of the curates of Down and Connor and a member of the central curates'
committee, Nov. 1799, 21 M 57/B35/5.

Newcome failed to report his sentiments to the bishops, with the result that some of them – or their registrars – refused to co-operate with the curates' committee when the latter was organising the diocesan petitions recommended by Newcome.[179] This created ill-will, and heightened the false impression that Newcome was more 'liberal' on the issue than the rest of the bench. It would have been wiser for Newcome to concert a response from the bishops and, until that was forthcoming, discourage the divisive and potentially dangerous agitation contemplated by the curates. Instead, by the weakness of his response he only encouraged what was particularly undesirable from the Church's point of view – an appeal to the Irish House of Commons. Clearly, the curates were fearful that Newcome was on the way out, and also that he lacked authority among his own bishops. They were right on both counts.

When Newcome died in January 1800, Lord Clare's epitaph was: 'The ... poor man was utterly unequal to' the primacy.[180] James Stuart does his best in his *Historical memoirs of Armagh* for all recent primates. But even he was forced into faint praise when he got to Newcome, whom he described as 'a man of mild, pleasant and unaffected manners, a pious, humane and deeply learned divine. ... [He] resided very much at Armagh and attended to the duties of his high office with becoming solicitude and zeal. His life terminated before he had an opportunity of conferring any very essential benefits on the city; but his gentleness, urbanity and benevolence secured him the respect and the affections of the people.'[181] Clare, however, would have denied Newcome even this much credit. Writing late in 1798, he had observed: '[The Primate] ... is now in the neighbourhood of Dublin where, much to his reproach, he has lived almost without intermission since his promotion to the see of Armagh. With a very meek and sanctified appearance, he pays less attention to the duties of his station than any man I know, and I detected him in as scandalous a job committed for a near relation as could well be executed.'[182] Nor is this an isolated reference to Newcome as a jobber: in December 1801, Primate Stuart referred disapprovingly to 'those solicitations which my predecessor almost daily carried to the Castle.'[183] Primate Stuart was given to censoriousness and Lord Clare to over-statement. But they certainly did not influence each other's judgements, so these must be regarded as independent condemnations of Newcome. The best reason for doubting Newcome's meekness and unworldliness is that he was so avid for the primacy that he was not deterred by the $c.£18,000$ required for the palace at Armagh. Would any man in his mid-sixties with 'twelve children now living' have acted thus unless he had plans for rapidly recouping his outlay?

Other verdicts on Newcome are more varied and even contradictory. At the end of his first year as primate, Dr Haliday of Belfast exclaimed: 'Literature and science, good morals and piety have served ... our new Primate ... in place of friends'; to which

179 Higginson to Agar's registrar, Samuel Cooper, 18 Nov. 1799, 21 M 57/B35/5. Cashel was, predictably, one of the dioceses which refused to co-operate.   180 Clare to Auckland, 14 Jan. 1800, Sneyd papers, Keele University Library: photocopy in PRONI, T/3229/1/25.   181 Stuart, *Armagh*, pp 359–61.   182 Clare to Auckland, 15 Nov. 1798, *Auckland correspondence*, iv. 67.   183 Stuart to Charles Abbot, 27 Dec. 1801, *The viceroy's post-bag*, p. 105.

Charlemont replied: 'If such wonderful precedents as this ... should chance to be imitated, even the bench of bishops would, O strange!, become respectable.'[184] Since both men were old-fashioned Whigs, to whom Catholic Emancipation was abhorrent, neither can have been aware that Newcome had more than nibbled at this forbidden fruit. Not so the co-editor of the *Memorials and correspondence of Charles James Fox*. Writing in the early 1850s, he asserted (most improbably): 'It was said at Dublin, when Lord Fitzwilliam was abruptly recalled, that Dr Newcome's appointment was the only lasting benefit he had been able to confer on Ireland.'[185] Mant took a different view. In a passage already partly quoted in connection with Robinson, Mant commented that Newcome 'like his immediate predecessor, ... appears not to have taken a prominent part in the political administration of affairs [!], but unlike him he has left few memorials to mark his episcopal character'.[186] From the perspective of Agar's career and the long-overdue lifting of the taboo against Irish primates, the appointment of Newcome is chiefly significant as a demonstration of the superior force of accident, or in this case a concatenation of accidents, over the designs and services of even so able a man as Agar, and of English trivia over Irish consequence.[187]

Moreover, even if Robinson, Fowler and Newcome had been better churchmen and abler Church leaders, they would still have laboured under the disadvantage of being alien to the Irish political class. Partly, this was because of their Englishness – although this point can be overstated: as one Englishman on the Irish bench had remarked in 1721, 'After our quarantine is over, we are all clean, and our posterity (of the very next generation) will be true-born Irishmen'.[188] Partly, it was because of their personal characteristics, which were mainly unattractive. But, mostly, it was because their initial promotion to the Irish bench had blasted the expectations of one, two or three senior Irish churchmen, and also those of a host of junior Irish churchmen below the level of dignitary, who had been candidates for the 'leavings'. Archbishop King had put this point, with gruff succinctness, in 1716. He argued that, if an Irishman had been appointed to fill a recent vacancy, 'ten clergymen would have been advanced and obliged, whereas by sending us a bishop out of England, all these were stopped and a damp put on the whole clergy.'[189] This 'damp' continued to operate towards the end of the century, in spite of intervening changes (see pp 188–92), because half the Irish bench of the 1790s were bishops like Robinson, Fowler and Newcome who had originally been 'sent out of England'. It affected not only 'the whole clergy' but – more ominously – their elder brothers in both Houses of the Irish parliament.

---

184 Haliday to Charlemont, 31 Dec. 1795, and reply, 4 Jan. 1796, ibid., p. 270.   185 Op. cit., i. 14.   186 Op. cit., ii. 747.   187 Earlier in the century, the problem had not just been that English trivia determined the selection of Irish bishops, but also that some potential English problems were solved at Ireland's expense. In 1727, 1730 and 1735 respectively, three heterodox English clergymen were deliberately and cynically consigned to Irish bishoprics – John Hoadly to Ferns, Robert Clayton to Killala, and Thomas Rundle to Derry – in order to get rid of them from the Church of England. See Johnston-Liik, 'Common problems', pp 27–8, Connolly, *Religion, law and power*, pp 188–9, and Walsh and Taylor, 'The Church and Anglicanism', pp 54–5.   188 Quoted in McNally, *Early Hanoverian Ireland*, p. 199.   189 Ibid., p. 152.

'Making such men bishops': the Irish episcopal bench, *c*.1760–*c*.1810

If Agar easily out-classes the three archbishops who were his nominal superiors in the period *c*.1780–*c*.1800, how does he compare with the generality of late eighteenth-century bishops – the men who were not sufficiently senior to be Church leaders (in the sense that Robinson and Agar were), but whose careers throw light on other issues – for example, ecclesiastical standards. What were these standards? Is Agar unenviably conspicuous among his contemporaries and near-contemporaries on the episcopal bench as a 'political prelate'? And if, as is hard to controvert, he excelled them all in ability and effectiveness as a Church leader, was he in turn excelled by them in other, perhaps more Christian virtues? To these, as to most fundamental questions, there are no conclusive answers. But the indications are that, like Agar himself, most of his Rt Reverend Brethren of the period *c*.1760–*c*.1810 were a complex mixture of good and bad, and need to be considered in the round and not condemned because of the odd misdeed or dubious action. One of them thought otherwise. In December 1798, the censorious Brodrick roundly declared: 'I firmly believe that tithes would never have been spoken of as an hardship, if the clergy had done their duty in any degree. The root of the disorder is in making such men bishops.'[1]

THE POLITICAL PRELATE, *c*.1760–1806

All bishops of both the Churches of Ireland and England in Agar's day were political prelates in that all were political appointees. Even when they were appointed or promoted on grounds of piety or learning, that was a political decision because a politician had made it. Referring to an earlier period, Professor Connolly has wisely warned that 'the assumption that political appointees were necessarily corrupt or negligent is a twentieth-century prejudice.'[2] The arguments used by Portland in 1798 to justify the further promotion of O'Beirne, his Irish political aide and former private secretary,[3] bear this out. In September he pointed out to the lord lieutenant that 'the particular circumstances of the see of Meath ... require no common hand to bring it into order ... . I ... cannot add to the weight of the testimony you have received in favour of the Bishop [of Ossory, as O'Beirne then was], and I will conclude by saying

---

1 Brodrick to Midleton, Dec. 1798, Ms. 1248, vol. 17, f. 97.   2 Connolly, *Religion, law and power*, p. 184.   3 See p. 561. For O'Beirne's letters to Portland on Irish political affairs, 1787–95, see *Irish*

that his promotion will make me very happy.' Later, in November, he asked 'that you should let it be understood that it was his behaviour and performance of the duties of his function ..., [as] represented to you by your predecessor, which had determined you to propose him to the King for the see of Meath.'4 Since no one on the Irish bench had been a more plainly political appointee than O'Beirne (a matter of obvious embarrassment to Portland), it is highly significant that his merits as a diocesan were equally plain.5

Agar (to say nothing of O'Beirne) was a political prelate in two further respects. One was his membership of a political connection, which it has been argued did him no good – at least after 1768 – wrecking his pretensions to the archbishopric of Dublin in 1778, and compromising his pretensions to the primacy thereafter. The other was his standing, in his own right, as 'infinitely the first ecclesiastic, if not in all respect the first man of business' in the House of Lords, or (as the well informed English politician, the 2nd Lord Walsingham, observed more succinctly in 1784) 'the ablest man in Ireland.'6 The two respects were distinct, but it would be unrealistic to suggest that they did not impinge upon each other. Agar himself mixed them up, and in the process diminished his stature as a Church leader. For example, he unsuccessfully used the influence of his political connection to advance his claims to Dublin in 1778 and to extract a reversionary promise of the primacy in 1784. He also made a discreditable proposal to Lord Clifden in August 1794 in relation to promotion in the Church for the latter's undeserving brother, John Agar:

> By the death of the Archbishop of Tuam, a vacancy will probably be made on the bench of Irish bishops. Surely this might very reasonably be an object to you for your brother, John? And I really know not any person in this country whose rivalship could defeat your claims. Lords S[hannon] and E[ly] would be formidable competitors, but I have no reason to think that either of them has any friend at present whom he would wish to promote in that line. ... If you don't succeed on the present occasion, try to lay claim to the next vacancy.7

This makes something of a mockery of the stand which Agar had earlier taken on the issue of Galbally glebe-house. Superficially, the proposal smacks of nepotism: in reality, the motivation was political – the strengthening of the Agar connection and of Agar's position in the House of Lords and on the episcopal bench. Fortunately for Agar's reputation, Lord Clifden did not pursue the matter and John Agar died young.

---

official papers, i, pp 143–5. 'Cardinal' O'Beirne's Roman catholic origins, which were considerably distorted by his political opponents, made him an object of additional suspicion, even to some Whigs. Although he was pushy, meddlesome and scheming, especially in his early days, there is no reason to doubt the impression of benignity and basic honesty conveyed by the portrait of him painted *c.*1815 by Sir Henry Raeburn. This, rather unexpectedly, is to be seen in the picture gallery in Dresden, captioned 'Lucius O'Beirne, Bischof von Meath'.   4 Portland to Cornwallis, 16 Sep. and 2 Nov. 1798, Portland papers, PRONI, T/2905/22/106 and 109. 5 Healy, *Diocese of Meath*, ii, pp 110–63. 6 [Welby?] to Agar, 10 May, 1784, T/3719/C/18/8. 7 Agar to Clifden, 10 Aug. 1794, 21 M 57/B23/20.

If, because he was a politician, Agar had his blind spots and aberrations, as a political leader of the Church and a legislator on its behalf (see pp 444–5), he was pre-eminent – partly because of his own energy and ability, and partly because of the supineness of his nominal superiors, Robinson, Fowler and Newcome. The diocese of Cashel, the board of first fruits and the Church of Ireland as a whole, were hugely indebted to him for the leadership he provided during the more-than-difficult decades of the 1780s and the 1790s. But it was inevitable that his very effectiveness as a political leader should have compromised his character as a churchman. To be a political prelate was, essentially, a contradiction in terms, and not one of Agar's making. It has been remarked *apropos* the Church of England: 'As far as politics is concerned, it was as difficult for eighteenth-century bishops to balance the duties of "prelate" and "pastor" as it had been for their predecessors. ... It must be recognised, however, that they ... were the representatives in parliament of both Church and clergy, a role doubly important in the absence of a sitting convocation after 1717.'[8] In Ireland, not only was there no sitting convocation, but convocation never met between 1711 and 1862. William Playfair, compiler of an immense, nine-volume *Peerage and baronetage* of the three kingdoms which was published in 1809–11, expressed the prelate/pastor paradox in its simplest terms: 'It may perhaps be difficult to explain why archbishops and bishops form a part of the legislature of this country, whilst all clergymen of an inferior rank are ... completely and expressly excluded from it.' Not even Agar could have bettered the complacent facility with which Playfair went on to explain the paradox: 'The example of the bishops has not, unfortunately, the full effect that it ought to have on their inferiors in the Church, whose characters and conduct are not in many instances equally correct.'[9]

Unfortunately for Playfair's argument, there is some statistical reason for thinking that the bishops attended the Irish House of Lords, not so much as 'representatives ... of the Church and clergy', as for the purpose of advancing their own careers. An examination of percentage attendances, by bishopric, at the 3,573 sittings of the Lords which took place throughout the eighteenth century, produces the following results: 'Clonfert 58%, Killala 55%, Dublin 50%, Cashel 49%, Armagh 49%, Dromore 49%, Ferns 48%, Tuam 47%, Cork 47%, Ossory 47%, Kildare 46%, Killaloe 44%, Kilmore 43%, Down 42%, Cloyne 40%, Meath 40%, Elphin 38%, Waterford 38%, Clogher 36%, Raphoe 33%, Limerick 31%, Derry 20%.'[10] Clearly there is a close correlation between high attendance and possession of one of the 'poorer dioceses, almost invariably served by the prelatical "freshmen" '; and, in most cases, this high attendance was motivated by hope of promotion. The pattern is confused by the inclusion of the four archbishoprics, whose incumbents were presumably expected to give a lead by being regular attenders. (But for Robinson in the period 1786–94 and the marginalised Tory primate, Thomas Lindsay, in the period 1714–24, it may be conjectured that the attendance-rate of the archbishopric of Armagh would have been

8 Walsh and Taylor, 'The Church and Anglicanism', p. 4.   9 Playfair, *British family antiquity*, v, appendix, pp lxxix–lxxxi.   10 Falvey, 'Eighteenth-century episcopate', p. 110.

higher.) However, if the archbishoprics are set to one side, it becomes apparent that the bishoprics which recorded an attendance rate of less than 40% were those in which all but the most ambitious of churchmen would have been content to die. The attendance rate of Derry, at 20%, must have been artificially low because of the notorious absenteeism of the long-serving Frederick Hervey; but it can be no coincidence that Derry was one of the richest bishoprics, and in Hervey's day *the* richest and richer than any of the archbishoprics except Armagh (see pp 388–91).

This correlation of attendance and expectancy was not significantly different from the behaviour of the Church of England bishops in the British House of Lords. In the years after 1715, Sir Robert Walpole had ensured, 'first, through his "Pope", Edmund Gibson, Bishop of London, and after 1736 through the duke of Newcastle, ... that all leading clerics should be political animals, trained to march into the appropriate lobby at need. So reliant was Walpole on episcopal votes in the Lords, ... that many of his creations were seen only rarely in their dioceses.'[11] Towards the end of the century, the bishops of the Church of England were still 'almost a laughing-stock for their subservience. They could not even stay away without exciting comment: when only 7 of the 26 appeared in parliament during the ticklish Regency Crisis of 1788, ... it was [taken as] "a proof that crows soon smell powder" .'[12] A year earlier, in November 1787, *The British Mercury* bluntly stated: 'There never was a minister more fortunate in the way of death than Mr Pitt. Bishoprics and regiments fall in every month – he has had four of the former within nine months.'[13] A constant threnody in the *Autobiography* of the reforming Richard Watson, bishop of Llandaff, 1782–1816, was the 'political pliancy' of all the Church of England bishops except himself.[14] In the spring of 1806, with a new government in power which included Charles James Fox and some neo-republican Whigs, and excluded the friends of the hitherto dominant but recently deceased Pitt, the 'thinness of the bishops' bench' in the post-Union House of Lords excited comment. Among the Irish bishops, Brodrick and the recently promoted bishop of Ossory, John Kearney, 'stayed away, though they are in general pretty constant attendants on the House.'[15] Brodrick later turned up for a somewhat controversial Church of England Curates' Bill, and was shocked at the rough usage which the bishops received in return for their want of 'political pliancy.'

> The Chancellor [Lord Erskine], after swearing at the Archbishop of Canter-
> bury, such is the way of English chancellors, told him that, if the bishops did
> not attend the committee on the bill, neither would he. ... Lauderdale [a leading

11 Eric J. Evans, *The contentious tithe*, p. 2.   12 Richard Pares, *King George III and the politicians*, pp 41–2. For confirmation of this traditional view, see John Cannon, *Aristocratic century: the peerage of eighteenth-century England* (paperback edition, Cambridge, 1987), pp 99–104.   13 *The British Mercury ...*, vol. iii for 1787, p. 293.   14 *Anecdotes of Watson*, pp 92–5, 159–63, 189, 224–5, 271, 343–4 and 372–3.   15 Fox to 6th duke of Bedford (the lord lieutenant), 16 June 1806, Holland House papers, BL, Add. Ms. 47569, ff. 297–9; 2nd Earl Spencer (the home secretary) to William Elliott (the chief secretary), 2[?3] May 1806, Jupp/Aspinall transcript from the Althorp papers.

Whig peer], as I am informed, gave a dressing to the bishops in general yesterday. On defending the petition against it and receiving a check from the Archbishop on account of the irregular introduction of his observations, [he] gave us to understand that we should be paid with interest hereafter.[16]

As *The British Mercury's* sneering reference of 1787 suggests, the circumstances leading to the promotion of men to the English bench were commonly regarded as suspicious. The suspicion of underhand political motivation seems to have been particularly well founded in the case of one promotion, that of Edward Willes, bishop of Bath and Wells, 1743–73.

> His elevation (putting his brother's [Sir John Willes, lord chief justice of the common pleas in England, 1737–61] influence out of the question) was attributable to his holding a situation, the duties of which appear somewhat incongruous with the functions of a priest. He was 'decypherer [*sic*] to the king' ... [and], as I find by the information of a respectable descendant, 'he recommended himself to the ministry of the day by important communications and services in the secret department about the time of Bishop Atterbury.'[17] The accomplishment of ... [this] truly orthodox prelate's ruin [in 1720] ... proved to the promoters of it ..., his brother bishops, ... the fruitful source of divers consecrations and translations. ... One of the points upon which Atterbury's condemnation turned was the very uncertain test of comparison of handwriting, ... after the pretended discovery of documents in the Bishop's close stool ...; and no doubt the decyphering faculty of Willes was here brought into action ... . This office [of decypherer to the king, which Willes held until his death, calls], I believe, for a very active, laborious and incessant exertion, admitting scarcely a moment's time for anything else.[18]

By the late eighteenth century, there was understandably a greater squeamishness about the qualifications for promotion to the English bench and about the secular occupations which were 'congruous with the functions of a priest.' One man who gave serious thought to the matter, and to what he believed to be a difference between English and Irish political morality in this regard, was Brodrick's brother, the half-English, half-Irish Lord Midleton. In June 1793, Lord Midleton was apprehensive that he might not be able to obtain an Irish bishopric for Brodrick without promising to support the government in return; this he regarded as 'a bargain and sale ... [and] dishonourable. Such is the opinion of correct men in England, but I know in Ireland the opinion is different.'[19] Perhaps he overestimated the proportion of 'correct men'

---

16 Brodrick to Midleton, 23 June 1806, Ms. 1248, vol. 19, f. 17. This Curates' Bill was not actually passed until the following year (*47 George III, cap. 75*).   17 Francis Atterbury, bishop of Rochester, 1713–23; deposed for Jacobitism and exiled.   18 Cassan, *Lives of the bishops of Bath and Wells* (London, 1829), pp 166–8.   19 Midleton to Brodrick, 17 June [1793], Ms. 8889/9.

in England. In 1806, the young Canning remarked cynically of the newly appointed archbishop of Canterbury, Charles Manners Sutton (the near-primate of 1794 and 1800): 'He is a good archbishop and votes right.'[20] Twenty years later, in June 1827, when Archbishop Manners Sutton and the 3rd duke of Northumberland voted against the government in the House of Lords on a corn bill, Canning, now prime minister, visited his displeasure on the Very Rev. Hugh Percy, an aspirant to a bishopric, who was son-in-law of the one and cousin of the other. Canning 'catechised' him (in Professor Pares' memorable expression) about the conduct of the Archbishop and the Duke, and extracted from him a promise of support before agreeing to recommend him for the bishopric of Rochester.[21] Lord Midleton would not have thought this 'correct', and nor was it – either in Canning for proposing, or in Percy for accepting, the 'bargain and sale.'

In both kingdoms, therefore, it was widely assumed – and expected by the government of the day – that the parliamentary conduct of the episcopal bench would be characterised by subservience to government. There was perhaps a slight distinction in that bishops of the Church of Ireland, after their initial appointment, usually gravitated towards a generalised support of the Irish government for the time being,[22] whereas bishops of the Church of England retained loyalties to and links with the political party, group or patron by whose influence they had first been appointed. To that extent, the Irish bench was somewhat less politicised than the English. But this may just mean that roughly half its members, being English, had not been appointed on the basis of Irish political affiliations in the first place. In 1793, one of the more thoughtful and conscientious of these English appointees, Richard Woodward, bishop of Cloyne, 1781–94, who by then had been living in Ireland for over thirty years, thought it 'hardly proper' for 'a stranger' to vote on political subjects in the Irish House of Lords; 'the arrangement of the kingdom' he added .'.. should be left to those who have a permanent interest in it.'[23]

This self-denying ordinance is the more remarkable granted that Woodward was, of all the bishops (whether English or Irish) on the Irish bench, the one most celebrated for his political defence of the Church of Ireland. He was a political prelate of a different type from Agar, whose sphere of activity was, essentially, the House of Lords. Woodward was a pamphleteer. In 1786, he published the persuasive and best-selling polemic, *The present state of the Church of Ireland, containing a description of its precarious situation and the consequent dangers to the public, recommended to the serious consideration of the friends of the protestant interest; to which are subjoined some reflections on the impracticality of a proper commutation for tithes, and a general account of the origins and progress of the insurrections in Munster*. It was in this pamphlet, of self-explanatory bias, that the emotive phrase 'Protestant Ascendancy' was, not first coined, but first

20 Canning to his wife, 31 May [1806], Jupp/Aspinall transcript from the Canning papers. 21 Pares, *George III and the politicians*, p. 186n.   22 Akenson, *Church of Ireland*, pp 16, 31–2 and 35–9. The Whig Bishops Newcome, Dickson and Marlay were important exceptions.   23 For this letter, written on 5 Mar. 1793, and its context, see pp 495–6.

given currency.[24] Convinced from mid-1786, however misguidedly, 'that the Rightboy disturbances were not simply a recurrence of the already common phenomenon of agrarian disorder ... [but what he called] "a deep and well conducted plan" to "extinguish the protestant religion in Munster and Connaught, raise the expectations of the papists, kindle a religious war and separate Ireland from Great Britain", Woodward set himself the object of opening "the eyes of the landed gentlemen" of Ireland to what was at stake.'[25] His well judged polemic 'caught the mood of the country and provided conservative protestants with the potent rallying cry they had palpably lacked throughout 1786.'[26] It achieved its purpose of rallying the Irish House of Commons and administration to support the rights of the clergy in the session of 1787 which immediately followed its publication,[27] and to that extent represents perhaps the most successful blow struck on the Church's behalf by any bishop (Agar not excepted) in the period under review.

No other English appointee to the Irish bench came near to Woodward's perhaps excessive zeal in defence of the Church of Ireland. Nor, when they absented themselves from the discussion of purely 'political subjects in the House of Lords', were the other Englishmen motivated by this scrupulousness: more probably, they were motivated by indifference. The distinction between a political and a Church issue was sometimes fine; and unfortunately for the Church, and for a political prelate of Agar's type who was trying to marshal its defending forces in the House of Lords, the English bishops' indifference extended to some issues in which the Church's interests were to a greater or lesser extent involved. There were so many distinctions between the Churches of Ireland and of England in the regulations pertaining to their spiritualities and especially their temporalities, that an English bishop on the Irish bench might well not attach to a particular issue the critical importance which an Irish bishop did. This lesser sense of relevance and urgency among the Englishmen on the Irish bench may help to account for one marked statistical discrepancy between the Irish and the British Houses of Lords. This was that, in the course of the eighteenth century, the overall attendance rate of the bishops in the former declined by almost 50%.[28] In view of the paucity of temporal Irish peers at the beginning and for the first two-thirds of the century, the government had greater need of an episcopal presence then than later in the century. But the Church's need of the bishops' presence and support was greatest in the later period. In particular, there was much scope and need

---

24 For Woodward's major part in the evolution of the concept of 'Protestant Ascendancy', see James Kelly, 'The genesis of "Protestant Ascendancy"' (op. cit.), and 'Eighteenth-century Ascendancy: a commentary', in *Eighteenth-Century Ireland*, v (1990), pp 173–87.   25 Kelly, The "Paper War" of 1786–8, in *Eighteenth-Century Ireland*, iii (1988), pp 54–6.   26 Kelly, 'The genesis of "Protestant Ascendancy"', p. 116.   27 Ibid., pp 119–22; MacDonagh, op. cit., pp 18–20. For the complete turnaround in Dublin Castle's attitude, and the gratitude to Agar of the clergy of his metropolitan province for his contribution to this outcome, see: Orde to Rutland, 28 Nov. 1786, Rutland to Agar, 12 Aug. 1787, and Sackville Hamilton to Rutland, 8 Sep. 1787, *HMC Rutland Mss.*, iii, pp 358–9, 405 and 412; and addresses from diocesan clergy of Munster to Agar, with copies of his replies, June–July and Sep. 1787, 21 M 57/B8/6–23.   28 Falvey, op. cit., p. 111.

towards the end of the eighteenth century for a bishop with Agar's particular skills as a debater and man of business – skills in which he excelled both Boulter and Stone and which had never been required of them. As Buckingham put it in 1789: 'Formerly [i.e. up to *c.* 1768], the House of Lords was very thinly attended – never by more than thirty members, of whom the bishops' bench composed the clear and decided majority: the education, the habits, the poverty of the lay peers depressed all idea of debate.'[29] Skills as a debater and man of business were additionally requisite in Agar's day because, after the constitution of 1782 had removed the powers of the Irish and British privy councils to *amend* Irish legislation, the Irish House of Lords became much more prominent both as a longstop for the Irish administration and as a last line of defence for the Church. Leadership and management of the Lords accordingly assumed an importance to the government which they had not had before; hence Chief Secretary Fitzherbert's pathetic description of Agar as 'the first feather on our wing.'

The new importance of the Lords as a last line of defence for the Church is also easily illustrated. Just before the winning of the constitution of 1782, in March 1782, Sir Henry Cavendish, 2nd Bt, moved for a return, to be furnished at the start of the next parliamentary session, of the figures for clerical residence and the performance of divine service, parish-by-parish throughout the country, between 1 June 1782 and 1 June 1783;[30] and one of the first uses to which the House of Commons put its greater procedural freedom under the constitution of 1782 was to pass a bill to better the position of the already pampered tenants of the episcopal estates, which ran out of parliamentary time in the Lords, but was not to be the last of such proposals (see p. 397). Obviously, Agar and most of the bishops had been quite right in 1780–82 to be fearful of constitutional change. An excellent example, fully documented by himself, of Agar's political role behind the scenes and in the Lords, post-1782, is his Barren Lands Act of 1793:

> Mr Grattan in the beginning of the session of 1793 having, according to cus-
> tom, signified his intention to bring in what he called a Barren Land Bill, and
> it being supposed that he would as usual bring in a bill under that specious title
> similar to those which he had produced before (the apparent and direct effect
> of which was to remove all suits for the recovery of tithe out of the ecclesi-
> astical courts and leave them to be decided by a jury, which in fact would be to
> render the recovery of tithe nearly impracticable), the Archbishop of Cashel
> was desired by Mr Secretary Hobart to prepare such a bill for that purpose as
> would really promote the improvement of barren land and at the same time
> secure the proprietors of tithe as much as possible against fraud and litigation.
> In compliance with the wishes of government conveyed through Mr Hobart,
> the Archbishop did prepare the present Barren Land Bill, *viz.* the 33rd George

29 Buckingham to Grenville, 13 May 1789, *HMC Dropmore Mss.*, i. 467.   30 *Irish parliamentary register*, i, pp 328 and 824, cited in Kennedy, 'Dublin and Glendalough', p. 242; copy order of the House, 9 Mar. 1782, Wickham papers, PRONI, T/2627/5/T/2.

III, cap. 25, which he gave to Mr Secretary Hobart, who introduced it into the House of Commons where only one slight alteration was made in it, and in that form it passed through the House of Lords and received the royal assent. The Archbishop then, in order if possible to prevent litigation on this subject, made a collection of all the cases arising out of the English act of the 2 and 3 Edward VI, cap. 13, sec. 5, etc., which had been decided in the English courts of law, as well as of the best explanations of that act, and caused the Irish act to be printed with marginal references to those decisions and explanations.[31]

Frederick Temple, archbishop of Canterbury, 1896–1902, famously remarked about his future successor, Randall Thomas Davidson, archbishop from 1903 to 1928: 'My only doubt is whether so much political sagacity is altogether compatible with perfect piety.'[32] In Agar's case, the methods he had become accustomed to using in order to establish and strengthen his influence in Dublin Castle and the House of Lords inevitably attracted him to the bad idea of adding to his own weight and that of the Agar connection a nephew on the episcopal bench. The politically naïve and inept Newcome found himself drawn into the political arena through the accidents of who his pupils at Oxford happened to be and of being placed in a diocese to which a borough was annexed (see pp 468–9). So the politically astute and active Agar was bound to succumb to the pollutions of politics. In his famous review of Lord Dover's edition of Horace Walpole's *Letters to Sir Horace Mann*, Macaulay likened Walpole's 'literary luxuries' to *pâté de fois gras*, because both owed their excellence to the diseases of the animal which provided them.[33] The language of the simile is designedly coarse. But, with some refinement, it can be applied to Agar's leadership of the Church, which undoubtedly owed its excellence to the diseases of the political animal which provided it.

THE ALLEGED SUPERIORITY OF THE ENGLISHMEN ON THE IRISH BENCH, *c.*1760–*c.*1800

As the earlier discussion (pp 174–84) of the issue of bishops' boroughs made clear, most British politicians thought that Irishmen on the Irish bench were much more likely than Englishmen to involve themselves in the murkier forms of Irish politics. Amazingly, the activities of Primate Stone were soon forgotten. Moreover, English prejudice went further even than this. Right up to, and indeed beyond, the Union, most English churchmen and members of the English ruling class thought that it was not only politically prudent but ecclesiastically proper that Englishmen should occupy the senior positions in the Church of Ireland. The commentator of 1765 who preferred 'the moderate principles of an Englishman', Robinson, to 'the early Protestant bigotry a Scotchman or an Irishman imbibes', was that very snobbish scion

31 Agar's 'state' of the diocese of Cashel, 1779–1801, 21 M 57/B6/1.   32 Quoted in Alan Clark (ed.), *'A good innings': the private papers of Viscount Lee of Fareham* ... (London, 1974), p. 236. 33 *The Edinburgh Review ... for July 1833–January 1834* (vol. lviii, Edinburgh, 1834), p. 227.

of old English nobility, the countess of Moira (*née* Lady Elizabeth Hastings). Similar
prejudices were voiced from time to time by people whose views ought to be entitled
to greater attention than Lady Moira's. In 1801–2, during a rumpus over the
translation of an Irishman to a better bishopric (see pp 610–11), Primate Stuart,
asserted that 'A bad moral character would in England be an insuperable obstacle' to
a man's elevation to a bishopric, whatever his 'rank, ... wealth ... or parliamentary
interest.' In 1806, Charles Lindsay, bishop of Kildare and dean of Christ Church (a
Scot), in his letter to Stuart about the act of parliament fraudulently passed by his
predecessor in 1792 (see pp 256–7), concluded with strictures on the Irish character:
'Upon the whole, there are many difficulties in this case – a few legal, but more of a
moral nature, considering the temper of the people we are among – for this case could
not at this time have happened in England.'[34] Most telling of all, Euseby Cleaver, when
trying to find arguments to support his request in late 1798 for a translation to the
English bench, had ascertained that no Irish bishop had been so translated since the
reign of William III, and was told 'that in the year 1788 the English bishops made
some application to Mr Pitt for the King, on the surmise of Bishop Preston's
[Cleaver's predecessor at Ferns] translation, and on the grounds that bishops were
appointed here with less attention to qualification and character than in England.'
Cleaver was also informed, by Buckingham, that the 'difficulty of translation from
hence ... arose from the King.'[35]

The King's opinion that the bishops of the Church of Ireland were inferior in
point of 'qualification and character' to their Church of England counterparts, comes
as no surprise. It was, after all, that view of the matter which led to the appointment
of Stuart as primate in 1800 (see pp 592–8). However, the King was thereby providing
another striking example of English double standards and hypocrisy, since he and his
predecessors had approved the choice, and signed the warrant of appointment, of each
and every one of the bishops of the Church of Ireland, and since his grandfather,
George II, had seen half a century earlier that 'all the [Irish] bishoprics must not be
given to chaplains' from England. In 1800, Brodrick complained, in his usual
exaggerated fashion, of the 'many instances ... of the negligence and indeed profligacy
of our clergy ... . But surely the blame of all this lies ultimately with those who
recommend to the highest offices in the Church.'[36] Since bishops were made in
England, the blame lay with English lords lieutenant, secretaries of state, prime
ministers and sovereigns. Furthermore, they were not so much blameworthy for
allowing Irish political interest to sway their selection – the cases of Agar and, still
more, of William Beresford show that they were actually not particularly responsive
to Irish political interest – as for placing Englishmen on the Irish bench for slight and
trivial reasons. Of these reasons, the proximate was usually that the Englishman
concerned had been brought to Ireland as a viceregal chaplain. Something has already
been said (pp 138–40 and 188–9) of viceregal chaplaincies. There was a good deal of

34 Lindsay to Stuart, 28 Jan. 1806, Bedfordshire RO, WY 994/48.   35 Cleaver to Egremont,
24 Dec. [1798], PHA/57/13.   36 Brodrick to Midleton, 23 Oct. 1800, Ms. 1248, vol. 17, ff. 136–7.

hyperbole (and not just from George II and Archbishop King) about them; but the fact is that Englishmen like Cleaver obtained bishoprics in Ireland on much the same grounds as they obtained them in England – most of them had previously been college or private tutors to the sons of influential men. Viceregal chaplaincies were a stepping-stone to preferment which was unique to Ireland: tutorships were not. Thus, John Moore, archbishop of Canterbury, 1783–1805, had begun his career as tutor to Lord Clifden's father-in-law, the 4th duke of Marlborough; and George Pretyman-Tomline, bishop of Lincoln, 1787–1820, and of Winchester, 1820–7, whom Pitt unsuccessfully proposed as Moore's successor, had started his career as tutor to Pitt. Even in the markedly more aristocratic Church of England of 1832, where 'Eight of the [26] bishops were the sons or near relatives of peers ..., most if not all [the rest] had been tutors to young nobles or future statesmen.' At their best, the ex-tutors represented scholarship; and a tension between scholarship and professional service was a feature of the upper reaches of both Churches.[37]

The tension was much stronger in the Church of Ireland. This was partly because the chaplains were English and the professionals were Irish. Moreover, very few of the chaplains had had much experience of parochial or cathedral duties in the Church of England prior to their arrival in Ireland. By contrast, almost all of the Irishmen who reached the Irish bench had had to work their way up through the ranks of the Church of Ireland and were known quantities when the decision to elevate them was taken. It was, as Professor Akenson calls it, a 'two-caste arrangement'.[38] It was additionally inequitable because the imported tutor-chaplains generally speaking did not bear comparison to the best Irish-born scholars in the Church of Ireland – certainly not to George Berkeley, 'the worthiest, the learnedest, the wisest and the most virtuous divine of the three kingdoms'[39], who was appointed bishop of Cloyne in 1734 . In the late seventeenth and early eighteenth century, provosts, fellows and ex-fellows of TCD, nearly all of them Irish, had been regularly promoted to Irish bishoprics: between 1735 and 1796, this ceased to be the case.[40] Yet, during this period, and indeed throughout the eighteenth century, the Church of Ireland did not obtain from England a transfusion of new scholarly blood. In George I's reign, for example, the bishops 'sent out of England' were, if anything, less well qualified academically than the Irish appointees; and in George II's reign, three of them were heterodox. The unity of the two Churches was a point of great importance to Irish churchmen. But the Englishmen who actually arrived did nothing to strengthen it and merely helped to sink the Irish Church in the estimation of the Church of England. And, needless to say, there was no reciprocal trade in bishops from Ireland to England.

Another tension within the upper reaches of the Church of Ireland derived from the fact that the Englishmen on the Irish bench had usually given up whatever

37 Mathieson, *English Church reform*, pp 52 and 66; Cowper, *Deans of Canterbury*, pp 185–6 and 204–5. 38 Akenson, *Church of Ireland*, pp 12–16.   39 Leslie and Swanzy, *Clergy of Down*, p. 22, quoting the 1st earl of Egmont.   40 McDowell and Webb, *TCD*, pp 23–4, 34, 50, 59–61, 64, 78 and 107–8; McNally, *Early Hanoverian Ireland*, pp 166–7.

preferments they possessed (if they possessed any) before coming to Ireland. An Irish act of 17 and 18 Charles II, presumably passed for the laudable purpose of combating pluralism, stipulated that spiritual preferment in the Church of Ireland was incompatible with spiritual preferment in the Church of England.[41] As Cleaver's case shows, a chaplaincy did not of itself constitute a spiritual preferment; but, as it also shows, only an 'uncommonly kind' English patron, lay or ecclesiastical, would have allowed an English clergyman to forsake his preferment in the Church of England for long enough to prospect for better things in Ireland (see p. 192).[42] So, broadly speaking, an English clergyman with anything worth losing would have hesitated before embarking for Ireland, and most of the English tutor-chaplains who did embark bore at least the appearance of needy and desperate men, and were disliked accordingly by Irish clergymen. They were also disliked because they were a numerous band. There was no actual limit to their numbers,[43] and each lord lieutenant usually appointed up to ten chaplains at any one time. Of these, only his first chaplain in seniority or – as happened in 1751 – his first two, had any realistic hope of a bishopric; but this did not soften the stereotype of the viceregal chaplain. The few well connected Irishmen who were able to obtain second or third chaplaincies for themselves, were not appointed to bishoprics almost immediately, as the (almost invariably English) first chaplains were, but had to queue in inferior dignities in the Church – Agar for five years, William Beresford for far longer. Against this background, the slur cast by Englishmen on the 'moral character' and the 'qualification and character' of the Irish bench was unfair. It was unfair because it implied that the doubtful bishops of the Church of Ireland were Irish, whereas they were more than likely to be English. It is highly significant that the demonstration supposedly staged by the Church of England bishops in 1788 against the translation from the Irish bench of William Preston, bishop of Ferns, was against an Englishman, the former tutor, private secretary and first chaplain to the Duke of Rutland.[44]

It is not easy to find a direct comparison between an Englishman and an Irishman on the Irish bench, or between an English and an Irish aspirant to the

41 Lord Chancellor Lifford to Buckinghamshire, 18 [Feb.] 1779, *HMC Lothian Mss.*, pp 345–6.   42 Rev. Carew Reynell, who came to Ireland as chaplain to the 3rd duke of Devonshire in 1737, retained the chancellorship of Bristol cathedral until he obtained an Irish bishopric in 1739 – Hon. H.B. Legge to Devonshire, 6 Mar. 1739/40, Chatsworth papers, PRONI, T/3158/142. Hon. and Rev. Charles Lindsay retained his English preferments while chaplain to his brother-in-law, Lord Hardwicke, 1801–3, and did not resign them until made a bishop – Addington to Hardwicke, 8 Sep. 1803, Hardwicke papers, BL, Add. Ms. 35708, f. 187. But this seems to have been because Hardwicke (like Cleaver's patron, Egremont) was patron of the English livings which Lindsay held.   43 Hardwicke to Hon. Charles Yorke, 7 June 1802, ibid., Add. Ms. 35393, f. 82.   44 Bishop Watson, an old friend of Preston and, like him, a *protégé* of Rutland, thought Preston should not have been made a bishop (*Anecdotes of Watson*, pp 231–2). Preston's background was academic, and he was possibly a ducal adviser and amanuensis before Rutland brought him to Ireland in that capacity. Preston was fond of shooting, which may have been regarded as an un-episcopal if not actually uncanonical sport – Thomas Gascoigne to Rutland, 10 Oct. 1787, *HMC Rutland Mss.*, iii. 428; G.P.V. Akrigg, *Jacobean pageant, or*

Irish bench, because no two cases are ever sufficiently alike, or if they are, they occur at significantly different points in time. This latter reservation applies to the two cases of irregular private life which will now be compared. While the oft-mentioned John Hotham was chaplain to his brother-in-law, Lord Buckinghamshire, in 1777–9, Hotham's private life was far from what it should have been. In 1779, Buckinghamshire, who was about to recommend him for a bishopric, reported gleefully that Hotham's 'chastity has been attacked. ... As yet, indeed, the attack has only been signified by words and eyes gloatingly fixed upon his lower drapery. But probably the hands will soon follow the eyes and rend the veil of the temple. ... [The lady] inhabits the best house, keeps the best table and cuckolds the most agreeable husband in Dublin.' Shortly afterwards, Buckinghamshire referred to the incipient bishop's 'miscellaneous attachments.'⁴⁵ Had he not been such a well connected, and protected, Englishman, the likelihood is that Hotham would not have been made a bishop. This was the fate of the mere Irishman, the Rev. Luke Godfrey (one of the relatively few clerical opponents of Brodrick's father-in-law, Bishop Woodward, in the pamphlet war initiated by Woodward's *Present state of the Church of Ireland*). Although Godfrey was politically well connected in Ireland (in 1790 his daughter, Barbara, had married the 1st marquess of Donegall, who controlled three seats in the House of Commons⁴⁶), and although it had been confidently asserted late in 1795 that he would be the next bishop, Godfrey was passed over. Following this disappointment, the home secretary, Portland, tried to assuage Lady Donegall's 'filial piety' by reminding her of the other 'marks of favour which have been successively conferred upon Lord Donegall with a rapidity hardly to be paralleled.'⁴⁷ However, the real reason for Godfrey's staying unmitred was revealed two years later, in 1797, by Lord Camden. He stated that it was impossible to make Godfrey a bishop because 'a supposed intrigue between him and a certain countess in Ireland is too much talked of to make the recommendation a proper one.'⁴⁸ This comparison confirms that good connections in England counted for more in the making of Irish bishops than strong parliamentary interest in Ireland. It also suggests that unsuitable Englishmen became Irish bishops because they were out of sight of England and out of mind of George III and of those conscientious British ministers and senior English churchmen who might have blocked their promotion back home.⁴⁹

William Bennet, bishop of Cork, 1790–4, and of Cloyne, 1794–1820, was not a notorious sinner like Hotham. Still, he was the English appointee whose behaviour had caused Brodrick to declare in 1798: 'The root of the disorder is in making such men

the court of King James I (London, 1962), pp 312–13. **45** Buckinghamshire to Hotham Thompson, 13 Mar. and 12 Sep. 1779, T/3429/1/42 and 48. **46** Westmorland to Pitt, 30 Apr. 1790, Stanhope/Pitt papers, U1590/S5 0.5/1. **47** Portland to Lady Donegall, 26 Dec. 1795, *Irish official papers*, i. 131. **48** Camden to Portland (letter marked 'most secret'), 4 Dec. 1797, HO 100/70, ff. 325–7. **49** These suggestions are supported by the (admittedly confused) correspondence over the appointment of Dean Christopher Butson, an English *protégé* of the very Church-minded Addington, as bishop of Clonfert in 1804 – Hardwicke to Charles Yorke, 3 May 1804, Hardwicke to Hawkesbury, 24 May 1804, and Hawkesbury to Hardwicke, 20 May 1804, Hardwicke papers, BL, Add. Mss. 35706, f.3, 35609, f.23, and 35709, f.33.

bishops.' He was the nephew and former chaplain/secretary of Lord Westmorland. Brodrick's complaint about him was that he intended to present to the living of Midleton a young relative who 'was, as is said, apprentice either to a silversmith or an attorney. I firmly believe he never had any education at all. His moral character is extremely bad, and as to religion, he has not a feeling on the subject.'[50] Bennet was, from the beginning, slapdash in the exercise of his episcopal functions.[51] He acquired notoriety during the last months of Westmorland's *régime* because of the latter's desperate efforts, while he still had the power, to obtain something even better than Cloyne for his newly promoted nephew – the archbishopric of Tuam, the bishopric of Clogher, an English bishopric, even the provostship of TCD. Referring to Clogher, Westmorland assured Pitt: 'Bennet would be the properest man for us ..., if he was not to be considered as almost too lucky. But he is a man of great character here.'[52] Burke thought not. Referring to the provostship of TCD, he castigated Bennet's 'odious and, at this time, ... portentous avarice and rapacity.'[53] Bennet was subsequently renowned for the regularity of his absenteeism.[54] When present, he later annoyed Brodrick (his metropolitan from 1801 onwards) by being a 'strenuous' party man in Co. Cork elections.[55] (This was not surprising, as he had been employed by Westmorland to fish in those troubled waters in the early 1790s.[56]) It must have been Bennet, as it certainly was Richard Marlay, bishop of Waterford, whom Brodrick had in mind when he wrote in 1802: 'You will not be surprised at the disorder I found [in the province of Cashel] when you recollect that for two of my suffragan bishops, I had *beaux esprits*. I must add that this was the least offensive part of their character as bishops.'[57] Nevertheless, the late nineteenth-century history of Bennett's old school, Harrow, records that he 'was, according to the general testimony of his contemporaries, an admirable scholar and a delightful companion.'[58] In Chart, he later found an inventive apologist:

> a noted antiquarian, ... [he] might perhaps have been the Reeves of the eigh-
> teenth century had he resided in his diocese. Unfortunately, however, he spent

50 Brodrick to Midleton, 5 Mar. 1798, Ms. 1248, vol. 17, ff. 38–9.   51 Sirr, *Archbishop Trench of Tuam*, p. 8.   52 Westmorland to Pitt, [pre-5 Sep. 1794, PRO, 30/8/331, ff. 311–12.   53 Quoted in Stubbs, *History of Dublin university*, p. 276; the negotiations leading to the filling of the provostship by a scholarly, clerical fellow of the college, Rev. Dr Richard Murray, are described on pp 271–8. See also a memorandum from Edward Cooke, Westmorland's special envoy to London, to Pitt, [16 Nov. 1794], *Later correspondence of George III*, ii, pp 264–8. For the archbishopric, bishoprics and provostship which Westmorland attempted, or was reputed to have attempted, to obtain for Bennet, see: Westmorland to Pitt, [pre-5 Sep.] 1794, PRO, 30/8/331, f. 312; Westmorland to Portland, 6 Oct. 1794, HO 100/46, f. 210; Bishop Marlay to Charlemont, 18 Oct. 1794, *HMC Charlemont Mss.*, ii, pp 250–51; and Hon. William Brodrick to Brodrick, 23 Dec. 1794, NLI, Ms. 8883.   54 Brodrick to Midleton, 5 Mar. 1798, Ms. 1248, vol. 17, ff. 38–9.   55 Brodrick to Midleton, [Apr./May 1817], Ms. 1248, vol. 19, f. 138.   56 Viscount Longueville to Lord Hobart, June 1803, enclosing a letter from Bennet to Rev. B. O'Sullivan, 13 Jan. 1801, Jupp/Aspinall transcripts from the Buckinghamshire papers, Bucks. RO, J. 346–7.   57 Brodrick to Midleton, 19 Sep. and 14 Oct. 1802, Ms. 1248, vol. 18, ff. 52–3 and 56. He presumably meant '*bels esprits*', which means 'wits' or, satirically, 'men of genius'. See also R.W. Bond (ed.), *The Marlay letters, 1778–1820* ... (London, 1937), pp 57–63.   58 Edmund W. Howson and George Townsend Warner (eds.), *Harrow school* ... (London, 1898), p. 185.

much of the later years of his life in London on the ground that family illness of a distressing kind obliged him to do so. His term of office lasted well into the Union [he died in 1820], but though he was sufficiently interested in Irish antiquities to peruse, illustrate and comment on the work of others ..., he seems to have published no considerable work on the subject. ... [He] was noted for his long and persistent advocacy of the Bible Society ... [and was one of] the most distinguished prelates at the time of the Union.[59]

Not even Chart, however, could have found anything good to say about Westmorland's next chaplain, 'a poor creature' from England[60] called John Whetham, whom Westmorland had made dean of Lismore and whom he wanted to make bishop of Ossory while the going was good. In early September 1794, the newly appointed Portland wrote to Pitt protesting at Westmorland's recommendation of Whetham for the bishopric. Surely, wrote Portland, 'other means might be suggested to him [Westmorland], by which Mr Whetham, with what he already possesses, might have an income equal to that of the bishopric, though I had rather see him removed from that country [Ireland] into this, because he would pass here more easily unnoticed and be lost in the mass, which cannot be the case in Ireland. But ... my object is to prevent his being placed on the bench.'[61] It is not altogether clear what these comments mean – apart from the obvious, that Portland wanted the job for a Whig. The implication is that standards were, or at the very least ought to be, higher in the Church of Ireland than in the Church of England, because clergymen of the former came under the hostile scrutiny of a non-Anglican majority of the population. For whatever reason Whetham was not made an Irish bishop,[62] and Westmorland's other improper recommendation – that of Fowler for the primacy – was not complied with either. Westmorland's successors, Fitzwilliam and Camden, between them made only one chaplain-cum-secretary a bishop; this was John Porter, bishop of Killala, 1795–7, and bishop of Clogher, 1797–1819. Lord Abercorn, who had wanted Clogher for an Irish *protégé*, referred dismissively to Porter as 'Lord Camden's Cambridge parson.'[63] But, in fact, Porter had been regius professor of Hebrew at Cambridge, and so was qualified on scholarly grounds for a bishopric, even if his translation from Killala to Clogher was indecently rapid. Camden's successor, Cornwallis, discontinued the practice of having a first chaplain/secretary,[64] so he made no bishop on that basis, and – with one immediately post-Union exception – Porter was the last of the line.

Meanwhile, scholarly clerics of Irish birth were once again being raised to the Irish bench: Hugh Hamilton in 1796, Joseph Stock in 1798 and Matthew Young in 1799. These were among the 'events which the King ... believed and trusted would be

59 Phillips, *Church of Ireland*, iii, pp 265 and 290.   60 John Beresford to Auckland, 23 Aug. 1794, Auckland papers, BL, Add. Ms. 34453, f. 12. I am indebted for this reference to Terence Finley. 61 Portland to Pitt, 6 Sep. 1794, Portland papers, PRONI, T/2905/22/8.   62 Pitt to Westmorland, 19 Nov. 1794, *Later correspondence of George III*, ii, pp 268–71.   63 Abercorn to his political manager, John Stewart, 18 Feb. [1798], Abercorn papers, PRONI, D/623/A/80/82.   64 Bishop O'Beirne to John Foster, 28 Mar. 1808, PRONI, D/207/50/4.

productive of very considerable advantage to the Established Church of Ireland.'[65] (If George III had genuinely been concerned to advance scholarly Irishmen to Irish bishoprics, he could have initiated that change of policy at any time since his accession in 1760.) It has been suggested, perhaps too cynically, that these promotions took place because 'in the disturbed years at the close of the century, ... Irish sees had become less attractive in English eyes.'[66] This would have been Euseby Cleaver's view (see p. 190), and it no doubt had some validity. But, following Westmorland's series of discreditable recommendations of 1794, there may have been a dawning realisation in government circles that the old system of preferring (in both senses) tutor-chaplains had been harmful to the character of the Irish bench, to the reputation of the British government and, ultimately, to the British connection itself.

In spite, therefore, of the difficulty of making direct comparisons, it is reasonable to suggest that, generally speaking, the Englishmen on that bench, in Agar's day and earlier, were inferior to the Irish-born. At the most senior levels, it is impossible to make a comparison because the most senior levels were reserved for Englishmen. But the evidence suggests that between the death of Boulter in 1742 and that of Stuart in 1822, the unfailingly English primates were not up to the job of leading the Church of Ireland (with the exception, perhaps, of Robinson during his first twelve years). During the dangerous years of Robinson's primacy – the period 1778–93 – the Church was led by Agar, and during the whole of Stuart's primacy, Stuart was led by Brodrick. The archbishops of Dublin of the period 1729–1801, all but one of whom were English,[67] were no more distinguished than the archbishops of Armagh, with Fowler combining obnoxiousness with lack of distinction. All the bishops of the eighteenth-century Church of Ireland whose promotion was indecently rapid were English; almost all the persistent absenters were English; the only three who were theologically suspect were English (Clayton was part-Irish by birth, but he was made an Irish bishop on English grounds and through English influence); and the three who were most flagrantly immoral, Stone, Hervey and Hotham, were likewise English.

It would be a little sweeping, granted some of the individuals in the sample, to characterise the Englishmen, Fowler, Hotham and Cleaver, as the most mercenary and 'sordid'[68] bishops of the century. But they would be hard to beat in those respects (Hervey being one bishop who would run them close, in spite – in his case – of acts of wild generosity early in his career[69]). In general, because most of the English bishops on the Irish bench had originally come to Ireland naked, or almost so, they were

---

65 Portland to Primate Newcome, 15 Dec. 1797, T/2905/22/96.   66 McDowell and Webb, *TCD*, p. 108.   67 Significantly, the one Irishman, Arthur Smyth, had been employed in the late 1730s as tutor and grand tour companion of Lord Hartington, the son of the lord lieutenant, Devonshire, and a future lord lieutenant himself – as the damaged and obscurely worded Latin inscription on Smyth's funeral monument in St Patrick's Cathedral, Dublin, records. Smyth acknowledged in June 1760 that 'I owe my rise entirely' to Hartington, now 4th duke of Devonshire (Chatsworth papers, PRONI, T/3158/1617). The duke was dead, but his friends were in power, when Smyth was made archbishop of Dublin.   68 This adjective, as has been seen (p. 389), was actually applied to Cleaver's brother, William, Bishop of Chester.   69 Beaufort's journal, 1787, MIC/250, pp 24–6.

particularly liable to the imputation of mercenariness. Dr Beaufort, for example, gleefully noted on his travels in 1787 that John Oswald, bishop of Raphoe, 1763–80 (a Scot), who had billed his successor for £4,000 for improvements to the palace kitchen, offices and demesne, was 'so minute as to charge every oak, laburnum, ash, etc., that he planted'; also, that Bishop Percy of Dromore, among other specimens of miserliness, dispensed with a diocesan registrar so that he could himself pocket the fees of the office, and made a clergyman ride five miles specially for the purpose of paying Percy ninepence, 'forgot in his institution charges'![70] One Englishman on the Irish bench who was a distinguished exception to this rule, or at any rate preconception, was Bishop Chenevix of Waterford.[71]

In fact, it rather looks as if Englishmen on the English bench were also conspicuous for avarice. In 1829, the historian of the bishops of Bath and Wells commented ruefully: 'Each individual churchman seems to think the Church will "last his time", little heeding what will become of its revenues afterwards. The hierarchy, by too much secularity, must eventually work the downfall of the temporalities of the Establishment. A bishop is not vested with those revenues solely for his own aggrandisement.'[72] When the winds of Ecclesiastical Enquiry blew open the arcana of both the Church of Ireland and the Church of England in the course of the 1830s, it was among the Church of England episcopate that the most embarrassing discoveries were made. While the practice of nepotism was more or less common form among the bishops of both Churches, the recently deceased Bishop Pretyman-Tomline had exceeded all bounds in the extent of the financial provision he had made for his family (two sons and a nephew).[73] So had Bowyer Edward Sparke, bishop of Ely, 1812–36, who in addition to the immoderate and nepotic abuse of his patronage, had most disgracefully anticipated it, to the considerable detriment of his successor. Archbishop Manners Sutton had also been guilty of this type of anticipation.[74] In Durham, in spite of the exceptional rise in the incomes of the bishop and cathedral dignitaries on account of their new-found mineral wealth, pluralism – for which there was no necessity whatever – was still prevalent among them.[75] There was no equivalent at senior levels in the Church of Ireland of such excesses, thanks to the progress of 'graceful reform', and particularly to Primate Beresford. The efforts of Archbishop Lawrence on behalf of his son-in-law, Henry Cotton (see p. 350), were mild in comparison and fully justified by Cotton's services to the Church as librarian and historian. In any case, both Lawrence and Cotton were English.

A MIXED BAG OF BISHOPS, 1758–1822

While a few Englishmen on the Irish bench were unenviably outstanding for immorality, absenteeism and avariciousness, and more were either over-promoted or

70 Ibid., pp 15 and 19.   71 *Remains of Mrs Richard Trench*, pp 9–11.   72 Cassan, *Lives of the bishops of Bath and Wells*, p. 176.   73 Cowper, *Deans of Canterbury*, pp 179–80, 182 and 187–8; Evans, *The contentious tithe*, p. 5.   74 Mathieson, *English Church reform*, pp 65 and 114–15.   75 Heesom, *The founding of Durham University*, pp 11–15.

at least promoted over-rapidly, most of them were not conspicuously inferior to the bishops of Irish birth and occupied with them the middle ground of the profession. These, the great majority of the episcopate, were men of mixed achievement and record. In general, they attained a higher mean standard of performance than the strictures of Brodrick (and Stuart) might lead one to expect; and in most cases the mean concealed some extremes of good and bad behaviour.

In his characteristically tolerant and civilised fashion, Hubert Butler makes a good case for a number of them, mainly for the already-mentioned Robert Fowler junior. He was of particular interest to Butler because when he was eventually[76] made a bishop in 1813 (in spite of the sexual transgression of his youth and of other doubts as to whether he could 'be conscientiously recommended'), it was as bishop of Ossory, and Ossory was the diocese in which Butler lived.

> On the eve of the Union, the Irish protestant hierarchy were more independent in their doctrines and behaviour than they have ever been before or since. ... In Mayo, the Bishop of Killala [John Law], despairing of converting the catholic majority to protestantism, was circulating among them such catholic literature as might elevate their morals and manners ...; [and, it might be added, his successor, Joseph Stock, distinguished himself during the French invasion of Connaught in the autumn of 1798 by his courage, moderation and compassion]. In Kilkenny, Dr O'Beirne, ... [then] Bishop [of Ossory], was both zealous and fashionable. He had promoted the association for discountenancing vice, and also, in collaboration with the Duchess of Devonshire, written a modish comedy for Drury Lane. ...
>
> Among the clergy after the Union there was certainly more earnestness and morality; there was less laxity about doctrine and as a consequence more sectarian bitterness. In the diocese of Killala, for example, where the protestant bishop had once circulated catholic tracts, a vigorous campaign of proselytism was initiated. In Kilkenny the Rev. Peter Roe ..., the [Evangelical] rector of St Mary's, an ardent crusader for Sunday schools and bible societies[78] ... [was at war with Fowler] ..., his lax and tolerant bishop, ... [who] was often wise where ... Roe was foolish. Men will usually respect those who have good humour, good nerves and a knowledge of human nature. They do not ask too searchingly how these virtues are nourished. Probably most of Fowler's contemporaries would have agreed with our diocesan historian that he made 'an excellent bishop.'[79]

---

76 Camden to 1st Viscount Mountjoy, and Fowler to Mountjoy, 31 Oct. and 1 Nov. 1796, Domvile papers, NLI, Ms. 9399.   77 Stuart to Brodrick, 19 May 1806, NLI, Ms. 8869/4; 3rd Earl Talbot to William Gregory, Dec. 1819, Talbot-Gregory correspondence, PRONI, D/4100/1/5 78 Ironically (in view of these far from Agarite enthusiasms), Agar may have helped Roe to obtain preferment in the diocese of Ossory – Henry Roe (Roe's father?) to Agar, 10 Jan. 1809, T/3719/ C/43/4.   79 Butler, *Escape from the anthill*, pp 32–45.

Although there was more than a generation between them, Agar did have a number of personal attributes in common with Fowler junior: he was polished, fashionable, music-loving, tolerant and wise in areas where religious enthusiasts were foolish. There, however, the likeness ends: there are few, if any, instances of Agar's being 'lax', either in his personal conduct or as a diocesan. At the time of Fowler's promotion, Bishop O'Beirne complained to Primate Stuart that it had 'produced more general indignation than ever has been witnessed in Dublin.'[80]

A better example of a bishop who was of both good and bad repute is John Garnett, bishop of Clogher, 1758–82. Garnett was Hotham's predecessor. To him must therefore be mainly due the tribute which the usually hypercritical Hotham paid following his first visit to Clogher: 'The diocese is in the highest order of any in Ireland. The clergy are a most respectable body of men, many of them very learned, all of them conscientious and exemplary, and except two or three for whom I must get houses to be built, strictly resident on their respective benefices.'[81] Garnett has been immortalised for his benevolence to the meritorious but ungracious Skelton, who was languishing in the rough and remote parish of Pettigo when Garnett was translated to Clogher in 1758. Garnett, 'a prelate of great humility and a friend to literature and religion ..., though he had but one eye, could discover ... men of merit as well as some people with two.' Quite unsolicited, he promoted Skelton twice, to Devenish, near Enniskillen, in 1759, and to Fintona, near Omagh, in 1766. 'Such a bishop was indeed an honour to the station he filled and a blessing to the clergy who had the good fortune to be under him.' Skelton's way of thanking him was to declare repeatedly 'My Lord, you are only a puppet in the hands of God Almighty', to which 'the good Bishop' replied 'You're right, Skelton, you're right.'[82] This attractive character is not the one met on pp 177–8, where Garnett appeared in the role of dogged exploiter of the patronage attached to his successive boroughs of Old Leighlin and Clogher. The incoming lord lieutenant in 1776, Buckinghamshire, also encountered the worldly and self-seeking Garnett. Before Buckinghamshire's appointment was even official, Garnett – clearly bent on preferment – pursued him to his parish church in Norfolk:

> Last Sunday, when prayers were advanced as far as the middle of the psalms [wrote Buckinghamshire], an ecclesiastical figure, followed by a respectful attendant, stalked up the centre of Blickling church and, stroking up a band from under his waistcoat, possessed himself of the parson's pew. My eyes were immediately attracted, and recollection suggested to me that it was one Garnett, whom I remember fellow of Sidney College, and some years afterwards saw presented at St James' as an Irish bishop. Church over, he honoured me with a visit ... . The conversation turning upon Ireland and my having been mentioned as destined to succeed Lord Harcourt, I took occasion to hint at the numberless applications which that probably ill-founded report had occasioned. Whether

80 O'Beirne to Stuart, 3 June 1813, Bedfordshire RO, WY 994/75.   81 Hotham to Viscount Sackville, 9 July 1782, *HMC Stopford-Sackville Mss.*, i, pp 279–80.   82 Adam Clarke (ed.), *Compendium edition of the lives of Bishop Newton, Rev. Philip Skelton, etc.*, ii, pp 392–407.

this hint prevented him, or he had not originally intended to ask for anything, the successor to the present Lord Primate is not as yet appointed.

In any case, 'the present Lord Primate', who had come as a viceregal chaplain to Ireland at the same time as Garnett, in 1751, outlived him by twelve years.[83]

Even Brodrick and his father-in-law and early patron in the Church, Bishop Woodward, were not above the imputation of worldliness and self-seeking. 'To put it mildly', writes Dr Kenneth Milne, 'Charles Brodrick was well-connected. He was the fourth son of the 3rd Viscount Midleton [a title which dated from 1717], and married [in 1786] ... Mary Woodward, daughter of the Bishop of Cloyne ... . Brodrick ..., though not Irish-born, was familiar with Irish society and politics long before his ... [appointment] to the bench. Having graduated from Cambridge, he came to Ireland [in 1784] to look after the family estates [at Midleton and in Cos. Waterford and Monaghan[84]]. It was at Cloyne, his father-in law's diocese, that he served the early part of his ministry.'[85] The connection with Woodward in fact ante-dated Brodrick's marriage, as Woodward had preceded Brodrick as head agent for Lord Midleton's estates, in the period 1780–4.[86] Probably it originated in England, where all the Brodrick family lived until Brodrick's move to Ireland; Woodward owned a (probably inherited) property in Gloucestershire, and his brother was a physician in Bath.[87] Following his marriage, Brodrick explained very unabashedly to his family's political ally, Lord Shannon, 'that my wishes would be to have a deanery of from £300 to £500 a year, and that if it exceeded that sum, I hoped the Bishop of Cloyne would permit me to exchange the archdeaconry which I am to have very soon.'[88] Woodward, in the event, was able to do even better for his son-in-law, for in June 1789 a vacancy in the rectory of Castrachore, alias Midleton, then held along with the treasurership of Cloyne, enabled him to appoint Brodrick to both.[89] This meant that he could also go on living, until challenged in 1793 (p. 212), at Cahirmone, the residence of the agent for the Midleton estate.

This sounds like a very cosy arrangement from Brodrick's point of view, and a nepotic action on the part of Woodward. Yet, an earlier letter from Brodrick to his brother, Lord Midleton, prior to the marriage connection and just after Woodward's promotion to Cloyne, gives a very different impression of Woodward:

> His Lordship [Woodward] has very explicitly informed me ... that he is determined to consider nothing but real merit in everything that comes within his patronage; that as to the living of Curryglass, he thinks himself bound to give it to a Mr King, who he says is fifty years of age and only a curate, and he

83 Buckinghamshire to Hotham Thompson, 26 Sep. 1776, T/3429/1/3.   84 Brodrick to Midleton, 22 Apr. 1784 and 27 June 1786, Ms. 1248, vol. 14, ff. 5 and 95.   85 Milne, 'Principle or pragmatism', p. 187.   86 Midleton to [Daniel?] McCarthy, 20 May 1781, and Brodrick to Midleton, 30 May 1784, Ms. 1248, vol. 13, ff. 164–7, and vol. 14, ff. 22–23.   87 Woodward to Brodrick, 21 Mar. 1792, Ms. 8870/2; Hotham to Hotham Thompson, 5 Oct. 1785, T/3429/2/9.   88 Brodrick to Midleton, 30 Oct. 1787, Ms 1248/14, f. 115.   89 Brady, *Records of Cork, Cloyne and Ross*, ii. 392.

mentions him as a person to be preferred to his own particular partialities because he has been for a number of years a most useful assistant to him in several of the public charities in Dublin, particularly that of the foundlings, previous to his obtaining a bishopric; and I find from the Bishop's discourse that there are others who from the same line of conduct have highly recommended themselves to his favour, and will take place of any other recommendations, in which I understand from his Lordship that even Mr Connolly [*sic*] had not interfered.[90]

Thomas Conolly of Castletown, Co. Kildare, was Woodward's Whiggish patron, through whose influence he had been made a bishop. Conolly controlled two boroughs, was MP for a county (Londonderry), and was a leading figure among the independent, not to say wayward, country gentlemen in the House of Commons. This placed his adherence at a premium in the eyes of Dublin Castle. His influence was particularly strong during the lord lieutenancy of Buckinghamshire, whose second wife was Conolly's sister; Conolly made the promise of a bishopric for Woodward (which did not materialise until after the close of the Buckinghamshire viceroyalty) one of the conditions of Conolly's support. So, Woodward – like all bishops – was a political appointee, and yet pursued a policy of promoting clergymen on merit, and did not exempt from its operation the nominees of both Conolly and Lord Midleton.

In more general terms, he was a pioneering exponent of practical Christianity. In 1768, when dean of Clogher, he had published (and dedicated to Conolly) *An argument in support of the right of the poor in the kingdom of Ireland to a national provision; in the appendix to which an attempt is made to settle a measure of the contribution due from each man to the poor on the footing of justice.* In this pamphlet he advocated 'the establishment of a system of county poor-houses in Ireland on the same lines as the houses of industry in the larger towns. He suggested in each county a poorhouse with fifty beds for a hundred paupers, ten beds for ten sick persons and a house of correction for vagrant beggars – ... reforms ... [which] were partially carried into effect by the institution of the Irish county infirmaries in 1769.'[91] This highly significant publication has been overshadowed by Woodward's famous or notorious *Present state of the Church of Ireland*, which has coloured him indelibly as a reactionary. Yet, he had supported the Catholic Relief Acts of 1782 (he had not been in the House of Lords in 1778), and said so in his pamphlet. He was a thinking man and, in most situations, a man of conscience, who was troubled – among other things – by the potential clash between his obligations to Conolly and Whiggery and his obligations to Agar and the Church. (There was no clash between them in 1786–7, because Conolly declared his opposition to tithe reform and support for coercion in Munster.) During the crucial and kaleidoscopic session of 1793, Woodward wrote an important letter on this theme to Conolly:

90 Shannon to Midleton, 3 Oct. 1783, Ms. 1248, vol. 11, f. 157.   91 Phillips, *Church of Ireland*, iii, pp 274–5.

The critical situation of the Ecclesiastical Establishment and the protestant religion in Ireland rendered it my indispensable duty to contribute my vote for their preservation. For this purpose, I have sent my proxy to the Archbishop of Cashel, on whose judgement on these questions I rely, as we have always concurred in opinion. At the same time, I have stated in the strongest manner my wishes that he would not produce my vote on any *political* question, unless he was forced to do it by the orders of the House. ... It would grieve me in any instance to give a vote in opposition to you. ... Yet ... [that risk] could not be avoided without a flagrant desertion of the immediate duty of that office with which I am entrusted by the Constitution and to the exercise of which I was raised by your protection.[92]

The letter shows extreme punctiliousness in Woodward. Perhaps it was this which dictated his self-exculpation to Archbishop Moore following the Henry Agar affair, although it is hard to believe that he was not also influenced by hopes of the primacy for himself and/or of the bishopric of Cloyne for Brodrick.

Brodrick was strongly influenced by his father-in-law's ideas;[93] and, thanks to the good start he had been given in Cloyne by Woodward and to the influence of the Midleton family, he became a bishop in his mid-thirties (only a little older than Agar had been when made bishop of Cloyne in 1768). Cloyne was the object of the Midleton family's ambition for him.[94] But he did not succeed Woodward there when the latter died in 1794 (that prize went to the 'almost too lucky' Bennet). In the following year, Brodrick became a bishop, although of 'infinitely ... the worst of all Irish sees', 'the bog of Clonfert', which was worth little more per annum than the rectory of Midleton.[95] Nevertheless, it was a start. In 1796, he was translated to Kilmore, and he succeeded Agar at Cashel in 1801. In Kilmore, Brodrick had given preferment to the newly ordained John Jebb, the future bishop of Limerick, who followed him to Cashel in 1802. In 1807, as a young and impressionable clergyman in that diocese, he described Brodrick as

a host in himself. He appears to me daily growing in wisdom, in disinterestedness, in spirituality and in humility. His perfect knowledge of the world, strong good sense and unimpeachable integrity, joined with that personal dignity which is at once so simple and so commanding, give him a wonderful weight in the world ... . I cannot, indeed, find words to express the delight I feel at having such a man for my patron and my friend, or my gratitude that our Church is blest with such a guardian in these awful times.

92 Woodward to Conolly, 5 Mar. 1793, Leinster papers, NLI (an unsorted and recently acquired archive). I am indebted for this reference and transcription to Sir Richard Aylmer. 93 Brodrick to Midleton, 5 Dec. 1798, Ms. 1248, vol. 17, f. 95. 94 Midleton to Brodrick, 4 Aug. 1794, Ms. 8889/11. 95 Bishop Butson to Agar, 17 Apr. 1809, T/3719/C/43/74; Bishop Marlay to Charlemont, 18 Oct. 1794, *HMC Charlemont Mss.*, ii, pp 250–51; Albinia, Dowager viscountess Midleton, to Brodrick, 18 Dec. 1794, Ms. 8885/11.

In later life, Bishop Jebb declared: 'I would not exchange the results and the remembrance of my connection with Archbishop Brodrick, now a saint in heaven, for the wealth of worlds.'[96] It must be suspected, however, that Jebb took Brodrick too much at face value and invested him with a religious enthusiasm which was actually Jebb's own. Brodrick was exactly a generation younger than Agar (he had been born in 1761), and the differences of generation and style between Agar and him are obvious: where Agar was occasionally to be seen in a tavern, and played his part in the political wining and dining which were characteristic of Dublin's 'parliament winter', Brodrick 'was strictly temperate and only drank water at dinner.'[97] But there was a coolly business-like side to Brodrick's (as to Agar's) character, which manifested itself particularly in the management of the affairs of his see estate. John Hare, when negotiating for the renewal of Lord Normanton's Cashel see lands lease in 1812 (see pp 418–20), spoke of Brodrick in terms which are hard to reconcile with Jebb's eulogia: 'he is a cunning, crafty, avaricious man, yet like all dissemblers he wishes to be thought what he really is not, a moderate, fair-dealing man, more devoted to the good things of the other world than this. He is vain and open to flattery.'[98]

Essentially, Brodrick too was a child of the eighteenth century, and his 'wonderful weight in the world' owed much to his aristocratic background (fig. 18). The son, brother and (although this could not have been anticipated in his lifetime) father of a viscount, Brodrick conducted his business affairs like a temporal rather than a spiritual peer. When, in 1809, his daughter, Mary, became engaged to Lord Bernard, son and heir of the rich Co. Cork magnate, the 1st earl of Bandon, and grandson of Agar's friend, Lord Shannon, the settlements were on the grand aristocratic scale: 'I thought' wrote Brodrick 'that in taking £5,000 per annum I had provided for every possible want Lord B. and M. could have.'[99] Some years later, in 1817, when Brodrick was having a row with Lord Normanton over the renewal, it was as a fellow-aristocrat, not as a bishop, that Brodrick spoke: '[I never] knew or heard of such a paragraph being penned by one gentleman when writing to another in the same sphere of life. ... It is language, as you very well know, perfectly inadmissible in the society into which your situation in life carries you.'[100] Attention has already been drawn to Agar's aristocratic preconceptions about the social class from which churchmen should be drawn – 'However exemplary and virtuous ... [a] curate might be, ... to one class of parishioners he too nearly approximated, and from another he was too far removed in situation, to excite for his representations or admonitions a necessary respect.' Brodrick, in spite of the generation gap, was (to a modern way of thinking) no more advanced in this respect. In 1818, his brother-in-law, the Rev. Dr Henry Woodward, rector of Fethard in the diocese of Cashel, suggested to him the winding-up of the Cashel widows' fund. His reasons were that the existence of the fund encouraged 'a low description of clergyman', improvident marriages and marriages to 'low women'

---

96 Forster, *Life of Jebb*, i. 54, and ii. 117.   97 Seymour, *Diocese of Emly*, p. 262.   98 Hare to Normanton, 5 Sep. 1812, 21 M 57, 2nd earl's unreferenced correspondence.   99 Brodrick to Midleton, 23 Jan. 1809, Ms. 1248, vol. 19, f. 38.   100 Brodrick to Normanton, 15 Feb. 1817, 21 M 57, 2nd earl's unreferenced correspondence.

– all of them misfortunes which he knew Brodrick did not want to 'multiply' in the diocese.[101] From his elevation to the archbishopric of Cashel in 1801 until his death in 1822, Brodrick was unquestionably 'one of the most effective reformers within the Irish Church.'[102] But even before 1822, his style of reforming churchmanship had become as outmoded as Agar's had begun to look in Brodrick's heyday. Actually, he had become gravely compromised as a reformer, under pressure from the political realities with which he had to contend.[103] In other words, and in spite of Jebb, Brodrick is just like the other bishops in the sample: the truth about him lies somewhere between the 'saint in heaven' and the 'cunning, crafty, avaricious man.'

Brodrick, like Agar, belonged to a borough-owning family. But he objected to any bargain over the seats for the family borough of Midleton as a *quid pro quo* for his own promotion – as did his brother, Lord Midleton (see p. 479). Such a transaction Brodrick actually called 'simoniacal'[104] – a term which was not peculiar to Brodrick and the 'graceful' reformers. In 1789, it was used by William Cecil Pery, bishop of Limerick, a man nearer to Agar's generation (actually, he was fifteen years older). The Perys were not a borough-owning family, although they as good as controlled one seat for Limerick City. This had been held from 1761 until 1785 by Bishop Pery's elder brother, the speaker, (pp 147–8). The great object of the Perys' ambition was the bishopric of Limerick, because the most important part of the Pery estate, Newtown Pery, adjoined the old city of Limerick; and in 1784, this was obtained for Bishop Pery on the strength of Speaker Pery's political influence. Against this background, particular significance attaches to a letter which the Bishop wrote to his brother, now Lord Pery, in 1789, sorrowfully but firmly reiterating his refusal to comply with Pery's request regarding a living in the diocese:

> It grieved me excessively, and still continues to do so, that I was obliged to refuse your request in favour of Mr Hoare's exchange with his son, but I got the young man appointed resident preacher at the cathedral, worth [to] him about forty guineas a year, which is pretty well for a young man but little more than two years in orders. I ... [have] made an absolute resolution never to agree to the resignation of his living, the best in the three dioceses [Limerick, Inniscattery and Ardfert], to his son; for if I did, I must do the same for others who had stronger calls on me than Mr Hoare, and [I] would not make a precedent that would be highly unjust and ungenerous to all the clergy in the diocese. But the matter of fact is this, that they are so eager for this change to get for the son a wife of £1,400 or £1,500 fortune, which the father is to put in his pocket, so that the business would be absolutely simoniacal ... . Let me then assure you that there is nothing on earth I would refuse you that I could do consistent with my conscience and honour, which I hope I shall never forfeit;

101 Woodward to Brodrick, 18 Sep. 1818, NLI, Ms. 8861/9.   102 Akenson, *Church of Ireland*, p. 74.
103 Milne, 'Principle or pragmatism', p. 193. This is the descent from principle to pragmatism which is the theme of the essay.   104 *Lord Shannon's letters to his son*, p. 1iii.

for, indeed, I love you more than all the world besides, and so I ought, for to you I entirely owe my present situation.[105]

This letter is another reminder that, while parliamentary influence made or contributed to the making of bishops, whether it be Pery, Woodward, Brodrick or Agar himself, it did not necessarily make bishops who were unmindful of the higher responsibilities of their calling. Unfortunately for the favourable impression of Bishop Pery (and of the late eighteenth-century Irish bench) which the letter creates, he is yet another example of a bishop who failed to maintain consistently the high standards of conduct of which he was capable. Only a few years later, he was the subject of a strong complaint to Agar (as Pery's metropolitan) from Lord Chancellor FitzGibbon, whose seat and estate were situated in the county and diocese of Limerick. Pery's 'conduct to his clergy' wrote FitzGibbon, 'has been for some years capricious and brutal in the extreme, but has now become so very arbitrary and oppressive that it cannot longer be endured. ... Yesterday, the Bishop held his ordinary visitation, at which he was guilty of a most unwarrantable and cruel act of oppression against a clergyman of exemplary good character and conduct ..., [whom] I am determined, so far as the law will bear me out, to protect.'[106] It may be that Bishop Pery is yet another instance of a churchman who remained too long in harness. He was seventy-two in 1793 (a mere trifle compared to Archbishops Cox and Robinson); and FitzGibbon's suggestion that the capriciousness and brutality were characteristics of only 'some years' standing, implies that Pery had not been always thus.

THE CASE FOR COADJUTORS, 1770–1819

Agar was not guilty (though this was a matter of luck, not rectitude) of the form of avariciousness to which Cox, Robinson and Fowler succumbed, that of lingering on in their archbishoprics, for the sake of the emoluments, long after their usefulness (not that Cox had ever had any) was at an end. This was a decision which should not have been left to the discretion of the individuals concerned. It was not left to them in the contemporary Roman catholic Church in Ireland, where a system of coadjutorship had, since the seventeenth century, existed routinely and fairly unacrimoniously. These catholic coadjutorships did not obviate all aspects of episcopal superannuation and neglect; for example, the Rev. Dr Anthony Blake, archbishop of Armagh, 1758–87, 'chose to live in Galway among his landed relations rather than in his diocese of poor and discriminated-against catholics', and did not submit to a coadjutor and retire to Galway 'on a pension out of the diocese' until 1782.[107] This mention of money is probably the key to the divergent practices of the two Churches. Tom Moore noted in August 1823 that Primate Stuart, 'whose income was £20,000 a year, ... left £130,000

---

105 This paragraph is taken from Malcomson, 'Speaker Pery and the Pery papers', pp 40–1. 106 FitzGibbon to Agar, 27 Aug. 1793, T/3719/C/27/7 (see pp 212–13).   107 Cullen, *New Ross church*, p. 6; Stuart, *Armagh*, pp 407–9.

behind him, and Troy, the R.C. archbishop of Dublin, whose income was £800 a year, ... died worth about a tenpenny.'[108] Catholic prelates were so poorly remunerated in comparison to those of the Church of Ireland, that a reduction in emolument held no great terrors for them, whereas it would have been unthinkable to Cox, Robinson and Fowler.

A few further examples of catholic coadjutorships will serve to illustrate their prevalence and also the important fact that most may have been, and some definitely were, established on the initiative and/or with the approval of the incumbent. In 1770, Dr Peter Creagh, bishop of Waterford, 'being in failing health, postulated for a coadjutor', and Father William Egan, P.P. of Clonmel, Co. Tipperary, was appointed in 1771, succeeding Dr Creagh as bishop in 1774.[109] Archbishop James Butler III of Cashel had been coadjutor to his predecessor and namesake between 1773 and 1774 although, since 'the same name was about all these two archbishops shared ..., he waited until the old archbishop had died before he proceeded to the diocese' (and presumably had not been appointed at 'the old archbishop's' behest).[110] In 1781, the Rev. Richard O'Reilly, parish priest of Kilcock, Co. Kildare, was appointed coadjutor to Bishop Keeffe of Kildare; but in the following year he was appointed instead to the much more important coadjutorship of Armagh, where he succeeded the errant Primate Blake in 1787.[111] 'Thomas Costello, bishop of Clonfert, 1786–1831, ... was named coadjutor, with *succession* [my emphasis], to the bishop of Clonfert on 4 July [1786, and] succeeded on the death of Bishop Andrew Donnellan towards the end of 1786.'[112] Sometimes, the succession thus established went wrong. 'On 1 March [1803] ... Florence MacCarthy ... was appointed coadjutor, with right of succession, to Francis Moylan [bishop of Cork], and permitted to retain the parish of St Finbarr [in Cork City] *in commendam*. [But] he died in 1810 without succeeding to the bishopric.'[113] Sometimes (as apparently in Cashel in 1773), there were difficulties with the incumbent bishop, not over the principle of, and the need for, a coadjutorship, but over the choice of the individual. In the diocese of Ferns, 'When Bishop Caulfield's infirmities rendered a coadjutor necessary' in 1803, he applied for one and Dr Patrick Ryan was appointed in 1804. Dr Ryan succeeded Caulfield in 1814, but by 1817 his health, too, had become 'much enfeebled.' The next coadjutorship did not proceed so uncontentiously. His clergy proposed Dr James Doyle, a Regular, as coadjutor. However, Bishop Ryan's 'eccentricities had not declined with his health' – in particular 'his ... prejudice against the Regulars ... . In deference to wishes so influential, the Rev. James Keatinge, a zealous curate of the diocese, was appointed coadjutor bishop of Ferns',[114] and succeeded as bishop two years later. In Clogher in 1816, the Bishop's

---

108 Wilfred S. Dowden (ed.), *The journal of Thomas Moore*, ii (Newark, Delaware, 1983), p. 667. I am indebted for this reference to the Knight of Glin.   109 Rev. William P. Burke, *History of Clonmel* (Waterford, 1907), p. 279.   110 Fagan, *The oath for Irish catholics*, p. 146.   111 Rev. M.J. Brennan, *An ecclesiastical history of Ireland ... to the year 1829* (Dublin, 1848), p. 387; Bolster (ed.), *Moylan correspondence, part 1*, p. 118n; O'Flaherty, 'Ecclesiastical politics and the Penal Laws', pp 44–5.   112 *Moylan correspondence, part 2*, pp 90–91n.   113 Ibid., *part 1*, p. 90n.   114 W.J. Fitzpatrick, *The life, times and correspondence of the Rt Rev. Dr Doyle, bishop of Kildare and Leighlin* (2 vols., Dublin,

'wishes' had caused a much more serious dispute, which ended up in Rome. In this case, the issue was the wish of the imperious Dr James Murphy, bishop of Clogher, 1801–24, to have his nephew, the Rev. Edward Kernan, appointed coadjutor, so that the succession would be secured to the nephew. In the end it was.[115] Generally speaking, however, the system of coadjutorships seems to have operated with surprising smoothness and goodwill. In Dublin in 1809, for example, Dr Daniel Murray was appointed Dr Troy's coadjutor (and given the parish of St Andrews' for his interim support) 'at the insistence of' Troy himself, whom he succeeded as archbishop in 1823.[116] In 1814, as has been seen (p. 328), Dr Patrick Everard became coadjutor of Cashel, succeeding Archbishop Bray in 1820; and when Everard 'spent some days ... in Cashel' just after his appointment as coadjutor, Bray 'received him in the most gracious and polite manner.'[117]

It was hardly to be expected that the Church of Ireland, or for that matter the Church of England, would willingly have acted on Roman catholic precedent. But the two Established Churches would have consulted their own best interests if they had made coadjutorships a regular component of their administrative structures. Ironically, the word 'coadjutor' was in common Anglican parlance. Robinson, in an already-quoted letter of 1780, called Agar (with transparent insincerity) the 'coadjutor' he had long been lacking; and a witty judge, writing to Agar in 1803, described Dr Troy as 'your Grace's *coadjutor*.'[118] But such loose and facetious usage only showed how far churchmen were from the serious consideration of a system of coadjutorship. They were not even ready to accept the possibility and principle of retirement.

> In the year 1763, ... [Zachary] Pearce, being seventy-three years old, and having held the bishopric of Rochester and deanery of St Paul's seven years, proposed to resign them both [apparently without a pension], in order to pass the remainder of his days in privacy and retirement and to dedicate himself solely to study and devotion. ... His Majesty's consent had been given, but upon further deliberation was withdrawn; for doubts and difficulties were raised by some of the Ministers concerning the legality and propriety of resigning a bishopric; and the bishops generally disapproving it, the design was laid aside [and Pearce soldiered on until his death in 1774].[119]

Only the egregious Lord Buckingham – ever-busy, but for once constructively so, and perhaps acting on a suggestion made by that bogeywoman, his Irish catholic wife –

1861), i, pp 40 and 71.   **115** Draft statements by Revs. Hugh O'Reilly and Peter Maginn to Rome, [May 1814], Clogher diocesan papers, PRONI, DIO (RC) 1/4B/17 and 19; resolutions signed by 24 priests of the diocese, 11 Feb. 1815, copy of a letter to a newspaper, [1816?], and note about the resolution of the quarrels within the diocese, 29 June 1819, DIO (RC) 1/4B/42, 45 and 52.   **116** D'Alton, *Archbishops of Dublin*, pp 488–9.   **117** Archbishop Bray to Bishop Moylan, [late? 1814], *Moylan correspondence, part 1*, pp 116–17.   **118** William Smith, baron of the Irish exchequer, to Agar, 26 Oct. 1803, T/3719/C/37/38.   **119** Adam Clarke (ed.), *Compendium edition of the lives of Bishop Newton, Rev. Philip Skelton, etc.*, ii, pp 149–50.

came up with a fairly formal proposal for semi-retirement and coadjutorship. The context was the premature plans of 1798–1800 for a new Clerical Residence Act for the Church of England (see pp 236 and 275–6). Buckingham urged on his brother, Grenville, the introduction of 'the system of coadjutors to bishops when infirm or incapable, and possibly some arrangement for the care of dioceses too large or populous' – i.e. the creation of suffragan bishoprics in the modern, not in the eighteenth-century sense, of the term, which then comprehended all bishops who were not archbishops.[120] Nothing came of this suggestion – although something short of, but resembling, a coadjutorship was nearly put in place during the last illness of Archbishop Moore of Canterbury in 1804–5.[121] In the absence of any such precedent, the most senior churchmen and the best ecclesiastical lawyers were perplexed as to what to do when the practical necessity for a coadjutorship looked like arising in the Church of Ireland, and eventually arose.

In the spring of 1804, the Hon. Thomas Stopford, bishop of Cork. 1794–1805, began to show signs of skittishness. Dr Duigenan, who was vicar-general of Cashel, advised Brodrick, as metropolitan of the province in which Cork was situated, that 'the vicar-general of Cork and Ross is a proper person to be appointed coadjutor to the Bishop, provided he be a doctor in divinity, as I believe he is.'[122] But the vicar-general, the Rev. Dr James Kenney, made difficulties. He urged, reasonably enough, the need to arm themselves with 'legal proofs [of] the incapacity of the Bishop', and went on to question the legality of the limitations which Brodrick intended to place on the powers of the coadjutor.[123] He also queried the financial implications of his assuming the coadjutorship. To this last query Duigenan responded testily: 'I do not know how Mr Kenn[e]y can be put to any expense in executing the office of a coadjutor. ... He will be entitled to the fees usually paid on collation and institution.'[124] Brodrick, who (as has been seen) prided himself on his superior grasp of ecclesiastical law, then put forward the suggestion that he himself should act as coadjutor. But Duigenan explained that this would be illegal, as an archbishop could not accept a commission from a suffragan. (This still applies in the present-day U.K. Civil Service, where an officer may 'act up' – as it is quaintly called – but may not act down!) The coadjutor, Duigenan continued, would collate to vacant benefices, but the management of the temporalities of the see (e.g. the see estate) would be conducted, not by the coadjutor, but by the Bishop's agent and friends.[125] Actually, the temporalities would fall to be administered by the lord chancellor of Ireland, if the Bishop were certifiably insane. Stopford cannot have been as far gone as that. He must have maintained a level of eccentricity acceptable in an Irish bishop, because the idea of a coadjutorship seems to have been dropped. He then died in January 1805.

120 Buckingham to Grenville, 9 Nov. 1799, *HMC Dropmore Mss.*, vi. 15.   121 1st Lord Henley to his brother, Lord Auckland, 6 Nov. [1804], *Auckland correspondence*, iv, pp 215–16. Moore was their brother-in-law.   122 Duigenan to Brodrick, 13 June 1804, NLI, Ms. 8861/4.   123 Brodrick to Stuart, 15 July 1804, Bedfordshire RO, WY 994/39.   124 Duigenan to Brodrick, 18 July 1804, ibid. 125 Duigenan to Brodrick, [July? 1804], Ms. 8861/8.

The problem recurred, however, in 1811, when Euseby Cleaver, Agar's successor as archbishop of Dublin, went unmistakably mad, and a coadjutorship for that diocese became quite unavoidable.[126] Primate Stuart complained: 'the Chancellor [of Ireland, Lord Manners] is entirely ignorant of the powers of that office and, what is still worse, they are not defined in any law book.'[127] The lord lieutenant, Richmond, who was anxious to persuade Brodrick to accept the coadjutorship (in addition to his duties as archbishop of Cashel), wrote despondently: 'The best lawyers and civilians of both England and Ireland have been consulted on the patronage of the see of Dublin ... . They have no doubt that it belongs entirely to the Chancellor. ... [So], the task [of coadjutorship] is arduous and without emolument or patronage.'[128] Stuart added to the despondency by warning Brodrick that 'The coadjutor would find great difficulty to maintain discipline in such a see as Dublin unless strengthened by an act of parliament.'[129] A special act was in fact passed, and Brodrick was appointed to the coadjutorship on 29 August 1811. However, as late as 1816 there remained doubt about which *ex officio* trusteeships and other functions of the archbishop of Dublin passed automatically to the coadjutor because they were 'merely episcopal', and which had to be otherwise provided for during the coadjutorship.[130] Moreover, notwithstanding the act, a very extraordinary situation developed in practice in regard to the administration of the affairs of the archbishopric. The wife of the incapable archbishop, Mrs Cleaver, who it might be thought would have had no standing in the matter, was in a position to offer to Brodrick the use of the Dublin house which had recently been purchased by Cleaver as a see house (see p. 381). She volunteered to have it fitted up and furnished to Brodrick's specification, and expressed her wish that all the expenses of the coadjutorship should be paid for out of the income of the see estate. She then explained that the Chancellor, who (because of his custodianship of the affairs of lunatics) had the right of presentation to vacant livings in the diocese, had 'kindly consented ... to present such persons as Mrs Cleaver has reason to believe would have been objects of the Archbishop's [Cleaver] patronage. She will from time to time submit to your Grace's [Brodrick] consideration those who may be proposed to her, or those whom she may wish to recommend to the Chancellor.'[131] The appropriate person to advise the Chancellor on the disposal of the ecclesiastical patronage of the diocese was, surely, the coadjutor, not the wife of the mad archbishop? Why did the entire income of the see (apart from fees on collations, visitations, etc.) remain with Cleaver? And why was Brodrick dependent for reimbursement of his expenses on the beneficence of Mrs Cleaver? In the event, her good intentions towards him were not actually honoured, because a protracted dispute arose after Cleaver's death in 1819 over whether Brodrick or Cleaver's executors were liable for the cost of the dilapidations to the see house during the coadjutorship (see p. 381*n*). Moreover, and much

126 Milne, 'Principle or pragmatism', p. 188.   127 Stuart to Brodrick, 1 Aug. 1811, Ms. 8886.   128 Richmond to Brodrick 20 July 1811, *ibid.*   129 Stuart to Brodrick, 23 July 1811, *ibid.*   130 William Downes, chief justice of the king's bench, to Brodrick, 26 Nov. 1816, Ms. 8861/8.   131 Rev. Richard Wynne [Mrs Cleaver's brother] to Brodrick, 1 Jan. 1812, Ms. 8861/6.

more importantly, the diocese of Dublin was reduced by the early 1820s to being 'utterly void of pastoral care.'[132]

This coadjutorship is thought to be 'the only example of such an appointment in the history of the Church of Ireland.'[133] In 1793, when Woodward was absent in England, Brodrick was described as having 'the care of the diocese of Cloyne.'[134] But this was probably as much an informal arrangement between father-in-law and son-in-law as it was a deputation from a bishop to his archdeacon: it was not a formal coadjutorship. Had coadjutorship been a well understood, properly remunerated and regularly implemented species of appointment – in particular, had it been resorted to in cases of illness, absence and old age as well as insanity – the Church would not have been weakened by the presence, sometimes at very senior levels, of men like the terminally hypochondriacal Robinson. 'Making such men bishops' may not have been a mistake at the outset: the mistake lay in allowing them to stay on until they died.

A DISRUPTIVE AND DIVISIVE SYSTEM OF PAY AND PROMOTION,
1772–1809

There were other serious mistakes in the mode of paying and promoting them. In late February 1798, Agar received what he called an 'anonymous plan for destroying the Church Establishment.' It was a curious mixture of *naïveté* and penetration. Based on incorrect statistical and financial assumptions, it unwittingly did a great injustice to the Church; it also made the unthinkably radical proposal of a secularization of a considerable proportion of the Church's wealth. To that extent, indeed, Agar's verdict was correct. But what was attractive about the plan was that it proposed a mode of paying bishops, cathedral dignitaries, beneficed clergy and curates in a simple and certain manner which relieved them from odium and litigation, from the burden of running see and oeconomy estates, and from that of building and maintaining palaces, deaneries and glebe-houses according to the current, complex system. The plan was

> to adopt a Land Tax in place of tithe. ... This new revenue should be received
> by government and ... the bishops and all descriptions of clergymen of the
> Established Church should be paid in like manner as the great officers of state
> are, and ... each bishop and ... clergyman should receive a sum equal to what
> their respective livings now produce; and ..., in case of a change in the value of
> land, ... an additional tax should be levied, so that at all times to give each man
> a sum equal to what the value of their living might increase to. ... The entire of
> the land, houses, etc., that are now in the possession of bishops and ... clergy
> should be disposed of in the most advantageous manner, and the income
> arising therefrom applied to defray the exigencies of the state. ... It may be said

132 Milne, *Christ Church Cathedral*, p. 289, quoting from the chapter act books.   133 Comerford, 'Church of Ireland clergy and 1798', pp 233–4.   134 Midleton to Brodrick, 1 Apr. 1793, Ms. 8889/7.

that the bishops and dignified clergy would by this plan in some degree lose their consequence and power. But let it be observed that they would ... [be] relieved from the indignation of the farmer and from a multiplicity of vexatious lawsuits.[135]

The 'vexatious lawsuits' which the writer had in mind were probably over tithes. But he may have intended, and certainly should have included, those over questionable see leases and over improvements and dilapidations. In a sense, his clumsy proposal anticipated by thirty-five years the setting up of the ecclesiastical commission. It contained some good ideas for the preservation, not the destruction, of the Church Establishment.

Other commentators on episcopal remuneration, in particular, were interested in making it, not only more simple and certain, but more equal. In part, this was to address the perceived problem of excessive episcopal mobility – 'the usual ... general change of quarters among the black coats' (p. 197). Writing from the perspective of the early twentieth century, the historian of one diocese exclaimed: 'During the eighteenth century, there were no fewer than thirteen bishops of Meath.'[136] Cork 'had five bishops during the eighteen years from 1789 to 1807.'[137] In fact, it has been shown that 'the popular concept of the Irish bishop as continually playing ecclesiastical leapfrog [in pursuit of promotion] is clearly unfounded. [In the second half of the century,] the typical bishop had only two sees in his career on the bench and spent an average of ten years in each diocese.'[138] So Cork was a freak and Meath had a turnover which was probably just a little above average. On the other hand, the average masked some extremes. There was greater stability in the senior sees and the archbishoprics, and more rapid turnover in the junior or climbing sees. Even this generalization, however, does not hold: there were three archbishops of Cashel in 1727[139] and there was only one bishop of Clonfert between 1804 and 1836. Every now and then, the impression of excessive mobility was reinforced by a flutter of simultaneous vacancies – for example, in 1794–5 and in the first couple of years of the nineteenth century. Moreover, the legislative code governing the building and improving of palaces and other clerical residences was based on an assumption of mobility and therefore tended to encourage that idea. It spread the cost of a new building over four bishops (after 1772 letting the first one, the original builder, off too lightly and thus encouraging excess), and over more than four if any of the successors served in the diocese for less than a year (see p. 344).

What mattered was the perception that turnover was rapid; it was this which gave rise to uncertainty, expectation and lobbying. The same perception existed in the Church of England. But in that Church, there were, if anything, too few bishops: in Ireland, there were too many, and to that extent the functioning of the Church of

135 Anonymous, printed plan addressed by 'a protestant' to Chief Secretary Pelham, pre–27 Feb. 1798, T/3719/C/32/9.   136 Healy, *Diocese of Meath*, ii. 92.   137 Acheson, *Church of Ireland*, p. 86. 138 Akenson, *Church of Ireland*, p. 18.   139 O'Regan, *Archbishop William King*, p. 326.

Ireland was disproportionately disrupted by vacancies and the rumours of vacancies at senior levels. Not until the Church Temporalities Bill of 1833 was a considerable, but on the whole not unreasonable, reduction in the number of Irish bishoprics proposed. In his speech on the second reading, the prime minister, the 2nd Earl Grey, 'showed that there was nothing new in the consolidation of Irish dioceses, their number having once been 33, and in the reign of James I as low as 18, and that half of the unions now proposed had previously been in force.'[140] (Agar, as archbishop of Cashel and bishop of Emly, and as archbishop of Dublin and bishop of Glendalough, himself represented two such consolidations.) While some such consolidation as was effected in 1833 was overdue, it is not unreasonable to suggest that it had not been effected by the Irish parliament because, in those days, half of the bishoprics were in alien occupancy. The strongest case for there to be four archbishoprics in Ireland (as compared to two in England) was the purely pragmatic one that at least two of the Irish archbishoprics were, in practice, earmarked for Englishmen.

To address the rather different circumstances of the Church of England, Bishop Watson of Llandaff proposed in 1783 a scheme of reform which had as its cornerstone a closer equality in the incomes of the bishoprics and a cessation of translation except to the two archbishoprics.[141] As part of the justification for his proposal, Watson argued 'that the prospect of being translated influences the minds of the bishops too powerfully, and induces them to pay too great an attention to the beck of a minister'; he added that, 'when the ... wish for translations were in a great measure removed, it would be natural for the bishops in general to consider themselves as ... wedded ... to a particular diocese.'[142] Surprisingly, he did not mention another advantage, from the moral and spiritual point of view: that the promotion prospects of bishops would no longer be dependent on the accidents of survivorship. In an age which, for example, regarded tontines as morally suspect, and in which they were periodically banned because they could be a virtual instigation to murder, it is surprising that this consideration did not have great weight. Watson even used the analogy of the tontine or lottery: 'Everyone hopes his own [ticket] will get some great prize in the Church, and never reflects on the thousands of blanks in poor, country livings.'[143]

One of the most unseemly characteristics of the higher clergy of both Churches in Agar's day was the ghoulish overtness with which they speculated on each other's mortality. 'It gives me great concern to hear that the Bishop of Clogher's health is precarious' (see p. 467), was a familiar preamble. Making not even this attempt to observe the decencies, the son of one bishop wrote in 1757 that 'two or three old men, ... the fattest deer in our herd, [were] just dropping into their graves.'[144] In 1787, parodying sentiments like these, Mrs Agar described as follows the impatience of Richard Marlay, 'the everlasting dean' of Clogher, to obtain a bishopric: 'The Bishop

---

140 Mathieson, *English Church reform*, pp 78–9.   141 Ibid., pp 25–6 and 68–9.   142 Watson, *A letter to his Grace the Archbishop of Canterbury* (London, 1783), pp 10–11 and 20.   143 Ibid., p. 33. For the banning of lotteries, see: Wilmot papers of 1–14 Sep. 1752 (PRONI, T3019/1963–4 and 1966); Legg, 'Money and reputation: the effects of the banking crisis of 1755 and 1760', in *Eighteenth-century Ireland*, xi (1996), p. 87.   144 Quoted in Barnard, 'Improving clergymen', p. 140.

of Kildare is panting *for life*, the poor Dean for death – I mean, the death of the Bishop of Kildare or indeed for that of any other bishop that will please to go to heaven.'[145] Although she was not to know it, Agar's own state of health (see p. 251) was later to give rise to similar expectations. Just after his translation to Dublin, in February 1802, a shameless poor relation of Lord Hardwicke wrote to Hardwicke's not-yet-mitred brother-in-law and chaplain, Charles Lindsay: 'the present Arch. B. [of Dublin] is by all accounts a bad life, and as Lord Hardwicke is now likely to continue long in his situation, he may very probably be able to place me, and two or three more after you, upon the Irish bench.'[146] Charles James Fox, too, was keenly interested in Agar's health. 'Pray let me know whether the Archbishop of Dublin is recovered', he wrote to his friend, Bedford, in April 1806. And again: 'it has been suggested here – and, as far as I am informed, properly – that the bench of bishops in Ireland does not afford any proper person to succeed to his see. I take for granted [Dean] Warburton could not be appointed to it at once?'[147]

Euseby Cleaver, bishop of Ferns, was also observing Agar's health, and the health of other senior prelates, with interest. Agar had contributed to the long deferral of Cleaver's hopes of better things than Ferns, where he had been stuck since 1789. Cleaver had been greatly agitated by his experiences, at the safe distance of Wales, during the rebellion. From mid-1798, he was resolved, if he had to stay in Ireland, to accept no bishopric or archbishopric which was not in a garrison town. He was not considered for Cashel in 1801, so Kildare and, later, Dublin became the *foci* of his ambition. Derry, where the palace itself was soon to be sold for use as a barrack, was another possibility. 'If I obtained it' he wrote to his patron in October 1798, 'I should then live in a garrisoned town, with an income that would assist my family. If you should at any time happen to hear anything interesting of that Bishop's [Frederick Hervey] health, I will thank you for early notice. He is advancing towards seventy, but may outlive many of his intended successors.'[148] The appalling Mrs Dickson had said the same ten years previously: 'Tell C[harles] F[ox] it is nonsense [for Bishop Dickson] to wait for Derry – the Bishop [of Derry] is likely to live many a year.'[149] Hervey's actual and eventual successor, Bishop Knox of Killaloe, wrote gleefully in July 1802 about 'the good news of [the] Bishop of Derry's [bad] state of health.'[150] But Hervey in fact lived until 1803. By that time, Cleaver had been disappointed of Dublin

145 Mrs Agar to Macartney, 16 June 1787, PRONI, D/572/9/9.   146 Rev. Charles Chester to Lindsay, 17 Feb. 1802, *The viceroy's post-bag*, p. 14.   147 Fox to Bedford, 13 and 26 Apr. 1806, BL., Add. Ms. 47569, ff. 270–2 and 275–8. The main barrier to Warburton's promotion, even to a bishopric, was the belief that his father had been 'an Irish harper'. Fitzwilliam had recommended him in 1795, but George III, having consulted Archbishop Moore of Canterbury (presumably because he now realised that Newcome was Fitzwilliam's yes-man), refused to make him a bishop. Moore died in 1805, and Fox made a very great point of Warburton's promotion in 1806 – in spite of Warburton's desertion of the Whigs over the Union (see p. 183). Accordingly, Warburton was made bishop of Limerick later in the year.   148 Cleaver to Egremont, 8 Oct. and 24 Nov. 1798, PHA/57/11–12.   149 Mrs Dickson to John Forbes, [late 1788–early 1789], PRONI, T/3391/68. 150 Knox to Alexander Marsden, 24 July 1802, NA, Official Papers, 620/62/57.

(because of Camden's and Cornwallis' prior commitment to Agar), and in general was finding that senior ecclesiastical appointments were heavily mortgaged to so-called 'Union engagements.'[151] In March 1805, Cleaver was assured of Pitt's high opinion of him. However, it was at the same time explained to him that Pitt had unfortunately promised the bishopric of Raphoe, when it fell vacant, to Lord John George Beresford (who became bishop of Raphoe in 1807). In any case, Raphoe was not a garrison town. When 'the Talents' came to power in 1806, Fox expressed doubts about Cleaver to Bedford: 'learning, ... you know, both with Lord G[renville] and myself, is a matter of great weight. ... [And] is his moderation on the Catholic Question quite certain?'[152] Fox was right to be doubtful, because Cleaver's cause was taken up by the 'No Popery' administration which succeeded 'The Talents.' 'He now conceives he is little likely to succeed to any good bishopric in this country [Ireland], and his family having been a good deal alarmed during the rebellion [!], he would readily take any English bishopric, even Bristol.'[153] In the end, he was given encouragement to look to the archbishopric of Dublin on the death of Agar, who was represented as being in declining health.[154] Cleaver, remembering Frederick Hervey, was sceptical. In March 1808, he complained bitterly that this perhaps remote contingency was no compensation for the losses he had suffered and the long years he had waited.[155] Then, in late May 1809, the duke of Portland, now prime minister, gave a positive assurance that the first vacant Irish see worthy of Cleaver's acceptance would be offered to him.[156] On 14 July, the very day of Agar's death, the Home Secretary wrote to the Lord Lieutenant asking him to send over a formal recommendation of Cleaver as Agar's successor.[157]

A system of promotion which encouraged churchmen to speculate and calculate on each other's mortality not only did obvious harm to religion and morality, but also had the practical disadvantage that it propagated rivalries and enmities – often needlessly, because tough incumbents like Hervey outlived many of their intended successors. Most promotion systems suffer from these deficiencies to some degree: what was unusually harmful about the promotion system in the Church of Ireland in Agar's day was that it was combined with a system of pay and perquisites which was labyrinthine. Thus, when promotions actually took place, they were almost invariably accompanied by wrangles over improvements and dilapidations to palaces (pp 337–40) and recriminations over the alleged milking of see estates (pp 401–4). If bishops had a choice in the matter, they tried not to leave a see where a desirable piece of patronage was about to fall in or a large renewal fine about to become due (see pp 434–5), or to go to a see where there were 'large demands for the house' (see p. 341). One churchman threatened with the worst of most worlds was George Chinnery, a

151 William Wickham to Cleaver, 24 Aug. 1802, Wickham papers, PRONI, T/2627/5/S/4. 152 Fox to Bedford, 13 May [1806], BL, Add. Ms. 47569, f. 284. 153 Richmond to Wellesley, 1 July 1807, *Wellington civil correspondence, 1807–9*, pp 103–4. 154 William Huskisson to Egremont, [Mar. 1805], PHA/58/1. 155 Cleaver to Egremont, 21 Mar. 1808, PHA/57/53. 156 Memo. by Egremont of an interview with Portland, 27 May 1809, PHA/58/4. 157 2nd earl of Liverpool to Egremont, 14 July 1809, PHA/58/5.

reluctant and temporary bishop of Killaloe, 1779–80. Promoted to Killaloe when Fowler was promoted to Dublin, Chinnery went thither in the expectation that the aged Cox would soon die, Agar would be promoted to Cashel, and Chinnery would be translated to the great object of his ambition, Cloyne. However, Cox failed to die; time marched on; and Chinnery knew well that if he was forced to tarry at Killaloe for more than a year, he would become liable for the £2,900 which Fowler had spent on the palace, of which £725 would not be recoverable from the next bishop of Killaloe. Observing his plight, various see tenants offered low renewal fines of £400–£500, which would go some way towards paying the £725, but would be 'detrimental' to Chinnery in the longer term, if for some reason he were stuck in Killaloe.[158] It looks as if he was translated to Cloyne just before the year was up. But then he, who had so eagerly speculated on the deaths of others, died within months of reaching the promised land.

Although this was not an issue at Killaloe, the management of bishops' boroughs was another activity with plenty of potential for recrimination and ill-will (pp 175–83): Bishop Dodgson of Ossory complained biblically in 1772 that 'at the last election [for St Canice], the sins of my predecessor were visited upon me.'[159] Thanks to Archbishop Bolton and the Pennefathers, Cashel was no longer a bishop's borough. But after Brodrick succeeded Agar at Cashel in 1801, they proceeded to fall out over almost everything else (see pp 364 and 416–17). The Henry Agar affair appears to have left no permanent scars;[160] the real antagonism between them began in 1801 and was caused mainly by the Cashel Palace and see estate – those very aspects of the system which were so regularly productive of bad blood. The effect of their antagonism on the Church was unusually serious, since Agar and Brodrick possessed the two best brains and the two most forceful personalities in the post-Union hierarchy. But in other respects the antagonism was typical of the jealousies, grudges and enmities which festered in the hermetic sanctum of Ireland's four archbishoprics and 18 bishoprics, into which – in the absence of any precedent or arrangements for the retirement of those 'dropping into their graves' – the 22 prelates were locked together until death. It would have been hard to devise a more disruptive system of manning the upper echelons of any institution. As individuals, the bishops were not saints, and only saints would have been uncorrupted by such a system.

---

158 Chinnery to Shannon, 28 Nov. 1779, Shannon papers, PRONI, D/2707/A2/2/58. This shows that the figure of £5,000 which Hotham had put on Fowler's expenditure (see p. 342) was exaggerated.   159 Dodgson to Lord Townshend, 2 June 1772, RCB Library, Ms. 20/52.   160 Brodrick to Agar, 7 Oct. 1799, 21 M 57/B35/1.

12

Emancipation, rebellion and union, 1795–9

Considering that the Act of Union was probably the most important single measure passed during Agar's political lifetime, and that he was 'a political character of great consideration'[1] and one of the most influential advisers of the Irish administration up to late June 1798, the uncertainty which envelops his views and actions between then and, in effect, January 1800, is remarkable. It has been asserted that he was opposed to the Union from the summer of 1798 until Cornwallis, the lord lieutenant who had been dispatched to Ireland with instructions to carry it, made it personally worth Agar's while to change his mind. Words like 'vehement' and 'strenuous'[2] have been used to characterise his opposition in the period July 1798 to July 1799. But he described himself as 'disinclined' rather than 'opposed', and no evidence has been produced to show that he exceeded the bounds of 'disinclination.' Nor has any attempt been made to investigate whether his misgivings were about the principle of a Union, about the terms (especially as regarded the tithe question and other matters vitally affecting the Church of Ireland), about the government's behaviour to himself personally in the second half of 1798, or about the policies of Cornwallis on Catholic Emancipation and law and order. Was he disinclined to matter or manner, measures or men? Is it possible that he was not so much disinclined to the Union as disenchanted with the government's tardiness in consulting him about it? Equally, is it possible that the government held back because of his known or presumed views on Catholic Emancipation, law and order, tithes, etc.? To try to find answers to these questions, it is necessary to bring into one focus the key issues and events in which Agar was involved in the years immediately preceding the Union.

AGAR'S UNIONIST TRADITION

Any student of Agar's previous political form would be sure to conclude that in 1798 he was a likely Unionist. In 1778, he had regarded a union as the only way left of 'parrying the impending evils' at that time.[3] In late 1779–early 1780, when Macartney was sent as Lord North's special and secret envoy to sound out the extent of unionist support in Ireland, Agar was closely associated with Macartney, by letter and in

1 'The state of the Irish House of Commons in 1791', p. 48.   2 Bolton, *Union*, pp 52 and 60.
3 Quoted in Kelly, *Prelude to Union*, p. 29.

(unrecorded) discussion. It is inconceivable that he did not, at this juncture, reveal himself to Macartney as a unionist. Union was, of course, not a static issue, and care has to be taken not to project on to 1798–1800 the circumstances of 1778–80. It should be remembered that one of the leading opponents of Union in 1798–1800 was the 2nd marquess of Downshire, whose father, Lord Hillsborough, later 1st marquess, had been its strongest serious advocate in the earlier period. On the other hand, the threat of invasion and the peril in which the connection of Ireland with Great Britain stood, were graver in 1798–1800 than they had been in 1778–80. Agar's unionism in the earlier period was founded on fear of and hostility to the measures which, when carried, came collectively to be known as the constitution of 1782. In two letters to Macartney of February and March 1780, he stated: 'from the moment the commissions of the judges shall be granted *quam diu se bene gesserint*, an English law will meet with no more countenance here than a French edict would. Our juries don't respect them much now and our judges will then support the practice.' If, he argued, the bill altering the tenure of Irish judges were not suppressed by the British privy council, 'justice will be worse administered here (if that be possible) than it is at present, and ... should appeals cease to be carried from our courts of law and equity to England, Irish property will soon become a very precarious tenure.'[4]

A bishop of the Church of Ireland had the further powerful motive for fearing the constitution of 1782 that it weakened the unity of the Churches of England and Ireland. Proof of this weakening seemed to manifest itself in the increasingly anti-clerical bias of the Irish House of Commons from the early 1780s onwards (see pp 190–1, 397 and 482). Professor Akenson has argued that 'the Irish parliament had been notoriously supine' in its attitude to the Church of Ireland, and that the Union constituted a danger to the Church by exposing it 'to the criticism of the British radicals.'[5] But this is essentially a hindsighted view. At the time, the great danger was seen by Irish churchmen as proceeding from the Irish landed class, both inside and outside the Irish parliament. Euseby Cleaver, with the perspective of an English churchman newly arrived in Ireland, specifically linked anti-clericalism and the constitution of 1782. He echoed Agar's anxiety about the administration of justice in Ireland 'since the appellant jurisdiction has been withdrawn' from the British House of Lords, and pointed to the doubts this had created in the minds of English lenders as to the value of Irish landed security. 'The outrages which ... Grattan encourages' he wrote at the end of 1788

> give a very ill impression on this side of the water [England] of the effect of law, and I believe the country gentlemen will lose more by their want of credit, than they can gain by [tithe] plunder. ... If the support of the government [for the clergy] be in any degree relaxed, riot will again hold up its head, and as long as it is directed against the clergy only, will find many advocates.[6]

4 Agar to Macartney, 17 Feb. and 26 Mar. 1780, *Macartney in Ireland*, pp 331–2.   5 Akenson, *Church of Ireland*, p. 73.   6 Cleaver to Charles O'Hara, 29 Sep. 1786 and 12 Dec. 1788, PRONI,

During the negotiations of 1798–1800 over the Union, the Church of Ireland 'bishops ... knew the antagonism to the Church which prevailed, and they believed that once organically united to the protestant nation and Church of England the position of the Irish Establishment would be unassailable.'[7] Under the Union, the Church of Ireland would be confirmed as 'the Church of England in Ireland.' Hence the automatic support tendered by Thomas Barnard, bishop of Limerick, in January 1799: 'Your Lordship [Castlereagh] knows that I am an Englishman and a bishop of the Church of Ireland, and therefore you cannot doubt my wishes to support any measure that may best secure the ascendancy of the protestant religion in Ireland and cement forever the connection of the two kingdoms.'[8] Brodrick, at this stage bishop of Kilmore, remarked at roughly the same time: 'It cannot be denied that many will be the inconveniences and indeed injuries to Ireland by an Union. On the other hand, we shall render more secure, I trust, our properties, our lives and our religion.'[9] As a churchman, Agar had a strong professional bias towards a union.

Moreover, his Westminster and Christ Church education, his family tradition and the recent anglicising influences which were being brought to bear on his nephew, Lord Clifden, all inclined rather than disinclined Agar to a union. In a letter to him of mid-June 1800, Lord Mendip described the 'approaching' Union as 'the measure which I have considered from my youth as the most likely to give power and permanence to this now great empire.'[10] Since he was writing to a favourite nephew and political disciple, with whom he had had decades of opportunities for discussion of the subject (it being a subject which was discussed rather than written about), these sentiments must be taken at face value. Mendip called himself 'a native of Ireland', even though he was strictly speaking no more than the son of an English churchman who had made his career in Ireland (as indeed was Bishop Barnard, who called himself an Englishman!). Apart from one sale very early on in his career (see p. 30), he retained until his death all the estates he had inherited in Ireland, but he had no house there and three in England. The proposed Absentee Tax of 1773 had threatened his pocket but – much more seriously – had challenged his conception of the relationship between England and Ireland. For this reason his arguments against the tax are both autobiographical and passionate: 'How preposterous must this be, when this restraint or fine is laid upon those who reside in the mother country, the seat of government and of their sovereign. ... Is the residence of great and powerful men, members of both Houses in the parliament of Great Britain, and who have lands in Ireland, of no use to that country, whose most material interests come so frequently under the consideration of this parliament and of these councils?'[11] Agar, too, took the side of the absentees when the tax was again mooted in 1780, although he urged the absolute necessity of the absentees coming over in person to employ 'the full exertion of their eloquence to dissuade the Irish parliament from' passing it.[12]

T/2812/18/13 and 16.   7 Phillips, *Church of Ireland*, iii. 287.   8 Barnard to Castlereagh, 20 Jan. 1799, *Castlereagh correspondence*, ii, pp 124–5.   9 Brodrick to Midleton, 5 Jan. 1799, Ms. 1248, vol. 17, f. 100.   10 Mendip to Agar, 17 June 1800, T/3719/C/34/25.   11 Ellis to Agar, 5 Nov. 1773, T/3719/C/7/5.   12 Agar to Macartney, 26 Mar. 1780, *Macartney in Ireland*, p. 332.

With this view of England as 'the mother country' and 'the residence of great and powerful men' from both kingdoms, it is not surprising that Mendip had counselled early on that his great-nephew and ultimate heir, the Hon. Henry Welbore Agar, should not be coarsened – indeed 'destroyed' – by the rough-and-tumble of electioneering for Co. Kilkenny (as Lord Clifden had been).[13] Instead, H.W. Agar should be educated and groomed for polite English society (and perhaps a seat for a close borough in England as well as Ireland). Though himself in opposition at the time, Mendip took pains to get him presented at court in 1786.[14] Lord Clifden, it should be added, assisted in this civilising and anglicising process, for example taking H.W. Agar to visit Horace Walpole at Strawberry Hill (near Pope's Villa) in July 1788.[15] In March 1792, H.W. Agar, now 2nd Lord Clifden, married Lady Caroline Spencer (1763–1813), eldest daughter of the duke of Marlborough, an English ducal connection which clearly delighted Mendip. In January 1793, he remarked snobbishly: 'I am not surprised that the Viscount [Clifden] has been inveigled by the splendour of Blenheim and the charms of his amiable wife to delay his journey to Bath.'[16] It was almost certainly Archbishop Agar who had been the means of introducing Clifden into the Marlborough family. In no sense was Lady Caroline Spencer's marriage 'arranged', because she was a strong-minded young lady who had already turned down, and been allowed to turn down, two much better offers.[17] But she would not have fallen for Clifden if she had never met him, and she must have met him through Agar's friendship with Lord Auckland, a former member of the duke of Marlborough's following in the British House of Commons.[18] Another member of the ducal circle and intimate at Blenheim was Archbishop Moore of Canterbury, which explains why Agar's correspondence with Moore (see pp 58, 260 and 347) dates from 1792.

In May 1793, Clifden was returned for the borough of Heytesbury in Wiltshire,[19] in which his father-in-law had the controlling interest. Auckland had previously sat for Heytesbury, and Clifden was to sit for it until he succeeded as 2nd Baron Mendip in the peerage of Great Britain in February 1802. Clifden's marriage and seat at Westminster added another string to his political bow ('I have some force in myself, ... Lord Mendip at Burlington House, and the duke of Marlborough in Downing Street'). 'At Westminster he supported Pitt's administration. In his only known speech, he moved the Address, in favour of the prosecution of war with France, on 21 January 1794. On 24 November 1795 he was a government teller.'[20] The worsening security situation in Ireland, the [Irish] Yeomanry Act of late 1796 and his own decision to raise the Gloucester (Co. Kilkenny) yeoman horse, obliged him temporarily

13 Ellis to Agar, 28 Nov. 1775, T/3719/C/9/3; Diana Agar to Ellis, 7 Jan. 1777, T/3719/C/11/1. 14 Ellis to Agar, 14 Aug. 1786, T/3719/C/20/22. 15 W.S. Lewis (ed.), *The Yale edition of Horace Walpole's correspondence*, xii (New Haven, 1944), p. 231. 16 Ellis to Agar, 5 Aug. 1792 and 14 Jan. 1793, T/3719/C/26/9 and C/27/1. 17 A.L. Rowse, *The later Churchills* (London, 1958), pp 157–8. One of the offers was from someone whom Rowse calls 'the duke of Sutherland', who did not exist until 1833, nor was the future duke or any other member of his family looking for a wife in the early 1790s. 18 Ibid., pp 150–56; Eden to Agar, 21 Aug. 1784, T/3719/C/18/26. 19 Thorne, *House of Commons, 1790–1820*, iii. 52. 20 Ibid.

to abandon Westminster and return to his Irish estates. 'On 18 February 1797 he wrote
to Pitt announcing his departure for Ireland, where he felt he could be of more service
"in support of the government and in defence of the country". ... [However, he was
back] in England to vote for Pitt's assessed taxes [on] 4 January 1798.'²¹ In mid-
February, he wrote from London to Agar about one of the periodic renewals of the
Absentee Tax proposal, and his letter is as unionist (with a small 'u') in its preconceptions as Mendip's letter of 1773:

> I am much obliged to you ... for the steps you have taken to secure the atten-
> dance of my friends [the MPs for Gowran and Thomastown] to resist the
> insane measure of an Absentee Tax. ... At the moment that the internal and
> external defence of Ireland depends on Britain, and that the finance by which
> her government from day to day is carried on is procured by the British
> parliament, without the security of which not a shilling could be obtained, to
> adopt a measure in its principle and effect so completely hostile to Britain,
> appears to me perfect insanity. ... It is pretended that men spending incomes
> drawn from Ireland in Britain do not contribute to the defence of the country
> in which their property lies. Of every pound spent in Britain, ten shillings goes
> into the exchequer from the multiplied taxes on consumption, the assessed
> taxes, etc., out of which exchequer some twelve to fifteen millions flows annu-
> ally for the maintenance of the fleet, without which, in one month from this
> day, 50,000 Frenchmen would overrun Ireland and subvert the whole property,
> real and personal, of the island. ... Were the tax to be really raised, I should ...
> sell my boroughs and all other disposable property I possess in Ireland and vest
> it on this side.'²²

From the tone of this letter, it is obvious that Clifden was writing to someone who was
of like mind on the issue; and Agar had earlier assured Camden 'that he was always of
the opinion that such a tax would be impolitic.'²³

A still clearer indication of Agar's views on the *principle* of a union in 1798, is
provided by two letters written to him in February and March 1798 by his vicar-
general and right-hand man, Pat. Hare, both of which contain two short sentences
(clearly the pith of previous conversations) stating that union was the only means of
salvation for Ireland. (Somebody, perhaps Agar, stroked out the sentence in the first
letter, presumably for reasons of secrecy.)²⁴ On the eve of the first mention of a

---

21 Ibid.   22 Clifden to Agar, 14 Feb. 1798, T/3719/C/32/5. A year earlier, when the tax had been
last proposed, Lord Midleton had said much the same to Brodrick: 'if even a tax of one penny in the
pound is laid on absentees, [I am determined] to withdraw the first convenient opportunity all the
property I can from that country, ... from ... the insecurity of all that would be left' – Midleton to
Brodrick, 11 Mar. 1797, NLI, Ms. 8889/18.   23 Endorsement by Agar, 5 Feb. 1798, on a letter of
the same date from Camden, T/3719/C/32/4. Interestingly, his usual associates, Ely, Shannon and
Waterford – all future Unionists – were sympathetic to the tax – Camden to Portland, 1 Mar. 1797,
HO 100/69, ff. 115–18.   24 Hare to Agar, 26 Feb. and 21 Mar. 1798, T/3719/C/32/7 and 29.

concrete measure of Union (which was made to Agar in mid-July 1798, although he must have known about it earlier), his long-standing and partly inherited unionist predilections were as strong as ever.

AGAR AND CATHOLIC EMANCIPATION, 1791–5

In Camden's view, expressed in the course of a long memorandum on the Union which he submitted to Pitt in July or August 1798, it was the prospect of its being accompanied by Catholic Emancipation which deterred Agar from supporting the Union. 'The person alluded to' wrote Camden 'is amongst the most anxious for the measure. But it is supposed the idea of his alarm proceeds from the apprehension it is imagined he may entertain from the admission of catholics; and most remarkable prejudice exists there – not too strong, however, if Ireland remains as she is.'[25] This connection between political concessions to catholics and a union had been made some years previously. In September 1792, for example, Bishop Woodward had speculated (*apropos* the Catholic Relief Act of that year and the further instalment of catholic relief rightly believed to be impending): 'If the minister has an union in view, he plays deep: if he has not, he is mad.'[26]

Agar's 'most remarkable prejudice' on the Catholic Question had been well known, if somewhat exaggerated, since late 1791, when the Irish administration of Lord Westmorland, under extreme pressure from the British government, espoused a policy of political concessions to Irish catholics. At the beginning of February 1792, Bishop Woodward – aghast – wrote to Agar: 'The outrages of White Boys [*sic*] were children's play to this wretched compromise of the Protestant Ascendancy, endeavouring (in vain) to conceal real fear under affected liberality, and increasing the danger by betraying cowardice.'[27] Agar's response to the Catholic Relief Bill of 1792 was to yield his vote, but not to sacrifice his opinion – this unheroic expression was actually used by him in his speech on the bill in the House of Lords.[28] The more celebrated, or rather notorious, expression which he allegedly used in this speech was that Roman catholicism was 'a religion held only by knaves and fools' – a sentiment which he later repudiated and endeavoured to explain away in a letter to *Faulkner's Dublin Journal* later in the year. 'I spoke not one word of the Roman catholic religion in general, nor of the papists as religionists. I only mentioned ... one practice of their Church – [that of] ... discouraging ... the lower orders of the people ... from reading the bible ... – as contributing to the priests' influence, and affording an opportunity to crafty and designing men of imposing upon the weak and ignorant.'[29] In December 1792, he got up a public meeting in Cashel to pass resolutions against further concessions to the

---

25 Pitt/Pretyman papers, PRONI, T/3319/60; Patrick M. Geoghegan, *The Irish Act of Union: a study in high politics, 1798–1801* (Dublin, 1999), pp 44 and 237. 26 Woodward to Brodrick, 28 Sep. 1792, NLI, Ms. 8870/3. 27 Woodward to Agar, 2 Feb. 1792, T/3719/C/26/2. 28 Malcomson, *John Foster*, p. 416. 29 *Faulkner's*, 15 Nov. 1792, 21 M 57/A33/9. Because this newspaper was owned by Agar's *protégé*, John Giffard (see p. 254 and 268), it was a natural outlet for Agar.

catholics,[30] and when the Catholic Relief Bill of 1793 (which, among other things, re-enfranchised catholic forty-shilling freeholders) came before the House of Lords, he both spoke and voted against it on 19 March. 'A very great misrepresentation of the Archbishop of Cashel's sentiments on the Popery Bill having been published' – yet again – Agar once more used *Faulkner's* to set the record straight:

> The Archbishop of Cashel said, if the only objects of this bill were to grant to the Roman catholics of this kingdom a more extensive dominion over their property, [or] personal security in a more perfect degree than they now possess it; a free toleration of religion, which in his opinion belongs of right to every man upon earth when not incompatible with the good government of the country he inhabits; or to concede to them the advantages of the blessings of education – he believed there would not be a dissenting voice within those walls. ... But, said his Grace, ... while the Roman catholic acknowledges a foreign power superior to the sovereignty of a kingdom, they [*sic*] cannot complain if the laws of that kingdom will not arm them with the political power of the state. This power, and this alone, would I withhold from them; and while the bill tends to grant this, I certainly cannot vote for it, however anxious I may be to concede to them everything else.[31]

The initial moderation of Agar's language (if his explanation of the 'knaves and fools' utterance is to be believed), his conciliatory conduct in making use of his *protégé*, John Giffard's, newspaper to set matters straight and defuse tension and, above all, his holding aloof from concerted opposition to either relief bill – won golden opinions from Westmorland (a perhaps biased commentator since he privately disapproved of the bills himself). In August 1793, he paid tribute to Agar, who had just left for England, in a letter of recommendation to Pitt:

> He desired me to represent him to you as I found him, which I told him I should have great pleasure in doing, as I've always found him invariably attached to his Majesty's government, giving his opinion fairly, his advice with peculiar ability, and giving the government every assistance he could, even when we were acting against what in his opinion we ought to do. I should be glad if you would show him that you entertained these sentiments of him.[32]

This assessment was highly relevant to Agar's probable line of conduct on the Union, a measure to which, on even the most pessimistic prognosis which could realistically be made in the summer of 1798, he was much less averse than the Catholic Relief Bill of 1793.

---

30 21 M 57/A33/11–12.   **31** *Faulkner's*, 19 Mar. 1793, 21 M 57/A33/16.   **32** Westmorland to Pitt, 29 August 1793, Pitt/Pretyman Papers, University Library, Cambridge: photocopy in PRONI, T/3313/32.

In early 1795, when Westmorland's successor as lord lieutenant, Lord Fitzwilliam, openly espoused a Catholic Emancipation Bill (which, among other things, made catholics eligible to sit in parliament), the political situation was much more fluid, not to say confused, than it had been in 1792 or 1793. In January, and up to the middle of February, the attitude of the British government to Fitzwilliam's Emancipation Bill was uncertain, as was the degree of authorisation and support which he had from London. The members of the Irish cabinet must have been aware of the likelihood of Fitzwilliam's being disavowed, and Agar, for one, was a much freer agent in 1795 than he had been in 1793, because he had nothing much to lose, having just been disappointed of the primacy. 'In the beginning of the business' – which presumably means January – FitzGibbon and Speaker Foster had prevailed on Fitzwilliam to declare that the Emancipation Bill was 'open for both Houses, and that it was not a measure of government.' However, it was not in the Irish parliament but at St James' that the Irish cabinet, or rather those members of it with the best English connections, made their big *démarche*. FitzGibbon, Beresford and Agar acting through their friend, Auckland, and Auckland's brother-in-law, Archbishop Moore, sought to catch the conscience of the King by representing to him that granting Emancipation would be a violation of the Coronation Oath enshrined in the English Act of *1 William and Mary, cap. 6.*[33] This 'Coronation Oath argument' is usually associated with Fitz-Gibbon, who certainly was one of its most active exponents, and with the representations made to George III in March 1795. However, FitzGibbon's biographer suggests that Agar 'may have been responsible for one of its first public appearances, in the *Freeman's Journal* of *10 October 1792* [my emphasis]. That edition included a paragraph claiming that the king would violate his Coronation Oath if he agreed to the catholic franchise. Agar had *protégés* at the *Freeman's* and it is possible ... that he wrote the paragraph himself.'[34] Earlier still, Woodward had come close to the Coronation Oath argument: one of the 'very material additions' which he interpolated in the first London edition of his *Present state of the Church of Ireland* (see p. 480) was 'an extract from the Act of Union between England and Scotland, which secures *for ever* the ecclesiastical Establishment in *Ireland*.'[35] Even the politically naive Fitzwilliam knew, well before he set off for Ireland, about the Coronation Oath argument, and had obtained the views of a leading English catholic on how best to refute it.[36]

Agar's most effective ally in propagating the argument early in 1795, as his correspondence reveals, was not Auckland, but the recently recalled and still-smarting Westmorland. As early as 2 March, Agar had sent Westmorland two letters, one 'public' and the other 'private', about the implications of the Coronation Oath. The shorter, 'public', letter, Agar asked him to show to Pitt; 'and your Lordship may safely assure him that no circumstances can lessen my obligations to him, my gratitude to my sovereign and my attention to whatever may contribute to promote the united interests of Great Britain and Ireland.'[37] Westmorland responded enthusiastically and asked for more:

33 Malcomson, *John Foster*, pp 417–18.   34 Kavanaugh, *Lord Clare*, p. 312.   35 Woodward to Brodrick, 7 Jan. 1787, Ms. 8870/1.   36 9th Lord Petre to Fitzwilliam, 20 Sep. 1794, Fitzwilliam papers, PRONI, T/3302/2/76.   37 Agar to Westmorland, 2 Mar. 1795 (both letters of the same date), T/3719/C/29/6–7.

I received your letter and shall certainly communicate it to Mr Pitt. The reasoning it contains is much admitted here, and it is certainly necessary some final settlement should, if possible, be made. The argument used *a contra* is that the parliament of King William could not bind the future parliaments of the country, that there must exist an omnipotent power of legislation in every state, and that the Coronation Oath, etc., etc., only bind to the maintenance of such Establishment as the laws in existence and formerly made shall direct. Tell me your answer to this reasoning.

Three days later he urged: 'I am anxious for your answer to [the] reasoning against your opinion of the Catholic Bill.'[38] On 18 March, Agar obliged with a lengthy paper in which he attempted to refute the argument that the Coronation Oath could not limit the sovereignty of parliament.

He began by reiterating part of the argument of his previous letter:

To capacitate ... [catholics] to sit in both Houses of Parliament without making and subscribing the declaration against popery [i.e. against transubstantiation] or taking the oath of supremacy ... appears to me to be a direct violation of the English act of the 14th of Charles II [the Act of Uniformity], cap. 2, sec. 1 ..., [which] is now made the law of Ireland by the Irish act of the 21st and 22nd of George III, cap. 48, sec. 3. It also appeared to me to be a repeal of the Declaration and Bill of Rights, which are expressly enacted and established 'To stand and remain and be the law of the realm *forever*'; also a repeal of the Act of Settlement, 'whereby all the laws and statutes of the realm for *securing the Established Religion were ratified and confirmed*' ...; also a direct violation of the Act of Union (the 5th Anne, cap. 8), by which the inviolable maintenance and preservation of the Established Religion in Ireland is secured by providing that all and singular the acts of parliament *then in force* for the establishment and preservation of the Church should remain and be in full force *forever*; and it is further therein enacted that this act and all and every the things therein contained be and shall *forever* be holden to be a fundamental and essential part of the Union. ...

It is notorious that the protestants of Ireland, at least nineteen parts in twenty of them, are utterly averse from the Popery Bill now in agitation, and that it never will pass the Houses of Lords and Commons except that the influence of the crown is very effectually exercised on the members of both Houses to prevail upon them to pass such a bill; and what minister will advise his Majesty ... to use all the influence of the crown to procure the passing of a bill through both Houses of Parliament subversive of the Church?[39]

38 Westmorland to Agar, 7 and 10 Mar. 1795, T/3719/ C/29/8–9.   39 Agar to Westmorland, 2 and 18 Mar. 1795, T/3719/C/29/6 and 10.

Agar's argument was shown to the King (which he must have expected) as well as to Pitt (which he had specifically requested). By 14 March, the King had received from the Lord Chancellor of England, Lord Loughborough, a former Northite and associate of Mendip's, what was described as a supplementary 'state of the question, as drawn up by a Right Reverend Prelate' of the Church of Ireland.[40] Loughborough was a self-seeking man and gifted intriguer,[41] as he was to show in late 1800 to early 1801, when he fanned the King's prejudice against Pitt's post-Union Emancipation Bill for the whole United Kingdom. But Loughborough had approved of the Irish Catholic Relief Act of 1793 and in 1795 had not yet found his anti-Emancipationist voice.[42] In consequence, his reaction to Agar's 'state of the question' was a constitutional lawyer's – that the Coronation Oath argument was 'derogatory to the legislative power, insofar as it implied a doubt of the competence of the legislature.'[43] On 19 March, Archbishop Moore asked the King for an audience to discuss Agar's paper and the responses to it of Loughborough and others.[44] Presumably, he had no difficulty in countering Loughborough's (cogent and forceful) reasoning, because the King's mind was now pre-possessed by the congenial Coronation Oath argument. (His enthusiasm for it, and gratitude to Agar, explain his new-found interest in Agar's promotion to the barony of Somerton – see p. 174 – and his speaking 'so decidedly to the duke of Portland that the duke wrote to Mr Pitt giving his acquiescence to it' in early April.[45]) In mid-May, Westmorland used 'some of your [Agar's] arguments' in a speech in the British House of Lords 'on the debate on D. of Norfolk's motion relating to Lord Fitzwilliam's removal.' 'The eyes of the world', wrote Westmorland, 'are opened upon the conduct of all concerned, and I should conceive the Roman Catholic Question is now fully understood here.'[46] In other words, Agar was not only one of those engaged, or suspected of being engaged, in secretly influencing George III against Emancipation, he was also an open advocate of the anti-Emancipationist case with Pitt and, seemingly, influential in that quarter, and well known as the brains behind the anti-Emancipationist party in the British government and parliament.

Meanwhile in Ireland, following the recall of Fitzwilliam and the arrival of his successor, Camden, and Camden's chief secretary, Pelham, the Emancipation Bill was being persevered in by Grattan, the Ponsonbys, and others. The Camden administration allowed it to remain an 'open' question (a precedent later adduced by the anti-Unionists, who urged that the Union was a similar question of conscience[47]), and although the government made its opposition to the measure plain, no office-holder was dismissed, or threatened with dismissal, for supporting it. Having obtained the

40 Malcomson, *John Foster*, p. 427.   41 Scott's first impressions of him, when they met in 1781, are memorable: 'a person of a mean appearance, short and slight, with an ordinary face, a full eye animated and impudent, and a strong provincial brogue ..., [who] came from Scotland to London in desperate circumstances' – *Clonmell diary (TCD)*, p. 295.   42 Geoghegan, *Union*, pp 138–9 and 141–2.   43 Loughborough to the King, 10 Mar. 1795, *Later correspondence of George III*, ii, pp 317–20.   44 Moore to the King, 19 Mar. 1795, ibid., p. 322.   45 Westmorland to Agar, 8 Apr. 1795, T/3719/C/29/21.   46 Mendip to Agar, 17 May 1795, and Westmorland to Agar, 13 June 1795, T/3719/C/29/30 and 32.   47 Malcomson, *John Foster*, pp 421–4.

substance of his wishes, Agar – as he had in 1793 when defeated in the substance – gave 'the government every assistance he could, even when we were acting against what in his opinion we ought to do.' On 30 April he made a significant memo. of an audience with Camden:

> Lord C. saw me alone to say it was the wish of the English cabinet that the R[oman] C[atholic] B[ill] should be defeated on the second reading. The impossibility of passing such a bill to be fully expressed by Mr P[elham] as subversive of the present constitution in Church and State, but not to be followed by any resolution [against future concession] except *some general one*. To which the Archbishop objected as useless; adhered to his former opinion that resolutions are necessary, but said he should acquiesce in the opinion of the English cabinet, though contrary to his own judgement.[48]

This was followed by a further demonstration of flexibility on the question of the setting up of Maynooth – the Camden administration's sop to the catholics for the defeat of the Emancipation Bill. Agar recorded:

> May 1795. A bill was introduced into the House of Commons by Mr Pelham to establish an university in Ireland for the education of popish ecclesiastics, and it was sent up to the House of Lords, requiring the objects of it to take only the oath of the 13th and 14th George III. The Archbishop had signified to Mr P. ... the propriety of requiring the making also of the declaration and taking of the oath in the 33rd George III, to which opinion Mr P. acceded. However, he forgot or omitted to make that alteration, and the Archbishop made it in the House of Lords without Mr P.'s previous consent in the committee. But Mr P. changed his mind, in conformity to the opinion of others, as was thought, and wrote a letter to the Archbishop requesting him to alter the bill again on the third reading and omit the declaration and oath of the 33rd of George III, which he did to oblige Mr P. though against his own judgement. The Archbishop also suggested to Mr P. the propriety of inserting a clause into the bill to have said university at thirty miles at least from Dublin; but it was not acceded to.[49]

Pelham wrote to him on 12 May expressing the hope that 'you will not think it necessary to persist in your amendment to the Education Bill, and will consent to its rejection on the third reading, as I am sure that any alteration after all that has passed would take away the grace of the measure, and I am sure that you will agree with me

48 Endorsement by Agar on a summons to Dublin Castle from Camden's private secretary, 30 Apr. 1795, T/3719/C/29/27. For the full story, from the Dublin Castle side, see Pelham and Camden to Portland, 20 Apr. 1795 (two letters), Portland to Camden, 24 Apr. 1795, and Camden to Portland, 30 Apr. 1795, HO 100/57, ff. 148–55 and 227–8.   49 Agar's political memoranda, 1782–95, 21 M 57/A18.

in thinking that a multiplication of oaths in a case of this sort is not desirable, and that those which are already required are sufficient.' Agar, who obviously did not agree with him, endorsed the letter: 'answered instanter that I would move the rejection if he wished it.' In reply, Pelham thanked him for his 'kind answer and ready acquiescence' and for all his 'marks of attention and regard ... ever since I first landed.'[50] Pelham, according to his brother-in-law, Lord Midleton, was 'the only Englishman without any Irish concerns of his own whom I have conversed with who seems to have any decided opinions favourable to the protestant interest.'[51] This helps to explain Agar's deference to Pelham's wishes. However, the episode also shows the extent of Agar's flexibility and pragmatism, even on issues which to him were issues of conscience, and suggests that there was every likelihood of his being recruited successfully and usefully to the cause of the Union in 1798.

AGAR AND SECURITY POLICY, 1795–8

It is generally assumed that Agar was a hard-liner on security policy (and therefore, by implication, likely to be hostile to the policy of 'lenity' adopted by Cornwallis from his arrival in Ireland in June 1798). However, when put to the test of hard evidence, this notion of Agar the hard-liner seems to rest on the assertion made by Henry Grattan junior in his hagiographic *Memoirs* of his father, that Agar was one of the three 'sanguinary' members of the Irish cabinet in 1795–8.[52] There are one or two snippets of evidence which could be interpreted as corroboration of this view. In March 1798, Clifden declared to Agar, who he presumably thought would endorse these sentiments: 'it is only by military courts and commissions [that] these miscreants [the United Irishmen] can be tried, and such ought to be created, and must, or the country is undone!'[53] A letter from Lord Shannon to his son, Viscount Boyle, dated 12 May 1798, details the contents of a very gung-ho letter from Clifden, of which Agar apparently approved: 'The Archbishop of Cashel showed me a letter from Lord Clifden, in which he says that things are very bad in the county of Kilkenny, where he has burned thirty houses on his own estate, being more severe on his own tenants than on other people's; and he is proceeding at a great rate, and has written to know whether he may shoot a few, which would put an end to all rebellion.'[54] On 4 July, when the rebellion in the south was as good as at an end, a disgusted English officer reported that Clifden had just burned 450 cabins within view of his own house at Gowran.[55]

50 Pelham to Agar, 12 and 13 May 1795, T/3719/C/29/28–9.   51 Midleton to Brodrick, 20 Oct. 1793, Ms. 8889/8.   52 Grattan, *Memoirs of Grattan*, iii. 401 and iv. 390. The passage is perhaps more informative about the anti-clericalism of the Grattans than it is about Agar's attitude on law-and-order. Grattan junior goes on to remark: 'Feelings of this description are not peculiar to that archbishop alone, for, unfortunately, it may be observed that clergymen, when they become politicians, are by far the most violent; and theirs is the worst species of rage, for their profession protects them, and they can indulge their passions without fear, as they are out of the way of danger.' 53 Clifden to Agar, 7 Mar. 1798, T/3719/C/32/14.   54 *Lord Shannon's letters to his son*, p. 93.   55 Major R.[?T.] Wilson, Clonmel, to Lord William Bentinck, 4 July 1798, *Irish official papers*, i, pp

These allegations or suggestions of sanguinariness are at variance with the view expressed by Agar in his visitation charge of 1802 (pp 218–20) that 'the law of force is always less effectual in its operation than the law of opinion, will and habit, [and that] more benefits were to be expected to society from the influence of example than from the severest punishments of offence.'[56] Pat Hare said something similar in a strangely moving passage in a letter to Agar of April 1801: 'until men had rather be starved than hanged, you will not put down the insurrections and nightly depredations of those ruffians. ... I say no punishment is too heavy for them. But it will not do. They are so poor that the law can only reach their lives, and their lives they do not value.'[57] Clifden's sentiments, which like Hare's may be regarded as indicative of Agar' own, sound more sanguinary when quoted out of context, or for purposes of effect by the witty Lord Shannon, than in reality they were. Clifden was not an armchair advocate of blood-and-thunder measures: he was on active service at the head of his yeomanry corps trying, first, to pacify Co. Kilkenny and, next, to defend it from attack at a time when 'The United Men are in thousands about Thomastown, and [there is] not army sufficient to keep the rebels from the town [of Kilkenny].'[58] From his post of some danger, Clifden was advocating properly constituted courts martial and the execution of those sentenced by such courts – in other words, the line soon to be laid down by Cornwallis. While other officers and magistrates were shooting and torturing suspects (often suspects arrested on the flimsiest grounds), Clifden wrote to Dublin Castle requesting permission to make some well selected examples. Shannon's *précis* of the letter is misleading. The letter survives in Agar's papers, and the relevant passage is: 'We have several leaders in confinement. I have written to Lord Camden for leave to shoot them. I fear I shall not get it. Such an example would restore tranquillity.'[59]

The allegation that he burned 450 cabins at Gowran also seems to derive from misunderstanding, or misrepresentation. A letter he had written to Agar a little earlier, establishes his attitude to destruction of property unless accompanied by clear military advantage:

> Now for the [blowing of the] bridge of Graige [i.e. Graiguenamanagh]: a more wanton, scandalous or really injurious act I believe never was done. It is in the highest degree injurious to the force here and obstructs our quick co-operation with any force that may be sent on the other side from Borris. ... It ruins this town, my property, and deeply injures the country all round. All this should and must be nothing, if it answered any good purpose, but when it only obstructs the operation of the troops, I can hardly conceive an act of more shameful ignorance or more scandalous disregard of what officers owe to the

185–8. **56** Page from *The Dublin Journal*, 30 June 1802, recording Agar's visitation charge, 21 M 57/A2/22. **57** Hare to Agar, 2 Apr. 1801, T/3719/C/35/11. **58** George Frost, the agent, Kilcooley Abbey, [Co. Tipperary], to Sir William Barker, 14 June 1798, Barker Ponsonby papers, TCD, P1/11/28. For Clifden's concurring view of the gravity of the situation, see Clifden to Agar, 6 June 1798, T/3719/C/32/73. See also pp 107–8. **59** Clifden to Agar, 11 May 1798, T/3719/C/32/53.

country. ... No man has been more willing to sacrifice himself and his property than I have. I have burnt several houses in this town; I consented to Sir Charles Asgill's [the general commanding in the area] destroying the whole, if it were necessary; I have assisted in foraging without mercy those of my tenants who were guilty; and after all to have my estate laid waste in such a way ..., is not to be borne patiently.[60]

In other words, although willing to sacrifice his property at Graiguenamanagh (not Gowran) to any good end, and anxious to demonstrate his disinterestedness, he had only burnt 'several houses', not the alleged 450. In general, he was opposed to 'burning houses', because he considered that martial law (which had been introduced on 30 March) was 'more merciful ... . I would burn that house under the *floor* of which I found pikes concealed, but the *mud-floored* cabin I would spare for the sake of the women and children it holds.'[61] His line on amnestying defeated rebels who were prepared to surrender was Cornwallis' in microcosm and in anticipation: 'The Ro[w]er people [i.e. from Lord Callan's estate in south-east Kilkenny] have sent to Graige to offer to deliver up their arms and the persons who murdered Mr Annesley, Mr Cliff[e] and Mr Elliot about a week ago.[62] ... If they do this and remain quiet, we will trouble them no more. I hold oaths of allegiance to be of little use.'[63]

Tipperary, Agar's adopted county, 'had been described by Camden in 1798 as "the scene of most outrage and the most marked acts of rebellion". It had also figured as the scene of some of the most brutal reprisals.'[64] In late 1796, when most 'loyalists' and advocates of strong measures were seeking pretexts for having the 'proclaiming clauses' of the recent Insurrection Act implemented in parishes and baronies of their counties, Agar had merely sought advice from Dublin Castle as to 'what measures he should adopt in consequence of reports of the emergence of disturbances in Tipperary ... . Pelham advised him against proclaiming the county, recommending instead regular meetings of the magistrates to enquire into the nature and extent of the disturbances.'[65] In 1798, Tipperary was disturbed for months prior to the rebellion, 'more by the eccentric and violent behaviour of its high sheriff, Thomas Judkin Fitzgerald, than by United Irishmen. Fitzgerald appears to have taken it upon himself to save the country from subversives by an extensive and intensive campaign of public flogging. This tactic subsequently gave rise to a number of court cases and amnesty acts.'[66] Agar's views on Fitzgerald can only be inferred from those of his Tipperary associates and correspondents. At first, these were suspicious and sceptical.[67] Then, in

---

60 Clifden to Agar, 19 June 1798, T/3719/C/32/90.   61 Clifden to Agar, 12 Mar. 1798, T/3719/C/32/22.   62 For these murders, see Comerford, 'The Church of Ireland in Co. Kilkenny', p. 148.   63 Clifden to Agar, 12 June 1798, T/3719/C/32/80.   64 Bolton, *Union*, p. 148. 65 Gaynor, 'Politics of law and order in Ireland', p. 84.   66 Thomas Bartlett, 'Clemency and compensation: the treatment of defeated rebels and suffering loyalists after the 1798 Rebellion', in Jim Smyth (ed.), *Revolution, counter-revolution and Union: Ireland in the 1790s* (Cambridge, 2000), p. 109. I am grateful to Professor Bartlett for sending me a draft of this essay.   67 Hare to Agar, 21 Mar. 1798, and Samuel Alleyn to Agar, 28 Mar. 1798, T/3719/C/32/29 and 34.

mid-May, Agar's friend, Lord Hawarden, wrote to him in perplexity: 'Is it possible that government can authorise *any magistrate* to set fire to people's houses who have taken the oath of allegiance and never appeared in any shape deserving of the rigour of the law, which I believe is the case of all my [Tipperary] tenantry? ... The French, if they were landed in Ireland, can do no worse than to burn and destroy men's property, *without distinction* whether they are friends or foes.'[68] By the summer, Pat. Hare was ready to 'support efforts to remove ... Fitzgerald, for he was "absolutely *a madman*".'[69]

There are also some indications that Agar's views as an individual member of the Irish cabinet were on the moderate wing where security policy was concerned. In early April 1798, following the *furore* created by the general orders of the commander-in-chief, Sir Ralph Abercromby, reflecting on the state of indiscipline of the army, Agar wrote pointedly to Auckland, a member of Pitt's government, that 'some persons' thought that a further set of orders by Abercromby applying to Kildare and King's and Queen's Counties only, were not quite as strong as they should have been, and that Abercromby had been too liberal in allowing ten days for the restoration of stolen arms. 'However, if we get them back in that time, I shall be perfectly contented.'[70] The 'some persons' were clearly those of his colleagues in the Irish cabinet who had been whipping up alarm in government circles in London, and two of whom, Clare and John Beresford, had been using Auckland as a means of undermining Abercromby's position. In view of Clare's subsequent, sudden conversion to the pacific measures of Cornwallis in early July, it is significant that Agar should have been more moderate in his views than Clare in the admittedly very different, pre-rebellion circumstances of April. At about the same time, Agar compiled and the Irish government printed a paper of *Extracts from several acts of parliament made to prevent tumultuous risings in this kingdom*, from *29 George II, cap. 12*, to *36 George III, cap. 20*.[71] The purpose of this codification was presumably to give magistrates and military officers a ready-reckoner of the powers already at their disposal, so that they would neither exceed them nor keep clamouring for more. Auckland called it 'an important and efficient paper, well calculated to do good in the serious circumstances of Ireland. I gave one of your copies yesterday to Mr Pitt.'[72] Dublin Castle also received at least one demonstration of Agar's disposition to moderation at an individual and indeed personal level. In mid-June, Clifden had written to him asking him to obtain from Lord Castlereagh the release of a United Irishman from the Rower who was too old to constitute any threat. 'His daughter is young and pretty and she has gained all our officers, militia and yeomen, so that from morning till night I hear nothing but solicitation in favour of this old man. ... If I interfered, every man sent off [to the tenders] would have a daughter,

68 Hawarden to Agar, 13 May 1798, T/3719/C/32/54. 69 Hare to Agar, 19 July 1798, T/3719/ C/32/100, quoted in Bartlett, 'Clemency and compensation', p. 110. 70 Agar to Auckland, 5 Apr. 1798, Auckland papers, BL, Add. Ms. 34454, f. 204. I am indebted for this reference to Sir Richard Aylmer. See also Gaynor, 'Politics of law and order', p. 358, and – for Abercromby's original general orders – Auckland to Agar, 11 Mar. 1798, T/3719/C/32/21. 71 T/3719/C/32/39A. 72 Auckland to Agar, 11 Apr. 1798, T/3719/C/32/39.

sister or niece to raise a host of solicitors and applicants.'[73] This episode does not evince a very 'sanguinary' disposition in either Clifden or his uncle.

AGAR'S RELATIONS WITH CORNWALLIS

In a letter of compliment which Cornwallis wrote to Agar in February 1805 (towards the end of Cornwallis' life), Cornwallis observed: 'I shall ever remember with gratitude the favour and powerful assistance which I experienced from my numerous friends in Ireland, which could alone have carried me through the various difficulties which I had to encounter when I first entered upon the government of that country.'[74] Cornwallis was not given to flowery language – that was one of the criticisms made of him by huffy Irish notabilities. So it seems improbable that he would have written in those terms to Agar if there had been any major falling-out between them when he 'first entered upon the government of' Ireland. This simple point is worth making, because it is generally assumed that Cornwallis quarrelled on arrival with the entire Irish cabinet of the 1790s except Clare, and would have quarrelled with Clare if Clare had not made it his business to ingratiate himself with Cornwallis.

Cornwallis, the trouble-shooter of the British Empire, was a very experienced soldier-administrator. His years of distinguished service in India had developed in him proconsular habits which were not well-attuned to the management of a parliament, and his experience of non-Anglican, indeed non-Christian, troops and non-Christian subject peoples had developed in him an outlook which was religiously non-exclusive and which questioned the principle of a Church Establishment. In this respect, his chief secretary, Lord Castlereagh, whose family background was presbyterian, was even more suspect to Anglicans, particularly churchmen. As Brodrick growled in May 1800: 'Our Secretary was not educated to ... ecclesiastical matters.'[75] Cornwallis' principal and, after the initial defeat of the Union in the Irish House of Commons, his only, supporter in the British Cabinet was Henry Dundas, the secretary of state for war, a Scots presbyterian; Dundas was credited with the opinion that it was right 'to have the Church of England in England, Presbytery in Scotland and the Romish Church in Ireland.'[76] Cornwallis himself was supposed by the same writer, Bishop O'Beirne, to have 'hated churchmen.'[77] As a professional soldier, Cornwallis certainly deplored the idea of civilians – let alone a churchman – directing military policy and even tactics, as the Irish cabinet of his predecessor, Camden, had done.[78] He also deplored the idea of the regular army being carved up into small bodies and dispersed all over the country to overawe the local population and restore order by draconian means.

73 Clifden to Agar, 12 June 1798, T/3719/C/32/80. 74 Cornwallis to Agar, 1 Feb. 1805, T/3719/C/39/3. 75 Brodrick to Midleton, 9 May 1800, Ms. 1248, vol. 17, f. 122. 76 Bishop O'Beirne to Primate Stuart, 24 Dec. 1805, Bedfordshire RO, WY 994/47. In view of the role played by Dundas, as home secretary, in the Catholic Relief Acts of 1792 and 1793, this remark could as easily have been made about him in 1798 as in 1805. 77 O'Beirne to Foster, 28 Mar. 1808, PRONI, D/207/50/4. 78 For an earlier example of Agar trying to dictate military policy, see Sylvester

Over a year earlier, he had refused the lord lieutenancy of Ireland because it was not offered to him on the basis that Catholic Emancipation would be part of the agreed programme of his administration. He accepted the post in June 1798 without any such stipulation (but with good hope that Emancipation might yet form part of the Union) because of the gravity of the crisis facing Ireland and the Empire. In September 1798, after learning that the British cabinet had decided to proceed with the Union on what he regarded as a narrowly protestant basis, he commented : 'I feel the measure of so much importance that it is worth carrying anyhow, but I am determined not to submit to the insertion of any clause that shall make the exclusion of the catholics a fundamental part of the Union.'[79] He would not have been aware of Agar's compromise on just such an excluding clause in 1795, because he would not have sought information on the subject from his anti-Emancipationist predecessors, Camden, Pelham and Westmorland. Instead, he would have associated the doctrine of perpetual exclusion with Agar's interpretation of the Coronation Oath. Cornwallis had joined Pitt's cabinet as master-general of the ordnance in February 1795, at the time of Fitzwilliam's recall, the evolution of the Coronation Oath argument and the circulation round British ministers of Agar's anti-Emancipationist crib. From this, Cornwallis can only have concluded that, of all the former Irish cabinet, the most dangerous enemy to Emancipation was Agar. Clare, of course, was just as dangerous. But Clare 'was quite capable of appearing reasonable and temperate when he chose', and soon convinced Cornwallis that he was 'by far the most moderate and right-headed man amongst us.'[80] Clare's purpose in very publicly siding with Cornwallis at critical moments in July 1798 was, not only to further their mutual aim of the Union, but to dish his former colleagues in the Irish cabinet. Among these he must have perceived Agar as his most threatening competitor, particularly in the post-Union world of Westminster; which is why Clare's subsequent comments on Agar (pp 590 and 596) during the vacancy in the primacy which occurred in 1800, show extreme bitchiness and imply strong jealousy. Cornwallis was of course aware of Clare's hostility to Emancipation. 'All the leading persons here' he lamented in late September, 'not excepting the Chancellor[!], are determined to resist the extension of ... [the benefits of the Union] to the catholics.'[81] But lulled into a belief in the essential moderation of Clare, Cornwallis would have seen no need to involve Agar in the initial planning of the Union, since he already had Clare as his 'third man'; and he might well have seen great danger in giving Agar the opportunity to influence the content of the proposals.

On his side, Agar initially had some reason to welcome Cornwallis' appointment. Alone among the Irish cabinet, he had a personal association with Cornwallis prior to the latter's coming to Ireland. This necessitates a short digression. One of Cornwallis' sisters, Lady Elizabeth, had been married to an obscure Irishman called Bowen

Douglas to Pitt, 16 Oct. [1793], Chatham papers, PRO, 30/8/327, f. 347.   **79** Cornwallis to Major-General Ross, 30 Sep. 1798, *Cornwallis correspondence*, ii, pp 416–17.   **80** Geoghegan, *Union*, p. 28; Cornwallis to Portland, 20 July 1798, HO 100/66, ff. 350–2.   **81** Cornwallis to Ross, 30 Sep. 1798, loc. cit.

Southwell (MP for Downpatrick, 1755–60). In her widowhood, she had fallen physically or, more probably, mentally ill, and Cornwallis' brother, James, bishop of Lichfield and Coventry, having 'long been acquainted with your willingness to undertake friendly and charitable offices', had asked Agar to interest himself in Lady Elizabeth's welfare. 'Your plan entirely meets with my own and Lord Cornwallis' approbation', he wrote in March 1796. Agar's efforts were then frustrated by Lady Elizabeth's death,[82] but the Cornwallis family obviously remained under a considerable obligation to him for trying. On public grounds, too, Agar may not have been wholly satisfied with the Camden system of government. Clifden, who must again have been echoing things which Agar himself had said, had written to him in early March:

> I hear from good authority that some as hostile to rebels and traitors as you or I, are determined to join them if the government do not afford protection to them and their families. I assure your Grace, I don't write this as doubting your sense or vigour on this trying occasion. To you and the Chancellor and one or two more of the Irish cabinet ministers, the public look with confidence. To the English part of the Irish government, people here look with none.[83]

Clifden, for one, was 'truly glad to hear of the appointment of Lord Cornwallis.'[84]

From his arrival in Dublin on 20 June, however, Cornwallis took immediate steps to distance himself publicly from Camden's Irish cabinet. Ignorant or regardless of the differences of opinion and the personal rivalries and antagonisms which divided them, he treated them as a symbolic unit, set them aside and discontinued the summonses to them to attend at the Castle. Having made this important gesture, he sought authority in early July to offer an amnesty to all former rebels who had not been guilty of murder in cold blood (in the event, the British government extended the excepted category to rebel leaders and to deserters from the government forces). According to one anonymous squib, which can be dated to July 1798, 'some of the old cabinet wished to resent his [Cornwallis'] behaviour ..., [including] Michael Cassio [who must be Agar, in view of Agar's proverbial leanness] ... . After a very few days ..., [however,] Cassio found the ground hollow. He refused to go on, but sulked and retired.'[85] Judging from a comment dropped by the Hon. Thomas Ralph Maude, who was soon to become Agar's son-in-law and was the son of his friend and Cashel neighbour, Hawarden, Agar may not have been sorry about the discontinuation of the old cabinet system. Writing from the Cashel Palace in late June, Maude asked: 'May we not hope, from the change that has been lately made, your Grace's perpetual attendance at the Castle will not be required, and that there is a probability (for even that would be a great comfort) of your coming into this country?'[86]

Perhaps Maude was being either naïve or consolatory? In any case, Agar was given no chance to leave Dublin and 'retire.' Instead, at the beginning of July he was offered,

82 Bishop Cornwallis to Agar, 29 Feb. and 17 Mar. 1796, T/3719/C/30/8 and 10a; Cowper, *Deans of Canterbury*, p. 188   83 Clifden to Agar, 7 Mar. 1798, T/3719/C/32/14.   84 Clifden to Agar, 19 June 1798, T/3719/C/32/90.   85 Sheffield papers, PRONI, T/3465/90.   86 Maude to Agar,

and accepted, a congenial and important appointment as the senior of ten commissioners for the relief of 'suffering loyalists.'[87] This appointment might be regarded as a particular instance of a general phenomenon recently highlighted by Professor Bartlett. Bartlett writes: 'The compensation scheme devised by Dublin Castle for those loyalists who suffered losses in the rebellion has to be considered the counterpart of Cornwallis' policy on defeated rebels: both were crucial in bringing to a successful conclusion the stated objective of the Viceroy's policy – the adoption of a ... Union.'[88] But there is no good reason for thinking that Agar needed – as many other 'loyalists' did – the sop of a generous and expeditious compensation scheme to reconcile him to 'Cornwallis' policy on defeated rebels.' In late July, a couple of weeks after Cornwallis' controversial amnesty, Agar wrote to Auckland (in a letter which will be quoted at greater length on p. 530) that Cornwallis' measures to put an end to rebellion 'must, I think, partake of severity as well as conciliation and pardon.'[89] In other words, he was not prepared to throw in his lot unconditionally with Cornwallis (as Clare, for his own good reasons, was doing), but he was not opposed in principle to Cornwallis' policy of 'conciliation and pardon.' In practice, that policy amounted to what Bartlett has called 'measured severity': of the 400 courts martial which Cornwallis had reviewed by March 1799, he allowed 81 of the 131 death sentences to stand.[90] So, there is no reason to imagine that Agar would have disapproved very much of Cornwallis' proceedings.

Nor is it likely that he would have disapproved very much of the famous compact made by Cornwallis with the so-called 'state prisoners' – 78 imprisoned United Irish leaders, against almost all of whom there was insufficient evidence to procure a capital conviction[91] – whereby they would in due course be allowed to emigrate provided they made a satisfactory confession of their connection with the French and aim to set up an independent republic. While Clare volunteered his public and vociferous support of this bargain with the state prisoners, Agar is not recorded as approving or disapproving. Probably this is for the good reason that his opinion was not asked. What is almost certain is that Agar was as alive as Clare to the propaganda value of evidence from the United Irish leaders that their intentions had been treasonable from early on, and that the failure to grant Parliamentary Reform or Catholic Emancipation, to reform the tithe system, etc., were merely pretexts used by them to inflame the people. (Agar would have derived particular satisfaction from Thomas Addis Emmet's acknowledgement, in the state prisoners' 'confession', that if tithes were abolished, the only beneficiaries would be the landlords, who would increase rents accordingly.[92]) As has been seen (p. 77), Agar had been particularly associated with the policy of collecting publishable testimony through the medium of parliamentary secret committees. He had come high in the ballot for membership of the secret committees of the House of Lords of 1793 and 1797; autograph minutes by him of the evidence heard by those

24 June 1798, T/3719/C/32/95.   87 Castlereagh to Agar, 2 July 1798, 21 M 57/A41.   88 Bartlett, 'Clemency and compensation', p. 127.   89 Agar to Auckland, 24 July 1798, *Auckland correspondence*, iv, pp 35–6.   90 Bartlett, 'Clemency and compensation', p.107; Geoghegan, *Union*, p. 22. Geoghegan's figures are derived from Bartlett.   91 Cornwallis to Portland, 29 Oct. 1798, *Cornwallis correspondence*, ii, pp 425–6.   92 Pakenham, *Year of liberty*, p. 290.

committees and that of 1798 are present among his papers;[93] he went to considerable trouble in 1793 to try to find a British precedent for a committee of the House of Lords receiving evidence on oath;[94] the 1797 committee appears to have been set up at his suggestion;[95] and he certainly received letters of congratulation on its outcome.[96] Three years later, during his first session of parliament at Westminster, Agar referred to the report of the last of the secret committees in his speech in the House of Lords on the renewal of the Irish Martial Law Bill (*41 George III, cap. 61*): 'He stated that, when in 1798 the Irish parliament armed the crown with the authority of martial law, they did so upon the serious inquiries of the secret committee', and had conducted fresh investigations in 1799 and again in 1800 before renewing it.[97] Ironically, it was during this debate that Clare incurred Pitt's contempt (according to Wilberforce) by acknowledging with a shrug 'the practice of torture for the purpose of making discoveries.'[98]

THE ROUGH WOOING OF AGAR, JULY–NOVEMBER 1798

On 28 May,[99] Pitt and his innermost circle of ministers had decided to carry a Union. On 4 June, Agar's friend, Auckland (who was to prove a treacherous friend, and not just to Agar), had been brought into the secret and asked to join a small group of experts who would together work out some of the details of the measure, particularly in regard to finance and commerce. Auckland was a natural choice. Not only had he been chief secretary for Ireland in 1780–2, he had been the negotiator of the Anglo-French commercial treaty of 1787 (a precedent which did not augur well for Ireland). He was also, comparatively speaking, at leisure to devote some time to Irish affairs. He was a member of the government, but not of the cabinet, and therefore not subject to the distractions and disruptions of waging war. To Auckland was also allotted, probably after discussion with Pitt, the diplomatic assignment of drawing both Agar and John Beresford (also at this stage 'disinclined' or worse) into a discussion of the Union. With Beresford, who was never happier than when playing with statistics, Auckland achieved immediate success by asking for information about Irish revenue and debt.

93 21 M 57/A35/1–4. This is a so far unused source of great potential importance. For example, I am informed by Sir Richard Aylmer, who has compared the two, that the minutes of the 1793 committee differ radically from the version printed in the *Lords' journals*: Agar's minutes are far longer; they name names; and they come to the opposite conclusion – *viz.* that the United Irishmen *were* deeply involved with the Defenders. 94 Ellis to Agar, 10 and 30 Apr. 1793, T/3719/C/27/4–5. 95 Memo. by Agar of meetings in Dublin Castle, 25 Apr. 1797, T/3719/C/ 31/42. 96 Lords Westmorland and Hawarden to Agar, 24 and 25 May 1797, T/3719/C/31/62–3. Hawarden's letter specifically makes the point about propaganda value. 97 [Cobbett's] *Parliamentary history of England ..., vol. xxxv ..., from the 21st day of March 1800 to the 29th day of October 1801* (London, 1819), pp 1242–3. 98 Ibid. (the quotation comes from the speech of an opposition peer, the 1st earl of Carnarvon); Geoghegan, *Union*, p. 14; Kavanaugh, *Lord Clare*, pp 370–73. Perhaps significantly, Agar later became friendly with Clare's denouncer, Lord Carnarvon – Carnarvon to Agar, 24 Feb. 1806, T/3719/C/40/15. 99 Geoghegan, *Union*, p. 10.

He did not repeat this success with Agar; and the nature of some of his queries to Beresford helps to explain why:

> I am against changes, but it appears to me that the loyal catholics ought to be distinguished ..., giving to the sect, not an establishment, but respectable and responsible men of their own persuasion, paid handsomely from the public purse. Are you able to inform me, with respect to Irish tithes, what proportion of the whole you conceive to be paid by protestants, what proportion by the more opulent planters, and what proportion by catholics, potato grounds, etc., etc.[100]

However, the main reason for Auckland's more tentative, and indeed, blundering approach to Agar was surely that he received a false briefing from Clare. Clare, a closer friend of Auckland's than (in the light of events) was Agar, wrote to Auckland at the beginning of July: 'The Speaker will, I believe, be against the measure, and I know the Archbishop of Cashel will oppose it vehemently.'[101] This was not so much a bad guess as a piece of deliberate misrepresentation. Nor was it even Clare's consistently expressed opinion, because in mid-November he wrote, again to Auckland: 'The Archbishop of Cashel ... [is] much disinclined to the measure of a Union; but on this or any other subject he may be easily tamed by Lord Mendip.' He then added, as if to explain Agar's disinclination: 'I do not find that Lord Cornwallis has as yet communicated with a single gentleman of the country upon any subject.'[102]

Meanwhile, in mid-July, Auckland had begun his supposedly diplomatic offensive on Agar, to whom he wrote: 'You are now approaching to the moment when every wise man should wish to do something that may give a new and improved turn to the disposition of your people in general, and a consequent security and tranquillity to your government. But what is both practicable and proper for that purpose, I am utterly unable to conjecture or hitherto to learn. I wish that you could tell me. I saw Mr Pitt yesterday.'[103] In a guarded and huffy reply, Agar questioned whether Auckland's 'moment' was 'approaching' just yet:

> I wish I could say the rebellion was at an end, but, alas! it has only changed its appearance. ... The rebels are no longer in bodies of 16,000 or more, but they are divided into smaller parties ... How or when this will end, I cannot say; but the time, I believe, is at a distance, and the mode must, I think, partake of severity as well as conciliation and pardon. ... Wishing (as I sincerely do) that all the measures of government may succeed, I don't think myself at liberty to create even a doubt in any man's mind about their probable effects; and

---

100 Beresford to Auckland, 19 and 21 July and 2 and 9 Aug. 1798, and Auckland to Beresford, 1 Aug. 1798, *Beresford correspondence*, ii, pp 161–3 and 165–71. For the tithe commutation plan, see 'Heads of a Union with Ireland', Nov. 1798, *HMC Dropmore Mss.*, iv. 399.   101 Quoted in Bolton, *Union*, p. 60.   102 Clare to Auckland, 15 Nov. 1798, *Auckland correspondence*, iv. 67.   103 Auckland to Agar, 18 July 1798, T/3719/C/32/98.

therefore, whatever my opinion may be, since it is not called for by those who decide on such matters, I keep it to myself.[104]

Agar must have realized that a Union had been decided upon and that Auckland was already at work on the details. Apart from anything else, Lord Buckingham had been in the know since early June,[105] and a secret imparted to Buckingham was a secret no longer. Agar may also have taken the view that a secret imparted to Auckland was not much safer. Some years later, another of Auckland's Irish correspondents was warned: 'When you write ... to our friend, Lord Auckland, remember that he is gratified by being favoured with communications from you, and that he cannot refrain from further gratifying himself by communicating the substance thereof with comments.'[106] Nevertheless, Agar's reply, though guarded, was fairly explicit. He was making it clear to Auckland (as he had already done in April, long before Cornwallis came on the scene) that Agar's line on security policy was a combination of severity and concilia-tion, that he was willing to enter into the discussion of a Union (which, in the context, must have been one of 'the measures of government' which he hoped 'may succeed') and that he wanted to be back in the counsels and confidence of Dublin Castle.

Auckland, however, continued to hide his cards. Once again he referred to 'the moment ... for uniting wisdom to energy in the choice and use of means which may render Ireland hereafter a benefit and not a burthen to the empire of which she forms so important a part. It is on this subject that I wish much to hear from you fully and confidentially, certainly with a disposition to apply your suggestions to good purpose, and incapable at the same time of committing you in any use that I may make of them farther than you wish. Mr Pitt continues to regain health.'[107] In reply, Agar reported how Cornwallis had just had a miraculous escape from being shot by a sentry in Phoenix Park. 'It is *wonderful* how he could have missed him.'[108] As a churchman, Agar perhaps had a professional leaning towards parables. The meaning of this one may have been that far too much depended on Cornwallis and that he was not in the best or safest hands in Ireland. Adverting to Auckland's soundings, he responded with equal circumspection: 'These are great objects – too mighty, in truth, for me alone. But, with the assistance of some other men who are well known to your Lordship, I should, though with very great diffidence, venture to take my share in this most arduous undertaking. On some other occasion, I shall resume this subject; but at pre-sent it seems that a system is adopted, and will probably be pursued, which precludes such considerations.' There was no reply from Auckland, unless it has been lost, until 14 September, when he complained that Agar had not yet given his views 'on that essential subject.'[109] There is then a definite gap in the correspondence. The next sur-viving letter is dated 23 October, and came, once more, from Auckland. He concluded:

104 Agar to Auckland, 24 July 1798, *Auckland correspondence*, iv, pp 35–6. 105 Geoghegan, *Union*, p. 11. 106 1st Lord Eldon to Lord Redesdale, [early Oct.? 1803], Redesdale papers, Gloucestershire RO: photocopy in PRONI, T/3030/6/7. 107 Auckland to Agar, 2 Aug. 1798, T/3719/C/32/109. 108 Agar to Auckland, 14 Aug. 1798, T/3719/C/32/110. 109 Auckland to Agar, 14 Sep. 1798, T/3719/C/32/122.

'The subject is somewhat too large for a letter, and therefore I do not wonder that the intimations which I have occasionally given have not produced your Grace's opinion. Mr Pitt's health continues to gain ground from week to week. ... I understand that the Archbishop of Dublin [then in retirement in Essex] is gradually declining.'[110] Auckland though one of Britain's most senior diplomates had 'never been remarkable for his courtly accomplishments'![111] Even allowing for the unreliability of the post office (of which Auckland had inside knowledge because he was British postmaster-general) this was hardly a frank and open exchange of views. Indeed, the expectation that Agar would state his sentiments unreservedly while the most basic information was withheld from him, was insulting, as was the crude allusion to the impending vacancy in the archbishopric of Dublin.

All the time that Auckland had been pumping Agar, Agar had been in Dublin, struggling under the unmanageable burden of work which fell upon the active commissioners for the relief of suffering loyalists. But the Irish government had made no attempt to communicate with him. In mid-November, Agar (perhaps deliberately) gave them an opening by writing to Castlereagh to congratulate him on his appointment as substantive chief secretary. In reply, Castlereagh courteously acknowledged 'the very essential assistance' he had received from Agar since his entry into official business a year previously,[112] but said no more. It was not until Agar left for England on 19 November that Cornwallis first solicited his views on and assistance with the Union. It can be no coincidence that Cornwallis had just received from London 'the heads of a treaty of Union', by the terms of which catholics remained excluded from parliament and high office,[113] but which contained no clause 'that shall make the exclusion of the catholics a fundamental part of the Union.' This decision having, for the moment, been taken, Cornwallis no longer needed to fear Agar's involvement in the planning of the Union and, in particular, his influence with the anti-Emancipationist members of the government, Westmorland, Auckland and Portland (with the last of whom, via Mendip, Agar was now on friendly terms). Indeed, on the assumption that Cornwallis was aware of Auckland's abortive negotiations with Agar up to this time, his fear of Agar's involvement may have been fuelled by an unfounded suspicion that they contained elements of an anti-Emancipationist intrigue.

Cornwallis' letter to Agar, now that it was at last written, was not well judged. He 'apologised for not having notified him of the Union project before his recent departure from Ireland, and ... suggested that the intention had only recently been notified by the British ministry.'[114] He concluded with the foolish and tactless observation: 'I have had no opportunity of being acquainted with the general sentiments of the principal people here [!], but I trust that they will consider the matter dispassionately, and think it wise to make a small sacrifice of vanity in order to secure more substantial benefits.'[115] Agar, understandably, did not respond well to being lied to and patronised.

110 Auckland to Agar, 23 Oct. 1798, T/3719/C/32/150. 111 *The British Mercury ...*, *vol. iii for 1787*, p. 102. 112 Castlereagh to Agar, [*c*.15 Nov. 1798], T/3719/C/32/160A. 113 Portland to Cornwallis, 12 Nov. 1798, *Cornwallis correspondence*, ii, pp 436–7; Geoghegan, *Union*, p. 39. 114 Quoted in Bolton, *Union*, p. 76. 115 Cornwallis to Agar, 19 Nov. 1798, T/3719/C/32/162,

This being the first intimation I have had of such an intention being entertained seriously, and being quite ignorant of the terms and conditions to be
offered, it is impossible for me ... to say at this time what part ought to be taken
by a man determined to promote as far as he is able what shall appear to him to
be the true interests of his country. My past conduct is the best proof I can give
of my wishes to support his Majesty's government at all times.[116]

Cornwallis' overtures to others were no more auspicious. On 5 December, Ely wrote
from Dublin to Agar: 'I have been, with many others, called to his Excellency's closets.
They recommended it with great modesty, and I have with the same modesty declined
giving any opinion till the entire subject is more generally understood. ... I intend going
to London in about ten days ..., and hope by that time to have the honour of seeing your
Grace there.' He subscribed himself effusively 'with every good wish for your Grace,
yours always affectionately, Ely.'[117] A Unionist judge voiced the general opinion when
he wrote in late December: 'My Lord Cornwallis is too ingenuous and direct ... .
Whatever he may be in the field, he seems no general in the cabinet. No pains have been
taken to conciliate, and many of the old friends and the most attached partisans to the
British government, whom it would be easy to retain, are said to have fallen off in
disgust.'[118] Towards Agar, however, the conduct of 'this wonderful and extraordinary
lord lieutenant'[119] was disingenuous – indeed, that of 'a crooked politician.'[120]

TITHE COMMUTATION AND AGAR'S OTHER MISGIVINGS

Agar's visit to England in mid-November was the only one made by the inner group in
the former Irish cabinet – Clare, Beresford, Foster and Parnell – which was not made at
the invitation of the British government. Nor was it a put-up job of the kind which
Lord Carleton had ridiculed in 1788 when the Irish lord chancellorship looked like
falling vacant (see p. 72). Agar's daughter, Fanny, was due to marry the Hon. T.R.
Maude in mid-December (see p. 81); and the marriage was to take place in Bath, where
Lord Hawarden had property and was living, and whither Agar had sent his wife and
daughter well before the outbreak of the rebellion.[121] Agar's presence was necessary to
finalise the settlements, obtain a special licence from the Archbishop of Canterbury and,
presumably, solemnise the nuptials.[122] At this family event, or afterwards in London,

printed (from the original, which was lent by the 2nd earl of Normanton) in *Cornwallis
correspondence*, ii, pp 440–1.   **116** Agar to Cornwallis, 27 Nov. 1798, T/3719/C/32/162–3;
Cornwallis correspondence (where the original received by Cornwallis is printed), iii. 1.   **117** Ely to
Agar, 5 Dec. 1799, 21 M 57/A46/1.   **118** Robert Day to Lord Glandore, 30 Dec. 1798, MIC/639/
6/87.   **119** Bishop Barnard to his niece, Isabella, 18 July 1800, printed in Anthony Powell (ed.),
Barnard letters, 1778–1824 (London, 1928), pp 131–2.   **120** Hon. William Wellesley Pole to his
brother, 1st Marquess Wellesley, 10 Feb. 1801, Wellesley papers, BL, Add. Ms. 37416, f. 74.   **121**
Mendip to Agar, 29 May 1798, T/3719/C/32/64.   **122** Robert French (the Dublin K.C. advising
him on the settlements) to Agar, 16 and 17 Nov. 1798, and Mendip to Agar, 2 Oct. and 27 Nov. 1798,
T/3719/C/32/161A–B, 133 and 164. The special licence will be found at 21 M 57/D52.

Lord Mendip would have had every opportunity to 'tame' Agar (in Clare's memorable but misleading phrase). But, even supposing that Clare had been right in his analysis of the extent of Mendip's influence, Mendip in this instance would not have wished to exercise it. The proposed commutation of tithes mentioned by Auckland to Beresford at the beginning of August was intended to apply to England as well as Ireland; and Mendip's intimate crony, John Hatsell (the retired clerk to the House of Commons at Westminster), had written in great alarm to Auckland about it in late October.[123] It is impossible that Mendip did not know about it, did not share in the alarm and did not join in the opposition to it, which was headed by Archbishop Moore.[124]

The precedent and starting-point for the proposed commutation of tithes was English – the recent redemption of the obsolete and inequitable Land Tax and its absorption into the new Income Tax. There had never been a Land Tax in Ireland – a long-standing British grievance. But the read-across to Ireland had been almost instantaneous. In late February 1798, as has been seen (pp 504–5), an anonymous, printed plan had been addressed to Pelham advocating 'a Land Tax in place of tithe ..., that would produce a great revenue and at the same time would give a general satisfaction ...; [for] the present mode of levying ... [tithes has] been for near a century the cause of great tumult, disturbance and disorder.'[125] Auckland, too, who had been an advocate of tithe commutation in Britain since the early 1790s,[126] was quick to make the same connection. In mid-April, well before he first wrote to Beresford about the Union, he expressed to Beresford his 'great confidence in the success of ... the Land Tax Bill ... . Oh! that it were possible to do something similar as to the liberation of tithe [he meant the liberation of agricultural land *from* tithe] in both kingdoms. But the clergy would be alarmed.'[127] In late July, referring exclusively to the Church of England, Pitt formulated the following ideas:

> The plan adopted in the last session for the sale of the Land Tax, seems in its general principle to be in many respects equally applicable to tithes. ... The owner of every estate should be allowed to redeem that estate forever from tithe, with the consent of the incumbent pastor and ordinary, on transferring to trustees (probably the commissioners for the reduction of the national debt) a certain portion of stock ... (as in the case of the Land Tax) ..., the interest of such a stock to be for the benefit of the living or appropriation ... . An annual fund would [thus] be secured as a substitute for the tithe purchased, considerably exceeding it in amount; and the amount of tithes throughout the kingdom so much exceeds the Land Tax, and the number of years' purchase is so much greater, that this measure, if successful to any degree, might be expected to operate both more successfully and more rapidly than in the case of the Land Tax, as an aid to public credit.

123 Hatsell to Auckland, 24 Oct. 1798, *Auckland correspondence*, iv, pp 63–5.   124 Pitt to Auckland, [26? Oct. 1798], ibid., p. 66.   125 'A protestant' to Pelham, pre-27 Feb. 1798, T/3719/C/32/9. 126 Evans, *The contentious tithe*, p. 80.   127 Auckland to Beresford, 15 Apr. 1798, *Beresford correspondence*, ii. 155; Ehrman, *The younger Pitt: the consuming struggle* (London, 1996), p. 178.

It would also be attended with collateral advantages of themselves essentially important. It would tend materially to promote improvement and agriculture, would give the greatest relief and satisfaction to the whole landed interest (including both owner and tenant), and remove the *chief cause of jealousy between the clergyman and his parishioner*. The latter circumstance alone would go a great way towards giving *additional credit and influence* to the clergy, an object at the present moment peculiarly of the most urgent importance in every view in which it can be considered; and regulations might easily be engrafted on this measure which could render such an influence still more effectual by furnishing additional means of enforcing residence and perhaps by forming a fund for the *augmentation of small livings*, and even for new endowments if the increased calculation and population of the country should require it.[128]

The idea of obtaining 'additional means of enforcing residence' had been prompted by the recent harassment of the clergy of the Church of England under the Clerical Residence Act of 28 Henry VIII (see p. 236). But it soon assumed an Irish dimension. Castlereagh's private secretary, negotiating with British ministers in late September, reported back: 'Tithes need not be settled by the Union, but ... it is suggested that the principle of the redemption of the Land Tax should be extended, under proper regulations, to the tithes. This should be accompanied by a competent provision for a reasonable number of catholic clergy.'[129]

It was almost certainly Buckingham who promoted the idea that the (actually irrelevant) 'principle of the redemption of the Land Tax' should be applied to Ireland, and should form the basis for a commutation of tithes and a modification of the relations between Church and State in that kingdom. In Buckingham's mind, a sense of the unfinished business of 1788 must also have been prominent. Since June, he had been in Dublin, at the head of his militia regiment (which had volunteered for service in Ireland). Drawing on the information he collected there, he bombarded Grenville and (through him) Pitt with advice about the Union and Irish affairs generally. No doubt he leaked the content of these representations to his Dublin cronies, and did not fail to exaggerate the extent of his influence with his highly placed brother and cousin. Among Grenville's papers is a document dated November 1798 and titled 'Heads of a Union with Ireland.' This includes the provision that

a plan for the commutation of tithes ... should be submitted either to the Irish parliament previous to the Union or to the United parliament immediately after. This is to be accompanied with the strictest possible provision for enforcing residence by the authority of the bishops, but under the compulsion of positive laws, according to which the profits of the living ... are to be paid to the

128 Rough, autograph plan, 30 July 1798, Stanhope/Pitt papers, U1590/o.9/43–4.   129 Robert Marshall to Castlereagh, 26 Sep. 1798, *Castlereagh correspondence*, i, pp 378–80.

incumbent only in proportion to his residence, and the remainder to accumulate as a fund for the repair of the church, parsonage, etc.[130]

Needless to say, the additional 'compulsion of positive laws' would be bound to undermine 'the authority of the bishops', as Agar had argued in his confrontation with Buckingham in 1788, and as Sir William Scott was to argue in 1799 in his hostile response to the present proposal (see p. 237). This combination of compulsory tithe commutation and 'positive laws' to enforce clerical residence, both to apply equally to Britain and Ireland, must have been the 'system' to which Agar had alluded darkly to Auckland in mid-August, and the adoption of which, he added, precluded Agar's participation in 'this most arduous undertaking', the Union.

The Irish tithe question is a subject not to be enterprised lightly; and there is, fortunately, no necessity to make the attempt.[131] From the point of view of Agar, a churchman who sought as far as possible to keep matters of Church governance out of the parliamentary arena, tithes possessed the special sacrosanctness of Old Testament precedent. He would have appreciated the passage in a pamphlet addressed to him in 1793 in which the anonymous author referred to 'quacking politicians ... daily stunning the public ear with crude schemes to support the Church, instead of the revenues she has enjoyed almost since her infancy.'[132] In 1786, Agar had defended the moderation of the clergy of the Church of Ireland and, as in his confrontation with Buckingham, had taken

> much pains to convince government as well as others that the conduct of the clergy has in no respect given cause for the present disturbances [in 1785–6]. To provide this, nothing more is necessary than to ascertain the prices demanded by the clergy for each kind of tithe for many years past, and compare them with the real and true value of the commodity. I have done this carefully, and can show that the clergy in general have not demanded a moiety of the value of any kind of tithe, not a third part of some, and not a fourth part of the value of the tithe of other articles, and for many years [actually, since 1736] have not received one shilling for agistment or many other tithes regularly paid in England.[133]

He had sent a questionnaire round the clergy of the entire province of Cashel at the end of 1786 requiring detailed information about tithing practices and the value of the tithes collected in every parish.[134] In consequence, when a speech was published a year and a half later 'in several newspapers as the speech of Henry Grattan Esq., containing very

130 *HMC Dropmore Mss.*, iv. 399.   131 For essential background to what follows; see: Bric, 'The tithe system in eighteenth-century Ireland', *passim*; Erck, *Ecclesiastical register*, pp l–lxii; Akenson, *Church of Ireland*, pp 87–111.   132 *A letter to his Grace the Lord Archbishop of Cashel ...* (Dublin, 1793), p. 4. For this pamphlet, see p. 578.   133 Agar to Ellis, 26 Aug. 1786, T/3719/C/20/25. In an autograph paper of *c.*1794 (21 M 57/B15/1) headed 'Prices of tithes in the dioceses of Cashel and Emly' he commented: 'in every instance the clergy lose two-thirds of their legal dues and in most instances much more, and yet how grossly are they misrepresented and calumniated'.   134 Copy of Agar's circular, 20 Dec. 1786, and 'Queries' drawn up by 'the Clerical Society', 15 Jan. 1787,

exaggerated accounts of the prices demanded by the clergy of Munster, a manifesto against the misrepresentation thereof was drawn by Dr C. Agar, Archbishop of Cashel, signed by him, the several bishops and clergy of the province of Munster, and published' on 20 August 1788.[135] Unfortunately, the returns on which this 'manifesto' was founded do not survive in Agar's papers or, apparently, anywhere else.

It was characteristic of him to have collected such a corpus of parochial information, which he could then draw upon to counter generalised attacks or the imposition on Ireland of 'ideas ... very ill-suited to this country' (see p. 235). The latter seemed to be what was in contemplation in late 1798. Tithe composition was, in effect, a separate issue in the two kingdoms, mainly because they were at different stages of development in respect of tithe. A graphic illustration of this difference is Ellis' throw-away remark in a letter to Agar of October 1786: 'I am not sure that I rightly understand what a tithe-proctor is.'[136] Tithe-proctors were blamed for inflaming the situation in Munster by their exactions, but they would never have come into existence if tithes had been collectable in Ireland with as comparatively little difficulty as in England. Euseby Cleaver, who was familiar with the situation in both kingdoms, warned his Irish friend, Charles O'Hara, in September 1786: 'If [the Irish] parliament admit of any commutation for tithes, there is an end of protestant interest in your country.'[137] In Britain, great progress with, and experience of, commutation had ensued as a result of the parliamentary enclosure movement. Between 1660 and 1800, 2,321 private enclosure acts had been passed for England and Wales: in Ireland over the same period the figure was seven.[139] The British parliament had passed 74 in 1794 alone.[138] This activity gave rise, among enthusiasts for commutation in Britain, to an optimism which can only have been alarming to Irish churchmen. In January 1799, Bishop Watson, who was extreme in his enthusiasm and optimism, asserted: 'If acts of parliament for enclosing commons and open fields go on for twenty years more as they have done for twenty years past, the grievance of tithe will be almost wholly done away.'[140] The huge statistical difference between the two kingdoms in the matter of enclosure had little to do with the attitudes of their respective Churches (one-third of the tithes of England and Wales were in lay ownership anyway): the main reason was the virtual absence in Ireland of surviving common rights and common land. These had been very largely annihilated as a result of all the surrenders and re-grants, escheats and plantations, confiscations and sales, which had taken place in Ireland between the mid-sixteenth and the early eighteenth century.

Not all the enclosure acts for England and Wales included arrangements for the commutation of tithes.[141] But of those which did, Ellis had written to Agar in 1788 recommending him to study

T/3719/C/20/39 and 21/5.   **135** Agar's 'state' of the diocese of Cashel, 1779–1801, 21 M 57/B6/1.   **136** Ellis to Agar, 29 Oct 1786, T/3719/C/20/34.   **137** Cleaver to O'Hara, 15 Sep. 1786, PRONI, T/2819/18/12.   **138** I am grateful for these figures to Dr D.W. Hayton, who in turn received them from Dr Julian Hoppitt of the History Department, University of London.   **139** Ehrman, *The younger Pitt: the reluctant transition* (London, 1983), p. 469.   **140** *Anecdotes of Watson*, p. 309.   **141** Evans, *The contentious tithe*, pp 94–111.

some of the later, which are drawn with more accuracy from experience than some of the former, in order to form a general plan for enclosing and improving waste and cultivated lands in Ireland, and for assigning in such plans of enclosure, as in England, a certain quantity of such land so enclosed to the minister of the parish in lieu of and as a full consideration for the tithe which would otherwise become due upon such enclosed and improved lands. This in England amounts to a seventh or an eighth of such enclosures.[142]

A seventh or eighth part of the land in a parish (and the figure was not unrealistic) in compensation for an often disputed right to a tenth of the gross produce of the parish, was an attractive bargain from the point of view of the clergyman or lay tithe-owner; and he was in a position to hold out for it in England and Wales because tithe composition during enclosure was voluntary, and the tithe-payers of the parish were usually keen to be rid of the burden and complication of tithe. Incomes, particularly among 'the poorest clergy' of the Church of England, were rising in this period. 'By the early nineteenth century only one-third of livings fell below the clerical poverty line, now estimated at £150, compared with half in 1736'; and a major factor in this welcome change was 'favourable tithe commutation during enclosure.'[143]

In Ireland, prospects for 'favourable tithe commutation' were not rosy. There had been no gain in 'accuracy from experience' in the Irish situation. Indeed, with the current swing from tithe-free pasture to tithe-paying arable, much previous experience had ceased to be applicable. While the collection of tithe was often subject to local disputes and even 'affrays' in Britain, there was no equivalent there to the widespread combinations and violence of 1785–7 or, as will be seen (pp 548–9 and 577–8), of 1797–9. And, while there was great variation within Britain in the items titheable and in tithing-rates in different parts of the country, the situation in Ireland was in this respect more extreme. Brodrick described it as follows in a letter to Lord Midleton of October 1800:

> It is perfectly true that throughout the province of Ulster, and I believe through a great part of the provinces of Leinster and Connaught, no tithe is paid for potatoes. In very many places, particularly in my diocese [Kilmore], no tithe is paid for hay, and for flax only sixpence for whatever quantity, much or little, a man may have on his land. Tithe, then, is paid generally only for wheat, for barley and for oats; in some places hay and flax are charged according to the quantity sown; and through Munster generally potatoes and hay pay according to a valuation of the crop. We have also here a small annual charge payable out of every house under the head of house or family money. Some small sum is also paid in many places for cattle grazing. These are the chief, I believe I may say the whole, of what is tithed, and you will observe that in no part of the country, as I believe, are all these articles tithed together, but where one article

142 Ellis to Agar, 12 June 1788, T/3719/C/22/24.   143 Walsh and Taylor, 'The Church and Anglicanism', pp 6–7.

is made subject to tithe, another is left out: as for instance, where potato gardens are tithed, family money is not charged, and little or nothing is paid for flax. ...

What had been the origin of these variations in the modes of tithing, I cannot say: probably it will be found in the extremely unsettled state of the country, the fears of the clergy who have been edged out of their just rights by papists and presbyterians, and the natural disposition to purchase peace by the sacrifice of the property of unknown successors. ... Another cause which may have operated to make the clergy more negligent of the part of their property arising from tithe in this diocese, is that the county of Cavan [where most the diocese of Kilmore is situated], being one of the six which were escheated after Tyrone's rebellion, King James provided the clergy very amply with land.[144]

Even if Brodrick was correct in his suggestion about the escheated counties, such provision of land in their part of Ireland was more than offset by the point made by Agar – that many things which paid tithe in Britain (e.g. personal industry[145]) in Ireland went tithe-free.

One clear symptom of the differences between Britain and Ireland in respect of the tithe question, is that in the former it was often, perhaps usually, possible for clergymen to trust to the common law, rather than to the civil law and ecclesiastical courts, for the enforcement of their rights to tithe. In Britain,

> Common lawyers were hostile to ecclesiastical jurisdiction but not to ecclesi-astical property. This mattered a great deal when the clergy sought to claim their share of the improved agricultural profits available after 1750. John Rayner's summary of tithe judgements, published in 1783, revealed the high rate of success enjoyed by clergy who took their claims to law. A series of important cases, attracting much public interest, was decided in the 1770s, almost all of them to the advantage of the tithe-owners.[146]

In Ireland, by contrast, the clergy could hope for redress only from the ecclesiastical courts; and some of Agar's political battles had been fought in defence of this privilege – for example, his wrecking amendment to Grattan's Barren Lands Bill of 1788 (see p. 450), and his act of 1795 (*35 George III, cap. 32*) amending the Summary Tithe Acts of 1763 and 1767 (*3 George III, cap. 25*, and *7 George III, cap. 21*).[147] Very recently, there had been a reminder of how far Irish practice lagged behind British in this res-pect. In March 1798, Dr Duigenan reported to Agar in great alarm that a Co. Mayo gentleman hostile to the rights of the clergy had introduced into the Commons a bill by which

---

144 Brodrick to Midleton, 23 Oct. 1800, Ms. 1248, ff. 136–7. For the situation in the north Antrim part of the diocese of Down and Connor, see Macartney to Agar, 24 Sep. 1786, T/3719/C/20/30.
145 Erck, *Ecclesiastical register*, p. li.   146 Langford, *Public life and the propertied Englishman*, p. 16.
147 See pp 74 and 444.

he means to *oblige* the clergy, in all cases where the value of the tithes does not exceed forty shillings, to sue for them exclusively before two justices of [the] peace ... . The clergy have at present their option of the two judicatures, and generally sue before the ecclesiastical judge by petition, as the most expeditious and effectual method of recovering their tithes. ... In most parts of Ireland the tithes yearly payable by any one person seldom cums [*sic*] up to forty shillings, and ... this bill will therefore demolish all jurisdiction of ecclesiastical courts in cases of tithes, and transfer it to little country squires to the ruin of the clergy. ... Besides, in the present period [i.e. since the Catholic Relief Act of 1792], many papists are made justices of [the] peace

In a very thin House, and following the desertion of most of 'the government troops', the bill had not as yet been defeated or postponed, and Duigenan urged Agar to 'speak to some of your friends to attend', and also 'to the lord lieutenant and some leading members of the government in the House of Commons.'[148]

Agar considered it untimely as well as inappropriate to impose upon Ireland a general and permanent scheme of tithe commutation in 1798. Ten years earlier, he had acknowledged that 'An enclosure bill properly drawn, with provisions to secure a fair portion to the parson and to prevent him from setting it for a longer term than 21 years at the full value or reserving a rent nearly equal to the true value, may be very useful in this country.'[149] Such a general Enclosure Act for the whole United Kingdom was in fact passed immediately after the Union, in 1801 (*41 George III, cap. 109*), and established the future ground rules for particular, short-term, parochial enclosure bills.[150] Agar's wording is somewhat obscure, but his concern that no valuation should be permanent is manifest.[151] This was common form, in Britain as well as Ireland, granted the wartime experience of rising agricultural prices. It caused the only other bishop of the Church of England (besides Watson) who favoured commutation, Bishop Pretyman-Tomline, to embrace – and convert his tutee, Pitt, to – the idea of 'corn rents': i.e. a flexible commutation capable of re-valuation in the light of a rise or fall in the price of corn.[152] Later, an Irish clergyman suggested that, 'to prevent the mischief arising from any future fall in the value of money, ... [a] limit to bar tithe ... [of] sixty years [should be established], which would be the time necessary for barring any claim to an estate.'[153] In fact, it was agricultural prices which fell, from 1813 onwards, thus inverting the assumptions of the late 1790s.[154]

---

148 Duigenan to Agar, 18 and 21 Mar. 1798, T/3719/C/32/26–7.   149 Agar to Primate Robinson, 30 Oct. 1788, T/3719/C/22/39.   150 The act is obscurely worded and seems not to apply to Ireland. But a later act of c.1820, 'for enclosing lands in the parishes of Tallaght, Kilsallaghan alias Kilsoughan, and Lusk, in the county of Dublin' (TCD, OL8 X–1–801) was passed under its authority, so there can be no doubt that it did.   151 Bishop Woodward had rejected tithe commutation in his *Present state* because of the problem of inflation – see *A letter to ... the Lord Archbishop of Cashel*, pp 7–8.   152 Evans, *The contentious tithe*, p. 107.   153 Rev. Dr Thomas Elrington, provost of TCD (later bishop of Ferns), to Brodrick, 9 May 1814, NLI, Ms. 8861/7.   154 Evans, *The contentious tithe*, pp 116–18. Commutations which had taken the form of allocations of land were not liable to these problems. On the other hand, they turned the incumbents concerned

There was, however, more to Agar's sense of the untimeliness of the proposal than a worry about the mechanism of valuation. As he put it:

> The clergy, from motives of compassion and moderation, have been contented to take small prices for predial[155] tithes, aiming only at getting as much out of an union of many parishes as would afford them a bare subsistence. But were you now to pass any bill rendering the average of such income the whole that should in future be paid by the several parishes constituting such union, you would ..., first, render the perpetuity of such unions necessary, though an increased population might make it proper to dissolve them; secondly, you would put an end to the increase of churches (however they might be wanted) and the extension of the Established Religion.[156]

Cleaver had made the same point in 1786:

> The tithes which at present go to the subsistence of one rector arise frequently from five or six and sometimes ten parishes, ... having but one church among them ... . [As cultivation advances, they] may have churches and glebe-houses and tithes in proportion to the improvement and population. But if the value of a living of many denominations were now to be appreciated and a permanent value given in lieu of tithes, perhaps there would be £300 or £400 per annum allotted for the maintenance of one clergyman, where in the progress of improvement there ought to be £500 or £600.[157]

Like Buckingham's threatened reduction in the tithe income of the clergy, and his threatened 'presbyterian equality' in the value of livings, a general tithe commutation would have greatly complicated, if not wholly arrested, the church and glebe-house building programme of the board of first fruits, and with it the promotion of clerical residence.

In mid-December 1798, Agar was invited to Downing Street for a discussion – presumably about the Union – with Pitt.[158] Though Pitt, and Grenville, had decided in September to lay Catholic Emancipation aside, at least as an initial accompaniment to the Union, Pitt's attitude to tithe composition, statutory enforcement of clerical residence, payment of the catholic clergy, etc., seemed to be unchanged. Years previously, he had urged 'those who are at the head of the clergy [of the Church of England to consider composition] ... soberly and dispassionately ... [and] to promote

into either farmers or small landlords, and they also increased the possibilities of disputes over dilapidation. Farm buildings, obviously, could fall into dilapidation; but a lease which was unduly favourable to the tenant was also a form of dilapidation. **155** Predial tithes were those charged on what grew on the land; they were virtually the only species of tithe paid in Ireland. See Bric, 'The tithe system in eighteenth-century Ireland', p. 272. **156** Paper in Agar's handwriting on tithe commutation, [1790s?], 21 M 57/B31/23. **157** Cleaver to O'Hara, 3 Oct. [1786], T/2812/18/21. **158** Pitt to Agar, 16 Dec. [1798?], T/3719/C/32/165.

some temperate accommodation, ... [since] even the appearance of concession, which might be awkward in government, could not be unbecoming if it originated in them.'¹⁵⁹ In December 1791, he had again urged Archbishop Moore (in vain) to take the lead, so that the bishops might 'be enabled to give a proper direction to the business.'¹⁶⁰ Whether he would maintain this deference to episcopal wishes, and whether it extended to bishops of the Church of Ireland, was a moot point. Granted the optimistic faith in composition which had gripped strong Church of England men like Bishop Pretyman-Tomline, Grenville and Auckland, and the baleful influence of Buckingham, the prospects for Agar's forthcoming interview did not look bright. As far as the specifically Irish bearings of all these plans were concerned, it was particularly ominous that Pitt had very recently stated to Cornwallis his conviction that 'a provision for the catholic clergy and some arrangement respecting tithes ..., with some effectual mode to enforce the residence of all ranks of the protestant clergy, offer the best chance of gradually putting an end to the evils most felt in Ireland.'¹⁶¹

Infuriatingly, and anticlimactically, nothing is known about what passed during Agar's interview with Pitt. It is even possible that the meeting did not take place. In this instance, above all, Henry Carter's destruction of Pitt-Agar correspondence is keenly felt. A modern admirer of Pitt has observed euphemistically that 'the Prime Minister was not at his best in meetings of that sort.'¹⁶² He had recently mishandled a series of meetings with Speaker Foster¹⁶³ so abysmally that – with some help from Cornwallis – he drove Foster into bitter, proactive and almost systematic opposition to the government. As the already-quoted Unionist judge observed, 'The Speaker, who in my humble opinion has full as much weight and character with his country as he deserves, is likely to be most mischievous.'¹⁶⁴ Foster was always going to have opposed the principle and the single measure of a Union, so in his case Pitt and Cornwallis only made a bad business much, much worse. With Agar, the case was different. There is every reason to assume that he supported the principle, but strongly disapproved of some of the details and accompaniments. It is likely that his discussion with Pitt, assuming that it took place, focussed and foundered on the accompanying proposals for tithe commutation and clerical residence and, if it had not been laid aside by December 1798, payment of the catholic clergy.

The post-Union representation of the Church of Ireland in the House of Lords of the United Kingdom was another source of great concern to Agar, and an issue on which the government's proposals had been drawn up without reference to him. On 11 January 1799, Portland wrote to Cornwallis: 'The Archbishop of Cashel acknowledges himself disinclined, but professes great and earnest desire to support government. He thinks that the spiritual lords *should be represented by the four archbishops*.'¹⁶⁵ This sounds like a very attractive arrangement from Agar's point of view. But subsequent events (pp 560–3) showed that there was more to his advocacy

159 Quoted in Evans, *The contentious tithe*, p. 80.   160 Ibid.   161 Pitt to Cornwallis, 17 Nov. 1798, *Cornwallis correspondence*, ii, pp 441–3.   162 Geoghegan, *Union*, pp 44–6.   163 Foster to 1st Lord Sheffield, 18 Dec. [1798], PRONI, T/3725/12.   164 PRONI, MIC/639/6/87.   165 Portland to Castlereagh, 11 Jan. 1799, *Castlereagh correspondence*, ii, pp 88–9.

of exclusively archiepiscopal representation than self-interest. Nor was this a side-issue. A letter of 5 January 1799 from Brodrick, who in most respects took a different view of the matter from Agar, explains why the mode of representation in the House of Lords was of major importance for the Church (and also shows that an alternative scheme to Agar's had already been settled and, what was more, made public).

> An alteration has taken place since the arrival here of the terms, by adding two to the number of the peers and taking two from the [spiritual] peers. ... In whatever way it is settled, the expense of the attendance on parliament will be so enormous to us, and the inconvenience of voyage and journey so very great to those of us who have families, that many of the bishops must of necessity decline it, and except persons under particular circumstances of connection in England, very few indeed will seek it. ... I am glad, therefore, that they are to go in rotation, to attend only one session at once, by which they will involve themselves the less in political intrigue to urge their own interest, and that the number is reduced to four, by which the fewer dioceses will be neglected.[166]

Having frequently fought the battles of the Church in the Irish House of Lords, and having every reason to expect new battles in the House of Lords of the United Kingdom, Agar would have regarded Brodrick's indifference to post-Union representation as misplaced idealism.

For most of January, Agar's and – more particularly – Ely's views on the Union were a topic of discussion between Whitehall and Dublin Castle. Cornwallis, who thought that Agar was more hostile to the Union than did Portland, heard that Ely was 'living [in London] with the Archbishop of Cashel, from whom he would infallibly receive ... [anti-Unionist] impressions.'[167] At this stage, it must be said, more interest attached to Ely's nine votes in the House of Commons than to the value of Agar's counsels as an elder statesman. Ely returned to Ireland first, his conduct still unpredictable. Parliament was due to meet on 22 January, and the day before, Castlereagh wrote, in relation to the proceedings of the House of Lords: 'Unless the Archbishop and Lord Carhampton shall arrive in time, there seem no materials for debate. The violent part the Orangemen have taken up seems to have made a considerable impression in some of our most protestant supporters. Lord Shannon's opinion is materially changed, and I think the Chancellor is a little shaken.'[168] This coupling of Agar with the 2nd earl of Carhampton, and Lords Shannon and Clare, the 'most protestant' erstwhile or current supporters of government, tends to confirm that it was Agar's 'protestantism', combined with Clare's previous misrepresentations of Agar, which had led to his exclusion from Cornwallis' and Castlereagh's confidence.

In the event, Carhampton did not turn up, having 'availed himself of some pretence to stay away, in order to save his office [the mastership-general of the

---

166 Brodrick to Midleton, 5 Jan. 1799, Ms. 1248, vol. 17, f. 100.   167 Cornwallis to Portland, 11 Jan. 1799, *Castlereagh correspondence*, ii. 90.   168 Castlereagh to Portland, 21 Jan. 1799, *Castlereagh correspondence*, ii, pp 127–8.

ordnance].'[169] Agar returned to Ireland on the 22nd itself.[170] Almost certainly, he so timed his arrival as to make it impossible for the Castle to extract from him a decided 'yea' or 'nay.' He was present in the House of Lords, along with 75 other peers and bishops, when a somewhat anodyne set of resolutions was adopted, preparatory to an address to the King. One of them spoke of 'consolidating, as far as possible, into one firm and lasting fabric, the strength, the power and the resources of the British Empire.' There were two divisions on this resolution, and one protest signed by thirteen peers and one bishop was entered on the *Journals*.[171] The surviving descriptions of what went on in the Lords either do not mention Agar, or are inexplicit about how he voted, though they all dwell on the fact that Ely 'skulked.' The most circumstantial is that of the 1st earl of Carysfort, the Grenvilles' brother-in-law:

> In the House of Lords, an amendment was first proposed by Lord Powerscourt calling in question the competency of parliament. As the other lords in opposition were not prepared to go this length, he desired to withdraw it, but the Chancellor would not agree to it. There was a division on the question for withdrawing the amendment, 46 to 19, in which the Archbishop of Cashel was in the minority, Lord Ely going behind the throne [i.e. abstaining]. On the amendment afterwards proposed by Lord Bellamont, the numbers were 16 and 1 proxy to 49 and 3 proxies ... . I am not sure whether the Archbishop of Cashel voted at all. Lord Ely again went behind the throne. ... The Archbishop of C. had, I believe, a considerable influence upon him. ...[172]

Agar's first vote may have had no more than procedural significance. He is unlikely to have voted *against* the government on the second vote, since the resolution amounted to no greater commitment than to *consider* the question. He certainly did not join in the protest. He then absented himself until 31 January, by which time the address had been agreed and voted in the Lords (though narrowly defeated in the Commons on 24 January). For the remainder of the 1799 session, he attended badly (by his usual standards). Over the same period, it may be noted, Primate Newcome barely put in an appearance, and Archbishop Beresford of Tuam scarcely missed a sitting: intimation, perhaps, that the former was soon going to create a vacancy and that the latter was eager to fill it.

COMPENSATION FOR SUFFERING LOYALISTS AND THE CLERGY

Agar had plenty of important and politically uncontroversial work to do during the first half of 1799 in his role as a commissioner for the relief of suffering loyalists – a

---

169 1st earl of Carysfort to Grenville, 23 Jan. 1799, *HMC Dropmore Mss.*, iv, pp 449–50.   **170** Agar's pocket memorandum book, 1790s, 21 M 57/D56.   **171** *Lords' journals*, viii, pp 189–201. **172** Carysfort to Grenville, 23 Jan. 1799, *HMC Dropmore Mss.*, iv, pp 449–50. The other accounts of the proceedings are: Cornwallis to Portland, 23 Jan. 1799, *Cornwallis correspondence*, iii, pp 40–1; and

role which also had the tactical advantage of keeping open his lines of communication with Dublin Castle. The first, and interim, task of the commissioners had been to disburse, in 'sums not exceeding fifty pounds', an emergency grant of £100,000 voted by the Irish parliament on 27 June 1798.[173] Then, on 6 October, an act (*38 George III, cap. 68*) was passed formally establishing the commission and laying down the stringent (and time-consuming) procedures which the commissioners were required to follow in adjudicating claims and authorising payments. The act was avowedly based on the post-1783 American precedent, from which the very term 'suffering loyalists' derived. This inflamed Cornwallis' Irish opponents. It was an unfortunate reminder that he had been the British commander who had surrendered at Yorktown in 1781 and, more to the point, it ignored the essential difference in the two situations – *viz.* that 'compensation was the only object in the case of America, for the country was given up',[174] whereas reconstruction should have been the prime objective in post-rebellion Ireland. These were the sentiments of Speaker Foster, who advocated an extensive programme of public works and of 'employment for the disbanded rebels.' Pitt thought this idea 'a very judicious one',[175] but by this time the act had become law and nothing was ever done to set up public works. Agar was not an apostle of economic paternalism. But he shared Foster's objections to another aspect of 'Mr Pitt's mode of liquidating the claims of American loyalists' – its slowness. Agar's comments on 'Mr Pitt's mode' include: 'Sixty per cent deducted from American claims, and claimants forced to wait twelve years before they received compensation; paid by lotteries.'[176] In the case of Ireland, one of Agar's fellow-commissioners forecast in March 1799 that the commission would need fourteen years to complete even the case-work currently before it.[177]

In addition to excessively rigorous procedures, the commission was hampered by the fact that its active membership was too small. Of the ten people whose appointment was confirmed by the act, three were judges and never attended. The *Almanack* for 1799, which would have been finalised at the end of 1798, does not even give their names. The remaining seven were kept excessively busy, for the act stipulated a quorum of five. In terms of their composition, they were men after Agar's own heart – and appropriate to a remit which included the destruction of or damage to a great deal of clerical property. Two were bishops – Knox of Killaloe and Brodrick. Agar was and remained on close terms with the former and was not yet on bad terms with the latter; and together they constituted the most able and efficient trio on the then Irish bench. Another was the banker to the board of first fruits, the Rt Hon. David

Clare to Auckland, 23 Jan. 1799, *Auckland correspondence*, iv, pp 79–80.   **173** Bartlett, 'Clemency and compensation', p. 119.   **174** Foster to Sheffield, 11 Sep. 1799, printed in Malcomson (ed.), *An Anglo-Irish dialogue: a calendar of the correspondence between John Foster and Lord Sheffield, 1774–1821* (Belfast, 1975), pp 29–30.   **175** Quoted in Malcomson, *John Foster*, p. 363.   **176** Copy of a paper written by one of the commissioners for suffering loyalists in North America, endorsed by Agar 'Mr Pitt's mode of liquidating the claims of American loyalists', together with notes on the paper by Agar, [Sep.? 1799], T/3719/C/131–2.   **177** William Knox, bishop of Killaloe, to Lord Abercorn, 25 Mar. 1799, quoted in Bartlett, 'Clemency and compensation', p. 120.

Latouche, a staunch Anglican (see p. 431). The fifth was the Hon. Richard Annesley, elder brother of the zealous dean of Down (see p. 313); and the sixth was Sackville Hamilton, the highly respected and now retired under-secretary in Dublin Castle, with whom Agar had worked amicably for many years. (The seventh was the chancellor of the Irish exchequer for the time being.) Clearly, however congenial to Agar most of these commissioners were, they were liable to the unanswerable objection that there were too few of them for the volume of work and the procedural complexity involved. 'By July 1800, only some 113 claims had been processed out of approximately 5,750 which had been received; over 5,000 of these claims were for sums under £200.'[178]

Of the 'over 5,000 ... claims ... for sums under £200', one had been lodged by 'Stephen Hogan of Cashel', who sought compensation for his loss of 50 guineas in bank notes when the mail coach from Cashel was robbed at Red Gap on the Dublin road.[179] At the other end of the scale came the 2nd earl of Courtown. Courtown, a largely absentee Co. Wexford magnate, was a courtier at St James', and had many influential connections. During the rebellion, he had been 'a Sir Peter Grievous ..., petrified to a degree of stupidity'. His house at Courtown, near Gorey (and not far from Ferns), had been wrecked by the rebels, and Courtown himself, to judge from the letter he wrote Agar in late October 1798, had caught the Cleaver virus (see pp 360–61). He reckoned his total losses at not less than £20,000 in unpaid rents and damage to his own house and to farmhouses belonging to tenants on his estates.[180] Ironically, three weeks later, Agar received a letter from Courtown's local clergyman and chaplain, the Rev. James Gordon, rector of Killegny in the diocese of Ferns, alerting him to the existence of a racket in connection with the claims of the suffering loyalists of Co. Wexford. 'I [have] found' he wrote 'that certain persons have under-taken the office of agents for the claimants ... for the emolument of one shilling in the pound of the money received ..., [and] apprehend that people by such agents are induced sometimes to state their losses higher than they otherwise would. [It would be] ... easy to examine on oath any person found transacting for others, on what terms he acts.'[181] The need 'to examine [claimants] on oath' was already clogging the work of the commissioners. Furthermore, the need to adopt the same procedure in respect of Courtown's large and difficult claim and Stephen Hogan's claim for 50 guineas, meant that the small claims, which were numerically predominant and were many of them very urgent, would take years to be settled. Yet, the large and the small claims were inextricably intertwined; for, if Courtown's tenants were compensated for the destruc-tion of their farmhouses and their stock and crops, the size of Courtown's claim would be correspondingly reduced.

On 1 June 1799, an amending act (*39 George III, cap. 65*) was passed to speed up the proceedings of the commissioners. Its purpose was to 'authorise "a partial

---

178 Bartlett, 'Clemency and compensation', p. 121.   179 Memorial from Hogan to Agar, [1799?], T/3719/C/33/69.   180 Shannon to Boyle, 6 June [1798], *Lord Shannon's letters to his* son, pp 110–11; Courtown to Agar, 23 Oct. 1798, T/3719/C/32/149.   181 Gordon to Agar, 10 Nov. 1798, T/3719/ C/22/159.

liquidation of the claims as speedily as they are examined and certified by the commissioners". Those claiming under £500 could be immediately given a third of the sum
desired and this would leave "an ample latitude for such reductions as may be finally
determined on". ... Finally – and crucially – greater use would be made of magistrates
in the various counties to adjudicate on claims for under £200.'[182] Another crucial
change was that the quorum for the commissioners was reduced to three, and that the
number of commissioners (which could be changed by administrative action) was
increased by the end of 1799 to fifteen. The act succeeded in its purposes: by October
1800, 5,533 claims totalling £674,960 gross, but 86 per cent of which were for less than
£200, had been settled by the commissioners at a nett figure of £569,469 (or an
average reduction of 15.6 per cent).[183] Agar's individual role in this change of policy
and in the workings of the commission is undocumented. A letter of 29 March 1799
from Castlereagh to Pitt outlining the need for new legislation does not mention Agar
by name: on the other hand, when the first three additional commissioners were
appointed in mid-June 1799, Agar was accorded a leadership role by Castlereagh, who
asked him to meet with the new members and explain the business to them.[184] Since
Courtown had addressed his opening bid to Agar, Agar must have had to deal with
Courtown, and was the commissioner who from rank, age and experience was best-
qualified to do so. Wexford was later cited as the model for a successful deployment of
those magistrates 'best able and most willing honestly and effectually to aid in the
enquiry into the claims of the loyalists' – which was probably attributable to Agar's
close relationship with Ely, the head of the county magistracy.[185] By whatever process
of enquiry and negotiation, Courtown reduced his claim to £2,532 and the objects of
his claim to his mansion house only (the commissioners never paid compensation for
loss of rents); this sum the commissioners further reduced by £231.[186] There is an
appendix to the *Commons' journals*[187] listing claims lodged up to February 1800.
Significantly, it includes no claims in respect of 'big houses', though one at least – the
largest – had been lodged by that date. Instead, the largest claim listed is that of a
clergyman for *c.*£1,600, which represented the cost of replacing his glebe-house, stock
and crops. It looks as if, for propagandist effect, the printed record was doctored to
exclude the rich and concentrate on humbler claimants. There is no evidence to

---

182 Bartlett, 'Clemency and compensation', p. 121.   183 Ibid.   184 *Castlereagh Correspondence*, ii, pp
245–6; Sackville Hamilton to Agar, 12 June 1798, and Castlereagh to Agar, 13 June 1799,
T/3719/C/33/16–18.   185 W[illiam] D[ownes] to Colonel John Wolfe, [*c.*28 June 1799], Wolfe papers,
NLI: photocopy in PRONI, T/3474/2/26.   186 Suffering loyalists papers, 1799–1800, NA, OP 80/5.
This fragmentary documentation does not include official figures for Cleaver's claim; but, since the
c.£4,000 mentioned by Cleaver to Egremont seems to have related to contents only, it seems very high in
relation to Courtown's and to the documented claims (OP 61/4; Bartlett, 'Clemency and compensation',
pp 100 and 121) for some other country houses which with their contents were destroyed and/or damaged.
These were: £1,637, less a deduction of £219, for Lord Waterford's house at Hollywood, Co. Wicklow;
£2,318, less £15, for Richard Griffith's house at Millicent, Co. Kildare; £2,926, less £98, for the Rt Hon.
Denis Browne's at Mount Browne, near Westport; and – the largest single sum paid out by the
commissioners – £9,267 nett for Lord Downshire's Co. Wicklow seat at Blessington, which was totally
destroyed.   187 Vol. xix (Dublin, 1800).

support this hypothesis, but the example of the secret committee *Reports* suggests that this eye to propagandist effect might have originated with Agar.

What definitely originated with Agar was an act passed a month before the amending act for the benefit of the suffering loyalists, entitled 'An act to enable all ecclesiastical persons and bodies, rectors, vicars and curates and impropriators, and those deriving by, from or under them, to recover a just compensation for the tithes withheld from them ... [in 1797 and 1798] against such persons as were liable to the same' (*39 George III, cap. 14*). This extended back to 1797 because the 'very wise law ... [to enable] the protestant clergy [to] ... recover the full value of their tithes' which Agar had been preparing in January 1798[188] had not had time to reach the statute book. Compensation for unpaid tithes was on a different footing from compensation for other losses incurred by suffering loyalists: it was enforced by the act against those liable to pay the tithes, whereas the compensation for other losses was paid by the government. Moreover, tithes were a special case in another respect. What was owed in tithe was generally subject to annual valuation, and in 1797 and 1798 such valuation often 'could not be made by means of force or terror or unlawful oaths and combinations or the ... rebellion, or ... [when] such valuation was actually made, ... the notes or items of such valuation have been destroyed ... or lost'.[189] So, Agar's act prescribed a procedure for retrospective valuation and for specially expedited recovery of the amount of the tithes by chancery, exchequer or civil bill. Only if the titheable articles themselves had been destroyed by either the rebels or the king's forces, was the tithe-owner free to lodge a claim with the commissioners for suffering loyalists.[190]

The act was in fact based on the Clergy Compensation Act of 1787 (p. 444), which increases the suspicion that Agar rather than Hely-Hutchinson had been largely responsible for what had eventually reached the statute book in that year. In cases where valuation of tithes had been impracticable, the 1787 Act empowered tithe-owners 'to apply to the going judges of assize, and on their being sworn to the amount of what they received annually in the years before this disturbance, said judges are directed to issue their warrant to levy the whole from the parishes in the same manner that county cesses are levied.'[191] Because of intervening developments in the law, Agar's Act of 1799 relied for its implementation on civil bill process through special sessions presided over by the assistant barrister of each county.[192] But otherwise it was a re-enactment of the 1787 Act, which had only been 'intended as a present redress'.[193] An essential factor in the passage of both measures through the potentially hostile House of Commons was that the interests of lay tithe-owners were inextricably involved with those of the clergy. The act also contained in its final clause one mild piece of tithe reform: it prohibited the future sub-letting of tithes by any lessee of the clergyman or lay impropriator,[194] thus cutting out extra tiers of middlemen and lessening the burden falling on the tithe-payer and the odium falling on the clergy.

---

188 Sir Richard Musgrave to Agar, 16 Jan. 1798, T/3719/C/32/2.   **189** *39 George III, cap. 14, sec. 4.* **190** This at least is the implication of sec. 20.   **191** Bishop Barnard to Buckinghamshire, 1 Feb. 1787, NLI, Heron papers, Ms. 13047/5.   **192** Richard C. Carr to Agar, 29 June 1799, with enclosure of same date, 21 M 57/B34/3-4.   **193** Barnard to Buckinghamshire, 1 Feb. 1787, loc. cit.   **194** *39 George III,*

In spite of the act's careful and politic drafting and its appeal to lay tithe-owners, its implementation was problematical. Agar later had correspondence with Clare (in the latter's official capacity as lord chancellor) and, more particularly, with the assistant-barrister of Clare's native county of Limerick, about the holding of special sessions at Cashel to facilitate clergy of Cashel and Emly who wanted to make claims or bring actions under the act and about questions of interpretation and enforcement.[195] The experience of one clergyman of Emly was particularly bitter. 'In September 1799, ... Agar wrote to Dublin Castle stating that he had learnt that it had been represented to the government that the poor in the neighbourhood of Pallas Grean had been aggrieved by the arrears of tithe being collected at one period, and not by instalments, and enclosing a letter from Archdeacon [Garrett] Wall, the rector of that parish. He [Agar] proceeds:

> I have made every enquiry and have not been able to discover that there is the slightest foundation for the report. In conversation Mr Wall assures me that he never heard that such a complaint existed until I mentioned it to him. He seems, I think, to have exculpated himself perfectly, and he speaks to me of the neighbouring clergy as being as little liable to such a charge as himself. The legislature, as an act of justice and in truth of necessity (if the Established Church is to be supported), has passed a statute to enable the clergy to recover a just compensation for the tithes withheld from them in 1797 and 1798. Here is an admission, and everybody knows it to be true, that the tithes of these two successive years were withheld from the clergy, though the law afforded them the usual remedy for the recovery of them. Here, then, is a presumptive proof of great lenity and forbearance on their part. But as soon as they begin to avail themselves of the special remedy afforded them by the legislature, and to try to recover to themselves and their families a small part of what ought to have been entirely paid long ago, they are charged with being rapacious and unreasonable. ...

In the letter enclosed, Archdeacon Wall ... states the method he had adopted for years past for collecting his tithes. He called for half the amount of each man's tithe about March or April, and for the other half about September or October. ... He states that three hundred persons were his debtors for tithe, but that out of £500 due he only received £100. He only took out *nine* decrees, not one of which he executed, but he took these "merely to make others pay, by putting *an individual* of their neighbours in each quarter of the parish to cost." '[196]

cap. 14, sec. 23.   **195** Correspondence among Agar, Clare and the assistant barrister, 5 July–16 Dec. 1799, 21 M 57/B34/5–12.   **196** Seymour, *Diocese of Emly*, pp 159–60.

AGAR'S CONVERSION TO UNIONISM

The very fact that Agar was in a position to sponsor legislation successfully and with government support, and was not only retained but given the lead as a commissioner for suffering loyalists, shows that he was not regarded as a 'strenuous' or 'vehement' opponent of the Union. Because the Castle did not re-open the question of Union in the 1799 session, and because the anti-Unionists in the Lords, unlike those in the Commons, did not take the offensive on the issue, Agar was not again required to come down on one side or the other. Although there have been suggestions (p. 132) that the Agar connection was at this stage divided on the Union, the fact is that Lord Clifden's conduct was equally ambiguous. As has been seen, two of his members supported the government in late January 1799, but the other two stayed away and were not replaced with Unionists until March/April 1800. During the 1799 session, Clifden himself remained at Blenheim, initially 'arrested by an attack of rheumatism for two days' and then by 'those falls of snow which made his arrival in due time impracticable.'[197] At this stage, even Mendip, the lifelong unionist, could 'neither censure [n]or approve what I cannot understand.'[198] Of the Agar connection, only Lord Callan, who was independent of both Clifden and Agar, provided unequivocal support during the 1799 session. By late April, Mendip and, by implication Agar, may have been thawing towards the Union: on 22 April, the cautious and deferential John Hatsell wrote to Agar about speeches and pamphlets for and against.[199] From the tone of this letter, it is plain that Hatsell was writing to a Unionist, however lukewarm, and in so doing he must have been acting on information given him by Mendip. As far as Clifden is concerned, what probably brought him round was a letter which Castlereagh wrote to him in mid-June 1799 assuring him that the measure of a Union would be persevered with in the next session, and that there would be compensation for disfranchised boroughs.[200] Up to then, it looks as if Agar and Clifden acted broadly speaking in concert, and did their best to remain, at least publicly, uncommitted.

Between January and July 1799, Agar's correspondence is very thin (as it is for all of 1799 and 1800) and he is not significantly mentioned in the correspondence of others. Following the defeat in the House of Commons and the clear proof it afforded of Cornwallis' and, to a lesser extent, Castlereagh's failure to court and conciliate prominent individuals and political connections, Dublin Castle began to exert itself to gain recruits among the ambivalent or uncommitted. There must remain a doubt whether Cornwallis' neglect of anti-Emancipationists had not been deliberate rather than absent-minded. Buckingham, who hated him and always exaggerated his shortcomings, reported that Cornwallis was 'scandalously lukewarm' about the defeat, and behaved as if 'he expected it and did not care one farthing for the event of the question.'[201] Cornwallis would certainly have preferred a narrow to a comfortable

197 Mendip to Agar, 28 Feb. 1799, T/3719/C/33/4.   198 Ibid.   199 Hatsell to Agar, 22 Apr. 1799, T/3719/C/33/8.   200 Castlereagh to Clifden, 13 June 1799, Castlereagh papers, PRONI, D/3030/823.   201 Buckingham to Grenville, 25 Jan. 1799, *HMC Dropmore Mss.*, iv, pp 454–5.

majority, because he was most anxious for an opportunity to re-open the Catholic Question. But it is probably going too far to suggest that this consideration made him indifferent to defeat.

Be that as it may, it is clear from subsequent evidence that it was not Cornwallis, or Castlereagh, who successfully wooed Agar's friend, the elusive Ely. Some years after the event, Portland referred, in another connection, to the circumstances 'which made Lord Ely decline having any communication with the then lord lieutenant of Ireland or his chief secretary respecting the Union ... . But a common friend of his and mine interfered and was so fortunate as to prevail upon him to open that negotiation with me ... which he had positively refused to do with Lord Cornwallis.'[202] Portland and Cornwallis were on very bad terms. Portland, though home secretary and therefore the cabinet minister with responsibility for Ireland, had been largely by-passed in the planning of the Union. To that extent, he could empathise with Agar's situation; he also had a line of communication with Agar via Mendip. Under these circumstances, it would be surprising if Agar were not the 'common friend' of Portland and Ely to whom Portland later referred. How Agar himself was brought over is less clear. All that is clear is that Cornwallis did not take the initiative, but merely responded to a private intimation from a third party, possibly Ely or Shannon. In early July 1799, Agar received some characteristically blunt and homespun advice from his sister, Diana: 'I hope you do not declare much against the Union, for if it is to be, it can answer no end but to hurt yourself materially with the great folks here [England]. Could it be kept off by so doing, it might be another matter.'[203] She need not have worried. At about the same time, Cornwallis announced to Portland Agar's adherence to the Unionist cause.[204]

Because parliament was in recess in July 1799, the first manifestation of his change of heart and of the influence he could bring to bear on behalf of the Union, came during what has been called 'The appeal to the country',[205] and particularly the appeal to Co. Tipperary. Tipperary was an inviting target from Dublin Castle's point of view. Its two MPs, Colonel John Bagwell of Marlfield, Clonmel, and Lord Mathew (son of the 1st Viscount Landaff and his late wife, who had been Agar's first cousin), had so far opposed the Union, but it was thought might, under constituency pressure, recant. In Mathew's case, the pressure was also paternal, because Lord Landaff supported the measure.[206] Hitherto, there had been both an anti-Unionist meeting and a more impressively supported Unionist meeting in the county. Just in time for the latter, the chief Unionist activist in Tipperary, Richard Hely-Hutchinson, 1st Viscount Donoughmore, had secured the support of the 2nd earl of Dorchester (formerly Lord Milton, Fitzwilliam's chief secretary), a huge, absentee proprietor, whose adherence – so Donoughmore hoped – would demonstrate to the public on which side of the question the weight of property in the county lay.[207]

202 Portland to a subsequent home secretary, Lord Hawkesbury, 18 May 1804, partly printed in *The viceroy's post-bag*, pp 136–7. 203 Diana Agar to Agar, 5 July 1799, T/3719/C/33/20. 204 Cornwallis to Portland, 8 July 1799, *Cornwallis correspondence*, iii, pp 113–14. 205 Bolton, *Union*, pp 126–56. 206 Ibid., pp 148–9. 207 Donoughmore to Castlereagh, 25 Mar. 1799, Castlereagh

To follow up this success, Donoughmore got up a requisition to the Unionist county sheriff (his younger brother, Francis) to convene a second Unionist meeting on 10 August. As an important convert since the previous meeting, Agar was one of the first to be approached. But his initial reaction to this move was hesitant: 'I am a friend to a Union between Great Britain and Ireland, but I am by no means convinced of the expediency of calling a meeting of the county for that purpose.'[208] However, later in the same day he received a letter from Cornwallis explaining 'that our friends in the county of Tipperary are decidedly of opinion that a county meeting should be called and are under no apprehension about the success of the measure. I have therefore only to request that your Grace will allow your respectable name to be added to the requisition.'[209] Agar complied, adding that, 'since the friends to a Union who have means of judging of the expediency of this measure deem it both safe and advisable, I shall not set my judgement in opposition to theirs.'[210] Agar's friend, John Toler, who was a Tipperary squireen as well as the attorney-general, thought 'the squeamishness of the Marshal [John Bagwell] is the best justification for our meeting. He earnestly wishes to have an apology for his recantation [from anti-Unionism].'[211] The meeting gave him one. The Unionists present at it, according to Landaff, possessed 'upwards of £300,000 per annum landed property in the county', and the Unionist resolutions they agreed to, though not 'exactly' as Agar had suggested, but more 'particularising and diffuse', were satisfactory and were carried unanimously.[212] For the time being, 'Cornwallis seemed justified in stating: "The accession of Tipperary to those counties before declared, gives us the entire province of Munster."[213]

In parliamentary terms, however, this proved delusive. By mid-January 1800, Landaff was admitting to Dublin Castle that Lord Mathew remained staunch to the opposition, in spite of his previous assurances, and was not deterred by Landaff's resolve to oppose him at the next general election.[214] (Toler had been right to grumble that certain great men 'vapour[ed] at the Castle' but did little or nothing in the country to reconcile other branches of their family to the Union.[215]) Then, at the beginning of February, Cornwallis reported to Portland that Bagwell and his two sons had changed sides again, and were now going to oppose the Union.[216] To avoid further agitation of the county and potential disturbance of its peace, Lord Donoughmore and the Tipperary Unionists confined themselves to a grand jury address at the spring assizes of 1800.[217] This was followed, in mid-April, by an address from the numerous

papers, PRONI, D/3030/695.   208 Agar to Francis Hely-Hutchinson, 2 Aug. 1799, Donoughmore papers, PRONI, T/3459/D/6/23A.   209 Cornwallis to Agar, 2 Aug. 1799, *Cornwallis correspondence*, iii. 120.   210 Agar to Francis Hely-Hutchinson, 3 Aug. 1799, T/3459/D/6/23B.
211 Toler to Castlereagh, 5 Aug. 1799, D/3030/907. The nickname 'The Marshal' requires explanation: Bagwell's family had been corn-millers, so he was opprobriously called 'Old Bags', 'Marshal Sacks' and variants thereof.   212 Landaff to Castlereagh, 25 Jan. 1800, *Castlereagh correspondence*, iii. 180; Landaff to Agar, 11 Aug. 1799, T/3719/cc/34; and Stephen Moore of Barne, Clonmel, to Castlereagh, 11 Aug. 1799, D/3030/918.   213 Bolton, *Union*, p. 150.   214 Landaff to Castlereagh, 15 and 16 Jan. 1800, D/3030/1088-9.   215 Toler to Castlereagh, 5 Aug. 1799, D/3030/907.   216 Cornwallis to Portland, 5 Feb. 1800, *Cornwallis correspondence*, iii. 180.
217 Donoughmore to Agar, 13 Apr. 1800, and Agar to Donoughmore, 14 Apr. 1800, T/3719/C/

landowners of the county to the sheriff opposing a requisition 'for again convening the freeholders to agitate the question ..., as the sense of the county was fully ascertained by the respectable meeting held at the last assizes.'[218] The list of signatories was headed by Lord Clare who, as lord chancellor, took precedence over all archbishops, and after him came the Archbishop of Cashel, the earls of Ormonde, Roden, Dorchester and Landaff (the last a governor of the county), Viscounts Desart, Hawarden and Donoughmore (the last two governors of the county), the Bishop of Killaloe, Lords Caher and Callan, John Toler, Sir Henry Cavendish, sixteen members of the grand jury, headed by Francis Hely-Hutchinson, the foreman, and numerous untitled country gentlemen, two of them governors.[219] Lord Dorchester remarked, bluntly, that he trusted this address would 'make all the Bagwells in the county as sensible of their own stupidity as we are of their duplicity.'[220] However, neither John Bagwell nor Lord Mathew swerved again from opposition to the Union, in defiance of the sentiments of the great preponderance of the landed wealth of their constituency.

As is obvious from the foregoing, Agar's role in Tipperary's expressions of Unionist sentiment was minor and contributory. In his personal capacity, he was credited with having won Lord Hawarden over to support the Union;[221] and his recently acquired leases of Cashel see lands gave him influence over such tenant voters in county elections as could be fielded from the three Augmentation townlands (since leases for a term of years were not freeholds). But, basically, because he was a late convert to the Union, he found that the leadership of the Unionist cause in Tipperary was already in other hands. Clifden had much the same experience in Co. Kilkenny. In mid-August, reporting on the success of his missionary visit to that part of the country, Cornwallis wrote: 'Previous to my arrival at Kilkenny, Lord Ormonde had taken a most active part both in the county and city; and, with the exception of Mr Ponsonby's friends, succeeded most perfectly in his object. His Lordship was powerfully assisted by Lord Clifden.'[222] In Tipperary, the zealous and ambitious Donoughmore, who was actually not one of the great county magnates but surpassed them all in activity and officiousness, had easily stolen a march on Agar. The Hely-Hutchinsons also had great influence with the local catholics, which Agar – for obvious reasons – did not. Henry Carter admitted that he had destroyed letters from Lord Landaff, and it is just possible that some of them related to the Union and would have cast Agar's role in a different light. However, in the official commendations of Unionist supporters which Cornwallis transmitted to Portland, the individuals singled

34/14–15. **218** Cornwallis to Agar, 9 Apr. 1800, ibid., iii. 225. This, clearly, is a loaned original, not a copy, of Cornwallis' letter, since it is endorsed (characteristically) by Agar: 'Answered instanter that I readily consented to do what he requires. C.C.' **219** Newspaper cutting recording an address signed at Clonmel on 17 Apr. 1800 by sundry peers, grand jurors and gentlemen of Co. Tipperary, to the sheriff of the county, Pierce Archer Butler, urging him to ignore the requisition of Lord Lismore, Sir Thomas Osborne, William Bagwell, Thomas Barton and others to call a meeting on the subject of the Union, Donoughmore papers, T/3459/D/23. See also Agar to Donoughmore, 23 Apr. 1800, ibid., D/6/39. **220** Dorchester to Cornwallis' private secretary, Colonel E.B. Littlehales, 25 Apr. 1800, *Cornwallis correspondence*, iii. 231. **221** Burke, *History of Clonmel*, p. 164. **222** Cornwallis to Portland, 14 Aug. 1799, *Cornwallis correspondence*, iii, pp 124–5.

out were Donoughmore and, to a lesser extent, Landaff and Toler.[223] Agar's influence, after all, was mainly an *ex officio* influence over the clergy of Cashel and Emly, and the government had the right to expect that it would be exerted on the government's behalf. Moreover, the already-mentioned convention (which Archbishop Bolton had violated) that the archbishop did not take a political lead in a county in which he had no hereditary stake, was also a factor: Agar's (and Clare's) presence at the head of lists of addressors was a matter of precedence, not a measure of prominence.

Agar's influence, via the clergy of Cashel and Emly, was not confined to the county constituency of Tipperary. He had some influence in Co. Limerick, which sent up a Unionist address at roughly the same time as Tipperary, and rather more in Limerick City. Referring to a forthcoming by-election for Limerick City in 1794, Edmond Henry Pery, 2nd Lord Glentworth, its former MP (and Speaker Pery's nephew and heir), had commented to Agar: 'I know well your Grace's influence in this part of the world, whenever you please to exert it.'[224] But his influence was greatest in the town of Cashel itself, as has been seen (pp 294–5), particularly in the vacuum created by the indisposition of the borough's patron, Colonel Richard Pennefather, in 1799–1800. Agar's promotion of the Unionist address from the inhabitants of Cashel which was voted at a meeting on 29 July 1799, and his hosting of Cornwallis' propagandist visit to Cashel the following day, were probably Agar's most important contribution to the debate in the country about the Union.[225]

AGAR'S MOTIVES

Cornwallis' already-mentioned letter to Portland announcing in early July 1799 Agar's adherence to the Unionist cause is fairly well known, and was quoted by Lecky (p. 5) as 'amusingly characteristic' of the self-interestedness of leading Irish political figures at the time of the Union.

> It was privately intimated to me that the sentiments of the Archbishop of Cashel were less unfriendly to the Union than they had been, on which I took an opportunity of conversing with his Grace on the subject, and after discussing some preliminary topics respecting the representation of the spiritual lords and the probable vacancy of the see of Dublin, he declared his great unwillingness at all times to oppose the measures of government, and especially on a point in which his Majesty's feelings were so much interested, to whom he professed the highest sense of gratitude and the most perfect devotion, and concluded by a cordial declaration of friendship. The Archbishop is looked upon in this country as a wise and able politician, and I consider the acquisition of his support as an object of no small importance.[226]

223 Ibid.   224 Glentworth to Agar, 13 July 1794, T/3719/C/28/15.   225 For the text of the Tipperary, Limerick and Cashel addresses of late July–early Aug. 1799, see 21 M 57/A45/1–9. 226 Cornwallis to Portland, 8 July 1799, *Cornwallis correspondence*, iii, pp 113–14.

This is unduly satirical at Agar's expense. For one thing, Cornwallis does not acknowledge the obvious – that the change in his own behaviour towards Agar and his greater communicativeness had a good deal to do with the change in Agar's attitude. Second, the letter needs to be read in conjunction with Cornwallis' subsequent references to Agar, which become less and less hostile as time goes on, suggesting that Cornwallis had occasion entirely to re-think his initial opinion of Agar. Third, it gives the impression that the major factor in Agar's change of heart was the gratifying of his wishes for himself personally.

This last impression was not altogether fair. The offer to Agar of a place in the Irish representation in the post-Union House of Lords at Westminster (see pp 560 and 599) was indeed an important inducement to an ambitious man and experienced parliamentarian. But the virtual offer of the archbishopric of Dublin in the probable event of a vacancy (to which Auckland had already made clumsy allusion in late October 1798) was a different matter. This was not a new inducement but the confirmation of an unsolicited offer made by Camden on 5 February 1798. On that occasion, Agar had asked for time to think and to inquire into the circumstances of that diocese (presumably a reference to its decreased value thanks to Fowler).[227] With the worsening of the security situation and the consequent pressure of other business, nothing further seems to have passed on the subject of Dublin during Camden's time in Ireland. But, unless Agar had gone into actual opposition on the Union, it would have been impossible for him not to have been given first refusal. Apart from anything else, Camden was in constant use in late 1798 and 1799 as a Unionist go-between with Irish politicians whom he had got to know while lord lieutenant, so this would have been no time to cast doubt on the validity of an offer made by Camden. Besides, the archbishopric of Dublin was a rather doubtful inducement (which perhaps explains why Agar does not seem to have responded to Camden's offer). As has been seen (pp 365–6), Lady Somerton and almost certainly Agar himself had set their faces against Dublin in 1796. When Fowler died in 1801 and the vacancy was created, Welby wondered 'whether your partiality to Cashel might not induce you to decline the other.'[228] Ely, by contrast, was clear that 'in these times, ... Dublin is far more preferable.'[229] But, as Ely's words implied, it was the Union which had made it so: from 1801, the archbishop of Cashel had to be in three places at once, Cashel, Dublin and London, whereas the archbishop of Dublin had to be in only two.

Since the reasons and inducements mentioned by Cornwallis, even in conjunction with the rough logic of Diana Agar, are not of themselves sufficient to explain Agar's change of tack, the explanation must be sought, in part, elsewhere. It probably lies in the tithe question. In late January 1799, soon after the defeat of the government in the House of Commons, Castlereagh wrote to Portland outlining the probable topics which the anti-Unionists would now latch on to in order to keep their forces together

---

227 Camden to Agar, 5 Feb. 1798, with endorsement by Agar of the same date, T/3719/C/32/4.
228 Welby to Agar, 2 Nov. 1801, T/3719/C/35/26. 229 Ely to Agar, 30 Oct. 1801, T/3719/C/35/24.

and press home their advantage. 'Your Grace must be aware that the party will carry the feelings of the country more with them upon the question of tithes than upon any other. They will press government to bring it forward, and impute their refusing to do so to a determination to force the question of Union by withholding from the people advantages which might be extended to them equally by the Irish legislature.'[230] Even before the Union had become the all-absorbing issue of the day, the tithe question had been raised in 'the Irish legislature' by the attempt in mid-March 1798 to transfer jurisdiction in most title cases to 'little country squires' (see p. 540). In March–April of the following year, 1800, the old bogey of the tithe of agistment was again raised, initially as a tactical move to impede the Union (see pp 574–7), but ominous for the Church because of the hostile language used in debate by little and not-so-little squires in the Irish House of Commons. Agar knew that the tithe question was not safe in the hands of the Irish parliament, particularly an Irish parliament flushed with victory over the proposed Union. Meanwhile, it began to look as if the Grenville/Pitt/ Auckland proposals for an all-embracing scheme were running into opposition. Following the plans and discussion of September–December 1798 (and a disastrous harvest), Pitt submitted to Archbishop Moore in January 1799 his 'plan for the sale of the tithe of the country on the same principle that the Land Tax had been offered for sale in the previous session of parliament.'[231] 'The tithes [were] to be sold and the proceeds invested in the Funds as a maintenance for the clergy, with provision for its periodical adjustment to the price of grain'[232] – i.e. the 'corn rents' scheme proposed by Bishop Pretyman-Tomline. 'The plan was discussed by the episcopal bench, but with the solitary exception of Richard Watson of Llandaff – the leading practical farmer among the bishops – it received no support.'[233] The falling-off of Pretyman-Tomline may have had a disenchanting effect on Pitt, who in any case had always sought episcopal concurrence before proceeding further. Besides, following the defeat of the Union in the Irish House of Commons, the ideas of the British government narrowed into the single focus of how to ensure the carrying of that one great measure.

Tithe commutation is one of those issues which keeps appearing, disappearing and reappearing. Even John Ehrman, the recent and encyclopaedic biographer of Pitt, is unable to trace the course of Pitt's thinking on the subject.[234] Commutation re-appeared, after the carrying of the Union, in September 1800–February 1801. But by then it had assumed a less threatening aspect, even though Buckingham was still in the offing, and trying to promote a complex scheme based on 'corn rents.'[235] Alluding to this, Pitt wrote to Grenville in late October – perhaps in a tone of impatience? – 'Our last plan respecting tithe would, I think, answer every purpose Lord B. proposes.'[236] 'Our last plan' was probably one of 'the plans so interesting to the Church of Ireland

---

230 Castlereagh to Portland, 28 Jan. 1799, *Castlereagh correspondence*, ii, pp 139–41.   231 *Anecdotes of Watson*, pp 306–7.   232 Mathieson, *English Church reform*, p. 21.   233 Evans, *The contentious tithe*, p. 80.   234 *Pitt: the consuming struggle*, pp 177–8. See also Akenson, *Church of Ireland*, p. 99. 235 Akenson, op. cit., p. 200.   236 Pitt to Grenville, 23 Oct. 1800, *HMC Dropmore Mss.*, vi. 357.

for the commutation of the payment of our revenues' which Brodrick on the very same day wrote to thank Lord Midleton for sending him. He added: 'In such hands as those from whom you had it, it cannot fail of being conducted with wisdom and moderation.'[237] This can only have meant Midleton's brother-in-law, Thomas Pelham. While Agar would not have agreed with Brodrick that any form of commutation was to be welcomed, he too would have been reassured by the involvement of Pelham. Brodrick used the word 'plans' in the plural, because there were at least two of them (not counting Buckingham's). In the second half of September, Castlereagh had drawn up a lengthy paper which showed considerable tenderness for the situation of the clergy (especially in view of Castlereagh's much-mistrusted presbyterian background) and, quite as important, would last for only 21 years, after which time procedures were laid down for re-valuation.[238] Grenville, apparently in response, came up with an alternative. He 'now favoured a radical plan of converting ... Irish tithes ... into rents payable, under penalties, by landlords rather than tenants' – broadly speaking, the solution eventually found, after long travail, in 1838.[239] This not only portended greater ease of collection, but allayed a long-standing fear of Irish churchmen and well-wishers to the Irish Church. Boulter had observed in 1737, *apropos* the tithe of agistment, that the question was 'whether the parson shall have his due or the landlord a greater rent'; Lord Macartney told Agar in September 1786 that 'the poor tenantry' of Macartney's part of north Antrim 'seem sensible enough that it is the landlords who on the expiration of the leases would reap the chief benefit from the abolition of tithes'; and the anonymous author of a polemic which appeared in a Munster newspaper at about the same time declared: 'Tithes are a rent, though a fluctuating one, and it is probable that the proprietors of lands will in time charge rents equivalent to the abolished tithes.'[240] A measure transferring the responsibility for payment of tithe to 'the proprietors of lands' would not have passed the separate Irish parliament.

Whatever Agar's fears for a plan of tithe commutation enacted under Grenvillite influence by the post-Union parliament of the United Kingdom, they were exceeded by his fears for what the Irish House of Commons might perpetrate, and they were allayed by the impact on Pitt and others of the opposition expressed by the Church of England bishops early in 1799. Agar seems never to have accepted the idea of a permanent and country-wide commutation, no matter how apparently favourable the

237 Brodrick to Midleton, 23 Oct. 1800, Ms. 1248, vol. 17, ff. 136–7. **238** Akenson, *Church of Ireland*, pp 99–100. A similar scheme was allegedly favoured some time later, in 1803, by Agar's ally (in most things), Bishop Knox of Killaloe; Knox, it was reported, 'inclines to approve the plan of letting the tithes of every parish to the parishioners for 21 years, at a valuation to be made at the public expense and under the control of government, [and] to be renewed every seven years, so as always to leave at least 14 years to protect improvements. He particularly thinks this would quiet the catholics in a considerable degree, as it would more evidently throw the burthen of tithes on their landlords, mostly protestants' – Lord Redesdale to Pitt, 22 May 1803, Jupp/Aspinall transcript from the W.D. Adams papers. **239** Akenson, *Church of Ireland*, pp 189–94; Jupp, *Lord Grenville*, p. 274. **240** Kennedy, 'Dublin and Glendalough', p. 166; Macartney to Agar, 24 Sep. 1786, T/3719/ C/20/30; newspaper cutting, [Sep.? 1786], T/3719/C/20/31.

terms. In 1804, Lord Sligo wrote candidly to him: 'I am not of opinion that the mode of paying the clergy by tithes is that which tends most to keeping up that constant good understanding that should subsist between them and the people. Your Grace, I believe, is of a contrary opinion.'[241] However, once the proposals of late 1798, with their unacceptable concomitant of clerical residence by act of parliament, were shelved, and once the proposed clerical residence legislation for England and Wales began dwindling to nothing in the hands of Sir William Scott (see p. 275), Agar could permit himself some guarded optimism about the effect of the Union. Any future plan common to the two kingdoms was likely to be more favourable to the Church of Ireland than any plan exclusive to Ireland. This was, firstly, because of the recently demonstrated influence of the bishops of the Church of England. Secondly, tithes were intrinsically less unpopular in Britain because they supported a clergy who ministered to the majority of the population. Thirdly, lay presentation and lay impropriation were much more common in Britain than in Ireland, with the result that in Britain the interests of the clergy coincided with those of a much larger section of the influential laity, many of them members of parliament.[242] For these reasons, it looks as if the tithe question, which initially disinclined Agar to a Union, soon afterwards fused with all his existing predilections to make a belated Unionist of him.

241 Sligo to Agar, 30 July 1804, T/3719/C/38/37.   242 'Suggestions for the improvement of the tithe system in Ireland', apparently in response to a paper by Castlereagh dated Sep. 1800, *Castlereagh correspondence*, iv, pp 206–10.

13

Agar and the Union, 1800–1: 'a bright example to the Irish bench'

Agar's influence on the Act of Union, in cabinet and parliament, and particularly his efforts to improve the terms held out to the Church of Ireland, did not really come into play until the beginning of 1800. In mid-December 1799, Lord Castlereagh wrote urging him to travel from Cashel to Dublin as soon after Christmas as possible, so that Castlereagh could communicate to him 'the important objects which will be submitted to parliament in the ensuing session.'[1] A letter written on Christmas Eve by his sister establishes that Agar complied. Diana Agar's tone continued to be cynical: 'The Union is considered here as quite *bought and secured*. ... [We have only] to ... hear the last words and dying speech of the Irish parliament. No hangman necessary: they [are] their own executioners.'[2] She did Agar an injustice if she considered him 'as quite bought and secured.' When he obeyed the summons to Dublin to hear about the business of the forthcoming session, he had an agenda of his own to follow, most of it relating to the post-Union situation of the Church of Ireland. The first half of this Chapter discusses the (qualified) success with which he pursued that agenda. The second half discusses the effects of the Union on the composition of the Irish episcopal bench and the future leadership of the Church, starting with the filling of the primacy, which fell vacant in January 1800 at a moment of extreme untimeliness for all concerned.

THE CHURCH'S POST-UNION REPRESENTATION AND CONSTITUTION

Agar opened his campaign at the great disadvantage that he had not been privy to the early planning of the Union and therefore had had no influence on the very little which had been decided in relation to the Church. That very little principally comprised the system of rotating representation for the archbishops and bishops, as adumbrated in Brodrick's letter written as long ago as 5 January 1799 (p. 543). Clearly, these details had been made widely known in order to win episcopal votes for the Union. So, since Agar disapproved of the principle of rotation, his campaign was in this respect a decidedly uphill struggle. In particular, he was exposed to the imputation of Bishop

1 Castlereagh to Agar, 14 Dec. 1799, T/3719/C/33/62.   2 Diana Agar to Agar, 24 Dec. 1799, T/3719/C/33/65.

O'Beirne that 'some bishops ... on our bench ... oppose every arrangement that did not originate with themselves.'3

'His Grace', Cornwallis later explained, 'had my promise, when we came to an agreement [in July 1799] respecting the Union, that he should have a seat in the House of Lords for life.'4 From this form of words, it looks as if Agar had deliberately left Cornwallis with two alternative methods of fulfilling this promise: he could either secure Agar's election as one of the twenty-eight temporal representative peers (for which Agar was eligible because he was Lord Somerton); or, alternatively, he could accept Agar's argument 'that the spiritual lords *should be represented by the four archbishops.*' Making the assumption – probably for tactical reasons – that Cornwallis would go for the first alternative, Agar made his first move to raise the issue of representation in mid-January 1800. He now proposed to Cornwallis and Castlereagh that a clause be inserted in article viii of the Union (the very lengthy article relating to representation) providing that, if 'any lord spiritual, being a temporal peer, shall be chosen by the Lords temporal to be one of the representatives of the lords temporal, in every such case and during the life of such spiritual peer ..., the rotation of repre-sentation of the spiritual lords shall proceed to the next spiritual lord.'5 At this stage, and in article viii as it became law, the four archbishops were arranged in one rota, and the eighteen bishops in another. So, 'the Agar clause' (if so it may be termed) meant that, while Agar lived, there would always be two archbishops in the House of Lords, and the archiepiscopal rota would consist of three people, not four.

On 31 January, when he had received no response to this proposal, he wrote urging Castlereagh 'to insert it in its proper place in the first instance, ... for it is evidently a right and necessary regulation: whereas, if moved as an amendment, it may create debate, and difficulties may be started which would otherwise never occur.'6 But there was further dithering, and approval for the principle of the clause, subject to only verbal amendments, was not received from Portland until 9 March.7 Then, in late March, it was pointed out to the British government that there was 'no provision in your bill for the overslaugh [*sic*] in your episcopal roster of duty ... [of] a bishop who may be a peer of Great Britain.'8 Portland had not fully understood what he was approving, and British ministers got it into their heads that it was, not an Agar, but a Hervey, clause, intended to disqualify the earl-bishop of Derry from representing the Church of Ireland in the House of Lords. Portland accordingly wrote pointing out unnecessarily that it was not properly drafted for that purpose!9 This confusion persisted. In November 1801 Brodrick, who had just become archbishop of Cashel and was therefore personally affected by the clause, thought that it was meant 'to have included also those who are peers by descent, as in the case of Lord Bristol, but in the

3 O'Beirne to Castlereagh, 10 Mar. 1800, *Castlereagh correspondence*, iii, pp 253–6.   4 Cornwallis to Portland, 10 Mar. 1800, *Cornwallis correspondence*, iii, pp 208–9.   5 Proposed clause in Agar's handwriting, 12 Jan. 1800, T/3719/C/34/2.   6 Agar to Castlereagh, 31 Jan. 1800, T/3719/C/34/4.   7 Copy extract from Portland's dispatch on matters raised by Agar, 'Received 9th and answered 10th March 1800', 21 M 57/A46/14–15.   8 Buckingham to Grenville, 27 Mar. 1800, *HMC Dropmore Mss.*, vi. 182.

hurry and bungling a mistake was committed, and nobody now knows how the act ought to be understood.'[10] This was to prove true of many parts of the Act of Union, but not of article viii, clause 6, the Agar clause, which was intended to strengthen the representation of the archbishops *vis-à-vis* that of the bishops, and did so for the duration of Agar's life.

While this modest improvement in the archiepiscopal representation was worth contending for, it is probable that Agar's real reason for pressing for the clause (and for leaving open the mode in which his promised 'seat in the House of Lords for life' was to be guaranteed him) was that he wanted to re-open the whole issue of archiepiscopal and episcopal rotation. In late January 1800, Cornwallis reported that Agar thought such rotation 'rather derogatory to the dignity of the [Irish] bench', because the lay representative peers of Ireland were to sit for life, as did the English bishops. Agar was also 'of opinion that the representation of the spiritual lords should consist of the four metropolitans, who from the nature of their office and from the triennial visitation of the different dioceses of the kingdom (which is regularly performed), are necessarily best-acquainted with the situation of the Church of this kingdom.'[11] Portland countered with the observation (which he probably owed to O'Beirne) that 'the residence and superintendence of the metropolitans appears to be full as necessary to the general order and discipline of the Church as their attendance in parliament.' Agar acknowledged the force of this argument, but could not 'discover how their attendance in parliament after the Union is to prevent them from executing those duties more than it does at this moment.' As a veteran parliamentarian, he saw that a bishop sitting for five or six months every six years (or, on average, only twice in his life, if so often), could not possibly become 'acquainted even with the forms and rules of the assembly in which he sits, much less ... enabled, as an unacquainted, unconnected stranger, to plan and promote with effect any measures for the welfare of the Church of Ireland.'[12] He also echoed Brodrick's reservations about 'the inconvenience that several of the bishops with the smallest incomes will suffer by going to London to attend parliament, and the trifling object it will be to them to have a seat for one year in six in the House of Lords.'[13] Portland had already expressed the view that any change in the arrangements formerly proposed 'would give [such] great umbrage to all the suffragan bishops, [that] ... it would be impossible to reconcile them to the support of it.'[14] In this, too, he was almost certainly speaking the language of one of the 'suffragan bishops', O'Beirne. Brodrick warned his brother: 'Your friend [Portland] cannot possibly be under worse guidance than that of his *ci-devant* secretary. The very idea of complete influence, which is prevalent, does an infinity of mischief.'[15]

9 Portland to Cornwallis, 26 June 1800, *Cornwallis correspondence*, iii, pp 270–71.   10 Brodrick to Midleton, 26 Nov. 1801, Ms. 1248, vol. 18, ff. 42–3.   11 Cornwallis to Portland, 25 Jan. 1800, *Cornwallis correspondence*, iii, pp 171–2.   12 Draft of a paper on episcopal rotation sent by Agar to Portland, 10 Mar. 1800, 21 M 57/A46/17.   13 Cornwallis to Portland, 10 Mar. 1800, *Cornwallis correspondence*, iii, pp 208–9.   14 Copy extract from Portland's dispatch, received 9 Mar. 1800, 21 M 57/A46/14–15.   15 Brodrick to Midleton, 3 Feb. 1800, Ms. 1248, vol. 17, f. 116.

O'Beirne expressed his views direct to the Irish government at about the time when Portland and Agar were arguing the matter out. Reporting Agar's exposition of the case for exclusively archiepiscopal representation at a meeting of bishops (where Agar's openness, courage and leadership are to be commended, though they were not by O'Beirne), he wrote to Castlereagh:

> I found most of the bishops, indeed I may say all, agreeing with me, that ... nothing ... [could compensate the Church for] the flagrant neglect of ... [the archbishops'] pastoral functions, to which the Archbishop's regulation would necessarily open a door. Exclusive of their metropolitical jurisdiction, to which constant recourse must be had in this kingdom, the archbishops have each an extensive diocese to superintend; and, of all the bishops, the presence of the primate and of the archbishop of Dublin is the [most] essential. There is scarcely a great institution to which they are not acting trustees, nor a charitable board at which their attendance is not essentially necessary.[16]

It is not surprising that the bishops unanimously objected to Agar's attempt to exclude them from a representative role in the post-Union House of Lords (and this no doubt coloured their reception of his other proposals, which will be discussed in due course). 'The bishops with the smallest incomes', in particular, must have hoped for better things as a result of becoming personally known in the Westminster parliament and to British ministers. To anyone stuck in remote Killala or Clonfert, a jaunt to London must in itself have held irresistible attractions. Cornwallis, who had an interview with Agar on this subject just before the meeting of bishops,[17] would presumably have been happy to incorporate Agar's alternative if Agar had gained acceptance of it from that meeting. Agar having, predictably, failed, Cornwallis referred the decision of the matter to the British government,[18] who decided to adhere to the existing proposal, as modified by the Agar clause.

It was unfortunate that this issue divided the bishops, and Agar from the bishops, because something could still have been done to make the episcopal representation more efficient. An archbishop who was an Irish representative peer (Agar) was likely to be as much of a one-off as a bishop who was a peer of Great Britain (Hervey); and so indeed it proved. What was required was a flexible mechanism for substitution, in the event of an archbishop's or a bishop's not needing his place on the rota, not wanting to occupy it or not being able to occupy it. Even if he had not been a British peer, Hervey's place was lost to the Church of Ireland when his turn came in 1801: he had been abroad for the past ten years and he was to die abroad in 1803. Brodrick, for one, would have been glad to cede his first turn on the archiepiscopal rota. As he wrote in December 1801, 'I could be much more usefully employed in my archiepiscopal office by remaining this winter at Cashel than by crossing the water to attend at West-

16 O'Beirne to Castlereagh, 10 Mar. 1800, *Castlereagh correspondence*, iii, pp 253–6. 17 Endorsement of 7 Mar. 1800 by Agar on a letter to him of 6 Mar. from Cornwallis' private secretary, Littlehales, T/3719/C/34/7. 18 Cornwallis to Portland, 10 Mar. 1800, *Cornwallis correspondence*, iii, pp 208–9.

minster.'[19] However, it would have been difficult to devise a scheme of substitution which did not seem to threaten the right of the bishops to sit once every six years. The fault lay in the government's premature disclosure and establishment of that right even before the session of 1799, in order to win the bishops' support for the Union. Ironically, the only two bishops who opposed the Union, Richard Marlay of Waterford and William Dickson of Down, were 'as far as they personally are concerned, ... glad of so good a reason for spending their winter in London as a call of duty of parliament.'[20] Brodrick thought that 'The whole of the representation of the Irish Church in the Imperial Parliament is almost a farce, although it is liable to fewer objections than any other mode that could be proposed.'[21] The second half of the comment was probably incorrect. On balance, Agar's plan for the four archbishops to sit for life was the least objectionable of those put forward, particularly if accompanied by some provision for substitution by a bishop of the non-attending archbishop's province. It was not Agar's fault that his advice was not taken in December 1798.

In the same letter of late January 1800 in which Cornwallis stated to the British government Agar's views on episcopal representation, he reported Agar's wish 'that the article for incorporating the protestant Churches of Great Britain and Ireland should be made a fundamental article, and so expressed as in the article of the Scotch Union.'[22] 'Continuance of the present Church Establishment in each kingdom' had been made 'a fundamental article' in the draft of article v which had featured among the 'Heads of a Union with Ireland' back in November 1799.[23] But the same draft of article v had continued with a reference to post-Union tithe commutation in both kingdoms. At whatever stage the reference to tithe commutation was deleted, the reference to 'a fundamental article' may have been deleted also, and subsequently forgotten about. Agar was now stated to be 'particularly anxious' on this issue; and Dr Duigenan, the judge of the prerogative court, and he urged 'that an act of parliament shall be passed on the subject to be hereafter incorporated with the Act of Union.' This must be the act of which an undated draft exists among Agar's papers, 'for securing the Church of Ireland as by law established.' It re-enacts and perpetuates the Act of Uniformity 'and all and singular other acts of parliament now in force for the establishment and preservation of the Church of Ireland'; provides that 'an oath to maintain inviolably the said settlement of the Church of Ireland' shall be taken by every subsequent monarch at his coronation; and states itself to be a 'fundamental and essential part of any treaty of Union', which is to be 'inserted in express terms in any act of parliament which shall be made for settling and ratifying any treaty of Union.'[24] Cornwallis' view was that the object would be 'better accomplished by adding to the 5th article as it now stands the following words: "And that the continuance forever of the said United Church as the Established Church of the said United Kingdom shall be deemed and taken to be a fundamental article of the Union" .' Bishop Watson of

19 Brodrick to Midleton, 22 Dec. 1801, Ms. 1248, vol. 17, f. 144.   **20** Brodrick to Midleton, 2 Apr. 1800, Ms. 1248, vol. 17, f. 122.   **21** Brodrick to Midleton, 9 May 1800, Ms. 1248, vol. 17, f. 123.   **22** Cornwallis to Portland, 25 Jan. 1800, *Cornwallis correspondence*, iii, pp 171–2.   **23** *HMC Dropmore Mss.*, iv. 399.   **24** 21 M 57/A46/9.

Llandaff, to whom – among many others – Archbishop Moore referred the matter, declared roundly: 'I think the act of parliament proposed by the Archbishop of Cashel and Dr Duigenan to be wholly unnecessary, but I approve of the addition to the 5th article proposed by the lord lieutenant ..., merely as it may tend to conciliate those who entertain apprehensions for the security of the Irish Church.'[25] In the end, after a delay of over five weeks caused by Archbishop Moore's soundings,[26] something closely resembling Cornwallis' form of words was adopted.

Agar was perhaps unwisely provocative in including in his proposed act an explicit reference to the Coronation Oath. But he had logic on his side in stating the necessity of some act defining the essential characteristics of the Church of Ireland which were to be preserved forever in the United Church. Article v, as then drafted and as finally enacted, assumed that 'the doctrine, worship, discipline and government' of the Churches of England and Ireland were the same: whereas only the doctrine was the same; the worship was somewhat different because of different prayer books and canons; and, as Agar's argument with Buckingham in 1788 and the discussion in Chapters Five to Nine of unions, pluralities, faculties, non-residence, clerical residences, tithes, the administration of see estates, canon law, ecclesiastical courts, etc., etc., amply demonstrate, the 'discipline and government' were different in many important respects. O'Beirne made the same point (though he did not admit that he was supporting an argument advanced by Agar!): 'There are various statutes in force relative to the Church of Ireland, resulting from local circumstances, that must be continued and confirmed. Several regulations are at this moment necessary that ought to be added.'[27] Agar, and O'Beirne, had precedent as well as logic on their side. All the arrangements for the post-Union representation of Ireland at Westminster were first embodied in a separate act of the Irish parliament (*40 George III, cap. 29*) and then inserted in, and re-enacted as article viii of, the Act of Union. It was to this procedure that Brodrick referred when he wrote in mid-May 1800, 'The Representation Bill must receive the royal assent in order that it may be introduced into the body of the act.'[28] There would seem to have been no good reason for proceeding differently in respect of the Church of Ireland than in respect of the parliament of Ireland. Moreover, another discrepancy immediately apparent to the most casual reader of the Act of Union is that the part of article viii relating to episcopal representation alone runs to much greater length than the whole of article v, the article providing for the far more important matter of the uniting of the two Churches.

Since he received no encouragement to proceed by separate act of the Irish parliament, Agar concentrated on proposing insertions in article v which would meet the most important of his concerns. In this he received little support from the other bishops and unfair criticism from O'Beirne, who wrote in the already-cited letter to Castlereagh of March 1800:

25 Watson to Moore, 5 Mar. 1800, *Anecdotes of Watson*, pp 328–30. 26 Copy extract from Portland's dispatch, received 9 Mar. 1800, 21 M 57/A46/14. 27 O'Beirne to Castlereagh, 18 Nov. 1799, *Castlereagh correspondence*, iii, pp 2–8. 28 Brodrick to Midleton, 16 May 1800, Ms. 1248, vol. 17, ff. 124–5.

The Archbishop of Cashel, at a meeting of the bishops, ... took occasion to condemn the entire article respecting the identifying of the two Churches. He said, if the government wished to unite the two Churches, he would make no objection, but that it would be essentially necessary to change the whole article, so as to secure the Church of Ireland against all possibility of change or alteration. ... To me and to all the other bishops it appeared perfectly unintelligible how, in an article that was to abolish the Church of Ireland as separate or distinct from the Church of England, and to incorporate and identify the two Churches for ever under the name of the Church of England alone, the distinction of the Church of Ireland should still be preserved, and a stipulation made that it should be secure for ever against all change or alteration.[29]

The alternative plan offered by O'Beirne was radical and, in Chart's view, destructive of the 'national character' of the Church of Ireland. O'Beirne 'suggested that, instead of a "united Church", there should only be one Church, the "Church of England in England and Ireland", with the archbishop of Canterbury as primate, and all the Irish bishops his suffragans and subordinates. In support of this suggestion he cited the precedent of the Danish bishops of sees in Ireland who owed allegiance to Canterbury in the pre-Norman days [1074–1152].'[30] It was not left to Agar alone to oppose this idea. Bishop Watson advised Archbishop Moore: 'Above all things, I wish the Church of England to forbear affecting a superiority over that of Ireland, by attempting to obtain an appellant jurisdiction for the see of Canterbury.'[31] So, O'Beirne's plan came to nothing.

Undeterred, though weakened in his bargaining power, by the hostility or indifference of the other bishops, Agar proceeded with his proposals to amend article v. His first essay, on 29 January 1800, was to get more-or-less the whole text of his draft act incorporated into the article;[32] but this did not find favour, except for the passage about the 'fundamental article', which, as has been seen, Cornwallis himself took up. It was probably in relation to this that Clare wrote to Agar on 20 March: 'I understand from Lord Castlereagh that your Grace feels perfect satisfaction in an addition to the resolution ... which he has communicated to you.'[33] Agar then proposed an insertion 'saving to the Church of Ireland [after the Union] all the rights, privileges and jurisdictions thereunto now belonging.'[34] Possibly to meet Agar's point, wording of similar though weaker import appeared at the start of article viii (a part of that article not anticipated by the Representation Act): 'all laws in force at the time of the Union, and all courts of civil or ecclesiastical jurisdiction within the respective kingdoms, shall remain as now by law established within the same', unless subsequently amended by the parliament of the United Kingdom. This was a faint assertion of the legal and

29 O'Beirne to Castlereagh, 10 Mar. 1800, *Castlereagh correspondence*, iii, pp 253–6.   30 Phillips, *Church of Ireland*, iii. 288; O'Beirne to Castlereagh, 18 Nov. 1799, loc. cit.   31 Watson to Moore, 5 Mar. 1800, loc. cit.   32 Draft in Lady Somerton's handwriting, with a variant version of part of it in Agar's, endorsed by him as having been given to Castlereagh, 29 Jan. 1800, 21 M 57/A46/13. 33 Clare to Agar, 20 Mar. 1800, T/3719/C/34/8.   34 21 M 57/A46/10.

other rights of a venerable institution; but at least it met the point. However, the point would have been better expressed in Agar's form of words, and should have been made or repeated in article v which, taken in isolation, still seemed to make the assumption that the discipline and government of the two Churches were the same. Finally, Agar sought to insert a reference to the Church of Scotland and to the Act of Union with Scotland – probably a tactical device to introduce an implicit allusion to the Coronation Oath (see p. 518), without mentioning that controversial issue by name. Article v, as amended and counter-amended, in the end read:

> that the Churches of England and Ireland, as now by law established, be united into one Protestant Episcopal Church, to be called "The United Church of England and Ireland"; and that the doctrine, worship, discipline and government of the said United Church shall be, and shall remain in full force for ever, as the same are now by law established for the Church of England; and that the continuance and preservation of the said United Church as the Established Church of England and Ireland shall be deemed and taken to be an essential and fundamental part of the Union; and that in like manner the doctrine, worship, discipline and government of the Church of Scotland shall remain and be preserved as the same are now established by law and by the Acts for the Union of the two kingdoms of England and Scotland.

Lecky, who rightly attributed the 'essential and fundamental' clause to Agar, pointed out how, 'for more than a generation, it was regarded by English politicians as a binding force', and was enshrined in successive Catholic Emancipation bills between 1813 and 1829.[35]

In previous drafts of article v, including Agar's of 29 January 1800, a reference was made to arrangements for holding convocations of the United Church. In Ireland, convocation had last met in the period 1703–11, when its proceedings had been disfigured by faction and turmoil; so convocation had played no part in the recent history of the Church of Ireland. In England, convocation was regularly summoned at the same time as writs for a general election were issued, and met on the provincial basis of Canterbury and York. This distinction between summoning convocation (in the singular) and the holding of convocations (in the plural) was to give rise to considerable confusion in this proposed part of article v. Agar's draft of late January ran: 'when his Majesty shall summon a convocation, the archbishops, bishops and clergy of the several provinces in Ireland shall be respectively summoned to, and sit in, the convocations of the United Church in the like manner and subject to the same regulations as to election and qualification as are at present by law established with respect to the like orders of the Church of England.'[36]

The intent of this wording must have been that the representatives of the 'several provinces' of the Church of Ireland should sit in the two provincial convocations in

England – perhaps on the basis that Dublin and Cashel sat with Canterbury, and Armagh and Tuam with York. O'Beirne misunderstood – or perhaps misrepresented – Agar's views in his letter to Castlereagh. 'In a private conversation with myself, the Archbishop ... talked of the absurdity of calling so many of the Irish clergy to London; but he forgot that the convocations are provincial, and the clergy to be convened in their respective provinces.'[37] With his considerable knowledge of the workings of the Church of England, Agar was not likely to have forgotten such a thing. A subsequent letter from Brodrick to his brother establishes that the forgetfulness originated in England: 'As to the convocation, I must refer you for whatever explanation you may want, to your friend, Mr Pitt. Whatever *blunders* appear in the articles, originate on your side of the water.'[38] It is improbable that Pitt ever concerned himself personally in matters pertaining to convocation. Certainly, it was to Auckland that the task of correcting the '*blunders*' and rewriting that part of the article was delegated. On 1 May he transmitted to Castlereagh 'the Church article, in which there are many small alterations ... merely in style, and to obviate the inaccuracy of that part ... which supposed only one convocation to exist in this country.' Auckland's revised version also left it in no doubt that the convocation of the United Church would meet provincially.[39]

Agar valued convocation as a symbol of the unity of the Churches. So, from his very different perspective, did Bishop Watson. Writing to Archbishop Moore in March, Watson declared: 'An united convocation will sufficiently unite the Churches of England and Ireland, both at present and as to all future changes, if it should ever be thought expedient to make any.'[40] Brodrick thought the same: 'As to the whole question of convocation, I conceive it to be introduced solely for the purpose of making the bond of the two Churches appear more firm and compact.' But Brodrick also wanted to make convocation a working forum for the Church of Ireland alone:

> Supposing all difficulty out of the way on the score of forming one assembly with Canterbury or York or both, it is ridiculous indeed, the very idea of bringing the body of the Irish clergy to be represented in convocation at Westminster. ... I would wish, when our parliament was removed, that some opportunity should offer of bringing ... [the Irish clergy] together periodically. I think that the collecting the members of this now disjointed body, might be made highly useful under a prudent head – nay, perhaps necessary for bringing into action many exertions for the benefit of morality and religion, which otherwise would sleep.[41]

This certainly was not Agar's wish: the man who thought the Irish episcopal bench should be represented at Westminster by the archbishops only, was no democrat. Since

37 O'Beirne to Castlereagh, 10 Mar. 1800, *Castlereagh correspondence*, iii, pp 253–6.   38 Brodrick to Midleton, 9 May 1800, Ms. 1248, vol. 17, f. 122.   39 Auckland to Castlereagh, 1 May 1800, *Castlereagh correspondence*, iii, pp 293–5.   40 Watson to Moore, 5 Mar. 1800, loc. cit.   41 Brodrick to Midleton, 9 May 1800, loc. cit.

the holding of convocation in one body in Ireland had had democratic and disruptive consequences in the past, he would have had no wish to resuscitate such a forum – even 'periodically.' Instead, he can only have welcomed the idea of splitting the Church of Ireland into provinces, and the disincentive to the ordinary clergy which travelling to Canterbury or York would constitute. Since there was no agreement, especially within the Church of Ireland, as to the future form and role of convocation, all reference to the matter was deleted from article v.

A couple of years later, the lord chancellor of England, the 1st Lord Eldon, was greatly puzzled by this omission. 'The article which makes the Churches of England and Ireland one, is singularly acted upon, if we have our English convocations for the Church of England and Ireland has no convocation nor forms any part of any convocation.' It was not even possible, he pointed out, for the archbishop and three bishops representing the Church of Ireland in each parliament to attend one or other province of the English convocation, because attendance at the English convocation was founded on a bishop's writ of summons to parliament, and for some reason writs had never been sent to the Irish bishops![42] Presumably, Agar would have anticipated these problems if he had not thought that, on the whole, it was prudent to let convocation sleep. The sleep was to be prolonged. No form of convocation of the Church of Ireland was held until after Disestablishment. In England, too, convocation was 'practically dormant' by the early 1830s.[43]

COMPENSATION FOR THE BISHOPS' BOROUGHS

Having failed to get his way on the slightly abstract issue of convocation, Agar now directed his energies to the very practical business of what was to be done with the compensation money (ultimately set at £15,000 each) due for the disfranchisement of three out of the four bishops' boroughs. These were Clogher, Old Leighlin, and St Canice.[44] Agar's plan, which he accomplished in the end, was that the money should be paid to the board of first fruits, and not to individual bishops or their sees, or to worthy local causes within those sees; and his papers include a copy of a clause to that effect, undated except for the year, '1800', for insertion into an act of parliament.[45] It looks as if the thoughts of one of the most influential members of Pitt's government had been moving in a similar direction. In a letter of early October 1799, Grenville had reminded Pitt that the bishops' boroughs 'belong to government' and 'might certainly be so arranged' as government thought fit.[46] This was something of an oversimplification, as has been seen (pp 175–83). Nor is its meaning absolutely plain. Was Grenville

42 Eldon to Redesdale, 28 Sep. 1802, *Irish official papers*, ii. 365.   43 Mathieson, *English Church reform*, p. 69.   44 E.M. Johnston[-Liik], *Great Britain and Ireland, 1760–1800: a study in political administration* (St Andrews, 1963), pp 169–70 and 190–92.   45 21 M 57/B25/3. Professor Akenson attributes this outcome to the post-Union negotiations of Archbishops Stuart and Brodrick. But this is an injustice to Agar, and also incorrect in point of timing, since the decision was taken before Stuart was appointed primate.   46 Grenville to Pitt, 9 Oct. 1799, *HMC Dropmore Mss.*, v, pp 465–6.

arguing that, since the bishops' boroughs already belonged to government, no compensation need be paid by government for their disfranchisement; or did he mean that some uniform arrangement for compensation should be applied to all three? If, as is probable, he meant the latter, Agar's proposal would have entirely met his wishes. It had the great merit of simplicity, whereas the situations in the three boroughs were varied and complex, as the rival claims made for the compensation money would soon make plain.

First in the field with a claim was Charles Tottenham, MP for New Ross, Co. Wexford, who urged that a special case should be made of Old Leighlin, since Ferns, the diocese to which it was attached, had been the scene of much destruction by the Wexford rebels. Tottenham, writing to Castlereagh in June 1800, represented that, 'as some churches, particularly the church of Old Ross ..., were burnt and destroyed by the rebels, and as ... the parishioners are unable, from the variety of losses that they have sustained by the rebellion, to raise any money towards the rebuilding of their churches, it would be well to enable the board of first fruits to rebuild churches in the diocese of Ferns with part of the compensation money.' He also drew attention to the fact that 'the church of New Ross ... is in a ruinous state ..., [and] the board of first fruits cannot by the powers now vested in them give any money to rebuild a church where divine service has been performed within the last twenty years.'⁴⁷ The churches of Old Ross and New Ross may have been good causes. But there does not seem any reason why the parishioners of the former should not have made application to the commissioners for the relief of suffering loyalists (Agar among them). In the case of the parishioners of New Ross, Tottenham's special pleading ran counter to the board's cherished twenty-year rule – as Tottenham acknowledged. It may also be suspected that the parishioners of New Ross were anxious to evade the operation of the recent act sponsored by Agar (*40 George III, cap. 33*), which made it possible for a parish to be 'cessed' for the building or rebuilding (as opposed to just the repair) of a church.

In January 1801, the Bishop of Ferns (and Leighlin), who was of course Cleaver, associating himself with the portrieve and burgesses of Old Leighlin (then numbering eleven, because there were two vacancies), entered a rival claim for the compensation money for Old Leighlin. Surprisingly, they did not mention the rebellion – perhaps to avoid strengthening the case previously made by Tottenham. Instead, they argued that, as the thirteen electors for Old Leighlin were all clergy of Ferns and Leighlin and all had been nominated by the bishop, the money should be put to exclusively diocesan use. Cleaver's proposal was that it should be employed to set up a revolving loan fund for glebe-house building in the dioceses. He pointed out that, of the 74 parochial unions in the dioceses, only 8 were provided with glebe-houses, of which 3 had recently been erected by the present incumbents. Over time, it would be practicable to get all the necessary glebe-houses built on this revolving basis, and the fund could then be applied, first, to the building of a house for the diocesan registrar, next, to the

---

47 Tottenham to Castlereagh, 16 June 1800, *Castlereagh correspondence*, iii, pp 323–4.

setting up of a charity for the benefit of widows and orphans of the diocesan clergy, then to the building of a new parish church in Maryborough, Co. Leix (already 'begun upon an estimate of £1,600'), and, finally, to the enlarging of Ferns cathedral, 'now become parochial, ... [but] much too small for the congregation which should attend it ..., [and lacking any] oeconomy funds.'[48] All this was perfectly plausible, although it was hardly fair to the bishops, cathedral chapters and clergy of other dioceses that Ferns and Leighlin should be specially favoured just because they happened to have contained a disfranchised borough.

Meanwhile, in September 1800, a claim had been received for the compensation money for St Canice. This came from the bishop of Ossory, Hugh Hamilton, 'a prodigious scholar, ... [former] professor of natural philosophy ..., fellow of the Royal Society and member of the Royal Irish Academy',[49] and evidently a man who also had an eye to the main chance; for he now argued that all the compensation money should be paid to himself personally, on the ground that his former borough influence had reinforced his claims to promotion (as it certainly had Newcome's – see p. 468). He submitted the two surviving corporation books of St Canice, covering the period 1661–1799, adduced numerous precedents to show that the bishop had always been, and had always been regarded as being, the patron of the borough, and stated that the portrieve and burgesses (who numbered 24 in St Canice) and the much more numerous freemen, were all the nominees of successive bishops. He concluded

> That the circumstances above-mentioned have given the bishops of Ossory such additional consequence, and obtained for them so much attention from government, that the bishops of that see (with the exception of only two bishops, who lived a very short time after their appointment) for above a century past, have all been translated to much more eligible bishoprics; ... [so] that, by the Union, your memorialist ... considers himself as the only person who has sustained any loss ... on account of ... [St Canice] ceasing to return any member to parliament.[50]

Hamilton's claim conveniently omitted two important facts: first, that Ossory was a junior and 'climbing see', so that its bishops were likely to leave on promotion in any case; and, second, that the bishops of Ossory had earned 'so much attention from government' precisely because the borough was insecure. It was therefore not true to say that the bishop's was the only interest there or that he was the 'only person' to be disadvantaged by disfranchisement.

The last claims to be received were in respect of Clogher, and were made by four different parties – the Bishop (John Porter), the cathedral chapter, the citizens and inhabitants, and the seneschal of the manor of Clogher. The Bishop, whose claim was

---

48 *Report of the commissioners for compensation for boroughs disfranchised by the Act of Union, session 1805 (89)*, viii, pp 29–31.   49 Acheson, *Church of Ireland*, p. 85.   50 *Report of the compensation commissioners*, pp 32–5.

dated '24 February [1801]' – the others were undated – pointed to the state of his palace, and asked for a loan of £4,000 to make additions to it (that sum to be recovered from his successor). The chapter, whose members were all *ex officio* voters in the former parliamentary constituency of Clogher, asked for an outright gift of the money necessary to endow a choir for the cathedral and a charity for the widows and orphans of diocesan clergy. The citizens and inhabitants, who had enjoyed the vote if they resided within the vaguely delimited 700 Irish acres granted to the defunct corporation of Clogher in 1629, claimed that they had derived great benefits from the franchise, including leases of land at nominal rents, and asked for money to repair the cathedral, make a road to their turf bog, improve their water-supply, establish a free school and build a new market house. Finally, the seneschal of the manor of Clogher sought compensation for the loss of his salary of £30 per annum as returning officer for the borough.[51] These four claims were plainly collusive, because the parties each asked for different and complementary things. Significantly, the Bishop did not act on behalf of the other claimants, as Cleaver had done, or seek to exclude the others, as had Hamilton. This was because Bishop Porter had just been defeated in the last election in Clogher's parliamentary history, a by-election affecting both seats which had been held as recently as January 1800. There had been a tough contest on the occasion, inflamed, of course, by the contest raging at national level over the Union. The Bishop's candidates, both of whom had been recommended to him by the government, had been elected and returned but, following a petition to the House of Commons, had been unseated on 29 March in favour of their anti-Unionist rivals.[52] This embarrassingly recent demonstration that the bishop of Clogher did not control Clogher borough was in fact the sequel to the earlier opposition in 1783 (see p. 179).

These competing claims, all of them containing an awkward element of truth, omitted one important aspect of the history of the bishops' boroughs – that their representation had at times been used to advance the general interests of the Church. The argument that Edward Leslie, the government's candidate for Old Leighlin at the crucial by-election of January 1787, was the son of a bishop and 'very zealous in support of the Church', was not pure electioneering: the seats for the bishops' boroughs, when the needs of the government and the plans of individual bishops permitted, were not infrequently used to return spokesmen for or defenders of the Church. Agar was of the view that this should have been done more systematically. Writing to the absent Primate Robinson in June 1788, he had urged:

> I know nothing more necessary in these times to the defence and support of our Ecclesiastical Establishment than to place a few such men in the House of

---

51 Ibid., pp 25–8.   52 *Irish Commons' journals*, xix, pp 34, 54, 73–4 and 122. The successful election petition against their return in January 1800 cost the Bishop's candidates well over £1,000 – John Martin, the attorney for them, to Alexander Marsden, secretary to the law department of Dublin Castle, 29 Mar. 1800, NA, Official Papers, 515/85/5. For a spirited but completely misleading account of these events, see Sir Jonah Barrington, *Rise and fall of the Irish nation* (Dublin, 1843), pp 559–60.

Archbishop Charles Agar

Commons, where we daily experience the want of friends. Excepting Mr [Arthur] Brown[e], who represents the College,[53] we have not I fear an *able* and a *zealous* friend there. Were Mr Trant and Dr Duigenan in parliament, I really think we might expect great assistance from them, for they are as well informed with respect to Church matters as they are well disposed to the Establishment and its interests.[54]

Agar's *protégé*, Dominick Trant, who had been in parliament (for St Canice) between 1781 and 1783, died suddenly in 1790, before Agar's proposal could be acted upon. But Duigenan was to represent Old Leighlin from 1791 to 1797, and Armagh (which of course was not disfranchised at the Union) from 1797 until his death in 1816. Under the dramatic and exceptional circumstances of Pitt's threatened Catholic Emancipation Bill in January 1801, George III came out strongly in support of the view that the one surviving bishop's borough should be represented by 'a strong friend to the present Church Establishment' rather than of the government of the day.[55] Henceforth this was to be the shibboleth of post-Union MPs for Armagh.

Yet, even before the Union, there were more MPs for bishops' boroughs than Duigenan and the short-lived Trant who could be regarded as representative of the interests of the Church. These were more abundant in the first half of the century; but in Agar's day they included: Eland Mossom Senior, MP for St Canice, 1759–74, who, although regarded by the bishops of Ossory as a potential opponent, was the son of a clergyman who had been dean of Ossory from 1703 to 1747; his successor, Thomas Radcliff, MP for St Canice, 1774–6, who was vicar-general of the diocese and metropolitan province of Dublin, judge of the consistorial court of Dublin and a member of a family of civil lawyers;[56] Philip Tisdall, who sat for Armagh, 1776–7, and had been returned for it in 1768, and was not just a law officer and a star performer for government but a distinguished judge of the prerogative court; and Henry Meredyth (see p. 444), MP for Armagh, 1776–89, who was a Dublin Castle official, 1753–78, and deputy auditor-general but, more significantly, owed that position to the recommendation of Primate Stone, executed most of Stone's and Robinson's responsibilities as treasurer of the board of first fruits, was agent for the see estate, and had been a member of Armagh corporation since c. 1750.[57]

The use to which the bishops' seats had sometimes been put therefore lent weight to Agar's contention that the compensation money should be used for the good of the Church generally. Furthermore, his idea of institutional compensation was appropriate to the unique situation of the bishops' boroughs – that they were the only ones with an *ex officio* patron. Above all, his idea was simple and formulaic and avoided

53 For Arthur Browne, see McDowell and Webb, *TCD*, pp 71 and 81.   54 Agar to Robinson, 2 June 1788, T/3719/C/22/22. Woodward had thought it prudent for Agar and himself to distance themselves from Trant and cease to finance the publication of his pamphlets after Trant had killed Sir John Conway Colthurst in the notorious duel – see Woodward to Brodrick, 16 Feb. 1787, NLI, Ms. 8870/1, and pp 50–51.   55 The King to Lord Loughborough, [28 Jan. 1801], *Later correspondence of George III*, iii. 474.   56 Kennedy, 'Dublin and Glendalough', p. 203.

a number of awkward or unacceptable alternatives. The alternative of paying no compensation at all, if that was what Grenville had in mind, was possibly the most unacceptable. It meant an avowal that the Castle had hitherto nominated eight members of the Irish House of Commons and would hereafter nominate one (the member for Armagh) of the members of the House of Commons at Westminster – and this at a time when the British government was insistent that the Union disfranchisements should be carried out on principles which did not strengthen the case for parliamentary reform in Great Britain. In any case, granted the recent history of the three bishops' boroughs due to be disfranchised, the Castle could not have made good its claim to exclusive nomination. It would also have been hard to deny that a number of bishops, of Clogher and Ferns as well as Ossory, had advanced the interests of themselves and/or their families during the last third of the eighteenth century as the vicarious result of having boroughs attached to their sees. Moreover, if the cases of the three bishops' boroughs were to be treated on their separate merits, the compensation money for Clogher would have to be distributed among the electors, since the bishop had lost the last election, and there would be no future opportunity of reversing that decision. Agar's formula was therefore very convenient to the government politically, as well as very advantageous to the Church and to Agar's adopted child, the board of first fruits.

It is not clear how soon the government accepted that the compensation money should go to the board of first fruits. In May 1800, writing about his own family borough of Midleton, Brodrick reported: 'I know not what sum will be given. Report says £15,000 for two seats. Such matters as these are not much spoken of by government till the Act of Union shall be passed.'[58] This circumspection – so far removed from the 'orgy of corruption' of legend – contributes to the difficulty of tracing the sequence of events. In early September, Castlereagh wrote from England to Agar thanking him for his 'obliging suggestions as to the best means of making the compensation for the ecclesiastical boroughs contribute to the enforcing residence amongst the clergy. I shall hope for an opportunity of communicating further with your Grace on this interesting subject.'[59] This sounds as if Agar was at this stage raising the matter for the first time. However, over aspects of the Union which had implications for the Church he had previously experienced a fair degree of forgetfulness on the part of both Castlereagh and Cornwallis,[60] so too much should not be read into Castlereagh's response. A more important piece of evidence is Charles Tottenham's already-quoted letter to Castlereagh which began: 'As I find it is the intention of government that the compensation for the ecclesiastical boroughs shall be given to the board of first fruits.' Tottenham was a cousin of Ely, and Ely a likely source of information about Agar's plans; so, since Tottenham's letter is dated 16 June,

57 Lists of the burgesses of Armagh, 1747–96, PRONI, DIO 4/40/1/11–13; History of the Irish Parliament database, *sub* 'Henry Meredyth'.   58 Brodrick to Midleton, 9 May 1800, Ms. 1248, vol. 17, f. 123.   59 Castlereagh to Agar, 7 Sep. 1800, T/3719/C/34/36.   60 See endorsements by Agar on his copy of 'the Agar clause' of 12 January 1800, T/3719/C/34/2.

the board of first fruits scheme may be regarded as almost 'official' by that date. The act passed at the beginning of August 'for granting allowances to bodies corporate and individuals in respect to those cities, towns and boroughs which shall cease to send any member to parliament after the Union' (*20 George III, cap. 34*) did not include the clause which Agar had drafted. But it had presumably been decided that this was an inappropriate insertion. The main purpose of that act was to set up commissioners of compensation to carry its provisions into effect, and it could hardly have pre-empted their decision in the matter of the bishops' boroughs. In practice, however, the only – or almost the only[61] – body corporate which received compensation for a disfranchised borough was the board of first fruits (which had been incorporated in 1723). The rest of the £1,400,000 went to 'individuals' (of whom only Lord Downshire received more than the board, Ely coming second-equal with the board). The very mention of 'bodies corporate' was therefore an implied reference to the board.

Moreover, the composition of the commissioners of compensation looked promising from the point of view of Agar and the board. They included: Robert French, Agar's legal adviser; Sackville Hamilton, Agar's colleague as a commissioner for suffering loyalists and a former government-nominated MP for Clogher, 1783–95, and for Armagh, 1796–7; and Dr Duigenan. The presence of Duigenan was a sort of guarantee that the interests of the board would not be overlooked. The cases of the three bishops' boroughs were considered and decided on the same day, 22 January 1802, and Duigenan resigned from the commission later in that year.[62] The commission, which remained in existence until 1805, conducted its business in Dublin, which cannot have suited Duigenan, who represented Armagh at Westminster. So, it looks as if he extricated himself from it as soon as he decently could, following the satisfactory decision in the case of the bishops' boroughs.

TITHES AND CURATES

Agar's success in obtaining this unexpected and welcome windfall of £45,000 for the board – his greatest and only major success at the time of the Union – derived from the government's coyness in introducing the question of compensation, which was considered late in the day and long after Agar had rejoined the Castle ranks. Another late and, from Agar's point of view, much less welcome development was the situation in which he found himself placed by a tactical opposition motion in the House of

---

61 When the commissioners came to enquire into the affairs of the uniquely venal and complicated borough of Swords, Co. Dublin (which, like Cashel, had once been a bishop's borough), they decided that the only thing to do with the compensation money was to use it to endow a school at Swords 'for the purpose of educating and apprenticing the children of the humbler classes without any religious distinctions' (D'Alton, *History of Co. Dublin*, pp 285–6). The archbishop of Dublin was an *ex officio* trustee of the school. It was not opened until 1809, Agar's last year as archbishop, but its buildings were being planned and put up in the intervening years.   62 'An account of the expenses attending the execution of the commission for granting compensation ... from the commencement thereof to the 8th August 1804', Foster/Massereene papers, PRONI, D/207/10/40.

Commons respecting tithes. In late March 1800, Sir John Macartney, a satellite and connection-by-marriage of Speaker Foster, raised the 'very insidious'[63] point that the exemption of pasture from tithe (the so-called 'tithe of agistment') rested merely on a resolution of the Irish House of Commons passed in 1736, and 'could have no longer any effect or operation after a Union.' (It had not been given statutory force, because it would never have passed the then bishop-ridden House of Lords.) Macartney's motion, reported Cornwallis, caused alarm and threatened defections among the country gentlemen who supported the Union. So, 'His Majesty's chief servants then agreed, in which the Archbishop of Cashel acquiesced, that it would be highly politic to check at once the ferment which was rising on the subject, by a bill' (*40 George III, cap. 23*) giving statutory effect to the exemption.

It is not surprising that Agar's acquiescence was deemed worthy of special mention:[64] Brodrick, for one, was not disposed to acquiesce in the government's bill. To Lord Midleton, he described Macartney's speech as

> the testimony of an enemy ... to the moderation of the Irish clergy. His num-
> bers, indeed, are in the true spirit of *Foster* calculation! ... When you have read
> this attentively, turn over the page, and observe the minister [Castlereagh]
> grounding on that moderation a bill for taking from the clergy so large a part
> (according to Macartney) of what the legislature has appointed for the main-
> tenance of the clergy, not applying it to the same general purpose of piety and
> charity in any other way, but putting it into the pockets of the landlord without
> any kind of compensation ... [to] the poor parson's scanty pittance. I wish Lord
> Strafford were alive to make these Church cormorants disgorge, or else to
> choke them in the midst of their voraciousness.[65]

There was, of course, no realistic possibility of reversing so long-established an exemption from tithe. Moreover, it affected the incomes of the clergy much less in 1800 than it had in 1736 because the operation of market forces, stimulated by war and facilitated by Speaker Foster's Corn Law of 1784, had encouraged a massive swing to tillage. As Foster himself had written in 1786: 'Will any rational man refuse to plough when he will put nine shillings in his pocket, lest the parson get one shilling? A vote of the Commons stopped the tithe of agistment: has a total immunity from tithe encouraged pasturage? By no means ... . Its operation is too trivial to alter a farmer's schemes for the year. Give him a market and he will give corn.'[66] Nevertheless, the situation of the bishops was delicate: they did not want to be blamed by Dublin Castle for jeopardising the government majority for the Union, while they did not want to appear to be voluntarily surrendering even a long-forgone right.

63 Edward Cooke to Grenville, 28 Mar. 1800, *HMC Dropmore Mss.*, vi. 187.   **64** Cornwallis to Portland, 26 Mar. 1800, *Cornwallis correspondence*, iii, pp 220–21.   **65** Brodrick to Midleton, 2 Apr. 1800, Ms. 1248, vol. 17, f. 122.   **66** Foster to Rev. Dr Law, 29 Nov. 1786, Foster/Massereene papers, PRONI, D/207/50/17. This remained Foster's opinion – see Foster to Redesdale, 30 Jan. 1805, *ibid.*, D/207/C/50/19.

On 24 March Agar was summoned to the Castle and asked to negotiate on its behalf with the bishops.[67] The face-saving line of conduct which he agreed with them became apparent when the Tithe Agistment Bill reached the House of Lords on 12 April.

> The Lord Chancellor ... observed that very improper misrepresentations had been made on the subject of this species of tithe; that 20,000 hand-bills had been circulated through the country for the purpose of goading the peasantry into rebellion, founded on such misrepresentations ...; [and] that the object of the present bill was to silence all such attempts ... . His Grace the Archbishop of Cashel [then] observed that he had ... great ... objection[s] to the principle of the bill ..., but [that] he and a majority of his brethren whom he had consulted, were of opinion that under the existing circumstances of this country, it would be prudential in this instance to sacrifice their private interests to the public peace. His Grace observed, however, that it was his intention to assign his reasons for not opposing the bill, in the form of a protest, in order that posterity might be informed of the true motives which induced the clergy to make such a sacrifice.[68]

On 15 April, he headed the list of bishops and peers who entered this protest against the bill following its passage through the House of Lords.

> It has hitherto been deemed right and just, when individuals or any number of persons were deprived of their property by law, to make full compensation to the parties so deprived ... . Yet, while we lament that this principle should be forsaken in any instance, we are ready to admit that the right to agistment tithe surrendered by this bill (though such tithe had been heretofore wrested from the Church without the shadow of law) has lain dormant and unproductive for about sixty years, the clergy of Ireland during that long period, by an unparalleled forbearance and submission to general opinion, having declined to assert their undoubted right thereto. ... Actuated therefore by a sincere attachment to our sovereign and our country, we have studiously withholden any active opposition to this measure ..., under a perfect conviction that this measure will not be made a precedent at any future time.[69]

The protesters were Agar, the Archbishop of Tuam, Lords Drogheda and Lifford, and the Bishops of Meath, Kildare, Limerick, Dromore, Elphin, Ferns, Cloyne, Cork, Kilmore (Brodrick), Clogher, Killala and Raphoe (seven of them by proxy). One of the proxy-voters, Agar's previous detractor, O'Beirne, was warm in his praise of this somewhat convoluted proceeding: 'It is exactly the principle, it is exactly the spirit and

---

67 Castlereagh to Agar, 23 Mar. 1800, T/3719/C/34/10.   68 Page from *Faulkner's Dublin Journal*, 13 Apr. 1800, 21 M 57/B36/13.   69 Ibid., 17 Apr. 1800, 21 M 57/B36/14/1.

style, in which I would have wished to state my own feelings on the subject.' O'Beirne also rejoiced at the wrong-footing of the two anti-Unionist bishops, Dickson of Down and Marlay of Waterford, who had not joined in the defence of the clergy out of party-attachment to Grattan and the Whigs.[70]

Since by this stage there were comfortable government majorities in the House of Commons on all other issues relating to the Union, the 'ferment' and the '20,000 handbills' which the tithe question was capable of raising must have been further, and final, proof to Agar of the anti-clericalism of that House and of the Irish landed class. He cannot be blamed for not being able to see very far beyond the Union and into the nineteenth century, and he was right in thinking that, for as far into the future as he can reasonably be expected to have seen, the Church of Ireland would fare better (or, if anything, too well) at the hands of the parliament of the United Kingdom than it had at those of the Irish. This in itself justified his optimism about, and support of, the Union.

Meanwhile, in the immediate term, his moderation over the tithe of agistment paid dividends by disarming opposition to, and winning support for, an extension of his act of the previous session for recovering arrears of tithe. The already-mentioned (pp 548–9) threats and violence against clergy and tithe-proctors had persisted. In Agar's own diocese of Emly, for example,

> On Wednesday, the 12th day of February last [1800], the house of the Rev. Richard Cox, rector of Cahirconlish, was attacked by a large number of men armed with pikes, guns, and swords, and having broken into the same came upstairs into the room in which lay John Haneen, his steward, and James Evans, his servant-man, and did violently seize the said Evans and dragged him downstairs, and did whip, cut and abuse him in a barbarous manner, and threatened him with instant death, if he did not discover where his master's tithe-books and notes were, and upon his promising to do so he escaped from them.[71]

Bishop Barnard of Limerick had worried that, in spite of such well documented outrages, another bill for the relief of the clergy might run into trouble in the House of Commons. But, to his delight, when Agar's bill 'To enable all ecclesiastical persons, etc., and impropriators, to recover a just compensation for the tithes withheld from them in the year 1799' (*40 George III, cap. 81*) came before the Irish parliament, 'fears of hostility ... to the clergy of the Established Church were unfounded, as the ... Compensation Bill ... passed both Houses ..., supported by the whole weight of government, and those that meant to give it *much* opposition when it was first mentioned, have given it *none at all.*'[72] There was a subsequent victory for the clergy, of a similar nature, which was never claimed by Agar but with which it is tempting to

---

70 O'Beirne to Agar, 19 Apr. 1800, T/3719/C/34/16.   71 Quoted in Seymour, *Diocese of Emly*, p. 160.   72 Bishop Barnard to his niece, 12 July [1800], *Barnard letters*, p. 129.

associate him. Sec. 5 of *40 George III, cap. 96* – 'An act to revive, amend, continue or make perpetual certain temporary statutes' – made perpetual the Whiteboy Act of 1787 (*27 George III, cap. 15*). This latter, among other things, made combinations among farmers 'to prevent the clergyman from viewing, valuing, *etc.*, his tithes ... a misdemeanour', and punishable by fine, imprisonment or corporal punishment.[73]

The next issue of potential difficulty, or worse, for the bishops and the Church was the agitation of the curates of the Church of Ireland for an increase of salary. This has already been discussed (pp 472–3) in the context of Primate Newcome's mishandling of the matter. It did not simply coincide with the struggle over the Union, but was given urgency by the curates' assumption that 'we may probably never have another parliament to petition, and we are convinced that the Irish parliament will provide for the wants of the Irish curates, and place them in that respectability which they so manifestly deserve.'[74] Agar had for some time past been regarded by the campaigning curates as 'the steady and distinguished friend of the Church' and a potential ally. In 1793, an anonymous curate had published in Dublin *A letter to his Grace the Lord Archbishop of Cashel stating the hardships under which the curates of the Established Church labour and how equitable a claim they have to an augmentation of their salaries.*[75] Early in 1797, Agar as a diocesan had shown his goodwill towards the curates (or at any rate his concern to recognise merit) by giving to the Rev. Arthur Lord, 'an impoverished curate', the very good living of Ballintemple (Dundrum, Co. Tipperary), which had previously been held by a cousin of Agar; this had added 'greatly to the number of benevolent acts that you have done in your diocese.'[76] The Rev. Edward Labarte, curate of Thurles, Co. Tipperary, declared unctuously: 'We are situated under a bishop on whom we place the firmest reliance, confident that he will let no opportunity escape to render the situation of the curates of his diocese as comfortable as possible.'[77] In 1796, an act had been passed in Britain (*36 George III, cap. 83*) raising the salaries of curates, and that precedent, together with the events of the rebellion, had considerably strengthened the Irish curates' case. In June 1798, an anonymous curate, whose letter was post-marked Balbriggan, Co. Dublin, wrote to Agar stating the distressed condition of curates in the country parts of Ireland, many of whom were doing the duty of beneficed clergymen who had fled for safety.[78]

When he came to introduce a Curates' Bill in the House of Lords, Agar explained

> that it had been in his contemplation above three years ago to introduce a bill
> of this kind, but that upon serious consultation with several of his Reverend

---

73 Duigenan to Brodrick, 'received 30 Aug. 1815, NLI, Ms. 8861/8.   74 Printed circular letter from Rev. Thomas E. Higginson, chairman of the curates of Down and Connor, Nov. 1799, 21 M 57/B35/5.   75 I am grateful to Mr Peter MacDonagh for this reference. There is a copy of the pamphlet in PRONI, D/3167/2/98. Its author argued (pp 7 and 13–14) that a curate could have lived on £40 per annum fifty years ago but now needed £100, that presbyterian ministers received £50–100 (and more if they worked in Dublin), and that an indifferently educated ensign was paid £60 plus living expenses. See also Seymour, *Succession of clergy in Cashel and Emly*, pp 14–15. 76 Lord Hawarden to Agar, 7 Feb. 1797, T/3719/C/31/6.   77 Labarte to Higginson, 30 Dec. 1799, T/3719/C/33/67.   78 Letter of 7 June 1798, T/3719/C/32/76.

Brethren it had appeared to them that the unsettled state of the country was highly unfavourable, both to the success and the justice of such a measure. ... Within that period, a great proportion of the provision of the beneficed clergy had been annually lost, and it was thought unjust and impolitic to bring forward a measure of this nature just at a moment when that class of the clergy were suffering severe injury. The times appeared now more favourable, and he therefore embraced the earliest opportunity of submitting the bill to the wisdom of parliament.[79]

Although he did not say so, the times were in one respect less favourable. This was because the curates had recently harmed their own good cause by their belligerence and particularly by their appeal to parliament. Brodrick wrote to Agar in October 1799 that 'there is nobody who would not wish to see the condition of the curates mended ..., [but] there are circumstances in the mode of application which no friend to the constitution in general, and the Established Church as a part of that constitution in particular, can approve.'[80] Another of the loyal curates of Agar's diocese observed that the 'petition from the curates of Ireland ... has a mutinous appearance, when presented to parliament unsanctioned by the approbation of our spiritual heads.'[81] Clare, too, was angered by the news that the curates of Down and Connor (the most militant of the lot) were 'about to summon a convention of the curates of every other diocese, at Dublin, to procure an increase of stipend.'[82] On the other hand, 'Simplex' warned Agar that, although the curates of Down had behaved 'in very culpable imitation of the Jacobins of France and the United Irishmen of this kingdom', there was great danger that the bishops would be misrepresented by the enemies of the Church if they treated this behaviour as it deserved. It fell to Agar, in 'the present vacancy of the primacy and the absence of the prelate next in rank [Fowler]', to decide what to do.[83] He decided – in what order is unclear – to recapture the initiative for the hierarchy, prevent the 'measure from being brought forward ... as a question of fretful opposition',[84] and do an act of belated justice.

Faulkner's Dublin Journal, no doubt provided with copy by Agar, reported enthusiastically that the

> bill designed for this excellent purpose by his Grace the Archbishop of Cashel has adopted for its principle the English act of 1796, suited to the circumstances of Ireland. It provides that the bishop or ordinary may raise the salaries of curates to £75 per annum (by the law as it now stands, they can increase it to £50 at the utmost), and where the incumbent does not reside at least four months in the year, it empowers the bishop to give to the curate the use of the glebe-house, or in lieu of it £50 per annum in addition to his salary. ... From

---

79 *Faulkner's Dublin Journal*, 13 Apr. 1800, 21 M 57/B36/13.   80 Brodrick to Agar, 7 Oct. 1799, 21 M 57/B35/1.   81 Rev. Thomas Lockwood to Agar, 27 Nov. 1799, 21 M 57/B35/2.   82 Clare to Auckland, 14 Jan. 1800, Sneyd papers, PRONI, T/3229/1/25.   83 'Simplex' to Agar, 19 Mar. 1800, 21 M 57/B35/7.   84 *Faulkner's Dublin Journal*, 13 Apr. 1800, 21 M 57/B36/13.

the respect and influence due to the great character by whom it is now introduced, we trust that it will become a solid and efficient advantage to a class of men of exemplary morals and untainted loyalty.[85]

In the drafting of the bill, Agar had in fact performed a more delicate balancing act than this facile account would suggest. On the one hand, he had to safeguard the position of those incumbents who needed one or more curates because of the extent or awkward shape or populousness of their parishes, but whose parishes were not rich enough to enable them to afford the new rate of pay. This he did by ensuring that the £75 was the new maximum, but leaving the minimum at the £20–level which had been established by the previous act regulating the matter, *6 George I, cap. 13*;[86] what each curate was actually paid was left by sec. 2 of Agar's act to the discretion of the diocesan. On the other hand, Agar had to meet the point raised by the curates (two of whom wrote anonymously to him on the subject in May 1800[87]) that beneficed clergy-men would dismiss them rather than pay them at the new rates. This he also did under sec. 2 which, as well as leaving the amount to the discretion of the diocesan, made the new pay-scale applicable to 'any curate *heretofore* [my emphasis] nominated or employed' as well as 'hereafter to be nominated or employed.' Additionally, in sec. 4 he gave authority to the diocesan to license curates who had not been nominated by the incumbent, and set up an appeal procedure to the metropolitan. The general thrust of the measure was to make it much harder for incumbents to hire curates on the cheap. In other words, it advanced Agar's broader aim of a resident clergy of good social class. It became law as *40 George III, cap. 27*.

Granted the pains Agar took over the Curates' Act, it was quite unfair of D'Alton to accuse him of 'starving ... the curates of Dublin ... on £50 per annum', and then, in 1807, of showing 'a too long deferred regard for the working clergy [by directing] that the incumbents of the diocese should for the future pay to their curates £75 per annum, instead of [the] £50 hitherto allowed.'[88] Thanks to Agar, the £75 had been available as a maximum since 1800; and his 'acts' as archbishop of Dublin show that £75 was nearly always the salary paid in the diocese between 1800 and 1807.[89] Moreover – although this may have been an exceptional rate of pay – the two curates of the wealthy and populous parish of St Ann's, Dublin, were each receiving £115 in the latter year.[90] Agar's act had been prompted by the British act of 1796; but Agar for the time being put the curates of the Church of Ireland on a better footing than their Church of England counterparts. For example, 'at the end of the century ..., 40 curates received stipends of £50 or over [in the diocese of Worcester, while] ... no fewer than 113 still existed on £30 to £50.'[91] The remuneration of Church of England curates was supposedly improved, after a good deal of parliamentary contention (see pp 478–9), in the period 1808–13, and Primate Stuart and other Irish churchmen felt

85 Ibid. 86 Agar to Hon. and Rev. Percy Jocelyn, 21 Apr. 1800, 21 M 57/B35/9; *40 George III, cap. 27, sec. 2.* 87 Letters of 7 and 29 May 1800, 21 M 57/B35/11–12. 88 D'Alton, *Archbishops of Dublin*, pp 350–51. 89 Agar's 'acts', 1801–9, 21 M 57/B21a. 90 Kennedy, 'Dublin and Glendalough', p. 233. 91 Evans, *The contentious tithe*, p. 9.

aggrieved that the new Church of England legislation did not extend to the Church of Ireland.[92] However, 'as late as 1830, more than a third of all curates [of the Church of England] received less than £60 per living.'[93]

AGAR'S CONTRIBUTION TO OTHER ASPECTS OF THE UNION

An already-mentioned letter of 20 March from Clare to Agar shows that Agar was one of the managers of the Union proposals and other government business in the House of Lords.[94] Further evidence of his role in this regard is to be found in the quantity of drafts for Union resolutions and articles, many of them financial and commercial and most of them in the handwriting of the long-suffering Lady Somerton, which are to be found among his papers.[95] Another, more entertaining survival in her handwriting is a description given in a letter to her cousin, Lord Macartney, of the chairing of the '*amiable idol*', the anti-Unionist Henry Grattan, 'in his sedan chair by a most tumultuous and riotous [Dublin] mob, ...[who] proceeded to a Mr McClelland's (a northern member, I believe [James McClelland, MP for Randalstown, Co. Antrim]) whom they knew was a Unionist, and paraded before his house for a long time menacing and abusing and calling upon him to appear, ... and frightening all the poor females of the family into fits, etc., etc.'[96]

In spite of the formidable parliamentary performances of which he was capable, Agar – though he is mentioned – is not particularly singled out by Cornwallis in his reports to Portland on the course of debates in the Lords and the prodigies performed by government spokesmen there.[97] This is possibly because he was as much a debater as a set-piece orator. Most of the oratorical power in favour of the Union resided in the House of Lords, and the government – uneasy, like all eighteenth-century governments, when numbers alone were on its side – published these speeches in newspapers and pamphlets as a counterweight to the effusions of the slick young lawyers in the House of Commons.[98] Clare's magnificent orations were intellectually the most powerful. But the one major speech made by Barry Yelverton, Lord Avonmore, was of special symbolic significance, because he had more solid claims than Grattan to have been the author of the constitution of 1782.[99] Avonmore's was therefore one of a number of speeches in the House of Lords published by the government in pamphlet form.[100] No speech of Agar's was used in this way. His contributions were reported in the newspapers but, as usual, this was on his own initiative.[101]

92 Spencer Perceval to Primate Stuart, 2 Apr. 1808, and O'Beirne to Stuart, 3 June 1813, Bedfordshire RO, WY 995/14 and 994/75. 93 Evans, *The contentious tithe*, p. 9. 94 Clare to Agar, 20 Mar. 1800, T/3719/C/34/8. 95 21 M 57/A46/19–34. 96 Lady Somerton to Earl and Countess Macartney, 5 Feb. 1800, Macartney papers, PRONI, D/572/8/48. 97 For example, Cornwallis to Portland, 11 Feb. 1800 (two letters, one 'official' and one 'private', of the same date), *Cornwallis correspondence*, iii, pp 184–6. 98 Carysfort to Grenville, 17 Feb. 1800, *HMC Dropmore Mss.*, vi. 134. 99 For an amusing comment on this, see Edward Cooke to Grenville, 24 Mar. 1800, *HMC Dropmore Mss.*, vi. 173. 100 Malcomson, 'Irish peerage and the Union', p. 308. 101 See,

Although the proceedings of the House of Lords were important mainly because of their propaganda value to the government, and although the outcome of divisions there was generally not in doubt, issues relating to the post-Union representation and status of the Irish peerage proved inflammable and threatened to produce an open revolt on the part of otherwise pliant supporters of government in the Upper House. There was a basic clash of interests between the resident or largely resident Irishmen in the Irish peerage, on the one hand, and the non-resident and/or non-Irish holders of Irish peerages. The former were concerned for the status of the Irish peerage relative to that of the peerages of England, Scotland, Great Britain and the forthcoming United Kingdom; in particular, they were interested in being elected as Irish representative peers to the post-Union House of Lords. The latter, generally speaking, valued their titles for social reasons but were indifferent to the status of the Irish peerage as a whole and looked to continuing membership of the House of Commons at Westminster.[102] Agar was on close terms with the 2nd Lord Arden, a lord of the admiralty and the elder brother of Spencer Perceval, the future prime minister. Arden was an anomaly – an absentee Irishman with an Irish peerage who was yet concerned for the status of his order. He also had a good amateur command of the intricacies of peerage law. To Agar he wrote in January 1800:

> I own I cannot help lamenting that it should be thought necessary to deviate in any respect from the precedent of the Scotch Union with regard to the peerage, except in the point of choosing the peers for life, which I think a great and obvious improvement. That Union declares the peers of Scotland to be peers of the United Kingdom and to have all the privileges of the peerage except sitting in the House of Lords and sitting on the trial of a peer ... . It has in my opinion been too much the fashion to think of the peers merely as members of an House of Parliament and not as a distinct order of men in the state, possessed of privileges and rights which belong to them whether there is any parliament in existence or not, and which it is inconsistent with the dignity and honour of the whole body to suffer any of their members to divest themselves of upon any consideration whatever of private interest or advantage ... . Suppose a peer chooses to divest himself of the privileges of peerage in order to get into the H. of Commons, what is to become of his wife? Is she to ... be suffered to retain hers, which she holds in right of him?[103]

This last was actually a very good question, to which no answer was ever provided.

Among Agar's papers is a very rough, autograph draft of article iv, the article relating to the rights and privileges of the peerage. It embodies, as does the article iv which became law, Arden's point that the Irish peers should explicitly be called peers

for example, *Faulkner's Dublin Journal*, 13 Feb. 1800, recording (in the precise words of a draft in Agar's handwriting) the substance of a speech he made on 10 Feb., 21 M 57/A47/1. **102** Malcomson, 'Irish peerage and the Union', pp 296 and 309.   **103** Arden to Agar, 11 Jan. 1800,

of the United Kingdom, enjoying all the privileges of peerage except an hereditary right to sit in the House of Lords and on trials of fellow-peers. The precise paternity of parts of a complicated piece of legislation is notoriously difficult to establish, and normally not worth the effort; but it is tempting to regard this amendment as the result of Arden's representations to Agar. The same may be true of another amendment. Agar's draft provides that the peers of Ireland will be eligible for election to the House of Commons for any constituency (Irish constituencies, by implication, included):[104] Arden was strongly opposed to this principle, as his letter of January 1800 made plain, and in another letter to Agar of early March he particularly pressed the impropriety of allowing Irish peers to represent Irish constituencies.[105] Arden's was not an isolated voice on this issue, so it is much less clear than in the other instance that Arden, through Agar, brought about a modification of article iv. By whatever instrumentality, the article was amended and Irish peers made ineligible to represent Irish constituencies. This still left them eligible to represent constituencies elsewhere in the new United Kingdom; and in a debate in the Irish House of Lords on 12 June, the 2nd earl of Glandore, a prominent supporter of the Union in matters unconnected with article iv, 'said that the provision of the bill which rendered the peers of Ireland capable of being elected members of the House of Commons of the United Parliament he could not concur in, considering it as he did a degradation of the peerage and an anomaly in the constitution.' Agar, perhaps indoctrinated by Arden, did not attempt to defend the constitutional propriety of the clause, but justified it on pragmatic, patriotic grounds: 'The clause in question did not compel any Noble Peer to accept of a seat in the Commons, but by giving the option of becoming a candidate, bestowed a most valuable privilege on the individual who was qualified in point of property to accept it, and extended in a degree the proportion of influence which Ireland would enjoy in the Imperial Legislature.'[106]

The Irish peers were especially vehement in their opposition to the provision of article iv that the crown should retain the right, after the passing of the Act of Union, to create new Irish peerages, in defiance of the precedent set by the Scottish Union of 1707. Arden voiced the general sentiment when he pointed out that 'in consequence of the terms of Union with Scotland, the peerages of that country drop and become extinct, [and] those that remain are every day growing more valuable and important to their possessors.'[107] The argument over this issue, to which an inordinate degree of importance attached, went on behind the scenes rather than on the floor of the House of Lords; and behind-the-scenes management and negotiation were Agar's *forte*. Moreover, his unique position as both a temporal and a spiritual peer of Ireland was of tactical value to the Castle, because 'my lords, the bishops, seem to affect

21 M 57/A46/3.   **104** Rough draft of article iv in Agar's handwriting, [mid-Jan. to early Mar. 1800], 21 M 57/A46/37.   **105** Arden to Agar, 3 Mar. 1800, 21 M 57/A46/16.   **106** *Faulkner's Dublin Journal*, 14 June 1800, reporting a debate in the House of Lords on 12 June about the post-Union privileges of the Irish peerage.   **107** Arden to Agar, 11 Jan. 1800, 21 M 57/A46/3. For the contrary argument – that the peerage of a kingdom needed to be relevant rather than rare – see Malcomson, 'Irish peerage and the Union', pp 320 and 322–4.

squeamishness as to voting upon that point.'[108] Together with Clonmell's successor as chief justice of the king's bench, Arthur Wolfe, Lord Kilwarden, Agar strongly represented to the Irish government the almost unanimous hostility of the resident Irish peers to the proposal that the crown should retain the right to create Irish peerages.[109] The British government clung stubbornly to this exercise of the prerogative, because of the utility of Irish peerages as rewards for English political services – one of a number of examples of the double standards and hypocrisy which were prevalent at the time of the Union, when British ministers and politicians were particularly prone to complain of the jobbery of the Irish. In the end, the British government gave way,[110] and a compromise was reached. The crown was to retain the right to create one new Irish peerage for every three existing peerages which became extinct, or, if the total number of Irish peerages fell below the number in existence in 1800, until the 1800 number had again been reached. The right to make promotions in the Irish peerage was also retained and was not restricted in any way. It was to be exercised in 1806 to promote Agar to the earldom of Normanton.

A 'NEGLIGENT' AND NOMINAL UNION OF THE CHURCHES

Agar's contribution to article iv, like the rest of his contributions to the Act of Union, came late and in reaction to external events and pressures: only when the Union was at its 'blueprint' stage, between June and approximately December 1798, had there been scope for constructive initiative, and at that stage Agar's 'opinion' had not been 'called for by those who decide on such matters' (p. 530). The planning at the blueprint stage had not been much informed by local knowledge or by inside information about the likely responses of members of the Irish parliament; so belated tinkering like Agar's with the provisions relating to the Church, or like Arden's with those relating to the peerage, were the rule rather than the exception. The result was in many particulars a mess. The drafting of article iv, for which Agar must bear some share of responsibility, was particularly hand-to-mouth. In spite of eighteenth-century obsessiveness on the subject of precedence, it rather looks as if 'the precedency of the bishops' (i.e. in what order the archbishops and bishops of the Church of Ireland were to come in relation to those of the Church of England) was forgotten about until Euseby Cleaver raised the matter, directly or indirectly, with Pitt.[111] The main provisions of article iv, which related to the hereditary peerage, were vitiated by ignorance of peerage law – presumably because the peerage purists were opposed to the principle of post-Union creations and promotions and so were not directly consulted. A later expert, G.E. Cockayne, quipped that the parts of article iv relating to vacancies and

108 Cooke to Grenville, 15 Mar. 1800, *HMC Dropmore Mss.*, vi. 163.   109 Cornwallis to Portland, 25 Jan. and 10 Mar. 1800, and Portland to Cornwallis, 15 Mar. 1800, *Cornwallis correspondence*, iii, pp 171–2, 208–9 and 213–14. Portland in his reply refers to 'the great and highly respectable authority of Lord Kilwarden', but for some reason, or perhaps by mistake, does not mention Agar.   110 *Cornwallis correspondence*, iii. 209; Portland to Cornwallis, 7 Apr. 1800, *ibid.*, 226.   111 Pitt to Grenville, 8 Apr. 1800, *HMC Dropmore Mss.*, vi. 192.

promotions looked as if they had been drafted by the war office, not by an office of arms.[112] More seriously, the representative peerage arrangements were so opaquely expressed that in the period post-1920 the Irish peers were prematurely deprived of the rights intended for them under article viii.[113]

Other symptoms of 'strangely imperfect' drafting[114] manifested themselves much sooner. A very experienced Irish treasury official confessed in 1810 to ex-Speaker Foster, now back in office as chancellor of the Irish exchequer at Westminster, his 'total incapacity' to base calculations on the clause of article vii relating to Ireland's proportion of the contribution and debt of the United Kingdom. Foster, too, could form 'no satisfactory conception of the meaning of the clause. I have often enquired from those who were concerned in drawing it, and I never could find out that they had any.'[115] Part of article vi was also pronounced 'almost wholly unintelligible' in 1811.[116] As the to-ings and fro-ings over convocation reveal, there was an awareness at the time that blunders were being made. Brodrick wrote to Midleton in May 1800: 'Our articles are now gone over to you, and I trust that care will be taken not to introduce into them any *English bulls*, which would of course be charged on Ireland.'[117]

> Article [v] was more significant for what it omitted than for what it included. The Church of Ireland became part of the United Church of England and Ireland in name but in little else. The change was more verbal than structural, for the Irish Church remained intact and distinct as an administrative system. The hierarchies and clergy of the two Churches were not amalgamated. Only in matters of religious formularies did a merger occur ... . One of the most striking characteristics of the Union was the almost negligent ease with which ecclesiastical matters were decided. The union of the two Churches was carried out by enactment of the British and the Irish parliaments, without the summoning of a convocation or synod of either Church.[118]

In mid-March 1800, a commentator on the parliamentary scene reported: 'We went through, yesterday, the article respecting the Church, and the last article, almost without observation. The opposition did not attend.' The result was a union of the Churches which was indeed 'more verbal than structural.' O'Beirne had argued that 'Church and State are, in our ideas inseparable and, when the State becomes in all parts one, the Church should be but one.' But what he had feared actually came to pass: the Church of Ireland remained 'separate and distinct from the Church of England, and resting upon other laws and depending upon other jurisdictions.'[119]

112 Malcomson, 'Irish peerage and the Union', pp 319–20. 113 Ibid., pp 289–90 and 324–6. 114 Buckingham to Grenville, 23 Mar. 1800, *HMC Dropmore Mss.*, vi. 172. 115 McCavery, 'Finance and politics in Ireland, 1801–17', p. 168. 116 Ibid., pp 175–6. 117 Brodrick to Midleton, 9 May 1800, Ms. 1248, vol. 17, f. 123. 118 Akenson, *Church of Ireland*, pp 72–3 and 344. O'Beirne had urged: 'An assembly of the bishops, or a convocation, appears to be necessary' – O'Beirne to Castlereagh, 18 Nov. 1799, *Castlereagh correspondence*, iii. 8. 119 O'Beirne to Castlereagh, 18 Nov. 1799, loc. cit.

While the new prayer book issued post-1800 proclaimed the existence of a United Church,[120] the statute book did not. Between the Union and Disestablishment, it is almost impossible to find a piece of legislation relating to both parts of a Church whose 'discipline and government' were supposed to be the same; while on at least one important matter – the reduction of pluralities – separate legislation for the Church of Ireland was blocked because of the embarrassing precedent it would set for the Church of England (see p. 276).[121] Immediately after the Union, the new chief secretary, Charles Abbot (a stickler for rules), was surprised to find that qualifications and procedures for ordination in the two Churches were different.[122] So were their canons. In July 1803, Abbot's perplexed successor, William Wickham, who was trying to find out 'whether the ordinary has ... full power to appoint churchwardens where the parish has neglected to choose them at the appointed time', turned for advice to Agar, and also asked him 'whether the canons of the Irish Church are printed, and in what shape, and where I am likely to procure them.'[123]

On 1 March 1800, the King had commended to Pitt an English plan for uniting the Churches of England and of Ireland, 'which seems to me to obviate all the difficulties ... and to require much less to be done than ... any of the other plans suggested'[124] – presumably an allusion to O'Beirne's and Agar's rival proposals. The great and perhaps sole justification for article v was that it required 'much less' and indeed next-to-nothing 'to be done.' Bishop Watson made a virtue of this. He acknowledged the existence of 'a little difference' between the two Churches 'in doctrine, discipline and worship', but did not see 'the utility of aiming at a perfect coincidence in them' and dreaded 'the discussion of matters ... likely to produce religious dissensions between the two kingdoms. ... I fear some dissatisfaction may arise in the hearts of the bishops and clergy of Ireland, if we do not leave their Church entirely to their own management and as much as possible in the precise state in which it now stands.'[125] Actually, this was the object of Agar's rejected proposals, most of which Watson had disliked; but Agar would have defined 'the precise state in which' the Church of Ireland then stood, and also how it was to interact for the future with the Church of England (via convocation and an exclusively archiepiscopal representation in the Lords).

As things worked out in practice after the Union, it was difficult, even when the one Irish archbishop (plus Agar) and three bishops

> were in London, ... to get serious attention paid to Irish business. ... [In 1805, Primate Stuart] complained to Brodrick that 'they [the ministers] seem to think that everything in Ireland will settle of itself, without any interposition on their part', and the members of the House of Lords seemed to regard the union of

---

120 I am grateful for this point to Dr Kenneth Milne.   121 Spencer Perceval to Primate Stuart, 4 June 1810, Bedfordshire RO, WY 995/22.   122 Abbot to Stuart, 4 May 1801, and Cleaver to Stuart, 6 Apr. 1804, WY 993/2 and 994/30.   123 William Wickham to Agar, 6 July 1803, T/3719/C/37/11; Agar to Wickham, 7 July 1803, Wickham papers, PRONI, T/2627/5/S/25. 124 *Later correspondence of George III*. iii, 323.   125 Watson to Moore, 5 Mar. 1800, *Anecdotes of Watson*, pp 328–30.

the two Churches as nominal, not real, consisting 'merely in a free and friendly intercourse between the Irish and the English bishops.'[126]

Ministers, for their part, blamed the lack of serious attention to Irish ecclesiastical business on the Irish bishops. In February 1803, Stuart was described as a 'defaulter' on his parliamentary duty when important measures affecting both Churches were under discussion. Chief Secretary Wickham hoped 'that my lords, the archbishops and bishops, are not all useless', and that 'our good friend', Agar, would be able to 'stimulate them to exertion.'[127] Stuart certainly put board of first fruits business before his parliamentary business, and wrote to Brodrick (whose priorities were similar): 'I lament that this happens to be your year of attendance on parliament.'[128] This was an unfortunate attitude, and might have been corrected if Agar's proposal for greater continuity in the episcopal representation at Westminster had been adopted.

'THE VACANT PRIMACY'

The introduction of Stuart's name anticipates the outcome of the lengthy negotiations and delays which took place over who was to be appointed primate in 1800. These went on from January to July – indeed to October – and so formed the essential background to Agar's belated effort to effect improvements in the position of the post-Union Church of Ireland. In July 1799, Cornwallis had held out to Agar, 'when we came to an agreement respecting the Union', the probability of his succeeding on a vacancy to the archbishopric of Dublin. But the first vacancy unexpectedly occurred, not at Dublin but at Armagh, following the death of Primate Newcome on 11 January 1800. Because of this, and of the delay in naming a new primate, Agar's bargaining position in negotiations with the government over the Union was weakened. Indeed, a cynic would suggest that the vacancy at Armagh had something to do with his 'acquiescence' in the matter of the tithe of agistment. As time passed, and still Agar was not appointed, his ability to dominate the Irish bishops was also reduced – a contributory factor in his lack of success at the meeting of bishops in early March. It is actually to his credit that he continued to make a nuisance of himself to the government, and to make himself unpopular with the bishops, when he had every interested motive for self-ingratiation.

Back in 1796, in one of her spirited letters about the superior attractions of the archbishopric of Cashel over those of the archbishopric of Dublin, Lady Somerton had written: 'Some years hence I should not dislike to go a further journey [to Armagh], when matters are *quiet* and we have a good, well established *peace*, when *Orange* and all other Boys are unheard-of, etc.'[129] None of these conditions had yet

126 Milne, 'Principle or pragmatism', pp 189–90, quoting from NLI, Ms. 8869. 127 Wickham to Redesdale, 18 Feb. 1803, *Irish official papers*, ii. 335; Brodrick to Midleton, 11 Apr. 1803, Ms. 1248, vol. 18, ff. 67–8. 128 Stuart to Brodrick, 14 Mar. 1802, Midleton papers, NLI, Ms. 8869/1. 129 Lady Somerton to Agar, 13 Oct. 1796, T/3719/C/30/34.

been fulfilled and, apart from the '*peace*', were never likely to be. But this did not deter Agar from making a determined pitch for the primacy in 1800. A week after Newcome's death, Lord Mendip wrote: 'I had early intelligence of *the event* and I lost no time, but laid in immediate pretensions [presumably with Portland]. I also writt [*sic*] *immediately* to Mr Pitt. ... Be assured that nothing within the compass of my means, such as they are, shall be wanting to promote your success.'[130] By this stage, there is something comical about a retired politician of eighty-seven exerting his influence on behalf of a nephew of sixty-five who was now far more important politically than he was. Meanwhile, Cornwallis, too, had written to Portland about Agar's pretensions to succeed to the primacy. There was now no echo of Cornwallis' previous satirical tone but, on the contrary, a scarcely qualified recommendation of Agar:

> If the King should think proper to give the primacy in the line of Irish bishops, I do not think that he can, without much inconvenience, pass over the claims of the Archbishop of Cashel, nor do I know any other candidate whose merits would justify such a supersession; and it is my duty to add that his Grace of late has conducted himself in a manner to give him strong political claims for the support of this government.[131]

He then went on to recommend Euseby Cleaver, should the King decide to adhere to the long-established practice of conferring the primacy on an Englishman.

Cleaver would have been an unpopular and objectionable choice. On the eve of the rebellion in Co. Wexford, his diocese boasted a high proportion of resident clergy and appears to have been in a good state of discipline – no small tribute to Cleaver, who had been bishop since 1789.[132] But his subsequent behaviour constituted a complete disqualification from the senior position in the Irish Church – his flight to Wales in what, by his own previous admission, 'look[ed] like panic', his mercenary lobbying for compensation for his (much inflated) losses in the rebellion, his unsuccessful attempts to get himself shifted to the English bench, and his incessant moaning. '[Ireland] is so comfortless a country to live in' he wailed in November 1798, 'that I find it very difficult to reconcile my mind to it. In point of inhabitants, it is worse than Botany Bay for a loyalist.'[133]

In view of the importance of the primacy, it was inevitable that a number of unofficial communications to the British government – in addition to the official one from Cornwallis – would be made. One came immediately from Agar's 'friend', Clare, who had a particular aversion to Cleaver:

> I wish the Archbishop of Canterbury only to enquire into his character and dispositions, and if he does not find both a very striking contrast to his own, let

---

130 Mendip to Agar, 18 Jan. 1800, T/3719/C/34/3.   131 Cornwallis to Portland, 13 Jan. 1800, *Cornwallis correspondence*, iii, pp 160–1.   132 Comerford, 'Church of Ireland clergy and 1798', pp 223–30.   133 Cleaver to Egremont, 14 Dec. 1797 and 24 July and 24 Nov. 1798, PHA/57/5, 10 and 12.

him be at the head of our Church. He is the most intemperate, overbearing priest I have ever met with, and in managing the estate of his see, avows that he acts solely upon a table of calculation which he bought for half a crown. ... It is of the last importance to us to have a *meek* and *firm* man, who would exert himself with persevering moderation to correct the abuses which prevail in our Church. Placed at the head of it, he ought not to be a politician nor a rapacious man; either vice will induce him to acts of very serious and extensive public mischief.[134]

Interestingly, Cleaver was not long in finding out about these representations. 'I am sorry to say' he later complained 'that on the vacancy of the primacy some people thought it worth their while to endeavour to injure my character as a landlord. I was aware of it, and met the report where it might be of importance.'[135] His informant was undoubtedly his old patron, Buckingham. Buckingham rained letters about Irish affairs on his brother, Grenville, and 'on the vacancy of the primacy' was pro-Cleaver, as well as – predictably – anti-Agar.

> I do earnestly put it to your duty and conscience to resist Archbishop Agar's success; and I will fairly own that I think Archbishop Beresford [of Tuam] would (though not so objectionable on the score of his moral character or conduct) be an improper choice. As to the other Irish bishops [he meant Irishmen on the Irish bench], they are, I am persuaded, out of everybody's thoughts; and of the English on the Irish bench ..., you cannot look upon one of them ... . Euseby Cleaver ..., I verily believe, is very decidedly the most fit. But I very much wish it were possible to find an English bishop who would undertake it. ... Since writing this, I understand from another letter that the duke of Portland's Bishop O'Beirne talks confidently of succeeding. I do hope and trust that a nomination so very highly improper is impossible.[136]

O'Beirne's pretensions may explain his anxiety to belittle Agar in his long and much-quoted letter to Castlereagh. When first appointed a bishop in 1795, O'Beirne had turned to Agar for information about Agar's use of rural deans; and Mant records that 'O'Beirne, in a note on his first charge at Ossory [in 1796? observed that] ... "the

---

134 Clare to Auckland, 14 Jan. 1800, Sneyd papers, PRONI, T/3229/1/25. This was a characteristic attempt to exploit Auckland's connection with Archbishop Moore. Clare was not far wrong about Cleaver and 'the table of calculation', except that Cleaver used it, not so much in the management of his see estate (little of which would have been let for lives), but in the management of the Egremont estate in Clare and Limerick – Cleaver to Egremont, 6 Feb. [1798], (PHA/57/7). What had angered Clare was that Cleaver, as bishop of Ferns, had 'demanded' an 'exorbitant' fine from the governors of St Patrick's Hospital for the renewal of a see lease held by that charity.   135 Cleaver to Charles O'Hara, 17 Sep. [1800], O'Hara papers, PRONI, T/2812/18/20.   136 Buckingham to Grenville, 20 Jan. 1800, *HMC Dropmore Mss*, vi, pp 106–7. For a caricature featuring three contestants for the primacy, see fig. 21.

Church of Ireland is as much indebted [to Agar] as to any prelate of modern days" .'[137]
In 1801, with the issues of the Union and the primacy both out of the way, O'Beirne
called Agar 'one whose progress through the sees he has already filled has been
marked by improvements that will produce a lasting effect in them, and which I
should be most happy to be able to accomplish within my more limited sphere.'[138]

These plaudits contrast strikingly, not only with O'Beirne's strictures on Agar in
March, but also with the strictures of Buckingham and Clare in January. Buckingham's reference to Agar's 'moral character' and 'conduct' is perplexing. Apart from
the suspicion of youthful gallantries and the certainty of a spicy personal correspondence, Agar's character and conduct seem to have been unexceptionable from a moral
point of view, unless Buckingham had heard exaggerated accounts of the Henry Agar
affair or the much-misunderstood matter of the Cashel see leases. However, Buckingham's hatred of Agar had led him into gross untruthfulness in 1789 (see p. 168), so it
is needless to analyse further his allegations of January 1800. Clare's comments are
more telling. He does not mention Agar by name; but there can be no doubt that the
'meek' man he postulates is intended to be the antithesis of Agar, and that Agar is at
least one of the prelates whom he regards as 'rapacious.' Clare, of course, like
Buckingham, had his own agenda – he ardently desired to be the British government's
sole Irish adviser, and was jealous of Agar. However, rapacity, particularly in the matter
of the see lands, was a charge to which Agar was vulnerable. So, too, was the suspicion
of being a 'politician' in the pejorative sense of the term (see pp 167–9).

More significant than Buckingham's predictable vendetta with, and Clare's
predictable jealousy of, Agar, is Cornwallis' increasingly favourable opinion of him.
Cornwallis agonised greatly over the methods to which he was forced to have recourse
in order to carry the Union. His initial description of how Agar allowed his objections
to the Union to be overcome by promises or near-promises of a permanent place in
the representation of the Irish bishops in the House of Lords of the United Parliament and of promotion to the archbishopric of Dublin, is typical of his reaction to
Irish political morality or the lack of it. However, what is obvious is that over time
Cornwallis came to respect Agar's good qualities – his unswerving adherence to his
word, once given (in this instance his undertaking to support the Union), his force-
fulness and resourcefulness in debate, and his stubborn and at times inconvenient
defence of the post-Union interests of the Church of Ireland. Cornwallis could not
have failed to mark the contrast between the 'sheer mischief and mutiny of Lord
Clare', whom he had once called 'the most right-headed man in the country', in
ambushing and defeating the annual grant to Maynooth when it came before the
House of Lords in April 1799, and Agar's statesmanlike moderation over the tithe of
agistment a year later.[139] As a result of his altered opinion of Agar, Cornwallis actually
ended up a strong advocate for Agar's appointment as archbishop of Armagh. Nor

137 Agar's 'state' of the diocese of Cashel, 1779–1801, 21 M 57/B6/1; Mant, *Church of Ireland*, ii,
739.   138 O'Beirne to Agar, 9 Nov. 1801, T/3719/C/35/28.   139 Sir Robert Peel, 2nd Bt, to J.W.
Croker, 9 June 1845, printed in C.S. Parker (ed.), *Sir Robert Peel from his private papers* (3 vols.,
London, 1899), iii. 181; Geoghegan, *Union*, p. 28; Kavanaugh, *Lord Clare*, pp 358–63.

was his good opinion shaken when Agar, in late March, spirited up his entire political connection to lobby Cornwallis, while coyly staying away himself. The deputation comprised Lord Clifden, with his four

> Union votes, Lord Callan, who has two friends in the House of Commons, and Mr [John] Preston [soon to be created Lord Tara], member for Navan [and patron of one of its seats], all nearly related to the Archbishop of Cashel ... . The earnest wishes of these persons, from whom we have received such power- ful support in our arduous contest, added to the Archbishop's own merits in the cause, may perhaps induce his Majesty to think more favourably of his Grace's pretensions; and I must confess, after the kingdoms become united, I cannot see any objection to an Irish primate.[140]

This last point was unanswerable. Ironically, had O'Beirne's plan for bringing Armagh under the ultimate authority of Canterbury been adopted, any colourable 'objection to an Irish primate' would have been done away.

There was general agreement, even among Agar's enemies, that there were few credible competitors to him for the primacy. Grenville commented dryly that Primate Newcome's death was embarrassing 'from the difficulty of finding a good successor to him on either bench.'[141] Newcome's death was the most important event in the primacy of a 'poor man' who made so little impact that, according to one modern authority, it was Primate Robinson who died on 11 January 1800![142] For almost the last third of the eighteenth century, Agar had been the most talented and energetic of the archbishops and senior bishops (Chapters Five, Ten and Eleven). Indeed, for roughly the last twenty years of the eighteenth century, he had been primate in all but name. Ironically, his leadership was most in dispute when it was most needed – in January–July 1800. Writing with tongue in cheek to his brother at the beginning of April, Brodrick told him: 'You certainly have mistaken the bone of contention most likely to create bloodshed among ... [the bishops]. It is not the Union ... . No. The filling up of the vacant archbishopric is much more of a *pistol case.*'[143]

George III's irrational prejudice against Irish bishops generally, regardless of whether they had been born in England or Ireland, has been discussed (pp 484–6). So, it boded ill for Agar and his challengers on the Irish bench that the King now expressed particular concern about the filling of the primacy. Appointments in the Church, the army and the royal household often attracted his determined, personal attention. As far as the Church of England was concerned, 'Several of his letters to Lord North [prime minister, 1770–82] announce his intention to promote or translate bishops, in circumstances which seem to prove that he cannot have received any [ministerial] advice. ... He made an archbishop of Canterbury [Moore] in a ministerial

---

140 Cornwallis to Portland, 24 Mar. 1800, *Cornwallis correspondence*, iii, pp 217–18. 141 *Later correspondence of George III*, iii, 313n. 142 Akenson, *Church of Ireland*, p. 74. 143 Brodrick to Midleton, 2 Apr. 1800, Ms. 1248, vol. 17, f. 122.

interregnum [1783], and another against the advice of the younger Pitt [1805].'[144] The King's concern was for high personal character and also for orthodoxy on the Trinity. This latter consideration explains a number of his interventions.[145] For instance, 'When Pitt proposed the theologian, William Paley, for a bishopric, the King ... refused, muttering "Not orthodox, not orthodox".'[146] The King's influence, it must be acknowledged, was not necessarily exercised for the best: Bishop Watson damned Archbishop Moore with faint praise when he said that Moore filled the English primacy 'not eminently, but inculpably'; and a more recent verdict is that he was 'in nowise remarkable'.[147] In the Church of Ireland, the crown possessed in theory the sole right of nomination to vacant bishoprics and deaneries, although in practice 'the monarch himself did not dabble often in Irish ecclesiastical affairs.'[148] George II had dabbled unsuccessfully in 1745 by objecting to Lord Chesterfield's recommendation of the latter's chaplain, Richard Chenevix, for the bishopric of Waterford: the King asked him to 'look out for another bishop', and Chesterfield impertinently told the King to 'look for another lord lieutenant'![149] One of George III's rare interventions at episcopal level had been made in 1795, when he blocked the promotion of Dean Warburton (p. 507). However, there was always the strong possibility that the primacy would be disposed of by 'the special appointment of my sovereign' (as Bishop Hotham put it, hopefully, c.1785).[150] George III had been closely involved in its disposal in 1764–5 (p. 441), had been involved, though less closely, in 1794–5 (p. 470), and could be expected to regard an appointment which would inaugurate and characterise the Union as a matter for his personal determination.

Accordingly, he soon made it clear that, when it came to finding a successor to Newcome, he was not disposed to heed the views of either the Irish or the British government. By 1 March, he had proposed to Pitt the translation to Armagh of a bishop from the English bench, and on that date furnished himself with a fairly distant precedent, that of Primate Boulter, who had been translated from the bishopric of Bristol in 1724.[151] Why he thought this necessary, is unclear: bishops on the English bench had been offered, and had declined, the primacy in 1765 and again in 1794. For a time, it looked as if the same thing was going to happen in 1800. The progress of George III's negotiations was later described as follows to Agar:

> It would seem that they had decided (erroneously in my opinion) that the person should be appointed from this bench; but those who wanted to go, they did not like to send, and those they wished to send, did not like to go. Jackson of Christ Church, Sutton of Norwich and Randolph of Oxford and ... [Stuart of St David's] all refused it at the first blush, but I believe it was more strongly pressed on the latter than the others. ... [It] was never offered to either Watson

---

144 Pares, *George III and the politicians*, p. 144.   145 Ditchfield, 'Ecclesiastical policy under Lord North', p. 230.   146 Walsh and Taylor, 'The Church and Anglicanism', p. 40.   147 *Anecdotes of Watson*, p. 137; Cowper, *Deans of Canterbury*, p. 186.   148 Akenson, *Church of Ireland*, p. 11.   149 *The remains of Mrs Richard Trench*, p. 2.   150 Hotham to Hotham Thompson, 13 June [c.1785], T/3429/2/12.   151 The King to Pitt, [1 March 1800], *Later correspondence of George III*, iii. 323.

or Horsley, but it is said that they offered themselves for it, the first because he supposed himself acceptable to the dissenters, and the other because he was popular among the papists.[152]

In other words, the primacy went 'literally a-begging' round the English bishops.[153]

The irrepressible Buckingham now began to hope 'that it will end in Euseby Cleaver. ... It is my full persuasion that there is not an Irish bishop fit for it except him; nor do I believe that you are better provided from the English bench, at least of [*sic*] those that will accept it.'[154] At this point, Cleaver's own expectations soared, inflated by a previous assurance from Buckingham that 'the King, who had a very indifferent opinion of many members of our bench, ... had repeatedly signified to him his approbation of me.'[155] Though he later claimed that, 'whatever recommendations of me have taken place, ... none of them were at my instance',[156] Cleaver now tried to improve his chances of the primacy by writing a very artful letter to Egremont. In this he piously reported that he had instructed the clergy of Ferns and Leighlin to preach forgiveness of injuries, but not until 'political power shall be forever removed from the reach of the Roman catholics [by the Union].' He also implied that he had taken the lead 'in yielding the tithe [of] agistment', which he described as doing 'a proper thing in a handsome manner.' This letter looks as if it was intended to reach the King. Egremont certainly passed it to Pitt, citing it as an augury of the good effects to be expected from the Union, and proclaiming Cleaver to be 'a man who has ever been thought ... a proper person to succeed to the primacy of Ireland.'[157] Egremont and Cleaver deceived themselves. A few years later, Cornwallis' successor as lord lieutenant, Lord Hardwicke, described Cleaver as 'a very jobbing fellow, though an English bishop.'[158] It looks as if Hardwicke had been warned against Cleaver by the King.

George III had already made up his mind that the new primate should be the Hon. William Stuart, bishop of St David's. As a canon of Windsor since 1793, Stuart was well known to the King, and he was also the fifth son of the King's youthful mentor and early favourite, Lord Bute. (Ironically, this was the same Lord Bute whose influence had obtained for Agar the deanery of Kilmore in 1765.) Stuart's other qualifications for such a high office were less obvious. The five other bishops on the English bench who had been mentioned as possible primates were all men of letters

---

152 Macartney to Agar, 9 Aug. 1800, 21 M 57/A46/47. The English clerics mentioned by Macartney were: Cyril Jackson, dean of Christ Church (1783–1809), with whom Agar corresponded about the admission of Agar's sons; Charles Manners Sutton, bishop of Norwich (1792–1805) and archbishop of Canterbury (1805–28); John Randolph, bishop of Oxford (1799–1807), of Bangor (1807–9) and of London (1809–13); William Stuart, bishop of St David's (1794–1800), and archbishop of Armagh (1800–22); Richard Watson, bishop of Llandaff (1782–1816); and Samuel Horsley, bishop of Rochester (1793–1802) and of St Asaph (1802–6). 153 *Later correspondence of George III*, iii. 378n. 154 Buckingham to Grenville, 27 Mar. 1800, *HMC Dropmore Mss.*, vi, pp 182–3. 155 Cleaver to Egremont, 8 May and 24 Dec. [1798], PHA/57/7A and 13. 156 Cleaver to Charles O'Hara, 17 Sep. and 25 Nov. [1800], T/2812/18/20 and 22. 157 Egremont to Pitt, 22 May 1800, enclosing Cleaver to Egremont, 9 May 1800, Pitt/Pretyman papers, PRONI, T/3319/75–6. 158 Hardwicke to Hon. Charles Yorke, 13 Aug. 1803, *The viceroy's post-bag*, p. 124.

and of intellect: compared to them, Stuart was a nondescript. Dr Johnson, who had met him in 1783, described him as 'being, with the advantages of high birth, learning, travel and elegant manners, an exemplary parish priest in every respect.' Even Brodrick, later his closest ally in the Church of Ireland, was less than effusive in his praise: 'He seems to me to be of a character exactly suited to his station [as primate], firm, moderate and decisive, with a very good, plain understanding, very painstaking, and very anxious to place all matters under his guidance or influence on a proper footing.'[159] The *D.N.B.* notes his 'respectable accomplishments and character', but dismisses him as 'a common type of ecclesiastic and nothing more.'[160] A more recent authority concludes: 'He was in fact a worthy, if undistinguished, cleric, [whose] good behaviour and good connections [had] led to his appointment as bishop of St David's ... in 1793.'[161] These verdicts may be harsh; but, plainly, he was no intellectual match for Agar. Nor would he have found favour with George III if he had been.

Meanwhile, rumours had reached Cornwallis and 'others in this country [Ireland]' that the primacy had been 'offered to persons in England.' Cornwallis was indignant at not being kept officially informed about what was going on on the other side of the water, and as he was on bad terms with Portland anyway, was inclined to blame the latter. So, on 11 March, he wrote to Portland (who, for once, was not to blame), in terms reminiscent of those used by Agar to Primate Robinson:

> Your Grace has not taken the smallest notice, in any of your letters to me, of the vacant primacy ... . I hope there is no foundation for these reports, as I think it would have a very bad effect at this time to send a stranger to supersede the whole bench of bishops and I should likewise be much embarrassed by the stop that would be put to the succession amongst the Irish clergy at this critical period, when I am beyond measure pressed for ecclesiastical preferment. The Archbishop of Cashel's conduct of late has, as I before observed to your Grace, been unexceptionable; but if it should be thought improper to appoint an Irishman, and especially a political Irishman, to that high station, a more respectable candidate could not easily be found than the Bishop of Ferns. There are likewise other respectable prelates on the Irish bench, and I trust that his Majesty will not find himself under the necessity of looking to any other quarter on the present occasion.[162]

In spite of this strong representation, the King by 16 July had offered the primacy to Stuart. Stuart replied diffidently on that date urging 'that my infirm state of health renders me little fitted for an office which requires unimpaired vigour both of body and mind [possibly a reference to Robinson]. The humid climate of Ireland would probably further enfeeble a very weak constitution, and (were my life to be protracted

---

159 Brodrick to Midleton, 8 Nov. 1801, Ms. 1248, vol. 18, ff. 38–9.   160 Quoted in *The viceroy's post-bag*, p. 98.   161 W.A. Maguire (ed.), *Up in arms: the 1798 Rebellion in Ireland: a bicentenary exhibition ... at the Ulster Museum, Belfast ...* (Belfast, 1998), p. 27.   162 *Cornwallis correspondence*, iii, pp 209–10.

for some years) the great expense of taking possession of Armagh [i.e. of the palace] would utterly ruin my children.' The King took this for a 'yes'! Like Stuart, he had never been to Ireland, but he hastened to assure him that, 'though the Irish climate is certainly damp, it is uncommonly mild and therefore not void of real merit.' (This is a rare instance of the weather being held out as an inducement to anyone to go to Ireland!) He also urged Stuart to think of 'the advantages that must arise to the cause of religion and virtue in Ireland by his [Stuart's] promotion to the vacant primacy of that part of the British Empire.'

These arguments persuaded Stuart to make what he told the King was a 'cheerful submission' to the royal commands.[163] Lord Hobart, who as Major Robert Hobart had been chief secretary, 1789–93, thought that Stuart had all along been playing hard to get, as he amusingly reported to Auckland, who was his father-in-law:

> The *Primate of Ireland* has this moment left me, having brought his Majesty's mandate in his hand ... . The Primate could not conceal a smile, which accompanied all his expressions of regret at the heavy task which had been imposed upon him. ... In short, he had the appearance of a man (or perhaps of a woman) who ... was all joy upon the occasion, but who, having set out with the *nolo episcopari*, was determined to play the game through.[164]

Agar was perhaps better-informed about Stuart's real feelings. By an extraordinary coincidence, Agar's friend and connection, Macartney, was married to Stuart's sister; and Macartney took Stuart's *nolo episcopari* more seriously. In a letter to Agar written three weeks later (and tending to confirm the view that Stuart was 'a common type of ecclesiastic and nothing more'), Macartney reported:

> I have seen our new Primate but once since his call to that dignity, which he does not seem yet perfectly reconciled to. ... He has many objections [to it], and considering his age [Stuart was forty-five which was surely the optimum age for such an assignment], connections, pretensions, etc., I do not at all wonder that he would have preferred taking his chance here for some of the good things, to a distant settlement in a country not likely to be a pleasant residence to him at any time, much less at present, and attended with an immoderate expense, which can't but be very inconvenient to him.[165]

In late November, when Stuart at last set out for Ireland, Cleaver surmised 'that he cast a longing eye at Bangor as he passed, which I believe was within his reach if he had made application for it.' 'The situation [of primate]' wrote Cleaver to another correspondent 'is arduous and ... full of solicitude.'[166]

163 Stuart to the King, [16 July 1800], the King to Pitt, [17 July 1800], the King to Stuart, [18 July 1800], and Stuart to the King [18? July 1800], *Later correspondence of George III*, iii, pp 377–8.
164 Hobart to Auckland, [18 July 1800], *Auckland correspondence*, iv, pp 109–10.   165 Macartney to Agar, 9 Aug. 1800, 21 M 57/A46/47.   166 Cleaver to Egremont, 1 Dec. 1800, PHA/57/33, and to

It may actually have been small comfort to Agar to learn from Macartney, and no doubt from others, that his successful competitor was reluctant to accept that which would have been highly acceptable to Agar. His friend, Lord Shannon, was more forthright and direct in his commiseration. Agar's disappointment of the primacy, he wrote, was 'an event in which I felt myself to be deeply interested, both on the score of personal friendship and regard, and the anxiety which every good protestant [i.e. anti-Emancipationist] must *at this time* feel for the interest of the Established Church and a wish to see it under that superintendence where its true interests are best understood.'[167] Cornwallis' reaction at the time is unrecorded. But later, after Agar's translation to Dublin at the end of 1801, he wrote: 'I can take no merit to myself for a promotion to which your Grace in every sense was so eminently and so justly entitled.'[168] By contrast, Lords Clare and Auckland exulted in Agar's (and Cleaver's) discomfiture:

> I do most sincerely believe [wrote Clare to Auckland on 24 July] that the King is one of the most right-headed men in his own dominions, and in this instance he has certainly evinced it strongly in not yielding to the recommendation of Dr Cleaver ... . I find they have softened our little friend Cashel, and sure I am he will take care that he has full equivalents for his acquiescence in the promotion of any other man. What a blessing it is that we have succeeded so well in abolishing that system of universal jobbing and cabal to which every government in this country has been so long forced to bend, and certainly there is no more perfect master of the art than the aforesaid little prelate.[169]

Clare must have been referring to Agar's forthcoming election as an Irish representative peer. But he was, clearly, unaware that this derived from a year-old promise made by Cornwallis and was not a 'softening' of Agar for his disappointment over the primacy. The 'full equivalents for his acquiescence in the promotion of any other man' which Clare implies that Agar had received before, must have been the barony of Somerton, conferred on him in 1795 just after the promotion of Newcome. More treacherous than Clare's words was Auckland's action in passing this letter to the King – which he must have done, as it is today in the Royal Archives.[170] The King had also asked Auckland to write to Clare urging him to smooth Stuart's path after the latter's arrival in Ireland.[171]

O'Hara, 25 Nov. [1800], T/2812/18/22.   **167** Shannon to Agar, 26 July 1800, T/3719/C/34/30. **168** Cornwallis to Agar, 19 Jan. 1802, T/3719/C/36/5.   **169** Clare to Auckland, 24 July 1800, *Later correspondence of George III*, iii, pp 380–81.   **170** The friendships of politicians are notoriously febrile. But over the years Auckland had involved Agar in all the happinesses and sadnesses of his huge family, and can only be described as a personal as well as political friend. The treachery of this unpleasant careerist to Agar was therefore on a par with his treachery to Pitt (see Geoghegan, *Union*, pp 156–9), and unlike the latter was unprovoked, except that Auckland may have been piqued that Agar had not succumbed to his clumsy attempts at seduction in the second half of 1798. **171** Hobart to Auckland, [18? July 1800], *Auckland correspondence*, iv. 109.

In the event, Stuart's appointment was delayed from mid-July to mid-October. This was not a deliberate delay. Cornwallis had urged strongly that the appointment be deferred until 'after the completion of the Union', either from a machiavellian wish to see the Union safely carried before Archbishops Agar and Beresford were disobliged, or in the hope that by spinning things out, he might yet secure the primacy for Agar or at least for some bishop of the Church of Ireland. However, by *c.*25 July Agar knew that he had been passed over. This was because news of Stuart's appointment had transpired through a 'misunderstanding' in Portland's 'department', the home office.[172] Other things were also going on in Portland's department. Portland, who was later described by a ministerial colleague as having 'a most insatiable love of patronage',[173] was now trying to extract from Stuart an undertaking that he would continue Newcome's appointee, Dr Arthur Browne, in the agency for the archiepiscopal estate.[174] It is remarkable that the Union, which in the thinking of the King and of most British ministers was supposed to close 'the reign of Irish jobs',[175] and in the thinking of Clare was supposed to abolish the 'system of universal jobbing', should have been heralded by an English job of Portland's! To be fair, Browne had been a notable defender of the Church's interests in the Irish House of Commons (see p. 572), was a Civilian and had written *A compendious view of the ecclesiastical law of Ireland* (Dublin, 1797). To that extent, he was an excellent choice as agent. However, he was also a Whig, which gave Stuart the opening to claim that the appointment was 'intended as a reward for parliamentary services.' Giving early warning of the tendency to huffiness and overreaction which was his most serious shortcoming, Stuart now declared that he must decline the primacy. Portland did his best to mollify him. But, unfortunately, he gave an extraordinarily tactless explanation for the encouragement given to Dr Browne to expect to be reappointed; this was that the 'lord lieutenant, little doubting (as it was natural he should do) that it [the primacy] would be filled by some prelate on the Irish bench' had assumed that the new primate would be acquainted with Browne's 'merits and peculiar fitness for the employment.'

By mid-October, George III had got wind of the dispute, and wrote to Portland:

> I confess I should have been glad if the duke of Portland's natural desire of obliging [!] had not been carried so far as to interfere by recommending an agent to the future Primate of Ireland, which ... he certainly would not have done to any English bishop. The getting a proper archbishop of Armagh I look upon as an essential duty. I am convinced that in the Bishop of St David's I have found the most suitable person. I certainly trust he will do credit to my personal nomination and prove a bright example to the Irish bench. ... I certainly cannot accept the Bishop's desire of declining what I think to the

172 Portland to Cornwallis, 1 Aug. 1800, Portland papers, PRONI, T/2905/22/129.   173 Henry Dundas, now 1st Viscount Melville, to his son, Robert, 1 Apr. [1808?], Jupp/Aspinall transcript from the Melville Castle papers.   174 Portland to Stuart, 25 Sep. and 4 Oct. 1800, Bedfordshire RO, WY 995/9–10.   175 George III to the new prime minister, Addington, 11 Feb. 1801, quoted in Malcomson, *John Foster*, p. 86.

advantage of religion and good morals, and therefore desire the duke of Portland will acquaint him that I have ordered the warrant for his appointment to the primacy to be prepared, as also one as Prelate of the order of St Patrick.[176]

Very accurate information about this rumpus was soon 'leaked' (presumably by Buckingham) to Cleaver, who reported that Stuart 'had dropped all thoughts of' the primacy, 'in consequence of some applications from the duke of Portland which affected his patronage. He laid the correspondence before the King on his return from Weymouth, who *commanded* him to submit to no condition.'[177]

It is often difficult to interpret Portland's actions because, as Canning later remarked, he wrote letters which '*might* mean more than he intended, or recollects himself, to have expressed'![178] This may not have been simple jobbery. It is possible that Portland, aware of Stuart's supposed reluctance to take on the primacy, had deliberately been trying to put him off. Alternatively, he may only have been trying to help, by putting Stuart under the guidance of an experienced functionary who would also be well placed to educate Stuart in the realities of Irish life. Portland by no means sank under George III's rebuke, but instead wrote to Cornwallis:

I am sorry to think that this note [from the King] affords no reason to hope that the Bishop [Stuart] will receive much admonition at *Windsor* to assume a conciliatory tone on his arrival in Ireland, or to endeavour to acquire the confidence of government or of his clergy by condescension and complacency [*sic*] of manners. I wish with all my heart I may be mistaken, not only for your Excellency's sake, but for the general good which, however wanting reform may be in the conduct of the ecclesiastical matters, would probably be better promoted by good temper and firmness than by authority and reserve.[179]

However blundering his methods, Portland was essentially correct – as events would prove – in his misgivings about Stuart's 'temper' and about the heady effect on him of rhetoric from '*Windsor*.'

'THE MINISTRY HAVE MADE THE ARCHBISHOP OF CASHEL PRIMATE'

On the very day of George III's rebuke to Portland, Stuart wrote to the former: 'though the situation of primate is materially changed since your Majesty was graciously pleased to communicate your wishes, the difficulties of that situation increased, and its dignity and consequence considerably lessened, I do not for a

176 The King to Stuart and to Portland (two letters), 16 Oct. 1800, printed in J.H. Jesse, *Memoirs of the life and reign of King George III* (3 vols., London, 1867), iii. 233.   177 Cleaver to Egremont, 3 Nov. 1800, PHA/57/32.   178 Canning to Melville, 21 July 1807, Jupp/Aspinall transcripts from the Melville papers.   179 Portland to Cornwallis, [?1]6 Oct. 1800, T/2905/22/134.

moment hesitate to ... accept.'[180] It may be that Stuart had in mind the rota arrangements for bishops and archbishops (including the primate) to sit in the House of
Lords. But these arrangements, as Portland pointed out to him, 'were all in existence
and might all have been known to you' in mid-July.[181] It seems more likely that his
sense of the depression of the primacy was connected with the elevation of Agar. On
2 August 1800, Agar, for his support and assistance in carrying the Union, in
parliament, in cabinet and in the country, had been elected with government support
one of the original 28 Irish representative peers. Then, on 13 August, in fulfilment of
another undertaking which Cornwallis had given him, Agar was officially recommended for promotion to a viscountcy,[182] and was created Viscount Somerton on
30 December. Small wonder if Stuart felt up-staged and out-ranked by a junior
archbishop who was his senior in years and in political and episcopal experience, was
a temporal as well as spiritual peer, and was a peer of parliament for life. Cleaver
expressed a general view when he commented, immediately after Stuart's arrival in
Ireland: 'He will be archbishop of Armagh, but I think the ministry have made the
Archbishop of Cashel primate, by giving him a permanent seat in parliament, whereas
the primate sits but once in three years.'[183]

When Agar was translated to the archbishopric of Dublin late in 1801, his preeminence over Stuart was signalised in another respect. Although the archbishop of
Armagh was, by the statutes of the order of St Patrick, Prelate of that order, the
archbishop of Dublin held *ex officio* the more important office of its Chancellor, and
the archbishop of Dublin's cathedral of St Patrick's was the order's mother church.
Writing to congratulate Agar on his promotion, O'Beirne declared that he had

> ever considered Dublin to be of more importance to morals and religion in this
> country than even the primacy. The one is a place of more state and greater
> representation: the other, from the general influence which the manners of the
> capital are ever known to have over every other part of the kingdom, is without
> comparison of superior and more extensive utility, when placed in proper
> hands.[184]

O'Beirne's view of the relative importance of the two archbishoprics had certainly
been strengthened by the Union. Stuart's appointment, as Cornwallis had argued in
vain, was extremely odd in its timing. On the eve of the Union, and in the face of a
strong internal candidate of 'excellent government principles and strongly attached to
England', it was a slight on Ireland and the Irish bench that an Englishman (or was
Stuart a Scot?) was obtruded upon them. If George III had persevered in 1794–5 as
he did in 1800, he would have found an English bishop who was at least no less
unwilling than Stuart to take on the Irish primacy; and at that stage, with an autono-

180 Stuart to the King, [16 Oct. 1800], *Later correspondence of George III*, iii, pp 429–30.
181 Portland to Stuart, 4 Oct. 1800, WY 995/10.   **182** Cornwallis to Portland, 2 and 13 Aug.
1800, *Cornwallis correspondence*, iii, pp 286–7.   **183** Cleaver to Egremont, 1 Dec. 1800, PHA/57/33.
184 O'Beirne to Agar, 9 Nov. 1801, T/3719/C/35/28.

mous and potentially unmanageable Irish parliament in existence, such an appointment would have made some sense. But it made none in 1800.

Nor was it followed by a change of policy which would have made retrospective sense of it – quite the contrary. Because of the 'engagements' entered into to win political support for the Union, the Union did the opposite of closing 'the reign of Irish jobs', in both Church and State. As Professor Jupp has commented, the Union gave the movement towards Economical Reform in Ireland 'a temporary rebuff': it was not until the 1820s that a start was made in reducing the volume of Irish patronage. In the early years of the century, the Englishmen sent to govern post-Union Ireland set a very bad example by carrying away with them when they left some very plum provisions for life charged on the Irish establishment;[185] and, in consequence of changes in responsibilities which had not been thought through at the time of the Union, the military authorities in England were glad of the opportunity to absorb Irish patronage hitherto disposed of by Dublin Castle. As the Chief Secretary complained in 1807, 'We have nothing to say to the army, the ordnance, the commissariat, the medical department, the barrack department and the comptroller of the army accounts.'[186] This meant that Dublin Castle's ecclesiastical patronage, which was unaffected by the Union, was of proportionately greater importance to it now as a means of sweetening the Irish members. So, the demands of post-Union parliamentary management, in conjunction with the 'engagements' for ecclesiastical patronage made by Cornwallis at the time of the Union, had a marked tendency to make the Church of Ireland more exclusively Irish in composition than heretofore. Whatever the intention, the actual effect of the Union on the Church was therefore not to 'close the reign of Irish jobs', but the reign of English bishops. Logically, this ought to have been the case, because the original purpose of overloading the Church of Ireland with bishops from England had been political. However, in the current mood of phoney purification, an influx of English bishops might have been expected post-Union, or alternatively an interchange of bishops (as of militia regiments from 1811 onwards) between the two components of the now United Church and Kingdom. This latter was in fact fleetingly mooted. In July 1807, the King

> expressed to the Archbishop of Canterbury a desire to remove the Irish bishops occasionally to England and the English to Ireland, to which proposition the Archbishop stated no objection. There is certainly none at present on legal grounds since the Union, for the Churches are *one and indivisible*, and it is equally certain that such an arrangement would strengthen the protestant interests and establishments in Ireland more than any measure that could be devised.[187]

185 P.J. Jupp, 'Irish MPs at Westminster in the early nineteenth century', in *Historical Studies*, vii (1969), p. 80; Malcomson, *John Foster*, pp 240–2; Hardwicke to Yorke, 1 and 18 Jan. and 21 July 1805, Hardwicke papers, BL, Add. Ms. 35706, ff. 128, 149 and 259; Redesdale to Agar, 22 Mar. 1806, T/3719/C/40/23.   186 Sir Arthur Wellesley to Hawkesbury, 18 May 1807, *Wellington civil correspondence, 1807–9*, pp 52–3.   187 Wellesley to Richmond, 22 July 1807, *ibid.*, p. 123.

Instead, the only non-Irishmen[188] who joined Stuart on the Irish bench during the twenty-two years of Stuart's primacy were Charles Lindsay, successively bishop of Killaloe (1803–4) and of Kildare, who was Hardwicke's brother-in-law, first chaplain and private secretary, and Christopher Butson, bishop of Clonfert (1804–36), who was appointed because Henry Addington, Pitt's successor as prime minister, had 'known him at Oxford as an excellent scholar' 'between twenty and thirty years ago'.[189] Some years earlier, when Hardwicke had made his aspirations to the lord lieutenancy plain, the prospect had been greeted with dismay: 'If that takes place, we shall have the Scotch cawing at each other like rooks ... . Only think of the Lindsays in the pension list!'[190] A Lindsay in the deanery of Christ Church from 1804 onwards proved a sufficiently heavy affliction, not only to Agar, but to his successors in the archbishopric of Dublin.[191] Lindsay is in effect an isolated exception to the rule that the men raised to the Irish bench between 1800 and 1822 were all Irish. This was because Christopher Butson, very unusually for an English episcopal appointee,[192] had served a long apprenticeship in the Church of Ireland – as dean of Waterford, 1784–1804. In that capacity, he had written regularly and confidentially to Agar, as his metropolitan; and he later, as a bishop, looked to Agar for leadership and promotion.[193] Butson, who had never been a viceregal chaplain, was therefore liable to none of the objections justly attached to the chaplains of yore, and indeed can be regarded as almost Irish. Significantly, Hardwicke – except where the interests of his own brother-in-law were concerned – thought it 'inconvenient' to go back to the system 'of removing from England to Ireland'.[194]

Lindsay, as has been seen (p. 489), was the last churchman to remove from England to Ireland as a viceregal chaplain and thence to be promoted to an Irish bishopric. He was an anachronism, because that practice had become discredited even before the Union. It ought to have had the advantage, from the British point of view, of breeding hybrids who by combining Englishness with local knowledge, matured into potential primates. However, since none of these hybrids on the Irish bench had been deemed 'fit' for the primacy in 1800, even that justification could no longer be offered. Not surprisingly, the practice was never renounced in any formal policy statement. Indeed, the Home Secretary made the assumption in December 1805 – perhaps absent-mindedly – that Hardwicke's replacement as lord lieutenant 'may be desirous of promoting [to a bishopric] some English clergyman who may be his

188 This assumes that Robert Fowler junior counts as Irish by 1813, the year of his promotion to the bishopric of Ossory.   189 Hardwicke to Yorke, 3 May 1804, and to Hawkesbury, 24 May 1804, Hardwicke papers, BL, Add. Mss. 35706, f. 3, and 35709, f. 23; *The viceroy's post-bag*, pp 9, 109–11, 125–30 and 132–43; Wickham to Cleaver, 21 Oct. 1802, T/2627/5/S/12.   190 Midleton to Brodrick, 2 Dec. 1793, NLI, Ms. 8889/8.   191 Milne, *Christ Church*, pp 287–90.   192 The celebrated traveller and orientalist, Richard Pococke, bishop of Ossory, 1756–65, had served in cathedral and diocesan offices in Ireland, and never as a viceregal chaplain, for over thirty years before being made a bishop. Bishop Woodward of Cloyne had a similar record of service.   193 Cotton, *Fasti*, i. 141; Butson to Agar, 9, 14, 22 and 29 Apr. 1797, T/3719/C/31/30, 36, 39 and 47; and Butson to Agar, 17 Apr. 1809, C/43/74.   194 Hardwicke to Yorke, 13 Aug. 1803, *The viceroy's post-bag*, p. 124.

chaplain'.[195] In 1807, the duke of Richmond and his chief secretary, Sir Arthur Wellesley, had thoughts of giving the bishopric of Cork to an Englishman, Dr William Busby, a canon of Windsor (like Stuart) and a friend and, apparently, the private secretary of Wellesley, or to some other Englishman whose promotion would vacate something suitable in the Church of England for Busby.[196] But the proposal 'offended some of our Irishmen, and even the friends of the Church [!]. The former do not approve of the promotion of an Englishman, by which they will get nothing; and the latter don't like that a bishopric should be given away ... with a view to obtain a provision for another person.' Wellesley therefore concluded that the bishopric 'should be given to the most deserving Irishman that could be found',[197] who proved to be the Hon. and Very Rev. Thomas St Lawrence. Meanwhile, the intervening administration of the duke of Bedford in 1806–7 plainly had had no plans to make English private secretaries and/or chaplains Irish bishops. From March 1806, it was generally understood that 'Dean Warburton is to be the next new bishop. He was to have been the D. of Bedford's private secretary, but he has declined that post [though not a viceregal chaplaincy], and a young gentleman in orders (a Mr [Philip] Hunt), who was with Lord Elgin in Constantinople, is to officiate in that capacity.'[198] This establishes that Bedford had wanted an Irishman as his chaplain-cum-secretary, and one moreover whose seniority and other claims already destined him for a bishopric. The young English clergyman, Philip Hunt, was his second choice, and was presumably too young to entertain episcopal aspirations. In other words, there does seem to have been an understanding among most contemporaries that the era of the imported chaplains was over: which did not strengthen, or render less isolated, the position of the imported primate.

The other method of 'removing from England to Ireland' was to introduce into a senior level of the Church of Ireland English churchmen of a seniority similar to Stuart's and for similar purposes of purification or reformation. This method was again resorted to in order to fill the vacancy created by Brodrick (though not by Stuart) in 1822 (see p. 376), and on subsequent occasions, too – usually with benefit to the Church of Ireland. But in Stuart's day, there was little mention of such high-level removals. One exception was the archbishopric of Dublin in 1819–20, after Brodrick had over-hastily declined it (p. 434), and before it was offered to Lord John George Beresford. Another, very politically charged, exception was Charles James Fox's earlier plans of 1806 that Englishmen of 'moderate principles and general approbation of our [the Whigs'] views with regard to the catholics' should

195 Hawkesbury to Pitt, 9 Dec. 1805, Stanhope/Pitt papers, U1590/S5 0.2/16. The replacement was the 1st earl of Powis, who did not have time to take up the appointment. 196 Wellesley to James Traill [under-secretary, Dublin Castle], 22 June 1807, and to Richmond, 22, 28 and 29 June and 5, 13 and 14 July 1807, *Wellington civil correspondence, 1807–9*, pp 87–9, 97–8, 107 and 110–11; Wellesley to Richmond, 2 July 1807, Richmond papers, NLI, Ms. 58, ff. 31–2. Busby (1757–1820) was made dean of Rochester in 1808. I am grateful to Lady de Bellaigue for identifying him for me. 197 Wellesley to Richmond, 21 and 22 July 1807, *Wellington civil correspondence, 1807–9*, pp 122–3. 198 C.W. Flint to Agar, 11 Mar. 1806, T/3719/C/40/21; Leslie, *Armagh clergy and parishes*, p. 354.

be appointed, as soon as there were vacancies, to the archbishoprics of Armagh and Dublin and possibly Cashel.[199] Fox, however, had no official responsibility for Ireland; his ignorance of the Irish Church was exceeded only by his avidity for its patronage; and he died before any Irish archiepiscopal vacancy took place. Besides, any English prelate dispatched by Fox to Ireland would have done the opposite of seconding Stuart's efforts and strengthening his position. Stuart, naturally enough, in view of the degree of royal favour which he enjoyed, was an anti-Emancipationist, and from Fox's point of view, as bigoted as Agar and as most senior Irish churchmen. 'The Primate' wrote Fox to Bedford, 'though a very honourable man, is at least as likely as another to have his belief warped by prejudice or passion. His Grace's disposition, too, *was* against all *moderates* of every description, and if he has changed, it is very lately, for his language about the catholics last year [1805] was that they had got the upper hand and they now were the persecutors and the poor Church of Ireland the persecuted.'[200]

The main reason – at least up to 1806 – that only Irishmen were promoted to Irish bishoprics in the period 1801–22, was the pressure of, and the almost invariable priority given to, 'Union engagements.' These 'engagements' were all to Irishmen and, more specifically, to 'the powerful local interests of this country' (as Cleaver was discouragingly warned in 1802)[201] – Alexanders, Beresfords, Knoxes, Trenches, Tottenham Loftuses and so on. In the case of one of these, the Hon. William Knox, the 'Union engagement' was for a better bishopric, since Knox was already on the bench as bishop of Killaloe (where he was a definite associate of Agar, his metropolitan). Of the new, 'Union' bishops, two – Lord John George Beresford and Lord Robert Tottenham Loftus – owed and acknowledged their ecclesiastical apprenticeship to Agar. A later appointee, the Hon. and Rev. Percy Jocelyn (who did not become a bishop until 1809, in the re-shuffle consequent upon Agar's death), had written to him in April 1800: 'We flatter ourselves in this diocese of Armagh that we shall have the happiness of being under your Grace's protection and guidance [as primate].'[202] Stuart was an intruder into, and Agar the natural leader of, a Church whose 'valuable dignities' were dominated by younger men of like background and mind to Agar's.

Wakefield, writing of the period immediately prior to Agar's death, waxed sarcastic about the youthfulness as well as the powerful political connections of such clergymen. Perhaps, he asked rhetorically, these 'very young men' qualified themselves early for the profession 'by a regular and learned education. But this does not seem to have always been the case: one archbishop was, I believe, before his appointment a lieutenant in the navy; the dean of Clogher was a member of the Imperial Parliament; and a rector of a valuable benefice was lately an *aide de camp* at the Castle.'[203] Sir Arthur Wellesley spoke with similar exaggeration of Lord Robert Tottenham Loftus, 'a very young man and, for a bishop, not a very well conducted and reputable man.'[204]

199 Fox to Bedford, 26 Apr. [1806], BL, Add. Ms. 47569, ff. 275–8.   **200** Fox to Bedford, 16 June 1806, *ibid.*, ff. 297–9.   **201** Wickham to Cleaver, 24 Aug. 1802, T/2627/5/S/4.   **202** Jocelyn to Agar, 29 Apr. 1800, 21 M 57/B35/10.   **203** Wakefield, *Account of Ireland*, ii. 477. There was no 'young' archbishop at the time, let alone one who had been a lieutenant, RN.   **204** Wellesley to Richmond, 19 May 1808, NLI, Ms. 59, f. 120.

(Tottenham Loftus was unpopular in Dublin Castle through no fault of his own: the muddler, Portland, had entered into a Union engagement that he should be made a bishop, had failed to record it officially, and then had remembered it with embarrassing clarity when pressed by Tottenham Loftus' father, Lord Ely.)[205] All these pleasantries, if taken too literally, are in danger of obscuring two important points.

The first is that the 'Union engagements' were fulfilled by the end of 1805, yet exclusively Irish appointments were made until 1822. The first appointment which had nothing to do with the Union was of Dr John Kearney, the provost of TCD, who it was stressed at the time was not a man with 'family connections', and whose promotion to a bishopric was intended to have 'an excellent effect on the university.'[206] This was in fact a resumption of the immediately pre-Union practice of deliberately placing scholarly Irishmen on the bench, and Kearney was the first of four successive provosts to be so promoted between 1806 and 1831.[207] (William Magee, a fellow but not provost of TCD, was made a bishop in 1819 and ended his career as archbishop of Dublin, 1822–31; it was remarked in 1813 that his 'promotion to the deanery of Cork was well deserved by the *Treatise on atonement*', which had run into seven editions since he had first published it in 1801.)[208] The next bishop after Kearney, Dean Warburton, had supported the Union. But, since his principal backer for a bishopric was Fox, this was actually a disadvantage to Warburton. Fox favoured him, partly on Fox's usual Whig party-political grounds, but also – and more laudably – because Warburton had stuck to his post and behaved well during the 1798 Rebellion.[209] The third episcopal appointee after the exhaustion of the 'Union engagements' was the already-mentioned Hon. Thomas St Lawrence, bishop of Cork, 1807–31. Although an aristocrat, there is no reason to doubt that at the time he was 'the most deserving Irishman', since his family actually had almost no parliamentary interest. Many aristocratic churchmen were like him.

This leads on to the second important corrective to Wakefield's pleasantries – the fact that what the 'Union engagements' had done was to accelerate and concentrate in Ireland a process which had been under way more gradually in England since *c.*1750. 'The changing condition was the improvement in the vital statistics of noble life which, after 1750, placed larger numbers of younger sons on the job market. ... In the Church [of England], the appearance of peers and their sons on the bench, in cathedral chapters and not least in ordinary livings which would earlier have been bestowed on a tutor, a poor cousin or simply a local boy made good, was the subject of adverse comment.'[210] Indeed, it could be argued that this process, driven naturally by demographic change, had been artificially retarded in Ireland up to the Union, because the

205 Memo. by Hardwicke of an interview with Tottenham Loftus, 25 May 1804, Jupp/Aspinall transcript from the Liverpool papers, BL.   206 Hawkesbury to Pitt, 9 Dec. 1805, Stanhope/Pitt papers, U1590/S5 0.2/16.   207 McDowell and Webb, *TCD*, p. 78.; Hon. William Wellesley Pole (the chief secretary) to Stuart, 4 Oct. 1811, WY 993/27.   208 O'Beirne to Stuart, 3 June 1813, WY 994/75; McDowell and Webb, *TCD*, p. 83.   209 Akenson, *Church of Ireland*, p. 79; Leslie, *Armagh clergy and parishes*, p. 354.   210 Langford, *Public life and the propertied Englishman*, p. 532. See also Walsh and Taylor, 'The Church and Anglicanism', p. 4.

younger sons of the Irish nobility had often been beaten to bishoprics by viceregal chaplains from England, most of whom exactly answered the description of 'a tutor' or 'a poor cousin.' In 1780, 5 of the 22 archbishops and bishops of the Church of Ireland had been the son or brother of a peer or a peer in his own right: in 1810 (the year after Agar's death), the figure was 11, and 2 others were closely related to peerage families. The 2nd earl of Rosse was making a very topical assertion when he wrote to Wellesley in 1808: 'It ... seems to me to be more agreeable to the nature of our constitution that the aristocracy of the Church should be taken from among the upper orders.'[211]

Brodrick, with his aristocratic, borough-owning background, was typical of the new breed of Irish bishop – and would have concurred with Lord Rosse (see pp 497–8). Significantly, Brodrick's promotion to Cashel had been unconnected with the Union and with his family's parliamentary interest: it was grounded on an unsolicited recommendation by Cornwallis and on Brodrick's own 'excellence of character.'[212] Bishop Knox of Killaloe, who was Brodrick's almost exact contemporary and also a member of a borough-owning family, was promoted to Derry in 1803 in fulfilment of a 'Union engagement', but was described at the time by Hardwicke as 'really a respectable bishop and, except the Archbishop of Cashel [Brodrick], the most likely to be useful in promoting the interests of the Church.'[213] Initially, Knox was the 'bishop who, on public grounds, stands higher [than any other] in the opinion of the Primate',[214] although Stuart revised his opinion downwards after Knox's unilateral decision in 1803–4 to sell the Derry palace (see p. 367). Even Redesdale acknowledged patronisingly that Knox was 'one of the most intelligent of the native bishops.'[215] In due course, the younger Union bishops also acquitted themselves well. Lords John George Beresford and Robert Tottenham Loftus, especially the former, became exemplars of 'The era of graceful reform.'[216] Beresford's cousin, George Beresford, bishop of Kilmore, after a controversial *début* which will be discussed on pp 609–12, served usefully and irreproachably in that bishopric from 1802 to 1841.[217] The Hon. Power Le Poer Trench, successively bishop of Waterford and Elphin and archbishop of Tuam in the period 1802–39 (a churchman, it must be said, with no traceable connection with Agar except that Agar had bought part of his Co. Kilkenny estate from Trench's father), actually became an Evangelical, following a religious experience in 1816.[218] But, long before this religious experience – indeed, from his entering the Church in 1792 – Trench had acquitted himself so well as almost to justify his

211 Quoted in Malcomson, 'A variety of perspectives on Laurence Parsons, 2nd earl of Rosse', in William Nolan and Timothy P. O'Neill (eds.), *Offaly history and society* ... (Dublin, 1998), p. 450. 212 Brodrick to Midleton, 8 Nov. 1801, Ms. 1248, vol. 18, ff. 38–9; memo. on Irish affairs, Jan. 1802, printed in 2nd Lord Colchester (ed.), *The diary and correspondence of Charles Abbot, [1st] Lord Colchester* ... (3 vols., London, 1861), i. 291.   213 *The viceroy's post-bag*, p. 124.   214 Hardwicke to Pelham, 21 Oct. 1801, WY 994/9.   215 Redesdale to Pitt, 22 May 1803, Jupp/Aspinall transcript from the W.D. Adams papers, PRO.   216 Acheson, *Church of Ireland*, pp 113–14, 137 and 142–6; Akenson, *Church of Ireland*, p. 130; George Robert Dawson to Robert Peel, [14 Sep. 1825], Peel papers, BL, Add Ms. 40381, f. 267.   217 Acheson, *Church of Ireland*, p. 158; Akenson, *Church of Ireland*, p. 77.   218 Acheson, *Church of Ireland*, pp 115–16, 127, 136–7, 157–9 and 162–3.

biographer's Pharisaical comment: 'The patronage of the crown, whatever be the motives which lead to its exercise, is under the control of One who causes it eventually to promote His own glory.'[219]

The only one of the cohort who, notoriously, disgraced himself and the Church was Percy Jocelyn, who had to be deposed as bishop of Clogher in 1822. However, Jocelyn's promotion to his first bishopric derived much less from his family's influence in Ireland than from the English influence of – inevitably – the duke of Portland (!), who was related to the Jocelyns. Portland had recommended Jocelyn to Pitt in December 1805, 'not only as the most deserving candidate among the nobility of that kingdom [for the bench] ..., but as one who, if of a private family, would do credit to it even in this kingdom ... . I therefore cannot but congratulate you upon the discharge of the Union engagements as enabling you more immediately' to make him a bishop.[220] In the event, that distinction fell to Portland at the tail-end of his own premiership, in 1809. Jocelyn is an isolated case. The other nobly born Irishmen promoted to the bench in the period 1801–22 broadly speaking lived up to the earlier description penned (in another context) by the humbly born Thomas Newton, bishop of Bristol (and nearly archbishop of Armagh in 1765); they were men who 'were honourable in themselves as well as their families, and whose personal merits and virtues, if they had not been nobly descended, would have entitled them justly to the rank and preeminence that they enjoy.'[221]

Primate Stuart was therefore the odd-man-out during his own primacy, which explains why he became pathologically censorious about almost the whole Church of Ireland hierarchy except Brodrick.[222] One of his great handicaps at the outset was that, though wafted to Ireland on a stiff breeze of 'religion and morals' from '*Windsor*', he was given no definite agenda of reform (nor, under the circumstances, would such a thing have been possible). In mid-July 1800, he rather pathetically sought information from Lord Hobart (who was not a member of the government) about 'what ministers intended respecting the Church of Ireland.' Stuart, so Hobart reported,

> *seemed to know* the number of livings and houses belonging to them, which he stated to be one great obstacle to the residence of the clergy: to ... which I could only reply that I was not aware of any particular plan in the contemplation of government; that the object of ministers was to find a man to place at the head of the Church on whom they could rely, and that I was persuaded his sentiments would have their full weight; but that of course he would require information upon the spot before he would suggest anything.[223]

Brodrick, who at this stage was still a junior bishop and an onlooker on the high politics of the Church of Ireland, had no definite plan in mind either:

---

219 Sirr, *Archbishop Trench of Tuam*, p. 20 and, more generally, pp 9–40.   **220** Portland to Pitt, 20 Dec. 1805, Stanhope/Pitt papers, U1590/S5 0.3/13.   **221** Quoted in Langford, *Public life and the propertied Englishman*, p. 532.   **222** Acheson, *Church of Ireland*, pp 76, 81 and 83; Milne, 'Principle or pragmatism', pp 187–8.   **223** Hobart to Auckland, [18? July 1800], *Auckland correspondence*, iv. 109.

I must acknowledge that our Church Establishment has many things in all its departments which stand in need of a thorough reform. The effecting it, however, must be an [*sic*] work of time, if ever it should be taken in hand. Much, I think, might be done by a primate of a steady disposition, who would despise *popularity*, though not much indeed in comparison of [*sic*] what *ought* to be done. But he would stand in need of the countenance and exertions of his superiors to second his own exertions. By all accounts the Bishop of St David's is well disposed to do all that can be done in the present times.[224]

Cleaver likewise remarked unspecifically that Stuart was likely to 'prove useful in his station.'[225] But it still looked in 1800–01 as if Agar would continue to be virtual primate, simply because Stuart had no programme for the Church of Ireland other than the programme of church and glebe-house building which was uniquely associated with Agar. If, as has been argued (pp 240–41), the start of 'The era of graceful reform' ought to be pushed back to the mid-1760s, it follows that Stuart, in pursuing the same programme (as he did), could only be a continuator, not an initiator. He was not responsible for any policy or reform which Agar or any Irish primate would not equally have espoused or which was not under way prior to Stuart's appointment. That appointment, and the Union itself, were not of originating importance to the Church of Ireland, and only seem to be so because of the tendency for books on Ireland, unreconstructed by that over-worked concept, 'the long eighteenth century', to end or to begin in 1800.

It was another misfortune for Stuart that the first major event of his primacy, the Catholic Emancipation drama of January–March 1801, was enacted to a script largely of Agar's writing. It had been the dissimulated intention of Pitt and the majority of his cabinet, and of the Irish administration of Cornwallis and Castlereagh, to follow the Union with the passing of an Emancipation Act proposed and carried as a government measure. As primate, Stuart controlled the return for Armagh, the only bishop's borough to survive the Union (though with its representation reduced from two members to one). The chancellor of the Irish exchequer, Isaac Corry, a supporter of Catholic Emancipation, was without a seat at Westminster, and Stuart was now asked by the Irish government to bring him in for Armagh, which meant evicting the sitting member, Dr Duigenan. Stuart, who was in London at the time, may have heard rumblings of a dispute between the King and his ministers over Catholic Emancipation; in any case, having 'been chosen by the King and named [primate] without communication with Pitt or Portland',[226] he wanted to ascertain the King's view of the matter. Accordingly, he mentioned it both to Loughborough and Archbishop Moore on 27 or 28 January. So far was Stuart's query from bringing the issue of Catholic Emancipation out into the open that Loughborough, in his advice to the King as to the nature of the response to Stuart, warned him not 'to anticipate the decision your

224 Brodrick to Midleton, 23 Oct. 1800, Ms. 1248, vol. 17, ff. 136–7.   225 Cleaver to Egremont, 1 Dec. 1800, PHA/57/33.   226 Geoghegan, *Union*, p. 165.

Majesty may form' when the cabinet proposed Emancipation to him as a government measure.[227] In the event, the King did 'anticipate the decision.' However, this was not in any response to Stuart, but in his famous outburst to Henry Dundas, secretary of state for war, at a *levée* on the same day, 28 January, 'that he should consider every man as his personal enemy who should propose the Catholic Question to him.' Dr Geoghegan remarks: 'The King's anger was triggered by learning that Catholic Emancipation was being adopted as a government policy; the Corry incident was not significant.'[228] The ensuing crisis, which led to the collapse of Pitt's ministry and the abandonment of the Emancipation proposal, gave Stuart some opportunity to demonstrate that he was as good a 'protestant' as Agar. Not only did he save Duigenan's seat; he also allowed him to suspend the sitting of the prerogative court (in Dublin) and provided him with accommodation in Stuart's own London house, so that Duigenan would be on hand if needed to champion the protestant cause in parliament.[229] But all this was fairly peripheral. The central role assigned by Professor Bolton[230] to Stuart in the events of January–March 1801 proves now to be largely a mistake.

Among prelates of the Church of Ireland, it was Agar, not Stuart, who played an important role in these events, though Agar's role had in fact been played six years earlier. In his correspondence and conversations with Pitt and others in late January–early February, the King made repeated mention of his Coronation Oath. There had also been an earlier outburst at a *levée*, probably in August 1800, on the subject of the oath. The King had expressed his hope that 'government is not pledged to anything in favour of the Romanists', and when Dundas answered equivocally, the King asked 'What say you to my Coronation Oath?' Dundas replied that the oath applied to the King in his executive capacity, but not as part of the legislature – a distinction which the King dismissed as 'Scotch metaphysics.'[231] The distinction, however, had validity, as did the objection which had worried even Westmorland in 1795, that Agar's interpretation of the Coronation Oath Act involved an alienation of sovereignty. At that time, Loughborough had given the King the all-embracing advice 'That the Coronation Oath imposes no restraint on the royal assent to any bills that have passed both Houses of Parliament.'[232] The truth was that the Coronation Oath argument rested on emotion rather than logic[233] – although, even on Dundas' distinction between legislative and executive, there was force in Agar's argument (p. 518) that the oath precluded the King from using 'all the influence of the crown to procure the passing of a bill ... subversive of the Church.' Basically, the Coronation Oath argument derived its force and its long innings[234] from the fact that it rationalised George III's (and George IV's) deep-seated

227 Loughborough to the King, [28 Jan. 1801], *Later correspondence of George III*, iii. 475. See also pp 474–81 *passim*.   228 Geoghegan, *Union*, p. 165.   229 Anonymous letter to Agar, postmarked 24 Feb. 1801, and [Timothy Sullivan?] to Agar, postmarked 11 Mar. 1801, T/3719/C/35/4 and 8. 230 Bolton, *Union*, pp 210–11.   231 Ibid., pp 92–3; R.J. Mackintosh, *Memoirs of the Rt Hon. Sir James Mackintosh* (2 vols., London, 1835), i. 170.   232 Loughborough to the King, [10 Mar. 1795], *Later correspondence of George III*, ii. 317.   233 Malcomson, *John Foster*, pp 424–7; Kavanaugh, *Lord Clare*, pp 311–12.   234 It survived to produce a serious altercation in the House of Lords between Lord Grey and Henry Philpotts, bishop of Exeter, over the third Reform Bill in April 1832 –

feelings and prejudices, and was so straightforward and simple that, in comparison to it, alternative arguments did indeed sound like 'metaphysics.'

This raises the question why, if Agar's services to the King in 1795 had been so signal, was he not rewarded for them with the primacy. A number of reasons may be suggested. First, George III is unlikely to have forgotten Mendip's desertion to Fox in 1783 and both Mendip's and Agar's behaviour on the regency. Second – and partly because of this – he must have regarded Agar as too 'political' and too integral a component of a political connection. Third, some misinformation about the Cashel see lands lease had almost certainly been conveyed to him. Fourth, as all his exhortations to and about Stuart in 1800 emphasise, he had a distorted and prejudiced view of the bishops of the Church of Ireland. Finally, there seems to have been something in the royal psyche which made the King hostile to those who had done him good by stealth. He was a case of 'They love not poison that do poison need.' As has been seen, his greatest aversion was Buckingham, who by unorthodox means had saved him from the Fox-North Coalition in December 1783.[235] The principal backstairs conspirators in 1795 and 1800–01, Lords Auckland, Clare and Loughborough, were likewise not rewarded for their deeds or misdeeds. Auckland did not obtain the cabinet rank he craved, Clare was an object of suspicion to the King and Addington,[236] and Loughborough was superseded as lord chancellor of England. Agar was a similarly marked man, even though he had contributed only belatedly to the backstairs attempt to catch the conscience of the King in 1795, and then had openly and avowedly written two papers on the subject of the Coronation Oath for the benefit of Westmorland's cabinet colleagues. Nevertheless, the ultimate injustice was done him that, although he consistently showed himself in January–July 1800 to be 'a bright example to the Irish bench', the King reserved that epithet, and the primacy, for the fairly dim Stuart.

PRIMATE STUART IS NOT 'AS TEMPERATE AS COULD HAVE BEEN SUPPOSED'

Eventually, over a year after his appointment, Stuart found an opportunity to assert himself and to strike what proved to be an ill-considered blow in the cause of 'religion and morals.' It was not customary (see p. 157) for the primate to be consulted about the filling of Irish archbishoprics and bishoprics. However, it must have been mortifying to Stuart to see so much senior Church patronage disposed of or committed according to 'Union engagements' and without reference to him, when he had been specially chosen by the King to advance 'the cause of religion and virtue in Ireland.' Accordingly, he decided to oppose what was actually not a Union engagement, the promotion of John Beresford's son, George, from the bishopric of Clonfert to that of Kilmore, which was in Stuart's own metropolitan province of Armagh. In a series of letters to Addington, to Hardwicke, and to others, written between the end

Mathieson, *English Church reform*, p. 55.   **235** Jupp, *Lord Grenville*, pp 36–8, 77–8, 86–7 and 302. **236** Kavanaugh, op. cit., pp 373–5.

of November 1801 and the end of January 1802, Stuart denounced Bishop Beresford as 'one of the most profligate men in Europe', 'whose immoralities have rendered him infamous', 'whose character is indisputably infamous' and whose appointment would mean that the province of Armagh was manned by three 'inactive and useless' bishops and 'three ... reported to be the most profligate men in Europe' (the same expression used a second time in the one letter). The appointment would be 'the most fatal blow the Church has ever received', and if it were made, the clerical 'profession itself would shortly cease to exist' in Ireland. Should his protest be unavailing, Stuart sought permission to resign the primacy and retire to a private situation in England; or, if this was refused, to confine himself to his diocesan duties in Armagh, abandoning his primatial and metropolitan functions and his responsibilities for the boards and charities of which the primate was an *ex officio* member.[237] Agar was supposed to be 'of a very violent temper'; but it is hard to see how he could have out-Heroded Stuart's language on this occasion – not that he would have raised the matter in the first place.[238]

In some respects, Stuart had chosen his ground well. To attack a Beresford was to go to the root of alleged Irish jobbery: it echoed what Fitzwilliam had done in 1795 and it anticipated the celebrated aphorism of William Magee, archbishop of Dublin, 1822–31 – 'The production and maintenance of Beresfords is not the final cause of the Irish Church.'[239] The promotion of this particular Beresford could not be justified on the usual plea of Union engagements: rather, as Stuart put it, it was 'the first unfettered act of the present administration.'[240] Moreover, it would place the controversial Beresford under Stuart's own metropolitical superintendence. 'As emolument is the only object of this young man ...' Stuart argued, 'it might have been procured for him in the catholic part of Ireland, where he could do little mischief; but surely it was unnecessary to remove him to the protestant part, where he can do a great deal? It is certainly true that I am not responsible for his removal [i.e. translation to Kilmore], but I am unfortunately so for his conduct when he is placed in my province, and am bound by the laws and usage [i.e. metropolitan visitations] of this country to inspect it.'[241] (This was Stuart's only answer to the good question, why had he raised no objection to Beresford when the latter was first raised to the bench as bishop of Clonfert at the beginning of 1801. It certainly deserves to be quoted in the long-running debate over whether or not the Church of Ireland regarded itself as a missionary Church!) Finally, Stuart – though he did not appeal direct to the King, being 'unwilling to give ... [him] the uneasiness which I think a letter from me on such a subject would have given him' – took care to use arguments designed to move George III, to whom he knew the whole correspondence would ultimately be shown.

237 Stuart's letters, of 27 November and 27, 29 and 31 December 1801 and 14 Jan. 1802, are printed in *The viceroy's post-bag*, pp 98–100, 104–7 and 111–16.   238 Redesdale, too, rushed in where Clare would have hesitated to tread; and, ironically, Stuart was among the many who deplored Redesdale's intemperate language and injudicious violence (see p. 432–3). For Redesdale's out-Clare-ing of Clare, see Malcomson, *John Foster*, pp 439–40, and for Redesdale's 'over-imprudent letters', see C.W. Flint to Agar, 11 Mar. 1806, T/3719/C/40/21.   239 Quoted in Acheson, *Church of Ireland*, p. 76.   240 Stuart to Abbot, 27 Dec. 1801, *The viceroy's post-bag*, p. 106.   241 Stuart to Addington, 14 Jan. 1802, *ibid.*, p. 115.

By this measure ..., we are deprived of the advantage promised to us by the Union. In truth, the two Churches cannot be considered as united unless they are governed by the same principle. ... I sincerely wish to retire, and entertain [the] hope that his Majesty will be graciously pleased to allow me to resign a situation which he compelled me to accept and which I can no longer hold with advantage to the country or honour to myself.[242]

Where Stuart's position was indefensible was that, although he used this extreme language and proposed to take this extreme step, he was unable, though repeatedly asked with patience and forbearance by the Prime Minister and the lord lieutenant to do so, to substantiate his charges against Bishop Beresford's 'moral character' (see p. 484).

If Stuart expected support from the King, as he clearly did, he was to be disappointed. He was not the first to discover that George III, though often 'one of the most right-headed men in his own dominions', was also one of the most ruthless. Agar, for one, who 'had been a great favourite at court', had experienced 'some alteration there' – as a naive and euphemistic admirer put it.[243] The same royal determination which had blocked Agar's path to the primacy was now brought to bear on Stuart. To Addington, the King wrote:

The King ... has the highest opinion of the worth of the Primate, [but] he cannot think he has been as temperate as could have been supposed ... . To decline advancing Bishop Beresford ... in the present stage of the business is impossible on so general an assertion, which undoubtedly has been stated by someone to the Primate or he would not have reported it. But the Primate ought now to feel he has eased his conscience by communicating what he has been told, which can by no means be a reason for permitting him to resign his present situation. On the other hand, the King cannot agree with the Lord Lieutenant that, even if the Primate should take the ill-advised step of resigning the presidency of the charities, ... he should be indulged in giving up the primacy, a step unknown since the Reformation.[244]

In other words, George III had made Stuart's bed and Stuart must lie on it. But the King had also shown considerable shrewdness when he surmised that the 'general assertion' against Bishop Beresford's character had 'been stated by someone to the Primate.' That someone can only have been Brodrick. The Brodricks were in a state of clan rivalry with the Beresfords (and also with the Beresfords' rivals, the Ponsonbys). In 1797, when Brodrick had been bishop of Kilmore, the same George Beresford who was now Stuart's *casus belli* had been appointed to the deanery of Kilmore; upon which Brodrick, almost certainly before he had so much as met

242 Stuart to Abbot, 27 Dec. 1801, ibid., pp 105–6. 243 *The Farington diary*, vi. 98. 244 The King to Addington, 16 Feb. 1802, *Later correspondence of George III*, iv. 12.

Beresford, and in damning anticipation of Stuart's later language, wrote to Lord Midleton: 'They have given me a *Beresford*, and perhaps the very worst of the whole gang, both in his moral and his religious character.'[245]

Having received no support from the King, Stuart now found himself in the humiliating position of a man whose bluff had been called. In the end, he resigned from nothing. Hardwicke wrote him a surprisingly gracious and conciliatory letter (considering that he had come to regard Stuart as a crank[246] and was resigned to his resigning). Stuart buried himself in Armagh, where it looks as if he devoted his energies to reimbursing himself 'the great expense' of the palace. In late June 1802, Addington, clearly still concerned about the recent rumpus, wrote probingly to Hardwicke: 'You will probably be surprised to learn that I have heard nothing from, or of, the Primate since the beginning of February.'[247] Hardwicke did not mince his words in his reply:

The Primate's conduct is inexplicable and indeed inexcusable. He has never once been in Dublin during the whole winter, and the business of the charities has been neglected on that account. He has also counteracted, as far as he could by his example, all that we are doing to keep down the expense of discount [by insisting that all the tenants of the see estate pay their rents in cash], ... at a time when the banks of the United Kingdom are precluded by law from paying in specie.[248]

The coolness between Stuart and Hardwicke persisted until 1804, and indeed sharpened in the spring of that year, when Stuart took offence at the appointment to the precentorship of Armagh of an unsuitable clergyman who was the subject of a Union engagement. On this occasion, Hardwicke complained that Stuart should have used his own considerable patronage to form an alternative arrangement, 'instead of remaining by his fireside at war with all the world.'[249] In late September 1804, however, this was just what Stuart did. When asked for his comments on a proposed appointee to the bishopric of Down (and it was in itself a conciliatory gesture that he should have been consulted), he made a reasoned and flexible response which proposed alternatives and stated the pros and cons of each.[250] At last, he seemed to be learning the virtue of what Hardwicke earlier called – and what was instinctive in Agar – 'a sincere desire to do the utmost practical good that circumstances will admit.'[251]

Bishop O'Beirne thought not. Referring to Stuart's huffiness and hypersensitivity, he remarked in March 1808: 'The Primate is a very particular man, and I fancy expects that [all] the advances should be made [by others] to him.'[252] O'Beirne was

245 Brodrick to Midleton, 5 Feb. 1797, Ms 1248, vol. 17, ff. 4–5. 246 This is the word used, aptly, by the editor of *The viceroy's post-bag*, Michael MacDonagh (p. 110). Hardwicke would probably have said 'an impracticable man'. 247 Addington to Hardwicke, 29 June 1802, Hardwicke papers, BL, Add. Ms. 35708, f. 33. 248 Hardwicke to Addington, 29 July 1802, Jupp/Aspinall transcript from the Hardwicke papers, BL. 249 Hardwicke to Sir Evan Nepean (the chief secretary), 19 June 1804, *The viceroy's post-bag*, p. 143. 250 Stuart to Hardwicke, 28 Sep. 1804, *ibid.*, p. 147. 251 Hardwicke to Addington, 29 Dec. 1801, ibid., p. 110. 252 O'Beirne to John Foster, 28 Mar. 1808,

right in thinking that Stuart was unreconstructed, because in 1810 Stuart staged what looked very like a re-run of the bishop Beresford *fiasco*. At this time, the lord lieutenant was the duke of Richmond, an outspoken, hard-drinking military man, good-natured and humorous, well disposed to the Church and a strong anti-Emancipationist. Against Richmond, of all people, Stuart made the allegation that his exercises of ecclesiastical patronage 'have been peculiarly unfortunate and have thrown weight into the Roman catholic scale.' In reply, Richmond averred that none of the three new and the four translated bishops of his lord lieutenancy was objectionable as a churchman or in his politics, with the possible exception of Joseph Stock, in whose translation Stuart had acquiesced. Richmond also defended his other ecclesiastical arrangements.

> I believe I am as strong a party man as most, but I cannot carry party feelings so far as to refuse what appears an accommodation [i.e. an exchange] to a person who is highly spoken of as a clergyman, because he is the near relation of a person whose politics certainly differ widely from mine. ... Your Grace adds that most of the bishops have expressed their disapprobation at [*sic*] what you are pleased to call this system of bartering. I am rather surprised at it, as most of the exchanges have been recommended by someone or other on the bench.[253]

It was a serious encumbrance to the Church of Ireland to have at its head a cantankerous man so prone to unnecessary and ill-founded quarrels.

It is fortunate for Stuart's reputation that the period in which the Church enjoyed its bonanza of church and glebe-house building (pp 276–80) roughly coincided with the last two-thirds of his primacy. However, in the period 1803–8, when the forward movement of the board of first fruits was becalmed (pp 263–9), his loss of face and weak bargaining power as a result of the Bishop Beresford affair, added to the difficulties of the board's situation. There was also doubt as to whether he intended to stay on as primate. Euseby Cleaver thought he had cast a longing eye at Bangor on his way to Ireland in 1800; one possible interpretation of his extravagant behaviour over Bishop Beresford was that he had been trying to engineer his own return to the English bench; and Hardwicke later, in January 1805, thought he was casting a longing eye at the then vacant archbishopric of York.[254] Wakefield, basing his remarks on good Co. Armagh information, complained of Stuart's subsequent absenteeism in England: 'though in the summer of 1807 he enforced the duty of residence to his clergy, almost immediately after his [visitation] charge [he] quitted the island ..., though not this year a member of the Imperial Parliament ..., nor did he return till the following summer.'[255] Then, not long after his return, he was responsible for 'a very poor restoration' of Armagh cathedral in 1809. 'The altar was re-positioned at the west end of the nave, and a gallery for choristers was erected, together with a canopied pulpit.

PRONI, D/207/50/4. **253** Richmond to Stuart, 21 Apr. 1810, WY 995/18. **254** Hawkesbury to Hardwicke, 30 Jan. 1805, *The viceroy's post-bag*, p. 150. **255** Wakefield, *Account of Ireland*, ii, pp 473–4.

The chancel was furnished as a cathedral Choir for weekday services and the crossing was used as a vestry.'[256] All this had to be undone only twenty-five years later. The dismissive description 'a common type of ecclesiastic and nothing more' seems increasingly apt. Insofar as there is a popular image of Stuart, it is that created by William Owen (1769–1825) in a flashy, Lawrence-style portrait of him as a prince of the Church with a piercing intellect.[257] However, a small pastel portrait, attributed to Adam Buck,[258] portrays an entirely different and much more homespun character. This would seem to be another example of the familiar phenomenon that the lesser artist is the more reliable source for the historian.

In spite of Stuart's limitations and deficiencies, the bad timing and inappropriateness of his appointment, and the many difficulties of his situation, Agar never attained to that position of effective primacy which seemed to beckon in 1800–01. The numerous and complex reasons for this have been discussed (pp 257, 364 and 430–32). Nor was this disappointment peculiar to Agar. In the clashes of personalities and jurisdictions which were endemic in post-Union Ireland until 1807, if not until 1812, none of the warring politicians and churchmen achieved any sort of primacy; and ministerial instability in London, which really lasted until the Prince Regent's intentions were placed beyond doubt in 1812, contributed greatly to the general uncertainty. As far as the leadership of the Church of Ireland was concerned, the decisive factors were Brodrick's enmity towards Agar and the ascendancy which Brodrick acquired over Stuart. Agar in effect bowed out in 1803, with his resignation of the treasurership of the board of first fruits. It looks as if he might have been staging a come-back in 1805 and again in 1807–8 (see pp 267–8 and 279–81). But at both times he was not his old dominant self, but a junior partner to John Foster. Basically, Agar had – by politicians' standards – some pride. He knew when the time had come to obtrude himself no further and withdraw: unlike Clare and others of his acquaintance, he did not wait to be humiliated. Indeed, his resignation in 1803 was of a piece with his aloof 'disinclination' to the proposed Union in 1798–9. So, the two-man mutual admiration society of Stuart and Brodrick dominated the Church from perhaps 1811 onwards and for the rest of the natural lives of the two archbishops. They even contrived to die on the same day, 6 May 1822.[259]

256 Galloway, *The cathedrals of Ireland*, p. 15.   257 I am grateful to the Very Rev. Herbert Cassidy, dean of Armagh, for showing me the portrait, which hangs in the newly refurbished Synod Hall in Armagh. There is a contemporary copy of it, dated 1815 or earlier, in the Armagh County Museum (accession 150. 1958), and also an engraving of it, dated 1 Jan. 1817 (accession 122. 1959). 258 Armagh County Museum, accession 77. 1996, reproduced in Maguire (ed.), *Up in Arms*, p. 26. I am indebted to Ms. Catherine McCullough, curator of Armagh County Museum, for her help over this and the preceding portrait of Stuart.   259 Milne, 'Principle or Pragmatism', p. 193.

Conclusion

Agar was the outstanding figure in the Church of Ireland episcopate during the period *c.* 1760–*c.* 1810 because of his intellect, his energy, his administrative ability, his parliamentary street-wisdom and his political courage and leadership. In another respect, however, he is typical of that episcopate: he and they have been at the receiving end of an almost uniformly bad press. A few of the bishops of the period have fared better in reputation than they deserved – Robinson and Hervey being the best-known examples. But most have fared worse. In part, this is because they have been studied second-hand via the comments of those whose prejudices have not been fully appreciated – anti-clerical Irish parliamentarians and country gentlemen, English politicians either serving in Ireland or remaining at home and, of course, King George III. In part, it is because due allowance has not been made for all the drawbacks and distractions of their situation (most of which have been a major theme of this study) – an invidious and inefficient system of pay and promotion, an absence of any arrangement for retirement on grounds of age or ill-health, the requirement that the bishops run huge and complex see estates, the bishops' individual liability for the sometimes daunting cost of episcopal palaces, and the responsibility imposed on some of them for the political management of parliamentary boroughs. All these things consumed time and energy, bred jealousies, hostilities and litigation, did not conduce to spirituality or a concentration on pastoral activity, and yet left the material rewards of the bishops ill-proportioned even to their seniority.

In addition, the bishops of this period have had a bad press because their dull and humdrum work of church and glebe-house building has not attracted much interest, nor has the background of limited resources and of an 'egregious deformity in our Church Establishment' against which they operated, been fully appreciated. Dazzled by the wealth of '*the richest Church in the world*', subsequent commentators have failed to see that nearly all of that wealth was earmarked for purposes other than the curing of 'the egregious deformity', mainly for the remuneration of individuals (the bishops included). Subsequent commentators have also been misled into thinking that, just because huge sums of public money began to pour into more appropriate places in the Church of Ireland at the very end of the period under review, the years 1803–23, those years constituted a new era of commitment to episcopal duty. In fact, it was Agar and the Church leaders of the preceding decades, when money was tight, who showed a commitment to duty which, if not positively heroic, was certainly ingenious and persevering. Furthermore, among the Church leaders of the first decade of the nineteenth century, Agar stands out as the only one who tried to prevent the initial mess made in the years 1803–8 of the bounty which the parliament of the United Kingdom was ready to bestow.

Because he was, in terms of political leadership, 'infinitely the first ecclesiastic' of the period 1778–1801, Agar has been caught in a kind of cross-fire. To Watty Cox he was the picture of 'abject servility to the measures of the English cabinet', while to 'the English cabinet' he was an object of suspicion as 'an Irishman and especially a political Irishman.' This latter prejudice deprived him of the primacy in 1800, as it had in 1794. His career is an object lesson in how limited and indeed counter-productive Irish political influence was as a means of getting to the top in a Church supposedly crammed with political appointees. The political appointees who got to the top were the fortunate tutors and chaplains to influential Englishmen; and they, too, were mostly English. On the other hand, Agar's career shows how necessary to the Church political ability and leadership were – for example, in stymieing Buckingham's plans in 1788, in pulling 'the Archbishop of Cashel's Act' out of a hat in 1795, and in nego-tiating the Union in 1800. Agar was, of course, a political prelate, but mainly in the good sense of that term. Where earlier political prelates – Archbishops Bolton, Boulter and Stone, for example – had pursued some purely political agenda which, if anything, brought the Church into disrepute, Agar's political agenda almost always advanced, or at the very least coincided with, the Church's interests. Obtaining offices for the 1st and 2nd Lords Clifden, and generally seeking to strengthen the Agar poli-tical interest and connection, were exceptions; but trying to drive Lords Buckingham-shire and Buckingham from office were not, and nor was the formulation of the Coronation Oath argument.

Although Agar has generally been considered only in this high-political context, it is actually his work as a churchman which most repays study. As a diocesan adminis-trator, he was clearly unrivalled, deploying small sums of money to achieve remarkable results, recovering Church resources which looked as if they were lost for good, and where possible proceeding by negotiation and exchange rather than by expensive outlay. It looks as if he was guided by conscious restraint. The churches he built were 'simple, yet elegant'; he drastically *reduced* the internal scale of Cloyne cathedral; and his Cashel cathedral aimed only at 'correct proportions, chasteness and simplicity of design, goodness of materials and neatness of execution.' He did nothing to arouse the envy or hostility of the laity, and he did not saddle his sees or successors with debt. His 'music-madness' did not blind him to the necessity of putting cathedral music on a sound and permanent financial footing. In his improvements to his palaces at Cloyne and Cashel, he eschewed 'the extravagance of the showy.' In Dublin, he disposed of the palace of St Sepulchre with a ruthless pragmatism worthy of the modern Representative Church Body, and benefited the see by continuing to live in his own private house in Dublin. He also seems to have prevented the building of an unnecessary deanery of Christ Church. In his management of see estates, he showed similar business acumen. For all the notoriety of his Cashel trust leases, they had the effect of enriching his successors in the see no less than his successors in title. In

Dublin, he refrained from controversial methods of increasing revenue, and instead cut expenditure, not only by selling St Sepulchre, but also by not attempting to live in Tallaght Castle. In other words, though the acknowledged expert among the bishops in the mysteries of improvements and dilapidations and in other aspects of an over-complex system of pay and perquisites, he put his expertise to restrained and responsible use.

What he did as a diocesan is additionally significant as an indication of what he might have done for the Church as a whole if he had ever possessed the authority of the primacy. The importance he attached to clerical residence and the due per-formance of clerical duties was an earnest of the vigorous use he would have made of the primate's authority to restrict pluralities countrywide. His economical attitude towards his episcopal palaces also suggests that he thought that by 1772, if not earlier, the legislative encouragement for palace-building and improving had gone too far. Likewise, though he defended in the House of Lords the existing combination of 21-year leases and regular renewal fines which lay at the heart of episcopal estate management, his bitter personal experience of Dr Palliser's refusal to renew must surely have privately convinced him that more was needed than the cosmetic reform effected by 'the Archbishop of Cashel's Act' of 1795? Most facets of the far-from-transparent system of remuneration for the bishops exposed them to misrepresenta-tion and malice, contributed to the alienation of the laity, and did not conduce to the ease and not necessarily even to the emolument of the bishops: the inferences to be drawn from Agar's own behaviour as a diocesan, and everything else which is known about him, suggest that he recognised this reality and appreciated that a rationalisation and redistribution of the bishops' rewards were needed. In this respect, too, he may have been influenced by personal experience as a diocesan: he never drew 'a great prize' in the ecclesiastical lottery, because the two successive archbishoprics which he held were in his time conspicuously under-remunerated, in relation both to their seniority and to his own contribution to the Church.

The other main sphere of his administrative activity (outside his successive dio-ceses) was the board of first fruits. When he obtained parliamentary grants from 1778 onwards to support the board's programme of infrastructural improvement, he intended that these new resources for the building of glebe-houses and the acquisition of glebes should be confined to the poorer clergy and smaller livings. He expected amply beneficed clergy, his own near relations included, to fend for themselves, and he sought to pass a Benefice Mortgage Act which would have made it easier for them to do so and – more important – would have left them with no excuse for not doing so. It was no part of his policy that interest-free loans should be made to such clergymen, and it looks as if he resigned as treasurer to the board in 1803 in protest against that prodigality. At bottom, his object was quietly to redistribute wealth within the Church, by making over-rich incumbents pay for the infrastructural improvements required in their benefices, and by earmarking the new money obtained from parliament for infrastructural improvements in the benefices of the poorer incumbents. This was an approach which made eminent good sense in an era when clerical incomes were rising and there was slack to be taken up, and when the Irish House of Commons remained hostile to the clergy and watchful for signs of clerical affluence. It was also of a piece with his efforts, as diocesan and metropolitan, to ensure that clergymen resided on their benefices and did their pastoral duty. This, he hoped, would win lay endorsement of the board's receipt and expenditure of public money, and would keep parliament from intermeddling in the internal affairs of the board and, more generally, in the internal affairs of the Church.

The board was the agency for much of this policy because he could be treasurer and effective head of it without being primate. While there is no evidence of how it conducted its business in the 1780s and 1790s, there is sufficient casual evidence – particularly in Stuart's, Brodrick's and John Foster's correspondence – to show that in the years immediately after the Union, when the board either had or expected to obtain really substantial resources, it became a decision-making and even policy-making body which was surprisingly independent of primatial control. From 1803 onwards, Agar was no longer the dominant figure on the board which once he had been. But up to then, even though its resources were very much smaller than they later became, he was able to use them as a lever to prize activity out of the most unenergetic bishops and impose the beginnings of a pattern of infrastructural improvement across the country as a whole. What he failed to do, even at the height of his influence in the 1790s, was to get his key Benefice Mortgage Bill so much as presented to parliament. This persistent failure establishes the limits of what he could hope to achieve unless he achieved the primacy. Later, in 1800, with the primacy vacant and several other Irish bishops fancying themselves as realistic candidates, it was understandable that his influence should be limited. But in the early 1790s, with Robinson in advanced decline and every probability that Agar would be his successor, Agar still could not overcome the vested interests ranged against his scheme. Actually, he fell victim to his own argument that the wealth of the wealthier benefices had to be kept up, in order to provide an incentive to 'our nobility and gentry to educate their children for the Church.'

In his role as the Church's leader in parliament, as in these other roles, Agar showed restraint, pragmatism and a capacity for graceful reform. For an 'intemperate', 'uncontrolled', 'violent' and 'hot-headed Irishman', he was associated with some legislation of a surprisingly soothing nature. His Barren Lands Act of 1793 removed, with safety to the Church, a grievance against it which had been causing trouble since 1788. 'The Archbishop of Cashel's Act' of 1795 preserved 'the inheritance, rights and profits of lands belonging to the Church and persons ecclesiastical', but disposed of the most sinister charges which could be levelled at the bishops as landlords. His Curates' Act of 1800 performed an act of justice and at the same time deprived the Church's enemies of a hard-luck story which reflected badly on it. His acquiescence in the Tithe of Agistment Act of the same year avoided a pitched battle between the Church and the House of Commons which the former's enemies in the latter would have been happy to have precipitated. Of these legislative and parliamentary achievements, the most striking was 'the Archbishop of Cashel's Act', and particularly the united response he masterminded among the bishops in 1795. At that time, he had just been disappointed of the primacy, and to that extent was politically *passé*; the personal self-interest of all the bishops was engaged on the opposite side of the question; and the changes in their leasing powers which the House of Commons bill proposed would actually have brought those powers more nearly into line with the practice of the Church of England – the Church in which half the then Irish bench had started their careers. Under these circumstances, it is remarkable that his lead was followed unanimously, and that he even won the support of a number of lay peers 'not usually very friendly to the Church.' What was important about Agar in his political and, particularly, his parliamentary capacity was the fact that he was 'a gentleman as well as an archbishop', and specifically a member of the Irish landed class. He fiercely reprobated what Ellis called 'the alarming duplicity'[1] of that class on the issue of tithes and on the rights of the clergy generally. But his presence at a senior level in the Church, and the leadership role he assumed in its parliamentary affairs from the late 1770s onwards, were helpful in soothing animosities between Church and parliament, particularly between Church and House of Commons.

Even in Agar's day, the Church still bore the stigma of Boulter. Boulter's policy had been to anglicise high offices in the state as well as the Church, and it must be strongly suspected that the House of Commons was retaliating for this when it resolved against the tithe of agistment and generally wrecked his plans for clerical residence in the 1730s. Boulter was a man of ability and a good churchman; and his selection for the primacy had been a matter of deliberate policy. His immediate successor, Hoadly, is best forgotten. Then followed Stone and Robinson, both the accidental products of English court intrigue and just the sort of colonial appointments which at this time were contributing to undermine British rule in North America. The longevity of Robinson prolonged the anachronism: twelve years after the establishment of 'Grattan's Parliament', the Church of Ireland was still headed by an Englishman, and half its bishops were still English. This made the Church, not just an anomaly, but a target. Ellis, for one, specifically linked the attack on tithes in 1785–7 with the agitation which had extorted 'that fantom [*sic*] of independence'; 'these men have hitherto quietly submitted [to the payment of tithes] for many years, and so would have continued to do, if they had not been excited by both art and experience to try the same arts which have proved successful in other instances.'[2] In 1793, the year before Robinson's death, the Irish treasury – the last pocket of colonialism in the Irish administration – ceased to be headed by a trio of redundant vice-treasurers, at least two of them absentee Englishmen (like Ellis!), and was converted into a treasury board, composed exclusively of Irishmen and accountable for its operation to the Irish parliament. So, by 1794, the Church of Ireland was the only institution in Ireland which was still English-dominated. It was not 'a national Church' – not even a national institution in the sense in which the Irish parliament was entitled to that designation: it was still a colonial

1 Ellis to Agar, 29 Oct. 1786, T/3719/C/20/34.   2 Ibid.; Ellis to Agar, 22 Sep. 1786, T/3719/C/20/29.

institution. This goes far to explain the unusual (by contemporary British standards) anti-clericalism of the Irish House of Commons and landed class.

The failure to appoint an Irishman to the primacy in 1794 is not capable of rational
explanation. By then, the primacy was the only great office in the kingdom, except the
lord lieutenancy (the chief secretaryship did not then rank as a great office), which had
not passed to an Irishman. The primacy no longer had a political role. Robinson had
been a lord justice for two short periods only, and had been absent from Ireland on both
occasions. Indeed, he had been absent for the past eight years, and had not been missed
by the government (although the Church had missed him sorely in 1788). The government's fear of an Irish primate on account of 'the borough annexed to the primacy' was
fantastical. The idea that English churchmen were superior to Irish in 'qualification and
character' was untenable (though it still had some years to run in the disordered mind
of George III). The other vacancies of 1794–5 were filled by Irishmen, the flow of
viceregal chaplains from England into Irish bishoprics appeared to be stemmed (and,
with one subsequent exception, actually was stemmed), and a shift towards Irish
predominance in the Irish episcopal bench was beginning to be discernible. Moreover,
there was in 1794, among the Irishmen on that bench, an exceptionally strong
candidate for the primacy – which had not been the case in 1765. Finally, the Irishman
concerned was half English and had good political connections in England. Even the
lord lieutenant who did *not* recommend him acknowledged that he had 'excellent
government principles and [was] strongly attached to England.'

The appointment of Agar in 1794 would not have been marked by dancing in the
streets of Dublin. But, as his showing in successive House of Lords ballots for the
secret committees of the 1790s demonstrates, and as Lord Shannon's eloquent letter of
condolence to him in 1800 suggests, he was clearly the popular candidate of the political
elite (if that is not a contradiction in terms). Because he was also a member of that *élite*,
and a man whose ideas had been formed in an earlier epoch and under Ellis' conservative influence, he would certainly not have attempted radical reforms of the Church of
Ireland of a kind which might, by anticipation, have warded off the assault of 'critical
strangers' in the 1830s. Un-clairvoyant, and conditioned by the sort of anti-clericalism
he had long experienced in the Irish House of Commons, Agar took the view that the
Church would survive with its privileged position intact provided it kept its head well
down, put its house in order, made the most of its existing resources, and was wary of
parliamentary succours lest they entail parliamentary surveillance. Such an outlook
does not betoken myopia. After all, it is hard to find an instance of any privileged group
or institution which has committed suicide to save itself from slaughter. There have
been some instances of self-mutilation before worse befell; the endowing of the
Erasmus Smith schools by the sleazy Cromwellian land-speculator, Erasmus Smith, in
1657–69, or the endowing of Durham University by the embarrassingly coal-rich
bishop, dean and chapter of Durham in 1831, are striking cases in point.[3] But the late

3 Stephen S. Brown, 'A survey of the records available for the study of the Erasmus Smith
endowment' (unpublished QUB MA dissertation, 1982), pp 1–5; Heesom, *The founding of Durham
University, passim.*

eighteenth-century Church of Ireland was not yet faced with such grim alternatives. Indeed, it had good reason to think that it was already benefiting from a course of self-administered medicine which would make it by the 1830s, as Professor Akenson has argued, a healthier and more efficient body than ever before in its history. It was to be brutally reformed, not because of inefficiency (otherwise why did the Church of England escape largely unscathed?), but because of the new presence of militantly hostile Irish Roman catholic and/or O'Connellite MPs at Westminster following the enforced concession of Catholic Emancipation in 1829 and the passing of the Great Reform Act in 1832.[4] To that extent, Agar had not been incorrect in his view that the future of the Church depended on the preservation, inviolate, of that particular Constitution in Church and State to which the Coronation Oath gave some specious security.

Visibly and foreseeably, the late eighteenth-century Church needed remedial treatment in two major respects. It needed strengthening at its parochial base, a process well under way thanks in large measure to Agar; and it also needed strengthening higher up by the lopping of some of its episcopal excrescences. One of its great weaknesses was that, in comparison to many privileged institutions which have existed over time, it was ill-arrayed politically to meet its foes and defend its privileges. The division in its ranks, and particularly at its most senior level, which derived from the unjustifiable foisting of Englishmen on the Irish bench, was beyond the Church's control, and was in any case on the way out. Its other great source of weakness was that its rewards system was unnecessarily opprobrious, divisive, complex and uncertain. This was a matter which, subject to the sanction of government and parliament, was within the Church's own control and, in particular, within Agar's expertise to rectify. For example, all the existing arrangements for building palaces and administering see estates derived from statute law, and mostly fairly recent statute law at that. Unlike tithes, they had no semblance of biblical authority; they were marginal and mutable. The Church would have been strengthened by greater simplicity, predictability and transparency in these areas, and Agar – with his knowledge of the system and grasp of detail – would, if appointed to the primacy, have been the man to rationalise or at the very least codify[5] all the existing legislation.

Under an Agar primacy, the board of first fruits would have been one major vehicle for administrative reform. It was the nearest thing to a forerunner of the ecclesiastical commission set up under the Church Temporalities Act of 1833, and could have anticipated the ecclesiastical commission's role to a greater extent than it did. The commission was to be the means of achieving a huge and very beneficial redistribution of wealth within the Church of Ireland.[6] But the board of first fruits, whose remit already extended far more widely than its name, could earlier have been

4 Akenson, *Church of Ireland*, pp 143–7.   5 As has been seen (p. 347), he codified the numerous acts regulating the building and paying-for palaces and other clerical residences in 1792, and was hoping to introduce a comprehensive piece of consolidating legislation. This probably remained stillborn because it was part-and-parcel of his Benefice Mortgage scheme.   6 Akenson, *Church of Ireland*, pp 171–9.

developed in a similar direction. The proceeds from any rationalisation or greater equalisation of the incomes of see estates might have been placed in its hands. There were also considerable possibilities in Brodrick's suggestion, made in 1802 in connection with the loan scheme for glebe-house building, that the annual rate of repayment of the interest-free loan should be calculated on the basis of what rent the clergyman would have had to pay for such a house. This may or may not have been a new principle, but it was a good one, and capable of far wider legislative application. Instead of entitling the builder of a palace or glebe-house to recoup some fixed fraction, or the whole, of his outlay from his successor, why did the legislation not entitle him to recoup the whole, less whatever rent he would have had to pay for such a house during incumbency, and entitle his successor(s) to do likewise until the cost of the building was defrayed? In this way, the burdens and the benefits would have been equally spread and enjoyed, disputes and rancour avoided, and the lottery closed. The principle might have been applied more widely still. Once the building was paid for, why should the occupying bishop or clergyman not have continued to pay the equivalent of rent for it during incumbency, the money to go to the board of first fruits, and to be subject to deductions for necessary and authorised repairs and improvements. Refinements of this kind to the existing system, leading to the creation of a significant central fund, would not have been beyond the bounds of possibility under an Agar primacy starting in 1794.

Agar would also have been the man to navigate the necessary legislation through the Irish parliament. Because Robinson had proved to be 'a very tough incumbent in fine preservation', there would have been little time (as things turned out) for Agar to have formed a better relationship between the Church and the Irish parliament than existed at the outset of his putative primacy. But the cessation of chaplains from England, and the appointment of an Irish primate, would have signified to peers and MPs that the Church was now on course to become a homogeneously 'national' institution. In crudely practical terms, this meant that, much of its best patronage being no longer reserved to Englishmen, the Irish 'nobility and gentry' could now regard themselves as the main stakeholders in the Church of Ireland. This, in turn, would have appeased the vested interests hitherto threatened by Agar's Benefice Mortgage Bill and his generally 'Robin Hood' approach to clerical, including episcopal, affluence. It ought also to have permitted a reduction in the number of bishoprics, thus eliminating one of the most visible excesses of the Church of Ireland and releasing funds for 'parochial reformation', cathedral restoration and possibly even coadjutorships. An overhaul of the modes of letting see estates which went further than 'the Archbishop of Cashel's Act' in lessening the invidiousness of the bishops' situation as landlords, would also have tended to soften the anti-clericalism of the House of Commons. In 1798–1800, when the time came to negotiate a union of the Churches of Ireland and England, Agar – had he then been a primate of three or four years' standing – would have done so from a position of authority instead of the position of weakness in which he found himself in 1800. A Church of Ireland with Agar as its head would have vigorously defended those aspects of its constitution where history or practical reality had made it different from the Church of England, and would also have been led into a better-defined Union with that Church in 1801. And after the Union, when huge sums of money became available to address 'the egregious deformity in our Church Establishment', he would have been able to recognise the element of threat in the promise, and would have responded more subtly and wisely than did the chief leaders of the Church from 1803 onwards.

Much of this is speculation and 'might have been.' But there is good reason to conclude that the Church as well as the individual suffered a loss when 'infinitely the first ecclesiastic' in Ireland failed, mainly as a result of English prejudice, ignorance and envy, to become the first Irish primate since 1702. Ultimately, it matters very little whether Agar himself was a man of private religious conviction, or just a political prelate and a worldling. What matters is that he possessed, and never was fully able to exercise, the particular political and administrative skills which were required by the late eighteenth-century Church of Ireland. These skills, by liberating bishops and clergy from thraldom to a defective and counter-productive system, would have promoted greater harmony among churchmen and greater pastoral efficiency in their dealings with the laity. In this way, Agar – for all the human failings of a man of his class and of his personal and dynastic ambition – was likely, had he been put on, to have proved a powerful promoter of 'the religion which he professed and taught'.

Bibliography

MANUSCRIPT SOURCES

Bedfordshire and Luton Record Office
Primate Stuart papers (William Stuart, archbishop of Armagh, 1800–22), WY 993–5. There are photocopies of this material in the Armagh Public Library (i.e. the Robinson Library)

Bolton Library, Cashel
Working papers of Robert Wyse Jackson, dean of Cashel, 1945–61

British Library, London
Auckland papers (William Eden, 1st Lord Auckland, chief secretary, 1780–82), Add. Ms. 34419 and 34453–4
Egmont papers (John Perceval, 1st earl of Egmont, who received some letters about Cashel borough elections, 1733–4), Add. Ms. 46984
Fees on Irish patents, 1752–82, Add. Ms. 23711
Flood papers (Rt Hon. Henry Flood of Farmley, Co. Kilkenny), Add. Ms. 22930
Hardwicke papers (Philip Yorke, 3rd earl of Hardwicke, lord lieutenant, 1801–6), Add. Mss. 35609, 35705-6, 34709–10, 35716, 35718, 35750, 35759 and 35772
Holland House papers (Elizabeth, Lady Holland, and Charles James Fox), Add. Mss. 56182 and 47569
Macintosh collection (Sir James Macintosh, Whig historian), Add. Ms. 34523
Northington letter-book (Robert Henley, 2nd earl of Northington, lord lieutenant, 1783–4), Add. Ms. 38716
Peel papers (Sir Robert Peel, 2nd Bt, chief secretary, 1812–18, and home secretary, 1822–30), Add. Mss. 40229 and 40381
Pelham papers (Thomas Pelham, 1st Lord Pelham, chief secretary, 1783–4 and 1795–8), Add. Mss. 33100–02 and 33118
Rose papers (George Rose, joint paymaster-general, 1804–6), Add. Ms. 42773
Wellesley papers (Richard Wellesley, 2nd earl of Mornington and 1st Marquess Wellesley), Add. Ms. 37416
Windham papers (William Windham, chief secretary, 1783), Add. Ms. 37873

Down County Museum, Downpatrick
Down Diocesan papers (incorporating some correspondence of the 1st marquess of Downshire, 1792, about the rebuilding of Down cathedral), DB 505

Dublin Diocesan Archives
Troy correspondence (John Thomas Troy, Roman catholic archbishop of Dublin, 1786–1823)

Hampshire Record Office, Winchester
Normanton papers, 21 M 57
Sloane Stanley papers (the papers of the family who succeeded Lady Mendip in the Paultons estate in 1803), 46 M 48

History of the Irish Parliament, Belfast
Database of MPs' biographies, 1690–1800, kindly made available by the project's director, Professor E.M. Johnston-Liik

Huntington Library, San Marino, California
Stowe papers (George Nugent Grenville, 1st marquess of Buckingham, lord lieutenant, 1783 and 1787–9), STG, box 29

Irish Architectural Archive, Dublin
Photograph of the countess of Brandon's funeral monument, neg. S/859/5
Cashel press cuttings files

Centre for Kentish Studies, Maidstone
Pratt papers – see under Public Record Office of Northern Ireland
Stanhope/Pitt papers: a section of the papers, c.1785–c.1805, of Pitt the younger, which came into the possession of his kinsman and biographer, the 5th earl Stanhope, U1590. (Partly photocopied by PRONI, T/3401.)

Lambeth Palace Library
Moore papers (John Moore, archbishop of Canterbury, 1783–1805)
Estimates of the incomes of Irish sees, c.1715 c.1750, Ms. 2168

Limerick Regional Archives
Vere Hunt letter-books (Sir Vere Hunt, 1st Bt, of Currah Chase, Adare, Co. Limerick)

National Archives, Dublin
Clifden estate papers (Gowran, etc., Co. Kilkenny), D 20046, D 20056, D 20062, D 20069, D 20080, D 20097, D 20108A–20109, D 20121, D 20125, D 20127A–20129, D 20141, D 20149, M 3239, M 3242, M 3244 and T 10997
Canon James B. Leslie's notes on the dioceses of Dublin and Kildare, [c.1920], M 2818
William Monck Mason's notes on the archbishop of Dublin's liberties, c.1810, M 2545
Official Papers (i.e. from the chief secretary's office, Dublin Castle), OP 61, 80, 103, 126, 150, 172, 196, 515, 518, 520 and 620

National Library of Ireland, Dublin
Bolton papers (Thomas Orde, 1st Lord Bolton, chief secretary, 1784–7), Ms. 16350
Burgh papers, Ms. 8606
Cashel cathedral (on the Rock of Cashel): prints and single drawings, 1658TA and 1757TC
Cashel common council minute books, 1672–1825, Mss. 5575–8

Cashel: typescript notes on its early municipal and parliamentary history, N.D., Ms. 17978

Clifden estate papers, D 10685–92 and Ms 8796

Domvile papers (including some of the Gardiner family, Viscounts Mountjoy, mid-1740s and mid-1790s), Mss. 9399 and 11848

De Vesci papers (Sir Thomas Vesey, 1st Bt, bishop of Ossory, 1714–30), J/1, J/19–20 and J/23–4

Heron papers (Sir Richard Heron, 1st Bt, chief secretary, 1776–80, and incorporating papers of his principal, the 2nd earl of Buckinghamshire, both then and later), Mss. 13034–9, 13042, 13047 and 13061

Killadoon papers (2nd earl of Leitrim, 1820s), Ms. 36062 and 26064

Land Commission: finding list of the contents of the Irish Land Commission archive, ref. LC 1752

Limerick papers (i.e. papers, 1775–94, of the Pery family, later earls of Limerick), PC 875, bundles 8, 15, 19 and 22

Midleton papers, 1781–1820 (Charles Brodrick, archbishop of Cashel, 1801–22, brother of the 4th, and father of the 6th, Viscount Midleton), Mss. 8861, 8865, 8869–71, 8883, 8885–6, 8888–9 and 8892. See also Surrey History Centre, Woking

Ogle papers (George Ogle, M.P. for Co. Wexford, 1769–97), Ms. 8148

Ormonde papers, 1770s (John Butler, 17th earl of Ormonde, of Kilkenny Castle), Ms. 2480

Prior-Wandesforde papers, mid-1740s–mid 1770s (John Wandesford, 5th Viscount Castlecomer and only Earl Wandesford), Mss. 35457 and 35479–80

Riall papers, *c.* 1770–*c.* 1810 (Rev. Samuel Riall of Upham, Cashel), Ms. 8395

Richmond papers (4th duke of Richmond, lord lieutenant, 1807–13), Mss. 58–9

St Canice corporation book, 1692–1799, microfilm p. 5143

Townshend papers (4th Viscount Townshend, lord lieutenant, 1767–72), Mss. 8009 and 14299

National Photographic Archive, Dublin

Cashel palace: photograph of the garden front, *c.* 1880–1900, Lawrence collection, Cab 7964

Nottingham University Library

Portland papers, PWF 68 (the Irish material in the 3rd duke of Portland's archive has been photocopied by PRONI – *q.v.*)

Pennsylvania Historical Society

Gratz autograph collection, case 12, box 29 (letter of 1805 from Agar to John Foster)

Private Collections

Annaly/Clifden papers, *c.* 1700–*c.* 1900 (part of the scattered Clifden estate archive), in the possession of James King Esq., Rademon, Crossgar, Co. Down. (Through his mother, Mr King descends from the Clifden heiress, the Hon. Lilah Agar-Ellis, who married the 3rd Lord Annaly in 1884.)

Archbishop Fowler's 'state' of the diocese of Dublin, 1777–8, up-dated to 1788, in the possession of John Fowler Esq., Rahinstown, Rathmolyon, Co. Meath. There are probably many more Archbishop Fowler papers at Rahinstown, but they are currently inaccessible.

Holloden papers: miscellaneous 'autographs' formerly at Holloden, Bagenalstown, Co. Carlow, in the possession of the late Miss Faith O'Grady

Professor P.J. Jupp, Belfast: Jupp/Aspinall transcripts from numerous archives of the period, *c.*1790–*c.*1835, made by the late Professor Arthur Aspinall and Professor P.J. Jupp in connection with their work for the History of Parliament, and then continued and extended by Professor Jupp in connection with other research projects. His files for 1800–09 were kindly made available by Professor Jupp

A.P.W. Malcomson, Belfast Ms. civil establishment of Ireland, 1749; book containing Agar's bookplate as a student at Christ Church, *c.*1755; letter from Primate Newcome to Countess Fitzwilliam, 24 Feb. 1795; letter from George Pretyman-Tomline, bishop of Lincoln, to 'My dear Sir', 29 June 1803

George Mealy & Sons Ltd., Castlecomer: framed reward notice for the recovery of the stolen 'Irish crown jewels', 10 July 1907

The earl of Rosse: Rosse papers, Birr Castle, Co. Offaly, including papers of Henry Flood and of his political disciple, Sir Laurence Parsons, 5th Bt, 2nd earl of Rosse, *c.*1760–*c.*1815

Joseph Smith papers, in the possession of Mrs Ian Campbell, Moot Farm, Downton, Wiltshire

Tickell papers, in the possession of Major-General M.E. Tickell, Branscome, Devon

Public Record Office, Kew

Chatham papers (William Pitt the younger, prime minister, 1783–1801 and 1804–6), PRO 30/8

Colchester papers (Charles Abbot, 1st Lord Colchester, chief secretary, 1801–2), PRO 30/9

Probate of the 1st Lord Mendip's will, 1802, Prob. 11/1370

Public Record Office of Northern Ireland, Belfast

Abercorn papers, *c.*1790–*c.*1810 (1st marquess of Abercorn), D/623 and T/2541

Armagh diocesan registry papers, *c.*1750–*c.*1850 (mainly material deriving from Primates Robinson, Newcome, Stuart and Beresford and/or the board of first fruits), DIO 4

Agar-Ellis (Clifden) papers (originals in the Northamptonshire RO), principally comprising Irish estate correspondence of Welbore Ellis, *c.*1745–50, T/3403

Barrington & Son papers (incorporating Primate Robinson estate material, 1740s and 1820s 30s), D/3805/2

Beaufort journal: tour journal of Rev. Dr Daniel Augustus Beaufort, Aug.–Dec. 1787 (original in TCD), MIC/250

Bedford papers (originals in the possession of the marquess of Tavistock, Woburn Abbey, Bedfordshire), deriving from the 4th duke of Bedford, lord lieutenant, 1757–61, T/2915

Blenheim Palace papers: estimate of the rentals of members of the Irish House of Commons in 1713 (original in BL), T/3411

Burrows journal: journal of a visit to Ireland by the Rev. J. Burrows, 3 June–12 Aug. 1773 (original in NLI), T/3551

Castlereagh papers (Robert Stewart, Viscount Castlereagh, chief secretary, 1798–1801), D/3030

Chatsworth papers (originals in the possession of the duke of Devonshire, Chatsworth, Derbyshire), deriving from the 3rd and 4th dukes of Devonshire, lords lieutenant, 1737–44 and 1755–7 respectively, T/3158

Clifden papers (originals in the Cornwall RO), comprising letters from Welbore Ellis to the 4th Viscount Townshend, 1767–72, T/2930

Clogher, Co. Tyrone: copy extracts from the Clogher corporation book, 1783–98, T/1566

Clogher Roman catholic diocesan papers, *c.*1810–*c.*1825, DIO (RC) 1

Austin Cooper account books, 1788–92 and 1803–7, MIC/251/1–2

Donoughmore papers (originals in TCD), deriving from John Hely-Hutchinson, provost of TCD, 1774–94, and his son, the 1st earl of Donoughmore, T/3459

Downshire papers (correspondence of the 1st and 2nd marquesses of Downshire, principally about Down cathedral, 1791–3), D/607

Emly/Pery papers (originals in the collection of the late Walter Armytage, Moyvore, Co. Westmeath), deriving from E.S. Pery, speaker of the Irish House of Commons, 1771–85, T/3052

Emly/Pery papers (originals in the Huntington Library, San Marino, California), T/3087

FitzGerald (Knight of Kerry) papers, *c.*1760–*c.*1800 (originals in the possession of Sir Adrian FitzGerald, Bt, London), MIC/639

Fitzwilliam papers (originals in Sheffield Archives [the Sheffield City Library]), deriving from the 4th earl Fitzwilliam, lord lieutenant, 1794–5, T/3302

Forbes papers, *c.*1785–*c.*1795 (originals split between two separate Mss. in NLI), deriving from John Forbes, Whig MP for Drogheda, T/3391

Foster/Massereene papers (John Foster, speaker of the Irish House of Commons, 1785– 1800, and chancellor of the Irish exchequer at Westminster, 1804–6 and 1807–11), D/ 207 and D/562

Additional Foster/Massereene papers (originals at Springfield Castle, Drumcollogher, Co. Limerick), MIC/680/L

Gosford papers, *c.*1775–1800 (the 1st and 2nd Viscounts Gosford), D/1606

Grey/Ponsonby papers (originals in the Durham University Library), deriving from William Brabazon Ponsonby, 1st Lord Ponsonby of Imokilly (1744–1806), T/3393

Hertford papers (originals among the Egerton Mss., BL), deriving from the 2nd earl and 1st marquess of Hertford, lord lieutenant, 1765–6, T/3076/2

History of the Irish Parliament working papers: series of notes on all the constituencies, 1690–1800 (and thereafter), alphabetically arranged, ENV 5/HP

Home Office papers (originals in the PRO, HO 100/1–104), MIC/224

Hotham papers, 1776–87 (originals in Hull University Archives), deriving from Sir Charles Hotham Thompson, 8th Bt, and Sir John Hotham, 9th Bt, bishop of Clogher, 1782–95, T/3429

Kavanagh papers, *c.*1765–*c.*1800 (originals in the possession of Andrew Kavanagh Esq., Borris, Co. Carlow), T/3331

King-Harman papers, *c.*1760–*c.*1800, including material on Kingston college, Mitchelstown, Co. Cork, D/4168

Macartney papers, 1768–1806 (Sir George Macartney, Earl Macartney, chief secretary, 1768–72, and cousin of Mrs Agar), D/572

Montgomery of Benvarden (Bushmills, Co. Antrim) papers, *c.*1770s–90s, T/1638

Normanton correspondence (originals in the Hampshire RO – *q.v.*), comprising the correspondence section of Agar's papers, T/3719/C

Northumberland papers (originals in the possession of the duke of Northumberland, Alnwick, Northumberland), deriving from the 2nd earl and 1st duke of Northumberland, lord lieutenant, 1763–5, T/2872

O'Hara papers, 1783–1800 (originals in NLI), deriving from Charles O'Hara senior and junior, Nympsfield, Collooney, Co. Sligo, T/2812

Pelham papers: transcripts from the originals in BL, T/755

Perceval papers (William Perceval, an early eighteenth-century archdeacon of Cashel), D/906

Pitt/Pretyman papers, *c.*1790–1806 (originals in Cambridge University Library), deriving from Pitt the younger via his mentor and first biographer, George Pretyman-Tomline, successively bishop of Lincoln and Winchester, T/3313

Pitt/Pretyman papers (originals in PRO), T/3319

Pomeroy papers, 1780s (Arthur Pomeroy, 1st Viscount Harberton, and his brother, General John Pomeroy), T/2954

Pratt papers (originals in the Centre for Kentish Studies, Maidstone), deriving from John Jeffreys Pratt, 2nd earl Camden, lord lieutenant, 1795–8, T/2627/4

Register of Irish Archives: Donoughmore papers, TCD; Hamilton of Hamwood (Dunboyne, Co. Meath) papers; Leslie papers, Glaslough, Co. Monaghan; Rathdonnell papers, Lisnavagh, Co. Carlow; and Springfield Castle papers, Drumcollogher, Co. Limerick

Ross of Bladensburg (Rosstrevor, Co. Down) papers, D/2004

Shannon papers, *c.*1760–*c.*1800 (Richard Boyle, 2nd earl of Shannon), D/2707

Sneyd (Auckland) papers (originals in Keele University Library), comprising an addition to the Auckland papers in BL, T/3229

Stanley of Alderley/Sheffield papers, *c.*1770–*c.*1800 (originals in the Cheshire RO), deriving from John Baker Holroyd, 1st Lord Sheffield, T/3725

Staples papers (the Staples family of Lissan, Cookstown, Co. Tyrone, and Dunmore, Co. Laois), including papers about Edward Maurice, bishop of Ossory, 1754–6, D/1567

Transcripts of the State Papers (Ireland) in the PRO, T/448

Talbot-Gregory correspondence (between the 2nd Earl Talbot, lord lieutenant, 1817–21, and William Gregory, under-secretary, Dublin Castle), D/4100

Wickham papers (originals in the Hampshire RO), deriving from William Wickham, chief secretary, 1802–4, T/2627/5

Volume of typescript copies of some of the papers, *c.*1740–*c.*1820, of the Forward-Howard family, earls of Wicklow (original in NLI), MIC/246

Wilmot papers (originals in the Derbyshire RO), deriving from Sir Robert Wilmot, 1st Bt, secretary resident in London to the lords lieutenant of the period 1740–72, T/3019

Wolfe papers, *c.*1790–*c.*1810 (originals in NLI), deriving from Colonel John Wolfe of Forenaghts, Naas, Co. Kildare, T/3474

Wynne of Hazelwood, Sligo, papers, *c.*1750s, MIC/666

Registry of Deeds, Dublin
Memorials of deeds relating to the Agar family, nos. 1681, 2065, 2875, 3000, 36882, 42680, 43883, 50551, 50711, 62891, 83380, 90041, 132095, 179910, 276570 and 299308

Representative Church Body Library, Dublin
Cloyne: records relating to the diocese of Cloyne, D.16/8

Dublin diocesan archive: visitation books for Dublin and Glendalough, 1803 and 1806, MIC/20

4th Viscount Townshend letter-book, mainly 1767–72, Ms. 20

Royal Irish Academy, Dublin
Burrowes papers (incorporating some Henry Flood material), Ms. 23 K 53

Royal Society of Antiquaries of Ireland, Dublin
Corporation books of Gowran (1736–1800) and Thomastown (1693–1840), Co. Kilkenny, Mss. C7A5 and C7A1 respectively

Surrey History Centre, Woking
Midleton papers, c. 1790–c. 1815 (mainly letters to the 4th Viscount Midleton from his brother, Charles Brodrick, archbishop of Cashel), Ms. 1248. See also under National Library of Ireland

Trinity College Library, Dublin
Barker Ponsonby papers, c. 1760–c. 1800 (Sir William Barker, 3rd and 4th Bts, of Kilcooly Abbey, Fethard, Co. Tipperary), P1
Clements papers, 1794–5 and 1802–c. 1810 (Colonel H.T. Clements of Ashfield, Co. Cavan, and Austin Cooper, agent for the Cashel see estate in the early nineteenth century), Mss. 7308–9
Crofton (Earbery) papers, 1780s, Mss. 3575–3587a
First fruits: fragmentary accounts, 1737–1805, relating to the board of first fruits, Mss. 1744–5
Talbot-Crosbie papers, c. 1760s–c. 1810 (2nd earl of Glandore of Ardfert Abbey, Co. Kerry), Ms. 260

West Sussex Record Office, Chichester
Petworth House (Egremont) papers, deriving from the 3rd earl of Egremont, patron of Euseby Cleaver, bishop of Ferns, 1789–1809, PHA 57

Yale University Library
4th Viscount Townshend papers, Osborn collection, box 14

PRINTED SOURCES

Acheson, Alan, *A history of the Church of Ireland, 1691–1996* (Dublin, 1997)
Akenson, D.H., *The Church of Ireland: ecclesiastical reform and revolution, 1880–85* (New Haven, 1971)
Akrigg, G.P.V., *Jacobean pageant, or the court of King James I* (London, 1962)
Almanach de Gotha (1872 ed.)
Ashbourne, 1st Lord, *Pitt: some chapters of his life and times* (London, 1898)
Auckland correspondence: *The journal and correspondence of William [Eden, 1st] Lord Auckland, edited by [his son] the bishop of Bath and Wells* (4 vols., London, 1861–2)
Barlow, Stephen, *The history of Ireland from the earliest period to the present time* (2 vols., London, 1814)
Barnard, T.C., 'Improving clergymen, 1660–1760', in Alan Ford, James McGuire and Kenneth Milne (eds.), *As by law established: the Church of Ireland since the Reformation* (Dublin, 1995)
Barnard letters: [*Letters of Thomas Barnard, bishop of Limerick, etc.*], *1778–1824, edited by Anthony Powell* (London, 1928)
Barrington, Sir Jonah, *The rise and fall of the Irish nation* (Dublin, 1843)
Barrington, Sir Jonah, *Personal sketches of his own times* (new ed., Dublin, 1917)

Barry, Jonathan, 'Cultural patronage and the Anglican crisis: Bristol, c.1689–1775', in John
Walsh, Stephen Taylor and Colin Haydon (eds.), *The Church of England, c.1689–c.1833* ...
(Cambridge, 1993)

Bartlett, Thomas, *The fall and rise of the Irish nation: the catholic question, 1690–1830* (Dublin,
1992)

Bartlett, Thomas, 'Clemency and compensation: the treatment of defeated rebels and suffering
loyalists after the 1798 Rebellion', in Jim Smyth (ed.), *Revolution, counter-revolution and
Union: Ireland in the 1790s* (Cambridge, 2000)

Bateman, J., *The great landowners of Great Britain and Ireland* (4th ed., London, 1883)

Beaufort, Rev. Daniel Augustus, LL.D., *Memoir of a map of Ireland, illustrating the topography
of that kingdom, and containing a short account of its present state, civil and ecclesiastical*
(London, 1792)

Bence-Jones, Mark, 'An acropolis in Tipperary' and 'An archbishop's Palladian palace', in
Country Life, 24 and 31 Aug. 1972

Bence-Jones, Mark, *Burke's Irish family records* (London, 1976)

Bence-Jones, Mark, *A guide to Irish country houses* (revised ed., London, 1988)

Beresford correspondence: *The correspondence of the Rt Hon. John Beresford illustrative of the last
thirty years of the Irish parliament* ... (2 vols., London, 1854)

Beresford, Susan E. Pack-, *Christ Church, Carrowdore* (Belfast, 1994)

Blunt, Reginald (ed.), *Mrs Montagu, 'Queen of the Blues': her letters and friendships from 1762 to
1800* (2 vols., London, 1923)

Bolton, G.C., *The passing of the Irish Act of Union: a study in parliamentary politics* (Oxford,
1966)

Bond, R.W. (ed.), *The Marley letters, 1778–1820* ... (London, 1937)

Boughton, Peter, 'Ducal art [the Grosvenor collection]: a study in changing tastes', in *National
Art Collections Fund Art Quarterly, no. 12* (winter 1992)

Bowden, C.T., *A tour through Ireland in 1790* (Dublin, 1791)

Brady, W. Maziere, *Clerical and parochial records of Cork, Cloyne and Ross* (2 vols., Dublin, 1863)

Brennan, Monica, 'The changing composition of Kilkenny's landowners, 1641–1700', in
William Nolan and Kevin Whelan (eds.), *Kilkenny history and society* (Dublin, 1990)

Brennan, Rev. M.J., *An ecclesiastical history of Ireland ... to the year 1829* (Dublin, 1848)

Brett, C.E.B., *Buildings of Co. Armagh* (Belfast, 1999)

Bric, Maurice J., 'Priests, parsons and politics: the Rightboy protest in Co. Cork, 1785–8', in
Past and Present, no. 100 (Aug. 1983)

Bric, Maurice J., 'The tithe system in eighteenth-century Ireland', in *Proceedings of the Royal
Irish Academy*, vol. 86, sec. C, no. 7 (1986)

The British Mercury ..., by J.W. von Archenholtz, vol. iii for 1787 (Hamburg, 1787?)

Brocket, 2nd Lord, Letter to the editor of *Country life*, 10 Jan. 1963

Brown, Stephen S., 'A survey of the records available for the study of the Erasmus Smith
endowment' (unpublished Queen's University of Belfast MA dissertation, 1982)

Burke, John, and Burke, John Bernard, *A genealogical and heraldic dictionary of the landed gentry
of Great Britain and Ireland* (3 vols., London, 1846–8)

Burke, Sir John Bernard (edited and revised by various), *A genealogical and heraldic history of
the landed gentry of Ireland* (London, 1904, 1912 and 1958)

Burke, Sir John Bernard (edited and revised by various), *A genealogical and heraldic dictionary
of the peerage and baronetage* ... (91st ed., London, 1933)

Burke, Rev. William P., *History of Clonmel* (Waterford, 1907)

Burns, R. Arthur, 'A Hanoverian legacy?: diocesan reform in the Church of England, *c*.1800–1833', in John Walsh, Stephen Taylor and Colin Haydon (eds.), *The Church of England, c.1689–c.1833 ...* (Cambridge, 1993)

Burns, Robert E., *Irish parliamentary politics in the eighteenth century [1714–60]* (2 vols., Washington DC, 1989–90)

Burtchaell, G.D., *Genealogical memoirs of the members of parliament for [the] county and city of Kilkenny* (Dublin, 1888)

Burtchaell, G.D., and Sadlier, T.U. (eds.), *Alumni Dublinenses* (Dublin, 1935)

Butler, David, 'The meeting-house of the protestant dissenter: a study of design, layout and location in southern Ireland [mainly Cork and South Tipperary]', in *Chimera: The UCC Geographical Journal*, no. 14 (1999)

Butler, Hubert, *Escape from the anthill* (Mullingar, 1985)

Butler, James, Roman catholic archbishop of Cashel, *A justification of the tenets of the Roman catholic religion* (Dublin, 1787)

Butler, Samuel, *The way of all flesh* (Penguin ed., 1995)

[Campbell, John, LL.D.], *A philosophical survey of the south of Ireland, in a series of letters to John Watkinson, M.D.* (Dublin, 1778)

Cannon, John, *Aristocratic century: the peerage of eighteenth-century England* (paperback ed., Cambridge, 1987)

Casey, E.M.S. (Lady Casey), *An Australian story, 1837–1907* (London, 1962)

Cashel Palace: *hotel brochure*, [*c*.1965]

Cashel Palace: *hotel prospectus for 2001*

Cassan, Rev. Stephen Hyde, *Lives of the bishops of Bath and Wells from the earliest to the present period* (London, 1829)

Castlereagh correspondence: *Memoirs and correspondence of Viscount Castlereagh ..., edited by the [3rd] marquess of Londonderry* (first ser., 4 vols., London, 1848–9)

Chester, Joseph Lemuel, *The marriage, baptismal and burial records of the collegiate church or abbey of St Peter, Westminster* (London, 1876)

Childe-Pemberton, William S., *The earl-bishop ...* (2 vols., London, *c*.1925)

Clark, Alan (ed.), *'A good innings': the private papers of Viscount Lee of Fareham ...* (London, 1974)

Clarke, Adam (ed.), *[Compendium edition of the] lives of ... Dr Thomas Newton, bishop of Bristol [by himself] ..., the Rev. Philip Skelton by Mr [Samuel] Burdy [etc.]* (2 vols., London, 1816)

C[ockayne], G.E., Gibbs, Vicary, and others, *The complete peerage ...* (revised and enlarged ed., 13 vols., London, 1910–40)

Coleman, John, 'Sir Joshua Reynolds and Richard Robinson, archbishop of Armagh', in *Irish Arts Review* (1995)

Collins, Arthur: *Collins' peerage of England ... [edited] by Sir Egerton Brydges ...* (9 vols., London, 1812)

Collinson, Patrick, 'Geoffrey Rudolph Elton, 1921–94', in *Proceedings of the British Academy*, xciv (1997)

Colchester diary: *The diary and correspondence of Charles Abbot, [1st] Lord Colchester, edited by [the 2nd] Lord Colchester* (3 vols., London, 1861)

Colvin, Howard, and Craig, Maurice (eds.), *Architectural drawings in the library at Elton Hall [Peterborough] by Sir John Vanbrugh and Sir Edward Lovett Pearce* (The Roxburghe Club, Oxford, 1964)

Comerford, Rev. Patrick, 'The Church of Ireland clergy of Co. Wexford during the 1798 Rebellion', in Liam Swords (ed.), *Protestant, catholic and dissenter: the clergy and 1798* (Dublin, 1997)

Comerford, Rev. Patrick, 'The Church of Ireland in Co. Kilkenny and the diocese of Ossory during the 1798 rising', in *Old Kilkenny Review, 1998*

Connolly, S.J., *Religion, law and power: the making of protestant Ireland, 1660–1760* (Oxford, 1992)

Connolly, S.J., draft *New DNB* biography of John Scott, 1st earl of Clonmell

Cooper, Austin, *An Irish antiquary: the sketches, notes and diaries of ...*, edited by Liam Price (Dublin, 1942)

Corballis, Caroline, 'Castlefield House [Gowran]', in *In the shadow of the steeple [:the Journal of the Duchas-Tullaheerin Heritage Society, Co. Kilkenny]*, no. 5 (1996)

The Cork Chronicle, 14 July 1768

Cornwallis correspondence: *Memoirs and correspondence of Charles, 1st Marquess Cornwallis*, edited, with notes, by Sir Charles Ross (2nd ed., 3 vols., London, 1859)

Cotton, Rev. Henry, *Fasti Ecclesiae Hibernicae: the succession of the prelates and members of the cathedral bodies in Ireland* (6 vols., Dublin, 1845–78)

Cove, Rev. Morgan, *An essay on the revenues of the Church of England ...* (third ed., London, 1816)

Cowper, J. Meadows, *The lives of the deans of Canterbury, 1541 to 1900 ...* (Canterbury, 1900)

[Cox, Watty], *The Irish magazine or monthly asylum for neglected biography*, Feb. and Sep. 1809

Craig, Maurice, *Dublin, 1660–1860* (London, 1952)

Crean, Hugh R., 'Gilbert Stuart and the politics of fine arts patronage in Ireland, 1787–93 ...' (unpublished postgraduate dissertation, City University of New York, 1990)

Creevy, Thomas: *Creevy selected and re-edited from The Creevy papers (1903) ... and Creevy's life and times (1934), by John Gore* (London, 1948)

Croker, Thomas Crofton, *Researches in the south of Ireland ...* (Dublin, 1824)

Cullen, L.M., 'The politics of clerical radicalism in the 1790s', in Liam Swords (ed.), *Protestant, catholic and dissenter. the clergy and 1798* (Dublin, 1997)

Cullen, L.M., *The Irish brandy houses of eighteenth-century France* (Dublin, 2000)

Cullen, L.M., et al., *St Mary and St Michael parish church, New Ross, 1902–2002: a centenary history* (Dublin, 2001)

Cumberland, Richard, *Memoirs* (London, 1806)

[A curate of the Church of Ireland], *A letter to his grace the Lord Archbishop of Cashel ...* (Dublin, 1793)

Curran, C.P., *Dublin decorative plasterwork of the seventeenth and eighteenth centuries* (London, 1967)

D'Alton, John, *The history of the county of Dublin* (Dublin, 1838)

D'Alton, John, *The memoirs of the archbishop of Dublin* (Dublin, 1838)

Debates: *The parliamentary register or history of the proceedings and debates of the House of Commons of Ireland, 1781–97* (17 vols., Dublin, 1782–1801)

Debates : *The parliamentary history of England from the earliest period to the year 1803 ..., [edited by William Cobbett]*, vols. xxxv and lxxxv (London, 1819)

Debates : *Cobbett's parliamentary debates ...*, vol. v (London, 1805) and vol. ix (London, 1807)

De Burgh, Ulysses H.H., *The landowners of Ireland: an alphabetical list of the owners of estates of 500 acres or £500 valuation and upwards, in Ireland* (Dublin, [1879])

De Paor, Liam, 'Cormac's Chapel [Cashel]', in Etienne Rynne (ed.), *North Munster studies: essays in commemoration of Monsignor Michael Moloney* (Limerick, 1967)

Dickson, David, *New foundations: Ireland, 1660–1800* (2nd revised and enlarged ed., Dublin, 2000)

Dictionary of National Biography (revised ed., 22 vols., Oxford, 1917–49)

Ditchfield, G.M., 'Ecclesiastical policy under Lord North', in John Walsh, Stephen Taylor and Colin Haydon (eds.), *The Church of England, c.1689–c.1833* ... (Cambridge, 1993)

Dolan, Ana, 'The large mediaeval churches of the dioceses of Leighlin, Ferns and Ossory', in *Irish architectural and decorative studies (the Journal of the Irish Georgian Society)*, ii. (1999)

Donnelly, J.S., junior, 'The Rightboy movement, 1785–8', in *Studia Hibernica*, nos. 17–18 (1977–8)

Donnelly, J.S., junior, 'Irish agrarian rebellion: the Whiteboys of 1769–76', in *Proc. RIA*, vol. 83, no. 12 (1983)

Doyle, Joe, 'The Hewetsons of Thomastown', in *In the shadow of the steeple[: the Journal of the Duchas-Tullaheerin Heritage Society, Co. Kilkenny]*, no. 2 (1990)

The Dublin Evening Chronicle, 8 Apr. 1788

Duncan, G.I.O., *The high court of delegates* (Cambridge, 1971)

The Edinburgh Review, ... for July 1833–January 1834 (Edinburgh, 1834)

Ehrman, John, *The younger Pitt: the years of acclaim* (London, 1969)

Ehrman, John, *The younger Pitt: the reluctant transition* (London, 1983)

Ehrman, John, *The younger Pitt: the consuming struggle* (London, 1996)

Ellis correspondence: *Letters written during the years 1686, 1687, 1688, and addressed to John Ellis Esq., secretary to the commissioners of his majesty's revenue in Ireland, edited by Lord Dover* (2 vols., London, 1829)

Ellison, Canon C.C., *The hopeful traveller: the life and times of Daniel Augustus Beaufort, LL.D., 1739–1821* (Kilkenny, 1987)

Enclosure Act: *An act for enclosing lands in the parishes of Tallaght, Kilsallaghan, alias Kilsoughan, and Lusk, in the County of Dublin, [c.1820]* (TCD, OL8 X-1-801)

Erck, John C., *An account of the ecclesiastical establishment subsisting in Ireland, as also an ecclesiastical register of the names of the dignitaries and parochial clergy and of the parishes and their respective patrons; with a detail of the monies granted for building churches and glebe-houses ...* (Dublin, 1830)

Evans, Dorinda, *The genius of Gilbert Stuart* (New York, 1999)

Evans, Eric J., *The contentious tithe: the tithe problem and English agriculture, 1750–1850* (London, 1976)

Fagan, Patrick, *Divided loyalties: the question of the oath for Irish catholics in the eighteenth century* (Dublin, 1997)

'Falkland' [Rev. John Scott], *The parliamentary representation of Ireland* (Dublin, 1790)

Falvey, Jeremiah, 'The Church of Ireland episcopate in the eighteenth century: an overview', in *Eighteenth-century Ireland*, viii (1993)

Farington, Joseph, R.A.: *The Farington diary ..., edited by James Greig ...* (8 vols., London, 1922–8)

Faulkner's Dublin Journal, 12 Mar., 16 Apr. and 23 July 1765

Fife correspondence: *Lord Fife and his factor: being the correspondence of James, 2nd Lord Fife (1729–1809), edited by Alistair and Henrietta Tayler* (London, 1925)

Fisher, Joseph R., and Robb, John H., *Royal Belfast Academical Institution: centenary volume, 1810–1910* (Belfast, 1913)

FitzPatrick, Samuel A. Ossory, *Dublin: a historical and topographical account of the city* (London, 1907)

FitzPatrick, W.J., *The Life, times and correspondence of the Rt Rev. Dr Doyle, bishop of Kildare and Leighlin* (2 vols., Dublin, 1861)

FitzPatrick, W.J., *'The Sham Squire' [Francis Higgins] and the informers of 1798, with a view of their contemporaries* ... (3rd ed., Dublin, 1866)

FitzPatrick, W.J., *Ireland before the Union, with revelations from the unpublished diary of Lord Clonmell* ... (London, 1867)

Flannery, Judith, *Between the mountains and the sea: the story of delgany* (Delgany, 1900)

Flood, Rt Hon. Henry: *Original letters to* ..., *edited by T[homas] R[odd]* (London, 1820)

Forster, Rev. Charles, *The life of John Jebb* ..., *bishop of Limerick, with a selection from his letters* (2 vols., London, 1836)

Fox correspondence: *Memorials and correspondence of Charles James Fox, edited by Lord John Russell and others* (4 vols., London, 1853–7)

The Freeman's Journal, 18 Sep. 1783

Fryday, Rev. Barbara, *A tale of two cathedrals* (N.P., *c.* 1975)

Galloway, Rev. Peter, *The most illustrious order of St Patrick, 1783–1983* (Chichester, 1983)

Galloway, Rev. Peter, *The cathedrals of Ireland* (Belfast, 1992)

Gaynor, Tony, 'The politics of law and order in Ireland, 1794–8' (unpublished University of Dublin Ph.D. thesis, 1999)

Gentleman's and London Magazine, for 1787, 1788, 1794 and 1809

Geoghegan, Patrick M., *The Irish Act of Union: a study in high politics, 1798–1801* (Dublin, 1999)

George III: *The later correspondence of* ..., *edited by Arthur Aspinall* (5 vols., Cambridge, 1962–70)

Gerard, Frances, *Picturesque Dublin, old and new* (London, 1898)

Giffard, John: *Who was my grandfather: a biographical sketch [of John Giffard], by Sir A.H. Giffard and Edward Giffard* (London, 1865)

Gleeson, Rev. John, *Cashel of the kings: a history of the ancient capital of Munster* ... (Dublin, 1927)

Glenbervie diaries: *The diaries of Sylvester Douglas, [1st] Lord Glenbervie, edited by Francis Bickley* (2 vols., London, 1928)

Gordon, Rev. James, *A history of Ireland from the earliest times to* ... *1801* (2 vols., London, 1806)

Grattan, Rt Hon. Henry, *A full report of the speech of* ... *on Thursday the 14th of February 1788 in the debate on tithes, taken in shorthand by Mr Franklin* (Dublin, 1788)

Grattan, Henry, Junior, *Memoirs of the life and times of the Rt Hon. Henry Grattan, by his son* (5 vols., London, 1839–46)

Greene, Anthony, 'The Church of Ireland: Aghabullogue [diocese of Cloyne]', in *The Coachford record*, iv (Dec. 1993)

Grenville papers: *Correspondence of Richard Grenville, Earl Temple, K.G., and the Rt Hon. George Grenville, their friends and contemporaries, edited by William James Smith* (4 vols., London, 1852)

[Griffith, Richard and Elizabeth], *A series of genuine letters between Henry and Frances* (4 vols., Dublin, 1770)

Grindle, W.H., *Irish cathedral music: a history of music at the cathedrals of the Church of Ireland* (Belfast, 1989)

Hall, Mr and Mrs S.C., *Ireland, its scenery, character, etc.* (3 vols., London, 1841–3)

Hardwicke papers: *The viceroy's post-bag: correspondence hitherto unpublished of the [3rd] earl of Hardwicke, the first lord lieutenant of Ireland after the Union,* edited by Michael MacDonagh (London, 1904)

Hardy, Francis, *Memoirs of the political and private life of James Caulfeild, [1st] earl of Charlemont* (2nd ed., 2 vols., London, 1812)

Hart, A.R., *A history of the king's serjeants at law in Ireland: honour rather than advantage?* (Dublin, 2000)

Harris, Walter, *The history and antiquities of the city of Dublin* ... (Dublin, 1766)

Hayton, D.W., 'The High Church party in the Irish convocation, 1703–1713', in H.J. Real and H. Stover-Leidig (eds.), *Reading Swift: papers from the third Münster symposium on Jonathan Swift* (Munich, 1998)

Hayton, D.W., 'Dependence, clientage and affinity: the political following of the 2nd duke of Ormonde', in T.C. Barnard and Jane Fenlon (eds.), *The dukes of Ormonde, 1610–1745* (Woodbridge, 2000)

Hayton, D.W. (ed.), *The Irish parliament in the eighteenth century: the long apprenticeship* (*Parliamentary history*, Edinburgh, 2001)

Healy, Rev. John, *History of the diocese of Meath* (2 vols., Dublin, 1908)

Heesom, A.J., *The founding of the university of Durham: the Durham cathedral lecture for 1982* (Durham, 1982)

Herbert, Dorethea, *Retrospections of ..., 1770–1806, [with] accompanying commentary by L.M. Cullen* (new ed., Dublin, 1988)

The Hibernian Journal, 14 Aug. 1783

Hickson, M.A. (ed.), *Old Kerry records ..., second series* (2 vols., London, 1874)

Hill, Judith, 'Davis Ducart and Christopher Colles: architects associated with the custom house in Limerick', in *Irish architectural and decorative studies*, ii (1999)

Hill, Judith, *The building of Limerick* (new ed., Cork, 1997)

Hislop, Harold, 'The bishops and the schools, 1806–12', in *Search: a Church of Ireland Journal*, vol. xiii, no. 2 (winter 1990)

Historical Manuscripts Commission Reports
    Bathurst Mss. (3rd Earl Bathurst, secretary of state for war and the colonies, 1812–27)
    Carlisle Mss. (5th earl of Carlisle, lord lieutenant, 1780–82), *15th Report, Appendix vi*
    Charlemont Mss. (1st earl of Charlemont), *12th Report, App. x, and 13th Report, App. vii (2 vols.)*
    Donoughmore Mss. (John Hely-Hutchinson, provost of TCD, 1774–94), *12th Report, App. ix*
    Dropmore Mss. (W.W. Grenville, Lord Grenville), *13th Report, App. iii* (10 vols.)
    Emly/Pery Mss. (E.S. Pery, speaker of the Irish House of Commons, 1771–85), *8th Report, App. 11, and 14th Report, App. ix*
    Lothian Mss. (2nd earl of Buckinghamshire, lord lieutenant, 1776–80)
    Rutland Mss. (4th duke of Rutland, lord lieutenant, 1784–7), *14th Report, App. i (vol. iii)*
    Stopford-Sackville Mss. (Lord George Sackville/Germain, 1st Viscount Sackville), vol. i

Hoffman, Ross J.S., *Edmund Burke: New York agent* (Philadelphia, 1965)

Holmes, George, *Sketches of some of the southern counties of Ireland collected during a tour in the autumn of 1797* ... (London, 1801)

Howson, Edmund W., and Warner, George Townsend (eds.), *Harrow school* ... (London, 1898)

Hunt, William (ed.), *The Irish parliament, 1775* ... (London, 1907)

Ingamells, John, and Edgcumbe, John (eds.), *The letters of Sir Joshua Reynolds* (Yale, 2000)

Inglis, Henry D., *Ireland in 1834* ... (second ed., 2 vols., London, 1835)

Irish Art Associates: *Catalogue*, summer 2000

Irish Georgian Society: *The Georgian Society records of eighteenth-century domestic architecture and decoration in Dublin* (5 vols., original ed., 1909–13; reprint, 1969)

Jackson, Robert Wyse, dean of Cashel, untitled article on the Cashel Palace, *c.*1960

James, Francis G., *Lords of the ascendancy: the Irish House of Lords and its members, 1600–1800* (Dublin, 1995)

Jesse, J.H., *Memoirs of the life and reign of King George III* (3 vols., London, 1867)

Johnston[-Liik], E.M. (ed.), 'The state of the Irish House of Commons in 1791', *Proc. RIA*, vol. 59, sec. C, no. 1 (1957)

Johnston[-Liik], E.M., *Great Britain and Ireland, 1760–1800: a study in political administration* (St Andrews, 1963)

Johnston[-Liik], E.M. (ed.), 'The state of the Irish Parliament, 1784–7', in *Proc. RIA*, vol. 71, sec. C, no. 5 (1971)

Johnston[-Liik], E.M., 'Problems common to both protestant and catholic Churches in eighteenth-century Ireland', in Oliver MacDonagh, W.F. Mandle and Pauric Travers (eds.), *Irish culture and nationalism, 1750–1950* (London, 1983)

Johnston-Liik, E.M., *History of the Irish parliament, 1692–1800: Commons, constituencies, and statutes* (Belfast, 2002). This is cited in the footnotes as a 'database', because it was not yet published when the text was finalised.

Journals : *Journals of the House of Lords of the kingdom of Ireland* (8 vols., Dublin, 1780–1800)

Journals : *Journals of the House of Commons of the kingdom of Ireland, 1613–1800* (19 vols., Dublin, 1796–1800)

Journals: *General index to the journals of the House of Commons ...* (2 vols., Dublin, 1802)

Joyce, Weston St John, *The neighbourhood of Dublin, its topography, antiquities and historical associations ...* (Dublin, 1939)

Jupp, P.J., 'Irish MPs at Westminster in the early nineteenth century', in *Historical Studies*, vii (1969)

Jupp, P.J., 'Genevese exiles in Co. Waterford', in *Cork Historical and Archaeological Journal*, vol. 75 (1970)

Jupp, P.J., *Lord Grenville, 1759–1834* (Oxford, 1985)

Kelly, James, 'The Irish Parliamentary Reform movement: the administration and popular politics, 1783–5' (unpublished University College, Dublin, MA thesis, 1981)

Kelly, James, 'The context and course of Thomas Orde's plan of education of 1787', in *The Irish Journal of Education*, xx, no. 1 (1986)

Kelly, James, 'Inter-denominational relations and religious toleration in late eighteenth-century Ireland: the "Paper War" of 1786–8', in *Eighteenth-Century Ireland*, iii (1988)

Kelly, James, 'The genesis of "Protestant Ascendancy": the Rightboy disturbances of the 1780s and their impact upon protestant opinion', in Gerard O'Brien (ed.), *Parliament, politics and people: essays in eighteenth-century Irish history* (Dublin, 1989)

Kelly, James, 'Eighteenth-century ascendancy: a commentary', in *Eighteenth-century Ireland*, v (1990)

Kelly, James (ed.), *The letters of Lord Chief Baron Edward Willes to the earl of Warwick, 1757–62: an account of Ireland in the mid-eighteenth century* (Aberystwyth, 1990)

Kelly, James, *Prelude to union: Anglo-Irish politics in the 1780s* (Cork, 1992)

Kelly, James, *'The damn'd thing called honour': duelling in Ireland, 1570–1860* (Cork, 1995)

Kelly, James, *Henry Flood: Patriots and politics in eighteenth-century Ireland* (Dublin, 1998)

Kennedy, Joe, 'Callan: a corporate town, 1700–1800', in *Kilkenny history and society* (Dublin, 1990)

Kennedy, Raymond, 'The administration of the diocese of Dublin and Glendalough in the eighteenth century' (unpublished University of Dublin Ph.D. thesis, 1968)

Kiernan, T.J., *History of the financial administration of Ireland to 1817* (London, 1930)

Kinane, Vincent, 'The Fagel collection', in Peter Fox (ed.), *Treasures of the [TCD] Library ...* (Dublin, 1986)

King-Hall, Magdalen, *The edifying bishop [Frederick Hervey]* (London, 1951)

King-Harman, A.L., *The kings of King House* (Bedford, 1996)

King, Sir Charles Simeon, Bt (ed.), *A great archbishop of Dublin: William King, D.D., 1650–1729, his autobiography, family and a selection from his correspondence* (London, 1908)

King, Jeremiah, *A history of Co. Kerry, part two* (Liverpool, *c.*1910)

Kirwan, John, 'Mount Juliet [Thomastown, Co. Kilkenny]', in *Old Kilkenny Review, 1998*

Laffan, William (ed.), *The sublime and the beautiful: Irish art, 1700–1830* (London, 2001)

Lane Poole, Mrs Reginald, *Catalogue of portraits in the possession of the university, colleges, city and county of Oxford*, iii (Oxford, 1926)

Langford, Paul, *Public life and the propertied Englishman, 1689–1798* (Oxford, 1991)

Langford, Paul, 'Politics and manners from Sir Robert Walpole to Sir Robert Peel', in *Proceedings of the British Academy*, xliv (1997)

Lawlor, Very Rev. H.J., *The fasti of St Patrick's Cathedral, Dublin* (Dundalk, 1930)

Lecky, W.E.H., *Leaders of public opinion in Ireland ...* (new ed., London, 1871)

Lecky, W.E.H., *Leaders of public opinion in Ireland ...* (new [and much revised] ed., 2 vols., London, 1903)

Ledwich, Rev. Edward, *Antiquities of Ireland* (Dublin, 1st and 2nd eds., 1790 and 1804)

Legg, Marie-Louise (ed.), *The Synge letters: Bishop Edward Synge to his daughter, Alicia, Roscommon to Dublin, 1746–1752* (Dublin, 1996)

Legg, Marie-Louise, 'Money and reputation: the effects of the banking crises of 1755 and 1760', in *Eighteenth-century Ireland*, xi (1996)

Leslie, Canon James B., *Armagh clergy and parishes ...* (Dundalk, 1911)

Leslie, Canon James B., *Clogher clergy and parishes ...* (Enniskillen, 1929)

Leslie, Canon James B., *Ossory clergy and parishes ...* (Enniskillen, 1933)

Leslie, Canon James B., *Ferns clergy and parishes ...* (Dublin, 1936)

Leslie, Canon James B., *Clergy of Derry and Raphoe* (reprint, Belfast, 1999)

Leslie, Canon James B., and Swanzy, Dean Henry B., *Biographical succession lists of the clergy of [the] diocese of Down* (Enniskillen, 1936)

Leslie, Canon James B., et al., *Clergy of Connor from Patrician times to the present day* (Belfast, 1993)

Leslie, Canon James B., and Wallace, W.J.R., *Clergy of Dublin and Glendalough: biographical succession lists* (Belfast, 2001)

Lewis, Samuel, *A topographical dictionary of Ireland ...* (2 vols., London, 1837)

Lightbown, Mary, 'The Gores of Barrowmount [Goresbridge, Co. Kilkenny] and their memorials', in John Kirwan (ed.), *Kilkenny studies in honour of Margaret M. Phelan* (Kilkenny, 1997)

Lodge, John, and Archdall, Mervyn, *The peerage of Ireland ...* (8 vols., Dublin, 1789)

Macartney, A.G., *The organs and organists of the Cathedral Church of St Patrick, Armagh, 1482–1998* (Armagh, 1999)

Macartney, Earl: *Macartney in Ireland: a calendar of the chief secretaryship papers of Sir George Macartney, edited by Thomas Bartlett* (Belfast, 1978)

McCarthy, [Very Rev.] R.B., 'Cahir church and parish', in *The church yearbook for the united dioceses of Cashel and Emly, Waterford and Lismore* (Waterford, 1963)

McCarthy, [Very Rev.] R.B., *The Trinity College estates, 1800–1923* ... (Dundalk, 1992)

McCavery, T.R., 'Finance and politics in Ireland, 1801–17' (unpublished Queen's University of Belfast Ph.D. thesis, 1981)

McCracken, J.L., 'Central and local administration in Ireland under George II' (unpublished QUB Ph.D. thesis, 1941)

McCracken, J.L., 'The ecclesiastical structure, 1714–60', in T.W. Moody and W.E. Vaughan (eds.), *A new history of Ireland, iv: Eighteenth-century Ireland, 1691–1800* (Oxford, 1986)

MacDonagh, Oliver, *The inspector general: Sir Jeremiah Fitzpatrick and the politics of social reform, 1783–1802* (London, 1981)

MacDonagh, Peter, ' "Hostile, indigested innovations": official pressures for reform of the Church of Ireland in the 1780s' (forthcoming article)

McDowell, R.B., 'The acquisition of the Fagel library', in *Annual bulletin of the friends of the library of Trinity College, Dublin* (1947)

McDowell, R.B., *Ireland in the age of imperialism and revolution, 1760–1801* (Oxford, 1979)

McDowell, R.B., and Webb, D.A., *Trinity College, Dublin, 1592–1952: an academic history* (Cambridge, 1982)

Macintyre, Donald, *Admiral Rodney* (London, 1962)

McLanathan, Richard, *Gilbert Stuart* (New York, 1986)

McNally, Patrick, *Parties, Patriots and Undertakers: parliamentary politics in early Hanoverian Ireland* (Dublin, 1997)

McParland, Edward, *James Gandon: Vitruvius Hibernicus* (London, 1985)

McParland, Edward, 'Edward Lovett Pearce and the deanery of Christ Church, Dublin', in Agnes Bernelle (ed.), *Decantations* (Dublin, 1992)

McParland, Edward, *Public architecture in Ireland, 1680–1760* (Yale, 2001)

McParland, Edward, Rowan, Alistair, and Rowan, Ann Martha, *The architecture of Richard Morrison (1767–1849) and William Vitruvius Morrison (1794–1838)* (Dublin, 1989)

Maguire, W.A. (ed.), *Up in arms: the 1798 Rebellion in Ireland: a bicentenary exhibition* ... at the *Ulster Museum, Belfast* ... (Belfast, 1998)

Malcomson, A.P.W., 'The Newtown Act: revision and reconstruction', in *Irish Historical Studies* (hereafter *IHS*), xviii (1973)

Malcomson, A.P.W. (ed.), *Irish official papers in Great Britain: private collections*, vol. i (Belfast, 1973) and vol. ii (Belfast, 1990)

Malcomson, A.P.W., 'Speaker Pery and the Pery papers', in *The North Munster Antiquarian Journal*, vol. xvi (1973–4)

Malcomson, A.P.W., 'Absenteeism in eighteenth-century Ireland', in *Irish Economic and Social History*, vol. 1 (1974)

Malcomson, A.P.W. (ed.), *An Anglo-Irish dialogue: a calendar of the correspondence between John Foster and Lord Sheffield, 1774–1821* (Belfast, 1975)

Malcomson, A.P.W., 'The politics of "Natural Right": the Abercorn Family and Strabane borough, 1692–1800', In *Historical Studies*, x (Galway, 1976)

Malcomson, A.P.W., *John Foster: the politics of the Anglo-Irish Ascendancy* (Oxford, 1978)

Malcomson, A.P.W., 'The parliamentary traffic of this country', in Thomas Bartlett and D.W. Hayton (eds.), *Penal era and golden age: essays in Irish history, 1690–1800* (Belfast, 1979)

Malcomson, A.P.W., 'The gentle Leviathan: Arthur Hill, 2nd marquess of Downshire, 1753–1801', in *Plantation to Partition: essays in Ulster history in honour of J.L. McCracken* (Belfast, 1981)

Malcomson, A.P.W., *The pursuit of the heiress: aristocratic marriage in Ireland, 1750–1820* (Belfast, 1982)

Malcomson, A.P.W., 'Belleisle [Co. Fermanagh] and its owners', in *Clogher Record: 1998*

Malcomson, A.P.W., 'A variety of perspectives on Laurence Parsons, 2nd earl of Rosse', in William Nolan and Timothy P. O'Neill (eds.), *Offaly history and society ...* (Dublin, 1998)

Malcomson, A.P.W., 'A woman scorned?: Theodosia, countess of Clanwilliam (1743–1817)', in *Familia: the Ulster Genealogical Review*, no. 15 (1999)

Malcomson, A.P.W., 'The Irish peerage and the Act of Union, 1800–1971', in *Transactions of the Royal Historical Society, sixth series*, x (2000)

Malcomson, A.P.W., and Jackson, D.J., 'Sir Henry Cavendish and the proceedings of the Irish House of Commons, 1776–1800', in D.W. Hayton (ed.), *The Irish parliament in the eighteenth century: the long apprenticeship* (Edinburgh, 2001)

Malins, Edward, and the Knight of Glin, *Lost demesnes: Irish landscape gardening, 1660–1845* (London, 1976)

Mant, Richard, bishop of Down and Connor, *History of the Church of Ireland ... [to 1810]* (2 vols., London, 1840)

Marnane, D.G., 'Landownership in south Tipperary, 1849–1903' (unpublished University College, Cork, Ph.D. thesis, 1991)

Mathieson, William Law, *English Church reform, 1815–1840* (London, 1923)

Matteson, Robert S., 'Archbishop William King and the conception of his library', in *The Library, sixth series*, vol. 13, no. 3 (Sep. 1991)

Maxwell, Constania, *A history of Trinity College, Dublin, 1591–1892* (Dublin, 1946)

Maxwell, Constania, *Country and town in Ireland under the Georges* (revised ed., Dundalk, 1949)

Melvin, Patrick (ed.), 'Letters of Lord Longford and others on Irish affairs, 1689–1702', in *Analecta Hibernica*, xxxii (1985)

Milne, Kenneth, 'Principle or pragmatism: Archbishop Brodrick and Church education policy', in Alan Ford, James McGuire and Kenneth Milne (eds.), *As by law established: the Church of Ireland since the Reformation* (Dublin, 1995)

Milne, Kenneth, *The Irish charter schools, 1730–1830* (Dublin, 1997)

Milne, Kenneth (ed.), *Christ Church Cathedral, Dublin: a history* (Dublin, 2000)

Mitchell, L.G., *Charles James Fox* (paperback ed., London, 1997)

Mohan, Rev. Christopher, 'Archbishop Richard Robinson: builder of Armagh', in *Seanchas Ard Mhaca*, vol. vi, no. 1 (1971)

Monck Mason, William, *The history and antiquities of the collegiate and cathedral church of St Patrick's, near Dublin ..., 1190 to ... 1819* (Dublin, 1820)

Moore, Tom: *The journal of Thomas Moore, edited by Wilfred S. Dowden*, ii (Newark, Delaware, 1983)

Moran, Mary, 'The Agars of Gowran (Lords Clifden and Callan)', in *In the shadow of the steeple[: the Journal of the Duchas-Tullaheerin Heritage Society, Co. Kilkenny]*, no. 2 (1990)

Mount, Charles Merrill, 'The Irish career of Gilbert Stuart', in the *Quarterly Bulletin of the Irish Georgian Society*, vi, no. 1 (Jan.–Mar. 1963)

Mount, Charles Merrill, *Gilbert Stuart: a biography* (New York, 1964)

Moylan, Most Rev. Francis: 'The Moylan correspondence in Bishop's House, Killarney, edited by Evelyn Bolster', part 1, *Collectanea Hibernica*, no. 14 (1971), and part 2, ibid., no. 15 (1972)

Musgrave, Sir William, 6th Bt, *Obituary prior to 1800 (as far as relates to England, Scotland and Ireland) ...* (6 vols., Harleian Society, London, 1899–1901)

Namier, Sir Lewis, and Brooke, John, *The History of Parliament: the House of Commons, 1754–1790* (3 vols., London, 1964)

National Library reports on private collections, nos. 97 and 138

Neely, Rev. Dr. W.G., *Kilkenny: an urban history, 1391–1843* (Belfast, 1989)

Newcome, William, bishop of Waterford, *Observations on Our Lord's conduct as a divine instructor and on the excellence of His moral character* (Dublin, 1782)

Nockles, Peter, 'Church parties in the pre-Tractarian Church of England, 1750–1833', in John Walsh, Stephen Taylor and Colin Haydon (eds.), *The Church of England, c.1689– c.1833 ...* (Cambridge, 1993)

O'Connell, Maurice R., *Irish politics and social conflict in the age of the American Revolution* (Philadelphia, 1965)

O'Flaherty, Eamon, 'Ecclesiastical politics and the dismantling of the Penal Laws in Ireland, 1774–82', in *IHS*, xxvi, no. 101 (May 1988)

O'Flanagan, J. Roderick, *Lives of the lord chancellors of Ireland* (2 vols., Dublin, 1870)

Ollard, Very Rev. S.L., *Fasti Wyndesonienses: the deans and chapter of Windsor* (Windsor, 1950)

O'Regan, Philip, *Archbishop William King of Dublin (1650–1729) ...* (Dublin, 2000)

Pakenham, Thomas, *The year of liberty: the story of the great Irish rebellion of 1798* (revised ed., London, 1997)

Peel Papers: *Sir Robert Peel [2nd Bt] from his private papers*, edited by C.S. Parker (3 vols., London, 1899)

Penny, Nicholas (ed.), *Reynolds* [Royal Academy exhibition catalogue] (London, 1986)

Phillips, Walter Alison (ed.), *History of the Church of Ireland from the earliest times to the present day* (3 vols., Oxford, 1933)

Playfair, William, *British family antiquity: the peerage and baronetage of the United Kingdom* (9 vols., London, 1809–11)

Plumb, J.H., *England in the eighteenth century ...* (Harmondsworth, 1970)

Pococke, Richard, bishop of Ossory, *Pococke's tour in Ireland in 1752*, edited by George T. Stokes (Dublin, 1891)

Pool, Robert, and Cash, John, *Views of the most remarkable public building, monuments and other edifices in the city of Dublin ...* (Dublin, 1780)

Power, Bill, *White knights, dark earls: the rise and fall of an Anglo-Irish dynasty [the earls of Kingston]* (Cork, 2000)

Power, Thomas P., 'Parliamentary representation in Co. Kilkenny in the eighteenth century', in *Kilkenny History and Society* (Dublin, 1990)

Power, Thomas P., *Land, politics and society in eighteenth-century Tipperary* (Oxford, 1993)

Powicke, F.M., *Handbook of British chronology* (London, 1939)

Rankin, J. Frederick, *Down cathedral: the Church of St Patrick of Down* (Belfast, 1997)

Rankin, Peter, *Irish Building ventures of the earl-bishop of Derry (1730–1803)* (Belfast, 1972)

Refausse, Raymond, and Clark, Mary (eds.), *A catalogue of the maps of the estates of the archbishops of Dublin, 1754–1850, with an historical introduction by Raymond Gillespie* (Dublin, 2001)

Renehan, Very Rev. Laurence F., *Collections of Irish Church history ...* (vol. i, Dublin, 1861)

Reports: *Compensation for boroughs disfranchised by the Act of Union: report of the commissioners of compensation, session 1805 (89)*

Reports: *Municipal corporations (Ireland): Appendix to the first report of the commissioners, session 1835 (28)*

Reynolds, Thomas, junior, *The life of Thomas Reynolds ... by his son* (2 vols., London, 1828)

Rizzo, Betty, *Companions without vows: relationships among eighteenth-century British women* (Athens, Georgia, 1994)

Robbins, Helen H., *Our first ambassador to China: an account of the life of George, Earl Macartney* ... (London, 1908)

Roebuck, Peter, *Yorkshire baronets, 1640–1760: families, estates and fortunes* (Oxford, 1980)

Roebuck, Peter (ed.), *Macartney of Lisanoure, 1737–1806: essays in biography* (Belfast, 1983)

Rowse, A.L., *The later Churchills* (London, 1958)

Ryan, Rev. Edward, *A short but comprehensive view of the evidences of the Mosaic and Christian codes* ... (Dublin, 1795)

Ryan, Rev. Edward, *The history of the effects of religion on mankind, in countries ancient and modern, barbarous and civilised* (2nd ed., Dublin, 1802)

Sadleir, Thomas U., (ed.), 'Manuscripts at Kilboy, Co. Tipperary, in the possession of the Lord Dunalley', in *Analecta Hibernica*, xii (1949)

Sadleir, Thomas U., and Dickinson, Page L., *Georgian mansions in Ireland* ... (Dublin, 1915)

Scott, John, 1st earl of Clonmell, [*Unpublished diary*] (privately printed, *c.*1860)

Seymour, Rev. St John D., *The succession list of parochial clergy in the united diocese of Cashel and Emly* (Dublin, 1908)

Seymour, Rev. St John D., *A history of the diocese of Emly* (Dublin, 1913)

Shannon, Lord: *Letters to his son: a calendar of the letters written by the 2nd earl of Shannon to his son, Viscount Boyle, 1790–1802, edited by Esther Hewitt* (Belfast, 1982)

Simms, G.O., archbishop of Armagh, 'The founder of Armagh's public library: Primate Robinson among his books', in *Irish Booklore*, i, no. 1 (1971)

Simms, J.G., *The Williamite confiscation in Ireland, 1690–1703* (London, 1956)

Sirr, Rev. J.D., *A memoir of the last archbishop of Tuam* (Dublin, 1845)

Sleater, Rev. Matthew, *Introductory essay to a new system of civil and ecclesiastical topography* ... (Dublin, 1806)

Smith, E.A., *Whig principles and party politics: Earl Fitzwilliam (1748–1833) and the Whig party* (Manchester, 1975)

Smithwick, Peter, 'Georgian Kilkenny', in the *Quarterly Bulletin of the Irish Georgian Society*, vi, no. 4 (Oct.–Dec. 1963)

Smyth, C.J., *Chronicle of the law officers of Ireland* (London, 1839)

Somerville, E.O., and Ross, Martin, *An incorruptible Irishman: ... Chief Justice Charles Kendal Bushe* ... (London, 1932)

Speechly, William, *Treatise on the cultivation of the pineapple* (York, 1779)

Speechly, William, *Treatise on the cultivation of the vine* (York, 1790)

Spring, Eileen, *Law, land and family: aristocratic inheritance in England, 1300–1800* (Chapell, Hill, 1993)

Stanhope, Philip Henry, 5th Earl Stanhope, *Miscellanies* (London, 1863)

Stanley, Arthur Penrhyn, dean of Westminster, *Historical memorials of Westminster Abbey* ... (London, 1868)

Statutes: *The statutes at large passed in the parliaments held in Ireland, 1310–1800* (20 vols., Dublin, 1789–1800)

Statutes : *A collection of the public general statutes passed in the parliament of Great Britain and Ireland, 1801–69* (74 vols., London, 1801–69)

Stone, Lawrence, *The family, sex and marriage in England, 1500–1800* (New York, 1977)

Stopford, Edward A., *A hand-book of ecclesiastical law and duty for the use of the clergy of the Church of Ireland* (Dublin, 1861)

Strickland, Walter George, *A dictionary of Irish artists* (2 vols., Dublin and London, 1913)

Stuart, James, *Historical memoirs of the city of Armagh for a period of 1373 years* (Newry, 1819)

Stubbs, John William, *The history of the university of Dublin from its foundation to the end of the eighteenth century* ... (Dublin, 1889)

Sullivan Sir Edward, 1st Bt (ed.), *Buck Whaley's memoirs* ... (London, 1906)

Thorne, R.G. (ed.), *The History of Parliament: the House of Commons, 1790–1820* (5 vols., London, 1986)

Tighe, Joan, untitled article on Cashel and its palace, *c.*1965

Tighe, William, *Statistical observations relative to the county of Kilkenny* (Dublin, 1802)

Townland index: *Census of Ireland, 1901, consisting of a general topographical index to the [parishes,] townlands and towns of Ireland* (2 vols., Dublin, 1904)

Trainor, B., and Crawford, W.H. (eds.), *Aspects of Irish social history, 1750–1800* (Belfast, 1969)

Trant, Dominick, *Considerations on the present disturbances in the province of Munster* ... (Dublin, 1787)

[Trench, Richard Chenevix, archbishop of Dublin], *The remains of Mrs Richard Trench* (London, 1862)

Wakefield, Edward, *An account of Ireland statistical and political* (2 vols., London, 1812)

Wall, Maureen, 'The quest for Catholic equality, 1745–78', in Gerard O'Brien (ed.), *Catholic Ireland in the eighteenth century: the collected essays of Maureen Wall* (Dublin, 1989)

Wall, Maureen, 'The making of Gardiner's Relief Act[s], 1781–2', ibid.

Walpole, Horace: *The letters of Horace Walpole, [4th] earl of Orford, edited by Peter Cunningham* (9 vols., London, 1857–9)

Walpole, Horace: *The Yale edition of Horace Walpole's correspondence, edited by W.S. Lewis,* xii (New Haven, 1944)

Walsh, John, and Taylor, Stephen, 'The Church and Anglicanism in the "long" eighteenth century', in Walsh, Taylor and Colin Haydon (eds.), *The Church of England, c.1689–c.1833* ... (Cambridge, 1993)

Warburton, J., Whitelaw, Rev. J., and Walsh, Rev. Robert, *History of the city of Dublin from the earliest accounts to the present time* (2 vols., London, 1818)

Waterhouse, G., 'The family of Fagel', in *Hermathena*, no. xlvi (Dublin, 1931)

Watson, John, and Stewart, John Watson, *The gentleman's and citizen's almanack* (Dublin, 1747–1840)

Watson, Richard, bishop of Llandaff, *A letter to his grace the Archbishop of Canterbury* (London, 1783)

Watson, Rev. Richard, LL.B. (ed.), *Anecdotes of the life of Richard Watson, bishop of Llandaff, written by himself at different intervals and revised in 1814* (London, 1817)

The Weekly Irish Times, 2 Sep. 1939

Weiner, Margery, *Matters of felony: a true tale of eighteenth-century Ireland* (New York, 1967)

Wellesley, Sir Arthur, [1st duke of Wellington], *Civil correspondence and memoranda of* ...: *Ireland, from March 30th, 1807, to April 12th, 1809* (London, 1860)

Wesley, Rev. John, *The journal of* ... (4 vols., London, 1827)

Whelan, Kevin, 'The catholic Church in Co. Tipperary, 1700–1900', in William Nolan (ed.), *Tipperary history and society* (Dublin, 1985)

Wickens, David C., *The instruments of Samuel Green* (London, 1987)

Wilmot, Sir Robert, 1st Bt: *'The king's business': letters on the administration of Ireland, 1740–1761, from the papers of Sir Robert Wilmot, edited, with an introduction, by James Walton* (New York, 1996)

Wilson, C.H. (ed.), *A complete collection of the resolutions of the volunteers, grand juries, etc., of Ireland which followed the ... first Dungannon diet ...* (Dublin, 1782)

Wolfe, Charles, dean of Cashel, *Cashel: its cathedral and library* [N.P., *c.* 1965]

Wood, Herbert, *A guide to the records deposited in the Public Record Office of Ireland* (Dublin, 1919)

Woodward, Richard, bishop of Cloyne, *The present state of the Church of Ireland ...* (Dublin, 1786)

Woodworth, G.M.D., dean of Cashel, *A bishop, bogs and books*, N.P., [*c.*1985?]

Woodworth, G.M.D., dean of Cashel, *A short history of the [Bolton] library* (Dunmurry, Belfast, 1991)

Woodworth, G.M.D., dean of Cashel, *Cashel's museum of printing and early books: a short history of the GPA-Bolton Library* (Clonmel, 1994)

Woodworth,.G.M.D., dean of Cashel, 'In Cashel forever' (unpublished history of the Bolton Library, Cashel, 1994)

Wyndham, Hon. H.A., *A family history, 1688–1837: the Wyndhams of Somerset, Sussex and Wiltshire* (Oxford, 1950)

Young, Arthur, *A tour in Ireland ...* (London, 1780)

Young, John, *A catalogue of the pictures at Grosvenor House, London ...* (London, 1820)

Index

Abbot, Charles, 1st Lord Colchester, 586

Abercromby, Ralph, Sir, General, 524

Abington church, diocese of Emly, Co. Limerick, 209

absentee taxes (proposed), 512–13

absenteeism, lay and episcopal, 110, 120, 201–2, 383, 450–51, 482, 488–90, 512–13, 546, 562, 613; *see also* non-residence, clerical

Achonry cathedral, 303

Acheson, Arthur, Sir, 6th Bt, 1st Viscount Gosford, 180–81

Acheson, Arthur, 1st earl of Gosford, 180, 182

Acts and bills (parliament of England, Great Britain and the UK): for preventing non-residence of the clergy (1537), 233–7; for exempting barren lands from tithe (1549), 433; for the preservation of lands belonging to the Church (1559 and 1571), 299; of Uniformity (1662), 518, 563; Bill of Rights (1689), 518; Coronation Oath (1689), 74, 517–19; for settling the crown (1701), 518; Scottish Union (1707), 517–18, 566, 582–3; for building churches in London (1711), 225; Quebec (1774), 34; Regency (1789), 165; Church of England curates' pay (1796 and 1806–13), 478–9, 576, 580–81; Land Tax (1798), 504–5, 534–5; Copyright (1801), 250; general enclosure for the whole UK (1801), 540; indemnification of the Church of England clergy for non-residence (1801), 236; Irish Martial Law (1801), 247, 529; Irish board of first fruits (1803), 263–7; clerical residence in Great Britain (1803), 205, 239, 501–2; for the sale of the palace of St Sepulchre (1804), 266–7; augmentation of small livings in Ireland (1806), 276–7; to enquire into the state of Irish education (1806), 250; Irish board of first fruits (1807), 247; Dublin paving and lighting (1807), 253; Irish board of first fruits (1808), 223, 228, 253–4, 278–85; clerical residence in Ireland (1808), 271–5; Dublin police (1808), 253; Rev. Richard Daniel's

charity (1808), 256; for endowing and augmenting benefices in populous areas in Great Britian (1809 onwards), 225; for building churches in Great Britain (1818 onwards); for divesting the see of Dublin of Tallaght Castle (1821), 370; repealing the Test Act (1828), 155; Catholic Emancipation (1829), 325; Irish Church Temporalities (1833), 420, 506; Lord Campbell's for converting perpetuities in Ireland (1849), 420

Acts and bills (Irish parliament): for making incompatible spiritual preferment in the Churches of England and Ireland (1666), 485–6; for building clerical residences (1699), 338–9, 364 382; Kilkenny (1717), 94; curates' pay (1720 and 1800), 578–81; board of first fruits (1723), 221, 223; for allowing bishops to let boggy land for 60 years (1726), 400, 412; for building clerical residences (1726), 56n, 364–5; elections (1728), 97, 295; for changing the site of an episcopal palace and allowing bishops to let demesne land for 40 years (1742), 366–7, 399; Newtown (1748), 108–9n; for promoting the residence of the clergy (1758), 211n; board of first fruits and Primate Boulter's fund (1755), 224, 456m; Primate Boulter's fund (1758), 229; summary tithe (1762 and 1767), 444, 539–40; Octennial (1768), 176, 178; for building clerical residences (1769), 344; for erecting new chapels of ease (1772), 444; to prevent the burying of dead bodies in churches (1772), 445; for electing churchwardens, repairing churches, etc. (1772, 1785 and 1792), 194–5; for building clerical residences (1772 and 1774), 342–3, 445; Absentee Taxes (1773, 1780 and 1798), 512, 514; for enabling catholics to take mortgages (1773–4), 445–6; Catholic oath of allegiance (1774), 328, 520; Dublin custom house (1774–80), 144; Catholic relief (1778), 65, 154–5, 195, 224–5; for the further improvement of the city of Dublin

Acts and bills (Irish parliament) (*contd.*)
(1778), 413–14; for incorporating the
charitable music society (1778), 246; supply
(including appropriations to the board of first
fruits, 1778, 1783–9), 223, 226–7; Mutiny
(1780), 47; repeal of the Test (1780), 155, 195,
447, 468; Tenantry (1780), 393–6; Catholic
relief (1782), 154, 325, 327, 447–8; for
repealing the Declaratory Act of 1720 (1782),
518; to permit marriages by dissenting
teachers (1782), 447; for endowing perpetual
curacies (1784), 393, 445; for making usurious
interest illegal (1784), 327; Dublin police
(1786), 253; clergy compensation (1787), 444*n*,
548; Magistracy (1787), 292–4, 444; for fixing
the dates of assizes (1787), 69; to lower
interest rates (1788), 34–5; for exempting
barren lands from tithe (1788–93), 450–52,
482–3, 539; first fruits (1789), 224; Pension
(1789), 168–9; Benefice Mortgage (*c.*1790),
228, 230, 259–62, 618, 622; deanery of Christ
Church (1792), 256–7; manor courts (1792),
74; Catholic relief (1792–3), 77, 295, 454, 460,
515–16, 520; Militia (1793), 77; Place (1793),
180; Catholic Emancipation (1795), 517–20;
Maynooth (1795), 520–21; Insurrection
(1795), 72, 523; to explain the Summary Tithe
Act (1795), 75; Yeomanry (1796), 513; to
enable Christ Church to convey Dublin city
grounds to King's Inns (1798), 471; to
enquire into the state of education (1798), 250;
for the relief of suffering loyalists (1798), and
amending act (1799), 545–7; for the recovery
of tithes lost during 1797–9 and 1799 (1799
and 1800), 548–9, 577–8; board of first fruits
quorum (1800), 283; for the building of
churches (1800), 569; to make permanent
certain temporary statutes, including the
Whiteboy Act of 1787 (1800), 577–8;
Representation (1800), 564; for setting up
commissioners to award Union compensation
(1800), 574; Union (1800), 560
Adare, Co. Limerick, 378
Addington, Henry, 1st Viscount Sidmouth, 83, 248,
266, 487*n*, 609
advowsons: *see under* Church of Ireland, patronage
in
Agar, Anne (*née* Ellis), Mrs Henry Agar (Agar's
mother), 24–6, 30, 42, 99–100, 160
Agar, Lady Caroline (*née* Spencer), Viscountess
Clifden, 513
Agar, Charles, of Gowran, Co. Kilkenny (Agar's
great-grandfather, the putative Dublin livery
stable ostler), 13–17, 20, 95

Agar, Charles, 1st Lord and Viscount Somerton and
1st earl of Normanton, successively dean of
Kilmore, bishop of Cloyne and archbishop of
Cashel and of Dublin

summary of the career of, 1, 615; attitude of to his ancestry, 14, 16; influence of
Welbore Ellis on, 9, 30, 33–6, 39, 44, 55, 73,
103, 143, 159–61, 165, 170, 352–3, 512–13,
530, 550, 620; and the Agar family interest in
Kilkenny, 92, 110, 116, 119–20, 122–4, 133,
140, 142; political pamphlet by (1772), 41–3,
110–11, 127; as a member of the Agar political
connection, 92, 135–7, 141–3, 145–58, 161–75,
183–4, 476, 609, 616; relations of with his
siblings, 40–54, 57, 65, 125–6, 143, 148;
alleged screening of his younger brother, Rev.
Henry, 48–53, 212, 509, 590; alleged nepotism
of, 46–55, 80, 120, 137, 186, 218, 244–5;
relations of with the 2nd Viscount Clifden,
57–7, 65, 164–6, 550

views of on going into orders, 36–7, 55;
chaplaincy of to Lord Northumberland, 1, 60,
138–40; as dean of Kilmore, 1, 61, 140; as
bishop of Cloyne, 141–3, 197–9, 217, 296–8,
301–2, 355–6, 410; as archbishop of Cashel,
199–200, 202–21, 298–301, 303, 306–13,
317–34, 339–41, 343, 348–65, 371–6, 378–85,
391, 396, 402, 406–12, 422, 509; ambition of
to become archbishop of Armagh, 10, 51, 66,
137, 160–61, 163, 172–5, 183–4, 382, 406, 408,
430, 442, 466, 474, 476, 587–98, 620, 622–3; as
archbishop of Dublin, 242–7, 249–57, 314–15,
365–70, 391, 413, 415, 433; as chancellor of
the order of St Patrick, 315, 415

and Kingston college, Mitchelstown, 53,
112, 295–300, 433; and the city and
neighbourhood of Cashel, 292–5, 323–5, 333,
351–2, 362, 376; and Cashel cathedral (ancient
and modern), 5–6, 10, 303–12, 317–24,
329–31, 353; attitude of to antiquities and
ancient fabric, 5–6, 301–2, 306–7, 332*n*,
359–60; and the Cashel palace, 334, 339–41,
343, 348–66, 371–6, 378–83, 416, 424; and the
archbishop of Dublin's palaces, 365–70, 381,
433; love of music, 246, 301–2, 317–23, 616;
intellectual interests of, 37–8, 58–62, 91, 349;
relations of with Gilbert Stuart and other
painters, 62–4, 86–7, 300; interest of in *haute
cuisine*, 352–3

role of in the Irish House of Lords,
73–7, 142–3, 155, 166–9, 327, 379, 394–9,
444*n*, 445–54, 480–83, 515–16, 520–21, 543,
576, 581–4, 590, 618–20; position and role of
in the UK House of Lords, 218, 247–8, 277,

529, 542–3, 554, 560–61, 599; expertise of in the law, 73–4, 260, 346–7, 395; legislation certainly, probably or possibly sponsored by, 73–4, 185, 194–5, 224, 256, 283, 327, 346, 366–7, 397–9, 411–12, 419, 444–5, 449, 524, 539–40, 548–9, 560–69, 577–81, 618–19, 622; role of in the Irish Cabinet, 9, 74–5, 444*n*, 516, 519–21, 524, 526–7, 531; role of in the commission for the relief of suffering loyalists, 527–8, 532, 544–7

and the Penal Laws, 43, 154–5, 445–8; and Catholic relief/Emancipation, 295, 327, 495–6, 515–21, 526, 607–9; personal relations of with catholics, 26, 89, 324–8; and the Regency Crisis, 57, 164–75, 609; relations of with Lord Buckingham, 164–70, 230–37, 239–40, 448–54; and law and order/security policy in the 1790s, 6, 10, 292–4, 521–5, 527–9; and the Union, 10, 86, 295, 510–15, 527–33, 542–4, 550–58

views on and defence of the Church, 36–7, 56, 156–7, 160–61, 184–6, 218–20, 232–4, 240, 260–61, 280–81, 380, 384, 444–54, 480–83, 504–5, 536, 541, 543, 560–66, 571–4, 580, 585–6, 590–92, 616–23; and tithe reform, 450–52, 482–3, 504–5, 533–41, 548–9, 555–8, 618; and the board of first fruits, 220–21, 224–30, 240, 249, 430–33, 365–6, 614–15, 617–18, 621–2; abortive Benefice Mortgage Bill of, 228, 230, 259–62, 618, 622; revives and extends office of rural dean, 199, 204–6, 589–90; builds churches, 185–6, 198–9, 206–10, 252–4, 256, 296; builds glebe-houses, 206–11, 252–4, 256, 298, 307; promotes clerical residence, 54–7, 186–7, 211–20, 228–30, 243, 254–6, 261; and the pay and role of curates, 4, 216, 219–20, 578–81, 618; relations and comparison of with Primate Robinson, 149–52, 156–7, 190, 198–200, 210, 224, 232–5, 239–40, 444–54, 461; relations and comparison of with Primate Stuart and Archbishop Brodrick, 258–70, 282, 339–40, 364, 416, 430–36, 598–600, 607–8, 610–12

financial affairs of, 1, 4, 42–5, 85–6, 100, 310, 406–12, 417–19, 422–30; Kilkenny estate of, 10, 23, 25, 44, 394, 420*n*, 421, 423–4, 428; and the see lands of Cashel, 7, 9–10, 384–5, 391, 396, 402, 406–12, 553, 590; alleged 'love of lucre' of, 2–7, 10, 79–82, 310, 329, 364, 368, 384, 415–16, 422, 433–5, 590; dynastic ambitions of, 86, 382, 424; peerages conferred on, 16, 84–6, 167–9, 174–5, 519, 584, 596, 599; will of, 10, 418–19, 422–3, 426

family, domestic and private life of, 53–4, 83–6, 351–3, 356–9; friendship of with John Scott, Lord Clonmell, 59, 66–71, 76–8, 88–9, 91, 142–3, 148–50; physiognomy of, 68, 86–7, 186, 330, 527; character and personality of, 13, 54, 59–62, 80–84, 87–91, 282, 364, 394, 492–3, 521, 590, 610, 612, 614, 618; awareness of the need for self-publicity, 74–5, 153, 167–8, 220*n*, 242, 515–16; declining health of, 251–2, 432, 507–8; burial place of and funeral monument to, 39, 185–6, 330, 352; posthumous reputation of, 2–12, 59, 300, 352, 364, 368, 415–16, 430; archive of, 4–5, 7–10, 206, 252, 542, 550, 553

Agar, Charles (eldest son of Rev. Henry), 52–3

Agar, Charles, Rev., archdeacon of Emly (Agar's cousin), 40, 54–5, 117–18, 120, 164, 217–18, 424–5

Agar, Charles Bagenal, Hon. (Agar's nephew), 123, 425

Agar, Diana, Miss (Agar's sister), 23*n*, 25, 40, 42, 46, 53–4, 62*n*, 127, 244–5, 267, 425, 551, 555, 559

Agar, Elizabeth, Mrs Samuel Bradstreet, 17

Agar, Ellis (*née* Blanchville), Mrs Charles Agar (Agar's great-grandmother), 16–17

Agar, Ellis, countess of Brandon (Agar's 'aunty'), 18–19, 24, 90, 101, 104–5, 113, 119–21, 139, 423–4

Agar, Emmanuel Felix, 45, 47

Agar, Frances, Hon., Viscountess Hawarden (Agar's daughter), 81, 84, 125, 202, 533

Agar, George, of Ringwood and Westcourt, Co. Kilkenny, Lord Callan (Agar's cousin), 40, 55, 117, 119–20, 149, 366–7; interest of in Callan and Co. Kilkenny, 102, 114–16, 119–21, 123–5, 132–3, 163–4, 591; estates and houses of, 112, 125, 424–5; and the Union, 132–3, 550, 553, 591; character of, 113–14

Agar, George Charles, Hon. (Agar's second son), 78–9, 83–4, 426

Agar, Gertrude, Mrs Welbore Ellis Agar, 13, 30, 40, 45, 149

Agar, Harriet Hon. (Mrs John Ellis Agar), 57

Agar, Henry, of Gowran, Co. Kilkenny (Agar's father), 18, 23–5, 95–9, 145, 423–4

Agar, Henry, Rev. (Agar's brother), 25, 32*n*, 42, 47–53, 212, 217, 496, 509

Agar, Henry (third son of Rev. Henry), 53, 79

Agar, later (1802) Agar-Ellis, Henry Welbore, 2nd Viscount Clifden (Agar's nephew), 40, 55–8, 100, 120–21, 169, 251, 366–7; as head of the Agar family, interest and connection, 38–40,

Agar, later (1802) Agar-Ellis, (*contd.*)
44, 57–8, 86, 123–5, 127–33, 163–7, 171–2,
425, 476, 512–14, 616; and the rebellion and
Union, 131–3, 172, 513–14, 521–5, 527, 550,
553, 591

Agar, James, of Gowran (Agar's grandfather),
17–25, 93–6, 176

Agar, James, of Ringwood, Co. Kilkenny (Agar's
uncle), 9, 18, 23, 25, 30, 92, 96–102, 110–11,
139

Agar, James, 1st Viscount Clifden (Agar's brother),
1, 13, 15–18, 32, 47, 57–8, 82, 87, 92, 125–9,
156, 158–64, 513, 616; character and career of,
35, 40–45, 97–116, 120–23, 129, 162–3; as
head of the Agar interest and connection,
42–4, 97–116, 119–23, 125–9, 133, 143–9,
158–64

Agar, James, Hon. and Ven., archdeacon of Kilmore
(Agar's youngest son), 83–4, 186, 244–5, 419,
426

Agar, James, 'of the Temple', 45

Agar, James, 3rd earl of Normanton (Agar's
grandson), 4, 10, 415, 421

Agar, Jane (*née* Benson), Lady Somerton and
countess of Normanton (Agar's wife), 1, 40,
54, 62–3, 71, 78–80, 88, 91, 185n, 202, 208,
319, 353, 368–9, 379–80, 426, 459, 506–7, 555,
587; character of and relationship with Agar,
82–6, 365–6, 581

Agar, Hon. and Rev. John Ellis (Agar's nephew), 37,
40, 55–7, 123, 218, 476

Agar, Lucinda (*née* Martin), Viscountess Clifden,
41, 43–4, 82, 90, 123, 126–9, 147, 171

Agar, Mary (*née* Tyrrell), Mrs Henry Agar, 48,
52–3, 300

Agar, Mary (*née* Wemys), Mrs James Agar (Agar's
grandmother), 18, 42, 96, 98, 119

Agar, Mary, Mrs James Smyth (Agar's aunt), 18

Agar, Mary (daughter of Rev. Henry), 53

Agar, Peter, 17, 98

Agar, Welbore, Viscount Somerton, 2nd earl of
Normanton (Agar's eldest son), 3–4, 8, 10, 33,
38, 47, 83–6, 251, 301, 354, 380, 398–9, 427;
and the Cashel see lands lease, 415, 417–23,
434–5, 497

Agar, Welbore Ellis (Agar's brother, 'Welby'), 13, 25,
30, 40, 42, 45–7, 53, 62–3, 125–6, 129, 267–8,
394, 424–5, 555

Agar, Welbore Ellis, Rev. (second son of Rev.
Henry), 53, 137, 186

Agar, Welbore Felix, 45, 47

Agar, Mrs (wife of Rev. Charles Agar, archdeacon of
Emly), 55

Agar, family of, of Gowran, Viscounts Clifden, 11,
13–26; interest of in Kilkenny and the House
of Commons, 92–100, 102–16, 119–33, 151,
162, 166–7, 170, 183–4; estate of in Co.
Kilkenny: *see under* Kilkenny, County; as a
political connection (in conjunction with
Welbore Ellis), 136–7, 143–75, 183–4

Agar, family of, of Ringwood, Co. Kilkenny, 22–3,
112, 121, 125

Agar, or 'Eagar', family of, of Co. Kerry, 14

Agar's Lane, Cashel, 324

Agar-Ellis, George James, 1st Lord Dover, 13, 27–8,
47, 483

Aghabullogue, rectory and vicarage of, diocese of
Cloyne, Co. Cork, 48

Akenson, D.H., 240, 279, 485, 511, 568n, 621

Alexander, Nathaniel, bishop of Clonfert, 229–30,
283, 603

Alleyn, Samuel, of Golden, Co. Tipperary (Cashel
see under-tenant), 295, 409

Altamont, Lord: *see* Browne, John Denis

American War of Independence, 32–3, 80, 91, 147,
154–6, 511, 545

Andrews, Francis, Dr (provost of TCD), 406, 439

Aney, advowson of, diocese of Emly, Co. Limerick,
238n; glebe-house, 209, 217; vicarage of, 217

Annesley, Francis Charles, 1st Earl Annesley, 313

Annesley, Richard, 2nd Earl Annesley, 179, 546

Annesley, Richard, of New Ross, Co. Wexford
(loyalist murdered in south-east Co. Kilkenny
in 1798), 523

Annesley, William, Hon., dean of Down, 313, 546

Antrim, north, 557

appellate jurisdiction: *see under* parliament (British),
House of Lords, and parliament (Irish),
House of Lords

'Archbishop of Cashel's Act', the (1795), 297–9,
411–12, 419, 618–19

archbishoprics/archbishops: *see under* individual
archbishoprics and their archbishops
generally; for individual archbishops, *see under*
their surnames – e.g. Agar

Archdale, Nicholas, of Castle Archdale, Co.
Fermanagh, 181

archdeaconries, 205–6, 214, 244

architecture and building, 55–7, 59, 96, 116, 144,
146, 148, 158–9, 196–9, 201, 206–9, 246–7,
252–4, 282, 296–8, 299–318, 323–6, 329–83,
386, 613–14; *see also* individual cathedrals,
churches, glebe-houses, houses, palaces, etc.

Ardbraccan House, Navan, Co. Meath, 340

Ardfert, diocese of: *see under* Limerick, diocese of

Arklow church, diocese of Glendalough, Co.
Wicklow, 247, 254

Armagh, archbishopric of, 189, 214, 249–50, 332,
393, 477–8; succession to, 51, 66, 137, 145–6,
160–61, 163, 166, 172–5, 183–4, 189, 389,
440–42, 458n, 461–2, 464–5, 466–71, 496, 526,
562, 587–98;
archbishops of, 134–5, 197, 222–3, 477–8,
490; archdeaconry of, 457; precentorship of,
612; cathedral, 214, 286, 310, 316–7, 613–14;
diocese of, 222, 286, 444–5, 455–8; palace,
332n, 382–3, 405, 594–5; province of, 538,
609–10; see estate, 189, 383, 388–9, 612
Armagh city, 331–3, 455–8, 460; parliamentary
borough of, 137, 175, 177, 182–4, 459, 571–2,
607–8; observatory, 331; public library, 331, 337;
university (proposed), 331, 383, 445–6, 471–2
Armagh, County, 460
Armstrong, Anthony, Rev., vicar of Emly and
prebendary of Killardry, 211–12, 217
Armstrong, John, Rev., 206
army, 18, 31, 74, 84, 91, 109, 119, 154, 266, 361–3,
525, 578n, 591, 600
art history, 18–19, 30, 33, 38, 46–7, 62–4, 87, 105,
185–6, 461, 458, 464n, 476n, 614
Asgill, Charles, Sir, General, 523
Ashbourne, Lord: see Gibson, Edward
Ashbrook, Viscount: see Flower
Ashe, St George, bishop of Clogher, 343n
Aspinall, Arthur, 7
assizes: see under legal system
association for discountenancing vice, 492
Athboy, Co. Meath, rectory and rectorial tithes of,
393
Athenry, Lord: see Bermingham
Athlacca, parish of, diocese and county of Limerick,
212
Atterbury, Francis, bishop of Rochester, 479
Atterbury, Francis, Rev., vicar of Kilmahon, diocese
of Cloyne, 52
Auckland, Lord: see Eden
Augmentation of the army on the Irish
establishment, 31, 109
'Augmentation' lands (granted to the Church in
1666), 399–400, 402
augmentation of small livings: see Primate Boulter's
fund
Augusta, princess dowager of Wales, 441–2

Bacon, John, junior (sculptor), 185–6
Bacon, Roland, archbishop of Cashel, 287
Bagwell, John, Colonel, of Marlfield, Clonmel, Co.
Tipperary, 551–3
Bagwell, Richard, MP, for Cashel, Co. Tipperary,
later dean of Clogher, 552, 603

Bagwell, William, 552, 553n
Baldwin, Richard, Rev. Dr (provost of TCD), 406
Ballinard (near Cashel, Co. Tipperary?), 362
Ballintemple, rectory of, diocese of Cashel, Co.
Tipperary, 137, 216, 578
Ballinulta, near Cullen, Co. Tipperary, 294
Ballyhooly church, diocese of Cloyne, Co. Cork, 198
Ballymore Eustace church, diocese of Glendalough,
Co. Kildare, 247, 253–4; glebe-house, 253
Ballymote, living of, diocese of Killala, Co. Sligo, 216
Ballynaboley, barony of Gowran, Co. Kilkenny, 44,
80, 420n, 423–4
Ballypadeen, etc., Co. Tipperary (part of Agar's
Cashel see lands lease), 407
Ballyquirk, barony of Gowran, Co. Kilkenny, 20
Ballyscullion, Bellaghy, Co. Londonderry, 386
Ballyshanemore, barony of Gowran, Co. Kilkenny,
20
Bank of England, 224
Bank of England consols: see under investment in
the stockmarket
Bank of Ireland, 427, 432–3
Bank of Ireland stock: see under investment in the
stockmarket
Bannerman, Mr (Agar's gardener at Cashel), 358–9
Barberstown, Co. Dublin, 29, 207
Barker, William, Sir, 4th Bt, of Kilcooly Abbey, Co.
Tipperary, 207
Barnard, Thomas, successively bishop of Killaloe
and Limerick, 69, 226–7, 512, 576–70
Barnard, T.C., 240, 304n, 338–9, 351, 399
Barnes, Thomas, alderman of Kilkenny, 23n
Barren Lands Bills/Acts: see under tithes
Barrington, Shute, bishop of Durham, 468
Barry, Redmond (amateur artist), 353
Barton, Hugh, 295
Barton, Thomas, of Grove, Fethard, Co. Tipperary,
295, 553n
Bates, Joah/Josiah? (organist?), 321
Batwell, Lullum (surveyor?), 108n
Bayly, John, of Gowran, Co. Kilkenny, 22
Bayly, Joseph, of Gowran, 22
Bayly, Lewis, of Gowran, 96
Beaufort, Daniel Augusts, Rev. Dr, 203, 282, 305,
355, 367, 379, 491
Beaulieu, near Drogheda, Co. Louth, 378
Bellamont, earl of: see Coote
Bellamont Forest, Cootehill, Co. Cavan, 378
Belvedere, Drumcondra, Co. Dublin, 379n
Bence-Jones, Mark, 307, 335, 337, 351, 360
Bennet, William, bishop of Cloyne, 176, 313, 344,
355, 487–9, 496, 576
Bennetsbridge, Co. Kilkenny, 16, 60

Bennett, John?, Rev., curate of Athlacca, diocese and county of Limerick, 212–13

Benson, Arthur, Colonel, 80*n*

Benson, Edward, Rev., 79

Benson, Frances (*née* Macartney-Porteous), Mrs William Benson, 79–80

Benson, Francis, Rev., rector of Fethard, diocese of Cashel, Co. Tipperary, 137, 218

Benson, George, General, 79, 80*n*, 81

Benson, Henry, Lieutenant, 80*n*

Benson, Hill, Rev., 79

Benson, Jane (*née* Winder), Mrs Edward Benson, 79

Benson, Jane: *see* Agar, Jane

Benson, J. Bowes, 79

Benson, Mary, Miss, 80*n*, 426

Benson, William, of Downpatrick and of Abbey Street, Dublin, 79–80

Benson, William, Rev., successively chancellor and precentor of Emly, 80, 137

Bentinck, William Henry Cavendish-, 3rd duke of Portland, 231, 358, 456, 467–70, 475–6, 487, 489, 508, 519, 532, 606; career and character of, 161–3, 172–5, 248–9, 277, 597, 604; and the primacy, 174, 467–70, 588–9, 597, 607; and bishops' boroughs, 176, 180; and the Union, 542, 551–6, 560–62, 581, 584*n*, 597, 604, 607

Beresford, Barbara (*née* Montgomery), Mrs John Beresford, 145

Beresford, George de la Poer, 2nd earl of Tyrone and 1st marquess of Waterford, 65, 82, 133, 141, 145, 170–71, 298, 514*n*, 547*n*

Beresford, George, bishop of Kilmore, 266, 605, 609–12

Beresford, Henry de la Poer, 3rd marquess of Waterford, 135

Beresford, John, Hon., 6–7, 145–6, 156, 158, 162–3, 248, 300–01, 389, 429, 517, 524, 529, 533–4, 609

Beresford, Lord John George, archbishop of Armagh, 135–6, 145, 184, 216, 276, 317, 381*n*, 393, 435, 456, 491, 508, 602–3, 605

Beresford, Marcus, Colonel, 175, 178

Beresford, William, Hon., archbishop of Tuam and 1st Lord Decies, 135–6, 145, 215–16, 270, 346, 429, 450, 471, 484, 576; slow promotion of, 141, 484, 486; character of as a churchman, 141, 270, 450; and the borough of St Canice, 175, 178–9, 182; and the primacy, 175, 466, 544, 589, 597; fortune amassed by in the Church, 141, 216, 429

Beresford, family of, earls of Tyrone and marquesses of Waterford, 136, 141, 175, 603, 610

Berkeley, George, bishop of Cloyne, 199, 355, 485

Berkley, Miss (visitor to Agar at Cloyne), 62

Bermingham, Ellis: *see* Agar, Ellis, countess of Brandon

Bermingham, Francis, 21st Lord Athenry, 18, 24, 104

Bermingham, Thomas, 22nd Lord Athenry and earl of Louth, 414

Bernard, Francis, 1st earl of Bandon, 497

Bernard, James, Viscount Bernard, 2nd earl of Bandon, 497

Bernard, Mary (*née* Brodrick), Viscountess Bernard, countess of Bandon, 497

Bessborough, Pilltown, Co. Kilkenny, 110

Bessborough, earl of: *see* Ponsonby, Brabazon, and Ponsonby, William

Bible Society, the, 489

bishops (of the Church of Ireland); characteristics of, 11–12, 65, 76, 187–90, 192–7, 220, 233, 240–41, 283, 290–91, 340, 387–90, 435–7, 483–99; number of, 19*n*, 187–8, 505–6, 622; wives of, 84–5, 470, 507; as 'political prelates', 41, 65, 110, 134–8, 224–5, 290–91, 443–8, 477–8, 475–83; appointment and promotion of, 140–41, 150–51, 156–7, 200, 340–44, 390–91, 435, 441–2, 474, 484–6 (*see also* chaplaincies, viceregal); boroughs controlled by, 12, 137, 175–84, 287–92, 438–9, 509, 568–72 (*see also* under: Armagh, Cashel, Clogher, Old Leighlin, St Canice); see estates held by *ex officio*, 12, 152, 175, 189, 206, 314, 339, 342–3, 346–7, 384–406, 411, 414, 420–22, 424, 429, 434–6, 504–5, 508–9, 615, 617–19, 621 (*see also* individual bishoprics); palaces occupied by *ex officio*, 12, 187, 334, 338–47, 351–2, 364–8, 375–6, 381*n*, 382–3, 491, 504–5, 508–9, 615–17, 621–2 (*see also* individual palaces, e.g.: Cashel; Tallaght Castle); absence of retirement arrangements for, 197, 499–509; post-Union representation of in the UK House of Lords, 282–3, 542–3, 554, 559–63, 567–8, 586–7, 599

Bishopscourt, Co. Kildare, 110, 358

Blackabbey, Co. Down, rectorial tithes and advowson of, 393

Blackwatertown, Co. Armagh, 405*n*

Blake, Anthony, Roman catholic archbishop of Armagh, 499–500

Blanchfield: *see* Blanchville

Blanchfield's Park, barony of Gowran, Co. Kilkenny, 16

Blanchville, Ellis: *see* Agar, Ellis, Mrs Charles Agar

Blanchville, Peter, of Rathgarvan, Co. Kilkenny, 16

Blanchville, family of, of Co. Kilkenny, 14, 16

Blaquiere, John, Sir, 1st Lord de Blaquiere, 358

Blarney church, diocese of Cloyne, Co. Cork, 198

Blaymires, Jonas (artist), 304*n*

Blessington, vicarage of, diocese of Glendalough, Co. Wicklow, 80

Blickling church, Norfolk, 493

Blow, John (composer), 302

Bolton, Alice (*née* Foster), Mrs Thomas Bolton, 337*n*

Bolton, Anne (*née* Buckworth), mother of Archbishop Bolton, 287

Bolton, G.C., 608

Bolton, Theophilus, archbishop of Cashel, 134–6, 202, 287–92, 304–5, 334, 336–8, 340, 347–8, 382, 400–01, 409, 420, 456, 616

Bolton, Thomas, of Knock, Co. Louth, 337*n*

Bolton library, Cashel, 337, 347–50, 376, 382

Borrisoleigh church, diocese of Cashel, Co. Tipperary, 208
    glebe-house, 208

Boulter, Hugh, archbishop of Armagh, 5, 134, 138, 223, 229, 232, 241, 383*n*, 390, 441, 456, 482, 557, 592, 616, 619

Boulyduff, Co. Tipperary, 70

Bourke, Ellis: *see* Agar, Ellis, countess of Brandon

Bourke, Joseph Deane, archbishop of Tuam and 3rd earl of Mayo, 135, 177*n*, 470*n*, 476

Bourke, Richard, Hon., bishop of Waterford, 340

Bourke, Theobald, 7th Viscount Mayo, 18, 24, 105

Bourne, Richard, Rev., chancellor of St Patrick's Cathedral, Dublin, rector of St Werburgh's and Finglas, etc., 243–4, 255, 463

Bowden, John (architect), 370*n*

Boyce, William (composer), 302

Boyle, Catherine, countess of Shannon, 89, 115

Boyle, Henry, 1st earl of Shannon, 103, 105, 150, 289

Boyle, Henry, 2nd earl of Shannon, 521

Boyle, John, 5th earl of Orrery, 356

Boyle, Michael, archbishop of Armagh, 135, 404

Boyle, Richard, 2nd earl of Shannon, 64–6, 145, 152, 164, 198, 224, 238*n*, 296, 315, 361*n*, 497, 514*n*, 521–2, 543, 551, 596, 620; political interest and connection of, 108, 135, 476; offices held by, 115, 171, 361*n*; and the primacy, 66, 596, 620; and the bishopric of Cloyne, 135, 198, 296

Boyle-Walsingham, Lucinda: *see* Agar, Lucinda

Boyse, Thomas, of Bishopswell, Co. Kilkenny, 127

Bradstreet, Charlotte: *see* Butler, Charlotte

Bradstreet, Samuel, of Tinnescolly, Co. Kilkenny, 17, 111

Bramblestown, barony of Gowran, Co. Kilkenny, 20

Bray, Thomas, Roman catholic archbishop of Cashel, 328, 501

Brinkley, John, bishop of Cloyne, 393

Bristol, bishopric of, 392, 508

Brodrick, Charles, Hon., successively bishop of Kilmore and archbishop of Cashel, 231, 258, 270–71, 275*n*, 276, 290, 341, 350, 398, 427, 454, 478–9, 545, 579, 591, 594, 602, 606; family and marriage connections of, 135, 494, 496–8, 605, 611; and the estate and parliamentary borough of Midleton, Co. Cork, 135, 192*n*, 212, 325–6, 494, 496, 498, 573; as archbishop of Cashel, 328–30, 333, 340, 376, 416–21, 434–6, 488, 502, 605; as coadjutor archbishop of Dublin, 381, 503–4; and the Cashel palace, 339–40, 363–5, 370–78, 381; and Agar's Cashel see lands lease, 416–21, 434–6; and the tithe question, 190, 475, 538–9, 557, 575–6; and the state of the Church of Ireland, 194, 230, 261, 270–71, 275*n*, 475, 484, 488, 492, 579, 586–7, 606–7; and education, 250–51, 498*n*; and church and glebe-house building, 258–9, 261, 263–5, 268–9, 274, 276, 278–85, 568*n*, 618; and the Union, 512, 525, 543, 560–61, 563, 567, 568*n*, 573, 575–6, 585–7, 591; antagonism of to Agar, 258, 268–70, 282, 339–40, 364, 416, 430–36; ascendancy of over Primate Stuart, 258, 268–9, 364, 430, 490, 611–12, 614; character of, 268–9, 475, 496–8, 611–12

Brodrick, Charles, junior, 6th Viscount Midleton, 419

Brodrick, George, 4th Viscount Midleton, 190, 231, 268, 325–6, 370, 398, 416, 427, 479, 494, 514*n*, 521, 538, 557, 561, 567, 575, 585, 591, 612

Brodrick, Mary (*née* Woodward), Mrs Charles Brodrick, 374, 494

Browne, Arthur, Dr, MP for TCD, 264, 572, 597

Browne, Denis, of Mount Browne, Westport, Co. Mayo, 547

Browne, Jemmett, archbishop of Tuam, 437, 447

Browne, John Denis, 3rd earl of Altamont and 1st marquess of Sligo, 3, 229–30, 415*n*, 558

Browne, Thomas, titular 4th Viscount Kenmare, 238*n*, 328

Brownstown, The Curragh, Co. Kildare, 27

Brownstown, barony of Gowran, Co. Kilkenny, 427–8

Bruce, Henry, Rev., later Sir Henry Bruce, 1st Bt, 385–6

Bruce, Thomas, 7th earl of Elgin, 602

Buck, Adam (pastellist and miniaturist), 614

Buckingham House, later Palace, London, 321

Buckworth, Anthony, Rev., vicar of Magheradroll, diocese of Dromore, Co. Down, 287

Buckworth, Richard, of 'Ballycormuck', Co. Tipperary, MP for Cashel, 287–8, 290

Buckworth, Theophilus, bishop of Dromore, 287

Buckworth Carr, William, MP for Cashel, 287–8, 291

Burdett, George, of Heath House, Maryborough, Co. Laois, MP for Gowran and Thomastown, 128–9, 132

Burgess, John, Dr, member of the Cashel corporation, 289

Burgess, Thomas, bishop of St David's, 403

Burgh, Thomas (architect), 29

Burgh, Thomas, agent to the board of first fruits, 431

Burgh, Walter Hussey, 153

Burke, Edmund, 86, 488

Burnett, James, Lord Monboddo, 38

Burney, Frances ('Fanny'), 60

Burrows, J., Rev. (visiting tutor in Lord Dartrey's family), 195, 205, 261, 386–7, 405n

Burtchaell, David, of Brandondale, Co. Kilkenny, 15

Burtchaell, G.D., 14, 15, 18, 41, 93

Burtchaell, Peter (agent for Lord Clifden's estate), 15

Burton: *see* Conyngham, William Burton

Busby, William, Rev., canon of Windsor and dean of Rochester, 602

Bushe, Amyas, of Kilfane, Co. Kilkenny, MP for Thomastown, 99

Bushe, Arthur, MP for Thomastown, 98

Bushe, Charles Kendal, MP for Callan, 112, 132

Bushe, G.P., of Kilfane, MP for Kilkenny city, 102n, 110, 117

Bushe, Thomas, Rev., of Kilmurry, Co. Kilkenny, 112

Bushe, Worsop, of Derrynahinch, Co. Kilkenny, 98

Bushe, family of, of Kilfane, etc., Co. Kilkenny, 92, 99

Butler, Anne, countess of Ormonde, 118

Butler, Charlotte, Viscountess Mountgarret, 17, 111, 114

Butler, Edmund, 10th Viscount Mountgarret, 17, 106–7, 111, 114

Butler, Edmund, 11th Viscount Mountgarret, 110–12, 114, 117, 118

Butler, Edmund, 12th Viscount Mountgarret and earl of Kilkenny, 366

Butler, 'Dame Elizabeth', 21

Butler, Hubert, 60n, 492

Butler, James, 2nd duke of Ormonde, 17, 20, 26–8, 92–3, 138n

Butler, James II, Roman catholic archbishop of Cashel, 500

Butler, James III, Roman catholic archbishop of Cashel, 326–8, 500

Butler, Lord John, earl of Gowran, 20

Butler, John, 17th earl of Ormonde, 116–19, 121–4, 127–8, 130–31, 133

Butler, Mildred (*née* Fowler), Viscountess Mountgarret and countess of Kilkenny, 462

Butler, Pierce, Hon. 115, 119–21

Butler, Pierce Archer, 553n

Butler, Piers, 3rd Viscount Galmoy, 21

Butler, Richard, 10th Lord, Caher and 1st earl of Glengall, 553

Butler, Robert, of Ballyragget, Co. Kilkenny, 327–8

Butler, Samuel (Victorian novelist), 85, 238

Butler, Somerset Hamilton, 8th Viscount Ikerrin and 1st earl of Carrick, 105–7

Butler, Walter, of Garryricken, Co. Kilkenny, 116, 118

Butler, Walter, Lord Thurles, 18th earl of Ormonde, 124, 130–31, 133, 553

Butler, family of, of Kilkenny Castle, dukes, earls and marquesses of Ormonde, 20, 26, 116, 124, 130

Butler, family of, of Mount Juliet, Co. Kilkenny, Viscounts Ikerrin and earls of Carrick, 93, 122

Butler, family of, Viscounts Mountgarret, 20, 93, 122

Butson, Christopher, successively dean of Waterford and bishop of Clonfert, 249, 269, 325n, 487n, 601

Butterfield, family of (tenants of Cashel corporation property), 287

Butterfield, John (caretaker of the Rock of Cashel), 306–7

Byrnesgrove, barony of Fassadinin, Co. Kilkenny, 21n

Cabinet, the Irish, 9, 74–5, 153, 161–2, 248–9, 267, 524, 526–7, 533

Cahir parish, diocese of Cashel, Co. Tipperary, 207

Cahirconlish glebe-house, diocese of Emly, Co. Limerick, 209, 577

Callan, Co. Kilkenny, 23, 100, 108, 124–5, 238, 425; parliamentary elections for, 9, 42, 61, 92, 100–02, 106–7, 112, 115–16, 121, 124, 132

Callan, Lord: *see* Agar, George

Campbell, John, 2nd duke of Argyll, 19n

Camus, near Cashel, Co. Tipperary, 335n

Canning, George, 480, 598

Canada, 34

canon law, 37, 140, 222, 233–4, 271–3, 275–6, 465, 502; *see also* under ecclesiastical courts

Canterbury, archbishopric of, 391, 414; archbishops of, 188, 485; cathedral organ, 321; deans of, 188; province of, 566–8, 565, 591

Carleton, Hugh, Viscount Carleton, 63–4, 72–4, 76, 78, 217, 366–7, 380

Carlisle, bishopric of, 392

Carlow, County, 72

Carmichael, William, Hon., successively bishop of Ferns and archbishop of Dublin, 177, 441

Carpendale, Thomas, Rev. (master of Armagh royal school), 455n

Carr, William, 288

Carrick, vicarage of, diocese of Lismore, Co. Waterford, 255

Carrigaline, advowson of, diocese and county of Cork, 238n

Carrigallen, vicarage of, diocese of Kilmore, Co. Leitrim, 245

'Carroll, Lewis', 166

Carrowdore, Co. Down, 393

Carter, Henry (servant in the 2nd earl of Normanton's Dublin house), 8, 542, 553

Carton, Maynooth, Co. Kildare, 378

Carysfort, Lord: *see* Proby

Cashel, archbishopric of, 223, 296, 299–301, 303–33, 341, 390, 426, 555; succession to, 138, 142, 149–50, 157, 200, 291, 390, 446–7, 509; archbishops of, 197, 200–02, 287, 305, 505; cathedral (Agar's), 5–6, 10, 186, 286, 298, 303, 305, 307–13, 317–25, 329–31, 379n; cathedral (on the Rock), 5–6, 10, 304–7, 329, 336–7, 382; cathedral choir, 318–20, 323; chancellorship of, 137; deanery of, 214–15; deanery (i.e. dean's house) in, 377; treasurership of, 292; diocese of, 9, 185, 194, 199–221, 228, 242, 296, 309–10, 314, 549; diocesan registry, 337, 348; diocesan registry archive, 338, 340n; palace, 58, 91, 186, 334–8, 339–41, 345n, 347–65, 370–83, 416, 509; parish of, 309, 318; province of, 203–4, 212, 302, 449, 481, 536–8; see estate, 9, 341, 343–4, 376, 385, 391, 396, 400–02, 406–12, 416–17, 420–22, 426, 426–7nn, 434–5; Agar's lease under, 9–10, 384, 406–12, 416–22, 423, 509, 553

Cashel, city, etc.: city and neighbourhood, 286–7, 291–5, 303–6, 323–5, 333, 361–3, 376, 515–16, 554; parliamentary borough of, 287–92; charter school, 88, 200, 320, 337n; new (1795) Roman catholic church in, 324–5; John Street, 324; *see also:* Agar's Lane; Bolton library; Hacket's Abbey; St Dominick's Abbey

Cashel Volunteers: *see under* Volunteers

Cassan, Stephen Hyde, Rev., 491

Castle, Richard, 341

Castlebar, 'Race of', 131n

Castlecomer, Co. Kilkenny, 41, 107; collieries, 107–8; House, 107–8; Chatsworth Street, 107n

Castledermot church, diocese of Glendalough, Co. Kildare, 247

Castle Durrow, Co. Laois, 378

Castle Ellis, barony of Gowran, Co. Kilkenny, 20

Castle Hume, Churchill, Co. Fermanagh, 378

Castleknock church, diocese and county of Dublin, 253

Castlemartyr, Co. Cork, 198

Castletown, Celbridge, Co. Kildare, 378

Castletown Cox, Co. Kilkenny, 201, 381–2

Castlewarren, barony of Gowran, Co. Kilkenny, 21

cathedrals, 187, 196, 244–6, 268, 285, 301–3, 310–17, 331; *see also* individual cathedrals

Catholic Emancipation, 9, 71, 89, 189, 268n, 269, 325, 470–71, 474, 508, 517–21, 526, 532, 541, 550–51, 596, 603, 607–9, 621

Catholic relief, 9, 77, 154–5, 189, 195, 224, 231, 295, 325, 448, 454, 460–61, 463, 495–6, 515–16, 519; *see also* Penal Laws

Caulfeild, James, 1st earl of Charlemont, 111, 414, 469–71, 473–4

Caulfield, James, Roman catholic bishop of Ferns, 500

Cavendish, Georgiana, duchess of Devonshire, 492

Cavendish, Henry, Sir, 2nd Bt, 482, 553

Cavendish, William, 3rd duke of Devonshire, 486n, 490n

Cavendish, William, marquess of Hartington, 4th duke of Devonshire, 102–3, 107n, 490n

Caxton, William, 348

Chadwick, family of (tenants of Cashel corporation property), 287

Chaigneau, David, of Corkagh, Co. Dublin, 22, 96–7

Chaigneau, Lewis, 22

chancellorship, lord (of Ireland), 72, 75, 77, 160, 224, 272–4, 442, 502–3, 549

chancery, court of (of England), 403

chaplaincies, noblemen's, 275n

chaplaincies, viceregal, 26, 138n, 139, 188, 275n, 484–9, 592, 601–2, 604–5, 616, 620

Chappell, family of (Armagh see tenants), 405n

charitable donations and bequests, board of, 249

charitable music society, Dublin, 246, 249

charities, 10, 96, 187, 199, 226–7, 249, 256, 455–7, 494–5, 497–8, 562, 571, 610–12; *see also* individual charities, e.g. the charitable music society, Dublin; Erasmus Smith educational foundation; Kingston college, etc.

Chart, D.A., 331, 337, 443, 458, 468, 488–9

charter schools, 226–7, 249–51, 320

Chatsworth, Derbyshire, 107n

Chatsworth Street, Castlecomer, Co. Kilkenny: *see under* Castlecomer

Chearnley, Anthony, of Burnt Court, Co. Tipperary (artist), 305

Chenevix, Richard, bishop of Waterford, 298–300, 491, 592

Chester, J.L., Colonel, 5–6, 306, 310

Chichester, Arthur, 1st marquess of Donegall, 487

Chichester, Barbara (*née* Godfrey), marchioness of Donegall, 487

chief judgeships (of Ireland), 72–8, 224, 429

China, Lord Macartney's embassy to, 79

Chinnery, George, successively bishop of Killaloe and Cloyne, 135, 198, 508–9

Christ Church Cathedral, Dublin, 28–30, 144, 214, 245–6, 253, 256–7, 314, 317, 392, 471; deanery of (in Fishamble Street, Dublin), 256, 379; *see also* Kildare, bishopric of

Christ Church college, Oxford, 26, 28, 33, 36–7, 55, 84, 90*n*, 232

Church of England, 225, 232, 621; bishops of, 188, 190*n*, 193–6, 205–6, 391–2, 428, 477–81, 483–5, 491, 501–2, 505–6, 536, 540–42, 556–8, 584, 591–3, 604–5; clergy of, 261, 489, 538–40, 578, 580–81; non-residence and pluralism of clergy of, 194, 222–3, 232–40, 275–6, 535; deans and 'dignitaries' of, 214, 311–12; rural deans in, 205–6; first fruits in, 223–4; parliamentary grants to, 225; building of churches and glebe-houses in, 225, 259–60, 285, 347; cathedrals of, 285, 303, 311–12; *see* estates of the bishops of, 403, 414, 417–18, 619; union of with the Church of Ireland, 275–6, 512, 557–68, 584–7, 599–605, 610–11, 622–3; tithe reform in, 534–42, 556–8

Church of Ireland: patronage in, 11, 47–8, 80, 120, 136–42, 186–90, 193, 200, 203, 211, 213–17, 237–9, 244–5, 255, 303, 341, 397, 465–6, 600, 602–3, 609–10, 613 (*see also* chaplaincies, viceregal); reform of, 11, 160–61, 213, 232–5, 237–41, 272, 504–6, 589, 597–8, 6092, 606–7, 615–23 (*see also* under tithes); union of with the Church of England, 275–6, 512, 557–68, 584–7, 599–605, 610–11, 622–3; *see also* : absenteeism, lay and episcopal; archdeaconries; bishops; canon law; cathedrals; churches, building and repairing of; church plate; churchwardens; confirmations; convocation; deaneries; deaneries, rural; ecclesiastical courts; first fruits, board of; glebe-houses, building of; glebes, acquisition and augmentation of; non-residence, clerical; ordinations; pluralism; privy council (Irish), unions effected by; residence, clerical (enforcement of); tithes; visitations

Church of Scotland, 566

churches, building and repairing of, 185, 194–5, 198–200, 206–10, 221, 223, 227–8, 245–7, 252–6, 268, 278–82, 285, 464, 541, 569–70, 615–16; *see also* individual churches, e.g. Gowran; Whitechurch

church plate, 207

churchwardens, 194–5, 200, 281, 586

civil law: *see* canon law; ecclesiastical courts

Clanwilliam, barony of, Co. Tipperary, 292–4, 407

Clanwilliam, countess of: *see* Meade, Theodosia

Clare, County, 192, 589*n*

Clare, Lord: *see* FitzGibbon, John

Clarisford, Killaloe: *see* Killaloe palace

Clarke, Rosetta (mistress of Lord Callan), 113

Claude Lorraine, 46

Clayton, Robert, successively bishop of Killala and of Clogher, 356, 474*n*, 490

Cleaver, Catherine (*née* Wynne), Mrs Euseby Cleaver, 192, 503

Cleaver, Euseby, successively bishop of Ferns and archbishop of Dublin, 173, 283, 434, 486, 576, 584, 598–9, 607; views of on career prospects in the Church of Ireland, 189–92, 511; and non-residence among the Irish clergy, 196, 271; and church and glebe-house building, 258, 569–70; and tithe reform, 511, 537; and the Ferns palace, 344–6, 360–61, 546, 547*n*; aspirations of to promotion, 484, 507–8, 588–9, 593–6; insanity of while archbishop of Dublin, 503–4; character of, 345, 490, 588, 593

Cleaver, William, bishop of Chester, 173, 389

Clements, Nathaniel, 2nd earl of Leitrim, 387

Clifden, Co. Galway, 41

Cliffe, Bartholomew, of New Ross, Co. Wexford (loyalist murdered in south-east Co. Kilkenny in 1798), 523

Clifton, Bristol, 53–4, 451–2

Clive, Edward, 1st earl of Powis, 601–2

Cloghala, barony of Gowran, Co. Kilkenny, 25

Clogher, bishopric of, 175, 179, 343, 389–91, 429, 435, 467, 488; cathedral, 303; diocese of, 493, 571; palace, 343, 351, 356, 378, 571; parliamentary borough of, 175–80, 182–3, 570–71, 573; Volunteers: *see under* Volunteers

Cloghran church, near Swords, diocese and county of Dublin, 464

Clonbeg glebe-house, diocese of Emly, Co. Tipperary, 208–10

Clondalkin, manor of Tallaght, Co. Dublin, 413

Clondelee, Co. Meath, 27

Clonenagh, rectory of, diocese of Leighlin, Co. Laois, 255

Clonfert, bishopric of, 174, 341–2, 496, 505; diocese of, 229–30, 277, 505, 562; palace, 341–2

Clonmel, Co. Tipperary, 88, 290, 305; gaol, 55

Clonmell, earls of: *see under* Scott

Clonmell House, Harcourt Street, Dublin: *see under* Dublin city

Clonoulty church and glebe-house, diocese of Cashel, Co. Tipperary, 208

Clonrohid church, diocese of Cloyne, Co. Cork, 198

Clonshavoy, near Murroe, Co. Limerick, 210

Cloyne, bishopric of, 141, 150, 174, 197–9, 214, 296–8, 391, 405, 409, 496, 509; cathedral, 301–2; chancellorship of, 410; diocese of, 9, 48–51, 197–9, 203–4, 211, 261, 296, 494–5; palace, 61–2, 355–6; Roman catholic church of, 326

coadjutorships: *see under* Roman catholic Church

Cobbe, Charles, archbishop of Dublin, 404

Cobbe, family of, of Newbridge, near Swords, Co. Dublin, 404

Cobh, Co. Cork, 370

Cockayne, G.E., 584

Collon church, diocese of Armagh, Co. Louth, 282

Colthurst, John Conway, Sir, 2nd Bt, 49

Colthurst, Nicholas Conway, Sir, 3rd Bt, 49–51

Colvin, Howard, 335–6

commissions of review, 273

confirmations, 188, 197

Connolly, S.J., 12, 240–41, 262n, 475

Conolly, Thomas, of Castletown, Celbridge, Co. Kildare, 135, 153, 155, 163, 231, 495–6

Conolly, William, of Castletown, Co. Kildare, 338

constitution of 1782, 147, 397, 482, 511, 581, 619

convocation, 566–8, 585

Conyngham, William Burton, of Slane Castle, Co. Meath, 127, 359

Cooke, Edward (under-secretary, Dublin Castle), 488n

Cooke, John (member of the Cashel corporation), 289

Cooke, John, Capt. (member of Mrs Griffith's Bloomsbury 'coterie'), 60

Cooke, family and estate, of Cookestown, Co. Kilkenny, 201

Cooke, family of (tenants of Cashel corporation property), 287

Cooleroe, barony of Gowran, Co. Kilkenny, 21

Cooley, Thomas, 298, 316, 333, 382–3

Coolnambrisklaun, barony of Fassadinin, Co. Kilkenny, 20

Cooper, Austin, of Merrion Square, Dublin, 349n, 369–70, 373, 377, 409, 416

Cooper, Samuel, of Killenure, Cashel, Co. Tipperary, 295, 324, 349n, 408–9

Cooper, William (1721–69), of Killenure, 349

Cooper, William (1772–1850), of Killenure, 295, 349n

Coote, Charles, earl of Bellamont, 142, 544

Cope, Walter, successively bishop of Clonfert and Ferns, 180–83, 342, 345–6, 459

Cork, bishopric of, 602; cathedral, 303; County, 389, 488; diocese of, 203, 505

Cormac, Edmund, Rev. Dr, PP of Cashel, 89, 324–5

Cormac's Chapel: *see under* Cashel cathedral (on the Rock)

Cornwallis, Charles, 1st Marquess Cornwallis, 489, 508, 510, 552–5, 599, 605, 607; relations of with Agar in 1798–9, 4, 295, 510, 525–8, 530–33, 542–3, 550–52; and the Church articles of the Union, 560–65, 573; and the primacy, 4, 587–8, 590, 594, 596, 598

Cornwallis, Lady Elizabeth, 526–7

Cornwallis, Frederick, Hon., archbishop of Canterbury, 397, 447

Cornwallis, James, Hon., bishop of Lichfield and Coventry, 526–7

Coronation Oath, 9, 74, 517–19, 526, 564, 566, 608–9, 621

corporation records, 17–18, 97–9, 175n, 287–9, 570

Corry, Isaac, 607

Costello, Anthony, 89

Costello, Thomas, Roman catholic coadjutor bishop, then bishop, of Clonfert, 500

courts of delegates, 271–4

Cotton, Henry, Rev., dean of Lismore, 307, 340n, 350, 363, 491

Courtenay, Henry, bishop of Bristol, 392

Courtown, Gorey, Co. Wexford, 546

Courtown, earl of: *see* Stopford, James

Cox, Michael, archbishop of Cashel, 138n, 200–02, 217, 305, 309–10, 339, 345n, 349, 352, 381–2, 407, 433, 499–500, 509

Cox, Richard, Sir, 1st Bt, of Dunmanway, Co. Cork, 200–01, 389

Cox, Richard, of Castletown Cox, Co. Kilkenny, 433

Cox, Richard, Rev., rector of Cahirconlish, diocese of Emly, Co. Limerick, 577

Cox, Watty, 2–3, 6, 11, 87, 92, 329, 352, 368, 616

Cradock, John, archbishop of Dublin, 43, 152, 390n, 414

Craig, Maurice, 335–6

Crawford, Thomas, of New Ross, Co. Wexford, 22

Creagh, Peter, Roman catholic bishop of Waterford, 500

Creighton, Lady Mary (*née* Hervey), countess of Erne, 385–6 crime and punishment, 48–51, 67, 112, 294, 528, 577; *see also* : duelling; Rightboy Movement; Whiteboys

Croft, William (composer), 302

Croker, Thomas Crofton, 301, 355

Crosbie, John, 2nd earl of Glandore, 19*n*, 190–92, 583

Crosbie, family of, of Ardfert, Co. Kerry, Barons Branden and earls of Glandore, 19*n*

Crow, Charles, bishop of Cloyne, 355

Cuffe, James, Lord Tyrawly, 71*n*

Cuffe, John, Capt., 1st Lord Desart, 95, 98

Cuffe, John, 2nd Lord Desart, 23, 101

Cuffe, Maurice, 94

Cuffe, Otway, 3rd Lord and 1st earl of Desart, 106*n*, 116–17, 553

Cuffe, family of, of Desart Court, etc., Co. Kilkenny, 92, 101, 238

Cullen church, diocese of Emly, Co. Tipperary, 209

Cullen, prebend of, St Patrick's Cathedral, Dublin, 244

Cumberland, duke of: *see* Henry Frederick

Cumberland, Richard, 451, 458

curates, role and remuneration of, 4, 216, 219–20, 243, 472–3, 478–9, 494–5, 497, 578–81

Curraghmore, Portlaw, Co. Waterford, 298

Curran, John Philpot, 129

Curryglass church, diocese of Cloyne, Co. Cork, 198; living of, 494–5

custom house, Dublin: *see under* Dublin city

D'Alton, John, 3–4, 207, 245, 252, 368, 406–7, 423, 580

Damer, George, Viscount Milton, 2nd earl of Dorchester, 180, 324–5, 551, 553

Damer, Joseph, 1st earl of Dorchester, 294, 324–5

Damer House, Roscrea, Co. Tipperary, 378

Dance, George (artist), 87–8

Daniel, Richard, Rev. (charitable benefactor of the poor of St Luke's parish, Dublin city), 256

Davers, Charles, Sir, 5th Bt, 386

Davidson, Randall Thomas, archbishop of Canterbury, 483

Dawson, Richard, 95, 176

Dawson, Thomas, 1st Lord Dartrey, 195

Dawson, family of, Lords and earls of Dartrey, 405

Day, Robert, judge of the king's bench, 190–91, 533, 542

Dealtry, R.B., Rev. Dr, precentor of St Patrick's Cathedral, Dublin, 365, 462

Deane, Elinor, Mrs, 300

Deane, Hugh Primrose (artist), 300

Deane, family of, of Inistioge, etc., Co. Kilkenny, 92, 238

deaneries, 214–15, 392, 465–6, 592

deaneries, rural, 199, 204–6, 212, 464, 589

Defenders, 529

de Grey, Thomas, 2nd Lord Walsingham, 90*n*, 476

Delany, Mary Granville, Mrs Delany, 356

Delgany church, diocese of Glendalough, Co. Wicklow, 464

Derry, bishopric of, 188–9, 341, 478, 507; deanery of, 214*n*, 392; palace, 367, 386, 605; see estate, 341, 385–6, 388, 390–92, 400, 416

Desart, Lords: *see under* Cuffe

Devenish, prebend of, diocese of Clogher, Co. Fermanagh, 493

Devonshire, dukes of: *see* Cavendish, William

Dickson, Henrietta (*née* Symes), Mrs William Dickson, 470, 507

Dickson, William, bishop of Down, 256, 470, 480*n*, 507, 563, 577

dilapidations: *see under* bishops' palaces; glebe-houses, building of

Dillon, Charles, 12th Viscount Dillon, 399

dissenters, 154–5, 195, 225, 235, 237, 269, 271, 300–01, 446–7, 455–6, 525, 539, 578*n*; *see also* Test Act, repeal of

Dissolution of the Monasteries, 195–6, 203

Dodgson, Charles, bishop of Elphin, 166, 312, 404, 467, 509

D'Olier, Isaac (silversmith), 380

Donacavey, prebend of: *see* Fintona

Donaghadee, Co. Down, 393

Donegall, marquess and marchioness of: *see* Chichester

Dongourney church, diocese of Cloyne, Co. Cork, 198

Donnellan, Andrew, Roman catholic bishop of Clonfert, 500

Doon church, diocese of Emly, Co. Limerick, 206, 209

Dorset, dukes of: *see under* Sackville

Douglas, Sylvester, 1st Lord Glenbervie, 52, 179–80

Dovehill, Co. Tipperary, 70

Down, bishopric of, 390, 612; cathedral, 312–15; County, 314–15; curates of, 579; deanery of, 214*n*, 313, 392

Downhill, Magilligan, Co. Londonderry, 374*n*, 386

Downshire, marquesses of: *see* Hill

Doyle, James Warren, Rev. Dr, later Roman catholic bishop of Kildare and Leighlin, 500

Drew, Thomas, Sir, 317

Drogheda, Co. Louth, archbishop of Armagh's palace in, 383

Drogheda, Lord: *see* Moore, Charles

Dromore, bishopric of, 346–7, 389–90, 400 palace, 346

Drury, Capt. (Cloyne *see* tenant), 405

Drury Lane theatre, London, 492

Dublin, archbishopric of, 150, 152, 213–14, 243–7, 249–51, 365, 415, 433, 503, 562, 599; succession to, 83, 137, 142, 148–58, 219, 242, 390*n*, 434–5, 446, 490*n*, 507–8, 532, 554–5; archbishops of, 3–4, 28–9, 150, 197, 368–9, 390*n*, 437, 490; archdeaconry of, 244, 466; cathedrals of: *see* Christ Church; St Patrick's; diocese of, 9, 28–9, 213–14, 216, 243–7, 252–7, 456, 462–4, 503–4, 580; palaces of, 365–70, 381, 433, 503; province of, 538; *see* estate, 368, 370, 389, 391, 401–2, 412–15, 435, 503

Dublin city, churches and parishes in: *see* individual churches and parishes, e.g., St Ann's, St Nicholas-Without;

    houses in, 342, 380, 414; Agar's house in St Stephen's Green, 8, 54, 365, 379–81; Clonmell House, Harcourt Street, 413–14;

      institutions and public buildings in: custom house, 29, 143–9, 156, 158–60; foundling hospital, 226, 249, 495; Four Courts, 159; Hibernian school for the marine service, 226; house of industry, 226, 249; King's Inns, 471; Parliament House, 144, 158, 334, 338, 379; Rotunda rooms, 317; Royal College of Surgeons, 315; St Patrick's hospital, 589*n*; *see also*: Marsh's library, Dublin; Trinity College, Dublin

      regulatory bodies in: Dublin corporation, 29, 144; paving board, 145, 249, 253; police, 253; wide streets commissioners, 146, 158

        streets and spaces in: Arran Quay, 159; Beresford Place, 158; Capel Street, 144; Carlisle Bridge, 158; College Green, 144; Ellis Quay, 29; Essex Bridge, 143–4, 148; Fishamble Street, 256–7; Gardiner's Mall, 144, 158; Gardiner Street, 158; Harcourt Street, 413–14; Henrietta Street, 197, 383*n*, 440; High Street, 159; Holles Street, 243; Inns Quay, 159; Lazar's Hill, 24*n*; Merrion Square, 59, 246, 381, 424; Mountjoy Square, 158; Phoenix Park, 159, 358; Sackville Street, 144, 158; effect of the Union on, 159–60, 257; Ellis estate in, 29, 143–8, 158–60; population of and congestion and mortality in, 243

Dublin, County, 1783 election for, 463

Dublin Evening Post, the, 83, 159

Ducart, Davis (architect and engineer), 305

duelling, 9, 49, 65, 70–71, 102, 151–2

Duff, James, 2nd Earl Fife, 246

Duigenan, Patrick, LL.D., 151, 202, 259, 264, 276, 283, 410, 442, 502, 539–40, 563–4, 572, 574, 607–8

Duiske Abbey, Graiguenamanagh, Co. Kilkenny, 21

Dunbar, George, of Green Bank, Ballitore, Co. Kildare, MP for Gowran and Thomastown, 128–9, 166

Dunbell, barony of Gowran, Co. Kilkenny, 43

Dundas, Henry, 1st Viscount Melville, 77, 175, 525, 608

Dunleer, Co. Louth, 17, 457

Dunmore, Co. Laois, 404

Dunn, Mrs, of Bickley, Kent, 88–9

Dunn, William, 88*n*

Duntrileague church, diocese of Emly, Co. Limerick, 209; union of: *see* Galbally

Durham, bishopric of, 188, 391, 420*n*, 491, 620 cathedral chapter of, 491, 620

Eagar, Robert, Major, 14

Eagar, or Agar, family of, of Co. Kerry, 14

Earlsfort, Lord: *see* Scott, John, 1st Lord Earlsfort

ecclesiastical commission (of 1833 onwards), 196, 421*n*, 621

ecclesiastical courts, 48–50, 202*n*, 233, 271–4, 275*n*, 364, 404–5, 539–40; *see also* under canon law

Eden, William, 1st Lord Auckland, 7, 51, 87, 173, 248, 268, 513, 524, 534, 542, 556, 567, 609; as chief secretary for Ireland, 158, 161; behaviour towards Agar in 1798–1800, 524, 528–32, 555, 596

education, 232, 250, 327; *see also* : Armagh university (proposed); charter schools; Erasmus Smith educational foundation; Trinity College, Dublin

Egan, Darby, MP for Kilkenny city, 94

Egan, William, Roman catholic coadjutor bishop, then bishop, of Waterford, 500

Ehrman, John, 556

Elliot, Richard, of New Ross, Co. Wexford (loyalist murdered in south-east Co. Kilkenny in 1798), 523

Elliott, William (under-secretary, later chief secretary, Dublin Castle), 179–80

Ellis, Anne (*née* Stanley), Lady Mendip, 33, 83, 385

Ellis, Diana (*née* Briscoe), wife of Bishop Welbore Ellis, 30

Ellis, Elizabeth (*née* Stanhope), wife of Welbore Ellis, future Lord Mendip, 30

Ellis, John, Rev., 26

Ellis, John, 26–7

Ellis, Philip, Rev., Roman catholic bishop of Segni, 26, 28, 328

Ellis, Susanna (*née* Welbore), Mrs John Ellis, 28

Ellis, Welbore, successively bishop of Kildare and
Meath, 24–30, 138, 256, 379–80

Ellis, Welbore, 1st Lord Mendip (Agar's uncle), 9,
27, 48, 58, 63, 65, 142, 186n, 212, 226, 232n,
380–81, 461, 513, 519, 532; career and
character of, 30–35, 37–8, 46, 57, 82–3, 103;
influence of on Agar and Agar's career, 9, 30,
33–6, 39, 44, 55, 73, 103, 139–41, 143, 159–61,
165, 170, 174, 352–3, 512–13, 530, 550, 588,
620; houses and estates of in England and
Ireland, 29–30, 33, 35, 38–9, 143–8, 158–60,
512, 52, 61, 83, 425, 512; and absenteeism, 512,
619; and the Agar interest in Kilkenny, 97,
99–100, 102–4, 113–14, 127–8; delays the re-
location of the Dublin custom house, 143–8,
158–60; fails to obtain the archbishopric of
Dublin for Agar, 148–58; and the Fox–North
Coalition and Regency Crisis, 32, 161–6, 170,
172, 174, 609; and the tithe question, 57, 534,
537–8, 619; tries to put fight into Primate
Robinson, 450–53; and the Cashel cathedral
organ, 321–2; as a gardener, 33, 359; peerage of
(with special remainder), 31–2, 52–3, 172; and
the Union, 512, 530, 533–4, 550

Ellis, William, Sir, 27–8

Ellis correspondence, British Library, 27–8

Ellis estate in Ireland, 27–30, 33, 35, 38–9, 143–8,
158–60, 512

Elphin, bishopric of, 342–3, 392, 401–2, 404;
diocese of, 203; palace, 187, 343

Elton, Geoffrey, Sir, 12

Ely, bishopric of, 188

Emly, archdeaconry of, 54–5, 217–18; cathedral,
206–7; chancellorship of, 137; diocese of: *see
under* Cashel; glebe-house, 208, 211–12;
precentorship of, 137; vicarage of, 217

Emly, 'the west division of', Cos Limerick and
Tipperary (part of Agar's Cashel see lands
lease), 407, 410

enclosure acts: *see under* tithes

'Enniscorthy' (i.e. the rectory of St Mary's,
Enniscorthy), Co. Wexford, 256

Ensor, John (architect), 380

Erasmus Smith educational foundation, 208,
249–50, 269, 620

Erskine, Thomas, 1st Lord Erskine, 478–9

Este, Charles, bishop of Waterford, 348

Evans, Francis, of Rathcormack, Co. Cork, 16

Evans, James (servant in Cahirconlish glebe-house,
Co. Limerick), 577

Everard, Patrick, Rev. Dr, president of Maynooth
and Roman catholic archbishop of Cashel,
328–9, 501

Everard, Redmond, Sir, 21

exchequer, chancellorship of the (Irish), 266–9,
277–81, 546

exchequer, court of (Irish), 101–2nn, 323

Exeter, diocese of, 205

Eyre, John, Lord Eyre, 414

Fagel, Henry, Pensionary, 250

Fagel library, 250, 269

Falvey, Jeremiah, 187, 194, 197

Fane, John, 10th earl of Westmorland, 77, 83n, 171,
231, 248, 292, 466n, 487–90; and the primacy
in 1794, 51, 173–5, 465–6, 470; and bishops'
boroughs, 175–6, 179–80, 183; and Catholic
relief/Emancipation, 515–19, 526, 532, 609

Farington, Joseph, 45, 47, 423, 426–7

Fassadinin, barony of, Co. Kilkenny, 16n, 20

Faulkner's Dublin Journal, 198, 220n, 222, 242,
268n, 515–16, 579

Ferguson, Samuel, Sir, 6n

fees of honour and on passing patents, 86, 344

fencibles (1783), 119

Fennor, prebend of, diocese of Cashel, 137

Fermanagh, County, 65, 69

Ferns, bishopric of, 179, 183, 214, 341, 438–9;
bishops of, 344–6, 573; cathedral, 332n, 570;
diocese of, 258, 569–70, 588; palace, 344–6,
360–61; *see also* Old Leighlin, parliamentary
borough of

Fethard glebe-house, diocese of Cashel, Co.
Tipperary, 208, 218; rectory of, 137

Fife, Lord: *see* Duff, James

Finglas, rectory of, diocese and county of Dublin,
244

Fintona [recte: Donacavey], prebend of, diocese of
Clogher, Co. Tyrone, 493

first fruits, board of, 233, 257, 326n, 472, 541, 587;
history and role of (1711–63), 220–223;
history and role of (1778–c.1800), 220–21,
223–30, 311; assists Agar with grants for
churches and glebe-houses in Cloyne, Cashel
and Dublin, 57, 198–9, 207, 252–4, 309, 311,
313; Agar's promotion of and ideas for,
220–21, 224–30, 240, 249, 259–64, 430–33,m
365–6, 614–15, 617–18, 621–2; treasurership
of, 221–2, 225–8, 249, 263, 430–33, 618;
receives compensation money for the
disfranchisement of the bishops' boroughs,
568–9, 573–4; rival schemes for the building of
churches and glebe-houses by (1802–6),
257–9, 613; the 1808 Board of First Fruits Act
and its implementation and consequences,
274, 276–85; *see also* : churches, building and

repairing of; glebe-houses, building of; glebes, acquisition and augmentation of

Fitzgerald, Lord Edward, 244

Fitzgerald, James, 20th earl of Kildare and 1st duke of Leinster, 103

Fitzgerald, Pamela, Lady Edward Fitzgerald, 83

Fitzgerald, Thomas Judkin-, Sir, 1st Bt, 523–4

Fitzgerald, William Robert, 2nd duke of Leinster, 153, 163, 244, 315, 463

Fitzgerald, family of, earls of Kildare and dukes of Leinster, 135, 231

FitzGibbon, Anne (*née* Whaley), countess of Clare, 90, 131, 426

FitzGibbon, John, 1st earl of Clare, 6–7, 64, 160, 181, 185, 248, 272, 426, 465, 473, 499, 517, 524, 529, 549; ambivalent relationship of with Agar, 72–6, 87, 328, 526, 530; and the Regency Crisis, 169–71; and Catholic Emancipation, 517, 526, 609; relations of with Lord Cornwallis and support for the Union, 525–30, 533, 543, 553, 565, 576, 581; and the primacy, 66, 588–90, 596

Fitzherbert, Alleyne, 1st Lord St Helens, 75–6, 248, 482

Fitzmaurice, William Petty-, 2nd earl of Shelburne and 1st marquess of Lansdowne, 90n, 161, 300

Fitzpatrick, W.J., 68–71, 76

Fitzpatrick, family of, Barons Gowran and earls of Upper Ossory, 41

Fitzwilliam, Lady Charlotte (*née* Ponsonby), Countess Fitzwilliam, 467

Fitzwilliam, Richard, 7th Viscount Fitzwilliam of Merrion, 322

Fitzwilliam, William Wentworth, 4th Earl Fitzwilliam, 173–4, 176, 182–3, 324, 449, 468–71, 474, 489, 507n, 517, 519, 610

flax, tithe of, 191, 450, 538

Flood, Henry, 9, 26n, 41–3, 67, 69–70, 92, 101, 105–6, 109–12, 114–19, 121–4, 133

Flood, Nick (gardener recommended to Archbishop Brodrick for Cashel), 370

Flood, Warden, of Burnchurch, Co. Kilkenny, 92–3, 95, 101

Flower, Harriet, Hon.: *see* Agar, Harriet, Hon.

Flower, William, 2nd Viscount Ashbrook, 114

Fontstown church, diocese of Glendalough, Co. Kildare, 247

forcible possession, 294

Forde, John (agent for Welbore Ellis' Irish estate), 35

Forfeited estates, trustees of, 21

Forster, George (burgess of Thomastown, Co. Kilkenny), 99

Foster, Anthony, chief baron of the exchequer, 337n

Foster, John (speaker), 1st Lord Oriel, 6, 64, 153, 175, 181, 249, 337n, 585, 614, 618; similar ancestry of to Agar's, 13, 17; views of on tithes, 575; opposes Catholic Emancipation and the Union, 517, 530, 533, 542, 575; supports work of church and glebe-house building as chancellor of the Irish exchequer, 266–9, 227–83, 301–11, 614, 618

'Foster's Corn Law', 223, 575

Foster, William, bishop of Clogher, 182, 267

foundling hospital, Dublin: *see under* Dublin city

Fowler, Louisa, Hon. (*née* Gardiner), Mrs Robert Fowler junior, 463

Fowler, Mildred: *see* Butler, Mildred

Fowler, Robert, successively bishop of Killaloe and archbishop of Dublin, 160, 190, 358n, 447, 531–2; character of, 166, 257, 414–15, 448, 462–3, 465–7, 490, 499–500; as bishop of Killaloe, 342, 413, 436n, 462, 509; as successful competitor to Agar for the archbishopric of Dublin, 150–51, 156–7; as archbishop of Dublin, 226, 240, 243, 247, 252–3, 257, 314–15, 327n, 365–9, 404, 413–15, 429, 447, 462–7, 499–500, 555; Primate Robinson's patronage of and later disenchantment with, 149–50, 156–7, 448, 464–5; ambition of for the primacy and a peerage, 166, 448, 461–2, 464–6

Fowler, Robert, junior, successively archdeacon of Dublin and bishop of Ossory, 413, 463, 465–6, 492–3, 601n

Fownes, William, Sir, 2nd Bt, of Woodstock, Inistioge, Co. Kilkenny, 99–100

Fownes, family of, of Woodstock, 93

Fox, Charles James, 161, 163, 174, 256, 468–70, 474, 478, 507–8, 602–4, 609; *see also* : Fox-North Coalition

Fox, Henry, 1st Lord Holland, 31, 102

Fox, Luke, justice of the king's bench, 247

Fox-North Coalition, 32, 161, 164, 172, 470, 609

Foy, Nathaniel, bishop of Waterford, 347

Foyran church, diocese and county of Meath, 253

France, 134

Freeman's Journal, The, 41–3

Freighduff, etc., Co. Tipperary (part of Agar's Cashel see lands lease), 407

Freind, Grace (*née* Robinson), Mrs Freind (Primate Robinson's sister), 457

French, Robert (commissioner for the relief of suffering loyalists), 574

French Revolutionary War, 511, 513–14

Frizzell, Richard (land surveyor), 408

Froude, J.A., 6, 466

Fuller, Stephen, of St George's, Bloomsbury, 33

Gainsborough, Thomas, 33

Galbally glebe-house, diocese of Emly, Co.
Limerick, 55–7, 476; union of, 54, 137

Galloway, Peter, Rev., 301

Galway, County, 18

Galwey, William, Rev., rector of Abington, Co.
Limerick, 210

Gamble, George (agent to the archbishop of
Dublin), 365, 413

Gandon, James, 158–9, 301, 379

gardening and planting, 33, 38, 342, 353, 359–60,
369–70, 375–6, 491

Gardiner, Elizabeth (*née* Montgomery), Viscountess
Mountjoy, 145

Gardiner, Luke (d.1755), 99n

Gardiner, Luke, 1st Viscount Mountjoy, 145, 158,
327, 447–8, 463–4

Gardiner, family of, Viscounts Mountjoy, estate of
in north Dublin, 144–5, 158–9

Garnett, John, successively bishop of Ferns and
Clogher, 177–9, 303, 390n, 493–4

genealogy (of the Agar family), 13–17
(of the Ellis family), 26, 39

Geoghegan, Patrick, M., 608

George II, King, 104–5, 139, 484–5, 592

George III, King, 165–70, 177, 230–31, 276, 313,
315, 320–21, 439, 452, 460, 465, 476, 507n,
517–19, 572, 588, 609–12; has a low opinion of
Irish bishops, 177, 484, 487, 490, 507n, 591–4,
620; and the primacy (1764, 1794 and 1800),
140, 441, 470, 588, 591–600, 609–12, 620;
Welbore Ellis's relations with, 30–31, 170, 513;
Agar's relations with, 167–70, 174–5, 248,
430, 453–4, 519, 586, 596, 609; and the
Coronation Oath, 517–19, 607–9; and the
Union, 586, 610–11

George, prince of Wales (later prince regent and
George IV), 166–70, 248, 608–9, 614

Germain, Lord George: *see* Sackville, Lord
George

Gibbs, James (architect), 309

Gibbs, R. (water-colourist), 22n

Gibson, Edward, 1st Lord Ashbourne, 6

Giffard, John, 248n, 254, 268, 516

Gilbert, John T., Sir, 6n, 451

Glandore, earl of: *see* Crosbie

Glankeen glebe-house, diocese of Cashel, Co.
Tipperary, 208

glebe-houses, building of, 55–7, 185–7, 207–11,
221–3, 228–32, 237, 241, 252–6, 258–63,
275–9, 274, 276–80, 281n, 284–5, 311, 334,
338–40, 364–5, 382–3, 464, 504–5, 541,
569–70, 617–18, 621–2; *see also* under first
fruits, board of

glebes, acquisition and augmentation of, 186–7,
207–9, 221, 227–30, 259–61, 268, 276–7, 280;
see also: under first fruits, board of; Primate
Boulter's fund

Glenbervie, Lord: *see* Douglas

Glendalough, Co. Wicklow, 413
diocese of: *see under* Dublin, diocese of

Glentworth, Lords: *see under* Pery

Gloucester, bishopric of, 392

Gloucester, duke of: *see* William Henry

Gloucester, Co. Kilkenny, yeomanry corps (Lord
Clifden's), 513–14, 522–3

Godfrey, Luke, Rev., rector of Midleton, 487

Godwin, Timothy, archbishop of Cashel, 138, 288,
336–7, 340

Goldsmith, Oliver, 60

Gordon, James, rector of Killegny, diocese of Ferns,
Co. Wexford, 546

Gore, Ralph, Capt., of Barrowmount, Co. Kilkenny,
21

Gore, William, successively bishop of Elphin and
Limerick, 214–15, 391, 401–2

Goresbridge, Co. Kilkenny, 21, 108

Gowran, Co. Kilkenny, 41, 108–9, 522–4; almshouse,
96, 109; castle (ancient), 17, 20, 22; castle
(successive Agar seats called), 82, 358, 378;
church (St Mary's), 19, 43n, 98; parliamentary
elections for, 17, 42, 92, 95–8, 102, 116–18,
126–30; Volunteers: *see under* Volunteers

Grace, Oliver (Agar's principal architect while in
Cashel), 58n, 208, 298, 306–10, 349, 354, 358,
365, 372

Graiguenamanagh, Co. Kilkenny, 15, 19n, 21, 108,
522–3

Grand Canal, 413

Grange, Lower, barony of Gowran, Co. Kilkenny,
424; Old, barony of Gowran, Co. Kilkenny, 21

Grant, Charles, 1st Lord Glenelg, 435

Grattan, Henry, 6, 169–70, 189–91, 240, 397, 450,
470, 482, 511, 521, 536–7, 577, 581

Grattan, Henry, junior, 6, 521

Graves, Richard, Rev. Dr, 257n

Graves, Thomas, Very Rev., dean of Ardfert, 191

graveyards, 281

Green, John, bishop of Lincoln, 189

Green, Samuel (organ-builder to the king), 320–23

Greene, Maurice (composer), 302

Gregory, William, Sir, 1st Bt (under-secretary,
Dublin Castle), 435

Grenada, 80

Grenville, George, 188, 441

Grenville, George Nugent, 3rd Earl Temple and 1st
marquess of Buckingham, 75–6, 173, 192,
227, 269–70, 300, 482, 484, 609, 616; character

of, 165, 168, 230–31; as lord lieutenant of
Ireland during the Regency Crisis, 164–71,
240, 459–60, 465–6, 616; enmity and duplicity
of towards Agar, 165–9, 589–90; and Church
reform in England and Ireland, 205, 230,
232–7, 239–40, 269–70, 276, 448–50, 452–3,
501–2, 535–6, 541–2; and the tithe question,
191, 240, 535–6, 541–2, 556–7; and the Union,
531, 550; and the primacy (1794 and 1800),
389, 589–90, 593, 598

Grenville, Lady Mary Elizabeth, Baroness Nugent,
marchioness of Buckingham, 231, 501–2

Grenville, William Wyndham, Lord Grenville, 165,
205, 230, 232, 236, 269–71, 275, 465, 508, 535,
541–2, 556–9, 573, 589, 591

Grey, Charles, 2nd Earl Grey, 506

Griffith, Elizabeth, Mrs Richard Griffith, 60–62

Griffith, Richard, of Maidenhall, Bennetsbridge,
Co. Kilkenny, 60–62

Griffith, Richard, of Millicent, Co. Kildare, 547*n*

Grosvenor, Robert, 2nd Earl Grosvenor, 1st
marquess of Westminster, 47

Grosvenor House, Park Lane, 47

Guinness, Arthur, 357

Guinness, Benjamin Lee, Sir, 1st Bt, 315

Guinness, Richard, 357

Gunning, Elizabeth, successively duchess of
Hamilton and Argyll, 105

Gunning, Maria, countess of Coventry, 105

Hacket, John, Rev., vicar of Clonfert, Co. Galway,
229

Hacket, William, Sir (founder of Hacket's Abbey,
Cashel), 324

Hacket's Abbey, Cashel, 324

Haggard Street, barony of Gowran, Co. Kilkenny, 20

Hales, William, Rev., FTCD, 326

Haliday, Alexander, MD, 469, 473

Hamilton, C.W., of Hamwood, Dunboyne, Co.
Meath, 22*n*

Hamilton, Gavin (painter and picture-dealer), 46–7

Hamilton, Hugh, bishop of Ossory, 178, 489,
570–71

Hamilton, Hugh Douglas (painter), 62*n*

Hamilton, John (under-secretary, Dublin Castle),
156*n*, 446

Hamilton, John James, 1st marquess of Abercorn,
489

Hamilton, Sackville (under-secretary, Dublin
Castle, etc.), 179, 546, 574

Hamilton, William Gerard, 86

Hampshire, 61, 202, 232

Handel, George Frederic, 246, 302, 321–3

Haneen, John (steward at Cahirconlish glebe-house,
Co. Limerick), 577

Harcourt, Simon, 1st Earl Harcourt, 115, 142–4,
177*n*, 443, 493

Hardy, Francis, 67*n*

Hare, John (agent for Agar's private and Dublin
archiepiscopal estate), 369, 418, 420–21, 423,
427, 434–5, 497

Hare, Patrick, Rev. (vicar-general of the diocese and
province of Cashel), 88–9, 186*n*, 200–02, 212,
295, 362–3, 418, 514, 522, 524

Hargrave, Mr, of Cork City (chimneypiece maker),
374

Harleian Society, the, 5

Harman, Cutts, Very Rev., of Newcastle,
Ballymahon, Co. Longford, dean of
Waterford, 329–30*nn*

Harris, James, of Malmesbury House, Salisbury, 38

Harrison, family of (tenants of Cashel corporation
property), 287

Harrow school, 488

Hartstonge, John, successively bishop of Ossory and
Derry, 339

Hastings, Lady Elizabeth, countess of Moira, 483-4

Hatsell, John (retired clerk of the British House of
Commons), 534, 550

Hawarden, Viscounts: *see* Maude

Hawkins, James, bishop of Raphoe, 576

Hazelwood, Sligo, Co. Sligo, 378

Hely, John, of Foulkscourt, Johnstown, Co.
Kilkenny, 106

Hely-Hutchinson, Francis, Hon., 552–3

Hely-Hutchinson, John (provost of TCD), 64, 66,
72, 76, 151–3, 202, 406, 442, 444*n*, 446, 459,
548

Hely-Hutchinson, Richard, 2nd Lord and 1st
Viscount and earl of Donoughmore, 551–4

Hely-Hutchinson, family of, earls of
Donoughmore, 125

hemp, tithe of, 191, 232, 450

Henley, Robert, 2nd earl of Northington, 162, 181,
183, 211, 470

Henry Frederick, duke of Cumberland (brother of
George III), 439, 442*n*

Herbert, Dorothea, 91, 200, 210–11, 302, 319

Herbert, Nicholas, Rev., rector of Knockgraffon,
diocese of Cashel, Co. Tipperary, 211

Heron, Richard, Sir, 143, 151, 153, 156–7, 211, 224,
446

Hertford college, Oxford, 468–70

Hertford, Lord: *see under* Seymour-Conway

Hervey, Frederick, successively bishop of Cloyne
and Derry, 4th earl of Bristol, 215, 351, 507–8,

Hervey, Frederick (*contd.*)
   560–62, 615; rapid promotion of, 31, 140–41,
   189, 406; absenteeism and misconduct of, 49,
   201, 351, 398, 406, 478, 490, 562; supports the
   repeal of Penal Laws, 154*n*, 195; as a builder,
   298, 317, 367, 374*n*, 381*n*, 386; sharp practices
   of in relation to his see estates, 385–6, 401,
   404, 406, 416, 429, 436
Hervey, Frederick William, 5th earl and 1st
   marquess of Bristol, 385
Hervey, George, 2nd earl of Bristol, 31, 140–41, 385
Hervey, John Augustus, Lord Hervey, 385
Hewetson, Christopher, of Thomastown, Co.
   Kilkenny, 98
Hewetson, Jane, Miss, 100
Hewetson, family of, of Thomastown, Co.
   Kilkenny, 98–100
Hewitt, James, 1st Viscount Lifford, 69, 72, 75, 142,
   299, 394, 429
Hewitt, James, Hon. and Very Rev., dean of
   Armagh, 2nd Viscount Lifford, 576
Heytesbury, Wiltshire, parliamentary borough of,
   513–14
Hibernian school for the marine service: *see under*
   Dublin city
hides, tithe of, 33
Hill, Arthur, 2nd marquess of Downshire, 65, 129,
   511, 547*n*, 574
Hill, Wills, 1st earl of Hillsborough and marquess of
   Downshire, 150, 226, 312–14, 331, 333*n*, 437,
   442–3*nn*, 446–7, 458, 511
Hill, family of, earls of Hillsborough and
   marquesses of Downshire, 135
Hinchcliffe, John, bishop of Peterborough, 391
Hoadly, John, successively bishop of Ferns and
   archbishop of Dublin and Armagh, 368–9,
   383*n*, 474*n*, 619
Hoare, Deane, Rev. (well beneficed clergyman in the
   diocese of Limerick), 498
Hoare, John, Rev. (son of the foregoing), 498
Hobart, Caroline (*née* Conolly), countess of
   Buckinghamshire, 495
Hobart, John, 2nd earl of Buckinghamshire, 66, 74,
   115–16, 226*n*, 312, 437–8, 458, 463, 487,
   493–4, 616; hostility of to the Agars and Agar,
   126, 136, 147–58, 394–5, 446; weak
   administration of, 153–4, 157–8; favours the
   repeal of Penal Laws, 154–5, 224, 446, 468,
   616; promotes his immoral brother-in-law to a
   bishopric, 487
Hobart, Robart, Major, Lord Hobart, 4th earl of
   Buckinghamshire, 180, 248, 482–3, 595, 606
Hogan, Stephen, of Cashel, Co. Tipperary
   (claimant for loss sustained during the
   rebellion), 546

Hollow Blades company, 21–2
Hollywood church, glebe-house and vicarage,
   diocese of Glendalough, Co. Wicklow, 245,
   247
Holycross Abbey, Co. Tipperary, 359
Hopkins, Ezekiel, bishop of Derry, 456
Hoppner, John (portrait-painter), 62–3
Horsley, Samuel, successively bishop of St David's,
   Rochester and St Asaph, 205, 592–3
Hort, Josiah, successively bishop of Kilmore and
   archbishop of Tuam, 289
Hotham, Charles, Sir, 5th Bt, 40
Hotham, Gertrude, Mrs Welbore Ellis Agar: *see*
   Agar, Gertrude
Hotham, John, later Sir John, 9th Bt, bishop of
   Clogher, 13, 19, 87, 172, 175, 179, 182–3, 303,
   331–2, 342–4, 351, 382, 398, 451, 460, 487,
   490, 493, 592
Hotham, family of, of Beverley, Yorkshire, baronets
   and Lords Hotham, 149
Howard, Charles, 11th duke of Norfolk, 519
Howard, Frederick, 5th earl of Carlisle, 158, 160,
   164, 176
Howgan, Mr (architect or clerk of works, Cashel
   cathedral), 305
Howley, William, archbishop of Canterbury, 276
Howth church, diocese and county of Dublin, 247
Huguenot? weaving industry in Callan, Co.
   Kilkenny, 108
Hunt, Philip, Rev. (chaplain and private secretary to
   the duke of Bedford in 1806), 602
Huntingstown, barony of Gowran, Co. Kilkenny, 25
Hussey, Philip (portrait-painter), 18–19, 105
Hutchinson, Samuel, bishop of Killala, 216, 341
Hydon, manor of, Somerset, 38

Ida, barony of, Co. Kilkenny, 20
illegitimate children (Agar family), 45, 101, 113
improvements: *see under* bishops' palaces; glebe-
   houses, building of
Industrial Revolution, the, 34, 225
infirmaries, county, 331, 495
Inishcarra, prebend of, diocese of Cloyne, Co. Cork,
   48–50
Inistioge, Co. Kilkenny, 41, 100
insanity, 52–3, 502–4
interest rates, 34–5, 327, 401, 420–21
investment in the stockmarket, 422–3, 426–30
Irby, family of (tenants of Cashel corporation
   property), 287
Ireton, Henry, 20
Irish Magazine, the (Watty Cox's), 2–3
Irwine, John, Sir, General, 87, 91, 149–50

Jackson, Charles, bishop of Ferns, 438–9, 447, 506–7

Jackson, Cyril, Rev., dean of Christ Church, Oxford, 592

Jacobites, 15, 18, 21, 27–8, 92–4, 479

James II, King, 20, 27–8, 351

Jebb, John, bishop of Limerick, 210*n*, 274, 348, 350, 496–7

Jenkinson, Charles, 1st earl of Liverpool, 32

Jenkinson, Robert Banks, Lord Hawkesbury, 2nd earl of Liverpool, 376, 434, 508

Jenyns, Soame, 38

Jocelyn, Percy, Hon, successively bishop of Ferns and Clogher, 603, 606

Jocelyn, Robert, 2nd earl of Roden, 553

Johnson, Samuel, LL.D., 594

Johnston, Francis, 247, 316, 368, 382–3

Jones, George Lewis, bishop of Kildare and dean of Christ Church, Dublin, 256–7, 314, 576

Jupp, P.J., 600

Kearney, James, MP for Thomastown, 132

Kearney, John, bishop of Ossory, 478, 604

Keatinge, James, Roman catholic coadjutor bishop, then bishop, of Ferns, 500

Keeble, John (composer), 322

Keene, Edmund, bishop of Ely, 347, 441

Kemmis, Thomas (Agar's attorney), 410

Kendal, Charles, of Sutton, Co. Dublin, 112

Kennedy, Ann, of Rathmaiden, Co. Waterford, 67

Kennedy, Catherine, of Rathmaiden, Co. Waterford, 67

Kenney, James, Rev. Dr, vicar-general of the diocese of Cork, 502

Kelly, Thomas (law officer and judge), 446

Kernan, Edward, Roman catholic coadjutor bishop, then bishop, of Clogher, 501

Kerry, County, 14, 127*n*, 191

Kevin Street police barracks, Dublin: *see* St Sepulchre, palace of

Kiddal Hall, Leeds, 26

Kildare, bishopric of, 391*n*, 392–3m 507; *see also under* Christ Church, Dublin (of which the bishop of Kildare was *ex officio* dean)

Kildare, County, 243, 524

Kildress, living of, diocese and county of Armagh, 255

Kilfithimone glebe-house, Co. Tipperary, 208

Kilkenny Castle, 20, 116

Kilkenny city, 15, 20, 41, 93–4, 108, 116–17, 119, 131, 178, 423–4, 522, 553; corporation of, 15, 22; parliamentary elections for, 94–5, 106*n*, 116–18, 121–3; Volunteers: *see under* Volunteers

Kilkenny, collectorship of, 124*n*, 130

Kilkenny college, 17

Kilkenny, County, 15–25, 41–2, 99–101, 104–6, 119, 121–2, 130–33, 513–14, 521–3;
landed estates in: Agar of Gowran, 16–25, 43, 98, 107–8, 125, 425; Agar of Ringwood, 22–4, 101, 112, 125, 425; Ashbrook, 114; Bessborough, 23; Boyse of Bishopswell, 127; Fownes of Woodstock, 99–100; Hewetson of Thomastown, 100; Normanton, 10, 23, 25, 44, 394, 420*n*, 421, 423–4, 428; Ormonde, 118–19; Wandesford, 107–8, 118;
parliamentary elections for, 23, 42, 92–3, 95, 102–116, 118–24, 126–33, 164; militia, 131–2; Volunteers: *see under* Volunteers

Killardry, prebend of, diocese of Cashel, Co. Tipperary, 217

Killala, bishopric of, 190, 341; diocese of, 203, 492, 562

Killaloe, bishopric of, 150, 190, 342, 413, 509; diocese of, 203, 216; palace, 342, 413, 509

Killenelick, prebend of: *see* Galbally, union of

Killashandra, TCD living of, diocese of Kilmore, Co. Cavan, 326

Kilmacduagh, deanery of, 214; diocese of: *see under* Clonfert

Kilmanagh, near Callan, Co. Kilkenny, 428

Kilmastulla church, diocese of Cashel, Co. Tipperary, 208

Kilmocar estate, barony of Fassadinin, Co. Kilkenny, 20, 21*n*

Kilmore, archdeaconry of, 245; bishopric of, 389–90; deanery of, 1, 61; diocese of, 539

Kilmurry, near Thomastown, Co. Kilkenny, 112

Kilnamanagh, barony of, Co. Tipperary, 407

Kilsallaghan, Co. Dublin, 29–30, 540*n*

Kilsaran, advowson of, diocese of Armagh, Co. Louth, 238*n*

Kilvemnon church, diocese of Cashel, Co. Tipperary, 208, 209*n*; glebe-house, 208

King, Caroline (*née* Fitzgerald), Viscountess Kingsborough, 296, 299

King, James, 4th Lord Kingston, 296

King, Robert, Viscount Kingsborough, 2nd earl of Kingston, 296, 298–9

King, William, successively bishop of Derry and archbishop of Dublin, 28–9, 134, 136, 141, 188–9, 245, 339, 347, 349, 382, 456, 474, 485

King, Beather, Rev. (Dublin curate preferred by Bishop Woodward), 494–5

King's bench, court of (Irish), 69–70, 74, 76, 102, 466

King's College chapel, Cambridge, 282

King's Inns, society of, 471
Kingston college, Mitchelstown, diocese of Cloyne, north Cork, 53, 112, 295–30, 433
Kirwan, Walter Blake, Rev., later dean of Killala, 462
Knaresborough, William, 43
Knockgraffon glebe-house, diocese of Cashel, Co. Tipperary, 208, 211
Knocktopher, barony of, Co. Kilkenny, 22
Knox, William, Hon., successively bishop of Killaloe and Derry, 135, 216, 264, 266, 283, 367, 507–8, 545, 553, 557n, 603, 605

Labarte, Edward, Rev., curate of Thurles, diocese of Cashel, Co. Tipperary, 578
Lancashire, 225
Lancaster, Joseph, 251
Land Tax, purchase of: *see under* tithes
Landaff, earls of: *see under* Mathew
landlord-tenant relations, 35, 333, 386–8, 393–6
Lanhydrock, Cornwall, 425
Laois, County, 14, 243, 524
Latouche, David, 431, 545–6
Latouche & Co., bankers to the board of first fruits, 431
Latouche, family of, of Bellevue, Delgany, Co. Wicklow, 464
Laurence, Richard, archbishop of Cashel, 307, 350, 374n, 376–7, 381, 491
Law, John, successively bishop of Killala and Elphin, 312, 341, 471, 492, 576
law: *see* legal system
law and order, 18, 72, 77–8, 131, 210–11, 292–4, 521–5
Lawless, Margaret: *see* Scott, Margaret
Lawless, Valentine, 2nd Lord Cloncurry, 46n
Lecky, W.E.H., 5–6, 306, 554, 566
Leech, Arthur Blennerhassett, 6n
legal system, 48, 74, 76, 99, 253, 271–4; assizes and quarter sessions, 48, 69, 88, 99, 102, 105, 112, 115, 292–4, 548–9; *see also* under: canon law; ecclesiastical courts
Leighlin cathedral, Co. Carlow, 42n
Lennox, Charles, 4th duke of Richmond, 245, 255–6, 316, 503, 602, 613
Leslie, Charles Powell (the first of three of that name), of Castle Leslie, Glaslough, Co. Monaghan, 404n
Leslie, Edward (later Sir Edward, 1st Bt), of Tarbert, Co. Kerry, 181–2, 571
Leslie, James, bishop of Limerick, 181
Leslie, John, successively bishop of Clogher and Raphoe, 403, 404n
Leslie, J.B., Canon, 465

Leslie, family of, of Castle Leslie, Glaslough, Co. Monaghan, 403–4, 404–5nn
Levinge, Richard, Sir, 1st Bt, 94
Lewis, Samuel, 301, 409
libraries, 58–9, 61, 296, 331, 347–8; *see also*: Armagh public library; Bolton library; Marsh's library
Lichfield, bishopric of, 392
Lidwell, Ann, Mrs (distressed gentlewoman in debt to Agar), 90
Liffey, River, 143–4, 159
Lifford, Viscounts: *see* Hewitt
Limerick, bishopric of, 214, 296, 390, 401–2, 498; city, 148, 498, 554; county, 192, 202–3, 554, 589n; 1783 election for county of, 463; diocese of, 191, 203, 498–9; earl of: *see* Pery, Edmond Henry
'Limerick black marble' (1813), 373
Lincoln, bishopric of, 189
Lindsay, Charles, Hon., bishop of Kildare and dean of Christ Church, Dublin, 245, 256–7, 282–3, 314, 392, 484, 486n, 507, 601
Lindsay, Thomas, archbishop of Armagh, 317, 477–8
Linen board, 442
linen manufacture and trade, 191, 232, 332–3, 445
Linton, Robert (Cashel cathedral organist), 322n
Lintown industrial school, Co. Kilkenny, 457
Lisanoure, Ballymoney, Co. Antrim, 78, 402–3
Lismalin, living of, diocese of Cashel, Co. Tipperary, 211
Lismore, Lord: *see* O'Callaghan
Lisnafunshin, near Castlecomer, Co. Kilkenny, 23n, 423–4, 427–8
literature, 38, 60–62
Llandaff, bishopric of, 391–2
Lloyd, Thomas (of Beechmount?, Rathkeale, Co. Limerick, Cashel see under-tenant), 409
local government, 194–5, 281; *see also*: under legal system
Lockhart, Miss (visitor to the Agars at Cashel), 90
Loftus, Charles Tottenham, 1st Lord and Viscount Loftus and 1st earl and marquess of Ely, 72, 74, 315, 470n, 476, 514n, 547, 555, 573–4; character of, 65; political interest and connection of, 65, 476, 573–4, 603; friendship of with Agar, 64–5, 74, 543; and the Regency Crisis, 164–5, 171; as joint postmaster-general, 164–5, 171, 292; and the Union, 533, 543–4, 551, 573–4, 603–4
Loftus, Henry, earl of Ely, 65, 108
Loftus, Lord Robert Tottenham, bishop of Clogher, 65, 135, 362, 603–5
Loftus v Hume, 69, 74

London, bishopric of, 188, 391, 414; church-building in, 225; *see also*: St Paul's Cathedral; theatre (London)

Londonderry, County, 155

Lord, Arthur, Rev., rector of Ballintemple, diocese of Cashel, Co. Tipperary, 578

lord justiceship (of Ireland), 64, 99*n*, 134, 383*n*, 442, 460, 471*n*, 620

lotteries, 35, 427, 506

Louth, earl of: *see* Bermingham, Thomas

Loveday, John, 304, 335

Lower Grange, barony of Gowran, Co. Kilkenny: *see under* Grange

Luttrell, Henry Lawes, General Lord Luttrell, 2nd earl of Carhampton, 119, 181–2, 543–4

Luttrell, Simon, 1st Viscount Irnham and 1st earl of Carhampton, 87, 414

Lyons, Co. Kildare, 306*n*

Macartney, George, Sir, Earl Macartney, 63–4, 78–80, 82, 84, 87, 157, 177, 366, 402–3, 510–11, 557, 581, 595–6

Macartney, Jane (*née* Stuart), Countess Macartney, 78

Macartney, John, Sir, 1st Bt, 575

Macartney-Porteous, Frances: *see* Benson, Frances

Macaulay, Thomas Babington, Lord Macaulay, 483

MacCarthaigh, Cormac, king of Cashel, 304

McClelland, James, MP for Randalstown, Co. Antrim, 581

MacCuilennain, Cormac, king of Munster and bishop of Cashel, 348

MacDonnell, J.C., Very Rev., dean of Cashel, 330

McNeill, J.G. Swift, 138

McParland, Edward, 304*n*, 329, 333

Maddoxtown, barony of Gowran, Co. Kilkenny, 43

Magahy of Cork, Messrs (organ-builders), 322–3

Magdalen college, Oxford, 316

Magee, William, successively bishop of Raphoe and archbishop of Dublin, 415*n*, 604, 610

Magheralin, Co. Down, 346

Maitland, James, 8th earl of Lauderdale, 478–9

Malone, Edmond, 202

Manchester, 34, 225

Manners, Charles, 4th duke of Rutland, 59, 63, 123, 160–61, 163–4, 225, 260*n*, 406, 448, 451, 486

Manners, Isabella, duchess of Rutland, 82

Manners-Sutton, Charles, successively bishop of Norwich and archbishop of Canterbury, 173, 478–80, 491, 592, 600

Manners Sutton, Thomas, 1st Lord Manners, 503

Mant, Richard, bishop of Down and Connor, 443, 459, 474, 589–90

Marlay, Richard, successively dean of Clogher and bishop of Clonfert and Waterford, 345*n*, 450, 470, 480*n*, 488, 506–7, 563, 577

marriage settlements, 24–5, 42, 45, 70, 78, 80–82, 118, 425–6

Marsden, Alexander (under-secretary, Dublin Castle), 85, 571*n*

Marsh, Narcissus, successively archbishop of Dublin and Armagh, 347, 456*n*

Marsh's library, Dublin, 350, 456

Marshall, Robert (private secretary to Lord Castlereagh), 535

Martin, G. (relation of Lady Clifden?), 43

Martin, John, 'of Dublin' (Lady Clifden's father), 41, 147

Martin, Lucinda: *see* Agar, Lucinda, Viscountess Clifden

Massy, William, Rev., rector of Clonbeg, Co. Tipperary, 210

Mathew, Lady Elizabeth, 82*n*

Mathew, Ellis (*née* Smyth), Mrs Francis Mathew, 70–71

Mathew, Francis, 1st Viscount and earl of Landaff, 70–71, 551–4

Mathew, Francis James, Lord Mathew, 2nd earl of Landaff, 71*n*, 295, 551–3

Mathew, Thomas, of Annfield, later of Thomastown, Co. Tipperary, 70–71

Matthews, John (Cashel cathedral organist), 319, 322

Matthews, John (verger in Cashel cathedral), 362*n*

Maude, Cornwallis, Sir, 3rd Bt, 1st Viscount Hawarden, 14, 80–81, 349*n*, 362–3, 524, 529*n*, 533, 553

Maude, Cornwallis, 3rd Viscount Hawarden, 81, 339

Maude, Frances, Viscountess Hawarden: *see* Agar, Frances, Hon.

Maude, Isabella, Viscountess Hawarden, 81

Maude, Thomas Ralph, 2nd Viscount Hawarden, 80–81, 527, 533

Maudlins, the, barony of Fassadinin, Co. Kilkenny, 20

Maule, Henry, successively bishop of Cloyne and Meath, 347

Maurice, Edward, bishop of Ossory, 348, 404

Maxwell, Constantia, 331

Maxwell, Henry, Hon., bishop of Meath, 340, 414, 467

Maxwell, Robert, bishop of Kilmore, 403

Maxwell, Robert, dean of Armagh, 403

Maxwell, family of, of Farnham, Co. Cavan, Barons and earls of Farnham, 403

Maynooth, Roman catholic seminary at, 328–9, 520–21, 590

Mayo, County, 341

Mayo, earl of and Viscount: *see under* Bourke

Meade, Theodosia, countess of Clanwilliam, 90, 309, 311

Meath, bishopric of, 390–91, 496, 505; diocese of, 186, 193–4, 271, 475, 505; palace, 340

Meath militia, 363

Melsham, family of (tenants of Cashel corporation property), 287

Meredyth, Henry, MP for Armagh city, etc., 444, 459, 572

Middlesex, 225

Middlethird, barony of, Co. Tipperary, 292–4, 407

Midleton, Co. Cork; estate of, 190, 212; parish and rectory of, diocese of Cloyne, 190, 212, 488, 494, 496; parliamentary borough of, 498, 573; proposed Roman catholic church on the Rock of, 325–6

'Midleton marble chimneypieces' (1814), 374

Middletown estate, Co. Armagh, 456–7

Milne, Kenneth, 494

Mitchelstown, Co. Cork, 296–300

Mitford, John, 1st Lord Redesdale, 226, 264–5, 268, 272, 277, 432, 605

Mohan, Christopher, Rev., 317

Molyneux, Capel, Sir, 3rd Bt, 177

Monboddo, Lord: *see* Burnett, James

Monck, Charles Stanley, 4th Viscount Monck, 22

Monck Mason, John, 178

Monck Mason, William, 3

Moneroe, barony of Gowran, Co. Kilkenny, 43

Monkstown church, diocese and county of Dublin, 247

Montagu, Elizabeth (*née* Robinson), Mrs Montagu, 60, 440, 457

monuments (funeral and commemorative), 5, 19, 30, 42*n*, 59, 185–6, 202, 330, 352

Moore, Charles, 6th earl and 1st marquess of Drogheda, 193, 576

Moore, Henry (agent for Welbore Ellis' Irish estates), 35

Moore, John, archbishop of Canterbury, 51, 232, 237, 260, 347, 496, 502, 507*n*, 517, 519, 533, 588–9; career and character of, 188, 485, 591–2; relations of with Agar, 51, 260, 347, 513; and Lord Buckingham's plan of Church reform, 452–3; opposes Catholic Emancipation, 517, 519, 607; opposes tithe reform, 534, 542, 556; and the union of the Churches of England and Ireland, 564–5, 567

Moore, Stephen, of Barne, Clonmel, Co. Tipperary, 289–90

Moncrieffe (a 'Scotch [medical] doctor'), 54

Moore, Thomas, 499–500

Morres, Hervey, 1st Viscount Mountmorres, 126

Morres, Hervey, 2nd Viscount Mountmorres, 74*n*

Morres, Redmond, 126, 380*n*

Morrison, John (architect), 198, 296–8, 305

Morrison, Richard, Sir, 206, 208, 296, 298, 305, 308–9, 330

Morrison, William Vitruvius, 298

Moss, Charles, bishop of St David's, 428

Mossom, Eland, senior, of Mount Eland, Co. Kilkenny, 178, 572

Mossom, Eland, junior, of Mount Eland, Co. Kilkenny, 100, 178, 427

Mossom, Robert, dean of Ossory, 215*n*, 572

Mountainstown, Navan, Co. Meath, 378

Mountgarret, Viscounts: *see* Butler, family of, Viscounts Mountgarret

Mountgarret ferry, Cos. Kilkenny and Wexford, 22

Mount Ievers, Sixmilebridge, Co. Clare, 335, 378

Mountjoy, Viscount: *see* Gardiner, Luke, 1st Viscount Mountjoy

Mountmorres, Viscounts: *see* Morres, Hervey

Mount Norris estate, Kent, 457

Mealiffe church and glebe-house, diocese of Cashel, Co. Tipperary, 209

Moylan, Francis, Roman catholic bishop of Cork, 500

Moyne, barony of Fassadinin, Co. Kilkenny, 21*n*

municipal corporations commissioners (Ireland), 291–2

Munster circuit, 396

Munster, province of, 552; *see also* Cashel, province of

Murray, Richard, Rev. Dr, vice-provost and provost of TCD, 488*n*

Murphy, James, Roman catholic bishop of Clogher, 500–01

Murphy, John, Rev. ('Father John Murphy of Boolavogue', Co. Wexford), 361*n*

Murphy, Thomas, Rev., vicar of Stabannon, diocese of Armagh, Co. Louth, 472

Murray, Daniel, Roman catholic coadjutor archbishop, then archbishop, of Dublin, 501

music, 246, 302, 317–23, 329–30

Naas, Co. Kildare, collectorship of, 129

Nall-Cain, Arthur Ronald, 2nd Lord Brocket, 360, 377

Namier, Lewis, Sir, 149

Napier, Lady Sarah, 231*n*

Navan, Co. Meath, parliamentary borough of, 591

navy, 226, 232

Newcastle, Ballymahon, Co. Longford, 378

Newcastle, duke of: *see* Pelham-Holles

Newchapel glebe-house, diocese of Cashel, Co. Tipperary, 208

Newcome, William, archbishop of Armagh, 199, 383, 397, 455, 480n, 507n, 544, 578, 587, 597; career and character of, 466–74, 591; and the borough of St Canice, 178, 468, 483, 570; and the Regency Crisis, 175; and Catholic Emancipation, 183, 449, 470–71; promotion of to the primacy, 174–5, 182–3, 449, 466–71, 473–4, 483, 507n, 570; as archbishop of Armagh, 183, 199, 383, 397, 455, 471–4, 578

Newenham, Edward, Sir, MP for Co. Dublin, 436

Newenham, E.A. (architect employed on the Cashel palace, *c.*1960), 377

'New Geneva', Passage, Co. Waterford, 300–01

Newman, Henry, Rev., vicar of Aney, diocese of Emly, Co. Limerick, 217

Newport, John, Sir, 2nd Bt, 269–70

Newport charter school, Co. Tipperary, 320; glebe-house, diocese of Cashel, Co.; Tipperary, 208; union of, 292

New Ross, Co. Wexford, 23; church, diocese of Ferns, 569

Newry, Co. Down, 79; Repeal club of, 6n

Newton, Thomas, bishop of Bristol, 347, 441, 443, 606

Newtown ('otherwise Normanton', near Castlecomer), Co. Kilkenny, 16n, 428

Newtown Pery, Limerick city, 148

Nicholls, Mr (companion of Viscount Fitzwilliam on a visit to Cashel), 322

Nicolson, William, bishop of Derry, 188–9, 400

Nollekens, John (sculptor), 30

non-residence, clerical, 215, 217–18, 222, 229, 232–7, 243, 254–6, 271–5, 317, 377; *see also* absenteeism, lay and episcopal

'Nore navigation' (i.e. canal), Co. Kilkenny, 41–2

Normanton, Yorkshire, 16

North, Brownlow, Hon., bishop of Winchester, 188

North, Frederick, Lord North, 2nd earl of Guilford, 32, 46, 74–5, 142, 147, 149, 151, 153–8, 161, 171, 188, 510, 591; *see also* Fox-North Coalition

Northumberland, dukes of: *see* Percy

Nugent, Lady Mary Elizabeth: *see* Grenville, Mary Elizabeth

Nugent, Robert Craggs, Earl Nugent, 33, 231

Oakly Park, Celbridge, Co. Kildare, 338, 381–2

O'Beirne, Thomas Lewis, successively bishop of Ossory and Meath, 193, 216–17, 249, 312, 464, 492–3, 525, 589, 599, 612–13; record and standing of as a bishop, 186, 283, 475–6, 492;

and the borough of St Canice, 176, 468; and the bishop of Meath's palace, 340; builds churches and glebe-houses, 186; and the building programme of the board of first fruits, 265–6, 269, 278–83; and clerical non-residence, 271, 273, 275; and the Church articles of the Union, 559–62, 564–7, 585–6, 591; and the tithe of agistment, 576–7; candidature of for the primacy, 589; opinion of Agar, 589–90, 599

O Briain, Muirchertach, king of Thomond, 303

O'Brien, Marianus, archbishop of Cashel, 287

O'Callaghan, Cornelius, 2nd Lord Lismore, 553n

O'Connellites, 284

Offaly, County, 524

O'Flaherty, John Bourke, of Castlefield, near Gowran, Co. Kilkenny, 121, 124n, 130, 163

O'Flaherty, family of, of Eyre Connaught, Lemonfield, etc., Co. Galway, 18

O'Flanagan, J. Roderick, 6

Ogle, George, MP for Co. Wexford, 470n

O'Hara, Charles, of Nymphsfield, Collooney, Co. Sligo, 537

O'Keeffe, James, Roman catholic bishop of Kildare, 500

Old Grange, barony of Gowran, Co. Kilkenny: *see under* Grange

Old Leighlin, Co. Carlow, parliamentary borough of, 176–7, 179–82, 341, 438–9, 459, 568–73

Old Ross church, diocese of Ferns, Co. Wexford, 569

'Orangemen', 254, 543, 587

Orde, Thomas, 1st Lord Bolton, 75, 121–2, 163, 293, 451

ordinations, 36–7, 188, 197

O'Reilly, Richard, Roman catholic coadjutor bishop of Kildare, then archbishop of Armagh, 500

organs: *see* Green, Samuel; Snetzler, John; and under music

Osborne, Thomas, Sir, 9th Bt, 553n

Osborough, W.N., 272–3nn

Ossory, bishopric of, 94, 178, 214, 339, 341, 343, 400n, 402, 407, 424, 468, 492–3; bishops of, 570; deanery of, 215; palace, 302, 339, 341, 343, 345n; *see also* St Canice

Oswald, John, bishop of Raphoe, 491

Owens, Michael (schoolmaster, Cashel cathedral choir-school), 319

Owen, William (portrait-painter), 614

Paley, William, Ven., archdeacon of Carlisle, 592

Pallas Green glebe, diocese of Emly, Co. Limerick, 209

Palliser, John, Rev. Dr, 396n, 407–12, 415, 417, 421–2

Palliser, John, of Derryluskan, Fethard, Co.
    Tipperary, 295, 396
Palliser, William, archbishop of Cashel, 287–8,
    337*n*, 347, 396
Palliser, William, junior, of Palliser House,
    Rathfarnham, Co. Dublin, 337*n*
Palliser, Wray, of Derryluskan, 396
Palliser House, Rathfarnham, 337*n*
Palmer, Joseph, Very Rev., dean of Cashel, 215,
    377
Palmer, Mr (incumbent of Tulloh, diocese of
    Killaloe, *c.*1800), 216
Parke, Edward (architect), 315
Pares, Richard, 480
Parker, Robert (Agar's steward at Tallaght Castle),
    369
parliament (British and UK); House of Commons,
    31, 263, 283–5, 387, 512–14, 473, 583–4;
    House of Lords, 28, 218, 238–40, 247, 263,
    277, 387, 477–81, 511–12, 529, 582–4;
    limitations of in exercising the supreme
    appellate jurisdiction in Irish causes, 394; *see
    also* Acts and bills
parliament (Irish): House of Commons, 65–7, 181–2,
    189, 239, 387, 429, 481, 548, 550; measures
    hostile to the Church originating in, 190–91,
    213*n*, 222–3, 226–7, 341, 394, 396–8, 450,
    511–12, 539–40, 555–6, 557–8, 574–7, 619–20;
    sale of seats in, 96, 103, 126–8; frequency of
    elections to, 176, 178; election of minors to,
    96–7; clerical interference in elections to, 134,
    287–91, 463, 554; election petitions to, 96,
    106–7, 117–18, 289–91, 571; franchise for, 22,
    97, 108, 117, 178–9; expenditure on elections
    for, 109–10; reform of, 121–2, 573; vacating
    seats in, 104, 116, 180–81; frequency of
    sessions of, 187, 443; speakership of, 109,
    147–8, 181, 289, 338, 442;
        House of Lords, 34, 73–6, 77, 87, 146,
    181–2, 222, 344, 379, 387, 414, 429, 544, 550,
    581–4, 590; appellate jurisdiction of, 69, 74–5,
    511; management of, 75–7, 134, 136, 142–3;
    published debates of (1783–4), 73; role of Agar
    and other bishops in, 134, 136, 142–3, 187–8,
    197, 224–5, 226–7, 394–9, 443–6, 447–8, 450,
    459–60, 465, 476–8, 481–3, 495–6, 515–16,
    520–21, 528–9, 543, 548–9, 576–7, 583–4,
    618–19; secret committees of (1793–8), 77,
    528–9; speakership of, 136, 429; *see also* Acts
    and bills
Parliament House: *see under* Dublin city
parliamentary elections (Ireland): *see* individual
    constituencies, and under parliament (Irish),
    House of Commons

Parnell, John, Sir, 2nd Bt, 248, 533
Parsons, Laurence, Sir, 5th Bt, 2nd earl of Rosse,
    67, 429, 605
Passage, Co. Waterford, 300
Paterson, Marcus, chief justice of the king's bench,
    72
'Paull' (portrait-painter?), 62*n*
Paulstown, barony of Gowran, Co. Kilkenny, 22
Paultons, Hampshire, 33, 352
Pearce, Edward Lovett, Sir, 334–8, 340–41, 354,
    360, 371–4, 378–80
Pearce, Zachary, bishop of Rochester, 501
Pedlie, Mr (royal gardener at Hampton Court), 375
Peel, Robert, Sir, 2nd Bt, 284, 434
Peerages, 13*n*, 32, 38–9, 41, 52–3, 72, 84–6, 104–5,
    116, 124, 127, 161, 167–8, 171–2, 174–5,
    201–2, 429, 457, 465, 582–5
Pelham, Thomas, Lord Pelham, 2nd earl of
    Chichester, 219, 248, 397–8, 455–6, 519–21,
    523, 526, 557
Pelham-Holles, Thomas, 1st duke of Newcastle, 31,
    107, 140, 392, 463*n*
Penal Laws, 9, 43, 70, 97, 108, 154–5, 288, 325,
    445–8, 495; *see also:* Catholic relief; Test Act,
    repeal of
Pennefather, John, Rev., 292
Pennefather, Kingsmill (1671–1735), of New Park,
    Cashel, MP for Cashel, 288–90
Pennefather, Matthew, Capt., MP for Cashel, 288–9
Pennefather, Richard, of New Park, Cashel
    (1701–77), MP for Cashel, 288–91
Pennefather, Richard, Colonel, of New Park, Cashel
    (*c.*1756–1831, grandson and successor of the
    previous Richard), MP for Cashel, 295, 309,
    554
Pennefather, William (*c.*1760–*c.*1803), collector of
    Clonmel and MP for Cashel, 293
Pennefather, William (of Lakefield?, Co. Tipperary,
    d.1872?), 287*n*
Pennefather, family of, of New Park, Cashel, 287,
    290–92, 295, 333
pensions, 24, 128, 167–8, 224, 499–501
Perceval, Charles George, 2nd Lord Arden, 582–4
Perceval, Spencer, 276, 278, 432, 582
Percy, Anne (*née* Stuart), Countess Percy, 140
Percy, Hugh, 2nd earl and 1st duke of
    Northumberland, 1, 60, 138–40, 177, 346, 441
Percy, Hugh, Earl Percy, 2nd duke of
    Northumberland, 63, 91, 139–40
Percy, Hugh, 3rd duke of Northumberland, 480
Percy, Hugh, successively bishop of Rochester and
    Carlisle, 480
Percy, Thomas, bishop of Dromore, 50, 204, 313,
    346–7, 491, 576

Pery, Edmond Henry, 2nd Lord Glentworth and 1st
    earl of Limerick, 554
Pery, Edmond Sexten, Viscount Pery, 147–8, 159,
    327, 498–9, 554
Pery, William Cecil, bishop of Limerick and 1st
    Lord Glentworth, 135, 147, 192n, 212–13, 312,
    498–9
Pettigo, Cos. Donegal and Fermanagh, 404, 493
Petworth-cum-Tillington, living of, Sussex, 192
Philippe ('Egalité'), duc d'Orléans, 47, 83
Pickardstown, Co. Dublin, 29
Pitt, William, 1st earl of Chatham, 31, 141, 162, 165
Pitt, William, the younger, 86, 162, 165–6, 169, 205,
    248, 266–7, 268n, 269–70, 478, 488, 508,
    513–14, 524, 545, 547, 596n, 606; lack of an
    Irish political following of, 165; meetings of
    and relations with Agar, 169, 173–4, 541–2;
    and the primacy (1794 and 1800), 173–4, 466,
    468, 588, 592–3; and tithe and Church reform
    in GB and/or Ireland, 205, 236, 275, 451–3,
    534–5, 540–41, 556; relations of with Lord
    Buckingham, 165, 230–31, 535, 556; and
    Catholic Emancipation and the Union, 515–19,
    529–32, 535, 541–2, 567–8, 584, 586, 607–8
plantation of Ulster, 539
Playfair, William, 477–8
Plowman, Frederick Prussia (painter), 62
Plumb, J.H., 188
pluralism, 188, 215, 217–18, 222–3, 229, 232–7,
    243, 254–6
Pococke, Richard, bishop of Ossory, 302, 337,
    456–7, 601n
Pomeroy, John, Ven., archdeacon of Cork, 347
Ponsonby, Brabazon, 1st earl of Bessborough, 24,
    102–4
Ponsonby, Lady Charlotte: *see* Fitzwilliam, Lady
    Charlotte
Ponsonby, George, 270
Ponsonby, John, Hon. (speaker), 102, 104–6,
    109–11, 114–15, 118, 121, 127, 177–8, 358, 439
Ponsonby, Richard, Hon., 439
Ponsonby, William, Viscount Duncannon, 2nd earl
    of Bessborough, 95, 102–104
Ponsonby, William Brabazon, 1st Lord Ponsonby of
    Imokilly, 119–20, 122–4, 131, 163–5, 397
Ponsonby, family of, of Bessborough, Co. Kilkenny,
    Viscounts Duncannon and earls of
    Bessborough, 93, 100, 103, 105, 124, 130, 133,
    135
Pope's Villa, Twickenham, 33, 83, 139, 352, 513
population (Church of Ireland and other), 189, 194,
    225, 243, 252
'Portaferry' (i.e. the chancellorship of Down
    cathedral), Co. Down, 256

Porter, John, successively bishop of Killala and
    Clogher, 429, 489, 570–71, 576
Portland, duke of: *see* Bentinck
Portlemon, near Mullingar, Co. Westmeath, 358
postmastership-general (Irish), 163–5, 171, 292
Poussin, Nicholas, 47
Powell, Caleb (of Clonshavoy?, near Murroe, Co.
    Limerick, Cashel *see under*-tenant), 409
Power, John (chairman of a meeting of the Cashel
    Volunteers), 294
Power, Richard, baron of the exchequer, 428
Pratt, John Jeffreys, 2nd Earl and 1st Marquess
    Camden, 130, 146, 182–3, 248, 362, 487, 489,
    508, 514–15, 519–20, 522–3, 525–7, 540, 555
Prendergast, Thomas, of Golden Lane, Dublin
    (agent for Welbore Ellis' Irish estates), 35
presbyterians: *see under* dissenters
presentation to livings: *see under* Church of Ireland,
    patronage in
Preston, John, of Bellinter, Navan, Co. Meath, Lord
    Tara, 411–12, 416–18, 591
Preston, Joseph, Rev., rector of Ballintemple and
    prebendary of Killenelick, 57, 137, 416
Preston, William, bishop of Ferns, 165–6, 345, 484,
    486
Pretyman-Tomline, George, successively bishop of
    Lincoln and Winchester, 173, 428, 485, 491,
    540, 542, 556
Price, Arthur, archbishop of Cashel, 305, 337–8,
    357, 376, 381–2
Price, family of (tenants of Cashel corporation
    property), 287
primacy: *see* Armagh, archbishopric of
Primate Boulter's fund (for augmenting small
    livings), 229–30, 276–7, 280, 284
Prittie, Henry, 1st Lord Dunalley, 71
privy council (British), 65, 146–7, 155, 224, 447,
    482, 511
privy council (Irish), 73–4, 163, 224, 289, 391n, 482;
    clerkship to, 163, 171–2; unions of parishes
    effected by, 213, 229, 237, 254–5, 261
Proby, John Joshua, 1st earl of Carysfort, 544
Purcell, Henry, 302

quarter sessions: *see under* legal system

Radcliff, Richard, Rev., chancellor of Down and
    rector of St Mary's, Enniscorthy, diocese of
    Ferns, Co. Wexford, 256
Radcliff, Stephen, Dr, judge of the prerogative
    court, 240, 444n
Radcliff, Thomas, MP for St Canice, Co. Kilkenny,
    572
Raeburn, Henry, Sir, 476n

Raheendonore, barony of Gowran, Co. Kilkenny, 21

Randolph, John, bishop of Oxford, 592

rape, tithe of, 191

Raphoe, bishopric of, 491, 508; deanery of, 214n, 392

Rathfarnham, Co. Dublin, 253; church, diocese and county of Dublin, 247; *see also* Palliser House, Rathfarnham

Rathgarvan, alias Clifden, barony of Gowran, Co. Kilkenny, 16

Rawdon, Lady Elizabeth: *see* Hastings

Rawson, George, Colonel, MP for Armagh city, 459

Rayner, John (jurist), 539

rebellion (1798), 9, 107–8, 131–2, 218–19, 301, 334, 345, 350, 360–63, 490, 492, 507–8, 521–5, 527–30, 545–7, 569

Reeves, William, bishop of Down and Connor, 488

Reformation, the, 221; *see also* : Dissolution of the Monasteries

Regency Crisis, 121, 124, 164–72, 230, 313, 454, 459–60, 465–8, 478

regular clergy: *see under* Roman catholic Church

Renehan, Laurence, Very Rev. Dr, 327n, 328

Repeal (of the Union), 6n

residence, clerical (enforcement of), 54–7, 186–7, 211–20, 223, 232–7, 239–40, 243, 254–6, 261, 270–76, 542, 558, 613

revenue board, 26, 41, 109, 143–7, 158, 162

revenue patronage, 89, 110, 124n, 129–30

Reynell, Carew, successively bishop of Down and Connor and of Derry, 486n

Reynolds, Joshua, Sir, 46–7, 89, 215–16, 458, 461

Reynolds, Thomas, of Kilkea Castle, Co. Kildare, 73

Riall, Samuel, Rev., of Upham, Cashel, 281

Riby, estate of, north Lincolnshire, 428

Rigby, Richard, 438–9

Rightboy Movement, 9, 49, 160, 190, 232–3, 294, 444, 449, 481, 536

road presentments, 281

Roberts, John (architect), 297–8, 305, 329

Roberts, Mr (gardener from England wanted by Agar for Cashel), 359

Robinson, Celia (mistress of Thomas Mathew), 70

Robinson, John (Lord North's secretary to the treasury), 156, 162

Robinson (originally Freind), John, Rev., 1st Bt, archdeacon of Armagh, 457–8, 460

Robinson, Matthew, 2nd Lord Rokeby, 457

Robinson, Richard, successively bishop of Killala, Ferns and Kildare and archbishop of Armagh, 1st Lord Rokeby, 51, 156–7, 160, 202, 215, 344, 365, 414, 426n, 470, 472, 494, 499–501, 594, 615, 618; character of, 137, 352, 437–9, 458–61; rapid and controversial promotion of,

139–40, 440–42, 619; attachment of to the Sackville family, 149–50, 177, 438–9, 442; and bishops' boroughs (especially Old Leighlin and Armagh), 176–7, 182–3, 438–9, 459, 571–2; as primate and a diocesan, 199–200, 222, 233, 316–17, 331–3, 382–3, 393, 395–7, 437–8,440–61, 490; as vice-chancellor and visitor of TCD, 151–2, 202; hostility of towards, and comparison with, Agar, 9, 149–52, 156–7, 190, 198–200, 210, 224, 232–5, 239–40, 444–54, 461; secures the archbishopric of Dublin for, and his subsequent relations with, Robert Fowler, 149–50, 156–7, 448, 464–5; and the Penal Laws and Catholic Question, 189, 327, 446–8, 454, 461; and tithe and Church reform, 189–90, 232–5, 239–40, 443–5, 448–54; and the work of the board of first fruits, 198–9, 226–9, 263, 313, 572; last eight declining years of, 51, 201, 226, 239, 448–54, 477–8, 620; buildings and benefactions of, 229, 316–17, 331–3, 343–4, 352, 379n, 382–3, 393, 455–8, 460

Robinson, Septimus, Sir, General, 439, 442

Robinson, Thomas, Sir, 1st Bt, 457

Robinson, William, Sir, 2nd Bt, 451

Robinson, family of (tenants of Cashel corporation property), 287

Roche, Boyle, Sir, MP for Gowran, 127

Rochester cathedral organ, 321

Rodney, George Brydges, Admiral the 1st Lord Rodney, 294

Roe, Peter, Rev., rector of St Mary's, Kilkenny, 492

Rohan-Chabot, Charles-Rosalie de, comte de Jarnac, 71, 83

Rohan-Chabot, Louis-Guillaume de, vicomte de Chabot and comte de Jarnac, 81, 82n, 252

Rokeby Hall, Dunleer, Co. Louth, 457–8

Rokeby Park, Yorkshire, 457

Roman Catholic Church, 34, 324–9, 499–501; post-1782 church-building in, 324–6; state payment of the clergy of, 530, 541–2; regular clergy of, 327, 500; coadjutorships in, 499–501; *see also* Penal Laws

Romney, George, 62–3, 464n

Ross, Charles, Sir, 4

Roth, George, MP for Thomastown, 129

Rower, the, barony of Knocktopher, Co. Kilkenny, 22–3, 112, 124, 425, 523–4

Rubens, Peter Paul, 46

Rundle, Thomas, bishop of Derry, 474n

Russborough, near Blessington, Co. Kildare, 378

Russell, Francis, marquess of Tavistock, later 7th duke of Bedford, 248

Russell, John, 4th duke of Bedford, 177, 438–9, 441, 442n, 459

Russell, John, 6th duke of Bedford, 248–9, 251n, 254–5, 270–71, 315–16, 507, 602–3

Russell, family of (tenants of Cashel corporation property), 287

Ryan, Edward, Rev., prebend of Donoughmore, St Patrick's Cathedral, Dublin, 59

Ryan, Patrick, Roman catholic coadjutor bishop, then bishop, of Ferns, 500

Ryder, Henry, Hon., successively bishop of Gloucester and Lichfield, 392

Ryder, John, successively bishop of Down and Connor, and archbishop of Tuam, 390

Sackville, Charles, 2nd duke of Dorset, 177

Sackville, Lord George, 1st Viscount Sackville, 148–9, 155–6, 163, 442

Sackville, Lionel Cranfield, 1st duke of Dorset, 150, 177, 200

Sackville, family of, dukes of Dorset, 149, 438

St Andrew's church, Westland Row, diocese and city of Dublin, 247

St Ann's church, Dawson Street, diocese and city of Dublin, 465; curates of, 580

St Asaph, diocese of, 205

St Canice, Co. Kilkenny, 94, 341, 343, 509; cathedral of, 202, 215, 302; parliamentary borough of, 94, 175–6, 178–80, 183, 468, 570, 572; *see also* Ossory

St David's, bishopric and diocese of, 205

St Dominick's Abbey, Cashel, 354, 359, 371

St George, Thomas MP for Clogher, Co. Tyrone, 177–9

St George's Chapel, Windsor, 302, 321

St George's church, Hardwicke Place, diocese and city of Dublin, 247, 252–3, 309, 465

St Helens, Lord: *see* Fitzherbert

St Kevin's parish, diocese and city of Dublin, 253

St Lawrence, Thomas, Hon. and Ven., bishop of Cork, 602, 604

St Leger, James, Hon. and Ven., archdeacon of Emly, 281n, 410, 412, 416–18

St Leger, St Leger, 1st Viscount Doneraile, 353

St Luke's parish, The Coombe, diocese and city of Dublin, 256

St Mary's, Shandon, diocese and city of Cork, advowson of, 238n

St Mary's, Youghal, diocese of Cloyne, Co. Cork, rectorial tithes of, 393

St Michael's church, High Street, diocese and city of Dublin, 247, 252

St Michan's, Church Street, prebend of, Christ Church Cathedral, Dublin, 245

St Nicholas-Without-the Walls, diocese and city of Dublin; perpetual curacy of, 244; church, 247, 252; parish, 253

St Omer, 327

St Patrick, order of, 249, 315, 415, 464, 597–9

St Patrick's Cathedral, Dublin, 3, 144, 214, 242, 244–6, 314–16, 490n, 599; bell-ringers of, 246; chancellorship of, 244; choir of, 246; deanery of, 465–6; patronage of, 244–5; vicars choral of, 246, 253

St Patrick's hospital, Dublin: *see under* Dublin City

St Paul's Cathedral, London, 308; deanery of, 391–2

St Peter's parish, Aungier Street, diocese and city of Dublin, 247, 253

St Sepulchre, the archbishop of Dublin's liberty and manor of, 253; palace of, 365–8; farm of, 413–14

St Stephen's church, Upper Mount Street, diocese and city of Dublin, 247

St Werburgh's church, Werburgh Street, diocese and city of Dublin, 243–4; rectory of, 243–4, 456n

Salford, 225

Salisbury, bishopric of, 188

Sanguiser, Mary (mistress of Lord Callan), 113

Santry Court, Co. Dublin, 325

Saunders Grove, Dunlavin, Co. Wicklow, 335

Scott, Lady Charlotte, 63

Scott, John, 1st Lord Earlsfort and 1st Viscount and earl of Clonmell, 32, 45, 49, 64, 72–6, 87–9, 142–3, 152–3, 156, 161–2, 293, 327, 396, 425, 428–9, 446n, 448, 462; career and character of, 66–71, 77–8, 161–2, 171, 224, 313–14, 327, 425, 428–9, 446n; witticisms of, 32, 45, 66, 67–9, 86, 88, 91, 137, 162; friendship of with Agar, 59, 66–71, 76–8, 86, 88–9, 91, 142–3, 148–50; and Gilbert Stuart, 63; and Clonmell House, Dublin, 413–14; hostility of to the Buckinghamshire administration, 143, 149–50, 224; and the Tenantry and Archbishop of Cashel's Acts, 394, 397–9, 411; and the Regency Crisis, 164, 171

Scott, John, dean of Lismore, 255, 314

Scott, John, 1st earl of Eldon, 276, 568

Scott, Margaret (*née* Lawless), Lady Earlsfort, Viscountess and countess of Clonmell, 72

Scott, Thomas, of Mohudder, Co. Tipperary, 70

Scott, Thomas, 2nd earl of Clonmell, 63

Scott, William, Sir, 49, 193, 236–7, 272, 275–6, 536, 558

Scully, Edward, of Kilfeakle, Co. Tipperary (Cashel see under-tenant), 388, 409 secret committees of the Irish House of Lords (1793–8): *see under* parliament (Irish), House of Lords

Seymour-Conway, Francis, 1st earl and marquess of Hertford, 140, 468–9

Seymour-Conway, Henry, Hon., 468

Shanahan, Michael (architect; owner of marble factory), 374

Shannongrove, Pallas Kenry, Co. Limerick, 378

Simms, George Otto, archbishop of Armagh, 458–9

Singleton, Henry, later chief justice of the common pleas, 97

Skeffington, Chichester Arthur, 6n

Skelton, Philip, Rev., 443, 462, 493

Skreen, rectory of, Co. Meath, 216

Sleater, Matthew, Rev., 59n, 208–9, 252–3, 306

Sleveen, barony of Fassadinin, Co. Kilkenny, 21n

Sligo, County, 290–91

Sligo, Lord: *see* Browne, John Denis

Sloane, Hans, of South Stoneham, Hampshire, 33n, 359

Smallcorn, Mr (Lady Mendip's gardener at Pope's Villa, Twickenham), 359n

small livings, augmentation of: *see* Primate Boulter's fund

Smith, Charles, M.D., 292

Smith, Michael, Sir, 1st Bt, 410

Smithson, Hugh: *see* Percy, Hugh, 2nd earl and 1st duke of Northumberland

smuggling, 144

Smyth, Arthur, archbishop of Dublin, 150, 317, 390, 428, 490n

Smyth, Edward (sculptor), 19n, 43n

Smyth, Ellis: *see* Mathew, Ellis

Smyth, James, of Tinny Park, Delgany, Co. Wicklow, 18

Smyth, Skeffington, Sir, 1st Bt, 71

Snetzler, John, 317, 320, 333n

Somerley, Ringwood, Hampshire, 7, 47, 62–3

Southwell, Bowen, MP for Downpatrick, Co. Down, 526

Sparke, Bowyer Edward, bishop of Ely, 491

speakership (of the Irish Houses of Commons and Lords): *see under* parliament (Irish), House of Commons; House of Lords

Speechly, William (the duke of Portland's gardener), 358–9

Spencer, Lady Caroline: *see* Agar, Lady Caroline

Spencer, George, 4th duke of Marlborough, 172, 485, 513

Spofforth, Yorkshire, living of, 192

Spooner, Mr and Mrs (members of Mrs Griffith's Bloomsbury 'coterie'), 61–61

Stanhope, Lady Anna Maria, marchioness of Tavistock, 248

Stanhope, Elizabeth: *see* Ellis, Elizabeth, Mrs Welbore Ellis

Stanhope, Philip Dormer, 4th earl of Chesterfield, 136, 592

Stanhope, William, Sir, 33

Stanley, A.P., Very Rev., dean of Westminster, 5

Stanley, Anne: *see* Ellis, Anne, Lady Mendip

Stanley, Hans, of Paultons, Hampshire, 33, 149, 156

Stanley, John (composer), 322

Staples, John, of Lissan, Cookstown, Co. Tyrone, 397, 471

Stapleton, Michael (stuccodore), 380–81

Stearne, John, bishop of Clogher, 303, 343, 456–7

Stevens, family of (tenants of Cashel corporation property), 287

Stewart, James, of Killymoon, Cookstown, Co. Tyrone, 397, 471

Stewart, Robert, Viscount Castlereagh, 2nd marquess of Londonderry, 184, 272, 385, 422, 524–5, 532, 543, 547, 550, 555, 557, 559–60, 562, 565, 569, 573, 589, 607

Stock, Joseph, bishop of Killala, 81n, 340n, 341, 469, 472, 489, 492, 576, 613

Stokes, Mr (valuer of work done on Kingston college), 297

Stone, Andrew, 140

Stone, George, archbishop of Armagh, 140n, 177, 383, 442, 451, 482, 572, 616; cultivates the Agar political connection, 30, 97; immorality of, 135, 197, 440, 490; rapid promotion of, 140; enters into Irish factional politics, 135, 150, 160, 177, 197, 438, 442, 459, 483, 616; as unsatisfactory treasurer to the board of first fruits, 222; absenteeism from and neglect of Armagh, 317, 383; and the Armagh see estate, 389; contributes to the promotion of Primate Robinson, 438–42, 458n

Stopford, James, 2nd earl of Courtown, 546–7

Stopford, Thomas, Hon., bishop of Cork, 502, 576

Strickland, Walter George, 63

Strokestown, Co. Roscommon, 378

Stuart, Gilbert, 62–4, 83, 87, 141n, 462, 464n

Stuart, James (historian of Armagh city, 1819), 316, 455–6, 458, 473

Stuart, Lady Jane: *see* Macartney, Jane

Stuart, John, 3rd earl of Bute, 31, 78, 140, 441–2, 593

Stuart, William, Hon., archbishop of Armagh, 250, 255, 257–9, 270, 340, 344, 364, 366–7, 416, 429, 472–3, 484, 492–3, 499–500, 503, 586–7,

601–2, 613–14, 618; appointment of to the primacy, 344, 592–9, 606–7, 609; and archiepiscopal and episcopal authority, particularly to curb non-residence, 193–4, 222–3, 255, 270–71, 274, 276; falls under the influence of Archbishop Brodrick and imbibes his antagonism to Agar, 257–8, 268–70, 282, 364, 366–7, 369, 430–33, 490, 611–12, 614; flawed plans of for building glebe-houses and churches by parliamentary grant, 258–9, 262–9, 274, 276, 278–80, 282–5, 472; and the board of first fruits, 258–9, 263–9, 274, 278–9, 282–3, 285, 430–33, 568*n*, 587; and the Armagh and other see estates, 387, 499–500, 612; and bishops' palaces, 344, 364, 366–7, 369; and Catholic Emancipation, 603, 607–8, 613; defects of temper of, 609–13; other limitations of, 593–4, 613–14; portraits of, 614
suffering loyalists, commission for the relief of, 249, 360–61, 527–8, 532, 544–7, 569
Suffolk, County, 385, 428
Sullivan, Timothy (Agar's steward at Cashel), 362
Summerhill, Co. Meath, 378
surveying (land), 99, 108*n*, 206, 396*n*, 407–8
Sutton, Manners-: *see* Manner-Sutton
Sweeny, C., Mr (Cashel cathedral choirmaster), 319
Sweet, Stephen (speculator in Co. Kilkenny land), 99
Swift, Jonathan, dean of St Patrick's Cathedral, Dublin, 223, 281, 304, 465
Swords, Co. Dublin; parliamentary borough of, 100, 574*n*; school, 249, 574*n*
Synge, Alicia (daughter and heiress of Edward Synge, bishop of Elphin), 404
Synge, Edward, bishop of Cork, 303*n*
Synge, Edward, bishop of Elphin, 136, 138*n*, 187, 290–91, 404
Syon, Middlesex, 139

Talbot, Charles, 3rd Earl Talbot, 434–5
Talbot, Richard, duke of Tyrconnel, 15, 27
Tallaght, Co. Dublin, 253, 540*n*; Castle (country palace of the archbishop of Dublin), 365–6, 368–70
Taney church, Dundrum, diocese and county of Dublin, 254
Temple, Frederick, archbishop of Canterbury, 483
Templecarne, rectory of, diocese of Clogher: *see under* Pettigo
Templeneiry glebe-house, diocese of Cashel, Co. Tipperary, 208, 362
Templenoe glebe-house, diocese of Cashel, Co. Tipperary, 208

Templetuohy church and glebe-house, diocese of Cashel, Co. Tipperary, 208–9
Tench, Thomas (Agar's attorney; agent for Welbore Ellis' Irish estates), 35
Tenison, Richard, successively bishop of Killala, Clogher and Meath, 343*n*, 403–4
Termonfeckin, Co. Louth, archbishop of Armagh's palace at, 383
Test Act, repeal of, 9, 65, 154–5, 158, 195, 446–7, 468
Theatre (London), 61, 492
Theatre (Dublin), 68
Thomastown, Co. Kilkenny, 22, 108–9; parliamentary elections for, 42, 92, 98–100, 102–3, 126–30; Volunteers: *see under* Volunteers
Thompson, Benjamin, Count Rumford, 353
Thorpe, Charles, Alderman (Dublin builder), 369
Thurles, Co. Tipperary; glebe-house, diocese of Cashel, 307; house of the Roman catholic archbishop of Cashel in, 327–8
Thurlow, Edward, 1st Lord Thurlow, 160, 170
Tinnalinton, barony of Fassadinin, Co. Kilkenny, 21*n*
Tipper, prebend of, St Patrick's Cathedral, Dublin, 80
Tipperary, County, 70–71, 89, 202–3, 290, 292–5, 314, 396, 419, 523–4, 551–4; town, Co. Tipperary, 58; union of, diocese of Cashel, 120, 208, 217–18
Tisdall, Philip (attorney-general; MP for Armagh city), 151–3, 380–81, 459, 572
tithes, 33–4, 558; origins and history of, 196, 203, 230, 539; appropriations and impropriations of, 196, 203, 245, 392–3, 558; diocesan and regional variations in, 203, 229–30, 538–9; House of Commons resolution (1736) and act of parliament (1800) against tithe of agistment, 223, 262, 574–7, 618; enclosure acts, 537–8, 540; Summary Tithe Acts, 74, 444, 539–40; Rightboy and other agitation against, 189, 294, 444, 449, 475, 481, 511, 536–7, 548–9, 577–8, 619; reform/commutation of (Ireland), 33–4, 75, 191, 232, 234, 240, 262, 266–7, 270, 504–5, 511, 530, 534–42, 548–9, 556–8, 563; reform/commutation of (Great Britain), 232*n*, 234, 534–42, 556–8; Barren Lands Bills/Acts (Grattan's, Agar's, etc.), 433, 450–51, 482–3, 539; Land Tax, purchase of (as a precedent for commutation), 504–5, 534–5
Toler, John, 1st earl of Norbury, 64, 72–3, 251, 552–3

Tomakeany, barony of Fassadinin, Co. Kilkenny, 20

Tomline: *see* Pretyman-Tomline

tontines, 35

Toorbeg, barony of Fassadinin, Co. Kilkenny, 21*n*

Toormore, barony of Fassadinin, Co. Kilkenny, 21*n*

topography, 203, 208–9

Tories (early eighteenth-century Irish), 18, 29, 92–4, 134

Tottenham, Charles, MP for New Ross, Co. Wexford, 569, 573-4

Tottenham Loftus: *see* Loftus

Townshend, George, 4th Viscount and 1st Marquess Townshend, 66, 109, 112, 141, 177–8, 180, 462

Tralee Roman catholic church, Co. Kerry, 326*n*

Trant, Dominick (assistant barrister for Co. Tipperary; anti-Rightboy pamphleteer), 49, 127*n*, 293, 572

Trench, Power le Poer, Hon., successively bishop of Waterford and Elphin and archbishop of Tuam, 192*n*, 603, 605–6

Trinity College, Dublin, 144, 151–3, 249–50, 322, 326, 348, 406, 439, 442, 446, 456, 485, 488, 604

Troy, John Thomas, successively Roman catholic bishop of Ossory and archbishop of Dublin, 327–8, 470*n*, 499–501

Tuam, archbishopric of, 142, 150, 174, 387, 390–91, 429, 476, 488; archbishops of, 150, 437; diocese of, 203, 229–30; province of, 229–30, 481, 538

Tyrrell, Benjamin (north Cork gentleman; father-in-law of Rev. Henry Agar), 48

Tucker, Abraham (philosopher), 38

Tulloh glebe-house (near Nenagh), diocese of Killaloe, 216

Turvin, Mrs (poor relation of Lady Kingsborough), 299–300

Twyford, living of, near Stowe, Buckinghamshire, 192

Tylney Hall, Hampshire, 61

Tymothan, prebend of, St Patrick's Cathedral, Dublin, 244

Tynan, prebend of, Armagh cathedral, 457

Tyndale, William, 348

Tyrconnel, duke of: *see* Talbot, Richard

Tyrone, earl of: *see* Beresford, George

Union, 157, 446–7, 510–15, 525–6, 528, 530–32, 535, 541, 550–51, 554–8, 591, 593, 599–600, 610–11; terms of, 542–3, 554, 559–68, 572–4, 582–6; winning support for (1798–1800), 131–2, 529–33m 550–54; compensation

money for boroughs disfranchised by, 258–9, 279, 431–2, 550, 568–74; consequences of, 159–60, 257, 266, 272–3, 283, 430, 586–7, 599–607; *see also* bishops, post-Union representation of

'Union engagements', 86, 172, 254, 600, 603–6, 609–10

United Irishmen, 46*n*, 77–8, 388, 522–4, 528–9

Upper Ossory, earls of: *see* Fitzpatrick

Upton, Henry (diocesan and provincial registrar of Armagh), 444–5

Ussher, Henry, archbishop of Armagh, 405*n*

Vanbrugh, John, Sir, 335

Velazquez, Diego Rodriguez de, 46

Vernon, Edward Venables, bishop of Carlisle, 392

Verschoyle, James, Very Rev., dean of St Patrick's, 315, 466

Vesey, John, archbishop of Tuam, 404

Vesey, John Denny, Sir, 2nd Bt, 1st Lord Knapton, 96, 176*n*

Vesey, Thomas, Sir, 1st Bt, successively bishop of Killaloe and Ossory, 94–6, 176, 215, 339, 404

Vesey, family of, of Abbeyleix, Co. Laois, baronets, Barons Knapton and viscounts de Vesci, 404

'Veto Controversy' (1808–13), 327

vicars-general, 202; *see also* under ecclesiastical courts

Vigors, Bartholomew, bishop of Ferns, 345

Vincent, John, Very Rev. Dr, dean of Westminster (formerly headmaster of Westminster school), 38

visitations, 14, 28–9, 50, 82, 89, 187–8, 193, 201, 204–7, 212–13, 219–20, 239, 242, 246–7, 251–2, 254, 270, 280, 463–4, 499, 610

Volunteers: Cashel, 294; Clogher, Co. Tyrone, 179; Gowran, 42, 119; Kilkenny city and county, 119, 121–3; Thomastown, 42, 119

Waite, Thomas (under-secretary, Dublin Castle), 110

Wakefield, Edward Gibbon, 213–14, 262, 275, 340, 386, 389, 391, 403, 409, 416, 603–4, 613

Waldegrave, James, 2nd Earl Waldegrave, 439

Wall, Garrett, rector of Pallas Green, diocese of Emly, Co. Limerick, 217, 549

Wallace, James (British attorney-general), 146

Walpole, Horace, 4th earl of Orford, 58, 61, 440, 461, 483, 513

Walpole, Robert, Sir, 1st earl of Orford, 134, 478

Wandesford, Lady Anne: *see* Butler, Anne, countess of Ormonde

Wandesford, Christopher, 2nd Viscount Castlecomer, 107

Wandesford, George, 4th Viscount Castlecomer, 104

Wandesford, John, 5th Viscount Castlecomer and Earl Wandesford, 104–7, 111, 118, 126–7

Wandesford, family of, Viscounts Castlecomer, 20, 133

Warburton, Charles Mongan, successively dean of Ardagh and bishop of Limerick, 183, 507, 592, 602, 604

Ware, James, Sir, 304

Warren, Ebenezer, MP for Kilkenny city, 94

Warren, John, bishop of Bangor, 260

Waterford, bishopric of, 296,389; diocese of, 203; palace, 340–41, 345n, 376–7; cathedral (Church of Ireland), 298, 303, 308, 329; cathedral (Roman catholic), 325, 329

Waterford, marquess of: *see* Beresford, George, and Beresford, Henry

Watson, Richard, bishop of Llandaff, 38, 194, 223–5, 236, 238–9, 260n, 275, 391, 478, 486n, 506, 537, 556, 563–5, 567, 586, 592–3

Webb, Robert (brother-in-law of the rector of Abington, Co. Limerick), 210

Wedderburn, Alexander, 1st Lord Loughborough and earl of Rosslyn, 519, 607–9

Welbore, William, 28

Welch, Patrick, MP for Gowran and Thomastown, 129

Weldon, Anthony, Sir, 91

Welland, Joseph (architect), 370n

Welland, William (Lord Midleton's agent and Archbishop Brodrick's amateur architect), 370–76, 381

Wellesley, Arthur, Sir, 1st duke of Wellington, 4, 247, 278, 280, 283, 600, 602–3

Wellesley, Garrett, 1st earl of Mornington, 302

Wellesley, Richard, 2nd earl of Mornington, 1st Marquess Wellesley, 122n

Wells, deanery of, 392

Wemys, Henry, Sir (c.1640–1722), of Danesfort, Co. Kilkenny, MP for Co. Kilkenny, 18, 93, 95

Wemys, Henry (1703–50), of Danesfort, MP for Callan, 97, 99, 103

Wemys, James, (c.1710–1765), of Danesfort, MP for Callan, 101, 105–6

Wemys, James, junior (c.1750–1820), of Danesfort, MP for Kilkenny city, 106n, 119

Wemys, Mary: see Agar, Mary (*née* Wemy), Mrs James Agar

Wemys, Patrick, senior (1679–1747), of Danesfort, MP for Gowran and for Co. Kilkenny, 95–6, 176n

Wemys, Patrick, junior (1707–62), of Delville and, from 1750, Danesfort, MP for Co. Kilkenny and for Callan, 97, 99, 103, 105–7

Wemys, family of, of Danesfort, Co. Kilkenny, 60, 93, 101, 106n

Wentworth, Thomas, 1st earl of Strafford, 575

Wesley, John, Rev., 117, 462

Wesley: *see also* Wellesley

West, John (stuccodore), 380

West, Robert (stuccodore), 380

Westcourt House, Callan, 124

West Layton, Yorkshire, 457

Westminster Abbey, 5, 39, 185–6, 321; prebendaries of, 190, 392, 462

Westminster school, 26, 28, 36, 38, 41, 192

Westport, Co. Mayo, 229

Westport House, Co. Mayo, 378

Wexford, County, 243, 546–7

Whaley, Anne: *see* FitzGibbon, Anne

Whaley, Thomas ('Buck' Whaley), of Whaley Abbey, Co. Wicklow, 405

Wheeler, Jonas, bishop of Ossory, 404

Whetham, John, dean of Lismore, 489

White, Richard, 1st Lord Bantry, 361

Whiteboys, 42, 181; *see also* Rightboy Movement

Whitechurch church, diocese of Cloyne, Co. Cork, 198

Wickham, William, 259, 264–5, 277, 586–7

Wicklow church, diocese of Glendalough, Co. Wicklow, 322

Wicklow, County, 243, 389

Wilberforce, William, 252, 529

Willes, Edward, bishop of Bath and Wells, 479

Willes, John, Sir, chief justice of the common pleas (England), 479

William III, King, 14–15, 26–7

William Henry, duke of Gloucester (brother of George III), 439, 442

Willis, Wood, Percival & Co. (Agar's London stockbrokers), 433

Winchester, bishopric of, 188, 428

Winchester college organ, 321

Winder, Jane: *see* Benson, Jane

Wolfe, Arthur, 1st Viscount Kilwarden, 72–3, 584

Woodstock, Inistioge, Co. Kilkenny, 378

Woodward, Henry, Rev. Dr, rector of Fethard, diocese of Cashel, Co. Tipperary, 497–8

Woodward, Richard, bishop of Cloyne, 135, 167, 240, 504, 572n, 601n; family and connections of, 135, 494–5; views of on a provision for the poor, 495; views of on the part a bishop ought to take in the House of Lords, 480, 496; and see estates, 405, 417, 454; and the Rev. Henry Agar affair, 48–52, 212; champions the Church, 1786–8, 240, 294, 328, 480–81, 487, 495, 517, 572n; and the Catholic Question, 326, 328, 454, 495–6, 515, 517

Woodward, Richard, junior, 405

Woodward, Richard, Major, 349n, 419–20, 434–5

Woodworth, G.M.D., Very Rev., dean of Cashel, 347n

Worcester, deanery of, 392; diocese of, 580

Worth, Edward, chief baron of the exchequer, 16

Wraxall, Nathaniel William, Sir, 31–2, 161

Wyndham, George, 3rd earl of Egremont, 192, 360, 389n, 593

Wynne, Catherine: *see* Cleaver, Catherine

Wynne, Owen, of Hazelwood, Co. Sligo, 192

Wynne, Richard, Rev. (brother-in-law of Archbishop Cleaver), 435

Wyse-Jackson, Robert, successively dean of Cashel and bishop of Limerick, 138n, 185–6nn, 377

Yelverton, Barry, 1st Viscount Avonmore, 581

York, archbishopric of, 188, 613; province of, 566–9

Yorke, Philip, 3rd earl of Hardwicke, 85–6nn, 254–5, 265–8, 275n, 277, 311, 419, 486n, 507, 593, 601, 605, 609, 612–13

Yorkshire, 13–14, 16, 457

Youghal, Co. Cork, 199, 303n; *see also* : St Mary's Church, Youghal

Young, Arthur, 332, 391, 409. 458

Young, Rev. Dr (chaplain and confidant of Lord Townshend), 462

Young, Edward, bishop of Ferns, 345

Young, Matthew, bishop of Clonfert, 489

Zoroaster, 38